THE NEW OXFORD COMPANION TO ECONOMICS IN INDIA

'For years to come, this book will be an essential reading for anyone seeking to understand India's economic development and political economy.'
—Ashutosh Varshney

'Kaushik Basu has done a great job in giving economics a broader scope and assembling authors who write expertly but in accessible style.'
—Lord Meghnad Desai

'... a unique and important guide to the dynamic Indian economy, and also a collection of penetrating essays by many of the world's true experts.'
—Stephen P. Cohen

'... an indispensable and innovative addition to the library of economics, not only for economists but also those whose lives are affected by economics.'
—*India Today*

'The volume is a unique experience as it exposes readers to a variety of themes penned by the distinguished writers ... A must-buy for each and every college, university and public library ...'
—*Business India*

'This is a dictionary that explains fundamental concepts and leaves it for readers to explore on their own ... [A] clear, engaging and useful resource.'
—*Business Standard*

'Too many economists may spoil the policy broth, but they can certainly produce a good encyclopedia on the economy!'
—*Outlook*

'India's first companion to economics is certainly among the more impressive additions to the catalogue of Indian encyclopedias.'
—*The Financial Express*

THE NEW OXFORD COMPANION TO

ECONOMICS

IN INDIA

Volume II I–Z

EDITED BY
KAUSHIK BASU
ANNEMIE MAERTENS

OXFORD
UNIVERSITY PRESS

OXFORD
UNIVERSITY PRESS

Oxford University Press is a department of the University of Oxford.
It furthers the University's objective of excellence in research, scholarship,
and education by publishing worldwide. Oxford is a registered trademark of
Oxford University Press in the UK and in certain other countries

Published in India by
Oxford University Press
YMCA Library Building, 1 Jai Singh Road, New Delhi 110 001, India

First Edition 2007
Revised Edition 2008
This Edition 2012

ISBN-13: 978-0-19-807855-5
ISBN-10: 0-19-807855-2

Typeset in Plantin 9.5/12
by Eleven Arts, Keshav Puram, Delhi 110 035
Printed in India at Thomson Press (India) Ltd., New Delhi 110 020

Contents

Entries A–Z

Volume I (A–H)

Volume II (I–Z)

Preface to the New Edition

The Oxford Companion to Economics in India (OCEI), published in 2007, was conceived in recognition of the fact that the Indian economy is complex beyond any single person's comprehension. The editor of *OCEI* (Kaushik Basu) and the publisher (Oxford University Press, OUP) felt that there would be a large demand for a book that brought between two covers the entire swathe of important topics pertaining to the Indian economy, and also the opinions of prominent economists, policymakers, and politicians on various issues related to India. In the event, they underestimated the largeness of the large demand. The first print run was sold out in the same year, and a revised edition (with updates and a few fresh entries) was out in the market in early 2008. The *OCEI* turned out to be a landmark both in publishing as well as the economics discipline in India, being the first A–Z reference book on 'economics in India'. It received an overwhelming response and has been widely reviewed, read, referenced and, on occasion, reviled. It has been used by students, teachers, scholars, and practitioners not just in India but also abroad, reflecting the expanding interest in the Indian economy. This was gratifying but also somewhat daunting in terms of the responsibility it implicitly placed on us.

Keeping in mind the requirements of students of economics and business, OUP went on to bring out a student-friendly, concise version of the same book—*The Concise Oxford Companion to Economics in India* (eds Kaushik Basu and Annemie Maertens)—in early 2010. This had a selection of entries from the original, which were arranged sectorally, and catered to economics courses throughout the country. It also included new entries on topics that had gained salience since the publication of the *Companion* (for instance, the financial crisis of 2007–9 and the accompanying recession), in addition to an appendix with a selection of statistics pertaining to the Indian economy and society. The concise edition has also been extremely well-received and has gone through two reprints already.

The downside of the good reception has been a demand for more—both in terms of topics and topicality. With a little arm twisting from our editors at OUP, last year in September, we started working on updating the concise edition. This process, however, got all of us thinking about doing a revised edition of the original *Companion*. We realized that there continued to be a large demand for the original *Companion*, given its broader scope. OUP had also been receiving regular queries on an updated edition from several universities and institutions.

Also, much water had flown between 2007 and now: the great global recession, arguably the most traumatic global downturn since the Great Depression of the 1930s; the sub-prime crisis, bringing to the fore concerns about financial markets and how to regulate them; and the revival of G-20 and the effort to engage heads of states of multiple nations in coordinating global policy, in which India has found itself taking an active role. We decided that the time had come to read through all entries, revise and update many of them, and commission new essays, paying special attention to the growing complexity of financial and fiscal policies, and the role of India in international collective action. The *New Oxford Companion to Economics in India* is the outcome. The *New OCEI* includes a total of 232 entries, more than 80 substantially revised and updated entries, and 24 new entries on issues of current and ongoing relevance. The expansion in size has meant that what originally appeared between two covers, now needed four. The *New OCEI* thus appears in two volumes in a boxed set.

Between the time when the original *OCEI* was published and now, one of the editors, Kaushik Basu, had moved from academe to policymaking. With the other editor, Annemie Maertens, in academe, we had a team that could appreciate the needs of researchers and students in the university grappling with and trying to create new theory and researching into statistical regularities and micro realities, and also of the policymaker, grappling with inflation, macro-prudential risk, currency unions, and more. Taking advantage of this dual perspective we decided to draw on both kinds of contributors for the *New OCEI*.

In editing this book we had to keep in mind the fact that India is growing, and growing complex in leaps and bounds. Managing and making policy for this behemoth is truly a challenge. No one can understand it all. We have to rely on the decentralization of knowledge and the availability of compendia written by multiple authors, each with expertise in some slender aspect of the economy. The best that the student of India and the policymaker for India can do is to study and ingest these broad brush accounts of the multifarious aspects of the Indian economy and then develop specialization as and when he or she needs to. We hope that this *New OCEI* will go some distance in fulfilling this need.

The key criteria for selecting entries for revision were areas in which there have been new developments, more recent data is available, and there have been important changes in policy. We got an extremely good response from contributors. However, we were unable to contact certain contributors and some were not able to meet our deadline. Most of these entries we have carried in their original form because, we feel, they highlight issues and concepts that continue to be relevant for understanding the issues of today. For a few others, where the author was unavailable, we got fresh entries on the same subject by new contributors (for instance, 'Fiscal Deficit' by Supriyo De and Dipak Dasgupta [original entry by Amaresh Bagchi]; 'Financial-sector Reforms' by K.P. Krishnan [original entry by Charan Singh]).

Keeping with the tradition of the original *Companion*, the new entries were invited from experts in varied fields (academics and practitioners at the highest levels), and these further enrich the diversity of perspectives included. They are a testament to not just the dynamism of the Indian economy but also of the discipline of economics. We have included some new entries on areas already covered in the original *Companion*—but these compliment the existing entries with fresh ideas and new areas of focus. Thus we have an entry on 'Inflation' by Prabhat Patnaik, which is a theoretical piece and was part the original *Companion*, and now we have a new entry (by Kaushik Basu) on virtually the same topic, which focuses on policy and experience, and comments on India's travails with inflation over the last few months and years.

In closing we may remind the reader that the *New OCEI*, like the original *Companion*, is conceptualized as an encyclopaedia. Thus there were limitations on the length of the entry as well as the number of references that could go with each entry. Each entry, therefore, provides an overview of the topic and is not meant to cover all its aspects in detail. There are various ways in which readers can browse through the *Companion*—alphabetically (A–Z), by topic through the comprehensive index, or by contributor (the 'list of contributors' has cross-references to the entries). Above all, this is a reference volume, meant to sit on the shelf to be pulled out as and when it is needed. The detailed index at the end as well as the accompanying CD is meant to make it friendly for those using it as a reference encyclopedia.

Producing a mammoth work like this invariably means a mountain of debt. One has to depend not just on the authors for taking the task seriously and delivering their entries but there is a whole host of other players—copyeditors, proof-readers, designers, and the marketing team—that may not be as visible but is, nevertheless, critical. Oxford University Press provided us with unstinting managerial and intellectual support and chased with deadlines not just the authors but, on some occasions, even one of the editors, whose identity will remain undisclosed. As editors we are acutely aware of the help that we received from this large cast of characters and thank them all. The list is too long to name them individually but it would be amiss if we did not mention Supriyo De and Shweta in the Ministry of Finance, who both assisted Kaushik Basu in numerous ways.

KAUSHIK BASU AND ANNEMIE MAERTENS
November 2011

Introduction

Experts on the Indian economy are a vanishing tribe, and for good reason. The complexity of the economy has grown to such enormous proportions that its full comprehension is beyond the capacity of any single human mind. And the complexity continues to grow as the economy gathers steam. But, of course, policies have to be crafted, taxes designed, subsidies doled out or rolled in, exchange rates propped up or allowed to flag, and laws pertaining to the economy enacted, amended, or repealed. Given the multifarious tasks that Indian policymakers have to contend with, there is a growing need to collate and coordinate information and wisdom that is scattered across a large number of institutions and individuals. Then there are the students of economics and commerce—a growing tribe in India, who need information and analysis on contemporary themes, which are deeper than what is to be found in newspapers and magazines and for which they cannot be expected each time to go to the original source or data archive. This companion is meant to be a response to these pressing needs of our times.

As often happens with such ventures, this one began with the editor's own felt need. I take active research interest in the policies that guide this huge organism called the Indian economy and I consider myself an expert on some aspects of it. Yet I am acutely aware of large swathes about which I know next to nothing. When in 1992 India's most famous stock market scam—the Harshad Mehta scandal—broke, an economist and a top official of the Government of India admitted that he (or she, let me add, in the interests of anonymity) did not even know the meaning of the many things that the evil genius of Harshad Mehta had manipulated. No one can blame him (or her). Anybody interested in the Indian economy, whether a student, researcher, policymaker, corporate manager, or ground-level activist, will appreciate the need for a reference source, where one can find most of the basic information and ideas concerning the Indian economy and the best of contemporary thinking on the subject. As befits a reference, the entries are organized alphabetically. The titles were selected carefully, with help from the editorial advisory board, to cover the essentials of the Indian economy. It should be mentioned here that the editorial board consists of people who cover a diverse range of expertise—from fiscal policy, globalization, and governance to agriculture and basic needs programmes. In addition to the alphabetical search, the reader can use the book's elaborate index of subjects and names or the CD-ROM version to search for topics thematically and by the names of contributors and prepare their own reading lists.

In his essay, 'Economic Possibilities for our Grandchildren', John Maynard Keynes, no doubt slightly dizzy from the then-recent rapid advances in economics, had predicted that within the next few decades all the major problems of the economy would be solved, and economics would cease to be an important subject. For once, the self-assured Maynard Keynes was completely wrong. Implicit in his observation was a view of the economy as a static object, waiting to be dissected and diagnosed. In reality, the complexity of the economy grows in step with our understanding of it. As we have a scientific breakthrough and begin to fathom some of this complexity, that very understanding enables our entrepreneurs, managers, consumers, and workers to discover new strategies and actions; and that, in turn, gives rise to newer complexities in the economy. Hence, like Sukumar Ray's famous character, Chandidas's uncle, who when setting out on long journeys dangled his favourite foods in front of him, from a mast anchored to his shoulders, in economics, unlike in the natural sciences, our investigation and the object of our investigation have a tendency to move in tandem.

Even as this volume is being compiled and edited, the economy of India is evolving into an evermore intricate organism. An interesting testimony to the dynamism of the economy concerns the entry on 'software exports'. As we were finalizing the proofs, it struck me that India's 'current' software exports figure may need to be updated, since the entry had been received a while ago. On checking back with the author, it turned out that in that short time interval, India's software exports (per unit of time) had not just risen but done so by over 30 per cent. While software in India is no doubt special, change is a perennial feature of any economy. Hence, a project like this volume, while it has its intellectual excitement, also has its preordained frustrations, because one knows that it can never be comprehensive and be able to totally live up to the task.

In taking on this large project—though its enormity dawned on me only after I had waded into it beyond the point of no return (otherwise there may not have been this book)—I decided that the book had to achieve two tasks. It had to be a reasonably comprehensive reference volume on basic facts and uniformities that gird the contemporary Indian economy, and also be a record of the best contemporary thinking on the subject. I must admit I had in mind the *Palgrave Dictionary of Economics*, which has been a lasting source of reference and an intellectual treasure house for economists and related social scientists. Hence, I invited some of the leading economists, scribes, industrialists, policymakers, and politicians of or connected to India to write. And the response (close to a 100 per cent, though not without repeat phone calls, cajoling, and threats) has been overwhelming, as the list of authors who figure in the pages that follow must make amply clear. The reader will find in this companion the thoughts and reflections of individuals who have been directly involved in shaping the economy of contemporary India, through their pioneering entrepreneurship, by their stewardship of the country's monetary and fiscal policy, and through the publication of their scientific ideas. What I hope will give this volume an added edge is that the list of authors includes not just the éminence grise but also a small number of students of economics—from Cornell, Delhi, and Harvard.

Since the mid-1990s not only has the overall economy of India surged, with growth rates frequently crossing the 7 per cent per annum mark and occasionally rising above 8 per cent, there is also a clear and evident increase in the sophistication of our scholars and researchers. The old polarization of 'left' and 'right', where people took up positions not from facts and deductive reasoning, but from their chosen texts and pre-committed opinions, is less evident today. Barring a few diehards at both ends, most analysts approach the subject much more scientifically. We wanted the best of this new opinion, irrespective of ideology, to be represented in this volume. And to that extent the book is aimed at those interested in not just policy but also in the conundrums of the economy as an intellectual challenge per se. Moreover, while this companion is meant to span the recent cover stories of India's high growth, leadership role in software and information technology, and outsourcing success, it also acknowledges the gloomy backwaters—the widespread poverty, farmer suicides, child labour, and the large and impoverished informal sector where a vast majority of India's labourers work.

There is virtual consensus that while India has grown rapidly over the last decade and poverty, as measured by the percentage of population living below the poverty line, has declined, inequality—whether it be regional or personal—has worsened and employment has not grown in step with the growth of the labour force. Understanding the basis of these seeming anomalies is extremely important. A huge rise in inequality can create political upheavals, which can in turn spell doom for growth. Moreover, there are many (the present author included) who consider such huge inequalities to be innately unconscionable even if the disadvantaged are too weak to protest and destabilize the economy.

But even if one were not trying to think of policies to avoid such a predicament, understanding the diverse changes in India is an intellectual challenge of no mean proportion. Is the growth in inequality a consequence of economic liberalization or a necessary concomitant of global changes, and, hence largely beyond the reach of national governments? Are movements in stock prices reflections of underlying strengths and weaknesses of the economy or the moods and machinations of investors and speculators? This companion is aimed at providing readers with the basic facts and ideas that will help them form their own opinion about these difficult questions. Hence, my hope is that this companion will be of value to both policymakers and professional economists as well as to students—graduate and undergraduate—interested in the Indian economy, and development economics in general.

Reference companions like this, by their sheer weight in the hands of the reader, raise expectations that are virtually impossible to fulfill. There are invariably topics and entries that disappoint by their omission. The decision of what to omit can actually be very challenging. I thought hard, for instance, about biographical entries—whether to include them or not. Some members of the editorial board were against such entries, some in favour, and others non-committal, which meant that the decision was finally mine. It was evident that any list would draw criticism about why, if x was there, was y not? Quite early in the project it was decided to confine biographical entries to only the dead, thereby silencing the potentially most vociferous objectors—those among the living who might not have appeared in the book but believed that they should have. In choosing names from history there is first the advantage that, with the passage of time and the advantage of hindsight, we have better idea about who deserves to be in and who out; and the added advantage that even when we are wrong there is no worry about having to contend directly with offended parties.

While most choices and omissions are by design, some are inadvertent as in cases of missed deadlines that became evident too late to make replacements possible. Indeed, the final stages of a work like this, involving close to 200 authors and over 200 entries, are spent mainly in chasing truant authors and getting them to turn in their pieces. And this, in turn, means that the editor has to get used to the magic reality of finding economists he sees at a distance (for instance while walking up to a group at a dinner party) vanish by the time he gets there.

But all said and done, the pleasures of a task like this outweigh the costs. For one, there is an enormous amount of learning-by-doing and this happens effortlessly as one reads and edits the manuscript. Then there is the pleasure of human interaction, since one has to work not just with the authors numbering in hundreds, but with teams of editors, editorial assistants, copyeditors, proofreaders, and research assistants. What now remains is only the 'interaction' with the reviewers and readers and, for that, I fortunately have to do nothing but keep my fingers crossed.

My foremost thanks to the editorial team at Oxford University Press whose unstinting support helped move this mammoth project smoothly along the conveyor belt. During the approximately two years of work on this book I moved frequently between India and the US. Though I tried to do the bulk of my work on this project when in India, I invariably had to carry parts of it to Cornell University. There I was aided by a talented group of research assistants—Amanda Felkey, Hyejin Ku, and Anandita Mariam Philipose—and had remarkably smart secretarial assistance from Amy Moesch. Finally, I owe a special thanks to a most outstanding Board of Editors—T.C.A. Anant, Pranab Bardhan, Jean Drèze, Dilip Mookherjee, and M. Govinda Rao. These are individuals of outstanding intellectual strengths and I called on them liberally at several stages—about what kinds of entries to include and what to omit, about possible authors, and also to have them read and comment on several of the entries. But, in the end, the final decisions were mine; and, as the overall in-charge of this project, I am reconciled that the brickbats, no matter how much I would like to deflect them elsewhere, must perforce end up at my doorstep.

KAUSHIK BASU
January 2007

Postscript

While it may not speak well of one as a forecaster, there are few things as gratifying to an editor as that of stocks of the book running out quickly. The *Oxford Companion to Economics in India* was released in February 2007. The reception was overwhelming. My apprehension that journals and newspapers would either not find reviewers since virtually all potential ones were authors or would get bad reviews from the ones who were not authors for that very reason, fortunately turned out to be misplaced. The book was widely reviewed and, more often than not, praised. It was viewed as a much-needed guide to a newly vibrant and increasingly complex India. The demand for the book from readers, in India and abroad, matched this evaluation. Within months it was evident that stocks would run out before the year's end, and in June we took a decision to go for another print run.

This turned out to be a blessing in disguise. While this did not give us the time to do a full overhaul, as would be the case with a completely new edition, it provided a window of opportunity to make some essential changes. First, there were some topics that had grown in significance since the time that the original volume was planned and produced and which did not have an entry. *Special Economic Zones* and *Land Rights and Acquisition* are two such examples. From being themes on the fringes of economic discourse in India, they had moved to centre space, with strong voices of support for and equally strong ones of dissent against the policy of acquiring land to set up new industries and special economic zones. A few such new entries have now been included in this reprint version. Second, a book of this kind invariably has some entries that are especially prone to getting dated. In the case of today's India this is true of, for instance, information technology and foreign direct investment. We asked the authors of several such pieces to revise their entries taking account of any important new information that may have come to light since the entries were originally written. Finally, we took this opportunity to make large improvements to the subject index, which should make the book more reader-friendly. The book is meant to be used not just by students of economics but journalists writing on India, grass-roots activists preparing a plan, policymakers crafting an intervention, and managers of corporations trying to enhance their understanding of the Indian economy. The two indexes were prepared carefully to help all these diverse readers navigate through the multifarious entries and topics that form this companion.

KAUSHIK BASU
January 2008

I

IMF Conditionality*

The International Monetary Fund (IMF) is a revolving fund that is mandated by its Articles of Agreement to extend *temporary* financial assistance 'under adequate safeguards' to member countries facing balance-of-payments difficulties (Article I). Like any lender, the IMF needs assurances from its borrowers that the funds lent to them will be used for the purposes defined by the Articles of Agreement, and in a manner that does not jeopardize their contractual servicing and repayment. IMF lending in support of adjustment programmes is conditional on the borrowing countries adopting certain economic and financial policies. The conditions attached to these loans are commonly referred to as IMF conditionality (see Guitián 1995; IMF 2001; Polak 1991). Such conditionality is part of IMF monitoring to make sure that the borrowed funds are being appropriately used and that the country will be able to repay the IMF as agreed. IMF lending and its associated conditionality follow broadly the same principles as private financial contracts, though several dimensions make IMF lending qualitatively different.

A key aspect of IMF lending is that countries in need of IMF loans generally do not possess internationally valuable collateral. If they did, they could use it to borrow from private lenders and would not require IMF resources. In a crisis situation, however, even if a country had internationally acceptable collateral, it might not be able to use it to borrow from private capital markets. In the absence of collateral, private loan contracts typically would include various covenants, coupled with monitoring. Formally, a covenant is designed to protect the lender and prohibit the borrower from taking actions that could reduce the probability of repayment. Covenants can impose clear obligations on the borrower, impose limitations on or prohibit certain actions, and specify when the borrower is considered to be in default.

IMF conditionality can be viewed as a complex covenant written into the loan agreement. The policy prescriptions in IMF-supported adjustment programmes essentially provide safeguards that the country will be able to rectify its macroeconomic and structural imbalances and will be in a position to service and repay the loan. Thus the conditionality associated with IMF programmes can be viewed as a substitute for collateral. Additional safeguards are provided by the fact that IMF claims are de facto senior to claims of other creditors, and that it disburses funds in tranches, conditional on the implementation of satisfactory policies to correct the imbalances.

Agreeing to IMF conditionality is an imposition on a country even though the two parties may share the same objectives—external viability, price stability, sustained high growth, reduced systemic risk, and so on (for a recent survey on whether and to what extent conditionality is appropriate, see Dreher 2009). To be sure, the covenant in the loan agreement required by the IMF is far more complex and has different characteristics

*The views expressed in this article are those of the author and should not be interpreted as those of the International Monetary Fund.

than covenants in simpler private financial transactions. The challenge in designing IMF conditionality is to specify the optimal covenant—the best policy conditions given the circumstances of the country, the disbursement intervals for the loan, the type of monitoring involved, and so on—to achieve programme objectives while providing sufficient safeguards to the IMF.

IMF lending also differs from private lending in significant ways (Khan and Sharma 2003). First, conditionality in IMF lending is much more complicated than in private financial transactions and involves assessing the macroeconomic imbalances or structural deficiencies that led to a country's macroeconomic problems and then negotiating an agreement with country authorities that will address those issues.

Second, it is difficult, if not impossible, to establish the 'value' of IMF conditionality. The value of negotiated conditionality largely depends on the degree to which the authorities of the borrowing country adopt the programme and are willing to expend effort and political credibility to implement it.

Third, unlike private lenders—for whom it may be sufficient to deal with a firm's management—negotiations for an IMF-supported programme are conducted with certain government representatives of the central bank and finance ministry, while the success of the programme depends on many other stakeholders in society—other ministries, trade unions, professional associations, civic groups, and non-governmental organizations.

Fourth, the IMF is, by design, a cooperative that makes loans to its sovereign members (see Chami et al. 2004). In the event of default, there is no court to which it can appeal and no tangible collateral that can be used to cover lost resources. The enforcement mechanism for ensuring that borrowing countries live up to their obligations essentially amounts to a combination of moral suasion, the borrower's desire to maintain its reputation, peer pressure, and the threat of being shut out of international capital markets.

IMF conditionality is implemented through programme design and monitoring that tracks whether agreed policies are implemented in a timely and effective manner. Programme design begins with an in-depth analysis of the sources of a country's macroeconomic imbalances (see Mussa and Savastano 1999). The next step is to agree with the country authorities on policy objectives and on macroeconomic policies and structural reforms to achieve those objectives.

Monitoring takes various forms, depending on the borrowing country's circumstances and the IMF lending facility being used. It generally includes prior actions, performance criteria, macroeconomic and structural benchmarks, and reviews. Monitoring also prohibits actions inconsistent with the IMF's Articles of Agreement, such as the introduction of new foreign exchange restrictions. Releases of IMF financing are linked to compliance with monitoring arrangements.

Prior actions are required when up-front implementation is critical to programme success or to allay doubts about the authorities' commitment. Examples of required actions include passing an agreed budget, realigning the exchange rate, adopting structural reforms, or enacting relevant laws. Such actions must be taken prior to the approval of a programme by the IMF's Executive Board, which triggers the first disbursement.

Performance criteria normally include quantitative targets for specified financial aggregates (such as bank credit, net international reserves, or fiscal balance) and often include structural measures (such as tariff reductions, tax system revisions, or privatization of public enterprises). Meeting these criteria triggers the release of subsequent tranches of committed IMF resources.

Macroeconomic and structural benchmarks set targets for macroeconomic variables and structural policies important for effective programme implementation. They do not directly affect scheduled disbursements.

Finally, reviews are used to assess overall progress toward programme objectives, identifying any sources of slippage (resulting from lack of policy implementation, external shocks, or programme design issues), and taking corrective actions. Reviews are usually specified as performance criteria—further disbursements are delayed if the review is not concluded by the scheduled review date.

In 1991–3, India borrowed from the IMF under a stand-by arrangement in the context of a severe balance-of-payments crisis, which had reduced foreign exchange reserves to precariously low levels. The key aspects of the adjustment programme were a significant reduction in the fiscal deficit, a substantial devaluation of the rupee, tightening of monetary policy, and structural reforms to improve resource allocation by reversing decades of state intervention. The adjustment effort was by and large successful in restoring the confidence of external investors, rebuilding foreign exchange reserves, lowering inflation, and buoying the Indian economy in the face of a sharp reduction in imports.

The IMF programme also provided an impetus for structural reforms. It virtually dismantled the complex system of industrial licensing that had prevailed since the 1950s, and opened up the state-dominated economy to private investment. The price mechanism was given a greater a role in allocating resources, the trade and payments system was liberalized, foreign investment was allowed in more sectors of the economy, and many tax and financial sector reforms were initiated. However, not much progress was made in restructuring state-owned enterprises and reforming the legal and regulatory system that impeded the reallocation of labour and capital.

The last two decades of the 20th century saw a major increase in structural conditions in IMF-supported programmes (Goldstein 2000; IMF 2001). The expansion of structural conditionality appeared to limit the scope for domestic policy choices, and hence reducing country ownership. But there was considerable validity for this expansion, especially in the context of countries that were in transition to becoming market economies. Still, many structural reforms are of a microeconomic nature and so are likely to be more intrusive than macroeconomic policies. Country ownership of programmes is essential for the design and implementation of these microeconomic measures because they have different effects on various segments and vested interests in society.

Increased structural conditions pose two main dangers. First, they may reduce country ownership of programmes and so impair their effectiveness. Second, a failure to implement structural reforms not critical for macroeconomic stability may undermine confidence in the overall programme—possibly triggering reactions in domestic and international capital markets that could make overall programme objectives harder to achieve.

It would be difficult and undesirable to eliminate all structural conditions from programmes. But careful thought is being given to which structural reforms are essential for achieving a programme's main objectives. These reforms will vary by country, but pruning the list of structural conditions may be possible without jeopardizing a programme's success or the IMF's ability to be repaid. In other words, prioritizing or streamlining structural conditionality need not mean weakening overall conditionality.

In a recent review, the IMF's Independent Evaluation Office (2007) found that compliance with structural measures was much lower than with macroeconomic conditions, and concluded that it was at times difficult to see how structural conditionality contributed to ensuring adequate safeguards for IMF resources or providing predictability to borrowing countries about the availability of Fund resources. It noted that while structural measures had declined markedly and moved towards core areas of IMF expertise, the design of appropriate and focused structural conditions would remain a key challenge for IMF programmes. The IMF has now discontinued the use of structural performance criteria, and instead monitors the implementation of structural policies in IMF-supported programmes in the context of the periodic programme reviews.

Reforms of the IMF's lending and conditionality framework have also included: (i) the simplification of IMF's lending toolkit to eliminate facilities that catered to narrow balance-of-payment problems and (ii) a shift to greater reliance on pre-set qualification criteria (or ex-ante conditionality) rather than the traditional (ex-post) conditionality.

Countries now have access to three crisis-prevention facilities: the Flexible Credit Line (FCL) with only ex-ante conditionality for countries with sound fundamentals and policy track records; the High-Access Precautionary Stand-by Arrangement (HAPA) with focused ex-post conditionality to achieve programme objectives; and the Precautionary Credit Line (PCL) which bridges the gap between the FCL and the HAPA by combining a pre-qualification process (similar to FCL) and focused ex-post conditionality for countries with moderate vulnerabilities that prevent them from meeting the high qualification standards set for the FCL.

What is the evidence of the effectiveness of IMF conditionality? Specifically, have IMF-supported adjustment programmes achieved their objectives of improving current account balances, increasing international reserves, lowering inflation, and raising growth? This is essentially an empirical question that requires evaluating the effects that past programmes have had on the macroeconomic variables of interest. Such evaluations are conducted periodically by the IMF's Strategy and Policy Review Department and by its recently created Independent Evaluation Office, with the results reported to the IMF's Executive Board. In addition, a number of studies over the years, both inside and outside the IMF, have examined the question using a variety of empirical methods.

Almost all the empirical studies surveyed by Haque and Khan (2002) show that IMF-supported programmes have improved current account balances and the overall balances of payments in borrowing countries. The results for inflation are less clear. Most of the studies indicate that although inflation usually falls, the decline is generally statistically insignificant. For growth, output is generally depressed in the short run—that is, during the stabilization phase—but increases as macroeconomic stability is established. Overall, the most recent empirical results indicate that, on average, IMF-supported programmes and the conditionality they incorporate have been reasonably effective in achieving their main macroeconomic objectives.

In the recent global crisis, Fund-supported programmes in emerging markets have been reasonably successful in cushioning the blow from the worst downturn since the 1930s. Timely, higher, and more front-loaded financing combined with more focused programme conditionality has led to greater country ownership and much better compliance than in the past. Severe disruptions that accompanied past crises like currency overshooting and bank runs have so far been avoided. Preventing sharp spikes in interest and exchange rates has minimized negative balance sheet effects. Output losses in programme countries, though large, have not been significantly worse than comparable non-programme countries, once pre-existing vulnerabilities like current account deficits and credit booms are taken into account. In most cases, the stance of fiscal policy has been accommodative, though in some instances concerns about debt sustainability and weak structural fiscal positions have required limiting the full working of automatic stabilizers. However, it is worth noting that to protect the most vulnerable segments of society, programme conditionality in many cases has included government commitments to strengthening and expanding the social safety net (IMF 2009a, 2009b).

Periodically, the IMF evaluates the design and implementation of programme conditionality. The next review is expected to be completed by end-2011 and will make an assessment of the recent conditionality reforms.

SUNIL SHARMA

References

Chami, Ralph, Sunil Sharma, and Ilhyock Shim. 2004. 'A Model of the IMF as a Coinsurance Arrangement', IMF Working Paper 04/219, International Monetary Fund, Washington DC.

Dreher, Axel. 2009. 'IMF Conditionality: Theory and Evidence', *Public Choice*, 141(1–2): 233–67.

Goldstein, Morris. 2000. 'IMF Structural Conditionality: How Much is Too Much?', Institute for International Economics, Washington DC.

Guitián, Manuel. 1995. 'Conditionality Past, Present, and Future', *IMF Staff Papers*, 42(December): 792–835.

Haque, Nadeem Ul and Mohsin S. Khan. 2002. 'Do IMF-Supported Programs Work? A Survey of the Cross-country Empirical Evidence', in M.S. Khan, S.M. Nsouli, and C.H. Wong (eds), *Macroeconomic Management: Programs and Policies*, Washington DC, International Monetary Fund.

International Monetary Fund. 2001. *Conditionality in Fund-Supported Programs—Policy Issues*, Washington DC, International Monetary Fund, available at http://www.imf.org/external/np/pdr/cond/2001/eng/policy/021601.pdf.

——. 2009a. *Creating Policy Space—Responsive Design and Streamlined Conditionality in Recent Low-income Country Programs*, Washington DC, International Monetary Fund. Available at http://www.imf.org/external/np/pp/eng/2009/091009a.pdf.

——. 2009b. *Review of Recent Crisis Programs*, Washington DC, International Monetary Fund, available at http://www.imf.org/external/np/pp/eng/2009/091409.pdf.

International Monetary Fund, Independent Evaluation Office. 2007. *Structural Conditionality in IMF-supported Programs*, Washington DC, International Monetary Fund.

Khan, Mohsin S. and Sunil Sharma. 2003. 'IMF Conditionality and Country Ownership of Programs', *World Bank Research Observer*, 18(2): 227–48.

Mussa, Michael and Miguel Savastano. 1999. 'The IMF Approach to Economic Stabilization', IMF Working Paper 99/104, International Monetary Fund, Washington DC.

Polak, Jacques J. 1991. 'The Changing Nature of IMF Conditionality', *Essays in International Finance*, No. 184, Princeton, NJ, Princeton University.

■ Income Mobility

'Income-mobility' analysis involves following the same people for two or more points in time and studying the changes in their economic well-being. It is something of a cliché, but nonetheless true, that income mobility is multifaceted. These many facets can be categorized as follows.

One is the issue of mobility of what among whom. 'Income mobility' denotes change in economic well-being among suitably chosen recipient units. Economic well-being may be measured by income, consumption, or labour earnings, among others. The recipient units may be households, per capitas, adult equivalents, or individual earners.

Second is the context within which mobility is analysed. Inter-generational mobility studies look at parents and children, while intra-generational studies look at the same individuals from one year to another.

Third are the two levels of mobility analysis. Macromobility studies gauge how much mobility there is in an economy. Micromobility studies investigate what are the correlates and determinants of changes for different recipients.

Once agreement has been reached on the measure of economic well-being, the choice of recipient unit, the inter-generational or intra-generational context, and the level of analysis, analysts nonetheless mean different things when they speak of income mobility. Six notions may be distinguished.

Briefly, the six mobility notions are: time dependence, which measures the extent to which economic well-being in the past determines economic well-being at present; positional movement, which is what we measure when we look at changes in individuals' economic position (ranks, centiles, deciles, or quintiles); share movement, which arises when individuals' shares of the total income change; income flux, which is what we measure when we look at the size of the fluctuations in individuals' incomes but not their directional income movement, which is what we measure when we determine how many people move up or down how many rupees; and mobility as an equalizer of longer-term incomes, which involves comparing the inequality of income at one point in time with the inequality of income over a longer period.

In India, empirical mobility studies have been carried out using three principal data sources. These are the NCAER (National Council for Applied Economic Research) data, the ICRISAT (International Crops Research Institute for the Semi-Arid Tropics) data, and the Palanpur data.

The first source is panel data collected by the NCAER in the late 1960s, in the early 1980s, and again in the present. Using the earlier data, income mobility was studied by Coondoo and Dutta (1990). They found that income mobility in India acted to equalize the distribution of longer-term income relative to initial income, that poorer households' incomes increased at above-average rates, and that overall mobility was about one-fourth of its maximum possible value. Substantially similar macromobility findings were obtained in a later study by Bhide and Mehta (2004). In addition, in the micromobility part of their study, Bhide and Mehta found that the factors related to the persistence of poverty are scheduled tribe status, household size, number of dependent children, literacy, ownership of a house, size of cultivated area, and income from livestock. A new round of the NCAER was fielded recently; new studies using the newer changes should start appearing shortly.

The second source is the panel surveys of ICRISAT villages beginning in 1975. The surveys cover seven villages. One comprehensive study of income mobility using these data is made by Walker and Ryan (1990). Among their key findings are that two-thirds of the sample households moved into or out of poverty in their nine-year analysis period, 23 per cent of the households were chronically poor, and households need to be very well-off to avoid poverty in all years. New ICRISAT data have been fielded since 2001 and are now being analysed.[1]

A third source of data is the in-depth examination of Palanpur, a village in Moradabad district of Uttar Pradesh. Drèze et al. (1992) and Lanjouw and Stern (2003) report on a series of studies that have been carried out in Palanpur over the last three decades. The advantage of such studies is that the researchers could literally track every household by name and by personal acquaintance to ensure that accurate matches were made over time. The research shows that per capita incomes are only 'weakly correlated' across years. It also shows that important improvements have been made both in the farm and non-farm sectors of the economy. In the farm economy, the labour market has tightened, raising real agricultural wages. In the non-farm economy, new job opportunities have been created. The elites were the first to benefit; the poor benefited to a lesser extent and only within the less dynamic parts of the non-farm economy. The authors conclude that although one must be realistic about the potential of off-farm employment to improve economic opportunities for the poor, improvements in living standards of the poor have been made.

This entry has briefly surveyed the directions and findings of income mobility studies in India to date. As a complement to studies of changes in poverty and changes in inequality, income mobility studies offer a wealth of exciting possibilities.

GARY S. FIELDS

References

Bhide, Shashanka and Aasha Kapur Mehta. 2004. 'Chronic Poverty in Rural India: Issues and Findings from Panel Data', *Journal of Human Development*, 5: 195–209.

Coondoo, Dipankar and Bhaskar Dutta. 1990. 'Measurement of Income Mobility: An Application to India', in Bhaskar Dutta et al. (eds), *Economic Theory and Policy: Essays in Honor of Dipak Banerji*, Bombay and New York, Oxford University Press.

Drèze, Jean, Peter Lanjouw, and Nicholas Stern. 1992. 'Economic Mobility and Agricultural Labour in Rural India: A Case Study', *Indian Economic Review*, 27: 25–54.

Lanjouw, Peter and Nicholas Stern. 2003. 'Opportunities off the Farm as a Springboard out of Rural Poverty: Five Decades of Development in an Indian Village', in Gary S. Fields and Guy Pfeffermann (eds), *Pathways out of Poverty*, Boston, Kluwer.

Walker, Thomas S. and James G. Ryan. 1990. *Village and Household Economies in India's Semi-arid Tropics*, Baltimore, Johns Hopkins University Press.

[1]See www.icrisat.org for further information.

Industrial Clusters

Clusters and Their Diversity Introduced

There are several locations that are synonymous with a particular product, both industrial and artisan, besides being known for services. In Tamil Nadu, a small town of Tirupur has been known to export ready-made knitted cotton garments worth over Rs 11,000 crore. Ludhiana, a well-known industrial town of Punjab with an estimated 12,000 enterprises, accounts for the highest number of bicycles produced in the world while employing 5,00,000 people. An estimated 25,000 enterprises in Surat and Navsari towns in Gujarat cut and polish the maximum number of small diamonds in the world.

Besides these large and mature clusters, there are also several other locations with a much smaller scale of economic activity, which collectively provide very high employment and contribute to regional development. Pochampally, a small town in Andhra Pradesh, is known for its exquisite hand-woven Ikat sarees. Similarly, Kancheepuram sarees (Tamil Nadu), Bandha Ikat (Orissa), Banaras silk (Uttar Pradesh), Chanderi for its exclusive fabric (Madhya Pradesh), and Kota for kota doria fabric (Rajasthan) are a few other famous handloom-based clusters. There are hundreds of such locations in India where several weaver families make hand-made sarees, stoles, dress material, *dupatta*s, bed spreads, curtains, and *dhoti*s. Among handicrafts and rural industries, Moradabad in Uttar Pradesh is called the 'Brass City' and is famous worldwide for its brass metal giftware and is said to house around 29 per cent of the metalwork-artisans of India. Mysore *agarbatti* (incense sticks) in Karnataka, Madhubani paintings in Bihar, Nainital hand-made candles in Uttarakhand, Dokra tribal jewellery from West Bengal, Sanganer textiles block printing in Rajasthan, Kalpi hand-made paper in Uttar Pradesh, and Bhadohi hand-knotted carpets in Uttar Pradesh are a few illustrious examples of handicraft clusters in India.

In the recent past, specialized services, such as software development, business process outsourcing (BPOs), and the healthcare industry (also famous as medical tourism) have grown around specific towns and cities. Bengaluru (Karnataka), Hyderabad (Andhra Pradesh), Pune (Maharashtra), and Gurgaon (Haryana) are some of the well-known cities for software and IT-based services. In the healthcare industry, Kochi (Kerala), Mumbai (Maharashtra), and NOIDA (Uttar Pradesh) are famous destinations.

All these locations that readily relate themselves to a specific product or service may commonly be called clusters. A typical example of a cluster of knitted garments includes diverse enterprises that undertake operations, such as knitting, stitching, finishing, dyeing, and printing; it also includes related service enterprises, such as merchant houses, export units, banks, input supplier firms, transporters, consultants, training organizations, academic institutions, and several other service enterprises.

Clustering Explained and Its Spread in India Recognized

The phenomenon of enterprise clustering is prevalent both in economically developed and developing countries. Geographical proximity of enterprises may give rise to specialized labour, nurture subsidiary industries, stimulate innovations, enable technological spillovers, foster flexible specialization, and thus help make the economic activities more productive through economies of scale. An industrial cluster is understood not only as a physical agglomeration of industrial enterprises, but also by the relationships, social norms, and mutual trust among the different local stakeholders. Economists refer to and recognize this collective of soft relationships as social capital.

In India, 4,259 clusters have so far been mapped on an Indian cluster observatory by a not-for-profit development consulting organization 'Foundation for MSME Clusters' (www.clusterobservatory.in). Out of these, 1,086 are industrial clusters, 491 are handloom clusters, and 2,682 are handicraft clusters. In addition, it is estimated that 2,000 more clusters exist in the micro-enterprises sector. Similar clusters in agriculture, horticulture, and services are also known to exist but have not yet been mapped. Probably this is the largest number of clusters recorded in any single country in the world. The clusters vary significantly in terms of product diversity, economic size, industrial structure, and employment generation. Several factors, such as closeness to raw material sources, proximity to markets, availability of skilled human resources, location, presence of related support industries, and focused interventions for promoting ancillarization may have individually or collectively contributed to the unique historical evolution of these clusters. Against every ten clusters, nine are estimated to have evolved naturally without any policy support to specifically promote them at their current locations (Gulati 1997: 2).

Economic Significance of Clusters

According to the fourth all-India census on MSMEs completed in 2009, there are 2.61 crore enterprises employing 5.94 crore people. The micro, small, and medium enterprises (MSME) sector is known to contribute

45 per cent of the national industrial output and 40 per cent of industrial exports, and is responsible for 9 per cent of GDP. The estimates provided by the 'Cluster Observatory' lists details of 1,086 industrial clusters with estimates of 6,94,379 enterprises, employing 1,56,92,736 persons and generating an estimated output of Rs 12,36,755 crore in 2008–9. Similarly, the handloom census (NCAER 2009–10: 18–27), published by the Development Commissioner, Handlooms, Ministry of Textiles, states that there are 43.31 lakh persons employed on 23.77 lakh looms across the country. Most of these units are concentrated among 491 handloom clusters listed in the Cluster Observatory. While similar information is not available about handicrafts and other micro enterprises spread across rural and urban India, anecdotal evidence suggests that these types of enterprises are also concentrated around clusters. Awasthi (2005: 5) estimates that clusters account for 77 per cent units and about 72 per cent employment among all type of MSMEs, including handlooms, handicrafts, and micro enterprises. While the estimates may differ from one source to another because of a preponderance of dynamically changing unregistered enterprises, these figures do point out the high economic significance of industrial clusters in India.

Geographical and Sectoral Distribution of Clusters

The 1,086 industrial clusters produce 136 types of products which have been categorized across 14 sectors. The food products sector accounts for the highest proportion of clusters at 23 per cent, followed by textile products at 14 per cent, metal products at 13 per cent, and non-metallic mineral products at 10 per cent. These four sectors constitute 60 per cent of the industrial MSME clusters. It is interesting to note that the industrial states of India account for more clusters than the others. Uttar Pradesh with 159 clusters tops the list, followed by Tamil Nadu with 103, and Gujarat with 95 clusters. It may be noticed that the six states of Uttar Pradesh, Tamil Nadu, Gujarat, Maharashtra, Kerala, and Andhra Pradesh account for 57 per cent of the MSME clusters. A graphical distribution of industrial clusters across the different states is given in Figure 1.

Development Policy and Clusters

Cluster-based interventions have some of their fundamental underpinnings in Michael E. Porter's work (1998), the 'Competitive Advantage of Nations', as also in the well-researched and documented development experiences of SMEs spread across north and north-east Italy. The economic significance of industrial and micro enterprise clusters in India was first realized in a report prepared by a national committee headed by Abid Hussain in 1997. Consequentially, from 2000, various national enterprise development institutions and policymakers took note of the need to support clusters. Over these years, the development policy focus has increasingly shifted from enterprise focused assistance to local production systems and new public institutional delivery systems that recognize and support public–private partnerships for service delivery. This development model builds on the argument that small enterprises lack competitiveness not because of their size but due to

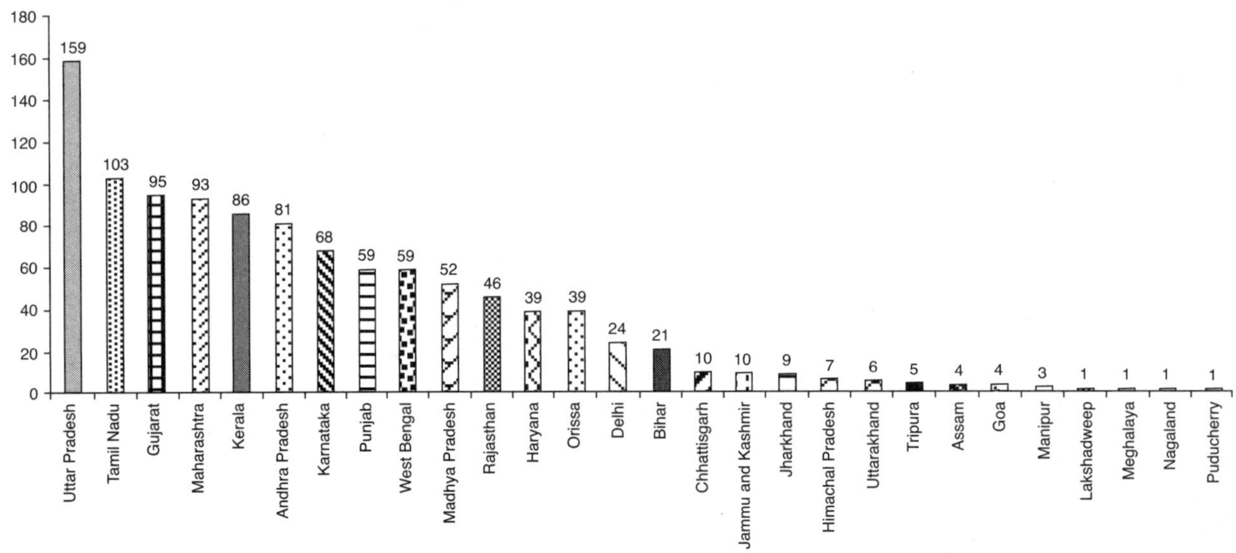

Figure 1 Industrial Clusters

isolation not only from other enterprises but also from service institutions, whether public or private. Existing clusters, therefore, provide a ready framework to engage different stakeholders, such as enterprises, their buyers, sub-contractors, raw material providers, machinery suppliers, business development service providers, local institutions, and relevant regulatory authorities to evolve a local system that works for the possible betterment of the entire cluster. It is now well-accepted that clustering leads to collective efficiency gains which individual firms can hardly achieve outside the clusters. A study on micro and small industries observed that the firms operating in industrial clusters have significantly higher productivity than those operating in isolation (Awasthi 2004).

As a result, a range of 'enterprise development institutions', other national and regional institutions engaged in research and development, training and banking have also started undertaking cluster-oriented initiatives in the recent past (Planning Commission 2004: 10). It is estimated that there have been 2,683 cluster-specific interventions mainly through 24 public support schemes for cluster assistance involving an estimated amount of Rs 7,000 crore during the Eleventh Five Year Plan (2007–12). Largely, these interventions have focused on productivity enhancement through efficiency gains leading to cost reduction. However, the success of these development initiatives has not been established unambiguously due to their recent origin and partially due to the lack of effective monitoring and evaluation systems. There is a lot of scope for improving the efficiency of enterprises through cluster development initiatives, improved cluster-level strategies, building cluster to cluster linkages, strengthening of local governance systems, building cluster-specific infrastructure, and fostering industry linkages with local, national, and international institutions. There is also space to work in the areas of innovation, poverty alleviation, greening, industrial ecology, and skill development through the cluster development approach.

Facilitating knowledge sharing and learning amongst industry stakeholders, facilitating the development of a 'clean development mechanism' (CDM), and providing inputs for transfer and diffusion of environmentally sound technologies in the context of climate change have become quite important for achieving manufacturing competitiveness. Fostering responsible businesses among clusters can also lead to improved working conditions for the labour, increased gender considerations, and improved governance systems through the clusters.

Mukesh Gulati and Amar Singh

References

Awasthi, Dinesh. 2004. 'Labour Process and Productivity in Micro and Small Enterprises, The Indian Experience', *The Indian Journal of Labour Economics*, 47(4): 871–988.

——. 2005. 'Dynamics of Cluster Development in India, Emerging Lessons and Future Strategies', Institute of Economy and Development, Observer Research Foundation (ORF), New Delhi, July (unpublished).

Gulati, Mukesh. 1997. 'Restructuring and Modernisation of Small Medium Enterprise Clusters in India', Report for United Nations Industrial Development Organisation, Vienna.

NCAER. 2009–10. *Handloom Census of India*, New Delhi, NCAER, pp. 18–27.

Porter, Michael E. 1998. 'Clusters and the New Economics of Competition', *Harvard Business Review*, November–December.

Planning Commission. 2004. 'Employment Creation and Skill Development through Development of Clusters of Small Establishments', A Research Report (unpublished).

Industrial Growth

In 1950–1, industry (mining; manufacturing; electricity, gas, and water; and construction) contributed 15.2 per cent of the gross domestic product (GDP), employing 9.4 per cent of the workforce. Five and half decades later, in 2004–5, it accounted for 26.6 per cent of GDP, employing 18.8 per cent of the workforce. During nearly six decades since 1950–1, annual growth rates of industry and GDP have been 5.4 and 4.5 per cent, respectively; manufacturing, which accounts for about three-fifths of industrial output, has grown roughly at the same rate as industry.

While the utilities and mining activities are mostly publicly owned and operated, construction is almost entirely in the private sector. Manufacturing is also predominately in the private sector: in 2007, the public sector's and foreign-owned enterprises' share in manufacturing GDP was 8 per cent each; while the public sector's contribution was mostly in 'heavy industry', foreign-owned enterprises were prominent in consumer goods and durables.

Registered manufacturing, that is, factories employing 10 or more workers using power or 20 or more workers without using power, contributes 70 per cent of the output, employing about one-fifth of the workforce; the unregistered sector (consisting of household enterprises and small workshops representing labour-intensive industries) contribute the rest, employing four-fifth of the workers.

Manufactures currently account for 67 per cent of India's merchandise exports, and 43 per cent of total exports.

During the last six decades, industrial composition has diversified significantly: basic and intermediate goods' share has gone up; capital goods' share peaked in 1970, but declined precipitously thereafter (Table 1). In other words, from producing simple consumer goods, India is now capable of designing and manufacturing sophisticated capital equipment, including much of the requirements of advanced industries like atomic energy, space communication, and defence equipment. Indian industry is predominantly domestically owned and managed, with high domestic content in its exports.

Table 1 Changing Composition of Industrial Output

Industry	1956	1960	1970	1980	1993–4	2004–5
Basic goods	22.33	25.11	32.28	33.23	35.5	45.7
Capital goods	4.71	11.76	15.25	14.98	9.3	8.8
Intermediate goods	24.59	25.88	20.95	21.33	26.5	15.7
Consumer durables	48.37	37.25	31.52	30.46	28.7	29.8
(a)Durables	–	5.68	3.41	3.81	5.4	8.5
(b)Non-durables	–	31.57	28.11	26.65	23.3	21.4

Source: *Economic Survey* (various issues); 'Quick Estimates of Industrial Production and Use-based Index for Month of July, 2011 (Base 2004–5 = 100)', Press Note, 12 September 2011, CSO.
Note: This is based on the weighting diagrams of successive indexes of industrial production.

While industrial growth since 1950 represents a significant departure over the colonial period (1.7 per cent per year in the first half of the 20th century), it is roughly comparable to the average of all developing economies, but distinctly slower than that in East Asia, and just about two-thirds of China's, with a much lower share of capital goods, and much slower growth in manufactured exports. In 2010, India was the world's ninth largest manufacturing nation, though the output per head was extremely modest, according to United Nations Industrial Development Organisation' *International Yearbook of Industrial Statistics* (2011).

Phases of Growth

The first 15 years of planning since 1951–2 witnessed an annual growth of about 7 per cent, with notable achievements in import substitution of all major basic and capital goods, mostly produced in the public sector (Table 2). To illustrate, three major steels mills, a heavy electrical machinery plant, a mining machinery plant, and four machine tool plants were set up during this period, laying the foundations for a diversified and self-reliant economy. By the late 1960s, Indian steel was probably one of the cheapest in the world, gaining a potential edge in the export of metal manufactures.

Table 2 Trends in Growth Rates of Output in Industry and Manufacturing

	Industry	Manufacturing	GDP
1951–65	6.9	6.9	4.0
1966–80	4.2	4.8	3.6
1951–80	5.4	5.3	3.6
1981–91	7.0	7.4	5.6
1981–2008	6.2	6.2	5.9
1992–2008	6.7	6.6	6.5
1951–2008	5.4	5.4	4.5

Source: *National Accounts Statistics* (various issues).
Note: Industry includes mining, manufacturing, electricity, gas and water, and construction.

The growth momentum, however, could not be sustained after the mid-1960s for a variety of reasons: consecutive crop failures in 1965 and 1966, border conflicts with neighbours, and freezing of US aid and consequent currency devaluation made it difficult to continue with the 'heavy industrialization' strategy. With food inflation in the 1960s and the oil crisis in the 1970s, the focus of economic policy shifted to attaining self-sufficiency in food grains and reducing import dependence in commercial fuels. This period also witnessed inclusion of a variety of 'distributive' considerations in policymaking that probably diverted the scarce physical and administrative resources in pursuing the development of backward areas, promotion of small industry, curbing of monopolies, and promotion of new entrepreneurship, and so on. Thus, industrial growth slowed down on a secular basis to around 4 to 4.5 per cent per year in the next 15 years (1966–80).

However, industrial growth has turned around since 1980–1 with improvement in public infrastructure investment and agriculture performance and with industry once again becoming the economy's 'leading' sector, regaining the rates of growth attained in the first 15-year period. Manufactured exports have also showed improvements after the mid-1980s with the depreciation of the real exchange rate. The revival is also associated with a gradual loosening of controls on imports, domestic output and investment, and greater openness to foreign capital and technology.

The pace of deregulation picked up speed after 1991, as part of the structural adjustment programme that sought to decisively shift the coordination of economic decision-making in favour of markets and away from the state, with much greater external orientation than ever after Independence. The reforms triggered an industrial boom during 1992–6, which however, was short-lived, signaling the onset of deceleration that persisted until 2002–3.

The following five years (2003–4 to 2007–8) witnessed yet another boom (along with an acceleration in the growth in the services sector), taking India to a higher growth path. Industrial growth since 1990–1 is best captured in Figure 1. A massive road building effort 'crowded-in' private investment in trucks and automobiles, and increase in credit to the household sector boosted demand for consumer durables and residential construction, which seem to largely 'explain' the recent growth episode (Nagaraj 2008). The boom in exports of IT services also seems to have contributed to demand for industrial goods and commercial real estate.

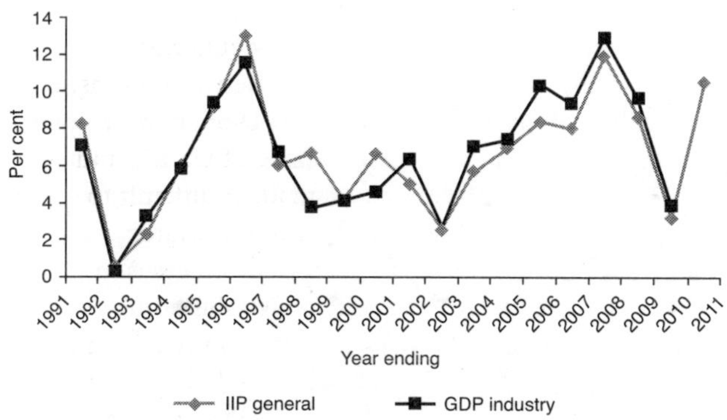

Figure 1 Industrial Growth, 1991–2010

Industrial Policy

Consistent with the professional opinion of the times, industrialization was the prime mover of India's development planning in the 1950s. Given its size, the stage of development, and natural resources endowments, import-substitution was seen as the 'natural' choice with a growing role for public sector in capital and technology-intensive industries. Moreover, for a large and diverse country, *a priori*, it was perhaps difficult to be sure where its dynamic comparative advantage, in fact, lay. The Mahalanobis model that provided the analytical underpinning for the strategy was premised on the view that the binding constraint on maximizing the economy's long-term growth potential was the lack of domestic machine-building capability, considering the widely held pessimism about export possibilities around that time. However, in order to meet the employment objective, an extended version of the model envisaged protection of traditional methods and organizations of production with fiscal and administrative measures.

To implement this strategy a large administrative machinery was set up to grant industrial and import licences. After the mid-1960s, as mentioned earlier, numerous 'distributive' objectives were superimposed on the import substitution policy that rendered licensing highly discretionary. With accumulating evidence on inefficiencies of the 'Licence Raj', and slower growth after the mid-1960s, there was a gradual dismantling of the regulatory regime since 1980 that culminated in the near complete 'bonfire' of control in 1991.

Financing of Growth

In the planning era, industrial investments were almost entirely domestically financed with public-sector commercial banks providing short-term (working) capital, development banks (IDBI, IFCI, and ICICI) supplying long-term credit, and the capital market playing a negligible role. However, after the reforms the sources of finance got diversified, with the coming in of private commercial banks, foreign direct investments, and portfolio investors, and the freedom granted to large domestic firms to tap international capital markets.

Yet, Indian industry remains predominantly domestically financed, and the financial system is bank-centric. With the demise of development financial institutions, and debt market yet to take their place, it is commercial banks that are now meeting most of the demand for long-term finance, with the maturity structure of the loans getting significantly shorter. Role of foreign-owned firms and foreign direct investment in Indian industry is as yet modest, though prominent in technology-intensive industries like pharmaceuticals and electrical machinery. For most of the period, despite a significant policy boost, the stock market has played a limited role—mainly financing large firms, while small- and medium-sized firms depended almost entirely on bank credit.

Industrial Labour

The industrial labour market remains dualistic: factory workers are part of the organized sector, with numerous laws protecting them and the extent of protection increasing with the factory size. However, the share of organized industrial labour in manufacturing employment has shrunk with growing competition, increasing sub-contracting of low value-added work to the unregistered sector, the spread of electricity, and access to credit and physical infrastructure.

Workers in the unregistered sector are part of the urban unorganized (informal) labour market that has grown significantly on account of the shift of the workforce from agriculture, and a decline in the share of organized labour. Given the excess supply of (unskilled) labour, wages in this sector tend to be close to the competitive equilibrium that is marginally higher than that for those in rural areas, adjusting for higher costs of living in urban areas. Yet, these workers have a better chance of getting formal education for their children, acquiring employable skills, and having access to rudiments of healthcare that could improve their potential earnings.

Explanation for Growth

What explains India's modest industrial performance over the long period? In other words, why has Indian industry remained undersized, despite industrialization being the centrepiece of its development strategy? There are broadly two kinds of explanations. Following classical economic percepts, in a large agrarian economy, the size of the industrial sector depends on the size and growth of agricultural surplus (after meeting farmers' food requirements) and of exports. Since the trade ratios for large economies tend to be small, it is agricultural productivity that mainly determines industrial demand. Further, inadequate public investment in irrigation and power could have restricted the breaking of the agrarian barriers for modernization and augmenting farm productivity (Chakravarty 1986).

However, the mainstream economic view holds that the small size of the industrial sector is mainly the result of policy-induced restrictions on output and investment that have constrained the supply response of domestic enterprises to exploit international markets for labour-intensive manufactures. Further, insulation from the international economy could have denied India the opportunities of trade and investment that have been historically important transmission mechanisms of augmenting demand and for technical progress (Bhagwati 1993).

After two decades of liberal reforms during which the much criticized state interventions were whittled down, industry has now become more competitive; quality and variety of domestic manufactures has improved significantly; and export composition has become more diversified. Yet, industrial growth rate at best has remained as good as it was in the 1980s, even after the recent boom is taken into account. Share of industrial output and exports has not moved in favour of labour-intensive goods, as expected in theory. Why? In other words, why have two decades of gradual market-oriented reforms not been able to accelerate industrial growth and export of labour-intensive manufactures, as advocated in reforms literature?

Again, the explanations can be broadly grouped into two categories. One, that the reforms have remained incomplete: industrial labour market remains rigid with little freedom for employers to hire and fire workers; infrastructure remains in short supply and of poor quality; and financial integration is incomplete without capital account convertibility. Freedom to hire and fire workers, for instance, could restrict employers' ability to set up large-scale factories, as is done in China, to reap the economies of scale in production. The alternative explanation emphasizes demand constraints originating from poor agricultural performance after the reforms, inadequate public infrastructure investment, and inadequate credit for agriculture and small enterprises (Nagaraj 2011).

There is unanimity on the need for stepping up infrastructure investment, but not on how it should be done, who should provide it, and how it is to be financed. Pointing to the alleged public-sector inefficiencies, policymakers are keen to bring in private participation (including foreign capital) into this sector and implement it through public–private partnership (PPP). Despite an improved tax–GDP ratio and sustained improvement in the financial performance of the public sector, there is a great reluctance to revive public infrastructure investment one suspects, on account of the fiscal orthodoxy (Nagaraj 2009).

R. NAGARAJ

References

Bhagwati, Jagdish. 1993. *India's Economy: The Shackled Giant*, Oxford, Clarendon Press.

Chakravarty, Sukhamoy. 1986. *Development Planning: The India Experience*, Oxford, Clarendon Press.

Nagaraj, R. 2008. 'India's Recent Economic Growth: A Closer Look', *Economic and Political Weekly*, 12 April, 43(15): 55–62.

——. 2009. 'Public Sector Performance Since 1950: A Fresh Look', in Gopal K. Kadekodi and Brinda Viswanathan (eds), *Agricultural Development, Rural Institutions and Economic Policy*, New Delhi, Oxford University Press.

——. 2011. 'Industrial Performance, 1991–2008: A Review', in D.M. Nachane (ed.), *India Development Report 2011*, New Delhi, Oxford University Press.

■ Industrialization

Before the Industrial Revolution, India accounted for a quarter of the world's industrial output. Rise of modern industry and trade in the 19th century had a complex impact on Indian industry. Some segments of traditional industry declined, and there was a fall in India's share of world industrial production. At the same time, some segments of traditional industry gained from the new economy, and a modern mechanized factory sector arose using low-cost labour, natural resources, and plentiful entrepreneurial talent. At the time of independence from British colonial rule in 1947, the indigenous business class was a strong force in economic and political terms, and played a leading role in the import-substituting industrialization regime that followed. The regime effectively ended in the 1990s, inaugurating a more open economy that has seen significant diversification in the nature of manufacturing activity and participants in a relatively short time.

This entry will deal with industrialization in the long run, with reference to modern industry, whereas traditional industry is discussed more fully elsewhere (see entry titled 'Handicrafts' in this volume).

Trends

In 1901, 13.9 million industrial workers formed 10.5 per cent of the entire workforce in South Asia. In 1991, 28.7 million workers made up 9.4 per cent of the workforce. The share of industry in national income grew somewhat faster from 11.1 per cent in 1900–10 to 16.4 per cent in 1940–6 and 27 per cent in 2000 in the Indian union. In terms of employment and income, the region did not industrialize rapidly. And yet this impression of very little structural change may be misleading. A combination of policy and market factors has ensured that job growth occurred mainly in small factories, whereas household industry declined, and growth of jobs remained small in large factories where much of the income growth was concentrated. In other words, in the long run, industrialization has been accompanied by institutional changes such that the average worker may now be working harder than a century ago, and under worse conditions. How this transformation came about is an interesting question.

'Modern' industry can be defined as manufacturing units that use machines and non-human sources of energy, employ wage labour, and are subject to some form of regulation. Modern industry tends to be approximated by the scale of 'factories' registered under the Factories Act. This is not a perfect measure, but it is the best available. By this measure, employment in modern India, in British India and the princely states, increased from 400,000 in 1891 to 1,570,000 in 1938. The corresponding figure for the Indian union stood at 10 million in 1991. Employment in modern industry as a percentage of industrial employment increased from 5 in 1891 to 11 in 1938 (it was 29 in the Indian union in 1991). The share of factories in real income generated by industry increased from about 15 per cent in 1900 to 45 in 1947 (it was 55–60 per cent in the mid-1990s in the Indian union).

History

Impressive as this record was, the growth was initially uneven. In colonial India, industries around Bombay and Calcutta accounted for about half of factory employment. Cities that pulled a number of key resources together—ports, a history of export trade, resident capitalists, European settlement, railway termini, water and power, financial markets, and labour markets—were very few in number in the mid-19th century, and these cities saw the beginning of industrialization. However, as key resources like capital, labour, knowledge, and infrastructure began to spread, so did industrialization. Thus by 1947, Ahmedabad, Madras, and Kanpur were also major industrial centres. Reflecting the crucial importance of cheap natural resources in Indian industrialization, nearly half of all factory employment was engaged in cotton and jute textiles. Other important groups included food, tobacco, and leather. The share of chemicals, metals, and machinery was small. Machinery and manufactured intermediate goods were largely imported. In this sparse landscape, a few bold import-substitution initiatives stood out. Tata steel of Jamshedpur was the most significant example.

The first burst of investment in cotton and jute mills occurred in the third quarter of the 19th century. The capital came partly from foreign investment and partly from capital accumulated by Indians in the early-19th-century trade in opium and cotton. The growth of India's trade with China after the East India Company's monopoly in China trade ended (1834–5) played an important role in the origin of mill enterprise. The steamship (from the 1830s), the telegraph (from the 1860s), and the Suez Canal (1869) brought the continents closer. The American Civil War (1865), which cut off supplies of American cotton to Lancashire, created a boom in Indian cotton trade and large profits, part of which found their way into cotton mills. This episode, together with a tea mania of a similar nature in Calcutta and a gold mania in Madras, stimulated the local stock exchanges.

The First World War was a landmark event. On the one hand, massive excess demand for Indian goods developed. On the other hand, machinery, raw materials, spares, and chemicals normally imported from Britain or Germany stopped coming in. The immediate impact of supply constraints was inflation from which cotton, jute, and steel emerged as gainers. The long-term impact was a change in official mindset. Until the War, the government followed a hands-off policy in respect of Indian industry and a buy-British policy in respect of purchases for defence, railways, or administration. After the War, the government began to look towards local sources and became more open to promoting such sources. The use of protective tariffs for industrial promotion was sanctioned. This measure led to dramatic growth in sugar, steel, cement, matches, paper, and woollen textiles, in some cases leading to overcapacity. However, problems of poor management and inefficiency had begun to show up in the older industries like textiles, and tariffs could not shelter industry from those problems. There were consequently attempts to introduce new technology and management practices, to voluntarily restrict supplies, and to squeeze labour a little harder.

Pioneers in modern industry came from communities that had specialized in trading and banking activities. On the western coast, the Parsis, Khojas, Bhatias, the Gujarati traders and bankers based in Ahmedabad, and the Bombay-based Baghdadi Jews, were the early millowners. Several of these communities had a history of collaboration with Europeans. Some had withdrawn from maritime trade as European firms based in London took control of this sphere. In Calcutta, and largely north and south India, Europeans dominated the import–export trade, banking and insurance, and eventually jute, engineering, mines, plantations, railways, power, and dockyards. Commodity trade, however, was not in European hands, but in the hands of Indian traders, chiefly the so-called Marwaris. By the end of the inter-War period, prominent Marwari firms in Calcutta had entered the jute industry and, on a smaller scale, sugar, paper, cement, construction, and share broking. The European capitalists did not welcome this trend. Consequently, a schism opened in Calcutta's industrial–commercial world that took a toll when large European firms became targets of hostile takeovers shortly after Independence. Seeds of Calcutta's precipitous industrial decline after 1960, thus, had their roots in the city's schizophrenic business culture.

Import-substituting Industrialization and Beyond

The shared experience of colonialism had created, in the 1950s, a consensus among economists and politicians on the need to restrain trade and build a strong government. It was then held that free trade and a non-interventionist state, tenets of liberalism to which colonial governments adhered, had impoverished and 'drained' the resources of the colonies. Emulating the Soviet model, industrial policy placed emphasis on the development of heavy machinery and material production. Since domestic production of goods which used a scarce and expensive resource like capital could lead to high cost of production, tariffs were steeply raised. On the other hand, scarce resources needed to be rationed, which led to industrial licensing.

This new economic policy depended for its success on comprehensive controls. To exercise command over financial capital, banking and insurance were nationalized and interest rates controlled. The government was the sole channel for import of essential raw materials and food. To reduce the fiscal burden, exchange rates were fixed and overvalued. Because the government had privileged access to scarce resources, government investment in capital-intensive industry became inevitable. The public sector established industries or nationalized them. Expansion in steel and heavy machinery was almost entirely in the state sector. A large part of the cotton textile mill industry was nationalized. The only area of 'free trade' was bilateral trade with the Soviet Union. Encouragement to export was provided by export bonus and entitlement schemes, often at high fiscal costs.

Import-substituting industrialization generated quick returns for about a decade and a half, followed by economic slowdown. The point of transition came when prospects of manufacturing growth by selling in the limited home market were exhausted. The high cost and poor quality of goods produced for the home market discouraged growth of demand. The extreme form of import protection practised in India, with average tariff rates close to 100 per cent, hurt export. Whereas freer trade in the colonial period had given domestic industry access to new technologies and helped it learn, restricted trade made learning difficult and reduced competitiveness. Poor export effort and high budget deficits worsened inflation and balance of payments. Inefficiency 'spilled over'. For example, the relatively high cost of locally produced machines raised the cost of goods made using those machines. Comparative advantages were ignored. As resources were channelled into non-competitive capital goods, potentially exportable labour-intensive manufactures were denied capital. Resources, thus, were made to move to sectors with lower return to capital and lower employment potential. The later years of import substitution, thus, were characterized by low levels of factor productivity and low employment potentials.

Between 1985 and 1995, a package of trade and industrial reforms was introduced in India. The reform package had a predictable composition: liberalization of exchange rates, reduction in tariffs, easing of industrial regulation, and rollback of state investment. The end of the regime saw a rise in income, employment, and export growth rates, and the avoidance of a serious macroeconomic crisis. But the greater role of markets in directing investment and the partial rollback of government spending increased inequality, especially regional inequality, in the pattern of industrialization.

Industry Illustrations

A few industry illustrations may be in order. One pattern that cuts across several broad industry groups in the 30-odd years of import substitution is the reorientation in several formerly exporting industries towards the domestic market. Three significant examples are tea, textiles, and steel. In the tea industry, the export–production ratio declined from 70 per cent in 1950 to 27 per cent in 1991. In textiles, despite having developed a mill industry almost soon after Britain, India retreated from the world market from the 1950s. At the same time, rates of investment and quality improvements also dropped. The domestic market, apart from being protected by very high tariffs, initially did not consume high-quality products, so that the existing producers were not under pressure to invest in quality and produce improvement or to compete on quality. But government policy also played a role in inducing a shift from exports to the home market. Price controls in tea exports, for example, discouraged potential buyers of Indian tea.

The textile policy in place between 1950 and 1985 is a notorious example of intervention. Designed to shelter handlooms from competition, it paralysed the mills with restrictions. Faced with a sluggish market and restrictions on the choice of techniques, mills withdrew from exports, whereas small weaving factories called 'powerlooms' captured the domestic market. Investments in new technology stagnated. The technological paradigm that came to rule the cotton textile industry until the late 1980s was one that used very old generic machines, produced generic cloths at very cheap prices, and catered to the home market. In steel, protection, discouragement of exports, and public-sector dominance led to very slow growth that failed to achieve the full potential of the industry, given India's abundant supplies of coal and iron ore, and a large unmet demand.

A second general pattern in pre-reform industrialization was a positive trend. In knowledge-based industries, principally pharmaceuticals, implicit protection such as a process patents regime fostered indigenous research and development, though largely of an imitative kind. This development stood India in good stead at the end of the millennium, as several firms emerged from this experience with superior research capability. In general, the accent on higher and technical education throughout the Nehruvian era, unfortunately at the cost of basic education, worked to the advantage of building capability in knowledge-based industries, which performed well in the post-reform period.

Conventional manufacturing industries saw relatively rapid growth in the 1950s and 1960s, followed by a long stagnation. With trade liberalization, all had to adapt to the sudden increase in competition and the opportunity to sell in the export market. This reintegration with the world market has helped labour-intensive industries such as textiles and clothing regain a 'leading-sector' role, a process in which the home and export markets have played broadly compatible roles. But, on the other hand, the reforms have also driven many weak overcapitalized firms to bankruptcy, and exposed areas of serious institutional deficiency. The transition is still ongoing.

TIRTHANKAR ROY

References

Gokarn, S., A. Sen, and R. Vaidya (eds). 2002. *The Structure of Indian Industry*, Delhi, Oxford University Press.

Krueger, A.O. (ed.). 2002. *Economic Policy Reforms and the Indian Economy*, Chicago, The University of Chicago Press.

Morris, M.D. 1983. 'The Growth of Large-scale Industry to 1947', in D. Kumar and M. Desai (eds), *The Cambridge Economic History of India*, Vol. 2, Cambridge, UK, Cambridge University Press.

Uchikawa, S. (ed.). 2002. *Economic Reforms and Industrial Structure in India*, Delhi, Manohar.

■ Industry

Industry accounts for about 27 per cent of GDP in the Indian economy. This is significantly smaller than the average share of 35 per cent for developing countries as a whole. The share of manufacturing in India's industrial value-added is 80 per cent. Textiles, chemicals including pharmaceuticals, and basic metals including steel are some of the major sectors in manufacturing. Software, pharmaceuticals, biotechnology, and auto components have emerged as the dynamic sectors in the post-1991 period. The electricity sector has been an area of major policy attention but reforms have been slow.

Indian industry experienced slow growth and poor productivity performance during the period from 1950 to 1980. The policy regime had strong preference for the public sector, extensive controls over private investment, a highly protective trade policy, and inflexible labour laws (especially after the mid-1970s). Promotion of the small-scale sector and regional balance were additional objectives of the industrial policy regime. Up to the mid-1960s, policy instruments were aimed at purposive diversification within the industrial sector and increased public investment. The period after the mid-1960s witnessed a marked deepening of the import-substitution regime and strengthening of domestic regulatory structures. This period witnessed a significant deceleration in growth to 4 per cent per annum compared to 6.1 per cent in the period from 1950 to 1965.

The decade of the 1980s witnessed some experimentation with domestic deregulation that yielded handsome dividends in productivity gains and acceleration in growth to 7 per cent per annum. In 1991, in response to a major balance-of-payments crisis, India made a radical shift away from its long-standing policy of inward orientation, and the subsequent reforms have moved the policy regime significantly towards market orientation, deregulation, and liberalization. Indian industry has responded to the increased competition—domestic as well as foreign—with significant restructuring, although the constraints arising from poor infrastructure, largely unreformed public-sector, slowly reforming banking sector, inflexible labour laws, and other barriers to exit stand in the way of faster adjustment to the new and emerging policy regime which is inspired by market orientation.

The Pre-reform Regime

The pre-reform industrial policy regime relied heavily on the development of a public sector to cater to the infrastructure needs of development and to provide direction to the process of industrial development within a mixed economy framework. Besides 'reserving' certain strategic areas of industrial production, for example, iron and steel, coal, transport, power, mineral oils, atomic energy, arms and ammunition, and allied items of defence equipment, in the public sector, the state also acted as the leading entrepreneur in machine tools, non-ferrous metals, fertilizers, and so on. Nevertheless, the private sector was expected to play a major role, especially in the provision of consumer goods and building up the small-scale sector.

Industrial licensing was a major instrument of control of the private sector under which central government permission was needed for both investment in new units and for substantial expansion of capacity in existing units. Licensing also controlled technology, output mix, capacity location, and import content. Large industrial houses needed separate permission for investment or expansion under the Monopolies and Restrictive Trade Practices (MRTP) Act so as to prevent the concentration of economic power. There were price and distribution controls in industries such as fertilizers, cement, aluminium, petroleum, and pharmaceuticals. Almost 800 items were reserved for production by small-scale units as a way of protecting the small-scale sector from competition from large-scale units. There were also barriers to industrial restructuring and exit of firms.

India's import tariffs were among the highest in the world, with duty rates above 200 per cent being fairly common and tariff rates being highly dispersed. Imports of manufactured consumer goods were completely banned. For the rest, only some goods were freely importable, and for most items where domestic substitutes were being produced, imports were only possible with import licences. The criteria for issuing these licences were non-transparent, delays were endemic, and corruption unavoidable. Policies towards foreign investment were quite restrictive, reflecting the general protectionist thrust of industrial policy.

The period from 1950 to 1980 experienced stagnant industrial growth at the rate of 5.5 per cent per annum. However, significant diversification of the industrial structure was achieved. But total factor productivity (a measure of the efficiency with which labour and capital are used in generating value added in the manufacturing sector) is estimated to have stagnated/declined during the period from 1960 to 1980. The high-cost industrial structure resulting from the heavily protectionist policy regime created an anti-export bias in the industrial sector. The erosion of competitiveness could be seen in the secular decline of India's share in global exports of manufactured goods from 1 per cent in 1950 to 0.4 per cent in 1980.

Beginning of Reforms in the 1980s

A central focus of the reforms was the improvement of industrial productivity. Some important features included selective removal of industrial licensing, import liberalization for exports, partial liberalization of trade policies and procedures, and changes in the foreign direct investment (FDI) regime for capital goods. However, the reservation of production for the small-scale sector continued even while it constituted an important hurdle in the way of developing export capability in labour-intensive sectors such as garments, leather products, and sports goods, where India has comparative advantage. Industrial policy in the 1980s also paid little attention to facilitating the restructuring of the industrial sector by removing the numerous barriers to exit.

Trade policies during the 1980s were consciously designed to improve efficiency and promote exports. The driving force for the reform was easier access to imported intermediate inputs to facilitate capacity utilization and modern capital goods for technological upgradation. Export subsidies were provided in order to offset the anti-export bias resulting from the protectionist regime.

The limited domestic deregulation and trade policy reforms were successful in creating conditions in which productivity in the Indian manufacturing sector grew at 2.7 per cent per annum in the 1980s compared to a growth rate of –0.5 per cent per annum in the earlier two decades. The industrial growth rate also accelerated to over 7 per cent per annum in the 1980s. Exports of manufactured goods grew at about 11 per cent per annum during the decade. A 45 per cent depreciation in the real effective exchange rate in the second half of the 1980s was one of the factors responsible for a significant acceleration in the growth of these exports from 4.5 per cent per annum in the first half of the 1980s to 21.7 per cent per annum in the second half.

The sustainability of the better growth and productivity performance of the industrial sector, however, was being put to test by a deteriorating macroeconomic environment, largely on account of the growing fiscal profligacy of the Government of India during the 1980s. The Gulf War of 1990 and the political instability at the turn of the decade further contributed towards a collapse of international confidence in the Indian economy. The result was the balance-of-payments crisis of 1991.

Economic Reforms since 1991

The response to the balance-of-payments crisis was to not only put in place policies for macroeconomic stabilization but also seize the opportunity to launch wide-ranging economic reforms to realize the potential of the Indian economy for higher growth. Beginning in 1991, policymakers attempted to take significant steps towards integrating the economy with the world and improving the macroeconomic environment from the deterioration of the 1980s. The transformation in the policy regime away from extensive control and a strong inward orientation in the decade and a half since 1991 has been attained through incremental/gradualist changes, occasional reversals, and without any big ideological U-turns. Coalitions of various political parties at the Centre and different political parties ruling the states have taken turns in moving the economic reform process forward, albeit in a haphazard manner.

The period from 1991–2 to 1996–7 saw rapid and wide-ranging reforms in industrial and trade policies, tax policies, and other policies impacting on macroeconomic management. There was a distinct slowing down of reforms after 1996–7 partly because of complacency at the favourable response to the early reforms, partly because of confusion resulting from change of government at the Centre, and also because by the mid-1990s, the competition had begun to pinch and Indian industry was becoming less supportive of change including external liberalization. In 2001 India regained the momentum of change towards improving the environment for private investment, opening the economy to foreign competition, and infrastructure development. However, macroeconomic management (after an excellent start when the consolidated fiscal deficit of the Centre and the states was brought down from 9.6 per cent of GDP in 1990–1 to 7 per cent in 1992–3) has been an area of weakness that could undermine the achievement of sustainable growth at high rates in the future.

The industrial policy reforms during the 1990s were bold in doing away with numerous barriers to entry, for example, removal of industrial licensing for investment, opening up all but a few strategic areas to other than the public sector, and, more recently, replacing the earlier MRTP Act with a new Competition Law to regulate anti-competitive behaviour. Even on the policy of reservation for the small-scale sector, a beginning was made by dereserving a number of items, although the task remains essentially unfinished. Also, the microeconomic reforms and judicial reforms which would make the factor markets more flexible and enable individual firms to benefit from the more competitive environment were slow to come.

Trade policy reforms made a radical break with the past by discontinuing with the complex system of import licensing and making an open commitment to lowering the tariff rates on imports. At the outset, import licensing was dispensed with for most goods other than consumer goods, thereby removing a major source of corruption and inefficiency. In 2001 India finally began to remove the quantitative restrictions on consumer goods and agricultural products over a three-year period.

Import duties were reduced gradually if not always steadily. After a sharp decline from an average of 73 per cent in 1991–2 to around 25 per cent in 1996–7, the import-weighted import duty crept up again to 36 per cent in 2000–1, reflecting a revival of protectionist pressure from established Indian industry. Subsequently there was a reversal of this trend and the government reiterated the objective of reducing India's tariff protection rates to Association of East Asian Nations (ASEAN) levels. However, even at 18 per cent in 2005, import duty rates in India are still the highest among the developing countries.

In the 1990s the FDI rules were liberalized with a view to gaining improved access to technology and world markets and also helping release the resource constraints on investment. Many industries were deregulated and opened to FDI. For others, the Foreign Investment Promotion Board was set up to expedite applications for foreign investment. As of December 2005, the FDI policy allows 100 per cent foreign ownership in a large number of industries and majority ownership in all except banks, insurance companies, airlines, and certain types of mining. In addition, the Indian stock market has been opened for investment in equity to foreign institutional investors (FIIs). These policy changes have led to a sharp increase in FDI flows from almost nothing in 1990 to over $5–6 billion, but the levels are still much below those in China.

A major challenge of the reforms was how to attract private investment into sectors such as electricity, telecommunications, roads, railways, ports, and airports, in order to meet the enormous investment requirements of upgrading infrastructure. These sectors were opened up to private investment at different times in the subsequent years with varying degrees of success.

Telecommunications is the area where reforms have been most successful, helped by the fact that pricing of telecom services (unlike that of power) was not uneconomic. Access to telecom services has expanded greatly, costs have come down, and quality improved as a handful of strong private-sector telecom service suppliers are competing effectively with the public-sector companies. Private investment has also been attracted in ports and more recently in airports. In roads, new investment has been dominantly in the public sector, as is the case in most countries, but there has been some limited private-sector involvement which could increase in future.

The biggest disappointment has been in the power sector, mainly because both the reform of the incumbent public-sector and the setting up of an effective regulatory framework have been slow to come. The expectations of attracting large investments in generation capacity were belied by the continuing financial problems of the distribution segment which remains unviable because of a combination of unrealistically low tariffs for some sections of consumers (households and farmers) and very large inefficiencies in collection. In recent years, attempts have been made to depoliticize the process of fixing power tariffs. The Electricity Act of 2003 lays out a broad legal framework of regulation for the sector and effectively empowers state governments to accelerate power-sector reforms through fostering greater competition, increased involvement of the private sector, and better governance. But many details remain to be put in place.

Profit-making public-sector units (PSUs) were allowed greater autonomy and larger freedom to raise resources in the capital market, but the relatively less well-performing PSUs languished for want of public funds and political will to restructure, privatize, or close down. A Disinvestment Commission was set up in 1997, but privatization was not seriously put on the policy agenda until 2001. A few public-sector enterprises were privatized with the transfer of management control during 2001–3, the most important being BALCO (Bharat Aluminium Company Ltd), which was sold to a 'strategic' private investor. But resistance surfaced strongly when privatization of two oil companies was attempted. Further brakes were put on privatization by the new government which came to power in 2004. The current policy is that profit-making public-sector enterprises will not be privatized although sale of government equity can continue as long as the government retains 51 per cent.

The increased market orientation of the policy regime generated a favourable investment response from the private sector up to 1996–7. Indeed, the rate of private fixed investment increased from a low of 12.9 per cent in 1991–2 to 15.9 per cent in 1996–7. Following a two-year period of decline, private fixed investments resumed an upward trend, reaching 19.1 per cent in 2004–5.

The slowdown in reforms after 1996–7, together with a worsening of the external economic environment after the Asian financial crisis, resulted in slowing down of industrial growth rate. From 12.3 per cent in 1995–6, industrial growth rate dropped to 7.7 per cent in 1996–7 and 3.8 per cent in each of the successive two years. The subsequent period has shown industrial revival with the growth rate accelerating to 6.8 per cent, 7.9 per cent, and 8.9 per cent in the latest three years for which data are available, that is, 2002–3, 2003–4, and 2004–5, respectively. Moreover, the software boom has continued and created a new brand image for India in world markets.

There is substantial evidence to suggest that Indian industry has been restructuring and reducing costs in a slow but steady manner since the mid-1990s. The pace of adjustment and adaptation has been slow in some of the important traditional industries, for example, textiles and garments which are facing new challenges of the competitive world market scenario after the end of the multi-fibre arrangement (MFA) in January 2005. On the other hand, pharmaceuticals and automotive components are examples of manufacturing industries that have successfully turned around and developed a global vision to penetrate world markets.

The Indian pharmaceutical industry currently has a global market share of 1 per cent, and the share of its exports in total output has increased from 32 per cent in 2000–1 to 35 per cent in 2004–5. While making inroads into the fast-growing generics market worldwide, the industry is also positioning itself under the new Intellectual Property Rights (IPR) regime through increased research and development (R&D) expenditures and strategic alliances to move up the value chain. With a more liberal foreign investment policy, multinational corporations and international generics companies have also been attracted to restructure their operations and increase their stakes in existing ventures in India and set up new ventures. The auto-components industry has also significantly improved its export orientation, having trebled its exports between 2001–2 and 2004–5 and increased its export share in output from 13 per cent to 16 per cent over the same period.

The post-reform era has also spurred the development of the biotechnology industry which is driven by new enterprise and new innovation. Skilled human resources, active government support, and increased investment—public as well as private—promises sustained growth of this industry with global orientation. India is emerging as the most favoured destination for collaborative R&D, bioinformatics, contract research and manufacturing, and clinical research as a result of growing compliance with internationally harmonized standards. Several states have taken steps to develop bio-clusters based on academic and entrepreneurial strengths.

Export performance of manufactured goods provides some indication of how Indian industry has fared in attaining global competitiveness. While data on India's penetration in world markets are not readily available, the trend growth of India's exports shows Indian industry on the move. Between 1991–2 and 2001–2, India improved its growth of manufactured goods exports to 11.8 per cent per annum from the 11.4 per cent per annum of the 1980s. This was significant as it came on the higher base of the 1980s and was attained after allowing for adjustment to the balance-of-payments crisis of 1991. The subsequent two years for which data are available show even higher growth rates of manufactured goods exports, that is, 22 per cent and 17 per cent, respectively.

Isher Judge Ahluwalia

Inequality

Inequality has been a key theme in the research agenda of economists because of: (i) the intrinsic ethical attractiveness of equality and (ii) the significant implications of inequality for many macroeconomic variables like growth and poverty. Although issues related to inequality can be analysed along several dimensions, we deal mostly with inequality in income or consumption and wealth.

Before undertaking a study of inequality one is always confronted with the issue of how to measure inequality. Since it is impossible to describe and compare the distribution of income of the whole population, it is necessary to have summary measures. One can get an idea of inequality by using rough measures like the share of the, say, bottom 10 or top 10 per cent of the population. However, such a measure ignores the intermediate 80 per cent of the population. There is now a large body of literature dealing with the measurement of inequality (Sen 1997).

One of the most commonly used measures of income or consumption inequality is the Gini coefficient. It measures the extent to which the distribution of income or consumption among individuals deviates from the equal distribution. A high value of this coefficient signifies a more unequal distribution. Let us consider a population of N individuals with incomes $Y_1, Y_2, \ldots, Y_N$. We can plot the cumulative percentages of total income received by cumulative percentages of the population starting from the poorest. Such a plot is called the Lorenz curve. Obviously, for equal incomes, X per cent of the population will always enjoy X per cent of the total income and the Lorenz curve is the diagonal straight line. Otherwise, the curve always lies below this line since the bottom X percentage of the population will always have less than X per cent of the total income. The Gini coefficient captures the gap between the actual Lorenz curve of the economy and the hypothetical equal distribution line.

Algebraically, the Gini coefficient can be computed using the following formula:

$$G = \frac{1}{2N^2Y^*} \sum_{i=1}^{N} \sum_{j=1}^{N} |Y_i - Y_j|$$

where Y^* is the mean income $Y^* = (\sum_{i=1}^{N} Y_i)/N)$ and $|Y_i - Y_j|$ is the absolute difference between incomes of individuals i and j. It considers differences over all pairs of incomes and there are N^2 such pairs of incomes. Hence, it can be viewed as one half of the mean of absolute values of differences between all income pairs. This measure of inequality has many desirable features.

In the Indian context, the consumption expenditure surveys (National Sample Survey [NSS]) constitute the most basic source of inequality measurement. These surveys are conducted on a regular basis and cover a fairly large sample of households. Recently, individual tax return data have been used to analyse income shares of individuals in the top earnings bracket. Since most of the population is exempt from income taxation, it is possible to look at only the top 1 per cent of the population. The various measures in Table 1 provide a snapshot

Table 1 Inequality in India Computed Using Various Measures, 1951–2004

Year	Gini[a,b]	Consumption[b] shares of bottom 20%	Consumption[b] shares of top 20%	Income[c] shares of Top 1%
1951	35.56	7.0	43.0	13.42
1960	32.59	8.4	41.4	12.31
1965	31.14	8.8	40.0	10.92
1970	30.38	8.8	39.5	10.02
1973	29.17	9.0	38.1	7.02
1977	32.14	8.5	40.9	6.18
1983	31.49	8.6	40.5	6.46
1986	32.22	8.5	41.1	8.64
1988	31.15	9.0	40.5	8.52
1992	32.02	8.8	41.10	6.96
2004	36.80	8.0	45.34	

Note: [a] in percentages (Gini index for consumption), [b] UNU-WIDER, [c] Banerjee and Piketty (2005).

of inequality in India. Because of space limitations, information is only provided for a handful of years.

Historically, inequality levels (wealth as well as income or consumption) in India during the 1950s were quite high. The average Gini index for consumption in the 1950s would be in excess of 35; the Gini index for land distribution for this period would also be in excess of 40. However, through the 1950s and 1960s, there was a steady (though not substantial) decline in all these measures. The Gini index fell from 35 to a lower level of 30. The consumption share of the bottom 20 per cent of the population went up and the corresponding share of the top 20 per cent declined. The income share of the top 1 per cent also showed a significant decline. Many scholars attribute this trend to the slower growth and socialist policies of this period.

However, inequality measures remained fairly stable during the 1970s and 1980s. There is no evidence of any clear increasing or decreasing trend. In fact, the absence of a trend is somewhat more pronounced if we look at the Gini coefficients for rural and urban households separately. Since inequality among urban households is greater than inequality among rural households, greater urbanization during this period could have led to a very small increase in overall inequality. This feature is observed in the early 1990s also. However, the income share of the top 1 per cent did a turnaround in the 1980s after falling steadily for nearly three decades. It is interesting to note that this coincided with the beginning of the more pro-business orientation of the economy and higher growth rates. In fact, some economists attribute the beginning of the higher growth phase in the early to mid-1980s to this shift in policy orientation.

While there is general agreement about the stable nature of inequality in the 1970s and 1980s, a different picture emerges after the 1990s. Two major rounds of surveys were undertaken in 1993–4 and 1999–2000 (NSS Rounds 50 and 55). The inequality measures estimated using the basic data from these two rounds do not show any significant increase in inequality. In fact, inequality amongst the rural households shows a slight decline over this period. However, as has been pointed out by many, these two rounds are not strictly comparable. A key difference between the two surveys is the use of different 'recall periods'. The 50th round uses (like all previous rounds) the 30-day recall period for all types of consumption expenditures; respondents are asked to report expenditures incurred over the previous month. The 55th round uses the same recall period for many items but it also introduced a longer recall period (365 days) for consumer durables. Consequently, many poor households who would have reported no expenditure over the last month (in this category of items) end up reporting some expenditure over the past year. Deaton and Dreze (2002) point out that this effectively improves the reported expenditure pattern of the poor households and gives a misleading picture of reduced inequality. After adjusting the basic recorded data of the 55th round, they find evidence of marked increases in inequality over these six years.

The most recent available estimates show that by 2004 inequality had increased to 36.8. From the distributional information, it is clear that while the bottom 20 per cent lost their consumption share, the rich 20 per cent now had over 45 per cent of the consumption share. In the estimates based on the National Council of Applied Economic Research (NCAER) data set, which collects household income information rather than consumption expenditure as is done in the NSS data, inequality for 2004–5 was much higher with a Gini of 0.535, which would place India among the high inequality countries in the world.

Inequality seems to have risen on several fronts. The broad trends in income distribution in India are reflected in regional inequality, particularly in inter-state inequality, which measures inequality between states. In measuring inter-state inequality, it is presumed that the distribution within a state is equal and inequality arises due to the difference in the mean income between states. While inter-state inequality was quite steady in the 1970s and 1980s, there was a sharp increase in the 1990s (Pal and Ghosh 2007). In 1988–9, inter-state inequality given by the Gini coefficient was 0.15, but by 1998–9 it had increased to 0.23, an increase of 50 per cent (Ahluwalia 2000).

Although the gap between states has been widening, the composition of the states in terms of the best and worst performers of growth has changed. Instead of Punjab and Haryana, it is now Maharashtra and Gujarat which have the highest growth rates. Although, Bihar and Orissa continue to be at the bottom, other poor performers such as Rajasthan and West Bengal have been able to significantly increase the pace of their growth.

According to a growing number of studies, the increase in inequality at the all-India level has been driven by the widening gap between rural and urban areas. While inequality in the rural sector stays the same, inequality in the urban sector shows considerable increase. This pattern is not just true at the aggregate all-India level but most states also exhibit a similar pattern. For some, both rural and urban inequality has increased (Deaton and Dreze 2002). Other studies based on NCAER data suggest even higher levels of disparity between urban and rural areas.

There is some evidence of increase in wage inequality too. The Gini coefficient of hourly wages for regular workers seems to have risen in 1999 after remaining fairly stable in the 1980s and early 1990s. The wage gap across various occupations too widened. While the real wages for agricultural labourers have grown at the rate of 2.5 per cent per year, the corresponding growth rate for public-sector employees is almost double.

A similar pattern is observed in the case of the income share of top earners. As mentioned earlier, the income share of the top 1 per cent has been rising since the mid-1980s. Apart from a brief decline in the early 1990s, it shows considerable increase from 1993 onwards. In fact the increase in the share of the ultra rich (the top 1 per cent of this 1 per cent) is much more striking. Within the richer section, the ultra rich have experienced a much larger growth in income since the 1990s. This suggests that inequality amongst the rich is also increasing. Though it is not possible to make sweeping generalizations, there are enough indications to worry about the growth process becoming increasingly pro-rich in its orientation.

As yet there is no clear causal explanation for this apparent increase in inequalities since the 1990s. One can argue that this is an inevitable consequence of the high growth phase in a development process. The famous Kuznets hypothesis postulates that inequality should follow an inverse-U shape along the development process. The early phase of development is associated with greater urbanization and industrialization resulting in greater income inequality. However, after a stage, as a large proportion of the labour force is absorbed in the industrial sector, inequality starts falling. Until recently, some of the developed economies of the West were believed to have exhibited such a pattern. For example, in the US the share of the top 10 per cent increased from 50 per cent around 1770, to about 75 per cent around 1870, and then fell to 50 per cent in 1970. Such a view could be comforting in the sense that rising inequality need not be a matter of concern (though the time scale is still a matter of concern). However, this hypothesis has not enjoyed immense support from empirical research. Moreover, the sectoral shift in the Indian context took place in the 1980s, and the rise in inequality can not perhaps be attributed to it.

It is important to recognize the rising inequality independently and seek proper causal explanations and not simply view it as by-product. If the growth process is highly uneven so that only a smaller section can benefit from it, it can have serious consequences for poverty reduction and further growth in the economy. For example, as Deaton and Dreze (2002) point out, the reduction in poverty over the 1990s was significantly moderated by the rise in inequality. For the same level of inequality (same distribution of consumption), the growth in the 1990s would have implied a much larger reduction in poverty.

One can also draw several lessons from recent research on inequality and growth. A traditional view suggests that rising income and wealth inequality fosters higher growth by generating greater incentives to save and invest. However, this view has come under scrutiny recently and a large body of empirical as well theoretical research shows that inequality can be harmful for growth. From a political economy perspective, higher inequality leads to social conflict and greater demands for redistribution. The effects of these outweigh the positive incentive effects of inequality and the end result could be lower growth. Inequality affects growth negatively through various other channels as well. In the presence of imperfect (credit) markets and limited financial development, higher (wealth) inequality leads to underinvestment in physical and human capital and hence lower growth. Given the imperfect nature of markets in India, there is the danger of the full growth potential not being realized in the future if inequality levels continue to rise.

In this context it is important to note that the inequalities with respect to dimensions other than income and consumption expenditure in India are even worse. For instance, the Gini coefficient of adult schooling in India, which can be thought of as educational inequality, was 0.56 for 1998–2000 (Bardhan 2008). This level is much higher than that in China or Brazil which stands at 0.37 and 0.39, respectively, for 2000; in fact it is one of the worst in the world. Land inequality in rural India was 0.73 in 2003. Given the importance of both physical and human capital in the growth processes these types of inequalities may act as severe bottlenecks for future growth.

The causal relation between inequality and growth runs both ways. The process of growth can also have implications for income inequality. The experience of many OECD countries shows that growth does not necessarily entail a reduction in inequality. To the extent growth is achieved through trade and skill-biased technological and organizational changes, the growth process leads to a widening of earnings among different sections of society. The widening of various wage gaps has already been observed in the Indian context as well.

In summary, though not alarmingly high, there is some evidence of rising inequalities in India in the last two decades. It is too early and premature to attribute this rise to the process of liberalization itself. However, inequality deserves a close watch and the rising trend has to be studied carefully. The uneven nature of the growth process has to be explored further so that policy actions can be taken to ensure relatively even access by different sections of the society to the benefits of growth in a liberalized and globalized India.

AJIT MISHRA AND INDRANIL DUTTA

References

Ahluwalia, M.S. 2000. 'Economic Performance of States in Post-Reforms Period', *Economic and Political Weekly*, 6 May, 35(19): 1637–49.

Banerjee, A. and T. Piketty. 2005. 'Top Indian Incomes, 1922–2000', *The World Bank Economic Review*, 19: 1–20.

Bardhan, P. 2008. 'Economic Reforms, Poverty, and Inequality in China and India', in K. Basu and R. Kanbur (eds), *Arguments for a Better World: Essays in Honour of Amartya Sen*, Vol. 2, Oxford, Oxford University Press.

Deaton, A. and J. Dreze. 2002. 'Poverty and Inequality in India—A Re-Examination', *Economic and Political Weekly*, September, 37(36): 3729–48.

Pal, P. and J. Ghosh. 2007. 'Inequality in India: A Survey of Recent Trends', DESA Working Paper No. 45, UN.

Sen, Amartya. 1997. (Expanded Edition). *On Economic Inequality*, Oxford, Oxford University Press.

UNU-WIDER. 2008. *World Income Inequality Database*, Version 2.0c, May.

■ Infant and Child Mortality

In *Mother India,* her patently West-centric 1927 diatribe against the idea of independence for India, the American journalist Katherine Mayo pointed to the high levels of infant mortality in the country, which she attributed to the excessive sexuality and premature maternity that Hinduism encouraged in its followers. Seventy-five years later, high infant mortality is used as a major indicator, not of excessive and early sex (though demographers do attribute at least some of it to excessive and early childbearing—the two are not the same thing at all, especially in the age of modern contraception), but of unacceptably slow progress in a country's economic development whatever its income growth has been.

While the infant-mortality rate (or IMR—the number of deaths during the first year of life per 1,000 live births) is a handy figure for all kinds of evaluations and comparisons, the more useful measure for policy purposes is probably the child mortality rate (the number of deaths in the first five years of life per 1,000 live births). This is because the years immediately after infancy also represent a particularly vulnerable stage in life, sometimes even more vulnerable than infancy. This is especially so in populations that practise prolonged breastfeeding and that therefore delay exposure to the gastrointestinal and other infections that cause such a large proportion of early childhood deaths. In the following paragraphs, I will, therefore, look interchangeably at levels and trends and differentials in infant and child mortality in India.

According to the best recent figures available, those from the second round of the National Family Health Survey (NFHS II—IIPS 2000), at the end of the 20th century the IMR for India as a whole stood at around 68 deaths per 1,000 live births. This is a big improvement from the figure of 134 in the early 1970s. But it is still a long distance from the single-digit figures for the IMR that characterize a society's transformation from a condition of high to low mortality. During the same period, under-5 mortality was 95 per 1,000 live births. That is, the probability of dying before the fifth birthday is still around 10 per cent for the average newborn in India. More worryingly, there is some indication that gains in lowering infant and child mortality have begun to slow down since the 1990s.

These national averages hide gross inequalities in the life chances of infants and children in different parts of the country and in different socio-economic categories. For example, the rural–urban divide continues to be significant in spite of apparently deteriorating living conditions for the poor in urban areas. In the NFHS-II data set, in the late 1990s, child mortality was nearly twice as high in rural as in urban areas and post-neonatal mortality (deaths between the ages of 1 month and a year) was as much as 73 per cent higher. The national IMR of 68 was a result of an IMR of 73 in rural areas and 47 in urban areas. But before we celebrate health conditions in the towns and cities, it must be pointed out that this same survey finds that the IMR for the poor urban population (what the survey classifies as the 'low-standard-of-living', or SLI population) was as high as 76—obviously the proximity to health services and the greater directly and indirectly acquired health knowledge in the towns is not enough to compensate for the overcrowding and pervasive poverty that kills so many slum children before they can celebrate a first birthday.

Other kinds of differentials are just as pernicious and imply that egalitarianism and equity are somewhat hollow slogans in India. The NFHS data are particularly revealing about differentials by caste, a category that is supposed to be unimportant in modern India. This same national average of an IMR of 73 hides a rate of 83 for the scheduled castes and 84 for the scheduled tribes. All these figures become even better contextualized if one looks at the unrealized potential by taking IMRs in economically or socially 'advantaged' populations in India. For example, compare 83 and 84 to a rate of 33 for high SLI urban Indians and a magically low 12 in Kerala for the children of women who have completed high school education or more.

Speaking of Kerala leads naturally to discussing all those geographical parts of the country that look as if they will never catch up with that state. Whatever the gloomy revisionist reappraisals of the Kerala model of development, the fact remains that for a range of social variables, it could just as well have been situated in Scandinavia as in southern India. The IMR in Kerala in NFHS-II stood at 16—note that this is not substantially higher than the figure for the children of well-educated women in the state, that is, socio-economic differentials *within* Kerala are unimaginably, at least to our limited imaginations, small. In contrast, the IMR in Rajasthan was 80, Madhya Pradesh 86, Uttar Pradesh 87, and Orissa 81; in Bihar, the figure was (a suspiciously low) 73. Rates in the rest of the large states in the country were in the 40s, 50s, and 60s, with only Himachal Pradesh doing itself a little proud with a rate of 34.

These regional differences lead one to an examination of the determinants of infant and child mortality. The large literature on the subject is best unravelled by classifying what have been called the 'proximate determinants' of infant and child mortality into those that arise from bio-demographic factors (to do with maternal age, parity, and intervals between births), environmental contamination (through the conditions of birth as well as the surroundings of life) affecting the exposure to infection, poor nutrition, injury, and what the authors of the proximate-determinants framework (Mosley and Chen 1984) call 'personal illness control' (those behaviours and attributes that rely on medical technology, both to prevent ill health as well as to cure it).

Whether one looks at trends in infant and child mortality in India or at contemporary differentials, all these factors come into play. To begin with, both over time as well as across regions (whether urban–rural or state-wise), bio-demographic factors have changed in the direction of improved prospects for child survival. High-risk births, as defined by very low or very high maternal age at birth or by a large number of siblings, have come down as a proportion of all births as the childbearing age has risen and fertility has declined. The only risky bio-demographic factor that has probably not changed much for the better is birth interval. Indeed, there is some evidence that as fertility has come down in India, there has been a compression of birth intervals—births to women have become more closely spaced. This has probably happened both because of involuntary reasons (to do with shortened breastfeeding and little use of birth-spacing contraception) as well as for voluntary reasons to do with wanting to get family size goals quickly met so that the demands of babies and young children can be more quickly dispensed with.

Environmental contamination continues to play havoc on young lives in the country. Whether due to poor public sanitation or poor household hygiene (fostered as much by poverty as by lack of knowledge), incidents of acute respiratory infections, fever, or diarrhoea in the two weeks before the survey were reported in about a quarter of children in morbidity surveys like the NFHS. Not surprisingly, these illness rates were higher in rural areas, among the poor, among the lower castes, and among children of non-literate mothers. But these figures need to be interpreted with caution, based as they are on reporting by mothers. This caution is suggested by the finding that Kerala reported above-national-average levels of childhood morbidity, leading to the speculation whether the state's low infant and child mortality are not in fact an outcome of prompt recognition (and treatment) of illness. In other words, actual morbidity levels in the country may well be much higher than these reported levels because, in an environment of constant risk, coughs and diarrhoea may often be considered 'normal' enough not to merit mention in surveys.

Poor nutrition is certainly implicated in infant and child health and mortality in India, both as a determinant as well as an outcome of illness. Incidentally, maternal nutrition is as important here as is the level of child nutrition—in NFHS-II, over half the married women tested had some degree of anaemia, an important predictor of poor delivery outcomes. And there must be something 'cultural' about the poor nutritional levels in India—we seem to have much higher levels of malnutrition than many poorer countries in Sub-Saharan Africa. In the NFHS survey of 1998–9, almost half the children under the age of 3 were *underweight* (as measured by weight for age), almost half were *stunted* (according to height for age), and about 16 per cent were *wasted* (according to weight for height). Each of these measures of poor nutritional status captures different aspects of food deprivation and illness prevalence; what is important here is to note that these figures are unacceptably high even by the standards of a poor country.

Finally, there is personal illness control, the use of medical technology to prevent as well as treat the many infectious illnesses that account for the high levels of infant and child morality in poor countries. In particular, there is the miraculous ORS (oral rehydration salts), which refers to the simple and inexpensive administration of a glucose and electrolyte solution to reduce deaths due to the dehydration caused by severe diarrhoeal disease. ORS packets are supposed to be routinely delivered by the national primary healthcare system but in NFHS-II, it was found that only 27 per cent of children below the age of 3 who had a bout of diarrhoea in the two weeks preceding the survey were given ORS packets, and about 40 per cent received some more traditional forms of oral rehydration such as extra fluid or gruel or home-made sugar and salt solutions. Worse, over half these children were treated with 'pills' or 'syrup'; 15 per cent even received an injection.

Of course it is better to prevent an illness than to cure it. And here too medical technology is a handy tool to overcome some of the disadvantages of poor environmental conditions. But in spite of the great publicity attending international and national universal immunization programmes, the fact remains that at the time of NFHS-II, only 42 per cent of children aged 12–23 months were 'fully' vaccinated (against tuberculosis, measles, DPT, and polio), and 14 per cent had not received any vaccinations at all. These figures are improvements from the levels found in the NFHS-I survey of five years earlier (when the respective figures were 36 per cent and 30 per cent) but far from a reason to boast of a successful immunization programme in the country.

Infant and child mortality in India cannot be discussed without touching upon gender differentials. Since Visaria's (1967) pioneering exploration of the unduly masculine juvenile (0–6 years) sex ratio of the 1961 Census, it has been increasingly clear that little girls face an 'unnatural' disadvantage in survival compared to little boys. Unnatural because this disadvantage does not exist in many much poorer regions such as the countries of Sub-Saharan Africa. In other words, the higher death rate of female children is being achieved with some effort—the effort needed to deny girls the same care as boys. What form this deprivation takes is debatable; at various points of time, discrimination in food allocation, healthcare, or even that elusive input, 'love', has been blamed (for example, Miller 1981). While all these kinds of selective neglect are plausible, the largest single factor is probably the healthcare provided to girls—this healthcare is often too sub-standard, too little, and too late.

For a short while, it appeared that sex differences in child survival were narrowing; indeed life expectancies are now frequently greater for women than for men, in spite of a continuing high burden of reproductive mortality in the country. But more recent data clarify that this convergence of male and female child death rates is not really a cause for joy. In district after district, state after state, the juvenile sex ratio in the 2000 Census is much worse than in 1991. Given the gender convergence in death rates, this means that the female disadvantage in survival has got converted into a female disadvantage in initial existence. It is the sex ratio of *births* rather than the sex ratio of *deaths* that now works against girls. The increased resort to foetal sex-determination tests, followed by selective abortion of female conceptions, was at first reported only anecdotally. But there are now sufficient quantitative data to confirm this anecdotal evidence. Worse, this rising masculinity of births shows little signs of abating in spite of its proclaimed illegality through the Pre-natal Diagnostic Techniques (PNDT) (Regulation and Prevention of Misuse) Act, 1994, and the PNDT Amendment Act, 2002, as well as the vast 'educational' campaigns to discourage sex-selective abortions. Moreover, whereas sex differences in child mortality in the past were predominantly a feature of north India, a masculine sex ratio of births has assumed virulent form in new parts of the country, the western states of Gujarat and Maharashtra in particular. The relative economic wealth of these states suggests that development is exacerbating gender differences in life prospects, if one considers sex-selective abortion as but one end of a continuum of discrimination against the girl child.

It is depressing to end on this negative note. But perhaps the third round of the NFHS, which is currently under way, will reveal that all this public and policy interest in and dismay about the life chances of children in general and girl children in particular has finally begun to pay off.

Alaka Malwade Basu

References

Basu, A.M. 1997. 'Anthropological Demography in the Understanding of the Determinants of Child Mortality', in G.W. Jones, J.C. Caldwell, R.M. Douglas, and R.M. D'Souza (eds), *The Continuing Demographic Transition*, Oxford, Oxford University Press.

International Institute for Population Sciences (IIPS). 2000. *National Family Health Survey, India 1998–99*, Mumbai, IIPS.

Mayo, K. 1927 [1998]. *Mother India*, New York, Harcourt Brace and Company; London, Jonathan Cape [*Mother India: Selections Edited and with an Introduction by Mrinalini Sinha*, New Delhi, Kali for Women].

Miller, B.D. 1981. *The Endangered Sex: Neglect of Female Children in Rural North India*, Ithaca, Cornell University Press.

Mosely, W.H. and L.C. Chen. 1984. 'Child Survival: Research and Policy', *Population and Development Review*, supplement to Vol. 10.

Visaria, P. 1967. 'The Sex Ratio of the Population of India and Pakistan and Regional Variations during 1901–1961', in A. Bose (ed.), *Patterns of Population Change in India 1951–61*, Bombay, Allied Publishers.

Inflation

Inflation rates in India have always been much lower than in Latin America. The reason is simple: with a vast majority of workers being unorganized and having no wage indexation, even moderate rates of inflation can bring great misery. Almost all inflation in other words is *inflation in terms of the unorganized workers' wage unit.* It is of the sort that monetarism, whose concept of *'non-accelerating'* inflation necessarily entails pari passu movements in money wages and prices occurring at an 'equilibrium' real wage, is theoretically incapable of cognizing.

The misery of unorganized workers has called forth urgent anti-inflationary government action not because of altruism, but because of the substantial voting strength that these workers enjoy and use to good effect. It is noteworthy that *every* major inflationary episode in India has caused a change in government: 1966–7 pushed the Congress Party out of power in several states (and eventually caused its split, reducing it to a minority even at the centre); 1973–4 threatened Mrs Gandhi with imminent loss of power, which was thwarted by the imposition of an Emergency, but only temporarily; and 1979–80 swept the Janata Party out of power.

In the early years after Independence, inflation was seen almost exclusively as being demand pull in nature. Rao (1952) argued that an increase in the investment rate in an economy like India, which was marked by supply-side rigidities, would have multiplier effects not on the level of real income but on the level of money income through price adjustment. Consumption, therefore, had to be fiscally restrained in order to allow an increase in the investment ratio, which was essential for more rapid development. Agriculture, especially food grains production, was an obvious constraint, a fact underscored by the Latin American Structuralists as well. But the early Indian planners set great store by land reforms and other institutional changes in agriculture which they felt would ease supply constraints even without much investment and keep the fiscal strain of non-inflationary financing of development within manageable limits. The need for land reforms was also underscored by Kalecki (1972) who argued that the 'main "financial" problem of development is of adequate agricultural production'.

The possibility of a cost push inflation, though recognized at the time, was not seriously considered until the mid-1960s, when the introduction of administered pricing for crucial agricultural commodities (and the fact that market prices moved in sympathy with administered prices even in the presence of adequate stocks) compelled its cognizance. A spate of 'competing claims' theories came up (Mitra 1977, for example), with implications for the analysis of inflation came to be recognized as the result of struggles over distributive shares. Indeed, instead of the simplistic 'demand pull–cost push' dichotomy, the 'competing-claims' framework made it possible to integrate the two conceptions and develop a composite theoretical framework within which not only the inflationary process but also the economy's longer-term contradictions could be fruitfully analysed.

A simple model will illustrate this approach. Dividing the economy into two sectors, agriculture and industry, and four classes, comprising workers and capitalists in each sector, we can distinguish for each class a 'claim function'. For all classes other than the (unorganized) agricultural workers the claimed distributive share is a function of the state of aggregate demand. If state intervention ensures that the outputs of the two sectors are always 'in balance', then the state of capacity utilization in industry can be a proxy for aggregate demand. We can then have the following price equations, assuming all claims are satisfied (and also for simplicity that the claims of the 'organized' classes are satisfied, on the basis of *current*, and not *lagged*, prices).

$$[\alpha \,.\, p'(t) + \omega(u) \,.\, \lambda \,.\, p'(t)]\ [1 + \pi(u)] = p(t)$$
$$[\alpha' .\, p(t) + w(t) \,.\, \lambda'][1 + \pi'(u)] = p'(t)$$
$$w(t) = \varpi \,.\, p'(t - \theta)$$

where primes refer to the agricultural sector which provides raw materials and wage goods to industry, w to the money wage rate of its workers which adjusts to inflation with a time lag θ to give them a real wage ϖ, α to the current material input requirement of each sector from the other, λ to the labour coefficients, p to the prices, π to the profit mark-ups which depend on the state of demand (the mark-up in the case of the agricultural sector is enforced through state-administered prices), and ω to the real wage claim of industrial workers which also depends on the state of demand. (The unorganized nature of agricultural workers manifests itself in the fact that their real wage claim is constant and achieved only intermittently.)

For any given u, and assuming for convenience that $\theta = 1$, the system gives steady inflation at the rate $[\{\varpi . \lambda'/F(u)\} - 1]$

where $F(u) = \{1 - [\alpha . \alpha' + \omega(u) . \lambda](1 + \pi(u))(1 + \pi'(u))\}/(1 + \pi'(u))$, whence $F'(u) < 0$.

This rate increases as u increases. Since a higher growth rate is generally associated with a higher level of aggregate demand in the economy (higher u), it follows that, for any given set of 'claim functions', the rate of steady growth and the rate of steady inflation are positively related, a conclusion highlighted by the Latin American Structuralists. The *position* of this upward-sloping 'growth inflation frontier' depends on the 'claim functions'. If the 'claims' increase (that is either $\omega(u)$ or $\pi(u)$ or $\pi'(u)$ or a combination of any of them increases for any given u), then the $F(u)$ curve *shifts* inwards for any given u; in such a case the 'growth inflation frontier' shifts outwards, and the rate of inflation increases for any given growth rate. We can thus distinguish between *a movement along the 'frontier'* and *a shift of the 'frontier'*. The former refers to alternative combinations of steady growth and steady inflation feasible for given 'claim functions'; the latter refers to the consequences of increasing claims, or outward-shifting 'claim functions'.

Several writers, notwithstanding their different ideological positions, have located the contradictions of the Indian *dirigiste* regime in an intensification of conflicts over competing claims, which eventually impinges adversely on growth. This, as first mentioned, can be seen as involving increases in 'claim functions' leading to an outward *shift* of the 'growth inflation frontier': the maintenance of any given growth rate becomes increasingly difficult over time since it entails increases in the rate of inflation, and hence a steadily worsening condition of unorganized workers in particular, which undermines the political viability of the system.

The efforts of the state to sustain the system can also be analysed in this framework. If the decade after the mid-1960s witnessed frantic efforts to push down the 'claim function' of the workers, culminating in the Railway Strike of 1974, the decade after the Emergency saw an equally determined effort to stabilize the polity by pushing down the 'claim function' of surplus producers in the agricultural sector, culminating in the massive peasant rallies of the mid-1980s at Delhi's Boat Club. The Rajiv Gandhi period accordingly tried to overcome the crisis by resorting to foreign borrowings, but these contributed, within a changed international conjuncture, to the collapse of dirigisme and the introduction of neo-liberal policies.

Under the neo-liberal regime, inflation control commands even greater priority, but for an altogether different reason, namely, to appease financial interests that are in the ascendancy (Chandrasekhar and Ghosh 2002) and that characteristically abhor inflation. Inflation control occurs inter alia through a squeeze on unorganized rural workers, whose purchasing power is reduced by sharp cuts in government expenditure in rural areas (Patnaik 2004). Instead of the earlier regime of an expansionary fiscal policy, pursued with the aim of promoting growth but restrained only by the fear of inflation which might politically alienate unorganized workers, we now have a contractionary fiscal policy that hurts precisely these workers while controlling inflation to the satisfaction of financial interests.

PRABHAT PATNAIK

References

Chandrasekhar, C.P. and J. Ghosh. 2002. *The Market That Failed*, Delhi, Leftword.

Kalecki, M. 1972. 'Problems of Financing Economic Development in a Mixed Economy', in *Essays on the Economic Growth of the Socialist and the Mixed Economy*, Cambridge, Cambridge University Press.

Mitra, A. 1977. *Terms of Trade and Class Relations*, London, Frank Cass.

Patnaik, U. 2004. 'The Republic of Hunger', *Social Scientist*, September–October.

Rao, V.K.R.V. 1952. 'Investment, Income and the Multiplier in an Underdeveloped Economy', *Indian Economic Review*, February.

■ Inflation: Experience and Policy

Introduction

Inflation is a sustained rise in prices across the board, that is, a phenomenon where the average price of all goods in an economy is on an increasing trajectory. For the common person, there is something threatening about this phenomenon, especially when the rise in prices of goods is not matched by a similar rise in wages.

We know from experience, combined with a little bit of cogitation that the prices of commodities will, over time, rise and fall, responding to the tugs and pushes of demand and supply. A failure of a particular crop or a sudden fashion for a certain kind of clothing will cause the price of that crop or that kind of clothing to rise, just as an unexpected glut in the production of onions will cause the price of onions to fall. These relative price movements are nature's way of signaling to consumers and other buyers that they should consume less of the commodity facing shortage and more of the good in glut, and to producers to produce more of what is in short supply and less of what is available in plenty. To even out these ebbs and flows of prices would be folly, as we know from countless examples of misdirected government interventions.

Inflation, on the other hand, refers to not such *relative* price changes but a generalized, sustained increase in the overall price level in the economy. The phenomenon of inflation has been with humankind ever since we moved away from barter to the use of various mediums of exchange, like paper money, precious metals, or even cigarettes, as happened in prisoners of war camps during the Second World War. While it is true that we do not fully understand inflation and to that extent it remains a threat, what is comforting is that years of research have given us deep insights into this troubling phenomenon. And even though we do not fully understand its origins, economists have developed techniques and policy interventions that can control it. For some of these antidotes there is good reason to use utmost caution in using them and in deciding what dosage to administer since each such policy intervention comes with side effects, like increased unemployment or slowdown in investment. But it is a testimony to the advance of economics that the spiraling hyperinflations that occurred ever so often till even half a century ago, now seem to be a matter of history.

Experience

Even as this entry is being written, India is in the midst of an inflationary episode. It began around December 2009, when the WPI inflation climbed to 7.15 per cent.[1] It continued to rise, was in double-digits for four months, starting March 2010 and peaking in April 2010 at 10.88 per cent. Thereafter, it was on a broadly downward trajectory, with a small pick-up in inflation in December 2010. The slow downward trend and the turnaround at the end of 2010 has caused some concern, mainly because compared to most emerging economies, India's inflation record has historically been quite low.[2]

Before this 18-month run of inflation, the Indian economy had one year of price stability, with inflation never exceeding 5 per cent since January 2009. But prior to that there was another rally of inflation from March 2008 to December 2008, when WPI inflation hovered in and around 10 per cent. Before these two rallies in quick succession, we had very little inflation for a dozen years. There were occasional months when inflation would exceed 8 per cent and not a single month when it was in double-digits during these 12 years of relative price stability.[3]

For completeness it may be mentioned that independent India's highest inflation occurred in September 1974, when inflation reached 33.3 per cent. Arguably our worst inflationary episode was from November 1973 to December 1974, when inflation never dropped below 20 per cent and was above 30 per cent for four consecutive months starting June 1974.

What is good performance and what is bad depends on our yardstick. Even during the dozen years of price stability we had more inflation than in virtually any industrialized country in recent times but, in comparison to most emerging market economies and developing nations in the world, India's performance since 1947 has been creditable.

One reason for the concern with the past 18 months inflation-run is that it looks relatively bad compared to the dozen years of price stability preceding 2006. There has been talk of runaway inflation and hyperinflation. It is, however, important to get the perspective right. We are nowhere near hyperinflation—usually described as inflation over 50 per cent per month (Cagan 1956). The world's biggest inflations occurred in Europe, once around 1923 and again around 1946. The record is held by Hungary from August 1945 to July 1946. During these 12 years, prices rose by 3.8×10^{27}. That is, what cost 1 pengo on 1 August 1945, would cost 3800 ...

[1]All inflation numbers, unless explicitly stated otherwise, refer to annual inflation, that is, the growth rate of the price index on a year-on-year basis.

[2]A more detailed analysis of the Indian experience and the theory underlying the policy used to control inflation occurs in Basu (2011). In writing this entry I have drawn considerably on this paper.

[3]When analysing inflation in India, I have used the WPI-based inflation numbers throughout this entry. On the few occasions when other indicators are used, this is made explicit. WPI inflation is the most widely used index of inflation even though it has been debated whether it is the most appropriate (see Patnaik et al. 2011).

(with another 24 such zeroes) pengos on 31 July 1946 (Basu 1997). From August the pengo was replaced with the forint in an effort to shed the trillions of zeroes that were needed to express prices in pengos.

Comparable hyperinflations occurred in Russia from December 1921 to January 1924, in Greece in 1943, in Zimbabwe in 2008, in Germany in 1923, and in many other instances. Germany's 1923 hyperinflation may well be the most analysed case of inflation. It played havoc with the economy, created political tensions which contributed to the rise of Nazism, and also caused psychological disturbances.

Not quite as large as these European inflations but nevertheless staggeringly large ones occurred till two or three decades ago in many Latin American countries (see Garcia et al. 2010). These being closer to our times, they may have greater relevance for India. One country that has coped with mega inflations, many times larger than what we have in India, and seems to have at last stabilized and is now among the forerunners of well-run economies among emerging market economies is Brazil.

A study of the Brazilian economy since 1962, shows that the nation did not have a single year where inflation was in single digits from 1962 to 1997. There were only two years (1973 and 1974) when inflation was below 20 per cent. The real bad period was 1988 to 1994. On average, prices were rising close to 2,000 per cent per annum during this time. Brazil's experience gives us a bit of an insight into what inflation does to growth. A pure eyeballing of the data suggests that when inflation is below 10 per cent, there is little correlation between the rate of inflation and the growth rate. But at higher levels, high inflation is usually associated with lower growth, especially when inflation, starting at a high level, rises even further, growth slows down. During the six hyperinflationary years mentioned earlier, growth had a real setback with GDP growing at negative rates in three out of these six years.

Asian countries have in general had more stable inflation. South Korea, which grew at astonishingly high rates from the late 1960s to recently, did have high inflation but nowhere near the experience of Latin American economies like Brazil. The average inflation in South Korea in the 1970s was in double-digits, with inflation peaking in 1980. While this coincided with high growth for quite some time, it eventually seemed to have had a dampening effect on GDP growth. Tighter monetary and fiscal measures brought inflation down in the 1980s and, eventually, restored high growth.

To complete the India story one may comment on food inflation, which is of special interest in an economy in which large segments of the population continue to be poor. In this episode of rising prices, food inflation rose well above the overall WPI inflation. It peaked at 20.22 per cent in February 2010 and remained around 20 per cent for four consecutive months. Such high food inflation

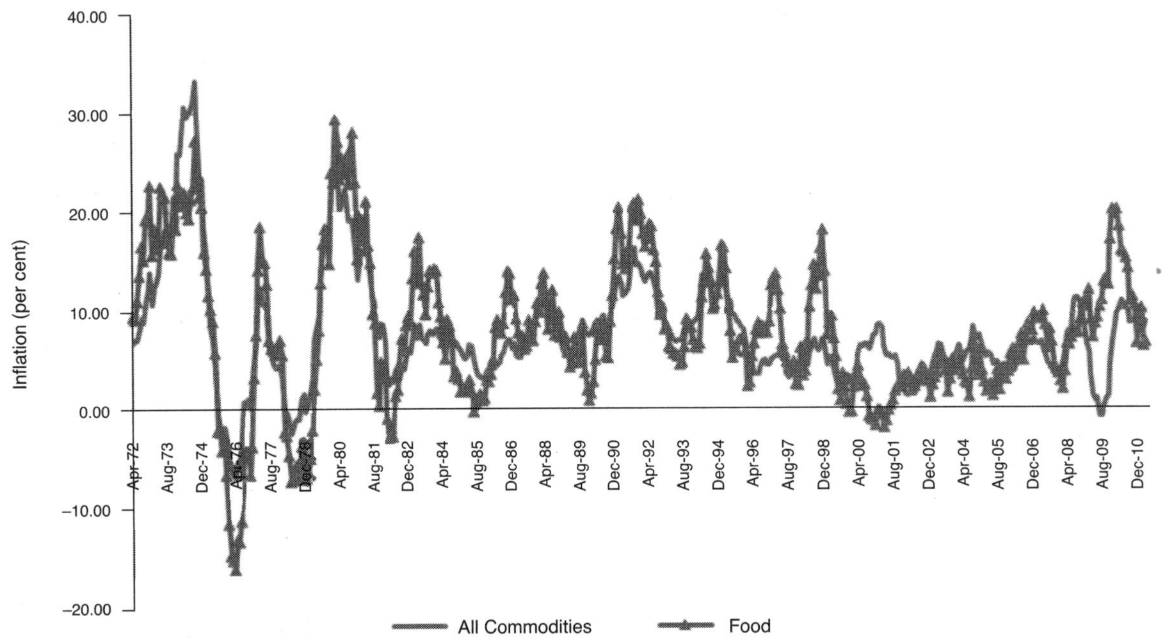

Figure 1 Y-o-Y Inflation for All Commodities and Food since 1972

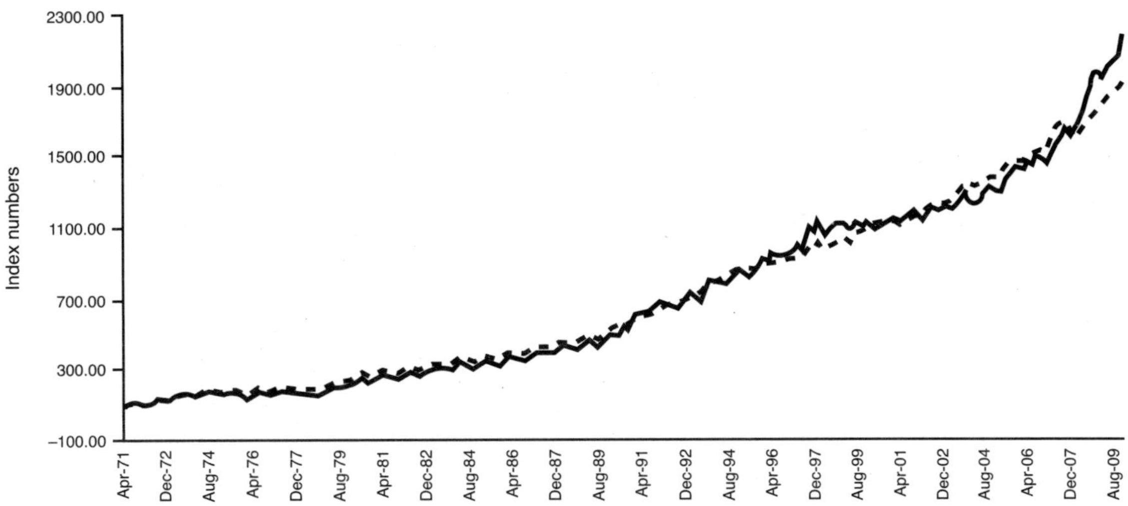

Figure 2 WPI Index for All Commodities and Food since 1971

is relatively rare in India. It happened in 1974, 1980, and a few other occasions.

Over the last few years there has been a sense that the inflation faced by emerging economies is changing some of its stripes, thereby demanding not just greater resolve but new ideas in order to have price stability. Rakshit (2011) points to the somewhat unusual divergence between CPI inflation and WPI inflation, even though they seem to have converged once again over the last six months. We can also see from Figure 1 that the volatility of inflation seems to have changed. While inflation, both for WPI and food, has clearly been on the rise since 2000, it seems to be less volatile than it used to be before the mid-1980s. Before 1982 we had some stretches of very low inflation but also peaks of a kind that, fortunately, we do not see any longer.

Figure 2 reveals another interesting change. The index of food prices used to be fairly firmly glued to the overall price index till the late 1990s. A careful examination of the two graphs shows that that is not the case anymore. The divergence between the two is especially pronounced over the last two or three years (see Figure 3). This explains why the difference between CPI inflation and WPI inflation has been more marked in recent times. However, this also points to a new-found resilience of the Indian economy. It is arguable that earlier our overall inflation was driven by the agricultural sector. What happened to food prices affected everything else and so the two indices moved in tandem. Over time, the share of agriculture in total GDP has fallen and the growing strength of the economy means that food prices alone may not be the driving factor.

This has an immediate policy implication that may be noted here. In controlling overall inflation, food prices may not be as important as they were in the past. Of course, controlling food inflation is important in itself since such a large segment of India continues to be poor and any inflation in food prices hurts it disproportionately. This is discussed at some length in this year's *Economic Survey* (Government of India 2011). But in controlling overall inflation, we have to turn our attention to macro demand management—fiscal and monetary—even while we try to augment the supply of food and other commodities.

Policy

For many ordinary people, inflation management is simply a matter of determination on the part of the government. The government has to simply decree price caps for various goods and deploy public servants to monitor prices in markets and punish those who break the law. We have enough evidence from around the world to know that this simple approach does not work. While the government may be able to control the prices of a few goods which are supplied by a limited number of large corporations (since these can be monitored relatively easily), to do so for all goods and services is a virtual impossibility. What happens when such across-the-board price controls are attempted is the flourishing of black markets. And also goods tend to vanish from store shelves. Queues form to buy goods at controlled prices,

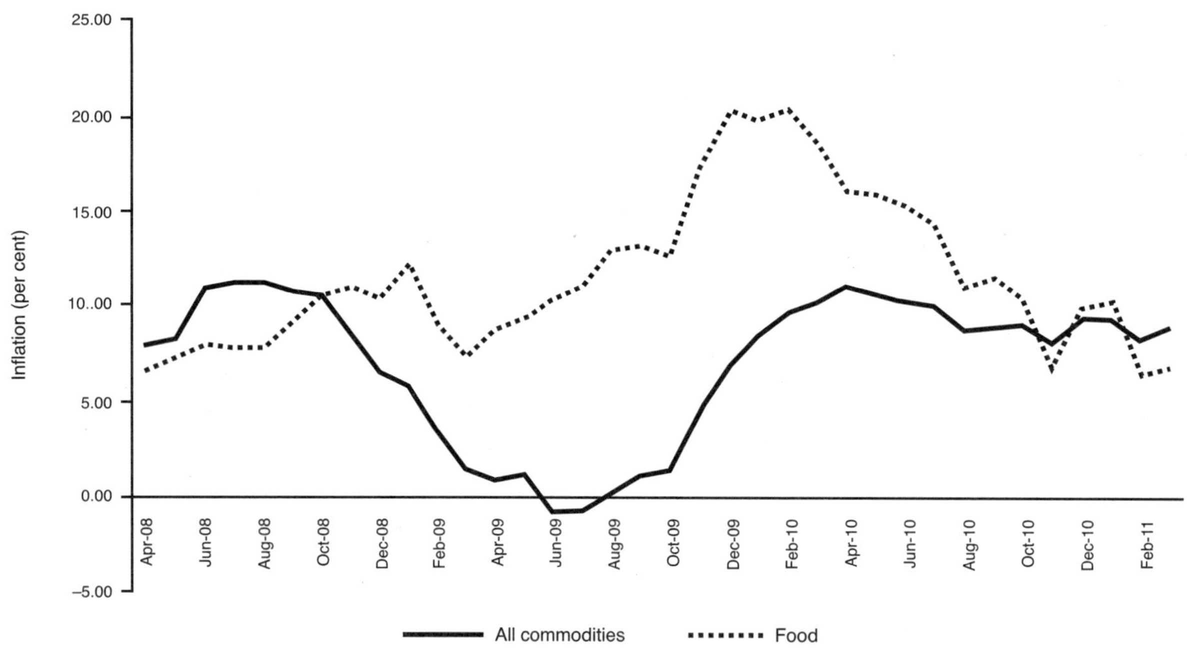

Figure 3 Y-o-Y for All Commodities and Food since 2008

with people waiting for hours to get ordinary goods like loaves of bread and other regular food items. The social cost of time wasted in standing in queues can be colossal. Fortunately, India has not resorted to administered pricing for most goods, even though there are occasional demands for this.

The standard method used to control inflation in India in recent times has involved controlling fiscal and revenue deficits, putting curbs on liquidity in the market through various monetary measures, and also trying to ease up supply bottlenecks, particularly when the inflationary pressure is especially high in a limited number of goods. Short-term measures such as banning exports of certain goods and cutting back on import duties on certain items are also used, though these may rightly be viewed as measures to contain sector-specific price increases.

When it comes to macro demand management, besides fiscal roll-back, the main measures used pertain to monetary policy variables controlled by the Reserve Bank of India (RBI). In India, RBI has mainly used the control of the repo and reverse repo rates, which are the rates at which the RBI does its overnight lending to and borrowing from banks, and the cash reserve ratio (CRR) which the banks are required to hold as cash. The latter puts a curb on on-lending by banks. Since January 2010, RBI raised the repo rate multiple times. Though CRR has also been tightened several times, of late the propensity has been to rely on tightening the repo and reverse repo rates. In its most recent monetary policy announcement, made on 3 May 2011, RBI announced that it would henceforth lock-in the reverse repo rate at one percentage point below the repo rate. Thus, from now on it will simply announce the repo rate.

In the latest monetary policy announcement, RBI has also instituted a new Marginal Standing Facility (MSF). The interest on this is 1 percentage point higher than the repo rate and banks are allowed to borrow a limited amount—up to 1 per cent of each bank's net demand and time liabilities. Clearly, banks will use this facility only after they have used their repo option. In addition, the interest rates paid by banks on their savings rate, which are fixed and normally left dormant, were raised from 3.5 to 4 per cent. This was announced as a monetary policy measure.

The aim of this whole exercise is to influence call money rates and tighten liquidity. But how well can a central bank control overall liquidity? From experience around the world, we know that these powers are there but limited. Overall demand in the economy, as well as total liquidity, comes from many sources—corporates, farmers, labourers, housewives, and the government. So what any single agent can do is limited. Also, actions by other agents can undo what one agent does. This is what contributes to making inflation one of the hardest problems to manage—the emperor of economic maladies.

At a very abstract, elemental level, inflation is the product of our ability to make contracts and deliver on promises. While we think of promises mostly in bilateral terms, the most important 'economic' promise, one that has made modern civilization possible, is the mysterious promise represented by money—the note in your wallet or the bank balance in your account, which in itself is of no value. Money is nothing but a generic promise from your society—the government being the most important representative of that—that you will be able to change these useless bits of paper for actual goods and services in the future. It is this which enables a worker who toils all day to not insist that his employer hand over to her food, clothing, and shelter material in the evening in exchange for the hard work. Instead, she accepts money. Money is a kind of pledge to her by society at large. She can redeem that pledge at leisure and in small measures—buying food, shelter, education, as and when she needs these. Money was not discovered one day in a moment of scientific triumph. It emerged gradually, in small measures and little innovations. But in terms of human achievement it must stand right there at the pinnacle of inventions. Without it we would have very little of what we know today as human society and life.

The trouble in controlling money supply arises from the fact that society has an ability to create 'near monies'. For years, the US Fed kept a control on prices by buying and selling government bonds or what are called 'open market operations', which are the other side of, respectively, releasing money into and absorbing money from the economy. However, money is not the only medium of exchange. People can use all kinds of other commodities and papers to trade goods. If, for instance, government bonds were fully acceptable as a medium of exchange, then the central bank selling bonds and collecting money would have very little impact on the economy. It is the appearance of 'near monies' that compels the US Fed to use other strategies for price stability. The US Fed nowadays, instead of trying to directly control money, tries to establish some control over liquidity by targeting market interest rates through changes in the 'discount rate'.

Another problem in controlling inflation occurs from the fact that increasing monetization and programmes of financial inclusion, which are concomitants of economic progress, imply that savings which people would have kept as money under the pillow may now be put in bank deposits and other small savings plans. This re-introduction of currency into the market which otherwise would have sat dormant can raise the velocity of circulation of money and give rise to inflationary pressures. This does not necessarily imply that inflation will be higher but that to keep inflation at bay the government and the central bank may have to keep its own demand creation under a tighter leash.

Another special problem associated with the inflation policy in our contemporary world has to do with globalization. It was realized (believed?) that, unlike most other products, where we encourage multiple producers to get into business and to have competition, money creation is one area where competition is not desirable. It was decided that this is one area where, far from boosting competition, what we want is a monopoly. Each economy must have at most one money-creating authority. It was with this principle in mind that the Bank of England was created in 1694, though its monopoly rights of creating money were firmed up much more clearly only at the time of renewal of its Royal Charter in 1742.

The problem with controlling inflation arises from the fact that the principle of one-economy-one-central bank has got weakened in recent times. With globalization, the world economy is increasingly beginning to look like a single economy, but to the extent that there are many central banks with the right to create money, we are tending to get back to the kind of world we worked hard to get out of (Government of India 2011: chapter 2). This is one factor that has been changing the nature of inflation in recent times. What we are increasingly beginning to see is a new kind of stagflation at a global level, where stagnation is afflicting the industrialized nations and inflation is high in emerging economies. To jump start their economies many central banks in industrialized nations are increasing money supply, the second round of quantitative easing, or QE2, by the US Fed being a case in point. This additional money, in today's flat world, is tending to flow to emerging economies, creating inflationary build-ups there.

It is arguable that inflation policy in our new world will require, in addition to all the usual instruments of within-nation control, such as CRR, repo rates, and discount rates, increasing coordination in monetary and fiscal policies across nations, especially the systemically important ones.

KAUSHIK BASU

References

Basu, Kaushik. 1997. *Analytical Development Economics*, Cambridge, MA, MIT Press.

——. 2011. 'Understanding Inflation and Managing It', forthcoming in *Economic and Political Weekly*.

Cagan, Philip. 1956. 'The Monetary Dynamics of

Hyperinflation', in M. Friedman (ed.), *Studies in the Quantity Theory of Money*, Chicago, University of Chicago Press.
Garcia, Marcio, Diego Guillen, and Patrick Kehoe. 2010. 'The Monetary and Fiscal History of Latin America', Princeton University, mimeo.
Government of India. 2011. *Economic Survey 2010–11*, New Delhi, Ministry of Finance.
Patnaik, Ila, Ajay Shah, and Giovanni Veronese. 2011. 'How Should Inflation be Measured in India?', *Economic and Political Weekly*, 46(16): 55–64.
Rakshit, Mihir. 2011. 'Inflation and Relative Prices in India 2006–10: Some Analytics and Policy Issues', *Economic and Political Weekly*, 46(16): 41–54.

■ Informal Labour

Informal labour is labour whose use is not governed either by state regulations or by collective agreements between workers and employers. Though negative, this definition is nevertheless meaningful and appropriate. For, it is the existence of formal labour in the context of a dual economy that isolates informal labour as a category. A dual economy, first conceptualized by Arthur Lewis in a classic paper (Lewis 1954), is composed of two distinct sectors—formal (or modern or organized) and informal (or traditional or unorganized).[1] All developing economies are dual economies in which state regulations and collective agreements govern the use and remuneration of labour only in the formal sector.

Lack of clarity on this point has been a source of much confusion in the literature. Informal labour has, in different instances, been viewed as labour engaged in urban small-scale enterprises, as self-employed labour, as labour engaged in 'traditional' activities, as wholly unskilled labour, as labour whose use is not subject to any rules or norms, and as labour which is illegal. None of this has any sound conceptual or empirical foundation. Informality does not imply a particular mode or location of labour use; informal labour can be in self-employment as well as in wage employment, just as it can be in urban or in rural areas. Informal labour need not be confined to 'traditional' activities; it can be engaged in both 'traditional' and 'modern' activities. Informal labour is not necessarily unskilled; it is just that its skills are acquired from outside the formal education system. It is not that there are no rules and norms that govern the use and remuneration of informal labour; only that these rules and norms reflect or derive from prevailing social values and institutions and generally differ from those established by the state for the formal sector of the economy. And informal labour cannot be illegal; for, outside the formal sector, there simply are no legal norms to violate.

A core characteristic of a dual economy is that the remuneration of formal labour is much higher than that of informal labour. One reason is that state regulations and collective bargaining set the remuneration of formal labour at a level that is considered adequate to ensure a 'decent' level of living for a worker and his/her dependants; this remuneration happens to be much higher than the average labour-income in the unorganized sector. The other reason is that the productivity of formal labour is much higher than that of informal labour; the former is employed together with capital and advanced technology, while the latter is performed with simple tools and natural resources.

The gaps in remuneration and productivity between formal and informal workers are even wider than the gaps between formal and informal labour. The reason is that the formal workers have full-time employment while informal workers are underemployed. Underemployment is a reflection of surplus labour for which the informal sector serves as a reservoir. Surplus labour is accommodated essentially through work-sharing arrangements that are intrinsic to the dominant systems of employment of informal labour—the systems of self-employment and casual wage employment. Work-sharing also means income-sharing. And it is the combination of extensive work-sharing and low productivity of labour that engenders high incidence of poverty among informal workers.

The existence of a large gap in labour income between the two sectors has important consequences for the functioning of a dual economy. It is evidently rational for most, if not all, workers to seek jobs in the formal sector in the first place. Labour supply to the formal sector is thus 'unlimited' so that formal employment gets determined by labour demand in the formal sector alone. Informal employment is thus largely a residual. All those who fail to find employment in the formal sector seek employment in the informal sector.[2] They find it because the possibility of work-sharing in the informal sector allows absorption of new workers and pre-empts

[1]A detailed discussion of the characteristics of a dual economy is available in Ghose (2010).

[2]Only a few young and educated persons from relatively well-off households can afford to wait in the queue for jobs in the formal sector; these are the unemployed in a labour-surplus dual economy. This explains why the unemployment rate is generally low in developing countries even while the incidence of poverty is high. The poor are not unemployed; they have bad jobs.

full-time unemployment. *Ceteris paribus*, an increase in the number of persons seeking employment in the informal sector leads not to full-time unemployment of some informal workers but to increased underemployment of all informal workers. This, of course, means a reduction in output per informal worker and hence an increase in the incidence of poverty. Such outcomes are pre-empted only if there is compensating growth of productivity of informal labour, that is, only if there is investment and growth in the informal sector.

It is obvious that the wage rate in the informal sector—the wage rate for casual labour—cannot be market-determined; the existence of work-sharing means that the supply of casual labour always exceeds the demand for it. There thus arises a question as to how this wage rate is determined. The short answer is that this wage is governed by the output per worker in self-employment.[3] This is easy to see once we recognize that the casual wage labourers and the self-employed (at least a large section of it) are not mutually exclusive categories. A casual labourer and a self-employed person can be and often are members of the same household. And a casual wage labourer periodically engages in self-employment just as a self-employed person periodically engages in casual wage employment.

What, then, does an improvement in employment conditions in a labour-surplus dual economy mean? It essentially means an increase in productivity, and hence of labour income of informal labour. This can come about in two possible ways. First, if the growth of the formal sector is such that the incremental demand for workers there exceeds the incremental labour force in the economy in each period, some of the informal workers move to formal employment in each period. Productivity and incomes of those who remain in informal employment then increase (even if output growth is zero) because of a decline in underemployment. Second, public investment in the informal sector, by generating substantial growth, can directly increase the productivity of informal labour.

In development theory, economic growth is expected to steadily improve employment conditions in a dual economy basically through the first route. In schematic terms, the formal sector, where formal labour and skills combine with modern technology and entrepreneurship, is the source of capital accumulation and hence the engine of growth, while the informal sector is merely the supplier of labour. As growth occurs, therefore, it seems reasonable to expect the formal sector to pull labour out of the informal sector so that the share of informal employment in total employment declines. However, a little reflection tells us that the rate of growth of the formal sector has to be impossibly high for this to work. The best that can be achieved is a rate of growth of formal employment that is higher than the rate of growth of the labour force in the economy. But this does not improve employment conditions in the economy. For, the rate of growth of the workforce in the informal sector still remains positive so that underemployment grows and output per worker declines. If employment conditions are to improve, therefore, there must also be output growth in the informal sector, which requires public investment in the sector.[4]

It is time to look into some facts (the relevant data are put together in Table 1). Informal labour is the overwhelmingly dominant form of labour in India. In 2004–5 (the latest year for which data are available), formal employees—the regular wage employees who work in the government/public sector, in the private corporate sector, and in other private-sector establishments with 10 or more employees, and also enjoy some kind of social security—constituted just 6.6 per cent of the prime-age workforce of 365 million. The percentage employed in the formal sector was higher because the sector employed informal labour to a significant extent; 39 per cent of those employed in the formal sector were informal workers. Of the 341 million informal workers (including the informal workers employed in the formal sector), 56 per cent were in self-employment, 33 per cent worked as casual wage labourers, and 11 per cent were regular wage employees. And informal workers were to be found in all production sectors of the economy: 59 per cent were in agriculture, 19 per cent were in industry, and 22 per cent were in services.

An average casual wage labourer, who is employed and paid on a daily basis, worked for 4.8 days in a week and sought but failed to find work on another 0.7 days; thus the rate of underemployment was 12.7 per cent. Even this high rate of underemployment is most likely to be an underestimate. For, given the high incidence of poverty among these workers, it is hard to believe that they were seeking work on only 5.5 days in a week. Underemployment of the self-employed (the incidence of poverty among whom is also high) is likely to be nearly as serious as that of the casual wage labourers, but the former is hard to measure.[5]

[3]For rigorous formulation of this proposition and elaboration of the implications, see Ghose (2010).

[4]For elaboration of the arguments, see Ghose (2010).

[5]This is because of the difficulty of distinguishing, in the case of the self-employed, between 'someone being in employment' and 'someone actually working'. This difficulty does not arise in the case of casual wage employees, who are in employment only when they are actually working.

Table 1 Informal Labour in India, 1983–2005

	1983	2004–5
Total employed workforce (in million)	238.0	365.4
As percentage of total employed workforce:		
Formal employees in formal sector	10.2	6.6
Informal employees in formal sector	3.4	4.2
Workers in informal sector	86.4	89.2
All informal workers	89.8	93.4
As percentage of all informal workers:		
Regular wage employees	6.6	10.6
Casual wage employees	35.2	33.3
Self-employed	58.2	56.1
Employed in agriculture	65.6	58.5
Employed in industry	11.6	19.0
Employed in services	22.8	22.5
Rate of underemployment (%)		
Casual wage employees	13.0	12.6
Number of days of work per week		
Casual wage employees	4.7	4.8
Wage per day worked (in 1983 Rs)		
Formal employees		65.2
All regular wage employees	19.7	44.5
Casual wage employees	7.1	11.4
All employees in the formal sector	27.3	53.6
All employees in the informal sector	8.6	13.9
Output per worker (in 1983 Rs)		
Formal sector	1844.7	6868.3
Informal sector	829.9	1737.0
Incidence of poverty (%)		
Formal employees		6.5
All regular wage employees	38.1	17.7
Casual wage employees	76.8	56.5
Self-employed	57.4	35.4

Source: Author's estimates based on data available from the 38th and 61st Rounds of National Sample Survey of Employment and Unemployment, and from National Accounts Statistics.
Note: The poverty lines used are: Rs 446.7 for rural areas and Rs 578.8 for urban areas in 2004–5 prices.

The gaps in productivity and wages between the formal and the informal sectors are large. In 2004–5, the average wage per worker in the formal sector was nearly four times that in the informal sector. And the output per worker in the formal sector was also about four times that in the informal sector.

Contrary to expectations, economic growth in India has been associated not just with increasing importance of informal labour in the economy but also with widening gaps between formal and informal labour. During the 22-year period between 1983 and 2005, the rate of economic growth was quite rapid: 5.6 per cent per annum.[6] Yet, the share of informal employment in total employment increased from 90 per cent in 1983 to 93 per cent in 2004–5. At the same time, the ratio of wage per worker in the formal sector to that in the informal sector increased from 3 to 4 and the same ratio for output per worker increased from 2 to 4. Economic growth in India has strengthened, not weakened, dualism.

The proximate reason is the very slow growth of demand for labour and high growth of labour productivity in the formal sector. Formal employment actually recorded zero growth. Even formal sector employment (which includes employment of informal workers) grew at a rate of only 0.9 per cent per annum while the labour force was growing at a rate of 1.8 per cent per annum. So the share of formal employment in total employment declined from 10.2 to 6.6 per cent. And the share of informal employment in the formal sector increased from 25 to 39 per cent. At the same time, output per worker in the formal sector increased at a rate of 6.3 per cent per annum.

How can these trends be explained? Research points to three broad factors. First, because India is a late developer, its formal sector uses technologies acquired from developed countries, which tend to be labour saving in character. Second, India pursued a development strategy that placed much emphasis on heavy industries, which are inherently capital-intensive.[7] Finally, the regulations governing employment in the formal sector have been such as to encourage growth of wage and output per worker rather than growth of employment. By placing excessive emphasis on protection of jobs of persons already in formal employment, these regulations effectively define the interest of formal employees in terms of growth of wages. At the same time, they generate rather strong incentives for employers to focus on capital-intensive activities as well as on capital-intensive techniques of production; for, the interest of workers (growth of wages) remains consistent with that of employers (growth of profits) so long as the output per worker rises steadily.

So the growth of the formal sector in India failed to generate a process of transformation of informal labour into formal labour. In consequence, the growth of the workforce in the informal sector was higher than the growth of the labour force in the economy. Fortunately,

[6]This refers to net domestic product (NDP) and not to gross domestic product (GDP).
[7]See Chakravarty (1987) for an insightful discussion of India's development strategy.

the growth of the informal sector was substantial so that output per worker in the informal sector still grew at a rate of 3.5 per cent per annum. It was this that brought about modest improvements in the employment conditions of informal labour. The real wage rate for casual labour increased at a rate of 2.2 per cent per annum while the rate of underemployment remained stable. The incidence of poverty among the self-employed as also among the casual wage employees declined by about a percentage point per year.

The growth of the informal sector also brought about some changes in the pattern of employment of informal labour. The importance of self-employment declined while that of wage employment correspondingly increased. The share of regular wage employees in all wage employees also increased. And informal workers were moving out of agriculture into industry; the share of agriculture in total informal employment declined from 66 to 59 per cent while the share of industry increased from 12 to 19 per cent. These are changes that economic growth is expected to generate in a developing economy in the aggregate. In the case of India, we observe them only in the informal part of the economy. Much of the employment in the formal sector was in services to begin with. And the share of services in formal sector employment increased over time while the share of industry declined.

The main point that India's development experience highlights is that while the conditions of informal labour will continue to improve (though rather slowly) so long as decent growth of the informal sector is sustained, dualism will steadily grow stronger so long as the growth of the formal sector fails to generate a process of transformation of informal labour into formal labour. Such a combination of outcomes is not just undesirable but is also unlikely to be sustainable. This is why government policies have to focus not just on sustaining a decent growth of the informal sector (and on implementing special employment and social security schemes for informal workers) but also on increasing the employment intensity of growth of the formal sector.

AJIT K. GHOSE

References

Chakravarty, Sukhamoy. 1987. *Development Planning: The Indian Experience*, Oxford, Clarendon Press.

Ghose, Ajit K. 2010. 'Reinventing Development Economics', *Economic and Political Weekly*, 45(42): 41–50.

Lewis, W. A. 1954. 'Economic Development with Unlimited Supplies of Labour', *Manchester School*, 22: 139–91.

Infrastructure

The stabilization of the Indian economy in 1992–3 was followed by major structural reforms. An important part of these reforms was the opening up of the infrastructure sector to private capital, and with some lag to foreign capital as well. Unlike in manufacturing, the entry of private capital in infrastructure necessitated regulatory and associated policy developments, given that the infrastructure sector shows varying degrees of market 'failure'. The report of the Expert Committee (GoI 1997) popularly called the Rakesh Mohan Committee (RMC) report set the agenda for reforms of the infrastructure sector. The electricity sector had witnessed the so-called independent power producer policy that 'encouraged' the private sector to generate power to be sold to state electricity boards (SEBs) through long-term contracts as early as in 1994. The report and the discussions that followed created a virtual consensus that the problem of India was that of poor infrastructure holding back development.

The RMC report served to highlight the importance of bringing in the private sector into most areas of infrastructure. Following the report and its wide influence, many states (Gujarat, Andhra Pradesh, Karnataka, Punjab, and Rajasthan) passed legislations that created umbrella organizations—typically infrastructural development boards (IDBs) that have the mandate (but not necessarily the power) to develop infrastructure, especially through private capital. Through enactments, the private sector's participation, typically in the form of BOT, was enabled in most states. Nevertheless, after an initial spurt, private investments petered out. The much hoped for investments in urban areas have yet to materialize. The creation of IDBs did not give these organizations sufficient power, and the new laws did not address issues emanating from consistency with past laws and authorities. Thus, turf wars between the IDB and the public works department (PWD), the irrigation department, and the roads and bridges department were not uncommon.

More than fiscal stringency several basic factors ensured that the movement towards reforms was very slow. It was only much later—in 2002—that the government was able to get the model for building roads right with the inclusion of the annuity form in public–private partnerships (PPPs), and the improvements in EPC for government-built roads. This led to fairly large investments in the arterial national highways (Golden Quadrilateral, the Port Connectivity and the East–West and North–South Corridors). Lately, investments are being generated in the power sector through the Ultra Mega Power Project (UMPP) framework. Following the success of Case I and II models of the UMPP framework, some states have mimicked them for adding capacities. While these are certainly steps forward, the core problems of subsidization, linking competition for the markets to competition in the markets, besides the immediate task of bringing about a national market remain.

Other more basic adverse factors that were operative in the pre-reform period have continued to constrain infrastructure. The problems of land acquisition have been, and continue to remain, a major constraint in infrastructural investment. The common perception is that India's democracy naturally makes land acquisition difficult while in China and elsewhere in East Asia the matter is easy since governments are not accountable. The reality though is very different. It is the continuation of the state's unmitigated control over land emanating from an 'imperial' law inherited from colonial rulers that is at the root of the problem. Besides incorporating the rents in agricultural use, land values in areas surrounding urban centres also include the value arising out of the probability of the land being used for non-agricultural purposes such as housing. But in India, since governments have a discretionary control over land use, the latter value does not uniformly accrue to all land surrounding an urban area. All of it would suddenly accrue to the land that is released by the government for non-agricultural use. This would depress the prices elsewhere while increasing them for the land released from agricultural use (and acquired or brought by an aggregator). Thus, post-acquisition the market prices are always very high, often by as much as five to ten times the pre-acquisition 'market' prices paid. Interesting ways of acquisition possible such as issuance of development rights to the ex-landowner, equity share in projects, re-mapping through town planning schemes, and compensatory transfer of development rights are not part of the practice.

The unfairness introduces large risks in the form of post-acquisition litigation and social movements that have delayed large infrastructure projects. Indeed many 'environmental' movements take place around land acquisition because the affected people have little recourse under the law. A less 'imperial' state would have attempted to limit the public purpose as arising when the land required is specific, such as the site of a deep water port or a dam, or for the expansion of a road between two towns, since these tend to be unique.

The institutional framework for acquisition is also problematic. There is far too much discretion and power available to the administrator and the government of the day. Moreover, it is the government that decides both the land to acquire and also its value. This creates a conflict of interest that acts against landowners who do not have contacts in high places.

Lately, the government has come up with the Land Acquisition Amendment (2007) Bill which in some ways attempts to rectify the worst aspects of the imperial 1894 law. Thus multiple valuation methods are allowed. Nevertheless, valuation is still not independent. While it includes a provision for private acquisition of land, this is not correctly drafted and has created much misunderstanding and opposition. A significant improvement is that public purpose has been better specified. Similarly, the valuation includes recognition of the future increase in value due to changing land use and as such provides a vehicle for correct valuation and overcoming pre-acquisition land use distortions if the government so chooses. However, the risks may not have been mitigated since the discretion available with the government of the day has not been reduced. The associated Rehabilitation and Resettlement Bill, 2007, though is highly problematic, having been driven almost entirely by NGO perspectives. Its most important lacunae are that it does not provide for closure of compensation during land acquisition/resettlement process, and is worded in ways that enhance the range of discretion, thus heightening the potential for politicization of the compensation and rehabilitation elements for the displaced. Risks are enhanced since the wording is such that there is no firmness to what the government needs to do, but many options are mentioned as what the government 'may' rather than 'will' do. Similarly, the insistence on profit share would delay closure.

A visible evidence of the country's infrastructure failure is in its cities. In planning with very low floor space indices (FSIs) (very low built-up densities) that have little relationship with locational economics, the land cost share in real estate infrastructure becomes too high. Similarly, since much urban infrastructure shows increasing returns to built-up density, this too becomes expensive to provide. As a result, the poor get pushed into 'illegal' spaces, and most others are spread out in sprawl development, with increased travel times and densities that are not high enough to make mass transport systems (metro rail) viable. Other network infrastructure too become like drinking water, and sewage systems become expensive as well.

Compounding this problem is the lack of organizational autonomy and authority of elected representatives in urban local bodies and their lack of control over staff which results in powerlessness to take on their responsibilities credibly. This is despite the 74th

Constitutional Amendment which provides autonomy to urban local bodies.

Overambitious standards in infrastructure, especially in the layout of townships have also been a cause of failure. Thus, the excessive provision of open and public spaces in the design invite violations since they are often 'unaffordable'. Such violations then spread (given the very high return to violations), so that the chance of holding on to reasonable standards is lost. Violation becomes rampant, especially by those able to influence officials. Similarly, the Ministry of Urban Development's insistence on very high standards for post-treated solid waste (not possible in India given the inevitable contamination with faecal matter), has kept interested foreign investors away.

Besides the Delhi Metro, which as a project is being well implemented, metros have been taken up in a number of other cities as well. However, the opportunity to generate vast social values and relax urban transport constraints through the linkage of the metro with other modes by increasing the densities in metro corridors through coordination with town planning authorities, and more generally to coordinate town planning with transport planning, are being missed. The potential to greatly reduce gross trips, especially motor trips by truly moving to the multimodal, and have populations reside and economic activity take place close to the metro and transport corridors in both the metropolitan cities and in the large second rung cities are being missed completely. This orthogonality of town planning from transport planning, the very FSIs that city planners use in India, and the inadequate release of land for urban use result in very high house prices. Options such as auctions of additional FSI, raising FSI and linking it to purchase of transfer of development rights (TDRs), award of TDRs to slum dwellers and to others upon whose land low FSIs need to be imposed or whose land is being used for infrastructure development in urban places, and use of clarity on property rights and titles are all being missed. Similarly, the ignorance and non-use of 'TP schemes'[1] to overcome hurdles in urban planning and releasing land for urban development with amenities is surprising. The most important failure here is the lack of coordination across the functions that constitute municipal services. And that has made Indian cities among the most disease-prone with public health engineering all but absent. Sewerage services have the characteristic of being a good, the consumption of which when not universal creates vast negative enternalities—unhygienic environment—when people who are not covered by the service use public and vacant spaces as their toilet. More than in any other public service, therefore, USO is most justified here. Yet this sector had high access charges and there are almost no public toilets. No wonder then that India has very high levels of morbidity in its urban places, well above that of its income peers.

Despite more than 15 years of 'reforms', the electricity sector continues to be plagued by policy and regulatory uncertainty. In the oil and natural gas sectors, the picture is no different with the system having moved from the earlier administered price mechanism to what is worse—adhocism in prices and tax rates. The oil sector continues to extract its toll through massive adulteration, diversion, short-selling, and an impossible governance situation where managers get murdered if they resist adulteration by dealers. In electricity the losses are astronomical. In oil and gas a new initiative to put oil and gas distribution on open-access common carrier mode has been put in place but the substantial regulations have yet to happen. The initial developments would suggest that neither the Petroleum and Natural Gas Regulatory Board (PNGRB) nor the Competition Commission are seriously concerned with the deleterious effects of price-based subsidies on the efficiency and the distortions and waste in the use of oil resources. Yet there is an attempt to regulate even segments of the business that are not strictly natural monopolies, such as tankage. The Electricity Act, 2003, attempts to bring in open access and competition for the market in generation, with trading as a distinct business, and reduction in cross-subsidies. Yet actual open access has not taken place on the ground and electricity distribution shows large losses.

The problem is that state regulators have been weak and have not used their powers (even) under the existing law (the Electricity Act, 2003). Thus, they have allowed unbundled distribution companies (DISCOMs) to buy power on a long-term basis at inflated prices from other state-owned companies. They have not sought to rule cost to serve prices, with the government then setting the subsidies, but have gone ahead and set different prices for different categories without explicitly determining the cross subsidy surcharge necessary under the law. Thus, despite 'independent' regulation, consumers still do not know their true cost to serve tariffs. They have also allowed government companies to hold on to the same

[1]These are most effectively used in Ahmedabad and some of the Gujarat cities to overcome the problem of urban extension without having to physically acquire land, through a process of land aggregation and remapping individual plots with internal offsets and transfers. Strangely, few of the other cities are even aware of the potential that is there in TP Schemes. Most urban commissioners being non-professionals are hardly aware of space planning techniques. And in the lack of clarity in the roles of the officer versus the elected, task performance suffers, and there is little coordination across functions and organizations, since there is no embedment of responsibility as well.

tariff for a class of consumers right across the state despite the fact that the DISCOMs' territory rather than the state boundaries constitute the basis of tariff setting. The behaviour of state electricity regulators raises the peculiarly Indian phenomenon of 'regulatory capture' of ostensibly independent regulators. It is remarkable that the tariffs of almost all segments of consumers other than for agricultural pump-set users is higher than there cost to serve.

Regulatory developments in infrastructure, with the notable exception of TRAI in the early phases, have proven to be an added retardant to not only private investments but also investments in general. The poor capacities and motivation of regulators to exploit the powers under the Acts to push for reforms are factors contributing to this situation. Since many of the appointees are retired civil servants who are attuned to thinking from the government's perspective of having to 'manage' rather than reforming a system, this behaviour is not surprising. Clauses empowering arbitrary government intervention are common in regulatory Acts.

Regulators have tended to choose the much discredited and non-workable cost plus regulation, in the late 1990s! In not choosing the obvious—incentive regulation—such as price cap and its variants for sectors like transmission and wires business in distribution of electricity or in pipelines, they have further enhanced the regulatory risk.

The fundamental problem in electricity and energy (and in the food and fertilizer sectors as well) emanates from the mode of subsidization. Price-based subsidization in lowering the allocative price of the service/commodity cause many perversities. Low prices for electricity (zero prices for use given the HP-based tariffs) that apply to agriculture result in major distortions on the user and utility side. The user side distortions include excessive use and wastage, environmental problems, including salinity ingress, destruction of aquifers, water-intensive crops being grown in dry areas, and cropping pattern distortions more generally. While these are sometimes mentioned in discussions, that they arise out of the near zero prices is not appreciated. Not surprisingly India draws out more groundwater than any other country by a wide margin. Similarly, the zero tariffs repel any investments in water saving technologies, such as drip and sprinkler systems, with much potential since the costs here are private. The eastern region with abundant water is discriminated against in the national market for grain and this is one of the important reasons for the continued poverty in the region since it hurts the region's comparative advantage to grow water intensive crops. Worse still are the utility side effects, especially in electricity and oil. In electricity the large price difference between consumers of various categories creates the scope for price 'arbitrage', that is, for the commercial staff to misreport consumption by various sectors to create rents, and loss of accountability.

Instead of eliminating the 'price arbitrage', the government and regulatory bodies try to work around the situation by having 'tamper proof' metres, 'armoured cables', separation of rural agricultural feeders from others, and mono-phase distribution, all of which are not only enormously expensive but also doomed to fail since fundamentally there cannot be an accountability to revenue in a situation of price arbitrage. What is even more remarkable is that there are central programmes that give funds and grants for such investments which are essentially wasteful. The story is not very different in oil distribution. The tragedy is that political commitment and administrative energies, both rare in India, have, in these sectors, been spent against an impossible task of overcoming losses when the price arbitrage is large.

In many states electricity distribution officials have been given magisterial powers since these powers are necessary to resist theft under the conditions described earlier. So a simple task like management becomes quasi-police and something that has to be monitored at the highest level—by the Prime Minister's Office. It goes without saying that in such situations the private sector would not enter unless the contracts are overly sweetened.

Some positive developments have taken place in distribution. The Bhiwandi experiment of handing over a particularly difficult distribution territory to a private operator who can use the carrot and stick approach to overcome theft is in the right direction. Here the private party, being able to appropriate a significant part of the gains brought about by better management of the distribution system and overcoming theft, had strong incentives to do so. The fact of low agricultural demand in Bhiwandi meant that the temptation to now indulge in price arbitrage was not strong. However, since this model cannot overcome this problem without tariff reforms, it has limited applicability. The electricity sector could overnight get rid of its problems with tariff reforms (near uniform prices) and direct endowment-based subsidies.

In Gujarat the feeder separation puts irrigation pump-sets (IPs) on separate feeders so that the supplies can be curtailed to eight hours or so.[2] Then the rest of the system can be held accountable to electricity flow on the other feeders improving the control and accountability of the system and giving the very large social value of

[2]Recognize that at zero use prices for electricity, the demand from farmers is technically 'infinitely' large and, therefore, needs to be rationed.

24x7 supplies to consumers at home and in rural areas. This programme—the JGY—has brought about benefits to rural households in Gujarat since the government, unlike in many other states, is willing to both contract for capacity and buy power to supply to other consumers. This also generates surplus since the charges here are well above costs. Other states by 'evenly' distributing the pain have denied value to all consumers and are unable to bootstrap to viability. But, of course, the better supplies to IP sets, enabled by the large surpluses generated from properly serving other customers at high tariffs, have only increased the wasteful use of electricity by farmers in Gujarat.

The central regulator also faces the challenge of bringing about proper market mechanisms for competition in the market. For a long time the regulator shared the false notion that one cannot have markets in a world of shortages, without realizing that when the tariff for a segment is zero then there would be shortages. In any case availability based tariffs, which linked short-term prices to the frequency deviation from 50 hertz, was already a market of sorts. Now the regulator has rightly decided that this needs to go with a proper day ahead market and a real time balancing market. The first consultation papers in this regard are apparently being worked out. Creating the right kind of markets is not easy since the market design has to ensure that despatch is on merit order and there are adequate incentives for adding to capacity. The latter more so for India since India is in the phase of infrastructural expansion. This would mean separate markets for capacity and energy, such that the competition for the market and in the market are linked. Additionally, transmission pricing would have to permit long-distance exchange, and congestion pricing would have to be non-distortionary. Right now the regulator is confronted with the problem of more than one power exchange with suboptimal trades taking place and trade itself being constrained by a dysfunctional preference being given to bilateral traders, when the regulator should have treated all trades, except those involving long-term power procurement contracts, on par.

The risks from government decision-making, which are often discretionary, hurt private investments. The government of the day has far too much discretion that is not adequately constrained by the legislature. Thus it was only in the late-1990s that the Centre and the Reserve Bank of India were able to place limits on state governments in their use of guarantees and contingent liabilities to incur expenditures that did not have the sanction of the legislature. State-level public-sector units are largely a vehicle for government spending that bypass the legislature. Similarly, the central government too has used central public-sector undertakings (PSUs) to finance infrastructural and related expenditures that did not have the formal approval of Parliament.

Associated with this tendency is the poor record of adhering to contracts by the state in its internal dealings, with its own enterprises and parastatals, and often with private contracting parties. PPPs, especially those that involve regular payouts—annuities, viability gap funding, shadow tolling, subsidy payment—that is, private finance initiatives (PFIs), are problematic because when governments change there is an irresistible tendency to open up/question the earlier government's deals. Where the agreements emerge out of law and the adherence to procedures and processes is under the law, and they are not purely commercial, the risk is much less. But few projects are so covered. The ex-ante effects of large risks have typically ruled out many otherwise possible PFIs. Irrigation, water supply and sanitation, city roads, and sewerage services, all of which have large asset lives or have excludability/appropriability problems, are affected.

It was the compositional and coordination economies that justified state intervention and planning in the late industrialization context, and herein the failure of the Indian state is most glaring. Where multiple agencies/departments have to work together failure is almost guaranteed. Thus, the new highways built under the National Highway Development Programme (NHDP) do not smoothly lead to city centres. So a large part of the total value of the vast investments on road construction, which would have otherwise been possible, is denied to society. Coordination among multiple agencies and authorities necessary for the seamless construction and management of a road, or in the realization of benefits from multimodal designs, has proven to be all but impossible to realize.

The problem is fundamental and lies in the nature of the accountability of the key managers within the state and its parastatals. Constitutional immunity to career bureaucrats and the conflicting allocation of powers and responsibilities between elected representatives and administrators are responsible for a situation of powerlessness among politicians (and the bureaucracy). Politicians cannot credibly promise to get a local road or the water supplies fixed. After all, they have to depend on administrators who are not essentially answerable to them. As a result they cannot make 'political capital' which is the raison d'être of politics. Nor can citizens demand accountability since the system makes them powerless. Not surprisingly, in a Darwinian sense, the situation has selected and created the irresponsible and corrupt politician. Administrative positions change with a rapidity that would prevent any firm and deep understanding of the problems, in essentially what are public management and policy tasks that increasingly demand specialist skills. A general belief in the power of 'leadership' to overcome hurdles, sanctified in the public image of a few successful bureaucrats, takes the attention away from the need to rewrite the rules, restructure organizations, redefine the budgetary process, and introduce competition for powerful positions in policymaking and administration by going outside the cadre to experts, and above all in making policies incentive compatible.

Procurement failure is another important reason for poor infrastructural performance. PWDs, railways, and other government parastatals with the significant exception of a few central public enterprises, have perverse contracting procedures and rules. Typically the tenets of good procurement are ignored. There is little flexibility to tailor procurement to suit the purpose or the nature of the good/service. Service contracts that attempt to shift all risks on to the private party, payment terms that do not recognize the experience nature of many goods and services, and frequent post bid changes in scope, besides poor specifications are typical. Too many packages that enhance coordination risks and make monitoring all but impossible have all taken their toll. Improvements have been slow, despite models being available.

Despite the existence of the Indian Supply Services (as a special civil service now abolished), procurement practices remain rudimentary and generally do not recognize the need to tailor procurement to the kind of goods/services being procured. Again, poor specification, often lack of separation of the price bid and the technical bid, the practice of ex-post change in evaluation criteria when complex items are being procured, and the lack of clarity on the requirements and valuation ex-ante have all acted to contribute to the problem. It is more a case of those in power being able to take advantage of these deficiencies rather than 'corruption per se' being the problem. Some of the leading public enterprises have far better procurement practices but are hampered by the onerous condition of necessarily having to tender for all procurement and processes that do not allow for reputational effects to be taken advantage of, besides the ubiquitous interference from the government.

Telecom, which has been on a relatively smooth path of unfoldment, thanks in many ways to the earlier TRAI and the light (price cap) regulation, has run into controversies. Spectrum allocation reached the high point of sophisticated and perversion-free allocation with the recently concluded 3G auction which created a bid framework for allocation based on joint equilibrium in all the circles with multiple (4) competing players in every circle. With reference to this auction, clearly the earlier 2G allocations were crude and would most certainly have generated some rents.[3] The most important issue here is the prevalence of the notion that first-come-first-served is a fair basis for awarding scarce resources, or project opportunities to private players. Its ill-effects in generating rents and in rent-seeking behaviour are not widely recognized within the government, especially in the civil service.

The coal block allocation process for the power sector has had the perversity that ex-post entry, some of the winning players have successfully interpreted the use of coal allocated to them to include not only for the power being procured (for which they had bid) but also for additional power generation which they can sell as merchant producers in the spot market or on a contractual basis to other parties. Therefore, this has resulted in those who did not make such interpretations to rightly go to the court.

The PPP challenge is essentially a procurement and contracting one where economics and especially ideas of incentive compatibility of the various actors, legal consistency, organizational feasibility, and political feasibility have to be recognized and built upon. This has proven difficult even in pioneering countries like the UK, so it is highly debatable if PPPs could be a panacea for the problems in the infrastructure sector, or that they can be used on a wide scale with an expanding scope that is hoped for. Yet, the importance of getting PPPs right cannot be overstressed in India because there is very little possibility of the state and administrative machinery reforming from within to improve the delivery of public services, and execute large infrastructure projects. The very few exceptions, most notably the Delhi Metro, only prove the rule since their success would hardly have been possible without the unique drive and capacity of its CEO. This dependence upon unique leadership, without a concomitant change in the process, rules, and framework would make only for a slow and inefficient addition to woefully required infrastructure.

It is hardly realized that much of the infrastructure in the now advanced countries was built by competing natural monopolies and the state, with the role of the state increasing in importance with the lateness of

[3]Yet the claims of lakhs of crores of rupees loss and transfer benefits are hardly valid since these benefits (the revenue loss to the state) would to a large extent be competed away by the new entrants having to fight for market share with the earlier incumbents and those winning the 3G spectrum as well. Consumers would be the ultimate beneficiaries through low tariffs and higher service quality and network expansion.

industrialization. In successful East Asia and China as well, the state has been at the forefront of infrastructural development, where the service has the characteristic of being a natural monopoly. And where there is appropriability failure the state's role has been paramount. The task of creating suitable frameworks for bringing in the private sector in such sectors as city roads, drinking water, and sewage and sanitation systems with multiple market failures (natural monopoly, additivity benefits of use, and value subtraction when there is non-use even by small segments) is important but the state has little ability to do so and certainly not in keeping with the enormous hope being placed on PPPs. The tendency to go in for PPPs and PFIs without appropriate bid structures is rife.

At the other extreme there is a tendency to constrain PPPs through the overemphasis on 'model concession agreements'. Not all PPPs that do well need to generate rents. The inability to distinguish between rents arising out of perverse agreements and profits that are true rewards for heightened performance, and for cost efficiency under regulation that has to award the same tariffs for the inefficient incumbent and the newly entering private player again leads to problems. It is also not realized that PPPs involve great variety depending upon the economic characteristics of the product/service, local conditions, the existence and extent of subsidization, and the constitutional framework. The problem is severe enough to have warranted the creation of Partnerships UK to whet and comment upon PPPs as a neutral body. India more than the UK would need this kind of institution but the government is yet to realize that such an organization can lead to risk reduction, true standardization, and lower the costs for both municipal bodies and private players and financiers. Due to the lack of such expertise and a referral body (and for other reasons) the recent privatizations of Delhi and Mumbai airports are not free of rents or risks, despite the obvious and large gains to users that the bringing in of private players has resulted in.

The idea of a development finance institution (DFI) to merely direct government funds to infrastructure was anathema in a liberalized financial environment. But the Infrastructure Development Finance Company (IDFC), which was set up in 1997, wisely interpreted its roles to be market development, project structuring, viability gap financing, and leveraging private investments through crucial investments. Policy advice covering details to enable the creation of appropriate frameworks was a role that IDFC took upon but which overlapped with the turf of the state. Expectedly, despite major gains, the experiment had only a limited life. Again the government has mooted the idea of a special finance company to direct funds borrowed abroad 'cheaply' to private projects, including PPPs, and more recently of a special purpose vehicle (SPV) to finance the viability gap component of infrastructure projects. These initiatives reflect a tendency to get at least some projects going even if core problems with policy and regulation that enhance risks and negate viability remain unaddressed. The India Infrastructure Financing Company Ltd has wisely set itself the correct mandate of doing more take-out financing (covering the interest rate change risk), helping structure projects appropriately, refinancing, lending long, and credit enhancement, all of which crowd in private and bank capital and leverage the original government contribution to resources.

Earlier, the government was prone to giving guarantees merely to cover avoidable risks emanating from poor policies and inadequate contractual frameworks, but now there is increased realization of arriving at the optimal risk allocation. Therefore, in seeking private investments very large costs and risks may be ultimately borne by the state. The worst example of this tendency is the framework that created IPPs (now mercifully abandoned) under which cash strung state electricity boards were encouraged to sign high-cost power purchase agreements (PPAs), which shifted most significant business risks on to the government, while taking over political risks. And to 'compensate' for this reversal, the private parties charged high risk premium returns. Returns in generation could, therefore, go as high as 30 per cent.

The state's failure in infrastructure and, more generally, in the provision of public services is systematically revealed. Development indicators that depend upon the state and its activities and where the public aspect is large do relatively poorly than others which depend less on the state. Thus, on infant mortality or death during child birth, both of which depend much more on the performance of public health and hygiene systems, India's score is far below that of other countries with similar levels of income. But on adult mortality which can be mitigated by a private health sector—India's low-cost doctors and medicines—the performance is significantly above that of its peers. Primary education and basic literacy, sanitation and sewerage, and airports are, respectively, more public in nature than higher education, at home sanitation, and operation of airlines. The limited access of the Indian state has made India's performance in the former set of services much poorer than in countries with levels of income comparable to India's.

Success has eluded reform efforts in many sectors. But when realized, the effects have been remarkably large. Thus NHAI got the essentials of the road construction contracts nearly right—a road fund sealed from the general government budget, independent engineers to certify road quality, good designs that erred on the side of higher specifications, linking payment to maintenance, clarity in risk allocation, appropriate package sizes, and turnkey basis for the award of contracts. Similarly, the BOT and annuity frameworks were also essentially incentive compatible though fewer stretches were to be built using these forms. The resulting investments were overwhelming and in a year or so more investments than in an entire decade flowed into the highway sector. The programme's economy-wide demand-side effects continue to be a force in the high growth of the economy since 2002. The approach and contract forms of NHAI are also sought to be imitated by many state governments.

Airlines were thrown open to the private sector without much regulation except on safety and technical aspects. Despite some major limitations in the policy, such as not allowing private airlines (until recently) to operate on international routes, the airline industry has completely changed from the vantage point of the consumer. New segments have been added and air travel is no longer a luxury; it also threatens to challenge an immovable railways in upper class travel. Some improvements in roads, especially in the western and southern parts of the county, have suddenly made possible multiaxle trucks with their superior efficiency. 'Fast' buses on roads now challenge the railways in all classes of passenger travel.

Much the same story holds in overnight postal packages delivery. A private sector, despite the higher cost of duplication of services on account of numerous players, has made it nearly impossible for the high-priced state owned carrier Speed Post to survive. In both airlines and posts, besides the superior operating efficiency of the private sector, the fact of significantly lower labour costs for the private sector is important. Unlike much of East Asia the long period of enclaved growth has created a schism in the labour market by which the competitive labour market is not usually to large firms or the state. Cost differences can be as high as eight times or more. So in privatization or in contracting out of services where competitive labour can be brought to bear there are enormous cost savings.

In telecom, on the other hand, the basics of the regulation (price cap tariffs, independence, shift from licence fees to revenue sharing to lower risk, and allowing multiple licensees to ensure competitive behaviour even if such entities were under-scaled, but with no bar on merger and alliances) was right. And the technology driver in reducing costs and increasing the coverage potential was high. For these two reasons the telecom sector has grown very rapidly through both private and public investment. Telecom promises to cover all except the bottom 20 per cent or so of the population over the decade. For cellular telecom, India has the lowest tariffs in the world. Internet access has also grown by leaps and bounds and the much lower penetration of both telecom and internet as compared to China is on account of factors that lie quite outside the sector (the income level in India being barely a fourth or less than that of China, much better income distribution in China, besides higher levels of literacy and education). Problems of quality, especially in mobile services have surfaced, but are being systematically addressed by the regulator.

Political difficulties in the reform of infrastructure have been overly highlighted in discussions. The reality is otherwise. Where reasonable policy and institutional frameworks could be developed and put in place success has been spectacular. In almost all cases of slow movement or failure, the policy, regulatory, and subsidy frameworks in creating perverse incentives for both consumers and service providers are the core causes of failure. Corrections can also be politically feasible. After all there is so much surplus hidden in the current deadweight losses that even vested interests could be overcome through innovative mechanisms that allow them benefits while avoiding the deadweight losses. Similarly, the subsidies currently being enjoyed by the genuinely deserving can be easily retained and even enhanced through reforms. Thus today state electricity boards incur losses than are in excess of Rs 60,000 crore annually. Only a part, perhaps no more that Rs 15,000 crore would be delivered to farmers. The latter sum if made available as a direct subsidy to farmers through coupons without distorting the allocative (use) price of electricity would avoid these large losses and also be politically rewarding.

The ubiquitous poor have been the excuse for resisting change. In the name of the poor, the government's subsidy burden is of the order of 15 per cent of GDP. In contrast, to correctly subsidize the poor all, it would take is no more than about 1 per cent of GDP. In infrastructure, the poor are the excuse for keeping prices so low that they often get excluded. This happens in many ways. In drinking water in Delhi, despite the total production of more than 200 lpcd of water, as much as 30 per cent of the population uses less than 50 and some as low as 20. The price of water is low enough to make the large elastic demand of the rich compete with the inelastic (life line) demand of the poor to create denial, that is, the non-availability of a necessity despite purchasing power. Large health losses and purchase of water in markets at prices that are many times the cost of production negate the large consumer surpluses in a necessity. Moreover, since producing entities are thereby starved of internal resources there is underinvestment that creates permanent denial or 'outsiders' who have little hope of getting on to networks. The problem is further compounded by the usually high access charges when the use charges are so low. The red-herring that the fundamental problem of lack of endowments can be solved by loading the problem on to infrastructure in the highly distortionary way of subsidizing use rather than access and that too through prices is nevertheless shared widely among policymakers.

SEBASTIAN MORRIS

References

GoI. 1997. *The India Infrastructure Report,* Vols I, II and III, The Rakesh Mohan Committee, New Delhi, NCAER and the Government of India.

Morris, S. (ed.). 2001. *India Infrastructure Report 2001: Issues in Regulation and Industry Structure,* 3iNetwork, New Delhi, Oxford University Press.

——. (ed.). 2003. *India Infrastructure Report 2003: Public Expenditure Allocation and Accountability,* 3iNetwork, New Delhi, Oxford University Press.

——. (ed.). 2004. *India Infrastructure Report 2004: Ensuring Value for Money,* 3iNetwork, New Delhi, Oxford University Press.

——. 2010. 'The Question of Land and Infrastructure Development in India—Urgently Required Reforms for Fairness and Infrastructural Development', WP No. 2010-03-02.

Morris, S. and Rajiv Shekhar (eds). 2002. *India Infrastructure Report 2002: Governance Issues for Commercialization,* 3iNetwork, New Delhi, Oxford University Press.

Raghuram, G., Rekha Jain, Sidharth Sinha, Prem Pangotra, and Sebastian Morris. 1999. *Infrastructure Development and Financing: Towards a Public Private Partnership,* New Delhi, Macmillan.

Pandey, Ajay and Sebastian Morris. 2009. 'Electricity Reforms and Regulations—A Critical Review of the Last 10 Years Experience', Indian Institute of Management Ahmedabad, 25 March, Report submitted to CERC.

■ Intellectual Property Rights

The generation, valuation, protection, and valorization of intellectual property are becoming critically important issues all around the world. Why is this so? First, we have the phenomenon of increasing dominance of the new knowledge economy over the old 'brick and mortar' economy. Generation and protection of new knowledge assume importance in this context. Then there is the exponential growth of scientific knowledge. There is also the increasing demand for new forms of intellectual property (IP) protection as well as access to IP-related information. Additionally, we also have to address the emerging complexities linked to IP in traditional knowledge, community knowledge, and animate objects. All these pose a challenge in setting up the new 21st-century IP agenda, especially for a country like India.

While setting up the agenda for a balanced and progressive intellectual property rights (IPR) regime in India, it needs to be realized that IP will no longer be seen as a distinct or self-contained domain, but rather as an important and effective policy instrument that would be relevant to a wide range of socio-economic, technological, and political concerns. The development of skills and competence to manage IPRs and leverage their influence will, therefore, need increasing focus in India.

Historically, the IP system has been divided into two main branches. One branch is concerned with industrial property. This deals with technological inventions providing new solutions to technical problems. These are registered as patents; utility models also known as 'petty patents' or 'utility innovations'; trademarks for goods and services; commercial names and designations; industrial designs; geographical indications or indications of source and appellations of origin; and layout designs of integrated circuits. The other branch deals with copyright and related rights that protect literary and artistic expressions or works of culture, which, in the broadest sense, relate to creative expressions of ideas. Copyright provides protection to literary, musical, artistic, photographic, and audiovisual works, computer programmes, software, multimedia creations, and so on. The protection of confidential business information of commercial value, often called 'trade secrets', is also an important and distinctive form of IP. The protection of growers' rights in relation to new varieties of plants is another distinct form of IP.

The adoption of the Trade Related Aspects of Intellectual Property Systems (TRIPS) Agreement has meant certain obligations on all countries within which they have to circumscribe their laws. Every nation always needs a robust IP Act. It should be designed to facilitate innovation and growth as well as development. In particular, TRIPS has entailed significant changes for the protection of pharmaceutical products and processes. The Agreement has not only made product patent protection binding on all member countries (Article 27.1), but also strengthened, inter alia, process patents (Articles 28 (b) and 34), narrowly defined the conditions for establishing exceptions to patent rights (Article 30), and limited the possibility of applying special modalities of compulsory licences to pharmaceuticals (for example, as provided for in Canada until 1993).

India has continuously evolved its IP laws. Several amendments to the Copyright Act, creation of a new Trademark Act, a new Designs Act, and amendments to the Patent Act show India's desire to change. New Acts have also been enacted covering semiconductors and layout designs, which are of considerable importance to the electronics industry. Similarly, India's Plant Variety Protection Act and Farmers Rights Act will impact its agriculture and food industry. The Geographical Indications Act will protect the interests of groups in the different geographical areas of India.

Although IP covers diverse aspects, it is the aspect of patents that has attracted greatest attention. The first patents law in India was enacted in 1856. The Indian Patents and Designs Act was enacted in 1911. The need for a comprehensive law so as to ensure that patent rights are not worked to the detriment of the consumer or to the prejudice of trade or the industrial development of the country was felt as early as in 1948. After several attempts, the Bill introduced in Parliament came on to the Statute Book as the Patent Act, 1970.

India needed the 1970 Patent Act, given its state of scientific, technological, and industrial development at the time. This Act did not allow product patents in the fields of drugs and pharmaceuticals, food, and agriculture. Only process patents were allowed. This allowed India to make use of its undoubted prowess in process chemistry and engineering. India would not have succeeded in having the drugs and pharmaceuticals industry that it has today without the Patent Act of 1970. In the 1950s, India was importing even formulations. Today, thanks to this Act, the Indian pharmaceutical industry is one of the most developed amongst the developing countries.

During the 1995–2005 period, India met its entire TRIPS obligations in various stages starting from providing mailbox applications in 1999 with retrospective effect from 1 January 1995, followed by a second amendment to the Patents Act, which was passed by the Parliament of India in 2002 and came into force on 20 May 2003. This amendment for the first time brought the Indian Patents Act more or less on a par with the developed countries by providing a 20-year patent term and 18-month publication and also safeguarding national interests by remodeling compulsory licence provisions and by introducing bolar and import provisions. The third amendment to the Patents Act came into force from 1 January 2005, providing product patenting in pharmaceuticals, food, and chemicals, rationalizing and reducing timelines for processing patent applications, and doing away with exclusive marketing rights (EMR). The amended Act also provides pre-grant and post-grant oppositions and also safeguards generic producers from patent infringement suits by providing protection through EMR only from the date of grant.

There is concern about limiting the impact of the monopolies that will result from the enforcement of the new Act. Here, one must understand the way in which licences are issued. These are of three types of licences—voluntary, automatic, and compulsory. A voluntary licence is the result of a negotiated arrangement between the patent holder and any other party interested in the commercialization of the patent product.

The patent holder gets a royalty payment and there is no state intervention. On the other hand, state intervention is needed in the case of automatic and compulsory licensing, which can be used by the government in special circumstances. If AIDS poses the threat of a serious epidemic, then a compulsory licence can be issued for AIDS drugs, even if the drugs are under patent. Therefore, such exigencies have been taken care of in India.

The greatest challenge is for the drugs and pharmaceuticals industry. This industry seems to be gearing up well to face this challenge. It is increasing its investment in research and development (R&D) several folds. It is moving from 'imitative research' to 'innovative research', including research on the discovery of new molecules. Other knowledge-based industries in India, such as the information technology (IT) industry, biotechnology, and microelectronics, will also have to gear up to the new IPR regime. The Indian IT industry will have to reduce the content of body shopping and move on to innovative IT products, which will need IP protection. The same is true of biotechnology. The Indian biotechnology industry now has a turnover of close to $3 billion, which is impressive. In recent years, there has been a spurt in the creation of new IP from Indian biotech and IT companies. However, this needs to be accelerated.

Before Indians protect IP, we must generate IP that is worth protecting. Indian institutions, national laboratories, and industrial R&D laboratories, will have to gear up for this. Nurturing a strong innovation base through a balanced system of recognition and rewards is the need of the hour. India will have to invest liberally to enhance the skills and knowledge base of scientists through structured in-house and external professional training programmes, even abroad, on understanding, interpreting, and analysing the techno-legal and business information contained in IP documents and in drafting of IP documents.

Some organizations have achieved remarkable results by understanding and developing strategies to meet these challenges. The Council of Scientific and Industrial Research (CSIR) has been a pioneer. During 2002–4 CSIR was granted 516 US patents, which is more than all the patents granted to it during its entire 60 years of existence! In the subsequent years (January 2005 and December 2008), CSIR continued to be the top patent filer from India with 2,050 patents filed in India, 388 in the US, and 297 in Europe during this period. The precursor to the CSIR initiatives in the IP domain was the articulation of its intellectual property management policy in 1996.

Skills in filing, reading, and exploiting patents will be most crucial in the years to come. We must properly protect our inventions. We must fully understand the implications of the patents granted to our competitors. Many of the patents written by our professionals can be easily circumvented. Manpower planning for IPR protection needs priority. IPR must be made a compulsory subject matter in law courses in Indian universities. A number of patent training institutes will have to be set up. Judicious management of patent information will require well-structured functioning of information-creating centres, information documenters and retrievers, information users, IPR specialists, and IT experts.

Monitoring national and international patents and other IP through access to online databases to ensure effective protection and to ward off infringements and threats to India's IP portfolio will be crucial. Analysing and assessing techno-legal and business information and market intelligence for identifying strategic alliances and exploiting potential uncovered niche areas of opportunities itself will give rise to new knowledge-based businesses.

Further, in order to ensure that the courts deliver judgements that meet the ends of justice, there is need for further exposure for those in the judiciary to deal with the evolving new developments in the IP field. In our country the delay in the courts is a great cause of frustration for patentees and as such it would be desirable to have the members of the judiciary exposed to the decisions and the guiding principles that emerge from them.

Its rich traditional knowledge base, in particular its great strength in traditional medicine, is a special area of concern for India. Indeed, traditional medicine plays a crucial role in serving the health needs of a vast majority of people in developing countries, including in India.

The grant of patents on non-original innovations (particularly those linked to traditional medicines), which are based on what is already a part of the traditional knowledge of the developing world, has been causing great concern in the developing world. It was CSIR that challenged US patent No. 5,401,504, which was granted for the wound-healing properties of turmeric. In a landmark judgement, the US Patent Office (USPTO) revoked this patent in 1997, after ascertaining that there was no novelty, the findings by the innovators having been known in India for centuries.

There was yet another case of revocation in May 2000. The patent granted to W.R. Grace Company and the US Department of Agriculture for neem (EPO Patent No. 436257) by the European Patent Office was quashed again on the grounds that its use was already known in India. India also filed a re-examination request for the patent on Basmati rice lines and grains (US Patent No. 5,663,484 granted by USPTO), and the Ricetec Company of Texas decided to withdraw the specific claims challenged by India and also some additional claims.

There is a problem regarding the grant of such patents linked to the indigenous knowledge of the developing world that needs to be addressed jointly by the developing and developed worlds. To mitigate this problem, a traditional knowledge digital library (TKDL) on traditional medicinal plants and systems has been set up by CSIR in partnership with the Department of Ayurveda, Yoga, Unani, Siddha, and Homoeopathy (AYUSH). TKDL has led to traditional knowledge resource classification (TKRC). Linking this to the internationally accepted international patent classification (IPC) system means bridging the gap between the knowledge contained in an old Sanskrit *shloka* and the computer screen of a patent examiner in Washington! So far, TKDL has transcribed 2,29,395 traditional medicine formulations from 150 books on Ayurveda, Unani, Sidha, and Yoga. This has eliminated the problem of wrongful grant of patents since the Indian rights to that knowledge are now known to the examiner.

Patent offices of the US, European Union, and UK now have access to TKDL; agreements with other international patent offices are now on the way. TKDL access agreements with the US and European Union have in-built safeguards on non-disclosure to protect India's interest. India now has a powerful institutional mechanism in the form of TKDL, which is able to prevent the grant of wrong patents not only within a few weeks but also at practically zero cost!

For instance, the US multinational company, Natreon Inc., had filed a patent application (EP 1906980) in July 2006, for the use of ashwagandha plant extract for treating or managing anxiety and depression-induced stress. The TKDL team submitted its third party submission in July 2009 with evidence from as far back as the 12th century from the then prevalent practices used in Ayurveda, Unani, and Siddha. After looking at the strong TKDL evidence, the applicant withdrew the claims in July 2009.

In a recent (November 2010) case, a California-based company, Juice Beauty, had to withdraw its EPO patent application EP 1942917 on compositions and methods for using organic juice–based skincare products.

Several companies from Kenya, China, Denmark, Netherlands, the US, and, interestingly, even from India have withdrawn their patents. So the power of TKDL is already in evidence.

Eventually the creation of TKDL in India would serve the larger purpose of providing and enhancing its innovation capacity. It could integrate widely scattered and distributed references on the traditional knowledge systems of the developing world in a retrievable form. It could act as a bridge between traditional and modern knowledge systems. Availability of this knowledge in a retrievable form in many languages will provide a major impetus to modern research in the developing world, as it can then itself get involved in innovative research to add further value to this traditional knowledge—an example being the development of an allopathic medicine from a traditional plant-based medicine. Sustained efforts for the modernization of traditional knowledge systems in India will create higher awareness at national and international levels and will establish a scientific approach that will ensure higher acceptability of these systems by practitioners of modern systems and the public at large.

India expects to be a major global knowledge production centre by 2020. For this to happen, the Indian strategy will have to rest not only on the generation of new knowledge, but also its protection and valorization. Indian strategy has to evolve around bringing IP protection into the mainstream of its endeavours in education, science and technology, legal and judicial systems, trade and economics, and so on. Several ongoing initiatives suggest that India is well on its way to achieving these objectives so that it can attain its rightful position in the emerging world dominated by the knowledge economy.

R.A. Mashelkar

■ Interest Rates

Interest rates are one financial variable that affects all sectors—consumers, corporations, financial intermediaries, investors, and policymakers.

One of the key factors that provided impetus to the strong growth that the manufacturing sector in India has witnessed in the recent past has been a steep fall in interest rates. Fall in rates contributed to the improved health of Indian corporations as well as banks. This phenomenon gave corporations the opportunity to pre-pay high-cost, legacy debts and replace them with fresh funds raised at lower rates. Similarly, banks used the opportunity to maximize profits on their treasury operations since bond prices increase as interest rates drop. Indian banks leveraged these hyper profits to clean up their balance sheets by making higher provisions for their non-performing assets (NPAs) or sticky loans. There was one more beneficiary of the low interest rate regime—the government. Low interest rates substantially cut its borrowing cost for the funds it raises from the market annually to bridge the fiscal deficit.

The scenario, however, has changed in the last two years. The unprecedented credit crunch in the wake of the collapse of the US investment bank Lehman Brothers Holdings Inc. forced all central banks across the globe, including the Reserve Bank of India (RBI), to pare rates and flood the financial system with money to prop up a sagging economy. But, with the economy returning to a high growth path and inflation staying at an elevated level for long, RBI has been raising its policy rates and making money more expensive to fight inflation in the world's second fastest growing major economy.

The one constituency that has traditionally borne the brunt of lower rates has been the saver. As bank deposit rates drop, the real interest rate (the nominal rate minus the expected inflation rate) sometimes turns negative, impinging on long-term financial savings. Even when the deposit rates are relatively high (such is the case now), if inflation is higher, the return becomes negative. When the rates rise, bankers are traditionally proactive in raising loan rates but they do not raise their deposit rates so fast.

There are rigidities in the interest rate architecture and the market rates do not have a correlation with the administered rates on small savings and a few other instruments. For instance, the yield on the 10-year benchmark government security (G-sec) dropped from 11.70 per cent in October 2000 to 4.94 per cent in October 2003. Around the same time, the interest rate on public provident fund (PPF) savings dropped by only 3 percentage points, from 11 to 8 per cent. The government, however, tried to iron out the distortions following the recommendations of two committees that examined the issue of administered rates and the tax concessions associated with them—the Reddy Committee[1] and the Rakesh Mohan Committee.[2]

Interest rate deregulation is a key component of financial sector reforms. In the 1970s, the government not only dictated the rates at which loans were to be given to companies but also the amount that could be disbursed to various sectors. It was, therefore, natural that deposit rates too were regulated; without an administered rate, banks would never have been assured of profitability.

From Repression to Liberation

The history of interest rates in India is that of a passage from repression to liberation. The Indian central bank is authorized to regulate the interest rates of banks under Sections 21 and 35A of the Banking Regulation Act. Historically, it used this authority to influence credit demand. For instance, in October 1960, RBI stipulated minimum lending rates. In September 1964, it announced ceiling rates to dampen credit growth. In March 1968, it announced a ceiling for export credit (Mohanty et al. 1997).

Interest rates in the financial sector were substantially regulated in India until the late 1980s. Following the recommendations of the Chakravarty Committee,[3] a gradual process of deregulation was initiated. This process gained momentum in the 1990s with the recommendations of the Narasimham Committee.[4]

Today, market forces determine interest rates in the money and government securities markets to a large extent. In the banking system, except for non-resident deposits, all deposit rates are free. On the advances front, all rates are now free except for 1 per cent of bank loans reserved for the poorer section of society who can raise money at 4 per cent under the so-called differential rate of interest or DRI scheme.

Let us first take a look at the deregulation of deposit rates. Before September 1964, the deposit rates were governed by voluntary agreements between the large public-sector and foreign banks operating in India. The only exception was a short period of six months, between September 1960 and February 1961, when RBI regulated the interest rates of deposits up to 14 days. Regulations of deposit rates came into being from September 1964.

Five years later, in September 1969, RBI banned interest payment on current accounts and deposits of up to 14 days. From 1979 onwards, almost all deposit rates were administered. In April 1992, banks were given the freedom to fix interest rates on term deposits of 46 days to three years and over within the ceiling prescribed by RBI.

In October 1995, the deposit rate structure was made more flexible by giving banks the freedom to fix rates on domestic term deposits over two years. The ceiling, however, continued to be prescribed for deposits between 46 days and two years. In July 1996, banks were given the freedom to fix rates on deposits over one year. In April 1997, interest rates on term deposits between 30 days and one year were linked to the bank rate. In October 1997, interest rates on term deposits were completely deregulated. In April 1998, the minimum maturity of term deposits was reduced from 30 days to 15 days and dropped further to seven days in 2001–2 only for wholesale deposits of Rs 15 lakh and above. Now even retail customers can keep any amount for seven days.

Now, a look at the lending rates. A major reform was initiated to simplify the complex lending rate structure from 22 September 1990. 'The structure was characterized by a multiplicity of rates with concessionality in the interest rate dependent on numerous criteria such as size of loan, priority nature of a sector, location of activity, programme-specific lending, incomes of borrowers and so on' (RBI 1991: 17).

In the revised interest rate structure, all sector-specific rates were abolished and banks were given the freedom to determine interest rates for loans above Rs 2 lakh, subject to RBI determining the minimum lending rates.

Six categories of lending rates were introduced—five slabs below Rs 2 lakh and a minimum lending rate for above Rs 2 lakh. These slabs were compressed into three, effective from 22 April 1992, and again into two from 8 April 1993.

With effect from 18 October 1994, RBI stopped prescribing the minimum lending rate and banks were free to fix the rates on all loans above Rs 2 lakh. At that time, the concept of the prime lending rate (PLR) was introduced—the rate at which banks were to lend money to top-rated clients. Barring small loans and certain categories of export credit, all loans were freed. Taking into account a very high spread over PLR (at least 4 per cent), since October 1996, banks were directed to announce a maximum spread over PLR for all advances other than consumer credit after approval from their boards.

[1]Expert Committee to review the system of administered interest rates and other related issues by Y.V. Reddy.
[2]Advisory Committee on the administered interest rate and rationalization of savings instruments.
[3]The Committee to review the working of the monetary system, chaired by Sukhamoy Chakravarty, was set up in December 1982 by RBI. It submitted its report in April 1985.
[4]Narasimham Committee on financial sector restructuring, 1991.

In 1998–9, RBI stopped prescribing the rate for small loans of up to Rs 12 lakh and instead banks' PLR was made the ceiling rate for small loans. Banks were allowed to charge fixed or floating rates at or above PLR for loans over Rs 2 lakh. The next year, the concept of tenure-linked PLR was introduced to give banks more operational flexibility. In 2001–2, following the international practice, RBI made PLR a benchmark rate and banks were allowed to lend below the PLR for loans above Rs 2 lakh. In 2003–4, in the interests of transparency, RBI directed banks to announce the benchmark PLR (BPLR) with the approval of their boards.

Loans to exporters were given at 2.5 per cent below a bank's BPLR while small loans of up to Rs 2 lakh given to agriculture, small-scale industries, and the so-called weaker sections of society were capped at BPLR. However, a bulk of the bank loans were given below BPLR when the system was slosh with money and banks did not have too many avenues to deploy extra liquidity.

The BPLR regime came to an end on 30 June 2010. It was replaced by the base rate. This is the minimum lending rate below which banks cannot lend to any borrower. Along with that, interest rates on rupee export credits as well as small loans of up to Rs 2 lakh also were freed. Rates of export finance, however, could be linked to the base rate. Till that time, export finance rates were 2.5 percentage points below BPLR. Under the base rate mechanism, RBI freed rates for all rupee loans, including those extended to farmers. Banks can, however, provide subsidized loans, provided the government offers budgetary support. Currently, all crop loans up to Rs 3 lakh bear an interest rate of 7 per cent and the government offers a subvention of 3 per cent to banks for such loans. Only public-sector banks offer such concessional loans.

RBI's decision to deregulate loan rates follows the recommendations of a panel headed by executive director Deepak Mohanty. The panel was formed in June 2009 to review the BPLR system and suggest an appropriate loan pricing system and it released its report in October 2009.[5]

Last Bastion of Mandated Rate

The interest rate spectrum in the banking system is market-determined today with RBI deregulating the savings bank rate, the last bastion of mandated rate, on 25 October 2011. Ahead of this, RBI issued a discussion paper on the pros and cons of deregulation of the savings rate.

A savings account is the most common operating account for individuals and others for non-commercial transactions. Banks generally put a ceiling on the total number of withdrawals permitted and stipulate a certain minimum balance to be maintained in such accounts. Before regulation, the rate was pegged at 4 per cent.

Till March 2010, banks were paying interest only on the minimum balance kept between the 10th and the end of a month in such an account but now they pay interest rates on a daily average basis.

The rates on small savings and provident fund too continue to be administered by the government under various Acts of Parliament. These rates were relatively high with attractive tax incentives until 1998–9 when the government started paring them to create a uniform interest rate architecture.

The Post Office Savings Bank is included in the Union List (item No. 39 of the Seventh Schedule) of the Constitution of India while small savings schemes are framed by the central government under the Government Savings Bank Act, 1873, the Government Savings Certificates Act, 1959, and the Public Provident Fund Act, 1968. For each scheme, statutory rules are framed indicating details, such as the rate of interest and maturity period.

The Deposit Scheme for Retiring Government Employees, 1989, and the Deposit Scheme for Retiring Employees of Public Sector Companies, 1991, have been introduced as non-statutory schemes with effect from 1 July 1989 and 1 January 1991, respectively.

The relief bonds scheme was introduced in 1987 to provide relief to drought-affected areas in that year through central government notifications. These kept getting re-issued with market-related interest rates till 2003 when they were finally discontinued. The scheme was, however, relaunched in the same year in the form of two Government of India savings bonds—the 6.5 per cent savings bonds 2003 (non-taxable) effective 24 March 2003 and the 8 per cent savings bonds 2003 (taxable) effective 21 March 2003.

Former finance minister Yashwant Sinha, in his budget speech for 2001–2, proposed an expert committee to review the system of administered interest rates. Accordingly, a committee was constituted under the chairmanship of Dr Y.V. Reddy, then RBI deputy governor (he later became governor). The committee submitted its report to the government on 17 September 2001.

According to the report, 'Regulation of interest rates in this segment has not only created distortions in the interest rate structure but has also adversely affected the allocative

[5]Report of the Working Group on Benchmark Prime Lending Rate. Following the announcement in the annual policy statement for 2009–10, RBI constituted the group (Chairman: Deepak Mohanty). It submitted its report in October 2009.

efficiency of resources. Integration of financial markets remains weak due to existing rigidities in the small saving rates and the consequent market segmentation.'

Not only were such high real interest rates putting an unsustainable burden on both central and state governments but the resulting high cost of capital was also inhibiting economic growth all round, the Reddy Committee noted.

The issues relating to small saving schemes are complex and intricate. They were introduced when the banking and capital markets were relatively underdeveloped and the government was regarded as a reliable trustee or banker for public savings.

Since then, the banking and capital market have developed significantly. However, the interest rates on these schemes, which were initially conceived to offer reasonable returns to savers, have theoretically become floor rates for deposits of banks and financial institutions, particularly when the policy rates are low. This has created distortions in the system and made it difficult for financial intermediaries to reduce their deposit rates.

Consequently, lending rates cannot drop either since banks need to maintain a spread between deposit and lending rates to stay viable. Incidentally, the spread or the net interest margin enjoyed by Indian banks is higher than those of their global counterparts because of high intermediation costs in India.

The Reddy Committee suggested that there should be progressive reduction in the number of administered instruments. The committee made two major recommendations to rectify the distortions in the interest rate matrix: (i) benchmarking the administered interest rates on small savings schemes and Government of India savings bonds to the secondary market yields of G-sec of corresponding maturity and (ii) abolition of income tax provisions on small savings schemes to ensure a level playing field in the financial market.

The government accepted the first recommendation. It had also taken a stance of gradually phasing out tax concessions on these instruments. Subsequently, on 24 January 2004, the government constituted another committee under the chairmanship of Dr Rakesh Mohan, then deputy governor of RBI, to review the implementation of the Reddy Committee recommendations. This committee, which submitted its report in May 2004, was in favour of continuing with the use of average G-sec yields as the suitable benchmark for small savings. It also recommended the abolition of certain schemes for which investments are primarily motivated to obtain tax benefits.

While the government is going slow on implementing the recommendations of these two committees, the fact remains that administered interest rates have come down. For instance, the public provident fund rate which was pegged at 12 per cent in 1999 now stands at 8 per cent through four cuts.

Similarly, the rate on National Savings Certificates-VIII has come down from 12 to 8 per cent. The fall in post office recurring deposit during this period has been four percentage points—from 11.5 to 7.5 per cent.

The government may be willing to align administered rates with overall market rates but this is easier said than done. Any cut in the administered rate will affect the saving community which is not politically acceptable, particularly since it has no safety net. For the same reason, not everybody is in favour of freeing the savings account rate. They argue that even though it pays only 3.5 per cent, an administered rate offers stable returns to savers. Most banks are also resisting it as they fear a rate war and their cost of funds going up following deregulation.

There is a clear distinction in the interest rate movement between two segments—the banking and markets turf where RBI plays the referee and the array of savings instruments offered by the government. There is an apparent disconnect between the two fields.

Even within the banking space there are different benchmark rates. These are the bank rate, repurchase or repo rate, and reverse repo rate. The bank rate was introduced in 1935 as a signal rate but lost its relevance in the later half of the century. Former RBI governor C. Rangarajan reactivated it in April 1997. Last changed in 2003, it has remained at 6 per cent and became defunct while the repo rate and the reverse repo rate have continuously been changed in sync with the stance of the monetary policy. The repo rate is the rate at which banks raise money from RBI, and they lend money to the central bank at the reverse repo rate.

The repo rate is now 8.50 per cent and the reverse repo is 7.50 per cent. The difference between the two rates is the liquidity corridor, technically known as liquidity adjustment facility (LAF). The rates of the overnight call money market—where banks lend to each other to help tide over their temporary asset-liability mismatches—are expected to rule between the two rates.

While keeping the bank rate unchanged for years, RBI has been using the repo and reverse repo rates as policy rates. In a tight liquidity situation—which has been the case for past two years—the repo rate is the policy rate. But when there is excess liquidity in the system and banks are parking money with RBI, the reverse repo rate becomes the policy rate.

An internal committee of the RBI[6] had recommended that the bank rate should be repositioned as a discount rate through which the central bank can inject liquidity in the system in exceptional circumstances against collateral of bonds. The committee wanted the repo rate to be the key policy rate and in order to do so, the system should, as far as feasible, run in a cash-deficit mode as has been the case with most developed markets. This will give RBI better grip of the monetary policy, and transmission will be quicker.

In its annual monetary policy review in May 2011, the RBI decided to reposition the repo rate as the single operative policy rate and keep the reverse repo rate always one percentage point below the repo rate. It did not tinker with the bank rate but introduced a new marginal standing facility (MSF), from where banks can borrow overnight up to 1 per cent of their deposits. The rate of interest on money raised through this facility will be 1 percentage point above the repo rate.

So in the revised arrangement, the repo rate is in the middle of a corridor in which the ceiling is the MSF rate, 1 percentage point higher than the repo rate, and floor is the reverse repo rate, 1 percentage point lower than the repo rate.

These changes symbolize a greater transformation that has taken place in RBI's monetary management strategy. But only rates are not the tools for monetary management. A key driving factor for monetary management and interest rate movement in India is liquidity management. When there is too much of dollar inflow, RBI purchases the greenback. With every dollar purchase, an equivalent amount of rupee gets into the system. Similarly, when the system runs too dry, the central bank buys bonds from the market under its so-called open market operation or OMO to infuse liquidity.

TAMAL BANDYOPADHYAY

References

Mohanty, Deepak, Amitava Sardar, and Abha Prasad. 1997. 'Perspective on Monetary Policy', *RBI Occasional Papers*, June–September, 18 (2&3).

Reserve Bank of India (RBI). 1991. *Annual Report 1990–91*, Mumbai, RBI.

[6]Report of the working group on operating procedure of monetary policy, released in March 2011.

International Finance

Four major ways in which international finance affects India are, first, the increasing availability of foreign savings; second, their use; third, the changing effectiveness of macroeconomic policy; finally, the effect of macroeconomic policy on capital flows, their use, and associated risks, in the context of India's economic structure. I examine each in turn, drawing on insights from new research, and taking a nuanced view between ideological positions that emphasize only the risks or only the benefits of capital flows.

Foreign Savings

India received some aid flows in the 1950s and the 1960s, and an influx of remittances started from the mid-1970s. But in the 1990s there was a large expansion of private capital flows due to changes in technology, markets, and liberalizing reforms in many parts of the globe, in which India participated. Capital inflows contribute to growth through technology spillovers and improvements in efficiency, but they also boost resources for investment. Using foreign savings to supplement domestic savings in this way requires an initial widening of the current account deficit (CAD) of the balance of payments (BOP), and for the widening to occur, investment must exceed savings.

It is a tautology that a CAD must equal the capital account surplus minus any rise in foreign exchange reserves. The latter is a balancing component which monetary and exchange rate policy affects directly and also indirectly, through effects on macroeconomic variables. The components of the BOP capital account are foreign investment, net commercial borrowings, net non-resident Indian (NRI) deposits, net external assistance, rupee debt service, and other capital. Foreign direct and foreign portfolio investments are non-debt-creating inflows. The first is the most stable of the various categories. Debt-creating inflows, and short-term debt in particular, carry a higher risk of reversal, but the share of short-term debt in India's total debt has been falling.

The current account (CA) is formally defined as the acquisition of foreign assets by domestic residents minus foreign residents' acquisition of domestic assets. If this is positive, the CA is in surplus. The basic macroeconomic identity, that income must equal expenditure, implies that the current account surplus (CAS) must equal both net exports of goods and services, and also gross national saving (GNS) minus investment. Subtracting income payments made abroad from gross domestic product gives gross national product. Subtracting consumption from the latter gives GNS. But the popular conception of CAS is identified with the net exports of goods and services.

Investment is the most volatile component of expenditure and expectations of the future can be particularly volatile in a reforming economy. Consumers would like to smooth consumption over time, if capital markets permit it. The modern intertemporal approach to the BOP (Sachs 1981) analyses this dynamic forward-looking behaviour. The new insight is that macro policies, savings and investment, and not only trade policies, affect the CA.

In a developing country with incomplete capital markets, forward-looking decisions will be severely constrained. Intertemporal optimization can give only a rough benchmark. Heightened uncertainty under reform may raise precautionary savings. But the associated positive productivity shock should raise investment and inflows that contribute to its financing. If incomes are expected to be higher in future, current consumption should rise towards higher smoothed levels. Therefore, although both savings and investment would rise together, the rise in investment would exceed that in savings (Goyal 2004). But the Indian CA moved into surplus at the turn of the century, and foreign exchange reserves rose rapidly. I turn to the effects of monetary policy in the Indian context to understand this.

Implications for Monetary Policy

Monetary policy affects the interest rate, and through it investment, savings, the current account and foreign inflows, but it was thought to have only short-run effects. What is known as the new International Finance or Open Economy Macroeconomics (Obstfeld and Rogoff 1996), however, emphasizes forward-looking expectations, with asset prices such as the exchange rate adjusting rapidly, and other sticky prices taking longer. The expectations congealed in the sticky prices give monetary policy persistent long-run effects. Changes in wealth in an open economy and shifts closer to potential output add to this impact of monetary policy.

In the workhorse open economy Mundell–Flemming model, however, monetary policy becomes ineffective under perfect capital mobility and a fixed exchange rate. A fall in money supply raises interest rates and invites more inflows, which raises money supply. Any differential between domestic and foreign interest rates reflects expected domestic currency depreciation plus country-risk premium. This is known as uncovered interest parity. If monetary policy and intervention keep the exchange rate undervalued (depreciated) on average, interest rates must also be low, otherwise capital will flow in to take advantage of higher domestic interest rates and a strong currency, creating conditions for a future reversal.

Capital mobility has risen in India but it is still far from perfect. There are now few restrictions on inflows, but domestic residents cannot easily hold foreign assets to diversify their portfolios. And the exchange rate is a managed float; it is not fixed. Monetary policy does have degrees of freedom. Under reserve accumulation and active sterilization of the resulting increase in money supply, the onus is on policy to minimize the interest differential.

Administrative restrictions on Indian interest rates are scaled down but have not completely gone. Banking spreads, prime lending rates, and savings deposit rates are difficult to decrease, partly for political reasons. But the gap between Indian and foreign interest rates now affects foreign inflows since the major restrictions left are only on domestic residents.

Aggressive sterilization, together with the rigidities, maintained positive interest gaps, attracting more inflows, but reducing the stimulus to activity that would have absorbed some of the inflows. A huge accumulation of forex reserves occurred partly due to arbitrage at different points of the interest rate spectrum.

The severe credit squeeze and rise in interest rates that followed the first episode of exchange rate volatility in 1995–6 helped trigger a sustained industrial slowdown. The Reserve Bank of India (RBI) shifted away from strict monetary targeting. The bank rate, which had been frozen, was activated as a benchmark for interest rates, and gradually brought down. The other prime aim of monetary policy was to prevent appreciation and volatility in the exchange rate. Reversals were carried out only during periods of exchange rate volatility, sometimes induced by fluctuations in foreign capital inflows. Since the late 1990s, policy committed to a soft interest rate regime, but steady softening of nominal interest rates occurred only after February 2001, with the fall in world interest rates. An upswing in activity followed. The response of spending to interest rates had risen. The fiscal deficit did not put pressure on interest rates because of large domestic savings and high foreign inflows.

High volatility of the exchange rate followed periods when it was almost static. Such reversals disturb markets and can lead to panic attacks on the currency; both market players and policymakers overreact. The RBI intervened to limit volatility but did not maintain regular limited volatility, which may have mitigated the burst of high volatility and the defensive rise in interest rates.

Reducing Risk and Absorbing Capital Inflows

Following Tirole's (2002) position that the fundamental failure is the inability of governments to credibly contract with foreign capital, a number of authors argue that crises are inevitable where financial institutions are weak. Hausman et al. (2002) suggest the basic problem is that a developing country cannot borrow in its own currency. Markets do not exist for laying off currency risk.

There are three ways to reduce risk associated with capital inflows: improvements in the international financial architecture, initiatives for regional cooperation, and improving own markets.

Limited exchange rate volatility around a trend competitive rate creates incentives for hedging and lowers exposure to currency risk, thus deepening and developing markets and reducing overreaction. Steady forex markets reform since 1995 has made more instruments available for hedging, but better incentives would contribute to their use. As long as policy credibly improves fundamentals, markets may help the RBI achieve targets. Changes in money supply should be sufficient for its purpose, but market intervention and announcements are additional tools available if necessary. The RBI has considerable clout to focus expectations in thin markets. Other benefits the exchange-rate policy has are as follows:

- It is consistent with encouraging trade and ensuring external balance over the long run.
- It frees monetary policy to better implement smoother and more counter-cyclical interest rates to stimulate the real sector.
- Higher activity allows more inflows to be absorbed.
- It keeps inflation low as it counters supply shocks and anchors expectations.

In order to maintain a competitive real exchange rate and encourage exports, a benchmark real effective exchange rate (REER) set after the devaluations of the early 1990s has been largely maintained. This is a valid strategy as long as India, like China, has large reserves of labour yet to be absorbed into higher productivity employment to which exports contribute. Since the informal labour market accounts for about 90 per cent of the workforce, large numbers available to work at low wages prevent the substantial rise in average real wages required for a major currency appreciation. Such a rise in real wages is possible only with a rise in labour productivity in agriculture.

This labour market structure implies that if foreign capital can be used to alleviate specific bottlenecks and supportive reforms are undertaken, supply may not be a constraint on output since output is below its potential. As long as monetary policy is able to anchor nominal wages and inflationary expectations, it can stimulate demand. A rise in credit will finance an expansion in output, capital, and capacity.

An economy at full employment requires an appreciation of the exchange rate to absorb foreign inflows since a rise in domestic absorption can occur only through a rise in imports. If there is excess capacity, the rise in absorption can occur at an unchanged real exchange rate, through output and capacity expansion, but low interest rates are a necessary complement to such a strategy. Some exchange rate appreciation would help to absorb inflows but it cannot be the major part of the adjustment. Full capital account convertibility, which allows domestic residents to acquire foreign assets, also absorbs reserves, but it raises the risk of capital outflows and crises unless markets and institutions are well developed. Therefore, it has to be introduced gradually and in a correct sequence.

Short-term movements in the exchange rate to counter temporary supply shocks, such as oil price hikes, can achieve the required limited volatility and pre-empt the effect of these shocks on the domestic price-wage process. As productivity rises, limited nominal appreciation is feasible without harming exports.

A large voting population whose wages are not formally indexed to inflation implies administrative restraints on prices of basic consumption goods. Since political pressure from farmers pushes up farm support prices, consumption subsidies are given. Since these are not complete, nominal wages respond with a lag to a rise in food prices leading to inflation. But with more openness, world prices restrain domestic food prices. An exchange rate policy that lowers food price inflation reduces the necessity for distorting subsidies and administered prices. Improvement in efficiency releases surplus, which enhances its political feasibility. Therefore, the policy is compatible with political constraints and macropolicy objectives to lower inflation and raise growth.

ASHIMA GOYAL

References

Goyal, Ashima. 2004. 'Puzzles in Indian Performance: Deficits without Disasters', in Kirit S. Parikh and R. Radhakrishnan (eds), *India Development Report 2004–05*, New Delhi, IGIDR and Oxford University Press.

Hausman, Ricardo, Barry Eichengreen, and Ugo Panizza. 2002. 'Original Sin: The Pain, the Mystery and the Road to Redemption', mimeo, November.

Obstfeld, Maurice and Kenneth Rogoff. 1996. *Foundations of International Macroeconomics*, Cambridge, Massachusetts, MIT Press.

Sachs, Jeffrey D. 1981. 'The Current Account and Macroeconomic Adjustment in the 1970s', *Brookings Papers on Economic Activity*, 1: 201–68.

Tirole, Jean. 2002. *Financial Crises, Liquidity and the International Monetary System*, New Jersey, Princeton University Press.

■ International Migration

International migration goes back a long time. Indeed, the migration of people is as old as humankind. And migration across borders and oceans is at least as old as nation states. The slave trade, which started in the mid-16th century, was the largest, enforced mass migration of labour in human history. It is believed that over two centuries more than 15 million people were taken from Africa to Europe, North America, and the Caribbean to work in households and on plantations. The abolition of slavery in the British Empire in 1833 was followed by the movement of indentured labour which was yet another form of servitude. Starting around the mid-1830s, for a period of 50 years, about 50 million people left India and China to work as indentured labour on mines, plantations, and construction in the Americas, the Caribbean, Southern Africa, Southeast Asia, and other distant lands. This was probably close to 10 per cent of the total population of India and China circa 1880. During this period, there was also some movement of people from Europe to the Americas. Most of them, however, were adventurers or refugees rather than migrants. The real exodus from Europe came later. Between 1870 and 1914, more than 50 million people left Europe, of whom two-thirds went to the United States, while the remaining one-third went to Canada, Australia, New Zealand, South Africa, Argentina, and Brazil. The migration was, in effect, driven by the push of labour-surplus Europe and the pull of labour-scarce America, as also other new lands with temperate climates that attracted white settlers. In making this distinction, the most plausible reference point, or denominator, is land, for it is the land–labour ratio that mattered. And, if the denominator has all inputs, rather than just land, the distinction between labour-scarce and labour-surplus countries conforms closely to the distinction between high-wage and low-wage countries. Such mass migration from Europe amounted to one-eighth of its total population in 1900. International movement of labour on this massive scale came to an end with the First World War. From 1919 to 1939, migration continued but at much lower levels as immigration laws were put in place and passports came to be needed. The Great Depression of the 1930s further dampened these flows as unemployment levels rose sharply everywhere.

International Context

It is possible to discern two phases of international labour migration in the second half of the 20th century. During the first phase, from the late 1940s to the early 1970s, there were two distinct streams of international migration. First, people migrated from Europe to the United States, Canada, Australia, and New Zealand. This movement was driven by a search for economic opportunities on the part of the migrants but was also shaped by laws, with the exception of the United States, which restricted immigration largely to Europeans. From 1951 to 1975, total immigration into the United States was 7.8 million; it was 3.8 million into Canada, and 2.8 million into Australia. Second, people moved from the developing world in Asia, North Africa, and the Caribbean to Western Europe, where economic growth combined with full employment created labour shortages and led to labour imports. From 1951 to 1975, total immigration into Western Europe, mostly from the erstwhile colonies, was about 10 million. During the second phase from the early 1970s through the late 1990s, migration to Europe slowed down for a while as immigration laws became restrictive almost everywhere. But this did not last long. Migration to Europe revived in the 1980s and gathered momentum in the 1990s, as latecomers to the European Union began to import labour. This time round, however, a significant proportion of the migrants came from Eastern Europe and the former USSR. There were, in addition, two different streams of migration. First, there was permanent emigration of people not only from Europe but also from the developing world to the United States. These were mostly persons with professional qualifications or technical skills. And, in the period from 1975 to 2000, total immigration into the United States was 16.3 million, more than twice what it had been in the preceding quarter century, while total immigration into Canada at 4.2 million and into Australia at 2.4 million witnessed little change. Second, there was temporary migration of people from labour-surplus developing countries, which was mostly of unskilled workers and semi-skilled or skilled workers in manual or clerical occupations. There were three sets of destinations for such people: the industrialized countries, the high-income labour-scarce oil-exporting countries, and the middle-income newly industrializing countries.

Dimensions and Composition

It is clear that international migration during the second half of the 20th century was significant, despite stringent immigration laws and restrictive consular practices. The database on international migration is slender. But available evidence shows that between 1960 and 2000, the number of international migrants rose from 44.3 million to 66 million in developing countries, from 28.6 million to 79.4 million in industrialized countries (excluding the former USSR), and from 72.9 million to 145.4 million in the world (excluding the former USSR). In this span of four decades, the proportion of international migrants in the total population fell from 2.1 to 1.3 per cent in developing countries and rose from 4 to 8.3 per cent in industrialized countries. For the world as a whole, this proportion declined from 2.58 to 2.44 per cent.

It would seem that international migration has gathered momentum during the first decade of the 21st century. The United Nations' estimates based on projections suggest that, in 2010, the proportion of international migrants in world population was higher at 3.1 per cent. Similarly, in 2010 as compared with 2000, the proportion of international migrants in the total population was estimated to be slightly higher at 1.5 per cent in developing countries and much higher at 10.3 per cent in industrialized countries. These United Nations' projections also estimate that between 2000 and 2010, immigration into the industrialized countries would have increased by about 20 million (8 million in the United States, 2 million in Canada, and 10 million in Western Europe), while immigration into the oil-exporting countries of the Middle East would have increased by at least 5 million (of which there were 2.2 million in Saudi Arabia and 1 million in the United Arab Emirates). In the coming decades, this momentum in international migration may be reinforced by demographic change. The ageing of the population in industrialized countries, which is a consequence of increased life expectancy and zero or negative population growth, carries an enormous potential for international migration on a larger scale.

These aggregate statistics do not reveal changes in the nature of international migration. In the contemporary world, it is possible to distinguish between five categories of migration across borders, of which two are old and three are new. The old labour flows are made up of emigrants and refugees. Emigrants are people who move to a country and settle there permanently. The principal destinations are the United States, Canada, and Australia. Most such people are admitted for their professional qualifications or for unification of families. Such emigration is estimated to be in the range of 1 million people per annum. Refugees are people who leave their homes because of famines, natural disasters, ethnic strife, religious violence, political persecution, or civil war, to seek a home or asylum so as to take up permanent residence in other countries. Such distress migration, which is involuntary, leads to the movement of 1 million people across borders every year. But refugees constitute a declining proportion of the stock of international migrants in the world. The new forms of labour flows are guest workers, illegal migrants, and professionals. Guest workers are people who move to a country on a temporary basis, for a specified purpose and a limited duration. Most of them are unskilled or semi-skilled workers. The largest number, estimated at more than 8 million, is in the Middle East. But they are also to be found in Western Europe. This category also includes seasonal workers employed in agriculture, particularly in the United States and Canada. Illegal migrants are people who enter a country without a visa, take up employment on tourist visas, or simply stay on after their visas expire. The largest number of such illegal immigrants is in the United States, estimated at about 11 million in 2010. Estimates suggest that the number of illegal immigrants is at least 5 million in Western Europe and more than 1 million in Japan. Professionals are people with high levels of education, experience, and qualifications, whose skills are in demand everywhere. Scientists, doctors, engineers, and academics are classic examples of such migrants. But there are more professionals such as lawyers, architects, accountants, managers, bankers, or designers who can emigrate permanently, live abroad temporarily, or stay at home and travel frequently for business. These people are as mobile as capital across borders. There is an emerging new form of cross-border movement of people described as body shopping. Firms in industrialized countries engage persons from low-income countries with standardized skills, particularly in computer software, construction activities, school teaching, or healthcare, to work on a contract basis with special non-immigrant status visas.

Causes and Determinants

The factors underlying international migration are manifold and complex. The most important among them, of course, is disparities in income levels and employment opportunities between countries. The population imbalances between labour-scarce and labour-abundant countries can also play an important role. There are both push and pull factors underlying the process. Demographic factors combined with unemployment and poverty are the obvious push factor. Differences in wage levels and employment probabilities are the basic pull factor. The process of economic development can both dampen and stimulate international migration.

As economic development provides more employment, higher wages, and better living conditions at home, it reduces the significance of the push factor even if differences in the level of income and the quality of life persist vis-à-vis the world outside. This is because people do not wish to leave their homes. Yet, even if economic development reduces the need to migrate, improved levels of education and higher levels of aspiration increase both the desire and the ability to migrate. Of course, it is not possible to understand international migration in terms of economics alone. The reasons are clear. For one, non-economic factors, such as explicit immigration laws or implicit consular practices which constitute barriers to entry and shape the composition of inflows, are significant determinants of cross-border movements even where the underlying reasons are economic. For another, there are cross-border movements of people, where the underlying factors are not economic. Migration in distress, which represents neither voluntary decisions nor economic decisions, is the most obvious example.

Implications and Consequences

From the perspective of home countries, or countries of origin, international migration has both positive and negative consequences for economic growth and development.

The most obvious positive consequence of international migration for economic growth is the remittances from migrants. The evidence is striking. Remittances to developing countries increased rapidly from $24.3 billion in 1980 to $66 billion in 2000 as did remittances to industrialized countries from $16.8 billion in 1980 to $44.7 billion in 2000. The first decade of the 21st century witnessed a phenomenal growth in remittances. In fact, remittances to developing countries rose to $167 billion in 2005 and $325 billion in 2010. For developing countries, taken together, remittances have become the second largest source of external finance, less than direct foreign investment but much more than official development assistance. What is more, remittances are a more stable source of external finance and are more evenly distributed among countries. On an average, in 2010, remittances were the equivalent of 2 per cent of GDP for developing countries, but this proportion was significantly higher in some developing countries. Remittances can enable an economy to realize an excess of investment over savings through a corresponding excess of imports over exports, thereby reducing the need for external resources. Therefore, remittances from migrants can alleviate either the saving constraint or the foreign exchange constraint, thus enabling an economy to attain a higher rate of growth than would otherwise be possible.

The most obvious negative consequence of international migration for economic growth, in the long term, is the brain drain. This has been recognized and emphasized for a long time. Brain drain represents an unrequited transfer of human capital which is bound to constrain growth. The problem may be accentuated in economies where international migration absorbs a large proportion of increments in the workforce or where labour surplus is small and skills are scarce. The export of workers in these circumstances may lead not only to qualitative but also to quantitative depletion of the labour force with serious repercussions for growth and development. In a labour-exporting country, the depletion of human capital constrains economic growth for several reasons. First, there is a loss of scarce skills that are not easy to replenish. Second, the education or training of professionals or skilled workers absorbs scarce investible resources, but the returns to public investment in education do not accrue to society. Third, the training of workers to replace emigrants imposes additional costs in terms of both resources and time. Fourth, the migration of people at the higher end of the spectrum of incomes means revenue forgone by the government, particularly in the sphere of direct taxes. There is, however, a silver lining to this cloud that appeared not so long ago. The spread and momentum of globalization, juxtaposed with the rise of emerging countries in the world economy, provides a stimulus for return migration that could reverse the brain drain. If so, it may create new opportunities for developing countries as it could, almost overnight, provide them with access to a workforce that is well educated and highly trained in the industrialized world.

The Indian Experience

For India, the migration of its labour across borders is nothing new. It began a long time ago. The contact with the Persian Gulf region and Southeast Asia, in terms of movement of people, goes back several centuries. Migration of workers on a significant scale came much later in the colonial era. It began with the migration of workers as indentured labour for plantations or mines to faraway places such as Guyana, Jamaica, Trinidad, and Fiji; to not-so-distant lands such as Mauritius, Malaya, and South Africa; and even to neighbouring countries such as Ceylon and Burma. This phase came to an end in the early 20th century. Thereafter, in the 1920s and 1930s, the migration of labour, which was entirely voluntary and sometimes on a contract basis, took Indian traders, skilled workers, and clerical personnel to East Africa and the Persian Gulf states. All the same, throughout this period, colonial ties remained the basic determinant of the nature and direction of migration.

Migration

There are two distinct categories in international migration from independent India: emigration to the industrialized countries which began in the early 1950s and labour exports to the Middle East which began in the mid-1970s. Migration to the industrialized world was permanent and a very large proportion of these migrants were persons with professional expertise or technical qualifications. Migration to the oil-exporting countries was temporary in nature, and most of these migrants were unskilled workers and semi-skilled or skilled workers in manual or clerical occupations. Emigration to the industrialized countries registered a steady growth between 1950 and 2000. During this span of five decades, total migration to the industrialized world, where the principal destinations were the United States, Canada, and the United Kingdom, was about 1.5 million persons. The United Kingdom was a major destination until about 1970 and the United States thereafter. Over the period as a whole, about 50 per cent of the migrants settled in the United States, another 30 per cent in the United Kingdom, and the remaining 20 per cent in other industrialized countries, mostly Canada. The massive differences in wage levels and the even greater differences in expected incomes over a life cycle obviously created a desire to migrate on the supply side. Yet the ability to migrate was almost entirely dependent on the possibilities of employment and the barriers to immigration in the countries of destination on the demand side. Export of workers to the Middle East began in the mid-1970s as dramatic increases in oil prices led to an economic boom in these labour-scarce economies. This outflow reached peak levels in the early 1980s but declined thereafter to stabilize at a lower level. Such temporary migration of workers to the Middle East reached high levels once again during the 2000s. At the crest of the wave, during the early 1980s, the average outflow was almost a quarter of a million workers per annum. Between 1975 and 2000, the total migration from India to the Middle East was about 3 million workers. Unskilled workers constituted almost 40 per cent of this migration, skilled workers accounted for somewhat less than 50 per cent, while white-collar workers and high-skill workers made up approximately 5 per cent each. The principal destinations of the migrants were Saudi Arabia, the United Arab Emirates, and Oman, which provided a home for two-thirds to four-fifths of the Indian migrant population in the Middle East. It is difficult to estimate the magnitude of return migration, which was inevitable given the temporary nature of this export of workers. Available evidence suggests that from 1975 to 2000, total return migration was in the range of 1.5 million workers. The size and the composition of these labour flows from India was determined in the Middle East, where governments, in consultation with employers, made basic decisions not only about the number of workers and skill composition but also about wage levels and working conditions.

Remittances and Capital Flows

International migration from India has been associated with two sorts of financial flows: remittance inflows which constitute unrequited transfers and capital flows in the form of repatriable deposits. These financial flows acquired significant dimensions beginning in the mid-1970s. The period since then has witnessed spectacular growth in remittances from migrants. The inflow of remittances increased from a mere $0.2 billion per annum during 1970–1 to 1974–5, to $1.2 billion per annum during 1975–6, to 1979—80, $2 billion per annum during 1980–1 to 1984–5, $2.5 billion per annum during 1985–6 to 1989–90, $4.6 billion per annum during 1990–1 to1994–5, $11.1 billion per annum during 1995–6 to 1999–2000, $17.8 billion per annum during 2000–1 to 2004–5, and $40 billion per annum during 2005–6 to 2009–10. In fact, remittances to India reached a level of $25 billion in 2005–6 and jumped to $54 billion in 2009–10. These inflows were substantial. In 2009–10, for example, remittances were the equivalent of 3.9 per cent of GDP, 7.2 per cent of private final consumer expenditure in the domestic market, 11.6 per cent of gross domestic savings, and 10.7 per cent of gross domestic capital formation. The significance of remittances was far greater in the external sector. In absolute terms, in 2009–10, remittances were $54 billion, as compared to exports at $179 billion, imports at $288 billion (so that remittances were large enough to finance half the balance of trade deficit), direct foreign investment inflows at $37 billion, and portfolio investment inflows at $160 billion with outflows at $128 billion (so that remittances were significantly larger than net portfolio investment inflows). It is worth noting that in 2009–10 external assistance in terms of gross utilization was just $6.8 billion, while net aid inflows were negative. There was a rapid increase in capital flows from migrants in the form of repatriable deposits during the 1980s, which stopped thereafter. The total amount outstanding in such deposits rose from $1.3 billion at the end of 1980–1 to $10.4 billion at the end of 1989–90. The major factor underlying the spurt in these capital flows was the interest rates on such deposits, which was at least one percentage point higher than interest rates in international capital markets and significantly higher than interest rates in the domestic capital markets of the countries where the migrants lived. The substantial differences in interest rates, however, were insufficient to sustain net inflows during 1990–1 and were unable to prevent the enormous net outflows of $1.7 billion during 1991–2 as India ran into an acute balance-of-payments crisis. Since then, interest rate differentials have almost vanished and, with the passage of time, so have foreign-currency-denominated deposits. Deposits from non-resident Indians are accepted either in external rupee accounts or in non-repatriable rupee deposits.

Economic Implications

The permanent migration of persons with professional expertise or technical qualifications mostly to the industrialized countries, described as brain drain, represents a privatization of benefits and socialization of costs where the benefits in the form of higher income accrue to the migrants as individuals, while the substantial costs of their higher education are borne by society as a whole without any tangible returns. Temporary migration of unskilled, semi-skilled, or skilled workers mostly to the Middle East is different insofar as the social cost of school education or vocational training is modest and the social benefits derived from remittances or skills formation are significant. The implications and consequences of return migration, however, are different. The return of those with professional expertise or technical qualifications could transform the brain drain into a brain gain. The return of semi-skilled and skilled migrants who have acquired new skills or upgraded old skills while abroad may also have a favourable impact on the economy. Return migration of unskilled workers may increase the incidence of open or disguised employment, even at the margin, by exerting pressure on the labour market where job opportunities are scarce. There can be no doubt that remittances are a real blessing, not only for the migrants' families at a micro level but also for the economy at a macro level. But there is striking asymmetry between social costs and private benefits, which is a function of the skill and education levels of migrants. Available evidence suggests that remittances, in the aggregate as also per capita, from unskilled and semi-skilled migrants are significantly higher than remittances from others. Such migrants are persons who are at the lower end of the spectrum of incomes before departure, whose remittances essentially support consumption of their households or extended families at home. These remittances also provide resources for investment in the rural sector, particularly agriculture, or help acquire assets for self-employment in the urban sector. In sum, such remittances create consumption possibilities and income opportunities for the poor or the less well-endowed. In contrast, remittances from educated and professional migrants, drawn from the upper end of the spectrum of incomes before departure, in the aggregate as also per capita, are much lower. This is because they do not need to support the consumption of their extended families at home and would much rather support the consumption of their households, or use their savings for investment, in the host country. It would seem that migrants who impose low social costs provide high social benefits, whereas migrants who impose high social costs provide low social benefits for the economy. In the context of balance of payments, the story is simpler at a macro level. Remittance inflows financed a large proportion of the balance-of-trade deficit and thus reduced the current account deficit to manageable proportions. Indeed, at this juncture, remittances are far and away the most important source of external finance for India. Repatriable deposits provided external resources to finance the current account deficit for a while, in much the same way as any other form of borrowing abroad may have done. These may have eased balance-of-payments difficulties in the 1980s but when large net inflows turned into massive net outflows, capital flight accentuated, if not precipitated, the crisis in the balance of payments. Such capital flows from migrants are now placed in rupee-denominated external accounts or non-repatriable rupee deposits, which is clearly a change for the better.

DEEPAK NAYYAR

References

Hatton, T.J. and J.G. Williamson. 1994. 'What Drove the Mass Migration from Europe in the Late Nineteenth Century?', *Population and Development Review*, 20: 1–27.

Lewis, W. Arthur. 1978. *The Evolution of the International Economic Order*, Princeton, Princeton University Press.

Nayyar, Deepak. 1994. *Migration, Remittances and Capital Flows: The Indian Experience*, Delhi, Oxford University Press.

——. 2002. 'Cross-border Movements of People', in Deepak Nayyar (ed.), *Governing Globalization: Issues and Institutions*, Oxford, Oxford University Press.

——. 2008. 'International Migration and Economic Development', in Narcis Serra and Joseph Stiglitz (eds), *The Washington Consensus Reconsidered: Towards a New Global Governance*, Oxford, Oxford University Press.

Stalker, Peter. 1994. *The Work of Strangers: A Survey of International Labour Migration*, Geneva, International Labor Office.

Tinker, Hugh. 1974. *A New System of Slavery: The Export of Indian Labour Overseas: 1830–1920*, Oxford, Oxford University Press.

United Nations. 1998. *International Migration Policies*, New York, United Nations.

——. 2009. *Trends in International Migrant Stock: The 2008 Revision*, and *International Migration 2009*, New York, United Nations, Population Division, Department of Economic and Social Affairs.

International Migration from India: Economic Impact

The first 100 years of migration from India since its modern inception in the 1830s was constituted largely of unskilled and low caste workers. Migrants in the 19th century came from poorer socio-economic groups, from poorer parts of the country, and went to (relatively poor) Southern countries. Between 1834 and 1937, 30.2 million people left India and 23.9 million returned, resulting in a net migration of 6.3 million (Davis 1951). A century later, international migration from India was starkly different in its selection characteristics. Migrants came from richer socio-economic groups, from wealthier parts of the country, and, with the significant exception of the large migration to the Middle East, went to industrialized countries. Post-Independence, an initial stream of unskilled and semi-skilled labourers migrated from Punjab and Gujarat to the United Kingdom (1950s to early 1960s). Another stream of unskilled and semi-skilled labourers went to the Gulf region (post-1973 oil shock) along with (for the first time) a substantial number of skilled labourers.

The latest stream has been high-skilled migration to the US following the liberalization of US immigration law in 1965. The large demand for information technology workers in the US in the late 1990s led to another wave of young professional immigrants and by 2003 immigrants from India emerged as the second largest group of legal immigrants to the US. This migrant stream has been the most highly educated, both compared to other immigrants into the US as well as to other Indian migrant streams abroad. Since the 1990s, increasing numbers of skilled emigrants from India have also been moving to Australia, Canada, New Zealand, and Singapore.

The impact of international migration depends critically on the magnitude and selection characteristics of migrating labour (including education, age, gender, vintage, and geographical and ethnic origins), the reasons for leaving, institutional features of the country of destination, and specific institutional features and policies to promote and harness these flows in the country of origin (Kapur and McHale 2005). The interaction of these factors in turn affects what aspects of the economy are most impacted by international migration and the mechanisms through which these impacts are amplified or attenuated. This entry focuses on three critical mechanisms that have most affected the Indian economy: financial capital, human capital, and reputational capital.

Financial Capital

For nearly half a century Indian policymakers operated under conditions of foreign exchange scarcity. Attracting inflows from non-resident Indians (NRIs) has been part of the official thinking since 1970 when the first scheme to attract NRI flows was mooted. Inflows from the NRIs have come through the current account (remittances) and capital account (NRI banking deposits). Financial remittances emerged as an important part of India's balance of payments (BOP) since the oil-boom-induced Gulf migration in the 1970s. Remittances which were virtually negligible in 1970, rose to $0.43 billion in 1975 and jumped to $2.76 billion in 1980. However, they stagnated during the 1980s, even dropping slightly to $2.4 billion in 1990. Since then they have climbed steeply to $11.1 billion in 1999 and $21.7 billion in 2003. As a percentage of India's gross domestic product (GDP), remittances grew from 1.2 per cent in 1991 to more than 3 per cent in 2003.

Paralleling the inflows of remittances have been NRI inflows in the capital account. Although schemes to attract the latter were introduced in 1970, a decade later deposits barely exceeded one billion dollars. During the 1980s, while remittances languished, deposits accelerated, growing to $12.4 billion by March 1990. Following the onset of the 1991 reforms, both remittances and NRI deposits grew rapidly in the 1990s with the latter totalling $35 billion by March 2006. This spurt has in part been due to the rapid growth in the stock of Indian citizens residing abroad (especially in North America) and the degree to which their earning power has increased. Policy changes including the large devaluation of the rupee and liberalization of gold imports have also made a difference, especially in bringing remittances from the Middle East through official channels rather than underground (*hawala*) markets.

In general NRI capital flows have been relatively stable and are comparable to portfolio equity flows, both exhibiting low volatility. They are influenced by standard risk and return variables, economic and political risk in the case of NRI capital flows, and the interest rate differential between deposit rates and LIBOR (London Inter-bank Offer Rate) in the case of portfolio equity flows (Gordon and Gupta 2004). The only significant behavioural difference between NRI capital flows and foreign portfolio investors is that the latter are much more sensitive to India's credit risk as assessed by foreign ratings agencies, while the former are more blasè about sovereign risk when they put money into India. The one clear case when NRI withdrawals amplified India's BOP crisis in 1991 appears to have been driven by the perception of an impending devaluation rather than credit risk per se. When storm clouds threatened, as in the aftermath of the Asian financial crisis in 1997 and India's nuclear tests in 1998, India raised funds from its diaspora: US$ 4.2 billion from the India Resurgent Bonds (RIBs) issued in 1998 and another US$ 5.5 billion from the India Millennium Deposit (IMD) scheme in 2000. In March 2006 NRI deposits accounted for 30 per cent of India's total long-term debt liabilities, exceeding even that owed to multilateral institutions. Together with remittances totalling $170 billion between 1991 and 2005, these inflows have been an important source of insurance, significantly contributing to India's burgeoning foreign exchange reserves and allowing the Government of India to retire multilateral debt prematurely and permitting Indian companies to refinance costly external borrowings.

In contrast to the large inflows in the current account and banking deposits in the capital account, NRI foreign direct investment (FDI) has been remarkably limited even controlling for low levels of FDI into India. Total NRI investment out of the total FDI approved since January 1991 to December 2003 was around 3.5 per cent. An oft-made comparison between the Chinese and Indian diasporas is that FDI from the former into China exceeds FDI from the latter into India 20–25 times over. During the 1990s annual average FDI flows into China as a share of gross fixed capital formation have exceeded 10 per cent while in India's case these have been barely above 2 per cent. Nearly 60 per cent of Chinese FDI (between 1978 and 1999) came from three ethnically Chinese economies (ECEs)—Hong Kong, Macao, and Taiwan—while the diaspora's share in FDI in India has been under 4 per cent. However, overall financial inflows (that is, remittances, NRI banking deposits, and diaspora FDI) from emigrants from the two countries are more comparable—with inflows into China being between two and four times those into India in absolute terms and roughly comparable as a fraction of GDP.

Despite their substantial size it is surprising how little we know of the macro and micro impacts of NRI financial inflows into India. There is considerable reporting confusion between inflows in the current and capital accounts and the RBI has been remarkably lackadaisical in revamping its statistical systems to better understand these inflows. Remittances have been much more important for some states than others. The most obvious case is Kerala where studies indicate that remittances now account for nearly a quarter of state net domestic product with wide-ranging economic and social consequences. Kerala's large investment in human capital, proximity and historical links to the Middle East, and the stagnation of the economy, all contributed to extensive international migration. Over time, migration, remittances, and return migration have transformed the state's economy, making it the most globalized of India's states—remittances are nearly a quarter of the state's economy. Remittances have fuelled a consumption boom and the resulting demand has driven growth in the service sector, most of which—such as transport, trade, and telecommunication—is non-tradables (Zachariah et al. 2003). While much of the demand boom for consumer durables has spilled over to other states, one sector that has grown on the back of investments is the hospitality industry (tourism, transport, hotels, and restaurants), and private institutions in health and education have also mushroomed.

Human Capital

International migration has affected human capital formation in India in several ways. First, the *prospect* of migration current affects behaviour by changing forward expectations. For instance, at individual level the possibility of emigration leading to a higher expected return to human capital could lead to greater human capital investments. There are some indications that the burgeoning demand for private engineering, IT, and medical education in India and for English-language education are at least in part being fuelled by the prospects of higher returns from working abroad. Second, the so-called 'brain drain' results in an *absence* of scarce human capital. India has one of most positively selected emigration rates in the world. Recent estimates of the emigration rate from India for those with tertiary education are 42 times those with primary and 14 times those with secondary education. The implications of this loss are manifold, ranging from negative effects on institutions of higher education in India to the quality of healthcare and innovation. Nearly 60,000 Indian physicians (more than 10 per cent of the stock in India) practice abroad, and by all indications these come from the upper end of physician quality (Mullan 2006). An indication of the severity of the flight of scientific and engineering talent is the fact that the ratio of patents filed by Indians in North America to that by Indians in India (when normalized by population) is about 28,000:1 (Kapur n.d.). Third, there are human capital effects of the *diaspora* stemming from the flows of ideas from the diaspora. Some of India's most distinguished economists residing abroad have long been active participants and contributors to debates on India's economic policies and a younger generation appears to be following suit. Increasingly, a large number of Indian-origin faculty in business schools abroad advise Indian firms. Fourth, *return migration* has augmented human capital through additional training, experience, and networks. Although financial flows resulting from international migration receive most attention, a potentially more important type of remittance is the flow of ideas, be it technologies, theories, world-views, beliefs, or new ways of doing things. For instance, economic policymaking in India has been singularly affected by returning economists who have studied and worked abroad and have then worked in the economic policymaking institutions. However, while returning human capital in the 1950s and 1960s sought employment mainly in public-sector institutions, this is rarely the case in more recent years.

Network and Reputational Capital

The Indian diaspora has had important trade-enhancing and investment effects through its brokering role and by acting as a reputational enhancement mechanism. Firms and institutions in less developed countries (LDCs) are severely handicapped in the global arena because of reputational handicaps arising from a 'country-of-origin' effect.[1]

The success of the Indian diaspora has also made it possible for Indian diasporic networks to act as reputational intermediaries and credibility-enhancing mechanisms. This role has been particularly important in economic sectors such as software where knowledge, especially ex-ante knowledge, of quality is tacit. Just as the Chinese diaspora played a critical role in the initial breakthrough of labour-intensive manufacturing exports from China, the Indian diaspora had a great role to play in the labour-intensive segment of IT—namely, software and IT-related services. The destination of skilled labour flows from India to the US had important reputation effects. For instance, the Indian diaspora's success in Silicon Valley influenced how the world views India, reflecting the reputational spillover effects of success in a leading sector in a leading country. Of course once Indian IT's reputation was established, the role of the diaspora shifted to a brokering and human capital one.

In India's emergence as a leading exporter of cut and polished diamonds too, the Indian diaspora's reputational and brokering role has been critical. In 1968, India exported US$ 40 million in cut and polished diamonds. By 2003, India's exports of cut and polished diamonds had multiplied to US$ 7.1 billion, constituting 17 per cent of its total exports. India accounts for 55 per cent of world net exports of cut and polished diamonds in value terms, 90 per cent in terms of pieces, and 80 per cent in terms of caratage, making it the largest exporter of cut and polished diamonds in the world. Over 90 per cent of these diamonds were processed in Gujarat, employing over 1 million people in that state. India's rise as a world leader in the diamond industry over the past 35 years has been driven by the ascent of Indian èmigrè diamond traders (mostly Gujarati Palanpuri Jains) in Antwerp, the centre of the world diamond trade.

Despite the sizeable flows of labour from India and the large India diaspora, data and analysis in this area are scant, hobbling our understanding of this complex issue. A major obstacle to understanding the economic impact of immigration on India is the lacuna in statistical systems commensurate with those that monitor the cross-border flows of capital and goods and services. While there are a host of potential statistical sources ranging from the National Sample Survey to visa and passport offices and the Protectorate of Emigrants, none have geared themselves up to collecting migration data that would lend themselves to analysis, perhaps because there is little external pressure from international organizations to do so.

DEVESH KAPUR

References

Davis, Kingsley. 1951. *The Population of India and Pakistan*, Princeton, Princeton University Press.

Gordon, James and Poonam Gupta. 2004. 'Nonresident Deposits in India: In Search of Return?', IMF Working Papers 04/48.

Kapur, Devesh. n.d. 'Democracy, Death and Diamonds: The Domestic Impact of International Migration from India', unpublished book manuscript.

Kapur, Devesh and John McHale. 2005. *Give Us Your Best and Brightest: The Global Hunt for Talent and Its Impact on the Developing World*, Washington DC, Center for Global Development and Brookings Institution.

Mullan, Fitzhugh. 2006. 'Doctors for the World: Indian Physician Emigration', *Heath Affairs*, 25(2): 380–93.

[1]'Reputation' here refers to prior beliefs of buyers of products and users of services.

Zachariah, K.C., E.T. Mathew, and S. Irudaya Rajan. 2003. *Dynamics of Migration in Kerala: Dimensions, Differentials and Consequences*, New Delhi, Orient Longman.

International Trade

Traditionally, India is viewed as a large, self-contained economy with few links with the outside world. Ancient evidence, however, attests to the historical importance of India's foreign trade. For millennia, India has been the world's greatest sink of gold: since not a grain of gold was produced in India till the Kolar mines were sunk in the 19th century, this mass of bullion represented her accumulated trade surplus with the outside world. Much data indicate India's flourishing exports to the Roman and Byzantine empires, originating in one of the most extraordinary events in history: in 305 BC, a Bihari king marched his army across the entire subcontinent and through the mountain passes into Afghanistan to defeat the Greeks in the shadow of the Hindukush and link India with the Silk Road, the highway of international commerce between East and West. From this unique episode emerged the first all-India empire, the Mauryan empire. Nor was maritime trade insignificant. Shore temples like Mahabalipuram and Somnath arose in part as banks financing the trade of south India with Southeast Asia or of Gujarat with the Middle East and Africa.

There was always, however, a tension between coast and interior, a delicate balance of power swayed by the relative contributions of each to the revenue and military capacity of the state. Land empires like the Mughal, rooted in river valley agriculture and defending a land frontier against north-western invaders, inevitably subordinated coastal interests to those of the hinterland. Well adapted to an age of land transport, they neglected maritime power and the technology of transport and defence at sea. From the 16th century, however, the world, particularly Western Europe, entered the age of open ocean navigation. By the 18th century, the sea was the primary avenue of international trade; continental regimes that, because of geography and consequent internal structure, faced landward, were gradually eclipsed and maritime powers, committed to ocean trade routes and their defence, came to dominate the world. The Pax Britannica now governed an 'empire of the sea' and an international trading network into which coasts everywhere were willy-nilly drawn.

The colonial system that evolved was dedicated, in principle, to free trade within the empire. In practice, it relegated India and other non-white colonies to the role of suppliers of primary products to Britain, 'the workshop of the world', and its trading hub. India exported opium and indigo in the 19th century, and tea, cotton, jute, and occasionally wheat and sugar in the 20th century. Manufactured exports were limited to cotton textiles. The scene was set for prolonged stagnation as an overcrowded agrarian economy trapped in the vicious circle of poverty.

Over the century preceding 1950, similar scenarios were enacted all over the colonial world and this experience shaped policymakers' attitudes in the 1950s, when these colonies attained independence. Free trade was viewed as a design for reducing poorer countries to 'hewers of wood and drawers of water'. Their major exports, of primaries, faced low price and income elasticities of demand, threats from synthetic substitutes and from recycling of scrap (for example, copper and tin) and consequently deteriorating terms of trade. Their manufactures could not compete with richer countries in the world market or indeed even at home. 'Export pessimism' fostered the belief that their development must necessarily be an autarchic process, based on import-substituting industrialization (ISI).

Nor was this entirely a prejudice born out of unfortunate experience. Before the 1960s, it had a solid economic basis. The populous low-wage countries had a labour cost advantage in manufacturing. But they also had low and inelastic domestic demand for manufactures: local producers could not achieve scale economies in home markets, while if they sought foreign markets, they ran into high distribution costs, political risks, and exchange rate volatility. Increasing returns were of course pervasive in industry, and in fact generally more important than unskilled labour costs. So low-wage economies could not realize the comparative advantage in labour-intensive manufacturing that neoclassical trade theory predicted on the assumptions of constant returns to scale and perfect mobility of goods.

If primary exports were inelastic and manufactured exports hopeless, growth had necessarily to be internally generated. And since growth shifts demand towards manufactures, self-sufficient growth involved industrialization. Industrialization in turn required protection from foreign large-scale producers located in affluent mass markets. It was also state-sponsored, not market-driven. Such a development strategy dominated Indian planning since P.C. Mahalanobis, author of the Second Five Year Plan.

Particularly from the late 1960s, protection of manufacturing became a comprehensive and Byzantine system: the highest tariffs in the world (averaging 117 per cent) topped off total quantitative control and licensing of imports with complex and opaque procedures. Indeed, such an evolution was inevitable once government became the arbiter of import policy with the implied power to restrict entry and generate rents. Competition for these rents endowed administrators with enormous powers of patronage that could be exploited or encashed if dubious deals were veiled in official secrecy or by unintelligible regulatory procedure.

More generally, state-sponsored ISI was inherently limited in effectiveness and potential. It constrained productivity in many ways. It sacrificed comparative advantage and the economies of scale that accrue from specialization. It excluded foreign competition, thereby diluting pressures for efficiency. It denied India new technology embodied in imports. It raised the prices and reduced the quality of capital goods and intermediates. While all these were direct consequences of restricted trade, productivity effects just as severe flowed from the large role of government in production and economic administration under such a regime. Vast administrative resources were needed by government for formulation and enforcement of policy and by firms for compliance or evasion. As vast were the resources diverted from productive investment and innovation to rent seeking, the effort to influence the politicians and officials who doled out contracts and licences or enacted laws that set the parameters of economic activity. In a heterogeneous society dominated by organized interests, government decisions reflected these sectional pressures: this undermined productivity when, for instance, industrial location was determined primarily by these pressures or recruitment guided by non-merit considerations. Equally damaging were the pressures of organized labour: these encouraged an approach to the public sector as an employment guarantee scheme rather than a productive element in the economy; they also perpetuated labour laws that eroded efficiency and ruled out quick exit for loss-making enterprises. Finally, there were the monumental delays of government decision-making, a cost that was critical in markets requiring adaptation to rapid change or in a growth process where time is of the essence.

The main, though not exclusive, focus of this inefficiency was the public sector, which, in the ISI regime, occupied 'the commanding heights of the economy'. Its low productivity hampered supply of crucial infrastructural inputs—power, steel, coal, cement, railway and air transport, telecommunications, roads and port facilities—to the economy at large, undermining output and growth. It also implied low profitability: public enterprises became a chronic drain on the exchequer.

ISI favoured capital- and energy-intensive industries with high capital cost. Public investment also implied cost inflation due to corruption and cost escalation due to the dilatoriness of government decision-making.

High cost of public investment, losses of public enterprises, and soaring salary bills in the public sector combined with vast subsidies extracted by organized interests from government to drive up public expenditure. Revenue, meanwhile, remained inelastic due to the low level and slow growth of income and the resistance of the same interest groups to tax increases. The initial response of government to these budgetary pressures was to curtail public investment. But this undermined infrastructure, creating interrelated crises in power, coal, steel, railways, cement, fertilizers, and so on, that restricted growth until 1980 to a mere 3.2 per cent per annum. The 1980s saw a restoration of infrastructural investment, essentially debt-financed, with growth accelerating to 5.2 per cent. But budget deficits became endemic, a public prodigality contrasting with the frugal 22–24 per cent rate of private saving. Government borrowed massively, driving up public debt and interest rates. With debt service rising more than proportionally to the rapid growth of the debt and becoming a growing and incompressible budgetary commitment, government fashioned a debt trap for itself.

Excess demand created by budget deficits was partially absorbed by crowding out private investment through higher interest rates. In part, however, it overflowed abroad in trade deficits, financed by foreign loans at the exorbitant rates of the debt-crisis-ridden 1980s. The growth of foreign debt gradually eroded confidence in the rupee. A succession of unstable (therefore, fiscally irresponsible) governments between 1989 and 1991, and the Gulf War of 1991, which imposed on government the cost of repatriating lakhs of Indian workers from the Gulf while depriving India of their foreign earnings, precipitated a crisis that drove India into the arms of the International Monetary Fund (IMF) and down the road of reform.

While in India the internal dynamics of ISI led to massive 'government failure', the international economy was changing. ISI was based on the assumed pervasiveness of scale economies in manufacturing and high distribution costs fragmenting the world market. From the mid-1960s, changes in tastes and technology and in the global distribution of wealth undermined these assumptions. Living standards rose worldwide: demand became more sophisticated and differentiated with quality, variety, and exclusiveness outweighing mere cheapness—so that the scale economies associated with long production runs and standardization dwindled in importance. Increased uncertainty of the business environment (due to intensified global competition) made investment in specific fixed assets (which are the basis of economies of long runs) unjustifiable. Technology evolved instead towards 'flexible specialization', using microelectronically controlled general-purpose tools to produce small batches of differentiated products almost as cheaply as long runs. Distribution costs too dropped. Higher degrees of processing reduced the material and mineral intensity of output and, therefore, the share of transport cost in delivery price. A unipolar world economy centred on the Atlantic was replaced by a polycentric system with the Pacific and the Middle East as its other foci: this reduced spatial and cultural gaps that poor-country producers had to bridge in reaching rich markets. Ocean transport costs fell due to containerization, warehousing costs due to 'just-in-time' management technology. Above all, the information and telecommunications revolution not only demolished barriers of ignorance that had segmented markets in the past; it also created an international market in labour services that none had dreamt were tradable at all.

While technology, tastes, and economic geography combined to create a potential for globalization, its realization was facilitated by a dismantling of trade barriers beginning with the Kennedy Round in the 1960s and culminating in the World Trade Organization (WTO). Poor countries could now access rich markets at little cost and could realize their potential comparative advantage. In particular, densely populated, low-wage Asia could exploit its labour cost advantage to capture markets for manufactures and services hitherto beyond its reach. The initial consequence was the East Asian miracle—the upsurge in growth led by labour-intensive manufactured exports from the Pacific rim and, eventually, China. South Asia followed. The labour surpluses of Asia were absorbed into the international economy much as the virgin land of the New World was in the late 19th century and the elastic supplies of fossil fuels were during the Industrial Revolution, and with similar consequences for the worldwide distribution of economic growth and potential economic power.

India was a latecomer to this process, its responses delayed by vested interests nurtured by ISI—in the bureaucracy, in protected industry, in organized labour in the public sector, and in large import-substituting enterprise. The crisis of 1991, however, made liberalization inevitable, paving the way for a retreat from quantitative controls and prohibitive tariffs. Liberalization also involved freer flow of capital and technology, a spectacular upsurge in exports and acceleration of growth (and consequently in developmental imports like oil and machinery) without accumulation of debt. India's recovery and transition to a high-growth trajectory were rapid, with only a minor blip between 1997 and 2000, a period when the Asian economic crisis abroad was compounded by domestic political instability.

In India, as elsewhere, accession to the WTO was a contentious issue. The WTO sets the framework for the international economy. It is not, however, a free trade system but only a forum for multilateral negotiation of the limits to trade restriction. The advanced West, concerned about slow growth, stagnant labour markets, and the threat from Asia to its economic ascendancy, has sought to negotiate a right to restrict trade on the plea of environmental or labour standards. It has tried to exploit existing clauses on quality and safety standards and against dumping to erect non-tariff barriers to imports. And it has pursued regional trading arrangements like the European Union (EU) and North American Free Trade Agreement (NAFTA) as alternatives to multilateral trade expansion over which it has less control. Protectionism in the West has changed its form but not its substance under the WTO. In India too, while Western protectionism is vigorously opposed, the government remains sensitive to the pressures of uncompetitive industries and their workers and has defended their interests through extensive anti-dumping action. Regional objectives like a South Asian free trade area have also been pursued—though fruitlessly, because of political constraints. Participation in the WTO has not, therefore, deterred protectionism—though protectionism is not the appropriate strategy for an economy that is expanding rapidly though trade.

While labour-intensive exports were the engine of growth throughout Asia, in India their expansion had its own distinctive features. These were shaped by comparative advantage that was partially a legacy of past policy. In most labour-abundant countries, traditional labour-intensive manufactures, in particular textiles, have spearheaded initial export expansion. In India, however, product reservation for small enterprise, supposedly for employment and equity, succeeded spectacularly in crippling the textile industry. And, while trade policy was being slowly reversed, interest group pressures ensured retention and reaffirmation of product reservations. The Abid Hussain Committee, appointed to re-examine industrial policy, recommended total dereservation, but its report was forgotten and India opted out of the world's mass market for traditional labour-intensive goods. The conquest of this market propelled China's stratospheric boom of the 1990s. India meanwhile was in dire peril of restricting itself to niche exports, cottage industry, exotica, and boutique products.

The effects of this quixotic industrial policy were reinforced by the neglect, particularly in the BIMARU states (Bihar, Madhya Pradesh, Rajasthan, and Uttar Pradesh), of primary education and health. This made it difficult to launch basic labour-intensive manufacturing with quality and productivity comparable to those of China where high literacy and health levels were inherited from the Maoist regime.

Fortunately for India, the advantage conferred by low labour costs is pervasive. It extends well beyond traditional labour-intensive goods into new industries and services not burdened by past legislation and well-organized interest groups. Further, in these new activities, India has been the fortunate beneficiary of historical accidents. The government's efforts to build up a large, university-educated middle class and its investment in science and technology education have created a labour force well equipped for the information technology (IT) and biogenetics booms. And its failure, despite its best efforts, to stamp out all vestiges of the knowledge of English that India had inherited from her colonial past has insured survival of an asset of incalculable value in an age of instant worldwide communication, basically in the English language. Thus, while China dominates the vast world market for traditional labour-intensive manufactures, new vistas are opening up for India in software and IT, biotechnology, basic pharmaceuticals, the export of higher education (particularly in technology and management) and of medical services and professionals, and long-distance communication-based services like data transcription and business process outsourcing (BPO). In these fields, India's assets are complementary to China's (and most of East Asia's). These advantages, however, may be transient; with some effort, they can be replicated in other countries and they can be irreparably damaged by unimaginative policy. Fortunately, electoral compulsions are forcing central and state governments to correct their most egregious policies: the West Bengal government, for instance, has been compelled by public pressure to recant on its earlier hostility to English education. The BIMARU states, however, unlike West Bengal, have not yet learnt their lesson.

Assuming that India maintains its existing pattern of comparative advantage, what will be the distributional consequences? Rapid expansion of IT and biotech, of BPO and similar services will mean an explosion in employment and incomes for the college-educated urban English-speaking population. It may also create incentives for upward mobility and opportunities for the less fortunate to climb the social ladder of absorption into the Great Indian Middle Class. Yet it is hardly an inclusive strategy of development. It emphasizes services performed by an educated middle class as the leading sector in growth—amidst an ocean of illiteracy and poverty. Income generated in this leading sector will eventually trickle down to the poor through increased demand for food and manufactures. But this is a process that raises mass aspirations and then fulfils them excruciatingly slowly. Not only is it inequitable in the extreme, it is also a prescription for political volatility. It is doubtful if it is a sustainable strategy in a democracy.

Contrast this with Chinese growth strategy. China began with the virtual dissolution of the communes, an institutional reform that doubled the per capita income of its 600 million farmers between 1978 and 1984. It followed it up by flooding the world market with the infinitely varied products of its raw, but literate and healthy, labour. The initial impact of expanding opportunity was distributed among hundreds of millions, creating an ever-widening internal market for basic manufactures that supplemented external demand. The momentum of growth became independent of fluctuations in the world economy. The superiority of this strategy in terms of income distribution and of economic and political sustainability is evident.

Whatever the specific locus of opportunity that trade opens up for India, her future indisputably lies in increasing engagement with the outside world, an engagement that promises to end her millennial stagnation and poverty.

Ashok Guha

References

Bhagwati, J.B. and P. Desai. 1970. *India: Planning for Industrialization: Industrialization and Trade Policies since 1951*, Oxford, Oxford University Press.

Bhagwati, J.B. and T.N. Srinivasan. 1975. *Foreign Trade Regimes and Economic Development: India*, New York, Columbia University Press.

Srinivasan, T.N. and S.D. Tendulkar. 2003. *Reintegrating India with the World Economy*, New Delhi, Oxford University Press.

■ Irrigation

Irrigation plays an important role in Indian agriculture. In 2002–3 nearly 45 per cent of the 175 million hectares (ha) of the country's cropped area was irrigated. On a rough estimate, irrigated areas accounted for more than 60 per cent of the total crop output in the mid-1990s.

Post-Independence Trends

The irrigated area has nearly quadrupled since the early 1950s: from around 24 million ha in 1953–4 to nearly 83 million ha in 2005–6. According to one recent estimate, nearly three-fourths of the increment in total crop output between the early 1970s and early 1990s came from expansion of irrigated area and increase in per hectare yields on irrigated land. Un-irrigated crop areas actually declined and the rate of yield improvement in these areas has been overall far slower compared to the irrigated areas (Table 1).

Expansion of irrigation has been central to the strategy for increasing agricultural production. During the second half of the 20th century, the government directly invested close to Rs 1,000 billion at current prices (equivalent to Rs 2,300 billion at constant 1996–7 prices) on irrigation and flood control. The bulk of it was for irrigation. By far the largest part of it was spent on construction of new reservoir-based canal systems and, to a much smaller extent, improvement of these systems. Substantial amounts were also spent on small-scale surface irrigation work (tanks, local stream diversions, and lift irrigation) as well as public tube wells. But these were much smaller than investments on large-scale surface work.

The government also encouraged and stimulated the exploitation of groundwater by farmers for irrigation by giving liberal credit at concessional rates of interest, by implementing a huge rural electrification programme, and providing 'cheap' electricity and diesel oil for pumping. These public-sector initiatives were greatly reinforced by two other factors: reduction in the costs of lifting water brought about by the advent of energized pumps, followed, in the 1960s, by the HYV–fertilizer revolution which greatly enhanced the potential for increasing yields. Both increased the private profitability of groundwater irrigation, which in turn stimulated a surge of private investment in wells and tube wells.

As a result, the importance of groundwater as an irrigation source increased from less than 30 per cent in 1951 to nearly 60 per cent in 2000–1 (Table 2). The number of dug wells increased from 4 million to around 10 million; over 80 per cent of wells now use electric and diesel pumps. This was also the period of the tube well explosion. Negligible in 1951, their number is now close to 9 million, irrigating two-and-a-half times the gross crop area under dug wells.

Table 2 Growth of Groundwater Irrigation, 1951–94

		1951*	1968*	1994 @	2001@@
Open wells	No 10^6	3.9	6.1	10.2	9.6
	Energized 10^6	Neg	1.4	7.2	8.2
	Net area irrigated 10^6 ha	6.0	8.0	12.4	13.2
Tube wells	No 10^6	Neg	0.4	5.1	8.8
	Energized 10^6	Neg	0.4	5.1	8.2
	Net area irrigated 10^6 ha	Neg	4.5	18.4	31.8

Source: * CBIP (1989).
Note: @ CWC (1998).
@@ Minor irrigation Census 2000–01 irrigated area relates to gross crop area

Compared to groundwater, the expansion of surface irrigation, though substantial, is considerably less both in absolute and relative terms. Practically all the increase has come from large reservoir-based canal systems. In the early 1950s surface systems consisted of several hundred thousands of traditional, locally managed small-scale tanks (collectively called 'minor' works) and some relatively large canal systems fed by anicuts and barrages across major rivers. Large storages were few. Since then there has been hardly any increase in the storage capacity of 'minor' surface works. The live storage capacity of reservoirs of more than 10,000 m3 (called 'major and medium works') has increased to more than

Table 1 Net Irrigated Area by Different Sources, India, 1950–1 to 1995–6

Source	1950–1		1995–6		2005–6	
	Million ha	Distribution per cent	Million ha	Distribution per cent	Million ha	Distribution per cent
Surface	14.9	71.3	23.7	44.3	24.7	41.1
Govt canals	8.3	39.7	17.5	34.0	15.5	25.8
Tanks	3.6	17.2	3.1	5.8	2.0	3.8
Other sources	3.0	14.4	3.5	6.5	7.3	12.2
Groundwater	6.0	28.7	29.8	55.7	35.4	58.9
All sources	20.9	100	53.5	100	60.1	
GIA all sources	22.6		71.5		82.6	

Source: GoI, Statistical Abstract of India (various issues).

175 billion cubic metres (bcm). They now account for the bulk of the total water utilization and area irrigated by surface sources. It needs to be noted that official land use statistics tend to understate the crop area being irrigated from surface sources.

The quality of irrigation has also improved to some extent mainly because of the emergence of groundwater as a major source. Losses in taking water from the source to the fields are far less in the case of wells and tube wells. Users have much greater flexibility to adjust irrigation according to the actual condition of crops. In the case of surface irrigation, large reservoirs have wider catchments and can, therefore, provide larger and more reliable supplies than works that depend on small local catchments. The spread of conjunctive use of surface with groundwater also helps improve overall water use efficiency in surface irrigated areas as well. Available evidence points to an improvement in efficiency of irrigation water use in all major river basins of the country.

Uneven Access to Irrigation

Given the size and diversity of the country it is not surprising to find much inter-regional variations in the extent and sources of irrigation and the their development over time. Available data suggest that inter-state disparity in surface irrigation (relative to cultivated area) is considerably less than in groundwater irrigation and that, while the former has progressively declined over the years, the latter has not. Disparity in the proportion of gross irrigated to total crop area has also been widening over the years.

Access to irrigation among the farming population is also unequal. For the country as a whole, there is a consistently positive association between the size of holdings and the proportion of households having access to any irrigation and a consistently negative relation of holding size to the proportion of irrigated to total operated area (overall and by major source). In other words, smaller holdings have less access to irrigation but are able to irrigate a higher proportion of their land.

The disparities in irrigation ratio, both overall and by source, have greatly narrowed during this period. This is because while the irrigation ratio has increased in all size classes, the rate of increase has been much higher in the larger holdings as compared to the smaller holdings. Expansion of irrigation has clearly favoured the bigger holdings far more than the small holdings (Table 3).

Table 3 Percentage of Operated Area Irrigated by Source, All-India, 1953–4 and 1991–2

	1953–4			1991–2			% Sample hhs with
	Surface	Ground	All	Surface	Ground	All	irrigation
<1 ha	18.5	8	26.6	19.8	21.8	41.6	40.0
1–2 ha	18	7.1	25.1	18.1	20.8	38.9	55.4
2–4ha	14.3	6.8	21	15.9	20.9	36.8	61.5
4–10 ha	9.8	5.4	15.2	13.8	19	32.8	65.8
>10 ha	4.4	2.4	6.8	15.5	12.5	28.1	62.7
All	10	4.9	14.8	16	19.3	35.4	51
Cv %	41	33	38	17	18	14.4	

Source: National Sample Survey.

Areas of Concern

Government strategy for developing and implementing irrigation attracts criticism on several grounds. The bulk of public investment in the water sector has gone into construction of large surface irrigation projects. Inadequate preparatory investigations and laxity of pre-clearance appraisals have resulted in serious underestimation of costs. Compounding this is the tendency to start far too many projects unmindful of the resources available to implement them. The result has been inordinate delays in completing projects, over capitalization, underutilization of their potential, and accumulation of a huge overhang of incomplete projects.

They also attract criticism for ignoring, at any rate to grossly underestimating, the adverse impacts of these projects (by way of displacement of human population, submergence of forests, and effects on riverine and estuarine ecosystems); the failure to design them so as to minimize these impacts; and ensuring that effective compensatory measures for unavoidable impacts and the costs involved are fully provided for in the project.

Depletion of groundwater is another major area of concern. Despite significant and increasingly widespread fall in the groundwater table, the government policy continues to encourage and finance private investment in wells/tube wells, their energization, and deepening. In this process, the distribution of access to groundwater is shifting in favour of larger farms at the expense of small holders. Whether and to what extent they increase the quantum of water extracted is also in doubt. To the extent they do, they are dipping into the static reserve whose loss cannot be replenished easily or fast. Present levels of use already exceed the sustainable limit in several areas and are likely to do so in more and more areas. The situation calls for major changes in the strategy and priorities of irrigation.

Needed Corrections

The potential for further expansion of water supplies for both surface and groundwater irrigation is strictly limited. In the case of surface water nearly 60 per cent of the utilizable potential of surface of water (690 bcm) is already being utilized and with the completion of projects under construction this proportion might reach 80–85 per cent. As the limits of potential are nearing, new projects are becoming more difficult and more costly. These constraints will not be overcome by inter-linking rivers. Apart from questions about its engineering aspects, there are serious concerns about its social and environmental impact, and its likely contribution to augmenting overall supplies relative to the costs involved.

In the case of groundwater there is growing evidence that its exploitation is already at unsustainable levels in many areas and this is becoming more widespread. As the number of wells and tube wells continues to grow apace, they are getting deeper and deeper, and more and more powerful pumps are being installed to chase falling water tables. There is a progressive decline in the area irrigated per well and per tube well. The Central Groundwater Board reports that in as many as 60 per cent of the districts in the country water tables have fallen by more than 4 metres over the 20-year period from the early 1980s. Scattered studies of wells and tube wells being used for irrigation show much larger long-term declines in groundwater levels.

The problem, therefore, is not just to check further increase in extraction but even reducing it in many areas to bring them within sustainable limits. Since a falling groundwater level indicates mining of groundwater reserves, it is necessary to explore ways, including artificial recharge, to increase effective recharge rates from their current or perhaps even natural recharge rates.

Improving Water Use Efficiency

Therefore, of necessity, the focus of irrigation programmers and policies has to shift to measures to facilitate and induce conservation and more efficient use of available supplies. The expansion of surface irrigation based on large reservoirs and the rapid growth of groundwater have no doubt led to considerable improvement in both technical efficiency of water use and in productivity per unit of water. But efficiency in both respects is considerably less than what is achievable by better water management with available agricultural technology. This has two components: (1) increasing the proportion of surface and groundwater drawn at source that is effectively available for consumptive use of crops and (2) flexible management of the timing and quantum of water application to crops to achieve higher yields per unit of consumptive use.

In surface systems, substantial volumes are lost due to evaporation in the reservoirs and canals, seepage and waste in the distribution network, and on farmers' fields. They contribute little to increased production of crops and useful biomass. No proper measurements of these losses are available. There is reason to believe that they are much higher than notional working assumptions used by engineers. Ensuring that the distribution network right down to the user level is properly laid and maintained in good physical condition can reduce leakages due to weak, breached, and porous banks. Lining of canals may also be desirable in some areas. The resulting reduction in seepage losses may increase the availability of supplies for consumptive use at the sub-basin or basin level but a part of it may simply result in a spatial redistribution of effective supply among the systems in the basin. Conjunctive use of surface and groundwater also increases the proportion of water let out of reservoirs that is effectively available for use for irrigated crops.

Productivity per unit water also depends on the extent to which the quantum and timing of irrigation can be managed flexibly to maintain an optimum soil moisture profile during crop growth. Surface irrigation systems have inherent limitations in this respect. In the Indian context, inadequate regulatory devices aggravate them. It is, therefore, essential to invest in installing appropriate physical structures at all levels of canal systems to enable better regulation of water deliveries to their different segments. Flexibility in water application can be increased by creating small ponds or other devices close to the user level and/or by more extensive recycling of seepage in canal commands.

The scope for and potential contribution of this option depends on sub-surface geology and the extent to which it is already developed, both of which vary from system to system and region to region. Also it is necessary to bear in mind that allowing unrestricted conjunctive use on an individual basis risks skewing the distribution of access to water in favour of larger farmers. Subject to this caveat, it is clearly important to explore and exploit all these possibilities.

This calls for a substantial shift in investment priorities in favour of improving physical facilities, controlling structures in existing systems, and moving away from new constructions. But it calls for much more. Radical changes are needed in institutional arrangements for water management and the way they function. They need to be complemented by measures to create strong incentives for more prudent and economical use of water.

Water Governance

That water governance is in serious disrepair is reflected in extensive violations of regulations regarding permissible crop patterns and groundwater extraction. Un-authorized and illegal tapping of canal water, and pumping of water from under riverbeds to areas outside the commands of public systems have become widespread. Institutional mechanisms meant to prevent and penalize such violations have been largely ineffective. Regulations prohibiting construction of new wells and tube wells in areas classified by groundwater boards as 'over exploited' and restricting new wells and tube wells in 'gray' blocks that are close to exploiting their potential are practically ineffective.

The need for radical institutional reforms to address these problems is widely recognized. But there are widely divergent views on its content. Some neo-liberals see water as a tradable commodity and consider property rights and market mediated allocations as the solution. However, (1) clearly defined 'property' rights are impossible to define in the case of a fluid common pool resource open to pervasive mutual interference by different users; (2) being a limited but vitally important common pool resource serving multiple users and uses for several ends (especially externalities, non-tradable outcomes, and long-term sustainability), balancing of competing claims has to be seen and accepted as fair end equitable; and (3) these tasks cannot be done through the market they have to be based on a social consensus, arrived at through a political process.

A very different approach—and one which takes cognizance of these compulsions—argues for redefining the role of the state to serve as a trustee of society in matters relating to water, leaving investment, management, and regulatory functions to autonomous organizations functioning within broad guidelines and legal framework defined by legislatures. The desirability of user involvement and active participation in management of irrigation is gaining acceptance. Some states have taken significant steps to implement this concept by entrusting water users associations with maintenance and collection of water charges at the tertiary level. A couple of states have also provided for induction of elected user representatives on management committees of different tiers of canal systems. But they have little effective role in deciding or implementing rules of allocation and scheduling. These functions continue to vest with the government. Institutional reforms clearly have a long way to go before they can make a significant impact on water management.

Economic Incentives for Efficient Use

Moreover, it is important to recognize that better laws, better enforcement of laws, and better management are necessary but not sufficient. But given that uses and users are numerous (running literally into millions), diffused, and connected in a complex network of inter-dependent, even the most competent, honest, and professional management cannot effectively monitor observance and enforce compliance of even properly designed rule systems. It is essential to complement them with strong economic incentives to induce individual users to behave in a manner conducive to achieving the overall objectives. Pricing of irrigation and inputs used for irrigation (especially energy for pumping) is critical.

Wasteful and inefficient use of water by farmers as well as the overexploitation of groundwater, which is a glaring feature of the Indian scene, is due in large measure to the policy of keeping water charges and the price of electricity and diesel oil at levels far below costs. This folly has been compounded by laxity in assessment and collection of dues, and by failing to adjust rates in the face of increasing costs and increasing output prices. With the effective cost of water relative to output prices falling progressively and steeply, users' interest in reducing waste and improving water use efficiency, already weak, has become weaker. But water pricing is a politically sensitive issue, which no government, irrespective of party affiliations, wants to even talk about. It is difficult to convince a politician or a farmer that improving efficiency and productivity that can come about with a combination of institutional reforms and higher prices would largely, if not wholly, compensate the effect of higher prices. With few takers for price reforms and anaemic interest in institutional reforms, it is difficult to be optimistic about the prospect for achieving prudent, efficient, and sustainable management of irrigation.

A. Vaidyanathan

■ IT-enabled Sectors

India's software services industry, which started in 1974, is one of the world's successful information technology (IT)-exporting industries. For the fiscal year ended March 2010, it generated $37.3 billion in export revenue, or 6.3 per cent of global IT services expenditure (NASSCOM 2010: 253), up from 3.4 per cent in 2007. A further $12.4 billion in export revenue was earned from IT-enabled services, such as call centres and back office work. As of March 2010, the industry employed 2.3 million people in software and IT-enabled export services. The US is the largest market, with a 61 per cent share, followed by Europe (30 per cent). Exports have grown at an average of 32 per cent annually over the decade to 2010.

The Indian software story is little understood, in part because its clients are firms rather than retail consumers. Most retail users and small firms buy 'product software', that is, software that is replicated in its original form across many users. Examples of product software include the popular Windows operating system that runs computers and computer networks, and Microsoft Word, an application that enables word processing.

While most large corporations use product software for purposes such as managing hardware (operating systems, utilities, drivers, and so on) as well as for standardized applications such as word processing, they usually need software customized to their needs for complex applications, such as software to automate an assembly line in a manufacturing company or software to manage students' course enrolment in a university. This is 'custom applications software'. It is part of a larger category called software services. This includes relatively simple work such as deploying hardware, software and websites, and training and system maintenance. It also includes more complex work such as integrating different pieces of product and custom software into a working system and the remote management of a range of services, such as email, network management, accounting, research and development (R&D), and customer care. Software services, a $588 billion industry worldwide, is a larger field than software products. Globally, software products had sales of $307 billion in 2009.

The Indian software success story is particularly interesting because it is a rare case of services rather than manufactured goods being exported from a developing country. Also unusual is that it happened in custom software rather than product software: most software-exporting countries develop product software. India and Ireland are the exceptions, but Ireland's exports are almost entirely to Europe and the work is simpler than India's software services, consisting of localizing American software to European requirements. The third unusual thing is that IT is considered one of the most difficult items to export due to the requirement of staying regularly updated with rapidly changing customer requirements and requiring the ability to respond quickly to the latest technological changes. These have tended to deter technology-oriented service exports, as documented by Hobday (1995).

Several factors enabled India's software success. We discuss the key role played by domestic policy and entrepreneurship but will also show that technological changes mattered too. Moreover, we argue that though India's software story is a story of success, it faces challenges as well.

Origins and Growth

The first Indian software exporting firm was TCS (Tata Consultancy Services), which was established in 1968 to serve the in-house data processing requirements of the Tata industrial group. In 1969, it started offering data processing services commercially to local clients on a Burroughs' mainframe. It became Burroughs' exclusive India sales agent in 1970. In 1974, Burroughs, attracted by the low costs of Indian engineers, asked TCS to send engineers to the US to install Burroughs' system software at Burroughs' clients' offices.

Thus started the software export business termed 'body shopping', that is, the export of programmers for assignments typically lasting a few months. The Indian firms initially did little other than recruit engineers, while the overseas client decided on the work that they would do. The engineers initially focused on systems installation and maintenance. Later, as IBM started dominating the global computer business, they converted clients' existing applications software into IBM-compatible versions. Thus, it was relatively simple work compared with developing operating systems and software.

By 1980, the industry had earned export revenue of $4 million, shared by 21 firms, of which TCS and a sister firm accounted for 63 per cent (Heeks 1996: 88).

As Table 1 shows, the industry grew substantially after 1984 when the number of firms increased from 35 to 700 by 1990. This was enabled by two factors. First, the government, after a period of hostility to the private IT sector, turned around and announced several incentives for exports, including the New Computer Policy in 1984. This led to substantially reduced import tariffs (on hardware from 135 to 60 per cent, and on software from 100 to 60 per cent), re-allowing of wholly owned foreign

Table 1 Growth of the Indian Software Industry

Year	Exports ($m)	No. of firms	No. of employees	Average revenue per firm ($)	Average revenue per employee ($)
1980	4	21	250	190,476	16,000
1984	25.3	35	1350	722,857	18,741
1990	105.4	700	6500	150,571	16,215
2000	5,287	816	162,000	6,479,167	32,635
2010	37,300	NA	993,000	NA	37,562

Source: NASSCOM, 2004–2010; Heeks, 1996.
Note: 1. Year refers to the fiscal year ending 31 March of that year. For example, 2000 refers to the period 1 April 2005–31 March 2000.
2. Figures are for software only and do not include IT-enabled services, such as call centres.

firms for exports, and exemption of export income from income tax.

Second, a major shift in technology globally, under way for some years prior to 1984, came to fruition in the mid-1980s. The new technology contained a hardware and a software component. The hardware component was the workstation, with its sophisticated graphics and numerical computation capabilities, which was invented in the US in the mid-1980s. The workstation, unlike the PC (introduced in the late-1970s), could run small business applications and could be used to write software for all kinds of computers, including mainframes. The software component was the widespread adoption of Unix as the standard operating system for workstations and mainframes. We term these latter two developments the U-W standard in subsequent text (Dossani 2004).

The U-W standard enabled programmes to be written on any workstation in a common language (C, which is the language of Unix). Earlier, programmers worked on mainframes with differing languages and operating systems, and so wrote programmes in the language of that mainframe. Thanks to the U-W standard and reduced tariffs, it became economical to write programmes in India, despite the relative absence of mainframes.

Thus began 'outsourcing', or the sending of work to India, a replacement of the earlier, more expensive paradigm of sending programmers to work in the US and other developed countries. An American firm, Texas Instruments (TI), was one of the earliest adopters of this approach. It set up a wholly owned subsidiary in Bangalore in 1986 (Sharma 2009).

Although several multinationals followed TI into India by setting up wholly-owned operations, it were the Indian IT firms that realized the potential for outsouring, that is, undertaking projects in India on behalf of overseas clients. TCS developed the first complete custom software project for an overseas client remotely, thus showing that outsourcing could tackle complex projects. Termed the 'remote project management model', TCS' approach was to remain the industry's mainstay for the next two decades.

TI's role was catalytic in more ways than one. By setting up in Bangalore at a time when the industry was still largely Mumbai-based, it demonstrated the advantage of locating work near engineers rather than near sources of capital. Note that the four southern states, Karnataka, Andhra Pradesh, Tamil Nadu, and Kerala produce 52 per cent of India's engineering graduates. Bangalore thus gained market share at the expense of Mumbai. Whereas in 1980 none of the top eight software exporters were from Bangalore and even by 1990, TI was the only Bangalore firm in the list (the rest were Mumbai-based firms), by 2000, there were two Bangalore firms in the list and Bangalore firms made up a quarter of the industry's exports.

Separating engineers from their clients came with one price: clients in developed countries no longer expected their programmers to acquire industry skills or knowledge of the latest technologies—how could they since they were remotely located? Remember that the internet was still a decade away. In consequence, India's software engineers primarily focused on programming. This led to a decline in revenue per employee by 1990, as shown in Table 1.

In the 1990s, the software industry entered a higher growth phase. Once again, domestic policy changes and global technology shifts were the drivers. First, India went through major economic reforms. These included tariff reductions and allowing exporting firms to open overseas marketing and delivery offices. The latter opened the mid-sized American firms to Indian outsourcers, while enabling 'blended' delivery, that is, both remote and proximate services, to larger clients.

The second factor was the second major shift in technology in as many decades. Once again, it consisted of hardware and software components. The hardware components were, first, a re-invention of the PC, due to its increasing computing power, as a business machine, thus replacing the ageing workstation with a dramatically cheaper alternative; and, second, the invention of routers and other networking gear that enabled the creation of networked computers over optic fibre. With the adoption of the software component, the internet, in the mid-1990s, the cost of transmitting information digitally (hence, the term 'the digital age') plummeted, enabling such networks to be global.

Whereas earlier India's software industry was restricted to preparing custom software programmes, the digital age enabled the offshoring of live services, that is, functions, such as book keeping, payroll, and customer care. Thus a large new industry—significantly larger than software programmes—opened up to off shoring. By 2010, India had become the developing world's largest supplier of such services to developed countries. Thanks to a stable and liberal policy environment, the sophistication of the work done in India is steadily increasing.

The period 2000–10 did see important technological shifts, though, with an impact on the Indian software industry. The rise in wireless computing, particularly on mobile platforms, was the key hardware shift of the decade. The rise of web-based applications, such as Gmail and Facebook, marked the primary shift in software. However, neither shift caused paradigm changes in the Indian software industry.

Sustainability

Several scholars and policymakers have questioned the sustainability of India's IT-enabled sector. Of course, the record over the past three-and-a-half decades speaks for itself, but the critiques need to be addressed. Their reasons for unsustainability are: the absence of domestic markets from which to acquire domain skills, lack of intellectual property (IP) protection, small firm sizes, migration of skilled IT professionals to developed countries, lack of R&D in universities and industry, limited involvement of a skilled diaspora, and the lack of clusters (Schware 1992).

Some of these factors lost relevance from the industry's early days due to high Indian domestic growth. To address some of these: domestic markets are increasingly important sources of revenue and domain skills, especially in industries that are globally sophisticated within India, such as telecommunications, finance, and logistics. IP protection is considered adequate, following India's commitment to WTO norms. The diaspora of skilled IT professionals, centred globally around Silicon Valley, is increasingly engaged with India through business connections. Small firm sizes are no longer a concern, given that the large Indian IT firms, such as TCS, Infosys, and Wipro, each profitably employ over 100,000 employees. Significant clusters of IT activity now exist, notably in Bangalore, Hyderabad, Chennai, Pune, Mumbai, and Delhi.

Perhaps the biggest remaining concern is the quality of skills possessed by engineers trained in India and among researchers in universities. The issue is not quantity but quality. The Indian engineering education system, as of 2010, is large and growing rapidly. About 3,000 engineering colleges—mostly private, enrol about 3 million students. The growth in enrolment is largely due to the establishment of new colleges, with a recent annual growth rate of 40 per cent.

While the quantity of graduates addresses any immediate concerns that may arise from migration, the big challenge is that the quality of graduates may not be adequate. Indian engineers are often considered to possess adequate basic technical skills, but lack project management and deep technical skills (Carnoy et al. 2010). Meanwhile, the faculties in engineering colleges are mostly not educated to doctoral levels, thus limiting their ability to undertake R&D.

This may help to explain why the Indian software industry earns considerably less than its multinational peers. While the Indian average is $37,562, by contrast, as an example, CSC, a large US-based IT oursourcer, which earned revenue of $16 billion in 2009 and employed 92,000 persons, had a revenue per employee of $173,000.

RAFIQ DOSSANI

References

Carnoy, Martin, Rafiq Dossani, and Jandhyala Tilak. 2010. 'Understanding the Expansion and Quality of Engineering Education in India', Working Paper, Stanford University.

Dossani, Rafiq. 2004. 'Origins and Growth of the IT Industry in India', Working Paper, Asia-Pacific Research Center, Stanford University.

Heeks, Richard. 1996. *India's Software Industry*, New Delhi, Sage.

Hobday, Michael. 1995. *Innovation in East Asia: The Challenge to Japan*, Cheltenham, Edward Elgar.

NASSCOM. Various Years. *The IT Industry in India*, New Delhi, NASSCOM.

Schware, R. 1992. 'Software Industry Entry Strategies for Developing Countries: A "Walking on Two Legs" Proposition', *World Development*, 20(2): 143–64.

Sharma, D. 2009. *The Long Revolution: The Birth and Growth of India's IT Industry*, Delhi: Harper Collins.

K

■ Raj Krishna

Raj Krishna (1926–85) was an influential agricultural and development economist who taught primarily at Delhi University and the University of Rajasthan. In addition, he held various short-term government posts, including that of member of the Planning Commission. He also held visiting positions at various universities in the US and at the World Bank. Upon his death, he was described by one of his colleagues at the Delhi School of Economics as a true 'political economist', in the sense of the term used to describe 18th- and 19th-century economists. Indeed, his writings reflect two persona: one, the serious academic and the other, the debater, policymaker, and polemicist par excellence. Moreover, he seemed to move seamlessly between these two roles—at various stages in his career, he took leave from teaching and research to dabble in policymaking, only to return inevitably to his academic roots.

His writings span a period of four decades—from a piece entitled 'Economic Planning for the People', published in the *Congress Souvenir* in 1946, when Raj Krishna was only 20, to 'Ideology and Economic Policy', published posthumously in 1988. He wrote on a wide variety of subjects for a wide variety of audiences. His writings range from a controversial piece advocating that India acquire nuclear capability[1] to the rather technical econometric paper entitled 'Policy Modelling of a Dual Grain Market', written in 1983.

[1]'India and the Bomb', *Seminar*, 1965.

Raj Krishna was wholly a product of Delhi University. He obtained both his BA—from Hindu College—and MA degrees in economics there. He then taught for many years as Lecturer at Delhi College (now known as Zakir Hussain College). At that time he also began a long association with the then fledgling Indian Cooperative Union. He became director of research of the organization, conducting studies on the efficacy of cooperative enterprises, especially that of cooperative farms.[2]

Although he wrote some pieces on the subject early on, Raj Krishna's work in agricultural economics began with his PhD thesis at the University of Chicago in 1961. It was there that he was exposed to the then newly developing econometric methodology for the estimation of agricultural supply functions and the measurement of productivity growth. Greatly influenced by the work of Marc Nerlove and Zvi Griliches (both at Chicago at the time) and guided by T. W. Schultz and D. Gale Johnson, he wrote his thesis on estimating the price response of farm supply in India and Pakistan, using data from the early part of the 20th century. This work proved to be quite influential as it demonstrated that the price elasticities of supply for farmers in India were not very different from those estimated for developed countries (for similar crops over similar periods of time). This work (Krishna 1963) was quite definitive in dispelling the notion that supply functions in underdeveloped countries were relatively unresponsive or even vertical. Indian peasants, it seemed, responded to price incentives much like farmers in the

[2]An account of this work may be found in Jain and Coelho (1996).

West. Returning to India, Raj Krishna joined the Institute of Economic Growth in Delhi. He continued to work in the general area of agricultural economics, extending the work from his thesis to other crops, data sets, and time periods. An interesting finding was that there was little difference in the price responses of large and small farms. In 1965 he was appointed member of the Agricultural Prices Commission. At that time it was an influential body responsible for the central government's agricultural policy, setting price supports and subsidies and controlling the movement of agricultural commodities. Raj Krishna resigned within a year, writing a memorable note of dissent calling for the free movement of food grains throughout India and the dismantling of the so-called 'food zones'. Much of his thinking on this subject was summarized in a 1967 paper, which was a scathing indictment of the government's agricultural policy. It is of some interest to note that food zones were not formally eliminated until 1993, although they had effectively lapsed because of a lack of enforcement. Raj Krishna continued to write forcefully on this and other issues concerning agricultural price policy during a 1967–8 stint at MIT and the Food Research Institute at Stanford.

Raj Krishna then joined the University of Rajasthan in Jaipur where he remained for six years or so. It was there that he began his work on the unemployment problem, beginning with some technical work on estimating the consequences of growth on employment and culminating in his classic paper, 'Unemployment in India' (1973). He addressed many of the problems associated with the measurement of the rural unemployed and provided detailed estimates and an econometric analysis of causes. This paper represents the best of Raj Krishna's work, ranging from esoteric measurement issues to examining the ethical basis of the 'right to work'. His research led him to develop the strong conviction that investment alone could not alleviate unemployment effectively—he calculated that it would take a 25 per cent savings rate to keep unemployment from growing—and that direct action on this front was called for. As a result, he became a forceful advocate of rural employment guarantee schemes of the kind that some states (notably Maharashtra) were experimenting with.

Raj Krishna then spent two years (1973–5) at the World Bank at a time when, largely guided by Hollis Chenery, it was also advocating direct attacks on poverty. He then returned to India in 1975 to the Delhi School of Economics. In 1977 he became member of the Planning Commission during the Janata Party government. During his tenure there the Commission wrote the draft Sixth Five Year Plan. Concurrently, he was also a member of the Seventh Finance Commission responsible for the disbursement of funds to the states. He pointed out some inter-state inequities present in the system and advocated a revision of the formulae used to allocate funds.

With the change of government in 1979, Raj Krishna resumed teaching at the Delhi School of Economics. He remained engaged in constant debate about economic policy and most of his written work of this period reflects this (for instance, Krishna 1980, 1981, and 1984). He also wrote frequently on economic issues for large audiences in newspapers and general interest journals. It is during this period that he coined the memorable phrase 'The Hindu Rate of Growth', a polemical device intended to draw attention to the meagre 3.5 per cent growth rate experienced by India over the long run. The fact that this rate of growth remained steady through changes in governments, wars, famines, and other crises, made it for him an inherently cultural phenomenon—hence the name. Raj Krishna then spent two years at Stanford's Food Research Institute again during 1981–3. This interlude allowed him to return to more academically oriented research and revisit some old questions on agricultural price policy, unemployment, and planning. He resumed teaching at the Delhi School of Economics in 1983 where he remained until his death in 1985. Since then, of course, food zones have been eliminated, India has the Bomb, and its economy has grown at two to three times the Hindu rate.

VIJAY KRISHNA

References

Jain, L.C. and K. Coelho. 1996. *In the Wake of Freedom: India's Tryst with Cooperatives*, New Delhi, Concept Publishing Co.

Krishna, Raj. 1963. 'Farm Supply Response in India–Pakistan: A Case Study of the Punjab Region', *Economic Journal*, 73: 477–87.

——. 1967. 'Government Operations in Foodgrains', *Economic and Political Weekly*, 16 September.

——. 1973. 'Unemployment in India', *Economic and Political Weekly*, 3 March.

——. 1980. 'India's Development Experience', *Scientific American*, September.

——. 1981. 'India's Sticky Economy and Some Non-economics of Non-performance', in *Democracy, Development and Social Justice*, Seventh Vikram Sarabhai Lectures, Ahmedabad, Dr V.A. Sarabhai Memorial Trust.

——. 1984. 'Ideology and Economic Policy', Coromandel Lecture, November 1984. Published in the *Indian Economic Review*, 23 January 1988.

L

■ Labour Laws

The intention of this entry is not to provide an exhaustive account of issues surrounding labour laws in general, but rather to critically describe some aspects of a significant law which acts as a metaphor for labour laws in general—the Industrial Disputes Act, 1947 (IDA). I concentrate in particular on the scheme to resolve labour disputes and examine the IDA as an ostensible social security system. Among the many labour laws in India, the IDA probably reflects some of the most significant idiosyncrasies, one of which is the fact that it has a lineal connection with legislation aimed to further the British war effort during the Second World War. By legislating the IDA in 1947, Rule 81-A of the Defence of India Rules was formally inducted as law to become the key legislation associated with 'industrial relations', covering labour disputes, strikes, lockouts, lay-offs, and retrenchments. These Rules were set up to ensure uninterrupted industrial production during the Second World War by structuring the role of both the executive and judicial arms of the state in a unique format to resolve 'industrial disputes'. Indian legislators at the time of Independence debated extensively on whether the labour legislation should be oriented towards a system where collective bargaining between unions and employers was encouraged or if a system should be developed that would emphasize state intervention in the resolution of conflicts. Protagonists favouring the latter, more paternalistic approach won on the grounds that this method would better serve the cause of social justice because a system of separate labour adjudication would keep in mind the 'power position and susceptibilities of workers' (Kennedy 1966).

The Industrial Dispute Resolution Scheme

The scheme elaborated in the IDA to settle a dispute can be summarized as follows. An industrial dispute, among other things, includes discharge or dismissal of workers, interpretation of standing orders, wages, bonus, rationalization, lay-offs, retrenchments, and conditions of work. The parties to a dispute have a couple of options open to them—they can set up a *Works Committee* consisting of representatives of the parties to the dispute and resolve the matter, but since the recommendations of such committees are not legally binding it is common practice to initiate a process referred to as *conciliation*, which involves the active participation of the executive branch of the government. The government steps into the picture if one of the disputing parties asks for intervention and the government considers the demand for such intervention valid. Alternatively, if a dispute appears to be persistent in the perception of the government, the government can also choose to intervene. Initially, if the dispute is particularly complex, a conciliation officer from the labour department or a Board of Conciliation appointed by the government is required to try working out a settlement. A settlement, though binding on all parties, is not as binding as a court order. As a consequence, it is widely held that conciliation is viewed merely as a stage before adjudication. If a settlement is not worked out, the conciliation officer or Board tables a failure report. At this point, parties to a dispute can ask for an arbitrator to resolve the conflict, but this again is not very common, as the award of the arbitrator does not have legal standing. Instead, proceedings then move to the final stage called adjudication, upon a reference being made by the government.

The IDA gives the government the power to appoint labour courts and tribunals to adjudicate disputes. There are three kinds of courts—labour courts, industrial tribunals, and national tribunals, structured in their inception, to conduct proceedings following inquisitorial methods. Labour courts deal with relatively minor matters—typically matters that affect less than 100 workmen, while industrial tribunals look after disputes of greater import and magnitude of workers involved. The judgements and awards of labour courts and tribunals are final and not subject to regular appeal. If some party to a dispute is not satisfied with the judgement or award, they can move for special leave appeal to the Supreme Court under Article 136 of the Constitution of India or seek writ jurisdictions of the relevant High Court under Articles 226 and 227 of the Constitution.

In this scheme, the role of trade unions is defined by the Trade Unions Act, 1926, which allows any seven adults to gather and register themselves as a trade union. As a consequence, independent of the size of membership, all registered trade unions enjoy the same legal rights, powers, and privileges. Very broadly, these rights include the right to hold property, to contract, to litigate, and to be exempt from criminal liability if the union calls for a strike. However, the Act has no clause that obliges employers to recognize a particular union or even a set of unions as being representative of the workers' interests. This is a point that has been ratified by court decisions that have made it very clear that the law does not support obligatory recognition of a particular trade union as a bargaining agent.[1] At the same time Section 36 of the Industrial Disputes Act states that when a dispute arises, a worker can be represented by *any* registered trade union. This implies that while it is the volition of the employer to decide who is a representative bargaining agent; even the smallest union can bring up the grievances of its members into the dispute resolution process. As a consequence, multiple unions can exist, each winning the support of a fraction of the labour force employed in the concern, and the employer is obliged to deal with all of them.

[1]See, for example, *T.C.C Thozhilali Union* vs *T.C.C*, 1982 I L.L.J 425. In this judgement it is explicitly stated, 'Recognition by an employer of a trade union as a representative of its members and as their bargaining agent is a matter of volition on the part of the employer.'

Under this framework, the relationship between a union and an employer cannot be characterized by the usual understanding of the term cooperative bargain. Neither side is confined to a framework where a direct confrontation decides what each side will give and receive, because each side can always initiate or threaten to initiate the conciliation–adjudication process with the added ambiguity of who precisely are the players. As described in the preceding discussion, the conciliation–adjudication process involves participation by the executive arm of the government at many of the crucial stages of dispute resolution. The process of conciliation, initially placed in the hands of the labour department, may later end up involving the labour minister or even a higher executive functionary. Also, as noted earlier, if conciliation is not successful, the next stage involves the government as well. It is entirely the discretion of the government whether the dispute is referred for adjudication or not. Such involvement of the government at various steps of dispute resolution causes large-scale political interference in the resolution process. In fact, prominent political parties control the bulk of union activity in India and the independent union movement is quite weak. A study based on a sample of dispute cases shows that unions affiliated to the ruling party were favoured by referring demands raised by them for adjudication, while reference of demands raised by rival unions was wilfully prevented (Saini 1993). As mentioned earlier, the adjudication process with respect to industrial dispute resolution was envisioned as being more inquisitorial rather than adversarial in nature. However, it is widely reported that in reality it is very much subject to standard adversarial procedures followed in most courts in India (Desai 1994). It appears that disputes get settled on the basis of legal norms and procedures rather than on particularities of the case, requiring unions to be represented by individuals who are conversant with legal procedures, to rebut employers who are represented by advocates. It has been observed that such considerations have given rise to the phenomenon of 'outsider union leaders' who man key positions in trade unions. These individuals, who are typically not workers, position themselves as having the requisite skill to see disputes through administrative, political, and legal hurdles. Such outsider union leaders may not have the interest of workers as their central objective and have been documented as being prone to working out underhand deals with employers that ultimately result in weaker unions (Saini 1995). Of course the exact orientation of such leaders would vary from case to case, but the overall point to note is that the relationship between workers and employers is not at all direct. Instead the relationship is mediated by a number of exogenous elements that include outsider union leaders, politicians, judges, and administrators.

One way of analysing this scheme is to perceive the intervention in a labour dispute by the executive and judicial arms of the state as resulting in an *exogenous contract*—termed so because bodies other than the contractors specify the 'contract' (Singh 2000). Though such a 'contract' is ostensibly driven by the concern to take into account the 'power position and susceptibilities of workers', the scheme described in the preceding paragraphs suggests such outcomes are clearly linked to the strategically engineered resources expended on the outcome, each party attempting a favourable outcome through the mediation of politicians, administrators, corporate lawyers, outsider union leaders, and judges. While all parties may be aware of such relations, in so much so as they are not able to simultaneously and precisely predict the exogenous contract—such outcomes are subject to the hazard of being inefficient. Such inefficiency arises from the fact that since each one of the parties functions with a set of tactical private information and networks which the other parties cannot be fully cognizant of, this structurally introduces agency problems that follow from the asymmetry of information across parties. This line of reasoning indicates that the idiosyncratic scheme of resolving industrial disputes encourages non-cooperative outcomes, where a structure that would encourage more direct relations between labour and its employers could support more cooperative results.

The scheme for industrial dispute resolution may not necessarily lead to equitable results either, particularly in the instance where employers have deep pockets, compounded by the endemic delays of the judicial system, a point that has been particularly stressed in the recent 'Report of the Second National Commission on Labour 2002' (SNCL, Government of India). The quest for equitable outcomes is possibly better met by giving workers rights that act to consolidate their bargaining power—the status of workers as a group could be influenced by a host of circumstances that can raise their well-being, say, by encouraging a framework that increases productive employment opportunities and by encouraging structures that favour collective bargaining. In this context the SNCL has very aptly, among other recommendations, suggested that the law be reoriented to encourage bipartite consultation at enterprise level and that disputes be resolved through voluntary arbitration rather than through adjudication. It is interesting to note that while India has signed some of the Conventions that form the 'ILO [International Labour Organization] Declaration on Fundamental Principles and Rights at Work', it has not ratified the critical conventions regarding Freedom of Association, Right to Organize, and Collective Bargaining.

Social Security

Apart from providing the scheme to resolve industrial disputes, the IDA also doubles up as a device to provide employment security to a class of workers employed in the formal sector. The IDA allows employers to lay off (temporarily severe the services of a worker) or retrench (permanently truncate the services of a worker) a worker only after they pay out a stipulated severance pay to the worker. However, in addition to this, 'large' employers are subject to further restrictions according to the stipulations laid down in chapter V-B of the IDA: they have to actively seek permission from the government before they can lay off or retrench workers or even close the establishment. This chapter is of comparatively recent vintage, having been added to the IDA in 1976 when it was legislated to cover establishments that employed 300 or more workers. Subsequently the Act was amended in 1984 to cover establishments employing 100 or more workers. Since labour legislation is in the Concurrent List of the Seventh Schedule of the Indian Constitution, amendments to the IDA at state level have resulted in further changes; for example, in West Bengal, establishments employing 50 or more workers come under the aegis of chapter V-B of the IDA. The adverse impact on the demand for labour in the organized sector on account of these laws has been widely noted (Fallon and Lucas 1993; Besley and Burgess 2004; and GoI 2001). However, the institutional change that is required to remedy the situation requires a wider discussion, not merely calling for 'greater flexibility' in the labour market. It is important to appreciate that this is ultimately an issue of rights, and one way of initiating a discussion is to approach the problem using the frame provided by successive court judgements in response to a series of contestations that claimed that 'Chapter V-B of the IDA violated the fundamental right to carry on business and was therefore unconstitutional'.[2]

In the first judgement of this series, the Indian Supreme Court held in the *Excel Wear* vs *Union of India* case that the requirement that large concerns should seek permission from the government before they closed down was an 'unreasonable' restriction on the fundamental right to carry on business and that additionally the law was procedurally flawed because the government had the power to pass arbitrary orders.[3] In response to this, both the Indian state and subsequently the judiciary

[2]For a more detailed account, see Singh (2001).
[3]*Excel Wear* vs *Union of India* AIR 1979 SC 25.

chose to interpret the judgement in a manner that diluted its intent. The 1984 amendment to the IDA translated the procedural objections raised in the Excel Wear case by merely requiring orders to state reasons for granting or refusing permission to close down, fixing a time frame within which an order had to be passed, and making provisions for review and/or appeal, while completely ignoring the substantial issues raised in the judgement. In the meanwhile, a series of High Court judgements also held the clauses pertaining to lay-offs and retrenchments unconstitutional, which again resulted in relevant procedural changes being incorporated in the 1984 amendment to the IDA.[4] In addition, in *Workmen of Meenakshi Mills Ltd.* vs *Meenakshi Mills Ltd.*, a Division Bench of the Supreme Court, in contrast to its earlier stance in the Excel Wear case, upheld the constitutional validity of the clause that requires employers to seek permission from the government before retrenching workers.[5] The decision was based on the argument that though the right to retrench is an integral part of the right to carry on business, the restriction imposed on this right by the law was justified because it protected the 'interests of the workers' which the state is obliged to guarantee according to the Preamble to the Constitution and the Directive Principles enshrined in it. The term 'interests of the workers' according to the judgement 'covers the interests of all workers employed in the establishment including not only the workers who are proposed to be retrenched but also the workers who are to be retained'.[6]

Translated into the language of economic analysis, it can be said that the rules governing the contract of employment under Common Law distribute the risk of an exogenous shock over both the employer and the worker who runs the risk of being potentially unemployed, whereas the structure of rights under the IDA compels the employer to bear all the risks of a downswing. To make a normative judgement across these alternate states, the Pareto criterion is quite unhelpful; instead one needs to get some sense of the costs and benefits associated with each structure of rights. In a sense the Supreme Court, in the Meenakshi Mills case, *did* perform a cost–benefit analysis while deciding whether the requirement that large firms should seek permission from the government before being allowed to retrench workers violates the fundamental right to carry on a business. To recall, the Supreme Court held that the requirement indeed violated the fundamental right to carry on a business, but such violation was justified in the interests of the workers. In other words, the implicit valuation was that the gains for workers from security of employment are far greater than the loss suffered by the employer. However, the crucial point to note is that in making this evaluation, the Supreme Court chose to perform the crucial evaluation over a very limited unit—a large employer and the workers who are employed in that concern. By ruling in favour of existing rights, the judgement sought to maximize social welfare over a very narrow domain of currently employed workers in large firms and their employers. The very limited domain taken into consideration allowed the ruling that the procedure of seeking permission from the government before retrenching workers is a fair requirement. While the allocation of rights and the procedure to implement these rights might be viewed as being just in the domain over which the Supreme Court has sought to maximize social welfare, once the domain is enlarged to include other effects and components of the economy, this position is less defensible.

The manner in which the rights of large employers have been curtailed has implications well beyond a particular enterprise and the workers employed in it. The retrenchment law forces an involuntary exchange on the employer in an attempt at redistribution; however, the consequences of this attempt are quite unlike the effects of more conventional schemes of redistribution such as taxation. Taxation might lower incentives, but it leaves agents free to participate in voluntary exchanges given their new asset positions. The scheme of redistribution sought by the retrenchment laws is to have a third party decide the outcome of what is essentially an exchange interaction, in the belief that the third party—in this case the labour department of the government—will only allow configurations that are in the interest of 'workers'. As employers are unsure of being given permission to retrench workers, they will plan in accordance with this anticipation, and as a result cut down on subsequent additions to their labour force—possibly substituting other factors of production for labour or plainly refusing to hire the labour that they might otherwise have hired.

[4]In *K. Gurumurthy* vs *Simpson and Co.*, Madras (1981) II L.L.J. 360, Section 25-M (which deals with lay-offs) was declared unconstitutional, while the Andhra Pradesh High Court in *General Industrial Society Ltd.* vs *Commissioner of Labour* (1980) I An.W.R. 92 held that Section 25-M was constitutionally valid. Turning to retrenchment, the Madras High Court in *K. V. Rajendran* vs *Dy. Commissioner of Labour Madurai* (1980) II L.L.J. 275 and the Rajasthan High Court in *J.K. Synthetics* vs *Union of India* (1984) 48 FLR 125 (Raj) held Section 25-N (which deals with retrenchment) to be violative of the Constitution, while the Andhra Pradesh High Court in *I.D.L. Chemicals Ltd.* vs *T. Gattiah* (Writ Appeal No 16 of 1981, decided on 4 December 1981) upheld the validity of Section 25-N.

[5]*Workmen of Meenakshi Mills Ltd.* vs *Meenakshi Mills Ltd.* (1992) 3 SCC 336.

[6]Ibid.: 377.

Thus, the law acts to pre-empt a number of strategies that producers might otherwise follow, but for the law.

To the extent chapter V-B constrains the growth of employment that could absorb the substantial workforce that resides outside the formal sector, the laws are inimical to the spread of the benefits of growth and are therefore unjust. However, if the relevant domain is enlarged to include all workers, current and potential, the remedy has to engage with the fact that economic justice, in the final analysis, is associated with the allocation of risk across society. Thus any process that aims to bring in the much-needed flexibility to the Indian labour market will have to engage with providing some security against risks of the market, by evaluating the possibilities of unemployment insurance or a social security system financed by a tax or a mix of both strategies.

JAIVIR SINGH

References

Besley, Timothy and Robin Burgess. 2004. 'Can Regulation Hinder Economic Performance? Evidence from India', *Quarterly Journal of Economics*, 119, February: 91–134.

Desai, D.A. 1994. 'Industrial Adjudication and Social Justice in India', in Debi S. Saini (ed.), *Labour Judiciary, Adjudication and Industrial Justice*, New Delhi, Oxford & IBH Publishing Co.

Fallon, Peter R. and Robert Lucas. 1993. 'Job Security Regulations and the Dynamic Demand for Industrial Labour in India and Zimbabwe', *Journal of Development Economics*, 40: 241–55.

Kennedy, V. D. 1966. *Unions Employers and Government*, Bombay, Manaktalas.

Government of India (GoI). 2001. Report of the Task Force on Employment Opportunities, Planning Commission, Government of India.

Saini, Debi S. 1993. 'Reference Power of State in Industrial Disputes Adjudication: A Study with Reference to Industrial Disputes in Faridabad', *Journal of the Indian Law Institute*, 35 (Part II) (4): 233–52.

———. 1995. 'Leaders or Pleaders: Dynamics of Brief-case Trade Unionism under Existing Legal Framework', *Journal of the Indian Law Institute*, 37(1): 73–91.

Singh, Jaivir. 2000. 'Judicial Intervention in the Contract of Employment: Some Reflections on Labour Adjudication in India', mimeo, New Delhi, CDE, Delhi School of Economics.

———. 2001. 'Some Aspects of Industrial and Labour Markets in India: Perspectives from Law and Economics', unpublished PhD dissertation, Department of Economics, University of Delhi.

■ Labour Turnover in the High-technology Sector

The last decade has witnessed an explosive growth in India's information technology (IT) sector, both in terms of revenue as well as employment. The Indian IT–BPO (business process outsourcing) sector grew by 15.5 per cent from US$ 28.1 billion in 2005 to US$ 71.7 billion in 2009. As a proportion of national GDP, the sector revenues have grown from 1.2 per cent in 1998 to 5.8 per cent in 2009. Knowledge professionals employed in this sector more than quadrupled during this period reaching more than 2 million in 2009 just in the software market (NASSCOM 2009). The IT sector and related activities contribute about two-thirds of total employment (OECD 2010) and are a major force in the emergence of the Indian economy as a global powerhouse. An important consequence of this transition to an 'information economy' is an increasing dependence of technological productivity on the accumulation of knowledge and human capital and a decreasing importance of physical capital in the production process. Since human capital is intrinsically embodied with the worker, the growth of knowledge-intensive industries will have unique implications for the labour market in general and labour turnover in particular.

The IT sector in India (as in other countries) has faced high rates of labour turnover. Job-hopping is very common with annual turnover rates sometimes greater than 40 per cent (ASSOCHAM 2011). Many in the industry have cited this high attrition rate as a significant threat to India's global competitiveness in the IT sector. While high turnover rates do impose non-trivial costs on the employer, it is important to recognize the positive role that labour mobility plays in transmitting knowledge across firms, particularly in research-intensive sectors like IT.

There are at least two interesting questions that arise for labour markets in the context of a knowledge-based economy. First, what drives labour turnover in this sector and how is it different from labour mobility in other traditional sectors of the economy? Second, how does labour turnover of highly skilled workers aid or impede economic efficiency and is there a positive role for restricting labour mobility through non-disclosure agreements between the worker and the firm or non-poaching agreements between competing firms?

Favourable Selection in Labour Turnover

Labour turnover in this sector deviates from traditional theory in two important ways. Much of the existing economic literature on labour turnover has used asymmetric learning models to predict that if the current employer has greater information about worker productivity than a new employer, then worker turnover should consist of low productivity workers or 'lemons' (Greenwald 1986). This adverse selection model, however, does not explain the nature of turnover in modern technology firms where highly productive workers change employers frequently and the traditional stigma associated with frequent change in employment is not observed. To the contrary, new employers often form a favourable opinion of workers who have changed jobs in their career. Second, while in traditional industries, labour turnover is less likely to occur among more senior employees with longer tenures in the firm, this correlation seems to be absent in the IT sector. Some firms have reported higher separation rates at the middle-manager levels among employees with more than five years of tenure than for employees with less than five years experience (*Business Standard* 2004).

Many of these labour market anomalies can be explained by two important features of high-technology industries. First, the returns to investment in IT are highly stochastic due to the high rate of technological obsolescence and the inherent unpredictability of innovation. Frequently changing technology creates a need for workers to switch jobs as new firms often provide more challenging opportunities for workers to use their technical skills when their current employment does not. Thus a firm that realized successful returns on its investment in the past may not have a good project that makes productive use of its investment in the current period. Workers in these firms can be more productive in other firms in the market that have successful returns on their investment in the current period. Hence turnover, driven by the resulting misallocation of worker productivity across firms in the industry, allows the worker's knowledge to be utilized efficiently. In such an environment, workers with a diverse employment experience develop a reputation for being dynamic and enterprising and are thus able to command higher wages than workers who remain with the same employer for long durations.

Second, an important function of labour movement in high-technology firms is the transmission of knowledge spillovers through worker turnover. Knowledge spillovers refer to the knowledge and experience gained by a worker from her past employment that has some applicability to production or investment utilization in another firm. These could represent direct use, in a rival firm, of innovations learned from past employment, or spin-offs and passive learning from that innovation. Studies have shown that much of the human capital acquired by workers in high-technology firms is general rather than firm-specific so that knowledge about research and production processes acquired by a worker in one firm can be easily applied to in another firm. Opportunities for acquiring knowledge and experience about innovation processes in the firm usually arise at higher job levels in the firm's promotion ladder. Since more productive workers have a comparative advantage in such jobs, they are more likely to be promoted and, hence, they are also more likely to shift their services to a new firm when their current employer receives bad returns on his investment.

This mechanism of labour turnover described earlier can also explain the absence of a negative relationship between tenure or job seniority and turnover. Traditional economic models of labour turnover predict that workers with longer tenure in the firm are less likely to change employers. This is presumed because the longer the worker stays in the same firm, the greater the employer's private knowledge about the worker's productivity and also the greater the accumulation of firm-specific human capital by the worker which is not transferrable to a new employer. Moreover, the longer tenure itself may be the result of a better match revealed between the worker and the firm (Jovanovic 1979). Hence badly matched employment relationships between the firm and the worker will be terminated early in the worker's career and well-matched relationships will endure. In high-technology firms, on the other hand, firm-specific human capital is not important and the quality of the employment match changes over time depending on the investment returns realized by the firm in each period. Thus a good investment return today may yield a highly productive match with a worker, while a bad return in the future will render the same match unproductive. This severs the link between tenure and turnover in high-technology firms.

Restricting Labour Turnover through Non-poaching Agreements

The transmission of knowledge spillovers through worker mobility has important implications for the efficiency of investment decisions undertaken by firms. Firms cannot appropriate all the gains from investment when workers can carry knowledge spillovers to a new firm. The presence of knowledge spillovers thus acts as a positive externality leading to underinvestment in technology by firms in the market. Incorporating non-disclosure agreements into wage contracts is a common policy employed by many high-technology firms to restrict the flow of knowledge through worker turnover. While such agreements enhance investment incentives by curtailing turnover, they exacerbate the misallocation of worker productivity by restricting the efficient flow of knowledge across firms that have varying success in research and development (R&D). The desirability of allowing such restrictive agreements in wage contracts then depends on which of the two counteracting effects on output is larger. When knowledge spillovers are significant, the effect of restrictions on spillovers on efficient turnover of workers is likely to be more important. In this case, non-disclosure agreements can reduce industry output even though R&D investment is higher (Shankar and Ghosh 2010).

Non-disclosure agreements are becoming an increasingly popular way of restricting the transmission of knowledge through employee turnover in Indian IT firms. However, many of these agreements are often hard to enforce in practice since much of knowledge gained by a worker is tacit and not easily contractible. A more restrictive but easily enforceable method of restricting knowledge spillovers through turnover is the use of non-compete clauses in wage contracts which prohibit a worker from accepting employment in a competing firm for a specified period of time. A variant of such clauses is the non-poaching agreement signed by competing firms in India. For example, in 2009, a group of IT companies in Pune formulated a non-poaching agreement to restrict lateral hiring among themselves (Kumar 2010).

It is also believed that NASSCOM is trying to design a non-poaching code for software and BPO companies in an attempt to address employee attrition (*Economic Times* 2010). Again as with non-disclosure agreements, allowing the use of such arrangements to restrict worker mobility will be desirable for enhancing industry output only if the gains from larger investment outweigh the loss from the possible misallocation of worker productivities across firms in the industry.

The pattern of growth in India's technology sector is often compared with the evolution of high-technology firms in Silicon Valley. While India's high-technology sector is still in its nascent stages of development, many aspects of the Silicon Valley experience have been observed in the Indian context. The flow of information and knowledge facilitated by the easy mobility of labour across firms, which was identified as a crucial factor in the success of firms in Silicon Valley (Saxenian 1994), characterizes the environment in India's IT industry. This is evidenced in the proliferation of start-ups most of which are spin-offs formed by enterprising employees from more established firms in the market. While current rates of employee turnover in the IT industry are frequently viewed as a cost to the industry, it is important to highlight the positive spillovers created by the free flow of ideas and knowledge across firms facilitated through this labour mobility (Kemme et al. 2009). In this context, the IT and software industry in India as well as lawmakers should exercise caution and carefully weigh the costs and benefits of agreements that restrict labor mobility.

KAMESHWARI SHANKAR

References

ASSOCHAM. 2011. 'Talent Crunch, Soaring Attrition Rate Might Push India behind Other BPO Giants', ASSOCHAM Press Release, 14 April.

Business Standard. 2004. 'Domestic Technology Firms Undergo Labor Pains', 18 June.

Economic Times. 2010. 'Anti-poaching Pacts are Back; Hiring Hits Fast Lane', 3 December.

Greenwald, B. 1986. 'Adverse Selection in the Labor Market', *Review of Economic Studies*, 53: 325–47.

Jovanovic, B. 1979. 'Job Matching and the Theory of Turnover', *Journal of Political Economy*, 87(5): 972–90.

Kemme, D., V. Lugovskyy, and D. Mukherjee. 2009. 'Labor Mobility, Knowledge Transfer and Productivity Spillover of Multinationals: Evidence from Indian Firms', Working Paper.

Kumar, Divij. 2010. 'Viability of Non-poaching Agreement', *PSA Legal Labour Bulletin*, October, XI.

NASSCOM. 2009. 'Indian IT–BPO Industry 2009: NASSCOM Analysis'.

New York Times. 2007. 'Indian Entrepreneurs Leave Outsourcing for Firms of Their Own', 30 November.

OECD. 2010. 'The Information and Communication Technology Sector in India: Performance, Growth and Key Challenges', OECD Digital Economy Papers, No. 174, OECD Publishing.

Saxenian, A. 1994. *Regional Advantage: Culture and Competition in Silicon Valley and Route 128*, Harvard University Press, Cambridge, MA.

Shankar, K. and S. Ghosh. 2010. 'A Theory of Worker Turnover in R&D Intensive Firms', Working Paper.

The Telegraph. 2006. 'Hop, Skip and Jump', 21 March.

■ Land Acquisition for Industry

Fast economic growth in the last two decades has increased demand for land from many sources, such as infrastructure, industry, resource extraction (such as mining), and urbanization, including real estate. Even when many of these activities are funded privately and seem to be driven by the profit motive, they serve a social purpose, as employment generation per unit of land is higher in non-agricultural uses than it is in agriculture. Growth through industrialization would not only increase labour productivity but also reduce pressure on farm land by pulling people away from land to non-farming occupations. However, land acquisition has emerged as the most important structural constraint in India on the process of fast industrialization and improvement in infrastructure. Delays in procuring land leads to uncertainty and cost escalation, and thus affects development.

Acquisition of land by the government has lately drawn resistance in many cases due to inadequate compensation for the land and loss of livelihoods of the affected people, as well as for involuntary displacement without proper rehabilitation. Moreover, people are not willing to give up their present dwellings and occupation of farming for a dark future totally dependent on the vagaries of the market. The land acquisition law has been quite hostile to the interests of the landowner, as it attempts to make land available to the government at a minimal price. So far the practice by most state governments has been coercing people to give up their land by using the legal powers of eminent domain, and in some cases even through the use of force. Thus the model followed has been, 'let some people lose out so that others[1] may gain'. Unfortunately the losers tend to be the poorest people with little skills, often tribals, who are unable to negotiate with market forces and cope with the consequences of their forced expulsion from land; they end up being much worse-off than they were before the acquisition.

Some estimates suggest that at least 60 million Indian citizens were displaced between 1947 and 2004, among whom at least 40 per cent were tribals and 20 per cent were dalits (Fernandes 2004). Of those displaced, less than 18 per cent were resettled (Fernandes 2008: 89). This has turned millions of independent producers into property-less labourers. This could have been avoided with imaginative land acquisition and rehabilitation policies.

Rising Conflicts over Forced Acquisitions

Before 1990, most land was acquired by the government for large irrigation projects, public-sector enterprises, and other explicit public purposes, such as the new townships of Chandigarh, Gandhinagar, and Bhubaneswar, and, therefore, the use of coercive legal powers carried at least some credibility in the eyes of the public. However, in the last two decades, the powers of eminent domain have also been used for acquisition for private industry, which is not driven by the 'noble cause of national development, but profit motive' (Ray and Patra 2009). Although the Land Acquisition Act, 1894, does not include acquisition of land for a private company as public purpose, this restriction has been bypassed by state governments (and supported by rulings of the Supreme Court), as the definition of public purpose in law includes acquiring land 'for planned development of land from public funds in pursuance of any scheme or policy of Government and subsequent disposal thereof in whole or in part by lease, assignment or outright sale with the object of securing further development as planned' (Gonsalves 2010). Thus, in all cases where compensation to the landowners was paid out of the government treasury the clause of public purpose was invoked,[2] irrespective of the fact that land was eventually used for making air conditioners or a housing colony for the affluent. Though such private enterprises may contribute to direct and indirect employment generation, people's perception of these activities being in 'public interest' is generally negative and, therefore, they are less tolerant of being made to leave the area or accept unfair compensation in such cases. Consequently, there have been growing protests and militancy leading to tension, conflict, and violence, besides increasing costs involved in the delayed acquisition of land.

It may be noted that in a recent case the Supreme Court held: 'Any attempt by the State to acquire land by promoting a public purpose to benefit a particular group of people or to serve any particular interest at the cost of the interest of a large section of people, especially of the common people, defeats the very concept of public purpose' (*The Hindu* 13 March 2011).

Low compensation is not the only cause for resistance. There is resistance also because of the trust deficit that exists today between the government and the peasantry because the promises for rehabilitation and settlement accorded to them on earlier occasions have not been fulfilled and the compensation amount has been uncertain and irregular. Thousands of families displaced by various projects are still awaiting compensation payments. In a few cases, those displaced in the early 1970s are yet to receive compensation (Sardana 2011). In many cases, the true beneficiaries are absentee landlords and intermediaries, but not the poor peasantry.

Public Purpose

With regard to limiting the scope of 'public purpose', the Government of India came up with a draft Land Acquisition Bill, 2009, where 'public purpose' includes only:

(i) the provision of land for strategic purposes relating to naval, military, air force, and armed forces of

[1]This includes some enterprising poor too.

[2]For instance, in Singur, the Government of West Bengal published 13 notifications under Section 4 of the Land Acquisition (LA) Act, 1894, in July 2006 declaring its intention to acquire roughly 1,000 acres of land stating 'that land is likely to be needed to be taken by Government/Government Undertaking/Development Authorities, at the public expense for a public purpose, viz., employment generation and socio-economic development of the area by setting up of Tata Small Car Project' (Bandyopadhyay 2008).

the union or any work vital to national security or defence of India or state police;

(ii) the provision of land for infrastructure projects of the appropriate Government, where the benefits accrue to the general public; and

(iii) the provision of land for any other purpose useful to the general public, for which land has been purchased by a person under lawful contract or is having the land to the extent of 70 per cent, but the remaining 30 per cent of the total area of land required for the project is yet to be acquired. *Explanation: The word 'person' shall include any company or association or body of individuals, whether incorporated or not.*

This clause may help farmers in the developed regions who are aware of market conditions, but may result in large-scale cheating and deception in tribal and remote areas where *goonda*s will be hired by the land mafia and the tribals will be forced to sign land transfer deeds to achieve the cut-off figure of 70 per cent. In any case, in many central India states, tribal land cannot be sold to non-tribals through market transactions. To get possession over such land, the industry would have to use extra-legal methods of showing sales in the name of some non-existent or compliant tribal. It may also legalize transfer of land that originally belonged to tribals, but is now alienated from them, and has not been restored back to them despite laws to the contrary. Moreover, land records are hopelessly out of date in many states, which will delay private transfer of land. Often, land is cultivated by the poor, especially tribals, but their possession of the land is not recorded in official documents. Such people would be compelled to give up their possessions without any compensation.

Further, 70 per cent of the land purchased under 'lawful contract' will not carry the responsibilities of resettlement and rehabilitation (R&R). Reducing the area of land acquired through the government will also reduce its responsibility to do social impact analyses, which are proposed in the Amendment Bill of 2009 when the number of families displaced exceeds 400 (200 in tribal pockets).

In the 1894 Act, the public purpose included provision of village sites, planned development or improvement of existing village sites, provision of land for town and rural planning, provision of land for residential purpose to the poor or landless, and for educational and housing schemes. These provisions have been removed by the proposed 2009 Amendment, which is unfortunate.

There is nothing in the Amendment Bill to suggest that land can be acquired for housing for rural and urban poor by the state, or that acquiring land for educational, health, and other such welfare needs will be covered under 'public purpose'.

If it is to be presumed that these can be covered under 'any other purpose useful to general public', under Section 3(f) (iii), a clause applicable only for private projects (and needing 70 per cent prior purchase by the private person), it would mean that the government is leaving all its functions, even those as basic as health, education, and housing for the poor, to be handled by private investors. If it is to be part of 'any other public facility as may be notified by central government' under the definition of 'infrastructure', then how will education, health, and housing for the poor by state governments or local self-governing bodies be covered? Thus, the proposed amendments exhibit a clear bias against the rural and urban poor, and the landless and rural areas in general.

I would suggest the following definition of public purpose:

(i) the provision of land for strategic purposes relating to naval, military, air force, and armed forces of the union or any work vital to national security or defence of India or state police, or safety of the people;

(ii) the provision of land for infrastructure projects of the appropriate government, including irrigation and power, where the benefits largely accrue to the general public;

(iii) the provision of village sites, acquisition of land for the project affected people, planned development or improvement of village sites, provision of land for residential purposes to the poor, educational, and health schemes; and

(iv) the provision of land for any other purpose useful to the general public, including land for companies, for which at least 70 per cent of the project affected people have given their written consent. *Explanation*: The project affected people will include people who would lose more than 50 per cent of their present income in addition to those who are likely to be displaced as a result of the implementation of the project.

Compensation

The main opposition to involuntary land acquisition is due to highly inadequate, uncertain, and delayed compensation that is paid one time[3] to landowners under the present law. It is calculated according to the market price, which means the average registered price

[3]This is often spent on non-productive items like marriages and motorbikes.

in that area for three preceding years. It is no secret that what is registered is never more than 40 per cent of the actual price paid. The 2009 Amendment to some extent acknowledges this, and suggests that:

11B. (1) The Collector shall adopt the following criteria in assessing and determining the market value of the land—

(i) the minimum land value, if any, specified in the Indian Stamp Act, 1899, for the registration of sale deeds in the area, where the land is situated; or

(ii) the average of the sale price for similar type of land situated in the village or vicinity, ascertained from not less than 50 per cent of the sale deeds registered during the preceding three years, where higher price has been paid; or

(iii) the average of the sale price, ascertained from the prices paid or agreed to be paid for not less than 50 per cent of the land already purchased for the project where higher price has been paid, for the purpose of item (iii) of clause (f) of Section 3, whichever is higher.

However, it is felt that even the proposed Amendment does not go far enough in offering attractive compensation to those who lose their land. This issue was considered by the National Advisory Council in 2006, and based on its recommendations I would suggest the following:

1. Compulsory land acquisition should be undertaken only when the government can ensure that all those who are displaced are brought above the poverty line and made significantly better off (say, their income becomes double)[4] than they were prior to the displacement, not just in economic terms, but also in terms of human development and security, in a reasonable time frame, and in accordance with their aspirations. Land acquisition policies should be prioritized in such a way that wastelands will be acquired first, and fertile land as well as land owned by the poor, irrespective of its quality (unless the poor are themselves keen to move out of agriculture and opt for doubling their incomes), should be acquired last (Reddy and Reddy 2007).
2. The principle of market value as laid down in Section 23 (1) should be substituted by replacement value inclusive of both land and other habitat entitlements. For example, if a poor person was paid only the depreciated value of his or her house, he or she would be unable to buy or build a new house with that sum and would become homeless. The person's house, however old or ramshackle it might be, provides shelter. When it is forcefully acquired, it must be ensured that the compensation is enough to provide an alternative and better shelter.
3. Consent award should be the primary mode of settling the amount of compensation. Payment of large sums of cash might not be in the best interests of project affected people (PAPs), such as tribals and the poor, who are unused to handling large amounts of money. It should not always be lumpsum, but could be in the form of monthly payments[5] of at least double the present income (adjusted for inflation) to extend for 20 years, and based on the informed choices of the PAPs.
4. Also, not only should lost property and assets be compensated for, but lost livelihoods and lost opportunities should also be compensated for. This would mean that the asset-less people, such as landless labourers, encroachers of government land, artisans, and gatherers should also be compensated by giving them either land or a compensation of at least 10 days of minimum wage per month for a period of 20 years. The definition of 'persons having interest in land' in Section 9 of the Act should include sharecroppers, tenants and sub-tenants, encroachers (occupiers), sharecroppers, and attached agricultural workers.
5. Communities must be adequately and appropriately compensated for common amenities and assets lost because of a project. Also, all those amenities and assets required for fulfilling the basic needs must be provided. This is especially important in order to prevent conflicts with host communities, whose common resources would otherwise be under pressure from PAPs.
6. No state action for compulsory acquisition should contravene constitutional protection for STs under Schedules V and VI of the Constitution and laws preventing tribal land alienation.

Whereas there have been many protests by farmers against land acquisition in Andhra Pradesh, Maharashtra, Orissa, West Bengal, and Uttar Pradesh, one has not heard of any such agitation in Tamil Nadu. The Tamil

[4]The difference in terms of costs between what is proposed here and what the present practice is would be much less than 1 per cent of the project cost, whereas the benefits to the project in terms of avoidance of delays, quick possession of land, and good relations with the local people are immense.

[5]The Haryana R&R scheme provides for payment of annuity in the form of royalty for a period of 33 years at the rate of Rs 15,000 per acre per annum which will be increased at the rate of Rs 500 per year. With respect to the land acquired for setting up of special economic zones (SEZs)/technology cities or technology parks, in addition to the R&R package, the rate of annuity will be Rs 30,000 per acre per annum for a period of 33 years, payable by private developers, to be increased at the rate of Rs 1,000 every year.

Nadu Acquisition of Land for Industrial Purposes Act (TNALIPA), 2001, is more flexible with regard to the compensation offered, as compared to the central Act, and the acquisition process can be completed in a much shorter duration, from about three years to less than 180 days, indicating fewer avenues for the dispossessed to negotiate outside the domain of monetary compensation. By following a policy that offers more generous compensation for the land acquired, while allowing some room for negotiation, landowners face powerful incentives to avoid legal contestations.

A case, which senior bureaucrats in Tamil Nadu hail as a model for land acquisition, is the Perambalur multi-product SEZ, where farmers came in large numbers (nearly 1,000) to sell their land when they thought that the prices offered were much higher than anticipated. Shortage of labour, depleting groundwater tables, rising input costs, and lack of good prices for output are repeatedly cited by farmers for their willingness to move out of agriculture (Vijayabaskar 2010).

There is a provision in Section 24 of the present Land Acquisition Act that the future value of the land would not be taken into consideration while determining compensation. As the completion of projects vastly increases the market value of land not acquired in that area, people who are forced to sell land feel cheated as the compensation that they get is sometimes not even one-tenth of the market value after a few years of acquisition. Section 24 should, therefore, be deleted. Instead, there should be a provision that whenever land acquired for public purpose is transferred to an individual or a company for a consideration, 25 per cent of the difference between such consideration and the compensation be given to the original landowner. For future transactions too, there should be a capital gains tax on land value, a part of it to be shared with the people who have lost their land, so that they too benefit from the increases in the future value of land (Marjit 2010). Fundamentally, the problem is one of guaranteeing a fair share in the augmented value of the land in future for at least 20 years to the original owner of the land, as the value can really shoot up once the land is put to non-agricultural use.

Large Projects

Each large development project (involving transfer or change in land use of a 100 acres of land or more, or affecting 100 families) must be first subjected to a legally binding holistic appraisal as to the desirability and justifiability of the project. The public, and particularly the people likely to be affected, must be given due opportunities of information and hearings, and allowed to examine all aspects of the project, including the 'public purpose', and also the possibilities of achieving the same objectives through non-displacing or less displacing alternatives.

Wherever the people are not willing to shift, it must be assumed that the fault is either in the package being offered, in the progress of implementation, or in the approach towards the displaced communities. Alternatively, it could be because the implementation of R&R programmes is so unsatisfactory that the affected people do not feel confident of receiving what they have been promised. In any case, this must be recognized as a failure of the rehabilitation process.

The provisions of an enlightened rehabilitation and compensation policy must have legal backing so that not only the concerned agencies of the government but also affected and interested citizens can ensure enforcement and legal intervention. Unfortunately the law pertaining to rehabilitation has been on the anvil since 1998, but it has still not seen the light of the day, though it is well established that more than three-fourths of the displaced people, especially tribals, become worse-off due to involuntary displacement.

For the displaced people, the new settlement must be as close to the factory site and new township as possible so as to ensure maximum access to the newly created economic opportunities. In such projects, a major responsibility of the project authorities should be training and capacity building of PAPs. In between decision and displacement, there is always a significant time gap. During this period, every PAP who consents must be made literate, and trained for semi-skilled or skilled jobs as per her choice and educational qualifications. If this policy is faithfully executed, it will reduce displacement because most jobs will then be taken up by PAPs and inflow of employees from outside will be minimal. So a big township would not be required.

To give an example, although the site for the Vedanta Bauxite plant was settled in the Kalahandi district as way back in 2000, the author found in 2010 that the primitive tribes living in uplands just 5 km away from the plant could neither understand the local language (Oriya) nor sign their names. Thus, no effort had been made by the state government or the project authorities to educate the tribals and improve their skills.

Acquisition of Land in Schedule V Areas

For the predominantly tribal Scheduled V area of central India, the government passed the Panchayat Extension to Scheduled Areas Act (PESA) in 1996, which is applicable to the panchayats of tribal areas in nine states—Andhra Pradesh, Jharkhand, Gujarat, Himachal Pradesh,

Maharashtra, Madhya Pradesh, Chhattisgarh, Orissa, and Rajasthan. Under Sub-section (i) of Section 4, the Act provides that 'the Gram Sabha or the Panchayats at the appropriate level, shall be consulted before making the acquisition of land in the Scheduled Areas for development projects'. Detailed executive instructions were issued by the government under my signatures as Secretary Rural Development, Government of India, sometime in 1998 to describe the modalities of consultation.

The procedure was deliberately made difficult so as to discourage projects from displacing tribals in Schedule V areas. For instance, it provided that the company requiring land must produce a letter of consent from each of the concerned gram panchayats, in favour of the proposed acquisition of land. In case, any of the gram sabhas expressed disagreement, the district collector was to arrange a joint meeting of the requiring body, land acquisition authorities, and the concerned gram sabha and attempt, through such consultative meetings, to arrive at a consensus for selecting the specified land agreed to for the acquisition. In case a disagreement still persisted, the collector's order would prevail, who would give detailed reasons why the gram sabha's objections were being overruled.

Unfortunately there has never been any monitoring of this order, with the result that most field officials are not even aware of this provision.

It may be mentioned here that PESA only provides for consultations for land acquisition; it does not require concurrence of the panchayats or the gram sabhas. However, what is recommended in this entry is concurrence of at least 70 per cent of the PAPs in case land is being acquired for industry both for scheduled and non-scheduled areas.

Diversion of Forest Land

Such diversion requires the central government's clearance under the Forest Conservation Act, but up to 2009 it did not involve any consultations with the communities that may have rights or be dependent on the land being diverted. Fortunately, in July 2009, the Ministry of Environment and Forests (MoEF) issued a circular stating that the completion of the process prescribed in the Forest Rights Act, 2006, and the consent of relevant gram sabhas were required for the diversion of forest land for any non-forest purpose. In order to ensure that these executive instructions are not flouted, it would be desirable to make them part of the Forest Rights Act.

Summing Up

The impoverishment and displacement of rural communities due to improper land acquisition and rehabilitation policies can easily be avoided through a more imaginative set of policies that insist on informed consent of at least 70 per cent of the affected people. Obviously they will agree only when they too benefit from such projects, both in the short and long run. If consent is made compulsory for transfer of forest land, surely the same principle should be extended to the acquisition of private land, at least for profitable private projects.

Moreover, the compensation should be liberal enough to double the incomes of the affected people and lift them above the poverty line. They should also benefit from the increased value of land in the future by receiving a share on capital gains tax on land sales. The policy should make the primary stakeholders partners by giving them at least 5 per cent of the shares of the company rather than being one-time beneficiaries or spectators of development. Establishing vocational training centres, and water, sanitation, and health facilities on the rehabilitation site should be done before the actual displacement. Demonstrative implementation of rehabilitation and resettlement measures would bring down the distrust of the people in the administration, which is at present not only creating conflicts but also delaying irrigation and power projects so essential for the prosperity of the poor landowners.

N.C. Saxena

References

Bandyopadhyay, D. 2008. 'Singur: What Happened, What Next and Time to Pay the Cost', *Economic and Political Weekly*, 29 November.

Fernandes, Walter. 2004. 'Rehabilitation Policy for the Displaced', *Economic and Political Weekly*, 39(12): 1191.

——. 2008. 'Sixty Years of Development-induced Displacement in India', in H.M. Mathur (ed.), *India Social Development Report 2008: Development and Displacement*, New Delhi, Oxford University Press.

Gonsalves, Colin. 2010. 'Judicial Failure on Land Acquisition for Corporations', *Economic and Political Weekly*, XLV(32): 37–42.

Marjit, Sugata. 2010. 'Guaranteeing Future Claims of Farmers in Land Acquisition: An Option-pricing Approach', *Economic and Political Weekly*, XLV(52): 80–2.

Ray, Sanjukta and Shreemoyee Patra. 2009. 'Evolution of Political Economy of Land Acquisition', available at http://www.scribd.com/doc/44959477/India-Infrastructure-Report-2009#.

Reddy, V. Ratna and B. Suresh Reddy. 2007. 'Land Alienation and Local Communities Case Studies in Hyderabad-Secunderabad', *Economic and Political Weekly*, 4 August.

Sardana, M.M.K. 2011. 'Land Acquisition Issues', ISID Discussion Notes, available at at http://isid.org.in/pdf/DN1002.pdf.

Vijayabaskar, M. 2010. 'Saving Agricultural Labour from Agriculture: SEZs and Politics of Silence in Tamil Nadu', *Economic and Political Weekly*, XLV(6): 36–43.

Land Reform

Land reform usually refers to redistribution of land from the rich to the poor. More broadly, it includes regulation of ownership, operation, leasing, sales, and inheritance of land (indeed, the redistribution of land itself requires legal changes). In an agrarian economy like India with great scarcity and unequal distribution of land, coupled with a large mass of below-poverty-line rural population, there are compelling economic and political arguments for land reform. Not surprisingly, it received top priority on the policy agenda at the time of Independence. In the decades following Independence, India passed a significant body of land reform legislation. The Constitution of 1949 left the adoption and implementation of land and tenancy reforms to state governments. This led to a lot of variation in the implementation of these reforms across states and over time, a fact that has been utilized in empirical studies trying to understand the causes and effects of land reform.

In this entry, I will briefly discuss the economic and political arguments in favour of land reform, and review the Indian evidence on the effects of land reform on agricultural productivity and poverty, and economic and political determinants of the speed and intensity of implementation.

Economic Arguments in Favour of Land Reform

The most obvious argument in favour of land reform is equity. In a land-scarce country with a significant section of rural population below the poverty line, the case for ensuring that everyone has access to some minimum amount of land seems compelling from this point of view. However, this is a general argument in favour of redistribution, not necessarily redistribution of land. To make that case, one needs to understand the economic forces that govern the allocation of land.

I begin with two empirical observations. First, small farms tend to be more productive than large farms. This inverse farm size–productivity relationship is widely documented (see Banerjee 1999 for a review of the literature). Another empirical regularity is that owner-cultivated plots of land tend to be more productive than those under sharecropping tenancy (Shaban 1987).

Given these observations, one could make an argument in favour of land reform based not only on equity considerations, but also efficiency. For example, the inverse relationship between farm size and productivity suggests that land reform could raise productivity by breaking (less productive) large farms into several (more productive) small farms. Also, lower productivity under sharecropping suggests that land reform could raise productivity by converting sharecroppers into owner-cultivators.

But then what prevents market forces from getting rid of the asymmetry and the resultant inefficiency? Saying that the inverse farm size–productivity relationship is driven by diminishing returns is not satisfactory, since that assumes that land cannot be sold or leased. For example, if a small farmer is more productive and a large farmer less productive, then the latter would be better off leasing some land to the former. Similarly, if sharecropping is inefficient relative to owner-cultivation, a landlord should sell the land to the sharecropper to make him an owner-cultivator, and get a share of the resulting productivity gains.

Clearly, an explanation of these facts must be based on some frictions in the operation of the land market, or some other input relevant for agricultural production.

A leading explanation of both these facts is based on incentives. A small farmer cultivates his land with own and family labour, while a large landowner uses hired labour which has lower incentives to put in effort. Similarly, a sharecropper effectively faces an income tax of 50 per cent (the most commonly observed sharing rule in the absence of tenancy legislation being 50:50) and naturally puts in less effort. This, however, raises a deeper question: why cannot these parties design contracts that would get rid of the incentive problem?

A key assumption here is that some inputs such as effort, care, and maintenance of land are inherently difficult to monitor. As a result, unless the party that is supplying these inputs is full residual claimant (that is, retains 100 per cent of the profits), it will undersupply these inputs.

A landowner can offer a fixed rent contract that has this property. According to this contract, the landlord simply gets a fixed fee and the tenant keeps all the residual earnings. If everyone lived for one period, this would be equivalent to selling the land to the tenant. However, if the tenant is poor, then even though this contractual arrangement would be efficient, it might not be in a landlord's interest to offer it.

Consider a simple example. Suppose, given the scarcity of land, the fixed rent that would induce the landlord to lease out a given plot of land is Rs 100. However, since the tenant is poor and does not have enough liquid wealth, he may not be able to pay this rent upfront, or guarantee to pay it irrespective of whether the output is high or low. He may be able to pay a guaranteed fixed rent of only Rs 50. It is in the landlord's interest then to ask for a share of output, even though that would reduce effort, since he gets a higher expected rent. He would not ask for too high a share of output though, since at some point reduced effort would start reducing his expected rent (this is like the Laffer curve in the context of income taxes: if tax rates are too high, cutting taxes may actually raise revenue via increased labour supply).

This rent extraction versus incentives trade-off (see Banerjee et al. 2002 for a formal analysis) can explain the persistence of inefficiency in the land market. This would explain both the stylized facts mentioned earlier and why market forces will not necessarily get rid of the implied productivity losses.

An alternative form of friction that can explain these facts is that, due to an imperfect legal system, the market for land does not operate well. For example, if leasing out land entails a risk that it might be hard to evict the tenant if the landowner wishes to withdraw land for owner-cultivation at some later point, then the land-leasing market would not work well. Indeed, in their cross-state analysis of tenancy laws in India, Conning and Robinson (2005) show that tenancy laws, though designed with the aim of helping tenants, actually reduced the extent of tenancy.

So far we did not consider the issue of heterogeneity of farmers in terms of ability and/or in terms of soil quality. For example, a key econometric concern is whether the empirical observations mentioned above control for unobserved heterogeneity. If these observations are purely driven by unobserved variations in farmer quality or land quality, then the efficiency case for land reform is weakened. For example, if higher-ability farmers prefer to cultivate smaller plots of land (as opposed to being constrained to do so) or landowners prefer to lease out lower-quality plots to sharecroppers, then in the absence of any other frictions such as those mentioned earlier land reform will not raise average productivity.[1] However, there is some evidence (for example, Rosenzweig and Binswanger 1993 on farm size and productivity; Shaban 1987 on sharecropping) to suggest that these empirical facts are not purely driven by heterogeneity in farmer quality or land quality. For example, Shaban (1987) finds, after controlling for land quality, that the same farmer puts in less effort in plots of land that he cultivates as sharecropper compared to plots of land that he cultivates as owner-cultivator.

To sum up, incentive problems and imperfect property rights are the leading explanations for distortions in the allocation of land. These arguments imply that land reform will raise productivity as well as serve the goal of equity.

As a matter of fact, redistributive policies that fall short of full-scale land reform can also have positive productivity effects. These include policies that increase the wealth or income of the rural poor or their bargaining power vis-à-vis landowners (Banerjee et al. 2002 refer to these as empowerment strategies).[2] Given that the loss of efficiency is due to the trade-off between rent extraction and incentive provision, any strategy that reduces the ability of landowners to extract rents will raise efficiency, even if it falls short of land reform, and will also serve the goal of equity. However, some of these strategies, such as regulation of tenancy, might have a negative effect from the point of view of reducing the incentive of landowners to lease out land. This is likely to be a particularly important concern for poorly implemented tenancy-reform legislation: the presence of the tenancy law would have the negative effect on the land lease market described earlier and at the same time the positive incentive effect on tenants may only be partially realized. I will return to this point in the discussion of empirical work on land reform in India.

The above arguments also suggest that even if equity is the only consideration, there may be a case for redistribution of land as opposed to any other form of redistribution. For example, if because of imperfect property rights the market for land sales and rental is very thin, then a direct intervention in the land allocation method may be required to improve the conditions of the rural poor. This would typically require a combination of reforming property rights in land (for example, formalization of land records and legal protection of ownership rights) and redistribution (stipulating a land ceiling and redistributing surplus land).

[1]Of course, heterogeneity combined with the frictions discussed earlier may accentuate or mitigate the loss of efficiency. For example, if land quality and effort are complements in the production function and landowners tend to lease out inferior-quality land, then reform that transfers land from landlord to cultivator will still raise efficiency, although to a lesser degree than if the land was of higher quality.

[2]Examples of the latter include tenancy laws that stipulate an upper bound to the share that can be charged as rent, or public works programmes that raise the rural wage rate.

Indian Evidence on the Causes and Effects of Land Reform

The two key empirical questions are: what is the effect of land reform on productivity and poverty, and what are the factors that drive its success? These are clearly interdependent: factors that affect the success of land reform are also likely to affect productivity and poverty. For example, if a left-wing administration comes to power, as it did in Kerala and West Bengal, it will implement land reforms more actively and also implement other reforms (for example, empowering local governments) that might have a direct bearing on productivity and poverty. The challenge is to isolate the effect of land reforms.

Land reform legislation in India consisted of four main categories: abolition of intermediaries who were rent collectors under the pre-Independence land revenue system; tenancy regulation that attempted to improve the contractual terms for tenants, including crop shares and security of tenure; a ceiling on landholdings with a view to redistributing surplus land to the landless; and finally, attempts to consolidate disparate landholdings.[3] Abolition of intermediaries is generally agreed to be one component of land reforms that has been relatively successful. The record in terms of the other components is mixed and varies across states and over time. Landowners naturally resisted the implementation of these reforms by directly using their political clout and also by using various methods of evasion and coercion, which included registering their own land under names of different relatives to bypass the ceiling and shuffling tenants around different plots of land so that they would not acquire incumbency rights as stipulated by the tenancy law. The success of land reform has been driven by the political will of specific state administrations, the notable achievers being the left-wing administrations in Kerala and West Bengal.

Besley and Burgess (2000) have used state-level data for the 16 major Indian states from 1958 to 1992 and exploited the variation across states and over time in land reform legislation to identify the effect of land reform on productivity and poverty. They generate a cumulative variable that aggregates the number of legislative reforms to date in any particular state. Controlling for state and year fixed effects, and a number of time-varying economic and policy variables, they find that the lagged version of their cumulative land reform variable has had a negative and significant effect on poverty. Interestingly, they find that this is due primarily to the tenancy reform component of land reform. However, this also seems to have had a negative effect on agricultural productivity, suggesting an equity–efficiency trade-off. Abolition of intermediaries had a negative effect on poverty, but no effect on productivity. Imposing a ceiling on landholdings does not seem to have had much effect on either poverty or productivity, while land consolidation had a positive effect on productivity without having any effect on poverty. The authors conclude that land reforms did not have much effect on the distribution of land and seem to have operated mainly through altering the contractual relations in agriculture.

The previous study takes land-reform legislation as the measure of land reform, and not its implementation. Given the widely acknowledged gap between the two, one concern is that, as discussed in the previous section, a poorly implemented tenancy reform may have a net negative effect on productivity by freezing up the land lease market even though it might improve the productivity as well as the income of some tenants. Indeed, a study by Banerjee et al. (2002) that focuses on West Bengal, a state where tenancy reforms were implemented very thoroughly, yields very different conclusions: tenancy reforms improved agricultural productivity. Within a year of being elected in 1977, the left-wing administration launched Operation Barga, a programme designed to implement and enforce the long-dormant agricultural tenancy laws that regulated rents and security of tenure of sharecroppers. Under these laws, if tenants registered with the Department of Land Revenue, they would be entitled to permanent and inheritable tenure on the land they sharecropped as long as they paid the landlord at least 25 per cent of output as rent. In the decade following the launching of Operation Barga, there was significant improvement in the terms of tenants' contracts and security of tenures.

The authors use two different approaches to estimate the effects of this reform on agricultural productivity.

Their first approach is to compare the growth in productivity in West Bengal districts with that of districts in the neighbouring country of Bangladesh. Except for religion and political boundaries, the two regions are very similar in most respects. This includes agro-climatic conditions, prevalence of tenancy, and agricultural technology and so we can expect technological shocks to agricultural yields to be similar between these two regions. Indeed, during this period agricultural productivity in both regions (and much of eastern India) grew in part due to the belated arrival of the Green Revolution permitted by the spread of a locally suited high-yielding variety (HYV) of rice, a fall in the price of fertilizers, and an

[3] See Besley and Burgess (2000) who also provide a systematic description of these laws and their amendments that were passed in individual states over time.

increase in small-scale private irrigation. However, the authors find that even though the rate of adoption of HYV rice was faster in Bangladesh than in West Bengal, the rate of growth in rice productivity was higher in West Bengal. They attribute this difference to the implementation of tenancy reform. There are two concerns with this approach: first, that the data collection method concerning agricultural production underwent some changes under the new administration that could have inflated West Bengal's growth performance relative to Bangladesh. Also, during this period a number of other policy reforms were undertaken in West Bengal, such as decentralization of certain public programmes, and this approach could be picking up the effects of these other policies.

The second approach utilizes the fact that this reform was implemented in different districts of West Bengal at different rates due to bureaucratic frictions. The authors use inter-district variations in the rate of implementation of this programme (captured by the fraction of sharecroppers who were registered under this programme) as exogenous changes in the availability of a new contractual regime. That is, districts that received the programme earlier are the 'treatment' districts and districts that received it later are the 'control' districts. The resulting changes in productivity are attributed to the reform, after controlling for a number of other policy and economic variables that also changed during the period when the programme was implemented. Since this approach studies inter-district variation in agricultural productivity, it is not likely to be affected by concerns about any possible upward bias in the level of agricultural productivity due to changes in the data-collection methods. Also, since it looks at variation in the intensity of implementation of tenancy reform, it is less likely to pick up the effect of other programmes. This approach yields similar results regarding the effect of tenancy reform on agricultural productivity as the previous one, suggesting that tenancy reform did have a positive effect on agricultural productivity.

To sum up, it seems likely from the studies discussed here that tenancy reform had a direct positive effect on tenants who were directly affected by it, but the indirect effects of this reform on the rural land market as a whole are less clear. This explains why Besley and Burgess (2000) find that tenancy reform negatively affected rural poverty and Banerjee et al. (2002) find it positively affected agricultural productivity. However, both these studies are based on aggregate data (state or district level) and cannot distinguish between the direct and indirect effects of land reform. Only micro-level studies can throw more light on this question.

So far the effects of land reform have been discussed. Now I turn to the question of what determines its success.

Besley and Burgess (2000) find that political factors had a significant effect. In particular, Congress administrations had a negative effect on the passing of land-reform legislation, especially tenancy reform. In contrast, left-wing administrations had a significant positive effect. Besley and Burgess use these political variables as instruments for their land-reform measure to address the concern that land reform is endogenous and could be driven by factors that also affect the dependent variables of interest.

Conning and Robinson (2005) further pursue the investigation of determinants of land reform and find that, after controlling for other variables including state and year effects, the likelihood of reforms increases when land inequality is higher and where peasants have greater political power. Bardhan and Mookherjee (2005) study village-level data from West Bengal and find that land reform activity is highest where left-wing parties hold a larger number of seats in the state legislature and, interestingly, where they face greater political competition.

To sum up, land reform is clearly driven by political factors. One important ingredient is the strength of left-wing parties in the state. We can think of the support for left-wing parties as 'demand' for land reform. The 'supply' of land reform seems to depend on the electoral success of left-wing parties, as well as how tight the electoral competition is.

In this entry, the economic arguments in favour of land reform were reviewed and it was shown that they are based on frictions in the allocation of land. These frictions could either be due to agency costs or imperfect property rights. The evidence on land reforms in India was then evaluated. The evidence suggests that land reforms had a negative effect on poverty, while the effect on productivity is mixed. In states where these measures were strongly implemented, the effect of land reform on productivity seems positive.

MAITREESH GHATAK

References

Banerjee, A.V. 1999. 'Prospects and Strategies for Land Reforms', in B. Pleskovic and J. Stiglitz (eds), *Annual World Bank Conference on Development Economics 1999*, Washington DC, World Bank, pp. 253–84.

Banerjee, A.V., P.J. Gertler, and M. Ghatak. 2002. 'Empowerment and Efficiency: Tenancy Reform in West Bengal', *Journal of Political Economy*. 110(2): 239–80.

Bardhan, P. and D. Mookherjee. 2005. 'Political Economy of Land Reforms in West Bengal 1978–98', Working Paper, University of California, Berkeley and Boston University.

Besley, T. and R. Burgess. 2000. 'Land Reform, Poverty Reduction, and Growth: Evidence from India', *Quarterly Journal of Economics*, 115(2): 389–430.

Conning, J. and J.A. Robinson. 2005. 'Property Rights and the Political Organization of Agriculture', *Journal of Development Economics*, 82: 416–47.

Rosenzweig, M. and H. Binswanger. 1993. 'Wealth, Weather Risk, and the Composition and Profitability of Agriculture', *Economic Journal*, 103: 56–78.

Shaban, R.A. 1987. 'Testing between Alternative Models of Sharecropping', *Journal of Political Economy*, 95: 893–920.

Land Rights and Acquisition

Land Rights in the Pre-colonial Period

Codified rights to land date back at least to the time of Manu. In Manu's code, land rights are awarded to the first clearer. The king did not claim ownership of all the land in his kingdom then. Manu prescribed a maximum share of one-sixth of the gross produce to the king as recompense for giving protection. The code prescribes the duties for the four varnas (literally colours, which later formed the basis for all castes).

Commentators on Manu's code have elaborated on the different modes of acquisition advanced in it. In Sen (1918: 53–4), we find:

> NARADA ... says that there are twelve different modes of acquiring wealth of which three are general (i.e.) open to all castes; and the rest are peculiar to the several castes. Succession, gifts of affection and marriage presents received with the wife—these are common to all the castes. There are three special cases of acquiring wealth in the case of brahmins which are free from stain, viz., acceptance of free gifts, performance of priestly duties and receipts from disciples; similarly there are three special sources of wealth in the case of kshatriyas, viz., revenue, gains of war and penalties of law; so the vaisyas acquire wealth in three distinct ways, viz., through agriculture, herdsmanship and commerce; and the sudras gain wealth by serving the aforesaid three castes.

The *avarna*s or 'untouchables' had no prescribed mode of acquisition: as near-slaves, they owned very little, and their masters could confiscate even that.

As it happens, custom could, and did, override the Sastric law. From the Gupta period onwards Sudras gained the right to acquire wealth through agriculture and animal husbandry. From this time on, all the four varnas owned land, though it was only the Sudras and avarnas who actually cultivated it.

In matters of succession, most of India followed the principles laid down in the *Mitakshara* of Vijnaneshwara. The *Mitakshara* allowed partition of ancestral joint-family property among offspring even when the father was alive. The *Dayabhaga*, written by Jimutavahana and Hemadri, and followed in West Bengal and Assam, permitted partition of joint family property only after the father's death. Marumakkathayam was a matrilineal system of inheritance that was unique to the state of Kerala: all family property was jointly owned, and among the liberties enjoyed by women was the right to property.

This multiplicity of succession laws in India made land rights a very complex affair. No female was allowed to be a member of the coparcenery[1] in the Mitakshara system. Joint-family property devolved by survivorship within the coparcenery. This meant that with every birth or death of a male in the family, the share of every other surviving male got either diminished or enlarged. Joint-family property or group property became the norm in India. Maine (1953: 305) observed the distinction between this form of ownership and the norm that prevailed in the West:

> A Hindu may start with nothing, and make self acquired fortune by dint of his own ability and exertion; and he is the absolute owner of the estate. But in a couple of generations his offspring would have ramified into a joint-family, exactly like a banyan tree which started as a single shoot. Absolute unrestricted ownership, such as enables the owner to do anything he likes with his property, is the exception. The father is restricted by his sons, the brother by his brothers, the women by their successors. If property is free in the hands of its acquirer, it will become fettered in the hands of his heirs. Individual property is the rule in the West; corporate property is the rule in the East.

Land ownership was very prestigious. An individual member of the joint family could not easily borrow funds since the family's property could not easily be attached or foreclosed. Further, an individual's borrowings for illegal or immoral purposes were not binding on the other members of the joint family. So those who lent money were kept on the defensive. This acted as a fetter on the development of new contractual arrangements in agrarian

[1] Coparceners are persons with the right of joint inheritance or heirship to property. Coparcenery was a narrower body of persons within a joint family, and consisted of father, son, son's son, and son's son's son.

land management and reinforced the continuance of subsistence agriculture for many centuries.

However, Hindu law did permit the *kartha* (head) of a vaishya joint family to pledge its properties in order to raise loans. It also permitted interest collection. The fetters of group interests were relatively weak here, and this resulted in the development of many contractual forms, including negotiable instruments and insurance, in commerce.

In both the Hindu and Mohammedan systems, the king was by no means the owner of all land in his kingdom. When Islamic rule came to India, the sharia was applied to settle disputes among Mohammedans and between Mohammedans and Hindus. But the Hindu law continued to be applied in the settlement of disputes among Hindus. The sharia, as in the Hindu system, also discriminated against women in matters of succession. It held that 'the share of one male is equal to that of two females'.

With the fall of the Gupta Empire, there was an increase in the collection of land revenue. When Mohammedan rule came to India, the right to collect revenue from specified regions was conferred on intermediaries who maintained and supplied troops for the rulers. These intermediaries, who were subject to transfer from one region to another, tried to extract the maximum revenue they could from the regions under their temporary control. About one-half of the entire yield was collected as land revenue.

In the forests that covered more than a third of the territory of India, neither Hindu nor Mohammedan law applied. Land was collectively owned and jointly cultivated. Barter exchange prevailed. No particular type of work commanded special esteem there and there was also little evidence of gender discrimination. In the hill tracts of India such tribal communes have survived until quite recently.

British Rule: Land Rights and Forests

The East India Company changed the land laws in India piecemeal and in stages. The Act of Settlement of 1781 preserved the personal laws of the 'Hindus' and 'Mohammedans' in matters of inheritance, succession, and contracts. But grouping all Indians under 'Hindu' and 'Mohammedan' was impractical (see Setalwad 1960: 9–10).

The Regulation of 1793 imposed the Permanent Settlement on Bengal, Bihar, and Oudh, and notified that the zamindars and independent *talukdars* were the actual proprietors of land (Field 1885: 515). This Regulation extinguished the property rights of hundreds of peasants and transferred them to a class of intermediaries.

Different experiments were tried out in different parts of India. The multiplicity of systems in British India included: (i) the *ryotwari* system (under which the owner paid land revenue directly to the state) in Madras, Bombay, and Berar; (ii) the ryotwari-in-principle system (though not so named officially) in Assam, Coorg, and Burma; (iii) the Permanent Settlement system (under which the owner paid revenue to an intermediary—with inheritable rights—who paid a fraction to the state) in parts of Bengal, Bihar and Orissa, Benares, and Madras; (iv) the Temporary Settlement system (under which the intermediary's rights were not inheritable) in Oudh and parts of Bengal; and (v) the effectively, though not officially so-designated, *mahalwari* system (under which the village collective paid revenue to the state) in most parts of the United Provinces, Central Provinces, Punjab, and parts of Agra and Oudh. Common to all the systems in force was the fact that the British had unfairly distorted the land rights of the peasants in India.

While in theory, the ryotwari tenure conferred rights on the actual landowners, in reality, the actual cultivator was often different from the owner. The landowners were from all the four varnas; however, the actual cultivators were almost exclusively from the sudra and 'untouchable' castes. The British rulers completed a scientific survey of land and recorded the rights of the owners in their revenue records, while leaving unrecorded the entitlements of the actual cultivators, sharecroppers, tenants, and lessees. During British rule, the owner's land could be attached and sold to collect revenue, and the purchaser could obtain sound title to the land. The burden of land revenue became unbearable in the 19th century. Distress sales of land became a frequent occurrence. The golden age for the moneylender dawned.

After India was taken under the direct administration of England in 1858, the British quickly imported their own principles of jurisprudence into Indian criminal, civil, and commercial law, by way of a series of enactments such as the Code of Civil Procedure (1859), the Indian Penal Code (1860), the Code of Criminal Procedure (1861), the Indian Registration Act (1866), the Indian Contract Act (1872), the Indian Trusts Act (1882), and the Transfer of Property Act (1882). Section 205 of the Criminal Procedure Code made land liable to attachment and sale in the execution of a court decree. Inviolability of private property and rule of law were introduced in India step by step. The Land Acquisition Act of 1894 brought the American principle of eminent domain into India.

For railway expansion between 1855 and 1880 great chunks of forest were destroyed. In 1864, the British established the Indian Forest Department. The department incorrectly assumed that all land not actually under cultivation belonged to the state. Unless it had been expressly recorded in writing, customary use was deemed a 'privilege', not a 'right'. The new Forest Act of 1878 divided the forests of India into three classes. The first, 'state or reserved forests', were meant for commercial exploitation. A legal settlement was made before constituting reserve forests which 'either extinguished customary rights of user, transferred them as "privileges" to be exercised elsewhere, or, in exceptional cases, allowed their limited exercise' (Guha 2001: 216). Millions of hill dwellers of India lost their land rights in reserve forests. In the second—'protected'—class of forests, rights and privileges were recorded but not settled. The third class—that of village forests—remained a 'dead letter'.

Constitutional Protection to Property Rights

India did not have a written constitution till 1935. Sections 299 and 300 of the Government of India Act, 1936 (GI Act), were introduced to protect property rights including those of zamindars and other vested interests.

Land right is a state subject under the Indian Constitution. Article (19)(1)(f) granted all citizens the fundamental right to acquire, hold, and dispose of property. By a curious and tangled process, Section 299 of the GI Act, 1936—drafted by the British to protect vested interests—was modified and incorporated as Article 31: as a fundamental right to property in independent India!

After Independence, the state legislatures passed land reform legislations. The affected parties approached the courts. The Patna High Court held the Bihar Act abolishing zamindari interests invalid in *Kameshwar Prasad* vs *Bihar* (1951) on the grounds that the compensation amount was inversely related to the size of the zamindari. The court held that this violated the 'equality before law' criterion of the Constitution. This necessitated the passing of the first amendment to the Indian Constitution. Articles 31A and 31B with the Ninth Schedule were introduced with effect from 18 June 1951. Acts placed in the Ninth Schedule were kept out of the judicial review prerogative of the courts.

The clash between the judiciary and the legislature continued. The court struck down the expropriation legislation as unconstitutional, and the state responded by amending the Constitution. The fourth and seventeenth amendments emerged through this route. The drastic twenty-fifth amendment to the Constitution followed the court's striking down of the bank nationalization of 1969 on the grounds of inadequate compensation. In *Keshvananda Bharati* vs *State of Kerala* (1973) 4 SCC 225, a full bench of 13 judges assessed the validity of the new amendment. Eleven judgements were delivered. The majority view upheld all the amendments related to property rights. However, property right was held not to be a part of the 'basic structure' of the Constitution which was declared inviolable (cf. Singh 2004).

The Forty-Fourth Amendment Act, 1978, removed property as a fundamental right and deleted Articles 19(1)(f) and 31 from the Indian Constitution. Article 300-A—'No person shall be deprived of his property save by authority of law' (bearing a close resemblance to Section 299 (1) of the GI Act 1936) was introduced as a statutory right.

A unanimous Supreme Court judgement of 11 January 2007 reiterates the Kesavananda Bharati decision forewarning continued confrontation between the judiciary and the legislature.

Land Reforms and Their Impact

P.S. Appu's comprehensive study of land reforms concludes (Appu 1996: 191):

> Of the three programmes considered in this study, the laws for the abolition of intermediary interests were implemented fairly well. But in the case of tenancy reform and ceilings on holdings, the policies adopted were ambivalent and there were large gaps between policy and legislation and between legislation and implementation. We have seen that as a result of the implementation of the tenancy laws, tenants became owners of or acquired lands in only about 4 per cent of the operated area. The enforcement of ceilings led to the re-distribution of less than 2 per cent of the operated area. Thus these two measures taken together led to the re-distribution of only about 6 per cent of the operated area. This is insignificant.... In the People's Republic of China between the years 1950 and 1952 about 43 per cent[2] of the agricultural land changed hands.
>
> Earlier [ibid.: 75], he laments: 'The worst consequence of the reform was the large scale ejectment of tenants-at-will, under tenants and share croppers.'

'Operation Barga' in West Bengal, in which the rights of sharecroppers were recorded, and Kerala's 'Kudiyiruppu' laws granting homestead land to agricultural labourers, were a few successes. The Task Force on Agrarian Reforms (1972–3) of the Planning Commission identified the reasons for the poor performance of land reforms as 'the lack of political will, absence of pressure from below, inadequacies of

[2]Professor N. Krishnaji estimates that the percentage is much higher.

the administrative machinery, judicial intervention, the absence of correct and up-to-date land records and the lack of supporting facilities for the beneficiaries'.

Unenforced and partially enforced land reform legislation increases the transaction cost of effecting transfer of land rights. It provides enormous scope for the unscrupulous exercise of discretion by bureaucrats and politicians. Litigation is costly. The transfer of surplus land at considerable cost to '*benami*s' (false substitutes) in order to evade ceiling legislation is widespread. With increasing uncertainty, there is no incentive for the landlord or the 'benami' to make improvements on the land. Oral tenancies have become the norm, and landlords are ready to leave their lands uncultivated rather than to allow their tenancies to be recorded.

Forests, Common Property Resources, and Tribal Lands

In 1998–9, government and forest departments owned 95.65 per cent of the recorded forest area. Sixty per cent of forest lands lay essentially in the adivasi-dominated regions of India.

Large-scale shrinkage of common property resources takes place through: (i) encroachments by big landholders and powerful vested interests at village level; (ii) state appropriation of common lands for 'public purpose', mainly, that is, for development projects and commercial and industrial use; and (iii) distribution to poor landless and agricultural labourers. Most distributed lands are subsequently purchased by the rich.

The present National Policy on Resettlement and Rehabilitation for Project Affected Families, 2003, compensates only assets, not livelihoods. Compensation is given only to persons with undisputed legal title. It is not considered necessary to grant compensation for loss of access to community assets like grazing lands and forests. Inadequate rehabilitation of the displaced tribals compounds their woes, making them asset-less, unemployed, and trapped in debt bondage.

Constitutional provisions have not done much for tribal communities. The romantics from the outside world plead for preservation of tribal life. But tribals who get an opportunity to walk out of the quagmire vote with their feet and leave. The dilemma regarding the right tribal policy still persists.

Gender Discrimination

In the past, family assets were apportioned almost exclusively among men (an exception being the Marumakathayam system). However, custom decreed that the returns from those assets be shared with women. During all life-cycle ceremonies associated with birth, puberty, marriage, and death and the festival of family deities, the male branches of the family were required to bestow gifts on the female branches.

In the Hindu law women had absolute ownership only over *stridhan* (property gifted by parents and relatives on marriage and other occasions). The Hindu Law of Inheritance Act, 1929, the Hindu Gains of Learning Act, 1930, and the Hindu Women's Right to Property Act, 1937, were British legislations conferring limited property rights on women.

The framers of the Indian Constitution took note of the discrimination against women in society. Section 6 of the Hindu Succession Act, 1956, hit at the ancient rule that property shall devolve by survivorship among the male members of the Hindu coparcenery. Till then, in Hindu Law, coparcenery was an exclusive male membership club. The aim of the 1956 Act was to mitigate gender discrimination in the Mitakshara coparcenery by including women in the system. The mother of the deceased, the widow, and the daughter were included as Class-I heirs along with the son. But the 1956 Act did not completely end gender discrimination. In a major blow to patriarchy, the Hindu Succession (Amendment) Act, 2005, has abolished discrimination between the son and the daughter in the matter of succession to coparcenery property. Whether this will be enforced or will suffer the same fate as land reforms is a matter for conjecture now.

Eminent Domain

The Land Acquisition Act of 1894 confers power on the government to compulsorily acquire land for public purposes or for a company on payment of compensation. Planned development, education, health, and other schemes are included as illustrations of 'public purpose'. Section 23 specifies the principles for computing compensation. A 'solatium' of 15 per cent of the market value of the land acquired is required to be added to the compensation in view of the compulsory nature of the acquisition. The Act makes no reference to rehabilitation. Since compensation is granted only to persons with legal title, tenants, sharecroppers, and wage labourers become ineligible.

Is it right for the state to expropriate land to advance private-sector development through schemes such as Special Economic Zones (SEZs) to correct India's 'infrastructure deficit'? There is mistrust that such schemes may do more for their promoters than for the country. Widespread opposition to expropriation of poor farmers at Singur and Nandigram stemmed from a felt sense of inequity.

Unless conversion of agricultural land for industrial use is permitted, all industries could be located only in deserts and desolate places! Normally, it is not necessary for the state to acquire private land and transfer it to private industry. The market is the proper channel for it, except to break hold-ups affecting the industrial development of an entire region. Sections 23 and 24 specify the principles to determine the amount of compensation. Section 23 states that 'increase in the value of land due to the new use' should not be taken into account. This is manifestly unfair since the sellers expect a substantial windfall after the setting up of major industrial projects on their lands.

Any practical solution should enable farmers whose lands are acquired to get cash compensation for a major portion (say, four-fifths) of their lands to meet their immediate obligations. They should be allotted an equivalent area for the balance of land (say, one-fifth) in the developed portion of the project area. That would give the landowners an opportunity to obtain a share in the possible future windfall gains. The promoters invest huge sums in these projects. They should be obligated to invest at least 5 per cent of the total project cost in construction of educational and health facilities to which the affected farmers and their children should have privileged access. In this way, the future health and educational needs of the farmers' families would be taken care of and their children would grow to be employable anywhere (cf: Sau 2007).

S. NEELAKANTAN

References

Appu P.S. 1996. *Land Reforms in India*, New Delhi, Vikas Publishing House Pvt. Ltd.

Field, C.D. 1885. *Landholding and the Relation between a Landlord and Tenant*, Calcutta, Thacker, Spint & Co.

Guha, Ramachandra. 2001. 'The Prehistory of Community Forestry in India', *Environment History*, 6(2): 214–26.

Maine, John D. 1953. *Treatise on Hindu Law and Usage* (ed. N. Chandrasekara Aiyar), 11th edn, Madras, Higginbothams.

Sau, Ranjit. 2007. 'Second Industrialisation in India: Land and the State', *Economic and Political Weekly*, 42(7): 571–7.

Sen, Priyanath. 1918. *The General Principles of Hindu Jurisprudence, Tagore Law Lectures (1909), Sri Krishna Tarkalankara: Commentary on Dayabaga*, Calcutta, University of Calcutta.

Setalwad, M.C. 1960. *The Common Law in India*, London, Stevens and Sons.

Singh, Jaivir. 2004. '(Un)Constituting Property: The Deconstruction of the "Right to Property in India"', *CSLG Working Paper Series*, CSLG/WP/04–05, Jawaharlal Nehru University, New Delhi, August.

■ Law and Legal System

The expressions 'law' and 'legal system' should be defined, as they are both used in more than one sense. In the sense used here, 'law' means statutory law and 'legal system' means the framework used for resolving disputes. But more explanation is needed. In the legal system, the bar (lawyers) and the judiciary also have a role to play. All disputes do not necessarily have to go through a process of adjudication. Conciliation, mediation, and arbitration are possibilities. The words 'conciliation' and 'mediation' are often used synonymously. However, there is a difference. Conciliation is an attempt to resolve the dispute before it becomes formal. It is nipped in the bud. Mediation is intervention when there is a formal dispute. When this mediation becomes a little more formalized, with a legal agreement stipulating who will mediate as a third party, we have arbitration. If none of this works, there is no choice but to resort to courts. There are around 12,000 courts—one Supreme Court, 21 high courts, and the remainder known as lower courts. Courts have to follow prescribed procedures and major statutes on procedures are the Indian Evidence Act, 1872; the Limitation Act, 1963; the Civil Procedure Code, 1908; and the Criminal Procedure Code, 1973. In addition, there are tribunals for specific purposes, such as land tribunals, industrial tribunals, tax tribunals, service tribunals, the Company Law Board, water pollution tribunals, and air pollution tribunals. Other quasi-judicial bodies include the Competition Commission of India, and other regulatory authorities or forums under the Consumer Protection Act, 1986. Tribunals and other quasi-judicial forums do not necessarily have to follow the rigid procedure followed by courts.

The law and the legal system should continuously change and adapt. However, since 1991, there has been an additional trigger because of economic reforms. The legal system must provide an adequate structure of incentives and deterrents for a market-based economy to function. Globalization also requires a legal system that conforms to global norms. Some recent initiatives for statutory law reform are directly linked to the World Trade Organization (WTO) agreements, intellectual property being a case in point. It must also be mentioned here that legal services might be opened up under fresh WTO negotiations, though temporarily the Doha negotiations are stuck. Other initiatives, such as in infrastructure or the financial sector, are directly linked to privatization, opening up to competition, and removal of historical government monopolies. However, over and above this, old statutes must change. India does not follow the legal principle known as desuetude, which simply means that all statutes are for a prescribed period of time and once this is over, statutes die a natural death, unless a fresh review establishes the need for their continuance. Therefore, dysfunctional and old statutes continue on the books unless they are specifically repealed.

How many statutes are there? This is difficult to answer, because there are both central and state-level statutes. There is also a counting problem. For instance, there may be a new statute that amends an existing statute. Is this going to be counted once or twice? Subject to this, there are between 2,500 and 3,000 central statutes. The earliest two go back to the year 1836 and these are the Bengal Indigo Contracts Act and the Bengal Districts Act. Thanks to computerization and use of information technology, it is now reasonably easy to access central statutes, that is, a listing of titles as well as the text. For instance, they are available on the Ministry of Law and Justice's website (under the head India Code) and private organizations have brought out CDs. Even hard copy versions are available. Unfortunately, this accessibility has not yet extended to all states. Consequently, no one has a handle on how many state-level statutes there are. Figures between 25,000 and 30,000 float around, but these may be an exaggeration. A few states have listings of titles on their websites (not always the text), and in a few more, hard copy versions have been published. These suggest that something like 15,000 may be a more reasonable figure. PRS Legislative Research has started compiling all state-level statutes.

The first element of statutory law reform is to scrap dysfunctional statutes. For the 2,500 to 3,000 central statutes, this identification has been made. The most visible of these identification exercises was the Jain Commission on Review of Administrative Law, which submitted a report in 1998. This Commission identified around 1,300 statutes for outright repeal.

Based partly on the recommendations of this Commission, around 350 central statutes were repealed in 2001–2. It is always easier to repeal a statute in its entirety. Part of the problem is that a statute often has dysfunctional and old sections that need repeal. The entire statute cannot be junked. Unfortunately, not much has been done to repeal old statutes at the state-level. Some have been repealed in Gujarat and an exercise has been undertaken to identify old ones in Rajasthan. Ideally, all states should have permanent law commissions.

Second, statutory law reform should have an element of unification and harmonization. Statutes have been enacted at various points in time in the same area, without taking cognizance of what already exists. Labour legislation is an example. There are 47 different central Acts that directly deal with labour and many more that deal with it indirectly. Among the 47, the Fatal Accidents Act was enacted in 1855 and the Public Liability Insurance Act was enacted in 1991. Given this time span, it stands to reason that concepts and definitions will disagree. Within labour law, there is lack of unanimity about definitions of wages, workman, employee, factory, industry, and child labour. Case law also differs, causing further confusion. Banking law is another example of such lack of harmonization. There is thus a case for unifying and harmonizing.

Third, there is the issue of over-legislation. India is over-legislated and under-governed. Over-legislation is correlated with the problem of reducing unnecessary state intervention; with reforms the views on what the state should do have changed. For example, controls used by the state under the Essential Commodities Act of 1955 are no longer relevant, or necessary, or even desirable. Incidentally, several such controls date to shortages under Second World War conditions. Temporary legislation under the Defence of India Rules, 1939 became permanent. Another spate of redundant economic legislation dates to the period between 1969 and 1976. Laws on bank, coalmine, and general insurance nationalization, the former Monopolies and Restrictive Trade Practices (MRTP) Act, the Contract Labour (Regulation and Abolition) Act, the former Foreign Exchange Regulation Act (FERA), the former Urban Land (Ceiling and Regulation) Act, and the Foreign Contribution (Regulation) Act are of this vintage. With views on statute interventions changing, these statutes have become redundant.

Fourth, despite the existence of thousands of statutes, there are areas where laws do not exist. Credit cards, automatic teller machines (ATMs), hire purchase and leasing, electronic data interchanges (EDI), some areas of intellectual property, regulatory bodies, or the government's liability in tort are instances. Statutory law reform must fill the gaps.

Administrative Law

The most important constraint on efficient decision-making is not statutory, but administrative law.[1] These rules, orders, and regulations are not even published.

[1]The body of rules, regulations, orders, and decisions created by administrative agencies of government (Barrons Law Dictionary © 2003).

Even when they are, the language is not citizen friendly, the Plain English movement having left India untouched. The last time such a collation of administrative law was attempted was in 1966. The labour market can be used to illustrate the difference between statutory law and administrative law. In labour markets, reduced state intervention is primarily interpreted as reduced intervention in industrial relations. Most problems relate to the Industrial Disputes Act (IDA), especially chapter V-B. These concern lay-offs, retrenchments, and closures, and chapter V-B requires prior permission from the 'appropriate' government before such action can take place. This permission is never obtained. Therefore, labour markets become rigid and employers adopt artificially high capital intensity and circumvent the legislation. Given the other provisions of labour legislation, the requirement of governmental permission can be dispensed with, without adversely affecting the interests of labour. This is a valid point and the IDA invariably figures when labour market reform is mentioned. However, the IDA only covers the organized labour force (8 per cent of the total) and, within that, only enterprises that employ more than 100 workers (2.17 per cent of the labour force).

In contrast, administrative law relating to labour issues covers many more people. Twenty-nine different inspectors can descend under 47 statutes. A system of a single inspector for all labour laws does not exist. While grave violations are ignored, minor errors provide scope for harassment. Rules under the Factories Act, framed in 1948, provide for whitewashing of factories. Distemper will not do. Earthen pots filled with water are required. Water coolers will not suffice. Red-painted buckets filled with sand are required. Fire extinguishers will not do. Nor are documentation requirements or time periods for which records have to be kept standardized. And so on. Such procedural problems characterize all three stages of an enterprise's operations, entry, functioning, and exit, and impose transactions costs that render Indian business uncompetitive. Part of the problem with administrative decisions is that they leave a large degree of discretion, often at petty functionary levels, and thereby encourage corruption and rent seeking. Corruption is not distributionally neutral and has an anti-poor bias. For example, this has been documented for urban vendors and rickshaw-pullers. The answer lies in removing scope for discretion and discretionary abuse. But that is part of the agenda of pending reforms, often at the state level. Quite often, administrative reforms are interpreted in the narrower sense of civil service reforms. The 2nd Administrative Reforms Commission was established in 2005 (the 1st is from the second half of the 1960s) and has produced 15 reports on improving governance and administrative delivery. However, many of the recommendations have not yet been implemented.

Speed of Dispute Resolution

The legal system will not be credible without speedy dispute resolution. There are 25.4 million cases pending in lower courts, more than 3.7 million in high courts. With the Supreme Court included, the pendency figure inches close to 30 million. And this is the backlog only in courts. With tribunals and other quasi-judicial forums included, backlog figures approach 40 million. Two-thirds of the backlog consists of criminal cases, and in criminal cases the rate of conviction is less than 6 per cent, though if one counts from the filing of the charge sheet, the conviction rate is higher. In lower courts, more than 800,000 cases are more than 10 years old, with special concentration in states like Gujarat, Madhya Pradesh, Maharashtra, Uttar Pradesh, and West Bengal. In high courts, more than 450,000 cases are more than 10 years old, with special concentration in Allahabad and Kolkata. The figure on under-trials is subject to some dispute. But of the figure of around 240,000 that is cited, three-fourths are under-trials who are in jail and are accused of petty offences, having been in jail for longer than the maximum mandatory sentences for those petty crimes. Some recent successful attempts at reform have been in releasing such under-trials. On an average, it takes more than 10 years to resolve a dispute. This does not make redressal credible.

There are 26 Supreme Court judges, 876 high court judges, and 15,917 subordinate judges. These are the maximum numbers of allowable judges, the sanctioned positions. In reality, most courts have vacancies and working strengths are lower. Not surprisingly, the total number of judges in India is on the low side. For every million population, the United States has 107 judges, Canada 75.2, Britain 50.9, and Australia 41.6. The figure for India is slightly over 10 and the Law Commission recommended this should increase to 50. There are 450,000 lawyers, all of whom are regulated by the Advocates Act of 1961. In addition, 2,000 judicial officers are posted in various tribunals. Tribunals came up because they were thought to be faster than the court system, being free of cumbersome procedures. However, things have turned out differently. Perhaps the most important reason is that there is no finality about decisions taken in tribunals, as there is always scope for appeal to high courts and the Supreme Court. In the late 1970s, to provide cheap legal services to the poor, the system of *lok adalats* was started. The Legal Services

Authorities Act, 1989, was enacted to give statutory backing to lok adalats. The experience varies across states. Other attempts at reform have involved fast-track courts, family courts, mobile courts, *gram nyayalayas*, *nyaya panchayats*, plea bargaining, shift systems in subordinate courts, people's courts, women's courts, and use of information and communications technology (ICT). While there are successes, these are not yet universal.

How does one ensure speedy redressal? There are many aspects, some of which concern improving procedures in the subordinate and appellate courts. Various reports of the Law Commission have highlighted these issues. These reports have also focused on problems concerning the bar and the judiciary. If one visualizes demand and supply curves for dispute resolution, these traditional remedies involve a shift of the supply curve to the right.

But first, let us mention demand-side solutions and these involve a shift of the demand curve to the left. When highlighting the backlog in courts, one has adjudication in mind. But adjudication is only one way of resolving disputes. There are other dispute resolution mechanisms like conciliation, mediation, and arbitration. If these can be made more efficient, the demand for adjudication will decrease. One of the problems with conciliation and mediation has been a lack of credible conciliators and mediators. Historically, arbitration has never taken off because it has not been freed from the apron strings of courts. A relatively new Arbitration and Conciliation Act was passed in 1996 and has made arbitration more efficient, as systems have become less open-ended.

One must also mention the role of the government as a litigant. Government litigation crowds out the private citizen from civil courts. This is especially so for appeals, which often fail. A sample survey found that in Karnataka, the government was a litigant in 65 per cent of the civil cases. A large chunk of government litigation was in the form of appeals against lower court judgements and the survey found that 95 per cent of government appeals fail. Apart from being a commentary on the quality of government legal counsel, such statistics also underline the procedure followed in appealing. Appeals have automaticity. That apart, the government is often a litigant on both sides. There are also too many general appeals.

The inefficient indirect tax system also leads to many court cases. For instance, the Supreme Court has adjudicated whether lemons, chillies, green ginger, betel leaf, turmeric, and coconut are vegetables! Once there is standardization and unification of taxes, especially indirect taxes, such cases should decrease and a Goods and Service Tax (GST) will eventually be implemented.

However, court cases will not disappear even if demand is reduced. Therefore, the efficiency of disposal also needs to improve. Many of the problems are procedural and delays are possible at each of the four stages a civil suit, say, goes through—pre-trial, trial, appellate, and execution. An amendment to the Civil Procedure Code, enacted in 2001–2, has improved matters in civil cases. In 2003, a committee submitted a report on reforming the criminal justice system. But nothing much has happened. Once those or similar recommendations are accepted, the Criminal Procedure Code, the Indian Evidence Act, and the Limitation Act can be amended. The criminal justice system cannot be dramatically improved without addressing the issue of police reforms. Between 1979 and 1981, there were eight reports of the National Police Commission. In 1998 there was the Ribeiro Committee and in 2000 there was the Padmanabhaiah Committee. The issue of police reforms has been examined in such detail that no further examination is needed. It is a question of implementing the recommendations. But this has not happened, despite the Supreme Court instructing state governments to do so. After all, the Police Act dates back to 1861. Indeed, the Prisons Act also goes back to 1894, and the recommendations of the All India Committee on Jail Reforms, going all the way back to 1980–3, have again not been implemented.

Many suggestions about the functioning of the judiciary have been reiterated in more than one Law Commission report, apart from the Justice Shah Committee Report in 1972 and the Justice Satish Chandra Committee Report in 1986. The argument for more judges and more benches is a valid one, although there is the issue of vacancies not being filled on time and sitting judges being co-opted to head commissions of inquiry. The Law Ministry has argued for 15,000 more courts, but this requires financial resources. Unfortunately, the judiciary has been under a cloud, with even Supreme Court judges accused of corruption. There are also issues connected with the judiciary refusing to declare assets and procedures for removal of corrupt judges being unclear. However, with the same number of judges, it is possible to improve productivity by using modern technology and the Supreme Court and some high courts have demonstrated how this can be done. There is also the issue of imposing working norms and accountability for judges. For instance, increasing the number of working days and cutting down on long vacations is equivalent to increasing the number of judges by 25 per cent. Accountability and transparency norms cannot, and should not, be imposed on the judiciary from outside. And the same principle also applies to the bar. Without the judiciary being seen to be interested in reforms and introspection, there cannot be much support for greater monetary resources or even financial autonomy.

The scenario is thus quite depressing. The only silver lining is that there is now much greater awareness about the need to reform the law and the legal system, with the political economy of vested interests being less serious than in many other purely economic reform areas. As a pure back-of-the-envelope kind of number, the incremental GDP growth from reforming law and the legal system has been computed to be 1 per cent.

BIBEK DEBROY

■ Liability Rules

The law of torts, popularly known as liability rules, is a body of law that deals with issues that involve unintended harm suffered by an individual due to an act of omission or commission on the part of somebody else. Analytically speaking, liability rules deal with accidents that may arise from the interaction of two or more parties who are otherwise complete strangers to each other; for example, disputes over road accidents and product-related accidents are litigated under the law of torts. Depending on the liability rule in force, there could be legally binding due-care levels for both parties, for only the defendant, for only the victim, or for neither of the parties. A liability rule typically specifies whether and how much liability (compensatory) payments are to be made by the injurer(s) to the victim(s). This decision typically depends on whether and by how much the care levels adopted by the parties at the time of the accident were less than the due-care levels. For example, the rule of negligence holds an injurer liable for accident loss if and only if at the time of the accident his care level was less than the due care. The rule of strict liability, in contrast, holds an injurer to be liable notwithstanding the levels of care opted for by the parties. As one would expect, courts in different parts of the world have applied different rules while fixing the liability for wrongdoings.

In India, tort cases constitute only a small fraction of the cases that are litigated. Nonetheless, Indian courts in some landmark judgements have applied and explained various doctrines of the law of torts. For example, the tort criteria of *cause-in-fact* and *foreseeability* have been explained in many judgements. In this exercise, courts have made repeated references to the principles of decision making that are prevalent in the common law countries. The question 'what constitutes a negligent act?' has been answered at length in many insightful judgements.[1]

Within the law of torts, disputes over road accidents constitute the bulk of the litigated cases. In some recently adjudicated cases though, the scope of liability rules has been expanded to include cases of violation of personal liberty and fundamental rights, illegal detentions, and negligent behaviour of public officials. Courts have used various versions of the negligence criterion as a basis of liability in most of the tort cases. This is particularly true for motor accident cases. Some of these versions, however, are different from those in the US and UK. For instance, in the US, the rule of negligence with the defence of contributory negligence holds an injurer to be liable if and only if at the time of the accident he was solely negligent. In contrast, in India, this rule requires a proportional sharing of liability when both parties were negligent.

Economic Analysis of Liability Rules

In the literature on law-and-economics, some of the most important results relate to the question of the economic efficiency of liability rules. While undertaking efficiency analysis of liability rules, the problem has generally been considered within the framework of accidents resulting from interaction of two parties who are strangers to each other. It is assumed that, in case of occurrence of an accident, the entire loss falls, to begin with, on one party. This party is aptly defined as the victim or plaintiff, the other party being the injurer or defendant. The probability of an accident and the amount of loss in case of an accident are assumed to depend on the levels of care taken by the parties. The social objective is to minimize the total social costs of accidents which are defined to be the sum of the costs of care plus the expected accident loss. It is assumed that the legally binding due-care level for a party is set at a level that is commensurate with the objective of minimizing the total social costs. It turns out that the last assumption is critical in establishing the economic efficiency or otherwise of a liability rule. Later, I shall discuss this issue further.

As far as the economic analysis of liability rules is concerned, there are too many works to be listed here. Calabresi's (1961) was a pioneering contribution. While Calabresi's work analysed the effect of liability rules on parties' behaviour, the first formal analysis was put forward by Brown (1973). Shavell (1987), Landes and Posner (1987), and Jain and Singh (2002) are some other contributions that contain systematic and detailed formal analyses of liability rules. The basic proposition emerging

[1]For illustrations, see Bangia (1997).

from this work is that if a solely negligent party is made to bear the entire accident loss, then both the parties will be induced to take efficient care. As a corollary to this general result, it has been shown that the rule of strict liability with the defence of contributory negligence, the rule of negligence, the rule of negligence with the defence of contributory negligence, and the rule of comparative negligence are efficient; these rules induce both victims as well as injurers to take optimal care. The rules of no liability and strict liability, on the other hand, have been shown to be inefficient.

Economics of Judicial Decision-making in India

Economic analysis of law in general and of liability rules, in particular, is a relatively new branch of research in India. As was remarked earlier, motor vehicle accidents constitute the bulk of the cases litigated under the liability rules. The Motor Vehicle Act, 1988 (MV Act), deals with accidents and related issues. While deciding on motor accident cases, Indian courts have applied the rule of negligence and the rule of negligence with the defence of contributory negligence. Section 140 of the MV Act, however, recognizes 'no fault liability' but only in cases of death and permanent disablement. Therefore, in the light of the findings of the economic analysis of liability rules, discussed earlier, it can be claimed that in most of the cases, Indian courts have applied rules that have been shown to be efficient. But this goes only thus far. Since economic analysis has also clarified that this claim about the efficiency of liability rules is valid only if the due-care levels are fixed at the efficient levels and courts do not make errors while estimating the harm. It has been argued that for a liability rule to be efficient, it is important that courts take into account the entire loss suffered by the victim.

One crucial factor that could affect the liability payments and, therefore, the efficiency characteristics of liability rules is the errors made by a court in assessing the harm. If a court overestimates (underestimates) the harm, it may entitle the victim to overcompensation (undercompensation). Such court errors can have various effects depending on the liability rule in force. For example, under the rule of strict liability, if due to court errors the liability payments are less than (more than) the actual harm, injurers will take less than (more than) the efficient care. If so, it will be interesting to see how Indian courts have fared on this count.

Compensation for motor vehicle accidents is dealt with under chapters X–XII of the MV Act. Under this law, the compensation is supposed to be 'full'. But in practice, there has been large variance in the compensation awards, even in very similar accident cases (Singh 2004). To make matters worse, even in the very same case, different courts have awarded different compensations, where an appeal was made against the initial awards. There are many such instances. One reason for this inconsistency is that different courts have used different criteria for assessing the damages.

It is widely known that the multiplier method for assessing damages is superior to other methods. This method and its superiority have been explained at length in a landmark judgement delivered by Justice Jagannadha Rao of Andhra Pradesh High Court in the case of *Bhagwandas* vs *Mohd Arif*. While Indian courts are increasingly using this method, there are serious problems with the way it has been done. Under this method, assessment of full compensation involves the calculation of the annual loss of dependency, and the number of years for which income has been lost due to the accident. Due to the lack of information, a court is likely to make errors in assessing 'full' compensation. But, with the help of tables prepared by the actuaries, the multiplier can be calculated with a fair degree of accuracy. The value of the multiplier depends on the age of the victim; the lesser the age the higher will be the multiplier and vice versa. Surprisingly, courts have used the same multiplier even for victims of entirely different age groups. Even more surprisingly, some courts have used a lower multiplier in the case of younger victims and a higher multiplier when the victims were older![2]

Apart from such errors, there are other factors also that can affect liability payments and, therefore, the efficiency of a liability rule. For example, if injurers can at times escape liability for the harm they have inflicted on others, then they will internalize only a part of the externality and will be less careful. A more comprehensive economic analysis of the Indian judicial system that addresses these issues is still awaited.

Policy Issues

As has been demonstrated here, there are various kinds of uncertainties regarding compensation awards. As a result, the damage awards in an adjudicated case cannot be taken as an indicator or precedence for similar cases that might be litigated in future. When compensation is different from the actual harm, the stated objective of the law, namely, to compensate the victims, remains unachieved. Moreover, legal uncertainties cause at least two types of economic inefficiency. Singh (2004) shows that in the presence of such uncertainties there cannot exist a liability rule that can induce injurers to take efficient care. That is,

[2]For details, see Singh (2004).

potential injurers will take less care. This, at least to some extent, explains the traffic misrule one witnesses in India.

To understand the second type of inefficiency, it is pertinent to explore the implications of clearer rules and more predictable court judgements. Certainty or the predictability is said to be the key for the efficacy and efficiency of legal rules. When the rules are clear, and the amount of compensation is predictable, parties to an accident are more likely to guess the judicial decision. This, in turn, increases the probability of pre-trial or out-of-court settlements. More out-of-court settlements would mean that fewer cases are actually litigated. This is efficient, since it saves society's time and resources that can be invested more productively elsewhere. Uncertainties, on the contrary, reduce the chances of out-of-court settlements, and result in more litigation. This is so because not only are more cases litigated, the very same case is litigated in different courts. There are no easy answers to the problem, but the inconsistency in judicial pronouncements is one of the several factors responsible for the backlog of cases besetting the Indian judicial system.

RAM SINGH

References

Bangia, R.K. 1997. *Law of Torts*, Faridabad, Allahabad Law Agency.

Brown, J.P. 1973. 'Toward an Economic Theory of Liability', *Journal of Legal Studies*, 2: 323–50.

Calabresi, G. 1961. 'Some Thoughts on Risk Distribution and the Law of Torts', *Yale Law Journal*, 70: 499–553.

Jain, S.K. and R. Singh. 2002. 'Efficient Liability Rules: Complete Characterisation', *Journal of Economics*, 75(2): 105–24.

Landes, W.M. and R.A. Posner. 1987. *The Economic Structure of Tort Law*, Cambridge, MA, Harvard University Press.

Shavell, S. 1987. *Economic Analysis of Accident Law*, Cambridge, MA, Harvard University Press.

Singh, Ram. 2004. 'Economics of Judicial Decision-making in Indian Tort Law', *Economic and Political Weekly*, 39: 2613–17.

Case

Bhagwandas vs *Mohd Arif, AIR 1988 A P 99.*

■ Licensing

The evolution of industrial policy since Independence offers a fascinating window into India's long obsession with mixed economy methods, the philosophical and theoretical foundations of which are often traced back to Mahalanobis' two-sector model (which formed the basis of the Second Five Year Plan) that demonstrated the importance of preferentially channelling savings into the capital goods sector. As originally conceived, and articulated in the Industries (Development and Regulation) (IDR) Act of 1951 and later in the Industrial Policy Resolution of 1956, the role of the state in the industrial economy was to orchestrate this canalization of savings by itself undertaking production in the capital goods sector while exercising control over private investment so as to enable a 'balanced' industrial development, where 'balance' was contemplated with respect to regional concentration as well as the relative rates of capacity creation in different sectors. In addition, controlling private investment flows was also considered crucial for keeping in check monopolistic tendencies and for protecting cottage industries and the small-scale sector. The policy of industrial licensing, whereby proposed investment projects were required to be vetted and approved by the state, arose naturally as a means of fulfilling these objectives.

In the immediate post-Second World War period, this did not appear too burdensome a set of responsibilities for the planning authority to take upon itself—the apparent 'success', at the time, of the Soviet Union in shouldering an even more complex system of controls provided grounds for optimism.

Accordingly, the original scope of the licensing policy was fairly broad: industries were divided into two schedules (or lists), with industries in the first schedule being subject to licensing requirements. The first schedule was an expansive list, spanning industries from fertilizers to industrial machinery. Licences were required for (i) opening new establishments, (ii) expanding capacity, (iii) changing the existing product mix, and (iv) relocating to another region. Subsequent amendments to the policy designated certain industries as being reserved for the small-scale sector and, therefore, off-limits for large investment projects, while creating size-based exemptions for investment projects.

A Licensing Committee was set up to handle applications. Approval was subject to a consideration of whether projected demand warranted the additional installation of capacity as well as a feasibility assessment of the particular project, the former being based on Plan targets and the latter being a discretionary judgement on the part of the Licensing Committee. As a preliminary stamp of approval for a project, the entrepreneur would be given a Letter of Intent (LOI), which he/she would then use to apply for separate licences for importing raw materials and capital goods, for raising funds in the capital market, and so on. Once these auxiliary clearances had been obtained, the entrepreneur would be issued an industrial licence. The actual enforcement of approved capacities was primarily achieved by means of limiting supplies of power, water, and raw materials, most of which were in the public sector.

An early and abiding emphasis was on conserving foreign exchange—projects that required importation of raw materials or capital goods were rationed, with the latter being further referred to the Capital Goods Committee (CGC), which would determine whether the capital goods in question could not have been purchased domestically.

The policy was also differentially restrictive with regard to foreign-owned firms (defined as firms in which foreigners held a majority equity share)—any project proposed by such a firm could be approved only if it did not crowd out a similar project proposed by a domestically-owned firm.

With the passage of time, administrative costs began to pile up and complaints from frustrated industrialists began to pour in. As a result, licensing policy went from being general to being extremely specific, embodying a veritable slew of provisions, exceptions, and exemptions, all of which were subjected to continual revision. At the end of the day, even the bureaucrats responsible for issuing licences admitted to being perplexed about the procedures in effect at any point in time.

The first significant attempts to rationalize the system were in the 1970s, based on recommendations outlined in a report by Professor R.K. Hazari and the report of the Industrial Licensing Policy Inquiry Committee (ILPIC). Both reports made the point that the licensing system was being gamed by the large corporate houses, who were obtaining licences for capacity without actually installing it, thereby pre-empting their competitors. On the basis of an analysis of the Licensing Committee's (partial) records on applications and approvals, Professor Hazari came to the mildly-stated conclusion that 'one might, in a rash mood, hazard the statement that Birlas do not follow up about *one-half* of their licenses' (emphasis mine). The Hazari Report also pointed out that the size distribution of proposed projects was heavily skewed and, from the standpoint of administrative cost, it did not make sense to monitor the investments of a large proportion of applicants. Partly as a result, in 1973 the procedures were amended to make licensing mandatory for large industrial houses (defined under the Monopolies and Restrictive Trade Practices [MRTP] Act as being corporations with more than Rs 20 crore in assets), while increasing the size-based exemption limit for all other firms.

As Mohan and Aggarwal (1990) have noted, both the Hazari report as well as the ILPIC were extremely critical of the performance of the licensing system, but neither of them went so far as to challenge the basic ideological premises underlying it. On the contrary, their recommendations constituted little more than ad hoc adjustments to the policy with a view to fine-tuning it. In their view, it was not that the basic notion of the state replacing the market mechanism as a determiner of the merits of private investment projects was flawed, but that the feasibility of government oversight of private investment could not be guaranteed without a narrower focus on monitoring priority sectors and large-scale projects.

This policy inertia persisted well into the 1970s and the early 1980s, but by this time a long period of industrial deceleration (see Bosworth et al. 2007) was beginning to cast grave doubts on the ability of the state to steer the market. The 1980s witnessed a series of mini-reforms of policies ranging from foreign-exchange controls to industrial licensing. A large number of industries were freed from licensing requirements in 1985. This period is often hailed as marking a shift in ideology in favour of the market, although it was by no means as decisive as the massive liberalization of 1991. The New Industrial Policy of 1991 represented a clean break from the past—it practically abolished the system of industrial licensing (although it was retained in a handful of industries).

What is telling, though, is that neither of the two waves of reform was purely the result of an accumulation of a critical mass of opinion against the old ideology. The death of Indira Gandhi in 1984 and the unprecedented balance-of-payments crisis in 1991 unexpectedly brought to the helm progressive elements of the Congress party (Rajiv Gandhi in 1984 and Narasimha Rao and Manmohan Singh in 1991) who were able to seize the opportunity to effect a change in policy direction.

For scholars looking back in the hope of trying to assess the consequences of the 'Licence Raj' (as it came to be called in its day), the challenges are formidable. In the first place, it may not be particularly meaningful to consider a counter-factual world in which the Licence Raj did not exist, to the extent that the latter was only one of an interlocking set of policy controls, whose joint direction was determined by a unifying ideology. From a theoretical perspective, however, it is not difficult to imagine the kinds of distortions that industrial licensing in isolation might have created through its effects on product variety, competition, and efficiency. For instance, the regulation of entry and capacity expansion can easily have large effects on aggregate productivity, by protecting inefficient firms from competition and by limiting the expansion of efficient ones. Kochhar et al. (2006) observe that in 1981, the average manufacturing firm in India was more than 10 times smaller than the average manufacturing firm in the US, although this may have been as much due to licensing regulations as to restrictive labour regulations that differentially affected larger firms. Of broader significance is the extent to which state intervention skewed the intersectoral allocation of investment, resulting in a manufacturing sector unusually (for a labour-rich country) concentrated in capital-intensive production (Kochhar et al. 2006).

Other consequences of the policy are worthy of mention: (i) The reservation of sectors for small industry is likely to have seriously undermined the export potential of some of these industries (see Gang and Pandey 2008). (ii) Foreign direct investment in India has also historically been pitifully low, due in no small part to the bureaucratic hurdles created by the licensing policy.

In conclusion, industrial licensing sounds anachronistic in this day and age, summoning up a vision of bureaucrats surrounded by files in dusty offices and money covertly changing hands, and it is truly fascinating that 60 years ago it was considered the instrument of choice for fulfilling the state's (well-intentioned) designs. That the policy, and to a greater extent, the overarching industrial programme that underpinned it, significantly shaped the current industrial landscape is indisputable. What the economy would have looked like today, and what its capabilities would have been had a different ideology prevailed at the time of Independence is, however, anyone's guess. But the one lesson that has emerged from India's 40-year-long experiment with state control is that it inevitably fosters rent seeking, whether in the form of bureaucrats seeking bribes for issuing licences, or in the form of industrialists trying to buy protection of one sort or another. This experience alone has arguably helped shape a strong consensus against eschewing the market mechanism in future policymaking.

Notes on Sources of Data

1. The text of the IDR Act and the Industrial Policy Resolutions of 1948 and 1956 and subsequent amendments to the licensing policy may be found, for example, in Iyer (1982).
2. A comprehensive list of industries de-licensed in different years may be found in various volumes of the *Handbook of Industrial Statistics* published by the Government of India.

A.V. CHARI

References

Bosworth, B., S. Collins, and A. Virmani. 2007. 'Sources of Growth in the Indian Economy', NBER Working Paper 12901.

Gang, Ira N. and Mihir Pandey. 2008. 'Small-scale Industries', in Kaushik Basu (ed.), *The Oxford Companion to Economics in India*, New Delhi, Oxford University Press.

Hazari, R.K. 1966. *Industrial Planning and Licensing Policy*, New Delhi, Government of India.

Mohan, R. and V. Aggarwal. 1990. 'Commands and Controls: Planning for Indian Industrial Development, 1951–1990', *Journal of Comparative Economics*, 14: 681–712.

Iyer, K.V. 1982. *Liberalization of Industrial Policy*, New Delhi, Indu Press.

Kochhar, K., U. Kumar, R. Rajan, A. Subramanian, and I. Tokatlidis. 2006. 'India's Pattern of Development: What Happened, What Follows', *Journal of Monetary Economics*, 53(5): 981–1019.

Literacy

Literacy refers to an individual's ability to communicate through reading and writing. The literacy rate for any population measures the fraction of the population, above some cut-off age, that is literate. Based on the most-recent statistics compiled by the United Nations Educational, Scientific and Cultural Organization (UNESCO), more than one in three Indians above the age of 15 years is unable to read and write. Further, the roughly 268 million adult illiterates in India constitute one-third of the global population of illiterates. International comparisons show that the Indian literacy rate is well below those for other populous countries like China and also below those for developing countries in general.

The main source of information on literacy in India is the decennial census. The census enumerates a person as literate if he/she can 'read and write with understanding in any language'. Currently the census reports aggregate literacy rates for the population aged seven years and above. As Figure 1 shows, the literacy rate has risen significantly, especially in the post-Independence period. From a low level of 18.3 per cent of the population in 1951, it rose to 65.4 per cent in 2001. The recorded improvement in the most recent decade is notable in that with a 13 percentage point increase in literacy, the absolute number of illiterate people fell for the first time since Independence (from 328 million in 1991 to 296 million in 2001).

This data carries some caveats. One, the determination of literate status is based on self-reporting by respondents, or on inference by the census enumerator, with little attempt to verify actual literacy skills. Literacy tests administered as part of household surveys carried out by the National Sample Survey Organisation (NSSO) in 1991 found that more than a third of self-declared literates in the sample were illiterate (Govinda and Biswal 2005). This suggests that the estimates provided by the Census of India may be biased upwards. Two, the current '7+ years' threshold for computing aggregate literacy rates differs from that used by the Census till 1971 ('5+ years') and from that used commonly in international comparisons ('15+ years'). The difference matters. Aggregate literacy can be viewed as a weighted average of age-specific literacy rates. If the age-specific literacy of 5–6 year olds is lower than the average literacy of the '7+' age groups, a switch to the higher threshold can overstate improvements in literacy. Despite these caveats, estimates of the trends may be broadly accurate.

The Many Dimensions of Disparity

The distribution of literacy in India is uneven. As Figure 1 shows, the literacy rate for males has been consistently higher than that for females. In 1951, less than 9 per cent females were literate while the corresponding number for males was over 27 per cent. The gender literacy gap has narrowed in recent decades, but remains large: in 2001, the female literacy rate of 54.2 per cent was significantly below the male rate of 75.9 per cent. Two, there is strong regional variation in literacy rates. Broadly speaking, the populous states of north India have lower literacy levels (and also greater gender disparity) than the southern states. Comparing states in 2001, Kerala had the highest literacy rate of 90.9 per cent (94.2 per cent for males, 87.9 per cent for females) while Bihar had the lowest with 47.5 per cent (60.3 per cent for males and 33.6 per cent for females).

Three, urban literacy is higher than rural literacy. In 1951, only 12.1 per cent of the rural population was literate relative to 34.6 per cent of the urban population. For 2001, the literacy rate was 59.4 per cent in rural areas compared to 80.3 per cent in urban areas. Four, literacy

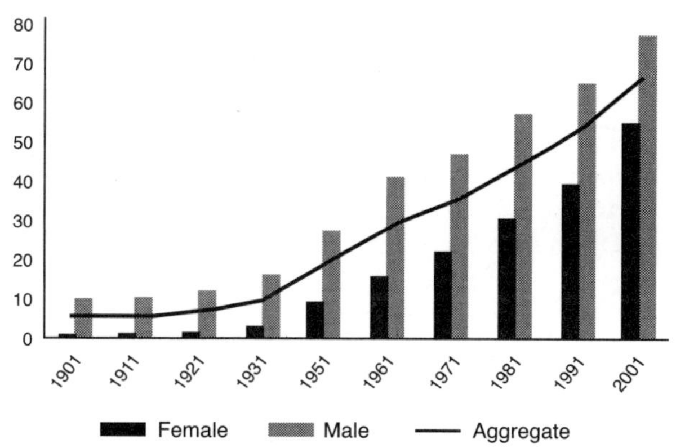

Figure 1 Trends in Literacy

Source: Census of India, various years.

rates vary across age groups: younger cohorts, such as those aged between 10 and 20 years have higher literacy rates than older cohorts because of recent improvements in access to education. There is also a strong socio-economic dimension to literacy. Current literacy rates for scheduled castes (SCs, 54.7 per cent) and scheduled tribes (STs, 47.1 per cent) are significantly lower than for the population as a whole, though STs in the north-eastern states are an exception. Lastly, the 2001 Census released literacy rates by religion for the first time—literacy among the Muslim population (both men and women) was found to be lower than the national average.

While Census statistics are built around a simple, self-reported, binary classification (literate or illiterate), broader notions of literacy exist. For UNESCO literacy is 'the ability to identify, understand, interpret, create, communicate, compute, and use printed and written materials associated with varying contexts. Literacy involves a continuum of learning to enable an individual to achieve his/her goals, to develop his/her knowledge and potential, and to participate fully in the wider society.' Notions of functional literacy focus on the ability to use literacy in daily life. Unfortunately, there is no good quality, systematic assessment of such broader notions of literacy in India at the state or national level.

Why Does Literacy Matter?

Arguably literacy is an essential determinant of the quality of life. By enhancing cognitive skills, literacy enables fuller development of human potential, and helps promote a sense of self-worth and dignity. As such literacy is often proclaimed as a human right and measures of literacy are included directly in indices of human welfare. For instance, a country's adult literacy rate is a significant component of UN's Human Development Index. Literacy also plays a prominent role in social development. In India, literacy, especially female literacy, is the single most important factor associated with lower fertility and higher child survival, far outweighing in statistical significance other factors commonly associated with economic development such as income and urbanization. Female children have significantly higher chances of survival relative to male children in districts with high levels of female literacy and, more generally, greater female empowerment (Murthi et al. 1995).

In addition to its intrinsic value and wider social benefits, literacy is essential to economic transformation. A minimal level of literacy and numeracy is essential for participation in market transactions and fuller realization of economic potential. In particular, it enables greater and more effective participation in labour markets. Literacy is often a prerequisite for the acquisition of many other skills. The extent to which illiteracy poses a barrier to economic participation may depend on other considerations: for instance, an illiterate person with access to at least one literate household member (proximate illiterate) may not be as disadvantaged as one who belongs to a household where all members are illiterate (isolated illiterate). Also, while literacy can be achieved in any one of many languages, it may be advantageous to be literate in a language that is commonly used in economic interactions. At the aggregate level, there is considerable evidence of a positive link between investment in human capital and rates of economic growth. More specifically for India, there is evidence that states with higher initial levels of literacy have experienced stronger poverty reduction since the 1960s, other things being equal, than states with weaker starting positions (Datt and Ravallion 1998).

The Need for Public Intervention

While these benefits of literacy seem self-evident, at least to those who are already literate, they can be less obvious to illiterate people. The acquisition of literacy requires sustained individual investment in time and effort to develop cognitive skills (to decipher written text) and fine motor skills (to be able to write). Such skills are more readily acquired at a relatively young age when learning is easier and the opportunity cost of time is low, but children themselves are not best placed to assess the merits of literacy. In many countries, cultural biases lead even parents to underestimate the benefits of literacy for their children, especially for girls. More generally, gaining literacy involves a beneficial externality in that others gain through enhanced communication possibilities with those who choose to become literate. If so, the social return to investment in literacy is likely to exceed the private return.

Not surprisingly, extension of literacy has been the subject of considerable effort around the world, both by the state and increasingly by non-state actors. 'Education for All', an international initiative, was launched in 1990 to accelerate progress with achieving universal primary education and raising adult literacy. Most countries around the world aspire to providing universal primary education, but in many cases the achievement of this goal has been limited by supply constraints (not enough schools and teachers) or less than universal take-up even in the absence of tuition fees. Governments have sought to make attendance at primary school level mandatory, or use other means to nudge the population to enrol. Incentives such as Conditional Cash Transfers (monetary payments made to households contingent on their children attending school regularly) and free school meals can enhance school attendance, especially in deprived sections of the population.

Why Has it Taken So Long to Reduce Illiteracy?

Addressing illiteracy in a population requires extension of literacy among the stock of illiterate adults (through adult education) and among the flow of entrants (via education of children). The relative size of the two populations determines the magnitude of effort and resources needed in each category. As listed in Table 1, in India roughly 263 million adults (those aged 15 years or above) and 33 million children of school-going age (7–14 years) were classified as illiterate in 2001. In addition, there were 164 million illiterate children between 0 and 6 years of age. Reducing illiteracy among children requires that the large cohort of children entering school-going age enrol and complete basic education. Helping the 33 million 7–14-year-olds who are illiterate is important, as is encouraging the 167 million literate 7–14-year-olds to complete school. But even with high enrolment and progression rates, aggregate illiteracy rate is likely to remain high without efforts directed specifically at reducing adult illiteracy. We review recent progress in each of these categories.

Table 1 Age Distribution of Population by Literacy, 2001

(in million)

Age (in years)	Population	Literate population	Illiterate population
0–6	164	0	–
7–14	200	167	33
15+	664	401	263
All	1,028	732	296

Source: Census of India 2001 for population totals and total number of illiterates. Age-specific literacy rates are not available from the 2001 Census, so we use estimates provided by Govinda and Biswal (2005) based on National Sample Survey and National Family Health Survey data.

In India, a recent surge in enrolment rates of children of school-going age has begun to reduce flows into illiteracy. As part of the worldwide 'Education for All' programme, a range of initiatives launched by the government and various non-government organizations (NGOs) pushed the school enrolment of children aged between 6 and 14 years to 79 per cent in 2000. Enrolment rates have since risen further under the Sarva Shiksha Abhiyan (SSA) launched in 2001 to raise enrolment of children in this age-group to 100 per cent and encourage all children to complete eight years of school. The SSA is financed in part by a surcharge of 2 per cent on tax receipts collected since 2004. Central government funding of the SSA has financed improvements in school infrastructure, and the recruitment and training of more teachers. Related schemes have encouraged school attendance in other ways, notably through mid-day meal schemes. By some estimates enrolment of children aged 6–14 stood at over 95 per cent in 2004. It is expected to be boosted further by the recent enactment of the Right to Education Act which makes education compulsory and free for all 6–14-year-olds.

Despite this surge in enrolment, learning outcomes remain weak. In part, this is because drop-out rates remain high. According to government statistics, over a third of enrolled children are estimated to drop out at the primary school level (Standards I–V), with the figure rising to over 50 per cent by the time students reach the lower secondary level (Standards I–VIII). Drop-out rates are even higher for categories such as SC and ST that are more vulnerable to the risk of remaining illiterate. Besides, there are questions of whether enrolled children are able to acquire basic literacy skills. There are no nationwide standardized assessments of learning outcomes at the primary level. However, non-official assessments such as the report series compiled by Pratham, an NGO, point to serious shortcomings in reading skills of rural children: in 2008 only 56 per cent of children in Standard V were found capable of reading a Standard II text (a short paragraph) with fluency.

What factors contribute to the poor learning outcomes of primary school students in India? A wide variety of factors come into play including the poor quality of schooling infrastructure, non-availability of textbooks, inappropriate curricula, and shortcomings in teacher competencies and effort. Of all these, teacher effort is the factor that has been the most widely studied. The *Public Report on Basic Education in India* (PROBE 1999) found teacher absenteeism to be a widespread problem. Even where the teacher is present, there is little reward (or punishment) for teaching effectively. Greater information—such as that provided by standardized assessments—could help stimulate public debate and pressure for change from parents and NGOs. Greater monitoring of teacher presence, tied with financial incentives to reduce absenteeism, has been found to have beneficial effects on both teacher presence and learning outcomes in pilot studies. It remains to be seen if these successes can be replicated in the many state-level initiatives that aim to improve learning in schools.

NGOs can help too, by improving incentives and supplementing public effort. The Learning Guarantee Program in Karnataka, supported by the Azim Premji Foundation, provides financial rewards to schools where students achieve certain levels of learning or improvements in learning. Such schemes have to be carefully designed: where teachers' unions oppose schemes that measure performance of individual teachers, structuring incentives at the level of schools may help. But even when such schemes succeed in eliciting greater effort from schools that choose to participate, they run the danger of increasing inequality between schools by targeting 'out' some of the weaker schools that chose not to opt into the scheme. Using such schemes to improve student learning would need to go hand-in-hand with other schemes to improve performance of weaker schools. Where weak learning outcomes within schools can be attributed to weaknesses in pedagogy, it may help supplement teacher effort with remedial instruction. The Balsakhi programme organized by Pratham in urban areas provides additional support teachers (Balsakhis) to schools to augment instruction to weaker students during school hours. As Balsakhis are local secondary school graduates trained by Pratham, their services cost a fraction of those of regular teachers. The programme has been found to improve basic literacy and numeracy skills (Banerjee et al. 2007). Once again, the challenge is to sustain and scale up such programmes, especially as many NGOs rely quite significantly on volunteer effort.

The progress on addressing adult illiteracy has been weaker. The National Literacy Mission (NLM) was launched in 1988 to impart functional literacy to non-literates in the age group of 15–35 years. Its principal tool is the Total Literacy Campaign (TLC), an area-specific, time-bound, volunteer-based, mass-mobilization style programme inspired by the TLC from Ernakulum, Kerala. In the Ernakulum campaign, under the leadership of the Kerala Shastra Sahitya Parishad, careful efforts were made to identify every illiterate person in the district between 6 and 60 years, and then volunteers were used as instructors to help them attain literacy. Standards were set for literacy and numeracy and a primer, called *Aksharam*, was developed which imparted information on a range of socially-relevant issues. While TLCs have expanded nationwide and are followed by Post-Literacy Programmes to deal with relapse into illiteracy among the newly literate, to date Kerala remains the only state for which every district has been declared wholly literate by the NLM. For the other states, there are pockets of progress but systematic progress remains elusive. However, even when TLCs have been less than successful in raising adult literacy, they may have had indirect benefits through encouraging adults to enrol their children in schools. The Continuing Education Scheme provides further learning opportunities for those who graduate from TLCs and Post-Literacy Programmes.

Progress on adult literacy has been impeded by various factors. The pressure from civil society to improve adult literacy and the flow of public resources is not as strong as in the case of primary education. Also, where literacy contributes to social and economic empowerment of marginalized groups, efforts to sponsor adult literacy may face resistance from those who benefit from the prevailing order. Finding creative channels to enhance adult literacy and to prevent relapse of literate adults into illiteracy would benefit from careful research and systematic evaluation of current programmes.

To summarize, the ability to read and write is an essential skill, both for human development and economic transformation. While literacy has improved in India especially since Independence, a third of the population remains illiterate. Policy effort must focus not only on extension of primary education and improvement in its quality, but creative means to reduce adult illiteracy.

Sandeep Kapur and Mamta Murthi

References

Banerjee, A., S. Cole, E. Duflo, and L. Linden. 2007. 'Remedying Education: Evidence from Two Randomized Experiments in India', *Quarterly Journal of Economics*, 122(3): 1235–64.

Datt, G. and M. Ravallion. 1998. 'Why Have Some Indian States Done Better than Others at Reducing Rural Poverty?', *Economica*, 65(257): 17–38.

Govinda, R. and K. Biswal. 2005. 'Mapping Literacy in India: Who are the Illiterates and Where Do We Find Them', background paper for the Education for All Global Monitoring Report 2006, Literacy for Life, UNESCO.

Murthi, M., A-C Guio, and J. Drèze. 1995. 'Mortality, Fertility and Gender Bias in India', *Population and Development Review*, 21(4): 745–82.

The PROBE Team. 1999. *Public Report on Basic Education in India*, New Delhi, Oxford University Press.

M

Prashanta Chandra Mahalanobis

Prashanta Chandra Mahalanobis (1893–1972) is a name that figures prominently in any discourse on the Indian economy. It is rather amazing that the person who made the most significant contribution to Indian planning and development during the post-Independence era was an economist neither by profession, nor by formal training. Professor Mahalanobis was a physicist turned statistician, whose acquaintance with economics as a subject came through his broader interest in applying statistical techniques to a variety of problems in different fields.

Mahalanobis graduated from Presidency College, Calcutta, with Honours in physics and subsequently went to Cambridge where he did mathematical tripos with Part I in mathematics and Part II in natural science (physics). Returning home, he joined the physics department of Presidency College as teacher. However, his keen scientific mind soon began to explore areas outside physics, particularly statistics. Influenced by the philosophy that 'measurement is science', Mahalanobis took up statistics as a tool to arrive at measures of various empirical subjects that were essentially associated with variability in observations. This latter exercise brought him to the realm of economics. He learnt economics by the way of solving specific problems from this field, which were intermingled with problems from other fields.

Mahalanobis's contribution to economics can be broadly divided into two categories: the first involves his contribution to the systematic collection and analyses of data on various socio-economic variables; the second relates to his contribution to India's national economic planning.

The Indian Statistical Institute was established in 1931–2 under the guidance of Mahalanobis and a number of important socio-economic studies were carried out by the Institute which included a rupee census, family budget and indebtedness surveys for industrial and rural workers, estimates of acreage and yield of various crops, pattern of expenditure and consumer preferences, and causes and after-effects of the Bengal famine in 1943.[1] The Central Statistical Organisation (CSO) was set up in 1949 and the National Sample Surveys (NSS) started in 1950 at Mahalanobis's initiative, for the collection and analyses of socio-economic data for computation of national income and to provide other statistical information needed by the government for policy purposes. The CSO and NSS remain the two most important sources of data for any researcher doing empirical work on the Indian economy.

A more far-reaching, albeit controversial, contribution of Mahalanobis came in the context of India's development planning. Mahalanobis established a close friendship with Jawaharlal Nehru—an association which began in the 1940s when Nehru was chairman of the National Planning Committee set up by the Congress Party.

[1]A detailed account of these works can be found in Mukherjee (1973). For a detailed account of Mahalanobis's life and works see also Rudra (1996).

They shared a common view about the strategy for development for post-colonial India. Influenced by the success story of the erstwhile Soviet Union, both believed that the escape route from poverty, unemployment, and underdevelopment lay in state-sponsored industrialization and modernization through science and technology. When Jawaharlal Nehru became the first Prime Minister of independent India, Mahalanobis was appointed Honorary Statistical Advisor to the Indian cabinet and became actively involved with the Planning Commission, which was set up by Nehru in 1950 with the aim of designing national economic policy through Soviet-style planning. Mahalanobis was the chief architect of the so-called Nehru–Mahalanobis development strategy which was adopted in the Second Five Year Plan in 1955. Identifying deficiency of physical capital as the root cause for underdevelopment, the plan document emphasized heavy investment in industrialization and modernization of technologies. Since private savings and private rate of accumulation were believed to be inadequate to finance such investments, the plan advocated a highly interventionist economic policy that would involve direct participation of the state in the production process, especially in the capital-goods-producing sector. Heavy industrialization was also seen as a solution to the unemployment problem, whereby a quickly growing industrial sector, characterized by increasing returns, would absorb the surplus labour from the agricultural sector and promote overall growth. While the stated objectives of the Second Plan were not much different in spirit from the First one (both bearing the imprint of Nehru's socialist way of thinking), what distinguished this Plan document was the underlying theoretical construct, which came to be known as the 'Mahalanobis model'. The basic Mahalanobis model is a two-sector growth model which was later extended by Mahalanobis to a four-sector one. The benchmark two-sector model is structurally close to the Harrod–Domar model.[2] However, unlike the Harrod–Domar model, Mahalanobis did not treat saving ratios as a constant. In fact, for Mahalanobis the savings or investment ratio was the key variable which the government could directly influence through public investment.

The Mahalanobis model is arguably the most important contribution of Prashanta Chandra Mahalanobis to the field of economics, specifically to the *theory* of development planning. It is a fine example of a theoretical construct which is simple and elegant, and at the same time readily applicable. However, a lot of debate has centred on the plausibility of the assumptions of the model. The Mahalanobis model has been especially criticized in recent years for its closed economy approach. Indeed, the Mahalanobis strategy goes against the traditional theory of comparative advantage which argues that a labour surplus country like India should specialize in production and export of primary products and import capital-intensive manufacturing goods. This criticism seems a bit misplaced though, in view of the fact that the static comparative advantage theory works only if there is unlimited possibility of trade at given prices. As Mahalanobis (and many others at that point of time) perceived, trade opportunities in primary products were rather limited, which necessitated a strategy of self-reliance through rapid industrialization. Second, the recent dynamic comparative advantage theories of trade have shown that from a dynamic point of view it is not always a bad strategy for a developing country to promote industrialization with an aim to increase productivity and eventually develop a comparative advantage in manufacturing export. In fact, Japan has successfully implemented such a strategy in the 1950s. If the Mahalanobis model did not work for India, it is not a reflection of the weakness of the model per se; the problem lies in its execution.[3] It is nonetheless fair to say that Mahalanobis erred in not adequately recognizing the political and socio-economic constraints that hindered successful implementation of such a strategy in India.

A more serious limitation of the model lies in its treatment of the agricultural sector. Mahalanobis underplayed the role of the agricultural sector in the development process. Indeed, a sluggish agricultural sector could seriously impede the growth process by limiting the supply of wage goods. Mahalanobis probably assumed that agricultural productivity could easily be improved by removing the institutional barriers to agrarian development through land reforms—an assumption that turned out to be wrong given the complex political economy of India. Whatever be the explanation, failure to incorporate an effective way of relieving the wage goods constraint is a major weakness of the Mahalanobis strategy.

The criticisms notwithstanding, the Mahalanobis model remains an important landmark in the history of Indian economic thought, not only because it brought about major changes in the national economy, but also because it ushered in a new way of analysing the Indian economy based on quantitative reasoning. At a time when most of the policy analyses on the Indian economy

[2]A similar model was developed independently by Soviet economist Feldman.

[3]See Chakravarty (1993).

were rather vague, the Mahalanobis model was one of the first instances where precise numbers were calculated to arrive at well-defined policy prescriptions. Thus the most significant contribution of Mahalanobis lies in moulding the approach to economic policy in India during the post-Independence period.

MAUSUMI DAS

References

Chakravarty, S. 1993. 'P.C. Mahalanobis—A Personal Tribute', in S. Chakravarty, *Selected Economic Writings*, New Delhi, Oxford University Press.

Mukherjee, M. 1973. 'Professor Mahalanobis, Contributions to Economics: A Condensed Survey of Research', *Sankhya*, December, 35: 45–62.

Rudra, Ashok. 1996. *Prashanta Chandra Mahalanobis: A Biography*, New Delhi, Oxford University Press.

■ Manufacturing Hub

At the time of Independence, Nehru articulated a bold new vision for an India of his dreams. He was aware of the vicious cycle of poverty, low savings, and a thin base for capital investment. Armed with theories of economic development which emphasized capital formation, more specially heavy industry and self-reliance according to his principal economic advisor Mahalanobis, his government embarked on a series of five year plans. What resulted was economic planning with a preponderance of the public sector, an apologetic private sector, and a hamstrung market economy. Exports were regarded as an enabler for imports and not a goal. The GDP (gross domestic product) growth rate for the first 30 years averaged just 3.5 per cent—also known as the Hindu rate—and crossed 5.5 per cent only in the 1980s. After 1990, however, the situation began to change with the process of economic liberalization and opening up of the economy.

The reforms of 1991–2, triggered some major initiatives along the lines of Akamatsu's 'wild geese' theory of economic development. The theory, in brief, divides economic development into three phases. The process begins with the import of new products in response to a growing domestic demand and the impulse is generated for their domestic production. Thus import substitution takes place through replacing imported items with domestic substitutes. Stage one is defined as the period in which domestic production equals domestic consumption. Over time, domestic costs tend to decline through economies of scale as well as import of technology within the framework of a protected market. Stage two is marked by a commencement of exports with the domestic cost structure reaching international levels. Thus domestic production becomes larger than domestic consumption. Stage three envisages a slowdown in the rate of growth of exports with a rise in the cost of domestic factors of production like labour as well as the operation of the 'catching up cycle' in other developing countries.

This theory largely explains the growth experiences of Japan, South Korea, and the other East Asian Miracle Economies and, as I will later argue, is relevant to the take off of India's manufacturing sector. The Japanese economy after the Second World War was in shambles and the development process had to commence afresh. With financial help from the US and the dissolution of the Zaibatsu, a number of new businesses began to take root. The national goal, which reflected the aspirations of most Japanese, was to become an economic superpower. Japan proceeded to do this not on the strength of domestic consumption, which was low on account of a paucity of incomes but on the basis of accessing the international markets. A low wage structure kept costs down and creative reverse engineering of a whole array of products like automobiles, cameras, watches, microchips, and computers led to Japanese brands flooding the world markets in the decades that followed. Japanese ingenuity lay not just in copying foreign goods but in analysing them component by component and producing better and cheaper products. By the 1980s Japan had arrived in the league of economic superpowers. Its standard of living and wage rate were comparable to those of the advanced Western nations.

South Korea is another striking example of Akamatsu's 'catching up cycle'. Korea, like Japan, was war shattered in 1950 with the difference that it was a poorly developed country before the War. It commenced its recovery by addressing the export market in consumer goods like shoes, garments, and sportswear. Soon it began an aggressive drive to develop more complex industries like shipbuilding, steel, construction, automobiles, and electronics. Like Japan, the population, though poor, had a high savings rate. Furthermore, its political system supported '*chaebols*', which were encouraged to specialize in select sectors of industry. Eventually brands like Hyundai, Samsung, and LG gave stiff competition to Japan.

Development impulses along these lines created the Asian Tigers who, besides Japan and South Korea, included Hong Kong, Taiwan, Singapore, Indonesia, Malaysia, and Thailand. Despite many differences in their political philosophies, they shared a similar approach to economic development, namely, high domestic savings, the encouragement of broadly based human capital, minimal price distortions, sound macroeconomic management, and, most important, an emphasis on exports. These countries were shining examples of sustained high growth spread over 30 years.

After the reforms of 1991–2 India rapidly entered stage two of Akamatsu's Theory. Further, one of the remarkable facts was that with the relaxation of exchange controls 1991 onwards, the rupee depreciated in relation to the US dollar by a 100 per cent over the next decade. Also, compared to the US, the relative difference in inflation rates did not change significantly and the difference in interest rates actually narrowed.

Consequently, import substitution and export received a major impetus leading to greater outsourcing of components, services, and finished goods. For example, between 1997–8 and 2002–3 the production of all types of motor vehicles went up by 50 per cent in numbers whereas the consumption of domestically produced auto components rose by 110 per cent in value. This would indicate that currency depreciation was a key driver of the replacement of imported components by domestic substitutes and the fact that in the same period the export of auto components went up by 135 per cent shows that there was significant increase in outsourcing from India by foreign auto companies.

In the pharmaceutical industry, interestingly, there was a move from the manufacture of bulk drugs to more value-adding generic products as well as to research process outsourcing in biotechnology. Information technology was already on a growth path through accessing global markets. Parallely there was rapid progress in the incorporation of electronics in manufactured products and the outsourcing of software for embedded systems used in areas like communications, robotics, and automobile safety. On the services front, the outsourcing of medical care, call centres, knowledge management, and research and development seem poised for fast growth. In most cases we see a move up the value chain, that is, from the relatively simple to the more complex components of goods and services.

India during the 1990s and thereafter has attracted a steadily growing portfolio of foreign direct investment (FDI) and a large number of multinationals have established production facilities to take advantage of a fast-growing middle class market.

In fact, the total investment, including FDI, in manufacturing between 1990 and 2002, after adjusting for the changing exchange rate, has been around $ 95 billion. Over a dozen leading automobile manufacturers have established their presence in India. The equivalent of $4 billion has been invested in this industry. Also, investments of $1.2 billion have gone into the two-wheeler sector, $500 million into domestic appliances, and $300 million into television and radio transmission. These industries, however, represent only the tip of the iceberg. Much of the balance investment has gone into the ancillaries sector, which represents a large number of small- and medium-scale businesses. The list of ancillaries is huge since in the auto sector alone 13,000 components go into building a car.

The Indian consumer is fast becoming an engine of growth with her rising purchasing power, which sustains an increasing variety of goods and services. India's demographic transition is supporting this trend with large numbers of youths entering the employment stream. Moreover, young people unlike their parents are tending to spend more and save less. These developments are not just relevant to the changing structure of international trade but also exciting in the context of growing global integration. They underscore the mobility of Indians across the world and the desire of firms to become globally competitive in the areas of quality, productivity, delivery, and new product development.

China is going through a similar transition but only faster. It is building its industry on the strength of its huge middle class and proactive investment policies, and pushing exports to the hilt. Indian manufacturing could do much better with a relaxation of labour laws, cheaper power, and better infrastructure. Nevertheless, sooner rather than later, India is poised to become a major manufacturing hub for outsourcing by the big international players. Growing exports in turn will lead to greater economies of scale, employment generation, and higher domestic consumption. The world will be the biggest gainer on account of both India and China.

VINAY BHARAT-RAM

References

Akamatsu, K. 1961. 'A Theory of Unbalanced Growth in the World Economy', *Weltwirtschafliches Archiv.*, 86(2): 196–217.

Automotive Component Manufacturers Association of India. 2003. *Automotive Industry of India—Facts & Figures 2002–03*, New Delhi.

Bharat-Ram, Vinay. 1997. *The Theory of Global Firm*, New Delhi, Oxford University Press.

Central Statistical Organisation (Industrial Statistics Wing), *Annual Survey of Industries* (Vol. 1), Department of Statistics, Ministry of Planning, Government of India.

■ Medical Care, Quality of

Health policy in India during the last 25 years has been driven by the desire to make basic healthcare accessible to all. Great strides have been made towards this goal: the average adult visits a doctor 6 times a year in rural Rajasthan and 6.1 times in Delhi compared to 3.5 times a year in the US.

The use of health services by the rich and poor is very similar. In Rajasthan, the poor visit doctors 5.2 times a year compared to 6.48 times for the rich; in Delhi, the poor visit doctors *more* than the rich (6.8 times versus 5.2 times a year). Even so, health indicators such as the infant mortality rate place India at the level of Kenya and Gabon and large differences persist between the rich and the poor—1 in 10 children born to poor families dies within 12 months compared to 1 in 26 among the rich (World Bank 2006).

Clearly the service that people receive from doctors is important. This entry summarizes the emerging literature on the quality of private and public doctors in India. We define alternative measures of quality, discuss recent findings, and suggest implications for health policy. Partly due to difficulties in defining and measuring quality, there is little country-wide evidence to rely on. The existing evidence, however, indicates that the quality of primary medical care is alarmingly low.

Defining Quality

Quality can be measured in three ways: (i) structure (tangible hardware such as infrastructure or consumables such as medicines); (ii) process (quality of medical advice); and (iii) outcomes (impact of care on patients' health).

Structural measures have dominated empirical work in economics and other social sciences that aim to make population-wide estimates of healthcare quality. This is understandable since large-scale surveys are confined to relatively quick and easily measurable variables. By far the most common measure has been availability of medicines (Collier et al. 2003).

Structural quality by itself provides an inaccurate picture of service delivery. For example, if a public facility gives free medicines, the stock of medicines measures subsidization of care, and is unrelated to the quality of advice. Prescriptions could just as easily be filled by the local pharmacy. Worse, insufficient drug availability may simply indicate 'stock-outs' at the most popular facilities, which could be inversely related to the quality of care. Other physical items in facilities are largely subject to the same criticism—the more 'tradable' a piece of equipment is, the worse it performs as an indicator of service.

At the other extreme, measures of quality based on health outcomes are still in their infancy even in developed countries. The data collection and analysis required for establishing causal relations between clinical service and health outcomes is limited. Moreover, the methodology adopted in these studies is unlikely to help in the analysis of Indian medicine, since the majority are done in rich countries (particularly the United States), where infectious diseases common to India are hardly ever observed.

Progress *has* been made on 'process' measures of quality that capture aspects of provider behaviour likely to result in better health outcomes. In addition, they respond quickly to medical education and incentives; collected over time they are a suitable candidate for assessing quality improvements in the country.

What We Know about Process Quality

When a person visits the doctor, the quality of care s/he receives depends on (i) whether the doctor is present (the 'extensive' margin of effort), (ii) what the doctor knows (competence), and (iii) what the doctor does (effort); the latter two reflect the 'intensive' margin of care.

The Extensive Margin: Absenteeism in the Public Sector

Problems of provider absence arise from unfilled vacancies and absenteeism. These are problems specific to *public* providers since a private provider is not paid if absent and is, therefore, making an efficient choice. By the same token, vacancies in public facilities are not as much a problem of quality as of access—not having a public health centre is the same as having one with all posts vacant.

The aspect of the 'extensive margin' that is a genuine problem in the public sector is the problem of absenteeism, since salaries are paid but the expected services are not delivered. A recent study measures absenteeism using a large, representative survey based on surprise visits to primary healthcare facilities (Chaudhury et al. 2005). On average, over 40 per cent of doctors employed at public facilities were not found when visits were made (after adjusting for all legitimate reasons for absence). For non-doctors, the problem was equally bad, with the average absence rate just under 40 per cent. Further, absenteeism was not confined to a few 'bad eggs'—researchers visited each facility three times and while 15 per cent were absent all three times (the bad eggs) only 22 per cent were present every time.

A more intensive study of one district of Rajasthan, which continuously monitored conditions in public facilities associated with 100 villages, found that sub-centres were closed 56 per cent of the time during regular hours. Absence rates were 45 per cent in sub-centres and 36 per cent in primary centres (Banerjee et al. 2004). If closings follow an established pattern, such as always being closed on Tuesdays, then the welfare loss may be small. However, long queues were seen at facilities that never opened. However capable the providers, they cannot give high-quality advice in absentia.

The Intensive Margin: Competence

Even when providers are at work, problems on the intensive margin arise in terms of quality of advice, which can be measured in two ways. First, the quality of medical advice depends on how much doctors know—measured 'knowledge' or 'competence' reflects the *maximum* quality a doctor can provide. However, if effort is costly, the actual quality of care could be substantially lower than this upper-bound. Second, one can also observe the provider in actual clinical practice to evaluate what doctors *do*. In both cases, relating knowledge and practice to established benchmarks of good-quality advice provides a measure of the quality of medical care.

Nationally representative studies of this type have not been done, but a recent study in Delhi revealed disturbing patterns (Das and Hammer 2005a). Hypothetical questions for five common cases or 'vignettes' were posed to a representative sample of public and private doctors in Delhi. Several results are noteworthy.

The overall knowledge of medical practitioners in Delhi was very low. For four out of five typical cases, the average provider was more likely to *harm* than assist. For example, less than one-third of observed providers asked questions or undertook examinations that would help identify pre-eclampsia in a pregnant woman; the remainder gave advice that would, in high probability, lead to the death of the mother, child, or both.

The study also addresses the long-standing debate on the relative quality of care in the public and private sectors. One side sees the private sector as 'quacks'; the other sees the public sector as staffed by less-competent doctors. The data indicate that both views have valid empirical grounding. On average, competence in the two sectors was similar. However, if private-sector providers are divided into those with and those without an MBBS degree (Bachelor of Medicine and Bachelor of Surgery) and the public sector is divided between staff at hospitals (mostly elite institutions in Delhi) and at primary healthcare centres (PHCs), differences emerge.

Doctors in public hospitals were nearly as competent as private MBBS providers—they may well be the same people at different stages in their career or, given the prevalence of 'dual practice', the same people, period. Doctors in small public clinics were substantially less competent than public doctors in hospitals and private doctors with an MBBS degree, although they were more competent than private providers without an MBBS.

The most striking feature though, was the variation in competence across poor and rich neighbourhoods. In the private sector, more competent MBBS *and* non-MBBS doctors were practising in richer areas; indeed, private MBBS doctors in poorer areas were sometimes worse than non-MBBS doctors in richer areas. The government does nothing to equalize these differences in the private market. The difference in competence across rich and poor areas was very similar in both the public and private sectors. Poor people go to PHCs and to the non-MBBS private sector, receiving advice from providers with very low competence in either case. Richer people go to competent private doctors or to competent public doctors in hospitals and obtain better advice.

The Intensive Margin: What Do Doctors Do?

Evidence on the quality of performance in clinical settings, or what doctors do, is thin. However, the same study included a component in which doctors were observed for one working day within a few weeks of the original study on competence (Das and Hammer 2005b). The amount of time, number of questions asked, examinations performed, medication prescribed, and advice for use of medications and follow-up were all recorded. An average interaction between a doctor and a patient in Delhi lasts 3.8 minutes; the doctor asks 3.2 questions, undertakes an examination 63 per cent of the time, and dispenses 2.6 medicines. These numbers are much worse than in Spain, Germany, or the UK, worse than in Tanzania, Paraguay, and Nigeria, but somewhat better than in Malawi.

Disaggregating the data further showed a number of patterns.

- What doctors knew (from the vignettes) had little to do with what they did (from observation). On average, doctors performed less than one-third of the critical procedures that they *had said they would perform* in cases of diarrhoea and viral pharyngitis.
- More competent doctors exerted more effort—a combination of time, questions, and examinations.
- Public doctors put in far less effort, spending half the time and doing only 60 per cent as many examinations as private-sector providers. These results remain after adjusting for workload, competence, and location.
- Non-MBBS doctors did about as well as they could—their behaviour approximately matched what they said they would do on the vignettes. MBBS doctors did less in practice than what they said they would do hypothetically. In the private sector, the difference was modest; in the public sector the difference was dramatic, particularly among doctors in small clinics.

Indeed, the difference in effort between the public and private sectors was so stark that people in poor neighbourhoods were *better off* visiting less-qualified private-sector doctors than their more-qualified public-sector counterparts, at least in terms of diagnostic abilities.

Even so, the private sector was not a panacea. In line with previous work (for instance, Patel et al.

2005), the study also found that the incentives to exert effort can be 'too strong'. Doctors in the private sector cater to patient expectations by overmedication, and poly-pharmacy (prescribing multiple medicines for a patient) is higher in the private compared to the public sector. In many cases, a private-sector doctor would accurately diagnose viral diarrhoea, but still prescribe anti-cholinergics and antibiotics. The former is contra-indicated, and the latter develops antibiotic resistance, raising the cost of future treatment.

The evidence on the 'extensive' and 'intensive' margins leads to some frightening conclusions for the quality of care in the public sector: a poor person visiting a primary healthcare centre is likely to find the doctor absent 40 per cent of the time. When the doctor is present, what s/he knows is just enough to ensure a 60 per cent chance of *not* harming the patient *if s/he did all s/he knew to do*. Unfortunately, the gap between knowledge and practice is large for public-sector doctors—typically, the doctor will ask the patient two questions and spend 2.5 minutes before sending him/her off with medication for the day. The rich will see a doctor who is more likely to be there, knows more, and acts more conscientiously. As an added bonus, the rich will probably spend *less* on unnecessary medicines and treatments than the poor.

These patterns combined with information on patients indicate deep-seated problems in the healthcare sector. First, the wide variation in quality of providers can be maintained for a long time—low-quality doctors are not driven out of the market, though they may be driven out of rich neighbourhoods. Second, choices between where to seek treatment (public or private facilities) can lead to better or worse outcomes depending on the nature of the disease involved. If the disease is self-limiting and, therefore, lack of effort is not a problem, it is better to go to a public clinic where the patient will not receive a number of unnecessary medicines. If the disease needs careful attention, the private sector is better. Unfortunately, people do not generally know a priori which type of problem they have.

Policy Options

Policy options for improving the quality of care in the healthcare market are limited. The first option is to increase information *to the public* about how to decide when a problem is serious and, therefore, sort themselves into public and private sectors. Further, better information and public action on *prevention*, either through public hygiene campaigns or large-scale sanitation programmes would go a long way to keeping people from having to make these choices.

Additional training for *providers* is unlikely to improve the quality of service delivery. On the extensive margin, it is unlikely that doctors are not aware that they are expected to show up for work. Similarly, on clinical practice, many doctors know what to do but simply do not do it, responding to their direct incentives (public doctors are on salary and have very little incentive to provide service; private doctors want repeat business).

Policies to change the image of primary healthcare in the public sector could improve the entire market, but require substantial investments. Setting benchmarks of service that people can trust and rely on would be a good start. This would include providing incentives to public-sector doctors (perhaps through 'bonus' schemes or empowering local authorities to hire and fire) and developing trust with the population. Both are likely uphill political battles. Another is to closely monitor and certify providers in the private sector. But simply expanding the scope of the 'inspectorate raj' is not something that can be done without first improving the capacity and honesty of public service providers.

In some countries the threat of litigation for malpractice serves as a disciplinary device. This has its own problems, especially with private, third-party payment schemes in which defensive medicine could drive up overall costs. In India the court system is already so overburdened that this is not a practical route to fixing the quality of healthcare problems. The challenge will be to improve healthcare performance under the set of currently existing institutions; this is a difficult task that first requires a systematic shift in the debate away from physical access towards the content of care.

JISHNU DAS AND JEFFREY S. HAMMER

References

Banerjee, Abhijit, Angus Deaton, and Esther Duflo. 2004. 'Wealth, Health and Health Services in Rural Rajasthan', *American Economic Review, Papers and Proceedings*, 94(2): 326–30.

Chaudhury, N., J. Hammer, H. Rogers, K. Muralidharan, and M. Kremer. 2005. 'Causes of Absenteeism in Public Health Workers and Teachers in Eight Countries', World Bank, processed.

Collier, Paul, Stefan Dercon, and John Mackinnon. 2003. 'Density versus Quality in Health Care Provision: Using Household Data to Make Budgetary Choices in Ethiopia', *World Bank Economic Review*, 16(3): 425–48.

Das, Jishnu and Jeffrey Hammer. 2005a. 'Which Doctor? Combining Vignettes and Item Response to Measure Clinical Competence', *Journal of Development Economics*, 78(2): 348–83.

———. 2005b. 'Money for Nothing: The Dire Straits of Medical Practice in Delhi, India', Policy Research Working Paper No. 3669.

Patel V., R. Vaidya, D. Naik, and P. Borker. 2005. 'Irrational Drug Use in India: A Prescription Survey from Goa', *Journal of Postgraduate Medicine*, 51: 9–12.

World Bank. 2006. *World Development Report: Equity and Development*, New York, World Bank and Oxford University Press.

■ Middle Class

In recent years, the discourse about the Indian middle class—by some accounts the largest in the world—seems to have caught the public's imagination. However, two different stories are simultaneously being told. According to one story, the high rate of economic growth over the past decade has resulted in a large number of people moving from poverty into the middle class. This broad-based economic boom has affected all sections of society and resulted in a growing market. It is expected that this growing market will increase opportunities for domestic and foreign companies, thereby augmenting the virtuous cycle of growth (Das 2000). The second story, however, focuses on the elitist nature of this growth and suggests that the Indian middle class has become increasingly insular, with the perks of middle-class existence reserved for the privileged sections of society (Varma 1998).

The exact size of this middle class remains difficult to estimate. There are few national surveys that collect data on income. The most-cited source, a household survey conducted by the National Council of Applied Economic Research (NCAER 2000), contained only one question on total household income and is considered an approximation at best. Moreover, the proprietary nature of this data does not allow for independent evaluation. National Sample Surveys (NSS) offer other sources of data for examining changes in consumption expenditure over time. While consumption data tend to underestimate certain types of consumption—such as of alcohol or tobacco—they still provide a good proxy for changes in consumption over time. Results from the NCAER surveys as well as NSS surveys are summarized in Table 1. These results suggest a steady increase in the households at middle- and upper-income levels in the past 20 years, particularly in urban areas.

The sheer size of the Indian middle-income group is important for estimating the size of the Indian market, but for social scientists the structure and composition of the middle class are even more important. While the definition of 'middle class' varies widely from Marxists to non-Marxists, much of the research on the 'middling sorts' has tended to focus on the nexus between education, occupation, and income. Changes in these three categories over the past 20 years in India paint a very interesting sociological picture.

While all segments of Indian society have benefited from a high rate of economic growth in the past two decades, the gains have been differentially captured by different segments of society. Table 2 summarizes the proportion among various occupational groups of households with an annual expenditure of Rs 60,000

Table 1 Changes in Household Consumption Expenditure and Household Income

Consumption expenditure above Rs 60,000*				Income above Rs 70,000**			
	Rural	Urban	Total		Rural	Urban	Total
1983	0.05	0.13	0.07	1985–6	5	22.2	9.5
1987–8	0.05	0.14	0.08	1989–90	8.8	28.2	14.2
1993–4	0.05	0.15	0.08	1995–6	13.7	37.2	20.4
1999–2000	0.06	0.22	0.11	1998–9	17.3	47.3	25.8

Source: *Author's calculations using data from NSS rounds 38, 43, 50, and 55.
**National Council of Applied Economic Research data.

Table 2 Growth in Proportion of Households Spending Rs 5,000 and Above per Month between 1983 and 2000 by Household Occupation

	Rs 5,000 and above			
Primary occupation of the household	1983	1987–8	1993–4	1999–2000
Upper professional	0.30	0.37	0.39	0.48
Lower professional	0.16	0.19	0.21	0.28
Manager & govt official	0.47	0.50	0.59	0.65
Proprietor—working	0.30	0.29	0.31	0.34
Clerical	0.17	0.18	0.19	0.28
Teacher	0.21	0.24	0.22	0.29
Merchant	0.10	0.11	0.12	0.17
Salesman	0.05	0.05	0.04	0.07
Service worker	0.06	0.05	0.06	0.11
Small farmer (≤5 acre land)	0.05	0.05	0.05	0.07
Large farmer (> 5 acre land)	0.19	0.17	0.16	0.23
Planter, poultry	0.12	0.12	0.11	0.14
Agricultural labour	0.01	0.01	0.01	0.01
Fisherman, forestry worker	0.03	0.03	0.03	0.03
Machine operator	0.09	0.11	0.11	0.14
Artisan	0.05	0.05	0.04	0.07
Transport worker	0.07	0.07	0.06	0.11
Labourer	0.04	0.03	0.03	0.04
No Occupation—retiree, unemployed	0.03	0.03	0.04	0.08
Occupation missing	0.05	0.03	0.02	0.09
All India	0.07	0.08	0.08	0.11

Source: Author's calculatons from NSS rounds 38, 43, 50, and 55.

or more, using data from the NSS. These data suggest that while all segments of society have gained over the past 20 years, the growth is greatest among professionals and government officials/managers. The proportion of households with a monthly expenditure level of Rs 5,000 and above has risen sharply for upper-level professionals—consisting of doctors, engineers, and lawyers, among others. Fewer than one-third of such households fell into an expenditure category of Rs 5,000 and above in 1983, whereas nearly half of the professional households had attained the expenditure level of Rs 5,000 and above by 2000. Managers and government officials seem to have been particular beneficiaries of the past two decades, with nearly 65 per cent of households attaining expenditure levels of Rs 5,000 and above. In contrast, manual workers and artisans show hardly any gains, and farmers and self-employed entrepreneurs only limited gains.

While there is no doubt that a higher rate of growth in the service sector and the entry of multinationals into India have played an important role in the income growths of professionals and managers, two other structural changes are far more important. Personal income tax rates in India steadily declined between 1985 and 2000. In the early 1970s, at its height, the maximum marginal tax rate was 85 per cent (which turned into a top tax rate of 97.5 per cent with the addition of surcharges). In 1985–6, the effective top tax rate dropped to 50 per cent, and it was further reduced to 30 per cent in 1997. High rates of taxation led to substantial tax evasion, but only farmers and self-employed people were able to evade paying full income taxes; employees and professionals had fewer such opportunities. Thus the decline in personal income tax rates raised their disposable incomes, but affected farmers and entrepreneurs, who paid fewer taxes to begin with, much less.

The second factor that played an important role in the growth of salary incomes was the growth in government salaries. In spite of the stagnation in government employment, the public sector continues to employ nearly two-thirds of the workers in the formal sector. Salaries of government workers were raised sharply in 1997, following the implementation of the Fifth Pay Commission Report. This increased the incomes of a variety of government servants, including government officials, clerical workers, and lower-level peons.

Thus, as we focus on income growth in India, it is important to note that much of this growth has been concentrated in the hands of educated workers in the formal sector, with some trickle-down effect for service-sector workers such as domestic servants, transportation workers, and merchants. In contrast, the two groups that were highly protected under the central planning and Licence Raj regime, middle- and large-scale farmers and entrepreneurs in small-scale industries (Raj 1973), have not gained proportionately.

These changes in the incomes of educated professionals need to be evaluated in the context of changes in educational and occupational distribution in India. The education level in India has risen steadily at all levels. The proportion of 30- to 50-year-old men with higher secondary and college education rose from 5 per cent in 1983 to 13 per cent in 2000; the proportion of women in this category increased from 1 per cent to 5 per cent (Desai and Das 2004). At the same time, occupational distribution has not changed substantially. Among 30- to 50-year-old men, about 10.5 per cent held professional, clerical, or other white-collar jobs, and this percentage had dropped to 9.14 per cent by 2000; among women, the proportion had risen slightly, from 1.5 per cent to 2 per cent.

These changes have led to increasing competition for white-collar jobs. While education remains a necessary condition for obtaining a professional or white-collar job, it is no longer a sufficient condition. Among 30- to 50-year-old men with higher secondary and college education, the likelihood of obtaining a white-collar job was about 0.73 in 1983, but it had dropped to 0.43 by 2000; the comparable likelihood for women dropped from 0.38 in 1983 to 0.24 in 2000.

These data paint an interesting picture of the social changes in India over the past 20 years. Incomes of educated urban professionals and white-collar workers have steadily risen, while these jobs have not grown as a proportion of the economy. At the same time, educational levels have gone up, creating high levels of competition for increasingly attractive white-collar jobs. In this, the growth in the Indian middle class differs from the growth of the middle class in Europe and the United States, where changes were driven by increasing jobs in white-collar occupations, not just by changing the occupational reward structure.

This dominance of educated professionals among Indian middle classes, even as competition for white-collar jobs is increasing, creates social tensions that have been of great interest to political scientists and social commentators (Varma 1998, Ahmad and Reifeld 2003). However, although much attention has been directed towards the consumer orientation of the growing middle class—some studies even define middle class in terms of consumer durable ownership—little attention has been paid to the social stratification processes that determine access to white-collar jobs and

thereby entry into the great Indian middle class.
Two areas of research require particular attention:
(i) stratification within the educational system; and
(ii) role of social networks in access to white-collar jobs.
With increasing education, a degree or a diploma is necessary but not sufficient for access to well-paying jobs in the formal sector. Consequently, quality of education—or perceived quality—is likely to become increasingly more important. Growth of private schools even in rural areas is a testament to this desire on the part of parents to obtain every possible educational advantage they can for their children. At the same time, it is possible that caste- and family-based social networks will become increasingly important in job searches.

Sonalde Desai

References

Ahmad, Imtiaz and Helmut Reifeld (eds). 2003. *Middle Class Values in India and Western Europe*, New Delhi, Social Science Press.

Das, Gurcharan. 2000. *India Unbound*, New Delhi, Viking.

Desai, Sonalde and Maitreyi Bordia Das. 2004. 'Is Employment Driving India's Growth Surge?' *Economic and Political Weekly*, 39: 345–51.

National Council of Applied Economic Research (NCAER). 2000. *India Market Demographics Report 2000*, New Delhi, NCAER.

Raj, K.N. 1973. 'The Politics and Economics of the "Intermediate Regimes"', *Economic and Political Weekly*, 7 July, pp. 1189–98.

Varma, Pavan. 1998. *The Great Indian Middle Class*, New Delhi, Penguin.

■ Millennium Development Goals

At the United Nations Millennium Summit held in New York in September 2000, the UN Secretary-General agreed to report annually to the General Assembly on the progress made towards achieving the millennium development goals (MDGs). Endorsed so far by 192 states of the world, MDGs are an ambitious agenda for reducing poverty, ending deprivations, and assuring citizens of their human rights. Eight MDGs have been specified (see Box 1), and for each goal one or more quantifiable targets (21 in all) and 60 indicators have been set, mostly for 2015, using 1990 as a benchmark. Effective partnerships between developed and developing countries are seen as fundamental to the realization of these inter-related goals and targets (United Nations 2011a).

Box 1 Eight Millennium Development Goals

Goal 1
Eradicate extreme hunger and poverty
Goal 2
Achieve universal primary education
Goal 3
Promote gender equality and empower women
Goal 4
Reduce child mortality
Goal 5
Improve maternal health
Goal 6
Combat HIV/AIDS, malaria, and other diseases
Goal 7
Ensure environmental sustainability
Goal 8
Develop a global partnership for development

Source: United Nations.

The MDGs derive their significance from the adoption of the Millennium Declaration at the historic Millennium Summit. The Declaration reiterates the importance of six fundamental values for advancing the well-being of humankind: freedom, equality, solidarity, tolerance, respect for nature, and shared responsibility. It also underscores, among other things, the importance of peace, security and disarmament, development and poverty eradication, protecting the vulnerable, as well as protecting our common environment, human rights, democracy, and good governance for making the world a safer and more secure place (United Nations 2011b).

Significance

Indian reactions to the MDGs were initially somewhat sceptical and lukewarm. The perception of MDGs as being promoted largely by experts from the United Nations Secretariat, International Monetary Fund, Organisation for Economic Co-operation and Development, and the World Bank led some to believe that this exercise was yet another imposition of the will of the 'first world' countries on 'third world' countries. Some questioned the choice of goals and asked why critical goals such as abolition of smoking, legalization of abortion, universal recognition of gay and lesbian rights, or reduction in sale of small arms by developed countries had not been included. Feminist and women's groups were unhappy with the narrow focus only on maternal mortality and not more broadly at least on reproductive health. Yet others wondered about the usefulness of prescribing so many narrowly defined technical targets. Some, especially in the government, scoffed at the MDGs because India had set even more ambitious goals for its own development. For instance, the goals of the Tenth Five Year Plan (2002–7) aimed at bringing all children to school by 2003, and for all children to complete five years of schooling by 2007. It also aimed at reducing maternal mortality to 200 per 100,000 live births by 2007 and to 100 by 2012 (GoI 2011a). Many of them believed that the MDGs were appropriate for the set of least developed countries in Sub-Saharan Africa, not for India which had started witnessing rapid economic growth following the initiation of economic reforms in the early 1990s.

In recent years, there has been, for good reason, growing acceptance of the MDGs within the government as well as among non-governmental organizations. First, it is not true that India's performance along many dimensions of human development is far superior to that of Sub-Saharan Africa. For instance, India's adult literacy rate (63 per cent) is the same as the average for Sub-Saharan Africa. On some counts, India fares even worse than Sub-Saharan Africa. For example, 43 per cent of India's children under five are malnourished (underweight) as against an average of 22 per cent for Sub-Saharan Africa (UNICEF 2011). Second, while goal setting by India might be ambitious, it has often been a case of misplaced optimism. For instance, as against the goal of attaining a maternal mortality ratio of 200 by 2007, recent estimates place the figure at 254 for 2004–6 and 230 for 2006–8, which is nowhere close to the target of reaching 100 by 2012. Third, comparative analyses of the success of many East Asian and other economies offer overwhelming evidence that India's economic growth as well as social and political stability remain seriously undermined, if not threatened, by pervasive poverty. India, despite emerging as one of the fastest growing economies in the world today and recording significant progress along many fronts (notably in science, information technology, medicine, and management), has a huge backlog of human poverty, inequalities, visible discrimination, and simmering conflicts. Most recent data from the Government of India, for instance, reveal that close to 450 million people live below the poverty line, 273 million Indians, nearly two-thirds of them women, cannot read and write, some 54 million children below the age of five are malnourished, and over 1.3 million infants die before reaching the age of one. Fourth, the pace of progress towards attaining the MDGs has been slow, uneven, and worrisome. India has much ground to cover on almost every goal. The *Millennium Development Goals—India Country Report 2009* identifies national efforts to reach goals relating to hunger, child survival, maternal mortality rate, and ensuring access to safe drinking water as being slow or off-track (GoI 2011b). The country's performance, for instance, is believed to be 'almost on track' for Target 1—halving the proportion of population below the poverty line between 1990 and 2015. This was the case when the old estimates of poverty showed improvements—from 36 per cent in 1993–4 to 27.6 per cent in 2005. However, according to the recently accepted estimates of poverty by India's Planning Commission based on a revised poverty line, 37.2 per cent of the country's population lives below the poverty line, which is not much different from the situation in 1993–4. Progress in halving, between 1990 and 2015, the proportion of people who suffer from hunger has also been slow. Some 43 per cent of India's children below the age of five are malnourished (underweight), which is among the highest figures in the world. Similarly, even though many positive steps have been taken to universalize primary education, India is far from ensuring that all children enrolled in school receive good quality basic education. Girls in particular face many barriers to education. Barely two out of three Indian children reach Grade 5, and of those completing five years of schooling, many cannot even read and write. In 2010, barely half (53.4 per cent) of the rural children in Grade 5 could read a Grade 2 level text. Similarly, two-thirds of the rural children in Grade 1 could not recognize numbers 1 to 9. Nearly 64 per cent of rural children in Grade 3 could not do two-digit subtraction problems and a similar proportion in Grade 5 could not do simple division problems (Pratham 2011). Again, the Government of India admits that, despite several steps to promote gender equality and empowering women (including the constitutionally mandatory reservation of one-third of seats for women in local elections), 'empowerment of women is still far too slow to reckon. Participation of women in employment and decision making remains far less than that of men and the disparity is not likely to be eliminated by 2015' (GoI 2011b). Girls and women face strong discrimination that manifests itself in significantly fewer freedoms for them. The most shocking finding of the provisional report of the Census of India 2011, for instance, has been the precipitous fall in the already adverse female–male ratio among children of 0–6 years from 945 in 1991 and 927 in 2001 to 914 in 2011 (GoI 2011c). Paradoxically, the decline has been particularly striking among affluent sections and in urban areas where higher literacy levels and higher incomes have gone hand-in-hand with easier access to medical technologies for pre-testing and aborting female foetuses. On Goal 4, namely, reducing child mortality, India's record on child survival remains poor. In 2009, India reported an infant mortality rate (IMR) of 50 deaths per 1,000 live births as against 6 in Malaysia, 13 in Sri Lanka, 12 in Thailand, 26 in the Philippines, 17 in China, and 41 in Bangladesh (UNICEF 2011). Within India, too, the IMR varies considerably from 12 per 1,000 live births in Kerala to 67 in Madhya Pradesh (GoI 2011d). From among the more populous states, only seven states—Delhi, Karnataka, Kerala, Maharashtra, Punjab, Tamil Nadu, and West Bengal—report IMRs that are equal to or less than the IMR for Bangladesh. It is also well-documented that chances of infant survival are lower in rural than in urban areas and among scheduled castes and scheduled tribes. Particularly disturbing is the failure to translate the acceleration in economic growth post-1990 into significant improvements in child survival. In 1990, for example, Bangladesh reported an under-five mortality of 148—25 per cent higher than India's. The situation is very different today. By 2009, Bangladesh reported an under-five mortality of 52—21 per cent lower than India's (66) even though over this period GDP per capita grew faster in India (on average by 4.8 per cent every year) than in Bangladesh (3.4 per cent). The possibility of India's GDP growth rate breaching 10 per cent continues to mesmerize many policymakers who seem to believe in the automatic conversion of growth into human development. Amartya Sen (2011) articulates the dangers of being obsessed with growth:

> My primary concern, however, is that the illusions generated by those distorted perceptions of prosperity may prevent India from bringing social deprivations into political focus, which is essential for achieving what needs to be done for Indians at large through its democratic system. A fuller understanding of the real conditions of the mass of neglected Indians and what can be done to improve their lives through public policy should be a central issue in the politics of India.

Constraints

What holds back India's efforts at addressing the huge backlog of human poverty and accelerating efforts to attain the MDGs? Broadly speaking, there are four serious constraints. The first is financial. No country can assure good quality education for every child, maternal benefits for every mother, safe drinking water, adequate nutrition or healthcare for all, and other basic amenities without adequate resources. It is true that considerable scope exists in India for improving the efficiency and effectiveness of public spending. Plugging leakages, eliminating corruption, and minimizing wastage can greatly enhance social outcomes. However, there is no denying that public expenditures in ensuring access to social services have been low. Take the case of health. Public expenditure on health in India is only around 1.2 per cent of GDP—among the lowest in the world—and nowhere close to the 'at least 2–3 per cent by 2012' pledged by the Government of India in 2005 (GoI 2011c). As a consequence, private expenditure accounts for 78 per cent of the total expenditure on health, which is among the highest in the world and much higher than the out-of-pocket expenditures incurred in China (61 per cent), Sri Lanka (54 per cent), and Thailand (36 per cent) (Shiva Kumar et al. 2011). At one level, the challenge of mobilizing additional domestic resources for development is definitely economic. But it has many political ramifications as well. Public protests and agitations linked to taxes have occurred in many instances. Major opposition often comes from the most prosperous business groups, property owners, and high-income earners. Powerful vested interests and influential lobbies distort patterns of public investment and expenditures, and this gets reflected in several biases that go against the interests of the poor and voiceless in society. Political opposition is also common when it comes to withdrawal of perverse subsidies or even rationalizing of bus fares, and water and electricity tariffs. Here again, corruption and malpractice prevent good governance. India is not such a 'poor' country that it cannot afford such levels of investment. Decisions on public finance need to be guided by economic wisdom and not by political opportunism.

The second serious constraint has to do with an adequate and effective leadership for championing issues of poverty, equity, social justice, and the dignity of human beings. The leadership gap is particularly evident in the government, within politicians and administrators, and in the corporate sector. Effective political, bureaucratic, and community leadership is needed to turn the situation around.

The third constraint has to do with poor monitoring and evaluation systems. Rampant corruption and poor accountability, manifest most starkly in high absenteeism, have greatly undermined the faith in the capacity of the government to deliver public services. India has failed to develop a strong culture of evaluation and public monitoring. Even today, for instance, there are no standardized measures of learning achievements by children, nor are specialized data on health readily available. As a result, public accountability remains weak, and possibilities of effectively restructuring policies and programmes are limited.

The fourth constraint has to do with weak participation. The attainment of the MDGs rests critically on people's participation and empowerment. Contributions by people and local communities in planning and shaping development outcomes have been limited. Particularly striking has been the lack of opportunities for women to participate in and contribute towards development. People get empowered when they begin to enjoy and exercise greater freedoms—economic, social, political, and cultural. This occurs with higher levels of education, improved health and nutritional status, greater economic freedom, improved access to employment and higher earnings, and more meaningful participation in decision making. But investments in these areas have been inadequate. As a result, capacity for local governance remains weak. Democracy received a strong boost with the 73rd and 74th Constitutional Amendments mandating local elections in order to promote local governance. Nevertheless, the practice of democracy leaves much to be desired. The voices of the poor and weak have remained muffled and their interests have often been compromised.

Looking Ahead

India's track record in ending human deprivations may appear somewhat depressing. But future prospects are not. India, unlike many other countries, is uniquely positioned to enjoy a rich demographic dividend from a large young population. The expansion in physical infrastructure is rapidly improving communications and connectivity. New technological innovations are being tapped to improve the quality of public management. Locally elected village-level governments (panchayats) are emerging as important actors in development administration. Women, in particular, are beginning to participate more actively in public decision-making. We also find positive developments in addressing the constraints. The country's economic position is sound. And judicious macroeconomic management is likely to ensure sustained and even accelerated economic growth over the coming decade. Financial allocations to social sectors are beginning to show an upward trend. There is renewed vigour and commitment among the economic and political leadership to eradicate human poverty and realign policies in favour of the poor. Evidence of this can be found in the slew of pro-poor legislations introduced recently, including the Mahatma Gandhi National Rural Employment Guarantee Act (2005), the Right to Information Act (2005), and the Right to Education Act (2009). Many more are in the anvil, including a Food Security Act that seeks to legally entitle different cross-sections of society to food at subsidized prices. Media, civil society organizations, and institutions like the Office of the Comptroller and Auditor General of India are increasingly focusing on and demanding better accountability and management of public resources. The challenge now is to ensure that the benefits of growth get distributed more equitably and contribute to enhancing the capabilities of the poor. Pursuit of the MDGs can contribute significantly.

Ensuring the attainment of the MDGs has implications for public policy, public management, and public action. Policy formulation and prioritization need to be grounded more firmly in a healthy respect for human rights and in the rights-based approach to development. This implies correcting many imbalances and inequities and reassigning priority to the concerns of the poorest and most disadvantaged in society. At the same time, it is important to ensure consistency and coherence in policies—between domestic and global policies, between macro and micro policies, and between private- and public-sector policies. Similarly, there is need to ensure alignment between commitments and strategies, legislation and policy, action plans and budgets. Equally important is to radically improve public management systems and create institutional structures that match new strategies for reaching the poor. Greater coordination and convergence in action are required. Establishing accountability has to become central to public management. Efforts at strengthening capacity at different levels ought to be backed by improved performance monitoring. Most important, a new work ethic and moral code that recognize and respect human dignity are needed to guide public administration. It is important for media and research institutions to intensify and politicize the quality of public discourse and hold debates around many of these issues. Finally, improved public dialogue, enhanced public participation, strengthened public vigilance, and sustained public pressure for improved accountability are essential if the MDGs are to be attained.

Attaining many of the MDGs by 2015 is still feasible; it is also necessary if progress has to be accelerated and sustained. Indeed, this is the only way India can emerge, over the next decade, as a true world leader.

A.K. SHIVA KUMAR

References

Government of India (GoI). 2011a. *Tenth Five Year Plan (2002–2007)*, New Delhi, Planning Commission, available at http://planningcommission.nic.in/plans/planrel/fiveyr/10th/volume1/10th_vol1.pdf, accessed on 21 May 2011.

——. 2011b. *Millennium Development Goals—India Country Report 2009*, Mid-term Statistical Appraisal, New Delhi, Central Statistical Organisation, Ministry of Statistics and Programme Implementation, available at http://www.un.org.in/UNDP/MDG/GOI%20MDG%20Report%202009.pdf, accessed on 21 May 2011.

——. 2011c. 'Provisional Population Totals Paper 1 of 2011 India Series 1', New Delhi, Office of Registrar General and Census Commissioner, available at http://www.censusindia.gov.in/2011-prov-results/prov_results_paper1_india.html, accessed on 21 May 2011.

——. 2011d. 'Sample Registration Bulletin January 2011', New Delhi, Registrar General India, available at http://www.censusindia.gov.in/vital_statistics/SRS_Bulletins/SRS%20Bulletin%20-%20January%202011.pdf, accessed on 21 May 2011.

Pratham. 2011. *Annual Status of Education Report (Aser)-2010*, Mumbai, Pratham.

Sen, Amartya. 2011. 'Quality of Life: India vs. China: The New York Review of Books', 12 May 2011, available at http://www.nybooks.com/articles/archives/2011/may/12/quality-life-india-vs-china/?pagination=false, accessed on 21 May 2011.

Shiva Kumar, A.K., Lincoln C. Chen, Mita Choudhury, Shiban Ganju, Vijay Mahajan, Amarjeet Sinha, and Abhijit Sen. 2011. 'Financing Health Care for All: Challenges and Opportunities', *The Lancet*, 377(9766): 668–79.

United Nations. 2011a. 'Official List of MDG Indicators', The Official United Nations Site for the MDG Indicators, available at http://unstats.un.org/unsd/mdg/Host.aspx?Content=Indicators/OfficialList.htm, accessed on 21 May 2011.

——. 2011b. 'The Millennium Declaration', Resolution Adopted by the General Assembly [without reference to a Main Committee *(A/55/L.2)*] 55/2, United Nations Millennium Declaration, available at http://www.un.org/millennium/declaration/ares552e.htm, accessed on 21 May 2011.

UNICEF. 2011. *The State of the World's Children 2011*, New York, United Nations Children's Fund.

■ Mobility of Population

Migration Trends at Macro Level

Population mobility in the Indian subcontinent has historically been relatively low. Researchers like Kingsley Davis (Davis 1951) have attributed this to the prevalence of the caste system, joint families, traditional values, diversity of language and culture, lack of education, and predominance of agriculture and semi-feudal land relations. By the Davisian logic, improvements in levels of education and in transport and communication facilities, shift of workforce from agriculture to industry and tertiary activities, and so on, would increase mobility. Interestingly, however, an analysis of the trend in population mobility in post-Independence India reveals that, despite significant improvements in education, transport and communication facilities, growth of industries, diversification of the economy, and modernization of norms and values, population mobility at the macro level has declined. A number of micro-level studies have come to similar conclusions (Racine 1997).

The pattern of internal migration (excluding international migrants) has been presented in Table 1 using data from the population census. It may be seen here that mobility of population has declined systematically from 1961 to 2001, both in rural as well as urban areas.

Table 1 Internal Migrants in Various Categories, 1961–2001

	Percentage to total population					Total migrants (in million)
	1961	1971	1981	1991	2001	2001
			Total Migrants			
Intercensal	15.0	12.4	12.2	9.7	9.5	98.3
Intercensal inter-state	2.0	1.6	1.6	1.3	1.6	16.8
Lifetime	30.6	28.7	29.4	26.5	29.2	301.1
Lifetime inter-state	3.3	3.4	3.6	3.3	4.2	42.3
			Male Migrants			
Intercensal	11.3	9.4	8.9	6.1	6.2	32.9
Intercensal inter-state	2.2	1.8	1.6	1.2	1.6	8.5
Lifetime	18.3	17.2	16.6	13.8	16.4	87.2
Lifetime inter-state	3.4	3.4	3.3	2.8	3.7	19.7
			Female Migrants			
Intercensal	19.0	15.7	15.7	13.5	13.2	65.4
Intercensal inter-state	1.7	1.3	1.7	1.5	1.7	8.3
Lifetime	43.7	41.1	43.1	40.3	43.0	213.7
Lifetime inter-state	3.2	3.4	3.9	3.8	4.6	22.7
			Rural Male Migrants			
Intercensal	8.4	7.1	6.3	4.2	4.0	15.2
Intercensal inter-state	0.9	0.8	0.7	0.5	0.6	2.3
Lifetime	13.9	12.9	11.5	9.4	10.5	40.2
Lifetime inter-state	1.4	1.3	1.2	0.9	1.1	4.4
			Urban Male Migrants			
Intercensal	23.8	18.5	16.9	11.7	11.7	17.7
Intercensal inter-state	7.9	5.6	4.4	3.3	4.1	6.2
Lifetime	37.5	33.6	32.4	26.0	31.2	47.0
Lifetime inter-state	12.3	11.2	10.0	8.0	10.2	15.3

Note: Lifetime migrants are by their place of birth, while intercensal migrants are by their place of last residence for reasons of temporal comparability.

Focusing on mobility of men, wherein economic factors are likely to be relatively more important, the decline in the percentage of migrants can be seen to be significant in case of lifetime migrants, intercensal (shifting place of residence during the last decade) migrants, and inter-state intercensal migrants. Recently released data from the Population Census 2001 reveal that the percentages of lifetime migrants have gone up marginally both for men and women during the 1990s. The 2001 figures are nonetheless less than those of the 1960s or 1970s.

Importantly, the share of intercensal migrants has continued to fall almost continuously in all categories during 1961–2001. This implies that the growth rates of (male) intercensal migrants have been less than those of the rest of the population. The decline is markedly steep in the case of male migrants, both in rural as well as urban areas, which can be attributed, besides the rigidities of the agrarian system, growing regionalism, and so on, to inhospitable environment in cities and towns. The share of (intercensal) migrants in the total incremental urban population was 22 per cent during the 1980s, which has come down marginally to 21 per cent during the 1990s. A fall in the rate of urbanization during 1991–2001 also confirms the decline in population mobility in the country. The pattern is similar for female intercensal migrants, although the rate of decline is less than that for males.

National Sample Survey (NSS) data for the past two decades also confirm the declining trend of migration for males, both in rural as well as urban areas, although the fall is less than that reported in the census. The migration rates had declined to all-time lows in 1993, whereafter there has been a slight recovery. The fact that percentages of migrants in 1993 are marginally higher than the figures for 1999 (but less than those for 1983) may be attributed to the more liberal definition of migrants adopted in the 55th round of the NSS (see Kundu 2003). For women, the percentage of female migrants as per NSS data has gone up marginally during the past couple of decades. The general conclusion that thus emerges unmistakably is that mobility of men, which is often linked to the strategy of seeking livelihood, has gone down systematically over the past few decades. Unfortunately, the ghost of overurbanization has weighed heavily on the minds of demographers and urban planners. This has been backed by the phenomenal urban growth observed during the 1950s and 1970s that is now believed to be partly definitional. As a consequence, all official projections of urban population during the 1980s and 1990s, including those of the Planning Commission and the Expert Committee for Population Projections, have erred on the higher side. The recent projections of urban growth made by the United Nations (UNO 1995) are somewhat lower but still not untouched by the overurbanization hypothesis. The current data on urban population and migration seriously question all these projections.

Migration Dynamics—The Regional Dimension

According to the neoclassical models of growth and labour mobility, spatial disparity in development, ceteris paribus, would result in migration from backward to developed states and regions which would help in bringing about optimality in the spatial distribution of economic activities. The mobility pattern observed in India fits well in these models. The analysis of inter-state migrants, attempted on the basis of census as well as NSS data reveals that the less-developed states report a high percentage of net out-migrants. The developed states, on the other hand, turn out to be in-migrating in character.

In recent decades, however, the migration pattern has been different. There has been a steep and consistent decline in the rates of net out-migration from backward states like Bihar, Rajasthan, and Uttar Pradesh. Importantly, Madhya Pradesh and Orissa stand out as exceptions as these report significant inflow of population. This could be explained in terms of massive public-sector investment, resulting in creation of job opportunities in industry and business. The local population, unfortunately, is not able to take advantage of these developments because of low levels of literacy and skills.

Developed states like Karnataka, Maharashtra, Tamil Nadu, and West Bengal that have been attracting large-scale in-migration, now report decline in in-migration rates. The state of Gujarat does not show this declining trend due to its growing dominance on the industrial map of India. Similarly, Haryana reporting high in-migration rates during recent decades can be explained in terms of migration from Punjab due to social instability and communal tensions in the 1980s.

Some scholars have explained the decline in inter-state migration (Mehrotra 1974) in terms of developmental programmes launched by the central and state governments in the post-Independence period. Furthermore, better transport, communication, and commutation facilities are supposed to have reduced the need to shift residence for employment or education, since people can now commute to neighbouring cities and towns. Undoubtedly, there is some truth in these arguments but they are not adequate to explain growing immobility. An analysis of the regional structure of development would discount the regional imbalances hypothesis since inter-state inequality in several dimensions of economic and social development has not declined and in many cases has gone up. A better explanation could possibly be found in the growing assertion of regional identity, education in regional languages up to high school, adoption of Master Plans and land use restrictions at city level, and so on; all these directly or indirectly discourage migration. This would discount the proposition that the mobility of labour, operationalized through market, would ensure optimal distribution of economic activities in space.

Changes in the Composition of Migrants

The most important change in the composition of migration is the sharp decline in the percentage of persons reporting economic factors as the reason for mobility. As many as 36 per cent of the recent rural male migrants (less than one-year duration) had reported new, better employment or transfer as the reason for their migration decision in 1983, as per the NSS data. This has come down to 25 per cent in 1999. For women, the percentage has declined from 5 to 3. Economic factors have become less important in migration decisions among urban migrants as well. For males, the percentage figure has gone down from 46 to 34 while the corresponding figures for women are 8 and 3.[1] The increase in the share of women among migrants under all categories and durations is yet another indication of the growing importance of non-economic factors since marriage and joining the family are the major factors responsible for their mobility.

A related conclusion is that economic deprivation is less of a factor in migration of males now than in preceding decades. The migration rate in rural areas is as high as 23.3 per cent in the category with the highest monthly per capita expenditure (MPCE), going down systematically with expenditure levels. The rate is as low as 4.3 in the lowest class (Table 2). The same is the case in urban areas as well, the corresponding percentages being 43.3 and 10.5. The pattern is identical for women both for rural as well as urban areas. It is important to point out that this is not clinching evidence that economically better-off people are more likely to migrate to avail of new economic opportunities elsewhere, since the expenditure levels reflect the post-migration situation. It is possible that people have moved to a higher consumption expenditure category *after* or *because of* the mobility. However, such post-migration upward movement may not be so high as to render the hypothesis that people in the high expenditure categories are more likely to migrate invalid. Also, the poor are unlikely to shift to top expenditure categories after migration where the percentage of migrants is very high.

Table 2 Percentage of Migrants across Monthly Per Capita Expenditure (MPCE) Classes, 1999–2000

Rural			Urban		
MPCE class (Rs)	Men	Women	MPCE class (Rs)	Men	Women
0–225	4.3	31.6	0–300	10.5	32.1
225–55	3.7	34.2	300–50	13.0	35.6
255–300	4.0	38.0	350–425	13.4	37.3
300–40	4.6	39.8	425–500	19.7	39.9
340–80	4.9	41.3	500–75	21.1	40.9
380–420	5.8	43.2	575–665	23.9	41.2
420–70	6.3	44.3	665–775	27.8	45.3
470–525	7.3	46.1	775–915	30.7	43.6
525–615	8.6	48.6	915–1120	37.1	48.3
615–775	10.7	51.5	1120–1500	41.2	48.6
775–950	14.5	53.0	1500–1925	38.8	47.3
950 & above	23.3	57.0	1925 & above	43.3	49.3
All	6.9	42.6	All	25.7	41.8

The share of in-migrating households to total households in different per capita expenditure categories does not show a clear pattern. The figure happens to be high in some of the low, middle, and high expenditure categories. A similar mixed pattern can be observed in case of percentages of households reporting out-migrating members, outside the state or the country. At best, one could say that the distribution is bimodal, high values occurring at the lowest and highest expenditure classes. From these, one would infer that both poor and rich households are reporting mobility. This, too, would question the proposition that poverty is the key factor in migration.

Interestingly, migration rates among rural households do not vary linearly with size of their landholdings, as per NSS data. Indeed, households having virtually no land (less than 0.01 ha) report the highest migration rate. But then marginal farmers with the smallest landholdings—between 0.01 and 0.20 ha—report low migration. The rates are high again in the middle-level (between 1 and 3 ha) landowning category. Above that, the figures are once again low. The same pattern is observed to hold among scheduled caste (SC) and scheduled tribe (ST) households as well.

Migration rates for SC/ST or for other backward castes (OBC) are around 6 per cent among rural males in 1999–2000 (Table 3). The rate for other (non-backward)

[1]There have been some classificatory changes, as far as the reasons for migration over various NSS rounds are concerned. This has rendered strict temporal comparison somewhat difficult. The definitions, however, have not changed in the last two NSS rounds which reveal that the share of all employment-related migration has gone down during 1993–9, except for urban males.

Table 3 Percentage of Migrants in Different Social Groups

	Rural			Urban		
Social groups	Male	Female	Person	Male	Female	Person
Scheduled tribe	5.6	35.7	20.4	28.2	41.1	34.5
Scheduled caste	6.4	43.4	24.4	22.5	39.3	30.5
Other backward caste	6.5	42.8	24.2	23.7	41.7	32.3
Others	8.1	44.3	25.9	27.6	42.6	34.7
All	6.9	42.6	24.4	25.7	41.8	33.4

castes is over 8 per cent. For women, too, the migration rate for the non-backward classes is marginally higher than that of the others. In urban areas, however, the rates for SC/ST, backward, and other castes are not very different. One may infer that poverty and immiserization, often linked with SC, ST, and OBCs, and push-factor[2] migration do not provide major explanations for population mobility.

In a fast-globalizing economy like India, new employment opportunities are coming up in selective sectors and in a few regions/urban centres. While the poor constitute a large proportion of migrants, a substantial number belong to the middle- and high-income categories, grabbing new opportunities thrown up in the process of globalization. It would, therefore, be erroneous to consider all migrants as destitutes or economically and socially displaced persons, moving from place to place as part of their survival strategy. Furthermore, the fact that the percentage of migrants has declined and their economic and social status is better than that of non-migrants and has even improved over time, reflects barriers of mobility for the poor. With growing regionalism, service provision being based on market affordability, and changes in skill requirements in the urban labour market, the emerging productive and institutional structure has become hostile to newcomers. This has made the migration process selective wherein the poor who are unskilled labourers are finding it difficult to access the livelihood opportunities coming up in developed regions and large cities.

AMITABH KUNDU

References

Davis, Kingsley. 1951. *The Population of India and Pakistan*, New Jersey, Princeton University Press.

[2]As per the 49th Round of the NSS, the percentage of migrant households among STs was as high as 2.7 per cent in rural areas in 1993. The figure for SCs is 0.9 per cent against the national average of 1.1 per cent. Correspondingly, in urban areas, the percentage figure for STs is 2.9 against the SC and national figures of 2.1 and 2.2.

Kundu, A. 2003. 'Urbanisation and Urban Governance: Search for a Perspective beyond Neo-liberalism', *Economic and Political Weekly*, 38(29): 3079–87.

Kundu, A. and S. Gupta. 2000. 'Declining Population Mobility, Liberalisation and Growing Regional Imbalances—The Indian Case', in A. Kundu (ed.), *Inequality, Mobility and Urbanisation*, New Delhi, Indian Council of Social Science Research and Manak Publications.

Mehrotra, G.K. 1974. Birth Place Migration in India, Census of India 1971, *Special Monograph*, No. 1, New Delhi, Government of India.

Racine, Jean Luc (ed.). 1997. *Peasant Moorings: Village Ties and Mobility Rationales in South India*, New Delhi, Sage.

United Nations Organization (UNO). 1995. *The UN Study of World Urbanization Prospects*.

Monetary Policy

Monetary policy refers to that part of public policy pursued by a central bank that influences monetary and other financial conditions with the broader objectives of price stability, sustainable growth, and high employment. The role of monetary policy, as an arm of broad economic policy, has evolved over time in tune with developments in economic theory and empirical findings on changing perceptions of the role of money and interest rates in economic activity with advancements in technology, institutions, and financial markets. The evolution of monetary policy in India is no exception to this general trend.

The conduct of monetary policy is generally assigned to the central bank. The central bank responds to the evolving economic activity within an articulated monetary policy framework, which covers: (i) the objectives of monetary policy; (ii) the analytics of monetary policy focusing on the transmission mechanism; and (iii) operating procedures focusing on operating targets and instruments.

Objectives

Traditionally, central banks have pursued the twin objectives of price stability and growth. A number of central banks have additional objectives of exchange rate stability and financial stability. While these objectives are interrelated, there are trade-offs as well. Faced with multiple objectives that are equally desirable, there remains the problem of assigning to each policy instrument the most appropriate objective.

Accordingly, there is broad consensus, both in academic and policy circles, that monetary policy is best suited to achieving the goal of price stability. Price stability is generally defined as a low and stable order of inflation. For developed countries, such an inflation threshold is considered to be around 2 per cent which could be higher for developing countries depending on their stages of economic development.

A number of prominent central banks including the European Central Bank, Bank of England, and Bank of Japan have adopted price stability as the single objective of monetary policy. However, the Federal Reserve System of the US continues to pursue multiple objectives of monetary policy—maximum employment, stable prices, and moderate long-term interest rates. Central banks in several developing countries have made exchange rate management another important policy objective. In recent years, particularly after the financial crises of the 1990s, the concern for financial stability is an integral part of the central bank's activism.

Historically, in countries which have experienced high inflation or hyperinflation, there is stronger public commitment to price stability as the primary objective of monetary policy. However, most central banks tend to operate on the golden mean of constrained discretion which takes the pragmatic view that within the objective of price stability, monetary policy has to stabilize swings in effective demand as well (Bernanke 2003).

The preamble to the Reserve Bank of India Act, 1934, has spelt out the objectives of the Bank as being 'to regulate the issue of Bank notes and the keeping of reserves with a view to securing monetary stability in India and generally to operate the currency and credit system of the country to its advantage'. Although there is no explicit mandate for price stability, as is the current trend in many countries, maintaining price stability and ensuring an adequate flow of credit to the productive sectors of the economy have evolved as the objectives of monetary policy in India. In essence, monetary policy thus aims to maintain a judicious balance between price stability and economic growth. The relative emphasis on price stability or economic growth is governed by the prevailing circumstances and is spelt out from time to time in the policy announcements of the Bank.

Of late, considerations of financial stability have assumed greater importance in view of the increasing openness of the Indian economy and financial reforms. In the Indian context, financial stability could be interpreted to mean: first, ensuring smooth and uninterrupted payments and settlement system; second, maintenance of a level of confidence in the financial system amongst all the participants and stakeholders; and third, absence of excessive volatility in financial markets that unduly and adversely affects real economic activity. The Reserve Bank of India thus strives to pursue its monetary policy objectives by creating an environment of financial stability.

The Analytics of Monetary Policy

The monetary policy framework largely depends on the underlying relationships between the relevant economic variables. It is also important to assess the stability of such relationships and the effectiveness of the various transmission channels. The transmission mechanism describes how monetary policy action affects output and inflation, the final objectives of monetary policy. In the literature, four sets of transmission channels have been identified: one, the quantum channel, especially relating to money supply and credit; two, the interest rate channel; three, the exchange rate channel; and four, the asset price channel. How these channels function in a given economy depends on the stage of development of the economy and its underlying financial structure. There can be considerable feedbacks and interactions among the various transmission channels which need to be carefully assessed for a proper understanding of the transmission mechanism.

In the design of monetary policy, another important consideration is that since the central bank may not be in a position to directly achieve its ultimate objectives, monetary policy is often formulated in terms of an intermediate target. For example, in a monetary targeting framework, a suitable monetary aggregate is considered an intermediate target based on the basic relationship between money, output, and prices. Exchange rate as an intermediate target can be suitable for small open economies, setting the exchange rate against a low-inflation anchor country. This would, however, entail loss of independence in steering domestic interest rates. The 'impossible trinity', that is, incompatibility between fixed exchange rate, open capital account, and independent monetary policy is well recognized by central banks world over. Direct interest rate targeting has been adopted in countries with higher levels of financial market integration. There have been attempts to combine both interest rate and exchange rate through the monetary conditions index (MCI).

In the context of improving transparency, the recent trend has been towards direct inflation targeting. Adoption of explicit inflation targeting as the final goal of monetary policy involves the preparation of an inflation forecast, which, in a way, serves the purpose of both an intermediate target and final objective. The prerequisites for inflation targeting include a considerable degree of operational autonomy or independence for the central bank, flexible exchange rate conditions, well-developed financial markets, and absence of fiscal dominance.

In view of the growing complexities of macroeconomic management, several central banks, including the European Central Bank, have placed reliance on a broad set of economic and leading indicators rather than focusing on an intermediate target or a direct inflation target. The Federal Reserve has traditionally been following a more broad-based approach to the conduct of monetary policy in the US.

Monetary policy in India used to be conducted till 1997–8 with broad money (M_3) as an intermediate target, which amounted to regulating money supply consistent with the expected growth in real income and a projected level of inflation. In practice, the monetary targeting framework was used in a flexible manner with feedback from developments in the real sector. Questions were raised about the appropriateness of such a framework with the changing interrelationship between money, output, and prices in the wake of financial reforms and opening up of the economy. The Working Group on Money Supply (RBI 1998) sought to address some of these issues. The most significant observation of the Group was regarding the changing nature of the transmission mechanism as it highlighted that the interest rate channel was gaining in importance. In line with this thinking, the RBI has switched over to a multiple-indicator approach from 1998–9 wherein interest rates or rates of return in different markets (money, capital, and government securities), along with such data as on currency, credit extended by banks and financial institutions, fiscal position, trade, capital flows, inflation rate, exchange rate, refinancing and transactions in foreign exchange available on high-frequency basis, are juxtaposed with output data for drawing policy perspectives.

Operating Procedures: Instruments and Targets

Operating procedures pertain to day to day implementation of monetary policy by central banks through various instruments that can broadly be classified into direct and indirect instruments. Typically, direct instruments include required cash and/or liquidity reserve ratios and directed credit and administered interest rates. The cash reserve ratio (CRR) determines the level of reserves (central bank money or cash) banks need to hold against their deposit liabilities. Similarly, the liquidity reserve ratio requires banks to maintain a part of their deposit liabilities in the form of liquid assets (for example, government securities). Credit and interest rate directives take the form of prescribed targets for allocation of credit to preferred sectors/industries and prescription of deposit and lending rates.

The indirect instruments generally operate through the price channel which covers repurchase transactions (repos), outright transactions in securities (open market operations [OMOs]), standing facilities (refinance), and market-based discount window. For example, if the central bank desires to inject liquidity for a short period, it could do so by providing liquidity to banks in exchange for securities at a desired interest rate, reversing the transaction at a predetermined time. Similarly, if the central bank desires to influence liquidity on an enduring basis, it could resort to OMOs involving outright purchase (and sale) of securities without any buy-back obligations.

While OMOs including repo transactions operate at the discretion of the central bank, standing facilities make available limited liquidity which could be accessed by eligible market participants (generally banks) at their discretion. Standing facilities can be of two types: uncollateralized deposit facility with the central bank and marginal collateralized lending facility by the central bank. A market-based discount window makes available reserves either through direct lending or through rediscounting or purchase of financial assets held by banks.

While direct instruments are effective, they are considered inefficient in terms of their impact on the financial market. On the other hand, the use of indirect instruments depends on the development of the supporting financial markets and institutions. These instruments are usually directed at attaining a prescribed value of the operating target, typically bank reserves and/or a very short-term interest rate (usually the overnight inter-bank rate).

The optimal choice between price and quantity targets would depend upon the sources of disturbances in the goods and money markets. In reality, it often becomes difficult to trace the sources of instability. Hence monetary policy is implemented by fixing, at least over some short time interval, the value of an operating target. In a single-period context, the choice of the level of the target amounts to setting a rule for monetary policy. However, in a dynamic context, the connection is less straightforward. Indeed, deviation from a target could occur, either intended or unintended, which may impart an inflationary bias when monetary policy is conducted with discretion (Kydland and Prescott 1977). In order to address the problem of dynamic inconsistency, rule-based solutions are emphasized in the literature, for example, monetary rule (changes in money supply at a predetermined rate) and Taylor-type rule (changes in interest rate based on deviation of growth and inflation from their potential/desired levels). While a rule-based system imparts transparency, providing certainty about future policy response, it becomes ineffective in its response to unanticipated shocks given its inflexibility. In practice, therefore, central banks follow an approach of constrained discretion.

The operating procedures of monetary policy of most central banks have largely converged on one of the following three variants: (i) a number of central banks, including the US Federal Reserve, estimate the demand for bank reserves and then carry out OMOs to target short-term interest rates (the Federal Funds Rate in the case of the USA); (ii) some other central banks, including the Bank of Japan, estimate market liquidity and carry out OMOs to target the bank reserves, while allowing interest rates to adjust; and (iii) a growing number of central banks, including the European Central Bank, modulate monetary conditions in terms of both the quantum and price of liquidity, through a mix of OMOs, standing facilities, and minimum reserve requirement and changes in the policy rate with the objective of containing overnight market interest rate within a narrow corridor of interest rate targets.

In the Indian context, reserve money was used as the operating target in the monetary-targeting framework until the mid-1990s. In the current monetary policy framework, with growing interlinkages in the financial market, reliance on direct instruments has been reduced and liquidity management in the system is carried out through OMOs in the form of outright purchases/sales of government securities and daily repo and reverse repo operations under the liquidity adjustment facility (LAF) (Reddy 2002). The LAF has enabled the Reserve Bank to modulate short-term liquidity under varied financial market conditions, including large capital inflows from abroad. In addition, it has enabled the Reserve Bank to set a corridor for the short-term interest rates consistent with policy objectives. This has also facilitated bringing down the CRR of banks without engendering liquidity pressure. These operations are supplemented by access to the RBI's standing facilities. In this new operating environment, changes in reverse repo/repo and/or the Bank Rate have emerged as interest rate signals.

Although there is no explicit interest-rate target in view of the evolving nature of the financial market and presence of nominal rigidities in determination of interest rates in certain segments of the market, a great deal of reliance has been placed in recent years on interest rates and exchange rates in the day-to-day conduct of monetary policy. In the context of increasing openness of the economy and a market-determined exchange rate, the large capital inflows witnessed in recent years have posed a major challenge in the conduct of monetary and exchange rate management. A critical issue in this regard is whether the capital flows are temporary or permanent in nature. The recent episode of large capital flows prompted a debate in India on the need for exchange rate adjustment. In a scenario of uncertainty facing the monetary authorities in determining temporary or permanent nature of inflows, it is prudent to presume that such flows are temporary till such time that they are firmly established to be of a permanent nature.

The liquidity impact of large inflows was managed till the year 2003–4, largely through the day-to-day LAF and OMOs. In the process, the stock of government securities available with the RBI declined progressively and the burden of sterilization increasingly fell on LAF operations. In order to address these issues, the RBI signed in March 2004, a memorandum of understanding (MOU) with the Government of India for issuance of Treasury Bills and dated government securities under the Market Stabilization Scheme (MSS). The intention of the MSS is essentially to differentiate liquidity absorption of a more enduring nature by way of sterilization from the day-to-day normal liquidity management operations. The ceiling on the outstanding obligations of the government under the MSS is initially indicated but is subject to revision through mutual consultation. The issuances under the MSS are matched by an equivalent cash balance held by the government in a separate identifiable cash account maintained and operated by the RBI. The operationalization of the MSS to absorb liquidity of more enduring nature has considerably reduced the burden of sterilization on the LAF window.

In its monetary operations, the RBI uses multiple instruments to ensure that appropriate liquidity is maintained in the system so that all legitimate requirements of credit are met, consistent with the objective of price stability. Towards this end, the Bank pursues a policy of active demand management of liquidity through OMOs including LAF, MSS, and CRR, using the policy instruments at its disposal flexibly as and when the situation warrants.

Emerging Challenges

The major challenge currently faced is the conduct of policy in surplus liquidity conditions. Given the increasing openness of the economy, the stance of monetary policy in major economies and the direction of international interest rates have assumed significance for the conduct of monetary policy. Globally, volatile movements in asset prices have posed challenges to financial stability. In India, given the conservative lending and investment policies of banks, it has not been a major issue. However, with the current trend towards diversified lending, credit penetration, and liberalized investments, asset prices would need to be closely watched for their implication for maintaining financial stability. Another factor which would have significant impact on the conduct of monetary policy is the ongoing modernization of the payments system with the introduction of real-time gross settlement (RTGS). The gradual e-monetization can shrink cash demand and thus the monetary authority's balance sheet, reducing seigniorage revenue. However, the central bank's ability to influence the nominal rate of interest is eventually an issue of political economy and the government can always require settlement through central bank money.

Conduct of monetary policy, even in the best of times, is complex since it has to be forward looking and based on current and sometimes inadequate data relative to rapid changes. Additional complexities arise in the case of an emerging market like India, which is transiting from a relatively closed to a progressively open economy. In an environment of increasing capital flows, narrowing interest rate differentials, and surplus liquidity conditions, exchange rate movement tends to have strong linkages with interest rate movements and poses the challenge of an integrated view on interest rates and exchange rate developments for monetary management. Therefore, policy coordination assumes greater significance in an increasingly synchronized business-cycle environment linked by trade and capital flows.

Y.V. Reddy

References

Bernanke, Ben. 2003. 'Constrained Discretion and Monetary Policy', *BIS Review*, 5.

Kydland, F.E. and E.C. Prescott. 1977. 'Rules rather than Discretion: The Inconsistency of Optimal Plans', *Journal of Political Economy*, June, 85(3). 473–91.

Reddy, Y.V. 2002. 'Monetary and Financial Sector Reforms in India: A Practitioner's Perspective', presented at the Indian Economy Conference, Program on Comparative Economic Development, Cornell University, 19–20 April.

Reserve Bank of India (RBI). 1998. *Report of the Working Group on Money Supply: Analytics and Methodology of Compilation* (Chairman: Y.V. Reddy), Mumbai, RBI.

Monsoon

A monsoon is defined as a seasonal shift in wind direction. It is a word derived from the Arabic '*mausim*', meaning season. In a true monsoon climate, there is a typical shift in seasonal wind patterns, causing a drastic change in the general precipitation and temperature pattern. There are two Indian monsoons: the *south-west monsoon* and the *north-east monsoon*. The south-west monsoon, which is the main monsoon, takes place during the four months of June to September, and it produces most of the annual rainfall in the country. The north-east monsoon begins by November. It, in contrast, supplies only a fifth of the country's rainfall, and it covers only the states of Tamil Nadu, West Bengal, and Karnataka.

The orography over India influences monsoon circulations and associated rains. The northern part is bounded by mountains: the Himalayas in the north; the hill ranges from Arakan Yoma to the Patkai hills in the east; and the Hidukush mountains to the Kirthar range in the west. A chain of ranges higher than 2,000 m runs between latitudes 30° to 40° north and from about 40° to 100° east. These ranges practically block the north–south movement of air and heat in the lower troposphere. There are two branches of the south-west monsoon: the *Bay of Bengal* branch and the *Arabian Sea* branch.

The Indian subcontinent begins to heat up in March. Land surface temperature tends to peak in May, and its large difference from sea surface temperature results in a reversal of winds from the sea towards land. This reversal is intensified by the location of the Himalayas and Hindukush mountains; consequently, during the monsoon period, a large low-pressure area exists over Southwest Asia. The winds blow from the south-west, and the orography traps moisture within the region, producing intense convective weather systems associated with widespread rainfall. The onset of the monsoon over Kerala is around 1 June, and it covers the entire country by 15 July. The monsoon starts withdrawing from the extreme north-west by the first week of September.

All-India summer rainfall from June to September is about 89 cm. The summer rainfall during this period is more than 100 cm along the entire west coast and in the north-eastern states, and peaks at more than 250 cm in Meghalaya, coastal Karnataka, and the Konkanpatti, Goa region. The seasonal rainfall is less than 100 cm over the rest of the country, and it is less than 20 cm over western Rajasthan, Jammu and Kashmir, and Tamil Nadu.

One of the main features of the monsoon is its variability; whether in absolute/national terms from year to year, or in temporal and spatial terms within a single year. This, of course, has important/drastic implications for Indian agriculture. As much as two-thirds of Indian crop land is unirrigated and hence completely dependent on rainfall. Total seasonal rainfall has varied between a low of 66 cm in 1918 to a high of 108 cm in 1917 (other records include 67 cm in 1972 and 107 cm in 1961).

The year-to-year variability depends upon two ocean atmospheric interaction phenomena. The first, El-Nino, is an abnormal warming of the eastern and central Pacific south of the equator that tends to occur towards the end of December and persists for several months. The second, called the Southern Oscillation (SO), refers to fluctuations in atmospheric pressure over the eastern and western Pacific Ocean in the southern hemisphere.

There is no one-to-one direct relationship between El-Nino/SO and all-India rainfall in the south-west monsoon. While all El-Nino years in the Pacific Ocean were followed by drought years in the Indian region, not all drought years have been El-Nino years. The opposite phase of El-Nino (La Nina), moreover, was generally, though not always, associated with abundant rains.

The distribution of monsoon rainfall over the four months from June to September can also be highly variable. There can be some nearly dry spells within the four monsoon months. Precipitation in July—the most important month for the *kharif* (summer) crop—has varied between 12.4 per cent (in 2002) and 32.3 per cent (in 1988) of the total rainfall during the year. Similarly, the regional distribution of rainfall across India's 36 meteorological subdivisions can also be erratic. During 8 of the 61 normal monsoon years within the period 1901–2005, more than 35 per cent of the sub-divisions received either deficient (–20 per cent to –59 per cent) or excess (+20 per cent or more) rains.

During winter, the air above the Indian landmass cools and begins to sink, forming a high-pressure area over most parts of the country. Dry and cold north-west winds from the north circumnavigate the Himalayas, and they emerge over the north-eastern parts of the country to flow south-west. This generates the north-east monsoon along the south-eastern coastline during November and December.

India has two crop seasons: kharif, or the summer crop, and *rabi*, or the winter crop. The kharif crop, particularly in the unirrigated areas, depends largely on the monsoon. Even the rabi crop depends quite a bit on the monsoon, including the south-west monsoon, because of its effect on water in the reservoirs during the winter months.

During the 1950s and 1960s, the Indian economy's growth rate was fairly close to the growth rate of the agricultural sector, which, in turn, was closely associated with the monsoon. This relationship, however, has become weaker over time, with the share of agriculture in overall GDP declining from about 57.4 per cent in 1950–1 to about 20.4 per cent in 2004–5. Consequently, the economy's growth rate has started to demonstrate considerable resilience to the vagaries of the monsoon. For example, in spite of drought-like conditions in 2004–5, the economy managed to grow at 6.9 per cent. This resilience, however, conceals a lot of the shadows that monsoon-related uncertainties cast on India's economic performance and welfare. About 57 per cent of the total workforce of India depends on agriculture for earning a livelihood, and erratic rainfall often leads to build-up of price pressures in some essential commodities, such as onions.

The relation between rainfall and agricultural yield or output is a complex one, and it involves the total amount of rainfall, and its temporal and spatial distribution, within the crop season. Furthermore, even the relationship between the amount of rainfall and yield, given other things, is unlikely to be monotonic (for example linear or logarithmically linear). There is an optimum amount of rain for every crop, and postulation of a monotonic relationship runs the risk of misspecification with no room for the harmful effects of either a flood or a drought. It is for this reason that some economists suggest the need for a crop-specific rainfall index with the harmful effects of both a drought and flood incorporated appropriately.

ASHOK K. LAHIRI

References

Lahiri, Ashok K. and Prannoy L. Roy. 1985. 'Rainfall and Supply Response: A Study of Rice in India', *Journal of Development Economics*, 18: 315–34.

Ramage, C.S. 1971. '*Monsoon Meteorology*', New York, Academic Press.

Rao, Y.P. 1976. 'Southwest monsoon', Meteorological monograph, Synoptic Meteorology No. 1/1976, June.

■ Monsoon and Economic Activity

However out of place it may seem in the present technology-driven 21st century world, the annual fate of Indian agriculture is still crucially decided by the quality of the monsoon. A good monsoon typically raises the prospects of a good harvest; a drought or a flood invariably depresses them. In itself this is undesirable enough, but what is worse is that some believe that through an agriculture–industry linkage, the state of the monsoon also determines the levels of activities in the rest of the economy. If this belief contains some element of truth, the Indian economy is prone to fluctuations at the whims of the rain god.

Probably this is a manifestation of underdevelopment. Developed countries, having a small fraction of their national income coming from the agricultural sector, are naturally protected from agricultural cycles. Even technologically, they are better at insulating their agricultural production from the vagaries of nature. Be that as it may, the Indian economy should also have exhibited a gradual decline in its dependence on the monsoon because over time there has certainly been a sharp fall in the importance of the agricultural sector in the country. After all, one must reckon with the fact that the share of agriculture and allied activities in Indian GDP was only 14.6 per cent in 2009–10 and 14.2 per cent in the year after as compared to 19 per cent in 2004–5 and about a quarter at the beginning of the new millennium. The fall in the share of agriculture, however, has not been reflected through a decline in the power of agriculture to shape the fate of the economy, for as a provider of employment, agriculture continues to be the single-most important sector, still employing more than 50 per cent of the employed labour force of the country. Consequently, the domination of the rain god continues to persist.

One can hardly doubt that in India the extent and nature of rainfall continues to be a major determinant of agricultural output. This, in turn, reflects the fact that irrigation facilities in the country have still been inadequate. Indeed, in 2007–8, only 54.5 per cent of the total land under cereals production and only 16.2 per cent of the land devoted to the production of pulses was irrigated. Consequently, food grains production, which comprises of cereals and pulses, was undertaken in land of which only 46.8 per cent was irrigated. This implies that the uncontrollability of agricultural output has remained a problem for the government and this volatility is also recognized in official documents like the annual *Economic Survey* of the Government of India where every year a whole section is devoted to the nature and extent of the current monsoon.

The quality of the monsoon, therefore, affects the livelihood of hundreds of people within the agricultural sector. But the more important question is whether the performance of the agricultural sector significantly affects economic activity in other sectors, especially the industrial sector, as well. Agriculture, so far as textbook economics goes, helps the industrial sector essentially in two different ways. First, it supplies inputs to be used in the industrial sector and, second, it provides a market for industrial goods. With the importance of traditional agro-based industries gradually going down, we shall ignore the role of agriculture as a supplier of inputs and focus only on the second aspect of agriculture–industry relationship.

How does agriculture work as an outlet for industrial goods? The standard argument is that higher output in the agricultural sector translates into higher agricultural income, which in turn, creates higher demand for industrial goods. The argument sounds apparently reasonable, but does not stand a closer scrutiny. The trouble is that there is no guarantee that agricultural income would rise if there is an increase in agricultural output. The reason is straightforward. An increase in output leads to a fall in prices and so the revenue or the income of the farmers, which is the product of the price and the quantity sold, may either go up or down. In fact, demand for agricultural goods is rather *inelastic*, that is, a fall in price leads to a relatively small increase in demand. So to make the market absorb the increased output, a large fall in prices is necessary. A large fall in prices, in turn, implies a fall in the income of the farmers. In other words, an increase in agricultural output is likely to *reduce* farm income instead of increasing it. Indeed, we do hear about farmers complaining about over production, low prices, and of too much supply in the market.

There is, however, an indirect channel through which an expansion in agricultural output may raise industrial demand. Given that demand for agricultural goods, especially that for food grains, is inelastic, an increase in output and a consequent fall in prices lead to a fall in the total revenue of farmers. But this also means that consumers outside the agricultural sector are spending less on agricultural goods. So they must be spending more on industrial goods. This, in turn, should increase industrial demand. This increase in demand, however, has to be weighed against the fall in demand coming from the agricultural sector. Demand for industrial goods coming from the agricultural sector should fall because farm incomes are falling due to a fall in farm prices. Demand coming from within is increasing because the buyers have to spend less on food. The net effect on industrial demand may still be positive, but the magnitude is not likely to be big, surely not as big as is needed to presume that agriculture is a strong determinant of industrial performance.

For the sake of completeness, it should also be mentioned that classical economists had identified a third channel through which agricultural production might possibly affect industrial output. In the classical scheme, wages in the industrial sector are indexed to the price of food grains. Classical economists like David Ricardo believed that an increase in the supply of food grains, reducing the price of food, reduces wage rates for industries and makes industrial production a more profitable business. This, in turn, tends to expand industrial output and employment. In fact, there was a long debate in 19th century England between David

Ricardo and his contemporary Thomas Malthus as to whether it was advisable to repeal the Corn Laws, which had imposed artificial barriers on imports of food grains from abroad. Repeal of the Corn Laws would have paved the way for cheaper imports of food grains from the colonies. Malthus was against such imports on the ground that they would hurt the farmers, but Ricardo was all for the repeal because he thought that it would reduce the domestic price of food grains, reducing industrial wages and increasing industrial production. Can we use the Ricardian argument to put forward the hypothesis that there is a strong relationship between agricultural production and industrial output in India? Can we simply say that a good monsoon leads to a bumper harvest, depresses the price of food, reduces industrial wages, and hence expands industrial production by making it more remunerative?

There are two problems with using this classical argument to establish the relationship between industry and agriculture in the Indian context, and probably in any real context. First, the classical argument presumes that industrial wages are tied to food prices, that is, real wages are fixed in terms of food. This may not be a good assumption; in India real wages in terms of food, both in the formal and the informal sectors, seem to be increasing over time. Second, at least formal wages, which are arrived at through collective bargaining, are indexed to a basket of goods in which food is just one item, though an important one. The two problems, taken together, would suggest that the simple mechanism of the agriculture–industry link as conceived by classical economists may not work.

There is yet another channel which could explain the co-movement of industry and agriculture. This is the channel of procurement of food grains and attempted price stabilization by the government. It is well known that before the harvest, the government typically announces a price for each important crop and after the harvest it procures the crop at the pre-announced price. Then over the year the procured food grains are distributed through the public distribution system. Procurement is an important economic activity and over the years procurement of food grains as a percentage of production has steadily increased. For example, procurement of rice and wheat as a percentage of total output increased from 14.6 per cent in 1992–3 to 25.74 per cent in 2001–2. After going down slightly in 2003–4 to 24.08 per cent, the proportion increased again to 25.26 per cent in 2004–5, and further to 36.56 per cent for rice and 31.44 per cent for wheat in 2009–10.

How does increasing procurement by the government explain the agriculture–industry linkage? Clearly, procurement of stocks in a year of bumper harvest prevents the market price from crashing. With the price remaining stable and the quantity produced going up, farm income unambiguously goes up in a year of good harvest. This leads to an increased demand for industrial goods. The supply side remaining more or less unchanged, the increased demand is translated into an expansion of the industrial sector. Similarly, in a year of bad harvest, the government should ideally release more stocks to the market than it would procure, thereby preventing the market price to increase. This, in turn, would reduce farm income and consequently the demand for industrial goods coming from the agricultural sector.

Whether this mechanism of price stabilization is actually at work to establish an agriculture–industry linkage is ultimately an empirical question. Now, if the government were seriously concerned with food price stabilization, one would observe that in years of good harvests government stocks are piling up while they are being run down when output is low. In other words, one should observe a statistically significant positive relationship between production and government stock holding. Unfortunately, by regressing government stocks on the level of production for the period 1971–2 to 2009–10, we find no statistically significant relationship between the two either for rice or for wheat. The same negative result is obtained for both rice and wheat when we regress change in stocks on change in output. This tends to imply that no serious attempt of price stabilization has been made by the government and, therefore, no mechanism can be established for agriculture–industry link in this regard.

In short, contrary to the common belief that in India a good monsoon and a consequent increase in agricultural output gives a big impetus to industrial demand, we find no compelling reason as to why economic activity in sectors outside agriculture would depend on agricultural performance and the monsoon. In the final analysis, however, the question is empirical. The empirical relationship between agricultural performance and the monsoon is quite strong. The real question is about the empirical link between agriculture and industry.

When we regress indices of industrial production on current and lagged output levels of food grains for 1981–2 to 2009–10, we find that statistically a very strong and positive relationship exists between the two. A moment's reflection, however, would tell us that since both industrial production and agricultural output have been growing over time, probably due to capital formation and technical progress, an OLS regression might give an erroneous result that the two variables are causally related. Once we de-trend the two series by taking first differences of the logarithms of the variables and then run an OLS regression, no statistically significant relationship can be established between the two. This verifies our theoretical arguments that the fate of Indian industry is not dependent on agricultural performance or the quality of the monsoon.

Two conclusions emerge from this analysis. First, the performance of the secondary and the tertiary sectors in India has no reason to fluctuate at the whims of the rain god. Second, within the agricultural sector, the fates of millions, more than half of the population to be more exact, still depend on the uncertain yearly monsoon and this uncertainty can be reduced partly by absorbing an increasing number of these people in the industrial sector and partly by providing more irrigation to the agricultural sector.

Abhirup Sarkar

N

■ National Income

The conceptual background, recommendations of the National Income Committee, methods of construction of the available time series on national income, the pattern of economic growth, sources of growth, and inter-state income inequality in India in the post-reform era are the subject matter of this entry.

National income and net national product (NNP) are synonymous. NNP is the value of the total output of the economy calculated without double counting, that is, GNP (gross national product), less allowance for depreciation (D) of the capital assets used in the production process. Hence, NNP = GNP – D.GNP may be distinguished from GDP (gross domestic product). National product is what is produced by normal residents of the country within the country or abroad. Domestic product is what is produced within the country by normal residents and foreigners. There has been a shift of interest first from NNP to GNP, and subsequently to GDP in academic discussions and official publications.

GDP can be calculated by totaling the gross value added, that is, value of gross output minus value of raw materials. This method of calculation is known as the 'output' or 'value added' approach. Alternatively, GDP can be calculated by summing up the returns to the different factors of production—labour, capital, and entrepreneurship. That is, GDP = wages and salaries + rent + profit. This method is known as the income approach. GDP at factor cost equals GDP at market prices minus taxes plus subsidies and other transfer payments. The variant, GDP at factor cost, is the commonly used measure of national income.

National income calculated from the relevant monetary magnitudes for the year in question is referred to as national income at current prices. For inter-temporal analysis, national income at constant prices is the appropriate measure. The contribution of each sector is valued at the base year prices to obtain the real output of the sector. The sum of the real outputs for different sectors is taken as the national income at constant prices. Such a method may not be entirely satisfactory. However, it may be better than using some overall price index as a deflator.

There are various complexities, qualifications, and ambiguities in applying general principles for a practical calculation of national income aggregates. The data requirements are very heavy. The quality of the estimates depends on the accuracy of the data sets and appropriateness of data adjustment procedures.

Recommendations of the National Income Committee

India has a long tradition of estimating national income by individual scholars. Sivasubramanian (2000: 426–7) briefly reviewed the exercises by Naoroji for 1867–8, Atkinson for 1875 and 1895, and Digby for 1898–9. He listed 29 point estimates by different scholars for individual years covering the period 1900–46. Several of these estimates did not cover the native states, their geographical coverage being limited to British India. Some estimates excluded the service sector. The estimates for a given year are not comparable on account of the differences in concepts, geographical coverage, and data bases. The quality of most of them leaves much to be much desired.

Recognizing the importance of national income data for formulating policy and development planning, the Government of India set up the National Income Committee (NIC) in 1949 with P.C. Mahalanobis as its Chairman and D.R. Gadgil and V.K.R.V. Rao as members. The committee had the benefit of advice from Simon Kuznets, J.R.N. Stone, and J.B.D. Derksen. It prepared the first set of official estimates of national income (NNP) for 1948–9 to 1950–1 at current and constant (1948–9) prices. It identified the data gaps and made a number of recommendations for improving the databases and for promoting further work and research on national income. It drew up a framework for national accounts. NIC thus laid the foundations for estimating national income and related aggregates in India on sound lines. The methodology adopted by NIC was on the lines of the approach devised by V.K.R.V. Rao for his estimate for British India for 1931–2.

Official Estimates for the Post-Independence Era

Official estimates of national income and related aggregates are available from the year 1948–9 onwards. The NIC methodology was adopted and refinements introduced continually. The Central Statistical Organisation, recently renamed as the Central Statistics Office (CSO), Government of India, has been in-charge of the preparation and publication of the estimates. The scope of the estimates has been progressively widened. Since 1975, the estimates have been published under the title, National Accounts Statistics (NAS). The base year of the estimates at constant prices was changed several times, from 1948–9 to 1960–1 in 1967, 1970–1 in 1978, 1980–1 in 1988, 1993–4 in 1999, 1999–2000 in 2006, and 2004–5 in 2010. At present, GDP estimates at factor cost by industry of origin at 1999–2000 prices are available for the years 1950–1 to 2003–4, and at 2004–5 prices for the years 2004–5 to 2010–11. Since 1999–2000, quarterly estimates of GDP have been published by CSO. Quarterly estimates are now available with a time lag of two months. CSO has been compiling estimates of rural and urban incomes in terms of net domestic product (NDP) for the base years of the National Accounts Statistics (NAS) series since the NAS 1970–1 series. These rural and urban estimates are now available for the years 1970–1, 1980–1, 1993–4, 1999–2000, and 2004–5. A detailed review of the methodology and databases is undertaken whenever the base year is changed. Workforce estimates available from the decennial population censuses and quinquennial surveys on employment and unemployment conducted by NSSO are used in the revision of the series. The 1993–4, 1999–2000, and 2004–5 base year series incorporated several of the recommendations of the 1993 System of National Accounts (SNA) framed by the UN.

For compiling GDP estimates, the economy is divided into three broad sectors: agriculture (primary), industry (secondary), and services (tertiary). The value added or output approach is adopted for the sub-sectors of agriculture, forestry and logging, fishing, mining and quarrying, registered manufacturing, and construction. The income approach is used for the other sub-sectors.

The domestic product estimates at factor cost by industry of origin fall into two broad categories depending upon the nature of the database: direct estimates and indirect estimates. Direct estimates are based on regularly available annual data. Indirect estimation is resorted to when regular annual data are not available. In such cases, periodic benchmark survey-based estimates are constructed for the survey year and they are extrapolated backward or forward on the basis of physical indicators of activity in the sector.

Direct estimates mostly relate to the 'organized' sector while indirect estimates relate to the 'unorganized' sector. 'Direct estimates' have a lower margin of error than 'indirect estimates'. The share of 'direct estimates' in aggregate GDP rose from 57.6 per cent in the 1970–1 base series to 63.7 per cent in the 1980–1 base series, and further to 89.6 per cent in the 1993–4 base series. For certain sectors, the share of direct estimates was as low as 26.6 per cent (forestry sector).

A very detailed and informative review of the methodology and data aspects of the 1993–4 NAS base year series is provided in Volume II of the Report of the National Statistical Commission headed by C. Rangarajan. The report, which was submitted in 2001, contained a critical account of the decline in the quality and reliability of the basic data sets and recommended several improvements. The permanent National Statistical Commission (NSC) established in 2005 has a major task to perform to improve the quality of data in different fields, including NAS.

CSO's annual NAS white paper presents current and constant price aggregates of GDP and NDP by economic activity, consumption expenditure, savings, capital formation, capital stock, public-sector transactions, and disaggregated statements, as well as four consolidated accounts of the nation.

Time Series Estimates: 1900–46

The credit for constructing a continuous and long time-series of national income estimates for the period 1900–1 to 1946–47 for undivided India including the native states goes to Sivasubramanian (2000) who presented his series in his PhD dissertation completed at the Delhi School of Economics in 1965. The concepts and methods employed by him were broadly similar to those adopted by V.K.R.V. Rao and the National Income Committee. He published his revised series in 2000 taking into account the suggestions and criticisms of well-known economists Heston and Maddison, among others. This is the best available series for the first half of the 20th century.

For estimating national income by industrial origin, the economy was divided into three broad sectors: primary, secondary, and tertiary. Each of these sectors was further sub-divided into a number of sub-sectors and their contribution was estimated separately. The 'value added' approach was followed for all the sub-sectors in the primary sector and for the mining, large-scale industry, and house property sub-sectors. The 'income' approach was adopted for the rest of the sub-sectors. Net factor income from abroad was estimated separately and added to net domestic product (NDP) to obtain NNP. For constant price series, 1938–9 was selected as the base year.

Pattern of Economic Growth

Economic growth, usually measured in terms of the growth in GDP of a country, has received considerable attention during the past two decades or so. The growth performance of the Indian economy and its three broad sectors since 1900 is summarized in Table 1.

Several important features of growth are noteworthy. First, in the pre-Independence period from 1900 to 1947, the average annual rate of growth was a mere 0.9 per cent and per capita growth was close to zero. The dominant agricultural sector fared the worst. Second, there was considerable acceleration of growth to around 3.5 per cent a year during 1951–80, but per capita income growth was only about 1.5 per cent. Third, there was further acceleration of growth in the 1980s and 1990s to 5.6 per cent and per capita growth to 3.5 per cent a year. Fourth, during 2001–6, growth increased by about 2 percentage points to 7.7 per cent. Fifth, in the most recent period, 2007–11, there was further acceleration to 8.2 per cent per annum. Sixth, in the post-reform period beginning in 1991–2, growth was led by the services sectors, which recorded growth rates of 7.6 per cent in the 1990s and 10.0 per cent a year in the most recent four-year period. Rakshit (2007) attempts an insightful and detailed analysis of this phenomenon. He examines the demand and supply factors behind India's 'services revolution' and the relative role of agriculture and industry vis-à-vis that of services in the growth process. He notes that the most important factor on the supply side has been growth in total factor productivity (TFP).

Sources of Growth

The sources of growth in organized manufacturing and agriculture have been analysed in many studies during the past four decades or so. In recent years several studies for the aggregate economy have been attempted. Bosworth et al. (2007) and Krishna (2007) list the relevant bibliography. The special merit of Bosworth et al. (2007) is that it covers the three broad sectors in a unified framework and incorporates the most recent data revisions. The relevant results of the study are given in

Table 1 Average Growth Rates of GDP by Sector, 1900–1 to 2010–11

Sector	1900–1 to 1946–7	1951–2 to 1980–1	1981–2 to 1990–1	1991–2002 to 2000–1	2001–2 to 2006–7	2007–8 to 2010–11
	(1)	(2)	(3)	(4)	(5)	(6)
Agriculture	0.4	2.5	3.5	2.7	2.9	2.9
Industry	1.5	5.3	7.1	5.7	7.9	7.6
Services	1.7	4.6	6.8	7.6	9.0	10.0
Total GDP	0.9	3.6	5.6	5.6	7.7	8.2
Per Capita GDP	0.1	1.4	3.4	3.5	5.8	6.4

Source: Sivasubramanian (2000); CSO (2001); *EPW* (2011).
Note: 1. The growth rates in column (2) relate to undivided India.
2. The growth rates for 2009–10 and 2010–11 used for column (7) are QE (quick estimates) and RE (revised estimates), respectively.

Table 2 Sources of Economic Growth by Sector, 1960–81 and 1985–2005 (annual percentage rate of change)

Sector/Period	GDP	GDP per worker	Contribution: Capital	Land	Education	TFP
(1)	(2)	(3)	(4)	(5)	(6)	(7)
Total economy						
1960–81	3.4	1.3	1.0	–0.2	0.2	0.2
1981–2005	5.8	3.8	1.4	0.0	0.4	2.0
Agriculture						
1960–81	1.9	0.1	0.2	–0.2	0.1	–0.1
1981–2005	2.8	1.8	0.5	–0.1	0.3	1.1
Industry						
1960–81	4.7	1.6	1.8	–	0.3	–0.4
1981–2005	6.4	2.9	1.6	–	0.3	1.0
Services						
1960–81	4.9	2.0	1.1	–	0.5	0.4
1981–2005	7.6	4.0	0.7	–	0.4	2.9

Source: Bosworth et al. (2007).

Table 2. Two sub-periods are distinguished: 1960–81 and 1981–2005.

At the aggregate economy level, while the first period achieved negligible TFP growth (0.2 per cent a year), the second period registered a TFP growth of 2.0 per cent a year, accounting for more than one-third of GDP growth. TFP growth was the most impressive in the services sector (2.9 per cent a year) in the period 1981–2005. Agriculture and industry too fared better in this period. However, the contribution of TFP to output growth in industry was quite meagre at about 15 per cent.

Inter-state Income Inequality

Individual states in India compile and publish annual estimates of State Domestic Product (SDP) following a more-or-less uniform methodology evolved in consultation with CSO. In the wake of the major economic reforms in the early 1990s, the states in India have become significantly autonomous in formulating and implementing policy. This policy autonomy is reflected in the differential growth patterns of the states. Growing inter-state income inequality has become a major issue of policy concern. Table 3 summarizes the growth experience of 19 major states in the country in the post-reform era, divided into two sub-periods, 1994–5 to 2001–2 and 2002–3 to 2008–9.

Table 3 Summary of the Growth Performance of 19 Major States in the Post-reform Era: Growth Rate of Gross State Domestic Product (GSDP) at Constant Prices

	1994–5 to 2001–2	2002–3 to 2008–9
All India	6.2	7.8
19 major states:		
Average	5.1	7.9
Standard deviation	1.4	3.9
Coefficient of variation (%)	27.0	49.6

Source: Based on GoI: Table 12.10 (2011).

Average growth performance across states improved markedly from 5.1 per cent during 1994–5 to 2001–2 to 7.9 per cent during 2002–3 to 2008–9. However, inter-state income disparity measured by the coefficient of variation (CV) widened substantially from 27 to 50 per cent. It is interesting that the rank correlation between the two sets of growth rates was negative, but close to zero at –0.033.

In the recent sub-period, 2002–3 to 2008–9, the 10 states above the national average of 7.8 per cent in descending order of growth performance were Gujarat (11.2 per cent), Bihar (9.8 per cent), Odissa (9.3 per cent), Haryana (9.3 per cent), Chhattisgarh (9.3 per cent), Uttarakhand (9.2 per cent), Kerala (8.7 per cent), Maharashtra (8.7 per cent), Andhra Pradesh (8.2 per cent), and Karnataka (8.1 per cent). Five states, namely, Madhya Pradesh (4.5 per cent), Assam (5.5 per cent), Punjab (5.6 per cent), Uttar Pradesh (5.8 per cent), and West Bengal (6.7 per cent) were at the bottom. Himachal Pradesh (7.8 per cent), Rajasthan (7.6 per cent), Jharkhand (7.5 per cent), and Tamil Nadu (7.3 per cent) stood slightly behind the national average of 7.8 per cent (see GoI 2011).

K.L. KRISHNA

References

Bosworth, B., S. Collins, and A. Virmani, 2007. 'Sources of Growth in the Indian Economy', NBER Working Paper No.12901, February.

Central Statistical Organisation (CSO). 2001. *National Accounts Statistics, Back Series, 1950–51 to 1992–93, and National Accounts Statistics, 2001*, New Delhi, CSO.

——. 2010. *National Accounts Statistics, 2010.*

Economic and Political Weekly (*EPW*). 2011. *GDP Estimates*, 5–11 March.

Government of India (GoI). 2001. *Report of the National Statistical Commission*, New Delhi, Government of India.

——. 2011. *Economic Survey, 2010–11.*

Krishna, K.L. 2007. 'What Do We Know about the Sources of Economic Growth in India?', in A. Vaidyanathan and K.L. Krishna (eds), *Institutions and Markets in India's Development*, New Delhi, Oxford University Press.

Rakshit, M. 2007. 'Services-led Growth: The Indian Experience', *Money and Finance*, February, 3(1): 91–126.

Sivasubramanian, S. 2000. *The National Income of India in the Twentieth Century*, New Delhi, Oxford University Press.

National Rural Employment Guarantee Act

Passed by the Lok Sabha on 23 August 2004 and signed by the President of India on 5 September 2005, the National Rural Employment Guarantee Act (NREGA) has been hailed as a major initiative in the Government of India's commitment to providing an economic safety net to India's rural poor. Data from 2002 show that 71.9 per cent of India's population still resides in rural areas, and coupled with the fact that the majority of India's poor also resides in rural areas, the NREGA can be thought of as a policy to boost rural income, stabilize agricultural production, and reduce population pressure on urban areas.

The NREGA extends to all rural areas of India, including Fifth and Sixth Schedule areas, except the state of Jammu and Kashmir. Among its provisions are the following: (i) Every household in the rural areas of India shall have a right to at least 100 days of guaranteed employment every year for at least one adult member, for doing casual manual labour at the rate of Rs 60 per day. (ii) Only productive works shall be taken up under the programme. The State Council shall prepare a list of permissible works as well as a list of 'preferred works'. The identification of preferred works shall be based on the economic, social, and environmental benefits of different types of works, their contribution to social equity, and their ability to create permanent assets. (iii) The programme may also provide, as far as possible, for the training and upgradation of skills of unskilled labourers. (iv) Wages may be paid in cash or kind or both, taking into account the guidelines and recommendations of the State Council on this matter as far as possible. (v) Employment shall be provided within a radius of 5 km of the village where the applicant resides at the time of applying. In cases where employment is provided outside such radius, it must be provided within the block, and transport allowances and daily living allowances shall be paid in accordance with programme rules. (vi) In cases where at least 20 women are employed on a worksite, a provision shall be made for one of them to be deputed to look after any children under the age of 6 who may be brought to the worksite, if the need arises. The person deputed for child minding shall be paid the statutory minimum wage. (vii) A proportion of the wages, not exceeding 5 per cent, may be deducted as a contribution to welfare schemes organized for the benefit of labourers employed under the programme, such as health insurance, accident insurance, survivor benefits, maternity benefits, and social security schemes.

The NREGA, as it stands, explicitly eliminates two important criteria inherent in Employment Guarantee Schemes (EGS), particularly those that have been instituted in the state of Maharashtra: (i) public works programmes should not compete with agricultural labour hiring decisions and (ii) public works programmes should generate a productive asset that directly impacts agricultural productivity (Basu 2005). However, with Indian agriculture largely characterized by seasonality—a slack/lean season when agricultural labour demand is low and a peak/harvest season when labour demand is high—it can be reasonably assumed that the public employment, guaranteed for at least 100 days, will be instituted during the lean season when the rural labour force is most vulnerable. By removing the constraint that productive assets must be created to impact agricultural productivity, the NREGA allows for a certain leeway regarding the location of public works programmes.

The operational dimensions of the NREGA are important and generate much of the debate about its efficacy. But equally important in the debate has been its conceptual basis, and whether the problem to which it is addressed, rural poverty, is in fact best addressed by such an Act. There has been considerable discussion, for example, on whether the employment will be targeted to those who are poor, or whether there will be leakages to those above the poverty line.

In this entry, we take a slightly different tack to the current extensive debate on poverty targeting. We consider the Act as an intervention in rural labour markets, and ask what the consequences of this are likely to be for wages and employment (Basu et al. 2006). We start with the presumption that rural labour markets in India do not conform to the classic competitive labour markets of economics textbooks. If they did, the arguments for the NREGA would be weaker. However, in our view agricultural labour markets in India exhibit a range of hiring arrangements, from sharecropping to seasonal spot wage labour demand and a variety of credit–labour–land contracts in between (Basu 2002). Thus, labour markets in rural India can best be characterized by imperfect competition with high costs on the part of workers to seek and to switch employment, and with elements of monopsony power that lead to low wages and, above all, to equilibrium unemployment.

Assuming the NREGA targets this latter group of unemployed workers, the possibility of an alternative source of income—call it the disposable income from public works employment calculated as the minimum agricultural wage paid in these programmes minus the cost incurred by workers in reaching and staying at the worksite—raises the reservation wage of all workers in the rural sector, and implicitly confers some bargaining power on to rural workers. Thus, apart from the provision of an analogue of unemployment benefits, the fact of a guarantee of employment at a given wage through the NREGA introduces contestability in the rural labour market. In other words, private firms/landlords in rural areas need to raise the disposable income of the workers they hire—once again defined as the private wage minus the transportation/search cost of seeking private employment—in order to ensure the same number of available workers as before.

The key question then boils down to whether the NREGA can raise both private-sector wages and employment. The answer lies in how the labour supply schedule available to private employers in agriculture reacts to the opposing effects of the NREGA: in effect whether or not the unemployment benefit aspect that provides workers the option of an alternative source of employment and leads to a reduction in the pool of workers available for private employment dominates the contestability effect of the NREGA that makes private employment options more lucrative subsequent to a rise in private-sector wages. Intuitively, if the disposable income generated by public works programmes is low enough relative to the disposable income generated from private employment, then the contestability effect should dominate, leading to an increase in both private-sector wages and employment.

With the wage guaranteed in the NREGA at Rs 60 per day, the implicit discretion over transportation and other costs, and over various benefits at the point of employment, is thus revealed as a key factor in determining the efficacy of the NREGA.[1] What, then, should be the guaranteed optimal disposable income for public works employees? The answer lies in the efficiency versus equity trade-off from government intervention. The efficiency argument dictates that the disposable income should be low enough such that the contestability effect should dominate the unemployment benefit effect of the NREGA. On the other hand, the equity argument dictates that disposable income from public works employment should be high since the NREGA is a tool to redistribute income (through the NREGA fund) to the rural poor. Thus the equity criterion is inexorably tied to the government's aversion to income inequality. In general terms, if productivity of private-sector workers is low and hence there is low disposable income from employment in agriculture to begin with, then the disposable income from public works should be low. Needless to say, the opposite should be the case when productivity of workers in the private sector is high.

Finally, the ability of guaranteed public works employment can be thought of additionally as a policy that stabilizes employment levels in the rural sector facing productivity shocks. However, the extent to which such programmes can insure workers depends largely on the ability of the government to write and commit to complete contracts. In other words, if the government can credibly announce the wage and the location of public works programme for each and every possible productivity level, then the Employment Guarantee Act can in principle provide complete insurance to workers. But, as stated earlier, the nature of the NREGA leaves considerable discretion for the locational choice of public works programmes and other benefits at the worksite. This, coupled with the inability of the government to fully anticipate productivity shocks, may be viewed as providing only partial stabilization.

Conceptually, in order to better understand the ability of a public works programme to stabilize the labour market, the sequence of events from the announcement to the execution of a public works programme needs to be pinned down. As the NREGA is written, first the government announces the wage to be paid in public works programmes.

Next, productivity shock, positive or negative, to the private sector is revealed. Subsequent to the revelation of the productivity shock, private employers and workers form expectations regarding the location, and hence accessibility, of public works programmes ex post, and private employment contracts are signed. Finally, having observed private employment, the government decides on the location of public-works programmes and other benefits, and thus determines the disposable income of workers who seek public employment. In effect, with ex-post discretion on the location of public employment, the government can act to either ration or encourage public works employment. During times when the productivity shock is positive, a location for public employment can be so chosen as to make the transportation cost high, and hence disposable income low from public employment while the opposite can be true when the productivity shock is negative. In this latter vein, it is worth noting that in the event where the agricultural sector specifically is exposed to a large negative shock, public works programmes can be instituted and productive assets created to directly dampen the level of unemployment in the agricultural labour market.

In the presence of labour market imperfections, an employment guarantee can improve both efficiency and equity. The key trade-off is between the unemployment benefit nature of the wage offered, and the contestability introduced into the labour market because of the employment guarantee. A conceptual cut at these issues reveals the key importance of the discretion embodied in the location of public works projects and various on-site benefits that can be made available to workers. While often seen as being 'merely' operational in nature, our argument shows that they are the counterpart to central

[1]See Basu et al. (2006) for an analysis of minimum wage laws, wherein the issue of ex-post policy discretion with respect to the enforcement of the minimum wage is once again key to the credibility of the law.

features of the conceptual argument on the efficacy of employment guarantees.

ARNAB BASU, NANCY H. CHAU, AND RAVI KANBUR

References

Basu, Arnab K. 2002. 'Oligopsonistic Landlords, Segmented Labor Markets and the Persistence of Tied-labor Contracts', *American Journal of Agricultural Economics*, 84: 438–53.

——. 2005. 'Labor Contracts and the Effectiveness of Rural Public Works Programs', processed, Williamsburg, VA, Department of Economics, The College of William and Mary.

——. 2005. 'Turning a Blind Eye: Costly Enforcement, Credible Commitment and Minimum Wage Laws', London, UK, Centre for Economic Policy Research, Discussion Paper 5107.

Basu, Arnab K., Nancy H. Chau, and Ravi Kanbur. 2006. 'A Theory of Employment Guarantees: Contestability, Credibility and Distributional Concerns', London, UK, Centre for Economic Policy Research, Discussion Paper 5784.

National Sample Surveys

National Sample Surveys (NSS) in India are carried out by the National Sample Survey Organisation (NSSO), an autonomous agency under the Ministry of Statistics, Government of India (GoI). Started in 1950, they provide representative estimates (at national level and for major states and often their size distribution around the mean level) of a wide range of socio-economic characteristics of the Indian population that are mostly comparable over time. The current cycle of regular surveys covers quinquennial household consumer expenditure (basis of widely discussed poverty estimates) and employment–unemployment surveys (both these surveys are also being repeated in other rounds with smaller or 'thin' samples), decennial surveys of household assets and liabilities, ownership and operational landholdings, and social consumption (education and health, reproductive and child healthcare, and problems of the aged). In addition, unorganized enterprise surveys are conducted in different groups of sub-sectors in manufacturing and services regularly to cater to the needs of national income accounts. This is necessitated by the numerical dominance of small unorganized and mostly self-employed enterprises in India that do not maintain regular books of accounts. The wider canvass of infrequently carried out surveys covers surveys of physical disabilities, use of common property resources, farming practices, situation assessment of farmer households, general housing conditions, internal migration, conditions of tribal communities, family living surveys, and many others. The Golden Jubilee volume (NSSO 2000) lists the topics covered in the first 50 years of the NSS. Described briefly but at the same time comprehensively by Murthy and Roy (1975), the 'NSS are a nationwide, large-scale, continuing, integrated multi-subject [more on this later] sample surveys conducted in the form of rounds of usually one year duration by a permanent, whole-time, trained survey staff that collects recall-based information by interviewing sample households.'

Large-scale sample surveys were pioneered by the Indian Statistical Institute (ISI), Calcutta, during the pre-Independence era. They were based on the fundamental statistical principle that a small random sample from a large population yields estimates of any desired precision of a population characteristic at low cost. Professor P.C. Mahalanobis who founded the ISI in 1930, along with his colleagues at the ISI, made major contributions to developing large-scale statistical sampling theory and survey methodology. Immediately after Independence, Mahalanobis was appointed Honorary Statistical Adviser to the Central Cabinet in January 1949. He was instrumental in establishing the Directorate of NSS in 1950 in Calcutta for the fieldwork and provided technical support from professional statisticians of the ISI relating to finalization of sampling design, schedules of enquiry (more on this later), training of field staff (warranted by multi-purpose, multi-subject nature), processing of data, and writing of reports. In a note submitted to the Government of India on 20 February 1952, Mahalanobis recommended that 'the NSS should be *organised on a permanent basis as a government but entirely independent authority* with necessary devolution of financial and administrative powers' (Rudra 1996: ch. 10). The Directorate of NSS remained with the ISI till 1969 when a three-member committee set up by the Government of India for the reorganization the NSS recommended entrusting all aspects of the survey to a single government organization in the Ministry of Statistics and governed by an autonomous Governing Council. This paved the way for the NSSO in its present incarnation.

Since its inception, being the first and the largest undertaking of its kind in the world, there has been emphasis on experimentation. The challenges in the initial years have been both organizational and methodological: setting up the vast network of field organizations for collection and processing of sample data from all corners of the subcontinent, devising rational but pragmatic survey practices and evolving sampling methods suited to a predominantly traditional, illiterate, and multilingual society and an underdeveloped economy. All this was subject to tight resource constraint. There has been experimentation with alternative sampling designs, schedules of enquiry, methods of data collection, and topics of enquiry.

Socio-economic Household Enquiries

The NSS socio-economic household enquiries adopt a personal interview method with a schedule of items on which data are collected from each sample household relying on retrospective recall. In the schedule approach, the task of eliciting information is left to the investigators who, backed by training and instructions, are expected to elicit reliable information after explaining concept and definition wherever needed. This approach minimizes non-response and works better when respondents are less educated. However, the length of schedule and time required for filling it may lead to possible respondent resistance or fatigue. A schedule of items for each round finalized by an expert working group is, therefore, revised suitably in consultation with inputs from the field based on earlier rounds. There has also been experimentation with alternative lengths of schedules of enquiry governing the time spent with informants, and multiple schedules for different subjects and canvassed in different sets of sample households, as opposed to an integrated schedule and alternative durations of recall periods.

The primary requirement of an optimal sampling design of any socio-economic household enquiry is to provide a quantitative and representative description of given socio-economic characteristics of households with a given level of precision at minimum cost. The sampling design of NSS socio-economic enquiries has been a two-stage stratified random sample in which villages or urban blocks (periodically updated by the NSSO through Urban Frame Surveys) constitute the first stage units (FSUs) and households in the selected villages/blocks are the second stage units (SSUs). It should be intuitively obvious that in an ethnically and culturally diverse society of continental dimensions like India, geographical dispersion in household characteristics across FSUs would be greater than that within FSUs. Consequently, the larger the number of selected FSUs, the greater, ceteris paribus, is the precision of the estimated characteristic(s). However, this raises the costs of movement of the field staff. Since demands on the NSSO to carry out surveys on different subjects far exceed the available resources of trained staff, integration of multiple subjects, not all necessarily closely related, became imperative. Integration saves on overhead costs including utilization of trained manpower and enables increasing the number of FSUs to improve precision. However, it overburdens investigators with multiple subjects and related concepts, definitions, code structures, and procedures, and results in lengthy or multiple schedules, long interviews, and possible respondent resistance and fatigue. In the same context, it may be noted that a sample design tailored to the main subject is not equally efficient with respect to supplementary enquiries. Finally, the availability of well-trained and motivated staff poses the biggest constraint given the budget provided by the government, the procedures of recruitment, and their geographical distribution in a multilingual country. It is, however, remarkable that the number of FSUs has gone up from about 1,400 villages/urban blocks in the 1950s to about 14,000 in the latest round. In order to facilitate easy assessment of sampling errors, the NSS usually take two independent sub-samples from each stratum, each of which is capable of giving a valid estimate of the population characteristic so that the difference between the two estimates provides an idea of sampling error irrespective of complicated procedures involved in selecting a sample or arriving at the estimates. If the two sub-samples are canvassed by two distinct sets of investigators, sub-sample-wise estimates provide an idea of investigator bias.

Two more survey practices in the NSS are important for intelligent understanding of the results. Most surveys collect *retrospective information* for a *pre-specified recall period* by paying a *single visit per sample household* in order to cover a larger number of households with a given team of field investigators. When the retrospective recall period is less than a year, as is usually the case (more on this shortly), the issue of seasonal variation in responses becomes important. Two practices in the NSS require mention in this context. One, all efforts are made to spread interviewed households reasonably evenly throughout the survey period so as to capture responses in all parts of the year so that average response over the year is free from seasonal bias. Two, a survey period of one year is usually divided into four sub-rounds of three months each and sample size is tailored to arrive at valid estimates of the characteristic for each sub-round separately so that seasonal variation in responses can be examined.

It is useful to dwell briefly on the recent controversy over the recall periods affecting comparability of poverty estimates across two quinquennial rounds of household consumer expenditure. The accuracy of retrospective recall of consumer expenditure is clearly shaped by the length of the recall period. A longer recall period leads to a recall lapse while a shorter recall period may be affected by what is known as a telescoping effect, that is incorrectly reporting purchases outside the recall period. The recall period for each item of household consumer expenditure has to balance these opposite tendencies in retrospective recall. For frequently purchased items that do not remain salient in memory like food grains, a shorter recall period is usually preferred in order to minimize recall lapse. For infrequently purchased items that remain salient in memory like durables, a longer recall period is deemed better.[1] Currently, the recall period is common for all the sample households. However, response would also be clearly shaped by the economic position of the household. For durable goods, for example, a shorter recall period would be better at the upper end with more frequent purchases while a longer one would be preferred at the lower end of the economic scale. Quinquennial surveys of household consumer expenditure have been using a uniform recall period of 30 days preceding the date of interview for all items except expenditure on (relatively) infrequently purchased items like clothing, footwear, durables, and institutional healthcare for which data are collected for two recall periods of 30 days and 365 days from each household. Non-comparability controversy arose because the 55th round for 1999–2000 made two departures. One, data were collected from the same sample households on two alternative recall periods of seven days (a common international practice) and thirty days (used traditionally in India based on experiments conducted in the 1950s) for some frequently purchased items in the food group. This created twofold difficulties for comparison. To start with, experience from earlier 'thin' rounds showed that seven-day recall-based food consumption is usually higher than that reported for thirty-day when canvassed on two independent sets of households. Given the higher share of food items in the consumption bundles of the poor, this would lead to a higher per capita expenditure on those items by the poorer households and consequently a lower proportion of persons below the same poverty line in comparison with the traditional 30-day recall. The non-salience of concerned items in respondents' memory also meant that a simultaneous canvassing of two recall periods on the same set of sample households was bound to lead to a possible 'contamination' that would make the results of this round non-comparable with those of all the earlier rounds. The second departure from the past was that for the infrequently purchased items, only a 365 days recall period was used in the 55th round. There is no objective method of resolving the non-comparability introduced by the two departures. Different procedures have been suggested for getting approximately comparable estimates of proportions of population below the poverty line for 1993–4 and 1999–2000.[2]

Finally, I may briefly dwell on some emerging challenges. The Indian economy has been growing at more than 3 per cent annually in per capita terms over the last two and a half decades in comparison with very low growth till 1980–1. This has several repercussions for the NSSO. Rapid growth has created a large number of new opportunities for the educated youth; this has not only increased difficulties in recruiting well-trained and motivated investigators but also resulted in rapid turnover. As far as respondent households are concerned, this has meant even shorter time to spend on interviews with investigators thereby raising non-response and resistance. Non-sampling errors resulting from these considerations have been a matter of concern. The same factors also have serious implications for the length of the schedules of enquiry. I have discussed this problem in the context of method of data collection. While the length of some of the present schedules of enquiry needs to be shortened, it would mean greater recall lapse and less comprehensive information with implications for multi-subject enquiries. In the household consumer expenditure surveys that have been in focus in recent times in connection with measurement of poverty, it is necessary to experiment not only with alternative recall periods for the same item(s) (some pilot studies have been carried out in this connection) but also multiple recall periods depending on the economic position of the household. Any one or more of these changes are bound to produce non-comparabilities with the past. How should these be brought about without losing the continuity with the past that has been the hallmark of the NSS? A small panel sample embedded in the usual independent sample is an innovation that needs experimentation. Demands have also been rising for more regionally disaggregated data. Should the NSS central sample be increased or should matching state samples that have not succeeded as yet in many states or small area sampling methods based on indicators be attempted? The multipurpose nature of the NSS has also been under the scanner as sample design for enterprise surveys has been found to be inefficient for household enquiries. All these are as yet unresolved questions. However, this largest sample survey organization of its kind in the world has proved to be resilient and dynamic and has been grappling with these difficult problems in search of solutions. At the same time, its continuing existence critically depends on increasingly

[1]See Deaton and Ghosh (2000) for discussions.

[2]A reference may be made to papers by Deaton, Sen, and Himanshu and Sundaram and Tendulkar in Deaton and Kozel (2005).

scarce willingness and response from the public at large while demands for data have been rising.

SURESH D. TENDULKAR

References

Deaton, A. and M. Ghosh. 2000. 'Consumption', in M. Ghosh, and P. Glewwe (eds), *Designing Household Survey Questionnaires For Developing Countries, Lessons from 15 Years of Living Standard Measurement Study*, Washington DC: World Bank, 91–134.

Deaton, A. and V. Kozel (eds). 2005. *The Great Indian Poverty Debate*, Delhi, Macmillan India Ltd.

Murthy, M.N. and A.S. Roy. 1975. 'Development of the Design of the Indian National Sample Survey during Its First Twenty-five Rounds', *Sankhya, The Indian Journal of Statistics*, series C, part I, 37: 1–42.

National Sample Survey Organisation (NSSO). 2000. *National Sample Survey, Fifty Years in Service of the Nation, Golden Jubilee (1950–2000)*, New Delhi, Ministry of Statistics and Programme Implementation, Government of India.

NSSO website.www.mospi.nic.in.

Rudra, A. 1996. *Prasanta Chandra Mahalanobis: A Biography*, Oxford, Oxford University Press.

Yogi, A.K. 1997. 'Methodology of National Sample Survey Organisation: An Appraisal', in *Indian Statistical System, Golden Jubilee of Indian Independence*, New Delhi, Department of Statistics, Ministry of Planning and Programme Implementation, Government of India, pp. 129–35.

■ NCAER's Household Survey

The National Council of Applied Economic Research (NCAER), headquartered in New Delhi, was founded in 1956 through the initiative of a group of public- and private-sector leaders. Designed to be an independent institution, run by a governing body and supported by corporate and individual members, its goal throughout has been to support informed decision-making both for public policy and the private sector through rigorous and objective empirical economic research. Since the beginning, the bulk of the Council's revenue has come from studies done on contract, and this remains the case.

The NCAER and Data Collection

It is not common for institutions concerned with empirical policy analysis to also engage in large-scale data collection; the NCAER is an exception. It seems that, more or less from the beginning, the NCAER found it necessary to establish its own capacity for large-scale primary data collection. Some of the impetus for this effort was no doubt provided by a series of techno-economic surveys for individual states that the NCAER was commissioned to undertake under its first Director-General, P.S. Lokanathan.

Over time the NCAER's activities, particularly in household surveys, have evolved parallel with those of the National Sample Survey Organisation (NSSO), also founded in the 1950s as a government entity. The characteristic product of the NSSO is repeated surveys ('rounds') on a core set of issues, collected by a large permanent field staff on a fixed schedule under the supervision of a government-appointed advisory council. The NCAER has complemented the NSSO by developing the capability to undertake more ad hoc data collection for a wide variety of sponsors on a broad range of topics. In addition, the NSSO has had a strong preference for information on consumption, while the NCAER has been more associated with measuring income and saving.

Sampling and Non-sampling Issues

Given the absence of accurate publicly available enumerations of households in India (as in most poor countries), ensuring a representative sample usually requires the prior construction of a sampling frame. In most cases a multi-stage sample design is adopted. Public data (such as from the decennial census) are used for the first few stages. For the final stage, where households are to be selected, customized sample frames are generated afresh through a household listing operation, which then guides the final sample selection and actual data collection.

In contrast to the NSSO's preference for permanent field staff, the NCAER has traditionally had fresh teams of young fieldworkers hired by local survey firms and trained and supervised by the NCAER's own staff. In view of the geographical and linguistic diversity of the country, the Council maintains regional offices. Data quality is ensured through pre-testing of survey instruments for content, flow, and likely response; centralized training of field officers/supervisors; and localized training of field interviewers both in terms of survey instruments and field exposure/testing by senior researchers of the Council. Responses during the first week of field operation are reviewed as part of the supervision. Completed questionnaires undergo complete editing and validity checks either at regional centres or at NCAER headquarters, depending upon the magnitude of the survey. Preliminary results are validated against available comparable information such as the census or national accounts.

Scope and Coverage

Since in any given year the NCAER can undertake as many as three or four national household surveys of differing size, scope, and complexity, it is difficult to provide a comprehensive overview of the range of findings and results. Also, not all data sets are publicly available as many are collected for individual sponsors, who differ in their willingness to make the underlying data publicly available or to finance their dissemination.

Despite these limitations, it is worth mentioning certain major data sets collected since the late 1960s which have proved to be important and fruitful sources of primary information for a range of researchers located both in India and abroad. Most of these data sets deal with the rural side of India's economy and society. A much smaller set deals with both urban and rural households. Between them, these data sets provide a major resource for understanding the evolution of Indian households and their welfare over a significant part of India's post-Independence history.

Perhaps the most distinctive among these is the sequence of panel surveys of rural households known as the Additional Rural Income Survey/Rural Economic and Demographic Survey (ARIS/REDS). These surveys were first undertaken in the late 1960s to track the impact of the intensive agricultural practices (later termed Green Revolution) on household behaviour through three consecutive rounds. The same households (including male children who may have set up their own households in the same village) were resurveyed in 1982 and again in 1999. A fresh round will be in the field in 2006. Sample sizes have expanded from around 3,000 households in the first round to around 10,000 in the 2006 survey. All these surveys have been undertaken in collaboration with US-based scholars, and with external financial support from a range of donors. These data have been utilized by a number of scholars and graduate students outside the NCAER to support a range of publications in working papers and refereed journals.

While the ARIS/REDS data provide a basis for longitudinal study of rural household behaviour, the so-called MIMAP data set provides a sound baseline for understanding the pattern of household and personal distribution of income in India at the beginning of the reform period. The reference year for this nationally representative survey of 5,000 households was 1995, and a distinctive feature of the data set is its careful enumeration of income and saving for both rural and urban households. This survey was designed as part of a global project supported by the International Development Research Centre (IDRC) of Canada, entitled Microeconomic Impact of Macro Adjustment Policies.

Mention should also be made of the India Human Development data set which surveyed 35,000 rural households in 1994, again with a focus on living standards, with associated information on the community as well as the household. A second round is being conducted in 2005 which resurveys many of the same rural households while adding an urban sample. The second round survey has been designed and executed in collaboration with scholars at the University of Maryland and supported by the National Institute of Health in Bethesda, Maryland.

These comprehensive household data sets are complemented by a large number of special-purpose surveys. Since the mid-1980s, the NCAER has conducted repeated surveys of ownership and expenditure patterns of a limited group of consumer goods. Called the Market Information Survey of Households (MISH) these surveys are primarily designed to assist decision making in the private sector. The income coverage of this survey is now being expanded to make it of greater academic interest. Other noteworthy data sets have included surveys of science education, domestic tourism, fuel use, and agricultural practices.

SUMAN BERY

■ Jawaharlal Nehru

Jawaharlal Nehru (1889–1964) was not a professional economist, yet no other individual has left a deeper imprint on independent India's economy. Not surprisingly, his economic beliefs, choices, and their often hard-to-determine consequences have attracted controversy. Leftists, liberals, the religious right, Gandhians, and environmentalists, all were critics of his economic policies, both during and after Nehru's lifetime.

In his youth Nehru adopted the Gandhian practice of the *charkha*, and he absorbed the ideal of self-sufficiency. However, he was never attracted by the Gandhian vision of small-scale, artisanal production, nor he did believe that moral virtue alone could regenerate India.

For Nehru, the economy was a central instrument for making India into a modern society; but he always subordinated economic ends to political ideals, and his own economic views were located within a broader conception of historical progress and political value. Three elements shaped his economic views: the historical experience of imperialism, the promise of the Bolshevik revolution, and the emergence, from the late 1940s, of the armoury of policies associated with development economics—which seemed to offer, here and now, a set of techniques to remedy the legacy of imperialism. The years of Nehru's political maturity coincided with a period—the middle decades of the 20th century (from roughly the 1930s to the 1960s)—that represented the zenith of the belief that human will and action could actively direct and shape the economic domain. This belief acquired two powerful expressions: the Soviet model, based on state control of the commanding heights of the economy, within a politically closed system; and in Western Europe, Keynesian and Swedish social democratic ideas of a mixed economy, regulated by an interventionist state operating within a liberal democratic system.

Early in his career, Nehru was associated with left-wing economic ideas. He played an important role in Congress's 1931 Karachi resolution on fundamental rights and future economic policy (which committed the party to state control of the economy, and urged a restriction of income differences in an independent India); and in works like *Whither India?* (1930), Nehru declared that India must progress towards 'the great human goal of social and economic equality, to the ending of all exploitation of nation by nation and class by class, to national freedom within the framework of an international co-operative socialist world federation'. While he came later to jettison such Marxist language, he did retain the Marxist analysis of imperialism (which anyway was a liberal argument, first developed by J.A. Hobson and assimilated by Lenin into Marxism), which viewed this as a system founded on structural dependencies.

This analysis defined his view of how an independent Indian state must preserve its autonomy. Nehru was convinced that India must not become dependent on foreign capital, and he early perceived the necessity of an independent defence capacity, which required an indigenous heavy industrial base. These imperatives shaped his policies during his years as India's first prime minister (1947–64).

These years were punctuated by a series of economic initiatives and declarations—for example, the Industrial Policy Resolution of 1948 (that committed India to a mixed economy and recognized the role of private capital), his speech at the 1955 Avadi Congress which spoke of a 'socialistic pattern' for India—some with less impact than others. None, though, was more important that the establishment in 1950 of the Planning Commission, a government agency that reported directly to the prime minister, and was not accountable to Parliament—a testament to Nehru's willingness to vest considerable policymaking powers in professional economists. Headed by the statistician P.C. Mahalanobis, the Planning Commission decisively shaped the Indian economy during the 1950s and beyond. And while Nehru was resistant to Western capital, he was not parochial when it came to ideas: the Planning Commission attracted a stream of distinguished Western economists, such as Ragnar Frisch, Jan Tinbergen, Joan Robinson, Nicholas Kaldor, and Charles Bettleheim, who came to advise and learn from the Indian experiment.

Its major achievement was the Second Plan (1956–61). Nehru played a major role in its drafting and it stands as the most elaborate statement of his economic policy. Unlike the more limited First Plan (1951–6), which aimed merely to direct fiscal flows and restrict entry of foreign capital, the Second Plan was an ambitious and systematic effort to create enduring structures. It directed investment towards physical infrastructure, inaugurating an era that saw the construction of steel plants and large dams, and of expanding bureaucracies required to manage these public-sector ventures. In tandem, Nehru also tried, ineffectually, to push through land reform, which he believed would serve to increase agricultural production and bring it more in line with the needs of a country that suffered from chronic food shortages. This agrarian strategy was stymied in the provincial state legislatures, and in the early 1960s a new policy was introduced, based on technological inputs to increase productivity—creating the basis of the 'Green Revolution' in selected parts of the country.

In judging Nehru's project of economic development, one must distinguish between assessing the design's coherence and evaluating its performance, and both must be again kept separate from judgements about subsequent (and often purely nominal) appropriations of his ideas Far from being doctrinal, Nehru's economic thinking was an effort to directly address India's problems as he perceived them. It had more in common with Keynesian ideas of a mixed economy than with Marxist or socialist theories. As with Keynes and other European social democrats, for Nehru the state had to create a habitat for economic expansion—through investment in a public sector that was expected to operate in tandem with a vigorous private economy. His particular approach was influenced by both domestic and international constraints.

Given the Congress Party's commitment to some redistribution, and given the scarce resources of the Indian state—historically a low taxer, and constitutionally constrained in its ability to tax India's vast agrarian economy—the state had no option but to generate its own resources, in the public sector, if it was to have anything to redistribute. That this essentially social democratic vision came to be seen as a Soviet derivative was a result of political chance. Nehru had initially expected that India's economic growth would be aided by the Western powers, and in the early 1950s there was significant American help. But the Americans soon made further aid conditional on the pursuit of a development path that invested in agriculture and light and consumer industries, which they argued would accelerate growth rates by making India an export-based economy. For Nehru rapid economic growth was never an end in itself; equally important were the values of autonomy and democracy. And, in the context of an international system polarized by the Cold War, Nehru was wary of India losing its political autonomy through economic choices.

Resting India's economic development on exports of consumer goods would, Nehru judged, weaken India's new-won independence (and on the evidence of those countries that did choose the American-sponsored path, such as South Korea or Pakistan, he was right). The Soviets, whom Nehru had earlier kept at arm's length, sensed a wavering of Western support for Indian development, and stepped forward with easy terms to support India's chosen strategy. Yet Nehru was equally convinced that, with India's commitment to democracy, industrial growth could not be forced Soviet or Chinese style. He refused the 'cruel choice' between democracy and economic development: both ends were fundamental to his vision of a modern India, and demanded simultaneous (if mutually hobbling) pursuit.

Nehru's real failures in the economic sphere lay in his inability to establish an effective system of primary education and to alter the rural property order—two achievements that proved essential to the economic surge that enabled other Asian countries to leap past India in later decades. Yet it is still perhaps early days to come to a final judgement about his legacy. Were the Indian economy to move into a sustained high-growth pattern in the 21st century, and if it is able to achieve a measure of redistribution, the choices made by Nehru, subject in recent years to much criticism, may ultimately be vindicated.

SUNIL KHILNANI

References

Chakravarty, Sukhamoy. 1987. *Development Planning: The Indian Experience*, New Delhi, Oxford University Press.

Frankel, Francine. 1978. *India's Political Economy: 1947–1977*, Princeton, Princeton University Press.

Hanson, A.H. 1966. *The Process of Planning: A Study of India's Five Year Plans 1950–1964*, Oxford, Oxford University Press.

Khilnani, Sunil. 2003. 'Temples of the Future', *The Idea of India*, 3rd edn, New Delhi, Penguin.

Planning Commission. 1956. *Second Five Year Plan: A Draft Outline*, New Delhi, Planning Commission, Government of India.

■ Non-banking Financial Companies

A non-banking financial company (NBFC) is a company incorporated under the Companies Act, 1956, and conducting financial business as its principal business. In contrast, companies incorporated under the same Act but conducting other than financial business as their principal business are known as non-banking non-financial companies. NBFCs are different from banks in that an NBFC cannot accept demand deposits, issue cheques to customers, or insure deposits through the Deposit Insurance and Credit Guarantee Corporation (DICGC).

In India, the non-banking financial sector comprises a multiplicity of institutions, which are defined under Section 45 I(a) of the Reserve Bank of India Act, 1934. These are equipment-leasing companies (EL), hire-purchase companies (HP), investment companies, loan companies (LC), mutual benefit financial companies (MBFC), miscellaneous non-banking companies (MNBC), housing finance companies (HFC), insurance companies (IC), stockbroking companies (SBC), and merchant banking companies (MBC). A non-banking company which conducts primarily financial business and belongs to none of these categories is called a residuary non-banking company (RNBC). An overview of NBFCs together with relevant supervising bodies is given in Figure 1. Since banking, insurance, and stock markets are covered elsewhere in this volume, HFCs, ICs, SBCs, and MBCs will not be addressed in further detail here.

While most institutions of India's non-banking financial sector are also found in other countries' financial systems, two of them, MBFCs and MNBCs, better known as *nidhi*s and chit fund companies, respectively, are genuinely Indian institutions and rarely found outside South Asia. Inside India, they are most popular in Tamil Nadu and Kerala, from where they have originated. A nidhi does business only with its equity shareholders. Much like a cooperative bank, a nidhi accepts deposits and makes loans, which are mostly secured by jewellery. A chit fund, in Kerala also known as *kuri*, is a particular form of a rotating savings and credit association

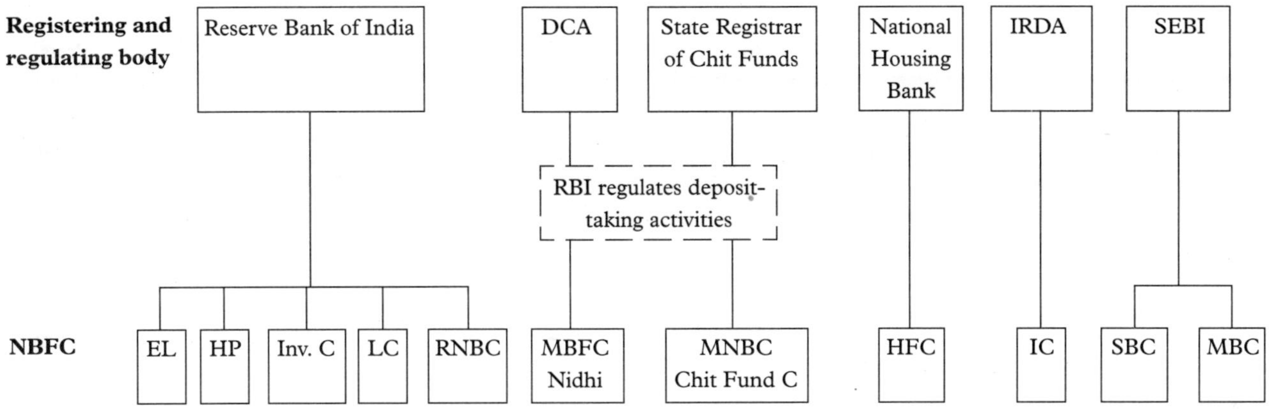

Figure 1 NBFCs and Supervising Bodies

Notes: Inv. C = Investment company.
DCA = Department of Company Affairs
IRDA = Insurance Regulatory and Development Authority
SEBI = Securities and Exchange Board of India

(ROSCA), which is most easily explained by means of an example. Twenty people, say, agree to contribute a fixed amount, say Rs 1000, every month. So the group pools in Rs 20,000 each month, the prize money. Every month an auction is held. In each auction, the bidder who offers the highest discount is given the prize money minus the discount. For example, when a member bids Rs 4,000, she will be paid Rs 16,000. The discount of Rs 4,000 is equally shared by all members. In this example, each member thus earns a dividend of Rs 200. The winner of an auction continues to pay the monthly contribution but is not eligible to bid in subsequent auctions. According to this system, after 20 months each member has received the prize exactly once, at which point the chit fund comes to an end. An MNBC or chit fund company acts as commercial organizer of chit funds. In 1999, the Reserve Bank of India (RBI) mandated net owned funds (NOF) of at least Rs 2 crore for registration of a new NBFC. Companies that were already in business in 1999 had to prove net NDFs of at least Rs 25 lakh to register. Companies that failed to meet this requirement by 2003 have to phase out their business. This led to numerous mergers of existing NBFCs and a considerable reduction in the number of NBFCs since the late 1990s after the sector had seen thriving growth throughout the 1980s and early 1990s. To illustrate, the number of companies monitored by the RBI increased from 7,063 in 1981 to 51,929 in 1996. At the same time the share of non-bank deposits tripled. In 2003, the number of NBFCs monitored by the RBI had come down to 13,849, of which 710 were authorized to accept public deposits.

Table 1 Profile of Public Deposits in the NBFC Sector as in End March 2003 (Rs crore)

	Number of reporting companies	Public deposits
Equipment leasing (EL)	58	511
Hire purchase (HP)	439	3539
Investment and loan (IL)	173	329
RNBC	5	15,065
MNBC and MBFC	200	656
Total	875	20,100

Source: RBI (2004).

Between 1998 and 2003, the ratio of public deposits with NBFCs to commercial banks came down from 3.4 to 1.5 per cent. A profile (as of 2003) of deposit-taking activities within the NBFC sector is given in Table 1. Among the 710 registered and 165 unregistered deposit-taking NBFCs, the majority operated as HP companies. The bulk of deposits was held by RNBCs. It should be noted, however, that these numbers understate the importance of NBFCs for savings mobilization for at least two reasons. First, financial intermediation in chit funds takes place instantly and members' contributions do not appear as deposits on Chit Fund Companies' balance sheets. For 2004, the turnover in registered chit funds is estimated at Rs 20,000 crore. Second, deposits in nidhis by nidhi members do not count as public deposits. Since the Department of Company Affairs (DCA), to which MBFCs report, does not publish statistics on nidhi operations, numbers on the volume of deposits in nidhis are not available. The number of

Table 2 Selected Assets and Liabilities of 870 NBFCs (excluding 5 RNBCs) as in End March 2003 (Rs crore)

Selected assets		Selected liabilities		
Equipment leasing	2011	Borrowings (by source)	Central and state governments	1,570
Hire purchase	13,031		Foreign sources	694
Investments	4,338		Banks and financial institutions	8,959
Loans and inter-corporate deposits	13,296		Inter-corporate	2,074
Bills	450		Issue of convertible or secured debentures	5,352
		Public deposits		5,053
		New owned funds		4,141

Source: RBI (2004).

nidhis was at 244 in 2004 and, according to conservative estimates, nidhi companies had lendings of about Rs 1,500 crore in 2001.

Selected items of NBFCs' (excluding RNBCs) balance sheets are displayed in Table 2. The majority of liabilities of these NBFCs are borrowings from various sources, whereas public deposits contribute less than 20 per cent. The majority of assets are loans and inter-corporate deposits, and HP assets, which mostly consist of retail funding of cars, commercial vehicles, and consumer durables. While NBFCs excluding RNBCs have a deposit to net owned funds ratio of 1:2, the five RNBCs that report to the RBI are much more leveraged with a deposit to net owned funds ratio of 18:6. The RNBC sector is dominated by two companies, which, in 2003, held more than 99.9 per cent of RNBC deposits. While they offer a variety of financial products including insurance, their main business is to accept term deposits, which are invested into mainly government-issued securities.

Are NBFCs essential to a country's financial system or, put differently, could their functions not also be performed by banks? In this connection, several arguments can be made. First, NBFCs provide services not well suited for banks. Banks primarily provide payment services and liquidity. Since banks have to maintain the value of deposits, they tend to have mostly debt-type, as opposed to equity-type, items on both sides of their balance sheets. In contrast, NBFCs can finance riskier borrowers and intermediate equity claims. They thus offer a wider range of risks to investors, which encourages investment and savings and creates a market for risks. Second, NBFCs unbundle services that are bundled within a universal bank, and thus foster competition, which benefits customers.

Third, through specialization, NBFCs can gain informational advantages over banks in their narrowly defined fields of operation. Fourth, NBFCs diversify the financial sector, which may alleviate a systemic crisis.

Are the functions performed by NBFCs important for economic growth? Recent research with cross-country data sets has established that development of the financial sector has the potential to accelerate economic growth. However, no research on the particular role of NBFCs in this process has yet been undertaken. Nevertheless, international comparisons show that economies with lower per capita income tend to have a smaller range of equity-type claims and a smaller market share of NBFCs relative to banks.

An important and widely discussed issue in the context of financial institutions is regulation. NBFCs are particularly important for facilitating storage of value and intermediation of risk. Moreover, like other financial institutions, they are sensitive to runs and herding behaviour. If the financial sector does not work smoothly, high transaction costs, lack of confidence and short-sightedness of economic factors, as well as a culture of corruption may result. The objectives of financial-sector regulation are protection against systemic risks (like depositor runs), consumer protection, efficiency enhancement, and social objectives.

Regulation may be structured as either institutional or functional. Under the former, each financial institution has its own regulatory agency, for example, one for each category of NBFCs. Under the latter, there are separate agencies for each function of an NBFC, for example, one for deposit-taking activities, one for lending, and one for market conduct. India's legislators have chosen a mix of these two models. As illustrated in Figure 1, the RBI regulates ELs, HPs, investment companies, LCs, and RNBCs. Similarly, HFCs, ICs, SBCs, and MBCs report to the National Housing Bank, the Insurance Regulatory and Development Authority (IRDA), and the Securities and Exchange Board of India (SEBI), respectively. All these are instances of institutional regulation. In contrast, nidhis report to the DCA and chit fund companies to the State Registrar of Chit Funds for their general operations, as well as to the RBI for their deposit-taking activities, an instance of functional regulation.

To achieve the objectives of efficiency enhancement and protection against systemic risks, regulation has to be neutral. This means that institutions providing the same or similar services should be subject to identical regulatory requirements. Regulatory neutrality fosters efficiency-enhancing competition between institutions as each service will be provided by the institution that can provide it at the lowest cost. Deviations from regulatory neutrality, on the other hand, most likely cause efficiency losses. Suppose that two institutions can provide a particular service at the same cost under regulatory neutrality but that, for no apparent reason, one of the two institutions is regulated less strictly. If regulatory requirements are costly to firms, that institution obtains a regulatory comparative advantage and will drive the more regulated one out of the market, an example of regulatory arbitrage. Moreover, if differences in regulatory requirements are big, less regulated institutions may drive out more efficient ones. In this worst case, the outcome will be both inefficient and fragile, as institutions that meet the lowest among all regulatory standards dominate the market. Much of the history of NBFCs in India over the last 50 years can serve as a case study of non-neutral regulation and consequent regulatory arbitrage. Before 1997, the RBI's supervision of NBFCs was limited to prescription of prudential norms and thus the structure of NBFCs' assets. No requirements were in place regarding minimum capital, amount and term structure of deposits, and interest rates on deposits and loans. At the same time the banking sector was heavily regulated through excessive statutory liquidity requirements, directed lending initiatives, and interest rate caps. NBFCs, which were not subject to any of these rules, thus enjoyed a substantial regulatory comparative advantage for several bank-type activities, most notably lending and deposit-taking. Consequently, between 1981 and 1996, the number of NBFCs grew more than sevenfold and the share of non-bank deposits increased from 3.1 to 10.6 per cent. Several companies were extremely leveraged and deposits-to-NOF ratio in excess of 40 were not uncommon. Numerous bankruptcies of NBFCs in the early 1990s prompted the RBI to take action. The measures sanctioned in 1997, most notably minimum NOF and a maximum deposits-to-NOF ratio of 1.5 and 4 (depending on the company's rating), brought NBFC standards closer to those of the banking sector. Subsequently the number of registered NBFCs shrank by 70 per cent between 1997 and 2003. Nevertheless, NBFCs continue to enjoy regulatory privileges. As of 2003, they can pay 11 per cent on deposits while the ceiling rate for banks is at 6.75 per cent.

The 1997 provisions were not applied uniformly across NBFCs. In particular, nidhis as well as RNBCs were exempt from maximum deposits-to-NOF ratios and, partly, from interest rate ceilings. Consequently, against the trend of a shrinking NBFC sector, the number of nidhis increased from 192 in 1996 to 244 in 2005 with instances where deposits amounted to 80 times the NOF. At the same time, insolvencies of major nidhi companies made it to national news. It was only in April 2004 that the DCA ruled nidhis to gradually reduce the deposits-to-NOF ratio to 20. The two main players in the RNBC sector have grown even more dramatically in response to the 1997 RBI initiative. As a share in total public deposits with NBFCs, deposits with RNBCs skyrocketed from less than 10 to 75 per cent between 1997 and 2003. The deposits-to-NOF ratio in the RNBC sector was at 116 in 2002 and improved to 19 in 2003 through a massive injection of capital. As one of the two large RNBCs continues to have weak financials, the RBI considers mandating a cap of 16, although no action had been taken by 2005.

As it stands, substantial deviations from regulatory neutrality and resulting inefficiencies continue to be common features of the NBFC sector. While the regulatory measures implemented over the last 10 years are steps in the right direction, regulators still have to go a long way to create an environment in which banking and non-banking financial institutions compete on even grounds.

Stefan Klonner

References

Carmichael, Jeffrey and Michael Pomerleano. 2002. *The Development and Regulation of Non-bank Financial Institutions*, Washington DC, World Bank.

Reserve Bank of India (RBI). 2004. *Report on Trend and Progress of Banking in India 2002–03*, Mumbai, RBI.

O

■ Oil

India's share of 3,882 million tonnes in the world oil consumption during 2009 was about 5 per cent, while its share in the 182 billion tonnes global oil reserves of proved quality was just about 0.43 per cent. During 2009–10, with domestic production of about 34 million tonnes, India could meet only about 18 per cent of its annual consumption of crude oil (Table 1). Even with India's per capita oil consumption at 113 kg in comparison to 302 kg in China and 2,732 kg in the United States during 2009, cost of oil imports constituted about 50 per cent of the total imports bill. The Eleventh Plan document has projected that the demand for oil will increase to 186 million tonnes by 2011–12 to meet 34 per cent of India's commercial energy needs. Thus, energy security is a major policy issue, which entails switching to alternative resources, such as clean coal technologies, gas, solar, wind, nuclear, and other unconventional sources of energy, and increasing efficiency besides reforming the oil sector. Roughly 40 per cent of petroleum goes to the transport sector, 30 per cent to industry, 8 per cent to agriculture, 16 per cent towards cooking, and the balance for miscellaneous use.

Already initiated reforms include private participation in exploration and production of oil and natural gas, dismantling of the administered pricing mechanism (APM), and allowing domestic companies to acquire international oils fields. However, the international arm of the Oil and Natural Gas Corporation, the ONGC Videsh Limited (OVL), spearheading the strategy of exploiting international reserves, is yet to acquire the status of a global operator in the true sense, while almost the entire marketing of petroleum products has remained with five major public-sector companies.

During recent years, India's exports of petroleum products have increased manifold (Table 1). With an output multiplier of 2.24, a forward linkage of 8.5 (2004–5 input–output table) and an employment multiplier of 2.3 persons per million rupees value of output (1998–9 prices), the petroleum products sector has the potential to offset pressure of crude imports and alter the strategic disadvantage into a major advantage if conducive policies are pursued. With a forward linkage of 6.82 (2004–5 input–output table), crude petroleum forms a vital input for a number of economic activities and accordingly, mineral oil prices remain a highly sensitive issue. Mineral oil as a group has a 9.36 per cent weightage in the new basket of goods considered for calculating the wholesale price index with the base year as 2004–5. Therefore, the direct impact of high oil price inflation on general wholesale price inflation is significantly high given the history of one-digit average inflation in India.

However, the indirect effect of oil price inflation through non-oil WPI is also significantly high with persistent effects for several months (Figure 1). Movement in international oil prices are reflected in domestic oil price inflation with a lag, which is mainly determined by the government's actions on the pass through programme (Figure 2). Interestingly, often only positive movements in international prices are passed through albeit with delay and lower magnitudes while losses are recovered during the slumps in the international market. During recent years, the prices have also been managed by maintaining a buffer stock and lower tariff.

Table 1 Key Statistics of India's Oil Sector

	Annual percentage change							
	1990–1	1995–6	2000–1	2005–6	2009–10	1990–5	1995–2000	2000–9
Recoverable reserves of crude oil (MMT)	739.0	732.0	703.0	786.0	775.0	-0.2	-0.8	1.4
Crude production (MMT)	33.0	35.2	32.4	32.2	33.7	1.3	-1.6	0.6
Gross imports of crude oil (MMT)	20.7	27.3	74.1	99.4	159.3	5.7	22.1	11.6
Consumption of crude oil (refinery throughput) (MMT)	51.8	58.7	103.4	130.1	160.0	2.5	12.0	6.4
Net imports of POL crude & products (MMT)	26.7	44.2	75.0	94.5	131.8	10.6	11.2	8.4
Consumption of POL products (MMT)	55.0	74.8	100.7	113.2	138.2	6.3	6.1	4.6
Export of petroleum products (MMT)	2.7	3.4	8.4	23.5	51.0	4.7	19.8	29.4
Self reliance in crude =100*production/ (Imports + production)	61.5	56.3	30.4	24.5	17.5			
R/P ratio (years)	22.4	20.8	21.7	24.4	23.0			
Percentage gross POL to India's total imports	33.1	22.7	38.3	44.5	49.5			

Source: Indian Petroleum and Natural Gas Statistics.

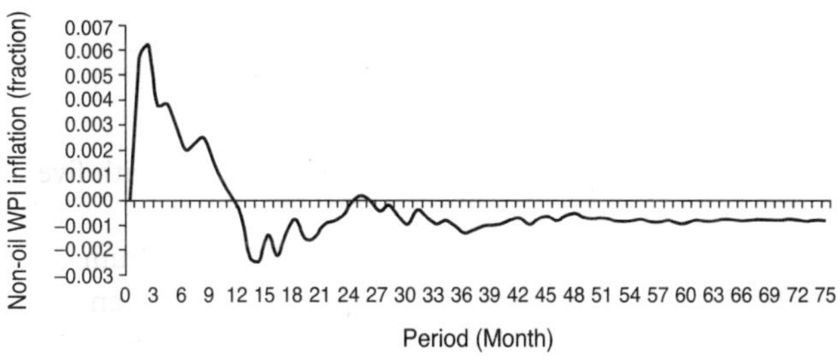

Figure 1 Effect of 10 per cent Permanent Increase in Mineral Oil Price in the Domestic Market on the Non-oil WPI (Y-o-Y basis) of India

Source: Author's simulation in a monthly model explaining almost 90 per cent variation in non-oil inflation during April 1995–December 2010.

In fact, India has attempted various forms of pricing mechanisms for petroleum products since 1948, including, inter alia, Valued Stock Account (VSA), import parity, and domestic production cost plus systems. The most durable APM based on domestic cost of production was introduced in November 1976 and it continued until the mid-1990s when it was perceived to be a stumbling block in accelerating investment to meet the production demands of a growing economy. Accordingly, during 1995–7, the government set up an industry study group to prepare a blueprint for deregulation and a strategic Planning Group for Restructuring of the Indian Oil Industry headed by Vijay Kelkar and an Expert Technical Group on phasing of reforms. Consequently, effective from 1 April 2002, APM was completely dismantled in

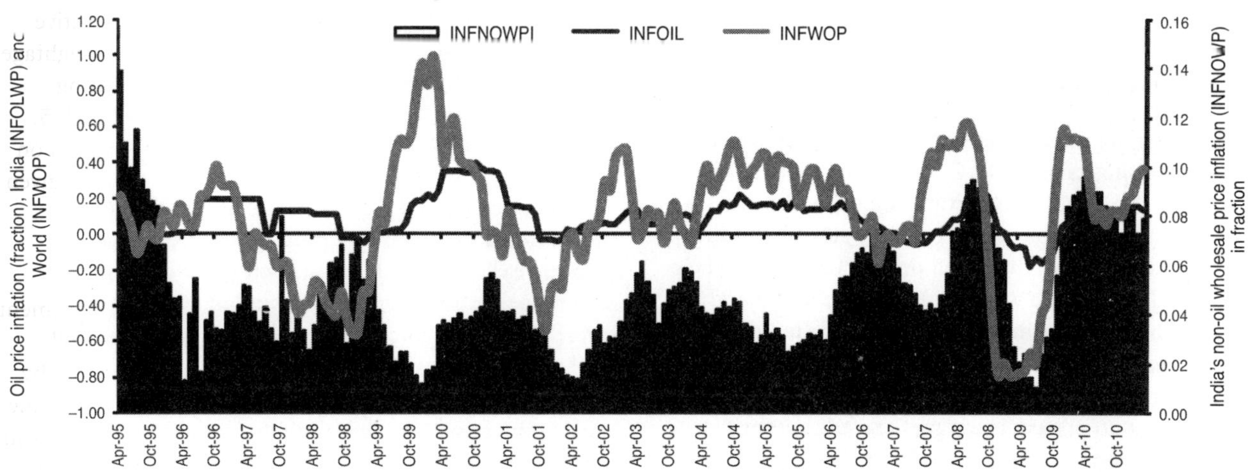

Figure 2 India's Response of Oil Price Inflation and Non-oil Price Inflation to the World Oil Price Inflation

Source (Basic data): NCAER database; Office of the Economic Advisor, Ministry of Industry, Government of India; International Financial Statistics (IFS) of the International Monetary Fund (IMF). The World oil prices are the UK Brent, light blend 38 API, fob UK.

favour of a system of Crude Oil Sales Agreement (COSA) between the producers and the refineries. However, with most of the oil companies still under the public sector, government intervention prevails. The mid-term review of the Eleventh Plan has expressed dissatisfaction with the progress made in achieving real competition in the marketing of petroleum products. It states: 'Persisting with a system of petroleum pricing that is not aligned with world prices is fundamentally unviable for a commodity which is 78 per cent imported. There is a clear need to ensure that prices of petroleum products are based on market price parity, and subsidies are given to BPL families only.' Sensing the urgency of reforms, another Expert Group on a Viable and Sustainable System of Pricing of Petroleum Products headed by Kirit Parikh was constituted in 2009, which submitted its report in February 2010 and recommended a market-determined pricing system for petrol and diesel. The report argues that the same can be sustained in the long run by providing a level playing field and promoting competition among all players, public and private, in the oil and gas sector, under adequate regulatory oversight to ensure effective competition. Subsequently, the Empowered Group of Ministers on deregulation, headed by Finance Minister Pranab Mukherjee, went ahead with partial implementation of the Kirit Parikh Committee report and petrol prices appear to have been decontrolled effectively but diesel prices are still controlled. However, given the effect of oil price shocks on the non-oil component of the wholesale price index, complete market aligned pricing of oil would remain a contentious issue.

Kanhaiya Singh

Oil Price Shocks

Economists are unanimous regarding the negative effects of oil price shocks on GDP, inflation, and balance of payments (BoP) of oil-importing countries. Since oil is an essential input and cannot be easily substituted in the short run, an increase in oil prices raises a country's import bill and hence worsens the trade balance and reduces income. The inflationary pressure emerges due to cost escalation arising from oil price pass-through—something which may trigger off a wage-price spiral if workers seek to protect real wages and the authorities follow an accommodating monetary policy. Restrictive monetary measures are not without their flip side either as interest rates rise and reinforce the depressionary effect of the initial worsening of trade balance. No wonder then that oil price shocks tend to cause stagflation, a combination of inflation and declining or stagnant GDP.

India's experience during the first three oil crises (in 1973, 1980, and 1990) was markedly different from the oil-importing Organisation for Economic Co-operation and Development (OECD) countries. The stagflationary impact in these economies was the largest in the wake of the first two shocks. In contrast, India's average growth did not dip below the trend during the two episodes. Growth rate did fall to 1.16 per cent in 1974–5, to 1.25 per cent in 1976–7, and to –5.2 per cent in 1979–80; however, these falls were not primarily due to oil price hikes, but due to monsoon failures in the three years and due to the fact that with agriculture accounting for around 40 per cent of GDP, climatic conditions had important effects on incomes generated in industries and services as well. The inflationary impact of the shocks was more pronounced but even in this respect the supply-side effect originating in agriculture played the major role, especially during the first shock.

One reason for the resilience of the Indian economy was low initial ratios of oil imports to GDP and exports so that the effects of the shocks were significantly less than those of (as yet low oil-intensive) agricultural production and public consumption and investment. Second, the cost-push inflationary consequences and demand-reducing impact were moderated by not allowing petro prices to rise in line with crude prices. Third, under the highly regulated trade-cum-exchange rate regime, severe restrictions on 'non-essential' imports prevented BoP from going haywire. Finally, and most important, the oil bonanza in the Middle East provided a major boost to exports, opened up large employment opportunities in the region for Indian workers, and led to a quantum jump in NRI (non-resident Indian) remittances. As a result, not only was there no significant deterioration in BoP, but over 1973–83 the average current account balance turned positive, contrary to the chronic (though modest) deficit in the pre-crisis years.

India also proved a contrarian during the 1990–1 shock. Being milder and of much shorter duration than the earlier ones, this shock left other oil-importing countries practically unscathed but landed India into a severe BoP crisis, forcing it to seek IMF assistance and initiate reforms à la the Washington consensus. However, the role of the oil price increase per se was not major in causing the crisis. The first Gulf war coming on the heels of the disintegration of the Soviet regime produced a major disruption in India's BoP. No less important was the inept management of the external account reflected in a large accumulation of short-term and easily reversible external debt (for example, NRI deposits); maintaining an overvalued exchange rate; and holding inadequate forex reserves relative to highly liquid external liabilities. Given the BoP vulnerability engendered by these factors, the oil price hike itself constituted only the last straw on the camel's back.

Compared with the three earlier shocks, the latest surge in oil prices seems *sui generis* in respect of its origins, nature, and economic consequences. In the first three episodes, abnormal price increases occurred over relatively short periods, 15–16 months during the first two shocks and only 4 months during the third. In sharp contrast, the steep northward trajectory of oil prices from early 1999 to end Q_1 2011 was punctuated by only two dips, the first in 2001 in the wake of the busting of the dotcom bubble and the second in 2009 following the outbreak of the global financial crisis. But despite the vertiginous fall on the two occasions (especially the second), over the 12-year period, the annual average increase in nominal and real (inflation-adjusted) oil prices amounted to nearly 19 and 16 per cent, respectively. What is more noteworthy, the steep rise in oil prices over such a long period did not, unlike the first two shocks, apparently have any stagflationary impact on the oil-importing advanced or developing economies. Notwithstanding the dotcom crash and the severest financial turmoil engulfing the global economy since the Great Depression, world output growth during the period averaged 3.8 per cent, with the advanced and emerging economies recording an exceptionally robust growth of 2.1 and 6.0 per cent, respectively. The high growth during the latest bout of prolonged oil price increases was also accompanied with quite moderate inflation: between 1999 and 2011 the average consumer price inflation was 4.1, 2.7, and 7.2 per cent, respectively, for the world economy, advanced countries, and EMEs.

Unlike in the three earlier shocks, the Indian experience during the latest one has been similar to that of most other oil-importing countries. Indeed, the phenomenon of accelerating oil prices accompanied with a vastly improved economic performance has been particularly conspicuous in the Indian economy. Over the period 1999–2011, when petroleum price increases averaged 19 per cent, India's average GDP growth (7.0 per cent) was one percentage point higher and CPI inflation (6.2 per cent) 100 basis points lower than the corresponding EME averages. The counterintuitive nature of the correlation between international oil prices and domestic macro behaviour was particularly striking before the financial crisis. During 2003–8 the average increase in international oil prices was about 24 per cent, but the period saw the best ever performance of the Indian economy with a 9.0 per cent GDP growth and an inflation of less than 5 per cent. In fact, remembering that over 1997–2003 inflation was higher (at 6 per cent) and growth significantly lower (at 5.1 per cent) even though the petro price increase was single digit (9.3 per cent), one is tempted to view the oil shock as positively salubrious for the country's economic health.

The clue to the conundrum of high growth with muted inflation in the face of rising petroleum prices lies in the sources of the shock and structural transformation in the global economy since the 1970s. The recent oil shock has not been supply-side but demand-side, as incomes have been rising at a fast pace in both advanced and emerging economies. Given the long gestation period of investment in hydrocarbon, economic logic suggests that: (i) growth-induced demand for petroleum products would push up oil prices in the short and medium run and (ii) this would moderate GDP growth but not make it negative. The main reasons why the demand-driven rise in oil prices during 1999–2011 did not cause a significant crowding-out of GDP or a rise in CPI seem to be the following.

Since the early 1970s the oil-intensity of world output has come down dramatically with technological improvements, substitution of gas for petroleum, and harnessing of alternative sources of energy. Again, over the last two decades total factor productivity has been boosted through dismantling of trade barriers; movement of enterprises to low-cost regions; development of global supply chains; outsourcing of a variety of services; and rapid diffusion across the world of both technical and organizational know-how. The associated rise in productivity along with intensification of competitive pressure helped greatly in sustaining growth and keeping inflation in check despite the galloping oil prices. No less important have been the roles of rising wage flexibility (with declines in both union membership and militancy) and of increasing dominance of inflation hawks in policymaking since the mid-1980s: the resulting 'great moderation' has had a decisive impact on inflation expectations and prevented the onset of wage-price spirals witnessed in the wake of the first two shocks.

Some of these factors have favourably affected India as well; even so her vastly improved macroeconomic performance during the latest shock is remarkable remembering that the country's energy efficiency is one-third of OECD nations'; over the 12-year period, oil imports as a share of GDP more than tripled; and since the turn of the century the importance of oil-rich countries as sources of export demand and NRI remittances have become much less than in earlier decades. Indeed, in the context of the steep rise in ratios of oil imports to export earnings and to GDP over 1998–2008, from 13 and 1.5 per cent to 31.5 and 6.5 per cent, respectively, India's robust growth sans high inflation and current account deficits appears highly counterintuitive. The main explanation lies in the fact that the demand-led growth of the world economy raised oil prices, but also boosted India's exports and NRI remittances. With exports–GDP and remittances–GDP ratios rising from 11.2 and 1.5 per cent to 21 and 3.5 per cent, respectively, and *net* oil imports' share in GDP growing from 1.5 to 4.2 per cent between 1998–9 to 2007–8, the benign impact of external factors outweighed the negative consequences of the oil shock. Again, while the increased openness of the economy (reflected in the 21.1 percentage point rise in the trade–GDP ratio to 45.3 per cent) and oil subsidies helped in moderating inflation, productivity growth fostered by the former was also non-negligible.

However, the post-crisis global scenario does not augur well for India's economic prospects. With the world growth driven almost wholly by oil-hungry EMEs rather than energy-efficient advanced countries, petroleum prices have been on a steeply upward trajectory since Q_2 2009. The implication for India is an ever increasing oil–GDP ratio (she is already the fourth largest consumer of petroleum) and a slowdown in export growth to and remittances from industrialized countries. Matters are not helped by the high (petro-based) fertilizer intensity of Indian agriculture and the overwhelming role of food prices in driving inflation. Hence arises the prospect of a growth slowdown with heightened inflationary pressure. The need of the hour is to align domestic fertilizer and petroleum prices to their international counterparts. While this would boost productivity growth in the long run, the associated cost would be a jump in inflation in the short and medium run.

MIHIR RAKSHIT

■ Outsourcing

Some time ago, British Airways announced its plans to get all its accounting done in Mumbai. Many hospitals in the US are getting X-rays read by medical technologists in India. No matter where you live, your cries for 'Help' with your DELL computer may be answered by a technician in Hyderabad. These are the examples of outsourcing that consumers in the West are well aware of because they are a part of their everyday experience. However, this is only the tip of the iceberg. Many businesses use software (for example, accounting, inventory control, marketing research) that needs to be customized for their own special needs. A significant part of India's software exports comprises such software services. The term 'outsourcing' has come to mean all such services traded internationally over electronic media such as Internet, fax, and telephones.

In this entry we will first ask what factors may have been responsible for the advent of outsourcing. Second, we will probe the source of anxieties generated in the West on account of outsourcing and examine arguments about whether these are warranted. We will then consider the history of outsourcing to India, followed by an analysis of whether outsourcing is of any significance to the Indian economy and if so 'how'.

While anxieties about outsourcing to locations abroad are a new development, outsourcing itself is not a new phenomenon. Revolutionary developments in information technology (IT), particularly in the past two decades, made it imperative for informational structures within business and government organizations to be overhauled. New databases for inventory control, market research, and other management tasks were created. However, this was a monumental task and in most firms the expertise for such informational overhaul was unavailable among the ranks of existing employees. Further, in many cases, it made little sense to add to the payroll of permanent employees those who were needed for a one-time job. As a result, the one-time job of an informational overhaul was typically contracted out to specialist local firms. However, what initially seemed like a one-time addition of software invariably required further support and service, especially as information needs changed and technologies evolved to meet them. Over time, firms came to think of database management as a separate function that could be contracted to independent local firms. This was the beginning of outsourcing at local level.

Outsourcing dramatically picked up pace in the 1990s as technology became capable of handling tasks of increasing complexity and costs of computing fell. Further, as the Internet became ubiquitous and costs of transmitting information dropped, it was a small step from a local specialized firm to a firm located in India or Ireland. What mattered was that the same job could be done abroad for significantly lower cost. Once cost savings were realized, it was natural for firms to be on the lookout for further cost savings and for more tasks to be contracted out to specialized firms abroad.

It is well known that India had invested what seemed like excessive amounts of resources into post-secondary education. For a long time now, Indian engineers and technical graduates had been overqualified for the domestic labour market. The demand for specialized software assignments matched the excess supply of engineers and programmers, and the economic reforms of 1991 removed some of the obstacles in the way of these international business contracts. A number of software firms emerged in India to take advantage of these opportunities in the American market. Initially, many Indian firms got their foot in the door of the US market by helping fix the Year-2000 (Y2K) software glitch primarily by on-site placement of Indian software professionals. Riding on the initial success with Y2K, Indian firms began to provide other low-cost software services to US companies and developed 'off-shoring' business models where a large fraction of a project's software design, development, and testing took place in low-cost India. The result was a software boom in India with a myriad of firms designing customized software for American companies. From here it did not take long for the off-shore market in a range of outsourced services to develop. From manning call centres to reading X-rays and processing of insurance claims, India's educated, low-cost, English-speaking workforce soon became an eager participant in the global service economy. Outsourcing from India had made a debut on the world stage in a noticeable way.

In the West, especially in the US and UK, the issue of outsourcing has created considerable anger and anxiety. In the US presidential debates during the 2004 election, the issue of outsourcing was given a lot of play. Leading media outlets such as *Time* ran cover stories on the issue and TV Networks such as CNN ran programmes that repeatedly highlighted the 'evils' of outsourcing. After all, outsourcing to India or China means that the jobs, whether existing or newly created, go to Indians or Chinese rather than to Americans.

It is legitimate to ask whether the phenomenon of outsourcing is essentially different from international trade in manufactured products. If Bangladesh can produce cheaper textiles than the US, then the imports from Bangladesh would drive American textile manufacturers out of business and consequently there would be similar sort of anxiety among American textile workers. Indeed, there was such anxiety vis-à-vis China in the 1990s and Japan prior to that, when cheap products manufactured in those countries posed a serious challenge to many segments of manufacturing industry in the US. What then is special about outsourcing?

International trade in any physical product, whether in textiles or automobiles, entails considerable shipping costs. Of course, they vary according to the product; they are reasonably small for textiles but quite high for autos. The greater the shipping costs, the less competitive are imports to domestically produced goods. However, when you think of services that can be sent over the Internet, the shipping costs are practically zero. An equally qualified programmer or a technician in India is able to do the job at a fraction of the cost of his or her American counterpart and ship the output over Internet. This is what has created the kerfuffle over outsourcing in the West.

Displacement of jobs may not be the only reason why outsourcing attracts so much discussion. Outsourcing may be breaking rank with history. There has always been a certain chronological pattern in the course of development across the world. As the labour force in low-wage countries develops skills in some industries—typically labour-intensive industries such as textiles—the comparative advantage in those industries passes on to low-wage countries. High-wage countries cannot compete anymore in those low-end industries. However, high-wage countries are typically also more technologically advanced and they have the advantage of a higher-skilled labour force. The capital in high-wage countries shifts to new products and new industries creating new jobs that require higher levels of skills. Thus there is a ladder of skills and jobs that the world keeps moving up, with high-wage countries leading and low-wage countries at their heels. When low-skill jobs are lost to low-wage countries, there is little to mourn for as long as much of the labour force can hope to climb the skills ladder and acquire high-end jobs. In other words, what one sees more explicitly through immigration, with menial and more 'dirty' jobs going to immigrants and migrant labour from less-developed countries, also happens indirectly through trade. Outsourcing, however, presents a clear break from this pattern. A fraction of the jobs lost in the US through outsourcing is clearly skilled. Acquiring higher levels of skills, it is feared, will no longer assure a secure future for an American worker.

Are fears about outsourcing voiced by many media commentators in the US warranted? We can try to address this question both theoretically and empirically. The most straightforward theoretical argument against the spectre of unemployment resulting from outsourcing is that any resultant unemployment is likely to be only a short-run phenomenon. As the jobs are outsourced to cheaper workers elsewhere, the production costs decline. The lowered costs and hence cheaper goods are a boon to domestic consumers; their real incomes rise. The rise in real incomes creates an increase in demand for other goods and services and hence in the supply of new jobs to produce them. The displaced workers take up the newly created jobs. Over time full employment is restored. Of course, the process takes some time to work and it is necessary to retrain the displaced workers. This theoretical argument invariably comes with a caveat that some workers are too old to retrain and some social insurance scheme may have to be provided for them.

The above argument is not specific to the consequences of outsourcing. It applies also to any job losses due to competitive imports or even to labour-displacing technical change. In fact, one could argue that the story of economic growth is very much a story of technological change, a large part of which consists of machines replacing human labour. The overall process has remained the same: the displaced workers have gone on to perform new activities created by a demand for a set of new goods and services. Essentially, there is little difference between a machine displacing local labour and a foreign worker doing the same.

Why then is there so much commotion about outsourcing when there is none at all about labour-displacing technical change? One reason is that the process of labour-displacing technical change is slow and continuous. The job losses come in trickles and it is difficult to attribute a big chunk of jobs lost to a specific event of technology adoption. Outsourcing, on the other hand, is easily noticed. An American company shifting its call centres or its accounting operations to India cannot fail to draw the attention of the American media. Outsourcing is very much in the public eye and, therefore, it provokes so much controversy. It is also easier to blame low-wage workers abroad for taking jobs away rather than assign responsibility to more abstract notions like technological change.

It has also been argued (Bhagwati et al. 2004) that the quantitative impact of outsourcing on the American labour market is insignificant and that very few high-end jobs have been lost as a result of outsourcing. Much of this debate is over future outcomes, so we can only examine arguments based on projections as in the following example. Bhagwati et al. use a much-cited Forrester Research report which estimates that slightly less than half of these jobs (43 per cent) can be classified as belonging to professions that may be subject to outsourcing and that 3.4 million jobs (roughly 300,000 per year) may be lost to outsourcing in the next decade (McCarthy 2004). Setting aside the question of whether such numbers will actually materialize, how one interprets these numbers becomes a matter of what they are compared with. Bhagwati et al. compare the average *annual loss* of jobs due to outsourcing with the *total* number of jobs in the vulnerable sectors and arrive at a small figure for outsourcing losses of 0.53 per cent. The same numbers can be interpreted as 17 per cent of the 20 million jobs the US economy is likely to *add* over the next decade, and jumps to 39 per cent of all *jobs added in the vulnerable sectors*. Thus whether you see job losses as small or significant may depend on the metrics you choose to apply.

It is often stated that many of the jobs being outsourced are low-skill, low-wage jobs and there is ample evidence that many outsourced jobs belong to this category. The current boom in relocation of call centres to India is a case in point. NASSCOM estimates that 95,000 of the 245,000 Indian workers employed in non-software outsourcing services work in call centres. Though some firms in India do high-end work such as patent application research, a majority of the remaining 150,000 workers are employed in relatively low-end jobs such as billing, payment processing, credit card services, and medical transcription. However, most software-related jobs in India cannot be so easily written off as being low end. It is true that in the mid-1990s Indian firms engaged in low-end software services such as fixing the Y2K bug. In recent years, however, the Indian software services sector has evolved to take on custom software of high complexity serving a diverse range of sectors. Examples abound: Infosys, Tata Consultancy Services (TCS), and Wipro, the big three Indian software firms, compete with IBM and Accenture for the accounts of Fortune 500 companies; a medium-sized Indian company, Mastek, was responsible for the IT infrastructure to manage the congestion charge for London's traffic system; Sasken is a Bangalore-based firm that supplies cutting-edge telecom software to many of the world's leading communication companies. A possible reason why Indian software continues to be seen as 'low end' is that no Indian company exports software products. Products have greater economic value than software services. Consequently, software services are seen as 'low end' in economic terms relative to software products. This does not mean that software services are provided by engineers with lower skills.

Increasingly, the distinction between Indian software companies and multinationals is being blurred as India offices of global software giants such as IBM, HP, and CSC (with 23,000, 13,000, and 5,000 Indian employees respectively in 2005) perform software tasks in India that they might in offices in the US. Given the range of skills and the complexity of services offered by Indian firms and MNCs (multinational corporations) in India, it is silly to write-off India's software services as primarily 'low end'. This is reinforced by the recent opening up of dozens of product development and research and development (R&D) centres in India, as well as Indian companies specializing in 'outsourced product development'. In 2005,

NASSCOM estimates that 25,000 engineers work in product development and R&D services in India employed in over 230 firms, primarily foreign, with product development offices in India. The number is expected to grow to 65,000 in three years. The list is impressive—Intel, Motorola, Sun, Oracle, Microsoft, SAP, Novell, Adobe, IBM, HP, GE, Google, Cadence, Yahoo, Amazon, Cisco, and TI all have product development and R&D facilities in India. Some of these facilities are recent while others such as those of TI (225 patents filed, 1,200 employees), Oracle (125 patents filed, 6,400 employees), and Intel (65 patents filed, 2,500 employees) have been operational for a long time. In addition to MNCs, numerous start-ups based primarily in Silicon Valley, the lifeblood of the US innovation system, do much of their product development in India.

Of course, none of the above has much significance for total levels of employment in the Indian economy. The entire software industry in India, of which outsourcing constitutes only a part, employs no more than 1 million workers in the total labour force of 450 million. Even the dramatic growth that is expected over the next decade is unlikely to change this picture by much. It is clear, therefore, that as a contributor to employment in India, outsourcing could hardly have made much of an impact. Its contribution to Indian economy is channelled through indirect ways.

First, the software sector has been the fastest-growing sector in India's exports that make a twofold contribution to the process of growth in a developing country. Exports generate the foreign exchange that enables purchases of productivity-improving foreign machinery and technology. In addition, the foreign exchange reserves generated by software exports have given Indian policymakers a comfortable cushion to withstand any sudden changes in its balance of payments.

Perhaps, the most noteworthy effect of outsourcing on the Indian economy has been an intangible one: it has caused a change in entrepreneurial culture. Gone are the days when the business leaders in India came exclusively from leading business families. The founders of India's software-exporting firms are self-made millionaires who started out with their technological knowledge as their capital. This is a very healthy development as India's future growth depends on young people with talent and expertise entering the entrepreneurial arena.

Outsourcing has been a learning experience for both Indian and Western firms. The word has spread that India has technical expertise of respectable quality that could be tapped and that business relationships could be established with Indian firms. Also, Indian firms have learned a lesson or two in doing business in the West. All this is bound to stand India in good stead for further expansion of exports. The rapid expansion of foreign firms in India's software service sector, as well as the recent growth in R&D and product development, reinforce this point.

Moreover, there have been management spillovers through which the management approaches learned through outsourcing and interaction with foreign companies have been put to use in Indian firms. For example, corporate governance practices such as employee stock option plans, developed within leading companies in the IT sector, have come to serve as exemplars for other companies to follow.

A legitimate question that one might ask is whether outsourcing is relevant to the lives of almost one-third of India's population that is below the poverty line. The answer is once again, 'Yes, but only indirectly and only slightly.' A large component of the 'poor' (those under the poverty line) in India make a living in agriculture. Outsourcing could have an impact on their lives only if it created significant employment for them outside agriculture. It is difficult to sustain a claim that outsourcing has done so either directly or indirectly.

In sum, outsourcing of services emerged globally when cost of telecommunications began to drop in the mid–late 1990s. India, with its large pool of science and technology professionals, quickly became a major provider of these services. Outsourcing to India continues to grow rapidly both in the 'low-end' (for example, call centres) and 'high-end' (for example, product R&D) segments. However, the impact of outsourcing has largely been through indirect means and not through direct employment. Consequently, while outsourcing will continue to be an important contributor to the overall economic picture, its role in poverty alleviation is likely to be small.

MILIND KANDLIKAR AND ASHOK KOTWAL

References

Bhagwati, J., A. Panagariya, and T.N. Srinivasan. 2004. 'The Muddles over Outsourcing', *The Journal of Economic Perspectives*, Fall, 18(4): 93–114.

McCarthy, J. 2004. 'Near Term Growth of Offshoring Accelerating: Resizing US Services Jobs Going Offshore', Cambridge, Forrester Research Inc., May.

P

■ Panchayats

Panchayats or village governments have informally existed in India for many centuries, but as formal institutions of local democracy are only just over a decade old. The British colonial authorities created some local administrative bodies (called union boards) in the 19th century, which were more of an effort to co-opt local elites into the colonial administration, rather than having any semblance of popular participation. The Constitution of the new Indian republic continued this tradition, recognizing state governments as the sole subnational units of government. The list of responsibilities was divided into the Union List (foreign affairs, defence, currency, income taxes, and so on), the State List (law and order, public health, agriculture, land reform, wealth tax, and so on), and the Concurrent List (electricity, newspapers, education, price controls, and so on) where both the Centre and states had responsibility.

Nevertheless, the Constitution encouraged decentralization to village governments, but left the responsibility for implementing such a system on state governments. In order to assist this process, the central government set up the Balwantrai Mehta Committee in 1957, which provided a detailed set of suggestions for a three-tier system of local government. The recommendations of this Committee have formed a model that has substantially impacted the actual process followed in India in the subsequent half century. Village panchayats were to form the bottom-most layer, to be elected directly, with reserved seats for scheduled castes and tribes (SC/ST) and women. Above them would be the *panchayat samiti* (PS) at block level, with members indirectly elected from representatives of the village panchayats, and also with special provision for representation of women and SC/ST residents. The top tier of the system was to be composed of the *zilla parishad* (ZP) at district level. Panchayats were to rely principally on grants and aid from central and state governments. Responsibilities to be devolved excluded administration of public education (above primary schools). The system was insufficiently detailed on its definition of public health responsibilities to be assigned to local bodies. In other words, the system was to be part of a top–down centralized state, where the role of local governments would be to provide municipal services and implement development programmes mandated by state and central governments. It reflected the consensus in the 1950s that the centralized state would be the principal agent of economic development.

The Balwantrai Mehta Committee left room for state governments to experiment with the system as they saw fit, consistent with the Constitutional assignment of responsibility, and was endorsed in this respect by the National Development Council in January 1958. The central government created a Ministry of Community Development, Panchayati Raj and Cooperation in 1958, and issued a publication in 1962 entitled *A Digest on Panchayati Raj* reiterating its encouragement to state governments to implement a three-tier system of local government. In the absence of any concrete political pressure from the Centre, state governments (with few exceptions such as Maharashtra and a Gujarat in the late 1960s, and West Bengal in the late 1970s) were unwilling to embark on any serious effort to devolve power to local governments.

Constitutional Design

A set of landmark (73rd and 74th) amendments to the Constitution passed in 1993 finally mandated the creation of a three-tier structure of local government, quite close to the structure advocated by the Balwantrai Mehta Committee. It established in all states (with population less than 2 million) governments at village, block, and district levels, to be directly elected at all levels once every five years. Reservations of seats and chairperson positions were mandated for SC/ST representatives on the basis of their demographic weight, in addition to one-third reservation for women. Two state-level commissions were also mandated—an election commission and a finance commission—to supervise the conduct of elections and devolution of finances. A District Planning Board was to consolidate plans from lower levels of panchayats.

The 73rd and 74th Amendments, however, did not mandate the pattern of devolution, and left this to the discretion of the concerned state government. They merely suggested that panchayats were to be devolved the responsibility for preparing plans for local development and implementing a host of schemes (listed in Schedule XI) with regard to agricultural extension, land reforms, health and family welfare, primary and secondary education, and promotion of small-scale industry. They also suggested gram sabhas—village meetings constituted of the electorate—be endowed with powers and functions to oversee the panchayats. No legislative authority was delegated to local bodies.

Implementation

The mandatory requirements of holding elections have been followed by and large in most states, though the timing of elections has often been sought to be manipulated by state governments. Mandated reservation of one-third of panchayat positions for women had been successfully implemented by 2000 (except in Punjab and UP), while for SC/STs it has been somewhat less than their demographic weight in some states: the ratio was below 70 per cent in Gujarat, Orissa, and UP (Chaudhuri 2005).

On the other hand, the implementation of the discretionary provisions has been highly uneven across different states, with only a handful of states embarking on any significant devolution of functions or finances. A Government of India 2001 Report of Working Group on Decentralized Planning and Panchayati Raj Institutions revealed that only Karnataka had transferred (that is, enacted legislation and passed government orders) functions, functionaries, and funds for 29 different Schedule XI items. West Bengal and Kerala had by then transferred 29 functions, but functionaries and finances for 15 or less items. The remaining large states (Bihar, Gujarat, Haryana, Punjab, Rajasthan, Tamil Nadu) had transferred functionaries and funds for not a single item. State governments held significant powers over panchayats in various respects. Six large states (Andhra Pradesh, Haryana, Karnataka, Orissa, Punjab, and UP) imposed restrictions on the powers of panchayats to approve expenditures above Rs 25,000. Own revenue generated by panchayats constituted only 3.7 per cent of their total income for the period 1995–8, down from 4.5 per cent for the period 1990–5. Gram panchayats in 10 out of 14 major states reported own revenues of less than Rs 10 per capita per year. Reports of State Finance Commissions were delayed in most instances, with the solitary exception of Kerala.

Nevertheless, some states have witnessed some meaningful devolution. In 1996, Kerala devolved 40 per cent of its development funds to panchayats, with the State Planning Board playing a key role in the implementation of discretionary components of the 73rd and 74th Constitutional Amendments. It organized a massive training exercise for panchayat officials. Gram sabhas have witnessed widespread popular participation; civil society organizations such as the KSSP (People's Science Movement) have organized presence in almost every village. Prior to the passage of the constitutional amendments, the Left Front government in West Bengal had created a mandatory three-tier structure of panchayats since 1978, directly elected every five years. These panchayats played a significant role in the implementation of land reforms, selection of beneficiaries of the Integrated Rural Development Programme (IRDP) credit programmes and various welfare assistance programmes, distribution of agricultural input mini-kits, administration of local employment programmes, and various community and cooperative projects. Since the 1990s, they have administered primary and secondary educational institutions, forming an alternative to the government-run schools that continue to remain under the state government.

Other states such as Rajasthan, Madhya Pradesh, and Karnataka have also witnessed some serious efforts at devolution. But for most of the country the general assessment is that the devolution has been de jure rather than de facto.

Detailed empirical data-based studies of the functioning and impact of panchayats have been restricted to a few states with some genuine devolution. *Gram sansad* (village meeting) attendance in 20 West Bengal panchayat constituencies as studied by Ghatak and Ghatak (2002) revealed 12–15 per cent attendance among voters, with representation of landless, marginal landowners, SC/ST groups, and Muslims more or less proportional to their population shares, but women and voters affiliated with the principal opposition party significantly underrepresented. Chattopadhyay and Duflo (2004) examine the effect of randomized reservation of gram panchayat positions in selected districts of West Bengal and Rajasthan. Reservation of *panchayat pradhan* positions for women was associated with a statistically significant shift in spending into areas favoured by women (drinking water and road maintenance).

Reservation of pradhan positions for SC/ST candidates, on the other hand, resulted in no discernible shift in composition of spending across different areas, but was associated with higher spending in the particular village in which the pradhan resided, at the expense of other villages administered by the same village panchayat. Bardhan and Mookherjee (2005) examine targeting of various programmes administered by West Bengal panchayats using a sample of 80 villages in 15 major districts. They find high levels of intra-village targeting of IRDP credit and agricultural mini-kits to the landless, marginal landowners, and SC/ST groups, which did not vary with shifts in local poverty, land inequality, illiteracy, or caste composition of villages observed over the period 1978–98. On the other hand, pro-poor targeting of employment grants and all other fiscal grants exhibited a tendency to deteriorate significantly when local poverty, land inequality, or low-caste status of the poor grew. They argue that this was the result of political discretion among state government and panchayat officials, a problem which could be avoided with the establishment of direct formula-based allocation of grants to village panchayats.

Agenda for Future Reforms

Much remains to be done to provide teeth to the 73rd and 74th Constitutional Amendments and transform panchayat bodies into genuine institutions for democratic decentralization of development programmes. Aiyar (2002), amongst others, has stressed the need for reforms in the following areas: (i) significant devolution of functions and finances to panchayat bodies (responsibilities, functionaries and funds for local infrastructure, agricultural development and development of small-scale industry; abolition of the the DRDA [Department of Rural Development and Aid], the arm of the state government bureaucracy traditionally responsible for administering development and welfare programmes); (ii) training of panchayat officials; (iii) direct formula-based grants to village panchayats and development of their capacity to raise local revenues; (iv) checks and balances over operation of village panchayats, including gram sabhas, audits by higher-level government officials, involvement of non-governmental organizations (NGOs), and disclosure rules for panchayat accounts; (v) conduct of elections, prevention of manipulation of timing of elections, voter lists, and vote counting by incumbents, law and order during conduct of elections, and rules governing electoral campaigns; and (vi) encouragement of local planning exercises based on popular participation. State governments have dragged their feet on these discretionary elements of the 73rd and 74th Amendments. To translate the intentions of the previous amendments into reality, perhaps another amendment is necessary.

Dilip Mookherjee

References

Aiyar, Mani Shankar. 2002. 'Panchayati Raj: The Way Forward', *Economic and Political Weekly*, 3 August, 37(31): 3293–7.

Bardhan, Pranab and Dilip Mookherjee (eds). 2005. *Decentralization and Local Governance in Developing Countries: A Comparative Perspective*, Cambridge, MA, MIT Press: particularly chapters by Shubham Chaudhuri for India and Bardhan and Mookherjee for West Bengal.

Chattopadhyay, Raghabendra and Esther Duflo. 2004. 'Impact of Reservation in Panchayati Raj: Evidence from a Nation-wide Randomised Experiment', *Economic and Political Weekly*, 28 February, 39(9): 979–86.

Chaudhuri, S. 2005. 'What Difference Does a Constitutional Amendment Make? The 1994 Panchayati Raj Act and the Attempt to Revitalize Rural Local Government in India', in P. Bardhan and D. Mookherjee (eds), *Decentralization and Local Governance in Developing Countries: A Comparative Perspective*, Cambridge, MA, MIT Press.

Ghatak, Maitreesh and Maitreyee Ghatak. 2002. 'Recent Reforms in the Panchayat System in West Bengal: Towards Greater Participatory Governance?' *Economic and Political Weekly*, 5 January, 37(1): 45–57.

Government of India. 2001. *Report of Working Group on Decentralized Planning and Panchayati Raj Institutions*, Ministry of Rural Development.

■ I.G. Patel

When I.G. Patel joined the Ministry of Finance, Government of India in 1954, as deputy economic advisor, the Indian polity was seized of the most formidable task of articulating an economic policy that could set India on a higher growth path and reduce widespread poverty and unemployment. There was no clarity then about how the existing economic theory should inform economic policy and what it would take to exercise it. J.J. Anjaria, the head of the economic unit, and Patel were fully aware of the inapplicability of the short-term Keynesian policy framework to resolve India's long-term development problems. While studying at Cambridge University in England and Harvard University, Patel was intellectually persuaded by the relevance for India of economic dynamics of R.F. Harrod and E. Domar, Rosenstein-Rodan's theory of the 'Big Push', and the insights of Michael Kalecki, as reflected in his advocacy of the need for a balance between the level of investment and the supply of consumer goods. What Patel learnt from these economists was a lodestar to his vision of economic policy but he modified it in the light of the Indian reality. In this, he drew inspiration from Joan Robinson's cryptic remark that 'economic model cannot tell us much more than what we tell it' (Patel 1986: 24).

Patel, shunning a scholarly career, chose to be a practitioner of economics because he relished dealing with reality with all its conflicts and compromises. He defined his role variously as an economic theorist who modifies theory when contradicted by facts, an economic analyst with quantitative acquaintance with the interrelationship among facts, an economic policymaker who teases out the essence from theories, and finally an economic administrator who translates economic advice into practice. In balancing these roles, Patel discovered that 'the route to the rational is not always direct' (Guhan and Shroff 1986: xi). In his own words, the economic advisor has to 'be Janus-like, saying one thing inside and the other outside' (Patel 1998: 72)—inside when economic reasoning is brought into free play and outside when it is diluted without losing its core to meet the popular perception of the economic strategy. An example of this tight-rope walking in economic policymaking was reflected in the expression, 'a socialistic pattern of society' concocted by Anjaria and Patel to dampen the socialist fervour of the politicians (ibid.: 73).

Patel had to start, around the time the First Five Year Plan (1952–6) was taking shape, from scratch as there was a glaring paucity of reliable statistics, essential for formulating economic plan or policy. The last finance minister of India before the transfer of power by the British said that he 'waged a war of five and half years without statistics, why must he want statistics to wage peace?' (Guhan and Shroff 1986: 37). Patel drew up a comprehensive balance sheet of the national economy, to the extent permitted by the available statistics, and improved the database by gathering around him a large number of economists and statisticians.

The First Five Year Plan was inspired by the economic theories of Harrod–Domar and Rodenstein-Rodan. While the former enabled the planners to see India's developmental problems in a long-term perspective with the emphasis on raising the saving rate, the latter emphasized the need to have broad-based industrial programmes conducive to learning by doing. However, given the incomplete information, the First Five Year Plan was no more than an indicative plan, with large public expenditure on infrastructure, targets for the private sector, and broad signals for macroeconomic fiscal and monetary policies.

Patel was more closely involved in thinking strategically during the preparation of the Second Five Year Plan which was modelled on P.C. Mahalanobis's vision of India's economic development. His model, comprising two sectors producing investment goods and consumer goods was not open to international trade. For a given targeted growth rate, it required a rising ratio of investment, which was ensured by the increasing proportion of investment goods to total output. The production of consumption goods, projected to grow more slowly, was in small-scale industries and agriculture, using more labour and less capital. However, the Second Five Year Plan was financially not feasible and was viewed with scepticism in the Ministry of Finance, the Planning Commission, and among the donor countries. Patel was chosen to be an interlocutor to reconcile the views of Mahalanobis, on the one hand, and those of the Ministry of Finance and the Planning Commission, on the other. As a result, he authored a 'Draft Plan Frame of the Five Year Plan II', showing in his subtle and persuasive way that Mahalanobis's plan implied an incremental savings rate of as high as 50 per cent which was, by any standard, impossible to attain without draconian policy measures. Further, India could achieve the same goal of a higher rate of growth as envisaged by Mahalanobis if it could export goods in which it had comparative advantage. His document received imprimatur both from Mahalanobis and the Ministry of Finance and Planning Commission, leading to the finalization of the Second Five Year Plan. However, the overlooking of Patel's caveats in his note and the inability of the administrative wing of the Government of India to clearly define the instruments of implementation of the plan strategy sowed the seeds of failure of the bold

Indian planning experiment. Inappropriate instruments like industrial licensing, reservation for small and cottage industries, choking exports, and promotion of inefficient import substitution subverted the political process resulting in rampant corruption.

Patel became the governor of the Reserve Bank of India (RBI), the central bank of the country in 1977. But the heyday of his role as the effective economic policymaker was over, not the least because the RBI functioned more as a fiscal agency under the tutelage of the Ministry of Finance and Patel worked with the severe handicap of the hostility of the then Prime Minister, Indira Gandhi. Patel greeted the advent of economic reforms in 1991, as it paved the way for a 'virtual bonfire' of industrial licensing and the panoply of other restrictive practices that had arrested India's economic progress for more than two decades.

DEENA KHATKHATE

References

Guhan, S. and M. Shroff. 1986. *Essays on Economic Progress and Welfare*, Delhi, Oxford University Press.

Patel, I.G. 1986. *Essays in Economic Policy and Economic Growth*, London, Macmillan.

——. 1998. *Economic Reforms and Global Change*, New Delhi, Macmillan.

——. 2002. *Glimpses of Indian Economic Policy: An Insider's View*, New Delhi, Oxford University Press.

Patents

Patents are legal rights that are granted by national authorities in each country separately over new, inventive, and otherwise eligible products or processes. These rights give their owners the authority to prevent others from commercially exploiting their inventions without their permission within that country. Up to 2005, India granted only process patents for food, medicine, and chemical inventions while allowing product patents in all other sectors. In compliance with its World Trade Organization (WTO) obligations on intellectual property, India has made a paradigm shift, making available both product and process patents for all eligible inventions. The history of the evolution of this regime in independent India is replete with battles fought between representatives of foreign right holders and domestic interests. By 2005, this picture had changed somewhat with some in Indian industry and government advocating strong patent protection, while others, including international civil society groups, backing minimal changes necessary to implement international obligations.

Patents Act, 1970

The Patents Act, 1970, which came into effect in April 1972, replaced the colonial Patents and Designs Act of 1911. The design of this law was the subject of at least three committees of inquiry over more than two decades since Independence, the most influential of which was the Ayyangar Committee set up in 1957 (Ayyangar 1959). The general philosophy underlying this long and complicated law was that patents should be used as industrial policy instruments to encourage industrialization and promote self-reliance. This was summed up in Section 82 (now 83) which stated inter alia that patents are granted to secure that inventions are worked in India on a commercial scale and that they are not granted merely to enable patent owners to enjoy a monopoly for the importation of the product.

One of the major changes introduced in 1970 was the virtual abolition of patents in the chemicals, food, and pharmaceuticals sectors through the use of four measures:

- First, the 1970 law limited the grant of patents for chemicals, food, pharmaceuticals, and agricultural chemicals to process inventions only. This meant that inventors of products such as new human or veterinary medicines, vaccines, diagnostic products, agricultural chemicals, or food (as well as their intermediate substances) could not obtain product patents in India, thus allowing anyone to manufacture and sell these products, using processes different from those patented, where necessary.
- Second, while patents over methods or processes for the production of such products could be granted if they were eligible, the rights of the process patent owner were limited to excluding others from using the process within India and did not extend to prohibiting them from selling the product directly obtained through the use of the process. Thus anyone could import the end product from a jurisdiction where there was no such process or product patent and compete in the market with the patent owner or his authorized agent.
- Third, the duration of the patent term was reduced from 14 years from the date of filing of the patent application given to all other eligible inventions to seven years for food, pharmaceutical, or agricultural chemical process inventions. This was done despite the fact that it is in precisely these sectors that patents are important and where substances have to undergo

long and expensive tests before obtaining marketing approvals from the national authorities. Thus, in reality, the term left for exclusive marketing of the product obtained from the patented process in India may have been negligible, if not negative.[1]

- Fourth, in the unlikely event that third parties needed to use such patents during their short lifetime, they were automatically allowed to use these inventions through the licences-of-right system applicable three years from the grant of food, pharmaceutical, and agricultural chemical patents. They had to only pay a statutorily fixed royalty of a maximum of 4 per cent of the sales price. In addition, in keeping with the underlying philosophy, the law strengthened the general provisions for compulsory licensing and use of patents by government.

This regime is credited by some with the growth and international competitiveness of India's generic drug industry, with medicine prices consequently moving from one of the highest levels in the world to the lowest.

International Obligations

Until 1995, India was not party to any international agreement on patents, although it was a member of the principal copyright treaties. As a founder member, India became bound by the agreement of the WTO on intellectual property known by its acronym TRIPS (Agreement on Trade-related Aspects of Intellectual Property Rights). TRIPS mandates, inter alia, the availability of process and product patents for eligible inventions in all fields of technology. Subsequently, in 1998, India joined two pre-existing treaties administered by the World Intellectual Property Organization (WIPO), the Paris Convention for the Protection of Industrial Property 1883 (as revised up to 1967), and the Patent Co-operation Treaty (PCT) 1970. Since the substantive provisions of the Paris Convention were already incorporated into the TRIPS Agreement, there were no additional changes in national legislation required on this account.

Joining the PCT, a subsidiary treaty of the Paris Convention that facilitates the work of patent filing internationally, made the task of filing of patents in India easier for foreigners and filing elsewhere easier for Indian residents.

The patent law of 1970 remained unchanged for more than 25 years until the process of implementing international obligations, notably the TRIPS Agreement, began—albeit with some delay—in 1999, was taken forward more substantially in 2002 and once again, more recently, in March 2005.[2] Given the very strong opposing interests trying to influence the content of the amendments, India availed itself of the grace period of 10 years up to 2005 allowed under this Agreement to introduce product patents for sectors excluded earlier.

Patentable Subject Matter

India introduced the extension of product patents to chemicals, pharmaceuticals, agricultural chemicals, and food, first through an executive ordinance in December 2004 and later, through a law that obtained the support of the left-wing parties, in March 2005. Earlier in 1999, having lost a WTO dispute, India introduced exclusive marketing rights (EMRs) that last five years—or less if a patent is granted or rejected in the interim—for patent applications covering pharmaceuticals and agricultural chemical product inventions filed from 1995 to 2004.

Confirming earlier patent office practice, chemical processes can be understood to include biochemical, biotechnological, and microbiological processes. However, any process for the medicinal, surgical, curative, prophylactic, diagnostic, therapeutic, or other treatment of humans, animals, and plants to render them free of disease or increase their economic value is excluded from patent grant.[3]

Inventions that are plants and animals, in whole or any part, including seeds, varieties, species, and essentially biological process for the production or propagation of plants and animals, are excluded from patent grant.[4] Inventions that are micro-organisms are not excluded and, according to official explanations of the law, this term could cover plasmids, viruses, bacteria, fungi, and algae.[5] Through the provisions on exclusion of parts of animals or plants and discoveries of any living thing or non-living substance occurring in nature, it may be that India excludes patent grant with respect to genes and recombinant DNA, but this is not clear.

In addition, mathematical or business methods, and algorithms or computer programmes per se are excluded. Although a move to clarify this was scuttled in 2005,

[1]If the invention was a chemical process, the patent term allowed was 14 years from the date of filing of the patent application.

[2]See http://ipindia.nic.in/ipr/patent/patents.htm for the text of the amendments to the 1970 law and rules.

[3]This is a broader exclusion than that under the 1970 law. TRIPS allows diagnostic, therapeutic, and surgical methods for the treatment of humans and animals to be excluded.

[4]Plant varieties are protectable in India through a different law, the Plant Variety Protection Act that was passed in 1999.

[5]However, at the time of passing the latest amendments in 2005, two issues (the definition and patentability of new chemical entities and micro-organisms) have been referred to a committee of experts by the government.

the technical application of a computer programme to industry or its use in combination with hardware, if otherwise patentable, would not appear to be excluded.

Criteria for Determining Patent Eligibility

According to the TRIPS Agreement, an invention that meets three separate and cumulative criteria, not further defined, must be eligible to be granted a patent: it must be new, involve an inventive step (or be non-obvious), and be industrially applicable (or useful). These criteria were followed in the 1970 law, which defined an invention as essentially meaning any product or process that is new and useful and which allowed obviousness as a ground for opposition.

The amended law retains this and further specifies that a new invention is one that is not disclosed through publication or use in the country or elsewhere before the filing date.[6] The requirement of 'inventive step', the most important criterion in judging patent eligibility, was defined in 2002 as a feature that makes the invention not obvious to a person skilled in the art. This requirement was changed in 2005 and is now met where the invention is non-obvious to a skilled person as before and either represents a technical advance over existing knowledge or is economically significant.[7]

In theory, under the Indian law, EMRs, or product patents, cannot be granted for existing or known products that have been in the public domain before the filing or priority date of their application. The case of an EMR granted to a multinational company in 2003 raised a controversy about claims of 'evergreening' of pharmaceutical patents. This is a reference to attempts by patent owners to extend their effective period of exclusivity through obtaining new patents on formulations, dosage forms, or minor chemical variations of an earlier patented product. In 2005, exclusions from patent grant were extended to cover trivial inventions. The provision makes it clear, however, that any invention that enhances the known efficacy of the substance or results in a new product or employs at least one new reactant is patentable (provided it is otherwise eligible) and that only the 'mere' discovery of a new form or of any new property or new use of a known substance or process is excluded. Some Indian pharmaceutical manufacturers who have just started down the Research and Development (R&D) path may also find it easier to make minor improvement inventions that meet these criteria.

Pre- and Post-grant Opposition

The law now lays down that patent applications will not be examined unless this is requested by the applicant or other interested party. Only abstracts of applications, as submitted by the applicants, will be published 18 months after their filing or earlier at the request of the applicant. The rights and privileges of the patent accrue to its owner from the date of publication, although infringement proceedings can only be instituted after grant. Pre-grant opposition is allowed to be filed by third parties, where applications have been examined, up to six months from the date of publication. In the absence of any opposition, and without any independent evaluation as allowed in the earlier law, the patent office must grant the patent without examination 'as expeditiously as possible' if the applicant has fulfilled all the procedural requirements of the law. The time given to an examiner to examine an application, where requested, is one to three months. If the patent gets granted before opposition proceedings are initiated, it can be opposed within one year after its grant, but there is no time limit prescribed for disposal of such proceedings.

Rights of a Patent Owner

As required by the WTO, the rights of the owner of a product patent exclude others from making, using, offering for sale, selling, or importing the product. The rights of process patent owners are extended from exclusive rights to use the process to rights over the product made through the process. The burden of proof of infringement of the rights of the process patent owner is shifted to the defendant in certain circumstances.[8] India has taken advantage of TRIPS flexibilities to allow parallel imports,[9] use of the patent for obtaining regulatory approvals, and other limited exceptions.

Patent Term

The patent term for both product and process patents is now 20 years from the date of filing of the patent application and is applicable to both new and unexpired patents as of 2002. Renewal fees have been made progressively higher—albeit still low in dollar values—so that only economically significant patents are maintained up to the end of the patent term allowed.

[6]The grounds for pre- and post-grant opposition, however, include publication in India or elsewhere but use or knowledge *only in India before the priority date*. Nonetheless, knowledge of the invention, oral or otherwise, within any local or indigenous community, whether located in India or elsewhere, is included.
[7]Some interpret this as a lowering of the standards of patentability. See Gopakumar and Amin (2005).

[8]Both the optional circumstances available under TRIPS are included instead of choosing one or the other.
[9]In 2005, the definition of parallel imports was broadened from importation from any person 'duly authorized by the patentee' to 'duly authorized under the law'.

Compulsory Licences and Use by Government

The licences-of-right system has been abolished as required but compulsory licences can be applied for and granted on a large number of grounds retained from the 1970 law three years from the grant of the patent, further extendable by one year on the grounds of non-working.[10] In emergency situations or public non-commercial use or use by government, such licences can be issued at any time even without first notifying the patent owner. There are no special expeditious procedures or prescribed time limits for the disposal of compulsory licence cases but six months has been accepted as the reasonable period that applicants have to first devote to attempting to obtain a voluntary licence from the patent owner on reasonable commercial terms. Three different standards of remuneration to be paid are applicable in case of general use of compulsory licences, emergency or public non-commercial use, and government use of patents. There is no prohibition of injunctions against use of the patent authorized by government, although this is provided for under the TRIPS Agreement. Compulsory licences can also be granted for export to countries without manufacturing capacity in the pharmaceutical sector, as permitted by the 2003 WTO decision.

In cases where there has been commercial exploitation of products covered by patent applications filed between 1995 and 2005, the patent owner is only entitled to get reasonable royalty provided that the manufacturer of the product has made significant investment and continues production up to the date of grant of the patent.[11]

The provision on the declaration of certain anti-competitive or restrictive conditions in contractual patent licences as null and void has been somewhat strengthened based on examples given in the TRIPS Agreement.[12]

Revocation

Revocation or invalidation of patents is provided for in cases where the patent is wrongfully obtained or where certain criteria or requirements are not fulfilled. One such requirement introduced in the law in 2002, both as a ground for opposition as well as revocation, is the disclosure of the source or geographic origin of biological material used in the invention and a declaration that the invention is not anticipated by any traditional knowledge. The clause allowing the government to suo moto revoke a patent which is 'mischievous to the State or generally prejudicial to the public' has been retained, subject to judicial review. The patent can also be revoked two years after the first compulsory licence if it has failed to remedy the situation that warranted the grant and a decision has to be taken within a year of such application.

A new Appellate Board has been established to hear certain patent appeals, including those covering grant, opposition, compulsory licences, and revocation on the grounds of non-working or public interest.

India's revised patent law represents a compromise between opposing interests—those who wanted to retain the 1970 law with minimal changes and those who wanted to strengthen patent protection and procedures beyond what was required by international obligations. While the law now reiterates the philosophy of the 1970 law and retains several of its provisions, the procedural and substantive changes make it clear that India would like to go some distance in tilting the balance back in favour of the patent applicant in the hope of promoting R&D. Only time will tell what effect the new law will have on location of R&D in India or on India's ability to supply cheaper medicines to the world. What is clear is that by 2005 India had made a break with the past and had begun a new era in patent law and practice.

JAYASHREE WATAL

References

Ayyangar, Justice N. Rajagopala. 1959. Report on the Revision of the Patents Law, September.

Gopakumar, K.M. and Tahir Amin. 2005. 'Patents (Amendment) Bill: A Critique', *Economic and Political Weekly*, 9 April, available at www.epw.org.in.

[10]This delay has been controversial as the Paris Convention limits this period of three years to compulsory licences granted on the grounds of non-working.

[11]It is not clear in how many cases this amendment made in 2005 will be applicable and whether or not this is compatible with WTO requirements.

[12]Some may argue that the TRIPS Agreement does not permit per se prohibitions and calls for a case-by-case analysis of the anti-competitive nature of these practices.

■ Pensions

A formal pension system existed in India even in the 19th century.[1] In its present avatar it is enshrined in the Central Civil Services (Pensions) Rules, from 1 June

[1]The earliest reference can be found in *Sukraniti*. In its modern form, see the Pensions Act, 1871 (Act No. 23 of 1871), to consolidate and amend the law relating to the Pensions and Grants by Government of Money or Land Revenue. The scope, coverage, and benefits under the pension system continued to be liberalized periodically, with the award of the benefits by the Royal Commission of Civil Establishment (1881, 1920, 1924) and the Government of India Acts of 1919 and 1935.

1972 (Muthuswamy and Brinda 2002). These rules, with certain modifications (for example, in the age of retirement, the proportion of commutation, period for restoration of the commuted amount, and so on), were also adopted by the rest of the public sector. The original intent of the system, endorsed by a landmark judgement[2] by the Supreme Court of India, recognizes the need for the old-age consumption security system to be largely a self-insurance system, guaranteeing some desirable stream of inflow. However, the ruling also indicates that pensions be largely treated as deferred (and adequate) compensation, thus linking pensions to the salary or wages drawn by individuals while in active employment. In the absence of clearly laid down social security taxes, such a system qualifies as a completely defined benefit (DB) system.[3]

In India, the combined (Centre and states) government expenditure on pensions and other retirement benefits (civil and defence) stood at Rs 403.21 billion in the year 2001–2 constituting 12.82 per cent of the total tax revenues (GoI 2004a). The total tax revenues constituted approximately 13.79 per cent of the gross domestic product (GDP) in that year. Note that this does not include payments to pensioners from statutory and commercial public-sector corporations.

Pensions were first introduced as a periodical allowance to individuals for meritorious work or service. Over time, their scope widened into a system of transfers to the elderly. Pensions metamorphosed into a system of social security, ushered in by Bismarck in Germany in 1891, encompassing the poor, retired elders, widow(er)s, orphans, the disabled, and destitutes.

Social security may be administered in several forms involving cash and non-cash transfers. In India, the former include enhanced interest payment and lower taxes for the elderly, and the latter include programmes for health, educational, nutritional and employment security, and subsidized transportation. These, however, do not form the core concern of pension reforms in India. The debate, in India, has concentrated on the narrow definition of pensions, focusing on employment-linked, post-retirement currency payments. These cover employees of:

(i) the public sector including government (central and state) civil service, defence, certain aided institutions, statutory and public commercial corporations (including railways, posts, telecommunications, banks, and financial institutions) under a pay-as-you-go (PAYG) system where pensions are paid out of current revenues (that is, either tax revenues or revenues from commercial operations), and
(ii) private-sector companies, governed by the Employees Provident Fund (EPF) and Miscellaneous Provisions Act, 1952, that extend a limited pension obligation under a largely funded (individual–employer) contributory system.

The total benefit payments, in the year 2003–4, from the employees pension scheme (EPS), administered by the Employees Provident Fund Organization (EPFO), amounted to Rs 23.55 billion (GoI 2004b). However, in contrast to a near-universal coverage in the public sector, there were only 1,758,841 pension beneficiaries (excluding beneficiaries from a few establishments operating their own pension funds), including 352,625 superannuation pensioners. Thus, despite registering the highest acceleration among the major items of government revenue expenditure in the past decade, the extant system of pensions does not cover a majority that is employed in the informal/unorganized sector.[4]

Demographically, India is favourably poised to expand coverage. According to the world population prospects (of the United Nations), assuming constant fertility (that is same as that between the years 2000 and 2005) the old-age dependency ratio in India in the year 2025 would be approximately 12. That is, there would be 12 elderly, aged 65 and above, for every 100 workers (workers are persons in the 15–64 age group), while in North America the old-age dependency ratio would be around 28 in that year. The presence of a larger number of workers in India is expected to bode well for growth in output and incomes and, therefore, government revenues.

Three policy parameters critically affect the sustainability of a pension programme. These are:

(i) the passivity ratio, the ratio of the number of post-retirement years (until death) to the number of working years,
(ii) the dependency ratio, the ratio of the number of old (non-workers) to the number of young (workers), and
(iii) the replacement ratio, the ratio of compensation or payment in old age (non-working years) to payment in youth (working years).

[2]On a writ petition filed by *D.S. Nakra* vs the *Union of India* (1982).

[3]As opposed to a defined contribution (DC) system where only payments by individuals are (usually) mandatorily defined but their receipts are not.

[4]According to the National Sample Survey Organisation (NSSO), there were 397 workers per 1,000 persons in the year 1999–2000, of whom nearly 360 were engaged in the informal sector.

In particular, an unfunded PAYG social security system can be welfare enhancing if $(1+m)*(1+g)$ exceeds r, where m, g, and r denote, respectively, rate of growth of population, rate of growth of productivity or output, and interest rate (Samuelson 1958).

The design of the Indian pension system has, however, led to a perverse redistribution of public monies,[5] induced rigidities in the labour markets, adversely affected the motivation to raise productivity, and fostered informalization of the economy. The principal issues facing the Indian pension system pertain to

(i) rationalizing the benefits of those covered by introducing the appropriate changes to influence the critical parameters, and
(ii) expansion of the coverage.

Recent changes in the pension system for central government civilian employees, joining service on or after 1 January 2004, have veered towards a completely DC system. Some state governments have also adopted the new system for their new recruits. Under this system, the individual and the government make an equal contribution of 10 per cent each of the individual's pay into that individual's retirement account (IRA). This is analogous to the EPF system. However, the new system differs from the EPF system in the treatment of cumulations into the IRAs and the withdrawals therefrom. The EPF system is similar to a bank account where a pre-announced rate of interest on the balance is credited to the individual's account. The individual is assured of a ratcheting-up of the balances. It is here that the new system is perceived to differ significantly. The monies accumulating in the IRA are to be invested by pension fund managers (PFMs) under the surveillance of a regulatory authority.

This new system is a major shift from the erstwhile system, where retired workers are entitled to guaranteed payments, to a system where the individuals or workers bear all the risk with no guarantees. It raises some doubts about whether the suggested system continues to qualify as a system of 'security'. Is it admissible to enforce a mandatory but unsecured DC system? Further, does this reliance on market bode well for the stability of financial markets and is there a need to have a separate regulator for the pension funds, when most of their funds are expected to be invested in markets under other regulators (Reserve Bank of India [RBI], Securities and Exchange Board of India [SEBI], Insurance Regulatory and Development Authority [IRDA])? In particular, the market for pension and life insurance products may be complementary.[6]

The new recruits in the defence services, however, continue to be administered under the erstwhile system of pensions. While the number of defence personnel in active employment is significantly smaller than of those in civilian employment, the pool of retirees and benefit recipients from the defence services constitutes a much larger share. The expenditure on defence pensions is more than twice that on central government civilian pensioners (excluding those with departmental commercial undertakings). The civilian employees of the central government constitute merely the head of the proverbial camel inside the tent that is almost certain to be uprooted when the camel decides to take to its feet.

The recent surge in interest in pensions was favoured by the effort to address the larger issue of poverty by distinguishing between the lifetime poor and those who fall into poverty upon retirement. It is generally hypothesized that the latter emerge due to lack of foresight (myopia) in contemplating loss of capacity to work and the corresponding decline in incomes. Myopia, however, is untenable as an argument to sustain pensions. As an example, consider two generations of persons. If the first generation is indeed myopic and provides inadequately for itself, then with hindsight (and increased literacy) this experience can easily be communicated to the next generation whereby for all subsequent generations the aforementioned short-sightedness ceases to exist. The nuclearization of the family system may aggravate the situation, but only for a trifle longer.

While the success of a defined contribution system in sustaining itself depends on participation and supervision,

[5]The average wage compensation to employees in the lower rungs in the public sector is significantly higher than the average wage in the private sector at an analogous level, while perhaps it is the opposite for those in the upper rungs of organizational hierarchy. The provisioning of pensions to public-sector employees, from a PAYG system, results in a substantially higher lifetime compensation as compared to employees in the private sector. A perception of high employment insecurity in the private sector as compared to fully secured employment in the public sector inhibits mobility of workers between the public and private sectors. It further depresses any incentives to raise productivity. Moreover, the absence of universal mandatory provisioning for retirement funds induces the expansion of the informal sector that can escape these costs. Of late, however, employment in the public sector has also seen an expansion in ad hoc or contractual appointments that are essentially designed to bypass the social security obligations.

[6]A profit-maximizing insurance company would rather pray that the insured lives a long life (so that it may collect annual premiums), while on the contrary a pension provider would expect to minimize its payments by praying for early demise of the pensioner.

social security must have the attribute of an unambiguous, risk-free guarantee. Security is perceived from a feeling of being cared for. The continued preoccupation with the narrow domain of income security has resulted in high rates of replacement (of income) for those already covered and severely constrained coverage expansion. The role of markets and governments should supplement that of the family and not foster perverse incentives that eventually encourage individualism bereft of the familial benefits. This crucial aspect was largely ignored, although it has now been recognized in the newly expanded approach of the World Bank (World Bank 2005). Rights and responsibilities of individuals, governments, and markets should be guided by ethical rectitude. This is crucial to minimize public-policy-induced distortions in choice of family, labour, and savings as well as in striking the correct balance between the roles of the government and the markets.

MUKESH ANAND

References

Government of India (GoI). 2004a. 'Indian Public Finance Statistics 2003–4, Ministry of Finance', Department of Economic Affairs, Economic Division, August.

———. 2004b. '51st Annual Report 2003–4 of Employees Provident Fund Organization', Ministry of Labour, New Delhi.

Muthuswamy, P. and V. Brinda. 2002. *Swamy's Pension Compilation Incorporating Central Civil Services Pension Rules*, Swamy Publishers (P) Ltd.

Samuelson, P.A. 1958. 'An Exact Consumption-loan Model of Interest with or without the Social Contrivance of Money', *Journal of Political Economy*, December, 66(6): 467–82.

World Bank. 2005. 'Old Age Income Support in the Twenty-first Century: An International Perspective on Pension Systems and Reform', 18 February, Web Version.

Petroleum Product Pricing

Background

Pricing of petroleum products has acquired significance due to the high and volatile price of crude oil in the international market. Figure 1 shows how world prices have moved since December 1990.

The average monthly price of the Indian basket of crude oil varies from the Brent crude price. It varied from US $36/barrel in May 2004 to US $132.5/barrel in July 2008, posing serious policy challenges to the government. High international price puts a significant burden on the Indian economy.

In 2010–11, India consumed 141.8 Mt of petroleum products. With refinery fuel consumption of 7 per cent of crude processed, these products were obtained from 152 Mt of crude. India's indigenous production of crude was 37.6 Mt that year. Thus our import dependence was 75 per cent.

A Brief History of Petroleum Product Pricing in India

Over the years, the government has followed a variety of policies for pricing of petroleum products, all of which have been found to have some deficiency or the other. The government's policy approach on pricing petroleum products since 1970s has moved between cost-based pricing, import parity pricing (IPP), trade parity pricing (TPP), and free market pricing to the administered price mechanism (APM). From 1976 till the mid-

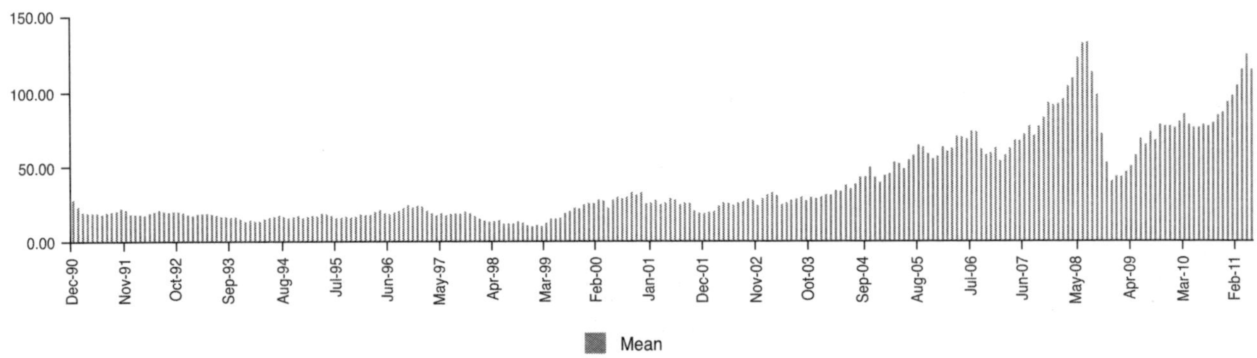

Figure 1 Monthly Mean Price of Brent Crude (US$ barrel)

1990s, the prices were based on a cost-plus basis and were fixed for the entire oil sector by the government under the APM. As long as world prices of crude remained stable and low, the cost-based pricing did not create any problem. However, the major weakness of APM was that it did not induce competition in the marketplace, so it did not fulfil consumers' interests for better products and services. Nor did it enable domestic oil companies to generate adequate financial resources for project development and capacity addition in this crucial sector.

From 1 April 2002, following the Kelkar group report, APM was dismantled but the prices were never fully decontrolled. The approach to pricing in this new policy framework was based on four distinct considerations:

(i) The price of indigenous crude oil would be market determined.
(ii) The prices of petroleum products produced by the refineries will be based on IPP.
(iii) Consumer prices of all other products except domestic LPG and PDS kerosene will be market determined.
(iv) There would be flat rate subsidies on PDS kerosene and domestic LPG.

India was largely a net importer of petroleum products till around 2002 and IPP made economic sense. However, domestic refinery capacity increased in early 2000 and India became a net exporter of many products. IPP in such a situation gave undue returns to refiners. IPP was no longer rational. In 2006, the Rangarajan Committee (MOP&NG 2006) recommended 'trade parity price' (TPP) as an upper bound on price. The committee recommended as TPP a weighted sum of IPP and EPP (export parity price) with weights of 0.8 and 0.2, respectively.

The integrated energy policy based on the recommendations of the expert group headed by Kirit Parikh (Planning Commission 2006) was approved by the Cabinet in December 2008 (Planning Commission 2008). It recommended trade parity pricing as one which reflects the opportunity costs of a consumer or a producer. It further stipulates that IPP is to be used for a product for which the country is a net importer and EPP for a product for which it is a net exporter. As long as the country is a net exporter of a particular product, EPP for that product equals TPP.

When the world crude prices started moving up rapidly from 2004, the government did not permit public-sector oil marketing companies (OMCs) to pass the full cost of imports on to domestic consumers of major oil products, that is, petrol, diesel, domestic LPG (that is, LPG used by households), and PDS kerosene (that is, kerosene sold through the public distribution system). Consumers of these products thus received large subsidies. As a consequence, OMCs had large under-recoveries, which were financed partly by the government through issuing bonds, partly by upstream public-sector companies ONGC and OIL, and GAIL through price discounts. OMCs also absorbed a part of the under-recoveries themselves. Since the government did not compensate the private-sector oil marketing companies, they went out of marketing these products. There was little competition in oil marketing. Over the years, under-recoveries of public-sector OMCs have grown as shown in Table 1.

In June 2011, before the government changed the prices of the four major petroleum products, the projected under-recovery for 2011–12 was Rs 1,72,000 crore. Apart from inefficiency in use of petroleum products due to subsidies, these under-recoveries have many consequences. They put stress on government finances. OMCs often do not receive compensation in time and are forced to borrow from banks, which further increases their financial burden. The reduced profitability of OMCs, ONGC, and OIL reduces their market capitalization, so any sale of their equity will bring in less to the government.

In August 2009, the government appointed an expert group under Kirit Parikh to recommend 'a viable and sustainable system of pricing petroleum products'.

Table 1 Under-recoveries of OMCs (in Rs crore)

Product/Year	2004–5	2005–6	2006–7	2007–8	2008–9	2009–10	2010–11
PDS Kero.	9,480	14,384	17,883	19,102	28,225	17,435	19,484
Dom. LPG	8,362	10,246	10,701	15,523	17,600	14,356	21,772
Petrol	150	2,723	2,027	7,332	5,181	5,155	2,227
Diesel	2,154	12,647	18,776	35,166	52,286	9,314	34,706
Total	20,146	40,000	49,387	77,123	103,292	46,260	78,189

Source: Petroleum Planning and Analysis Cell.

Objectives of Pricing Policy

The Parikh Committee (MOP&NG 2010) looked at the objectives and considerations that should guide pricing policy.

The very first question it addressed was: should the government intervene at all in the market and set prices?

A strong case can be made for intervention to protect poor consumers so that they can afford kerosene for lighting, which is a necessity for those who do not have access to electricity. Another objective may be to provide merit goods to consumers, such as clean cooking fuels like natural gas, LPG, and kerosene to replace use of biomass-based fuels, such as firewood and dung. These biomass-based fuels create indoor air pollution that causes respiratory diseases and eye infections, and results in many premature deaths, particularly of women and children. Also, use of firewood encourages deforestation and dung is better used as a fertilizer. Moreover, the task of gathering these fuels keeps girls away from schools. Thus, use of clean cooking fuels has many social and environmental externalities, and as merit goods the government may promote them through subsidies.

Another frequently reported reason for the government's intervention is insulating the domestic economy from the volatility of petroleum prices on the world market. It is feared that complete pass-through of increase in world oil prices may cause inflation which may persist even when oil prices come down. There is no clear evidence that in an increasingly open and competitive economy, price movements triggered by changes in the prices of oil products would persist over the medium-run. In addition, attempts to insulate the domestic economy against volatility require discriminating between a secular price rise due to demand–supply forces and a price rise due to transient causes, such as speculation in the world market. This is difficult to do.

To the extent that the level of self-sufficiency in domestic crude production increases, the impact of international oil prices on the domestic economy would be reduced. Thus, keeping domestic oil firms viable and in good financial health and providing an environment in which they can grow are also important policy objectives. It is equally important to keep domestic private-sector firms viable as it is to keep public-sector firms viable. A level playing field between public- and private-sector firms as well as among public-sector firms is desirable for promoting competition.

A major objective of policy is to have an efficient and competitive oil economy that promotes efficient use by consumers, appropriate choice of fuels among substitutes, and a proper choice of technique. This is best ensured by a competitive energy sector.

Intervention through price control necessitates that someone bears the financial costs. Price control means setting prices. If it is done on a cost-plus basis, it creates incentives for gold plating and creative accounting. Also, price calculations involve rigid specifications of items to be considered and their costs. This discourages innovation. For example, storage of LPG in large underground caverns facilitates imports by larger ships and reduces unloading time compared to storage in over-ground tanks. But, it may involve increase in operating costs. If the cost formula has set item-wise limits on operating costs, the project may be discouraged even if its total cost is much less.

If prices are to be fixed by the government, these have to be based on some principle. Prices can be fixed based on a predetermined formula, which is derived from principles like import parity (IPP), trade parity (TPP), or export parity (EPP). This approach is also fraught with major deficiencies. The formula often involves elements of cost-plus. In an industry that is continuously changing, a prescriptive and biased cost-plus pricing formula requires continuous monitoring and periodic adjustments in certain components of the formula. All these call for administrative and regulatory tasks to be performed by the government or its agency on a permanent basis. This increases administrative burden. A competitive price discovery process empowers companies to follow their own judgements of market conditions and results in fair pricing of products. In the event of any company adopting unfair pricing methods, such activities can be curbed by the regulatory authorities set up by the government.

Price control, subsidies, and taxes can introduce distortions which may not be desirable. Apart from inefficient use, they also lead to an erroneous choice of technique. For example, if diesel is cheap, it may encourage freight movement by trucks rather than by train. When the price difference between petrol and diesel is high, diesel-driven vehicles may be preferred. If there is a large difference between the prices of diesel and kerosene, kerosene may be used to adulterate diesel. In 2008, we even saw diesel being used in place of furnace oil. Intervention in pricing must be carefully thought out for its possible consequences.

A Viable and Sustainable Pricing Policy

India's oil imports are increasing and our import dependence is likely to keep growing. At the same time, 2008 saw an unprecedented rise in oil prices in the world market; 2011 seems to be heading for a repeat of this. Oil price volatility has also increased. Though future oil prices are difficult to predict, they are generally expected to rise. Given our increasing dependence on imports, domestic prices of petroleum products have to reflect international prices, and any subsidy given to poor consumers must be effectively targeted.

A viable long-term strategy for pricing major petroleum products is required. A viable policy has to be workable over a wide range of international oil prices and has to meet the various objectives of the government. It should limit the fiscal burden on the government and keep the domestic oil industry financially healthy and competitive.

While this final objective is clear, the major difficulty lies in designing an appropriate transition path from our present situation. With large price differences between cost of supply and consumer prices of diesel, domestic LPG, and PDS kerosene, a one step move to deregulated prices is politically difficult, to say the least. What can be done? The Parikh Committee reasoned as follows:

> Intervention through price control necessitates that someone bears the financial costs. The issue therefore is to assess the costs and incidence of the burden of alternative mechanisms on different groups in the society. On whom the burden falls depends on the policy and the instruments used. If the costs are financed by a general increase in taxes, or by increasing fiscal deficit or by cutting other government expenditure, all these affect certain sections of the people adversely. (Planning Commission 2006)

Petrol

Petrol is largely an item of final consumption. Table 2 gives the average annual consumption of petrol and diesel by vehicle owners.

Table 2 Average Annual Consumption of Fuel by Class of Vehicles

Type of vehicle	Average distance covered annually (KM)	Fuel efficiency (KM/litre)	Litres/ Vehicle/ Year	Monthly fuel cost at price on 1.1.10 in Delhi (Rs)
Two-wheelers (Petrol)	6,300 (10,000)	73.0	86	320
Three-wheelers (Petrol)	35,000 (40,000)	34.0	1,029	3,835
Cars (Petrol)	8,000 (15,000)	13.5	593	2,210
Cars (Diesel)	8,000 (15,000)	14.0	571	1,566
MPV* (Diesel)	7,800 (37,000)	8.7	897	2,461
Bus (Diesel)	55,000 (60,000)	4.1	13,415	36,802
Heavy trucks (Diesel)	55,000 (35,000)	3.6	15,278	41,913
Light trucks (Diesel)	20,000 (40,000)	4.5	4,415	12,112

Source: Orlando (2009).
Note: Figures in parentheses are estimates for Delhi, taken from the CPCB report (2000).
*Multi-purpose vehicle.

When the crude price increases to $120 compared to $70/barrel, the retail outlet price of petrol will increase by Rs 20/litre and the additional expenditure, assuming there is no reduction in use, will be around Rs 160/month for a two-wheeler user, the poorest of motorized vehicle owners, and less than Rs 1,000/month for a private automobile user (at the all-India level).

The committee considered this a bearable burden and recommended that petrol prices should be market-determined both at the refinery gate and at the retail level. The government accepted this and petrol prices have been deregulated.

Diesel

Many different users consume diesel. Trucks accounted for 37 per cent and buses 12 per cent, agriculture 12 per cent, passenger cars 15 per cent, railways 6 per cent, and power generation 8 per cent of the total diesel consumption in 2008–9.

Farmers get compensated for any increase in the cost of diesel as it is accounted for by the CACP while fixing the minimum support price (MSP) for major crops. Therefore, any increase in the cost of diesel will be reflected in the price and will not adversely affect farmers. However, those who use diesel relatively more may not get fully compensated by MSP. Higher diesel prices will induce them to use less diesel which may reduce over-use of groundwater, as is prevalent in many parts of the country. Of course, higher diesel prices resulting in higher MSP will increase the subsidy for PDS, but it would be much less than the reduction in the under-recovery on diesel.

Trucks and light commercial vehicles (LCVs) consume around 37 per cent of the diesel. In late 2009, long distance charge for a round trip between Delhi and Mumbai for a 9-tonne truck was more than Rs 40,000 whereas the cost of its diesel consumption was around Rs 22,000. There was some scope for absorbing the increase in the cost of diesel. Higher diesel prices also encourage fuel use efficiency as well as greater use of railways for freight movement. Railways consume around one-fourth as much diesel per net tonne kilometre as trucks.

Even assuming that truckers, power generators, industrial users, and so on (other than passenger car owners), are able to pass on the additional cost of diesel fully, the increase in the cost of diesel should be compared with the inflationary impact of subsidies, which would be similar.

Car owners who drive diesel vehicles, including sports utility vehicles (SUVs), should be able to bear the additional costs. There is no economic or social reason to subsidize them. In fact, diesel subsidy encourages use of diesel guzzling vehicles. Even though a diesel engine of the same capacity should give 35 to 50 per cent more mileage, because consumers in India buy more powerful and larger diesel-driven vehicles, the average km/litre of the passenger car fleet is lower for diesel-driven vehicles than for petrol-driven ones.

The implications of an increase in the retail price of diesel on various groups of consumers show no real compelling reason to subsidize them. Therefore, the committee recommended in February 2010 that the price of diesel should also be market-determined both at the refinery gate and at the retail level. Subsequently, world price of crude has increased substantially and deregulating diesel prices now would require a large increase in diesel prices. The way out of this would be to reduce taxes, raise the price of diesel by a modest amount, fix the subsidy on diesel as a flat per litre subsidy, and deregulate diesel prices. Over time when an opportune moment comes, the flat subsidy can be reduced.

Kerosene

The primary objective of subsidizing kerosene is for lighting purpose. In the absence of electricity, kerosene has, for long, been the only source of lighting (apart from more expensive vegetable oil-based lamps). With the progress of rural electrification the allocation of kerosene to states can be resuced and rationalized.

We can assess households' paying capacity for kerosene based on data given in Table 3.

A rural household in the poorest decile spends around 2 per cent of its monthly expenditure on kerosene. This is also around 13 per cent of what one might call its discretionary expenditure on entertainment, personal effects, toilet articles, sundry articles, consumer services, and conveyance. There is, therefore, some scope for increasing the price for PDS kerosene. Since incomes are increasing, kerosene prices may be increased in tandem with an increase in per capita income so that the share of expenditure on kerosene does not increase. Based on this the Parikh Committee had recommended an increase of Rs 6 per litre of kerosene.

However, 35 per cent of kerosene released for distribution through PDS gets diverted to adulterate diesel or is sold in the black market. A transparent and effective distribution system for PDS kerosene and domestic LPG can be ensured through the unique identification/smart cards framework. In such a system, a below poverty line household would be entitled to purchase 5 litres of kerosene at market prices per month from any shop. She will, however, pay only the ration price and the difference between the market price and the ration price will be electronically transferred from the government's account to the trader's account. This way there will be one price in the market for kerosene and there will be no incentive to divert it to the black market. The same scheme can also be used for targeting the LPG subsidy.

Table 3 Expenses on PDS Kerosene Consumption, Discretionary Items, and Total Household Consumption (Mean Values)

Decile	Quantity of kerosene consumed@ (litre/month)			Expenses (Rs/month)		
	Only from PDS	Only from other sources	From both sources	On consumption PDS kerosene	On consumption of discretionary items#	Total household consumption
			RURAL			
1	2.7	2.2	4.8	28.4	211.1	1,386.6
5	3.3	2.7	5.6	33.4	343.9	2,222.5
10	3.4	3.6	6.8	34.9	991.8	5,872.1
Total	3.3	2.8	5.7			
			URBAN			
1	4.0	3.4	7.4	41.0	335.7	2,016.0
5	4.5	5.2	10.1	49.1	642.1	3,444.5
10	3.9	4.6	9.2	42.2	2524.4	10,014.6
Total	4.2	4.6	9.5			

Source: NSSO Survey (Appendix 4, Parikh Committee Report).

Note: @ The figures relate to different categories of households.

Discretionary items include entertainment, personal effects, toilet articles, sundry articles, consumer services, and conveyance.

LPG

The price of domestic LPG should be market-driven and poor consumers can be subsidized through a smart card system. Even then the subsidized price should be increased periodically based on the increase in paying capacity as reflected in the rising per capita income. Based on this we had recommended a price increase of Rs 100/cylinder.

A Sustainable Mechanism for Financing Under-recoveries

With decontrol of petrol and diesel prices, a marginal increase in the prices of kerosene and LPG and rationalization of allocation of kerosene to states the under-recoveries would come down substantially. Still a mechanism for financing under-recoveries on PDS kerosene and domestic LPG is required. This mechanism involves mopping up a portion of the incremental revenue accruing to ONGC/OIL from production in those blocks, which were given by the government on nomination basis, at the rates that increase with the price of crude. The government's share will increase from 20 per cent at crude price above $60/barrel to 80 per cent at price above $90/barrel. In addition, there would be a need to provide cash subsidy from the Budget to meet the remaining gap. This is summarized in Table 4.

It is seen that the financial burden on the government Budget remains more or less stable at around Rs 23,000 crore, which is quite absorbable.

Finally, it should be emphasized that a market-determined pricing system for petrol and diesel can be sustained in the long run by providing a level playing field and promoting competition among all players, public and private, in the oil and gas sector. Adequate regulatory oversight is critical to ensure effective competition.

KIRIT S. PARIKH

References

Central Pollution Control Board (CPCB). 2000. *Annual Report*.

Himanshu. 2010. 'Analysis of Consumption Pattern of Kerosene and LPG', Appendix 4, in MOP&NG.

Ministry of Petroleum and Natural Gas (MOP&NG). 2006. *Report of Committee on Pricing and Taxation of Petroleum Products* (Rangarajan Committee Report), New Delhi, Government of India.

———. 2010. *Report of the Expert Group on a Viable and Sustainable System of Pricing of Petroleum Products* (Parikh Committee Report), New Delhi, Government of India, available at http://petroleum.nic.in/reportprice.pdf.

Orlando, Ernest. 2009. 'Residential and Transport Energy Use in India: Past Trend and Future Outlook', Lawrence Berkeley National Laboratory, USA.

Table 4 Financing of Under-recovery of PDS Kerosene and Domestic LPG

	Crude oil price level($/bbl)	70	80	100	120	140
	Sale volume—PDS SKO (million KL)	11.7	11.7	11.7	11.7	11.7
	Sale Volume— Domestic LPG (Million cylinders)	788.3	788.3	788.3	788.3	788.3
	Total under-recovery					
i.	PDS SKO (Rs crore)	20,300	24,200	32,000	39,800	47,500
ii.	Domestic LPG (Rs crore)	16,200	19,300	25,300	31,400	37,500
iii	Total (i+ii)	36,500	43,500	57,300	71,200	85,000
	Measures to reduce under-recovery					
iv	Reduction in SKO allocation by 20%	4,100	4,800	6,400	8,000	9,500
v	Increase in price of SKO by : Rs 6/litre	6,100	6,100	6,100	6,100	6,100
vi	Increase in price of LPG by : Rs 100/cylinder	7,600	7,600	7,600	7,600	7,600
vii	Sub-total: If all three measures adopted (iv+v+vi)	17,800	18,500	20,100	21,700	23,200
viii	Balance under-recoveries after (iii-vii)	18,700	25,000	37,200	49,500	61,800
ix	Contribution by upstream oil companies	1,660	4,980	16,600	29,880	43,170
x	Under-recoveries remaining (viii-ix)	**17,040**	**20,020**	**20,600**	**19,620**	**18,630**
	Subsidies provided through Budget*					
	a. PDS kerosene	960	960	960	960	960
	b. Domestic LPG	1,780	1,780	1,780	1,780	1,780
xi	Total (a+b)	2,740	2,740	2,740	2,740	2,740
xii	Total to be financed by government Budget (x+xi)	19,780	22,760	23,340	22,360	21,370

Source: MOP&NG (2010).

Note: *The amount of subsidy for PDS kerosene and domestic LPG from the Budget is a fixed rate of subsidy and, therefore, not impacted by different levels of crude prices.

Planning Commission. 2006. *Integrated Energy Policy: Report of the Expert Committee* (Parikh Committee), New Delhi, Government of India, available at http://planningcommission.nic.in/reports/genrep/rep_intengy.pdf.
——. 2008. *Integrated Energy Policy*. New Delhi, Government of India.

Pharmaceutical Industry

The pharmaceutical industry is one of the success stories of independent India. It has developed at a phenomenal rate since the 1970s. India has become self-reliant in drugs and has emerged as a major player in the global pharmaceutical industry. It is a source of low-cost quality drugs to the entire world including developed countries such as the USA.

The lessons that can be drawn from the Indian experience are relevant for the development of the pharmaceutical industry in other developing countries. They also have implications for the industrial policy debate about the role of the government vis-à-vis the market.

The patent system has played a very important role in the pharmaceutical industry. Globally the pharmaceutical industry is dominated by a small number of multinational companies (MNCs)—Pfizer, GlaxoSmithKline, Merck, Johnson & Johnson, for example. These MNCs develop new drugs or in-licence those developed by others and use the patent system to prevent others from manufacturing and selling them. They also use an elaborate marketing infrastructure to promote the new drugs and to maintain dominant market shares even after the expiry of patents. The large number of remaining pharmaceutical companies are not only much smaller in size compared to the MNCs, they primarily manufacture products for which patents have expired, and are known as generic companies.

But currently, the MNCs do not dominate the pharmaceutical industry in India. In fact, India and Japan are the only two countries in the world where Western MNCs do not dominate the pharma industry. Under the Patents and Designs Act, 1911, which was in force till 1972, India effectively had a product patent regime in pharmaceuticals. Under this regime, while the MNCs prevented the indigenous companies from producing the new drugs, using the then existing patent law, they themselves were more keen on processing imported drugs rather than developing the industry from the basics. As a result, on the one hand, because of lack of competition, drug prices in India were very high. On the other hand, in the 1970s, India was dependent on imports for many of the essential drugs. The import dependence constricted consumption in a country deficient in foreign exchange and inhibited the growth of the industry.

The 1911 Act was replaced by the Patents Act, 1970. This eliminated the monopoly power of the MNCs by abolishing product patent protection and providing only process patent protection in pharmaceuticals. The cost-efficient processes developed by the Indian generic companies—Cipla, Ranbaxy, Dr Reddy's Laboratories, and others—could be used for manufacturing the latest drugs, introducing them at a fraction of international prices, and dislodging the MNCs from their position of dominance in the domestic market.

The Indian pharmaceutical industry shot to international prominence when it started supplying drugs at low prices for HIV/AIDS. The price charged by the originator company for a three-drug combination (stavidi ne+lamivudine+nevirapine), which dramatically reduced AIDS deaths in developed countries, exceeded US$ 10,000 per patient per year till recently. Such pricing made it almost impossible to treat all the patients in developing countries. After Cipla offered the three-drug combination at US$ 350 (per year), the international prices have crashed making the drugs more affordable and accessible.

It was not only the revision of the Patents Act, however, that contributed to the success of the indigenous pharmaceutical sector. It is important to note that many other countries, for example, Ghana, Malawi, Pakistan, Uruguay, and Vietnam, did not provide product patent protection in pharmaceuticals. Despite that, the pharmaceutical industry remained underdeveloped in these countries because they basically lacked the entrepreneurial and technological skills to take advantage of the absence of product patent protection. India is different not only because of its long tradition of drug manufacturing. The entrepreneurial spirit of the indigenous private-sector was actively supported through public investments in research and development (R&D) and manufacturing.

The number of laboratories set up by the Government of India under the Council of Scientific and Industrial Research (CSIR) helped the development of the technological skills necessary for the pharmaceutical industry. In fact, a distinctive feature of the pharmaceutical industry in India has been the close collaboration between government laboratories and the private sector.

The setting up of the two public-sector companies—Hindustan Antibiotics Ltd and Indian Drugs and Pharmaceuticals Ltd (IDPL)—was another important factor in the development of the industry. Though both the companies are now sick, they gave a tremendous boost to indigenous efforts in the private sector and contributed to its success. The city of Hyderabad, where the synthetic drug plant of the IDPL was located, has actually developed into the main bulk-drug-manufacturing centre in the country and founders of many bulk-drugs units originally worked for the IDPL.

Basic manufacturing by the MNCs too accelerated after the industrial policy restrictions imposed by the government in the 1970s that stipulated that unless they produced bulk drugs in specified ratios they would not be permitted to expand in formulations. But in the 1990s, as these restrictions were withdrawn, the MNCs started closing down or selling off the plants that they had set up.

Contrary to the common view, India's experience shows that the state can play a very positive role in the development of indigenous industry. It shows how a country can benefit by regulating the MNCs and supporting the indigenous sector. It exhibits how favourable state policy can help the indigenous sector realize its potential and be competitive vis-à-vis the MNCs.

While the state in India has been successful in realizing the industrial policy objective of developing a strong indigenous sector, it has basically failed in pursuing the health policy objective of ensuring accessibility of drugs to those who need but cannot afford them. For drugs to be accessible, it is not enough that prices are lower than the patent-protected monopoly prices. If those who need them cannot afford even the lower prices, proper finances should be available to pay for the cost of the drugs. Purchase of drugs is financed by the consumers themselves, by the government, or through private or national insurance. Public-funded healthcare and/or subsidized insurance not only can counter the market power of the large firms and influence prices, it can also shift the financial burden from the poor who are unable to afford the cost themselves and hence can improve accessibility. But in India, the involvement of the government in healthcare is low and health insurance is underdeveloped.

It is true that the absence of product patent protection in India has not been associated with high accessibility of drugs. This does not mean that the presence or absence of such protection makes no difference. The absence of product patent protection and the presence of multiple producers and sellers provide opportunities that are not possible in a product patent regime. Even if public health and insurance facilities improve, it will be extremely difficult to ensure accessibility of drugs if the patent-protected prices are high.

Patents are mandatory in all fields including pharmaceutical products for a minimum period of 20 years under the Agreement on Trade Related Aspects of Intellectual Property Rights (TRIPS) of the World Trade Organization (WTO). In line with TRIPS, India has amended the Patents Act, 1970, and again introduced a product patent regime in pharmaceuticals since 1 January 2005.

The product patent regime will result in a monopoly market structure and high prices as in the regime before the Patents Act, 1970. After all, the basic rationale of product patent protection is that it will prevent others from manufacturing the product and hence enable the patent holders to charge higher prices to recoup their R&D costs. This will adversely affect not only consumers in India but also in other countries that depend on low-cost supplies from India.

But the protection of the private rights of the patentees is not the sole concern of TRIPS. It also recognizes the underlying public policy objectives and the special needs of the developing countries to permit flexibilities in implementing its provisions. Compulsory licensing is the most important flexibility permitted under TRIPS. A compulsory licence (CL) is an authorization by a government to non-patentees to use the patent without or against the consent of the patentee but on payment of royalties to the latter. A properly administered CL system is of vital importance in promoting competition and hence lowering prices while ensuring that patentees get compensation through royalties. In fact, CL is one of the ways in which TRIPS attempts to strike a balance between promoting access to existing drugs and promoting R&D in new drugs.

The Amended Patents Act has elaborate provisions on CL, but these have not been operationalized to have a simple and easy-to-administer CL system. The procedure is open-ended without any time limit imposed for the grant of CL. The entire process is excessively legalistic and provides patentees the opportunity to manipulate by litigation. The huge expenses involved in fighting the large pharmaceutical companies holding the patents may dissuade non-patentees from applying for licences in the first place.

The remarkable success of the Indian pharmaceutical industry has evoked the optimism that the growth in exports of patent-expired drugs will more than compensate for the decline in domestic opportunities as Indian companies are prevented from producing the new drugs developed abroad. But a steady and stable home market is of fundamental importance for success abroad. What is often not appreciated is that the remarkable export growth of the larger Indian companies in recent years has been accompanied by an equally remarkable domestic growth. It will be very difficult for Indian companies to sustain the export dynamism in the absence of a growing domestic market.

For the steady growth of the Indian generic companies, it is important to devise measures so that they can continue to manufacture and sell the new patented products in the domestic market. As mentioned earlier, this is possible within TRIPS by having a simple and easy-to-use CL procedure. So far as new drugs are concerned, apart from CL, the option is for Indian companies to develop new drugs themselves or collaborate with the MNCs. Some Indian companies have started R&D for new drugs. But because they do not have all the skills and the funds, the model they have adopted is to develop new molecules and license these out to the MNCs at early stages of clinical development. A number of Indian companies are very optimistic about the prospects of increasing marketing and manufacturing alliances with the MNCs in the new product patent regime. Outsourcing by the MNCs to Indian companies has started but the present size is still modest.

Both from the point of view of ensuring a competitive market structure and affordable prices and helping the growth of Indian generic companies, it is of fundamental importance to have a proper CL system, or better still to amend TRIPS and abolish mandatory product patent protection. But the MNCs are opposed to it. They consider exclusive patent rights as fundamental for earning profits for funding their R&D for new drugs. But it does not follow that patents are the best way to provide incentives for R&D. Arrow (1962), to whom much of modern economic theorizing on patents is attributed, did not consider patents the only possible incentive system. A number of alternatives have been mooted. If implemented, these can permit competition without adverse impact on innovation.

SUDIP CHAUDHURI

References

Arrow, Kenneth J. 1962. 'Economic Welfare and the Allocation of Resources for Invention', in *The Rate and Direction of Inventive Activity: Economic and Social Factors*, Princeton, Princeton University Press.

Chaudhuri, Sudip. 2005. *The WTO and India's Pharmaceuticals Industry: Patent Protection TRIPS and Developing Countries*, New Delhi, Oxford University Press.

CIPR. 2002. *Integrating Intellectual Property Rights and Development Policy*, London, Commission on Intellectual Property Rights.

Correa, Carlos M. 2000. *Intellectual Property Rights, the WTO and Developing Countries: The TRIPS Agreement and Policy Options*, London, Zed Books; Penang, Third World Network.

Govindaraj, Ramesh and G. Chellaraj. 2002. *The Indian Pharmaceutical Sector: Issues and Options for Health Sector Reform*, Washington DC, World Bank.

■ Planning

Most developing countries emerging from colonial rule in the middle of the last century adopted some form of economic planning reflecting a conviction, common even among non-communist countries at the time, that the state had to intervene actively to promote economic development. India was no exception to this trend—indeed it was in many ways a forerunner. The Indian National Congress, as early as 1938, although fully engaged in the struggle for Independence, had set up a National Planning Committee under Jawaharlal Nehru (later to become India's first Prime Minister) to work out concrete programmes of development covering major segments of the economy. The belief that planning and state intervention was necessary for development was shared even by the private sector at the time, as evidenced by the fact that in 1944 some of India's leading businessmen produced the so-called 'Bombay Plan', outlining a programme of economic development in which the state and the public sector were expected to play an important role.

Institutional Structure of Planning in India

Planning was institutionalized as a part of normal government activity when the Government of India, shortly after Independence in 1947, established the Planning Commission in March 1950 under the chairmanship of the Prime Minister.[1] This was followed by the setting up of the National Development Council (NDC) chaired by the Prime Minister and a membership consisting of all chief ministers of the states, members of the Union Cabinet, and full-time members of the Planning Commission. NDC is a deliberative forum which allows state governments to participate in the process of formulating plan objectives and strategies.

The nature of planning in India, and the role of the Planning Commission, has changed considerably over time. In earlier decades, planning relied on establishing

[1]The decision was announced by the Finance Minister Dr John Mathai in his Budget speech for 1950–1, but he resigned shortly thereafter largely in protest against what he felt was an undesirable innovation.

quantitative targets for individual sectors, derived from multi-sectoral planning models with a variety of executive instruments of control being deployed by the government to ensure that the targets were achieved. The government intervened to decide the scale of investment, location, choice of technology, ability to import, and so on. Over the years, it came to be recognized that investment should respond to market forces and entrepreneurs must have freedom to determine expansion plans, technology choices, and also the decision to import. While the practice of preparing Five Year Plans continued, the plans increasingly focused on broad national targets for growth, poverty alleviation, and the development of the social sector. Sectoral investment decisions were left largely to the private sector, although investment requirements of critical sectors such as energy and other infrastructure sectors received special attention in planning. These sectors were dominated by public-sector enterprises, and decisions taken by public-sector units were more amenable to government intervention, but even here progressively more freedom was given to public-sector units.

Changes in the political environment over the years inevitably had an impact on planning. The emergence of regional parties and the associated phenomenon of state governments being run by a variety of regional political parties, with the central government often being a coalition, led to a loosening of the control exercised by the central government on state governments. This has also generated pressures for greater financial devolution. As a result, state governments today have much greater freedom of manoeuvre relative to the Centre. A more recent development is the pressure for further decentralization to local governments—the level of government relevant for delivering essential services in health and education. Since the role of the government is increasingly being focused on service delivery in these areas, implementing devolution to the local level has become a very important issue for plan implementation.

The Planning Commission has changed over time to reflect these changes. It performs several different functions, operating much like a ministry in some respects, but with some important differences. It is responsible for preparing Five Year Plans which outline broad economic and social targets and the strategy to be followed, including the mix of public and private investment necessary to achieve the objectives. The Plan indicates in some detail the requirements of public expenditure on plan programmes in individual sectors for both the Centre and the states. Since the role to be played by the private sector has increased greatly, there is much more focus on the policy environment that is needed for the private sector to perform its expected role. The Plans also indicate the manner in which public-sector expenditures are to be financed, including the extent of assistance from the Centre to the states.

In terms of technology of planning, the Commission does not rely on in-house input–output type models which characterized the planning methodology in the 1960s and 1970s. Instead, several different research institutes have been commissioned to work on different models, which have somewhat different characteristics and strengths. Results from these models are used to evolve a synoptic view, keeping in mind the limitations of each model.

The Five Year Plans are implemented year by year through the central government's annual budgets and the budgets of the governments of states and union territories. The Planning Commission negotiates with the Finance Ministry the total volume of financial resources which can be provided in the central budget to support the central government's plan programmes and the volume of central plan transfers to state governments. This involves an intense process of negotiation and interaction to reduce the large initial demands of ministries to the scale of resources available, keeping in mind the Plan's original intentions and evolving budget constraints. Once the annual budgetary provision for the Plan is finalized, the Planning Commission is responsible for dividing this total between the Centre and the states, reflecting the broad pattern approved in the Five Year Plan, and also distributing the central share among central ministries. Investments made by public-sector corporations financed by their own resources, or by borrowed resources, no longer require direct approval of the Planning Commission except for large projects which need Cabinet approval, where the Commission also comments, along with the Finance Ministry.

The Commission also holds discussions annually with the states, when it reviews the states' performance and approves the level and sectoral composition of state plans. In practice, the approval of state plans is a formality which is a precondition for clearing the central assistance provided to the states. The Commission does not undertake detailed project by project approval of individual projects in the state plans. It comments on intersectoral allocations made by the state governments to draw attention to possible anomalies. In effect, discussions with individual states are an annual exercise which reviews the performance of the state and also advises the states on key issues.

The Commission also acts as a think tank for the government, exploring and proposing policy initiatives that are necessary to achieve plan targets and providing advice and critical evaluation of the effectiveness of policies in all sectors. This aspect of its role has also evolved considerably. In the early years, it was the only forum in the central government, other than the Finance Ministry, which articulated economic strategy and policy. Over the years, other economic ministries have developed independent capability and also become much more active in designing policies in their sectors. As a result, policy decisions relating to major sectors are evolved through inter-ministerial groups, in which the Planning Commission also participates. However, unlike other ministries, each of which typically takes a sectoral view, the Planning Commission is expected to inject a broader cross-sectoral perspective on formulating policy, viewing policies in individual sectors in the light of other sectoral policies also in a longer-term time frame. At times the Planning Commission also plays a key role in initiating policy papers, as it did in formulating the Integrated Energy Policy which was approved by the Cabinet in December 2009. Since energy covered many ministries, the Planning Commission was tasked with preparing an integrated policy on all energy sectors.

Early Experience with Five Year Plans

The First Five Year Plan (1951–2 to 1955–6) was little more than a collection of ongoing public investment projects, most of which were taken from the programme for post-War reconstruction which was fairly well-defined even before Independence. The Plan aimed at a general increase in the standard of living and also emphasized wider objectives, such as full employment and removal of inequalities, but there was no specific analytically directed strategy for development.

The Second Five Year Plan (1956–7 to 1960–1) was the first plan to articulate a strategy for development based on analytical work by Professor P.C. Mahalanobis using a two-sector model which distinguished between the capital goods producing sector and the consumer goods producing sector. Economic growth was viewed as a function of investment, and investment was seen to be constrained by the availability of capital goods. Since it was assumed that India could not expect to import capital goods freely because of limits on its ability to earn foreign exchange—an assumption which reflected export pessimism that was fairly common at the time—the availability of capital goods for investment depended on domestic capacity to manufacture capital goods. Given these assumptions, the best strategy for accelerating growth was to build up domestic capacity in the capital goods sector (and the associated metals producing sectors) as quickly as possible. Hence, the strategy implied directing large parts of the investment to the expansion of capacity in the capital goods sectors.

Since these sectors were both capital and technology intensive, and since private-sector entrepreneurial capacity was limited and in any case was more likely to be directed to the production of consumer goods, it was felt that public-sector units should be set up in the capital goods and metals producing sectors. Political developments at the time also favoured the expansion of the public sector. The Congress Party in 1955 had adopted a resolution in favour of the 'socialistic pattern of society' which was later also adopted by Parliament. It was also felt that the strategy of expanding the public sector had the advantage that surpluses generated by the public sector would be directed entirely to increasing the rate of investment whereas profits in the private sector would partly lead to higher consumption.

The Second Plan strategy ran into difficulties in the late 1950s because of severe balance-of-payments problems and food shortages, both of which were arguably linked to the neglect of export possibilities and of agriculture. Inflationary pressures intensified. Population growth also turned out to be a larger problem than was originally anticipated. The Third Plan (1961–2 to 1965–6) recognized these problems, but it did not propose any change in the basic strategy. Development was equalled with pursuing industrialization, based on promoting the so-called 'heavy industries' with a strong emphasis on the public sector, while providing protection from import competition through quantitative restrictions on imports.

The planning methodology in the 1960s was dominated by two considerations. The first was the perception that certain sectors were of strategic importance and investment resources must, therefore, be consciously directed towards expanding capacity in these sectors. This produced a natural suspicion of market forces, which were more likely to draw investment into 'non-priority sectors', such as consumer goods. The desire to define quantitative targets for individual sectors led to the adoption of more disaggregated planning models, expanding more accurately from four sectors in the Second Plan, to 60 in the Third Plan, and 186 later. Sectoral targets in turn provided the intellectual basis for the system of investment licensing, which sought to direct resources towards expansion in strategic areas and also prevent expansion in others. In practice, the system of industrial licensing proved to be highly inefficient, often leading to suboptimal scales of production, and forced adoption of suboptimal technology. It also served to protect existing private-sector investors who, having obtained permissions to create capacity, were then able to argue against licensing additional capacity to others on the grounds that this would promote wasteful competition.

The second consideration dominating Indian planning methodology was the perceived need to deal with the scarcity of foreign exchange. Export pessimism led to unwillingness to address this problem by depreciating the exchange rate in the hope of generating more exports. Instead, a twofold approach was adopted of mobilizing external assistance to meet foreign exchange needs and rationing scarce foreign exchange by restricting import demand through import licensing. Import licences were typically not given if domestic production capacity had been set up, which effectively gave tailor-made protection to domestic industry. Not surprisingly, the industrial structure that emerged was high cost and highly inefficient.

Although the Planning Commission provided the intellectual justification needed for introducing various controls over investment allocations, technology choices, and imports that evolved in the 1960s and 1970s, the actual controls were administered by the ministries concerned, with little effective linkage to planning methodologies. In any case, the quantitative targets mentioned in the Plan were much more aggregative than the level at which the controls actually operated.

In the early 1960s, Indian planning came under criticism on the grounds that the benefits of development had not accrued to the masses whose essential needs remained unmet.[2] Responding to this criticism, the Perspective Planning Division of the Planning Commission produced an influential paper in 1962 outlining a strategy for guaranteeing a minimum level of living to everyone within 15 years, that is, by 1975 using 1961 as the base year.[3] Recognizing that income distribution tended to be relatively stable, the paper argued that rapid growth of GDP would have to be a major part of the solution. Accordingly, it suggested a GDP growth target of 6 per cent per year which, with a relatively stable distribution, would lead to a broad-based improvement in living standards. Even so, the paper concluded that growth would not be sufficient for lifting the bottom 20 per cent above the minimum standard and they were likely to be left out and it would be necessary to have special employment generation programmes and income support for these groups. This strategy of 'growth plus distribution and poverty alleviation' became popular internationally, and was also was subsequently adopted by the World Bank and other multilateral development banks in the 1970s.

While India's planning strategy in the 1960s clearly emphasized the need to accelerate growth, it did not actually succeed in generating faster growth as targeted. Unfortunately, not enough effort was made to question why growth targets were not being achieved and whether changes in economic policies were needed. There was constant focus on the need for higher levels of investment, especially in the public sector, but factors affecting the efficiency of investment were ignored. As shown in Table 1, performance in the Third Plan period (1961–2 to 1965–6) deteriorated significantly compared to earlier years with the growth rate collapsing to 2.7 per cent per year. This was partly because of a succession of poor harvests, especially in the terminal year, and also partly because of two disruptive wars, first with China in 1962 and then with Pakistan in 1965, which forced an increase in allocation to defence and weakened India's capacity to mobilize resources for development.

Table 1 Growth Targets and Achievements (% per year)

	Target	Actual
1. First Plan (1951–2 to 1955–6)	2.1	3.6
2. Second Plan (1956–7 to 1960–1)	4.5	4.2
3. Third Plan (1961–2 to 1965–6)	5.6	2.7
4. Fourth Plan (1969–70 to 1973–4)	5.7	3.4
5. Fifth Plan (1974–5 to 1978–9)	4.4	4.9
6. Sixth Plan (1980–1 to 1984–5)	5.2	5.5
7. Seventh Plan (1985–6 to 1989–90)	5.0	5.7
8. Eighth Plan (1992–3 to 1996–7)	5.6	6.5
9. Ninth Plan (1997–8 to 2001–2)	6.5	5.5
10. Tenth Plan (2002–3 to 2006–7)	8.0	7.8
11. Eleventh Plan (2007–8 to 2011–12)	9.0	8.1*

Note: The growth targets for the first three plans were set with respect to national income. In the Fourth Plan it was net domestic product. In all plans thereafter it has been GDP at factor cost.
*Estimate assuming 8.5 per cent growth in 2011–12.

The war with Pakistan in 1965 was followed by two severe droughts which delayed the formulation of the Fourth Plan. However, this period saw a major restructuring of policies in agriculture, triggered largely by political developments. In 1966, India was highly dependent on imports of food grains from the United States under PL 480. President Lyndon Johnson, irritated

[2] The issue was raised by Dr Ram Manohar Lohia in his maiden speech in Parliament in 1962 and led to the appointment of a committee under Dr P.C. Mahalanobis to examine how the gains of development in the 1950s had to be distributed.

[3] 'Perspectives of Development: 1961–1976, Implications of Planning for a Minimum Level of Living', Perspective Planning Division, New Delhi, Planning Commission.

by India's criticism of the US position on Vietnam, imposed a strict policy under which each shipload of food required separate Presidential approval. Determined to overcome the country's humiliating vulnerability on this score, Prime Minister Indira Gandhi, gave top priority to achieving food self-sufficiency, and based on the advice of C. Subramaniam, then Minister for Agriculture, authorized experimenting with high-yielding wheat varieties, based on the import of high-yielding wheat seeds developed by Norman Borlaug under a Rockefeller Foundation grant in CIMMYT in Mexico. C. Subramaniam, in his memoirs, has recorded that there was opposition from three sources. The Communist Party was opposed to the move because it involved use of imported wheat varieties evolved from grants from the Rockefeller Foundation. The Planning Commission opposed it on the ground that existing domestic programmes for increasing agricultural productivity were good enough. Finally, the Finance Ministry opposed it because the programme involved an outgo of foreign exchange to import the wheat seeds. The Prime Minister overruled these objections and the programme went ahead. The high-yielding wheat was successfully adapted to Indian conditions by Indian agricultural research scientists and, together with supportive market support policies, led to the Green Revolution in wheat in the early 1970s.

An important episode in industrial and trade policy in the second half of the 1960s was the devaluation of the rupee in 1966 combined with measures of import liberalization as part of an agreement with the World Bank and the IMF aimed at mobilizing a much-needed external assistance from the international donor community. As it happened, the additional assistance promised by the World Bank and the aid donors did not materialize, leading to a considerable resentment at being forced to devalue. The import liberalization was reversed and the resentment at being forced to devalue lingered for many years, contributing to a prolonged suspicion of all advice on liberalization.

The problems of managing foreign exchange scarcity dominated policy agenda in the 1970s. The denial of external assistance, promised as part of the devaluation package, led to the Fourth Plan (1969–70 to 1974–5) emphasizing self-reliance and reduced dependence on external aid, which in practice meant a tightening of import controls and increased inward orientation. However, the performance in the Fourth Plan period was again disappointing (see Table 1) and this also meant little progress in achieving the minimum needs objectives laid down 10 years earlier.

The inability to reduce poverty was obviously linked to the failure of achieving rapid growth and should have led to a re-examination of the growth strategy itself. Instead, it led many participants in the public debate to argue that rather than pushing for elusive targets of growth, greater attention should be paid to implementing a direct attack on poverty through targeted schemes to help the poor. A number of targeted anti-poverty schemes were evolved in this period, including special programmes for rural employment and small and marginal farmers; these were incorporated into the Fifth Plan (1975–6 to 1979–80). As it happened, this Plan was terminated after the third year as there was a change of government when Mrs Indira Gandhi lost the election in 1977. This was followed by two years of Annual Plans in 1978–9 and 1979–80.

Economic Policy in the 1980s

The 1980s saw the beginning of changes in economic policy, prompted by the recognition that the East Asian countries, which followed somewhat different policies with greater outward orientation, were performing much better. This led to some important modifications in policy, with greater flexibility being given to the private sector, and freer access to imports for exporters, combined with a conscious effort at managing the exchange rate to avoid exchange rate appreciation in real terms.

These changes were reflected in the Sixth Plan (1980–1 to 1984–5) but it is important to note that the planning process had changed significantly by this time. Policy formulation was no longer the outcome of a planning process centralized in the Planning Commission. Instead, it came from multiple inter-ministerial committees, which also took into account the views of ministries and non-government experts. The Planning Commission was actively involved in all these deliberations, but it was not the principal policymaking body.

The policy changes introduced in the Sixth Plan were associated with a markedly improved performance in the Sixth Plan period and the growth rate of the economy exceeded the target for the first time (see Table 1). These policy changes were further intensified in the Seventh Plan period (1985–6 to 1989–90) when Shri Rajiv Gandhi was the Prime Minister. Policies towards the private sector were made more supportive and the tax system was rationalized, including reducing the income tax rate to 50 per cent. Import licensing was eliminated in a growing range of areas where domestic protection concerns were not significant. More important, in areas where import licensing remained in place, the licences were given much more freely. Import availability to exporters was liberalized very significantly and the exchange rate was managed in a way which brought about a significant but gradual real depreciation. This helped exporters and also made restrictions on import licensing less binding. The overt commitment to a strong public-sector remained unchanged, but there was a distinct shift away from the earlier policy of nationalizing loss-making private-sector units to protect employment, and there was much less pressure to expand public-sector investment in areas where private investment was forthcoming.

The Seventh Plan period saw continued strong economic growth, further reinforcing confidence in the new approach to policy. However, an important weakness in performance in this period was the steady increase in the fiscal deficit accompanied by unsustainable short-term external borrowing in an environment where export performance remained weak. These weaknesses led to a balance-of-payments crisis in 1991.

Economic Reforms after 1991

The balance-of-payments crisis in 1991 was triggered by the sharp, though temporary, increase in oil prices on account of the Gulf War in 1990. There was a loss of confidence leading to a reversal of external flows, reflecting the winding down of short-term external debt, which had built up in earlier years. The crisis became an opportunity for unveiling more systemic economic reforms by Dr Manmohan Singh, then the Finance Minister, who later became the Prime Minister in 2004.

The reforms of the 1990s were broadly similar to those attempted by most developing countries, but with some important differences. The thrust of the reforms was: (i) placing greater reliance on the role of the private sector in building on India's considerable entrepreneurial tradition, (ii) opening the economy to foreign trade and foreign direct investment, (iii) restructuring the role of the government to concentrate on functions not likely to be performed by the market (for example, expanding supply of public goods, such as primary health services and education, and also developing infrastructure) and also to regulate markets where necessary to ensure competition, (iv) maintaining an active role for the government in promoting livelihood-supporting activities relevant for the poor (for example, raising land productivity in agriculture and various types of support for small-scale industry), and (v) ensuring that macroeconomic parameters remained in balance and the financial sector was well run.

While these features are common to reform efforts elsewhere, there were also important differences. First, India's reforms were much more gradualist than in other countries, reflecting the compulsions of India's highly pluralist and participative democratic policy. The resulting slow pace of change meant that it took time for the reforms to be seen as well-established, leading to changes in economic behaviour as a result of which benefits were also derived more slowly. Second, privatization of existing public-sector enterprises was not a major feature of the reform effort, which focused instead on selling only minority stakes in profit-making public enterprises while trying to close down chronic loss makers.

Economic performance in the post-reform period showed a definite improvement. The balance-of-payments crisis of 1991, which led to the reforms, was quickly overcome and economic growth resumed strongly after 1992, yielding an average growth rate of 6.7 per cent for the Eighth Plan period (1992–3 to 1996–7). However, the economy slowed down thereafter, partly because of a global slowdown following the East Asian crisis of 1997 combined with a string of poor monsoons which depressed agricultural performance, and partly also because of a slowing down in the pace of reforms. As a result, the growth rate dipped to 5.5 per cent in the Ninth Plan period (1997–8 to 2001–2). Interestingly, the GDP growth rate in the 1990s was almost the same as in the 1980s, leading some observers to conclude that the bolder market-oriented reforms of the 1990s did not really add anything to the growth that had been generated in any case by the more limited reforms of the 1980s. However, this view does not allow for the fact that reforms were implemented only gradually and their full impact was, therefore, felt only in the next decade.

The Tenth Plan (2002–3 to 2006–7) called for a renewed effort at pushing economic reforms to achieve a growth rate of 8 per cent. After an initially weak start, the economy accelerated significantly and the growth rate in the Tenth Plan period was 7.8 per cent. The improvement in economic performance reflects the gradual maturing of the economy in response to economic reforms. Encouraged by this performance, a target of 9 per cent growth was set for the Eleventh Plan period (2007–8 to 2011–12) and the Commission also called for growth to be more inclusive.

The Eleventh Plan emphasized the importance of a much better performance in agriculture for achieving greater inclusiveness. Agricultural GDP growth had decelerated from around 3.6 per cent in the period 1980–96 to less than 2 per cent thereafter and this was undoubtedly a factor behind the perception that the benefits of progress had not spread to rural areas. The Plan emphasized the need for a comprehensive re-look at agricultural policies to achieve 4 per cent growth in agriculture. Upgrading infrastructure facilities (electric power, roads, ports, airports, railways, and so on) was another critical element in the Eleventh Plan strategy as lack of good quality infrastructure had been widely identified as a constraint. It was recognized that this would require a large increase in investment and this could not be done through the public sector alone. The Plan emphasized the need to involve the private sector in developing infrastructure through public–private partnerships, and much effort was directed at evolving policies to make this possible.

The Eleventh Plan also emphasized the need to pay much greater attention to the role of the government in the social sector—health and education—especially in rural areas. India lags behind other developing countries in this respect and corrective steps are urgently needed. Since these are areas where the agencies responsible for delivering services are those of state governments, much of the planning for service delivery would have to shift to the states and local governments. However, the central government would have to extend substantial assistance to the state governments for this purpose.

The performance of the economy in the Eleventh Plan period looks likely to average 8.1 per cent—growth which is less than the target of 9 per cent and only marginally better than the Tenth Plan average of 7.8 per cent. However, it is a remarkable achievement given that this was a period when the world economy was hit by a crisis of exceptional severity.

To summarize, Indian planning has changed considerably from the early years when it was part of a system of extensive direct intervention in an economy much more closed to global influences. The economy is much more open and growth is recognized to be much more private-sector-driven. The planning process is now aimed at setting broad goals, given domestic and external constraints, and also identifying critical areas for policy action to remove these constraints. It also serves to guide substantial government resources devoted to development, including independent evaluation of the effectiveness of the programmes.

In recognition of the importance of vigorous evaluation of government programmes and policies an Independent Evaluation Office, operating at an arms length from the Planning Commission, is being established. It will undertake detailed studies of the effectiveness of government programmes with a view to providing inputs for redesigning to increase efficiency.

MONTEK S. AHLUWALIA

Political Economy

Political economy refers to the distribution of political and economic power in a given society and how that influences the directions of development and policies that bear on the latter. In India, where the vast masses of people are poor and often socially disadvantaged, a relatively small minority holds much of the power, although in recent years democratic expansion has started to loosen the grip of elite control.

In terms of economic interests, the groups that have often been identified as powerful include large and medium business houses, large and medium farmers, the upper echelons of the salaried class, and the top layer of unionized labour. There have been learned, and sometimes intense, debates, particularly among Marxist scholars, on the nature of class formation and mode of production in India. Since empirical data on different categories are often limited to size groups of landholdings, or to asset-holding groups and to corporate market shares, it is not easy to clearly demarcate the different economic interest groups, and it is even more difficult to delineate the cross-cutting cleavages of economic and social stratification. And on how the groups get organized and exercise their power, we usually have mostly anecdotal and case-study evidence. We have more quantitative evidence on wealth distribution, which, of course, is highly unequal in India. According to National Sample Survey data, in 1991, while more than half of the households had less than Rs 50,000 in assets (physical, including land, and financial), only about 10 per cent of rural households and 14 per cent of urban households had assets exceeding Rs 2.5 lakh. (The Market Information Survey of Households carried out by the National Council of Applied Economic Research [NCAER] suggests that in terms of income, about 12 per cent of households in India in 1998–9 had annual income of above Rs 1.05 lakh, while 40 per cent of households had annual income less than Rs 35,000.)

But the inequality in human capital (for example, education) is much more than in physical or financial capital. According to World Bank estimates, inequality in adult schooling years among people in India is much higher than that in not just Sri Lanka, China, Vietnam, or Indonesia, but also most Latin American countries including Brazil and Mexico. The gulf between the educated and the uneducated in India is largely reflected in the social and economic disparity between those who do manual work and those who do not. This is the big dividing line in India, and is much too frozen over time, as education (particularly at secondary level and above), which is the main route of inter-generational mobility, is available (or affordable) to a small group of people, whose boundaries expand much too slowly. In terms of occupation categories, the earlier-mentioned

NCAER data suggest that salary earners, professionals, and businessmen constituted the heads of about 22 per cent of households in 1998–9 (since this excludes some unmeasured number of those described as cultivators who may also avoid manual work, the actual proportion of households with heads in non-manual occupations is likely to be higher). Since the overwhelming majority of manual workers are not organized, they hold little political power as workers. Of course, they are at election times often mobilized as social groups (divided along caste, community, religion, or regional lines) that give them some intermittent collective electoral power.

Even when social and economic interest groups (belonging largely, say, to the top two deciles of population) are influential, their influence is somewhat dissipated by extreme fragmentation. In terms of social and economic divisions, the Indian elite may be more fragmented than the elite in most other countries, reflecting the fact that India has one of the world's most heterogeneous societies. This gives rise to what political scientists call a 'collective action' problem, that is, the actors find it difficult to get their act together. It is more difficult for them to agree on a goal, and even when they agree on one, it is difficult for them to coordinate their actions to achieve that goal. This becomes a particularly acute political–economic problem in the matter of long-term public investment in infrastructure (power, roads, transport, telecommunication, ports, irrigation, and so on). Infrastructure is widely regarded as the crucial bottleneck for Indian economic growth, and the Indian elite is to largely benefit from any improvement in infrastructure. Yet substantial public investment in infrastructure that takes a relatively long time to fructify may require, in the current situation of fiscal deficits, giving up on the part of the elite of government subsidies or benefits of underpriced public goods and services (like water, electricity, fertilizer, cooking gas, and university education), or of major raises in salary or perks in government jobs. But coordinating on short-run sacrifices or curbing particularistic demands on the public fisc (it has been estimated that about two-thirds of all government subsidies go to the relatively rich) for the sake of long-term elite goals has been very difficult to achieve in India. Over the years, this collective action problem has become more severe. As more and more of hitherto subordinate social groups have come up to be politically important, particularly at state level (in a welcome expansion of political equality and democracy in India), the sources of demands on the polity have become more diverse. In the first two decades after Independence, the massive countrywide organization of the Congress Party used to coordinate the transactional negotiations among different groups and leaders in different parts of the country. That organization has fallen into disarray. The proliferation of small and regional parties and their increasing importance for the survival of coalition governments at the Centre have often meant that catering to particularistic demands overrides coordination for the long haul. At any given moment an important election somewhere in the country is never too far off, and the short-run issues trump the long-run ones.

When the interest groups are socially and economically fragmented, pulling in different directions with none dominating the whole show, state policies get buffeted around, and any steps towards economic reform are likely to be halting and hesitant. But such fragmentation may also give the state somewhat more autonomy, in the sense that it does not have to march to the tune of one dominant interest group, and an astute political leadership can play off one group against the other to some extent and earn its own rent in the form of special power and privileges. In any case, as the old debates among Marxist scholars on the 'relative autonomy of the state' made clear, in most countries the state leadership retains a great deal of potency as an organizational actor in goal formulation, agenda setting, and policy execution, even when it acts within the broad constraints of interest group politics. In India, over the years, the state has accumulated a great deal of power in direct ownership and regulation of the economy, and in spite of economic liberalization still controls the production, assets, and employment in large parts of the organized non-agricultural sectors. There is a growing body of public opinion that the state should reorient its role away from public ownership and control of business enterprises and more towards health, education, and other basic social services for the poor, and even when the state is to be the major funding agency for some of these services, it does not necessarily mean that the actual provision of the services has to be bureaucratically managed instead of being contracted out to the private sector or as some form of private–public partnership. But the political implementation of this view in India has been slow.

The paradox is that while the state in India has been powerful (and often heavy-handed) in its regulatory and interventionist role, it will not be described as what the political economy literature calls a 'strong state'. The latter essentially refers to a state that can credibly commit to, for example, a long-term policy and not deviate from it under short-term populist pressures. In the recent history of development, South Korea in the 1960s and 1970s is often cited as an example of a strong state which stuck to its commitment, for example, to export performance as a pre-announced criterion for helping industries, thus using international market discipline in raising cost and quality consciousness in an economy otherwise marked by a great deal of state intervention. Of course, South Korea was then an authoritarian state, and one may think democracies are prone to succumb more to populist pressures. But authoritarianism is neither necessary nor sufficient for credible commitment. That it is not necessary is illustrated by democratic Japan and the Scandinavian countries often successfully committing to pre-announced long-term policies; that it is not sufficient is, of course, amply illustrated by many African authoritarian regimes. But the success of Japan and Scandinavian countries as 'strong' democratic states and the failure of democratic India to be one may have something to do with the fact that social homogeneity and relative economic equality in the former enable them to resolve some collective action problems more easily and coordinate on long-term policies in a way that is much more difficult for extremely heterogeneous and unequal India.

But there is clearly a trade-off between credibility and accountability in state affairs. The institutional insulation that may be required to follow through on commitments may over time make the leadership impervious to the felt (and changing) needs and demands of common people. Even well-intentioned state-directed technocratic development projects, which do not involve the people at ground level but simply treat them as objects of the development process, often end up primarily as conduits of largesse for elite groups—middlemen, contractors, officials, and politicians—and very little reaches the intended beneficiaries. Even when a significant amount reaches the latter, the benefits are sometimes of the wrong kind, inappropriate technologically and unsustainable environmentally, corrosive of local institutions of community bonding and self-help, and always leaving untapped the large reservoir of local initiative, ingenuity, and information.

Of course, accountability can be exercised through the periodic elections in which common people give their verdict on politicians' performance, and the Indian electorate has been quite assertive in throwing out incumbents. But general elections constitute a rather blunt instrument for economic performance monitoring. Elections are fought on multidimensional platforms, and even vital economic issues often do not get salience in electoral mobilization. A particular leader who is perceived to uphold a hitherto marginalized caste group's dignity may win election after election, even though the same leader's policy neglect may be responsible for the dismal education and health environment of most children in that caste group.

One can say that federalism and decentralization are ways of making the state more responsive to local needs. The rise of regional parties and the strength of local autonomy movements at state level certainly reflect that, although the major Indian states are larger than most countries in the world, and as such the state governments are still quite distant from local communities, Indian federalism is currently afflicted by two major dilemmas. One is that while the regional governments are becoming more important in national politics, their fiscal dependence on the central government is steadily increasing: catering to the various particularistic demands, many of them are near fiscal bankruptcy which certainly limits their economic power and ability to carry out various important social service functions. The other dilemma is that with economic liberalization and increased regional competition, the disparity between economically advanced and backward states is growing: the advanced states increasingly resent the redistributive functions of Indian federalism (through the dispensations of the Finance Commission and the Planning Commission) that to them look like rewarding inefficiency and creating dependency, and yet no Indian polity can ignore the fact that some of the populous backward states hold a very large number of seats in the Lok Sabha and a coalition government is unlikely to survive any large-scale withdrawal of their support. How the Indian polity tackles these two dilemmas will shape the political economy of Indian federalism in the near future.

The 73rd and 74th Constitutional Amendments in the early 1990s have given some potency to the movement towards decentralization below state level, all the way down to gram panchayats. While this is a major step towards local accountability, as yet effective decentralization is largely absent in most parts of India (outside three or four states). Very few administrative functions (and even fewer sources of independent finance) have been devolved to the local governments, and state-level bureaucrats and politicians still largely hold sway. That in states like Kerala and West Bengal this decentralization has been somewhat more effective than in other states has much to do with the fact that prior land reforms and political awareness movements in these two states have made capture of local governments by the oligarchic local elites somewhat more difficult. While fiscally responsible and locally accountable governments at panchayat level remain one of the major ways of deepening Indian democracy, much will depend on how far we can proceed in our campaigns for land reform to weaken the powers of the local oligarchy, expansion of education, a more vigorous devolution of finances to the local governments, and regular auditing and activation of local non-governmental organizations (NGOs) and media as watchdogs on local-level corruption. There is some evidence that the active freedom-of-information movement and reservation of panchayat leadership positions for women and scheduled castes is having some salutary effects in this respect in some areas.

PRANAB BARDHAN

Population Policy

Any textbook or discussion on population policy finds it necessary to acknowledge that India was the first country to officially have both a population policy as well as a family planning programme—the two are not necessarily the same thing, though they get equated in practice as well as in popular discourse. This happened as far back as 1951, when the rest of the world took either or both of two approaches—bemoaned the burgeoning populations of the developing world (and in the case of the United States, fretted about what this implied for the Cold War) and/or (except for a few loud pioneers like Margaret Sanger and Marie Stopes) acted coy about or downright hostile to the idea of its own women using contraception.

But while India is held up as the trailblazer in all discourses on population policy and family planning programmes, this must not be taken to imply a purely home-grown and home-sustained affair. For one thing, even if an 'official' interest in population and family planning was expressed in India before it was anywhere else in the world, this interest was in many ways a natural outgrowth of the intense non-governmental and popular interest in these matters in the Western world in the early and mid-20th century. Independent India's official position on the population question was also directly encouraged, funded, and technically supported by an increasingly aggressive international population control movement that saw the country both as a testing ground for family planning efforts and new contraceptive technology, as well as central to any attempts to reducing developing country population growth rates.

In any case, the earliest native proponents of population policy in India were all heavily exposed to and influenced by both neo-Malthusian debates as well as the arguments of women's health advocates in the West. And within India itself, the population and family planning question was by no means a post-colonial preoccupation—the London-based neo-Malthusian League had several Indian vice-presidents, a branch was established in Madras as early as in 1928—the population theme was repeatedly discussed in pre-1947 legislative assemblies, primarily by upper-caste members decrying the unbridled fecundity of the poor masses.

All these pre-Independence preoccupations with the population problem, well before there was actually any significant rise in population growth rate, meant that by the time of the First Five Year Plan, the country was ripe for an official policy. At this time, the Ministry of Health was allotted Rs 6.5 million by the Planning Commission for a family planning programme. The Commission also recommended further research on population issues. While the promotion of artificial birth control was opposed by some individuals, including the Health Minister Rajkumari Amrit Kaur, Prime Minister Nehru was able to overrule these objections. And since that time, population has remained a major subject in planning documents and on-the-ground operations in one form or another, often controversial, but never abandoned fully. Among the major policy instruments[1] that the country took a lead in promoting must be mentioned the drastic liberalization of its abortion laws through the Medical Termination of Pregnancy Act of 1972, a piece of legislation which made abortion available virtually on demand. Whatever the population control and/or women's welfare motives behind this Act, it is today one of the facilitators of the increasing practice of sex-selective abortions in the country.

What kinds of arguments have motivated and continue to motivate the very existence of Indian population policy? The 1994 Cairo Conference on Population and Development somehow gave the impression that earlier advocates of population policy were motivated solely by demographic, as opposed to individual, concerns. But any serious history of the population movement in India cannot fail to discern at least three parallel streams of concern that egged on government action in the form of policy statements, even if these 'ideological' streams were not equally strong or equally effective at all times. Nor were these three streams necessarily mutually exclusive in individuals or groups—it was all too common for more than one of them to motivate the same person.

The first (but not necessarily the FIRST) such openly stated support for official population policy came from the neo-Malthusians, from those who saw the rapid population growth unleashed by mortality declines in

[1]For a detailed description of these instruments, see Visaria and Chari (1998).

mid-century India as a serious drag on development and a serious impediment to poverty eradication. The Coale and Hoover (1958) text that became compulsory reading in undergraduate economics courses in the 1960s and 1970s was a formal attempt to demonstrate the ways in which economic growth would be hampered by rapid population growth in India. The arguments advanced in it influenced Indian planning in the 1960s and continue to haunt even the more individual-centred population policy documents of today. Note, for example, the slipping in of phrases to do with 'sustainable development' in the 2000 National Population Policy, which is otherwise explicitly centred on a reproductive health agenda. In fact, within the framework of this 'national' policy, several states continue to devise measures that have more or less explicit fertility control agendas. Incentives and disincentives, the bad words of the 1970s, are important parts of this promotion of supposedly voluntary birth control.

But alongside this population control (the currently fashionable phrase is population stabilization) agenda, there has always been a genuine advocacy of family planning services for the sake of women's health and freedom. In fact, it was this motive that justified the original creation of an official family planning programme in the 1950s, with a slower growing population being viewed as an additional benefit rather than the central goal (Visaria 2000). To be fair, even after the programme gained momentum for population growth reasons, there was always a stream of support for it that focused on the need for contraceptive access for women and children's welfare. The integration of the family planning programme with the maternal and child health programme in the mid-1960s was a reflection of this perspective, at the same time as the population growth rationale was used to introduce time-bound, method-specific targets into the programme.

In other words, at least two of the rationales for a national population policy were arguably less distasteful than later projections of them made them out to be (Basu 1997a). Often enough they ended up with their more distasteful ends being privileged, especially on the ground, but there is nothing *inherently* objectionable in concerns about the implications of high fertility and rapid population growth for women's welfare and/or national development. However, there is a third and continuing stream of support for an aggressive population policy that has always existed in some form or the other and is difficult to condone on either empirical or ethical grounds. This support takes the form of wanting the state to run a coercive or semi-coercive family planning programme so that the fertility of the 'other' may be curtailed. This is one kind of eugenics argument because it is concerned with changing the us-versus-them distribution of the population. Who this other is has varied with time and place—sometimes it is the poor that have too many children, at other times it is the lower castes, sometimes it is the uneducated, most often it is the minorities. Never is it us—those who would thrust family planning upon the other—who need to do anything about our own fertility or anything directly about the poverty or illiteracy or minority status anxiety that fosters high birth rates in these others.

This attitude is completely analogous to the Western world's push to bring down Third World birth rates which so regularly riles Third World elites. It is also this attitude that was expressed in the growing coerciveness of the Indian family planning programme which culminated in the excesses of the Emergency, when several parts of the country witnessed the forcible mass sterilization of men too old or poor or weak or unorganized to protest. The 1976 National Population Policy explicitly espoused legislation to make family planning compulsory. It is especially ironical that the Minister for Health and Family Planning at this time was the very person who had made history at the United Nations International Population Conference in Bucharest in 1974 by declaring that the Western world was mistaken in pushing birth control in the developing countries when in fact 'development is the best contraceptive'.

The nature of population and family planning policy during the Emergency brought down the government. In addition, it had one serious effect that has in fact now become somewhat institutionalized. Because of the severe backlash that the Emergency experience created against contraceptive acceptance, post-1977 the distribution of acceptors suddenly changed completely—from being something that focused on male sterilization, the family planning programme became entirely targeted at female acceptors and that too almost exclusively at female acceptors of sterilization, even though vasectomy is a much simpler and safer procedure than tubectomy and even though in principle the programme is committed to offering a cafeteria of methods (Basu 1985).

The target-driven, female-centred family planning programme that characterized Indian policy was an important source of the growing resentment against government-sponsored population programmes worldwide by all kinds of activist groups and the Cairo Conference on Population and Development at last gave these groups the clout to completely change the paradigm—'reproductive health' rather than population control or family planning became the new goal of population policy in international documents as well as in government policy statements. While many of these national policies began as little more than rhetorical documents, thanks to continued monitoring and pressure from a variety of international and domestic non-governmental organizations, population policy in India does seem to be making some real transition to a more women-friendly approach. Method-specific targets were abolished in 1996 (unfortunately interpreted in some places to mean that services are not provided even to women who want them); local institutions became increasingly more responsible for programme needs assessments and design; a Reproductive and Child Health Programme was launched in 1997; and a National Population Commission was set up in May 2000 (with a whopping 100 members), as envisaged in the new National Population Policy of February 2000.

And while the fertility question continues to be politicized by many groups (Basu 1997b), there are also more restraining voices. For example, while the Rashtriya Swayamsevak Sangh continues to officially (at least in the statements of its leaders like K.S. Sudarshan) exhort Hindus to have more children to avoid being outnumbered by Muslims, at the silver jubilee celebrations of the Bharatiya Janata Party in December 2005, party President L.K. Advani actually openly promoted the two-child family norm for all Indians.

All these are good portents. But no consideration of population policy is possible without some reflection on the r-vs-R problem. By which I mean the rhetoric-versus-Reality question. Like most policy documents that emerge from the Planning Commission or other agencies of the Indian government, especially the central government, successive versions of population policy have also been articulate, well reasoned, reasonable, and often literary. Reading one of these versions, and especially reading post-Cairo versions, if one foolishly equated policy formulation with policy implementation, one would think that all India's population and reproductive health-related needs were being well taken care of by capable hands.

But, as scores of studies demonstrate, the ground reality is often totally disconnected from the rhetoric of these policy statements. If the policy statement proclaims its intent to address the contraceptive needs of adolescents and nulliparous married women, in reality, hardly ever does a family planning worker touch base with these categories of persons. Population policy may stress the need for a 'cafeteria' approach to the contraceptive methods it offers, but the bulk of family planning practice continues to consist of female sterilization. Policy statements may recognize the need for well-staffed primary health centres and may even lay down detailed staffing norms; but the vast majority of these centres do not have a female medical officer, a large number do not have any doctor at all, and a sizeable proportion do not even have an auxiliary nurse midwife (and whether these functionaries, when they do exist on the rolls, actually exist in person on any given day is another matter altogether).[2] On all these matters, the pessimist shakes his head in despair, but the optimist sees teething problems that will be overcome, that must be overcome.

ALAKA MALWADE BASU

References

Basu, A.M. 1985. 'Family Planning and the Emergency: An Unanticipated Consequence', *Economic and Political Weekly*, 20(10): 422–5.

——. 1997a. 'The New International Population Movement: A Framework for a Constructive Critique', *Health Transition Review*, 7: 7–31.

——. 1997b. 'The "Politicization" of Fertility to Achieve Non-demographic Objectives', *Population Studies*, 51: 5–18.

Coale, A. and E.M. Hoover. 1958. *Population Growth and Economic Development in Low Income Countries: A Case Study of India's Prospects*, Princeton, Princeton University Press.

Santhya, K.G. 2003. 'Changing Family Planning Scenario in India: An Overview of Recent Evidence', The Population Council South and East Asia Regional, Working Paper No. 17, New Delhi, The Population Council.

Visaria, L. 2000. 'From Contraceptive Targets to Informed Choice: The Indian Experience', in R. Ramasubban and S.J. Jejeebhoy (eds), *Improving Quality of Care in India's Family Planning Programme*, New Delhi, Rawat Publications.

Visaria, P. and V. Chari. 1998. 'India's Population Policy and Family Planning Program: Yesterday, Today and Tomorrow', in A. Jain (ed.), *Do Population Policies Matter: Fertility and Politics in Egypt, India, Kenya and Mexico*, New York, The Population Council.

■ Ports and Shipping

Ports

India has a long coastline (around 7,517 km), with 13 major and 176 non-major ports. Playing a vital part in India's economic development are its ports, which account for 90 per cent by volume and 70 per cent by value of the country's international trade. India's ports comprise 13 major ports including the Port Blair Port

[2]For empirical evidence on all these points, see the review by Santhya (2003).

Trust and around 175 non-major ports along the coast and islands. The former are under the jurisdiction of the central government and the latter of the respective state governments. There are nine maritime states.

Indian ports have been lacking sufficient investments for increasing capacity and efficiency. Loading and unloading times are longer than at most international ports. The Ministry of Shipping has initiated many reforms to increase private investment, improve service quality, and make the ports more competitive. These measures include the revision of various operational policies, preparing perspective plans for the major ports, commissioning two more major ports (one each on the east and west coasts), and introducing a Port Community System (PCS). Apart from a central policy, each state government also has its own maritime policy. In January 2011, the Ministry of Shipping drew up a maritime agenda for the decade 2010–20. The agenda acknowledges that

> Indian ports have to lay their emphasis and focus on improving berth productivity for container vessels as also the turnaround time of ships. Indian ports, as of now, irrespective of public or private, are not comparable to world-class ports due to various reasons. The broad strategies to make Indian ports achieve international standards are capacity creation, increase in the drafts, massive mechanisation, the development of adequate storage areas, providing seamless hinterland connectivity and attaining cost efficiency.

This document aims to navigate and steer the Indian maritime sector realistically into the premier maritime nations of the world. Hence, the attention is focused on improving infrastructure, modernizing existing facilities, better logistic chains, doing away with the licensing system, more openings in the domestic retail market with entry for world class players, and increased avenues for special economic zone type of projects. Under the programme, 276 projects were identified to be implemented between 1 April 2005 and 31 March 2012. The total investment under the programme is estimated to be Rs 1,00,339 crore at 2004–5 prices. Out of this, Rs 55,804 crore is for the port sector with the balance for the shipping and inland water transport sectors. These 276 projects cover the entire gamut of activities, namely, construction/upgradation of berths (76 projects), deepening of channels (25 projects), rail/road connectivity projects (45 projects), equipment upgradation/modernization schemes (52 projects), and other related schemes (78 projects) for creating backup facilities. Based on this exercise, the projected traffic of the major ports is 615.70 million tonnes. To meet this traffic by 2011–12, an estimated capacity of around 800.41 million tonnes was required. Following the implementation of NMDP, the capacity of major ports increased to 616.73 million tonnes as on 31 March 2010 as compared to 397.50 million tonnes during 2004–5.

However, for this, an analysis of the major and non-major ports is needed. The Planning Commission suggested a Mid-Term Appraisal document that would include the non-major ports and a monitoring system of all ports.

In 2009–10, Indian ports handled 849.9 million tonnes of traffic, with non-major ports accounting for around one-third of the total seaborne trade. In the same year, the growth of cargo handled at major and non-major ports was 5.8 and 35.4 per cent, respectively, compared to 2.2 and 3.3 per cent in the previous year. During 2009–10, the major and non-major ports saw a total cargo throughput of 849.89 million tonnes, an increase of 14.27 per cent over the previous year. The growth in cargo handled at major and non-major ports in 2009–10 was 5.76 and 35.44 per cent, respectively, as compared to 2.16 and 3.31 per cent achieved in 2008–9. In the recession year of 2008–9, India's seaborne cargo traffic grew by a mere 2.49 per cent but recovered sharply to 14.27 per cent in 2009–10. The deceleration in 2008–9 was mainly due to external factors rooted in global and domestic growth dynamics.

Shipping

The Indian shipbuilding industry grew rapidly during 2002–7 because of government subsidies. When the subsidies were removed in 2007, the Indian shipbuilding industry started losing new orders and its market share declined. In shipping, India lags far behind its potential. In terms of fleet size, the Indian shipping industry contributes just 1 per cent to the global fleet. Despite the growth in India's seaborne trade, at 12.25 per cent, the share of Indian ships in carrying out the country's overseas trade has been declining over the years—from around 40 per cent in the late 1980s, it fell to around 8.4 per cent in 2008–9. More than anything else, this underscores the immense potential for growth in the shipping industry. One of the main reasons for this declining trend has been that the Indian fleet has not been growing fast enough as compared to the growth in India's seaborne trade. There are several other problems in the related areas of coastal environment, skills, and human resources which the government is trying to solve.

T.C.A. Srinivasa-Raghavan

Poverty

The UNDP's annual *Human Development Report* (HDR) is a major source of information on various aspects of global well-being and deprivation. According to HDR 2005, India is ranked 127th among 177 countries in terms of the 'Human Development Index', and 58th out of 103 developing countries according to the 'Human Poverty Index'. Employing data for the most recent year between 1990 and 2003 for which they are available, it emerges that the proportion of the Indian population with an income less than the international poverty line of two purchasing power parity dollars a day is nearly 80 per cent: only 12 countries have fared worse in this regard. India, with an estimated adult illiteracy rate of 39 per cent in 2003, ranks 94th in a field of 115 countries for which data are available. The gender gap in illiteracy rates is pronounced: 27 per cent for males, and nearly twice this figure, at 52 per cent, for females. From statistics relevant for specific years between 1995 and 2001, one learns that the proportion of women victimized by sexual assault in the city of Mumbai was of the order of 3.5 per cent: only four cities, from a list of thirty-six, had a worse record. The proportion of the population that had been asked or was expected to pay a bribe to a government official was 22.9 per cent in Mumbai, a figure exceeded in only five other cities from a list of thirty-two. In a study done by Abu Saleh Shariff (2001) for the National Council of Applied Economic Research, we find that, in 1994 the proportion of the population that was deprived in terms of a 'capability poverty measure' was in excess of 60 per cent for the scheduled castes and tribes, and of the order of 52 per cent for the population at large. The 18th Congress Resolution of the Communist Party of India (Marxist)[1] records:

> [Between 1992 and 2000] about 77 crimes against dalits were reported every day and ... on average, three dalit women are raped and six dalit women disabled every day. These figures however are a gross underestimation because a large number of cases of sexual assault do not get registered. Dalit women face the triple burden of caste, class, and gender oppression.

These limited and unsystematic statistics provided in the preceding paragraphs are nevertheless sufficient to provide confirmation of the known (but increasingly less acknowledged) dominant reality of India: that it is a country of large absolute and relative deprivations, with a disproportionate burden borne by identifiable sections of the population. These statistics, despite the apparent randomness of their selection, also suggest that three useful analytical categories in terms of which deprivation in any society—including India—can be appraised are those of *positive freedom, negative freedom*, and *discrimination*.

The notion of 'positive freedom' is best captured in what Amartya Sen (1985) has referred to as the *capability to function*. The reference here is to the ability which human beings have to lead the 'good life', and the practical question is one of the power which individuals enjoy, or which they are enabled by society to acquire, in order to achieve various valued human 'functionings', a functioning being what Sen again calls a 'state of being or doing'. The notion of 'negative freedom', or 'liberty', is linked to the acknowledgement that each individual is entitled to what John Stuart Mill called a 'personal protected sphere', such that, within her or his protected sphere, the individual is in no way subjected to any hindrance in the pursuit of her or his desired goals, including the goal of avoiding deprivation. While positive freedom is concerned with 'enablement', negative freedom is concerned with 'absence of restraint' and 'protection from coercion'. If the extent to which positive and negative freedoms are secured for its citizens is an index of a society's achievement in avoiding capability failure and deprivation, then of comparable concern should be the *equitableness* with which such freedoms are distributed across the population. A society is subject to the charge of discrimination if it is one that presides over an inequitable distribution of freedoms across individuals on the strength of their group affiliation—where the grouping in question corresponds to some partitioning of the population on the basis, by way of example, of gender or caste or religion or age or geographical sector of origin.

In what follows, deprivation in India is assessed with respect to the aforementioned categories of positive freedom, negative freedom, and discrimination.

First, positive freedoms. A selective, and very largely non-quantitative, survey of the record suggests something like the following picture.[2] As Amartya Sen has pointed out, there has been no large-scale famine in independent India, unlike in colonial India, whereas, on the other hand, there is still a great deal of persistent and endemic hunger in the country. Undernourishment is still an integral aspect of the socio-economic profile of India's population: the incidence of low birth-weight babies, and of stunting and wasting among children, continues to be disquietingly large in comparison with

[1]See *People's Democracy*, 29(16), April 2005.

[2]For relevant facts and figures, the reader is referred to Planning Commission (2002: Statistical Appendix).

the record of neighbouring countries like China and Sri Lanka. The record of the last five years or so has been especially harsh: the coexistence of starvation deaths, agrarian distress, rural indebtedness, and farmer suicides in states like Orissa, Andhra Pradesh, and Maharashtra, on the one hand, with the phenomenon of bursting public granaries, on the other, must be seen to be a particularly unacceptable face of the recent regime of hunger and suffering.

The expectation of life at birth has increased from the early 1930s over 1941–50 to the early 1960s over 1991–2000, and yet lags behind the Chinese and Sri Lankan figures. The trends in the crude death rate and in infant mortality have been definitely declining ones, but their absolute levels are still such as to cause anxiety. In terms of guarding against child morbidity and mortality through elementary precautions such as oral rehydration therapy, there have been secular improvements, but at a pace so retarded as to cause India still to lag behind the global average.

Unemployment, which is intimately linked to poverty, continues to remain a major block to socio-economic development: joblessness, intermittency, seasonality, and sporadicity of employment, retarded rates of skill learning and segmentation of the labour market, casualization of the labour force, and depressed wage rates are not ideal guarantors of the right to livelihood.

Income poverty levels, in terms of the headcount ratio and other more sophisticated measures of poverty, are reported to have registered a steady decline from about the end of the 1970s to the turn of the millennium. All too often, 'poverty' has tended to be interpreted almost exclusively in terms of income deprivation. A reportedly steady decline in the headcount ratio, placed alongside a reportedly increasing profile of growth in per caput gross national product (GNP), not to mention the remarkable (and persistently visible) advances made by a relatively 'enclave' sector of the economy like information technology, has played a major role in fostering the impression that India's development experience over the last quarter of a century has been outstandingly promising. In this connection, it is markedly pertinent to review the conceptual basis of India's official poverty statistics, with specific reference to the 'identification' problem in poverty measurement, namely, the problem of fixing the poverty line.

Various rounds of the National Sample Survey Organisation's (NSSO) consumption expenditure surveys provide a remarkable time-series and cross-section database on the distribution of consumer expenditure across expenditure size-classes, together with detailed information on the quantity and value of commodity-wise consumption in each expenditure size-class. In the mid-1980s, the Union Planning Commission, employing NSSO data for 1973–4, fixed the rural and urban poverty lines at those levels of consumption expenditure at which the calorific norms of 2,400 and 2,100 kilocalories per caput per diem in the rural and urban areas, respectively, were observed to be achieved (a rough description of the exercise of 'inverting an Engel function'). The resulting poverty lines, in terms of monthly per person consumption expenditure levels, were approximately Rs 49 and Rs 56 in the rural and urban areas, respectively, at current (1973–4) prices. The commodity bundles corresponding to these levels of consumption expenditure in 1973–4 were identified; and in subsequent years, the poverty lines were fixed by revaluing the 1973–4 commodity bundles at current (that is, relevant year-specific) prices.

In performing time-series comparisons of poverty, it is important to get one's price indices as nearly 'right' as possible, as well as to ensure comparability across different rounds of the NSSO surveys, such as in terms of reconciling inter-round variations in reference periods of recall. The Indian poverty literature reflects much ingenuity in addressing these problems.[3] While these are necessary issues demanding attention, it is also true that, for the most part, the official procedure of identifying the poverty line has gone largely unchallenged. At the poverty lines compatible with the Planning Commission's suggested procedure, one notes that over time there has been an expanding divergence between actual calorific intake levels and the recommended norms. If consumer behaviour is taken to be explicable in terms of standard demand theory, then the 'price-updated' commodity bundles corresponding to the poverty line consumption expenditure level of 1973–4 would simply ignore (i) the possibility of preference changes in favour of 'non-food' over 'food' (necessitated, perhaps, by inter-temporally changing perceptions of what is called—even in relation to something as basic as footwear, for instance—to 'live without shame'); (ii) the possibility of differential rates of inflation for 'food' and 'non-food'; and (iii) the possibility of a dwindling availability of common property resources such as firewood for fuel and, therefore, of increasing involuntary reliance on the market for the consumption of such commodities. If the poverty line in any year were fixed at that level of consumption expenditure

[3]The reader is referred to Deaton and Drèze (2002) and Sen and Himanshu (2004), two crucial contributions (among others) to the charged debate on whether poverty has or has not declined over the reform period of the 1990s.

at which the calorific norm is actually observed to be achieved (as was done by the Planning Commission for 1973–4), instead of in terms of the price-updated value of the 1973–4 'poverty line commodity bundle', then the resulting time-trend of headcount ratios becomes an increasing rather than a declining one. Briefly, the Planning Commission procedure, which has been widely and uncritically accepted, is compatible with two highly questionable implicit judgements: (i) that, somehow, the 1973–4 pattern of consumption expenditure must be privileged as the only one with normative significance and (ii) that inter-temporal poverty comparisons are meaningful only if the poverty line consumption bundle is unvarying over time. In sum, it is—or should be—very hard to accept poverty trends deduced from the official approach to the identification problem. Even so, and taking these sorts of estimates at face value, one finds that more than a quarter of the country's population was in consumption expenditure poverty in 1999–2000 (Planning Commission 2002).

Additionally, one imagines the aggregate headcount ought also to matter in the scheme of things; and with something like 260 million poor persons in the country today, India has the dubious distinction of being the largest contributing country to the world's poor.

The country is far removed from a state where the absence of homelessness can be regarded as a routine aspect of everyday existence for an overwhelming majority of the population; and where housing is available, it is often of the semi-*pucca* or *kutcha* variety in rural areas, or of the type of shanties in urban slums. What of freedom from ignorance? The constitutional guarantee of universal mandatory primary education within the first decade of Independence continues to remain a promise unfulfilled. While literacy levels have gradually risen over time, with about two-thirds of the population now reported to be literate, this still leaves behind a third of a vast population unable to read or write a short statement on their everyday lives. Apart from the intrinsic importance of access to knowledge, literacy also has many instrumental advantages such as in being associated with lower levels of child labour and with declines in fertility, which later can only be for the good in the context of population stabilization and an alleviation of the reproductive burden borne by women.

The public provisioning of aids to mobility—railways, roadways, transport vehicles, and subsidized travel—has improved gradually over time, but nowhere near extensively enough to suggest that shortages in connectivity are not, even now, a major bottleneck for freedom of movement. Despite repeated encounters with the forces of nature (like floods and cyclones), identifiable sections of the population in identifiable parts of the country (like the north-east and Orissa) continue to be predictably vulnerable to natural disasters.

Briefly, an un-severe assessment of India's track record in the matter of positive freedoms would be: 'not bad'; but not bad only in relation to historically very high levels of illfare. It is, unhappily, not good—in relation to the country's needs, in relation to its potential, and in relation to the record of other comparably income-poor countries. It must be emphasized that this diagnosis of inadequate state success is not intended to seek a replacement of the state by the market or civil society, but rather to seek enhanced levels of public pressure on the state for significantly better delivery and accountability.

Second, negative freedoms. How unfettered a citizen is, is reflected in the extent of her or his legal entitlements, and the extent to which these are protected. There are two issues to be considered here: first, the prospect of securing the positive freedoms of the disadvantaged sections of society must sometimes be predicated on limiting the negative freedoms of the advantaged sections of society; and second, the positive freedoms of the latter class are often better secured simply because of both the immunity and influence enjoyed by it as a consequence of its superior status in respect of negative freedoms. A considerable prevalence of deprivation must be expected to be an outcome of a socio-political system which is largely unprepared to disturb the settled weight of vested interests in a deeply stratified society. For example, India's poor record of land redistribution is a reflection of far greater concern for the negative right of private property for the few than for the positive right of a minimally decent standard of living for the many. In an important related context, budgetary resources for securing an improved quality of life for the many are severely compromised by the inability or unwillingness to deal effectively with the crime of undeclared wealth and incomes perpetrated by the few. Even so, it is sobering to note that the picture might have been so much worse without a (even if qualifiedly) free press and parliamentary democracy. The verdict of the 2004 General Elections is a case in point.

Third, discrimination. Objectivity must compel the conclusion that here, more than anywhere else, the country's experience of socio-economic development and deprivation has been acutely dispiriting. Consider the distribution of positive freedoms across well-defined social groupings, effected on the basis of caste, sector of origin, or gender, for instance. Whether we speak of hunger or health or mobility or knowledge or income poverty, the scheduled castes and tribes are systematically and significantly worse off than the rest; people of rural origin are worse off than those of urban origin; and females are worse off than males. The picture is a faithful reflection of the group-wise distribution of personal liberties. Dalits are still subjected to caste atrocities; religious minorities are the victims of state-abetted genocide; women are discriminated against in the intra-family distribution of resources, in the intra-family allocation of work burdens, in the acquisition and utilization of skills in the labour market, in the payment of wages, and in the display of respect towards their privacy and their bodies, as reflected in the phenomena of rape, forced prostitution, dowry deaths, and sex-selective foeticide and infanticide. If one accepts the philosopher John Rawls' criterion of reckoning the welfare of a society in terms of the welfare of its most deprived member, then India's achievement on the deprivation front, as crystallized in the predicament of an income-poor, landless, illiterate, rural, scheduled caste woman, is a matter of shame.

India's poverty, like that of many other developing countries, is explicable in terms of the effects of colonialism, the terms of international trade, external debt, the self- or other-inflicted burden of military spending at the expense of social-sector spending, structural adjustment, and both the niggardliness and capriciousness of international aid flows. These factors, however, do not exhaust explanation: a more complete account must also take stock of the fact that the opportunities which reside in the unfulfilled potential for fair, reasonably egalitarian, and democratic internal governance are still waiting to be exploited. State policy in combating deprivation has been deployed on a number of fronts: these have been comprehensively analysed, in terms of performance with respect to growth and to social justice, direct anti-poverty programmes, and programmes for the satisfaction of basic needs, by S. Guhan (2002), whose overall assessment (p. 39) is telling: 'Whatever might have been the rhetoric of planning or politics, poverty alleviation has been an *adjunct* to India's development plans and policies rather than the *core* of their purpose.'

The following are some ingredients of a broad anti-poverty campaign that could be implemented. First, a strong pro-poor and anti-corruption message can be sent out by recovering—at least in a few 'obvious' and egregious cases—unpaid taxes on income and wealth, and earmarking the proceeds specifically for poverty-alleviation purposes, and likewise by imposing a 'poverty surcharge' on personal and corporate income, with this component of direct taxation again set aside for anti-poverty measures. Second, rural India needs special and renewed efforts at raising agricultural productivity, relieving debt distress, expanding agricultural credit, and increasing the coverage of extension activities. Other special groups in need of specifically targeted assistance are women, children, and the disadvantaged castes. Third, food security is critical: the public distribution system must be restored and improved. Fourth, poverty is not just a matter of income deprivation: to address it in its more generalized forms, it would help to draw a district-wise map of India, with the colour red reserved for those districts displaying acute inadequacies in access to drinking water, energy for cooking, elementary health facilities, a school, and a road; and, on the basis of such a map, some prioritized effort at infrastructural development must be initiated and sought to be implemented under a reasonable time-frame. Fifth, the plethora of anti-poverty employment schemes must be rationalized and streamlined. Indeed, the principal merit of employment schemes resides in their property of 'self-selection', which obviates the necessity for costly targeting; but, often, employment schemes incur large administrative, overhead, and material costs, are subject to the machinations of corrupt contractors, and do not result in the creation of durable assets. There may, therefore, be a strong case for preserving the 'self-selection' property of wage employment schemes while reformulating some of them as adult literacy programmes, which can result in the creation of a durable social and human asset and at the same time have a beneficent effect on fertility and child labour. Sixth, the 1991–6 Congress-led government was already in possession of a complete blueprint of a National Assistance Scheme, which is a feasible and affordable package of social security measures covering old age pension, survivor benefit, accident compensation, and disability relief, which should be dusted, aired, implemented, and given the widest possible publicity, both to inform potential beneficiaries of their entitlements and to advertise serious intent. Finally, and as distinct from specific anti-poverty policy, strategies for the macroeconomic desideratum of pro-poor growth must also be attended to.

These ingredients of state policy have all been informed by an appreciation of the centrality of bolstering positive freedoms, protecting negative freedoms, and reversing discrimination in any approach to the redress of deprivation.

What is called for is a massive effort at reforming governance, with key reference to the problems, as Dilip Mookherjee (2004: 54) lists them, of 'law and order, tax collection, infrastructure, environmental control, education, health, and anti-poverty programmes'. Most important, the challenge of poverty redress is a matter that requires infinitely more urgent attention than any which stems from the presumption that India is already well on its way to becoming a superpower.

S. Subramanian

References

Deaton, A. and J. Drèze. 2002. 'Poverty and Inequality in India: A Re-examination', *Economic and Political Weekly*, 7 September, 37(36): 3729–48.

Guhan, S. 2002. 'Rural Poverty Alleviation in India: Policy, Performance, and Possibilities', in S.Subramanian (ed.), *India's Development Experience: Selected Writings of S. Guhan*, New Delhi, Oxford University Press.

Mookherjee, D. 2004. *The Crisis in Government Accountability: Essays on Governance Reform and India's Economic Performance*, New Delhi, Oxford University Press.

Planning Commission, Government of India. 2002. *India: National Human Development Report 2001*, New Delhi, Oxford University Press.

Sen, A. 1985. *Commodities and Capabilities*, Amsterdam, North-Holland.

Sen, A. and Himanshu. 2004. 'Poverty and Inequality in India—I & II', *Economic and Political Weekly*, 18 September, 39(38): 4247–63 and 25 September, 39(39): 4361–75.

Shariff, A.S. 2001. *India: Human Development Report—A Profile of Indian States in the 1990s*, New Delhi, Oxford University Press.

Poverty and Exclusion

About one-quarter of the Indian population is estimated to be living in poverty. This entry explores the role of state programmes in reducing poverty and also illustrates some of the biases inherent in using household consumption data to arrive at poverty estimates. Available evidence on the distribution of household consumption and public spending leads me to two main conclusions. First, that some types of spending can substantially raise household consumption and reduce poverty. Second, that the benefits from public programmes are spread unevenly, both across and within regions, and these benefits are not well captured by measures of household consumption typically used to estimate poverty. As a result, there is likely to be some misclassification of poor and non-poor households and regional differences in poverty may be larger than current estimates suggest. It appears, ironically, that the poor in India are often excluded from the benefits of state redistribution. In this sense, poverty and exclusion go together and an accurate assessment of poverty requires an understanding of the nature of this exclusion.

Historically, two types of public programmes have been important in redistributing national income: direct transfers to the poor and the expansion of public services. Poor relief first became sizeable in England and Europe in the late 18th century while public education began somewhat later and expanded fastest in the United States (Lindert 2004). For countries that started to industrialize in the post-War period, direct transfers were relatively unimportant and the bulk of public welfare spending took the form of expansion in education, health, and physical infrastructure. This continues to be true of poor countries today: the provision of public goods and price subsidies on essential commodities are central components of policies aimed at reducing poverty. In addition, there has been a growing interest in schemes that transfer assets and provide credit for self-employment to families who are neglected by formal credit institutions.

I begin with an overview of state redistributive programmes in India. I examine the spatial distribution of public spending and the extent to which such spending has been directed towards the poor. At the regional level, I find a close and positive association between per capita domestic product and the benefits from public goods, services, and transfers. Within regions, there appears to be very little targeting of state subsidies towards the poor. The next section considers the implications of these findings for poverty measurement and is followed by brief concluding remarks.

State Redistributive Programmes

Food Subsidies

The public distribution system (PDS) was the first nationwide transfer programme introduced after Indian Independence. It began during the First Five Year Plan in the early 1950s and was based on the rationing schemes put in place by the British government during the War. The system functioned primarily to provide food security in the presence of fluctuating agricultural output and entitled all households to specified quantities of food grains and essential commodities at subsidized prices. It was not explicitly targeted towards the poor until 1997, at which stage a wedge was created between the prices paid by households listed as being below the poverty line and the others, with the poor paying prices that were about half the cost of provision and households above the poverty line paying close to cost prices. In December 2000, the Antodaya Anna Yojana (AAY) was introduced and the poorest 15 per cent below the poverty line were targeted for further subsidies. Those covered under the

AAY pay Rs 2 and 3 per kg of wheat and rice, respectively, and each household is currently entitled to a maximum of 35 kg per month of each of these.

There have been several studies of the PDS which document differences in take-up rates and coverage across regions and households. There are two principal sources of data on the distribution of food grains through the PDS. The Department of Food and Public Distribution publishes administrative data on the prices and quantities of each commodity distributed through the system. Household data on the consumption of these commodities can be had from the National Sample Surveys (NSS) which cover over 100,000 households across the country every five years and separately record the consumption of items from PDS and non-PDS sources. The last NSS round before the introduction of the targeted PDS scheme was in 1993–4. The data for that year show that many of the poorer states had very low rates of PDS participation and food subsidies through the system were generally higher in urban than in rural India. Bihar and Orissa were the two poorest states in that year, whether measured by poverty headcounts or the poverty gap ratio and less than 5 per cent of the households in these states bought food grains from the PDS. By contrast, in each of the four southern states, poverty rates were much lower and over 80 per cent of households bought subsidized rice and wheat. Within almost all states, the programme was not targeted towards poor households in that the value of food subsidies was increasing in household expenditure over a wide range of expenditure levels in the bottom half of the expenditure distribution (Tarozzi 2000). The 55th round of the NSS in 1999–2000 allows an evaluation of the effectiveness of the targeted PDS introduced in 1997. The survey records commodity-wise quantities and values which can be used to calculate prices paid by each household. The data show very little variation in either participation rates or prices paid across consumption quartiles. Participation rates rise slowly and prices paid fall slightly with expenditure. About one-third of surveyed households purchased some rice or wheat from the system and the corresponding figure was 30 per cent for those in the bottom expenditure quartile. This positive relationship between participation and consumer expenditure at national level could, in principle, arise from a dysfunctional PDS in some of the poorest states. This, however, is only part of the story because even within several states, participation is flat or rising in household expenditure. Most households paid prices that were a little above Rs 5 per kg (for both wheat and rice), which is fairly close to the issue prices for families below the poverty line. Administrative records on prices charged to those above and below the poverty line suggest that many states used funds from other sources to subsidize purchases by households above the poverty line.

There has been no major NSS round after the Antodaya scheme for the ultra poor began in 2000. In the relatively small sample surveyed in the annual consumption survey in 2004, only 1.6 per cent of all households and 3 per cent of the bottom expenditure quartile paid prices for wheat and rice that are stipulated under the scheme. Given the overall size of the scheme, its proper assessment requires much larger samples, yet these numbers suggest that its impact is still fairly marginal.

The overall picture with regard to food subsidies is one of substantial regional variation in outreach and very little targeting towards the poor within regions. Anecdotal evidence suggests that targeting may have improved under the AAY. Consumption data from the 61st NSS round (the first large one since the introduction of the scheme) will allow a more careful evaluation of this scheme.

Public Goods

Transfers by the Indian state in the form of increased access to public goods have been sizeable relative to other spending programmes, although overall levels of provision are still very low by international comparison.

The earliest reasonably systematic evidence on village-level access to public goods for the Indian states is available from the 1961 Census. More than four-fifths of the Indian population at that time lived in villages, yet village access to public goods in most of rural India was severely limited. A little over 40 per cent of Indian villages had primary schools, though many of these were constructed and managed by religious and other social organizations. Only 1 per cent had high schools, less than 2 per cent had health centres, 3 per cent had electricity connections, and 8 per cent had post offices.

In the first half of the 1970s, public good provision appeared, quite suddenly, in political speeches and policy documents. The Minimum Needs Plan introduced guidelines for rural access to clean water, schools and health facilities, electricity, and roads. Within this broad agenda, states differed in their priorities and in the rates at which they increased overall provision. Primary schools mushroomed in all states, and by 1991 over three-quarters of villages in most states had a local school. High schools expanded more gradually but steadily throughout the 1961–2001 period. Rural electrification was most rapid in states with commercial agriculture (in Haryana and Punjab coverage went from less than 10 per cent of villages in 1961 to 100 per cent by 1981) and piped water became widespread in the northern hill districts of Himachal Pradesh and what is now the state of Uttarakhand. Rural roads were relatively neglected until the 1990s, but expanded rapidly after that and by 2001 more than half of all Indian villages could be approached by a paved road. In contrast to the above changes, publicly funded health facilities have remained largely unavailable to the rural population. Primary Health Centres (the smallest facility with a trained doctor) were available in only 3 per cent of Indian villages in 2001 and no state, other than Kerala, had coverage of more than 10 per cent. The number of Primary Health Sub-centres (which house a trained nurse and provide immunizations) did increase substantially in south India and the 2001 Census indicates that these have spread to about a third of all villages in the southern states.

The foregoing discussion is not meant to suggest that the goods provided were of high or reliable quality—evidence on leaking school buildings, absent teachers and doctors, dry taps, and irregular power supply is now plentiful. The new facilities did, however, represent substantial expenditures, mostly by the state, that in some cases at least, reached those without wealth or political power. These investments also appear to have influenced social outcomes. Infant mortality rates are now roughly half of what they were in 1971. The gap in literacy between both males and females and urban and rural areas has been shrinking (at an increasing rate) and school attendance rates reported by the most recent census for scheduled castes and scheduled tribes are very similar to those for the rest of the population. States such as Rajasthan and Andhra Pradesh that invested in education have jumped from the bottom of the distribution of state literacy rates to the middle over the past 30 years. Even with large reporting errors and grossly inflated attendance rates, the trends in these outcomes are unmistakable.

An examination of the spatial distribution of public goods in 2001 shows that richer states had much better access, especially to those facilities that were relatively scarce at the national level. This relationship is often blurred by the case of Kerala which, over the past century at least, has consistently had the greatest access to educational and health facilities accompanied by an unremarkable economic performance. If we ignore Kerala, we find a positive and surprisingly systematic relationship between the availability of social and physical infrastructure and state domestic product per capita. A single standard deviation change in per capita state domestic product is accompanied by a one-third increase in the proportion of villages with high schools and a 40 per cent increase in village access to piped water and bus services. In this descriptive sense, much of the variation in public goods access between, say, Bihar, Rajasthan, and Punjab (representing the bottom, middle, and top of the range of state domestic product) is 'explained' by differences in incomes. These patterns are important for assessments of regional poverty differences as discussed in the next section.

Have differences in public good access been important for recent reductions in poverty? Deaton and Drèze (2002) present state-level poverty estimates for poverty headcounts and the poverty gap ratio based on NSS consumption data. The surveys in 1987–8 and in 1999–2000 are closest to the census years of 1991 and 2001. Matched in this manner, we find that changes in the availability of some public goods over the 1991–2001 period are highly correlated with declines in measured poverty. In fact, once we control for the expansion of public goods, changes per capita state domestic product seem to have very little to do with changes in poverty. These numbers, though rough and preliminary, suggest the absence of large trickle-down effects that did not operate through improved infrastructure.

Other Programmes

There are a large number of other programmes aimed at poverty reduction that have been introduced since the 1970s. Some of these, such as the Integrated Rural Development Programme (IRDP) started in 1978, were designed to encourage self-employment among the poor by providing them assets, often in the form of livestock. The IRDP, together with other self-employment schemes that were subsequently introduced, have come together under the banner of the Swarnajayanti Gram Swarozgar Yojana (SGSY). A major focus of the SGSY has been the promotion of small credit groups, known as self-help groups. Non-government organizations are funded and encouraged to promote the formation of these groups and nationalized banks are directed to provide them credit for self-employment activities. Other programmes include subsidized house construction under the Indira Awas Yojana and schemes that provide state funds to the unemployed for work on village infrastructure (the Jawahar Rozgar Yojana and, more recently, the National Rural Employment Programme).

Budgetary allocations to these programmes are sizeable and have been rising. Little, however, is known about the composition of recipients and, therefore, the extent to which these programmes have been successful in reaching the poor. The limited evidence available suggests little or no targeting towards the poor. The 55th round of the NSS in 1999–2000 questions respondents on assistance received by them under the IRDP. About

5 per cent of respondent households had received such assistance during the five years prior to the survey and, remarkably, we observe no difference in this proportion across household expenditure deciles.

Public-sponsored micro-finance seems to have had better success in reaching the poor although destitute households do not appear to participate in the self-help groups that are now significant actors in rural credit markets (Somanathan 2005). The success of these institutions relative to other government subsidies probably owes much to the fact that a sizeable fraction of public funds is routed through energetic and competent non-government organizations and state funds complement those given by external donor agencies who also independently monitor this sector.

Implications for Poverty Measurement

Poverty estimates for India are based on the value of monthly per capita consumption expenditure obtained from the consumption surveys described earlier. Official poverty lines are defined in terms of a threshold level of monthly per capita consumption expenditure that was linked to food adequacy in the early 1970s. Since then, poverty lines are updated based on changes in general price level and, since prices vary across states and urban and rural areas, so do poverty lines.

How might benefits from public programmes be reflected in poverty estimates? Income transfers are likely to be reflected quite well in household consumption expenditure because they do not directly influence relative prices. Food subsidies are a different matter. Households with the same consumption expenditure would have different levels of real consumption based on whether or not they were receiving food subsidies through the PDS. This has implications for estimating regional differences in poverty and for the listing of poor households within regions. Households in states with a well-managed PDS would, on average, pay lower average prices for food. If we adjust the state-level poverty line to incorporate this lower average price level, we are more likely to misclassify poor households as non-poor if they do not have access to state subsidies. So, paradoxically, errors in household listings could be larger in areas with higher coverage if the subsidies in question are not well-targeted.

One possible solution would be to create a set of price indices based on actual prices paid by households. We could estimate prices for each good as a function of household characteristics (state of residence, land possessed, household demographics, and any other relevant characteristics) and then construct household-specific price indices as functions of these predicted prices. The real consumption expenditure for a household would then be obtained by deflating observed expenditure by the index appropriate to that household. This procedure would, for example, use different price indices within regions for groups that are favoured by the state and those that are not. Poverty measures could then be based on the deflated consumption data obtained in this manner.

This procedure would work quite well for commodities and services that are consumed in well-defined units of reasonably uniform quality. In such cases, consumption survey data report both values and quantities consumed and the implicit prices are easy to interpret. Unfortunately, this is not the case with expenditures on education, health, transport, and many other expenditure categories for which consumption units are not standard and surveys record only total expenditures. In such cases, useful adjustments to consumption data cannot be made without information on the types of services to which each household has access. In this sense, it is relatively difficult to arrive at accurate measures of real household consumption when there is variable access to public goods.

This entry has outlined the major types of interventions used by the Indian state to alleviate poverty. The public spending programmes described here are found to vary enormously in their coverage and average effectiveness across states and have, in general, performed badly in terms of targeting poor households. I have considered some implications of these findings for the measurement of poverty differences across regions and for the proper identification of poor households. Of these, I believe that the misclassification of poor households is by far the more serious issue. Most consumers of poverty data are aware that differences in governance and the availability of public goods across Indian states must be kept in mind when comparing differences in private consumption. In contrast, Indian policymakers are increasingly restricting the availability of public benefits to households they place below the poverty line. Inaccurate lists of such households can compound the targeting problems that have historically plagued poverty-alleviation efforts. A careful characterization of the poor needs much more attention than it has so far received.

ROHINI SOMANATHAN

References

Banerjee, Abhijit and Rohini Somanathan. 2007. 'The Political Economy of Public Goods: Some Evidence from India', *Journal of Development Economics*, 82(2): 287–314.

Deaton, Angus and Jean Drèze. 2002. 'Poverty and Inequality in India: A Re-Examination', *Economic and Political Weekly*, 7 September, 37(36): 3729–48.

Lindert, Peter. 2004. *Growing Public: Social Spending and Economic Growth since the Eighteenth Century*, Cambridge University Press.

Planning Commission. Government of India, Tenth Five Year Plan.

Somanathan, Rohini. 2005. 'Poverty Targeting in Public Programs: A Comparison of Alternative Statistical Tests', Working Paper.

Tarozzi, Alessandro. 2000. 'A Bird's Eye View of PDS Utilization using the 50th Round of the Indian National Sample Survey (July 1993–June 1994)', Working Paper, Princeton University.

■ Power Industry

Introduction

Electric power has been one of the most powerful instruments of social and economic transformation in a developing country like India. Electrical energy is the most refined secondary form of energy which is produced out of a range of alternative primary energy resources in India such as coal, lignite, and petroleum products (for example, naphtha and diesel), natural gas, water pressure, and fissile elements (uranium, thorium sources), biomass, wind, and sun, whose respective availabilities and costs of conversion vary across resources.

Against the advantages, electric power also suffers from the following serious shortcomings:

(i) Non-storability of electricity, which requires the capacity of power generation in power load units (mega watt) to match with the peak demand in society.

(ii) High capital costs and high conversion, transmission, and distribution (T&D) losses. The component of conversion loss varies across the primary resources used and the concerned resource-linked technology as is accessible in a country.

(iii) High dependence on exhaustible and air polluting fuels for thermal power and site-specific availability of hydro potential for power generation causing environmental concerns for the sustainable development of the power sector in India.

The supply of electric power involves three stages of operations—generation (production), transmission (transportation), and distribution (retail sales). While these operations involve losses of energy, such losses are supposed to be offset more than substantially by the relative higher efficiency of the use of electricity as compared to other fuels for any given final use (or work to be done). This is explained by variations in the efficiency of end-use appliances and technology linked with respective fuels. Since these three activities have to be simultaneously and instantaneously coordinated, such coordination has been institutionally challenging and complicated, historically necessitating the emergence of a vertically integrated organization structure in the electric power industry in many countries, including India. Therefore, in India most of the electric power was supplied by vertically integrated power utilities—state electricity boards (SEBs) and electricity departments (EDs) at the state level till the introduction of power sector reforms. There are also captive power generation and supply facilities for many industrial and service sector units to take care of shortfalls and the unreliability of supply by the utilities.

As electrical energy is crucial for meeting the basic needs of the people, removing income as well as energy poverty, employment generation, and socio-economic transformation, and as it requires large indivisible investment, the Indian public-sector has historically dominated the development of this sector. It has also been under political pressure for charging low tariffs for the household and agriculture sectors since the inception of India's development planning. In view of these priorities and the consideration of balanced regional growth, the Indian Constitution put power as a subject under the concurrent list. A large part of its development has been financed by the central plan allocation for the sector through grants to the states as well as to the central sector owned by the union government (for example, the National Thermal Power Corporation [NTPC], the National Hydroelectric Power Corporation [NHPC], the Power Grid Corporation of India Limited [PGCIL], and the Nuclear Power Corporation of India Limited [NPCIL]). The importance of rural electrification and greater power connectivity to rural households have led to the emergence of the Rural Electrification Corporation Limited (REC)—a public-sector institution, which is engaged in expanding and strengthening the distribution of power in rural areas. Besides, the electrification of remote villages is also being done through the Ministry of New and Renewable Energy in association with the Indian Renewable Energy Development Agency Limited (IREDA), by mobilizing non-conventional technologies for exploiting alternative energy resources.

The political–economic compulsion of providing cheaper power at a subsidized rate to certain sectors of the economy led to persistent shortfall in average

Table 1 Growth of Energy Supply and Electricity during 1980–81 to 2008

Year	Total primary commercial energy available (mtoe)	Final energy available (mtoe)	Total primary energy used in electricity (mtoe)	Final electrical energy used (mtoe)	Share of electricity in total final energy (%)	Conversion and total T&D losses (%)
1980–1	92.623	68.764	28.824 (31.1)	6.953	10.1	75.9
1991–2	193.8	130.7	75.4 (38.9)	17.5	13.4	76.8
2001–2	300.44	171.37	122.82 (40.8)	27.2	15.9	77.9
2008	457.41	245.13	231.55 (50.6)	51.74	21.11	77.65

Source: TERI (2004) and IEA (2010).
Note: Figures in brackets shows percentage share of total primary commercial energy supply.

power tariff from the average cost of power supply for most of the Indian states over time; this is in spite of some cross-subsidization by the industry and the commercial sector. The average cost of power in India has also been high due to serious inefficiencies of the state monopoly suppliers (SEBs), and has been induced by the absence of horizontal competition at all the stages of the operations and by the over-manning of the sector. The short fall of revenue over costs has not been fully offset by budgetary transfers at the state level, resulting in commercial losses. Commercial losses of SEBs and EDs and the overall macroeconomic resource constraint of the Indian economy has led to chronic shortages of financial resources for the growth and modernization of the power industry. As a result, there have been chronic shortages of power supply and there has also been unreliable power supply which surfaces in the form of load shedding and power rationing, fluctuations in voltage, and forced outages of generation plants. As a consequence, consumers have been forced to invest in high cost captive power generation over the last three decades which has added to the overall cost of supply of electrical energy and led to the wasteful and polluting use of our scarce natural resources. The financial non-viability of the sector and the macroeconomic financial crises in the early 1990s led to the introduction of power sector reforms as a part of the government's structural adjustment programme, which is still ongoing during the current Eleventh Five Year Plan.

Growth of the Power Industry of India

The development of electrical power started in 1897 in India when the first unit of 130 kW generator was installed at Sidrapore in Darjeeling. In the pre-Independence era, power supply was mostly in private hands and was confined to urban areas. The total installed capacity all over the country (utility plus non-utility) increased from 2.3 thousand MW at the end of 1950 to 78.4 thousand MW in 1991–2, to 1.22 thousand MW in 2001–2, and 175 thousand MW in 2008–9. The corresponding gross generation rose from a meagre 6.6 billion kWh[1] in 1950 to 315.6 billion kWh in 1991–2, 579.1 billion kWh in 2001–2, and 839.8 billion kWh in 2008–9. As per the energy balance sheet of India for 2008 (IEA 2010), the share of electrical energy in the final commercial energy use when both are measured in oil equivalent units was approximately 21.11 per cent, involving the use of 50.6 per cent of the total primary commercial energy sources (see Table 1).

It may be further noted that the total installed capacity and gross generation of electricity by the utilities reached levels of 173 thousand MW and 811.1 billion kWh, respectively, in 2010–11. While Table 1 shows the growth of energy supply over the period 1980–1 to 2008–09, Tables 2 and 3 show the growth of capacity and gross generation of electrical energy in India from 1950–1 to 2008–9, separately for utilities and non-utilities. The mode-wise figures for installed capacity and gross generation are also indicated in the tables.

Table 2 Growth of Electrical Generation Capacity in India (in thousand MW)

Sector and mode	1950–1	1990–1	2008–9	Annual average growth rate 1950 to 1990–1 (%)	Annual average growth rate 1990–1 to 2008–9 (%)
Total utility (a+b+c)	1.7	66.1	148.0	5.5	4.58
(a) Hydro	0.6	18.8	36.9	4.8	3.82
(b) Thermal	1.1	45.8	107.0	10	4.83
(c) Nuclear	–	1.5	4.1	5.2	5.75
Non-utility	0.6	8.6	25.0	8.07	6.11
Total installed capacity	2.3	74.7	175.0	5.8	4.84

Source: Government of India (2005a, 2011).

[1]kWh is kilo watt hour.

Table 3 Growth of Gross Generation of Electricity (in billion kWh)

Sector and mode	1950–1	1990–1	2008–9	Annual average growth rate: 1950 to 1990–1	Annual average growth rate: 1990–1 to 2003–4
Total utility (a+b+c)	5.1	264.3	740.1	10.4	5.89
a) Hydro	2.5 (49)	71.7 (27.1)	110.1 (14.9)	8.75	2.41
b) Thermal	2.6 (51)	186.5 (70.6)	615.1 (83.1)	11.3	6.85
c) Nuclear	–	6.1 (2.3)	14.9 (2.0)	–	5.09
Non-utility	1.5	25.1	99.7	7.3	7.96
Total gross generation	6.6	289.4	839.8	9.9	6.10

Source: Government of India (2005a, 2011).

Hydro-thermal Mix

However, it is important to note that after the introduction of economic reforms in 1991, the growth rates of both installed capacity and gross generation of power declined substantially and the share of non-utility power increased. So far as the mix of generation modes is concerned, the share of all kinds of thermal power (that is, steam, gas, diesel, and so on) in the total gross generation of power in the utility system increased from 51 per cent in 1950, to 70.6 per cent in 1990–1, and 83.1 per cent in 2008–9, while that of hydroelectricity declined from 49 per cent in 1950, to 27.1 per cent in 1990–1, and 14.9 per cent in 2008–9. As non-utility power generation has been mostly thermal-based, there has been an imbalance of hydro-thermal mix from the point of view of efficiency for meeting the varying load of power demand, hydropower being known to be more convenient and efficient in meeting fluctuating peak load. However, while coal is an unclean fuel which leads to high CO_2 per unit of energy, that is, 3.75 kg per kg of energy in oil equivalent units, its relative higher availability makes it the cheapest option of power generation and supply in India, which had raised the share of coal thermal in total gross power generation of electricity to a level of around 69 per cent in 2008. While oil with the CO_2 coefficient of 2.47 kg had a share of around 4.5 per cent of the total gross generation, the cleanest fossil fuel of natural gas with the similar CO_2 coefficient of 2.31 had a share of approximately about 9 per cent in the total generation in the same year, being constrained by its limited availability from indigenous sources. The reasons for the declining share of hydro are the long gestation lag of storage dam projects and various socio-ecological constraints of such projects like displacement of human settlements, degradation of the ecological landscape due to inundation of the catchment and dam areas, and disturbances in the riverine water flow with a consequent adverse impact on the flora and fauna in the upstream as well as downstream areas.

Nuclear Power

The share of nuclear power produced out of a carbon-free and otherwise clean fuel has been till now very low at 2 per cent because of the earlier nuclear policy of the Government of India necessitating almost complete indigenization of its own plant and equipments and very limited supply of uranium fuel from the domestic sources, due to India not being a signatory of nuclear non-proliferation treaty. However, with the Government of India's new nuclear policy approach and the initiative of the bilateral agreement with the US and other countries for civil nuclear cooperation, India may be able to enter the international market for nuclear fuel, light water reactor, and uranium enrichment and reprocessing technology. This would enable it to raise the share of nuclear power in the total generation and contribute towards making the growth of the power sector low carbon. This would also enable India to utilize her vast thorium resources for power generation by developing a thorium–uranium cycle technology subsequent to the emerging faster breeder reactor technology and provide nuclear power a prominent role on the supply side of the Indian power industry in the long run (Government of India 2006).

All these would be viable subject to the conditions of resolution of all political–economic conflicts and constraints in entering the nuclear trade market and to the availability of adequate sites of plant locations which are safe from the point of view of seismic disturbances and nuclear waste disposal.

T&D System

On the side of T&D, the total length of T&D lines increased from 29,271 circuit kilometres (ckt km) at the end of 1950 to 6,344,858 ckt km at the end of 2003–4, and 7,278,946 ckt km in 2008. The share of distribution up to 500 volts in the total T&D line length was 59.5 per cent in 2008. It is interesting to note that while the installed generation capacity increased 76 times during this period (1950–1 to 2008–9), the length of T&D lines increased by 249 times. However, it is not just the line length in ckt km, but also the technological strengthening of the T&D system, which is important for the efficient evacuation of power. The Government of India has given a normative ratio of 1:1 for investment in generation to that in the T&D system, while the historical experience has been one of bias in favour of investments in generation over those in T&D for prolonged periods, which contributed to the weakness of the distribution system and the low quality of power supply.

Electricity Consumption

Energy Poverty

In spite of a 76-fold increase in the capacity of power generation in India, the per capita electricity consumption, which had been 15.6 kWh in 1950, could reach only the level of 528 kWh in 2008–9. The per capita electric power generation was 714 kWh for India in 2007, while the world average of per capita electricity production was 2,959 kWh per annum, with that in China and the US being 2,487 kWh and 14,338 kWh per annum, respectively, in the same year. India, in fact, suffers from energy poverty as is evident from such low availability of electrical energy when compared with other countries and the world average. In fact, electricity has not adequately penetrated the different sectors of the Indian economy as a result of which the share of electricity in the total final energy consumed was only 24 per cent in India while the share of the same at the global consumption level was 40 per cent in 2005 (Sengupta 2010). In 2004–5 only 54.9 per cent of the households had electricity as the primary lighting fuel in rural areas; this figure was 92.3 per cent for urban area (Government of India 2007). As 70 per cent of India's population still lives in rural areas, this implies huge inadequacy of electrical energy for the electrification of all homes and providing at least the lifeline requirement of energy in the form of electricity which is the cleanest fuel.

Energy Efficiency and Conservation

The total aggregate consumption of electricity increased from 51.74 TWh in 1971, to 211.74 TWh in 1990–1, and 601.6 TWh in 2008. The annual average growth rate of consumption of electricity, which had been 7.7 per cent per annum over the period 1971–2 to 1990–1, thus dropped to 6 per cent per annum in the post-reforms period, implying a decline of GDP elasticity of electricity consumption from 1.83 in the pre-reforms period to 0.77 in the post-reforms period. This sharp decline of GDP elasticity of electricity consumption shows an increase in the efficiency in the use of electrical energy, particularly in the declining electricity intensity of GDP in the post-reforms period, although there still remains substantive scope for improving such efficiency through further energy conserving technological changes. The industrial, domestic, and agricultural sectors are the major consumers of electricity in India constituting about 37.1, 24.7, and 20.4 per cent of consumption, respectively, accounting for 82.2 per cent of the total electrical consumption as supplied by the utility system in 2008–9.

Rural Electrification

The expansion of the T&D network system in the country had resulted in the electrification of 90.6 per cent of the total number of villages till February 2011, although 55 per cent of rural households in the country had not been connected with reliable supply sources of electricity and the development of power-based economic activity remained quite low even in the electrified villages.

Supply-side Efficiency Issues

In view of the high capital intensity of the order of about Rs 3.85 crore per MW for the generation capacity only, the capital productivity or capacity utilization is of crucial significance for the cost-effectiveness of electrical energy. The plant load factor (PLF)—which is the ratio of the total gross energy generated by all the plants of a utility system to the total maximum energy that can be generated by all the generating units together at full capacity for the entire calendar period—is the indicator of capacity utilization for generation. This was as low as 44.2 per cent in 1980–1, which improved to 53.8 per cent in 1990–1, 69.9 per cent in 2000–1, and 75.07 per cent in 2010–11. PLF as an efficiency parameter is determined by the net availability of power plant units (that is, net calendar time after allowing for maintenance downtime and forced outages due to operational inefficiencies), partial outages due to shortage of fuel/coolant in thermal plants and hydro resources in hydel plants, and finally the systems load factor (SLF), which is the ratio of the peak load to the average load demand for the utility system over a period. The SLF influences the extent of backing down of plants in off-peak hours.

There are also serious problems of inefficiency in the Indian power industry, which results from losses of energy in the process of conversion of energy resources into electrical energy, auxiliary losses due to own consumption of electricity by the power plants, and T&D losses. The totality of such losses accounted for 78 per cent of the energy throughout in the total system (see Table 1). The overall conversion efficiency of India's power industry for all kinds of fuel or resource use as indicated in the energy balance sheet for India was 69 per cent in 2008. Out of the gross energy generation, the auxiliary losses were of the order of 6.6 per cent, and out of the balance energy despatched at Busbar, the T&D losses were 25 per cent in the same year (2008), whereas T&D losses were about 23 per cent in the early 1990s. T&D losses include all losses due to transformer operations, transportation, and all unaccounted for consumption, including thefts and un-metered supply of electricity which have been high in India partly because of governance failure, which account for approximately in the range of half to two-thirds of what is booked against T&D losses. All these supply-side inefficiencies have resulted in both peak and energy deficits in India which were of the order of 10.8 and 7.6 per cent, respectively, in 2011–12.

Financial Performance

The financial health of power selling agencies like SEBs has been chronically poor in India because of uneconomic tariffs for agriculture and domestic consumption, high T&D losses, and other supply-side inefficiencies as mentioned earlier. While the average cost of electricity supply from the utilities was Rs 3.40 per kWh, the average revenue without any subsidy was Rs 2.62 per kWh causing a revenue expenditure gap of Rs 0.78 per unit in 2008–9 at the national level. This gap has been rising over time and the rate of recovery of costs through tariffs in terms of average tariff to cost ratio declined from 82.2 per cent in 1992–3 to 77.1 per cent in 2008–9, in spite of the introduction of power sector reforms during the period. As the average agricultural and domestic sector tariffs have been lower than the overall average tariffs and costs, sectors of industry, commercial users, and railways have been charged at rates higher than the average cost of supply effecting some cross-subsidization, although the extent of such under-recovery of costs and cross-subsidization has varied from state to state.

The substantive shortfall of tariffs from the costs for the agriculture and the domestic sectors, however, is not fully compensated by such cross-subsidization by the industry, commercial, and railway sectors in any state. State governments provide some budgetary subsidies by way of transfers in the form of grants to their respective SEBs, or EDs, or any distributive agency. In spite of such subventions, the financial performance of most of the state utilities or distribution companies has been quite alarming and the rate of return on capital employed has been quite low. The gap of under-recovery of cost could come down from Rs 0.78 per kWh without subsidy to Rs 0.33 per unit with subsidy, but only to Rs. 0.60 per unit in terms of revenue and subsidy as actually realized in 2008–9. Such gaps have also varied across states depending on state-level policies and efficiency in the management of the power sector. As a result of all these, the total financial losses without subsidy of the power distribution companies, particularly SEBs and EDs, increased to a staggering amount of Rs 52,623 crore in 2008–9. The distribution of utilities in India according to the rates of return on capital employed is given in Table 4.

Table 4 Rate of Return on Capital-wise Distribution of Utilities for 2008–9.

Rate of return on capital	Number of utilities
Negative value	32
0 to less than 1%	3
1 to 12%	46
Above 12%	8
Total	89

Source: Power Finance Corporation, Report on the Performance of the State Power Utilities 2008–09.

Power Sector Reforms and Institutional Changes

Given the chronic deteriorating financial condition of the SEBs, the fiscal crisis of the Indian economy in 1990–1 forced the government to introduce economic reforms in the state-dominated power sector for its efficient growth and modernization to meet the growing power demand. Although power in India was delivered by governments of the states and union territories, the policy guidelines had mostly been laid down by the central government. In the initial phase of the reforms, the government liberalized only the generation sector and invited independent power producers (IPPs) to bid for setting up generation capacities with up to 100 per cent foreign equity participation and for selling power to SEBs through power purchase agreements (PPAs). One of the first and the most controversial PPA signed was between the Maharashtra State Electricity Board (MSEB) and the Dhabol Power Corporation (DPC), an Indian subsidiary of the US-based multinational company Enron, which turned out to be a major failure as MSEB started incurring huge losses because of the high power purchase bills received from DPC. Other subsequent PPAs in other states also met with similar problems. As such, generation bidding could not induce competition because of the inadequate number of players in the bidding process and also because the generation bidding was often restricted with reference to the choice of fuel/technology type, location of new capacity, and so on. Besides, the privatization of generation investment contributed to the reality of a high capital servicing cost because of the high discount rate prevalent in the private capital market as compared to that used by the state for such investments in public utilities, and the cost plus pricing agreement which tended to inflate the capital base.

In the second phase of the reforms, the government introduced comprehensive structural adjustment reforms in power, which broadly involved the following three major changes.

1. *Unbundling of the SEBs*: This made possible the introduction of competition in potentially competitive businesses like generation and distribution to retail consumers. The unbundling of the SEBs was completed in 15 states till April 2011 most of which established separate distribution companies.
2. *Introduction of Independent Regulatory Commissions*: This was made imperative by the unbundling of SEBs for the following purposes:
   (i) To help coordination among the separated entities in the areas of generation, transmission, and distribution, with each area having several players on the supply side of a region.
   (ii) To set power tariffs, taking into account the interests of all the stakeholders.
   (iii) To act as a dispute settlement body.

   The State Electricity Regulator Commissions (SERCs) have been set up in all the states to implement these. A Central Electricity Regulatory Commission (CERC) has also been established to supervise inter-state issues in the transmission of power and in transactions between the generating units owned by the central government and state-level utilities. In addition, CERC also acts as an advisory body to SERCs and the Government of India.
3. *Privatization*: Privatization of entities in each of the unbundled areas was initiated in order to resolve the problem of inadequate investments in the power sector. In the second phase of reforms, in addition to generation, the privatization of the distribution areas also received attention. While the transmission area was corporatized at the state or regional grid level, corporate entities remain state-owned. Unfortunately, private investment has not adequately flowed into the electricity sector in either generation or distribution. Till 2010, the share of the private sector in the total generation capacity of 173.6 GW was 36.76 GW, that is, 21 per cent only. Private capital has been hesitant to enter the generation industry in view of the financial non-viability of the major purchasers of power. Besides, the privatization process has been initiated in the distribution area, but it has not yet yielded encouraging results in terms of remunerative power tariffs and physical efficiency parameters.

Electricity Policy

In view of these reforms, the Electricity Act, 2003, was passed to provide an enabling framework for accelerated and more efficient development of the power sector by implementing the agenda of reforms as outlined earlier. The National Electricity Policy (Government of India 2005b) along with a Tariff Policy were also notified in 2005 and 2006, respectively. These aim at providing access to electricity for all households in the next five years and meeting both energy and peaking demand by 2012 with per capita availability over 1,000 kWh per annum with adequate provisions for a spinning reserve. The policy emphasizes a reliable supply of good quality power at reasonable rates.

Delicensing Captive Generation

For the adequacy of power, the Electricity Act, 2003, and the Electricity Policy have delicensed the creation of generation capacity and promoted the captive generation of power, allowed open access to the T&D system, and recognized trading in electric power as a legitimate economic activity for better management. The generation of power has been completely delicensed with the exception of hydropower projects which have inter-state ramifications. However, all projects have to take certain statutory clearances, including one from the Ministry of Environment and Forests. These clearances are time consuming and contribute to delays and constraints in the growth of power supply. The Electricity Act also encourages industries to set up their own power plants in order to reduce dependence on government utilities by exempting them from paying various charges and dues which are otherwise applicable for any open access customer.

Open Access for Consumers

The new Electricity Act also allows open access to any consumer or distributing agency at the retail end and with a connected load of 1 MW and above to freely buy power from anywhere in the country. Regulatory commissions have to determine the wheeling charges and other surcharges, including a cross-subsidy surcharge. As the national power grid for the inter-state and inter-regional flow of power has now been established, such open access should be technically feasible. However, this open access for distribution consumers has not as yet been successful because of the non-availability of surplus power for such flow in most of the states and because of the restrictive policies of state governments.

Trading in Power

The Electricity Act also recognizes trading in electric power as a distinct legitimate activity for which licences are to be granted by electricity regulatory commissions—central or state—depending on whether inter-state or intra-state trading would be involved. Although such trading is supposed to facilitate better and more efficient management of the demand–supply balance at the regional and national levels, such trading is at present limited to only 4 per cent of the power generated since most of the power has been tied up by PPAs. Apart from trade licensing, CERC has given licences to two power exchanges set up in Delhi and Mumbai for similar trading.

Tariff Policy and Subsidy

The tariff policy as announced stipulates that in order to rationalize the power tariff structure, the regulatory commissions have to adopt a multi-year tariff approach, which means a prior announcement of the principles which would be governing the tariff in the following three to five years so that consumers and investors may adjust their plans and minimize any losses due to tariff uncertainty.

In order to remove energy poverty, the new tariff policy further recommends a special lifeline tariff for the poorest of the poor who may be allowed to pay 50 per cent of the average cost of supply. The minimum lifeline consumption for which such low tariff would be applicable has been fixed as 1 kWh/household/day. For all other consumers the tariff will be fixed within a band of +/− 20 per cent of the average cost of supply in order to limit cross-subsidization, which should also be phased out in the future. The Electricity Policy, however, allows the government to announce subsidies for any class of consumers whatever be the reason, with the rider that the subsides should be paid upfront to the concerned utility, avoiding situations which arose in the past where the subsidies remained as promises and were never fully realized.

Fuel Policy: Correcting Hydro-thermal Imbalance and the Role of Renewables

In view of the imbalance in the fuel composition of the generation of power in favour of coal thermal, the new policy emphasizes correction in the choice of energy resources by way of the full development of the hydro potential of the country and significant increase in the share of nuclear power by stepping up public investments and encouraging private partnership in the latter area. The recent changes in India's nuclear policy are likely to facilitate nuclear technology transfers in the future to achieve such objectives. Besides, the nuclear research and development policy is giving a thrust to the development of fast breeder reactors of higher capacity and thorium-based technologies.

In order to encourage the development of carbon-free renewable resource–based power so that India fulfils the responsibility of controlling climate change, the electricity policy stipulates SERCs to dictate a minimum percentage share of power that has to be procured from renewable sources of energy. Most of the SERCs have indicated this percentage share.

It may be noted here that the power generation capacity based on renewables (other than hydro) was 15.5 GWe, constituting 9.7 per cent in a power system of a total capacity of 1,60,000 MW as on 31 March 2010. Among such renewable resources, the share of wind in the total grid-interactive renewable energy capacity was 70 per cent, followed by small hydro with a share of 16.27 per cent, while that of solar photovoltaic power was a negligible 0.06 per cent. It is the relative higher availability of wind resources in India and the high cost of solar photovoltaic power which explain such resource-wise distribution of new renewable, resource-based power capacity (3i Network 2010). Further investments in research and the development of renewables technologies and entrepreneurial initiatives in the deployment of these technologies are of crucial importance to make the growth of the Indian power sector low carbon and sustainable.

The Indian power industry is going through an important transition. The process of reforms and the implementation of policies are yet to yield adequate or desired results and are being reviewed and debated from time to time to ensure that they end up achieving policy targets.

RAMPRASAD SENGUPTA

References

3i Network. 2010. *India Infrastructure Report 2010: Infrastructure Development in a Low Carbon Economy,* New Delhi, Oxford University Press.

Government of India. 2005a. *All India Electricity Statistics General Review 2005,* New Delhi, Central Electricity Authority, Ministry of Power, Government of India.

——. 2005b. *National Electricity Policy,* New Delhi, Ministry of Power, Government of India, available at http://powermin.nic.in/whats_new/national_electricity_policy.htm.
——. 2006. *Integrated Energy Policy,* Report of the Expert Group, Planning Commission, Government of India.
——. 2007. *Energy Sources of Indian Households for Cooking and Lighting 2004–05, Report on the NSS 61st Round,* New Delhi, National Sample Survey Organisation.
——. 2011. *Economic Survey 2010–11,* Ministry of Finance, New Delhi, Oxford University Press.
International Energy Agency (IEA). 2010. *Energy Balances of Non-OECD Countries 2008,* Paris, IEA/OECD.
Sengupta, Ramprasad. 2010. *Prospects and Policies for Low Carbon Economic Growth of India,* National Institute of Public Finance and Policy, New Delhi.
TERI. 2004. *TEDDY 2003/04: TERI Energy Data Directory & Yearbook,* New Delhi, TERI.

Power Sector and Regulation

It is common knowledge that the poor power situation in India is one of the principal impediments to economic growth and development. The statist strategy of public provisioning has failed: growth of coverage is dismal, quality of service is appalling, and operational inefficiencies are ubiquitous. What is to be done? Wherever commercial competition is feasible, the state should simply retreat, encourage private provisioning, and let the market allocate resources. However, for a variety of reasons, competition is unsustainable in many dimensions of the power systems and commercializing the functioning of state-owned providers is the feasible option, especially when private entry is limited. In dimensions where competition is unlikely to yield socially desirable outcomes, the state needs to regulate. A common rationale for the regulation of public utilities is that they are natural monopolies.[1] A natural monopoly situation implies that given the cost structure of the firm a single firm can meet the entire demand for the output and no two firms can exist simultaneously and still be profitable. Thus it is unlikely that we can get competitive prices and allowing unfettered competition with pervasive natural monopoly characteristics may result in socially inefficient entry. Moreover, if the natural monopoly's product or service is also essential to the public, the government cannot rely on the operation of markets to prevent abuse of monopoly power.

Direct regulation by the state is not viable as it amounts to the fox guarding the chicken coop: it invites state actors (politicians and bureaucrats) to capriciously frame regulations to suit their ends, which are not necessarily congruent with the larger public interest and the commercial interests of the service providers. The fear of such draconian regulations will inevitably keep private players out since entry involves large sunk costs. So attracting the private sector requires the state to credibly pre-commit to not behaving in a capricious way once the private entry has been made. The creation of independent regulatory institutions is a way for the state to credibly tie its hands.

In this background, I briefly analyse the performance of the Indian electricity regulators. In 1996, a conference of Chief Ministers approved the CMNAP (Common Minimum National Action for Power), which included the establishment of the Electricity Regulatory Commissions (ERCs) at central and state levels. Moreover, the reforming states were under considerable pressure from multilateral lending agencies to create ERCs; a state government that created ERC was in a better position to get large funding from them. The Government of India enacted the Electricity Regulatory Commissions Act, 1998 (ERC Act 1998). The Act paved the way for the establishment of the Central Electricity Regulatory Commission (CERC) at central level and State Electricity Regulatory Commissions (SERCs) at state level. Twenty-two states have already constituted SERCs. Prior to the enactment of the Act the regulatory function at central level was performed by the Central Electricity Authority (CEA) and the Government of India, and at state level by the State Electricity Boards (SEBs) and/or state government. There were some obvious drawbacks of the erstwhile regulatory framework. The foremost was the manner of setting tariffs, which lacked transparency at the very least. Though this anomaly has been corrected by the creation of these new regulatory institutions, the experience has been mixed.

Creation and sustenance of independent regulatory institutions requires a substantial degree of political and judicial maturity. Ultimately, the state actors have to forbear from routine interference in areas that they have hitherto considered to be a part of the state's (that is their own) eminent domain. The Indian political class has hitherto been unwilling to part with this fiefdom. Legitimate mandated regulatory functions are routinely compromised by the issuance of 'policy' directives.

Experience has shown that regulation is only one part of the reform story. Successful regulation requires complementary reforms, including the introduction of competition and encouragement of private participation.

[1]However, some components (like generation) of the sector may in fact be highly competitive and should ideally be deregulated.

It is argued that regulation itself will discipline and improve the performance of state-run corporations, and entry of private entities is unnecessary. This view implicitly assumes that these corporations will respond to incentives in the same way as private firms. The regulator's ability to bring about desired outcomes depends on the regulated entity's sensitivity to financial incentives in the form of tariffs, transfers, penalties, and so on. Historically, Indian state-owned entities have been motivated by myriad considerations, many of them of the non-commercial and non-financial kind. These considerations have been used as an alibi for poor commercial and financial performance by the managers of these entities and the political class that oversees and exploits these entities. Alibis of the 'social responsibility' variety are routinely seized upon by the political class to open the public purse to provide open-ended non-performance-related subsidies to these state-owned entities. Consequently, they face soft budget constraints and are unlikely to respond to regulatory incentives in the same way as private firms.

Moreover, there is insufficient institutional distance between the regulator and state-owned firms, especially when there is no firewall between the state actors and the regulator. Being two aspects of the same entity, namely, the Indian state, it is not credible that the regulator is even-handed when private firms compete with state-owned firms. Regulatory capture by state-owned firms is a very real threat. The only way to have good regulatory outcomes when state-owned firms are involved is to make these firms very like private firms, thereby destroying their public-sector character: have similar employment policies and similar managerial and labour incentives, deny them budgetary hand-outs, and empower management to make commercially sensible decisions. Although such pronouncements are piously incanted every time public-sector reform is proposed, the political class is clearly loath to part with the milch cow fattened over decades. For India to benefit from the liberalization process, its government must convince the entrants that the regulatory environment will provide no special favour to the publicly owned incumbent. Till the government solves this commitment[2] problem the future of independent regulation is bleak.

[2]These questions closely parallel questions that have long been considered in the macroeconomic policy literature as to whether governments that face elections every few years can commit to maintaining a low inflation policy, and if not, whether governments can effectively tie their own hands by installing an independent central bank charged with maintaining a pre-determined inflationary target.

Experts recommend a variety of institutional arrangements to enhance the quality of regulatory governance: clarity of regulatory roles, objectives, and powers; a credible firewall between the regulator and state actors to guarantee the regulator's independence; participation in the regulatory process by interested parties such as consumers; and accountability of the regulator for his decisions. Yet, and here is the rub, the creation of institutions meeting these criteria and the implementation of complementary reforms is in the hands of the very political class that stands to lose the most from these changes. Slow and hesitant attempts to untangle the mess are under way in the face of pressure from consumers and other interested parties. However, rapid improvement in infrastructure regulation requires a statesman to rise above myopic political interests and cut the Gordian knot.

Payal Malik

Primary Education

Introduction

Despite the progress India has made in primary schooling since Independence, there is much yet to be accomplished. Household data from the National Sample Survey (NSS) for 2004–5 reveal that 23 per cent of the children between the age of 12 and 15 years had not completed primary school. Gender, caste, and regional gaps, while narrowed, remain significant. Thus, the percentage of rural boys between the age 12 and 15 years with primary schooling in 2004–5 was 77 per cent, but this figure was only 72 per cent for girls. Only 72 per cent of scheduled caste and scheduled tribe children between the age of 12 and 15 years reported completing primary school, as compared to 79 per cent of the children of other castes. Comparing states, this percentage varied from 96 per cent in Kerala to a low of 58 per cent in Bihar. Indeed, despite the fact that the figure for Kerala approached the ceiling of 100 per cent by 2004–5, the difference in this completion rate between Kerala and Bihar in 1999–2000, at 38 per cent, *exceeded* that of rural adults of older cohorts in the two states. For example, the primary school completion rate for adults between the age of 45–50 years in 1999–2000 was 71 per cent in Kerala and 37 per cent in Bihar, yielding a gap of 34 per cent. Finally, education quality, as reflected in the results of standard achievement tests, is very low. Data from the Annual Status of Education Report (ASER) for

2009 reveal, for example, that only 33 per cent of Class V students in rural India could perform subtraction and that 53 per cent of these students could only read at the level expected in Class II.

In this brief entry it is not possible to fully describe the research on the determinants of primary schooling in India. Instead, the focus is on the role of policy in explaining schooling outcomes. The entry starts by describing the constraints which shaped the formation of schooling policy in India, and the broad features of this policy. It then goes on to discuss how schooling policy explains some of the features of schooling in India.

India's Educational Policy: Historical Origins and Current Status

At Independence, India inherited a very weak system of primary education. In 1835, the British authorities decided that publicly funded education should only be provided in English, a policy which was adhered to until almost the end of the colonial era. Available funds were also primarily used to subsidize fee-charging private schools, rather than public schools. Consequently, popular primary education, particularly in rural areas, received scant support (Myrdal 1968). In 1950–1, at the primary level there were only 211,071 schools and 537,918 teachers in the country, of whom over 40 per cent were untrained. Not surprisingly, schooling levels were low, with only 42 per cent of the 6–11 years age group and 14 per cent of the 11–14 years age group enrolled in school in 1950–1. And, disparities in schooling attainment were large: across states, across urban and rural areas, across castes, and across boys and girls. In 1950–1, girls constituted only 28 per cent of primary school enrolments, even though they constituted roughly half of the school-age population. Similarly, whereas 83 per cent of the population lived in rural areas in 1950–1, rural students constituted only 60 per cent of primary school enrolments.

Recognizing the importance of universal elementary schooling, the Constitution included a directive which sought to ensure universal elementary schooling by 1960. Though this deadline was not met, the objective of universal elementary schooling has been repeatedly upheld, most recently in the 93rd Constitutional Amendment which makes education for children between the age of 6 to 14 years a fundamental right.

This goal has been difficult to achieve, in part because of the country's very poor resource base. At the time of the First Five Year Plan, the Committee on the Ways and Means of Financing Educational Development in India estimated that the development of a national system of education would require an *annual* expenditure of Rs 400 crore, and an additional Rs 472 crore for teacher training and investment in buildings, yielding a total of Rs 2,472 crore over the five year period. However, India's total tax revenue in 1950–1 amounted to only Rs 625 crore. As a consequence, the Plan restricted *total* outlays by the central and state governments to only Rs 2,069 crore. As against the estimated requirement of Rs 2,472 crore, expenditure on education was restricted to only Rs 152 crore for the Plan period. Allocations to education have consistently fallen short of the government's target of 6 per cent of national income.

The limited resources of the central government combined with the assumption that lower-level state governments could more efficiently deliver 'local' public goods such as schooling resulted in education being placed on the Constitution's 'State List', that is, amongst the areas which state governments are responsible for. This decision effectively decentralized decisions relating to schooling resources and expenditure. Though the central government recognized that it nevertheless bore responsibility 'for helping, co-coordinating and guiding the work of the States', it admitted that it was unable to do much in this direction due to the shortage of funds (Government of India, First Five Year Plan). In 1976, education was shifted from the State List to the Concurrent List by the 42nd Amendment to the Constitution, thereby formalizing a role for the central government in framing educational policies and providing central support for nationwide schooling schemes. However, individual states remain free to evolve and frame their own policies and structures within this broad framework, as also to determine their schooling budgets and the allocation of state expenditures.

A majority of the schooling expenditure continues to come from state governments, which in 2006–7, bore 76.5 per cent of the total budgeted expenditure on education. The central government primarily funds 'plan' investment in physical capital such as school buildings, while state governments finance 'non-plan' expenditure on teachers and other forms of working capital. However, the central government also supplements state-level funding through centrally sponsored educational programmes, such as Operation Blackboard and, more recently, the Sarva Shiksha Abhiyan, which frequently include components for working capital expenditure, including teacher salaries.

Commitment to a decentralized framework was reiterated in two important policy documents, the 1986 National Policy on Education and the follow-up 1992 Plan of Action, which laid down a framework for utilizing decentralized political institutions, the Panchayati Raj

Institutions, for strengthening school decentralization. Since this period, the district is treated as the unit of educational planning, with district boards of education being responsible for teacher training, teacher allocations across schools, and a host of other administrative tasks. Village education committees were also set up to monitor investments at the school level and to ensure local participation in the educational planning process.

The resource constraint also led the government to advocate a large role for the community and private funding, with the First Five Year Plan stating explicitly that 'in the context of prevailing conditions a larger share of responsibility for social services will have to be borne by the people themselves'. This was accomplished by requiring even students enrolled in government schools to pay for tuition and other inputs. It was also achieved through a relatively liberal policy towards the growth of private schools.

In 1985–6, NSS data (42nd round) reveal that the average household expenditure per student enrolled in elementary schools was Rs 1,205, while the average expenditure per elementary student by the central and state government combined was only Rs 338.72—private expenditures was approximately four times that of public expenditure. Since then, most state governments have abolished fees in elementary schools and increased their expenditure on schooling. Data from the 2004–5 (NSS 61st round) document that the average per student expenditure by households with students enrolled in elementary school was Rs 1,269, with average government expenditure per student being Rs 2,264 (2006–7).

The continued high-level of household expenditure per elementary school student is largely a consequence of the rapid growth in private schools. For India as a whole, the percentage of primary school students enrolled in private schools increased from 15 per cent in 1986 to 21 per cent in 1995, to 28 per cent in 2004–5 (NSS, rounds 42, 52, and 61, respectively), though the relatively large number of private unrecognized schools generates considerable variation in this percentage by source (the 7th All-India Education Survey [AIES 2002] estimates private primary enrolments at about 15 per cent). The corresponding percentages for urban India were as high as 36 per cent in 1986 and 47 per cent in 1995, which dropped fractionally to 46 per cent in 2004–5. Restricting attention to households with at least one child in a private elementary school, average per student household expenditure on education in 2004–5 was Rs 2,058.

The poor infrastructural base that the country inherited combined with the shortage of funds also led the government to implement a 'step' approach, focusing initially on improving primary schooling facilities. Decisions regarding the number of schools and their locations were, however, guided by the constraints placed on the system by the nation's existing socio-economic fabric. It is frequently stated that India is primarily a nation of villages. In reality, however, India is a nation of habitations within villages, with habitations generally being defined along caste lines. Because of the residential segregation of households and the unwillingness of parents to allow their daughters to walk relatively long distances to school, the government adopted an *extensive* policy, with the goal of providing a primary school 'within easy walking distance' from each home (Third Five Year Plan). This goal was formalized by the 1986 National Policy on Education and the follow-up 1992 Plan of Action, which stated that every habitation with a population which exceeded 300 should be provided with a primary school within 1 km. This population norm was relaxed to 200 for scheduled caste and tribe habitations. As a consequence of this policy, the scarce resources available for primary schooling have primarily been used to finance growth in schools. The number of primary schools almost quadrupled between 1950–1 and 2007–8, increasing from 2,10,000 to 7,85,950.

Recent policy initiatives have been aimed both at ensuring access and improving quality. Most notable is the Right of Children to Free and Compulsory Education Act (RTE), 2009, which came into effect on 1 April 2010. The Act makes education a fundamental right of every child between the age of 6 and 14 years. It also seeks to ensure school quality by specifying norms for infrastructure in all schools, including a teacher–pupil ratio of 1:30, and by requiring teachers to regularly assess student learning levels and provide this information to parents. The Act also affects private schools: it prohibits unrecognized schools and requires all private schools to reserve 25 per cent of their seats for children from poor families, with the state reimbursing schools for this expenditure.

How effective the Act will be in ensuring school quality and learning is open to question. Far more effective in this regard are likely to be the recent efforts by the government and by non-government organizations to generate and collect information on learning levels and on school quality through surveys such as DISE (District Information System for Education) and ASER. This, however, is a first step. Real progress requires this information to be used to initiate the reforms necessary to ensure quality.

Effects of an Extensive Approach: Quantity versus Quality

Research has shown that the substantial growth in the number of schools and the policy of providing schools within walking distance of households have significantly contributed to the growth in primary school enrolments, particularly for members of scheduled castes and tribes (Kochar 2004). It has, therefore, contributed to the narrowing of schooling gaps.

However, the growth in the number of schools may have been at the expense of improvement in the quality of schooling infrastructure and other schooling inputs, including teachers. The 2009 ASER revealed that of the surveyed schools, only 52 per cent had a usable toilet, and as many as 25 per cent of the schools lacked water facilities. And, growth in the number of teachers has not kept pace with growth in student enrolments. Thus, India has witnessed an *increase* in the primary school student–teacher ratio over the years, from 24 in 1950–1 to 44 by 2002 (7th AIES).

The extensive approach has also made it difficult to exploit economies of scale in schooling. In 2002 (7th AIES), the average student size of a government primary school was 120, well below the range most educationalists consider to be optimal. As many as 60 per cent of the nation's schools had an enrolment of less than 100 in 1993 (6th AIES). In fact, a quarter of the rural schools had student populations of less than 50. Such small school sizes means that multi-grade instruction is the norm in most of the nation's schools, with teachers simultaneously providing instructions to students of several grades. This is also reflected in data on the number of teachers per school. In 2002, 28 per cent of the rural schools had one or less teachers, while 64 per cent of the schools had two or less teachers.

Do indicators of quality such as student–teacher ratios, class size, and schooling facilities affect schooling quantity and quality? While the evidence from developed countries remains ambiguous, a significant body of research demonstrates that they do matter for schooling in developing economies. The policy of creating a large network of schools, each of relatively small size and with inadequate supporting inputs, may therefore have implied a vote for quantity over quality.

Effects of Decentralization: Efficiency and Equity

It is widely believed that a primary advantage of a decentralized system of schooling is greater efficiency in input use, including the accountability of teachers. This has not been the case in India, as documented by several studies, including the PROBE report (1999) and Dreze and Sen (1995), which record the considerable wastage of teaching time in several states. This may, however, not be a failure of decentralization, but rather reflect the limited degree of school decentralization in India. For example, despite recent experiments with 'contract teachers', the accountability of teachers who are regular government employees to the community remains low.

Decentralization has, however, resulted in considerable variations in government allocations to schooling across states. For example, average budgeted expenditure per elementary school student in 2006–7 was Rs 1,375 in Uttar Pradesh, Rs 1,476 in Madhya Pradesh, and Rs 2,021 in Bihar. These expenditure levels are low relative to high-performing states such as Kerala (Rs 4,743) and Himachal Pradesh (Rs 6,626).

Reflecting this variation, data from the 7th AIES (2002) reveal a commensurate variation in student–teacher ratios across states. Compared to the national average of 42, the student–teacher ratio was 19 in Jammu and Kashmir, 22 in Himachal Pradesh, 55 in Uttar Pradesh, and as much as 83 in Bihar. Given administrative decentralization to the level of the district, it is no surprise that state-level variations in per student resources is mirrored by similar variations at the district level, *within* a state. For example, in Bihar, data from the 7th AIES (2002) reveal that the student–teacher ratio varied from 59 in Nalanda district to 100 in Gaya.

Effects of Privatization: Support for Government Schools

Why has decentralization not resulted in greater efficiency of input use in India? Relatedly, what explains the low level of public expenditure on primary schooling and the variations in this expenditure across states? Many believe that low schooling budgets and the poor quality of government schools reflect the apathy of local elites—not towards schooling, but towards *government* schools (Weiner 1991).

This may, in turn, partly be a consequence of the combination of policies of administrative decentralization and the government's tacit support for private schooling. Researchers have argued that competition from private schools and the consequent reduction in enrolments in government schools may cause the latter to improve their quality. However, an increase in private schooling within a community is also likely to decrease overall community interest in, and support for, government schools. If control over schools is decentralized, with communities exercising some level of control over school administration, this decreased interest in government schools may inhibit improvements in their quality. Differences in the socio-economic status of those who attend private and government schools may exacerbate this problem. If the private school population consists of the relatively influential and wealthy members of the community, public schooling communities may be singularly ill-equipped to ensure improvements in budgets for government schools.

Establishing a causal relationship between the growth of private schools and the quality of government schools is difficult. The data do reveal that the rich are far more likely to attend private schools than the poor, suggesting a high degree of schooling segregation by wealth and hence reduced support within a community for government schools. Dividing households by per capita expenditure, the percentage of primary school children attending private schools in 2004–5 (NSS 61st round) was as high as 48 per cent for households in the highest per capita expenditure quartile (37 per cent in rural areas and as much as 64 per cent in urban areas). In contrast, 13 per cent of primary school students from the lowest per capita expenditure quartile attended private schools (6 per cent in rural areas and 21 per cent in urban areas).

The data also reveal that in states characterized by high levels of private schooling, schooling attainment levels of the poor are particularly low. For example, private school enrolments at the primary level are amongst the highest in the wealthy states of Punjab and Haryana. For rural areas of these states, data from the NSS 61st round (2004–5) reveal that 38 per cent of the primary school students in Punjab and 46 per cent in Haryana were enrolled in private schools, relative to the national average of 20 per cent. In these same two states, the percentage of poor rural children between the age of 12 and 15 years who reported completing primary school was only 49 per cent in Punjab and 59 per cent in Haryana, just marginally higher than the average of 56 per cent for India's major states, despite the fact that these two states are amongst India's wealthiest.[1] These correlations are only suggestive. While they suggest that high rates of private schooling may reduce the quality of the government schools which cater to the poor, they could also be evidence of causality in the reverse direction, from poor government schools to increased enrolment in private schools.

[1]The poor are defined as households with expenditure below NSS state-specific poverty lines.

Conclusion

This necessarily short entry cannot do justice to the many issues that arise regarding primary schooling in India. Rather than attempting to be comprehensive, it focused on identifying a few policy constraints on improvements in primary schooling in India.

India's poor resource base resulted in an extensive approach, and in a decentralized schooling system with tacit support for private schools. While this approach has succeeded in increasing enrolments, and other measures of school quantity, the difficult task of improving school quality and achievement levels remains. The government has advocated further decentralization of school administration to village governments as a means of ensuring improvements in quality. Enhancing local accountability of schools and schooling staff is likely to generate some efficiency gains. However, it is unlikely that communities characterized by significant levels of private schooling will devote themselves to improving the quality of government schools. Improvements in school quality, as well as reductions in schooling inequalities and regional schooling gaps, may require a mix of centralized and decentralized control, with the extent of each varying with the socio-economic characteristics of the region. A necessary first step in improving quality is developing a monitoring system which provides accurate and timely information on learning levels and school quality. The steps taken by the government and by non-governmental organizations in this direction may provide the building blocks for ensuring a high-quality elementary school system in India.

Anjini Kochar

References

Dreze, Jean and Amartya Sen. 1995. *India: Economic Development and Social Opportunity,* Delhi: Oxford University Press.

Government of India. 2007. *Analysis of Budgeted Expenditure on Education 2004–05 to 2006–07,* New Delhi, Ministry of Human Resource and Development, Government of India.

Kochar, Anjini. 2004. 'Reducing Social Gaps in Schooling: Caste and the Differential Effect of School Construction Programs in Rural India', Stanford University, Manuscript.

Myrdal, Gunnar. 1968. *Asian Drama: An Inquiry into the Poverty of Nations,* New York, The Twentieth Century Fund.

PROBE. 1999. *Public Report on Basic Education,* New Delhi, Oxford University Press.

Weiner, Myron. 1991. *The Child and the State in India,* Princeton, Princeton University Press.

Privatization

The past quarter century has witnessed a significant move towards privatization in economies across the globe. Several industrial countries have embraced it as have most of the transition economies of East Europe and large parts of the developing world. After the initial push received in the early 1980s during the Thatcher–Reagan era the process appears to have gathered momentum after the decline of communism in the erstwhile Soviet bloc. In India, privatization or disinvestment of the public sector emerged as a major public policy option after the country embarked on a process of economic reforms in 1991.

Even though the question of the appropriate balance between public and private enterprise is one of the foundational issues in political economy, it has received relatively little attention in mainstream economic analysis until quite recently. In the past two decades there has emerged an appreciable literature that examines the diverse theoretical and empirical issues pertaining to privatization (Shleifer and Vishny 1994; Sheshinski and Lopez-Calva 2003, among others).

Privatization may be broadly defined as the transfer of various activities from the public to the private sphere. Specifically, it could mean the sale by government or state-owned enterprises (SOEs) to private economic agents. It could refer to a sale that is effected in full or in part. It can also mean a partnership between the public and private sectors through a transfer of responsibilities from the public to private sector. In terms of broad political economy it could also simply mean a shrinking of the welfare state.

It would be tempting to assume that since privatization has been accepted as a legitimate, and even a core, tool of statecraft by more than a hundred governments in the past two decades, its economic merits are firmly settled. There is in fact a widespread perception that privatization brings about outcomes that are superior from the point of efficiency in terms of resource allocation as compared to the situation under public ownership. However, these conclusions are without any firm basis either in theory or in empirical analysis.

In the following section, I shall briefly review the theory of privatization that has emerged in the past two decades. This will be followed by a brief account of the rather large body of empirical work that has developed in recent years. I shall then consider the strategy of disinvestment that has been followed by the Government of India in the past decade and a half.

Privatization: Theory

Within the standard microeconomic literature, it is well established that under perfectly competitive conditions, absence of information asymmetries, and complete contracts, it does not matter whether one is operating under private or public ownership. The original arguments for government intervention come up in the context of market failure that can arise due to myriad factors. Under conditions of natural monopoly, denoted by decreasing average costs in the relevant range of demand, the possibility of monopoly power by a private owner created the rationale for public ownership.

Yet it is widely contended that public ownership brings about efficiency losses that are non-negligible (see, for example, Sheshinski and Lopez-Calva 2003). They could well be higher than the gains that may be ensured by solving a market failure problem. This comes about especially when the scope of competition becomes larger with an increase in the size of the market, with the economy possibly getting opened up to international trade and adopting higher levels of technology. The emergence of the theoretical work on regulatory mechanisms that examines their allocative as well as distributive properties has also prepared a rationale for seeking an alternative to public ownership.

There are two broad perspectives, namely, the managerial and the political, that may be used to explain the presence of inefficiency under the public sector. The managerial perspective holds that monitoring is poorer in publicly owned firms and, therefore, the incentives for efficiency are weak (Vickers and Yarrow 1988).[1] The argument here is that monitoring under the public sector is imperfect vis-à-vis the private sector. This is often, though not always, due to the fact that these firms are not traded in the market, unlike private firms. This eliminates the threat of takeover should the firm perform poorly.

The political perspective contends that it is political interference that distorts the objectives and brings in the possibility of soft budget constraints faced by public-sector managers (Shleifer and Vishny 1994). The possibility of soft budgets protects public-sector managers from the threat of bankruptcy. Using simple game theoretic tools it is possible to demonstrate that the political loss in closing a publicly owned company is greater than the cost of using taxpayer money or public debt to bail out a public-sector company. It is argued that privatization would effectively drive a wedge between politicians and managers and would make restructuring more likely by making it too costly for politicians to subsidize firms.

In a seminal paper Sappington and Stiglitz (1987) examine the choice between public and private provision

[1]Vickers and Yarrow have analysed this in one of their books on privatization.

of goods in a context where both modes involve significant delegation of authority. They argue that the main difference between the two modes concerns the transactions costs faced by the government when attempting to intervene in the delegated production activities. It is shown that such intervention is generally less costly under public ownership than private. They then proceed to put forward what they call the fundamental privatization theorem. The theorem specifies the conditions under which privatization is optimal. It focuses on the special concerns introduced by imperfect information about the productive environment. It provides conditions under which all of government's objectives may be attained by an appropriately designed auction of the rights to produce a given product or service. It is shown that the conditions under which privatization is optimal are rather stringent. The authors conclude by emphasizing that neither public nor private provision can fully resolve the difficult incentive problems that arise when considerations of imperfect information result in the delegation of authority.

This leads to the position that it is not ownership, but the degree of competition, that ultimately matters for improving monitoring possibilities, and hence for productive efficiency. Major gains in efficiency can be expected by increasing market contestability via deregulation policies. Competition implies not only free entry into the market, but the freedom, especially on the part of SOEs, to fail. Competition also facilitates performance comparisons that can generally improve trade-offs between incentives and risk when several agents, or managers, facing uncertainties are being monitored.

In addition to the above micro-theoretic issues one needs to also consider the macroeconomic implications of privatization. Privatization may be used as a tool for improving the government's fiscal condition. When carried out through public offerings and mixed sales it can help increase the level of stock market capitalization and the development of the financial sector generally. The literature on the macroeconomic effects of privatization is not quite as rich from the theoretical perspective as that on the microeconomic effects.

Privatization: Empirical Evidence

In recent years a large body of empirical investigations has been carried out to assess the impact of privatization programmes in diverse settings (see, for example, Megginson and Netter 2001). There are several methodological problems with research in this area in addition to the problem of data availability and consistency. Some problems arise due to the nature of the accounting or stock data. One needs to determine the correct measure of operating performance, selecting an appropriate benchmark with which to compare performance, and to decide the appropriate statistical tests to be employed. Many of the studies on performance changes after privatization examine the effects on groups such as workers, but few examine the impact on consumers. Empirical studies on privatization may be broadly divided into three categories, (i) case studies, (ii) cross sectional comparisons of public- and private-sector performance, and (iii) statistical analysis of pre- and post-divestiture performance of enterprises. Both transition and non-transition economies have been studied. The conclusions obtained are diverse. In a study conducted to examine the performance of several British firms that were privatized in the 1980s, it was revealed that there is little evidence of any systematic improvement in performance, and promises made in political speeches remained unfulfilled. This is to be contrasted with the conclusion that Megginson and Netter (2001) come up with: 'Research now supports the proposition that privately owned firms are more efficient and more profitable than otherwise comparable state owned firms.'

In an important study Galal et al. (1994) compare actual post-privatization performance of 12 large firms, mostly airlines and regulated utilities, in the UK, Chile, Malaysia, and Mexico to predict performance if the firms remained SOEs. They capture the net change in welfare, defined as the sum of the changes in welfare of consumers, enterprise profits (including effects on buyers, the government, and other shareholders), the welfare of labour, and welfare of competitors. They document net welfare gains in 11 out of the 12 cases, which equal, on average, 26 per cent of the firms' pre-divestiture sales. In no case were workers worse off, and in three instances they were significantly better-off. They, therefore, conclude that divestiture makes the world a better place.

Yet it is important to apply caution in drawing unqualified support for privatization. Most statistical analyses of pre- and post-privatization performance are marred by the failure to control for the economic environment. These could contribute to improved performance in the post-divestiture period and, therefore, need to be factored out. In many cases where privatization appears to have resulted in efficiency enhancement, one finds that there has actually been contemporaneous deregulation or other competition-enhancing measures.

Kalyuzhnova and Andreff (2003) provide a valuable assessment of the privatization experience in Eastern Europe and Russia now that more than a decade has passed since the end of communism there. There were several experts who had advocated overnight mass privatization programmes in the early 1990s. Many of these measures were simply 'robbery by the old elite and the new oligarchs'. It is very important to consider whether it is desirable to go in for a 'big bang' policy of massive overnight asset transfer, or whether one should not promote an evolutionist and organic transformation of business enterprise. The first purports to ending state ownership in a drastic manner, using giveaway through voucher schemes and tolerating takeover by managers and management buyouts. The latter may be described as a bottom-up development of a new private-sector but no giveaway of state property. The emphasis here is on consolidation and stability so as to make growth sustainable.

Privatization: Indian Experience since 1991

A consideration of the privatization experience in India may well focus on the period after 1991, when the government embarked on a comprehensive process of economic reform and liberalization. At that time the public sector in India accounted for more than one-fifth of the country's GDP. Since a large number of public-sector enterprises (PSEs) regularly showed negative profit margins the government was keen on a programme of privatization, calling it disinvestment instead.

Data from the Department of Disinvestment, Government of India (2006),[2] reveal that the profit margins of manufacturing PSEs are systematically lower than the figures for manufacturing firms in the private sector. This is at least partly due to the fact that the expenditure on power and fuel, wages, and interest as a fraction of net sales are all systematically higher than the corresponding figures for similarly placed private-sector manufacturing firms.

In the interim budget of 1991–2 the government took a policy decision to disinvest up to 20 per cent of the equity in selected PSUs in favour of mutual funds and financial or investment institutions in the public sector. The disinvestment, which was to broad base the equity, was to improve management and enhance the availability of resources for these enterprises. The Rangarajan Committee report on the Disinvestment of Shares in PSEs in April 1993 emphasized the need for substantial disinvestment, and recommended that the percentage of equity to be divested could go up to 49 per cent for industries especially reserved for the public sector. It recommended that in exceptional cases, such as enterprises that had a dominant market share or where separate identity had to be maintained for strategic reasons, the target public ownership level could be kept at 26 per cent, that is, disinvestment could take place to the tune of 74 per cent. In all other cases it recommended 100 per cent divestment of the government stake. Holding of 51 per cent or more equity by the government was recommended only for six scheduled industries: (i) coal and lignite, (ii) mineral oils, (iii) arms, ammunitions, and defence equipment, (iv) atomic energy, (v) radioactive minerals, and (vi) railway transport.

In 1996, the government established a Disinvestment Commission. The purpose of this body was to formulate procedures so that any decision to disinvest would be taken and implemented in a transparent manner. The revenues generated from such disinvestment were to be allocated for education and health and for creating a fund to strengthen PSEs. By August 1999, the Disinvestment Commission made recommendations on 58 PSEs. The recommendations indicated a shift from public offerings to strategic/trade sales, with transfer of management. The Commission also observed that the essence of a long-term disinvestment strategy should be not only to enhance budgetary receipts, but also to minimize budgetary support to unprofitable units while ensuring their long-term viability. By 1998, government was of the view that 'in the generality of cases its shareholding in PSEs will be brought down to 26 per cent'. In PSEs involving strategic considerations, namely, arms and ammunitions, atomic energy, and railway transport, government was to retain majority voting.

By 2000–1 the government's policy regarding privatization and public-sector restructuring comprised the following considerations: restructure and revive potentially viable PSEs, close down PSEs that cannot be revived, bring down government equity in all strategic PSEs to 20 per cent or lower, if necessary, and fully protect the interests of workers. The entire receipt from disinvestments and privatization was to be used for meeting expenditure in social sectors, restructuring of PSEs, and meeting public debt.

The Ministry of Disinvestment was converted into a Department under the Ministry of Finance with effect from 27 May 2004 after the UPA (United Progressive Alliance) government headed by Dr Manmohan Singh as Prime Minister assumed office. From this point on, the disinvestment programme had to be in conformity with the National Common Minimum Programme. All privatizations were from now on to be considered on a transparent and consultative case-by-case basis. It was made explicit that the UPA would retain the existing 'navaratna' companies, which include the BHEL (Bharat Heavy Electricals Limited), in the public sector and that these will be permitted to raise resources from the capital market. The government constituted a 'National

[2]See http://divest.nic.in.

Investment Fund' in January 2005 into which the realization from sale of minority shareholding of the government in profitable PSEs would be channelized. This fund would be maintained outside the Consolidated Fund of India and the income from this Fund would be used for the following purposes: (i) invest in social-sector projects that promote education, healthcare, and employment and (ii) capital investment in selected profitable and revivable PSEs that yield adequate returns, in order to enlarge their capital base to finance expansion or diversification.

The total quantum of receipts on account of privatization during 1991–2005 is Rs 49,214 crore. This is just a little above the half mark figure of the target receipts of Rs 96,800 crore for this period. Even though there is a strong reform lobby that calls for rapid mass privatization in India from time to time it would be well to remember that the experience in Russia and Eastern Europe alluded to in the earlier section is far from reassuring.

After the initial phase of enthusiasm in the 1980s and then the onrush during the 1990s, we are now at a stage where we can take a more measured approach to privatization. There is certainly no clear superiority of private vis-à-vis public ownership from the standpoint of economic theory. More than ownership it would seem that the degree of competition and the regulatory environment are more relevant to productive efficiency. The empirical evidence presents a mixed picture. As the world environment gets more competitive it would be necessary to put the sizeable assets of the PSEs in countries like India to more productive use. Ultimately it is this consideration that should be of relevance rather than the simplistic presumption that the public sector is necessarily inefficient or that privatization is an all-purpose panacea.

PULIN B. NAYAK

References

Galal, Ahmad, Leroy Jones, Pankaj Tandon, and Ingo Vogelsang. 1994. *Welfare Consequences of Selling Public Enterprises*, Oxford, Oxford University Press.

Kalyuzhnova, Yelena and Wladimir Andreff. 2003. *Privatisation and Structural Change in Transition Economies*, Basingstoke, Palgrave Macmillan.

Megginson, William and Jeffry Netter. 2001. 'From State to Market: A Survey of Empirical Studies on Privatization', *Journal of Economic Literature*, 39: 321–89.

Sappington, David and Joseph Stiglitz. 1987. 'Privatization, Information and Incentives', *Journal of Policy Analysis and Management*, 6: 567–82.

Sheshinski, Eytan and Luis Felipe Lopez-Calva. 2003. 'Privatization and Its Benefits: Theory, Evidence, and Challenges', in K. Basu, P. Nayak, and R. Ray (eds), *Markets and Governments*, New Delhi, Oxford University Press.

Shleifer, Andrei and Robert Vishny. 1994. 'Politicians and Firms', *The Quarterly Journal of Economics*, 109(4): 995–1025.

Vickers, John and George Yarrow. 1988. *Privatization: An Economic Analysis*, Cambridge, MIT Press.

Public Distribution System

The public distribution system (PDS) refers to a network of retail outlets (popularly known as 'ration shops') through which the government sells grain (principally, rice and wheat) and kerosene. The scope of this entry is restricted to the public distribution system for grain. Grain sales occur at a fixed price called the 'issue' price that is typically lower than the market price. Two conditions govern the sale of subsidized grain. First, the buyer of grain must possess a 'ration card'. Second, grain purchases are subject to a quota. PDS is supported by a procurement operation that procures and funnels supplies to the public distribution system. Through the Food Corporation of India (FCI), the government procures grain at the 'procurement' price and then stores and transports it to various consuming locations.

Till the late 1960s, the principal policy question was how food could be procured cheaply. Towards this end, the government imposed mandatory levies on rice mills, instituted zoning regulations on movement of grain from surplus to deficit areas (so that prices were lower in the surplus zones), prohibited external trade except on the government account, and severely curtailed large trading operations through 'anti hoarding' controls on stocks.

The food policy context changed in the 1970s with the technological breakthroughs of the Green Revolution. Earlier concerns about movements in intersectoral terms of trade adverse to industry faded away. With large food surpluses, declining real prices of food grains, and greater political clout of farmers, the emphasis of food distribution shifted to support of farmgate prices, stabilization, and subsidy for lower-income groups. Food subsidy as a major item of government expenditure made its appearance around this time. Over time, the principal policy issue became finding acceptable ways to cap the food subsidy. In this background, the idea that subsidies ought to be targeted to the poor gained support in the late 1990s.

With rapid economic growth, the policy environment shifted in the late 2000s. There is concern that the income gains from growth have not been shared evenly. Ensuring that the poorest groups benefit from growth will require many things; one of them is using the expanding resources of the state to directly help the poor with basic goods and services, such as food, education, and health. The United Progressive Alliance (UPA) that came to power in 2009 promised a National Food Security Act that would create legal entitlements to subsidized food for the poor. The scope and form of such an Act is the subject of current debate.

Issues in Intervention

In principle, food market interventions are supposed to enhance the efficiency of food markets as well as improve the equity of food market outcomes. The efficiency effect arises from price stabilization. As private storage of food grains is typically unprofitable across years, markets do not supply price stabilization even though it is socially desirable, as poor risk-averse food consumers cannot obtain credit or insurance against crop failures. The reduction in risk is beneficial for producers as well. Even with stabilization, the market outcome involves unacceptably low food consumption for the poor. The equity objective of food market intervention is to augment the food consumption of such target groups by offering subsidies.

Both these goals can be achieved by procurement, storage, and distribution. To meet the equity goal, the government offers limited quantities of food to poor consumers at subsidized prices. Suppose this requires an annual distribution of 15 million tonnes of grain. The supply of this grain is secured by procurement. However, annual procurement could vary depending on the size of the harvest and available stocks. In times of abundant supplies, the government will wish to procure more than 15 million tonnes (and build stocks) while the procurement target would be lower than the distribution target (drawing down stocks) in times of a shortfall. Such a scheme could smooth out the inter-temporal variability in crop harvests with the exception of very unusual circumstances, such as a sequence of record harvests or a series of disastrous crop failures.

In practice, food market interventions rarely approximate the ideal. The goal of stabilization is to stabilize prices around their mean. However, technological progress and Engel's law (that demand for food grows slower than income) typically tend to decrease the relative price of food. As a result, interventions that try to stabilize with reference to historical supply levels tend to carry too much stock. A greater difficulty is that price stabilization of food crops leads producers to allocate resources away from non-food crops to food crops. Such a supply response also calls for adjusting interventions to higher supply levels. However, as market interventions develop political interests, price stabilization is eroded by the politics of supporting producer incomes.

On the distribution side, the issue is that while the poor can be counted (by means of surveys), it is not easy to identify them. The difficulty is that the criteria to identify the poor cannot be those that can be claimed or mimicked by the non-poor. Targeting schemes usually involve a trade-off between errors of exclusion (when some members of the target group are excluded from subsidies because of stringent targeting criteria) and errors of inclusion (when some members of non-target groups receive subsidies because of minimal targeting criteria). Subsidies with universal access (as was the case with the PDS prior to 1997) minimize exclusion errors but maximize inclusion errors.

The Food Subsidy

The food subsidy arises from government procurement and distribution of two commodities: wheat and rice. Significantly, coarse cereals (bajra and jowar) do not receive subsidies even though in some states they are major components of food budgets of poor households. In the past, subsidies have been offered on other commodities, such as edible oils and most notably sugar. These are now unimportant. The food subsidy consists of two components. The first component is the distribution subsidy that comes about from the fact that the difference between the issue price (at which the government sells) and the procurement price is not enough to cover the costs of distribution. The second component is the cost of carrying buffer stocks.

In the 1970s, the food subsidy averaged about 0.45 per cent of GDP. It rose to 0.54 per cent in the 1980s and was at about the same level (0.52 per cent) in the 1990s. In the 2000s (up to 2007–8), the food subsidy averaged 0.8 per cent of GDP and about 7.5 per cent of tax revenues of the central government. This indicates the pressure of the food subsidy on central government finances, as it is an expenditure of the central government alone.

The division of the food subsidy into the distribution and buffer stock subsidy varies from year to year. However, it is not uncommon for the buffer stock subsidy to exceed the distribution subsidy. Indeed, this was the typical pattern in the late 1990s. This happens whenever the government carries large stocks.

Stabilization

In an economy where the government stabilizes annual supplies, procurement and public distribution sales should balance over the span of a crop cycle (typically about 5–6 years). This was the case over the two decades between 1972–3 and 1991–2. However, since 1992–3, procurement has been consistently larger than public distribution sales and the government has had to cope with higher than desired grain stocks. The late 1990s and the late 2000s are two periods when government stocks exceeded 50 million tonnes.

The failure of stabilization and the accumulation of stocks are commonly attributed to the political clout of the farm lobby. Grain surpluses are regionally concentrated—in Punjab, Haryana, Uttar Pradesh, and to a lesser extent in Andhra Pradesh. It is argued that in the 1990s these states were able to exercise greater influence over the procurement prices determined by the central government because of the formation of coalition governments at the Centre. While political interests have undoubtedly developed around the government's market intervention, there are other factors as well.

Once public stocks get large it can be hard to get back to sustainable levels because of price expectations. For a grain seller, the opportunity cost of sale to the government is the market price of grain but at a later point in time (as the procurement price is fixed at the same level throughout the year). Price expectations are, in turn, dependent on future government actions. When government stocks are large, it is natural to expect future sales from these stocks (open market sale is one of the ways by which the government brings down stocks from unwanted levels) which reduce private storage. Indeed, these stocks can be so large that private storage might be negligible, as happened in the wheat market in 2001. At that time, the wheat stocks with the government were equivalent to the annual market supplies. Grain stocks were brought down by a combination of special measures, including subsidized exports, expanded welfare programmes, and open market sales, as well as the fortuitous circumstance of a drought in 2002–3.

Targeted PDS

Prior to 1997, entitlement to the PDS was not contingent on household characteristics. The most significant policy initiative in reforming food policy was the introduction of the targeted PDS (TPDS) in 1997. Subsidies depend on whether the household is classified as above poverty line (APL), below poverty line (BPL), or poorest of the poor (POP) identified by the Antayodaya Anna Yojana programme.

Presently, all households are entitled to a monthly quota of 35 kg of rice or wheat per month. In principle, the prices of subsidized grain are supposed to be fixed with reference to the government's 'economic cost', that is, the cost incurred by government agencies in procuring, storing, transporting, and distributing grain. BPL households are supposed to receive 50 per cent subsidy (that is, 50 per cent of the economic cost) while APL households are not supposed to be eligible for any subsidy. The prices for POP households are fixed below that of BPL households and not with reference to economic cost.

In practice, the subsidized prices fixed in 2002 have not been revised despite increases in economic cost. As a result even APL households received a subsidy in excess of 50 per cent of economic cost in 2008–9. The qualification to this is that the central government does not guarantee full grain supply to state governments for their APL requirements. The actual allocation depends on past purchases and ad hoc considerations. As a result, the grain quota for BPL households ranges between 10 and 35 kg per month across different states. The total number of households within a state that are eligible to be classified as BPL is made through an expenditure sample survey administered by the central government.

The list of BPL beneficiaries is prepared through a separate BPL census. In the latest census of 2002, households received scores based on 13 criteria. BPL households were identified as those which fell below a cut-off score (which was decided by the respective state governments). If the total identified BPL households exceeds that which is estimated by the central government, the subsidy on the excess households has to be borne by the state government.

Failure of Targeting

The National Sample Survey (NSS) of consumption expenditures of households in 2004–5 showed that only 40 per cent of rural poor households and 27 per cent of the urban poor households (that is, households with expenditures less than the official poverty line) possessed either a BPL or a POP entitlement. This is the exclusion error of targeting. The remaining poor households either had no entitlement or an APL entitlement.

The inclusion error of targeting is the proportion of BPL and POP beneficiaries that are non-poor—68 per cent in rural areas and 51 per cent in urban areas. High inclusion errors are to be expected. First, since there are benefits from being categorized as BPL or POP, the process of identification of poor is vulnerable to manipulation and capture by non-poor groups. Second, it is hard in practice to distinguish households who are just above the poverty line from those just below it. India's official poverty line measures bare subsistence and so households above this threshold may also exhibit signs of income stress. Indeed, 70 per cent of BPL and POP beneficiaries in rural areas and 78 per cent in urban areas are households with expenditures less than 1.5 times the poverty line.

Efficiency of the Public Distribution System

Among the poor that have BPL or POP entitlement, only 61 per cent use PDS. This suggests that many poor households do not find PDS convenient. Case studies have thrown up a variety of reasons, such as the limited liquidity of poor households (as ration entitlements can be accessed only once every fortnight rather than continuously), uncertain ration supplies, inferior quality of PDS grain, irregular hours of PDS shops, and their inconvenient location as the reasons. Ramaswami and Balakrishnan (2002) show that consumers perceive PDS grain to be of lower quality even though the government does not set out to procure such grain. This is a deadweight loss that occurs due to inefficiencies in the government marketing chain.

PDS has also been criticized for illegal diversions and for excess costs of state agencies. Illegal diversions happen as agents in the government marketing chain sell the subsidized grain in the open market and profit from the difference between the market price and the subsidy price. Excess costs occur when the cost of procuring and distributing grain is higher for state agencies than for the private sector. Jha and Ramaswami (2010) show that in 2004–5, 55 per cent of the subsidized grain was illegally diverted. They also show that only 29 per cent of the total food subsidy expenditures by the government reached the households. The remaining 71 per cent was absorbed by excess costs (28 per cent) and illegal diversions (43 per cent).

Future Directions of Food Policy

The coalition of political parties, the United Progressive Alliance (UPA), that came to power in 2009 is committed to a food security safety net. It is proposed that the poor have legal entitlements to subsidized grain. The debate is about the content of this legislation. Essentially, there are two issues. The first issue is about the scale of the food subsidy programme. Should it continue as a targeted programme or should it have universal access? The second issue is about the form of the subsidy programme. Should the subsidy programme be modelled on the public distribution system or are there alternative forms of delivery?

The massive exclusion errors of PDS targeting question the continuance of targeted programmes. Till a reliable way of identifying the poor is found, near-universal coverage will be necessary to avoid exclusion errors.

The staggering inefficiency of PDS means that alternatives to it will have to be tried. Chhattisgarh has claimed significant reduction in corruption by computerizing the supply chain from paddy procurement to the distribution of rice and making public the movement of grain from warehouses to retail outlets. It is suggested that this has improved transparency and governance.

Food coupons or food stamps are an alternative way to deliver food subsidies. Smart card technologies can also be employed for this purpose. Under such systems, the food subsidy is directly transferred to the beneficiaries. Households use this transfer to buy grain from designated retail outlets. Incentives for illegal diversions are eliminated because the dual price (market and subsidized price) system is abolished. Excess costs are reduced because of greater competition.

A food coupon alternative has other advantages as well. Because of limited volumes, the viability of PDS retailers is an endemic issue. This is not a problem with the food coupon system because it eliminates the dual marketing system (of private and government). Second, a food coupon system could easily accommodate additional food staples without the need for physical and institutional infrastructure (procurement and distribution) that is specially set up for that purpose. In parts of India, the poor consume 'inferior' coarse grains, such as sorghum and pearl millet, which are not subsidized by the current regime. Food coupons could allow consumers to spend their budget on their preferred commodities and would, therefore, be less distortionary in consumption. Third, there would be greater economic access as consumers would be able to use these coupons at more convenient retail outlets. Poor consumers will be able to readily use food coupons without worrying about timing their purchases with wage payments. While there are potential issues of fraud in food coupons as well in terms of counterfeiting and improper use, it seems far easier to track and audit numerically coded coupons than to do so for physical stocks of grain. Governments sometimes balk at the costs of investing in technologies such as smart cards. The payoffs must, however, be seen in relation to the resources lost in diversions and excess costs.

The future of effective food subsidy programmes is unlikely to lie in a centralized PDS. A regionally differentiated safety net of food subsidies (but financed primarily by central government funds) is likely to offer more opportunities for designing and delivering subsidies appropriate to local consumption patterns and capabilities.

BHARAT RAMASWAMI

References

Jha, Shikha and Bharat Ramaswami. 2010. 'How Can Food Subsidies Work Better? Answers from India and the Philippines', ADB Economics Working Paper Series, No. 221.

Ramaswami, Bharat and Pulapre Balakrishnan. 2002. 'Food Prices and the Efficiency of Public Intervention: The Case of the Public Distribution System in India', *Food Policy*, 27: 419–36.

Public Goods

For a country that calls itself both socialist and democratic, India has historically been remarkably comfortable with dramatic inequalities in access to public goods. In 1991, after, as discussed later, considerable narrowing of the gaps, rural populations in the southern state of Kerala had more than 10 times as many hospital beds per head as those in the eastern states of Orissa and Assam. The fraction of people in rural Orissa with access to medical facilities in their village in 1981 was less than 11 per cent compared to 96 per cent in Kerala. In 1991, 93 per cent of villages in Kerala had a middle school but the corresponding figure in Orissa and Assam was less than 25 per cent, and in Uttar Pradesh, the largest northern state, it was less than 15 per cent. Disparities within most of these states are equally striking: according to the 1991 Census, less than 7 per cent of the villages in Vishakhapatnam district in Andhra Pradesh had middle schools and just over 46 per cent had some educational facility, as against 55 per cent and 100 per cent in Guntur. In the district of Rangareddy, in the same state, only 6 per cent of villages had primary health sub-centres as against almost 40 per cent in Anantapur. Less than 1 per cent of villages in Vishakhapatnam had tapped water as compared to 59 per cent in West Godavari.

In part this reflects our colonial legacy: in British India, it was almost a rule that public goods were only to be built where there was some commercial benefit to be had. This, not surprisingly, led to almost complete neglect of most villages.

Village India also did not have much of a place in the Nehruvian vision of development through heavy industry. Moreover, the Gandhians in the Congress were uncomfortable with bringing change too rapidly to rural India. As a result, villages were, for the most part, left to their own devices.

The obvious result of this was that by the end of the 1960s the villages that had relatively decent access to public goods tended to be either places that could afford to fund them out of their own resources or those that had enough political clout to extract them from a recalcitrant state.

This is clearly borne out by data from the 1971 Census on the correlates of access to public goods (Banerjee and Somanathan 2006). We use data on 15 of the facilities that are classified as public goods in the census, which include various types of health and education facilities, water sources, and other types of infrastructure such as electricity, post offices, and paved roads. Since the census does not distinguish between private and community government-owned facilities, it is not clear that all of these deserve to be called *public* goods. Our best guess is that until the 1990s there were very few private education facilities in rural areas, while the power, transportation, and communication infrastructure continues to be in public hands. We are on weaker ground when we talk about hospitals and water tanks, and, especially, wells and dispensaries. The measure of access we use is the fraction of villages in a parliamentary constituency that have the particular public good.

We obviously need to be careful about possible sources of spurious correlation. We, therefore, only compare constituencies within the same state and include a range of geographical controls (rainfall, climate, whether on the coast, whether mountainous, sandy, or rocky, and so on) as well as controls for population density (it is easier to serve a denser population).

Our regression results are depressingly consistent with the conventional wisdom about who has power and influence in rural India. Among the 15 goods for which we have 1971 data, scheduled tribe-dominated areas have significantly less of ten (and more of none) while scheduled castes have less of eight and more of two. As is well known, these are the groups that are at the bottom of the Hindu caste hierarchy. We also see that the largest religious minority, the Muslims, have less of seven public goods and more of none. And, strikingly, areas dominated by Brahmins, the group that is at least nominally at the top of the caste hierarchy, have more of all the goods we would expect them to especially value given their traditional role as the repositories of written knowledge—all kinds of schools and post offices.

We also see some evidence that could be interpreted to mean that social capital matters. Areas where the population is more fragmented along caste and religious lines do worse, raising the possibility that these areas are particularly ineffective in asserting their collective claim to public goods. On the other hand, places with more land inequality do better, consistent with Mancur Olson's view that the presence of an elite with a strong private stake helps alleviate collective action problems.

Unfortunately, few of these results survive when we compare what happened to access to public goods in places where the values of explanatory variables (say, share of scheduled castes) went up between 1971 and 1991, with places where they did not change or went down. We find, for example, that there is no systematic relation between the improvement in access to public goods and changes in either land inequality or socio-religious fragmentation. The most interesting contrast between the two sets of results is what we find for scheduled castes. Our results suggest that areas where scheduled caste concentration went up did better in terms of improvement in access than other areas. We do not find the same pattern when we look at scheduled tribe areas. Indeed, the evidence suggests that they may have fallen behind. There is no clear pattern with respect to Muslim areas.

What should we make of the contrast between these two sets of results? One possible interpretation is that the cross-sectional results are simply wrong. There could easily have been other things that are different about these constituencies we were comparing that were driving our results and, therefore, we only get the right answers when we compare the same area over time. If this were the only explanation, it would suggest that historical/structural factors (like fragmentation and inequality) are perhaps much less important in determining access to public goods than we might have thought, except in some extreme cases such as that of scheduled tribes.

This may, however, be going too far. After all, both the Gini coefficient and the measures of fragmentation (especially given that they are measured at the parliamentary constituency level, which is not necessarily the domain within which all political competition takes place) are just proxies for the specific factors whose influence we are trying to capture. In addition, they change quite slowly, so it is not unlikely that the changes in these variables that we put into our regressions may be dominated by measurement error (the fact that what we measure only approximately captures what we really want). Therefore, it may not be surprising that they do not do very much in the regressions.

Indeed, there is some quite robust evidence that specific historical/structural factors do make a big difference. In Banerjee and Iyer (2005), we make the case that a key factor in understanding present-day rural India is the land tenure system it was assigned under British rule. Districts where an intermediary (usually called a zamindar) collected the land taxes do systematically worse than districts where the peasant directly paid the colonial state. Since the choice of the system was, to a significant extent, based on date of conquest in a quite specific and non-linear way, it is possible to make a strong case that what we are capturing is really the effect of the choice of the particular system and not something else about the district. While these systems were formally abolished in the 1950s (indeed, there is no land tax in India today) our results suggest that villages in non-landlord districts in 1981 were 15 per cent more likely to have a primary school, 30 per cent more likely to have a middle or high school, and 50 per cent more likely to have a primary health centre. While the mechanism underlying these effects is less easy to pin down exactly, our evaluation is that the history of the zamindari system (particularly the many instances of abuse of power by zamindars) created a political climate of class-based resentments, which continues to make these districts ineffective in their collective quest for public goods.

Iyer (2005) makes the case that another important historical influence on access to public goods is whether the district was under direct British rule or whether it was part of a princely state. She argues that the enforcement of the so-called Doctrine of Lapse under Lord Dalhousie, whereby the British annexed princely states where the king had died without having a male child, resulted in some districts being annexed for no reason other than the fact that the king happened to have died without an appropriate heir at an inconvenient time. When districts that got annexed in this way are compared to otherwise similar districts, they fare worse in terms of public goods, at least relative to British non-landlord districts. She argues that this might reflect the fact that the local elites in the princely states were much more directly concerned about public goods within their state while the elites elsewhere in British India were much more connected to the metropolitan cities of Calcutta, Mumbai, and so on.

This is not to say that access to public goods is entirely determined by historical/structural factors. By far the best predictor of change in access to public goods between 1971 and 1991 turns out to be the 1971 level of access. Places that had worse access in 1971 catch up quite rapidly over the intervening period. This would not be surprising if access to these goods was close to complete in most places at the start of the period—in fact, it would be mechanical. This was, however, very far from true. Half of the goods we consider were available in less than 5 per cent of Indian villages in 1971 and in less than 10 per cent of villages in 1991.

This strong tendency towards convergence in the 1970s and 1980s is entirely consistent with political agendas of that period. Under Indira Gandhi's 'Garibi Hatao' (eradicate poverty) programme, first put forward during her election campaign in 1971, the Indian state, for the first time, made an explicit pledge to provide public goods to everyone; other, even broader commitments were made by subsequent governments. These results suggest that these commitments, once made, were relatively binding. The government also made additional specific commitments towards the scheduled castes, which echoes the finding reported here earlier, that scheduled caste-dominated areas catch up during this period, over and above the broader tendency towards convergence.

The natural reading of these results is that the structures of society are not entirely binding. They do permit the state and other individual actors to have a considerable degree of autonomy. Once there is governmental commitment towards delivering public goods, for example, the public goods do get built, even where the population is politically unable to claim them.

One should, however, be careful not to read this finding too optimistically. Building public goods and appointing people to work there is relatively easy. Indeed, bureaucrats may have a strong private stake in both. Getting the most out of these public facilities, by making sure that teachers teach and health workers show up to work, is harder. According to Chaudhury et al. (2006), 24 per cent of teachers and 40 per cent of health providers in government facilities are absent on any given day. Moreover, even when the teachers are present they are often not teaching. This problem is significantly worse in landlord areas (Pandey 2004). Problems may be even worse in other areas for items such as power supply, with many rural areas only getting supply once in two days.

The issue here is precisely that the natural tendency of the bureaucracy is not to take on these issues, in part because it requires them to confront other bureaucrats. While more popular control has been offered as the solution to these problems of agency, the evidence so far is, at best, mixed (Banerjee and Duflo 2006). In my opinion, this is one of the greatest challenges facing India as a nation today.

ABHIJIT V. BANERJEE

References

Banerjee, Abhijit and Esther Duflo. 2006. 'Addressing Absence', *Journal of Economic Perspectives*, 20(1): 117–32.

Banerjee, Abhijit and Lakshmi Iyer. 2005. 'History, Institutions and Economic Performance: The Legacy of Colonial Land Tenure Systems in India', *American Economic Review*, 95(4): 1190–213.

Banerjee, Abhijit and Rohini Somanathan. 2006. 'The Political Economy of Public Goods: Some Evidence from India', *Journal of Development Economics*, 82(2): 287–314.

Chaudhury, Nazmul, Jeffrey Hammer, Michael Kremer, Karthik Muralidharan, and F. Halsey Rogers. 2006. 'Missing in Action: Teacher and Health Worker Absence in Developing Countries,' *Journal of Economic Perspectives*, 20(1): 91–116.

Iyer, Lakshmi. 2005. 'The Long-term Impact of Colonial Rule: Evidence from India', Harvard Business School Working Paper, No. 05–041.

Pandey, Priyanka. 2004. 'Are Institutions Malleable? Effects of History, Mandated Representation and Democratization on Public Schools in North India', mimeo, World Bank.

Public Health

What is Public Health, and Why Invest in It?

Public health services are conceptually distinct from medical services. Reducing a population's *exposure* to disease is their key goal—for example, through assuring food safety and other health regulations; vector control; monitoring waste disposal and water systems; and health education to improve personal health behaviours and build citizen demand for better public health outcomes. Thus they involve such disparate activities as improving slaughterhouse hygiene and cattle-keeping practices, cleaning irrigation canals to discourage vector breeding, and applying public health regulations.

Public health services produce 'public goods' of incalculable benefit for facilitating economic growth and poverty reduction. Consider, for example, the long-term growth possibilities generated by draining the malarial swamps of Washington DC. And conversely, consider the global economic costs imposed by the avian flu and SARS (severe acute respiratory syndrome) epidemics, emanating from poor poultry-keeping and health practices in a few Chinese localities. In India, the 1994 plague epidemic following poor municipal sanitation in Surat is estimated by the World Health Organization (WHO 2000) to have resulted in losses totalling up to $2 billion.

Poor public health conditions take economic toll in various ways, including reduced attraction for investors and tourists; continued expenditures on combating diseases which should have become history; and labour productivity losses. The poor pay a high price in debility, reduced earning capacity, and death. The rich suffer little mortality from communicable diseases, but nevertheless suffer repeated episodes of morbidity which are reflected in high rates of stunting amongst their children.

It has long been accepted that the most effective approaches to improving population health are those that prevent rather than treat disease. Moreover, they account for a small fraction of the total health budget in most countries. But in India, public policies and programmes have focused largely on the provision of curative care and personal prophylactic interventions such as immunization, while public health activities have been relatively neglected. This helps explain why India's health indicators are so much poorer than those of East Asia and much of the rest of the world. Since communicable diseases remain the primary sources of ill-health in India, this discussion will focus on them.

The Evolution of Public Health Services in the Developed World

In developed countries, the need for effective public health services was triggered partly by military concerns, since army casualties from disease were far higher than from battle. Elites also had a stake in disease control because cure was uncertain until antibiotics began to be mass produced in the mid-20th century. Besides, business interests were at stake, as illustrated by the massive business losses following a cholera epidemic in Hamburg in 1892.

In the last decades of the 19th century, scientists began to identify germs and learn how they cause disease. This led to the 'sanitary movement', which involved radical changes in citizens' health behaviours and private lives, including forgoing keeping livestock in urban areas. Protests arose, ranging from mass protests to the case of the incensed butcher chasing a sanitary inspector down a Chicago street with a knife. The changes had to be implemented not only rigorously (sometimes coercively), but with much attention to persuading citizens as to how better sanitation improved their well-being.

Much effort was devoted to building the organizational and technical infrastructure of public health services and public health engineering. Japan studied European public health services and moved early to emulating them as part of its preparation for becoming a world power, and applied similar measures in its colonies in Korea and Taiwan.

By the mid-20th century, the institutions and procedures for preventing exposure to communicable diseases had become well established in the developed world. They had brought about rapid declines in mortality and morbidity. Non-communicable diseases became the major source of ill-health, and the scope of public health services was broadened to control these through lifestyle changes and checking environmental pollution. Nevertheless, public health services continue to be highly successful at communicable disease control, and are overhauled periodically in response to changing circumstances.

Public Health Services in Colonial India

During the colonial period, public health measures were focused largely on protecting British civilians and army cantonments. There is much debate about whether this resulted from parsimoniousness where Indian well-being was concerned, or fear of triggering hostility by imposing alien practices. In any event, a series of measures ensured that the British lived in residentially segregated areas with good environmental sanitation. Municipal areas were privileged with machinery to assure good sanitary conditions, including the management of water, solid waste, and liquid waste. For towns and rural areas, the services were focused largely on early detection and control of outbreaks of contagious diseases with high fatality rates—such as cholera and the plague—before they could spread and even menace the more privileged populations.

Yet, even for these limited purposes, the colonial authorities built impressive capacity for delivering public health services:

- Institutions for public health training and research, which ranked amongst the best in the world—most notably the All-India School of Public Health and Hygiene and the Calcutta School of Tropical Medicine. These conducted basic research such as discovering how malaria is transmitted; developed and tested vaccines; and provided technical leadership and support as well as training for the public health authorities.
- Public health legislation along lines then current in Europe.
- Sanitary Departments at national and provincial levels for civilian public health services, while military hygiene was under military medical officers. They were answerable directly to the government, and administratively separate from the Indian Medical Service (IMS) which provided medical services.
- Policymaking and planning for public health services, done systematically to address all major threats to public health. The Sanitary Departments published annual reports with information on disease patterns and associated factors such as seasonal conditions and population movements, and analysed this information to extrapolate the potential for outbreaks for which

advance planning might be necessary. Periodic Sanitary Conferences were convened to discuss and refine overall policy thrusts and coordinate policies and implementation between provinces.

The Sanitary Departments were tasked with ascertaining local sanitary conditions and improving them; vital registration; monitoring disease trends; providing technical advice on disease control; and carrying out vaccination programmes. They were expected to detect outbreaks early, trace them to their source, and extinguish them quickly. Their medical staff was on average better qualified and better paid, and had faster promotion avenues than the IMS staff. Municipal governments hired their own public health staff, consisting of medical doctors, and 'a small army' of supervisors and sanitary inspectors to enforce sanitary regulations. Municipal planning was designed to avert public health threats, for example, an elaborate system of drainage in and around the city of Calcutta reduced the risk of malaria.

The spare but systematic colonial approach to public health service provision is reflected in its successes and failures. During the first half of the 20th century, the mortality spikes from epidemics were sharply reduced. By the end of the colonial era, mortality from diseases such as cholera and the plague had fallen sharply, but diseases such as malaria and gastroenteric infections continued to take a heavy toll. Independent India's First Five Year Plan notes that only 3 per cent of households in India had toilets, and that much of the population lacked basic water, drainage, and waste disposal services.

Public Health in Independent India

Little remains of the colonial public health arrangements, beside an impressive capacity to control outbreaks once they have occurred. The capacity to *prevent* outbreaks has atrophied. By 1950, much had changed both globally and in India, which led to this atrophy.

- Techniques for mass production of antibiotics were refined during the 1940s. This made it possible for local elites to protect themselves from dying of communicable diseases, without having to maintain rigorous environmental hygiene to prevent exposure to disease for rich and poor alike. The developed world also became better able to protect itself from the prospect of epidemics spreading from the developing world, and the focus of medical research shifted away from finding new technologies for communicable disease control—except when threatened by newly emergent diseases against which they have no protection, such as avian flu.
- The public health successes achieved in the developed world meant that by the 1940s their main causes of death shifted from communicable to non-communicable diseases such as cardiovascular diseases and cancer. At the same time, advances in medical technology offered the promise of managing these diseases through clinical and surgical interventions. The glamour and status earlier accorded to public health authorities were now accorded to medical doctors. The intellectual cutting edge shifted from improving public health systems to improving curative technologies and methods of healthcare financing.
- Multilateral and other donor agencies have encouraged creation of separate institutional structures and programmes for controlling specific communicable diseases, thereby facilitating the clear identification of project inputs and outcomes but discouraging the building of health systems that seek to use resources as they are needed to improve public health outcomes.
- The spread of democratic institutions also affected public health services, because electorates typically prefer public funds to be used to provide private goods (such as medical care), rather than public goods (such as sanitary measures to protect the health of the population as a whole). Selling a public health success electorally requires creativity, since the successes are by nature negative ('no cases of typhoid last year' does not hit the headlines, while advances in surgical techniques is big news). In the developed world, this means that public health authorities have to fight to ensure adequate funding, while in the developing world it can lead to serious neglect of public health services. It is notable that the non-democratic regimes of East Asia were the most successful in the developing world in improving health outcomes, by focusing their scarce resources on public health measures rather than on providing advanced medical care.
- Elite capture also plays a role. In India, more than in most developing countries, public funds for health and education have been funnelled towards tertiary rather than primary levels. Substantial proportions of the health budgets have been spent on expanding subsidized medical training, public-sector employment for medical graduates, and high-end tertiary medical services—all of which largely benefit the middle classes and detract from the provision of public health services.

Several policy thrusts of the newly independent India also detracted from public health service provision. To begin with, the overarching policy vision emphasized developing heavy industry rather than health and education. Public health services were merged with the medical services in the 1950s. Qualifications in specialty curative skills became far better rewarded than public health qualifications, and attracted the best talent. Gradually senior positions were filled by people with no training or experience in public health, poorly equipped and poorly motivated to manage public health activities. The demand for as well as supply of public health training atrophied. The atrophy was further sped by the fact that it is politically much easier to respond to budget constraints by cutting (the relatively invisible) public health positions and activities, while expanding the curative services for which there is strong electoral demand.

Moreover, an inconsistency in constitutional provisions starved public health systems of funds. Public health services were designated as the responsibility of the state governments, except for issues such as port quarantine and provisions relating to the spread of diseases between states. At the same time, the constitutional fiscal provisions require states to hand over the bulk of their tax revenues to the central government. The central health authorities leverage their funds by requiring states to provide co-financing for many of their programmes. This leaves little fiscal room for states to operate programmes for which there is little support from the central government, such as assuring environmental sanitation and other core functions of a public health system.

The resulting atrophy of public health services is manifested in many ways, including the following.

(i) *Neglect of public health regulations and their implementation*: Public Health Acts, which constitute the legislative framework for public health service provision, have not been updated and rationalized since the colonial era. For example, five decades after Karnataka state was created out of several contiguous kingdoms and provinces, it has not developed a unified and updated Public Health Act—those for each constituent part from the colonial era are still on the books. In Tamil Nadu, the Madras Presidency's Public Health Act of 1939 was still in place in 1999. The central government developed a Model Public Health Act in 1950 and revised it in 1987, but did not influence the states to adopt it. As in the colonial period, major municipal areas continue to be privileged, in that they still have public health regulations in place, and some staff and facilities for implementing them. These are much less in evidence in small towns, and even less in rural areas.

The Prevention of Food Adulteration Act is one of the few pieces of public health legislation that is still widely known to be in force. However, the Act has several serious deficiencies that prevent it from effectively ensuring food safety, not the least the fact that it focuses almost exclusively on food adulteration. In a large volume of detailed regulation, only a few paragraphs pertain to food hygiene. Besides, the Act is geared more towards punishing offenders than towards helping businesses understand and comply with the regulations. Given the very limited funds available to inspectors for purchasing food samples for testing, and the slow disposal of court cases, it is apparent to food sellers that the law is short on credibility. Food inspectors are also a shrinking category of staff, as they are of low priority for cash-strapped states.

(ii) *Diversion of funds from public health services*: The distortionary implications of the fiscal and planning regime are illustrated by the effects of the family planning programme. In the mid-1960s, the Indian government embarked on a massive effort to reduce population growth in the country, following some years of food shortages and census results showing that population growth rates had accelerated sharply. To deliver sterilization and other contraceptive services, the network of public clinics was rapidly expanded. The central government is generous in supporting the family planning programme, for example, by covering the salaries of female outreach staff. The proportion of the central government health budget spent on this programme has risen sharply, at the expense of other health programmes. However, the states have to pay for maintaining the clinics and the salaries of doctors and other staff.

This heavy financial burden for the states has led to a progressive strangulation of funds for what ought to be routine public health services, to the point where these are often vestigial at best. For example, in West Bengal, the posts of Sanitary Inspectors are largely vacant. Across the country, there is a trend for the posts of male health workers also to be vacant, since their salaries have to be met by the state governments.

Unfocused labour policies add to the problems, with the emphasis often more strongly on protecting labour than on assuring an appropriately qualified workforce. For example, in West Bengal, malaria workers' job security was assured by absorbing them into the cadre of male health workers. Thus many of the precious slots left in this important but underfinanced and dying cadre of public health staff are occupied by people who lack the required qualifications. Moreover, the staff suffers from the atrophying of public health training. For example, the District Sanitary Inspector of a large district said that in 33 years of service he had received almost no training in public health.

(iii) *Organizational changes inimical to maintaining public health*: Other problems arise from making health primarily a state responsibility, while building a 'command and control' framework of centralized planning backed by fiscal dependence of the states on the Centre. The central government is the key actor in designing health policies and programmes, partly because state budgets are highly constrained as already described. However, the central government focuses on planning specific programmes, such as malaria eradication or family planning. This means that the bulk of the funds allocated by the central Health Ministry to the states is tied to specific programmes and categories of expenditure within those programmes, and states are not free to reallocate the funds to issues that may be of higher local priority.

A related problem is that there is very limited scope for making overall reviews of public health policies, fine-tuning their implementation, and rationalizing the use of resources, which had been done in the colonial era through forums such as the Sanitary Conferences. The demise of a public health system means that there is also inadequate intersectoral coordination, which further wastes resources. For example, the health department has limited recourse if the irrigation department generates malaria by leaving a canal half-finished and waterlogged, but once an epidemic breaks out it will be called in to step up clinical services to handle the problem. A multiplicity of agencies is able to work on parallel tracks or even at cross-purposes. These trends are further encouraged by donors, as discussed earlier.

Public health planning and implementation have become ad hoc in ways deeply inimical to effective functioning. For example, it quickly became the norm for health programmes to be conducted on a 'campaign' basis. This means, in practice, that when a specific issue enjoys high priority a lot of resources are diverted towards it, and the obverse. However, public health cannot be sustained on a 'campaign' basis. Much can be achieved in a campaign, but the benefits can be short-lived without continuing arrangements for identifying and responding to any remaining or imported threats. For example, there are a few cases of many communicable diseases every year in the US, but through constant vigilance they are confined and stamped out.

The history of public health since 1950 in India illustrates that the organization of services is conducive to successful campaigns followed by unsuccessful 'maintenance' phases of disease control programmes. For one thing, with the exception of female health workers (who are earmarked for family planning service delivery), other health personnel are considered to be 'multipurpose'. In principle this is a good idea, but in practice it means that they are allocated to whatever is deemed a priority at the time and discouraged from other activities such as maintaining the gains from earlier efforts.

This is searingly illustrated by the fact that India came very close to eradicating malaria through a highly successful campaign in the 1950s—but then the programme was put into a 'maintenance phase' and malaria resurged. This resurgence has often been attributed to the emergence of DDT-resistant strains of mosquitoes, though it is clear that the government does not really believe this since it continues to use DDT as a main line of defence against malaria. Less attention has been paid to the shortcomings in programme design. In the 1950s, the malaria control programme was carefully organized, but attention to programme organization suffered subsequently. For example, the current programme is formulated such that the central government provides the DDT, drugs, and other supplies, while the state government is primarily responsible for the manpower costs. Not uncommonly the states are unable to afford the manpower to adequately supervise the spraying activities and prepare communities in advance so that they can plaster their homes before the spraying rather than plastering over the DDT. Besides, manpower is diverted: for example, an ORG (Operations Research Group) study found that frontline staff was preoccupied with family planning work at the expense of malaria supervision at critical times.

The Five Year Plans document the rapid shift away from a public-health-oriented focus in independent India. Even though little was done on sanitation in the 1950s, the Plans clearly recognized its importance for controlling communicable diseases. Water and sanitation were an integral part of the chapter on health planning, and sanitary inspectors figured as an important cadre of frontline staff. By the 1960s, water and sanitation had been separated out as belonging outside the health sector, and there was little further mention of sanitary inspectors in the Plans.

The reduced focus on public health outcomes was also reflected in other ways in the Plans. For example, there is a striking difference between the discussions of the health programmes and of the high-priority family planning programme. In successive Plans, the sections on health are concerned with inputs and the current priority thrusts such as universal immunization. For the rest, there is a typically desultory account of policies and programmes. Analysis of shortfalls is often devoid of suggested remedies, as in the case of the Ninth Plan on malaria. Even lip-service ceases to be paid to important issues—for example, the new strategies for malaria control make no mention of environmental management.

By contrast, the sections on family planning begin with a careful review of programme performance, reasons for shortfalls, and how to overcome them. The need for operational research is highlighted, as well as creative suggestions for generating greater demand for family planning. Indeed, the programme developed a highly successful Information, Education and Communication (IEC) campaign to change people's desired family size and bolster programme success. Similar efforts have been made in the health sector only sporadically, and typically to bolster campaign efforts such as immunization, rather than seeking to radically alter people's health behaviour to reduce their exposure to communicable diseases.

Encouraging Trends for the Future

There are many reasons to be hopeful that public health may receive more attention in the near future. Financing is available through large programmes, for example the Rural Health Mission, National Sanitation Mission, and the renewed support for the Employment Guarantee Scheme. If implemented creatively, these programmes can be used to improve public health outcomes. For example in the US, the Depression era food-for-work programmes were used to eradicate malaria from large parts of the south. The success of this effort resulted from careful planning and overseeing of the work by teams of sanitary engineers, entomologists, and administrators.

Institutions are also being built at local and national levels which can play powerful roles in public health. The Panchayati Raj Act has placed emphasis on building local government and devolving health activities to it. This makes it possible to build institutions for managing public health activities on the ground, with the requisite inter-sectoral coordination. States such as West Bengal and Kerala are experimenting with these possibilities in ways that can serve as models for other states.

At the national level, a new thrust is to build an institution modelled on the US Centers for Disease Control. This model has been adapted across the world, most recently by China and the European Union; the latter recognizes that the public health systems of its component countries need to be coordinated and supported by a 'federal' authority. If designed creatively, this could transform the way that the central government shapes and supports public health services in India. In a large federal country, the key roles of such a central agency include monitoring trends, research, advocacy, and helping states fill specific service gaps with targeted financial and technical help.

India has exceptional capacity to deliver services, as evidenced by its smooth conduct of elections and censuses across a vast population including pavement dwellers and remote villages. Its inattention to public health is taking a large toll on its economy, as well as on the lives of its citizens, and it is time to recognize that public health is a key part of its development infrastructure.

MONICA DAS GUPTA

References

Das Gupta, Monica and Manju Rani. 2005. 'How Well Does India's Federal Government Perform its Essential Public Health Functions?', The World Bank Policy Research Working Paper No. 3447, Washington DC.

Easterlin, Richard A. 2004. 'How Beneficient is the Market? A Look at the Modern History of Mortality', in *The Reluctant Economist: Perspectives on Economics, Economic History and Demography*, Cambridge, Cambridge University Press.

Harrison, Mark. 1994. *Public Health in British India: Anglo-Indian Preventive Medicine 1859–1914*, Cambridge, Cambridge University Press.

Institute of Medicine. 2002. *The Future of the Public's Health in the 21st Century*, Washington DC, National Academy Press.

Jeffrey, Roger. 1988. The *Politics of Health in India*, Berkeley, University of California Press.

World Health Organization (WHO). 2000. 'The Hidden Cost of Outbreaks', *Bulletin of the World Health Organization*, 78(11), available at http://www.who.int/doestore/bulletin/Thismonth/november.htm.

Public-sector Enterprises

... in many cases the ideal size for the unit of control and organization lies somewhere between the individual and modern state. I suggest, therefore, that progress lies in the growth and the recognition of semi-autonomous bodies within the state-bodies whose criterion of action within their own field is solely the public good as they understand it, and from whose deliberations motives of private advantage are excluded. (J.M. Keynes, 'The End of Laissez Faire', 1926)

India adopted the mixed economy framework in 1947 at the time of Independence, which allowed for the role of both the public sector and the private sector in the economic development of the country. Public-sector investment during the various Five Years Plans has been made to bridge the gap between the required investment in the economy and the investment forthcoming from the private sector.

Public-sector Enterprises (PSEs) were given primacy of position through the Industrial Policy Resolutions to serve the nation's development goals and to fulfil the objectives of rapid economic growth and industrialization, employment generation, creation of infrastructure, self-sufficiency in production, balanced regional development, spread of small-scale and ancillary industries, low and stable prices, and long-term equilibrium in balance of payments. These enterprises have played a critical role in the country's economic growth and development.

Central PSEs and State PSEs

PSEs, both at the central and state levels, have played their distinct roles in the development of the country. While the Central Public-sector Enterprises (CPSEs) have been established largely in areas that are delineated under the Central or the Concurrent List of the Constitution of India, the State Public-sector Enterprises (SPSEs) have been set up in areas that fall under the State List of the Constitution.

The CPSEs, in turn, comprise statutory corporations which are set up under Acts of Parliament and Government Companies, as defined under Section 617 of Companies Act, 1956, wherein more than 50 per cent equity is held by the central government. The subsidiaries of such government companies are also categorized as CPSEs. The CPSEs do not, however, include departmental undertakings and public-sector banks and insurance companies.

Five Year Plans and CPSEs

The Second Five Year Plan was launched in April, 1956 coinciding with the Industrial Policy Resolution (IPR). The IPR declared that 'the State will progressively assume predominance and direct responsibility for setting up new industrial undertakings and for developing transport facilities'. The Plan thus became the instrument to implement the IPR. Consequently, both the number and total investment in PSEs saw an overwhelming increase. The subsequent Five Year Plans followed the lead of the Second Plan and PSEs were established in different sectors.

The number of CPSEs went up from 5 on the eve of the First Five Year Plan, with a total investment of Rs 29 crore, to 249 as on 31 March 2010, with a combined investment of Rs 5.80 lakh crore. Quite often, socio-economic considerations have been instrumental in the establishment of PSEs. All PSEs are not the result of plan investment. Some of them were taken over/nationalized from the private sector on their falling sick (for example, National Textile Corporation) or for reasons of not maintaining adequate safety standards (for example, private coal mines). At the same time, some of the PSEs have seen dilution of equity holdings by the government and have been privatized (for example, Maruti Udyog Limited).

Initially, the major portion of CPSE investment was financed through Plan Budgetary Support of the central government. As the CPSEs have matured, the proportion of budgetary support has come down and 'own sources of financing' (termed as Internal and Extra Budgetary Resources [IEBR]) have increased. The total plan investment made in CPSEs during 2009–10 amounted to Rs 1,55,072 crore, of which only 2.88 per cent constituted Budgetary Support. Increasingly (and especially so since the Tenth Plan), the new CPSEs are being set up at the initiative of CPSEs as subsidiary companies, rather than those of the government. The Approach Paper to the Twelfth Five Year Plan targets IEBR at 2.84 per cent of GDP to finance the public-sector plan.

The CPSEs have been set up in diverse sectors of the economy which include agriculture, mining, construction, manufacturing, electricity, and service sectors. As on 31 March 2010, the share of 'manufacturing CPSEs' in aggregate investment (in terms of gross block) was the highest at 27.11 per cent, followed by 'services' (25.54 per cent) , 'electricity' (25.02 per cent), and 'mining CPSEs' (22.76 per cent). The top 10 CPSEs in terms of investment, as on 31 March 2010, have been Oil & Natural Gas Corporation Limited (ONGC), Bharat Sanchar Nigam Limited (BSNL), NTPC Limited (NTPC), Indian Oil Corporation Limited (IOC), Power Grid Corporation of India Limited (PGCIL), Steel Authority of India Limited (SAIL), Nuclear Power Corporation of India Limited (NPCIL), NHPC Limited (NHPC), National Aviation Company of India Limited (NACIL), and Mahanagar Telephone Nigam Limited (MTNL). The share of CPSEs in national income, furthermore, stood at around 6 per cent in 2009–10 and they provided employment to 14.91 lakh people on a regular basis (that is, excluding the casual workers).

Performance of CPSEs during 2009–10

The total income/sales turnover of all CPSEs during 2009–10 stood at Rs 12.72 lakh crore. This showed a decline of 3 per cent, in comparison to the turnover in the previous year. The global slowdown impacted CPSEs, especially the petroleum and the steel sectors. Despite the decline in turnover, the profits went up as the oil marketing companies (OMCs) benefitted from fall in price of imported crude oil.

While the profit of profit-making CPSEs during the year stood at Rs 1,08,435 crore, the losses of loss-making CPSEs stood at Rs 15,842 crore. The reserves and surpluses of all CPSEs, on the other hand, stood at Rs 6,05,648 crore as on 31 March 2010. The net worth of all CPSEs, similarly, stood at Rs 6,60,245 crore as on 31 March 2010, which was four times the paid up capital invested in all the CPSEs.

In terms of profitability ratios, such as net profit to turnover, net profit to net worth and dividend payout as well, the CPSEs compared very well at the aggregate level with their counterparts in the private corporate sector. This is notwithstanding the oil marketing CPSEs (OMCs) being subjected to administrative control on prices of petroleum products. The CPSEs have been also contributing significantly to the central exchequer by way of excise duty, customs duty, corporate tax, interest on central government loans, dividend, and other duties and taxes, which amounted to Rs 1.40 lakh crore in 2009–10.

Restructuring of Loss-making CPSEs

Some of the CPSEs have been incurring losses continuously for the last several years. There were 45 CPSEs (out of 249 CPSEs), as on 31 March 2010, which had their accumulated losses more than their net worth. The reason for sickness varies from one enterprise to another. The cause for sickness in some cases has been historical. For instance, textile companies that were taken over from the private sector on their falling sick could not be modernized quickly enough. High input costs of naphtha made the fertilizer units, such as FCI and HFC, unviable. Cheaper imports and competition in the market have adversely affected the CPSEs like HMT, Hindustan Photo Films, and IDPL. Similarly, advent of new technology has eroded demand for CPSEs like Hindustan Cables Limited and ITI Limited. The global recession of 2007–8 (and competition from cheaper airlines) adversely impacted public-sector companies like Air India/NACIL.

Board for Reconstruction of PSEs

In order to provide state support and revive these loss-making CPSEs, the government constituted the Board for Reconstruction of Public-sector Enterprises (BRPSE) in 2004.

So far the government has approved 42 revival proposals recommended by the BRPSE and winding up of two CPSEs. Out of the 40 cases recommended for revival, 15 were approved in 2005–6, 11 in 2006–7, 6 in 2007–8, 5 in 2008–9, and 3 in 2009–10. A portion of income from disinvestment proceeds are set apart to meet the capital investment requirements of profitable and revivable CPSEs. A number of CPSEs which have been through revival packages have now turned around, and have been making profits continuously for the past several years.

Ownership, Form, and Corporate Governance in CPSEs

The CPSEs, set up over the years, have had either of the two organizational forms of: (a) limited liabilities companies/public corporations or (b) statutory corporations. The limited liability or Joint Stock Company form has been the most preferred type of organization in the case of CPSEs as it is simpler to set up and provides the possibility of raising capital from the stock exchanges.

CPSEs fall under the administrative control of the relevant ministries. The Department of Public Enterprises (DPE), being the nodal department for CPSEs in the Government of India, formulates the broad guidelines on a number of policy issues common to all the CPSEs. The Ministry of Finance, in turn, lays down the disinvestment (and dividend) policy for CPSEs. In addition, the Public-sector Enterprises Selection Board (PESB) advises the government on appointments to top management positions at the board level in CPSEs through a fair and objective selection procedure.

CPSEs are subject to robust parliamentary supervision through the Committee on Public Undertakings (and SPSEs are under the umbrella of the respective state legislatures). The companies are required to place before Parliament their annual audited accounts and reports. CPSEs and SPSEs are subject to the audit of the Comptroller and Auditor General of India (C&AG). Auditors of government companies are appointed by C&AG in terms of Section 619(2) of the Companies Act, 1956. C&AG is also expected to comment upon the audit reports as well as conduct supplementary audits through its Commercial Audit Wing. CPSEs are also subject to the oversight of the Central Vigilance Commission, while SPSEs fall within the jurisdiction of the Lokayuktas in the states.

Listing of CPSEs has added another layer of compliance to improve corporate governance. Before a company is listed, it is required to have at least 50 per cent independent directors on its boards besides having an independent audit committee. The listing agreement obligates the companies to ensure periodic disclosure of information related to board meetings, performance, shareholding pattern, and other parameters. Listed CPSEs, therefore, become subject to greater transparency and market discipline due to disclosures and scrutiny by the investors on a continued basis. Both listed and unlisted CPSEs are also covered under a set of Guidelines on Corporate Governance issued by DPE in 2007.

These guidelines cover issues such as composition of the board of directors, the specialized committees of CPSE boards, and the frequency of board meetings in a year. They mandate that boards of CPSEs with an executive chairman should have at least 50 per cent members as independent directors. In the case of a non-executive chairman, the board needs to have one-third the total strength of the board as independent directors. The eligibility criteria of independent directors has been also laid down, to include ex-CMDs of CPSEs, CMDs of private corporate sector with turnover above a threshold limit, or retired senior officers from the government. The selection of independent directors is done by a Search Committee chaired by the Chairman, PESB, which is an independent body.

To monitor the performance of CPSEs, the government uses a system of Memorandum of Understanding (MOU), a negotiated document between the government and the respective CPSE that clearly specifies the targets, both financial and non-financial, and the obligations of both the parties. Having agreed to these objectives at the beginning of the year, the performance of the CPSE is evaluated at the end of the year with reference to these targets. With CPSEs collectively being among the largest provider of employment in the country, the need to efficiently use this human capital has been widely recognized. The MoU ratings of CPSEs provide the basis for performance related pay (PRP) of the chief executives and senior officials of the CPSEs. An employee stock option plan has been recently introduced by the government to enable individual CPSEs to allocate a portion of the PRP to its employees through this method.

In order to incentivize CPSE performance in an increasingly competitive environment, the government has adopted a set of norms on the basis of which these enterprises are conferred (in ascending order), 'Miniratna', 'Navratna', and 'Maharatna' status, which allow the firms differential but additional levels of significant operational freedom and flexibility. There are 63 Miniratna CPSEs, 16 Navratna CPSEs, and 5 Maharatna CPSEs (IOC, NTPC, ONGC, SAIL, and CIL) as of July 2011.

Economic Reforms and Industrial Policy of 1991

The Industrial Policy Resolution of 1956 (and subsequent modifications made therein over the years) was subjected to review in July 1991. The Statement on Industrial Policy (SIP) announced in 1991 heralded the liberalization of the Indian economy, stating, 'Portfolio of public sector investments will be reviewed with a view to focus the public sector on strategic high-tech and essential infrastructure. Whereas some reservation for the public sector is being retained, there would be no bar for areas of exclusivity to be opened up to the private sector selectively.' Along with the de-reservation of sectors that were the exclusive preserve of CPSEs, the tariffs on imports have been progressively reduced over the years. This has led to the CPSEs facing greater competition in the market. Despite this competition, the overall performance of CPSEs has improved.

Disinvestment and Listing on Stock Exchanges

The decision for disinvestment in CPSEs began with the announcement in 1991 to divest up to 20 per cent of government equity in select CPSEs in favour of public-sector institutional investors by way of strategic sale. The policy of disinvestment has been pronounced through the statements contained in the Budget Speeches of Finance Ministers. The disinvestment policy, as it has evolved over the years, can be divided into three distinct phases:

(i) 1991–2 to 1998–9: The focus was on disinvestment of minority shareholding in favour of financial institutions.
(ii) 1999–2000 to 2003–4: The focus was on disinvestment through strategic sale.
(iii) 2004–5 onwards: The focus was on partial disinvestment, that is, disinvestment of minority stakes through public market offerings, sometimes in conjunction with issue of fresh equity by CPSEs.

The government's current policy on disinvestment, which was adopted in November 2009, prescribes open market sale of minority shareholding to encourage 'peoples' ownership' of PSEs. The policy seeks, first to list all unlisted CPSEs, which have a positive net worth (no accumulated losses) and have earned profit in the three preceding years. Second, it aims to correct a historical legacy, which has left several listed CPSEs with small public floats. All such profitable listed CPSEs are required to meet the mandatory public shareholding of at least 10 per cent of their total equity. And third, if profitable listed CPSEs need to raise funds from capital market for their capital expenditure, the government could disinvest a part of its shareholding in conjunction with such issue of fresh equity by the CPSE. The government will, however, continue to retain at least 51 per cent shareholding and management control.

As on 31 March 2010, 50 CPSEs were listed, with a combined market capitalization of around Rs 15 lakh crore, accounting for around 22 per cent of the total market capitalization on the Bombay Stock Exchange. In terms of market capitalization, 7 CPSEs (ONGC, NTPC, Coal India Limited (CIL), Bharat Heavy Electrical Limited (BHEL), NMDC Limited (NMDC), IOC, and SAIL) are among the top 20 companies. The strength and potential of these CPSEs was demonstrated in the listing of CIL through India's largest IPO (Rs 15,199 crore) in October 2010. In mid-August 2011, CIL became the country's largest company in terms of market capitalization, being valued at Rs 2.51 trillion.

International Investment by CPSEs

International investment by CPSEs comprises off-shore investment by CPSEs through joint ventures, mergers and acquisitions, and operation of Indian subsidiaries abroad. There is an increasing realization among CPSEs that in view of liberalization, they have to leverage their inherent strengths and the potential to compete globally to become large multinationals, and that mere organic growth is not enough to propel them towards growth. Several CPSEs have either formed joint ventures or have set up subsidiaries abroad for consolidating their international operations. In the upstream hydrocarbon sector, ONGC Videsh Limited (OVL), a wholly owned subsidiary of ONGC, has been successful in acquiring oil and gas assets abroad. OVL has been acquiring overseas oil and gas assets through various routes such as direct purchase of equity stakes in assets, corporate acquisitions, participating through bidding rounds, direct negotiations, and advised acquisitions. As on 31 March 2011, OVL has participation directly or through wholly owned subsidiaries/joint venture companies in 33 exploration and production projects in 14 countries, comprising 9 producing assets, 4 assets under development, and 19 exploration assets. OVL also has equity participation in one petroleum product pipeline in Sudan. During the first four years of XI Plan, OVL has produced 35.915 MMTOE (million metric tonne of oil and oil equivalent) from overseas. In the year 2010–11, OVL produced 9.45 MMTOE, which accounted for 10.5 per cent of India's total domestic oil and gas production. Other CPSEs are increasingly following the lead given by OVL in international investments. International Coal Ventures Pvt. Ltd. has been set up as a joint venture company with SAIL, CIL, Rashtriya Ispat Nigam Limited (RINL), NMDC, and NTPC as the promoter companies for acquisition of coal assets abroad.

Corporate Social Responsibility

The Government of India issued the Guidelines on Corporate Social Responsibility (CSR) for all the CPSEs in 2010. Accordingly, it is mandatory for CPSEs to assume responsibility for the impact of their activities on customers, employees, shareholders, community, and environment. CSR projects are closely linked with the principle of sustainable development. The CSR budget of CPSEs are created through a board resolution as a percentage of net profit of the previous year. While the CSR budget is fixed for every financial year, the funding does not lapse if it is not spent during the year, and the unspent amount is to be transferred to the CSR fund. CPSEs may choose CSR projects in areas such as pollution control, disaster management, non-conventional energy sources, health and family welfare, education, and promotion of art and culture.

State Public-sector Enterprises

At the sub-national level there are around 1,160 SPSEs with a total investment of over Rs 3.7 lakh crore in the form of equity and loans as on 31 March 2008. Around 850 of these enterprises are in operation as others have been earmarked for closure or are in the process of being wound up. While Kerala led all the states in terms of number of SPSEs (88), Gujarat had the highest investment amongst all the states (Rs 55,227 crore). Total investment in SPSEs is around 80 per cent of the total investment in all CPSEs. Maximum investment in these enterprises has gone into public utilities, such as power generation, warehousing, and road transportation. Some of the SPSEs are bigger than Schedule 'D' and 'E' category CPSEs. The SPSEs, moreover, provided employment to 18 lakh people as on 31 March 2008, which is higher than the total number of people employed in CPSEs.

Although the SPSEs occupy an important place in the national economy, their performance has lagged behind those of the CPSEs. While 358 SPSEs showed profit in 2007–8, SPSEs of only 9 states have earned aggregate profits in the year. The accumulated losses of loss-making SPSEs stood at Rs 65,924 crore as on 31 March 2008. A study conducted by the Thirteenth Finance Commission found that while the budgetary (capital) support in terms of equity participation of states increased by almost 27 per cent from Rs 52,198 crore in 2002–3 to Rs 66,333 crore in 2007–8, the budgetary (revenue) support in terms of subsidies/grants to PSEs increased by 22 per cent during the same period. A large number of SPSEs are promotional entities/development corporations, which have been set up to channelize grants and subsidies from either the central government or the state government to the target population/unorganized sector for cheaper finance or for marketing support.

The SPSEs, in general, have failed to meet the Finance Commission norm of a minimum dividend payout of 5 per cent on government equity. However, efforts have been made across states to reform and restructure these government enterprises and close down the loss-making companies, with varying degrees of success. Currently, only six SPSEs are listed. Corporate governance in SPSEs could significantly improve if these companies are listed on the stock exchanges.

Sumit Bose and Sharat Kumar

References

Department of Disinvestment, Government of India. 2011. *Handbook of Disinvestment through Public Offering*, New Delhi, Government of India.

Department of Public Enterprises, Government of India. 2007. *Guidelines on Corporate Governance*, New Delhi, Government of India.

——. 2009. *Central Public Sector Enterprises—Leading Companies of India*, New Delhi, Shipra Publications.

——. 2010. *Guidelines on Corporate Social Responsibility*, New Delhi, Government of India.

——. 2011. *Public Enterprises Survey [2009–10]*, New Delhi, Government of India.

Kelkar, V. 2010. 'On Strategies for Disinvestment and Privatisation', 26th Sir Purshotamdas Thakurdas Memorial Lecture, Mumbai, January.

Keynes J.M. 1931. 'The End of Laissez Faire', reprinted in *Essays in Persuasion*, Macmillan, London.

Prasad P. 1957. *Some Economic Problems of Public Enterprises in India*, Leiden, HE Stenfert Kroese.

R

■ Railways

Railway transport in India began on 16 April 1853, with the passage of a train from Mumbai to Thane. In the century and a half since then, the railway network in India has grown to cover virtually all parts of the country. Only in the hilly regions of the north and north-east of India is the network relatively sparse. When India attained Independence in 1947, the total length of routes covered by the network was about 53,000 km, of which a meagre 388 km was electrified. From then until 2004, about 10,000 km have been added, not a very significant expansion over more than half a century. Obviously, much of the country had already been covered by the time of Independence. However, the total length of electrified segments has increased to over 17,000 km, almost 28 per cent of the total.

While the total length of the network remained relatively constant in the half century after Independence, its utilization increased manifold. Capacity expansions were achieved by a combination of factors—electrification, double lining, and increasing the number of wagons or coaches per train. Freight volumes carried by the system increased by about 8.7 times during the period 1950–2004. In the same period, the number of passengers carried increased by about 7.3 times. This growth in traffic was achieved on the basis of increases in the number of freight wagons and passenger coaches by multiples of 2.6 and 2.7, respectively, reflecting the importance of the other factors mentioned in the increased productivity of the system. One aggregate measure of productivity is 'train density', which is the ratio of total train kilometres operated to track kilometres. This parameter increased from 7.1 in 1950 to 15.2 in 2004.[1]

These magnitudes need to be viewed against the backdrop of aggregate changes to fully understand their significance. Over the 1950–2004 period, real gross domestic product (GDP) increased by a multiple of 10.2. Over the same period, the country's population increased by a multiple of 3. In proportion to GDP, therefore, railway freight traffic became a little less significant over the five decades. There is a very good reason for this. For the last two decades and more, the share of industry in GDP has remained stagnant at about a quarter. The share of agriculture has declined from about four-fifths to less than a quarter. Consequently, the share of services has risen from slightly over a third to over half of GDP. They have been by far the most significant contributor to GDP growth over the second half of the last century. Services, as a whole, are obviously far less dependent on commodity movements than industry. It is, therefore, not surprising that the growth in railway traffic has not kept pace with GDP growth.

By contrast, the growth in passenger traffic far outstripped the growth in population over the five decades. Clearly, as the significance of agriculture in the economy declined, more and more people felt the need to move out in search of employment. The railways met this

[1]The data used in this paragraph are taken from various publications of the Ministry of Railways, Government of India and extracted from www.indiastat.com.

need, allowing people to travel longer distances at lower costs than other modes of mass transport. They played a significant role in creating a highly integrated national labour market, an important factor in the growth of the services sector.

An Economic Perspective

An economic perspective on the railways would have two broad components. One would address the causal relationships between railway activity and economic growth. The other would look at the organization and operation of the railway system in terms of its economic viability. Specifically, is the system as it is currently run able to generate resources adequate to maintaining operations as well as investing in maintenance, capacity expansion, and safety enhancement? In this entry, I take the first perspective as given and, having accepted the importance of the railways as a contributor to economic performance, focus on the second component, that is, economic viability.

In recent years, many concerns have been expressed about the economic state of the Indian Railways. The essential problem is that the system is simply not generating adequate resources to fulfil the three critical objectives of maintenance, capacity expansion, and safety enhancement; in fact, it is barely able to meet its operating expenses. It is, therefore, quite dependent on transfers from the government to meet these objectives and, unless remedial steps are taken at once, this dependence will come sharply in conflict with the broader move towards fiscal discipline.

There are two main causes of this problem. First, operating as it does under persistent political compulsions, the system does not price its services on economic logic, with adverse consequences for revenue generation. Second, the system, despite the significant gains in productivity over the last 50 years, discussed earlier, currently operates relatively inefficiently, which, apart from other factors, is itself a consequence of inadequate maintenance and investment.

Pricing and Revenues

A 'rational' pricing benchmark would require that the price of each of the services provided by the railways should reasonably reflect its costs. Within these constraints, there are various economic arguments for subsidizing one or more classes of consumers, either directly by way of transfers from the government or in the form of cross-subsidies from other classes of consumers. There are several practical lessons that have emerged from experience for the design of a viable subsidy mechanism that reasonably satisfies the combined interests of consumers (access to services), the system (financial viability), and the government (fiscal discipline). These lessons will undoubtedly influence the future course of the system and will be addressed in the concluding section. The fact, however, is that, historically, pricing decisions by the railways have generally tended to prioritize political objectives over economic ones. This has led to two major 'distortions'—departures from the benchmark.

First, pricing has tended to favour passenger traffic over freight traffic. Low-cost passenger transportation has been a high-priority objective for successive governments, a fact reflected in the discussion on relative magnitudes in the preceding paragraphs. In order to keep passenger fares as low as possible and still earn enough money to survive, freight rates have tended to be higher than the benchmark would warrant. As a result, freight customers have looked for substitutes and, over the years, many have shifted to road because of railway freight rates. Typically, rail freight is considered to be more efficient for distances in excess of 250 km. Internal studies carried out in the mid-1990s revealed that a significant proportion of the freight traffic in the 250–700 km range had shifted to road, largely because of relative prices (Report of the Expert Group on Indian Railways 2001). One of the most important practical lessons on pricing is that it should take into account the availability of good substitutes. When these are there, raising prices will lead to declining revenues, as customers switch loyalties.

Second, within the passenger segment, lower class services have been underpriced, while upper class ones have been overpriced. For example, in 2003–4, lower class passengers constituted an overwhelming 98 per cent of the total, but contributed only 75 per cent of the revenues. Within this segment, the lowest service category, the 'second class ordinary', accounted for 71 per cent of the total passengers carried but only 16 per cent of total revenues. The last Railway Fare and Freight Committee, which made its recommendations as far back as 1993, had advocated a highest-to-lowest passenger fare ratio of 9.6. This ratio was as high as 14.4 in the late 1990s (Report of the Expert Group on Indian Railways 2001). Subsequent reductions in premium service fares have brought it down somewhat in recent years, but the impact of these discounts on revenues has been diluted by the steady increase in the affordability of air travel, which is the obvious substitute for potential upper class travellers.

Determining an optimal fare structure is obviously beyond the scope of this short entry, but it is obvious that the railways' earnings will always be constrained if it does not raise lower class fares. Equally obvious, there are significant political risks inherent in that move, which make it very difficult for any government to do so.

Efficiency and Costs

The other dimension of financial viability is the cost of operating the system. As mentioned earlier, a key objective is to not only cover operating costs, but also generate enough surpluses to maintain assets in working condition, fund expansions where necessary, and continually enhance safety. One measure of the ability of the system to meet these multiple objectives is the 'operating ratio', which is the ratio of operating costs to total revenues. The lower this is, the larger the surplus left over to address the other critical objectives. This ratio was in the 80–90 per cent range in the early to mid-1990s, but increased sharply to 97 per cent in 2000–1, before coming down to around the 90 per cent mark in recent years.[2] The fact is, however, that at these levels, there is very little left over after meeting expenses to cater to the future. Maintenance slackens, reducing effective capacity of the system and the quality and safety levels it can offer its customers. This reinforces the movement towards road by shippers and towards air by travellers.

A discussion of specific parameters of productivity is beyond the scope of this entry, but one very important reason for the high burden of operating costs is the wage and salary bill of the system. Employment in the railway system peaked at around 1.6 million in the late 1990s; since then, there has been steady, if slow, attrition. However, attrition does not immediately reduce costs, because of lifetime pension commitments. Since the Indian Railways, like the rest of the government, used a 'pay-as-you-go' pension scheme until 2004, all pension commitments are paid out of general revenues. In the 2005–6 railway budget, the provision for pensions was Rs 7,000 crore, almost 20 per cent of the 'ordinary working expenses', or operating costs (Ministry of Railways 2005). This commitment is unlikely to decrease in the foreseeable future, given the large number of retirees and increasing life expectancy. As an expenditure commitment, it dilutes the financial impact of any other efforts to increase efficiency and, through this, the pool of resources available to meet maintenance, investment, and safety objectives.

Reforms and the Future

Through all this, Indian Railways has been continuously attempting to deal with its problems, either directly or through by-pass solutions. Dramatic improvements may not have resulted, but the system continues to operate at some minimum acceptable standard of service delivery. In the freight business, value-added services were initiated through the Container Corporation of India, which provides a door-to-door service combining road and rail. In recent years, significant efforts have been made to realign the freight rates for a variety of commodities to the competitive situation in the marketplace. On the passenger side, expanding the premium services offered by the Rajdhani trains over long distances and the Shatabdis over short hauls has enhanced revenues, reinforced by more realistic pricing of these services.

However, the record shows that in the face of continuing resistance to a substantial adjustment of lower class passenger fares to more closely reflect the costs of providing them, the three critical objectives beyond merely keeping the trains running are elusive. The reform blueprint drawn up by the Expert Group on Indian Railways envisages the setting up of an independent tariff regulator to take political discretion out of the process of deciding fares. Once a 'rational' structure of freight tariffs and passenger fares is achieved and credibly managed by the regulator, the commercial viability that this induces will be able to attract private resources to make critical investments. Maintenance and safety will, of course, benefit from the increased flow of resources. Within this framework the government can, if it chooses, subsidize certain classes of customers on the basis of equity or regional development objectives, but persisting with the current emphasis on cross-subsidies is clearly at odds with revenue-enhancement objectives.

Given the importance of the railways for the country, providing the system the capability to meet the four objectives of operations, maintenance, investment, and safety is consistent with broader development objectives. This is not possible with marginal and peripheral changes. The core issue of rational pricing has to be tackled head on. If this is done, a system that has served the country for over a century and a half will get a new lease of life with a greater ability to meet the growing and evolving transportation requirements of the economy. If not, it will degenerate into a service used only by people who have no other choice and shunned by the rest, and find it increasingly difficult to live up to even the lowest expectations of quality and safety.

SUBIR GOKARN

References

Ministry of Railways, Government of India. 2005. Railways Budget 2005–6, presented on 25 February.

[2]Railway financial performance indicators extracted from tables appearing on www.indiastat.com.

Report of the Expert Group on Indian Railways. 2001. *The Indian Railways Report—2001: Policy Imperatives for Reinvention and Growth*, New Delhi, NCAER and IDFC.

Krishna Raj

More than a year after Krishna Raj's death on 17 January 2004, the intellectual community in India finds it hard to accept that he is no longer with it. For nearly three-and-a-half decades, he had edited the *Economic and Political Weekly* (*EPW*) with such devotion and competence that by the time he departed, it had become a highly respected international journal devoted to constructive discussion of current and theoretical issues of global relevance.

Born in 1937 in Ottapalam in Kerala (India) Krishna Raj did most of his schooling in Delhi, where his father Raghavan Nair worked for the British Information Services prior to 1947. He quit the service that year and started editing his own paper called *Delhi Times*. Though not an enduring or major publication, it apparently lasted long enough to enable Krishna Raj to complete his studies, including postgraduation in the Delhi School of Economics. By 1958, he was looking around for an opening in economic journalism—for which he had apparently a yen. By happenstance Sachin Chaudhury, founder editor of *The Economic Weekly* (*EW*) (and later of *EPW*) was also in Delhi, looking for an able youngster to 'cover' the nation's capital. They met through common friends and Krishna Raj's long career in economic journalism began. His dedication and perceptive coverage of economic and political events won over Sachin completely; and before long Krishna Raj moved to the *EW*'s office in Bombay, as the editor's factotum and principal assistant.

Whether or not Krishna Raj (and his parents) had leftist associations early in life is not known. However, the 1950s were the heyday of 'socialist planning' in India, and institutions like the Delhi School of Economics and the Indian Statistical Institute were at the time major 'think tanks' concerned with theoretical and policy issues of planning and development. Sachin was in contact with a good many of the scholars and practitioners in social sciences, in India as well as abroad; and, in time, Krishna Raj, as Sachin's right-hand man, also came to know such people well enough to get them to contribute regularly to *EPW*. By the time he shifted to Bombay, he had earned a good reputation for himself as a perspicacious reporter who could be trusted and who would be fair in criticism.

When Krishna Raj started as Sachin's apprentice in Bombay, he found himself in a very different environment from that of New Delhi. As the leading commercial and corporate centre of India, it was a city dominated by businessmen, financial institutions, and the market, as against the bureaucrats, politicians, and administrative system of Delhi. As editor of the *EW*, Sachin had started out to fill a long-standing need in economic journalism—that of 'an independent weekly to deal primarily with economic problems of the country, and then, with the broad political ones in so far as they issue on the former' (Chaudhury 1949: 10).

The journal sought to assess problems and policies of political economy in terms of their relevance to national progress and welfare, rather than in support of any particular economic constituency or ideology. The *EW*'s columns were thus open to everybody who had a good idea, and could express it clearly and succinctly. There was, however, an underlying commitment to democracy, social justice, individual freedom, and objectivity. Sachin was also a staunch liberal, who valued ethics and aesthetics probably more than material benefit. Krishna Raj, working in close proximity with the editor, soon acquired a tolerance of diverse views and an eye for fairness and facility of expression, which were to give his editorship in later years a uniqueness.

Despite its reputation among the knowledgeable, the *EW* was not a financial success and ceased publication in the mid-1960s. But Sachin would not give up and under the auspices of the Sameeksha Trust started publication of the *Economic and Political Weekly* in August 1966. However, he passed away in December that year. When his successor Dr R.K. Hazari left a couple of years later, the Sameeksha Trust invited Krishna Raj to take charge as editor of the *EPW* in December 1969.

Prior to the publication of the *EW* there were a few weeklies devoted to reporting on commercial or financial matters of interest to the business community. The *EW* had struck a new line in this milieu, opening its columns for comment by both scholars and laymen on basic economic, social, and political issues. The objectives were, besides promoting public awareness of the implications of current issues, to provide space to young and upcoming students of social sciences to publish their scholarly outputs. These objectives continued with the *EPW*, and under Krishna Raj's gentle but firm editorship, it soon became internationally respected as a dependable source of news and views on national affairs as well as a technical journal of excellence.

Krishna Raj's own position on many issues was, as mentioned earlier, fairly left of centre, even Marxist. But he was also a staunch democrat who valued individual rights and freedoms even as he disliked exploitation and capitalist arrangements. In his view, the state had an inescapable responsibility to secure for its citizens, alongside of law, internal order, and defence against external aggression, a life of dignity, free from poverty, disease, and ignorance. If this required the state to intervene in or regulate the economic and social spheres, he was willing to accept it, provided the policies remained within constitutional limits.

Despite his leftist leanings, as reflected in his editorials and accompanying shorter notes, Krishna Raj kept the journal views open to contributors holding diverse views, as long as the views were well written and well argued. He enlarged the scope of the journal progressively by providing space for special sections on agriculture, women's issues, management, energy policy, industrial questions, and so forth, apart from review articles, discussions, or reflections on literary or cultural matters. By the 1990s the *EPW*'s reputation was such that the editor's problem was one of abundance rather than lack of significant contributions.[1]

Towards the end of the 1980s, Krishna Raj's intellectual position had changed considerably. He recognized that the market is a useful instrument for resource allocation; but, left to itself, it could not meet the society's needs of economic justice and civilized levels of living for all its members. He also felt that while the state had a clear responsibility to provide economic and social justice to its citizens, it could also become a vehicle for oppression and exploitation. Likewise, he was fully conscious of the need to promote GDP growth to enlarge employment opportunities and assist poverty alleviation; but he did not accept that growth was sufficient in itself to attain employment or anti-poverty objectives. From his editorials during that period, it was patent that he was looking for a via media which would enable society to allocate its resources 'efficiently', that is, with the best social cost–benefit ratio.

It was not until the end of the 1990s that *EPW*'s financial position improved sufficiently to enable Krishna Raj to add gradually to his supporting staff, equip it with computers and DTP technology, and seek paid contributions to the journal. Until the end, his own lifestyle remained spartan, a fact not reflected in his demeanour or relations with others. Within his office, he practised whatever he preached in his writings—hard work, moral and intellectual integrity, respect for the individual, and total absence of discriminatory treatment of others. Until the Sameeksha Trust decided in early 2001 to revise his and his staff's salary scales upwards, they remained unbelievably low by Bombay standards or in relation to the amount and quality of output of the editor and his associates. Even today, they are nowhere near what the large community of economic and other journalists receives in other establishments in India. But the quality of Krishna Raj's leadership was such that, far from complaining about work status or conditions, the *EPW* staff felt a sense of fulfilment. His successor to the editor's chair, Rammanohar Reddy, has brought similar qualities to his task and the extraordinary spirit that pervades 'Hitkari House', the headquarters of the *EPW*, continues—in itself a continuing tribute to Krishna Raj.

In the months following Krishna Raj's death, many wrote to the *EPW* remembering him fondly. One such tribute said:

> In the continued two-front warfare against populist simplification on the one hand and technical esotericism on the other, *EPW* has presented an exemplar that can serve as a guide for many academic communities. We hope that the spirit of Krishna Raj will continue to preside over the *Economic and Political Weekly* (Rudolph and Rudolph 2004: 388).

K.S. KRISHNASWAMY

References

Chaudhury, Sachin. 1949. 'Light without Heat', *The Economic Weekly*, 1 January, 1(1).

Rudolph, Lloyd I. and Susanne Hoeber Rudolph. 2004. Under 'Reminiscences', *Economic and Political Weekly*, 31 January–6 February, 39(5): 388.

■ V.K. Ramaswami

V.K. Ramaswami (1929–69) was a career civil servant who acquired a great reputation as a theoretical economist of unusual originality and immense analytical skill. The motivation for his analytical research stemmed from his everyday work as an economic administrator in the service of the Government of India.

Ramaswami was born in the princely state of Baroda (now called Vadodara), where his father Sir V.T. Krishnamachari was Diwan. After Independence Sir V.T. joined the Government of India as Deputy Chairman of the newly formed Planning Commission. Ramaswami had his early education at home in Baroda and then graduated from Madras University and went to Oxford to study politics, philosophy, and economics. On his return to India, he first joined the Research Department of the Reserve Bank of India at

[1]It was not unusual for aspiring contributors to complain about lack of response by the editor—even to accuse him of bias against non-leftist contributions!

Mumbai, and then moved to New Delhi to work for the Government of India. He served as Economic Advisor to the Ministries of Industry, Commerce, and Finance. At the time of his untimely death in 1969, he was Chief Economic Advisor in the Ministry of Finance.

During Ramaswami's tenure as Economic Advisor to the government, investment planning came to occupy a predominant position in the conceptual framework of economic policy formulation for the Government of India. Five Year Plans produced targets of production, investment, consumption, export, and import of different commodities. These targets were expected to be achieved primarily by direct controls, public-sector investments, licensing of private investments, quantitative restrictions over (and licensing of) imports, along with a regime of tight exchange control. The primary function of fiscal policy was to meet the target of additional resource mobilization for meeting the required government expenditure.

During this period, the Government of India had in its employ a number of highly qualified and able economists, such as Ramaswami's senior colleague Dr I.G. Patel. Patel used his considerable talent mainly for mobilizing foreign and soft loans from external donors. In his memoirs, Patel wrote eloquently about his frustrations as an economist and made a plea for 'Making a Bonfire' of those licensing regulations (see Patel 2000).

Ramaswami, on the other hand, used his talents to educate policymakers and informed citizenry about the virtues of using regulatory fiscal policies to guide the economy in the desired direction. In a series of imaginative (and highly influential) research papers, he built a case for using taxes and subsidies to influence economic behaviour. His collected scientific papers edited by three eminent economists—Jagdish Bhagwati, Harry Johnson, and T.N. Srinivasan—are testimony to the quality and range of Ramaswami's research output (see Bhagwati et al. 1971).

Ramaswami's theoretical research began with explorations in the field of international economics. In this, he was lucky to have as his friends two outstanding economists—Jagdish Bhagwati and T.N. Srinivasan—who were doing creative research in this area. Many of Ramaswami's research papers in the early phase of his career were authored jointly with Bhagwati and/or Srinivasan.

Although Ramaswami had done insightful theoretical work on several problems, his major contributions were in the field of optimal policies in the presence of distributors in the market process. His work established that although tariffs remained the effective policy intervention in the presence of monopoly powers, for the case of production externalities, optimal policies were production tax-cum-subsidies. More important, this research showed that where there were distortions in production, consumption, or factor-use in the domestic economy, optimal domestic polices were also similar kinds of taxes and subsidies (see Ramaswami and Bhagwati 1963).

Perhaps the most influential among Ramaswami's various papers on optimal trade policy is the one in which he deals with the complications associated with imported intermediate goods. These researches were not only useful in formulating India's economic policies, but also significantly advanced our knowledge in the theory of effective protective rates (see Ramaswami and Srinivasan 1968).

These and several other papers on optimal trade and industrial policies, for which Ramaswami is justly acclaimed, were conceived within the framework of temporal theories of production and exchange. Towards the end of his brief career he moved on to study problems of economic growth and of monetary policy. His paper on two-sector growth models provides an elegant exposition of contemporary research in this field (see Ramaswami 1969). He also started working on models of economic growth in the presence of money. He left an unfinished paper on this at the time of his accidental death. He was then only 40 years old.

Ramaswami's research on international trade has influenced a whole generation of researchers including such eminent trade theorists as Max Corden and Ronald Jones. This should have been a matter of great satisfaction to Ramaswami, far greater satisfaction would have been to see his friend Dr Manmohan Singh, an eminent economist in the tradition of Ramaswami, introduce far-reaching reforms in India's economic policies in the 1990s, for which Ramaswami's research efforts in the earlier era provided valuable intellectual support.

MRINAL DATTA CHAUDHURI

References

Bhagwati, J.N., H.G. Johnson, and T.N. Srinivisan (eds), 1971. *Trade and Development: Essays in Economics*, by V.K. Ramaswami, London, Allen & Unwin.

Patel I.G. 2000. *Glimpses of Indian Economic Policy: An Insider's View*, New Delhi, Oxford University Press.

Ramaswami, V.K. 1969. 'On Two-sector Neoclassical Growth', *Oxford Economic Papers*, July, 21(2): 142–6.

Ramaswami, V.K. and J.N. Bhagwati. 1963. 'Domestic Distortions, Tariffs and the Theory of Optimal Subsidy', *Journal of Political Economy*, 71(1): 44–50.

Ramaswami, V.K. and T.N. Srinivasan. 1968. 'Optimal Subsidies and Taxes When Some Factors are Traded', *Journal of Political Economy*, Part 1, July/August, 76(4): 940–3.

V.K.R.V. Rao

Vijayendra Kasturi Ranga Varadaraja Rao was born in 1908 in south India in a Brahmin family of six children and very modest means. His father went to Bombay to earn a living, leaving the family behind in Srirangam. He sent for his family when V.K.R.V. was 13.

An outstanding student, munificent industrialists and lawyers in Bombay financed V.K.R.V.'s education. He received his Master's in economics by thesis from Bombay University in 1929. His was the first study on taxation of income in India and received favourable attention including reviews in the *Economic Journal* and the *Journal of the Royal Statistical Society*.

As a student and then a young teacher in Bombay University, V.K.R.V. was active in the Swadeshi League and the Congress Party, for which he wrote innumerable pamphlets and spoke at public meetings. By the time he went in 1933, at the age of 26, to study economics in Cambridge, he was a recognized public figure in Bombay. Despite his public fame, postgraduate degree, and teaching experience in India, he initially enrolled for a BA (Hons) programme wanting to sharpen his analytical and technical skills.

At Cambridge he was soon invited to the Political Economy Club of J.M. Keynes who was then working on his 'General Theory'. He became close to many eminent Cambridge economists who went on to guide his PhD In his PhD thesis he pioneered a methodology for estimation of the national income in the absence of adequate data. It was the first systematic effort to estimate the national income of a developing country and remains an important basis for the official series of India's national income and many other developing countries.

His work as an economist emphasized that economics is not neutral between ends and means. He built bridges between economics and other disciplines and between social science and policymaking. He argued for development to create employment. The World Employment Programme of the International Labour Organization was a result of his work. His influential article on economic development in underdeveloped economies in the *Indian Economic Review* of 1955 critiqued the blind application of Keynesian models in the context of developing country planning and gave a theoretical foundation for centralized economic planning. He was a strong supporter of centralized planning, of a leading role for government in investment in industry, and of supporting the weak and marginalized segments of the poor, farmers, and industry. His ideas shaped policy in the international aspects of the attack on world poverty and human needs. They helped shape Indian economic thinking and policies in the 1940s, 1950s, and 1960s. However, he is best remembered for building institutions that have enduring reputations to this day. The Delhi School of Economics, founded in 1943, has produced generations of superior economists and sociologists; the Institute of Economic Growth in Delhi has made major contributions for decades to economic policy formulation in India and has contributed many faculty members and students to top policymaking positions in governments in India and abroad; the Institute for Social and Economic Change in Bangalore has sought to integrate the social sciences and has been particularly effective in building rural community institutions of governance. As member of the Planning Commission and Cabinet Minister, his initiatives in developing new ports, training and research institutes, adult education programme, and so on, made an impact. As Minister of Education he created the Indian Council of Social Science Research to fund basic social science research. In the international arena, as Chairman of the United Nations Sub-Committee on Economic Development, along with Hans Singer, Michael Kalecki, and others, he helped lay the intellectual foundations for UN's approach to development policy, and generated the thinking that led to the soft loan window of the World Bank, the International Development Agency.

His contributions as an economist and institution builder were made through the many roles he took on: as the first Professor of Economics in Delhi University, founding-director of three new social science institutions, Vice Chancellor of Delhi University, and then in the Indian government (as Director of Food Statistics, Head of the Programme Evaluation Organization, and later as Member of the Planning Commission and Minister for Shipping and Transport and, later, of Education). In all these positions he identified and nurtured young talent, many of whom became eminent social scientists.

S.L. Rao

Regional Disparities

Since its inception Indian planning has been concerned with the idea of balanced growth, an idea that came naturally from the Solovian framework according to which economies can reach a balanced growth path that optimizes their use of resources. The fact that a large economy with considerable heterogeneity can have different regions growing with widely different trajectories gave rise to concerns about 'unbalanced growth' and regional disparities. Since the opening up of the Indian economy in 1991–2 and its fairly impressive growth over the past decade, led essentially by a certain number of Indian states, increasing concern has also been raised about the fact that some states are growing too slowly or not at all, and thus falling behind or failing to benefit from the opening up of the Indian economy and the dynamism of certain sectors and regions. Specialists of growth economics have also tried to verify in the context of large economies like India as to whether one of the predictions of growth theory that less developed regions or countries will 'catch up' with the more developed ones (through faster capital accumulation) is confirmed or not. This is often referred to as the 'convergence' debate, and in the Indian context empirical evidence points to the 'divergence' in the growth path between Indian states, which is influenced by initial conditions of social and economic infrastructure and human capital.

The UNDP *Human Development Report* (UNHDR) for 2010 has India in the 119th position on the Human Development Index in world rankings, a very marginal improvement on its 127th position in 2005. Physical, social, and economic infrastructure varies widely between regions in India. These are inputs into the economic process which subsequently affect the process of growth. However, it is obvious that we should not focus exclusively on growth when talking about regional disparities. The modern approach to development increasingly considers good health, a high level of education, equal rights for women or of previously oppressed social categories, and possibilities for individuals to participate in social and political processes to be an integral part of development goals. Hence, understanding the full complexity of regional disparities implies that we not only look at income (or growth of income) disparities between regions, but also at the disparities in the indicators mentioned earlier between social categories and classes in the *same* region. In almost all regions, be they growing rapidly or slowly, social and spatial segregation is widespread, in urban agglomerations between rural and urban areas (often separated by a just a few kilometres or tens of kilometres), and between areas that are easily accessible by transport and those that are not, such as hilly areas or remote interiors. Now the Multidimensional Deprivation Index is being increasingly used by international agencies and scholars (see UNHDR 2010 and the references therein) to compare international development. However, this approach, like the Human Development Index, still needs further theoretical and empirical refinement in order to understand long-term trends in growth and development, because the underlying linkages and causality between growth and its potential explanatory social, economic, and political variables is still a matter of considerable debate in the academic and policy community.

Hence, the term 'regional disparities' cover many inequalities; we try to cover the principal ones here. Ram and Mohanty (2005), in one of the most extensive studies on human development indicators for the states and districts in India, use a composite index of reproductive, child health, and census indices on literacy and gender to classify India's districts and states. Based on this index, the 100 worst-off districts in India are concentrated in the states of Bihar (35 out of 37 districts), Uttar Pradesh (32 out of 70), Jharkhand (formerly a part of Bihar) (12/18), Rajasthan (9/32), Madhya Pradesh (9/45), Arunachal Pradesh (2/13), and Orissa (1/30). Considering Jharkhand as a part of the former state of Bihar, 79 of the 100 worst-off districts in terms of the Ram–Mohanty index are concentrated in two of the most populous and poorest states in India. Among the 100 best-off districts, there is heavy concentration in southern and western India. For the south there is Tamil Nadu (25 districts out of 30), Karnataka (11/27), Kerala (14/14), Andhra Pradesh (6/23), and Puducherry (4/4). For the west, there is Maharashtra (12/35), Gujarat (1/25), Daman and Dui (1/2), and Goa (1/2). These nine states make up 75 districts out of 100. In the north, Delhi (9/9), Punjab (1/17), Chandigarh (1/1), and Himachal Pradesh (2/12) make up 13; West Bengal (2/18), Assam (2/23), Mizoram (4/8), and Manipur (1) make up another nine. Hence, according to these social development indices we find that the south and the west are clearly doing much better than the north and the east. So this helps us to shed light on the controversy: is there an east–west divide or a north–south divide? In fact, both divides exist.

Now, if we rank the states according to the Ram–Mohanty index, we have the following ranking (from the bottom upwards): Bihar (25.31), Jharkhand (30.77), Uttar Pradesh (32), Rajasthan (35.13), Arunachal Pradesh (35.13), Madhya Pradesh (40.18), Meghalaya (45.32), Chhattisgarh (45.07), Nagaland (45.24), Orissa (47.39), Assam (47.96), Jammu and Kashmir (48.76), Manipur (49.75), Haryana (50.02), Uttaranchal (50.78), Sikkim (53.70), West Bengal (54.29), Gujarat (54.84), Tripura (55.90), Punjab (58.92), Mizoram (61.17), Maharashtra (61.41), Karnataka (61.53), Andhra Pradesh (62.02), Daman and Diu (63.83), Himachal Pradesh (64.67), Chandigarh (70.30), Tamil Nadu (71.49), Delhi (71.72), Andaman and Nicobar Islands (73.27), Goa (76.22), Puducherry (78.82), and Kerala (83.45). The ranking of the states follows the ranking of the districts (that is, the poorest districts are in the poorest states, and so on), with the following caveat—some of India's economically advanced (high per capita income) states such as Punjab, Haryana, and Gujarat are in the middle range as far as social development is concerned. Several middle-ranking states in terms of per capita income are among the major performers in terms of social development (Karnataka, Andhra Pradesh, Puducherry, and Kerala). Maharashtra and Tamil Nadu are the only two large states in the top of the league on both counts.

Since this entry was written, the publication of the 2011 provisional census results makes it imperative to mention regional disparities in the sex ratio, even if gender issues are treated elsewhere in the volume. Mary John (2011) highlights that in the previous census (2001), several states in north-west India had a sharp fall in the child sex ratio, with Punjab at the top in the negative sense of the term, with the child sex ratio falling below 800. Gujarat, Haryana, Delhi, and Himachal Pradesh also had declining sex ratios. These northern and north-western states have been peaking or levelling off the practice of sex selection, and John emphasizes that these states have not yet come back to their 1991 levels of the child sex ratio, which was already a fairly unfavourable figure. Further, the practice of sex selection is probably widening, even if it is less dramatic than in the north-west, to states and districts in western, southern, and eastern India. Further analysis of district-level data from the 2011 Census in the coming months will enable greater in-depth analysis of this question, but the slowness of social change in India and the persistence of male preference in relatively richer states of the north-west, aided by technologies of sex screening, also highlight that economic growth will not necessarily lead to better social indicators in the absence of both governmental policy at the federal, state, and local levels, and a stepping up of societal debates on such questions. The availability and use of technology, in spite of government bans on sex screening shows the state–society divide in India on such questions.

As far as the growth of per capita income and physical and economic infrastructure is concerned, a considerable body of work demonstrates the role of infrastructure in growth (Bandyopadhyay 2002; Nagaraj et al. 1998). In fact, one finds that the rankings of per capita income and physical infrastructure correspond closely. The per capita income ranking goes like this for India's largest states (2002–3): Punjab, Maharashtra, Haryana, Tamil Nadu, and Gujarat have consistently been the rich states; Karnataka, Kerala, Andhra Pradesh, West Bengal, Rajasthan, and Madhya Pradesh are in the middle; and Assam, Uttar Pradesh, Orissa, and Bihar are the poorest states. This ranking is very close to the ranking generated by Chaudhuri et al. (2006) using the CART (Classification and Regression Trees) method that endogenously generates 'clubs' of states (clubs in the sense that they have similar characteristics) according to the trajectories of their growth of per capita income. One observes the following phenomenon in these groups—rich states stay rich, poor states have stayed poor, but states that are in the middle can progress or regress. Over the last decade, Karnataka, Kerala, Andhra Pradesh, and West Bengal have shown distinct signs of moving upwards towards the richer states albeit along different growth trajectories, whereas Madhya Pradesh and Rajasthan, in spite of occasional progress, fell behind and became poorer. Also, in the long period, states have *changed* their relative positions *within* the groups. Kar et al. (2011), in an important and recently published paper, also using convergence models of distribution dynamics, emphasize the rather disquieting fact that in post-reform India, especially in the period after 2000, there is evidence of a polarization around two groups of rich and poor states. They point out that high- and middle-income states of Gujarat, Kerala, Himachal Pradesh, Karnataka, Tamil Nadu, and West Bengal have a tendency to move up in the group of richer states while Punjab and Maharashtra, which are part of the same richer group, tend to fall behind. Bihar and Uttar Pradesh are members of the 'poorer' club along with some middle-income states like Assam, Madhya Pradesh, Jammu and Kashmir, and Rajasthan, and these states have actually moved down in the income and growth ladder, while Bihar has moved up within the poorer group in terms of income growth rates. This also highlights the fragility of the Indian growth story. Even if the overall growth story at the macroeconomic and aggregate level is a positive one and internationally and nationally visible, it also highlights the fact, as André Gunder Frank had famously stated that before there was development, there was no underdevelopment. Growth can be fragile, temporary, or cyclical, if the underlying economic fundamentals are not strong. Competition between states, regions, and agglomerations can stimulate capital movement and flight of human resources as the Tata Nano–Singur story or internal migration trends in India are showing, with the south, west, and north-west of India continuing to lead the way and attracting the bulk of investible resources.

If one considers the percentage of the poor living below the poverty line, one finds that India's poorest states in per capita income terms, that is, Bihar (43 per cent),

Uttar Pradesh (31 per cent), Orissa (47 per cent), Assam (36 per cent), and Madhya Pradesh (37 per cent) are again the worst performers according to the 1990–2000 official calculations. The performance of the high- and middle-income states is mixed (Ram and Mohanty 2005: 32). Poverty and its reduction for these two groups seem to be related more to the effort at social development rather than directly correlated with income levels in terms of per capita income. Kozel and Parker (2005) carried out an important study in Uttar Pradesh, India's most populous state, and they point out that this state, which has a population of 175 million, of which approximately 60 million (34 per cent according to the authors, who contest the official calculations) live below the poverty line, constitutes approximately 8 per cent of the world's poor. Their article underlines the varied dimensions of poverty (see also Ravallion and Datt 2002; Besley et al. 2005) related to lack of employment opportunities, property rights, and access to finance and public goods and services (notably education and health) that help build up human capital, caste and gender related oppression, governance failures, and the lack of political voice. They stress the multidimensional nature of deprivation and the wide variations that exist in the conditions of the population that live below the poverty line within the state. This problem of intra-state disparities is also evident when we examine, for example, educational disparities within the states. Consider, for example, West Bengal, a middle-income state that has recently been growing rapidly in per capita income terms. Based on data from Census 2001 and the 7th All India Educational Survey of the Human Resource Ministry (2005), we note that over the two census periods, the district of Kolkata has the highest overall literacy rate in West Bengal (at over 80 per cent); what is reassuring is that the male–female gap is the lowest as one would expect for a major urban metropolis, of just 6–5 (83.8–77.3). In considering gender differentials, it is particularly interesting to look at the difference between urban male (UM) and rural female (RF) literacy rates rather than just the rural–urban or the male–female gap as this gives an idea of the combined effect of the two divides. And the gap is enormous—the most important gaps for West Bengal's poorest districts are: Malda (84.4–38.4), that is, 46 points, Puruliya (85–33.2) 52 points, and Uttar Dinajpur (85.5–30.8) 55 points. That is, one can say without fear of exaggeration that within India there is the coexistence of regions that compare with the most successful regions of Asia along with regions that compare with the poorest in Africa, but this divide also exists *within* the same states, and even in some fast growing ones (such as West Bengal or Andhra Pradesh). The heterogeneity *within* and *between* states, and the *possible* reasons for the differences in performances that have been raised here, are also reviewed by Sachs et al. (2002).

In a work on social development similar to the Ram–Mohanty index analysed in the previous version of the paper, Banerjee (2010) provides a well argued synthetic indicator of social and demographic variables, including the prevalence rate of contraceptives, total fertility rate, infant mortality rate, health indicators, educational attainment indicators, indicators of basic amenities, and social and economic deprivation indicators. The overall results give the ranking of India's states in 2008 and 2010, with the 2010 social development ranking being: Kerala, Punjab, Tamil Nadu, Maharashtra, Andhra Pradesh, Karnataka, Gujarat, Haryana, Assam, West Bengal, Orissa, Rajasthan, Chhattisgarh, Madhya Pradesh, Uttar Pradesh, Jharkhand, and Bihar, taking into account only India's largest states. In this list, Andhra Pradesh, Karnataka, Orissa, and Punjab have slightly improved their positions; Chhattisgarh, Gujarat, Haryana, Rajasthan, and Tamil Nadu have moved down slightly; and the positions of Assam, Bihar, Jharkhand, Kerala, Madhya Pradesh, Maharashtra, Uttar Pradesh, and Bengal remain unchanged. It should also be remembered that these are synthetic indicators that average out opposing movements in their individual components some of which, such as income growth, demography, health or education, are extensively commented on in public debate where individual states are often highlighted.

This entry would be incomplete without a mention of the demographic dividend, which has been much commented on in recent debate. Projections from the census (see Aiyar and Mody 2010) seem to suggest that India's poorer states, which have not yet attained the population transition fully, are more likely to contribute to the working age (15–59) population in the coming decades as compared to better-off or more socially developed states. This implies that if educational and job opportunities and infrastructures are not substantially developed in these states (and in the neighbouring states) in the coming decades, the demographic dividend might boomerang into a Malthusian handicap.

All the empirical information presented here according to us shows a demarcation of the Indian economy into separate groups or clubs of states, depending on the variables chosen. As pointed out earlier, the evolution in principal indicators and in the relative positions of the states between 2005 and 2010 has not been massive. Social development is slow and uneven across India. The worrying trend is that these demarcations also exist within the states themselves, a fact that has become more prominent in recent times because of the greater availability of district-level economic and social data. The research agenda in this area probably needs to delve into the following question: Do regional disparities reflect underlying long-run structural differences in the initial economic conditions of the growth process, or are they more related to social, cultural, or political differences between the states? The answer might be a combination of all these factors, but they need to be singled out in increasing detail.

BASUDEB CHAUDHURI AND VELAYOUDOM MARIMOUTOU

References

Aiyar, Shekar and Ashoka Mody. 2010. 'The Demographic Dividend: Evidence from Indian States', IMF Working Paper WP/11/38.

Bandyopadhyay, Sanghamitra. 2002. *Convergence Club Empirics: Some Dynamics and Explanations of Unequal Growth across Indian States*, London, London School of Economics.

Banerjee, Kaustav. 2011. 'Social Development Index 2010', chapter 19, in Manoranjan Mohanty (ed.), *India, Social Development Report 2010*, New Delhi, Council for Social Development and Oxford University Press.

Besley, Timothy, Robin Burgess, and Berta Esteve-Volart. 2005. *Operationalising Pro-poor Growth: India Case Study*, London, London School of Economics.

Chaudhuri, Basudeb, Hélène Chevrou-Séverac, and Velayoudom Marimoutou. 2006. 'Growth and Convergence Clubs in Indian States, 1965–2002', Working Paper, GREQAM.

Government of India. 2001. Census Report.

——. 2005. 7th All India Educational Survey, New Delhi, Ministry of Human Resource Development, Government of India.

——. 2011. Census Report.

John, Mary E. 2011. 'Census 2011: Governing Populations and the Girl Child', *Economic and Political Weekly*, XLVI(16): 10–12.

Kar, Sabyasachi, Debajit Jha, and Alpana Kateja. 2011. 'Club Convergence and Polarisation of States: A Nonparametric Analysis of Post Reform India', New Delhi, Institute of Economic Growth, Working Paper 2010, published in the *Indian Growth and Development Review 2011*.

Kozel, V. and Barbara Parker. 2005. 'A Profile and Diagnostic of Poverty in Uttar Pradesh', chapter 23, in Angus Deaton and Valerie Kozel (eds), *The Great Indian Poverty Debate*, Macmillan.

Nagaraj, R., A. Varoudakis, and M.A. Véganzonès. 1998. 'Long Run Growth Trends and Convergence across Indian States', Technical Paper No. 131, Paris, OECD.

Ram, F. and S.K. Mohanty. 2005. *State of Human Development in States and Districts of India*, Mumbai, International Institute of Population Studies.

Ravallion, M. and Gaurav Datt. 2002. 'Why has Economic Growth been More Pro-poor in Some States of India than Others', *Journal of Development Economics*, 68: 381–400.

Sachs, Jeffrey, N. Bajpai, and A. Ramiah. 2002. 'Understanding Regional Economic Growth in India', Harvard University, Centre for International Development, Working Paper No. 88.

UNDP. 2010. *United Nations Human Development Report (UNHDR) 2010*.

■ Religion and Economic Well-being

In this entry, guided by the need to be succinct, I focus on adherents of the two major religions in India: Hindus and Muslims, constituting 83 and 12 per cent of India's population, respectively. This immediately raises the question of who is a Hindu? Embedded among Hindus are the scheduled castes (hereafter referred to by their preferred name, 'dalits'). Around 16 per cent of India's population comprises dalits and they are persons whom 'caste Hindus', that is, Hindus within the four-*varna* caste system, regard as being *outside* the caste system.

The most practical manifestation of this is the social stigma associated with being a dalit: in many instances dalits are those with whom physical contact is regarded by caste Hindus as unclean. Given the 'outsider' status of dalits within the Hindu religion, a major consequence of which is their social and economic backwardness, I adopt, in this entry, a tripartite division of persons: caste Hindus (hereafter simply Hindus), Muslims, and dalits.

This then raises the question of how economic welfare is to be defined. Here I define it in terms of the following components: the nature of employment, education and literacy, and health outcomes.

A striking feature of employment patterns in India is the preponderance of Hindus in regular salaried or wage employment; Muslims in self-employment; and dalits in casual wage labour. The National Sample Survey (NSS) for 1999–2000 shows that of men aged between 25 and 45 (that is, prime age men): 25 per cent of Hindus, compared to 18 per cent of Muslims and dalits, were in regular employment; at the other extreme, 47 per cent of dalits, compared to 24 per cent of Muslims and 18 per cent of Hindus, worked as casual labourers. Nearly half of Muslim men, between 25 and 45 years, compared to 28 per cent of dalits and 40 per cent of Hindus, were self-employed.

It should be remembered that the Constitution of India allows for special provisions for dalits in terms of reservation of a certain proportion of government jobs for them. Notwithstanding these provisions, which have been in force for half a century, less than one in five dalit men aged between 25 and 44 years was in regular employment. According to one analysis (Borooah et al. 2005), job reservations contributed less than one-third to the low proportion of regularly employed dalits. The same analysis also argues that when job reservation was extended it should have been to Muslims rather than to the other backward classes.

These differences in employment patterns are reflected in the educational achievements of the three groups. The NSS data show that in 1999–2000, over 73 per cent of Hindus over the age of 7 years were literate, compared to 65 per cent of Muslims and 54 per cent of dalits. The advantage in literacy had a gender dimension: 63 per cent of Hindu females above the age of 7 were literate, compared to 56 per cent of Muslim and 41 per cent of dalit females. At the other end of the educational scale, 11 per cent of Hindus above the age of 21, compared to 5 per cent of Muslims and 3 per cent of dalits were graduates.

Differences in educational achievement between Hindus, Muslims, and dalits could be ascribed to differences between the proportions of children from these groups enrolled in school. The National Council of Applied Economic Research (NCAER), on the basis of a 1994 survey, showed that enrolment rates of children between the ages of 6 and 14 were: 84 and 68 per cent for Hindu boys and girls; 68 and 57 per cent for Muslim boys and girls; and 70 and 55 per cent for Dalit boys and girls. In terms of reasons for non-enrolment, 23 per cent of Muslim parents (compared to 16 per cent of Hindus and 17 per cent of dalits) thought that education was not important while 34 per cent of dalit parents (compared to 29 per cent of Muslims and 22 per cent of Hindus) faced financial constraints and/or wanted their child engaged in non-school activity.

A recent analysis of school enrolment rates in India (Borooah and Iyer 2005b) argues that sending children to school depends upon attitudes to education: of the children, of their parents, and of the communities to which they belong. These attitudinal differences between the communities are sharp when the parents are illiterate but they tend to narrow substantially, if not disappear altogether, when literate parents, regardless of their religious community, appreciate the value of education.

Outcomes regarding health are many and varied and here I consider just a few. First, in terms of fertility the NCAER survey showed the total number of live births to currently married women as: 3.19 for Hindus, 3.82 for Muslims, and 3.38 for dalits. The higher fertility rate of Muslim women can, at least in part, be ascribed to their reluctance, compared to their Hindu counterparts, to use contraception: a much larger proportion of Muslim women, relative to Hindu and dalit women, did not use any contraception and, among the Muslim women who did use contraception, there was relatively greater reliance on spacing than on terminal methods. However, it has also been argued (Borooah and Iyer 2005a) that the higher Muslim fertility can, in part, be ascribed to the possibility that Muslims value daughters more than Hindus (have less 'daughter aversion' than Hindus).

Another aspect of health is the vaccination of young children. Complete immunization involves vaccination of children, within the first year of life, against six diseases: diphtheria, pertussis, tetanus, tuberculosis, poliomyelitis, and measles. The NCAER Survey shows that there were considerable differences between Hindus and Muslims in the proportion of children who were fully immunized: 60 per cent of children from Hindu households, compared to 40 per cent from Muslim households and 47 per cent from dalit households, were fully immunized. After controlling for non-community variables, the likelihood of boys and girls being fully vaccinated would fall by six and nine points, respectively, if they were dalits, and by 10 and 12 points, respectively, if they were Muslim. So not only did dalit and Muslim parents have, relative to Hindus, a lower propensity to fully immunize their children, they also embedded a gender bias into this lower propensity (Borooah 2004).

Vani K. Borooah

References

Borooah, V.K. 2004. 'Gender Bias among Children in India in Their Diet and Immunisation against Disease', *Social Science and Medicine*, 58: 1719–31.

Borooah, V.K., A. Dubey, and S. Iyer. 2005. 'How Effective Has Job Reservation in India Been? Caste, Religion, and Economic Status', University of Ulster, mimeo.

Borooah, V.K. and S. Iyer. 2005a. 'Religion, Literacy, and the Female-to-Male Ratio', *Economic and Political Weekly*, 60: 419–28.

——. 2005b. '*Vidya, Veda,* and *Varna*: The Influence of Religion and Caste on Education in Rural India', *Journal of Development Studies*, 41: 1369–404.

Rent Control Acts

The Rent Control Acts (RCAs) enacted in the various states of India were intended to restrict the increase of rent in certain premises situated within the urban areas and to regulate and control the eviction of tenants by landowners. The RCA was a piece of ameliorative legislation in the interest of tenants in urban areas. Historically, it was felt that the low degree of urbanization and development pressures immediately after Independence would lead to a gap in urban housing supply. The current owners could use this demand gap to charge exorbitant rents and displace current tenants who may not be able to pay these high rents.

Though each state enacted its own version of the Act, there are broad similarities among them. All of them impose two types of restrictions—on allowable increases in rent and on the conditions for eviction. The two are obviously related. First, as long as tenants paid the permitted increase in rents, there was no need to sign a fresh contract. Second, as long as they paid the rent, tenants could not be evicted unless they indulged in subletting, misuse of tenanted premises, non-use of the premises, or unless there was bonafide need of the landowner. In principle, the Act extended protection from eviction to a tenant even after determination of contractual tenancy so long as he or she paid, or was ready and willing to pay, the permitted increases and observed and performed other conditions of the tenancy consistent with the provisions of the Act.

Unfortunately, this is an instance of an Act gone horribly wrong. Tenants, taking advantage of the protection afforded them under the Act, continue residing in palatial houses by complying with the terms of the lease, paying in court the nominal/standard rent, while eviction proceedings take years to culminate in eviction. This has led to two types of responses by landowners. First, they have stopped investing in the upkeep of their houses resulting in broken-down premises and urban decay. Second, new house owners find it safer to keep their houses locked till they move in rather than rent them out in the intervening period.

Indeed, the rent control legislations are to a certain extent responsible for the decline in the quality of living and supply of rental housing. Taking advantage of the law, tenants refuse to vacate property they had taken on rent. Landowners respond through inadequate maintenance, poor repairs, and grudging provision of services. The enjoyment a tenant can derive out of the dwelling space ultimately tends to be reduced to a level commensurate with the controlled rent. The dilapidated conditions of Mumbai *chawl*s are ample proof of the adverse effects of the rent control legislation.

Importantly, this protection was extended to commercial properties also. The rent control legislations enacted throughout the country restricted the sale or transfer of commercial properties. This was responsible for the growth in *pugree*, the illegal institution of a one-time lump-sum payment to the landowner by the tenant, primarily to offset the low rents. It became a major source for the generation of black money in India. Visible instances of this counterproductive law are the famous Chawri Bazaar, Old Delhi, and Connaught Place shops that are worth millions but are still being rented out for as low as a few hundred rupees a month. This too has obvious consequences for real estate development and modernization of existing facilities for commerce and business.

In addition to landowners not spending sufficient amounts for the upkeep of assets, this also indirectly prevents the city municipalities from public spending on urban amenities. First, much of the tenancy is under the legal scanner. Landowners are unwilling to leave any record of tenancy so that tenants cannot claim as much in a court of law. This obviously means that there are no records of rents paid and hence no taxes collected either from rent income or from increased valuation of property. Second, property valuations are no longer driven by the market and property tax collections are below what they would have been were they to be valued at market prices.

The RCAs also laid the burden of proof on the owner. This essentially meant that tenants went to court. Given our court system, this meant long delays in case resolutions. Usually, an eviction proceeding is disposed of within a period of five to seven years. This is mainly because of a technical reason. For instance, the Delhi RCA is applicable only in cases of a pre-existing landowner–tenant relationship. Therefore, the determination of the jural relationship between the tenant and landowner at a preliminary stage is mandatory, and the same would entail appreciation and recording of evidence, trial, and arguments. Ordinarily, it is for the civil courts to determine whether and, if so, what jural relationship exists between the litigating parties. However, the Act postulates that the relationship of landowner and tenant must be a pre-existing relationship. The remedy for a landowner where there is no existing relationship is to move to the civil court by way of a suit for ejectment, untrammelled by the provisions of the Act. Therefore, it has become standard practice, or a line of argument, by every tenant to challenge this relationship causing protracted delay in adjudication of the eviction proceedings. Not surprisingly, landowners take recourse to extra-legal methods in most cases.

Over the years, the courts have done their bit to redress the situation. In particular, they started acknowledging the rights of landowners. In 2002, the

Delhi High Court struck down three sections of the Delhi RCA, 1958, which had virtually 'frozen' the rent of residential and commercial properties. The Court decreed Sections 4, 6, and 9 of the Act as 'ultra vires' and stated that these provisions were 'arbitrary and unfair' to landowners. It held these sections to be violative of the Constitution as they 'affect landlord's right to livelihood, right to life and avocation'.

In 1992, the central government announced the National Housing Policy and proposed amendments to the State Rent Control Laws to bring about uniformity in their application. The purpose of the model Act was:

- to regulate the availability of space at fair rents;
- to facilitate accommodation to all classes of society;
- to provide fair and equitable return on property investment; and
- to provide due and fair protection to tenants against landowners.

However, the states are yet to follow suit. For instance, a new Delhi Rent Act was introduced and approved by Parliament in 1995, but the Delhi government has not implemented it till date.

JUGNU BAGGA AND SHUBHASHIS GANGOPADHYAY

■ Repo Market

Repos, or repurchase agreements, are contracts for the sale and repurchase of government securities and short-term treasury bills at a future date. In this transaction, the seller repurchases the financial asset at the same price at which it was sold and pays interest on it. In other words, a repo is a short-term, interest-bearing loan against the collateral of government securities.

Unlike in the US and some other developed markets, corporate bonds, bonds of public-sector undertakings, commercial paper, and certificates of deposit are not eligible as collateral for repo deals in India. Since there are limits on the instruments that can be pledged as collateral as well as restrictions on the players in this market, the repo barely exists as a funding mechanism.

In fact, in the Indian context, the repo rate is considered an interest rate signal from the Reserve Bank of India (RBI) and the repo per se is a monetary stabilization mechanism that the central bank uses as a daily liquidity management tool.

The annualized rate of interest paid on the loan is known as the repo rate. The interest rate on repo deals is normally lower than the rates in the overnight call money market.

The repo rate is negotiated by counter-parties independently of the interest rate (or 'coupons') of the underlying securities and is influenced by overall money market conditions. Repos can be of any duration—between one and 14 days or even longer—but are most commonly overnight loans.

Inter-bank repos in India are permitted under regulated conditions. After serious irregularities in securities transactions in 1992, eligible participants and instruments in this market were restricted but the rules were subsequently liberalized in phases.

In 1995–6, the RBI partially reopened the market only for specified government securities. Virtually all new securities, auctioned by the Indian central bank, were made repoable but only banks and primary dealers (entities that trade in government securities) were allowed to strike repo deals.

In 1997–8, all government securities and treasury bills were made repoable. Finally, in 2003, mutual funds were allowed into this segment. In its annual policy, announced in April 2005, RBI Governor Y.V. Reddy allowed the entry of listed corporations and non-scheduled cooperative banks into the government securities repo market 'subject to eligibility criteria and safeguards'. The repo or reverse repo could be entered into by corporate entities and non-banking finance companies (NBFCs) for a maturity period of seven days and the counter-party could be either a bank or a primary dealer. To be precise, they cannot enter into direct repo or reverse repo deals with the RBI. Moreover, in order to avoid conflict of interests and mismanagement of funds, the Indian central bank has prohibited repo/reverse repo deals between NBFCs and corporations as many corporations have their own NBFC arms.

There have been plans to permit repos in bonds of public-sector undertakings and private and corporate debt securities, provided they are held in dematerialized form in a depository and the transactions are done through a recognized stock exchange. In 1999, Dr Y.V. Reddy had said, 'This can be operationalized after the government issues a clarification regarding applicability of stamp duties on transactions in dematerialized instruments.'[1] However, this has not yet been done. Reddy, at that time deputy governor, had admitted that the inter-bank repo market in India needs to be made more transparent and standardized better.

[1]Inaugural address by Dr Y.V. Reddy at seminar on 'Fixed Income Markets', organized by the National Stock Exchange and ISMA in Mumbai on 11 February 1999.

The development of the repo market is linked to the development of the overnight call money market as a pure inter-bank market. In its October 1998 review of monetary policy, the RBI had announced that the call/notice/term money market would be purely an inter-bank market with additional access only to primary dealers.

This implies that non-bank players have to be encouraged to deploy their short-term surpluses in the repo market where they should be allowed to borrow and lend freely through repos in both government and non-government securities. The RBI has been restraining the entry of non-banking players into the overnight call money market but it is yet to become a pure inter-bank market. Once this is done, the repo market will get a leg up.

Parallel to a thin repo market runs a tradable repo market called collateralized borrowing and lending obligation (CBLO). This unique instrument was developed by the Clearing Corporation of India Ltd (CCIL) about two years ago. While the repo is a bilateral deal in which both parties (the borrower and the lender) are obliged to follow the terms of the contract, the CBLO is a tradable repo in which either side can change the contract by using the CCIL's trading screen.

In other words, if a borrower has raised seven-day money through this route by using government securities as a collateral and does not need the funds after three days, it can snap the contract. Similarly, if a lender needs the money after two days, it can pull out of the contract even though the money has been lent for seven days. This is possible because of the tradable nature of the instrument. It is similar to any anonymous order-matching screen with real-time information. The CCIL addresses the settlement risk and provides guaranteed settlements.

The volume of CBLO is on par with the repo market. For instance, the daily average volume of CBLO for the week ended 4 March 2005 was Rs 4,563 crore on 135 trades. The daily average trading volume of the repo market was Rs 4,555 crore on 90 trades during the same period.

Dr R.H. Patil, chairman of the CCIL, says, 'In view of the advantages that the CBLO offers in terms of liquidity, transparency and flexibility, it is expected that it will eventually overtake the repo market in terms of volumes.' Here too banks, mutual funds, and primary dealers and insurance companies are the major players; corporations are yet to enter this segment.

The development of the repo as a liquidity management tool is a fallout of a fundamental change in the conduct of monetary policy made by the Indian central bank with the introduction of the liquidity adjustment facility (LAF) on 5 June 2000. This marked a migration from direct instruments of monetary control to indirect instruments in a market-based economy. The LAF operations are conducted through repo/reverse repo auctions.

As a prelude to the introduction of the LAF, an interim liquidity adjustment facility (ILAF) was introduced in April 1999. The RBI's monetary policy statement of April 2000 announced the introduction of the LAF through a system of repo and reverse repo auctions.

> The LAF enables the RBI to modulate short-term liquidity under varied financial market conditions.... It [the LAF] operates through daily repo and reverse repo auctions thereby setting a corridor for the short-term interest rate consistent with policy objectives. Although there is no formal targeting of overnight interest rates, LAF operations have enabled the RBI to de-emphasize the targeting of bank reserves and focus increasingly on interest rates [Report of Internal Group on LAF].

Till recently, the use of the terms 'repo' and 'reverse repo' in the Indian context differed from the way they were used in advanced economies. In international parlance, 'repo' denotes an injection of liquidity by the central bank against eligible collateral securities, while 'reverse repo' denotes absorption of liquidity by the central bank against eligible collateral. In contrast, in the Indian context, 'repo' denoted liquidity absorption by the Reserve Bank and 'reverse repo' liquidity injection. To achieve uniformity and facilitate international comparisons, the RBI changed the usage of the terms 'repo' and 'reverse repo' from 4 November 2004. So now, when the banks park their surpluses with the RBI and earn interest, it is called reverse repo. The banks earn an annual interest rate of 4.75 per cent on such a deal. If they want to draw down liquidity from the RBI, they resort to repo deals at an annual interest rate of 6 per cent.

One direct result of the emergence of the repo rate as the main signal rate is the diminishing importance of the bank rate—the rate at which banks theoretically can draw down refinance from the RBI.

The bank rate was used to signal the RBI's policy stance in association with other supporting instruments. The same objective is broadly achieved now with the repo rate. The repo rate has started reflecting the RBI's medium-term outlook and is partly assuming the role of the bank rate. In the process, the repo rate has gained wider acceptance in the market as a policy signalling rate.

TAMAL BANDYOPADHYAY

Reference

Report of Internal Group on Liquidity Adjustment Facility—An Internal Group of the RBI, available at http://www/rbi. org. in/scripts/Publication Report Details, aspx? From Date = 12/02/03 & SECID = 21 & SUBSECID = 0.

■ Reserve Bank of India

The Reserve Bank of India (RBI) is India's central bank. It manages India's monetary and exchange rate policies and public debt, that is, the borrowings of the central and state governments. The regulation of commercial banking is another of its key responsibilities. Between 1935 and 1949, when it was nationalized, RBI was a private entity. Until 1950, since 'finance' was a 'reserved' subject for the Government of India, monetary policy was made by the government, while the Imperial Bank of India (nationalized and renamed the State Bank of India in 1955) exercised much the greater influence on the money market. It was only in the first decades after Independence, that RBI came into its own as the primary institution in India's fledgling financial sector. RBI has since then viewed its wider activities as an 'institutional' dimension of its monetary policy role.

But even as it sought to follow a more active monetary policy from the 1950s, the Bank could ill-afford to ignore the longer-term needs of the planning and public investment process that had meanwhile got under way. From 1956, RBI loosened the reins of its lending to the government against ad hoc treasury bills, and its lending to government now came to account for a significant part of plan financing, for example, almost a quarter of the Second Five Year Plan's outlay. This undermined RBI's monetary policies and for the next three decades it mainly sought to adapt the financial system to the needs of the central government, increasingly by forcing the private sector to trim investment and consumption expenditures. RBI also deployed sectoral policies, notably selective credit control measures to check demand in specific sectors, and 'liquidity' instruments that boosted government securities as an investment destination for banks' funds.

The other pillars of the Indian central banking edifice were built on rather strong foundations, and despite several problems and setbacks helped expand and deepen India's financial system over the next five decades. Rural credit was a priority for RBI from its earliest years. In subsequent years RBI also took upon itself the development of long-term industrial finance when it helped in establishing national industrial financing institutions, such as the Unit Trust of India and the Industrial Development Bank of India in 1964. It maintained close links with these two institutions until 1976.

RBI has also been responsible for promoting and regulating the banking system. Consolidating banks and instituting sound licensing, management, and supervisory norms and procedures have been important priorities. Following RBI's efforts, an unwieldy banking arrangement comprising 566 banks in 1951 was reduced to a more homogeneous and manageable system made up of 91 institutions by 1967. At the same time the reach of the banking system widened, with offices of commercial banks increasing from about 4,000 in 1951 to over 7,000 in 1967.

In 1969, Prime Minister Indira Gandhi decided to nationalize 14 of India's largest private-sector banks. This one act dominated the 1970s. The issue in contention was basically sound: banking was not reaching the rural areas rapidly enough. RBI was entrusted with the supervision of the nationalized banks. This transformed RBI's role in ways that had never been envisaged. Its autonomy in monetary policy was further eroded not merely by fiscal dominance but also because of greater government involvement in banking affairs. It was not until the mid-1980s that monetary policy was gradually restored as an important policy instrument.

RBI has also been playing an important role in arranging short-term financing to tide over balance-of-payments problems, and the management of the exchange rate. However, since the abolition of exchange controls, RBI's role in this is now confined to interventions in the market to smoothen volatility.

But it is mainly in the reforms of the financial sector since 1991 that RBI has played a leading role. These reforms extended in three main directions. Monetary control has moved towards greater reliance on bank rate changes, open market operations, and repo auctions. This has been accompanied by greater discretion to banks to set deposit and lending rates and manage loan portfolios. These reforms have been accompanied by a steady decline in retail bank lending rates, with predictable effects on investment and consumer demand for credit. With regard to the external sector, in the early years stress was laid on freeing up trade and current account transactions from unnecessary and counterproductive controls.

The rapid growth in India's external reserves also encouraged RBI to relax restrictions on capital account transactions. Restoring the soundness of India's banking system has been another major priority. Here the focus has been on stricter lending norms, accelerated recovery or writing-off of non-performing assets (NPAs), speedy recapitalization whenever necessary, and the modification and implementation of risk-weighted norms of capital adequacy. Not surprisingly against the background of a rapidly liberalizing economy, the relations between RBI and the government have also been changing.

A major development here was a 1996 agreement limiting the monetization of government debt which has helped increase elbow room for monetary policy. Its control of inflation and management of the external sector, including through the 1997 Asian financial crises, represent important recent successes for RBI.

However, liberalization has not come without problems: RBI was caught napping twice, once over a stock market scam in 1993 and again in a 1998 bank collapse. In some parts of India, non-banking financial institutions also suffered crises and collapse. The cooperative banking system is another potential source of financial instability, and remains in need of reforms and rehabilitation.

For the last few years, RBI has been gradually moving towards liberalizing the financial markets even more with a view to deepening and broadening them, especially by a more rapid growth of the corporate bond market and a greater role for foreign players. It has been criticized for being too slow in this regard but its policy gradualism was vindicated after the global financial crash of 2008.

Its current focus is mostly domestic, aimed at financial inclusion so that more of the domestic savings can be brought into the banking system.

G. Balachandran and T.C.A. Srinivasa-Raghavan

References

Balachandran, G. 1998. *The Reserve Bank of India, 1951–1967*, New Delhi, Oxford University Press.

Reserve Bank of India (RBI). Various Years. *Annual Report*, Mumbai, RBI.

——. Various Years. *Report on Currency and Banking*, Mumbai, RBI.

■ Roads

The entire road network in India currently stands at 3.3 million km spanning the entire country, making it the second longest road network in the world behind the United States of America. The network includes national highways, state highways, major district roads, and other village roads. Use of the road network has increased dramatically throughout India's history with approximately 87 per cent of all passenger traffic and 65 per cent of all freight traffic currently on roads. However, despite this importance of roads for India, problems have plagued its infrastructure, including poor maintenance and inaccessibility of many villages.

India's oldest road is the Grand Trunk Road, which was built in the 16th century. Sher Shah Suri, the Emperor of India, attempted to link regional provinces for administrative and military purposes by building the road, which was at first called Sadak-e-Azam. After being used for transport and conquests, British rulers improved and renamed the road, sometimes calling it the 'Long Walk'. Today the road stretches for over 2,500 km, connecting Calcutta with Kabul in Afghanistan, making it the longest road in the country.

Currently, expenditure on the road sector in India is approximately Rs 211 billion, accounting for less than 3 per cent of union and state government expenditures. However, the total tax revenue from the road sector amounts to 15.5 per cent of revenue, resulting in a revenue surplus of Rs 289 billion. The government's total tax revenue is composed of taxes on initial vehicle purchases, fuel, road freight and passengers, and collections from tolls. However, while the union and state governments' tax revenue from the road sector was Rs 500 billion, only 30 to 40 per cent was accounted for by annual road user charges (for example, tolls).

The road network in India remains poorly funded for meeting the maintenance requirements for current roads. While the doubling of trucks on Indian roads has caused more extensive damage to the infrastructure, expenditure to improve and maintain roads has lagged behind. One of the major problems is the excessive expenditure on labour, which amounts to 60 to 70 per cent of expenditure on road maintenance. In addition to labour, asphalt, the dominant material in road construction, is produced by a few major oil companies, leaving very little production of other maintenance products. The government is beginning to use advanced materials, construct hot asphalt mix toll roads, and move towards less labour-intensive mechanized road maintenance, contributing to the creation of long-lasting all-weather roads. The cost for removing deficiencies in roads is extremely steep—removing deficiencies from National Highways would require Rs 1.65 trillion. Effort in expanding the road network has also lagged; the number of vehicles has grown by over 50 per cent, while the road network has grown by around 5 per cent. In order to keep up with the current rate of traffic growth, India would need to build 15,000 km of roads, costing Rs 1.5 trillion.

Of the 3.3 million km of roads in India, only 2 per cent or 65,569 km are national highways, yet they carry 40 per cent of the traffic in India. A particular problem is the width of highways, of which only 2 or 3 per cent are four-laned and almost 15 per cent have only a single lane. In fact, only 34,298 km of national highways are actually suitable for speedy transportation.

In 1998, Prime Minister Atal Bihari Vajpayee launched the government's National Highway Development Project (NHDP) to remove capacity constraints and improve all-weather connectivity. The funding for the NHDP comes from a Re 1 cess on each litre of diesel and petrol, amounting to Rs 20 billion per annum. On 9 December 1998, a Planning Commission task force decided on two components for the NHDP: a Golden Quadrilateral measuring 5,846 km and the North–South and East–West Corridors measuring 7,300 km. The Golden Quadrilateral consists of four major national highways connecting the four major regions of India: Delhi–Kolkata, Kolkata–Chennai, Chennai–Mumbai, and Mumbai–Delhi. Each of these highways is developed by Indian firms, joint ventures, and foreign firms. The North–South Corridor is designed to stretch from Kashmir to Kanyakumari, passing through major cities like Delhi, Hyderabad, and Bangalore. The East–West Corridor will begin in Silchar and end in Porbandar, passing through Lucknow, Udaipur, and Rajkot. Although many segments have been started between 1999 and 2001, much of the two highways still remains to be constructed. The first phase of the project was approved on 12 December 2000 at a cost of Rs 303 billion. The National Highways Authority of India predicts the majority of roads will be completed between 2005 and 2006.

The Pradhan Mantri Gram Sadak Yojana (PMGSY) programme was launched by the Government of India on 25 December 2000 to connect the 200 million people, or 330,000 habitations, lacking all-weather road access in India. The PMGSY programme was designed to further integrate the rural sector into the economy and allow easier access to healthcare and education services. On 23 September 2004, the World Bank Group approved a loan of US$ 400 million for the India Rural Roads Programme, which includes the PMGSY. By 2007, the government plans to provide all-weather road access to all habitations with population over 500, still leaving 50 million people without all-weather roads. The total cost for the project is estimated at just under US$ 600 million, of which almost two-thirds is in loans from the World Bank.

The Indian roads network stands to provide the country with great economic benefits if appropriately and quickly developed. According to the World Bank, the poor roads in India cause the nation an annual loss of between Rs 200 billion and Rs 300 billion. Development of India's road network should focus more on mechanizing road maintenance and continuing to provide tax incentives for private partnerships in road construction. However, at the same time there must be coordination in the government bureaucracy, as responsibility for roads spans several agencies and ministries. In addition, the road network in India must shift towards user charges through tolls and fuel taxes that are specifically used for road maintenance and construction, while encouraging further development of other transportation mechanisms, including the faltering railroad system.

PRITAL SAILESH KADAKIA

References

Choudhary, Ajeet K., Deepak Dangayach, Prashant Dwivedi, Tarun Sharma, and P. Venu Madhav. 2001. 'A Report on Road Sector in India,' Ahmedabad, Indian Institute of Management, 24 August.

National Highways Authority of India, Government of India, available at http://www.nhai.org/.

World Bank Group. 'Highway Sector Financing in India', available at http://www.highwayfinindia.org/.

——. 2004. 'Project Appraisal Document on a Proposed Credit in the Amount of SDR 206 Million (US$ 300 Million Equivalent) and Proposed Loan in the Amount of US$ 100 Million to the Government of India for a Rural Roads Project', 16 August.

■ Ashok Rudra

Ashok Rudra (1930–92) was not only a fine economist but also a great scholar and a 'public intellectual' in the best sense of the term. From the mid-1950s onwards, he conducted many pioneering studies of India's economy and society. Rudra's professional writings, based on painstaking research and strong value commitments, often challenged established theories and conventional wisdom. He was equally creative and fearless in his interventions in public debates. Rudra also wrote prolifically on literary and cultural subjects, and became an eminent Bengali writer, with a distinct style of his own. Few Indian economists achieved this remarkable blend of technique, scholarship, and creativity.

Biographical Sketch

Ashok Rudra was born in Rangoon in 1930. His parents came to Calcutta from Rangoon and later moved to

London. Rudra graduated in statistics from Presidency College (Calcutta) in 1950 and obtained his doctorate in statistics from London University in 1953.

After returning to India in 1953 with his wife Colette, Rudra joined the Indian Statistical Institute (ISI), Calcutta, as Research Officer. From then on he worked with many academic institutions in India. He served the Government of Kerala as Director, Bureau of Economic Studies, from 1958 to 1960 and after that joined the ISI, Delhi. He was a Professor of Economics at Bombay University (1965–7), Delhi University (1967–8), and Visva-Bharati University (1968–73). He worked as Senior Fellow of the ICSSR from 1974 to 1977 and as a Professor at the ISI, Calcutta, in 1978–9. In 1979, he joined Visva-Bharati again as a Professor of Economics, and retired in 1990. In 1991, he became National Fellow of the ICSSR, in which capacity he worked until his death on 29 October 1992.

Rudra had a lasting association with Visva-Bharati University in Santiniketan, starting in 1968. Santiniketan's proximity with rural areas was ideal for purposes of field surveys. He liked the natural and cultural atmosphere of Santiniketan and had a deep love for Rabindra Nath Tagore. He built a house in Santiniketan and made it his home.

During his first spell in Visva-Bharati, from 1968 to 1973, Rudra participated actively in Santiniketan's cultural life. He initiated a music circle, 'Sangeet Chakra', and also a Marxian study circle in which various issues would be discussed from a Marxian point of view but without partisanship or dogma. During the 1980s he started 'Mukta Manus' (free human being), an organization to promote scientific thought in rural areas and help people overcome superstition.

P.C. Mahalanobis played an important role in Ashok Rudra's professional life. Rudra wrote a biography of Mahalanobis, which was published posthumously. He also had close associations with many distinguished Indian economists: A.K. Dasgupta, K.N. Raj, Amartya Sen, Sukhamoy Chakravarty, Pranab Bardhan, T.N. Srinivasan, Krishna Bharadwaj, and Nikhilesh Bhattacharya, among others.

The main areas of Rudra's research include development planning, agricultural economics, political economy, Marx's theory of history, and field survey methods. A small sample of his wide-ranging contributions is discussed next.

Development Planning

In the early 1960s, Rudra was associated with the Perspective Planning Division of the Planning Commission, after joining ISI, Delhi. Under his guidance, the ISI team did pioneering work on economy-wide model building, and also played a key role in the estimation of poverty lines. Together with Alan Manne, Rudra developed a consistency model for the Fourth Plan, relating sector-wise output and investment levels to the demand for consumer goods based on alternative assumptions about future changes in the distribution of income as well as normative concepts of minimum levels of living.

Rudra was ahead of his time in his appraisal of the strengths and limitations of the planning process (Rudra 1975, 1988b). He criticized plan models (including his own) not only in terms of assumptions or content, but also with respect to their underlying economic philosophy. He argued that in a multi-sector model there is an implicit planner who decides patterns of investment allocation and choice of technology as well as the social welfare function. Rudra wondered 'how one could possibly have made such a preposterous assumption, as that of a single decision-maker commanding all the decisions in this vast overwhelmingly private sector economy'. He was also disillusioned about the efficacy of the planning process in reducing economic inequality, as envisaged in the plan documents.

In one of his last essays, 'In Defence of Planning and Socialism', Rudra (1992) observes that though the public sector in India has an unenviable record of inefficiency and corruption, 'it does not follow that the remedy lies in doing away with planning or the public sector or even reducing government intervention in economic affairs'. He feared that the New Industrial Policy (NIP) might lead to the disappearance of a whole range of industries, the use of more capital-intensive techniques, rising unemployment, and a greater concentration of economic power. He outlined a socialist alternative, based on 'co-operative institutions with effective worker participation in management'. 'There is no question,' he argued, 'of having an unplanned free market economy. What we require is a Welfare State strongly influencing private decision-making and taking care of direct delivery of welfare services for the needy.'

Agricultural Economics

Rudra's work on agricultural economics drew on the numerous field surveys he conducted in West Bengal and elsewhere. These include Farm Management Studies for the Ministry of Agriculture, a Survey of Agrarian Relations completed in 1975, and village surveys initiated jointly with Pranab Bardhan. Here, as in other fields, Rudra often challenged conventional notions.

He was particularly critical of the application of neoclassical economic theory to Indian agriculture and in

Indian Agricultural Economics: Myths and Realities (1982), he presented a critique of neoclassical theory. One of the central 'myths' exposed in this study is the myth of allocative efficiency in Indian agriculture, especially the proposition that product and factor markets are competitive. Rudra also took issue with the alleged inverse relation between farm size and productivity.

Aside from 'efficiency myths', the book criticized various 'inefficiency myths'. For instance, Rudra debunked the 'myth of semi-feudal inefficiency', attributed to Bhaduri (1973), whereby semi-feudal landowners 'have an economic interest in perpetuating the economic misery of the tenants'. He also challenged the myth of 'tenancy inefficiency', whereby tenant farms perform less well than owner-operated farms.

Rudra felt that understanding class relations was crucial to understand historical processes and contemporary realities. He defined class as 'a set of individuals who have similar relations with means of production ... and who are such that they have no contradictions among themselves, but have contradictions with members of other classes' (Rudra 1988a). Based on this definition he argued that there are two classes in rural India: big landowners and agricultural workers (though in some areas there may be a third class, that of 'subsistence farmers'). This reading of the class structure in rural India was similar to that suggested by Daniel Thorner and Alice Thorner in 1962.

Research Methodology

Ashok Rudra had an abiding interest in research methodology and developed original research methods of his own, particularly for field surveys. As a first-rate statistician he had a deep concern for technical rigour and often exposed methodological 'short-cuts' in statistical investigations.

For instance, his 1969 and 1982 publications discuss common misuses of statistical methods in economic analyses. Rudra points out that carrying out tests of significance of a null hypothesis without properly defined alternative hypotheses may be misleading. He also discusses the difficulty in applying methods of statistical inference with small samples, or when repeated observations are not possible. In such cases, 'a parametric test has to be necessarily carried out on the basis of a whole battery of assumptions regarding the population; and the test by itself does not throw any light on the validity or otherwise of the assumptions regarding the population'.

Similarly, while discussing problems of goodness of fit or functional forms, Rudra notes that it is rare for a model maker to have prior empirical knowledge and theoretical reasoning for fully specifying a model. Under such circumstances a common practice is to smuggle into the model certain pre-specified functional forms. Many results of model-making exercises depend on arbitrary mathematical properties of such assumed functional forms.

Rudra's (1989) article on 'field survey methods' is an enlightening example of his ability to combine statistical theory with field experience. He discusses, for example, how sampling with clustering and stratification gives better results than complete enumeration, how random sampling and purposive sampling can be complementary rather than rivals, and how the efficiency of a sampling scheme depends on the combination of sample size and population variance. He also discusses various aspects of respondent bias as well as biases related to scrutiny and feedback, questionnaire design, and stratification.

Rudra's 'subjective judgement' as a statistician, or his 'illumined common sense' as he sometimes described it, often guided his choice of statistical methods. In the 1970s, he conducted many quantitative statistical analyses of the agricultural economy. But later on he also studied qualitative aspects of agrarian relations using purposively selected samples and case studies, in which his personal observational skills played a key role.

Other Writings

Apart from his scientific writings, Rudra often contributed to popular journals and newspapers. He felt that his efforts as a social scientist would remain fruitless unless he was able to reach the common people.

These writings often focused on contemporary political and social issues. For instance, when the 'Naxalbari uprising' erupted in West Bengal at the end of the 1960s, Rudra wrote several articles in the weeklies *Frontier* and *Desh*, attempting to interpret this movement. He also argued that the officially accepted land reform measures were grossly inadequate. Later on, however, when the movement turned into a programme of individual annihilation of 'class enemies', Rudra distanced himself from it. Though he felt that some violence might be unavoidable in the context of class struggle, he did not hesitate to criticize the cult of violence.

Rudra's non-academic writings spanned an astonishing range of subjects: the relations between middle class men and women in West Bengal, the literary writings of Albert Camus, Satyajit Ray's films, Ram Mohan Roy's contributions to social progress, the ethical foundations of Marxism, to cite a few examples. A short story titled 'A Spring Evening in Paris' describes the chance meeting of the writer with a young lady who narrates the touching story of her lover being sent to a concentration camp.

Ashok Rudra wrote nine books in Bengali, including two books on agricultural economics, one on the contemporary influence of the Brahminic tradition, three on the middle class in West Bengal, one on Tagore's plays and songs, and two novels. In one of these novels, *Jasmine*, Rudra narrates in an autobiographical manner a somewhat complex love affair of a professor with one of his research students.

Rudra's writings reveal some important traits of his personality. As an intellectual, his basic aim was to influence the thought process of social life around him. He combined an idealist outlook with a scientific appraisal of social conditions. His personal life reflected the ideals he advocated. As a matter of fact, he always regarded it as important to avoid a hiatus between his values and his personal ways.

SUMAN SARKAR AND JEAN DRÈZE

References

Bhaduri, Amit. 1973. 'A Study in Agricultural Backwardness under Semi-feudalism', *Economic Journal*, 83: 120–37.

Rudra, Ashok. 1969. *Measurement in Economics*, New Delhi, Allied Publishers.

——. 1975. *Indian Plan Models*, New Delhi, Allied Publishers.

——. 1982. *Indian Agricultural Economics: Myths and Realities*, New Delhi, Allied Publishers.

——. 1988a. 'Emerging Class Structure in Rural India', in T.N. Srinivasan and P. Bardhan (eds), *Rural Poverty in South Asia*, New Delhi, Oxford University Press.

——. 1988b, *Non-Eurocentric Marxism and Indian Society*, People's Book Society.

——. 1989. 'Field Survey Methods', in P. Bardhan (ed.), *Conversations between Economists and Anthropologists*, New Delhi, Oxford University Press.

——. 1992. 'In Defence of Planning and Socialism', *Indian Economic Review*, Special Number, 27: 187–8.

■ Rural Credit

In 2000, over 70 per cent of India's population, and roughly three-quarters of its poor, lived in rural areas. The principal livelihood in rural India remains agriculture, an activity characterized by significant time lags in production and a high degree of sensitivity to weather conditions. These features of agricultural production make access to financial instruments critical to a rural household's ability to withstand income shocks and make long-term productive investments. However, as is well known, lenders' inability to perfectly identify the creditworthiness of potential borrowers and the cost of enforcing repayment place severe restrictions on rural households' access to credit. These problems are potentially more severe for the rural poor who are less able to reduce lender risk by providing collateral. This also has implications for the geographical distribution of formal credit lenders. Anticipating insufficient profits, lenders such as commercial banks may choose not to set up branches in relatively poor rural areas. This, in turn, by giving lenders in the informal sector monopoly power may further raise the interest rates the rural poor have to pay and restrict their access to affordable credit. Banerjee (2004) provides evidence that informal interest rates in India are high and exhibit significant variation.

A belief that the welfare costs of exclusion from the banking sector, especially for the rural poor, are high, has led to widespread government intervention in the banking sector of low-income countries. Examples of such intervention range from interest-rate ceilings on lending to the poor to state-led branch expansion in rural areas. India has witnessed some of the largest policy interventions aimed at providing banking for the poor. The motivation for the Indian interventions can be traced to the *All-India Credit Survey Report* (RBI 1954). This report showed that four years after Independence, the informal credit sector accounted for the bulk of rural lending, with moneylenders contributing close to 70 per cent of the total. The average annual interest rate on these loans exceeded 20 per cent. In contrast, less than 1 per cent of the borrowing was accounted for by commercial banks. Commercial banks remained confined to urban areas and geared towards the financing of trade and commerce. The survey data also showed a strong positive relationship between asset ownership and borrowing. The report concluded that financial backwardness was a root cause of rural poverty and that commercial banks needed to be harnessed to enhance formal credit in rural areas—both to enable poor rural households to adopt new technologies and production processes, and to displace 'evil' moneylenders who exploited their monopoly power to charge high rates of interest.

The conclusions of this report have guided the Indian government's policy towards rural credit markets. By 1991, according to the All-India Debt and Investment Survey, the share of moneylenders in total credit had declined to 15 per cent, and the share of commercial banks soared to 29 per cent. Equally striking is the fact that by 1991 the probability of a rural household having a formal loan was only weakly correlated with the amount of land it owned. At the same time, the total number of locations with at least one bank branch had increased from under 2,000 in 1951 to over 30,000 by 1991. By the year 2000, the Indian rural banking sector accounted for the rupee equivalent of 26,768 million dollars as deposits and 10,834 million dollars as loans outstanding. In terms of population reached, the rural sector accounted for 125 million savings accounts and 25 million borrowings accounts.

A proximate reason for these changes in borrowing practices was the fact that the Indian government and central bank followed an aggressive policy of state intervention in rural credit markets, often described as 'social banking'. The policy instruments to achieve these objectives included the expansion of the institutional structure of formal-sector lending institutions, directed lending, and concessional or subsidized credit.

In 1969, the 14 largest Indian commercial banks were nationalized, at which point they came under the direct control of the Indian central bank and were formally incorporated into the planning architecture of the country. Bank nationalization was intended to allow the state to target financial backwardness as a means of promoting social objectives. A central aim was to reduce and equalize the average population per bank branch across Indian states. To achieve this the Indian central bank adopted an area approach whereby unbanked locations—census locations with no prior presence of commercial banks—were targeted. The Indian central bank, however, still needed to coerce commercial banks to expand into unbanked rural locations, in particular in states where unbanked locations were remote and/or unprofitable. Under the Banking Regulation Act of 1949, commercial banks have to obtain a licence from the central bank in order to open a new branch. On 1 January 1977, the Indian central bank announced that to qualify to open a branch in an already banked location a commercial bank must open four in unbanked locations. This licensing rule was frozen in 1990 when India began liberalizing the economy, and was formally repealed in 1991. At this point it was deemed that future branch expansion should depend on 'need, business potential and financial viability of location'.

A second feature of the Indian social banking programme was an emphasis on directed bank lending towards sectors deemed as priority sectors (these included agriculture and small-scale industries), and within these sectors to individuals belonging to weaker sections of society. The latter included members of the historically disadvantaged scheduled castes and scheduled tribes. In 1980, the Indian central bank formalized its directed lending policy by requiring that, by 1985, 40 per cent of all bank lending go to priority sectors. Moreover, 25 per cent of this lending must go to individuals belonging to the weaker sections. While these targets remain in place to date, bank compliance with them fell sharply after financial liberalization.

The success of the Indian social banking programme in expanding the presence of commercial banks in rural India is incontrovertible. What is debatable is whether commercial banks in rural India affected the extent and type of economic activity in rural areas and whether they affected poverty and inequality. The extent to which credit disbursements by the banking sector were based on need rather than political power is also a matter of debate. Finally, the extent to which any economic gains were due to productive investments associated with credit provision, rather than simply attributable to the redistribution of resources through the banking sector, remains unclear.

Burgess and Pande (2005) use panel data for Indian states from 1961 to 2000 to examine whether the bank branch expansion programme affected state output and poverty outcomes. The typical problem with examining this relationship is that banks are prone to opening more branches in richer states. Not accounting for this fact can lead to biased estimates of the relationship between branch expansion and economic outcomes. Burgess and Pande address this problem by exploiting the fact that between 1977 and 1990 more bank branches were opened in financially less developed states. The opposite was true outside this period. This change in the trend relationship between a state's financial development and branch openings allows them to isolate the policy-driven part of branch expansion and to use that to examine how this expansion affected the Indian economy. They show that branch expansion was associated with an increase in the shares of rural credit and savings. In keeping with earlier studies, they also find that the branch expansion increased non-agricultural, but not agricultural, output. In a companion study, Burgess et al. (2005) used household data from the National Sample Survey to show that the simultaneous enforcement of directed bank lending requirements was associated with increased bank borrowing among the poor, in particular low-caste and tribal groups.

On the flip side, it is also true that commercial banking in rural India remained unprofitable. The average default rate for commercial banks during the 1980s stood at 42 per cent (as a share of all loans due for repayment). Default rates were very similar across types of borrower—a finding consistent with poor monitoring of borrowers at all levels, and the fact that large-scale loan defaults were very often politically condoned.

In the end, it was the relative unprofitability of rural banking that led to the demise of social banking in India. In 1991, at the outset of liberalization of the Indian economy, the *Report of the Committee on the Financial Sector* (GoI 1991) stated that redistributive objectives 'should use the instrumentality of the fiscal rather than the credit system' and that directed credit programmes be phased out and branch-licensing policy be revoked. As a result, post-1991 rural branch expansion has been limited and multiple studies suggest that access of the rural poor to the banking sector has declined. The share of rural banks in total banks has fallen from 58 per cent in 1990 to under 50 per cent by 2000 and the share of total bank credit that went to rural areas has declined from 15.3 per cent in 1988 to 10.6 per cent in 2000. The policy recommendation is that this reduction in formal-sector lending be met by micro-credit institutions. Despite impressive advances by the Indian micro-credit sector, it is still unclear whether it will be able to achieve a mobilization of rural savings and a credit outreach to equal that achieved by the Indian social banking experiment in the 1970s and 1980s.

ROHINI PANDE

References

Banerjee, Abhijit. 2004. 'Contracting Constraints, Credit Markets and Economic Development', in M. Dewatripont, L. Hansen, and S. Turnovsky (eds), *Advances in Economics and Econometrics: Theory and Applications*, Cambridge, Cambridge University Press.

Burgess, R. and R. Pande. 2005. 'Can Rural Banks Reduce Poverty? Evidence from the Indian Social Banking Experiment', *American Economic Review*, 95(3): 780–95.

Burgess, R., R. Pande, and Grace Wong. 2005. 'Banking for the Poor: Evidence from India', *Journal of the European Economics Association Papers and Proceedings*, April–May, 3(2–3): 268–78.

Government of India (GoI). 1991. *Report of the Committee on the Financial Sector*, chairman M. Narsimhan, New Delhi, Ministry of Finance.

Reserve Bank of India (RBI). 1954. *All-India Rural Credit Survey: Report*, Report of the Committee of Direction of the All-India Rural Credit Survey, Mumbai.

S

■ Savings and Investment

India is a high savings economy when viewed in the international perspective. Reflecting India's savings growth, investment has been high. The economy's savings and investment rates grew steadily from 21.5 per cent in 1991–2, at the point of India's deep financial crisis when the economy was opened up, to 36.4 per cent of gross domestic product (GDP) in 2007–8. The overall savings performance is remarkable when one considers India's per capita income in a cross-country comparison. India's high savings–investment profile was achieved in the early years through policy changes, including nationalization of banks in 1969 that multiplied the number of bank branches in rural India, facilitating and increasing financial savings. It was also the result of the beneficial effects of growing incomes on household savings and investment. However, the spurt in the 2000s mainly reflects a growth in private business savings as well as reduction in government deficit as a consequence of the Fiscal Responsibility and Budget Management (FRBM) Act, 2003. However, the strong impact of the global financial crisis led to fiscal relaxation and a significant decline in public-sector savings. As a result, the overall savings rate fell to 32.5 per cent in 2008–9 but should catch up as the crisis recedes and fiscal discipline is restored. As will become evident, all the indicators suffered a reversal in 2008–9, the last year of this analysis of savings and investment.

During the early Five Year Plans, the government, considering itself the engine of growth, took a leading role in investing in core strategic, infrastructure, and industrial sectors, confining private-sector activity to only the residual sectors. Further, private-sector activity was circumscribed through licensing and controls, such as a restrictive exit policy. Public-sector activity was considered so important that most financial savings instruments—banks, contractual savings institutions, such as pension and provident funds, and mutual funds—were stipulated, or strongly encouraged through the tax structure, to invest predominantly in the government. A high incremental capital–output ratio implied low marginal efficiency of investment and a lower than achievable rate of economic growth.

The dismantling of the supremacy of the public sector in commandeering financial resources gathered pace with India's 1991 financial crisis. Steadily the financial sector was liberalized together with a gradual removal of licences and controls on private-sector activity. Banks could lend more liberally, with a scaling back of directed lending, and at deregulated interest rates, while micro-finance was encouraged at the same time. Foreign banks could open branches, catering to the private sector. Foreign direct investment (FDI), virtually impossible during the early Plans, was welcomed in specified sectors. Even disinvestment from non-performing as well as profitable public-sector enterprises became acceptable as a concept and was attempted by successive governments, albeit with limited success.

The story recounted so far is the one that possibly represents, by and large, the prevailing view. While history—including economic history—is an analytical interpretation of human events, it should nevertheless be considered with perspicuity. Those economies in East Asia or Latin America which did not opt for a planning framework in the post-Second World War era may have experienced economic growth rates that were initially higher than India's. This reflected their exclusive export orientation, while India favoured the costlier option of self-sufficiency. But their strategic interests had to be set aside. Not those of India. In hindsight, the choice of a development path by the founding fathers which enabled rapid growth of the large industrial sector through public investment and meticulous management of the nation's scarce resources turns out to have been justified in today's international environment in which a nation's strategic global reach is crucial.

Like every overdrawn policy structure, however, this stance had outlived its purpose by 1991 and the moment had arrived for it to be dismantled in order to energize much-needed private-sector investment and economic activity. Since then, there has also been a secular increase in gross domestic investment, from 22.1 per cent of GDP in 1991–2 to 37.7 per cent in 2007–8. Private-sector activity comprised the major increase, from 57 per cent of the total investments to 74 per cent during this period. It thus increased by 17 per cent of GDP. Private corporate investment reflected the grand part of this increase, from 28 per cent of total investment in 1991–2 to 43 per cent in 2002–3, remaining in that range until 2007–8. Thus, it increased by 15 per cent of GDP. Of course, private corporate investment suffered in 2008–9 declining to a 36 per cent share (Chaudhuri 2007; EAC 2010; Government of India 2005a, 2005b; ICRIER 2010). And, as in the case of savings, the investment to GDP ratio fell to 34.9 per cent in 2008–9 reflecting the global economic environment.

A comparison of the evolution of public and private savings rates is useful in assessing the increase in public consumption *pari passu* with the decline in public investment. Total gross domestic savings (that is, before mortgage and other loans) in proportion to GDP more than tripled in modern India's economic experience, from 10.3 per cent of GDP in 1950–5, to 21.6 per cent in 1976–80, surging to 24.1 per cent in 1991–6 (Athukorala and Sen 2002). They continued to increase, to 28.1 per cent in 2003–4 and, remarkably, to 36.4 per cent in 2006–7 (ICRIER 2010). The public-sector component of savings was always small, indicating that the public sector was barely meeting its own revenue expenditures. Of course, some of it may well have been due to development expenditure. But, as administration and interest expenses climbed, dissavings emerged in 1998–9 and peaked in 2001–2. Thus, the public savings ratios to GDP were 1.7 per cent in 1950–5, 4.3 per cent in 1976–80, 1.7 per cent in 1991–6, –2.0 per cent in 2001–2, and –0.6 per cent in 2003–4. A turnaround began after this with the central government strictly adhering to a roadmap for reduction in both the fiscal and revenue deficits, with many state governments following suit. Positive public savings improved steadily until they reached 5 per cent of GDP in 2007–8, but fell to 1.4 per cent in 2008–9.

Private-sector savings have thus represented the overwhelming share of savings. Within this, the growth in private corporate savings has been faster. Thus, the share of household savings has continued to decline from around 85 per cent of total savings in the first part of this decade to 70 per cent in the second part. Despite this slide, total household savings continue to far exceed private corporate savings. Nevertheless, private corporate savings represent only about two-fifths of the former. There remains no doubt, therefore, that households have been the overwhelming source of India's savings, though their share in total savings is diminishing.

This savings growth was propelled by the expansion in the opportunity to save in non-physical assets as population per bank branch fell from 90,000 in the mid-1950s to 14,000 in the early 1990s. Household financial savings experienced phenomenal growth from 1.6 per cent of GDP in 1950–5 to 10.3 per cent in 1991–6, and then remained stable at about 10.6 per cent. The share of financial savings in total household savings also grew commensurately, from 21.7 per cent in 1950–5, to 38 per cent in 1976–80, and 54.2 per cent in 1991–6. This declined somewhat, to 47.2 per cent during 2000–4, remaining essentially at the same level during 2004–8. This was a period of relatively faster growth in physical assets.

Empirical evidence (Balakrishnan and Babu 2007) points to various favourable influences on savings, including the maintenance of positive real interest rates (the nominal rate being mainly administered), a low inflation rate within an anti-inflation policy framework, positive economic growth (even if somewhat low by Asian standards), fiscal factors (Shome 2002, 2006), and a steady rise in per capita income (though perhaps slow, reflecting the rate of growth of population). But it is clearly the growth in financial intermediation that stands out most as the main driver of savings. On the negative side, a worsening of the terms of trade—relative price of exports over imports—as well as remittances from abroad appear to have wielded an adverse influence.

Authors have postulated a robust relationship between economic growth and capital accumulation. For example, Chandra and Sandilands (2001) claim that growth has been the causal factor in capital accumulation. While public investment has been mainly policy-driven, private investment has had a long-term relationship with GDP and economic growth. Athukorala and Sen (2002) also find that increased availability of credit and lowered cost of capital encouraged private corporate investment, in particular during the reform-oriented 1990s, once again bringing to the fore the role played by the financial sector in the savings–investment process. Interestingly, based on such evidence, the continuing cutback in public investment during and after the 1991–4 fiscal tightening seems to have affected private corporate investment adversely, pointing to a possible complementary relationship, and reflecting a widely prevalent view that relative inadequacy in the public provision of economic infrastructure had stunted growth in private investment. The decline in the share of public investment in total investment over time is striking, from 44.8 per cent during 1986–91, to 38.6 per cent during 1991–6, 29.8 per cent between 1996–2003, and 23.5 per cent during 2003–8. It should be recognized, however, that during the current decade, the private sector has accelerated its participation and leadership in infrastructure projects.

The transmission mechanisms and channels that converted financial policy into instruments for successful investment performance have been detailed in various studies. The role of directed credit in safeguarding investment in priority sectors has been mentioned. With time, as the need emerged for an efficient financial architecture, institutional changes comprising an array of financial reforms were undertaken. Improving the allocative efficiency of resources by deregulating lending rates assisted private investment to penetrate further. At the other end, financial intermediation in the informal sector has also served as a catalyst in unlocking investment funds for those who would not have had access to loanable funds otherwise.

The government has played a crucial role in the development, regulation, and functioning of life insurance and provident funds as long-term savings instruments. It has also accessed, for its own needs, these contractual savings that comprised more than 30 per cent of household financial savings by the early 1990s, increasing to over 35 per cent by the early 2000s. Indeed, experts have opined that such funds have been pre-empted by the public sector. While liberalization of the sector has occurred subsequently, rigidities remain. The capital market, on the other hand, has been a major vehicle for converting savings into private investment. It has experienced phenomenal growth and the risk and exigencies associated with its formative years have been controlled with the establishment and functioning of an appropriate regulatory authority. There are increasing pressures to open the insurance market to international competition but its attitudes towards risk are a good reason for the government to take a cautious stance on the matter. There has been significant growth also in the derivatives market and its offshoots, and foreign institutional investors are being allowed flexibility, albeit regulated, to submit appropriate collateral when trading in derivatives.

With the opening up of the economy, an additional source of funds has been capital inflows. External-sector policy and monetary policy have been closely coordinated. Capital inflows have generally been absorbed in the country's reserves despite their monetary impact, in order to avoid an untoward currency appreciation, with the objective of maintaining export competitiveness. High investment has typically been an enabling factor in the export-led growth, with a supportive tax structure as its backdrop, and financed mainly from domestic savings. This policy mix is being tested somewhat, with the onset of the 2008–9 global financial crisis and India's relatively successful management of it. Capital inflows have surged, appreciating the rupee and challenging export performance. Against this, the current account deficit in the balance of payments has widened while inflation rates have lurked at levels higher than those of inflationary expectations. The Reserve Bank of India, therefore, faces crucial decisions between opening up or controlling capital inflows even as the Indian economy becomes more globalized.

To conclude, what has been the nature of economic processes in India in terms of savings, investment, and economic growth? Was it demand-driven as John Maynard Keynes viewed the world, where an x amount of expenditure—whether backed always by savings or not—would lead, through spin-off effects, to yx amount of income where y was a multiple of x? Was it the neo-classical process associated with the names of Robert M. Solow and T.W. Swan who emphasized the role of savings—translated into investment—for economic growth? Was it economic growth and rising incomes that triggered savings and investment, in line with the hypothesis propounded by W. Arthur Lewis based on the concept of capitalist surplus? Or was it technological innovation that shifted up the trajectory of the growth path and endogenized technical change itself, as Paul Romer and other contemporary economists have theorized?

Each of these linkages partially explains India's economic processes. During the early Plans, India opted for an expenditure-oriented development strategy based on imported technology in mega infrastructure projects. At the same time, specific policy measures facilitated a rapid growth in savings. As economic growth occurred and incomes increased, further enhancement in savings and investment was realized. As the economy was liberalized and opened in recent years, unrestricted importation of new technology in manufacturing sectors such as textiles and automobiles shifted the trend rate of growth upwards, while the share of international trade in GDP grew significantly.

India's annual growth rates reached 9.5 per cent in 2005–6 and 2006–7, the last years of the Tenth Five Year Plan, and 9.2 per cent in 2007–8. The global financial crisis resulted in a step down in the growth rate, to 6.7 per cent in 2008–9 and 7.4 per cent in 2009–10 (Government of India 2010). For the immediate future, the need for higher investment, including public investment, could not, therefore, be clearer and, commensurately to keep up the savings effort. Further, even during the high growth years, agricultural growth reached barely 2 per cent, compared to 10–11 per cent for manufacturing and services. As a majority of the arable land remains un-irrigated, agricultural-sector growth is determined by the vagaries of the monsoon. Volatility in agricultural growth translates also into unwarranted variations in overall growth. Investment in irrigation, perhaps in a public–private partnership, is imperative to lift India out of the limiting effects of its agricultural cycles since the government has essentially failed to uplift this sector adequately. Investment is also needed in other economic infrastructure, including highways, ports, internal waterways, railways, and, last but not the least, utilities, including electricity and gas. These challenges can be met by even higher private—both household and corporate—savings, continued pushing up of public-sector savings, and judicious accessing of funds from international capital markets.

PARTHASARATHI SHOME

References

Athukorala, Prema-Chandra and Kunal Sen. 2002. *Savings, Investment and Growth in India*, New Delhi, Oxford University Press.

Balakrishnan, Pulapre and M. Suresh Babu. 2007. 'Trends in Savings, Investment and Consumption', *Economic and Political Weekly*, 5 May, 42(18): 1591–4.

Chandra, Ramesh and Roger J. Sandilands. 2001. 'Does Investment Cause Growth? A Test of Endogenous Demand-driven Theory of Growth Applied to India 1950–96', United Kingdom, University of Strathclyde, mimeo.

Chaudhuri, Saumitra. 2007. 'Sustainability of Economic Growth', *The Economic Times*, New Delhi, 29 June.

Economic Advisory Council (EAC) to the Prime Minister. 2010. *Economic Outlook for 2010/11*, New Delhi, July.

Government of India. 2005a. *Economic Survey 2004–05*, New Delhi, Ministry of Finance.

——. 2005b. *Mid-Year Review*, December, New Delhi, Ministry of Finance, Economic Division.

——. 2010. *Mid-Term Appraisal of Eleventh Five Year Plan 2007–12*, New Delhi, Planning Commission.

Indian Council for Research on International Economic Relations (ICRIER). 2010. *Macro-economic Indicators*, New Delhi, ICRIER.

Shome, Parthasarathi. 2002. *India's Fiscal Matters*, New Delhi, Oxford University Press.

——. 2006. 'The Control of Tax Evasion and the Role of Tax Administration', in Luigi Bernardi, Angela Fraschini, and Parthasarthi Shome (eds), *Tax Systems and Tax Reforms in South and East Asia*, Oxford, Routledge.

■ Scientific Research

Science has been practised in India for several centuries. However, modern science may be considered to have started in India with Aryabhata, although western scientists would claim that it started with Galileo. In modern times, science in India has seen some singular achievements. In pre-Independence India, from the late 19th century to 1947, we had a number of scientific giants. In physical sciences, the biggest name was that of J.C. Bose who discovered radio wave propagation, but was unfairly denied a Nobel Prize. Another of the early scientific giants from India was the great mathematician Ramanujan, who is today ranked as one of the three greatest mathematicians ever in the world—remarkable for a man who did not even go to college. Several people are working even today on the theorems and conjectures of Ramanujan. C.V. Raman made great discoveries in acoustics and light scattering, and received the Nobel Prize in 1930 for his discovery of the Raman effect. He established a prestigious school of physics in India that produced many outstanding physicists, of whom K.S. Krishnan was one. Meghnad Saha and S.N. Bose, who were students of J.C. Bose, are other Indian physicists of note. The outstanding contribution of S.N. Bose along with Einstein is considered one of the fundamental aspects of physics. P.C. Ray in Kolkata promoted chemical research and industry. Although India did not have many major research laboratories, Indian universities carried out research in different areas of the physical and biological sciences. Two notable institutions devoted to basic scientific research in the pre-Independence period were the Indian Institute of Science, Bangalore, and the Indian Association for the Cultivation of Science, Kolkata. The discovery of the malaria parasite in India was a major landmark. Pre-Independence Indian science was thus well and truly flourishing and had many big names and achievements to boast of. The Indian Science Congress had notable contributions from Asutosh Mukherjee,

C.V. Raman, and others. All the science academies of India were established around the year 1934.

After Independence, our first Prime Minister Pandit Jawaharlal Nehru was a great votary of science in India. Nehru was responsible for establishing major scientific institutions such as the laboratories of the Council of Scientific and Industrial Research (CSIR) with the help of S.S. Bhatnagar, and the Tata Institute of Fundamental Research and the Department of Atomic Energy with the help of Homi Bhabha. The first Indian Institute of Technology was started in the year 1951 with J.C. Ghosh as its director. A large number of laboratories and educational institutions have since been set up, some of which are mission-oriented, the notable ones being the the Space Organization and the Defence Research and Development Organization. Science got its biggest boost under Pandit Nehru because of his conviction that science was intimately related to national development. The science policy resolution passed by Parliament bears testimony to this faith of Nehru. Two of the basic underlying principles that guided the country's course of development after Independence were self-reliance and self-sufficiency.

Since Independence, Indian scientists have made numerous contributions in the physical, mathematical, astronomical, biological, chemical, earth, space, and engineering sciences. During the early years, there was much work accomplished in the country, specially in the basic sciences although the facilities were far from comparable to those in the advanced countries. The funding for scientific research was meagre in those days, a situation that has progressively improved over the years, especially under Prime Minister Indira Gandhi and Rajiv Gandhi. Mission-oriented agencies such as the Department of Atomic Energy and the Department of Space carried out significant work showing great success in their endeavours. Agricultural research and implementation made quantum progress towards achieving self-sufficiency in food production. India acquired the capability to build its own atomic reactors and carry out other important work in the area of nuclear technology. The space programme succeeded in building its own satellites and in launching indigenous rockets. The giant millimeter-wave radio telescope near Pune built by the Tata Institute of Fundamental Research is a mammoth symbol of the progress of Indian science. New efforts in science and technology have received considerable support since the 1970s, the biological sciences and biotechnology being important fields of such support. There have been significant accomplishments in fundamental research as well, and several Indian scientists have received international recognition through election to major academies in the world. One example of an extraordinary post-Independence Indian scientist is G.N. Ramachandran who initiated molecular biophysical research in the country.

Our national policy for science and technology has generally been guided by a committee or council of scientists appointed by the Prime Minister. The Science Advisory Committee to the Cabinet (SACC) gave way to the very successful National Committee on Science and Technology (NCST) in 1971 with C. Subramaniam as chairman during Indira Gandhi's regime. The NCST produced fine plans for the various sectors, including the socio-economic, where science and technology play a role. The Department of Science and Technology (DST) was created on the recommendation of the NCST. The DST also initiated new modes of funding scientific research. The Department of Biotechnology and the Department of Ocean Development were later created on the basis of recommendations made by the SACC. The DST has been most forthcoming in funding research for scientists. The Science Advisory Council to the Prime Minister under Rajiv Gandhi succeeded in bringing about many significant changes, a crucial factor in the growth of scientific research in the country in that period being the direct involvement of our Prime Ministers who personally held the science and technology portfolio.

The science academies in India have become fairly strong and today have large enrolment. The number of universities has increased over the years and we have nearly 500 universities. Till about 10–15 years ago, our universities contributed about 50 per cent or more of the scientific research in the country. In a typical subject like chemistry, the Indian contribution to world research was around 8–9 per cent around 10 years ago. The total number of research papers from India has been 10,000–14,000, although of variable quality. Because of the large number of institutions and their vast numbers of students and researchers, India got increasing recognition in the world for competence in science, though not equal to the most advanced countries such as the US or Japan. It is this reputation that has helped India gain prominence in the fields of information technology and biotechnology where a number of foreign countries and companies are interested in investing in the country, in establishing facilities, and in making use of trained manpower. Over the years, however, a large number of young people educated in India have found it desirable to leave the country and establish themselves elsewhere, and they have made a name for themselves in the countries where they have settled. For example, in the US, Indian scientists and engineers have achieved great success in areas such as computer science, and some of them have got recognition as outstanding academicians.

Industrial research in the country was till recently carried out with the objectives of self-reliance and self-sufficiency. Import substitution, therefore, was an important goal that governed our R&D efforts. The CSIR laboratories have worked for many years with these objectives in view. There have been several contributions of indigenous research and development (R&D), although many of them can be considered to be incremental improvements of known technologies. The investment of industry in R&D till recently was marginal, and almost all the research was government-funded.

By the 1980s, the general feeling in the country was that our laboratories had come of age. However, by the early 1990s, the winds of change that swept the geopolitical and economic scenarios in the world were felt in India as well. Globalization has become a reality. Competitiveness has emerged as the key mantra. The intellectual property regime has dawned. The country has made much progress in areas such as information technology, biotechnology, and automotive industry, thanks to the availability of the large-scale manpower. There has also been considerable presence of foreign companies and multinationals in the R&D scenario of the country. The scientific scenario has undergone a sea change. The quality of science that needs to be carried out today to become competitive is rather high. Countries like China and South Korea are taking major strides in scientific research. India now publishes around 12,000 research papers and produces around 5000 PhDs in science per year, numbers that are lower than those of China. We are now at a stage where major efforts are needed to improve the infrastructure of our educational institutions and increase investment in science so that we become competitive in basic science and can generate intellectual property. There is little doubt that the country will have to lead in science if it is to be a 'major' knowledge base and an economic power. There is increasing realization in industry today that investment in R&D is essential to make real progress in the present-day scenario. With such public–private partnerships, India can indeed become a science (knowledge) power in the next two–three decades, if it can take the necessary promotional measures.

In the last four to five years, investment in science as well as higher education has increased enormously. The Science Advisory Council to the Prime Minister has come out with major recommendations on improving the science scenario in the country and some have been given effect to. For example, the five Indian Institutes of Science Education and Research will certainly help India to produce excellent scientific manpower. The new National Science Engineering Research Board is expected to bring in major changes with respect to funding scientific research. Dr Manmohan Singh has promised to increase the investment in science to 2 per cent of GDP from the present 1 per cent. The main problem that remains has to do with the quality of education and research. It is hoped that India will do everything possible to emerge as a major player in science by improving quality in these spheres.

C.N.R. Rao

■ Secondary Education

While much has been written about the problems and achievements of primary education in India, far less is known about secondary education, largely because the latter has not benefited from large-scale investment programmes such as the District Primary Education Programme or the Sarva Shiksha Abhiyan which have targeted primary grades. Yet, evidence suggests that secondary education is more important than primary for productivity and earnings: the wage increment from an extra year of secondary schooling is significantly higher than that from an extra year of primary schooling, that is, the pattern of returns to education is convex, with low returns at primary level and progressively greater returns at the secondary and tertiary levels of education in India. Presumably the Indian government's increased attention to secondary education in the Eleventh Plan (2007) is a result of several factors: the recognition that prosperity increasingly comes from post-primary education; primary school enrolment having become close to universal (notwithstanding the acute problem of poor learning levels); and the disadvantageous comparison with countries in the BRIC grouping (Brazil, Russia, India, China) with which India is increasingly compared. For example, evidence in Kingdon (2007) shows that India's youth literacy rate in the early 2000s was 22.5 percentage points behind China's and the proportion of its population with completed secondary and post-secondary schooling is more than thirty years behind China's (that is, China achieved India's current level more than 30 years ago). India's secondary school net enrolment rates are 27 percentage points behind Brazil's and Russia's and 28 points behind China's.

While the base of India's education pyramid (primary and secondary education) may be weak, it has emerged as an important player in the worldwide information technology revolution on the back of substantial (absolute) numbers of well-educated computing and other graduates. The challenge now is to strengthen the base, without neglecting tertiary education.

Access to Secondary Education

Table 1 shows gross enrolment ratios (GERs) in lower and upper secondary education in India in 1999 and 2005. It shows a rapid increase of 10 percentage points in both lower secondary GER (from 61 to 71 per cent) and upper secondary GER (from 31 to 41 per cent). It also shows a great improvement in gender equity, particularly at the lower secondary level where girls' participation increased by 14 points over this short six-year period.

Table 1 Gross Enrolment Rates in Secondary Education, India

	Total	Male	Female	Gender parity index
Lower secondary				
2005	70.5	74.9	65.7	0.88
1999	61.2	70.1	51.5	0.73
Upper secondary				
2005	40.9	46.4	35.0	0.75
1999	31.0	37.0	24.5	0.66

Source: Table 8, Statistical Tables from 2009 'Education for All', Global Monitoring Report, UNESCO, Paris.

Demand for secondary education has risen rapidly because it has high economic payoffs in the Indian labour market, and because these payoffs have been increasing over time. Estimates based on National Sample Survey (NSS) data from 1999 and 2005 find that the wage increment from each extra year of secondary education (around 20 per cent) and from each extra year of tertiary education (15 per cent) is significantly greater than that from each extra year of primary education (8 per cent) (Kingdon 2007). Moreover, the returns to higher secondary and tertiary education have *risen* consistently over time, while the returns to primary education have fallen (for women) or remained static (for men) (Riboud et al. 2007). Finally, the non-market returns to girls' secondary education (in terms of lower fertility and infant mortality) are much higher than those to girls' primary education.

The very high returns to secondary education raise the puzzle why secondary school participation is not higher in India. It seems there are some supply-side barriers. According to the Seventh All India Education Survey, in 2002, there were only one-fifth as many secondary schools (those with Grade 10 classes) as the number of primary schools. Thus, it seems likely that secondary school enrolment rates are low partly because of the lack of supply of nearby secondary schools. A demand-side factor that likely militates against higher secondary school participation is the high cost of schooling. Table 2 shows that households incur a great deal of expenditure in educating a child even in the government school sector which is meant to impart free tuition, and that the expenditure rises steeply with the level of education. Expenditure on private tutoring is important, constituting 13 per cent of total education expenditure in government and aided secondary schools and 10 per cent in private schools. Given a national per capita income of Rs 10,149 in 1995–6 (see http://planning.up.nic.in/ annualplan0607/vol1/Annex-chap-28.pdf), household expenditure on a child's lower secondary education in a government school (Rs 1,058) was about 10 per cent of per capita income. At the upper secondary level, it constituted 18 per cent of per capita income. Expenditure on a child's education in aided and private schools is even greater. This suggests that even in the publicly funded part of the schooling system, private costs are an important barrier to secondary schooling participation for those from poor backgrounds. The poor may not be able to borrow for secondary education despite its high returns because of imperfect credit markets.

Table 2 Annual Household Expenditure on Education, 1995–6 (in rupees, by level of education)

	Govt	Aided	Private	Total
Primary	269	1,186	1,431	507
Upper primary	639	1,350	2,159	921
Secondary	1,058	1,565	2,759	1,333
Senior secondary	1,831	2,553	3,698	2,257
Tertiary	2,683	3,416	5,509	3,164

Source: Author's calculations from National Sample Survey 52nd Round, 1995–6.

Inequality in Access to Secondary Education

While gender inequality in secondary access has fallen over time (see Table 1), there is much inter-state variation in the size of the gender gap. The gender parity index is the female to male secondary school enrolment ratio. A ratio of 1 represents gender equality. States such as Bihar and Rajasthan have grotesque gender inequality: girls are only half as likely to enrol in secondary school as boys. Uttar Pradesh, Madhya Pradesh, Jharkhand, and Chhattisgarh also have severe gender inequality but, on the bright side, many states have gender parity or even slightly pro-female secondary enrolment rates, for example, Kerala and

Tamil Nadu. Apart from the possibility of gender bias within the schooling system which may discourage girls' secondary school participation, an important part of the reason for gender inequality is to be found within the household itself. Using statistical analysis, Kingdon (2005) finds strong within-family pro-son bias in terms of both secondary school enrolment and educational expenditure. The persistence of these large gender inequalities appears not to reflect gender discrimination in the labour market since the rate of return to education is actually significantly larger for women than men in India (Riboud et al. 2007). Instead, gender inequalities in education more plausibly reflect the fact that some parents continue to believe in traditional gender roles, do not envisage daughters' participation in the labour market, and thus perceive it is futile to invest in girls' secondary education. Conservatism and concern for safety may also play a part in girls' attendance of distant secondary schools.

There is also a good deal of inter-state variation in the extent of *economic* inequality in access to secondary schooling, using NSS data for 1999–2000, as seen in Figure 1. The inequality (measured as the difference in access to secondary education among those in the top and bottom quintiles of the distribution of household per capita income) is greatest in Haryana, Andhra Pradesh, and the socially challenged states of Bihar, Madhya Pradesh, Rajasthan, and Uttar Pradesh. It is lowest in the left-leaning states of Kerala and West Bengal.

Learning Achievement Levels in Secondary Education

Indian states have their own separate exam boards and set their own curricula; there are no national-level data based on a common standardized achievement test in India. While the Council of Boards of Secondary Education provides pass rates in the High School and Intermediate (senior secondary) examinations in different states (and pass rates in the 2004 High School exam varied from 37 per cent in Manipur to 80 per cent in Andhra Pradesh), such inter-state comparison is meaningless since curricula, exam papers, passing requirements, and so on, all differ from state to state. In any case, the high school pass rates cannot be taken at face value as they are much inflated due to the phenomenon of widespread cheating. For example, when a reformist Uttar Pradesh government brought in an anti-cheating rule and installed police at all examination centres in 1992 to prevent the mass cheating that routinely takes place, the pass rate in the UP High School exam fell from 44–57 per cent in the previous four years to a pitiful 14.7 per cent in 1992 (Kingdon 2007). The policing order was withdrawn in later years and the pass percentage has crept back to the mid-40s. This suggests the extent of the problem of low achievement levels in secondary education,

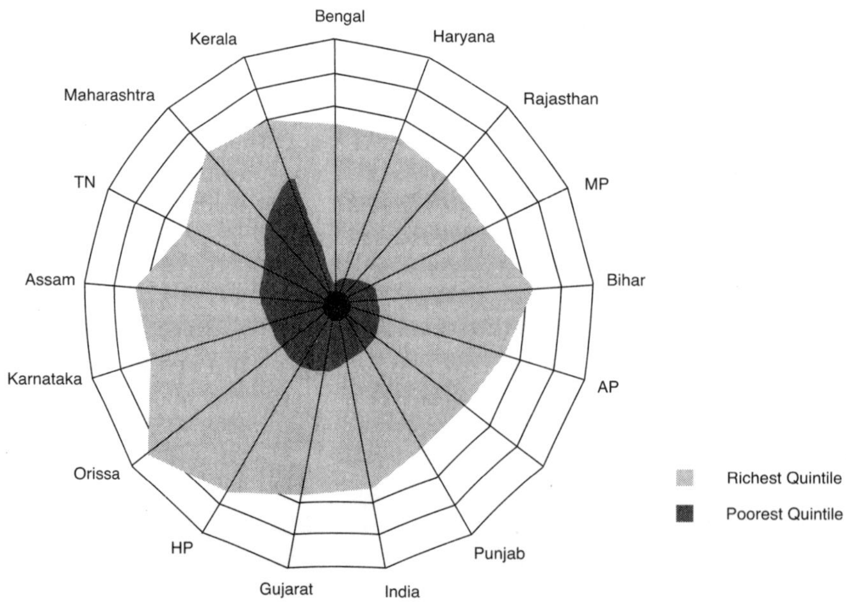

Figure 1 Differential Access to Secondary Schooling, India, 1999–2000 (between the top and bottom income quintiles)

Source: World Bank (2009).

Table 3 Enrolment Share of Different School Types at Secondary Level (by region and year)

Type	Rural				Urban			
	1978	1986	1993	2002	1978	1986	1993	2002
Govt	34	45	49	44	39	37	39	33
Aided	64	52	44	40	57	54	49	43
Private	2	4	7	16	4	9	11	24

Source: All India Education Surveys, various years.

though it is possible that learning achievement levels in Uttar Pradesh are lower than in other states.

India has not take part in any international tests of learning achievement levels since the early 1970s but recently the Ministry of Human Resource Development gave permission for items from the international TIMSS test[1] to be applied in two states. Based on data collected by Kin Bing Wu (World Bank 2009; Wu et al. 2009), Das and Zajonc (2008) place secondary students from Orissa and Rajasthan on a worldwide distribution of mathematics achievement. Tested one year further in school (ninth grade) than their international counterparts (who were tested in eighth grade), they find that India falls below 43 of the 51 countries for which data exists. But not all students test poorly. A proportion of Indian 14-year-olds pass the highest international benchmark and these, in absolute terms, constitute more students than in all but four of the other tested countries taken together. The authors conclude that 'the combination of India's size and large variance in achievement justify both the perceptions that India is shining even as *Bharat*, the vernacular for India, is drowning'.

Role of the Private Sector in Secondary Schooling

There are three main types of secondary schools in India: government, private aided, and private unaided. Aided schools in many states are like government schools because although they are nominally under private managements, their teachers are generally appointed and paid directly by the government, at government school salary rates. Unaided schools are truly private in the sense of having autonomy over hiring/firing and pay decisions.

There is little evidence on the quality of public, aided, and private schools at secondary level in India except for two recent World Bank surveys of secondary schools: a 2004 survey of 253 schools in Rajasthan and Orissa and a 2008 survey of 1,400 private aided and unaided schools in nine states. The latter shows no major difference in school facilities (classroom infrastructure, laboratories, toilets) between aided and unaided schools, and reveals that teachers in unaided schools are equally qualified academically as peers in aided schools, though they are slightly less likely to have pre-service teacher training. However, the average salary of unaided school teachers in 2007 was one-third that of aided school teachers (Rs 5,000 versus Rs 15,000 per month). Given that school costs are primarily driven by teachers' salaries, this suggests that overall unit costs of unaided schools are considerably lower than those of aided schools. At the same time, students in unaided schools did better in Board Examinations than their peers in aided schools, and were more likely to score in the first division, though this may partly be due to their better home backgrounds. Moreover, principals in unaided schools were less likely to cite any constraints or limitations to improving educational quality in their school (World Bank 2009). Unfortunately, no private–public comparisons are available of other indicators of school quality, for example, data on teacher attendance rates and teachers' time on task for secondary schools.

Perceived better quality of education in private schools is presumably what explains the steep increase in the share of private schools in total secondary school enrolment over time seen in Table 3. The increase in private secondary school demand is higher in urban than in rural areas. By 2002, 16 per cent of rural and about a quarter of all urban secondary students attended private unaided schools.

The growth of private schooling—though slower at the secondary than at primary education level—signals growing inequality of educational opportunity. The expansion of private schooling suggests not only that the quality of public education is poor but also that inequality (both in terms of access and quality of education) must be growing since the poor cannot afford private school fees.

Public Policy towards Secondary Education

After decades of post-Independence focus on elementary education, the Indian government in its Eleventh Five Year Plan (2007–12) gave special attention to secondary education. The Eleventh Plan has seen the launch of the Rashtriya Madhyamik Shiksha Abhiyan (RMSA) or National Secondary Education Mission. This centrally sponsored scheme aims to (i) universalize access to

[1]For TIMSS, see http://nces.ed.gov/times/. For PIRLS, see http://timss.bc.edu/pirls2001.html. For SACMEQ, see Southern and Eastern Africa Consortium for Monitoring Educational Quality, http://www.sacmeq.org/.

secondary schooling in the age group 15–16 by 2015 by providing a secondary school within 5 km and a higher secondary school within 7 km of all habitations, and (ii) universalize retention in secondary education by 2020. The strategies that have been laid down for the achievement of these goals are to upgrade upper primary schools and strengthen existing secondary schools through construction of classrooms, labs, computer rooms, separate toilets for girls and boys, and the appointment of additional teachers; the provision of special incentives to girls, minority groups, and other 'weaker section' groups—these could be freeships, scholarships, free uniforms, and so on, as in primary education; and quality improvements via providing in-service training of teachers, curricular reforms, computer-aided education, teaching-learning aids, leadership training of school heads, and science and maths education. The central government has committed Rs 20,868 crore for non-recurring and Rs 35,567 crore for recurring expenditures related to the RMSA by 2012. By 2020, the requirement will be greater.

Increasing access without quality is meaningless and quality does not come from mere construction of classrooms and provision of inputs such as teachers and books: it is well known that despite these inputs, learning levels are extremely low in primary education. Accountability and incentive structures need to be re-thought. To the extent that private schools provide better accountability mechanisms for teachers, it is encouraging that of the planned 11,000 new schools in the country's 6,000 blocks, those in 3,500 blocks will be supervised by the government and in the remaining 2,500 blocks through private–public partnership (PPP) arrangements, engaging the private sector and civil society. But there are different designs of PPPs around the world, some successful, others not, so the challenge is to choose the right type of PPPs for the Indian institutional context. Moreover, availability of comparable learning achievement data across the whole country is a necessary building block for ensuring that quality of secondary education can be tracked. At present, due to different exam boards and the lack of a common standardized examination, there is no official mechanism to monitor learning levels in secondary education. Thus, while the RMSA provides an exciting opportunity for advancing secondary education in India, its modalities need to be carefully thought if it is to deliver quality secondary education for all.

GEETA KINGDON

References

Das, J. and T. Zajonc. 2008. 'India Shining and Bharat Drowning: Comparing India to the Worldwide Distribution in Mathematics Achievement', Policy Research Working Paper, 4644, World Bank, Washington DC.

Kingdon, G. 2005. 'Where has All the Bias Gone? Detecting Gender Bias in the Intra-household Allocation of Educational Expenditure in Rural India', *Economic Development and Cultural Change*, 53(2): 409–52.

——. 2007. 'The Progress of School Education in India', *Oxford Review of Economic Policy*, Summer, 23(2): 168–95.

Riboud, M., Y. Savchenko, and H. Tan. 2007. 'The Knowledge Economy and Education and Training in South Asia', Human Development Unit, South Asia Region, World Bank, Washington DC.

World Bank. 2009. 'Secondary Education in India: Universalizing Opportunity', Human Development Unit, South Asia Region, World Bank, Washington DC.

Wu, K., P. Goldschmidt, C. Boscardin, and D. Sankar. 2009. 'International Benchmarking and Determinants of Mathematics Achievement in Two Indian States', *Education Economics*, September, 17(3).

■ Securities Markets

After the early 1990s, there has been a decline in price and quantity controls by the state in many parts of the economy, accompanied by major progress in trade liberalization. The role of the state in the allocation of capital has diminished. Firms have faced more competitive conditions. The financial sector has been increasingly called upon to engage in complex information processing, to make judgements about the future prospects of alternative firms, and shape resource allocation.

A far-reaching reforms programme on the securities markets in the 1990s complemented and supported the pro-competitive reforms in trade and industry. As described ahead, these policy initiatives on the stock market have been highly successful in fostering sound institutional development. India stands out when compared with most developing countries on the sophistication of securities markets, and in the prominent role of markets as opposed to banks in resource allocation.

Components of the Securities Markets

The term 'security' refers to a tradable instrument which has financial payoffs. India's securities markets comprise:

1. Corporate equity
2. Corporate debt
3. Corporate equity derivatives
4. Government bonds
5. Derivatives on government bonds

6. Commodity futures
7. Derivatives on currency

India has a fragmented regulatory architecture for addressing these components. The first three categories are regulated by the Securities and Exchange Board of India (SEBI). The Reserve Bank of India (RBI) plays a major role in government bonds and derivatives on interest rates. The Forward Markets Commission (FMC) regulates commodity futures. Finally, the RBI plays a major role in currency derivatives.

Corporate Equity and Equity Derivatives

The market for corporate equity is India's most sophisticated financial market. It works through the following elements.

Firms are incubated using the traditional approach, of capital from friends and family, or using the venture capital (VC) industry. There is a large industry comprising both foreign and domestic VC firms operating in the Indian market. Successful firms go on to sell shares to the public in an 'Initial Public Offering' (IPO). Roughly two IPOs per month took place in 2005. The IPO market works through a screen-based anonymous auction.

After the IPO, secondary-market trading commences, where there is competition between two exchanges, the National Stock Exchange (NSE) and the Bombay Stock Exchange (BSE). Both have member firms spread all over the country. Only 40 per cent of equity market turnover comes from Bombay. Roughly 7 million investors participate in the market, along with foreign investors. There is no separation between domestic and foreign investors, or between 'retail' and 'wholesale' investors: all price discovery takes place on unified electronic order-matching systems at the NSE and BSE. There are roughly 30,000 trading screens spread across the country, which are directly connected to the NSE, in addition to Internet access provided by many brokerage firms.

Two vital elements of the spot market are risk management and settlement. On the NSE, risk management is done by the National Securities Clearing Corporation (NSCC). Settlement is done using 'dematerialized' securities at the National Securities Depository Limited (NSDL) and the Central Depository Services Limited (CDSL).

The secondary market for equity is extremely active by world standards. The NSE and BSE are ranked 3 and 5 in the world by the *number* of transactions, with roughly 1 million to 2 million transactions per day on each exchange within the trading day of 5.5 hours. Annual spot market turnover works out to 107 per cent of end-year market capitalization. This is close to the value seen in market-dominated financial systems, such as the US (119 per cent).

India has complete unification between the equity spot market and the equity derivatives market in terms of brokerage firms, exchanges, and regulation. Futures and options are traded on 119 individuals stocks and on four market indexes. The 'Nifty' index is the biggest single underlying on which derivatives are traded. Index funds and exchange-traded funds are also available on major indexes.

The equity market thus has a strong set of institutional mechanisms over the full life cycle of firms, from VC to IPO to secondary market, to index funds and derivatives.

While there is a broad range of investors who operate on the equity market, it is dominated by small investors. The average trade size on the NSE in 2004 was Rs 27,715 on the equity spot market and Rs 488,790 on the equity derivatives market. Gross equity market turnover is computed by summing across the NSE and BSE, across spot and derivatives, and across buyers and sellers. In 2004, gross equity market turnover was Rs 86 trillion. Of this, just Rs 5.5 trillion was by all institutional investors, domestic and foreign, put together. Foreign investors made up the bulk, with Rs 5 trillion of gross turnover.

The two weaknesses of the equity market are:

1. In keeping with a long tradition of financial repression, institutional investors such as banks, insurance companies, trusts, and pension funds are prevented by the state from participating in the corporate equity market.
2. While the equity spot market has achieved Organisation for Economic Co-operation and Development (OECD) levels of turnover ratio, the level of derivatives turnover is miniscule by world standards, when expressed as a ratio to the size of the spot market.

Corporate Debt

When a company issues shares and bonds, both these are 'derivatives' on the cash flows of the company. There are direct relationships between the share price and the bond price. Hence, when there is active speculative price discovery on the corporate equity market, this should easily carry forward to the bond market.

However, India does not have an active corporate bond market. This failure derives from five factors:

1. Lack of screen-based auction for bond issuance (unlike the equity market).
2. Lack of nationwide electronic trading (unlike the equity market).

3. Foreign investors are permitted to lend to Indian firms through the banking channel, but are essentially prohibited from participating in the corporate bond market.
4. There are severe difficulties in credit recovery procedures when a company shuts down.
5. There is a bias in banking regulation, which gives banks incentives to disfavour bonds and hold loans instead, even though loans are more illiquid and more opaque than bonds.

The strong success of the equity market and the relative failure of the corporate bond market may have given firms an incentive to emphasize equity financing. The debt–equity ratio of Indian manufacturing dropped sharply from 1.995 in 1991–2 to 1.237 in 2003–4.

Government Bonds and Interest Rate Derivatives

Given persistent large fiscal deficits, the government has been a substantial issuer of government bonds. As of end 2004, the market capitalization of the government bond market was roughly Rs 10 trillion. However, there are many difficulties in market design which have inhibited liquidity and market efficiency. There is a narrow club of bond market participants, primarily located in Bombay. The RBI controls entry into the club. The RBI runs the depository. There is a fledgling exchange, also run by the RBI; however most transactions are as yet bilateral and not taking place on the exchange. The number of transactions observed per day is less than one-thousandth that seen on the equity market.

One modern element in the government bond market is the Clearing Corporation of India Limited (CCIL), which is a modern clearing corporation that has been placed outside the RBI. The CCIL is an innovation in market design, whereby counterparty credit risk is eliminated even though the transactions are themselves opaque. The RBI has started outsourcing some of the exchange operations work to the CCIL, which has resulted in improved efficiency and service quality.

There is a limited market for interest-rate derivatives. However, it is an opaque 'over-the-counter' market, where transactions are negotiated bilaterally, with severe entry barriers.

Commodity Futures

The FMC is an office of the Department of Consumer Affairs, which is charged with regulation of the commodity futures markets. It is not an autonomous regulator like SEBI.

In recent years, the FMC has permitted three entities to start nationwide commodity futures exchanges: the National Commodity Derivatives Exchange (NCDEX), the Multi Commodity Exchange (MCX), and the National Multi Commodity Exchange (NMCE). Turnover has risen dramatically to Rs 1.7 trillion in the first half of 2004–5.

There are many difficulties with the existing framework of commodity futures trading. For example, the present legal framework prohibits two fundamental tools of the derivatives market: cash settlement and options trading. More importantly, the universal international practice is of 'convergence' between commodity futures markets and securities markets, so as to exploit economies of scale and scope in securities firms, exchanges, and financial regulation. India is unusual in attempting to set up a separate regulator, exchanges, and securities firms for this narrow area.

Derivatives on Currency

As with derivatives on interest rates, currency derivatives trading does not take place on the transparent exchange platform. It is negotiated bilaterally between members of a small club.

There is a fairly active currency swap and currency forward market, with maturities going out to one year. However, market access is supposed to be restricted to 'hedging transactions only'. Participants have to demonstrate currency exposure in order to trade on these markets. This inhibits the development of information-based speculative price discovery. The weaknesses on the domestic market have fuelled the growth of an offshore 'non-deliverable forwards' market, which now constitutes an important alternative to the domestic forward market.

Under normal circumstances, currency forwards are priced by covered interest parity (CIP). However, the RBI rules block the ability of banks to engage in CIP arbitrage. This induces large deviations between the fair price and the observed price of forwards and swaps.

Role in Resource Allocation

Measurement of the *flow* of resources through alternative allocative mechanisms of the financial sector is fraught with methodological problems. In contrast, measurement of the allocation of the *stock* of financial capital is easier.

The non-food credit of the banking system measures the stock of credit given out by banks to big firms, small firms, and individuals. It constitutes an upper bound for the stock of capital which firms obtained from banks. The true market value of bank credit is likely to be slightly smaller than the book value, reflecting the incidence of distressed debt.

This can be compared against the market value of equities and bonds. In order to improve the accuracy of measurement, we exclude the shares of companies where trading takes place for less than 75 per cent of the days. This is achieved by focusing on the market capitalization of the COSPI index.

In July 2005, non-food credit stood at Rs 11.4 trillion. The market value of equity of the 2550 companies in COSPI stood at Rs 19.6 trillion. The market value of corporate bonds was estimated at Rs 4 trillion. If we conservatively assume all non-food credit as being borrowings of firms, out of the stock of financial capital of Rs 35 trillion, 67 per cent came from markets and 33 per cent from banks. This relationship is not an artefact of a specific date of measurement. Over a 13-year time series ending in July 2005, there were only seven months (4.6 per cent probability) where non-food credit was larger than COSPI market capitalization. The median value of the ratio of non-food credit divided by COSPI market capitalization over this period was 68 per cent.

Policy Issues

As argued in the preceding discussion, the market design of the equity market has been an outstanding success, in contrast with the policy failures in other areas. The policy agenda for the remaining six components of the securities industry consists of replicating the ideas and outcomes of the equity market. The four key elements that have induced success in the equity market are: (i) an arms-length separation between the focused regulator (SEBI) and competing firms that offer trading services (NSE, BSE, NSDL, CDSL, etc.), with a clear legal framework, (ii) lack of entry barriers into either financial intermediation or exchange infrastructure, (iii) price discovery driven by a heterogeneous mass of traders including foreign and domestic institutional investors and a large number of households from across the country, and (iv) lack of trading on the market by the government.

There are important problems of market structure and competition policy in the securities markets that have inhibited the diffusion of ideas and prevented the other components from matching the success of the equity market. Securities trading is fragmented across three groups of firms: SEBI-regulated exchanges, RBI-regulated exchanges, and FMC-regulated exchanges. Efficiency gains will be obtained through (i) competition and (ii) returns to scale if these three areas are unified, as is the international practice. This will require making SEBI the regulator of the entire securities industry.

In this difficult situation, the most awkward problems are posed by the RBI's operation of a monopoly financial exchange for bonds. As India's experience in sectors such as telecom has shown, there is merit in moving away from monopoly state production. The modern strategy consists of separating out the state function of regulation from production of services in a competitive market, with an arms-length relationship between the regulator and the competitors in the market. Further, a comparison with well-structured central banks such as the Bank of England does not suggest that running an exchange or regulating an exchange is the task of the central bank.

The second fundamental question that the securities markets face is that of global competition. Indian equities are now listed on foreign exchanges. This exerts limited competitive pressures in the domestic securities markets, by giving foreign investors an alternative venue where transactions can go. However, domestic investors, who account for the dominant fraction of transactions and particularly information-based speculation, have no alternative but to buy the services of local exchanges. The removal of capital controls that inhibit local households is required to bring competition to bear on this important industry.

Ajay Shah

References

Ministry of Finance. 2004. 'Securities Markets' (chapter 4), in *Economic Survey*, New Delhi.

Rajan, Raghuram and Ajay Shah. 2005. 'New Directions in Indian Financial Sector Policy', in Priya Basu (ed.), *India's Financial Sector: Recent Reforms, Future Challenges*, New Delhi, Macmillan, pp. 54–87.

Thomas, Susan (ed.). 2003. *Derivatives Markets in India 2003. Invest India*, Tata McGraw-Hill Series, New Delhi, Tata McGraw Hill.

———. 2005. 'Agricultural Commodity Markets in India: Policy Issues for Growth', in Priya Basu (ed.), *India's Financial Sector: Recent Reforms, Future Challenges*, New Delhi, Macmillan, pp. 176–96.

■ Self-employed Women, The Organization of

Poor self-employed women from the informal sector are engaged in jobs that operate outside any Labour Laws or regulations. These are jobs without definition. Yet the self-employed women workers of India form a large and important category of the country's labour market. The Self-Employed Women's Association (SEWA) was formed to give recognition and voice to these workers. As such, SEWA is a trade union of poor self-employed women workers from the informal economy. Founded in 1972, it is today the largest national union of informal-sector workers. From a membership of 1,017 it has grown to 7,18,000 members across seven states in India and fourteen districts in Gujarat. SEWA follows the Gandhian philosophy of truth, non-violence, respect for all religions, and dignity of labour. Here all members are recognized as workers.

Goals

SEWA's goals are full employment and self-reliance—full employment in terms of work, income, and social security like healthcare, childcare, shelter, and nutrition for the members and self-reliance in terms of economic self-reliance at household level and collective self-reliance at organization level. At SEWA, women workers strive for a 'Second Freedom'—which is economic freedom—through their collective and organized strength.

Integrated Approach

The belief that poverty has numerous facets and cannot be eliminated by financial assistance alone has lead to SEWA's integrated approach to poverty eradication, namely capital formation, capacity building, social security, and organizing. All these four components are required simultaneously and in a combination that is viable and manageable by the workers themselves. One without the others does not yield results.

Rural Organizing

Nearly two-thirds of SEWA's members belong to the rural areas. Its approach is area specific and demand driven. In rural areas there is surplus of labour and few employment opportunities. SEWA identifies the local issues or demands and organizes rural women workers around those issues. It strategically links up with the existing government programmes and schemes to address the demands. In order to generate employment opportunities, SEWA initiates economic programmes based on the available local skills or resources. Thus the rural workers of SEWA are organized into primary village-level producer groups or collectives. These groups are arranged into district-level federations—members' own economic organizations. In the process, SEWA has built 3,500 local producers' micro-enterprises and groups, a federation of 110 cooperatives, and 9 economic federations, representing members across 125 different trades.

SEWA's members evoke the image of a banyan tree in describing their activities and their interactions. SEWA is the central trunk that draws its strength from the roots. The trunk puts out branches that cater to the needs of poor women in one trade or another, or in providing a service that is much needed. Each branch then lets down roots that connect it to the soil, nurturing and sustaining the branch and at the same time strengthening the whole tree.

Informal Economy

SEWA's members belong to the informal economy and are beset by poverty, lack of access to information and technology, outdated tools and equipment, no assets, and high vulnerability to risk. Despite the fact that the informal sector comprises nearly 92 per cent of the total workforce in India, hardly any regulations exist that benefit it.

In its efforts to link its members to the mainstream economy, SEWA has grown from a family of organizations, into a movement. It is a confluence of three movements: labour, cooperative, and women's. The SEWA movement is building national and international alliances of workers in the informal sector (National Alliance of Street Vendors of India, Women in Informal Employment: Globalizing and Organizing, Homenet, Streetnet, and so on) for voice and representation.

SEWA has built a network of institutions like SEWA Academy, SEWA Trade Facilitation Centre, SEWA Gram Mahila Haat, and the Global Trading Network that provide various kinds of training, capacity building, and marketing facilitation support needed by its members to access newer and better economic opportunities and face the challenges of globalization. As an organization, SEWA is highly dynamic. As needs change and new challenges are thrown up, it shall continue to build a cadre of barefoot managers and economic institutions to help its members.

The major activities undertaken by SEWA are as follows.

1. Organizing the informal Sector
2. Capacity Building
3. Livelihood security activities
   - (a) Artisan Support Programme
   - (b) Weavers Support Programme
   - (c) Salt Farming
   - (d) Poultry Farming
   - (e) Gum Collection
   - (f) Masonry Training
   - (g) Dairy and Animal Husbandry Activities
4. Support Activities
   - (a) Healthcare
   - (b) Childcare
   - (c) Savings, Credit, and Insurance
   - (d) Housing Support
5. Eco-regeneration Activities

Box 1

Bhavnaben Mangabhai Kali is a salt worker from Kuda village, Surendranagar. Bhavnaben says: 'In order to start work, we took a loan from a moneylender and bought a salt pan. He exploited us all the time. He would not let us go to other moneylenders also. We had five children and we did not even have money to feed them. One day I learnt about SEWA and became a member. I attended a SEWA meeting and told the organizers that I wanted a loan for salt production. They explained to me that the next day one of the organizers from SEWA will come, do the assessment, and fill up the loan form. I then opened a bank account and got a loan. We were very happy. In the next season we did not have to go to the moneylender for a loan. I had known how to produce salt for years but never so scientifically. I got my salt tested for the first time and came to know about a salt lab.

It was decided at one meeting that we go to Vadodara. My husband encouraged me to go there. We went to Gujarat Alkalis Chemicals Ltd (GACL) along with our samples. We discussed the rates and our salt was purchased by them. It was for the first time that we learnt the real value of salt.

I feel quite satisfied now. I get so much of information and am not dependent on the trader. I still need to learn how to calculate the financial requirement before I apply for loan.'

(a) Nursery Raising
(b) Forestry Campaign
(c) Water Campaign
(d) Watershed Activities
(e) Fodder Security

6. Marketing

The case described in Box 1 highlights SEWA interventions.

REEMA NANAVATY

Self-help Groups

The Origins of SHG–Bank Linkage

In the 1970s an ambitious credit scheme called the Integrated Rural Development Programme (IRDP) with a considerable element of subsidy was launched in India to alleviate poverty. It was a supply-led, not demand-led credit programme, and the clients did not have choice of 'purpose' and 'amount'; the underlying assumption was that the poor lacked productive assets and by providing them credit, they would acquire assets and cross the poverty line. Loan and subsidy became the central points and the programme did not have the desired effect (Dasgupta 2001). In 1982–3, Development of Women and Children in Rural Areas (DWCRA) was launched as a sub-scheme of the IRDP. The focus of the DWCRA was on economic activities for rural women to be undertaken in groups. The concept of group was to enable women to take a larger amount of loan, so that by pooling their individual loans they could start viable non-farm activity. The DWCRA too met with limited success.

Since the 1970s, numerous non-government organizations (NGOs) had begun experimenting in micro-finance to address poverty issues and create self-employment for women. Official interest in informal group lending took shape during 1986–7 when the National Bank for Agriculture and Rural Development (NABARD) supported and funded an action research project on 'Savings and Credit Management of Self-Help Groups' of an NGO in Karnataka (Dasgupta 2001). Following a survey of 43 NGOs in 11 states in India to study the functioning of self-help groups (SHGs) in 1988–9, NABARD impressed upon the Reserve Bank of India (RBI) the need to advise commercial banks to extend credit to the SHGs under a pilot project of NABARD. The results of the pilot project run by four NGOs[1] extending credit to 1,706 SHGs were found to be quite encouraging. The RBI constituted a working group in 1994 to review the functioning of NGOs and SHGs and, accepting its recommendations, advised the banks that lending to the SHGs should be considered an additional segment under priority sector advances. The SHGs, thus, became a component of the Indian financial system, heralding the unique SHG–bank linkage.

Salient Features of the SHGs

The SHGs have been the focal point of rural credit, self-employment programmes, and poverty alleviation in India since the early 1990s. In 1999, the Ministry of Rural Development of the Government of India restructured the numerous programmes and introduced the new self-employment programme called Swarnajayanti Gram

[1]Interestingly, three of the NGOs were located in south India and one in Orissa: Association of Sarva Seva Farms, Madras—214 SHGs; People's Rural Education Movement, Behrampur—829 SHGs; Assistance for Development Action, Madurai—313 SHGs; and Community Development Society, Alappuzha—350 SHGs.

Swarozgar Yojana (SGSY), which is implemented through the SHGs.

The SHGs have some interesting features. One of the important features is the homogeneity in the group in terms of social and economic status. The group has a membership of between 10 and 20, and the majority are women's groups. The basic functions envisaged are mobilization of savings, creation of a common fund out of savings, availing of credit from banks, and advancing loans to members. Generally, the SHGs are targeted at people from poor and weaker sections in rural areas and particularly women. Elected leaders run the management of the group and duty is generally rotated. Meetings are held regularly—weekly or monthly—and minutes are kept of meetings.

The SHGs create a common fund out of their savings, interest earned on loan, donations, and so on. Savings mobilization is ensured in some cases by a regular and fixed rate of savings, in some by no fixed rate of savings, and in other cases as per capacity of members. Loan advances are decided on the basis of the purpose, quantum, and the resources available with the SHG. Purposes of loans for individuals include consumption, clearing outside debt, medical, education, business, and agriculture, and for common production activities. The repayment period of loans is generally shorter than that prescribed by banks and the rate of interest varies from 12 to 20 per cent.

Until NGO–micro-finance institutions began lending to SHGs, NGOs were self-help promoting institutions and banks were the providers of finance. The separation of facilitator and banking roles has worked to the advantage of poor and illiterate women. The 'social engineering' role performed by the NGOs has empowered women and led to social development (as discussed later). The banks grade groups according to their financial management and extend loans without appropriating women's savings; the women use their own money for their priority needs. The public-sector banks, regional rural banks, and cooperatives have made the SHG–bank linkage programme of India the largest in the world, possibly at the lowest cost of administration.

Growth of the SHGs in India

As already mentioned, in 1999 the Ministry of Rural Development launched a new self-employment programme named SGSY, which has been devised keeping in view the positive aspects and efficiencies of earlier programmes such as the IRDP and DWCRA. The SGSY has been launched with a view to achieving the desired linkages among the programmes and the much needed focus on the substantive issue of sustainable income generation. The number of SHGs formed under the SGSY in the Indian states till date has been 22.52 lakh covering 35.54 lakh swarozgaris.[2]

The number of SHGs has continued to grow in the 1990s and 2000s and by March 2010 there were about 69.53 lakh SHGs linked to banks in India (the total may be larger as there may exist SHGs without linkages and waiting for it). The bank loans advanced to the SHGs amount to over Rs 14,450 crore, which is about 1 per cent of the total bank loans (Reserve Bank of India 2005–6). Over 80 per cent of the groups are women's groups. Interestingly, 46 per cent of the linked SHGs are located in south India.

The formation of the SHGs has taken some innovative forms. In Kerala, a new dimension was added to the SHG movement by the decentralization of governance since 1996. The panchayats, or local self-government institutions, have begun sponsoring the SHGs (called Kudumbasree), largely of women, to channel poverty alleviation scheme funds. Almost every village now has a large number of Kudumbasree units. The panchayat programmes as well as central government self-employment programmes are implemented through the Kudumbasree units. These units are clustered at ward level as Area Development Societies (ADS), which are federated into Community Development Societies (CDS) at the village panchayat level. By May 2011, Kerala had around 2.05 lakh SHGs, 17,578 ADS, and 1,061 CDS covering over 37 lakh families. The savings of the groups had reached Rs 1,668 crore and the loans Rs 4,195 crore.[3] The Kalanjiyam programme of DHAN foundation in Tamil Nadu also has a similar structure of organization of SHGs, clusters, and federations. Kalanjiyam reaches out to 8.10 lakh women covering 9,757 villages in 51 districts in 12 states of India. These community organizations go beyond micro-finance to address social development. It has been claimed that the Kalanjiyam programme has nurtured leadership qualities among over 1,00,000 poor women (DHAN Foundation 2010). Kudumbasree has seen similar nurturing of leadership qualities among poor women as is evidenced by many of them contesting the panchayat elections in Kerala in 2005 and 2010.

The SHGs and Banking Habits

In a largely rural economy, such as India, the banking habit of the rural population plays a major role in mobilizing financial savings by commercial banks. Due

[2]See http://india.gov.in/sectors/rural/swarna_jayanti.php, accessed on 16 May 2011.

[3]See www.kudumbashree.org/?q=ataglance, accessed on 16 May 2011.

to the high transaction costs and the tardy expansion of banking network, the drawing of rural population, and especially women, into the banking fold as deposit holders and borrowers has not made much progress. For instance, in 2000 the number of bank deposit accounts held by men and women (per 1,000 population) in India were 570 and 213, respectively. Financial-sector reforms since 1991 had led to a fall in the number of credit accounts and hardly any increase in the number of deposit accounts (all per 1,000 population). However, the overall stagnancy in the number of deposit accounts was achieved by an increase in the number of accounts held by women countering the fall in the number of accounts held by men. This was surprising in a situation when the banking sector was narrowing the scope of its activities to urban and semi-urban areas and away from agricultural and rural banking. Could it be that the growth of women's SHGs and the bank linkage programme had an impact on deposit holding by women?

At the level of Indian states, the association between the per capita number of SHGs and the growth rate of per capita accounts held by women is positive, controlling for the prevalence of SHGs per 1,000 women at some point of time in the 1990s (Varman 2005). A study of two villages in Tamil Nadu showed that at individual level the likelihood of an individual holding a deposit account is more if she is the head of the household and/or if she has been a leader of an SHG at least once—'an individual who has been a leader of SHG is 23 times more likely to hold a bank account than a person who has not' (ibid.: 1712).

Analysing the impact of higher exposure to the SHGs on opening deposit accounts in banks—by comparing account opening before and after joining the SHGs—it was seen that in the two villages, at least 75 per cent of the SHG member account holders have opened their accounts only after joining the SHGs. The impact of the duration of exposure to the SHGs on opening deposit accounts was also clear—the longer the duration, the higher the proportion of SHG members opening deposit accounts. Out of those SHG members with individual bank accounts, 83.3 per cent have been in a position of leadership in the group. Leadership gives the member more opportunity, as she is responsible for operating the group accounts. Regions with more experience with and longer duration of SHG operations will have more members with leadership experience as the leadership rotates in democratically functioning SHGs (Varman 2005).

Overall, while bank linkage provides the SHG members access to a formal source of credit without collateral security, the democratic functioning of the SHGs leads to the development of banking habits among members of the SHGs.

The SHGs and Women's Health

Does participation in the SHGs—in the absence of formal health programmes—have positive effects on health? A study of 928 women from households below the poverty line in Kerala found that women who participated in the SHGs were less likely to face exclusion from healthcare than non-participants, which is important in the Kerala context, which has an ageing population accompanied by increasing prevalence of chronic illness and disability, rising healthcare costs, and lack of social protection (Mohindra et al. 2008). This study further demonstrated that compared to non-participants, women who had been members for two or more years reported lower rates of emotional stress and poor life satisfaction. Over time, female participants may have the opportunities to achieve better mental health through a variety of channels, such as income-generation activities, social participation and group sharing, and assuming new leadership roles in the self-help group and the community.

The SHG–bank linkage unique to India took almost ten years (1986–94) to take shape. The salient feature of the linkage is that NGOs sponsor the SHGs, and banks rate them and provide the link, that is, access to mainstream financial services. The 'social engineering' by NGOs goes beyond micro-finance, empowering poor illiterate women. The growth of bank-linked SHGs is the coming into mainstream banking of that segment of population which was hitherto kept out of it. NGO-sponsored SHGs have themselves evolved into nurturing women into leadership roles—Kalanjiyam is the best example—and local governance roles—Kudumbasree is an example—with large impact on their lives. The SHG–bank linkage has led to financial deepening by inculcating banking habits among women and has reduced exclusion to healthcare by making available timely credit.

Since about 2000, NGOs are being turned into micro-finance organizations (MFOs) to carry out the functions of financial intermediation. When NGOs are turned into MFOs financed largely by private-sector banks with a view to meet regulatory obligations, or by equity funds with an eye on profits, 'social engineering' functions could be taking a back seat. With the MFOs being driven by profit motives, women's empowerment will also take a back seat. Adapting Hulme and Mosley (1996), it may be said that when the need of the hour is further institutional experimentation and innovations to empower women and to extend financial services further down the socio-economic scale, 'replication' of the so-called successful models is leading to uniformity in financial interventions.

D. NARAYANA

References

Dasgupta R. 2001. 'An Informal Journey through Self Help Groups', *Indian Journal of Agricultural Economics*, 56(3): 370–86.

DHAN Foundation. 2010. *MDG Matters: Localising Millenium Development Goals*, Annual Report, Madurai, DHAN Foundation.

Hulme, D., and P. Mosley. 1996. *Finance against Poverty*, Vol I. Routledge, London.

Mohindra, K.S., S. Haddad, and D. Narayana. 2008. 'Can Microcredit Help Improve the Health of Poor Women? Some Findings from a Cross-sectional Study in Kerala, India', *International Journal for Equity in Health*, 7(2).

Reserve Bank of India. 2005–6. *Handbook of Statistics on the Indian Economy*, Reserve Bank of India, Mumbai.

Varman, M. 2005. 'Impact of Self Help Groups on Formal Banking Habits', *Economic and Political Weekly*, 23 April, 40(17): 1705–14.

Services-led Growth

Introduction

The Indian economy has undergone major macroeconomic and structural reforms since the balance-of-payments crisis of 1991. Trade, foreign direct investment (FDI), and industrial policies have been liberalized. Institutional, legislative, and regulatory measures have been undertaken to improve macroeconomic management. The liberalization of the economy has helped put India on a higher growth trajectory, with the compound annual growth rate rising from 5.8 per cent during the 1990s to 7.3 per cent in the post 2000 period.[1] India has been one of the fastest growing economies in the past two decades. The country's external sector performance has also improved post-liberalization, with an increase in India's share in world trade as well as FDI flows over the past decade.

The service sector has played an important role in enabling this improved economic performance during the post-reform period. Services have been the fastest growing sector of the Indian economy in recent years and have helped accelerate the overall growth rate of the economy. Services have also facilitated India's integration with the world economy through trade and capital flows. The phenomenal growth and export performance witnessed in services like information technology (IT) and business process outsourcing (BPO) has placed India on the global map. Services have also helped improve productivity in other sectors of the economy, thus contributing to an improvement in the economy's overall competitiveness.

This entry provides an overview of the trends in growth, employment, trade, and capital flows in India's service sector in recent years. It highlights the case of specific services where India is highly competitive and services which have undergone significant liberalization and structural change in the post-reform period. The entry concludes by assessing the sustainability of services-led growth in India and underlines the close link between the service sector's prospects and the success of the overall economic reform process in India.

Growth Trends in India's Service Sector[2]

The service sector has exhibited phenomenal growth rates in the past two decades. Its average annual growth rate rose from 7 per cent during the 1988–8 period to 9.2 per cent during the 2002–9 period, exceeding overall GDP growth of 7.5 per cent during this period. The average growth rates in agriculture and industry were lower at 2.2 per cent and 7.7 per cent, respectively, during this same period. Table 1 provides the overall as well as sectoral growth rates in India for the 2002 to 2009 period and the superior performance of services compared to the rest of the economy.

Services have exhibited an upward trend in growth over the past few decades, registering a compound annual growth rate (CAGR) of 8.95 per cent over the 2000–9 period, up from 6.3 per cent in the 1980s and 7.5 per cent in the 1990s, and exceeding the CAGR of 7.3 per cent for total GDP for the 2000–9 period. Figure 1 illustrates the superior performance of the services sector and its role in raising overall economic growth in India.

Growth performance within the service sector has, however, been uneven. The driving segments have been communication, banking and insurance, construction, and trade and distribution services, which have grown

[1]Based on Central Statistical Organization statistics, Government of India.

[2]Most of the statistics and estimates provided in this section are based on the UN National Accounts Statistics Database, unless otherwise mentioned.

Table 1 Growth in Sectoral and Overall Output at Factor Cost and Constant Prices, 2002–9 (%)

Sector	Growth rate								
	2002	2003	2004	2005	2006	2007	2008	2009	Average 2002 to 2009
Agriculture and allied activities	−7.3	9.8	0.2	5.3	3.7	4.7	1.6	−1.0	2.2
Industry	4.9	6.1	9.3	8.7	13.3	9.2	3.2	7.2	7.7
Services	7.1	8.6	9.9	11.4	10.3	10.4	9.2	6.7	9.2
GDP at factor cost	3.3	8.3	7.8	9.6	9.7	9.2	6.7	5.6	7.5

Source: Based on UN National Accounts Statistical Database, available at http://unstats.un.org/unsd/snaama/resQuery.asp.

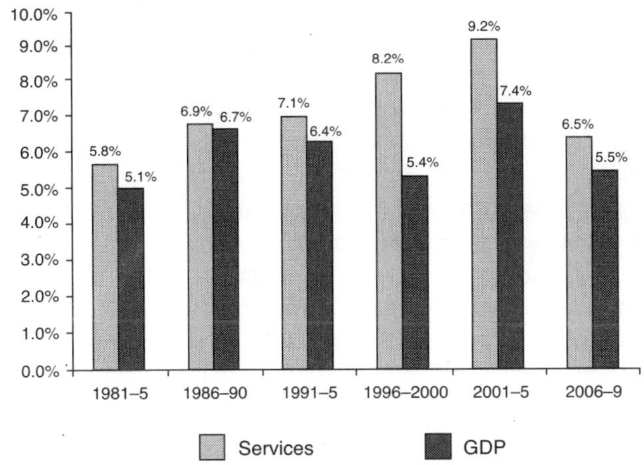

Figure 1 Compound Annual Growth Rate for Services and GDP in India, 1980s, 1990s, and 2000s (%)

Source: Based on UN National Accounts Statistical Database, available at http://unstats.un.org/unsd/snaama/resQuery.asp.

at over 7 per cent in CAGR terms during the 2000–9 period, while services such as railways and public administration services have grown at less than 4 per cent. These sub-sectoral trends reflect differences in policy and regulatory trends across different services and the role of rising incomes and domestic demand in driving growth in some services. Communication services have been the fastest growing service segment, reflecting the significant liberalization and deregulation in this sector since the 1990s.

The high growth rate of services has contributed to its rising share in the overall economy. Between 1950 and 1990, agriculture's share in GDP declined by around 25 per cent with the corresponding increase in the share of services and industry being distributed roughly evenly. However, the average share of industry in overall GDP has declined from around 22 per cent in 1990–4 to 20 per cent in 2005–9 and the share of agriculture has declined from around 30 per cent to about 18 per cent of GDP over this same period. This has been matched by a corresponding rise in the share of services in the economy. In 2009, services constituted around 64 per cent of GDP, up from around 48 per cent of GDP in 1990. This is in contrast to many other developing economies, where the decline in the share of agriculture in GDP has been followed by a corresponding rise in the share of industry, in particular manufacturing, and later in services. Thus, there has been a leapfrogging of the economy from dependence on the primary sector to the tertiary sector. Figure 2 shows the relative contributions of the primary, secondary, and tertiary sectors in India's GDP and the

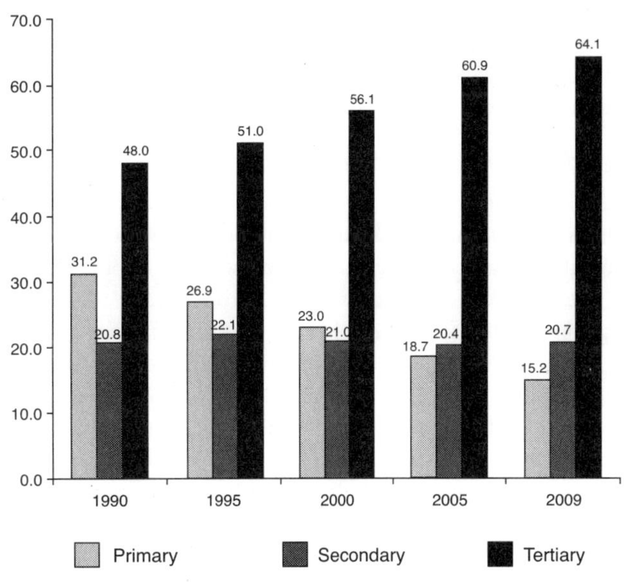

Figure 2 Composition of GDP across Sectors (%)

Source: Based on UN National Accounts Statistical Database, available at http://unstats.un.org/unsd/snaama/resQuery.asp.

steady shift in this composition between 1980 and 2009 towards services.

The service sector's contribution to overall employment has risen, though this has not been commensurate to the growth in services output. According to the 2001 Indian Census statistics, its share in employment rose from 20.8 per cent to 25.1 per cent between 1991 and 2001, while during the same period, its share in GDP increased by over 10 per cent, implying a low employment elasticity. According to the latest *Economic Survey*, the tertiary sector's share of employment has increased rather modestly, from 21.2 per cent in 1993–4 to 24.8 per cent in 2004–5 and 25.4 per cent in 2007–8, while its contribution to GDP has increased from less than 50 per cent to around 60 per cent over this same period. Most of this employment is concentrated in trade and distribution, construction, hotel and restaurants, and community and personal services segments. The employment trends reveal that very rapidly growing service segments such as communication and financial services have had relatively lower employment elasticity, indicating that their growth has mainly been based on productivity gains and technological improvements.

It is worth noting, however, that Indian data on services output and employment are subject to problems of data collection, disaggregation, and coverage. There is also no information available on price indices for India's service sector, as India's Wholesale Price Index does not cover services. There are efforts underway to improve statistical measurement and coverage of services under the aegis of a National Statistical Commission.

Trade in India's Service Sector[3]

The contribution of services to India's trade and FDI flows has also been growing over the past decade, facilitating India's integration with the world economy. India's services exports have grown from a mere $2.9 billion in 1980 to $16.7 billion in 2000 and further to $116.3 billion in 2010. Services imports have also risen significantly, from $2.9 billion in 1980 to $19.2 billion in 2000, and further to $108.6 billion in 2010. India has moved to a slight services trade surplus over the years, which has in part helped offset its otherwise persistent and growing trade deficit in goods. The average annual growth rate of India's services exports has accelerated significantly in the past decade, rising from 19.5 per cent in the 1995–9 period to 25.2 per cent in the 2000–9 period. The CAGR for services exports stood at 18.4 per cent during the 2000–9 period, far exceeding the CAGR for services output during this same period. These trends highlight the export-oriented nature of services growth in the Indian economy as well as India's growing competitiveness in the world services market and its liberalization of services imports, especially in the post-2000 period. As a result, the share of services in India's total exports has risen from 18.1 per cent in 1995 to over 34.9 per cent in 2010.

India has also outperformed other economies, including China, in the case of services exports. During the 1990s, India had the highest growth of services exports among all economies, with an average annual growth rate of 17.3 per cent, compared to China at 15.8 per cent and a world average of 5.6 per cent. In the recent decade, India's services exports have accelerated further, posting an average annual growth rate of 22.2 per cent in the 2000–10 period, outperforming all other economies. Figure 3 highlights India's superior services export performance in the latest decade.

Rapid growth in services trade has led to India's increased penetration of the world services market over the past two decades, reflecting India's growing competitiveness in the world services market, especially in the post-2000 period. As shown in Figure 4, India's share in world services exports has risen from less than 1 per cent in the 1980s and 1990s to 3.1 per cent in 2010. Its share in world services imports has similarly increased from 0.7 per cent in 1990 to 3.1 per cent in 2010.

It is worth noting that India's services exports have in general grown much more rapidly than its merchandise exports. Further, India's penetration of the world services markets not only exceeds that for goods but has also risen more rapidly, particularly in the latest decade. Figures 5 and 6 illustrate the relatively superior performance of services exports compared to merchandise exports.

Thus, the evidence indicates India's growing competitiveness in services relative to goods. This is also supported by estimates of India's revealed comparative advantage (RCA) in services versus goods, which show that between 1990 and 2009, the RCA for services increased by 82 per cent, while that for goods actually declined by around 10 per cent. Figure 7 illustrates the trends in India's RCA for services relative to goods.

There has been a shift in the structure of India's services exports away from traditional services such as transport and travel towards emerging areas such as business services, with computer and information services constituting the predominant segment. The contribution of transport and travel services to total exports declined from over 50 per cent in 1995 to around 30 per cent in 2000 and further to around 12 per cent in 2010. In contrast, software services increased their contribution

[3]Most of the statistics in this section are based on UNCTAD Handbook of Statistics Online, unless otherwise mentioned.

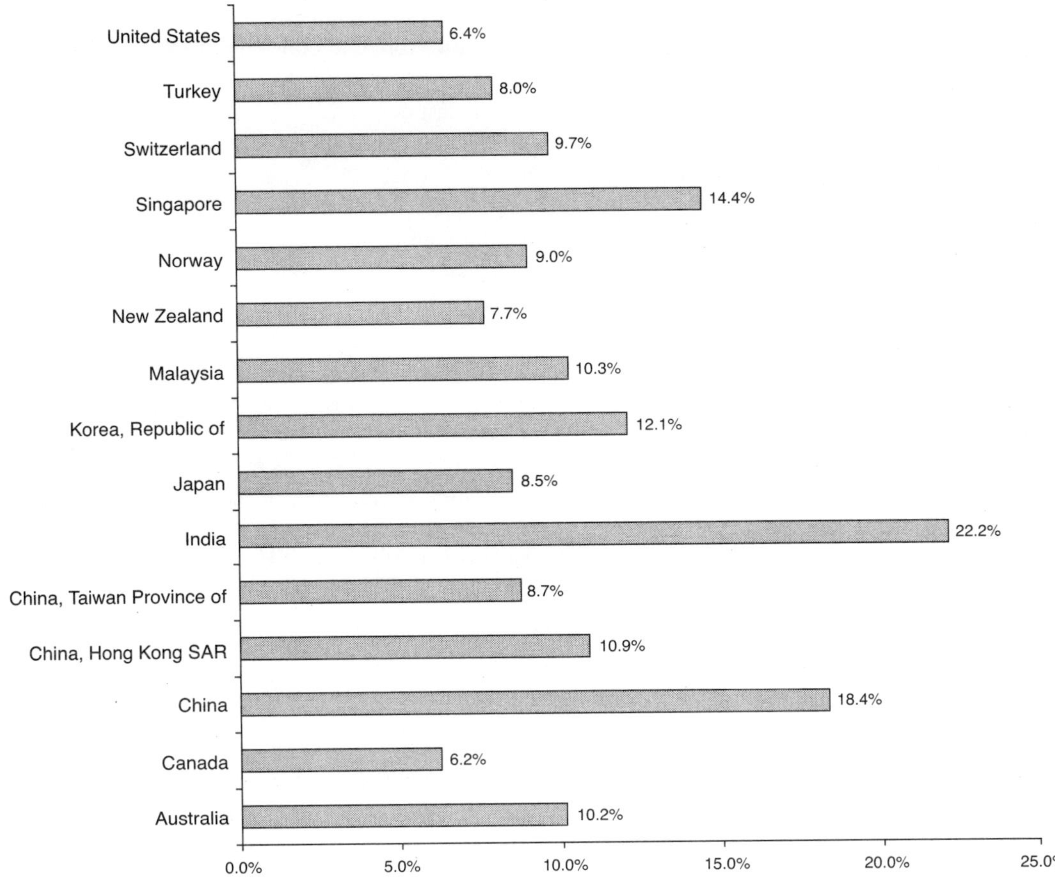

Figure 3 Average Growth Rate of Services Exports for Selected Countries, 2000–10 (%)

Source: Based on UNCTAD Handbook of Statistics Online, available at http://www.unctad.org/Templates/Page.asp?intItemID=1890.

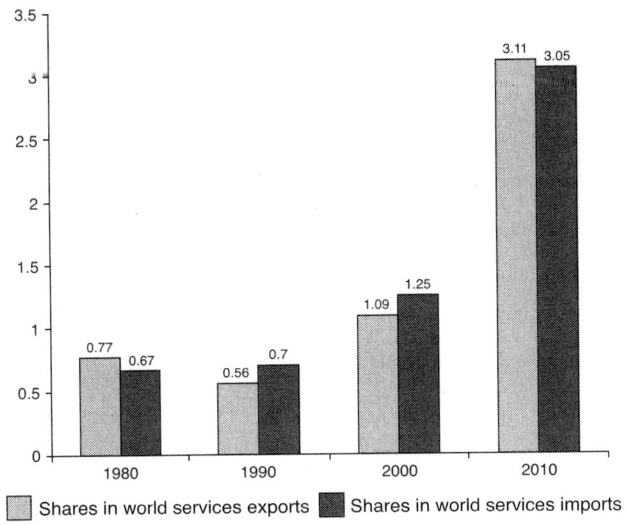

Figure 4 India's Share in World Services Exports and Imports, 1980–2010 (%)

Source: Based on UNCTAD Handbook of Statistics Online, available at http://www.unctad.org/Templates/Page.asp?intItemID=1890.

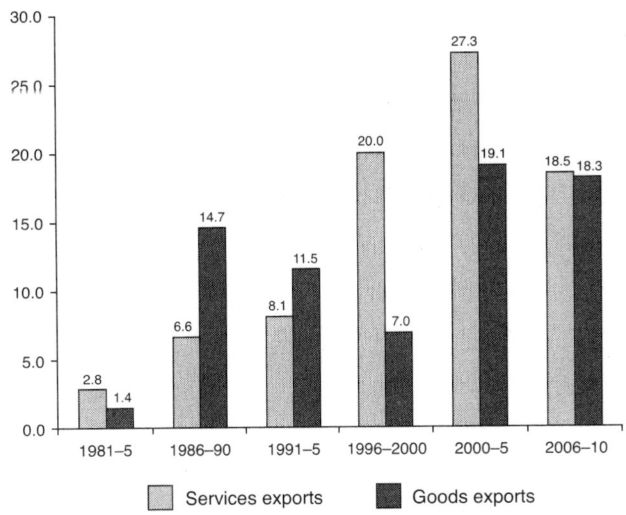

Figure 5 Average Annual Growth Rate of Goods and Services Exports, 1980–2010 (%)

Source: Based on UNCTAD Handbook of Statistics Online, available at http://www.unctad.org/Templates/Page.asp?intItemID=1890.

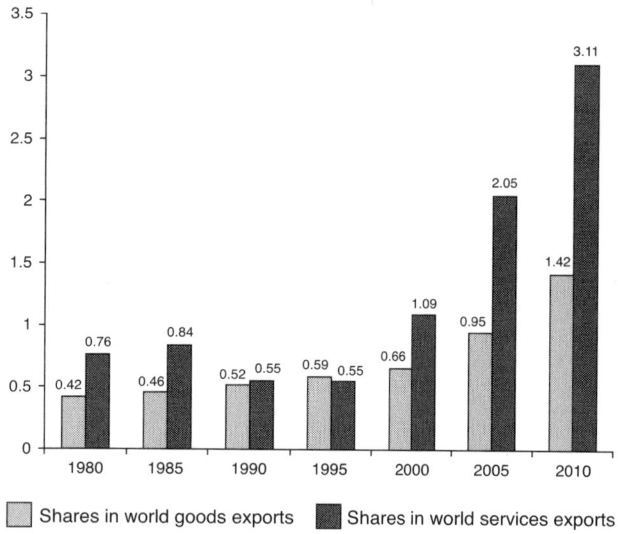

Figure 6 Share in World Exports of Goods and Services, 1980–2010 (%)

Source: Based on UNCTAD Handbook of Statistics Online, available at http://www.unctad.org/Templates/Page.asp?intItemID=1890.

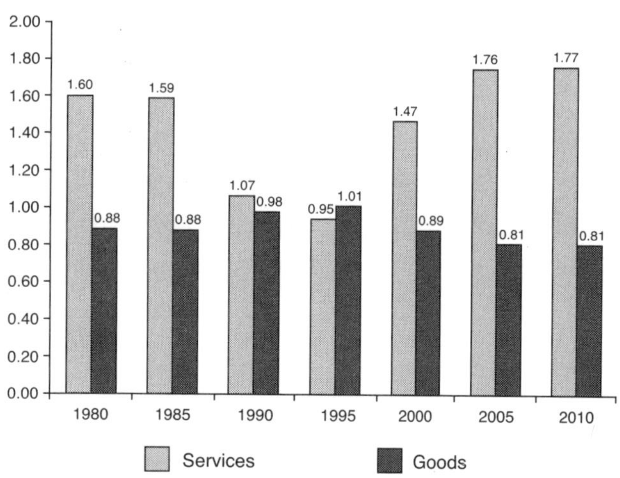

Figure 7 India's Revealed Comparative Advantage in Services and Goods Exports, 1980–2010

Source: Based on UNCTAD Handbook of Statistics Online, available at http://www.unctad.org/Templates/Page.asp?intItemID=1890.

from zero in 1995 to 28 per cent in 2000 and to 51.5 per cent in 2010, reflecting the segment's phenomenal growth over the past decade. The share of other business services (which include advertising, exhibitions, engineering, accountancy, and health services) has, however, declined over the 1995–2010 period. There has also been a diversification of the services export basket with the emergence of segments such as financial, insurance, communication, and construction services. Overall, India's services exports have become more broad-based over the last decade.

The disaggregated estimates for export growth of different service sub-sectors explain this shift in the composition of India's services exports. The fastest growing segment has been IT and BPO services which has registered double- digit growth rates annually in the past decade, resulting in its rapidly growing share in India's services exports.

The RCA estimates for different service segments similarly reveal India's competitiveness in the software services segment compared to all other service sub-sectors, as shown in Figure 8. This characteristic also holds if one takes a time series trend for RCA for the 2001–10 period, thus reflecting the sustained competitiveness and highly export-oriented nature of India's software services sector.

Given India's comparative advantage in skilled and labour-intensive services, cross-border labour mobility has played an important part in India's successful export performance in software and other business services. Indian computer professionals accounted for 68 per cent and 63 per cent of all specialty occupation visas granted in the United States (or non-immigrant H-1B visas given to persons with professional qualifications) in the computer services category in 2001 and 2002, respectively. In 2009, temporary admissions from India constituted 36.3 per cent (123,002) of all H-1B admissions (339,243) in the US. India has consistently remained among the top five source countries for temporary skilled workers admitted into the US across a variety of professional services, including healthcare, architecture, engineering, and education services.[4] India is also an important supplier of low and semi-skilled service suppliers to the Middle East in activities such as construction, transport operations, domestic help, nursing, and paramedical services.

India's services exports remain constrained by domestic and external barriers. The main domestic barriers are in the form of infrastructural, financial, regulatory, technical, and standard-related constraints. The main external barriers are in the form of immigration and labour market regulations, which limit India's ability to deliver services through the temporary cross-border movement of service providers. There have also been periodic backlashes against outsourcing in key markets

[4]See http://www.migrationinformation.org/USfocus/display.cfm?id=801#22 and http://www.dhs.gov/files/statistics/publications/YrBk09NI.shtm.

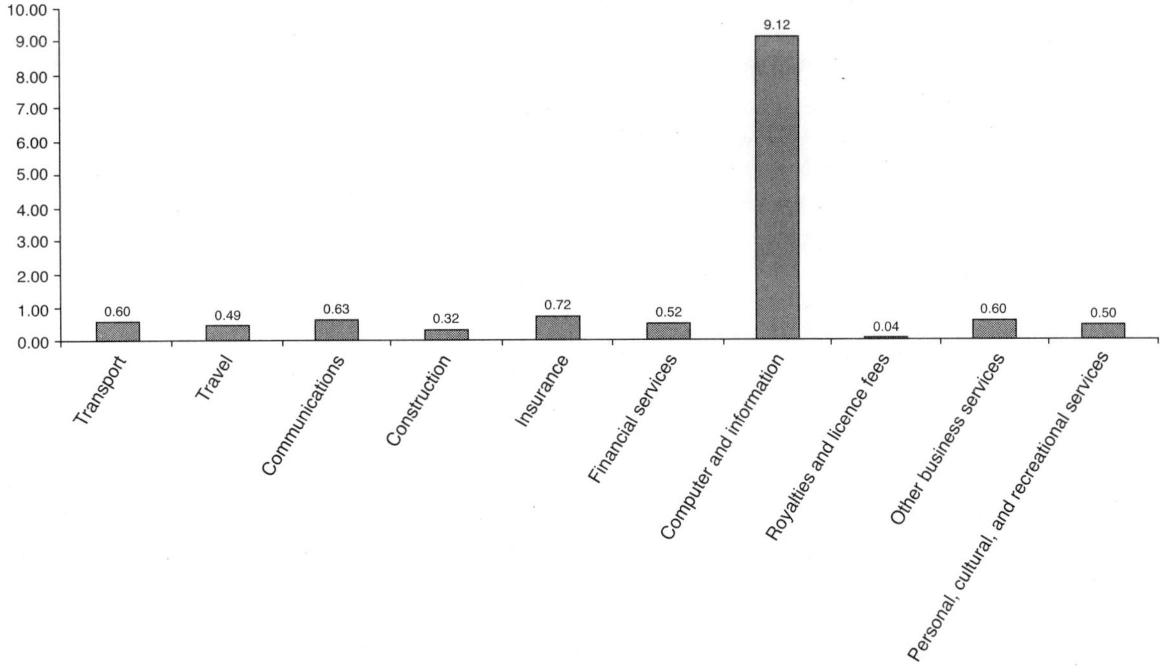

Figure 8 India's RCA for Selected Categories of Services Exports, 2009

Source: Based on UNCTAD Handbook of Statistics Online, available at http://www.unctad.org/Templates/Page.asp?intItemID=1890.

like the US. In 2009 and 2010, several protectionist bills have been introduced in the US to ban outsourcing of government contracts to third countries and to hike fees for specialty occupation visas. India's services exports have also been affected by the presence of data privacy laws, licensing and certification requirements, liability issues, and opposition from regulatory bodies and associations in overseas markets.

Trends in India's IT BPO Services[5]

The IT and BPO services segment has been the growth driver in India's service sector. IT and BPO services exports have risen from a mere $754 million in 1995–6 to $9.6 billion in 2002–3, to an estimated $59 billion in 2010, with the industry's total turnover reaching $88.1 billion or 6.4 per cent of GDP in 2010. Within the industry, IT services accounted for over half of export earnings ($33.5 billion) in 2010, BPO services for around 24 per cent ($14.2 billion), and engineering services and software products for another 19 per cent of export earnings in this industry.

The US has been the most important market for India's IT–BPO exports, with a projected share of 61 per cent in 2010 followed by the UK (18 per cent). In recent years, new markets have emerged in the Asia-Pacific and the Middle East, where the Indian IT–BPO industry is yet to realize its potential.

In line with the growth in IT–BPO revenues, there has been rapid growth in employment in the IT–BPO sector. The industry employed an estimated 2.3 million people in 2010 directly and another 8.2 million indirectly. Growth has been driven by a mix of companies in this sector, involving a variety of delivery models, including captive subsidiaries and offshore development centres of foreign companies as well as large, small, and medium-sized Indian companies.

India's IT–BPO exports are in a variety of verticals, including the banking and financial services industry (BFSI), telecom, manufacturing, retail, healthcare, and travel and tourism. Despite the financial crisis of 2008, BFSI remains the most important vertical. However, segments such as healthcare and retail have shown rapid growth in recent years. There has also been a gradual movement up the value chain, with a growing number of offshore R&D centres being established in India and a shift towards higher-end services such as business analytics, equity research, and market research. Some Indian companies are also engaging in reverse outsourcing by offshoring part of their operations to other countries.

[5]Much of the discussion in this section draws on the NASSCOM Strategic Review Reports for various years, unless otherwise mentioned.

Exports in this sector take the form of onsite delivery through the temporary movement of software professionals to other markets, and offshore delivery of services through data, voice, and information flows over the internet and phone. There has, however, been a shift from a predominantly onsite mode of delivery to a primarily offshore mode of delivery in order to further leverage India's labour cost advantage. The current offshore–onsite mix stands at 85:15.[6] According to the AT Kearney Offshore Location Attractiveness Index, India has consistently ranked highest among offshoring destinations, due to the combination of its skill availability, favourable business environment, and low cost.[7] Today, India accounts for around half of the global offshore IT–BPO market. It is expected to remain an important part of the global outsourcing market in future, notwithstanding emerging competition from other developing countries and regions.

FDI in India's Service Sector[8]

There has also been a structural shift in FDI flows into India towards the service sector. The average share of services in FDI rose from 10.5 per cent for the 1990–4 period to 28.3 per cent during the 1995–9 period. In 2009, services accounted for nearly 75 per cent of FDI inflows. Cumulative FDI inflows into services for the January 2000–May 2010 period stood at $76.9 billion or 63.6 per cent of total cumulative FDI inflows for this entire period. Service-sector FDI has grown rapidly in India, registering a CAGR of 36 per cent between 1992–3 and 2001–2 and a CAGR of 36.7 per cent between 2006 and 2009.

The range of service sub-sectors attracting FDI has expanded over time, with a growing share of 'other services' (which include business, financial, consulting, and miscellaneous services) in total FDI inflows. Certain services such as telecommunications and construction have remained important throughout the period, while some such as housing and real estate services have become more attractive destinations for FDI flows in recent years. The importance of segments such as telecommunications and real estate services reflect India's internal growth and liberalization dynamics which have driven the expansion of these services. The decline in the share of computer services in part reflects the impact of the recent global economic slowdown and the saturation of this sub-sector.

Services also account for a growing share of outward FDI flows from the Indian economy, as shown in Table 2. Services accounted for over 50 per cent of total FDI outflows for the 1999–2008 period, with non-financial services such as communication, software, and business services constituting the main segments.[9] In areas like software and health services, Indian firms are increasingly emerging as exporters of capital, setting up overseas establishments in developing and developed economies.

Liberalization of Services in India[10]

Services have been a critical part of the overall economic reform and liberalization process in India. Much of the recent structural and institutional reforms as well as the liberalization/deregulation strategies have involved the opening up of key services, such as telecommunications, banking, and insurance to attract much needed foreign capital and technology, and to encourage competition and efficiency in these areas to induce positive externalities for the rest of the economy. Many services, including, construction, housing and townships, hospitals and diagnostics, wholesale cash and carry trade, and computer-related services, for instance, have been put on automatic approval route for FDI and have been fully liberalized (albeit subject to certain conditions and regulatory requirements).

Perhaps the most significant feature of service-sector liberalization in India has been the elimination of government monopoly and the establishment of independent regulators in critical services. Telecommunication services have experienced the most liberalization and regulatory reforms in the past decade. Today, wholly foreign-owned firms are allowed in some segments of the telecom sector. Government monopoly in long distance telephony and internet has been eliminated. FDI has been permitted in most segments with a ceiling of 74 per cent foreign equity participation and even 100

[6]See 'No Major Reversal in Onsite-offshore Recruitment Mix: Infosys CEO', available at http://www.thehindubusinessline.com/2010/09/09/stories/2010090953150700.htm and RBI Survey (2009)

[7]http://www.atkearney.com/index.php/News-media/geography-of-offshoring-is-shifting.html?q=offshoring+india

[8]Data and estimates in this section are mostly based on http://www.indiastat.com, unless otherwise mentioned.

[9]Athukorala (2009), based on RBI Annual Reports for various years.

[10]Most of the discussion concerning FDI regulations in different services is based on http://www.dipp.nic.in/FDI_Circular/FDI_Circular_02of2010.pdf.

Table 2 Composition of Approved Outward FDI from India (million US$)

Category	1999–2000	2000–1	2001–2	2002–3	2003–4	2004–5	2005–6	2006–7	2007–8	1999–2008
Manufacturing	31.2	26.8	73.1	71.9	52.8	72.3	59.9	24.9	43.7	42.7
Financial services	0.2	1.2	1.6	0.1	2.4	0.3	5.9	0.2	0.2	0.7
Non-financial services	65.1	63.4	18.7	19.1	30.2	19.5	24.8	54.7	12.1	30.3
Trading	3.3	6.5	4.6	4.8	5.3	2.5	4.7	8.3	3.2	5.1
Other	0.1	2.1	2.0	4.2	9.2	5.4	4.7	12.0	40.7	21.3
Total	100.0	100.0	100.0	100.0	100.0	100.0	100.0	100.0	100.0	100.0
	1,767	1,406	3,051	1,464	1,430	2,781	2,866	15,053	22,480	52,299

Source: Reproduced from Athukorala (2009), Table 3, p. 136 (based on RBI Annual Report, various years).

per cent in the case of other service providers engaged in call centres and business process outsourcing. An independent regulator, the Telecom Regulatory Authority of India (TRAI) has also been established. Similarly, government monopoly in the insurance services sector has been eliminated and the sector has been opened up to private players, with foreign equity ceiling of 26 per cent on an automatic route basis. Further liberalization of this sector is under consideration. An independent regulator, the Insurance Regulatory Development Authority (IRDA) has been set up. Banking services have been liberalized with foreign equity participation (including by Foreign Institutional Investors) permitted up to 74 per cent in private banks and up to 20 per cent in public-sector banks, though conditions continue to apply in terms of restrictions on voting rights, licensing requirements, approvals from regulatory authorities, and the form of establishment permitted. Alongside the liberalization of capital markets and the banking system, the role of financial-sector regulators has been enhanced to ensure prudential management and ensure macroeconomic stability.

Services liberalization has, however, not been a smooth process in India. In several sub-sectors there has been considerable national debate. One such segment is retail, which to date remains only partially open to FDI in the single brand (not multi-brand) segment, owing to strong trader lobby opposition and concerns about displacement of small retailers by multinational retail chains. Likewise, legal services remain closed to foreign firms and service providers due to resistance from the concerned regulatory body. Another service sector where there has been much debate recently is higher education. Legislation has been proposed to permit Foreign Education Providers to set up campuses and grant degrees in India, subject to certain conditions. This Bill has raised concerns over issues of standards, equivalence, consumer protection, regulation of foreign players, and likely impact on public-sector institutions.

Overall, the debate concerning services liberalization has centred around issues of equity–efficiency trade-offs and impact on domestic players. It has also become evident that services liberalization needs to be accompanied by supporting domestic regulations and reforms and development of regulatory frameworks and regulatory capacity, if the gains from liberalization are to be realized and the potential adverse effects mitigated.

There is evidence to suggest that services liberalization has yielded efficiency gains to the Indian economy. A 2004 study by the World Bank finds a positive correlation between the degree of liberalization in a service sub-sector with regard to trade and FDI policies and its access to external markets, and growth in output and employment opportunities in that sub-sector. The study highlights that segments such as business services (mainly IT and IT-enabled services), communication, banking, and insurance, which have been liberalized, have exhibited higher growth rates, with wider efficiency and growth benefits to the rest of the economy while services where there has been limited opening have grown much more slowly.

Productivity estimates also corroborate the efficiency gains arising from competition and integration with global markets in the service sector. Estimates by McKinsey indicate that telecommunications and software services have much higher productivity levels than other service sectors in India, owing to factors such as global and domestic competition and changes in ownership structure, which have enabled technological externalities, knowledge spillovers, improved management practices, and technology diffusion. Liberalization in certain services has also impacted positively on export opportunities. The liberalization of segments such as telecommunications has had a positive impact on export opportunities in IT and

BPO services. Evidence also indicates increased usage of services in manufacturing and resulting productivity gains in India's manufacturing sector. Hence, as several studies point out, further liberalization of the service sector is likely to yield sector-specific and economy-wide gains in terms of growth, export, efficiency, and competitiveness.

India's Multilateral and Regional Engagements in Services

India has been actively involved in the WTO services negotiations. It has taken a proactive position in the services negotiations on temporary cross border movement of service providers (mode 4) and cross-border supply of services (mode 1) under the General Agreement on Trade in Services (GATS). In 2004, India made a joint submission along with several other developing countries for a Service Provider Visa under the GATS, with the aim of expanding and ensuring more predictable and transparent market access for intra-company transferees, contractual service suppliers, and independent professionals. India also submitted a joint proposal on mode 1 in 2004 to secure market access in outsourcing across a wide range of services, so as to pre-empt potential protectionism in this area.[11]

In the Doha Round request-offer process, there has been pressure on India from key WTO member countries to make binding and more liberal commitments on commercial presence (GATS mode 3) across a wide range of services. India has received requests from several developed countries to multilaterally bind in the liberalization it has undertaken autonomously in sectors such as banking, insurance, and telecommunications, where India's commitments fall short of the existing levels of liberalization. India has also received requests to open up other services such as retail, higher education, legal and accountancy services to foreign commercial presence. India has largely taken a quid pro quo approach to the services negotiations, that is, exchanging commitments on foreign commercial presence in return for market access in modes 1 and 4. In its August 2005 revised services offer, India significantly improved upon its earlier commitments on commercial presence, aligning its offer more closely with its autonomous liberalization initiatives in services. However, the extent to which this offer will be converted into legally binding commitments remains unclear, given the stalemate in the Doha Round.

India has meanwhile been pursuing its interests in the service sector through bilateral and regional agreements. In recent years, India has entered into broad-ranging trade negotiations which go beyond goods to cover services, investment, labour mobility, and other issues which have a bearing on services trade. Some of these include the India–Singapore Comprehensive Economic Cooperation Agreement (CECA) and the India–Korea Comprehensive Economic Partnership Agreement (CEPA) signed in 2005 and 2009, respectively. Several agreements are at different stages of negotiation, including with the EU and Australia. In all these agreements, India's aim is to facilitate investments in various services from its partner countries and to secure its interests in sectors such as IT–BPO and various other professional services, in particular through easier access for Indian service suppliers to these markets. There is also a growing recognition that India's main interest and competitive advantage lies in services and that the concessions it makes on goods can be traded off against concessions it can secure from partner countries in services and on key issues such as mode 4 and mode 1.

Conclusion

The preceding discussion highlights that the service sector has not only outperformed other sectors of the Indian economy, but has also played an important role in India's integration with world trade and capital markets. India's liberalization of services has been a challenging process in several sub-sectors but clearly those services where integration through trade and FDI has gone further are also the ones that have exhibited more rapid growth along with positive spillovers on the rest of the economy.

There is, however, concern about the sustainability of a services-led growth process and the current pattern of services growth, which largely stems from exports of skill-based services. The prevailing view is that for services growth to be sustained, the sector cannot remain dependent on external demand. It must also be driven by internal demand. More broad-based growth *within* the service sector is also required to ensure balanced, equitable, and employment-oriented growth, with backward and forward linkages to the rest of the economy. In this regard, further infrastructural and regulatory reforms and FDI liberalization in services can help diversify the sources of growth within India's service sector and provide the required momentum.

RUPA CHANDA

[11]Discussion of India's strategic interests in the WTO services negotiations is based on Chanda (2004).

References

AT Kearney, http://www.atkearney.com/index.php/News-media/geography-of-offshoring-is-shifting.html?q=offshoring+india

Athukorala, P. 2009. 'Outward Foreign Direct Investment from India', *Asian Development Review*, 26(2): 125–53.

Central Statistical Organisation. Various Years. National Accounts Statistics.

Chanda, R. 2004. 'Movement of Natural Persons: A Case Study of South Asian Countries', Research Report, Jaipur, CUTS Centre for International Trade, Economics, and Environment.

NASSCOM. Various Years. *The IT Industry in India: Strategic Review*, New Delhi.

Reserve Bank of India. 2009. *RBI Survey on Software & Information Technology Services Exports: 2008–09*, available at http://rbidocs.rbi.org.in/rdocs/PressRelease/PDFs/IEPR224RB0810.pdf.

——. Various Years. *Annual Report*.

World Bank. 2004. *Sustaining India's Services Revolution: Access to Foreign Markets, Domestic Reform and International Negotiations*, New Delhi, World Bank.

Sex Work

Sex work in India, as in the rest of the world, employs a large number of people who operate on the fringes of legality. It is difficult to know how many sex workers there are in India, but it is estimated that about 1 per cent of adult women in the country could be engaged in sex work (Dandona et al. 2006). Sex work is arguably even more stigmatized in India than in most other parts of the world because of strong social restrictions on sexual behaviour. Nag (2006) provides a detailed account of sex workers in India beginning with the Vedic age in the 8th century BC to the present day, illustrating the enormous diversity in Indian prostitution ranging from sex workers in the guise of *devadasis* to more commonly known brothel and street-based workers. A majority of the women enter the profession involuntarily, most of them being forced into it either because of poverty, abandonment or violence by husbands, or other family problems (Sleightholme and Sinha 1996). They are usually contractually obligated, in a form of bonded labour, to work in a brothel under the ownership of a madam or pimp. However, a growing number of newer sex workers are entering sex work relatively voluntarily (Kotiswaran 2008)

Much of what we know about sex work in India comes from studies of Sonagachi, Kolkata's oldest and best established red-light district, with over 4,000 sex workers working in 370 brothels that service about 20,000 clients a day. However, this is changing as more research is being conducted in other regions of India, such as in Andhra Pradesh where the spread of HIV is a concern (Dandona et al. 2006). Because of the intense level of stigma, the sex workers' sub-culture is often self-contained, shaped by a pervasive sense of exclusion from the mainstream, as well as conditioned by the market for sex work—selling a diversity of services to different clients for prices which in 1993 ranged from Rs 15 to Rs 600 per sexual act in Sonagachi; and from Rs 10 to Rs 900 per sexual act in 2003–4 in Andhra Pradesh. The average weekly income of a Sonagachi sex worker in 1993 was Rs 984 with an estimated hourly wage rate of Rs 8.20, which was approximately double the hourly wage rate of women in urban India. Thus, despite the considerable hardships they face, sex workers are in a rather lucrative profession and this perhaps explains why more women are entering the occupation voluntarily, despite its extremely stigmatized status. While this occupational 'choice' may stem from poverty and lack of better alternatives in the labour market, an important finding, especially for those attempting to implement effective policies which influence both entry and exit into the sex market as well as risk behaviour, is the recognition that sex work is not always involuntary and that sex workers do respond to economic incentives.

An interesting fact in the economics of sex work is that returns to education are comparable to those of women who work in more conventional occupations. Sex workers with primary schooling make about 4.2 per cent more than those with no education, while those with middle schooling make about 22 per cent more. This reflects the segmentation of the market with more educated sex workers catering to more educated clients. However, unlike other professions, age shows a sharp negative relationship with earning capacity, indicating that there is a relative premium for youth in this market (Arunachalam and Shah 2008; Rao et al. 2003).

The profession has received increased attention from social scientists in recent years because of the AIDS epidemic. This is particularly true in India where sex workers are at very high risk for contracting HIV and of transmitting it among their clients, who then have the potential of transmitting it to their wives and other family members. For example, HIV prevalence was estimated to be 16 per cent amongst female sex workers in 2004 (Andhra Pradesh State AIDS Control Society 2004) though national prevalence is estimated to still be low (less than 1 per cent among adults). Promoting the use of condoms and other safe sex practices among sex workers is, therefore, considered perhaps the most effective method to prevent the spread of the disease.

A major challenge in implementing this strategy comes from the strong preference that Indian men tend to have for sex without a condom. This results in a 'compensating differential' for safe sex; sex workers who insist on using condoms stand to lose a lot of money resulting in a major disincentive for practising safe sex. However, estimating this compensating differential with an ordinary least squares regression that regresses sex worker earnings against condom use results in a serious statistical bias, even after controlling for a variety of other characteristics that could affect income. This is because sex workers who are able to persuade clients to use condoms are also likely to be those with the most bargaining power, perhaps because they are particularly attractive to clients. This attribute of 'attractiveness' is not easy to capture in survey questionnaires—a problem that is known in the language of econometrics as 'unobserved heterogeneity'. Since attractiveness is positively correlated both with condom use and with sex workers' income, it causes a spurious positive correlation between condom use and income that sharply underestimates the extent of the income lost by using condoms.

One way of correcting for this bias is by using a 'natural experiment' that assigns condom use among sex workers in a manner that is not correlated with income. Rao et al. (2003) used 1993 data from Sonagachi with information on an HIV/AIDS intervention that went to sex workers in a relatively random manner providing them with graphic descriptions of the consequences of unsafe sex. This was highly correlated with a sex worker's propensity to use condoms, but uncorrelated with her income. Rao et al. (ibid.) were, therefore, able to use instrumental variables to correct for unobserved heterogeneity by using the HIV/AIDS intervention as an instrument for condom use. Using this method, they estimated that the average sex worker faced a loss in wages of between 66 to 79 per cent by using condoms.

Studies in other developing countries have found similar results with male clients paying a premium for non-condom use in Mexico (Gertler et al. 2005), Ecuador (Arunachalam and Shah 2010), and Kenya (Robinson and Yeh forthcoming). In fact, sex workers in Kenya often engage in riskier sex as a way of coping with unexpected non-labour income shocks, such as someone in the household getting sick (Robinson and Yeh forthcoming). Arunachalam and Shah (2010) show that the premium men pay for non-condom sex increases in locations with higher disease rates. The loss in earnings associated with condom use clearly represents a major disincentive in initiating safe sex programmes. The problem comes from the fact that clients, most of whom do not want to use condoms, are able to exploit competition among sex workers to bargain down the price of a sex act with condoms. If a sex worker insists on having sex with a condom, the client can simply go to the next brothel where he will find a sex worker who is more pliable. The solution to this can come either by educating clients about safe sex, or by creating an agreement among sex workers to collectively agree to refuse condom-free sex, which eliminates the possibility of competition.

The Sonagachi intervention achieved remarkable success by primarily following the second strategy (Gooptu 2000). Instead of using health extension workers for spreading the message of safe sex, which was the conventional practice in Indian public health interventions, this intervention decided to train a small group of 12 sex workers as peer educators to pass on information to their co-workers. The only thing that distinguished peer educators from other sex workers were the green medical coats that they wore over their sarees when they engaged in public health functions. The green coats also gave the peer educators a sense of self-worth and a 'respectable' identity. At the same time, as members of the community they were permitted easy access to brothels and had the credibility associated with being intimately aware of the hazards of the profession.

This process of educating sex workers and mobilizing them for the HIV-AIDS intervention, along with the increasing media attention brought about by the success of the project, led, over a period of two or three years, to a metamorphosis in sex workers' aspirations. The sex workers in Sonagachi founded a union to fight for legalization, reduction in police harassment, and other rights. A norm also developed among them of using condoms in sex acts, and by 1995 almost all the sex workers were using condoms at least some of the time. As a result, HIV incidence in Sonagachi was about 6 per cent in 1999 compared to 50 per cent in other red-light areas (including Mumbai's) that did not pursue such a culturally sensitive approach.

Vijayendra Rao and Manisha Shah

References

Andhra Pradesh State AIDS Control Society. 2004. *VIII Round of National Annual Sentinel Surveillance for HIV*, Andhra Pradesh, Hyderabad.

Arunachalam, Raj and Manisha Shah. 2008. 'Prostitutes *and* Brides?' *American Economic Review: Papers & Proceedings*, 98(2): 516–22.

——. 2010. 'Compensated for Life: Sex Work and Disease Risk', Working Paper.

Dandona, R., L. Dandona, G.A. Kumar, J.P. Gutierrez, S. McPherson, F. Samuels, and S.M. Bertozzi. 2006. ASCI FPP Study Team. 'Demography and Sex Work Characteristics of Female Sex Workers in India', *BMC International Health Human Rights*, 14(6): 5.

Gertler, Paul, Manisha Shah, and Stefano Bertozzi. 2005. 'Risky Business: The Market for Unprotected Commercial Sex', *Journal of Political Economy*, 113(3): 518–50.

Gooptu, Nandini. 2000. 'Sex Workers in Calcutta and the Dynamics of Collective Action', WIDER Working Paper No. 185, United Nations University.

Kotiswaran, Prabha. 2008. 'Born unto Brothels—Toward a Legal Ethnography of Sex Work in an Indian Red-light Area', *Law & Social Inquiry*, 33(3): 579–629.

Nag, Moni. 2006. Sex *Workers of India: Diversity in Practice of Prostitution and Ways of Life*, New Delhi, Allied Publishers.

Rao, Vijayendra, Indrani Gupta, Michael Lokshin, and Smarajit Jana. 2003. 'Sex Workers and the Cost of Safe Sex: The Compensating Differential for Condom Use in Calcutta', *Journal of Development Economics*, 71: 585–603.

Robinson, Jonathan and Ethan Yeh. Forthcoming. 'Transactional Sex as a Response to Risk in Western Kenya', *American Economic Journal: Applied Economics*.

Sleightholme, Carolyn and Indrani Sinha. 1996. *Guilty without Trial: Women in the Sex Trade in Calcutta*, Kolkata, STREE.

■ Slums

Over 50 per cent of the population of two of India's largest cities, Mumbai and Delhi, lives in housing settlements that are widely acknowledged to be slums. Despite the magnitude of the phenomenon, the concept of slums, while referencing dwellings deemed unfit for human habitation, escapes a precise definition. The term encompasses a range of living conditions attributed to housing settlements of the urban poor. While the popular assumption is that all slums infringe property regulations, many settlements, like some of the *chawl*s and *gaothan*s of Mumbai, have legal tenure but may be considered to be slums because of their degraded environment or population density.

The state's definition of slums typically rests on three principal factors: the illegality of the dwellings' tenure, the density of population, and the lack of hygienic conditions. The legal definition of slums, and legislation pertaining to them, is determined by each state government, as housing and urban development are subjects of state and not national governance. *Zhopadpatti, basti, jhuggi-jhopdi,* and *cheri* are some of the regionally-inflected terms referring to slums that are defined principally by their tenurial insecurity. For people living in these settlements, the fact of living in a slum is made manifest in the myriad experiences and practices of daily life, perhaps never more so clearly defined than through the ever-present threat of eviction, in the anxieties over the possible demolition and destruction of the investments that they have made in their housing, in the negotiated nature of their access to water, electricity, and toilets, and in the indignity of having to defecate in public.

The absence of conceptual and legal uniformity on what constitutes a slum, means that quantitative data on the magnitude and dimensions of slums at the all-India level is largely inconsistent and partial. The 2001 Census of India, the first to enumerate the living conditions of the population, where data was gathered on access to water, sanitation, sewerage, and electricity, and on the number of rooms a single household occupies, is thus an extremely valuable first step towards assessing the quantitative dimensions of the increasingly widespread phenomenon of slums in India. While not employing the term 'slum' as an organizing category, the census data reveals the shocking lack of affordable and adequate housing in urban India: over half of all households live in dwellings comprising of two rooms or less. In Mumbai, India's largest city, with a population of over 12 million, it is estimated that over 60 per cent of this population lives in 'slums' or on the pavements (the living conditions of the latter population, it is important to note, are not included in the effort to enumerate houses and household amenities and assets in the 2001 Census). Over a million people live in Dharavi alone, a slum that is widely recognized to be Asia's largest. The absurd ratio of toilets to people in Dharavi leads residents to joke that if you stood in line for a toilet, you would be facing a 15 day wait! However, despite the proportion of the population living in slums and on pavements and the apparent ubiquity of slums in Mumbai, slum settlements only occupy 8 per cent of the city's land.

Today's 'slum problem' is by no means a recent phenomenon. Slums have been part of the urban Indian landscape and an object of policy intervention from at least the late 1800s. After Independence, the influx of refugees from East and West Pakistan, compounded pre-existing housing shortages in cities. Recognizing the shortfall in housing stock, the national Five Year Plans made budgetary allocations to redress these shortages. Not only were these allocations woefully short of the demand for low-income housing in Indian cities, they were also never fully utilized, thereby aggravating the already yawning gap between the supply of and the demand for low-income housing. Likewise, areas demarcated for low-income housing in city plans were rarely used for that purpose. Slums thus were, and continue to be, a self-help response of the urban poor to the absence of affordable housing, and are built with little access to housing finance.

By 1970, the state had recognized its failure to provide low-income housing on the scale that was required, and so adopted a policy of *in situ* improvement of the environmental conditions of existing slum settlements. While this policy shift was indeed welcome, and some slums benefited from this initiative, for the vast majority of slums, the predominant state policy continued to be that of eviction and demolition. Indeed in the 1970s, slum dwellers were victims of some of the most brutal exercises of state violence as Indira Gandhi's populist politics of *garibi hatao* ('remove poverty') mutated into a license to *garib hatao* ('remove the poor') with the institution of Emergency rule in 1975. The violent evictions of the urban poor from Turkman Gate (Delhi) in April 1976 and from Janata Colony (Mumbai) in May 1976 stand out as sites of some of the worst excesses of the Emergency period. The scale and violence of the evictions quickened nascent mobilizations of the urban poor, such as the National Slum Dwellers' Federation, which today is probably the single largest organization of slum-dwellers in the country. The restitution of democratic rule did not, however, signal an end to forced evictions and mass displacements of the urban poor, quite to the contrary. Even in instances where slum-dwellers have been able to negotiate for an alternative location for their settlement, there is little guarantee that there will be no further eviction from the new site; given the Indian state's frequent recourse to its powers of eminent domain, the state could requisition the land in the future should it deem it necessary to do so.

In recent years, as cities vie with each other to provide a 'home' for foreign direct investment, issues of urban infrastructural development have increasingly found their way into policy agendas and statements after decades of neglect. States and corporate consortiums have enlisted the services of global consultancy firms to chart out a vision of how to transform their cities into what are deemed 'world-class' cities, visions that are informed by the needs and desires of a small, upwardly mobile business community which has achieved or aspires to success as global entrepreneurs rather than those of the entire city. In 2005 these efforts received a fillip as the central government launched the Jawaharlal Nehru National Urban Renewal Mission (JNNURM), a Rs 50,000 crore urban development effort to spur the transformation of select Indian cities into 'world-class cities'. While the bulk of this effort is directed towards the development of infrastructure and revamping of urban governance structures, 35 per cent of the budget has been allocated for the provision of basic services for the slum-dwelling urban poor. The mission certainly brought some much needed attention and investment to a rapidly urbanizing India, however, the singular focus on financial sustainability, and the concomitant desire to institute user fees for utilities, such as water and sanitation, suggests that access to public services will be informed by a notion of urban residents as consumers rather than as citizens. Such a formulation of urban residents, on the basis of ability to pay, will mean that the infrastructural facilities that are developed as a result of public investment may not be accessible to the most impoverished urban populations and will thus perpetuate the development of slums. Compounding this exclusion, is the policy of 'cut-off' dates practised in many cities to determine who among the urban poor is 'eligible' for access to public services and schemes. Only those slum-dwelling populations who can prove that they were residing in the city before a particular date are considered to have any basis for laying claim to public services and engaging the state over the provision of housing. Those who cannot provide such proof are thus unable to benefit from JNNURM investments. Nor is JNNURM able to anticipate and accommodate the needs of these 'ineligible' residents, or those who will be produced by the ongoing processes of urbanization, consequently compromising the mission's aim of realizing slum-free cities. The recent model Property Rights to Slum Dwellers' Act proposed by the central government, while a step in the right direction, is limited by its insistence on determining eligibility via 'cut-off' dates, a condition that flies in the face of evidence that urbanization is an ongoing process that will add increasing numbers of people to Indian cities many of whom will need access to low-income housing and affordable basic services.

In terms of the availability of land to house the urban poor, with the recent opening up of the real estate market to foreign direct investment, and the repeal of the Urban Land Ceiling Act, slum-dwellers find themselves on an increasingly asymmetrical playing field. On paper, provisions have been made to reserve areas for developing low-income housing, but more often than not these policies have not been realized, and increasingly revanchist sentiments are expressed towards any attempt to accommodate the shelter needs of slum-dwellers, who while providing the foundation of the economy of urban India are not seen to be legitimate denizens of its cities.

Indeed, the presence of impoverished populations in cities is often seen as detracting from each city's claim to be a 'world-class' city, yet, instead of addressing the structural causes of urban poverty, and the insecurities that mark the growing informal labour market, the attempt has been to move the urban poor out of sight, through evictions and legislative action, from both the physical and political landscape of the city. The discourse of the 'world-class' city has thus emerged in tandem with parochial, anti-migrant sentiments (directed primarily at slum-dwelling populations), contributing to the creation of a hostile urban environment in which impoverished populations are finding it increasingly hard to have their claims on the city recognized as legitimate.

From the perspective of its slum-dwellers, Indian cities constitute a palimpsest of multiple displacements and experiences of eviction and exclusion. The tenurial insecurities and other vulnerabilities that bring the rural poor to urban areas in search of livelihood are eerily echoed in the experiences and anticipations of eviction that they face once in the city, and which produce and reproduce their marginality. It is estimated that by 2025 half the population of India will be urban; unless investments are made to provide low-income housing options and affordable basic services in cities, slums will continue to be the housing solution for a vast majority of these new migrants.

GAYATRI AMBIKA MENON

References

Appadurai, Arjun. 2001. 'Deep Democracy: Urban Governmentality and the Horizon of Politics', *Public Culture*, 14(1): 21–47.

Banerjee-Guha, Swapna. 2009. 'Neoliberalising the "Urban": New Geographies of Power and Injustice in Indian Cities', *Economic and Political Weekly*, 44(22): 95–107.

Census of India 2001. 2003. *Series 1, India: Tables on Houses, Household Amenities and Assets*, Delhi, Controller of Publications.

Conlon, Frank. 1984. 'Industrialization and the Housing Problem in Bombay, 1850–1940', in K. Ballhatchet and D. Taylor (eds), *Changing South Asia: Economy and Society*, Hong Kong, Asian Research Service, pp.153–68.

Kundu, Amitabh. 1993. *In the Name of the Urban Poor: Access to Basic Amenities*, New Delhi, Newbury Park; London, Sage.

Prashad, Vijay. 2003. '"Shelter" in Modern Delhi', in K. Sivaramakrishnan and Arun Agarwal (eds), *Regional Modernities: The Cultural Politics of Development in India*, New Delhi, Oxford University Press, pp.143–61.

Ramanathan, Usha. 2006. 'Illegality and the Urban Poor', *Economic and Political Weekly*, 41(29): 3193–7.

Roy, Ananya. 2003. *City Requiem, Calcutta: Gender and the Politics of Poverty*, Minneapolis, University of Minnesota Press.

Singh, Andrea Menefee and Alfred de Souza. 1980. *The Urban Poor: Slum and Pavement Dwellers in the Major Cities of India*, New Delhi, Manohar.

Tarlo, Emma. 2003. *Unsettling Memories: Narratives of the Emergency in Delhi*, Berkeley, University of California Press.

Small-scale Industries

Small-scale industries (SSI) bear a great deal of responsibility in developing economies. A few of the roles they are expected to play include: a source of employment, a dynamic sector capable of quickly responding to changing incentives, a training ground for entrepreneurial talent, a safety net, a bastion of cultural heritage. In this entry we focus on some measurable aspects of India's SSIs: (i) defining SSIs, (ii) the importance of SSIs in India and their role in economic development, and (iii) policy towards SSIs and its impact.

What is Small: Availability of Data Sources

While firms can be defined as small in relative or absolute terms, absolute measures have greater appeal, particularly in cross-industry studies. A number of such measures have been used: number of employees, capital investment, and value of output, independently or combined with measures of organization level, technology, source of power, and type and quality of products. Typically the measure chosen is dictated by data availability and ease of collection.

One of the primary sources of data is the Census of Small Scale Industrial Units, conducted by the Development Commissioner Small Scale Industries, Ministry of Small Scale Industries, which includes all firms permanently registered with the State/Union Territory Directorates of Industries. The census has been undertaken three times, in 1972, 1987–8, and 2000–1; limited sample surveys gauging specific trends have been conducted in other years. However, the definition of a small-scale unit has changed over time, making inter-temporal comparisons difficult: increasing from a maximum of Rs 0.75 million invested in plants and machinery in 1966 to Rs 10 million in 1997. In part, the changes are necessitated by inflation. However, one consequence of the change in definition is that many firms move from the medium to small sector. Moreover, there is a high mortality rate in the small-scale sector. As a result the three censuses overstate the small-scale growth rate. The concept of tiny establishments was introduced in

1977 and was defined in 1999 as one where investment in plants and machinery does not exceed Rs 2.5 million. Also, there is a large unregistered sector that was covered only in the third census. Nevertheless, the three Censuses of Small Scale Industrial Units provide 'almost consistent' data and are important sources of information for analyses. The results should be used with appropriate caution.

Two other major data sources on SSIs are also based on data from the Ministry of Small Scale Industries. Since 1984 the Ministry has published data annually based on a 2 per cent sample of all working units which has been used by the Central Statistical Organisation (CSO) to calculate the contribution of the small-scale sector to industrial production. The Economic Survey also publishes data on the performance of the small-scale sector based on the data supplied by the Ministry. Unfortunately, there is large discrepancy between the Economic Survey data and the data from the censuses. For example, the Economic Survey shows less employment and more output as compared to the Third Census on Small Scale Industries for the year 2002–3.

The National Sample Survey Organisation (NSSO) conducts periodic economic censuses for different categories, one of which is non-directory manufacturing establishments (NDME), employing less than six persons with at least one hired worker. The surveys were conducted in 1978–9, 1984–5, 1989–90, 1994–5, and 2000–1. However, despite similar methodologies over the years, there are huge differences in the numbers over the years, especially in the number of enterprises, making this data set suspect.

The Annual Survey of Industries (ASI) conducted by the CSO covers the organized manufacturing sector, that is, factories registered under the Factories Act of 1948. The ASI covers all factories employing 10 or more workers and using power and those employing 20 or more workers if not using power on any day of the preceding twelve months (there are exceptions to this criterion, for example bidi- and cigar-manufacturing units and electricity undertakings). Factories are classified into two sectors, the census sector and the sample sector. Factories employing 100 or more workers constitute the census sector while the remaining constitute the sample sector.

Firms that are in the sample sector—currently all factories employing 99 persons or less—are a convenient and ready definition of small firms in organized manufacturing. While the ASI is quite good data, again comparability difficulties present themselves. For three years, 1997–8, 1998–9, and 1999–2000, the census sector included factories employing 200 or more workers. Also, until 1986–7 all factories employing 50 or more workers and using power and those employing 100 and more if not using power were under the census sector. The changing definition and scope of the sample sector over the years, different classifications for the ASI sectors, and the different presentations of the ASI data make the analysis of small firms based on this data difficult. In particular, there are no separate published reports for the census and factory sector after 1982–3. Availability of unit-level data in recent years may be useful in studying small industries. Despite several limitations such as underreporting of value-added and employment and incomplete coverage of factories, the ASI remains the best source for industrial data.

Analysis of small-scale industry in India suffers from data availability and access issues, data-set-specific definitions of small, and, where data are collected in the same manner over time, modifications of the definitions. This latter problem, while understandable, is particularly irksome. Moreover, the above data sets on the small-scale sector in India are all based on detailed surveys, but are presented in aggregated form. Many of the problems can be solved by making easily available to researchers establishment-level data. Appropriate precautions to ensure anonymity can be applied, and are especially easy to implement in the small-scale industrial sector. This has begun to happen, but there is still a proprietary element to data dissemination.

Role of the Small-scale Industries

During the post-Independence period, small firms were expected to play an important role in the development process, especially in absorbing surplus labour and achieving an equitable income distribution. This is the traditional stylized role assigned to small industries in the literature. At the beginning of the industrialization process, flexibility in production and the ability to offer differentiated products allow smaller firms to grow rapidly. Later, large-scale firms come to dominate the size distribution, making up a greater share of output, employment, and value-added because of scale economies, managerial efficiency, better access to finance and infrastructure, and a favourable tariff structure. Some small firms expand into medium- and large-scale firms; some die; others remain competitive.

Has this stylized role been borne out in India? In the fiscal year 1982–3 small units defined in terms of employment produced 17.5 per cent of organized-sector manufacturing output, and 12.4 per cent of value-added, and provided 22.4 per cent of employment; this represented almost no change over the previous decade in value-added or output share, and a minor increase in the employment share. There was also significant inter-industry variation: small firms were more important in some industries than in others; and this changed over time. It is estimated that the total share of village and small-scale industries in *manufacturing* value-added decreased from 47.3 per cent in 1984–5 to 44 per cent in 1994–5. In more recent years, in 2002–3, the share of the small-scale sector in *industrial* value-added was 39 per cent, according to the Small Industries Development Organization. During 1980–8, the growth rate of SSIs has been significantly lower than that of large-scale industries.

The small-scale sector is very heterogeneous. There are an excessively large number of inefficient units. According to the Second All India Census of Registered SSI Units, items reserved for production by small-scale industry only accounted for 11.3 per cent of the items and 28.3 per cent of the production in the SSI sector. Moreover, only 68 reserved items were found to account for 80 per cent of the production under the reserved category. According to the Third All India Census, 89 per cent of the units had gross output less than Rs 1 million; while only 1.88 per cent of the total number of units (units with more than Rs 10 million output) had an output share of about 70 per cent. Also, the registered sector within SSIs was small in terms of size, representing 13 per cent of the units, but had a large share in investment and total production, both standing at 59 per cent.

There has also been a steady increase in the capital intensity of the average unit in the small-scale sector. Between the First and Second Censuses the employment size of the average unit fell much more than the investment in plant and machinery. Between the Second and Third Censuses the employment per unit decreased

Table 1 Performance of the Small-scale Sector

	First Census 1972–3	Second Census 1987–8	Third Census 2001–2
Number of units enumerated	139,577	582,368	1,374,974
Production (Rs billion)	26.03	429.72	2,032.55
Employment ('000)	1,653	3,666	6,163
Net value-added (Rs billion)	0.84	102.61	not reported
Investment in fixed assets (Rs billion)	7.97	92.96	917.92
Investment in plant and machinery (Rs billion)	5.37	55.43	303.29

Source: M.R. Saluja. 2004. 'Industrial Statistics in India: Sources, Limitations and Data Gaps', *Economic and Political Weekly*, 27 November: Table 4, p. 5174.

Table 2 Performance of the Small-scale Sector

Year	No. of units (million)	Production (Rs billion) constant 1993–4 prices	Employment (million)	Exports (Rs billion) current prices
1994–5	7.96	1,091.16 (10.4)	19.14 (4.8)	290.68 (15.0)
1995–6	8.28	1,216.59 (11.5)	19.79 (3.4)	364.70 (25.6)
1996–7	8.62	1,353.80 (11.3)	20.59 (4.0)	392.48 (7.6)
1997–8	8.97	1,478.24 (9.2)	21.32 (3.5)	444.42 (13.2)
1998–9	9.34	1,594.07 (7.8)	22.06 (3.5)	489.79 (10.2)
1999–2000	9.72	1,707.09 (7.1)	22.91 (3.9)	542.00 (10.7)
2000–1	10.11	1,844.28 (8.0)	23.91 (4.4)	697.97 (28.8)
2001–2	10.52	1,956.13 (6.1)	24.91 (4.2)	712.44 (2.1)
2002–3	10.95	2,106.36 (7.7)	26.01 (4.9)	860.13 (20.7)
2003–4	11.40	2,287.30 (8.6)	27.14 (4.3)	NA
2004–5	11.85	2,457.47 (7.4)	28.28 (4.2)	NA

Source: *Economic Survey*, 2004 and 2005, based on information from the Development Commissioner, SSI, Ministry of Small Scale Industries.
Note: Figures in parentheses represent percentage growth over the previous year.

Table 3 Small-scale Industries, 2002–3

Estimated no. of units	3.57 million
Employment	19.96 million
Share in industrial value-added	39%
Share in total exports	34%
Total number of items produced	Over 8000
Number of reserved items	675

Source: Small Industries Development Organization, http://www.laghu-udyog.com/ssiindia/statistics/economic.htm#Employment, accessed 21 July 2005.

Table 4 Growth Rates of Small-scale and Large-scale Sectors

Year	Small-scale sector	Large-scale sector
1980–90	6.33	8.39
1990–8	5.36	9.84
1980–98	5.87	9.07

Source: Rakesh Mohan. 2002. 'Small Scale Industry Policy in India: A Critical Evaluation', in Anne O. Krueger (ed.), *Economic Policy Reforms and the Indian Economy*, Chicago, University of Chicago Press, pp. 213–97.

further from 6.29 to 4.8 persons, while per unit fixed investment increased.

Policy towards Small-scale Industries

It appears that the objectives of policies stressing the role of SSIs are not being realized. Small industries were recognized as important for employment generation and equitable distribution of income from the earliest days of Indian Independence. Policy measures included fiscal concessions, subsidized and directed bank credit, and technical and marketing support, along with reservations of products for exclusive production by the SSI sector. The policy of reserving products for exclusive manufacture in the small-scale sector was started in 1967 with 47 items; the list of reserved items rose to 873 in 1984. These policy measures were in tune with the other polices such as the domestic investment and foreign trade policies that became more restrictive over the years.

Since the mid-1980s there has been a gradual turnaround in policy, including reforms in the tax system and liberalization of import policy. The number of items on the reserved list for the SSI sector was brought down to 836 by 1989. The pace of reforms accelerated after 1991: average tariff rates have been steadily lowered, quantitative restrictions have been removed, and domestic investment policies have been liberalized. Over time, the number of items on the reserved list has also been reduced and stands at 605 in 2005. However, since all the items on the reserved list can now be imported, SSIs face competition from foreign enterprises even though large-scale industries in India cannot produce these products! The Censuses of the SSIs also suggest that the policy of reserving goods for production by SSIs has not been very effective. The number of units making reserved products is small compared to the overall size of the SSI sector, and the reserved products account for a small share of the total value of output in the SSI sector.

Finally, it appears that the export performance of India may have suffered because of the reservation policy. Most growing economies witness a changing structure of exports, with a high growth of exports of labour-intensive and resource-based industries. The export structure of India has not changed much in the last two decades, and this may be because many commodities in the potential high-growth category come under the reserved list.

Large-scale or Small-scale?

Despite all the hype and the apparent share of output and employment generated by SSIs, it appears that SSIs have not played a very special role in the development process in India. Employment generation has not been as high as expected, there is inequitable distribution within the small-scale sector, and exports have suffered. Moreover, the policies of reservation and subsidized credit do not appear to have had the desired effect; in fact, the performance is worse *because* of these policies. It appears that the policies towards SSIs need a radical overhaul. However, we cannot be sure, as the data available to the general research community are riddled with difficulties.

IRA N. GANG AND MIHIR PANDEY

References

Anderson, Dennis. 1982. 'Small Industry in Developing Countries: A Discussion of Issues', *World Development*, 10(11): 913–48.

Development Commissioner, Small Scale Industries, Ministry of Small Scale Industries, Government of India. 2004. *Third All India Census of Small Scale Industries 2001–2002*, New Delhi.

Gang, Ira N. 1995. 'Small Firms in India: A Discussion of Some Issues', in Dilip Mookherjee (ed.), *Indian Industry: Policies and Performance*, New Delhi, Oxford University Press, pp. 322–50.

■ Social Protection for Informal-sector Workers

Jaitunbibi sews readymade garments from her home. She sews sari petticoats and is paid a piece-rate of Rs 24 per dozen sari petticoats. Finally, Jaitunbibi gets about Rs 30 per day in hand for eight to ten hours work.

Madhuben is a construction worker. For a day's hard labour, Madhuben earns Rs 70 a day; her husband earns a little more—Rs 80 for the same work. She has to climb several flights of steps with a wooden plank on her head on which she carries bricks all neatly stacked. Workers like her often slip or trip, with fractures or even worse being part of the day's work.

Leelaben has been selling fresh vegetables in Ahmedabad's main marketplace since she was in her teens. She earns a net Rs 50 after deducting all her costs, including the cycle rickshaw that transports her goods to her place in the market.

Raniben Ahir is an agricultural worker, dairy farmer, and embroiderer. She lives in the dry and drought-prone Patan district in north Gujarat, earning Rs 50 a day to feed her family.

Jaitunbibi, Madhuben, Leelaben, and Raniben are all workers in the informal economy of India. Their lives, like those of million others across India, are full of toil and struggle. They work hard and are economically very active, but earn barely enough to keep their families going.

In India, 93 per cent of all workers are engaged in the informal economy (Chen et al. 2004), with a net contribution of about 63 per cent of GDP (Unni 2002). The vast majority of Indian women workers—more than 94 per cent—are in the informal economy. Most of these workers fall into four major work categories:

- Piece-rated home-based workers like Jaitunbibi who produce many different products from home;
- manual labourers and service providers like Madhuben who sell their labour for a living;
- street vendors and other self-employed business people like Leelaben; and
- small producers like Raniben who produce a variety of products.

Chen et al. (2004: 26) have noted:

> Informal employment comprises one half to three quarters of non-agricultural employment in developing countries: specifically, 48 per cent in North Africa; 51 per cent in Latin America; 65 per cent in Asia; and 72 per cent in sub-Saharan Africa. If South Africa is excluded, the share of informal employment in non-agricultural employment rises to 78 per cent in sub-Saharan Africa; and if comparable data were available for other countries in South Asia in addition to India, the regional average for Asia would likely be much higher.
>
> Some countries include informal employment in agriculture in their estimates. This significantly increases the proportion of informal employment: from 83 per cent of non-agricultural employment to 93 per cent of total employment in India; from 55 to 62 per cent in Mexico; and from 28 to 34 per cent in South Africa.

Further, the authors have noted that most informal workers—about 60 per cent worldwide—are women. Other than in North Africa, where 43 per cent of women workers are in informal employment, 60 per cent or more of women workers in the developing world are in informal employment (outside agriculture) (Chen et al. 2004). Finally, the authors have noted that since a growing number of workers are engaged in the informal economies of their countries, and because most of these are low paid workers, there is a close connection between informality and poverty, and given that the maximum number of informal workers are women, there is also a strong connection between gender, informality, and poverty (Chen et al. 2004: 29–55).

The Changing World of Work in India

The current trends in India suggest further informalization as the formal workforce shrinks for various reasons, including closures, lay-offs, and new contract-based production systems.

Perhaps one of the biggest examples of this shift from formal to informal work systems comes from the city of Ahmedabad. In the late 1970s and 1980s, more than 60 textile mills shut down, rendering more than 80,000 workers jobless. Most of these workers obtained re-employment in the city's informal economy—as street vendors, construction workers, loaders and unloaders in the market place, and ragpickers. Today 79 per cent of the city's economy is accounted for by informal workers (Unni and Rani 1999: 5).

The trend towards informalization preceded globalization and liberalization in India but has certainly been expedited by them. Export-oriented garment units and mechanization have already affected the employment of women like Jaitunbibi and Madhuben. In the garment sector, major changes have occurred—both in the product line which favours dresses, shorts, jeans and other apparel geared to export markets, and in the production process itself. This has shifted to factories with machines suited to the new markets. Mechanization in the construction industry, brought in by globally competitive multinational construction companies has resulted in a marked decrease in the demand for labour. Of course, globalization also presents some opportunities for small producers like Raniben. Her embroidered products now have the opportunity to reach new markets overseas, giving her the chance of earning a higher income.

Disasters like the earthquake of 2001 in Gujarat and persistent drought also affect women's work, not only because they always suffer the most in terms of losses and damage, but also because they alter their world of work. The impact of the earthquake on the construction industry has been particularly significant, with new stricter zoning laws and basic construction standards that have accelerated mechanization and thus redundancy of workers.

Similarly, drought forces thousands of families to migrate to cities, where they seek some informal employment. Finally, human disasters like sectarian violence also result in shifting of employment and new work systems as both workers and contractors or employers can no longer move freely in different neighbourhoods and often migrate to other areas or states for work.

Of course, the changes are more in the nature of a continuum with formal systems giving way to contractual ones and often one worker moving in and out of formal and informal work.

Social Protection in the Changing World of Work

All of the rapid changes in employment and work systems have a direct bearing on how social protection can be organized for informal workers. In any case, these workers barely had any social security. But in the new context, with the struggle for work and work security more acute, the increasing trend of multiple economic activities undertaken by one worker, and migration in search of employment, social protection poses both a challenge and an opportunity, as we shall see later, to organize workers.

But first the challenges. Perhaps the most vexed issue of all is that of identifying informal workers who are, especially if they are women, still invisible, geographically dispersed, and moving in and out of different economic activities. Unions in India, including the Self-Employed Women's Association (SEWA), have been pressing for the issuing of identity cards by the labour department. Not only does this give each worker a name and a face, it also gives her or him recognition as a worker.

This brings us to the next issue—how does one classify a worker's work when she is engaged in multiple activities or trades? Studies reveal that most of the women workers are involved in at least two economic activities and up to four or five are not uncommon. So, for example, do we call Raniben an agricultural worker, dairy farmer, or embroiderer?

In trade unions organizing formal workers this was never an issue, as by definition they were organized on trade lines. But for informal workers, the multiplicity of work and occupations does pose some, though not insurmountable, problems. These come up when we try to create structures or platforms where workers, government officials and employers come together to design, implement and monitor social protection programmes. Resources and financial contributions are involved and employers generally do not want to contribute from their earnings to a worker who is not wholly identified with their particular industry.

The changes in the world of work also challenge existing concepts of employment and work. An example of where this leads us in terms of social protection for workers is that of salt workers in Gujarat. These are among the poorest of informal workers, manufacturing 80 per cent of India's salt by pumping out brine from the dry desert. Entire families live in the desert for eight months of the year and return to their villages for agricultural work when it rains.

When salt workers organized into their own union, childcare emerged as a strong need. This was provided with the support of the Salt Workers Welfare Board which decides on social security programmes and resource allocations from a fund developed by levying a cess on large merchants in this industry. The Board approved of crèches for children for only eight months in a year, arguing that for the remaining four months, when they worked as agricultural labourers or small farmers, these women were no longer salt workers! Since childcare is a perennial need, the union, SEWA, stepped in to fill the gap and continue to negotiate with the Board to change its approach.

Childcare

Despite the maze of issues that have to be navigated to provide social protection to informal workers, unions, cooperatives, and NGOs in India have developed new ways and have used various opportunities to meet workers' needs and to organize them into membership-based organizations. To continue with childcare, Mobile Creches, an urban-based NGO, is providing quality childcare and early childhood education to children of construction workers. It obtains support from building contractors, the government, and others, organizing childcare at the construction sites. When a building is complete, the crèche moves to the next site, following the children there.

SEWA has also adopted this mobile approach, providing childcare for salt workers' children in the desert and then following them to their home villages in the monsoons. For other informal workers, most of whom have no fixed workplace, childcare is organized by workers' cooperatives in women's urban neighbourhoods or in villages in rural areas. The crèches are run by the workers themselves, usually enlisting neighbours and friends of the women who go out to work, and timings are adjusted to the working hours of the mothers in a particular area. While run by the women, contributions in cash and kind come from parents, employers, government programmes, and the union.

Insurance

As most informal workers have no access to protective insurance—for sickness, accidents, assets, work tools, and even life—organizations working with them have developed various risk coverage systems. In an insurance programme for agricultural labourers in central India run by the Medical College at Sewagram, insurance premiums are paid in kind—in kilograms of millet harvested which are then converted into cash. The 'millet premia' are fixed village-wise and according to landholding. The workers then get health insurance coverage through a linkage with the local hospital run by the medical college nearby.

From the very beginning at SEWA, it was seen that the members faced frequent risks and even major disasters. These not only caused immense suffering but also eroded their carefully accumulated assets, resulting in indebtedness and their sinking deeper into poverty. Hardly had a woman saved to buy her house or reclaim mortgaged lands through a loan from SEWA Bank, when she had to sell or mortgage it again to cover the costs of a new crisis.

Thus SEWA began to experiment with insurance as a buffer and support to plug the economic leakages women experienced during crises. Initially, the nationalized insurance companies were wary of collaboration. But as the workers organized and grew in strength, a partnership developed, and by 1992, a full-fledged insurance programme was developed with insurance companies.

Today 140,000 women, who are the policy holders, their husbands, and children have insured themselves. As the unfamiliar concept of insurance becomes acceptable to informal workers, SEWA Insurance or VimoSEWA has to expand to meet their demand for services.

Many of those who are insuring themselves—roughly a third—are first-time members of SEWA. Thus insurance offers a new way of organizing informal workers, and around a concrete economic benefit.

Today VimoSEWA operates like a cooperative, working closely with local insurance companies. The insurance sector has been privatized recently in India, and there is a mandatory condition which requires all the new companies to insure rural workers. As a result, they are trying to develop competitive products that could potentially be useful to informal workers.

SEWA's insurance package covers life, accident, widowhood, sickness, and damage to assets—homes and work tools. Husband's life, accident, and sickness coverage are also covered as an option, as is children's sickness.

In addition, insurance has been linked to other financial services like savings and credit. Women save through their village-based savings and credit groups, and then set aside some of their savings to pay for their insurance premium. Of the currently insured members, 30,000 have saved enough to put down a lump sum as fixed deposit in SEWA Bank. The interest accrued on this deposit then goes towards the premium every year, ensuring continuous and long-term coverage.

Thus, building on existing solidarity networks and the fact that all informal workers need insurance regardless of their nature of work, workers are seeking this kind of risk coverage.

Healthcare

Healthcare is the most widespread of services provided to informal workers everywhere today. Despite considerable public health infrastructure in India, informal workers do not have access to services for a whole host of reasons ranging from poor quality, inappropriate or inadequate services and sheer absence of these, especially in remote rural villages. The upshot of this is that most of the working poor—an estimated 80 per cent or more—seek care from private practitioners. While the services may be more prompt, they are not necessarily of good quality and are always three to five times as expensive as the public health services.

Small wonder then that there is a huge demand for affordable and good quality healthcare, and at workers' doorsteps. This demand has given rise to thousands of community-based health programmes run mainly by NGOs but also by some workers' organizations, both unions and cooperatives. In the Rajasthan desert, NGO URMUL, has organized primary healthcare, and especially tuberculosis care, for nomadic shepherds, craft workers and agricultural labourers, bringing down TB prevalence in this endemic and remote area.

In Gujarat, thousands of traditional midwives or *dai*s have formed their own state-level association. Some have even formed district-level cooperatives. Through these, they are both providing their health services and obtaining some fees as income.

Housing and Infrastructure

Housing and basic services like water, sanitation, and electricity is yet another area of social protection where organizations of informal workers have broken new ground. Since informal workers cannot always be organized on the basis of one trade, the alternative is to organize them in their own neighbourhoods, and around basic needs like housing, water, and sanitation.

In Ahmedabad, informal workers joined hands with the local municipal authorities to develop a programme aimed at transforming urban neighbourhoods by providing basic amenities: water, sanitation, individual toilets, garbage removal, streetlighting, and landscaping and paving. This programme, called 'Parivartan' (meaning change), is one based on partnership between government, workers, and the corporate sector, with each also contributing funds towards basic services in a neighbourhood.

Currently, through this process, families engaged in informal employment have not only obtained basic amenities but also organized their own neighbourhood committees for maintenance and overall community development. They have also joined their union. This is a still small but growing initiative in urban renewal and organizing.

A final example of organizing social protection comes from the Indian government's labour department. As a response to organizing by workers and also to offer them some protection, several workers' welfare boards have been established in India. The resource base for these is a cess levied on the final products which employers must contribute to a fund. The fund is administered by the government. But the approach is tripartite, with government, workers', and employers' representatives on the board. This is then a forum for planning, developing, and monitoring the implementation of social protection including maternity benefits, health insurance, childcare, and housing to mention a few. Often the implementation is undertaken by unions, as in the example of salt workers' crèches. But the responsibility of identification and registration of workers, ensuring that social protection actually reaches them, and also monitoring their working conditions, in general, rests with the board.

The largest example of this workers' fund approach is the bidi (Indian cigarettes) workers' 'welfare fund. But there is also a salt workers' fund, one for coir workers, head loaders, and others.

Studies commissioned by the Indian Labour Commission some years ago showed that these boards do serve their purpose— to support workers and encourage organizing—to a considerable extent. Since concrete economic and social security benefits are offered, workers are encouraged to identify themselves or join unions that help to ensure that they get access.

These multiple, varied, small, and some fairly large experiences in social protection offer some lessons to meet the challenges in the changing world of work. Some of these are discussed next.

Organizing Social Protection for Informal Workers—Some Lessons

First, these approaches are a good way to organize informal workers. While categorization of workers by occupation and following them in their different workplaces is challenging, the provision of social security services is actually an opportunity to identify workers and promote their organizing.

Since they get a useful service, workers have an incentive to come forward to identify themselves, register, get an identity card and even join a union, cooperative, or other local organization.

We saw how providing insurance services, healthcare, childcare and housing meant that workers were registered and even developed new forms of organizing and solidarity—like neighbourhood committees in the case of the 'Parivartan' urban infrastructure programme and the midwives' cooperatives for healthcare.

Second, social security services when provided, offer a way for informal workers to link up with formal systems and government and employers. Whether we recall our example of crèches for salt workers' children, insurance, healthcare, or basic amenities in urban areas, workers' interface, many for the first time, with the mainstream. This recognition and inclusion is vital—for their own self-worth and also for building their organizations, for 'voice' and representation.

Third, running their own social protection programmes is empowering, builds up workers' confidence and leadership, and ensures that all services remain relevant and affordable to all working people. Midwives, crèche teachers, insurance and housing promoters can and have developed into strong leaders. They have served their communities and also become organizers, both struggling against injustices and developing alternative, constructive activities for workers. They have also built and led their own representative organizations like cooperatives and producers' associations.

Fourth, many of the social protection programmes are sustainable—both financially and in terms of human resources—in the long term. The experience of SEWA Insurance shows that with a large membership base and risk-sharing measures like reinsurance, coverage of the poor normally considered 'too risky' is viable.

Further, if contributions from government, employers, private trusts, and workers are collected, then social protection programmes—whether health or child care, insurance or housing—are sustainable in the long term.

The key is that these services must be appropriate, timely, affordable, flexible, and managed and owned by the people themselves. Once local people see that these 'work' and are useful, they are ready to pay from their earnings towards such social protection.

Fifth, social security programmes, must be developed according to workers' varied and multiple needs and include elements that hitherto may not always be included in social protection, like childcare, for example. Informal workers need as comprehensive an approach to social security as possible. Thus, along with health insurance, for example, workers need life and accident insurance and also insurance for their work tools and assets.

Further, there are several ways in which informal workers have built up their own social security systems, including savings, risk funds, and grain banks. These need to be understood and built upon. Asset building through savings and credit is one of the most important ways in which workers secure their lives. The burgeoning micro-finance movement worldwide is strongest among informal workers and is already well established.

Sixth, special organizations and institutions must be created for the social protection of informal workers.

Multiple and varied forms of organizations exist in different countries. Unions, villages-based producers' and/or savings groups and their district-level associations, cooperatives and their state-level associations, and urban neighbourhood committees or associations are ideal for organizing workers, including for social protection.

These organizations are membership based and worker owned and managed, leading to credibility, accountability, increased solidarity, and also leadership of the workers.

Seventh, we have seen that work security and social security or social protection are two sides of the same coin. One cannot be attained without the other. If informal workers are to be strengthened and supported in their struggle for justice and against poverty, then work security is essential. Without regular work and income, they can neither feed themselves and their families nor have any measure of health security, insurance coverage, or housing, for example.

At the same time, work security can never be achieved without meeting the social security needs of informal workers. In sum, it is an integrated and holistic approach to informal workers' overall well-being that will minimize the risks that they face, strengthen them economically, and help lead to a better future.

Eighth, there are several spin-off effects, some quite unexpected, when organizing social protection for informal workers. The services themselves can provide self-employment or at least additional employment and income to workers. Now midwives trained in a special programme which SEWA runs, are earning a couple of hundred rupees extra per month from women in their villages. The special skill upgradation training has resulted in an elevated status in their villages and people's willingness to pay for their services.

Finally, since many of the examples of social protection involved partnerships—with government, employers and other outside agencies—workers became visible, legitimate and even respected for their significant economic contributions. They were able to enter the national mainstream on equal terms in many instances.

Further, organizing social protection and service delivery cannot be the sole responsibility of the government. While government undoubtedly has the primary responsibility—especially in terms of developing appropriate policies and programmes with suitable resources—it is the active involvement of workers and others right from the conceptualizing stage to the planning, implementation, and monitoring that makes all the difference.

Tripartite or multipartite structures, processes, and partnerships are called for today to meet the growing challenges for social protection. These include public and private decision-makers, as well as workers' or people's representatives. Multiple fora boards, committees, task forces, and commissions lend themselves to partnerships. It is in these spaces that modalities and constraints to full coverage of the poorest of workers can be discussed and worked out.

Coming together to work on concrete programmes is of course a 'win-win' situation for all involved. Most of all it strengthens informal workers and their movements, and gives them hope, energy, and courage to face the challenges that lie ahead in the changing world of work, particularly in the informal economy.

MIRAI CHATTERJEE

References

Chen, Martha Alter, Vanek Joann, and Marilyn Carr. 2004. *Mainstreaming Informal Employment and Gender in Poverty Reduction: A Handbook for Policy Makers and Other Stake Holders*, London, The Commonwealth Secretariat.

Unni, Jeemol. 2002. 'Supporting Workers in the Informal Economy: A Policy Framework', paper, SEWA-GIDR-NCAER.

Unni, Jeemol and Uma Rani. 1999. 'Urban Informal Sector: Size & Income Generation Process in Gujarat', research paper, SEWA-GIDR, August.

Software and Services Exports[1]

The Indian economy has transitioned from an inward-looking economy to a more liberalized and export-oriented one. Software and services exports in particular, have had impressive growth, and have grown over 32 per cent annually between FY2002 and FY2007.[2] Exports are estimated to reach between US$ 58 billion and US$ 60 billion by 2010.

Today, Indian software and services exports stand at approximately US$ 32 billion. The share of software and services exports in India's exports increased from 3.2 per cent in 1996 to almost 25 per cent in 2006.

In 1981–2, India exported US$ 12 million in software and services. At the time, the sector faced significant

[1]Software and services include (i) information technolgy (IT) services, (ii) IT-enabled services (ITES), and (iii) software products and engineering services.

[2]The fiscal year for the Indian economy follows a 12-month cycle spanning April–March.

challenges to growth. There was distrust of the private sector among policymakers. Imports were restricted and the corporate sector faced numerous bureaucratic hurdles. Business had difficulty accessing even basic infrastructure such as phones or data communication lines.

The economic reforms introduced in 1991 laid the foundation for the growth of the software sector in the country. The reforms decentralized power to regional and state offices—companies could now call on their local Software Technology Parks of India (STPI) offices with requests, instead of contacting Delhi. This increased the velocity of decision making in organizations, and reduced friction to business. The government's decision to allow 100 per cent ownership of subsidiaries by their multinational parents also brought several well-known multinational companies (MNCs) into India. They brought with them world-class technology, customer orientation, and employee orientation. The MNCs enhanced the competitive environment, forcing Indian companies to benchmark against global standards.

Market-determined pricing of initial public offerings (IPO) made equity a viable financing option for corporations. The reforms also introduced current account convertibility, which made it easier to hire foreign consultants and facilitated international brand building and overseas travel.

Another beneficial outcome of liberalization was easier and cheaper availability of data communication facilities. This made offshoring viable. The difference in time zones between India and North America is between 9.5 and 12.5 hours. Indian IT companies capitalized on this time difference to offer a 24-hour virtual workday, and achieved efficient project execution and higher project productivity. Thus the industry pioneered the global delivery model (GDM) that envisages a substantial amount of value addition being done in India. The benefits of offshore delivery are now widely accepted around the world.

The Software and Services Exports Market

Software and services exports are the dominating factor in the overall growth of the Indian IT industry. North America and Europe remain the key markets accounting for over 90 per cent of the total Indian software and services exports, with Europe accounting for 23 per cent of the total. This market poses challenges for Indian companies, due to both cultural and linguistic differences. The Asia-Pacific region accounts for about 8 per cent of all exports. It is predicted that demand from Latin America, Africa, and the Middle East will grow substantially in the coming years.

The level of IT investment varies widely across industry sectors. It is estimated that the financial services sector accounts for the largest share of investment. This includes spending by banks, insurance companies, and securities firms. Rapid changes in telecommunication technology, increase in mobile communications, and intense competition in the global telecom service and equipment markets have spurred IT expenditure in the telecom sector. Other sectors that spend strongly are manufacturing, retailing, healthcare, utilities, travel, and various governments.

Globalization is a Key Driver for IT Growth

The world continues to witness the powerful effects of globalization. The broad range of products and services available, coupled with the information revolution, has raised customer expectations. Today, customers expect services at ever-greater speed. They demand quality services at reduced costs.

The dual pressures of competition and a knowledgeable customer are forcing companies to revamp their business models. Consequently, corporate strategies are increasingly focused on efficiency, discipline, cost control, and leaner operations. There is a need to increase productivity and efficiency by investing in IT.

As a result of these pressures—customer, competition, cost, and core—more companies are looking outside their walls, to outsource their operations to value-for-money destinations. Outsourcing exploits technology to achieve collaboration across company boundaries over activities which, earlier, would have had to be conducted within a single company.

In this context, India has established itself as the premier offshore destination for IT services. Recently, Gartner (2005) declared India 'unequivocally the global leader in offshore IT and process services' based upon a survey conducted across selected organizations in North America that are either currently outsourcing or planning on outsourcing in the future. Additionally, India has been ranked No.1 according to the recently published Global Services Location Index (2006) by the global consulting firm A.T. Kearney.

India Offers Several Advantages

The basic business model of the Indian software industry is based on globalization. Globalization is sourcing capital from where it is cheapest, producing where it is most cost-effective, and selling where it is most profitable without being constrained by national boundaries. The Indian software and services export industry has pioneered the GDM, which leverages talent and infrastructure in different parts of the world. It enables Indian companies to deliver rapid time-to-market solutions, optimizing cost efficiencies.

The software development life-cycle tasks are partitioned to maximize those that can be taken up in cost-competitive, talent-rich, process-driven destinations such as India, and minimize those that have to be taken up at customer site. The GDM allows Indian vendors to capitalize on the time difference between India and the client location to achieve efficient project execution. This leads to lower cycle time with seamlessly integrated cross-border teams working on projects round the clock. Thus the GDM approach leverages the power of asynchronicity for fast and efficient execution.

The growth of the software and services industry has been largely driven by its knowledge professionals. The country has a huge base of highly qualified, English-speaking, analytically strong technical talent. According to Ministry of Human Resource Development, Government of India, there are close to 350 institutes of higher education and approximately 17,000 colleges in India. Collectively they produce 495,000 technical graduates,[3] 2.3 million other graduates, and over 300,000 postgraduates every year.

Indian companies quickly realized that securing the clients' confidence required them to have world class quality processes that were better than those of their global competitors. In fact, there have been several instances of clients upgrading their processes when working with Indian IT firms. Today, over 440 Indian companies have acquired quality certifications with 90 companies certified at SEI CMM Level 5—higher than in any other country in the world.[4]

The availability of a good communications infrastructure has helped Indian companies effectively implement the offshore development model. Further, a number of policy initiatives in the telecom sector, including privatization, have led to easier and cheaper availability of data communication facilities. For instance, the cost of an E1 line has decreased by nearly 50 per cent over the past five years.

Finally, as India grows into a knowledge-based economy, protection of knowledge capital becomes essential. India has a strong Intellectual Property Rights (IPR) regime and legal framework. India is a signatory to the Berne Convention, Universal Copyright Convention (UCC), and Trade-Related Aspects of Intellectual Property Rights (TRIPS) at the World Trade Organization (WTO).

However, the Indian software and services industry cannot afford to be complacent. It faces stiff competition from East Asian countries such as China and the Philippines, and from Eastern Europe. These destinations offer significant cost advantages. As the overall cost of offshoring increases due to reasons such as higher cost of operations, it is imperative that the Indian industry continuously innovate and move up the value chain. Companies should focus on acquiring better project management capability and deeper knowledge of business domains and improving both cost and quality with superior tools and methodologies.

Indian Companies are Moving Up the Value Chain

Outsourcing relationships have become of long-term strategic importance. Hence, for global corporations, it is important to find a service provider who understands the business needs and IT goals. In response to this challenge, Indian service providers are shifting from being programming shops to becoming patent creators and mission-critical solution providers.

Indian companies are rapidly expanding their breadth by foraying into emerging and high-growth areas like Engineering Services, Bioinformatics, and Nanotechnology. These areas represent global growth avenues for the IT industry. Service lines like infrastructure management and testing are estimated to grow more than other services. Gartner estimates that the worldwide market for testing services will be close to $13 billion, with 45–50 per cent being outsourced (NASSCOM Strategic Review 2007). Also, according to a recent study by Booz Allen Hamilton, engineering outsourcing services alone present an opportunity of over $150 billion by 2020, primarily due to firms seeking access to new growing markets and quality manpower. The study estimates the potential for Indian IT services firms to be over $40 billion by 2020.

Additionally, many Indian companies have started providing end-to-end services to their clients, by introducing business process management and transitioning services. Consequently, clients have a one-stop shop for all their requirements. Value addition comes from continuous process improvement for clients and from implementation of automation opportunities. Clients benefit from a common framework for shared services, built out of the experience of working with multiple clients and by leveraging technology. They have already started

[3]Including engineering degree and diploma holders and MCAs (NASSCOM Strategic Review 2007).
[4]As on December 2006 (NASSCOM Strategic Review 2007).

seeing measurable value in terms of increased productivity, reduced cycle time, and decrease in transaction costs. In India, the BPO (business process outsourcing) industry has grown from US$ 550 million in 1999 to over US$ 8 billion in FY2007. It is estimated that by 2010, this sector will be worth US$ 18–20 billion, providing direct employment to over one million Indians.

At the same time, the industry is also concentrating on optimizing and refining the existing GDM, and taking it to the next level. This includes extending the current GDM to all tasks from business process improvements, systems integration, knowledge management, and consulting to collaborating for the entire software lifecycle. Companies are now focusing on a process-driven approach with standardized solutions that increases the business effectiveness of IT. They are also enhancing productivity through a tools-based approach, while providing employees with world-class infrastructure.

Indian companies, aware of the changed business environment, have realized the need to expand their global presence. The number of overseas offices of Indian IT companies has increased from 167 in 1995 to over 800 today. These IT companies are diversifying their focus in the global marketplace—Europe, Asia-Pacific, and Latin America.

Today, the stakeholders—clients, partners, suppliers, investors, and employees—for Indian companies come from across the globe. Companies must learn to work in distributed, multicultural teams. In this context, Indian companies are working towards creating multicultural organizations, sensitive to local cultural issues in all countries. Indian firms now recruit talent from the best universities around the world. They also focus on instituting cross-cultural training programmes that sensitize managers to the issues involved in dealing with such a diverse environment.

Challenges to Future Growth

At the same time, some basic challenges remain to be addressed. India has to make large social investments in order to sustain the basic building blocks of a knowledge economy. Education is fundamental for the growth of an industry like software. University-based research in India, a critical factor for innovation in the industry, remains low. Industry–academia partnerships are also weak. It is predicted that India will need approximately 2.3 million IT and BPO professionals by 2010 to maintain its current market share. India's education supply chain has proven to be remarkably responsive to market needs. However, by 2010, the supply of professionals is estimated to fall short by over 500,000 (NASSCOM-Mc Kinsey Report 2005). India has to ensure an adequate pipeline of 'English-speaking' graduates. To date, this has been one of our strong advantages over the competition.

The industry has to ensure that a larger section of the population gets training in basic IT skills. Unfortunately, India is increasingly getting divided into people who do and people who do not have access to—and the capability to use—modern IT. Increasing access will help tap large talent pools across the country. However, a major problem in bridging the divide is the lack of infrastructure—both in terms of basic infrastructure issues and IT infrastructure.

If software services companies are to effectively implement the offshore delivery model, the country will need robust communication infrastructure and bandwidth. In this context, increased investments are necessary in optical fibre networks, telecommunications networks, and broadband IP networks. Another important challenge faced by the industry is shortage of quality infrastructure. Growth in the IT industry has so far outpaced the development of infrastructure in several cities. The need for creating integrated townships and developing Tier-2 cities is much greater than ever before. Developing such townships and cities would add to the existing infrastructure in Tier-1 cities like Bangalore and Chennai. It is necessary to create multiple hubs for growth for the IT industry.

Today, countries and organizations globally are looking for partners who will bring in unique value, cost savings, and productivity. India has demonstrated unique strengths in terms of quality, efficiency, and rapidly scalable skills. Benchmarking globally, creating international brands, having a relentless focus on the customer, and learning to operate in a multicultural environment are key success factors for the future of the industry.

The software and services exports industry is now entering a critical phase of growth. The next 10 years mark a time when the most innovative, competitive companies will pull ahead and dominate the global market. In the last decade, the Indian software and services industry has already helped change the way the world does business. Indian firms have had a great beginning, and we must not fritter away the advantages we have gained. Bill Gates spoke of India as the 'next software superpower'. I believe this goal is well within our reach. To achieve this, we must aspire higher than the status quo, and seize the opportunities ahead.

N.R. NARAYANA MURTHY

References

Gartner, A.T. Kearney, IDC, JMS Research, NASSCOM Strategic Review (2007) and NASSCOM-McKinsey Report (2005).

Space Satellites

India initiated a modest rocket-based space research programme in 1963 for carrying out basic scientific research in aeronomy and astronomy, but it soon embarked upon the development of a vibrant, totally self-reliant application-driven space programme, realizing the vast potential of space technology for tackling identified national tasks in the areas of communication, broadcasting, education, disaster management, weather forecasting, and management of natural resources. During the 1970s, the Indian Space Research Organization (ISRO) carried out a unique Satellite Instructional Television Experiment (SITE), using NASA's ATS-6 satellite, for regularly broadcasting developmental and educational programmes on health, hygiene, better agricultural practices, and family planning to 2,400 remote villages in six clusters. A number of selected aerial remote-sensing surveys with multi-spectral and infra-red cameras were also conducted to demonstrate the potential of space remote sensing for agricultural and environmental monitoring, land-use planning, and forest management. ISRO took a major step in 1972 when it signed an agreement with the USSR Academy of Sciences to launch an Indian-built satellite on a Soviet rocket, which resulted in the establishment of the ISRO Satellite Centre at Bangalore, for the development and application of satellite technology.

The successful launching of Aryabhata, India's first satellite, weighing 360 kg, in April 1975, from Kapustin Yar near Volgagrad, established India's capability to design, fabricate, and launch space satellites. This was followed by the launch of two experimental remote-sensing satellites Bhaskara-1 and Bhaskara-2 in 1979 and 1981, respectively, each carrying a TV camera system for imaging at 1 km resolution and passive microwave radiometers for studying the dynamics and temperature distribution over the oceans. Parallelly, ISRO undertook the development of a three-axis stabilized communication satellite called APPLE, weighing 670 kg and carrying two C-band transponders, which was launched into the geostationary orbit by the Arianne rocket in 1981 for communication and video broadcasting. The end-to-end experience gained from the design, fabrication, orbit raising, operation, and utilization of these experimental remote-sensing and communication satellites paved the way for India to emerge as one of the leading nations in satellite technology, capable of designing and launching state-of-the-art application satellites.

In order to achieve total self-reliance, parallel efforts were initiated at the Vikram Sarabhai Space Centre, Trivandrum, in the early 1970s, for the development of a modest launch vehicle SLV-3 which launched a 40 kg Rohini Satellite into a near-earth orbit. Sustained effort by ISRO scientists since then has enabled ISRO to develop a state-of-the-art PSLV (Polar Satellite Launch Vehicle) rocket capable of launching 2 tonne remote-sensing satellites into a polar orbit and GSLV (Geostationary Satellite Launch Vehicle) rocket that can launch 2 tonne satellites into a geostationary transfer orbit, making India totally self-reliant in space technology.

Communication Revolution through INSAT

Instead of following the conventional path of building separate communication and meteorological satellites, ISRO, from the start, decided to build cost-effective, multipurpose satellites combining all these services in a single geostationary spacecraft. To meet the immediate demand for nationwide TV broadcasting, ISRO decided to procure the INSAT-1 series of first-generation geostationary satellites from the Ford Aerospace Communication Corporation (FACC). These satellites weighing about 1,150 kg carried 12 C-band communication transponders, two high-power S-band transponders for national TV coverage, and a Very High-Resolution Radiometer (VHRR) for meteorological imaging in the visible and thermal infrared bands over the Indian continent. Even though INSAT-1A built by the FACC failed within four months of its launch, the successful launch of INSAT-1B in August 1983 initiated a communication revolution in India. INSAT-1B was followed by two more first-generation INSATs for providing nationwide services in communication, broadcasting, and meteorological services in the 1980s.

With the experience gained from the successful design, fabrication, launching, and operation of APPLE, ISRO decided to indigenously design and fabricate the second-generation INSAT-2 series of satellites, weighing over 1,900 kg and having much higher capacity than the first-generation INSATs. These satellites carried 12 C-band and 6 extended C-band transponders, 2 high-power S-band transponders, a data-relay transponder, and an improved VHRR with a resolution of 2 km in the visible and 8 km in the infrared. After the successful launch and operationalization of INSAT-2A in 1992, ISRO followed up with three more second-generation satellites, which, apart from the payloads launched on INSAT-2A, carried additional payloads for providing mobile communication, fixed satellite services, and Charge Coupled Device (CCD) cameras for augmenting meteorological capability. Growing requirement for fixed satellite services to address the communication needs of closed user groups resulted in the development of Very Small Aperture Terminals (VSAT), for receiving large volumes of data, audio, or video information directly from space. Rapid expansion of VSAT services and a growing demand from conventional communication and broadcasting services necessitated the development of third-generation INSATs. Since 2000, four third-generation INSAT-3 series of satellites, each weighing in excess of 2,700 kg, have been launched to provide extensive communication capability in C, extended C, and Ku bands and also enhance the sensitivity of meteorological imaging. In addition, a dedicated meteorological satellite weighing 1 tonne and carrying meteorological imaging payload with water vapour channels, named Kalpana after astronaut Kalpana Chawla, was also launched on our indigenous launch vehicle GSLV, from the Satish Dhawan Space Centre, Sriharikota (SDSC) in 2002. The latest member of India's communication satellite fleet is Edusat, a dedicated satellite for the spread of education, which was launched from Sriharikota in 2003 on GSLV.

India, as of now, has one of the largest domestic communication satellite systems, with 150 communication transponders on eight satellites, providing a variety of communication and meteorological services to the country. With over 5,500 two-way speech circuits covering about 143 routes and linking 704 earth stations of various sizes, the vast reach of INSAT satellites has been advantageously used for providing nationwide radio networking, administrative, business and computer communication, VSAT networking, and emergency communication services. More than 54,000 VSAT terminals including those installed by the National Informatics Centre (NICNET) are operating today to cater to the fast-growing requirements of both public and private closed user groups.

The most dramatic impact of INSAT has been in the rapid expansion of TV dissemination in India through the installation of about 1,400 transmitters, providing 90 per cent of India's population access to national as well as regional services through 60 channels of telecasting. Use of transportable earth stations and Satellite News Gathering Vehicles now allows extensive real-time coverage of important events anywhere in the country. Recognizing the importance of the interactive communication system, a number of experiments have been conducted for imparting developmental education to target audiences of different types both in the rural and urban areas. Six developmental communication channels are being operated to broadcast programmes on technical education, agriculture, and vocational training, with the active involvement of state educational administrators and eminent teachers. The launch of Edusat, a dedicated educational satellite for broadcasting curriculum-based lessons to students and teachers in universities and technical institutions, has given a big boost to the expansion of the tele-education service.

Telemedicine, which extends specialized medical facilities even to people in remote rural areas by connecting them with medical experts located at specialty hospitals in major cities, has emerged as another major satellite application. Telemedicine consists of linking customized medical software integrated with computer hardware, at each rural location, with a super specialty hospital through satellite-based VSAT. The medical history of the patient including X-ray, ECG, and other diagnostic records is transmitted to specialist doctors, who can diagnose and advise on the course of treatment through videoconference with the doctor and paramedic at the patient's end. Since the establishment of ISRO's telemedicine network 18 months ago, it has already expanded to cover 88 remote area hospitals in several states, which are connected to 27 Super Speciality Hospitals, and has helped over 100,000 patients receive tele-consultation treatment.

Remote Sensing for National Resource Management

With the successful launch of its first operational Indian Remote-Sensing Satellite IRS-1A in 1988 from Bikonur, ISRO became the fifth country in the world to carry out remote sensing from space. Both the first-generation remote satellites IRS-1A and 1B, carried CCD cameras for taking multispectral imageries with a resolution of about 36 m, matching the capability of contemporary US-operated LANDSAT satellites. The second-generation IRS-1C and 1D launched in 1995 and 1997, respectively, carried improved cameras with a resolution of 23 m in the multispectral and just 5.6 m in the panchromatic bands, the best available in the world at that time. The successful launch of the highly sophisticated technology satellite in 2001, capable of imaging at a resolution of just 0.8 m, and the subsequent launching of RESOURCESAT in 2003 and CARTOSAT in 2005, which in addition to very high-resolution and frequent revisit facilities also includes the capability to take three-dimensional images, have fully established India as a world leader in space remote sensing.

The IRS system has become invaluable for mapping spatial as well as temporal changes in soil characteristics, land-use patterns, forest resources, agricultural inventories, fisheries, and wastelands in the country. IRS imageries are now regularly employed to identify underground water aquifiers, map surface water bodies, estimate snow melt run-off, delineate water-logged regions, and predict acreage and yield of all major crops. Regular bi-weekly bulletins demarcating potential fishing zones in the ocean, based on ocean temperature and phytoplankton distribution, are routinely distributed to all the fishing centres to help fishermen obtain improved fish catch. Space remote sensing has become the most important tool for urban planning, wasteland mapping, mineral prospecting, coastal monitoring, and environmental management. A unique application of IRS data has been in the Integrated Mission for Sustainable Development (IMSD), for generating locale-specific prescriptions to enhance agricultural productivity on a sustainable basis, using space and biotechnological inputs, and thus usher in the new Ever Green Revolution.

Since the 1980s, ISRO has been regularly monitoring cyclones, floods, and other natural disasters and providing advance warning wherever possible. Remote-sensing imageries have become invaluable in identifying and demarcating hazard-prone areas. Locale-specific advance warning on drought using space data on vegetation index, a measure of vegetation vigour, is now regularly transmitted to all drought-prone districts of the country. India's remote-sensing satellites have also been regularly mapping environmental pollution including forest fires, oil spills, and land degradation. While predictions of earthquakes and to some extent tsunamis are still far from being exact, remote-sensing imageries are extensively employed for disaster assessment and post-disaster rehabilitation. India was the first country to develop a comprehensive cyclone-warning system to provide locale-specific disaster alerts to areas likely to be affected by cyclones and floods, which has saved thousands of lives and livestock over the years, in the coastal areas of our country.

The Indian Space Programme, which had a modest beginning in 1963 has, over the last four decades, built up impressive capability and a high degree of self-reliance in the development and application of space technology. Space technology applications now encompass communication, TV broadcast, education, meteorological prediction, management of natural resources, agriculture, environment, disaster management, and sustainable integrated development, practically touching all aspects of human endeavour. ISRO has so far launched 40 satellites, half of them from Sriharikota using its own indigenously developed rockets. The cumulative expenditure of the Indian Space Programme during the last four decades since its inception—including the vast infrastructure build-up of extensive test facilities, launch pads, control centres, tracking network, and regional centres for promoting application of space technology for a variety of national tasks—is a modest Rs 22,000 crore (US$ 8 billion), just about half of NASA's annual budget, which makes the Indian Space Programme a very cost-effective one.

U.R. Rao

■ Special Economic Zones

Special Economic Zones or SEZs refer to areas within a country where some of the economic laws and restrictions of the land are relaxed with the purpose of giving incentives to investors. The usual relaxations are with respect to taxes, import and export duties, and labour laws. At present, an ever-increasing number of less developed countries all over the globe are finding the SEZs an integral part of their development programmes. Undoubtedly, the success of the Chinese SEZs in the 1980s has led other less developed countries to set up their own. According to World Bank estimates, as of 2007 there are more than 3,000 projects taking place in the SEZs in 120 countries worldwide.

India is no exception to this general trend. In 2005, the Special Economic Zones Act was passed in the Parliament with the purpose of establishing, developing, and managing SEZs in the country. By June 2006, there were eight functional SEZs in India located at Santa Cruz (Maharashtra), Cochin (Kerala), Kandla and Surat (Gujarat), Chennai (Tamil Nadu), Visakhapatnam (Andhra Pradesh), Falta (West Bengal), and Noida (Uttar Pradesh) and 18 more were approved, waiting to become functional. By May 2007, the number of notified SEZs in the country after the passing of the SEZ Act of 2005 had reached one hundred. In addition to exemption from import and export duties, units in the SEZs get incentives in terms of benefits in income tax, service tax, and other obligations to the central and state governments. So it is not at all surprising that a large number of enterprises have queued up either to develop an SEZ or to enter an already established SEZ in India.

What are the advantages of having the SEZs? One major advantage is that an SEZ makes concentration of a number of similar production units within a small geographical area possible. This, in turn, has a number of well-known benefits. When similar firms are located together there is immense possibility of learning from one another, both directly and indirectly from the successes and failures of one's neighbours. This flow of knowledge improves technology, reduces costs of production, and makes each production unit more competitive. Moreover, it is a lot easier to ensure uninterrupted supplies of inputs and a steady flow of demand for the final output if a firm is located in a zone specially designated for firms producing a particular type of product. Raw materials and other types of input-supplying firms know exactly where to go to sell their products. So is true for specialized labour. On the other hand, consumers and distributors of final products also find it convenient to find a number of production units located in one place ensuring variety, competition, and efficiency.

But while it is hard to deny the advantages of localization of any particular type of industry, the question remains as to whether the advantage deserves tax breaks and subsidies of such magnitude as are being offered in the SEZs. Indeed, industries have been observed to be naturally localized throughout recorded history without much incentive or enticement. The Manchesters, Sheffields, or Silicon Valleys of the world were formed not out of any conscious government endeavour, but simply because firms in those places found it worthwhile to stay together. In similar manner, one can argue that in India and elsewhere, investments would have been forthcoming in any case if the investors found them profitable. Why then special incentives to form economic zones?

The objections against the SEZs do not end here though. In most cases, the firms that are getting the tax breaks and subsidies to form the SEZs are multinationals or large domestic players. One can certainly question the justification of giving economic incentives to these very rich enterprises at the cost of the common taxpayer. Indeed the tax structure implied by the SEZ Act looks regressive and unfair. One may perhaps argue in reply that these enterprises need to be initially subsidized to exploit potential gains from increasing returns. That would be reminiscent of the old infant industry argument. The trouble with this argument is that these big enterprises are not credit constrained. So if they can foresee potential gains from increasing investment, in order to exploit those gains they would go ahead with their investment even without any incentives offered to them.

Stricter proponents of free trade feel that the idea of the SEZs violates the very basic principles of a free market economy. According to them, India, which was imprisoned by the shackles of economic controls for a long period of time, was gradually emancipating itself from the chains through liberalization and globalization. It was a journey towards achieving efficiency. The SEZ Act is likely to reverse the process. To the liberals, building up the SEZs is equivalent to bringing back discretionary controls with all their evils and inefficiencies. The liberals apprehend that as industry houses will start competing with one another to get into the SEZs to appropriate the special benefits, the old licence raj with widespread lobbying and selective distribution of political favours might come back.

The more imminent problem, however, is related to the acquisition of land for the SEZs. Given that employment-wise, India is still a predominantly agricultural country, about two-thirds of the labour force being still dependent on the agricultural sector, and given that the land–man ratio is adverse in general, the available land is mostly cultivated. So a significant part of the land required for the SEZs must come from the agricultural sector. This has led some people to believe that indiscriminate land acquisition for the SEZs will jeopardize food security of the country.

A little reflection should, however, convince us that the fear about food security is ill founded. This is because of at least a couple of reasons. First, the land required for the development of the SEZs, though not small in absolute magnitude, is likely to be a negligible fraction of the total cultivable land in India. Acquisition of this land for building up industries and infrastructure is not going to affect the total food production in the country in any significant way.

Second, industrialization aided by the SEZs is likely to have a favourable effect on agricultural productivity. With industrialization, as more and more people shift to the industrial and the services sectors, pressure on agricultural land will fall and average landholding will increase as some of the emigrants going away from the rural sector will sell off their land to the people who would stay back. An increase in average landholding in the agricultural sector would, in turn, help consolidate fragmented pieces of landholding, which again would make possible the use of modern technology. Indeed, excessive fragmentation of land in India is one of the main constraints to the introduction of advanced methods of production. If land is consolidated, this constraint would be relaxed. It may be mentioned that in the advanced countries 2 to 4 per cent of the population is engaged in agriculture. But this small fraction of people is able to feed the entire country. This is made possible by the very high levels of productivity of labour in the agricultural sector, which again is the result of advanced technology.

If a similar pattern can emerge in India, the increase in the productivity of labour in the agricultural sector can indeed compensate for the loss of production due to loss in acreage. That the level of productivity in the Indian agricultural sector is abysmally low is clearly borne out by the fact that about two-thirds of the labour force engaged in the agricultural sector is unable to contribute more than 21 per cent of the gross domestic product. Only large-scale exodus from the agricultural sector can increase this productivity.

The real problem of land acquisition is not macroeconomic but arises at the microeconomic level. When land is acquired for the SEZs, people lose their livelihoods. Moreover, those losing their livelihoods are among the least likely to get immediate jobs in the newly built SEZs simply because they would usually lack the education and training required for a job in the industrial sector. As a result, these displaced people would fight land acquisition tooth and nail unless they are properly compensated for their assets and livelihood.

Struggles over land acquisition, ranging from political rallies, demonstrations, and small riots right up to widespread conflicts leading to massive manslaughter, are taking place in West Bengal, Orissa, Uttar Pradesh, and other places. This simply indicates that compensations have been inadequate. State governments have so far proceeded to acquire land mainly on the basis of the Land Acquisition Act, 1894. The Act empowers the government to acquire any land for a public purpose or for the purpose of use by a company by prior notification by paying a compensation to the owner. The problem is that there is no provision to compensate the other stakeholders of land including the landless labourers and share-croppers. In many cases, the owner of the land is an absentee landlord who is only too happy to sell off his land, the production of which he could not monitor and hence was being deprived of his just share. It is the other stakeholders who are the actual tillers and are truly losing their livelihoods. If land is to be smoothly acquired for the SEZs, these people are to be properly compensated. Some states, notably the state of Orissa, have come up with elaborate resettlement and rehabilitation packages for the displaced. But again these packages have been so far limited to the owners of the land and have not been extended to the other stakeholders.

Is there any moral ground of compensating the labourers? After all one can argue that land acquisition does not rob the labourer of his labour power and so there is no need to compensate him. This is not true of the landowner who is certainly losing his asset, namely land, after the acquisition. But the point to note is that the agricultural labourer often has a very specific kind of expertise which has no use in other sectors. So with acquisition of land the value of this expertise is greatly reduced, which is equivalent to a fall in the value of his human capital. For this he needs to be compensated. Also, when a government factory closes down, the worker whose job is terminated is usually compensated through a retirement package. Why should the government not follow the same practice when it is acquiring land and making people jobless?

But then the question arises as to why governments are reluctant to pay compensation to all stakeholders, especially if it is generally understood that such an act would make land acquisition for the SEZs undeniably smoother. In my opinion, one should look for an answer in the recent competition between the state governments to attract investment. Indeed, the SEZs have emerged as one of the primary avenues through which this competition is taking shape. To remain competitive, the states are trying to provide land for the SEZs at the lowest possible costs. On top of that various other subsidies and incentives are provided. In fact, so much money is spent to woo the investors that very little is left for compensation, rehabilitation, and resettlement. In fact, the competition is not confined to the Indian states alone. An intense competition is now developing between countries to woo multinationals. This competition explains the emergence of a large number of SEZs all over the world.

The problem is one of adopting a long-run feasible policy for India. The so-called East Asian model of economic development, which has produced miracles in terms of growth, though not always in terms of human development, can hardly work in India even towards increasing the rate of growth. The East Asian model puts the entire policy emphasis on the investor, giving him all the incentives possible. In the process, humanitarian considerations are largely ignored, farmers are uprooted from their land and livelihood, and savage labour laws are implemented within the SEZs. But even though such coercive methods could work in authoritarian regimes like China, they are unlikely to work in India where, however faulty, we have a democracy.

This is amply clear from the growing discontent all over the country against the SEZs and land acquisition. If the discontent grows, the process of industrialization will be in jeopardy. Paying too much attention to investors and too little to workers and the displaced is morally wrong. But more important, as a long-run strategy it is untenable.

Abhirup Sarkar

References

Krugman, Paul. 1995. *Development, Geography and Economic Theory*, Massachusetts, MIT press.

Land Acquisition Act, 1894. Government of India, Ministry of Law and Justice.

Orissa Resettlement and Rehabilitation Policy, 2006. Government of Orissa.

Sarkar, Abhirup. 2007. 'Development and Displacement: Land Acquisition in West Bengal', *Economic and Political Weekly*, 21 April, 42(16): 1435–42.

Special Economic Zones Act, 2005. Government of India, Ministry of Law and Justice.

■ State Bank of India

Genesis and Organization

The State Bank of India is India's oldest and largest commercial bank. It is lineally descended from the Bank of Calcutta, which was set up in 1806 (27 March) (Bagchi 1987: part I, p. 66) as a purely government-owned bank run by officials of the (English) East India Company. The latter had by then become the paramount power in the subcontinent. It was transformed into the Bank of Bengal, a joint-stock bank with limited liability, with effect from 2 January 1809 (ibid.: 97). The privilege of limited liability for shareholders was obtained by virtue of a charter granted by British Parliament, since under British law no limited liability could be claimed by a joint-stock company without special permission of the government. The Bank of Bengal had a minority government shareholding and a directorate on which government officials were represented. Two other banks of a similar composition, and with limited liability granted by Parliamentary charter, were founded in 1840 and 1843. They were the Banks of Bombay and Madras, respectively. The speculative boom and bust attending the US Civil War raised the price of cotton in India and property values in the city of Bombay to dizzying heights, only to dash them to the ground when the Civil War ended. The Bank of Bombay went bankrupt through reckless lending to speculators in real estate and phony companies. A New Bank of Bombay was established under the new Indian company law authorizing the setting up of joint-stock banks with limited liability. This became the Bank of Bombay in 1876 when the Presidency Banks Act was passed. That Act ended government shareholding in all three banks, of Bengal, Bombay, and Madras. But since they conducted much of the banking for the government and received interest-free deposits of government balances, they were strictly regulated by it.

The three banks were merged to form the Imperial Bank of India, which began functioning from January 1921. The Imperial Bank was privately owned and managed but remained the banker to the government. It was ultimately nationalized in 1955 and renamed the State Bank of India (SBI). From then on, the appointment of the chairman and managing director of the bank has been the prerogative of the Government of India. Subsequently, a number of banks that had been established by the so-called 'Native Princes' during the period of British rule were also taken over by the government and became subsidiaries of the SBI.

Functioning under Colonial Rule

This brief sketch cannot capture all the motivations for the founding of the different ancestors of the SBI or the chief characteristics of the way they functioned. I shall highlight only some of the more salient features of that history. Behind the founding of the Bank of Bengal was the goal of creating a market for loans to the East India Company's government in India and the correlative objective of bringing down the rate of interest on such loans. Initially, 'Company's paper' was virtually the only security against which Indian borrowers such as Dwarkanath Tagore could obtain loans from the bank. Another, unstated, objective was to create an institution for European businessmen in India that would extend them credit on privileged terms. When the system of cash credit was introduced, Europeans generally had much easier access to it than Indians. Moreover, except in the case of the Bank of Bombay, even large Indian firms rarely enjoyed clean credit from the Presidency banks.

The three Presidency banks had different structures and different policy stances towards Indian customers. The Bank of Bengal's head office was located in Calcutta, the capital of British India, and eastern India was the most important business base of Europeans, and that bank was the most discriminatory in its treatment of Indians. After 1809, it had no Indian directors on its board. Southern India was almost equally dominated by European capital; but from the late 19th century, Indian capital found profitable areas of operation in Ceylon (Sri Lanka), Burma (Myanmar), and the Straits Settlements (Peninsular Malaya and Singapore). Moreover, the Government of Madras kept some distance from the rather smaller-sized British enterprises in southern India. So even though the Bank of Madras had no Indian directors until the very last year of its existence as a separate entity, it discriminated less against Indian borrowers than the

Bank of Bengal. The Bank of Bombay in both its old and new incarnations had a number of Indian directors, the economy and the external trade of western India were less dominated by Europeans, and that bank followed a more even-handed policy with regard to its European and Indian customers.[1] But Indians were denied managerial positions in all three lands until the Bank of Bombay altered the practice from World War I. The salaries and emoluments of Indian staff vis-à-vis European staff of all three banks were grossly unequal. An exclusively European managerial cadre made for further discriminatory treatment of Indian customers.

The differences between the three banks had implications for regional differences in the spread of state-backed banking in British India. For example, in 1920, just before the birth of the Imperial Bank, the Bank of Bengal had only seven branches in the provinces of Bengal, Bihar, and Orissa, whereas the Bank of Madras had 18 branches in an area with less than half the population of Bengal, Bihar, and Orissa (Ray et al. 2003: Table 1.3). These differences persisted into the era of the Imperial Bank: at the end of 1941, for example, that bank had forty-three branches in the Madras Circle that covered Madras Presidency alone (with a population of 49.3 million), whereas in an area stretching from Mandalay in Burma to Lahore in Punjab, and covering a population that was more than four times the population of Madras Presidency, the Imperial Bank had only seventy-one branches. On that date, the Bombay Circle had 63 branches in an area covering Bombay and Sind and the Central Provinces and Berar. The intensity of bank penetration in the Bombay Circle was higher than in the case of the Bengal Circle, but most of the branches of the Imperial Bank were concentrated in the coastal region and cotton tracts of the Bombay Circle.[2]

The Presidency banks were strictly excluded from dealing in foreign exchange or borrowing on the London market. Prudential considerations (such as possible embarrassment because of sudden changes in exchange rates) as well as the pressure of the British exchange banks operating in India dictated this choice (Bagchi 1989: ch. 3). This restriction was also imposed on the Imperial Bank of India and was relaxed only after the establishment of the Reserve Bank of India in 1935 (Ray et al. 2003: 37).

In his book, *Indian Currency and Finance*, Keynes had recommended the setting up of a State Bank of India and he followed it up with a note on the same subject, jointly authored with Ernest Cable, that was published as an annexure to the Report of the Chamberlain Commission just before World War I (Keynes 1913; Bagchi 1989: 162–7). The Imperial Bank was not the State Bank as conceived by Keynes and Cable: it remained in private hands, whose interests would receive priority in case of any conflict with public interest. It also failed to impart the elasticity to money supply through deep penetration into the Indian exchange networks. From the 1930s many Indians demanded the nationalization of the Imperial Bank (Ray et al. 2003: ch. 9). The main grounds for those demands were that while the bank enjoyed a number of privileges as banker to the government, it was relatively insensitive to the needs of Indian economic development, it was controlled by a self-perpetuating management consisting entirely of British managers, and it was used as the handmaiden of British imperial policy and often inhibited Indian industrial and commercial growth. Demands for nationalization became more insistent after Independence, partly because the incumbent British managers stonewalled all suggestions for extending the branches of the bank and for inducting Indians into top management. The Government of India was cowed by the threat held out by the advocates of the Imperial Bank that its nationalization would send wrong signals to foreign investors in India and produce a crisis in the economy of the newly independent country. On the grounds that branch extension would prove to be unprofitable and harm the interests of the shareholders, the Imperial Bank management turned a deaf ear to the recommendation of the Rural Banking Enquiry Committee, 1950, for rapid extension of the branches of the bank to towns and taluq headquarters with no modern banking facilities.

In 1954, the Estimates Committee of Indian Parliament and the All India Rural Credit Survey Committee both recommended nationalization, on the grounds that most government business could then be conducted by the State Bank and that the stonewalling by the Imperial Bank of branch expansion could be ended. The Government of India accepted the recommendation and an Act was passed in 1955 to give it effect. From 1 July 1955, the nationalized institution began functioning as the State Bank of India.

Belying the self-serving predictions of the British management of the Imperial Bank, the taking over of all the monetary transactions of the government and the rapid extension of branches to unbanked centres of trade and industry in India led to a fast growth of income and profits of the newborn SBI. For example, while the annual net profits of the Imperial Bank from 1948 to 1954 fluctuated between Rs 11.3 million and Rs 13.6 million (Ray et al.

[1]For an analysis of the reasons for these regional differences, see Bagchi (1972: ch. 6; 1987: part I).
[2]The population figures are taken from the *Statistical Abstracts for British India* and the branch data from Ray et al. (2003: 315)

2003: Table 6.5), the net profits of the SBI increased from Rs 15.6 million in 1956 to Rs 27.1 million in 1961. Over the same period, the number of branches and sub-offices of the bank increased from 502 to 944. In contrast, the total number of branches of the Imperial Bank had expanded from 177 to 191 over the whole decade of the 1940s and from 191 on 31 December 1951 to 229 on 31 December 1954, despite all the pressure exerted by the Indian government (Ray et al. 2003: Table 4.1).

The State Bank of India from 1955

A number of the former 'native states' had opened government banks of their own. By an Act passed in 1959, these banks, such as the State Bank of Bikaner and the State Bank of Travancore, were converted into subsidiaries of the SBI. With the onset of economic liberalizing policies in India from the late 1980s and their acceleration in the 1990s, the SBI created a number of new subsidiaries or entered into joint ventures such as SBI Capital Markets Limited, State Bank of India (California), SBI Life Insurance Co. Ltd., and GE Capital Business Process Management Services Pvt. Ltd. The SBI, in line with the economic liberalization package, has also introduced several product innovations, especially in the area of personal banking. The floating of the Indian exchange rate has provided the SBI with a new arena of business. Because of its sheer size, it has become the single most important player in the foreign exchange market (of course, under the general supervision of the Reserve Bank of India). During 2003–4, for example, it commanded a market share of 35.63 per cent with a forex turnover of Rs 2,655 billion.

The SBI grew into a massive institution, spreading its branches into every corner of India. This expansion was facilitated by the requirements of priority-sector lending imposed on all scheduled commercial banks from 1969. The number of offices of the SBI increased to 8,422 and the number of employees to 219,000 at the end of March 1990. This was the period in which the SBI served the development of the real economy most closely. From the 1990s, despite the opening of a number of foreign branches, the rate of branch opening slowed down. The number of branches stood at 9,093 on 31 March 2004. Priority-sector lending constituted 43 per cent of the advances of the State Bank Group in 1989–90. In 2003–4, it came down to 38.69 per cent and the advances to agriculture fell to 12.79 per cent of the net bank credit, far short of the prescribed limit of 18 per cent.

From the 1980s, an increasing proportion of the shares of the SBI has been sold to individuals and companies, so that by 2003–4, the Reserve Bank of India as the representative of the government, held 59.73 per cent of the share capital and the rest was held by individuals, other financial institutions, and non-financial companies. This change in ownership structure has also impelled the SBI to look for profitability as the major criterion in taking up new products and ventures.

The SBI has undergone several transformations in its evolution—from being a family of banks partly owned by the government to being a bank owned by private individuals, to a bank that was almost fully owned by the government, and finally to one with considerable private participation in its shareholding and decision-making processes. But throughout its history, it has remained a dominant presence in the Indian money, and in recent years, the foreign exchange market as well. It would be a great pity, if under the pressure of generating more profit, this national institution ceases to be a bank that caters to the needs of all—from a villager who needs assistance to fill up a slip to an e-savvy customer.

AMIYA KUMAR BAGCHI

References

[*Note*: Apart from the references specifically cited below, all the information is taken from the Annual Reports of the State Bank of India from 1956 to 2003–4.]

Bagchi, A.K. 1972. *Private Investment in India 1900–1939*, Cambridge, Cambridge University Press.

——. 1987. *The Evolution of the State Bank of India, The Roots 1806–1876, Parts I and II*, New Delhi, Oxford University Press.

——. 1989. *The Presidency Banks and the Indian Economy 1876–1914*, Calcutta, Oxford University Press.

——. 1997. *The Evolution of the State Bank of India*, Vol. 2, *The Era of the Presidency Banks*, New Delhi, Sage.

Keynes, John Maynard. 1913. *Indian Currency and Finance*, London, Macmillan.

Ray, A., S. Das, J.S. Mathai, S. Roy, and U. Sarker. 2003. *The Evolution of the State Bank of India*, Vol. 3, *The Era of the Imperial Bank of India 1921–1955*, New Delhi, Sage.

■ Steel Industry

Indian Steel Industry in a Global Perspective

Steel is the largest metal industry and the second largest man-made material industry, after cement, in the world. Iron and steel provide the basic material needed for building the physical infrastructure of an economy as it grows into a mature developed one. Steel consumption has, therefore, been regarded as one of the basic indicators of an economy's state of development. The total world crude steel production increased from 28.3 million tonnes in 1900, to 696.4 million tonnes in 1973, and 1,227 million tonnes in 2009.

Since the end of the Cold War, the growth of the industry in the Asia-Pacific region, with China emerging as a major player, has been a significant phenomenon. The share of the Asia-Pacific region (excluding Japan) in global crude steel production increased from 28 per cent to 60 per cent during 1999–2009. China's crude steel output increased from 25.2 million tonnes in 1973, to 127.24 million tonnes in 2000, and to a spectacular 567.8 million tonnes in 2009.

India, on the other hand, is now the third largest crude steel producer in the world and the second in the Asia-Pacific region, after China and Japan. The production of crude steel and finished steel in India was 64.8 million tonnes and 36.91 million tonnes, respectively, in 2009. However, unfortunately, in spite of its being one of the largest producers of steel in the world, India is one of its poorest consumers in terms of finished steel. In the absence of reliable data on stock changes every year, we take the apparent consumption of steel for measuring consumption and demand for steel, the apparent consumption being defined as domestic production plus imports minus exports and the total demand facing the Indian steel market being domestic sales from own production and imports plus exports. India's per capita apparent consumption of finished steel was as low as 47.8 kg while that of China, Japan, and South Korea was 405.2 kg, 418.9 kg, and 936.1 kg, respectively, in 2009.

The finished steel intensity of the gross domestic product (GDP) was also 0.042 kg per dollar of income, which is quite low in comparison with other major steel-producing economies like China and South Korea (see Table 1). The steel intensity of GDP depends on the structural composition of GDP since steel use in the material commodity or industrial sector is substantially higher than that in the services or agricultural sector. The major use of steel in an economy is in the infrastructural construction of rail, roads and bridges, buildings (residential and non-residential), electricity supply and production of capital goods, and in the production of automobiles and consumer durables. The growth of these sectors and spending on them would get reflected in the changes in the share of the secondary sector in GDP and the rate of gross domestic fixed capital formation (GFCF). A cross-country comparison of the stages of development, the GDP share of the secondary sector, the GFCF rate, and the availability of domestic savings for financing such capital formation, as given in Table 1,

Table 1 Comparative Absorption of Steel by Major Asian Economies, 2009

	India	China	South Korea	Japan	Brazil
GDP per capita in $	1,134	3,744	17,078	39,738	8,121
GNI per capita in PPP($)	3,250	6,890	27,310	33,370	10,200
Domestic savings rate (2009) %	34	54	30	24	15
Gross domestic capital formation as % of GDP	35	48	26	20	17
Share of secondary sector (2009) %	29	49	37	30	28
Finished steel consumption per capita (in kg)	47.8	405.2	936.1	418.9	93.1
Finished steel intensity of GDP in kg per $ income	0.042	0.108	0.055	0.011	0.011
Finished steel intensity of GNI in kg per PPP $ income	0.015	0.059	0.034	0.013	0.009

Source: World Steel in Figures 2010; World Bank (2010).

would explain the relatively low rate of absorption of steel by the Indian economy in comparison with the other major Asian economies.

It may further be noted that the construction component of GFCF has a higher steel usage than the other components. The relatively slow rate of GFCF growth, that is, at 6.3 per cent and particularly the construction component which was 4.2 per cent during the 1980s and 1990s explains the erratic absorption of steel by the Indian economy to a large extent (Sinha and Suri 2003). India's low steel intensity of GDP does not provide evidence of the efficiency of its steel use, but only indicates an inadequate pace of industrialization and infrastructural development which is supported by the growing share of the service sector in GDP.

History and Growth

From the pre-Independence period to the Third Plan, at the very start, it must be mentioned that unlike other developing countries, India's modern steel industry is quite old and dates back to 1907 when the Tata Iron and Steel Company (TISCO) was registered as an iron and steel-making company. It represents the most important instance of entrepreneurship of Indian private capital in the 20th century. It started producing pig iron in 1911 and ingot steel a year later and grew without any tariff protection. Besides TISCO, the Indian Iron and Steel

Company (IISCO), and the Mysore Iron and Steel Works came into existence in 1918 and 1921, respectively. IISCO first produced pig iron and then steel. The Steel Corporation of Bengal was floated in 1937 to produce steel using pig iron and service utilities from IISCO; the two companies were subsequently amalgamated in 1953.

Post-Independence Period: First Phase of Development

The steel industry in India experienced its major growth after the Second Five Year Plan (1956–7 to 1961–2). Unlike the colonial period, the growth of the integrated steel plant sector during the period of planned development till 1991–2 took place mainly at the direction and initiative of the Indian state as per the Industrial Policy Resolution of 1956. This policy reserved the expansion of the integrated steel plant sector (that is, the route of steel making via pig iron making, starting with iron ore as raw material in a single production establishment) in the public sector. TISCO and IISCO were, however, allowed to carry on their business as private steel-making companies.

In view of the inelasticity of India's traditional exports and the shortage of domestic savings and foreign exchange, the growth of the steel industry took place under a policy regime of industrialization by import substitution. This was characterized by heavy tariff protection, import control, and state control of both domestic selling prices and the distribution of products of integrated steel plants.

In the Second Five Year Plan, three steel plants of 1 million tonne capacity each in terms of crude steel were set up under the public sector Hindustan Steel Limited (HSL) at Rourkela, Bhilai, and Durgapur; later their capacities were expanded to 1.8 million tonnes, 2.5 million tonnes, and 1.6 million tonnes, respectively. These plants were later merged into the Steel Authority of India (SAIL).

Second Phase of Planned Development of the Industry: Change in Government Policy and Deceleration of Growth

After the Third Plan (1962–3 to 1966–7) expansion programme, the growth of the steel industry decelerated because of the financial resource constraint faced by public-sector companies, long gestation lag due to indigenization of plant and capital equipment of projects, as well as some change in government policy regarding the priority of the steel sector in the central sector's plan investment allocation. The inefficiency of the public sector in absorbing foreign technology, low administered steel prices, and physical control of distribution resulted in a low rate of internal surplus generation in the steel industry in this period (Sengupta 2004). This period also saw a shift in the resource allocation policy of the government as a result of which the share of steel in the public-sector plan outlay declined from 7.81 per cent in the Third Plan to 3.57 per cent in the Eighth Plan ending in 1996–7.

The constraint in the availability of finances due to low profits, inadequate plan resource allocation, and also the non-availability of soft loans from other foreign sources left the Indian government with no choice but to depend on the Soviet Union alone for SAIL's new Bokaro Steel Plant (BSP) project, the Bhilai Steel Plant's 4 million tonnes expansion project, and Rashtriya Ispat Nigam Limited's (RINL) Vishakhapamam Steel Plant project, which were the major integrated plant projects during 1967–8 to 1991–2. This phenomenon obviously constrained the country's range of choice of technologies.

This period of slowdown in the expansion of steel capacity under the state initiative in the integrated steel plant route, however, saw the emergence of a secondary sector in the industry which produced steel out of steel scrap in electric arc furnaces due to a demand–supply gap. Many entrepreneurs also reoriented their induction furnaces (IF) to steel making by just melting steel scrap without any refining. India is possibly the only country in the world today using IF units on a large scale for producing steel.

The Third Phase of Development: Economic Reforms, Market Orientation, and Technical Change

There has been a significant structural break in the development of the Indian steel industry since the announcement of a series of economic reforms by the Government of India (GoI) in 1991–2. The new economic policy of the government and the policies attendant on it argued that the Indian state should, in principle, largely withdraw from direct investment in production. The production economy and the pattern of investment should hereafter be guided by domestic as well as the global market forces, in order to make the industries efficient as well as cost competitive. With reference to the steel industry, supply-side considerations induced the government to dismantle state control on the industry by delicensing private investment and decontrolling distribution and prices of steel.

Besides, the new government policy de-reserved the integrated steel-making sector from the public domain and decided that no new steel plant would be built at greenfield sites in the public sector. The government has also started privatizing public-sector steel companies by partly divesting their shares in the capital market. All these have basically opened up vast opportunities for the growth of the industry in the private sector. Foreign investment and foreign technologies have also been allowed to flow in at the same time.

Structure of the Indian Steel Industry and the Steel Market

The dynamics of change that followed economic reforms led to the emergence of the following structure in the steel industry:

1. Large integrated steel plants that combine primary steel-making and rolling of steel into semi-finished and/or finished products for sale. These plants produce steel out of iron which is extracted from the virgin iron ore with the help of coal, coke, limestone, and other fluxing materials. These plants mostly use blast furnace (BF) and basic oxygen furnace (BOF) technology.
2. Electric arc furnace (EAF) units using steel scrap and directly reduced iron (DRI) obtained by reducing iron ore with the help of non-coking coal or natural gas. Some of the plants combine DRI making from iron ore with EAF and also have rolling facilities. These medium-scale plants are often called midi plants. There were three major midi steel companies as in 2004–5—Essar Gujarat, Ispat Industries Limited, and Jindal Vijayanagar. Recently Essar Gujarat, Jindal Steel Limited at Bellary (JSW), and Jindal Steel and Power (JSPL) at Raigarh have set up blast finances and BOF furnaces as additional facilities warranting their reclassification into the integrated steel plant sector. However, Ispat Industries and more recent steel plants like Bhusan Steel Limited and Bhusan Power and Steel Limited have no blast furnaces and have only EAF as steel-making technology and describe medium-scale plants
3. Induction furnace (IF) units that are normally of a small size and primarily melt steel scrap, DRI, and pig iron in such proportions that no refining is needed to produce steel, which of course is not of high grade. Some of these have rolling mills for forward integration.
4. Stand-alone rolling mills which do not produce crude steel, but finished steel out of semi-finished steel like billets, blooms, or slabs produced by integrated steel plants, EAF units, or IF units, or imported from abroad, or ship-breaking scrap and other re-rollable scrap generated in the country.

The integrated steel plant sector presently thus consists of SAIL, into which the erstwhile IISCO, a subsidiary of SAIL, has been merged, RINL, TISCO, ESSAR Gujarat, Jindal Steel at Bellary, and Jindal Steel and Power at Raigarh. The segment of the industry comprising midi plants, EAF units, IF units, and stand-alone rolling mills is called the secondary sector and is entirely in the private sector with respect to the ownership of capital invested. The route-wise production of steel among the different segments in the last three years is shown in Table 2.

Table 2 Routes of Steel Production in India, 2006–7 to 2009–10

(million tonne)

Route*	2007–8	2008–9	2009–10
BF-BOF	22.4	22.8	29.2
EAF	20.8	25.7	15.6
IF	10.7	10.9	20.1
Total crude steel production	53.9	58.4	64.9
Total crude steel capacity	59.8	66.3	72.9
Capacity utilization (%)	90	88	89
Share of BF(%)	42	39	45
EAF(%)	39	44	24
IF(%)	19	17	31

Source: Joint Plant Committee (JPC).
Note: * Currently India has approximately 70 BFs, 40 mini blast furnaces, 350 EAFs, and 970 IFs of varying capacity.

The distribution of steel capacities as described in Table 2 implies that the secondary sector now has a 55 per cent share of the total production of crude steel in India. The share of the secondary sector in exports was 62.3 per cent in 2001–2. With reference to the pattern of ownership of capital assets, the private sector's share was around 58 per cent in crude steel-making capacity and 66 per cent in finished steel-making capacity around the beginning of the first decade of the 21st century. However, the share of crude steel-making in the private sector substantially increased to approximately 78 per cent approximately in 2009–10. The long-run growth of the industry would be driven more by private capital flows, both in the integrated and secondary sectors, with the secondary sector playing a major role on the supply side. However, given the uneven size distribution of the different plants or company units, the main producers, that is, the integrated steel plant sector, will continue to provide a leadership role in the market, particularly in the context of pricing.

In the initial phase of industrialization, the share of long or non-flat products was higher while the share of flat products went up with the attainment of higher levels of development. In India, the share of non-flat products is now approximately 53 per cent and that of flat products is 47 per cent. If we look at the shortfall in our domestic supply that is met by imports, we find it to be higher for flat products, at between 9 and 10 per cent of the total domestic consumption, a part of this belongs to special categories like plates of API grade for the oil and gas sector, CR coils for the auto sector, CRGO sheets for the power sector, and also HR coils which are imported on price consideration from the CIS countries and from China. Imports are negligible for non-flat products for which there exists substantive excess capacity in the industry.

Pricing of Steel and Globalization

The government's new economic policy since 1991 has liberalized the import of steel by abolishing the canalization of steel import and reducing tariff rates, and has encouraged domestic competition by delicensing steel capacity creation. Domestic steel prices in India are now very much linked to the price movement in the international market. The global business cycle in steel seriously affected the Indian steel industry in the late 1990s and early years of the first decade of the 21st century. It is only in recent years that the Indian steel industry has emerged from a period of long stagnation of demand and restricted supply. However, it would be inappropriate to say that the global trend in production and consumption as well as in prices has impacted the Indian steel industry uniformly during the post-reform period. For HR coils, adequate domestic capacities have been created with the setting up of capacities by Essar, JSW, JSPL, and Ispat, and subsequently by Bhusan Steel and with the modernization and expansion of the pre-existing flat capacities by all the private players, including Tata and the public-sector SAIL. Import requirements for HR coils have now substantially come down. However, hot rolled products at a cheap price are being imported from the CIS countries and China for price advantage. As a result, the fluctuations in the landed price of imports of flat products like HR coils and plates directly impact the domestic prices as import duties of 30–35 per cent effective earlier have now been brought down to 5 per cent in line with WTO commitments and all imports have been put under OGL. Although the import volume of non-flat categories of bars and rods, structurals, and rails would be negligible, India is a major importer of melting scrap, the basic input for semi-finished steel by the EAF/IF route. As a result, variations in the landed cost of scrap from the US and the Middle East, and those in the international prices of billet and slab directly influence the domestic prices of non-flat steel categories. It is seen that the fixing of domestic prices by major steel producers for both flat and non-flat categories broadly follows an import parity pricing principle.

However, the domestic market in Indian steel is not one of perfect competition because of the varying sizes of supplying companies. The six main producers with integrated plant technology, which have a 52 per cent share of the total actual supply of finished steel, occupy a position of price leadership in the market. The finished steel market in India has thus some dualistic features, with the main producers, on the one hand, setting prices and optimizing scale and product mix in the short run on oligopolistic principles, and the secondary producers, on the other, taking the open market prices as given and supplying steel on competitive principles. However, while open market prices can fluctuate from day to day and be influenced by the price leadership of the main producers, the pricing decisions of the main producers are in turn influenced by demand conditions, import prices, and open market price movements.

Export Orientation and International Competitiveness

The Indian steel industry ignored the export market for a long time because of the import-substitution orientation of India's industrialization. However, the situation started changing after the introduction of economic reforms in 1991 and India started exporting steel on a sustained basis; investments are being planned targeting the export market. The total steel export increased from a meagre 0.373 million tonnes in 1991 to 3.4 million tonnes in 2009–10, the latter figure representing only about 6 per cent of the total steel production in that year. Expansion of exports of a common variety of steel in the 1990s was possible for a host of reasons, including the devaluation of the rupee, full convertibility of the rupee on the trading account, and sluggish domestic demand coinciding with a boom in the world market, particularly an upsurge of demand in China and Southeast Asia. While the export market was very sluggish till 2001–2, following the economic crisis in East and Southeast Asia in the late 1990s, there was a subsequent upswing because of the spectacular growth in demand for steel in China and reduction in the flow of steel exports from the CIS countries due to the consolidation of their economies among other factors. This has enabled India to expand her steel exports. In the recent period the fall in international steel prices and recessionary conditions in major markets of Europe and the US following the widespread financial meltdown, coupled with the upward trend in the domestic demand for steel in the country primarily from the construction and the automobile sectors, have led the export volume from India to decline sharply. Indian steel firms have also been making substantive profits for the last two years, with SAIL reaching a record profit after tax (PAT) of Rs 67,54 billion in 2009–10. This happened at a time when steel prices were not quite high because of its movement along with the international prices. While all this implies the competitiveness of Indian steel in terms of the dollar cost of production, it does not necessarily reflect competitiveness in terms of technological efficiency or real factor productivity and quality (Sengupta 1994).

Further, the high ash content of Indian coal, high aluminia content of iron ore, and non-availability of good-quality fluxes (limestone and dolomite) offset part of the benefits of low factor prices. The productivity of labour is also substantially low for Indian steel plants, varying in the range of 300 to 400 tonnes of crude steel per man year for integrated plants as against 800 to 1,000 tonnes per man year for industrialized countries.

So far as technology and the capital productivity are concerned, a significant part of the Indian steel industry is relatively inefficient due to its outmoded technology. This is immediately apparent from the fact that the outmoded open hearth/twin hearth furnaces produced about 1 per cent of the total crude steel produced in the country in 2009–10 and the induction furnaces, which can do no refining, another 31 per cent of low grade crude steel. Most blast furnaces in India are old and small. The productivity of SAIL and RINL plants' best furnaces in terms of tonnes of hot metal (iron) output per m3 of working volume per day is around 1.75 and the same for TISCO's best furnace is around 2.2, while for any typical Japanese blast furnace it ranges between 2.5 and 3.3.

One of the major disadvantages that the Indian steel industry suffers from is the high overall energy cost of its steel-making technology. Energy constitutes about 33 per cent of the total cost of steel making in India while the comparable figure for most major steel-producing countries is around 20 per cent. The high energy cost is explained by the high energy usage per tonne of steel in India on account of obsolete technologies. However, the modernization of integrated steel plants since the 1980s has involved the replacement of the energy-inefficient open hearth process by the BOF process and the ingot casting by the continuous casting into slabs, blooms, or billets.

Future Prospect of the Indian Steel Industry

The current growth of India's GDP in the range of 8 to 8.5 per cent is likely to lead to the consumption of finished steel to around 66 million tonnes in 2011–12, that is, at the end of the Eleventh Five Year Plan. The National Steel Policy targets availability of domestic finished steel in India to 110 million tonnes in 1919–20 which would imply a growth in domestic demand in the range of 7.5 to 8 per cent per annum—with GDP—elasticity of finished steel being around unity. The strong pull of indigenous demand will come from the growth power, energy (oil and gas), ports, airports, roads, railways, urban development, automotive, and white goods sectors to make up the massive infrastructural deficit and to meet the growing demand for durable consumer goods with increase in incomes. While growth of activity in the infrastructural and construction sectors would induce growth in demand for reinforcement bars, structurals, plates, hot rolled coils, electrical sheets and pipes, growth in the automotive and white goods sectors would fuel growth of demand for cold rolled coils and galvanized and coated sheets and tin plates produced in the steel sector. However, there have been alternative estimates of steel consumption in 1919–20 on alternative assumptions. An econometric model-based estimate puts India's finished steel consumption in 2019–20 in the range of 166 to 171 million tonnes on the assumption of annual average growth rates of GDP, GFCF, and the Index of Industrial Production in the range of 8 to 9 per cent, 12 to 15 per cent, and 10 to 11 per cent, respectively, over the period 2010–11 to 2019–20 (Banerjee 2011). Indian steel exports are also projected to grow from 3.4 million tonnes in 2009–10 to a level in the range of 15 to 20 million tonnes by 2019–20. This would necessitate the production level of finished steel in the range of 125 to 130 million tonnes on the assumption of domestic consumption at the level as assumed in the National Steel Policy. In case Indian steel imports balance with Indian steel exports, the production level can be planned at the level of 110 million tonnes of finished steel production or 130 million tonnes of crude steel production. Otherwise, the country may need a capacity level of around 120 million tonnes of finished steel and 140 million tonnes of crude steel by 2019–20 to meet both domestic and export demands as per the assumptions of the National Steel Policy.

To meet such demand for steel, India's crude steel production capacity is projected to grow from 73 million tonnes in 2009–10 to 121 million tonnes in 2012–13 as per the initiatives on the supply side. Of this growth of 48 million tonnes of crude steel capacity, an addition of 12 million tonnes to capacity would take place in the form of greenfield new plants mostly of existing steel companies and the balance growth of 30 million tonnes capacity would take place through the expansion and modernization of existing plants. However, the existing major steel producing companies and global players, like ArcelorMittal POSCO (Pohang Steel Corporation) have announced their plans of capacity expansion to take advantage of the growing Indian steel market beyond the Eleventh Five Year Plan. While SAIL and RINL in the public sector will complete their expansion plans by 2012–13 reaching capacity levels of 21.4 million tonnes and 6.3 million tonnes of crude steel, respectively, major private producers like Tata Steel, Essar Steel, Jindal Steel and Power, and Ispat Industries have plans of reaching a total capacity of about 93.15 million tonnes with greenfield plant capacity expansion of 12.25 million tonnes. While the public-sector unit of NMDC has plans of setting up a capacity of 3 million tonnes of crude steel beyond 2012–13, Indian private steel companies and global players like ArcelorMittal and POSCO may together set up capacity at greenfield sites in the range of 100 to 120 million tonnes of crude steel in the time horizon up to 2019–20, with the shares of POSCO at 12 million tonnes, ArcelorMittal at 24 million tonnes, Tata at 20.5 million tonnes, Essar Steel at 18.2 million tonnes, Jindal Steel and Power at 15 million tonnes, and Ispat Industries at 11.6 million tonnes apart from several other small units. This would lead to the total installed capacity in the range of 210 to 230 million tonnes of crude steel and correspondingly finished steel availability in the range of 155 to 162 million tonnes in 2019–20 on the assumption that 70 per cent of the proposed greenfield new capacity addition will actually materialize, there will be 95 per cent of total capacity utilization, and 90 per cent yield from crude steel to finished steel. While such availability would be adequate for meeting demands as per the projections of the National Steel Policy, it would fall short of the alternative projected demand in the range of 166 to 171 million tonnes as per the econometric model developed in the industry source as referred to earlier (Banerjee 2011).

In order to achieve substantive addition to greenfield capacity, major constraints are being faced in land acquisition for plants and developing mines, coal and iron ore linkages, availability of water, and in obtaining environmental and forest clearances. It is now widely recognized that the acquisition of land for steel or other industrial development cannot be obtained by one time lumpsum payment at the market asset price of the land, but is to be acquired by an appropriate compensation for the loss of livelihoods of the owners of the land, most of whom are farmers and such compensation has to take care of such losses of all the persons displaced by the project. The compensation package, besides an initial payment needs to include a regular flow of income to make up for the loss of future earnings. This may be in the form of equity shares in the plant/mine unit, or regular employment for one member of each family, or an annuity payment of an assumed period, say, for 33 years. Payment of a certain share of profit from raw material mines may be spent on giving equities to displaced persons over a long time horizon. It is now being well-recognized that the engagement of the people displaced by construction and the local population has to form an essential component of the policy of land acquisition. Involving the local population as a major stakeholder is also required for the smooth functioning of a plant in both the construction and the development phase and this can be achieved by undertaking both welfare schemes on education, health, and housing and local infrastructural development as part of corporate social responsibility.

So far as the availability of financial resources for greenfield expansion of steel capacity is concerned, the high growth needs to be accompanied by a high savings rate and inflow of foreign savings, particularly through foreign direct investment which would not be difficult to attain. However, public–private partnership would be important for finance, technology, and management of the basic infrastructural development of water, power, highways, and other link roads and railway connections for the new plants.

In the recent period, increasing raw material prices, particularly of coal and iron ore are posing challenges of competitiveness for the new Indian steel capacity. This is likely to prompt investments and entrepreneurial initiatives in the exploration and development of new mines, and in owning new sources of such raw materials in India and abroad through joint ventures or equity participation. The major steel plants in India are now regularly hunting for joint venture opportunities in Australia, Indonesia, Mozambique, and South Africa.

The growth in demand for India's finished steel in the future is likely to be characterized by an increasing share of higher quality steel requiring access to special technologies of producing such high grades and quality. Such a need has prompted tie-ups or joint ventures with foreign companies which have developed and possess such technologies. Tata Steel's collaboration with Australia's Bluescope Steel Limited for producing coated steel through the formation of Tata-Blue Scope Steel Limited, Tata Steel with Nippon Steel for producing autograde high tensile strength steel, JFE Steel of Japan with JSW Steel of India for autograde steel, and that of SAIL with South Korea's POSCO for finex technology for making iron using coal fines without coking coal are some of the examples of collaborative or tie-up arrangements for technology transfer so that the growth of steel can be value adding as well as technologically and economically efficient.

The mega merger and acquisition events in the global steel industry, like the formation of ArcelorMittal, the merger of Corus Steel with Tata Steel, that of NKK with Kawasaki to form JFE of Japan, and a host of other such mergers leading to new formations in China (for example, Baosteel and Hebei) have also induced the Indian steel industry to look for partners abroad to reap the benefits of competitive supremacy, supply chain management, and raw material security. For example, Corus' superior R&D specializing in advanced steel products and heavy structurals, including parallel flange beams, have enhanced the value of Tata Steel's product-mix. Although the growth of the Indian steel industry is mainly driven by its buoyant demand in the home market, it has become outward looking on the supply side of technology and high-quality raw materials for supporting the growth. While the economic reforms process has now created the enabling environment for technology transfer, and restructuring and modernization of the Indian steel industry, the sustenance of its competitiveness in the long run would require continuous human resource development for the absorption of all new technologies so acquired through transfer as well as India's greater participation in R&D activities in steel (Banerjee 2010a, 2010b).

The first decade of the present century has been a watershed in the history of the Indian steel industry. The global recession and the severe financial crisis completed the process of shifting the fortunes of global steel from the advanced and developed markets of industrialized countries to East and South Asia. The shift has taken place not only in terms of relative growth of volume of steel but also in terms of value. This explains the interest of some of the major players in developing collaborations in the form of joint ventures or tie-ups. However, one should be cautious here and note that the big steel producers of the Organisation of Economic Co-operation and Development (OECD) countries have not as yet chosen to locate investments in general in the developing countries with a view to relocating their steel-making activities on a large scale. POSCO and ArcelorMittal are planning to produce steel for both India's domestic market as well as for exports. It should be noted that the advanced industrialized countries, in general, would not like to lose their market potential for the secondary export of steel to the developing countries in the form of engineering goods. India will, therefore, have to take dynamic initiatives in modernizing the industry and promoting R&D activities as well as develop human resources for achieving sustained competitiveness and for becoming an important player in the global steel market.

RAMPRASAD SENGUPTA*

References

Banerjee, Sushim. 2010a. 'Crossing the Bridge', mimeo, Kolkata, INSDAG.

———. 2010b. 'Consolidation: A Driving Force for Indian Steel', mimeo, Kolkata, INSDAG.

———. 2011. 'Demand Scenario and Domestic Crude Steel Availability', mimeo, paper for the conference of Indian Institute of Metals, 12–14 February 2011, New Delhi. Institute of Steel Development and Growth (INSDAG), Kolkata.

Sengupta, Ramprasad. 1994. 'The Indian Steel Industry: Investment Issues and Prospects, Part I: Market Demand and Cost Competitiveness', New Delhi, Investment Information and Credit Rating Agency of India Ltd.

———. 2004. 'The Steel Industry', in S. Gokarn, A. Sen, and R.R. Vaidya (eds), *The Structure of Indian Industry*, New Delhi, Oxford University Press.

Sinha, R.K. and S.C. Suri. 2003. *Indian Steel Perspectives 2005*, Delhi, Shipra Publications.

World Bank. 2010. *World Development Report 2010*, Washington DC, World Bank.

Stock Exchange

'...through the interplay of demand and supply of securities, a properly organized stock exchange assists in a reasonably correct evaluation of securities in terms of their real worth....through such evaluation of securities, the stock exchange helps in the orderly flow of distribution of savings as between different types of competitive instruments.'

—Shri Chintaman Dwarakanath Deshmukh
Hon'ble Minister of Finance, Government of India, 1950–6
(While introducing the Securities Contracts (Regulation) Bill, November 1955)

History of Stock Exchanges in India

The stock market in India has had a very fascinating and checkered history. Even in the 18th century, there was some trade in securities, when laissez faire was

*I am greatly indebted to Shri Sushim Banerjee of the Institute for Steel Development and Growth, Kolkata, for helping me with data and other information for updating the entry and for his comments and observations.

the dominant economic philosophy. A banyan tree in Bombay (now Mumbai) and a neem tree in Calcutta (now Kolkata) served as trading venues where the loan securities of the East India Company were traded towards the close of the 18th century and the shares of a few banks were traded during the early 19th century. However, the real beginning came in the 1850s with the emergence of joint stock companies with limited liability. With the Indian Companies Act being enacted in 1866 and the ensuing flow of British capital and enterprise into India, a number of tea and coffee plantations, jute mills, and mines had come up. These companies issued shares at huge premia and there were feverish dealings in securities and reckless speculation in the 1860s.

With the end of the American Civil War, the share mania suffered a setback, when people were left with a huge mass of unsaleable papers. The brokers suffered ignominy and were hounded out from place to place till about 300 of them organized an association on 9 July 1875 with its office on Dalal Street 'to support and protect the character and status of the brokers and to further the interest of both brokers and public in dealing in Bombay in stocks, shares and like securities and in exchange, to promote honourable practices, to discourage and suppress malpractices'. This laid the foundation of the oldest stock exchange in Asia (Tokyo Stock Exchange was founded in 1878.).

A number of textile mills came up in Ahmedabad in 1880s, which created a need for trading of shares of these mills. The brokers of Ahmedabad formed the Ahmedabad Share and Stock Brokers' Association in 1894. Eastern India witnessed a boom in the prices of jute, tea, and coal. As the boom ended, there were differences and disputes among brokers which paved the way for the establishment of the Calcutta Stock Exchange Association in 1908 with 150 brokers. The First World War and the *swadeshi* industrial revolution in the early 20th century prompted the establishment of the Madras Stock Exchange in 1920 with 100 brokers. Driven by market forces, several stock exchanges came up and disappeared in India in the 20th century.

Evolution of Securities Laws

The stock market crash of 1921 led to the formation of a committee under Sir Wilfred Atlay in 1923 to enquire into the working of the 'Native Share and Stock Brokers' Association'. The committee observed several deficiencies and the association agreed to rectify most of them. While action was under contemplation, another crash hit the market in 1925. The government offered to assume the rule-making power of the Association in lieu of its monopoly of organized trading in securities. As the association refused to accept this offer, the government had to enact the Securities Contracts (Control) Act, 1925, to regulate the working of the stock exchanges. Despite the Act, the market witnessed crises in 1928, 1930, 1933, 1935, and 1936. This led to another enquiry in 1937 by a committee under Mr Walter B. Morison. The Association implemented some of the recommendations of the committee through a new set of rules under the existing law. The major recommendations requiring legislative changes could not go through due to the outbreak of the War, when the stock markets were closed for weeks, forward trading was banned, and minimum prices were fixed for all shares.

To cope with such a situation, the Defence of India Rule 94C was promulgated on 24 September 1943 to prohibit all dealings other than ready delivery contracts; it also limited the period of such contracts to seven days. *Badla* transactions and options were banned. This drove trading out to venues outside the stock exchanges, leading to unbridled speculation. Share prices started booming in September 1945 and had reached serious proportions by the middle of 1946. With the lapse of Rule 94C with the end of the War, the government set up an enquiry committee under Mr P. J. Thomas to decide on the regulation of the stock market. The committee suggested a central legislation and a competent public authority to administer the legislation. The Capital Issues (Control) Act, 1947, came into being in 1947.

In the meantime, the Constitution of India had come into force in 1950 under which stock exchanges and future markets came under the exclusive authority of the central government. Following the recommendations of the A.D. Gorwalla Committee in 1951, the Securities Contracts (Regulation) Act, 1956 (SCRA), was enacted to provide for the direct and the indirect control of virtually all the aspects of securities trading and the running of stock exchanges and to prevent undesirable transactions, including options, in securities. Subsequently, there were some calibrated developments regarding the introduction of derivatives on stock exchanges.

Establishment of SEBI

The Securities and Exchange Board of India (SEBI) was initially constituted as a non-statutory body on 12 April 1988 through an Extraordinary Notification of the Government of India. In the aftermath of extensive liberalization in early 1990s, it was considered necessary to create a statutory agency, which would ensure fair play in the market, develop fair market practices, and prescribe and monitor conduct of issuers and intermediaries so that the securities market enabled efficient allocation of resources. Accordingly, the Securities and Exchange Board of India Act, 1992, was passed by the Parliament of India in April 1992. The Office of the Controller of Capital Issues was abolished. The statutory powers and functions of SEBI were strengthened through amendments at different points of time between 1995 and 2010. The preamble to the SEBI Act, 1992, states that SEBI has been established 'to protect the interests of investors in securities and to promote the development of, and to regulate, the securities market and for matters connected therewith or incidental thereto'.

Important Reforms since 1992

Screen-based Trading

Traditionally, trading on the stock exchanges in India took place in 'trading rings'. This was time-consuming and inefficient and imposed limits on trading volumes and efficiency. In the early 1990s, the exchanges ushered in an online fully-automated screen-based trading system (SBTS) which electronically matched orders on a strict price-time priority and cut down on time, cost, and risk of error, as well as on fraud, thereby, resulting in improved operational efficiency. It allowed faster incorporation of price sensitive information into prevailing prices, thus increasing the informational efficiency of the markets. It enabled market participants to see the full market on a real-time basis, making the market transparent. It allowed a large number of participants irrespective of their geographical locations, to trade with one another simultaneously, improving the depth and the liquidity of the market. It provided full anonymity by accepting orders, big or small, from members without revealing their identity, thus providing equal access to everybody. It provided a perfect audit trail, which helped resolve disputes by logging into the trade execution process in its entirety. At the end of 31 March 2011, the National Stock Exchange of India (NSEIL) and the Bombay Stock Exchange (BSE) Ltd. had 215,385 and 118,583 active trading terminals.

Dematerialization

The settlement of trades in the physical mode faced the problems of delays and bottlenecks due to expanding volumes, costs, risks of bad delivery, fraud/theft/forgery of certificates, objections due to signature differences, delay in receipt of share certificates on allotment, and so on, which came in the way of shorter settlement cycles or rolling settlement. The Depositories Act, 1996, was enacted in August 1996 and the National Securities Depository Limited (NSDL) started the process of dematerialization in the country in November 1996. Subsequently, the Central Depository Services Limited (CDSL) started operations in July 1999. The other facilitating measures that were adopted included exemption from payment of stamp duty to transfers of equity shares through electronic book-entry and abolition of market lots. As on 31 March 2011, there were 11.54 million active investor accounts with NSDL and 7.48 million active investor accounts with CDSL.

Rolling Settlement

Trade done on the stock exchanges in India accumulated over a trading cycle which varied from 14 days for specified securities to 30 days for others and settlement took another fortnight. Many things could happen between the execution of trade and its performance, providing for incentives for either of the parties to go back on its promise. This had on several occasions led to defaults and risks in settlement. In 1989, the Group of 30 had recommended that all secondary markets across the globe should adopt a rolling settlement cycle on T + 3 basis by 1992 to bring about efficiency in settlement and reduce settlement risks. In view of all these, SEBI first contracted the fortnightly carry forward system to a weekly carry forward system. The stock exchanges, however, continued to have different weekly trading cycles, which enabled shifting of positions from one stock exchange to another. Rolling settlement, which was introduced on a voluntary basis in the dematerialized segment of the stock exchanges in 1998, was made compulsory for all scrips by end-2001. The rolling settlement cycle was shortened to T + 3 with effect from 1 April 2002. With effect from 1 April 2003, SEBI introduced the T + 2 rolling settlement. With this, India joined a select league of six economies—Chile, Israel, Mexico, South Korea, Taiwan, and Turkey—which moved to a T + 2 rolling settlement.

Derivatives

To assist market participants to manage risks better through hedging, speculation, and arbitrage, SCRA was amended in 1995 to lift the ban on options trading. It was amended further in 1999 to expand the definition of securities to include derivatives so that the regulatory framework applicable to other securities could apply to derivatives as well. A three-decades-old ban on forward trading was withdrawn. SEBI granted approval to derivatives trading at NSEIL and BSE Ltd. on 25 May 2000. The Indian securities market witnessed a phased introduction of different equity derivatives with index futures being introduced in June 2000, index options in June 2001, individual stock options in July 2001, and individual stock futures in November 2001. The equity derivatives market has grown by leaps and bounds in India since then. During 2003–4, the turnover in the equity derivatives segment surpassed that in the equity cash segment. The equity derivatives segment clocked a turnover 2.02 times the cash market turnover during 2005–6, 3.20 times during 2009–10, and 6.25 times during 2010–11. Besides, a variety of non-equity derivatives, such as currency derivatives and interest rate derivatives, are now available on the stock exchanges.

Risk Management

To pre-empt market failure, stock exchanges developed a comprehensive risk management system encompassing capital adequacy norms of trading and clearing members, adequate margin requirements, limits on exposure and turnover, online position monitoring, and automatic disablement. They also administer an efficient market surveillance system to curb excessive volatility and to detect and prevent price manipulation. The fact that an anonymous electronic order-book does not allow members to assess the credit risk of the counterparty necessitated some innovation in this area. This brought in the concept of novation whereby a clearing corporation/house assumes counterparty risk of each member and guarantees financial settlement. The market has now full confidence that the settlement of trades would take place as scheduled, irrespective of any default by isolated members. The robustness of the risk management systems was tested during the global financial crisis of 2007–9 and the Indian stock exchanges have not experienced a settlement default for close to a decade now.

Corporatization and Demutualization

The joint committee of the Parliament of India constituted to look into the stock market scam (of early 2001) and matters relating thereto (Chairman: Lt General [Retd] Shri Prakash Mani Tripathi) noted that the stock brokers who held positions in the management of stock exchanges had acted in their own interests rather than in the interest of the stock exchange as a business entity and recommended demutualization and corporatization of the stock exchanges. SEBI set up a group on corporatization and demutualization of stock exchanges (Chairman: Justice M.H. Kania) in March 2002. At the end of March 2005, only 3 exchanges (Mumbai, Ahmedabad, and Madhya Pradesh) had been organized in the form of 'association of persons', while the remaining 20 were organized as companies—either limited by guarantee or by shares. Except one exchange (NSEIL), all exchanges, whether corporates or association of persons, were not-for-profit organizations. Of the 23 exchanges, two (NSEIL and the Over-the-Counter Exchange of India [OTCEI]) had adopted demutual structures from their inception. Hence, stock exchanges (except two stock exchanges—NSEIL and OTCEI—which were already demutualized) were mandated by the Securities Laws (Amendment) Act, 2004, to demutualize and corporatize by an appointed date. SEBI accordingly approved the corporatization and demutualization schemes of 19 exchanges in 2005.

Besides providing a trading platform, the stock exchanges provide the first line of supervision and oversight, have rule-making powers on matters like risk management, admitting companies for listing, compliance with the code of conduct by the members, and resolution of disputes between the brokers and their customers. As such, the governance and ownership structure of stock exchanges assumes wider significance. According to the Securities Contracts (Regulation) (Manner of Increasing and Maintaining Public Shareholding in Recognized Stock Exchanges) Regulations, 2006, no person shall directly or indirectly or together with persons acting in concert hold more than 5 per cent of the equity share capital of a stock exchange. However, a stock exchange, a depository, a clearing corporation, a banking company, an insurance company, and a public financial institution may hold, either directly or indirectly, either individually or together with persons acting in concert, up to 15 per cent of the paid up equity share capital of a stock exchange, with the prior approval of SEBI. Combined foreign investment up to 49 per cent is also permitted. In January 2010, SEBI constituted a committee to examine issues arising from the ownership and governance of market infrastructure institutions (Chairman: Dr Bimal Jalan) (see Table 1). The report of this committee is now subject to public debate and consultation.

The number of stock exchanges had shot up from 11 in 1990 to 23 by 2000. As on 31 March 2011, there were 19 stock exchanges (equity cash segment). With the coming of age of electronic trading with pan-India terminals and abolition of compulsory listing on regional stock exchanges, 17 stock exchanges in the equity cash segment have become inactive and 4 stock exchanges have not been granted renewal of recognition. There have been attempts to provide some kind of lifeline to inactive exchanges, but these have not proved effective. In order to provide an exit route, in December 2008, SEBI came out with guidelines with respect to exit option to regional stock exchanges whose recognition is withdrawn and/or renewal of recognition has been refused by SEBI and for regional stock exchanges who may want to surrender their recognition.

Market Outcome

As on 31 March 2011, BSE Ltd.'s market capitalization stood at $1,532 billion. The equity market capitalization ratio—defined as total BSE full market capitalization as on 31 March 2011 as a percentage of GDP at market prices

Table 1 Major Committees on Matters Related to Stock Exchanges and Main Outcomes

S. No.	Name of the committee	Chairman	Year	Main outcome
1.	Bombay Stock Exchange Enquiry Committee	Sir Wilfred Atlay	1923	Securities Contracts (Control) Act, 1925
2.	The Stock Exchange Enquiry Committee	Mr Walter B. Morison	1937	New set of Rules for the Native Share and Stock Brokers' Association
3.	Enquiry Committee on the Regulation of the Stock Market in India	Mr P. J. Thomas	1947	Capital Issues (Control) Act, 1947
4.	Committee on the Securities Contracts (Regulation) Bill	Shri A. D. Gorwalla	1951	Securities Contracts (Regulation) Act, 1956
5.	High-powered Committee on Stock Exchange Reforms	Shri G. S. Patel	1984	Strengthening the governance of stock exchanges
6.	High-powered Study Group on Establishment of New Stock Exchange	Shri N. J. Pherwani	1991	Creation of NSEIL
7.	Joint Committee to Enquire into Irregularities in Securities and Banking Transactions	Shri Ram Niwas Mirdha	1992	Regulations governing insider trading, inspection of stock exchanges, reforms to the functioning of stock exchanges
8.	Joint Committee on the Stock Market Scam and Matters Relating Thereto	Lt General (Retd) Prakash Mani Tripathi	2001	Amendment to SEBI Act, 1992
9.	Group on Corporatisation and Demutualisation of Stock Exchanges	Justice Shri M. H. Kania	2002	Demutualization of stock exchanges
10.	Committee on Ownership and Governance of Market Infrastructure Institutions	Dr Bimal Jalan	2010	Under consultation

at current prices for 2010–11—stood at 86.81 per cent, as against 30.40 per cent during 1992–93. During the last 20 years, blue chip indexes have grown at a CAGR of 15.10 per cent.

During 2010–11, the combined turnover of the cash segments of both NSEIL and BSE Ltd. amounted to $1,028 billion. The stock market turnover ratio stood at 68.47 per cent during 2010–11. The surge in liquidity has drastically reduced the market impact cost. Select indicators of the stock exchanges are presented in Table 2.

Access to stock markets has improved vastly. A host of domestic institutional investors, including scheduled commercial banks, mutual funds, pension funds, insurance companies, development financial institutions, and more than 1,700 foreign institutional investors invest in India through the stock exchanges. About 12 million people invest through the Indian stock exchanges from more than 1,500 towns. However, the participation of the household sector in the stock market is very low. Today, only a little more than 8 per cent of the domestic equity market capitalization is held by Indian households.

Some trends pointing to geographical and institutional concentration are evident. The top-5 cities accounted for 85 per cent of the stock market turnover (Mumbai's share: 59 per cent). The top-10 cities accounted for three-fourths of the resources mobilized by mutual funds (Mumbai's share: 41 per cent). In 2010, foreign institutional investors (FIIs) alone accounted for 13.95 per cent of the total turnover as against the combined share of domestic institutional investors (7.03 per cent). Likewise, FIIs, which held 14.54 per cent of the total domestic equity market capitalization, accounted for 56.93 per cent of the total institutional shareholding in listed Indian companies. Despite the government's permission, domestic provident funds do not invest in the Indian stock markets, whereas foreign pension funds/endowment funds are among the SEBI-registered FIIs. Small and medium enterprises (SMEs) still find it difficult to raise money from the securities market and a large majority of those which have done so in the past now enjoy very low liquidity.

Global Comparison

The Indian securities market has risen in prominence as a result of the two generations of reforms implemented under SEBI's aegis. India is ranked first in terms of the number of listed domestic companies. As at end-2010, India ranked as the 7th largest stock market in the world in terms of market capitalization. India now accounts for a larger share in the total world market capitalization

Table 2 Stock Exchanges in India—Select Indicators ($ billion)

At the end of financial year	Cash segments of stock exchanges: No. of brokers	No. of listed companies	Market capitalization	Market cap ratio (%)	Turnover	Turnover ratio (%)	Equity derivatives turnover	Currency derivatives turnover
2000–1	9,782	5,869	122.55	27.19	512.11	409.33	0.88	–
2001–2	9,687	5,782	125.46	26.86	172.05	134.03	21.77	–
2002–3	9,519	5,650	120.45	23.31	192.59	162.89	91.40	–
2003–4	9,368	5,528	276.49	43.61	348.66	133.38	466.38	–
2004–5	9,062	4,731	388.17	52.43	369.18	97.67	570.46	–
2005–6	9,269	4,781	677.55	81.54	538.84	78.94	1,089.65	–
2006–7	9,384	4,821	813.18	82.75	640.72	81.85	1,637.47	–
2007–8	8,517	4,887	1,284.99	103.84	1,274.79	99.84	3,313.23	–
2008–9	8,652	4,929	605.77	55.36	838.93	124.82	2,400.47	67.75
2009–10	8,804	4,975	1,366.04	98.95	1,163.48	89.48	3,725.26	786.08
2010–11	9,235	5,067	1,531.71	86.81	1,027.53	68.47	6,418.34	1,806.99

Source: SEBI.

and in the total market capitalization of all the emerging markets. India's global rank, share in the total world market capitalization (2.96 per cent), and the share in the total market capitalization of all the emerging markets (10.61 per cent) are at all-time highs.

During 2010, India improved its last year's world rank in terms of stock market turnover (Rank: 10). The ranking on all these parameters during 1993–2010 are given in Table 3.

Looking Ahead

Major reforms in the last one-and-a-half decade have led to stronger institutions, removal of arbitrariness, robust risk management and settlement systems, and clear dispute resolution mechanisms. However, there are still concerns by way of geographical and institutional concentration and less than optimal participation by retail individual investors (Table 4).

Table 3 Stock Exchanges in India—A Global Comparison

Parameter	India's rank: 2010	2009	2008	2007	2006	2005	2004	2003	2002	2001	2000	1999	1998	1997	1996	1995	1994	1993
Number of listed domestic companies	1	1	2	2	2	2	2	1	2	1	2	2	2	2	1	1	2	2
Total market capitalization	7	11	13	8	15	17	18	17	19	25	23	23	21	20	20	21	22	22
Average company size	55	55	68	55	67	69	70	74	79	85	80	81	77	78	69	70	60	59
Total turnover	10	11	13	15	18	18	18	16	17	15	14	17	19	21	18	31	23	24
Turnover ratio	22	12	26	31	21	20	15	6	7	6	4	17	27	39	11	60	40	35
Share in world market capitalization (%)	2.96	2.49	1.85	2.82	1.53	1.28	1.02	0.87	0.56	0.40	0.46	0.51	0.39	0.56	0.61	0.72	0.84	0.70
Share in world stock market turnover (%)	1.65	1.34	1.30	1.12	0.95	0.92	0.96	0.95	0.52	0.59	1.07	0.92	0.67	0.84	0.71	0.21	0.31	0.30

Source: Standard & Poor's.

Table 4 Stock Exchanges in India: Some Lopsided Patterns

Narrowness		
• > 8,000 scrips, but only about 3,000 actively traded		
• Top 10 securities account for 23% the stock market turnover; top-50 for 54%		
Geographical concentration		
• Mumbai accounts for 59% of the stock market turnover; top-5 cities: 85%		
• Mumbai accounts for 41% of the equity AUM of mutual funds; top-10 cities: 75%		
Investor-oriented market versus trading-oriented market		
• Cash: Derivatives	1: 6.25	
• Delivery: Non-delivery	1: 2.33	
Institutional concentration		
• Share of the leading stock exchange		
	Equity Cash Segment	– 76%
•	Equity Derivatives Segment	– 100%

The future agenda for the government and for SEBI, therefore, will include avoiding conflicts of interests between trading and management rights of brokers, achieving wider retail participation, strengthening and continuously upgrading risk management systems, effective supervision and enforcement action, programme for investor education and financial literacy, and effective grievances redressal and dispute resolution mechanisms. The Indian stock exchanges also need to carefully analyse the developments that are taking place across the globe, like the globalization and consolidation of stock exchanges, competition in trading services emanating from electronic communication networks and alternative trading systems, and the evolving revenue model for stock exchanges.

U.K. Sinha

References

Annual Reports of SEBI. Various Years.

Emerging Stock Markets Factbook, International Finance Corporation & Global Stock Markets Factbook. Various Years.

Final Report of the High Powered Committee on Stock Exchange Reforms (Chairman: Shri G.S. Patel). 1985.

Handbook of Statistics on the Indian Securities Market, SEBI. 2010.

High-powered Study Group on Establishment of New Stock Exchanges (Chairman: Shri M.J. Pherwani). 1991.

Report of the Enquiry Committee on the Regulation of the Stock Market in India (Chairman: Mr P.J. Thomas). 1948.

Report of the Joint Committee to Enquire into Irregularities in Securities and Banking Transactions (Chairman: Shri Ram Niwas Mirdha) (10th Lok Sabha). 1993.

Report of the Joint Committee on Stock Market Scam and Matters Relating Thereto (Chairman: Shri Prakash Mani Tripathi) (13th Lok Sabha). 2002.

Stock Market Indexes

Stock market indexes traditionally served as a benchmark to measure the performance of equity portfolios. In recent decades, they have additionally come to prominence through their direct role in financial products, including index funds and index derivatives. In India, in the last decade, there has been considerable new work leading to improved stock market indexes.

The oldest and most prominent index in India is the Bombay Stock Exchange (BSE) Sensitive Index, known as the BSE Sensex. The BSE Sensex was created in 1986. The set of companies that formed the index was chosen by a committee. It was a market-capitalization weighted index of 30 listed firms. Daily data are available from April 1979 onwards, where the returns prior to 1986 were back calculated keeping the set of companies fixed for the seven-year period from 1979 to 1986. The committee was likely to have chosen firms which did well in the 1979–86 period. This probably generated an upward bias in the apparent returns on the BSE Sensex.

The index set that was selected in 1986 was held fixed till 1996. This is likely to have generated a downward bias in index returns during the 1986–96 period. In a substantial reshuffle of the index components in 1996, as many as 13 of the 30 stocks were changed on one day. After 1996, the index set has been monitored and maintained on a regular basis. As of 31 March 2005, the index set covered 43 per cent of the market capitalization of active Indian equity.

In 2002, the BSE Sensex shifted from market capitalization weights to 'floating stock weights'. Here, the weightage of a company in the index is proportional to a subjective judgement about the shares held by investors who might possibly sell them.

The events of 1986, 1996, and 2002 imply that while the BSE Sensex has a long time series going back to April 1979, it suffers from inconsistencies in methodology. An additional difficulty when using the Sensex is that a 'total returns index', which incorporates capital gains and dividends, is not available.

The most important alternative to the BSE Sensex is an index published by the National Stock Exchange (NSE). Since 1995, the NSE has been India's biggest stock market. In 1996, a new index named the NSE-50 or 'Nifty' was released (Shah and Thomas 1998). This was calculated as a market-capitalization weighted portfolio containing 50 stocks. By virtue of using fifty stocks instead of 30, this index covered 56 per cent of the market capitalization of active Indian equity as of 31 March 2005. The full name of the index is now 'S&P CNX Nifty', reflecting the involvement of Standard & Poors from 1999 onwards. While the BSE Sensex is calculated using prices from the BSE, the NSE-50 is calculated using prices from the NSE.

The 50 firms that go into the NSE-50 index are chosen using a methodology that focuses on liquidity. The stocks are required to deliver low transactions costs while doing portfolio (or 'basket') trades to buy or sell the index portfolio. Basket trades of Rs 5 million at a time are simulated for these computations. Basket trades are simulated using four snapshots of the limit order book every day on the NSE. Firms with a higher market capitalization naturally have bigger transaction sizes in these simulated baskets. The simulations use exact data from the NSE, and thus accurately measure the transactions costs associated with doing basket trades. This mechanism ensures that the index series is not contaminated by illiquid stocks, and that index returns are genuinely attainable to an investor who would have to implement such basket trades on the market.

The time series for the NSE-50 from March 1996 onwards consistently uses these rules and is hence an internally consistent time series. The time series was pushed back to July 1990, where high trading frequency was used as a proxy for low transactions costs. Through this imputation strategy, a time series of the NSE-50 index is available from July 1990 onwards.

Another useful index which uses the same methodology is 'Nifty Junior'. This contains the set of fifty stocks that satisfy the liquidity criteria, but are not big enough to qualify for inclusion into the NSE-50 index. The sets of stocks in Nifty and Nifty Junior are guaranteed to always be disjoint sets. It is hence easy to compute a composite index of the 100 most liquid firms of India, as a weighted average of the two returns, with weights proportional to the market capitalization.

The two major financial-sector applications of market indexes are in index funds and index derivatives. Derivatives based on the NSE-50 trade at the NSE in India and at the Singapore Exchange Limited (SGX) in Singapore. In India, over 99 per cent of the index derivatives trading volume in 2005 was based on the NSE-50 index. The NSE-50 is the largest single underlying on exchange-traded derivatives in India. The BSE Sensex has been more successful in the index fund market, where it had 7 per cent market share as of July 2005.

A comprehensive set of stock market indexes, spanning different sectors as well as the entire economy, comes from the Centre for Monitoring Indian Economy (CMIE). The CMIE indexes are calculated using a consistent methodology from 1990 onwards. The largest of the index portfolios calculated at the CMIE (called COSPI) recomputes a set of eligible stocks every day, containing all firms with a historical trading frequency of above 75 per cent. The number of firms in the COSPI index fluctuates over time, reflecting the contours of the economy. As of March 2005, COSPI consisted of 2,500 stocks, which had a market capitalization of Rs 16.8 trillion, which constitutes the universe of 'actively traded equity' in India. This captures a substantial fraction of the total market capitalization of India which stands at Rs 20.6 trillion.

The CMIE releases COSPI and a detailed breakdown of 254 industry indexes organized in a tree structure. The CMIE also releases the daily time series of the number of stocks in COSPI, the market capitalization of COSPI, and the P/E of the index. The strengths of COSPI are that a single consistent methodology is in place from 1990 onwards, a large universe of stocks is captured, and a detailed range of industry indexes are available. The weakness of the COSPI family is that these index sets are relatively illiquid, which introduces noise in the index time series and impedes the direct utilization of the indexes in financial products such as index funds and index derivatives.

Susan Thomas and Ajay Shah

References

Shah, Ajay and Susan Thomas. 1998. 'Market Microstructure Considerations in Index Construction', in *CBOT Research Symposium Proceedings*, Chicago Board of Trade, pp. 173–93.

■ Street Vendors

Street vendors form a very important component of the urban informal sector in India. It is estimated that that there were around 10 million street vendors in the country comprising around 2 per cent of the total population in metropolitan cities (GoI 2004, 2006). Mumbai and Delhi have around 250,000 street vendors each, Kolkata has around 150,000, and Ahmedabad and Patna have 80,000 each. A street vendor is broadly defined as a person who offers goods for sale to the public at large without having a permanent built-up structure from which to sell. Street vendors may be stationary in the sense that they occupy space on pavements, or other public/private spaces, or they may be mobile in the sense that move from place to place carrying their wares on push carts or in baskets on their heads. The terms 'street vendor' and 'hawker' have the same meaning and they are often interchanged. In this entry we deal with specific problems of street vendors.

For the urban poor, street vending is a means of earning a livelihood, as it requires minor financial input and low skills though the income too is low. A large section of street vendors in urban areas are low-skilled migrants who came to the larger cities in search of employment.

There is another section of the urban population that has taken to street vending—those who were once engaged in the formal sector (see Breman 2001; Bhowmik 2000; Bhowmik and More 2001). These people, or their spouses, were once engaged in better-paid jobs in textile mills in Mumbai and Ahmedabad and engineering firms in Kolkata. Formal-sector workers in these three metropolises had to face large-scale unemployment due to closure of these industries. Many of them became street vendors in order to eke out a living. A study on street vendors conducted in these cities shows that around 30 per cent of the street vendors in Ahmedabad and Mumbai and 50 per cent in Kolkata were once engaged in the formal sector (Bhowmik 2000). A study conducted by SEWA in Ahmedabad shows that around half the retrenched textile workers are now street vendors.

The total employment provided through street vending becomes larger if we consider the fact that street vendors sustain certain industries by providing markets for their products. A lot of the goods sold by street vendors, such as clothes and hosiery, leather and moulded plastic goods, and household goods, are manufactured by MSM industries. These industries employ a large number of workers and they rely mainly on street vendors to market their products. In this way street vendors help sustain employment in these industries.

Street vendors are mainly those who are unsuccessful or unable to get regular jobs. This section of the urban poor tries to solve its problems through its own meagre resources. Unlike other sections of the urban population street vendors do not demand that the government create jobs for them, nor do they engage in begging, stealing, or extortion. They try to live their lives with dignity and self-respect through hard work. A study on street vendors in seven cities (Bhowmik 2000) shows that their average earnings range between Rs 40 and Rs 80 per day. Women vendors earn even less. These people work for over 10 hours a day under gruelling conditions on the street and are under constant threat of eviction. A study of street vendors in Mumbai conducted by SNDT Women's University and the International Labour Organization shows that an overwhelming majority of them (85 per cent) suffered from ailments related to stress—hyperacidity, migraine, hypertension, loss of sleep, and so on. A study by Bhowmik (2011) on street vending in 10 cities shows that incomes of street vendors have increased as compared to 2000. In 2010, when the study was conducted, street vendors in the metros earned an average of Rs 175 a day. In smaller towns like Indore, Ahmedabad, and Imphal, the average earnings were Rs 150 a day. This may look like a high increase in earnings but the notified minimum wage at that time was Rs 217 a day. It was found that Bhubaneswar (Orissa) was the only city where there was legal recognition of street vending. The incomes of street vendors in Bhubaneswar were higher than in the metros.

The poorer sections too are able to procure their basic necessities through street vendors, as the goods that they sell are cheap. The study on street vendors in seven cities mentioned earlier (Bhowmik 2000) shows that the lower-income groups spend a higher proportion of their income in making purchases from street vendors mainly because their goods are cheap and thus affordable. Had there been no street vendors in cities the plight of the urban poor would be worse than what it is. In this way, one section of the urban poor, namely, street vendors, helps another section to survive. Hence, though street vendors are viewed as a problem for urban governance, they are in fact a solution for some of the problems of the urban poor. By providing cheaper commodities, street vendors are in effect providing subsidy to the urban poor, something that the government should do.

Street food vendors are often regarded as carriers of diseases because of their lack of hygiene. This may not always be true. In fact this section of hawkers could play a vital role in the food distribution system. The Food and Agricultural Organisation (FAO) has undertaken a number of researches in different Asian cities to assess the utility of food vendors in providing cheap and nutritious food to the common people (see FAO 1999). FAO feels that if food vendors are provided training in hygiene and nutrition and are provided basic necessities like drinking water they could play an important role in supplying the basic dietary requirements of the urban poor.

Besides FAO's interest in street vendors, the corporate sector too has used street vendors to promote its sales. Sucheta Dalal (2002) in her column on investment on rediffmail.com has shown how large corporations producing food rely on street vendors to advertise and market their products. Roadside tea-sellers advertise tea sold by the corporates and sandwich sellers advertise bread. Ice creams manufactured by business houses are marketed (and advertised) by roadside ice-cream sellers. Bottled mineral water is also marketed by street vendors at traffic signals. Apart from selling the products, street vendors are given t-shirts and umbrellas that advertise the company.

Despite their growing numbers and their positive contributions to the urban economy, street vendors are regarded as illegal traders and encroachers. The illegal status of street vendors makes them vulnerable to rent seeking by the authorities (police and municipality). These officials extract money from them under threat of eviction. It is estimated that in Mumbai around Rs 400 crore is collected as bribes annually from street vendors (Bhowmik 2000). In Delhi, a study by Manushi (2001) shows that the police and municipality collect Rs 50 crore every month from street vendors.

The condition of street vendors in most cities in Asia, Africa, and Latin America are similar (Bhowmik 2010). There are some exceptions, such as Thailand, Columbia, Venezuela, Malaysia, and the Philippines where the governments and municipal authorities are tolerant of street vendors. Malaysia and the Philippines have national policies on street vending that are implemented.

In India, the issue of legalizing and regulating street vendors has been taken up by the National Policy for Street Vendors adopted by the government in January 2004 and in its revised version in 2006. It is believed that street vending can be regulated only if it is legalized. The policy lays down that ward committees, comprising all stakeholders, should be formed in each municipal ward which will designate and regulate hawking areas. The vendors will be issued identity cards and will have to pay a fee. The policy also provides for social security schemes for street vendors and their families. The National Commission on Enterprises in the Unorganized Sector was asked to review the national policy; it has some minor changes in the original policy (GoI 2006).

The opposition to legalizing street vendors comes from several quarters. There are the so-called 'citizens' groups who view them as encroachers on public space and departmental stores and shopping malls regard them as competition and want them removed. Municipal and police officials find it profitable to keep them as illegal entities so that they can extract rents from them. However, despite the opposition, which at times is very stiff, street vendors continue to exist mainly because they provide services to common citizens. The government's attempts to legalize street vending by passing a Bill has been pending since 2006. The government drafted a model Bill in 2009 but no serious attempts have been made to make it an Act.

SHARIT K. BHOWMIK

References

Bhowmik, Sharit K. 2000. *Hawkers in the Urban Informal Sector: A Study of Street Vending in Six Cities*, mimeo, Delhi, National Alliance of Street Vendors of India.

——. (ed.) 2010. *Street Vendors in the Global Urban Economy*, Delhi and London, Routledge.

——. 2011. 'Study of Street Vendors in Ten Cities', mimeo, Delhi, National Alliance of Street Vendors of India.

Bhowmik, Sharit K. and Nitin More. 2001. 'Coping with Urban Poverty: Ex-textile Mill Workers in Mumbai', *Economic and Political Weekly*, 36(52): 4822–7.

Breman, Jan. 2001. 'An Informalised Labour System: End of Labour Market Dualism', *Economic and Political Weekly*, 36(52): 4804–21.

Dalal, Sucheta. 2002. 'Hawkers: Need to Get Corporates into the Loop,' Rediffmail.com, 22 January.

FAO. 1999. 'Regional Seminar on Street Food Development', Bangkok, 29 September–1 October.

Government of India (GoI). 2004. *National Policy for Urban Street Vendors*, New Delhi, Ministry of Urban Employment and Poverty Alleviation.

——. 2006. *National Policy on Urban Street Vendors*, National Commission on Enterprises in the Unorganized Sector.

Manushi Nagarik Adhikar Manch (tr. Manushi Citizens' Rights Forum). 2001. 'Memorandum Submitted to the Lt. Governor of Delhi on Behalf of Delhi's Street Vendors and Rickshaw Pullers and Owners on 2 October 2001'.

■ Sustainable Development

The concept of sustainable development was popularized by the Report of the Brundtland Commission, *Our Common Future* (1987), and the global conferences organized by the United Nations at Rio (1992) and Johannesburg (2002). The concept provides a bridge between an ecologist's view of natural systems as integrated wholes, of an engineer's willingness to intervene in these systems to meet human needs, and an economist's concerns about balancing costs and benefits and choosing optimally between alternatives. Add to this a concern for equity within and between generations and what we have is sustainable development.

The need for this bridge arose because nature has to be treated not just as an input but also as an object of value in its own right. There are also concerns about risks because the scale and depth of human interventions in nature have increased greatly after the industrial revolution. Between one-third and one-half of the earth's land surface has been transformed by human action and humanity puts to use more than half of all accessible surface freshwater. Human activity is leading to loss of species, changes in the chemistry of the atmosphere, and other irreversible changes in natural systems. The depth of intervention increased with the introduction of genetically modified organisms and other exotic substances into the atmosphere.

The Report of the Brundtland Commission (1987: 42) describes sustainable development as a goal when it posits the aim of policy as 'meeting the needs of the present without compromising the ability of future generations to meet their needs.' But it also describes it as a process when it states that (1987: 46): 'Sustainable development is a process of change in which the exploitation of resources, the direction of investments, the orientation of technological development and institutional change are all in harmony and enhance both current and future potential to meet human needs and aspirations.'

Development policy can be viewed as being derived from some process of optimal choice amongst policy options. The qualification 'sustainable' can be viewed as a constraint on this process specifying that the choices made should conserve some quantity, say, the natural resource base, or the quality of the environment, or the discounted value of consumption. However, 'sustainability' could also be viewed as a quality of the choices that emerge from an optimization exercise when it stretches over many generations and a long period of time and which treat current and future needs in an integrated framework. Depending, of course, on the weights attached to current and future needs, such a multigenerational optimum meets current needs and conserves the capacity to meet needs in the future.

The sustainable development path that emerges from such an optimization exercise cannot conserve the quantity of every exhaustible or renewable natural resource. Every act of production or consumption necessarily uses up some natural resource and, as the second law of thermodynamics tells us, generates some waste. What 'sustainability' requires is that the generation, which thus depletes natural capital, compensates future generations by investing in activities that maintain the options required in the optimum path for meeting future needs. In this view it is not wrong to use up resources. But it is wrong to consume away the rent.

Environmental resources like biodiversity or the delicately balanced chemistry of the atmosphere are resources, which are critical to the maintenance of life on earth. In such cases the objective of sustainability would require conservation in a stricter sense since compensation to preserve options may not be possible.

A description of sustainable development in terms of the 'thought-experiment' of optimization suggests an organized determination of interdependent choices of production and consumption. By implication it also presumes an ethically acceptable distribution of consumption within and between generations. But in practice these choices are made separately by millions of producers and consumers and, in the world of today, in a framework of relatively unconstrained markets. The departure of market outcomes from what the optimum path requires is the central problem of public policy at the local, national, and global level. Hence, sustainable development has to be thought of not just as a characterization of an optimum path but also as a framework of norms or rules to guide atomistic decisions towards the optimum.

This more practical approach is reflected in the extensive work that has been done by economists on the valuation of environmental amenities, including the work on adjusting national accounts to reflect gains and losses in these amenities, social cost–benefit analysis of investment projects, and the analysis of economic instruments like pollution charges and emissions trading for controlling pollution. In a poor country like India, with a large agrarian population, the more practical dimensions of sustainable development have to focus much more on the nexus between poverty, ill health, population growth, and the deterioration of land, water, and biotic resources at the local level.

The actual practice of development policy is seldom as coherent as theory would require. Hence, a looser use of the term 'sustainable development' would simply require that policy planners and analysts are more mindful of the link between natural resources, production possibilities, and distributive justice. Thus, if a forest is to be protected or conserved, the most useful points of intervention may be in energy policy or agricultural policy. Equally the goal of raising rural incomes may require more systematic attention to the protection of the resource base on which production and well-being depend. How well has this nexus been reflected in Indian economic policy?

Planning in India was conceived as a way of using its natural endowment of land, water, and mineral resources more intensively and this approach dominated the first three plans. The primary focus remained, in the words of the Third Plan (1961–6), 'the maximum increase in production physically possible' (Third Five Year Plan

1961: chapter 2, para 6). But even at this early stage the natural environment appeared in two ways. First, the planners recognized the need to focus on conservation as a goal for soil and forests. Second, public works were always an important component of scarcity relief and the planners did try and direct these relief works to soil conservation, contour bunding, and other local conservation activities. By the Third Plan the problem of uneven regional development had been recognized, but the link with ecological disadvantages or neglect had not been fully realized.

The Fourth Plan (1969–74) marked a more substantial change, perhaps because of the influence of Mrs Indira Gandhi who was the Prime Minister then. The chapter dealing with long-term perspectives has a separate section on environmental quality and comes close to articulating sustainable development as a goal when it speaks about the 'obligation of each generation to maintain the productive capacity of land, air, water and wild life' (Fourth Five Year Plan 1969: chapter 2, para 46). Apart from setting up the institutional arrangements for environmental policy, the Plan also launched a social cost benefit analysis as a tool for project selection. It is worth noting that much of this took place several years before the Stockholm Conference on the Human Environment (1972) which Mrs Indira Gandhi attended and where she made her famous speech about poverty being the worst form of pollution.

The Fifth Plan (1974–9), dominated by the energy crisis of 1973–4, discussed the depletion of non-renewable resources explicitly and spoke about optimum depletion rates, recycling, and imports as an option for conservation. But it was the Sixth Plan (1980–5) which saw the full flowering of sustainable development in the rhetoric of the Plan. The statement of objectives included, for the first time, a clear reference to the environment when it stated that one of the objectives was: 'bringing about harmony between the short and the long term goals of development by protection and improvement of ecological and environmental assets' (Sixth Five Year Plan 1980: chapter 3, para 9). The Plan contained a separate chapter on environmental programmes which stated quite explicitly that: 'a concern for environment is essentially a desire to see that national development proceeds along rational sustainable lines' (Sixth Five Year Plan 1980: chapter 20, para 1). Note that Indian planners spoke about sustainable development before it was popularized globally by the Brundtland Commission.

The rhetoric of sustainable development continued but three decades after environment found a place in Indian planning, the Tenth Plan (2002–7) came to the sad conclusion that: 'Ecological issues, unfortunately, have not been adequately incorporated into our development strategy, despite the fact that there has long been recognition of the importance of environmental and ecological factors in Indian planning and policy' (Tenth Five Year Plan 2002: chapter 1, para 13).

The acceleration of growth in the first decade of the new millennium sharpened the conflict between economic growth and environmental protection, particularly where the exploitation of natural resources required access to forests and protected areas. The response in terms of 'no-go' and 'go' areas emphasized the difference between growth and environmental compulsuons whereas a sustainable development approach that systematically looks at the ecosystem services that are provided and balances them against the returns from resource exploitation may provide answers that address both growth and environmental concerns.

The greatest challenge of sustainable development in India in the near future lies in the rural economy. Public spending programmes for agriculture and rural development must be organized around agro-climatic regions, an approach that started in the 1980s but floundered thereafter. Irrigation planning must move away from civil engineering projects to becoming an element in integrated land and water management. Technological interventions must work *with* the climate and topography of each area and focus on providing sustainable livelihood for all. Employment guarantee and anti-poverty programmes must be folded into this. Such a transformation of public intervention will combine the compulsions of decentralization, employment generation, and environmental protection.

However, in the medium term, with urbanization and intensifying energy use, sustainability will need to be factored into the policies that govern all sectors. In a market economy the most important challenge is getting the prices right so that they reflect full social costs from the beginning to the end of the production and consumption process, including, most particularly, the costs of waste disposal. Getting prices right must include measures that shift the burden of environmental management on to the account books of the entities that are responsible for the problem and have the capacity to pay. This is a formidable challenge in a situation where water, power, and waste management services are heavily subsidized and where land and water markets are severely distorted and often inequitable.

As energy and material use intensify and as development brings into play new technologies, environmental risks will multiply. This will require stronger arrangements for technology assessment, for example, for the testing and approval of new seeds, chemicals, and pharmaceuticals, and in the examination and approval of safety provisions. Codified standards and prior approval and consent can take care of many risks. But there will always be some residual risks involved. And this is where liability and compensation come in. In fact, Indian law courts have perhaps done more to ensure greater attention, at least to safety and environmental management, than the standards set by statutes.

Looking beyond these national concerns, countries like India will also have to take into account the consequences of global environmental changes, most notably in climate, and expect to contribute to sustainability at the global level. The acceleration of growth makes this an urgent concern. This is reflected in the gradual shift of policy away from the view that developed countries are responsible for the accumulation of greenhouse gases in the atmosphere and they should take the steps required for their mitigation. There is now an acceptance that India cannot repeat the energy growth path of the developed world and has to look for low-carbon development options. There is also the recognition that some degree of climate change is inevitable and as a seriously affected country sustainable development requires more attention to adaptation strategies.

The gradual recognition of environmental and social compulsions as constraints on the pursuit of growth is a useful but incomplete approach. Sustainable development needs more than this. It calls for the integration of economic, environmental, and social objectives in a unified policy frame that addresses all three issues simultaneously and on an equal footing. Indian economic thinking and public policy still have a long way to go to reach this goal.

NITIN DESAI

References

Arrow, Kenneth J. and Anthony C. Fisher. 1974. 'Environmental Preservation, Uncertainty and Irreversibility', *The Quarterly Journal of Economics*, 88(2): 312–19.

Dasgupta, Partha. 2001. *Human Well-being and the Natural Environment*, Oxford, Oxford University Press

Dasgupta Partha, Simon Levin, and Jane Lubchenco. 2000. 'Economic Pathways to Ecological Sustainability: Challenges for the New Millennium, *BioScience*, 50(4): 339–45.

Planning Commission. 1961, 1969, 1981, and 2002. *Third Five Year Plan, Fourth Five Year Plan, Sixth Five Year Plan*, and *Tenth Five Year Plan*, New Delhi, Planning Commission, Government of India.

———. 2011. 'Low Carbon Strategies for Inclusive Growth: An Interim Report', New Delhi, Planning Commission, Government of India.

Solow, Robert. 1982. *An Almost Practical Step towards Sustainability*, New York, Resources for the Future.

Vitousek, Peter M., Harold A. Mooney, Jane Lubchenco, and Jerry M. Melillo. 1997. 'Human Domination of Earth's Ecosystems', *Science*, 277: 494–9.

World Commission on Environment and Development. 1987. *Our Common Future,* Oxford, Oxford University Press.

T

■ Tariffs

External-sector policies in India can been broadly classified into three phases: 1950 to 1975 was the period of tightening controls; 1976 to 1991 a phase of slow but limited liberalization; and 1992 onwards when systematic liberalization was undertaken. The reduction in tariffs, along with the removal of quantitative restrictions in April 2002, has resulted in significant import liberalization in India. The discussion here is organized around the four themes of rates, structure, exemptions, and issues for reform.

Rates

Customs rates in India, which were amongst the highest in the world in 1991, are still high by world standards. This is conveyed by the evolution of the 'peak rate' over the last 15 years. The 'peak rate', which applies for almost all manufactured goods, has dropped from 150 per cent in 1991 to 15 per cent in 2005. This was one of the most significant elements of economic reform in the recent period, one that has transformed the dynamics of domestic industry.

However, we have to be careful in the interpretation of the term 'peak rate', since in India, it is perhaps a 'median rate' and not the peak rate that is applicable for manufactured goods. Numerous tariffs for manufactured goods continue to be well above the 'peak rate' of 15 per cent.

One easily accessed measure of the extent of tariffs is tariff collections divided by imports. This was 11 per cent in 2004–5. However, we have to be careful in the interpretation of customs tax collections, since they reflect the summation of customs duty and the value-added tax (VAT) on imports. In India, the term 'countervailing duty (CVD)' is used for VAT on imports. In 2005–6, 43.4 per cent of the apparent customs collections is to be on account of VAT on imports.

Structure of Tariffs

The structure of tariffs is biased towards providing higher protection to finished goods. As a consequence, the duties on raw materials, intermediate inputs, and capital goods are generally lower than those on finished products. As is well known, modest differences in apparent tariffs can imply very big differences in the effective rates of protection. This results in immense lobbying by firms, and a complex structure of tariffs. The government uses highly detailed control of the tariff structure to promote one or the other industry. While 'industrial policy', defined as the process of government choosing certain industries and promoting them, has faded away in the Indian context in many aspects, tariff setting continues to be an area where it has a place. For example, in his Budget Speech, 2005, the Finance Minister said:

> For most textile machinery, I propose to reduce the duty from 20 per cent to 10 per cent, in order to help the textile industry acquire a competitive edge in the post-quota regime. Similarly, to encourage the food processing industry, I propose to reduce the duty on refrigerated vans from 20 per cent to 10 per cent. To give a leg-up to the leather and footwear industry, I propose to

reduce the customs duties on seven specified machinery from 20 per cent to 5 per cent. The duty on ethyl vinyl acetate (EVA), an input for the footwear industry, is also proposed to be reduced from 20 per cent to 10 per cent.

The full text of the Budget Speech contains numerous paragraphs of this activist-style tariff setting. Such moves are inevitably rooted in dubious political economy.

Exemptions

Going beyond the issue of rate dispersion, when two different consignments of the same item are imported into India, they could encounter very different tariffs. This is because there are a large number of exemptions. These exemptions are based on who is importing, or why he is importing. If the imports are for defence, police, training, education, oil exploration, exhibitions, expeditions, for export purposes such as packaging materials, durable containers, by charitable institutions, for handicapped persons, or for sports-related activities, exemption from custom duty is given after due paper work. The list of items where such exemptions exist runs into nearly 2,000. The importer gives the appraising officer the relevant literature and a certificate from one of the 33 approved certifying agencies such as the Director General of Foreign Trade, the Director of Vanaspati, Vegetable Oil and Fat, the Council for Leather Exports, or the Sports Authority of India.

The importer has to get a Bill of Entry from the appraising officer. These steps involve multiple contact points with the government and enormous costs of compliance, since appraising officers have to engage in questions of both valuation and end-use.

Policy Directions

The minimal agenda in reforms is the elimination of exemptions, which should ensure that no two consignments of a given product encounter different taxation rules or procedures. This would also serve to remove the involvement of all agencies external to the customs administration.

The second issue in reforms is identifying all goods with a rate above 'the peak rate' and bringing them down to the peak rate.

The third issue is the removal of rate dispersion, and the continued process of bringing down the peak rate from 15 per cent. A uniform rate is the best way to avoid the large dispersion of effective rates of protection, and the consequent political economy of tariff reform. Deficiencies of domestic taxation, however, pose an impediment against the move to uniform rate. There is a case for differential taxation of 'raw materials' and 'finished goods'—even though these terms are imprecise—given that domestic producers suffer state-level taxes that are not imposed on imports as part of VAT.

In the immediate future, the Vijay Kelkar FRBM Implementation Report has suggested that duty rates should be 5, 8, and 10 per cent for 'raw materials', 'intermediates', and 'finished goods', respectively. This is proposed as an interim solution until India is able to implement the goods and services tax (GST) in place of the various state sales taxes, state VAT, and so on. After the GST is in place, the next phase of tariff reform can commence—of moving to a uniform rate, and of going further down to a uniform rate such as 2 per cent.

ILA PATNAIK

References

Ministry of Finance. 2002. Report of the Task Force on 'Indirect Taxes', Government of India, December.

——. 2004. Report of the Task Force on 'Implementation of the Fiscal Responsibility and Budget Management Act, 2003', Government of India, July.

Mukhopadhyay, Sukumar. 2005. 'Proposals for Customs Reform in Budget 2005–06', *Economic and Political Weekly*, 15 January, 40(3): 199–202.

Panagariya, Arvind. 2004. 'India's Trade Reform', *India Policy Forum 2004*, NCAER, New Delhi and Brookings Institute, Washington DC.

Union Budget, 2005–6. Ministry of Finance, Government of India.

Virmani, Arvind. 2004. 'Customs Tariff Reform', *ICRIER Policy Brief*, December, 1(1), New Delhi.

■ Tata, The House of

The Tata Group was founded in the second half of the 19th century by Jamsetji Nusserwanji Tata, a leading industrialist of his time. Jamsetji believed that India would have truly laid aside its imperialist yoke only when it realized the full potential of its natural resources and became a modern, industrial nation. Over 100 years later, as India still continues on that journey, his vision remains the Group's guiding force.

Jamsetji saw disciplines such as medicine and science, and industries such as energy and steel as building blocks in the emergence of a brave and bright new country. After creating the most modern textile mills—his mills were using ring spindles long before Lancashire's mills—he committed the Group to setting up India's first steel plant and the first hydroelectricity plant and bestowed half his personal wealth to found the country's first institution of higher learning—the Indian Institute of Science. He set up an endowment in 1892 to send the country's best minds abroad for higher studies. He pioneered labour practices that were revolutionary for his times, instituting a pension fund in 1886 and paying compensation in 1895.

Thus did he set the mandate for the Group: to look beyond the generation of products and profits to serving the communities in which Tata companies functioned. Under his successors, the Group would align its growth plans with national priorities; it would be a pioneer; it would be technology-driven; and, above all, it would be ethical in its conduct.

After Jamsetji's death, his elder son Dorabji became the chairman, and with the help of Jamsetji's other son, Ratan, completed his unfinished projects: Tata Steel's plant at Jamshedpur, Tata Power's hydro-based power plants for Bombay, and the Indian Institute of Science in Bangalore. The late J.R.D. Tata became the Group Chairman in 1938 (and continued till 1991 when I succeeded him). Under his tenure, the Group expanded into many new businesses, many of them pioneering, and continued to be the country's premier business house.

Tata Airlines ushered civil aviation to the country in 1932, later evolving into Air India, which was nationalized by the government of independent India in 1953. In the early 1950s, Tata Chemicals cracked the technology for making synthetic soda ash, hitherto the preserve of a clutch of six companies. Tata Motors signed a joint venture in 1954 with the then Daimler-Benz to make commercial vehicles and Tata Consultancy Services (TCS) marked India's debut into information technology (IT) services way back in 1968.

However, in the heydays of the controlled economy of the 1960s and 1970s, the Group's plans did not always find favour with the socialist-minded government uncomfortable with 'big business'. The Group's plans to modernize a range of industrial sectors were repeatedly thwarted, none more prominently than the passenger car sector which the Group tried twice, in vain, to enter in partnership with Daimler-Benz and Honda, but also in aluminium, paper, and fertilizers.

But in the last 25 years, as the Indian economy has been opened up, the Tata Group has regained momentum. When multinationals were re-invited to India in the 1980s, the Group brought in best-in-class technologies through joint ventures with MNCs in automobile engines (Cummins), industrial controls (Honeywell), computer hardware (IBM), and telecom equipment (Lucent Technologies). Around the same time, Tata Motors' leadership in commercial vehicles was challenged by a spate of Indo-Japanese joint ventures, but the company successfully managed to hold its own innovative and competitively priced products in a convincing demonstration of the country's engineering expertise.

When telecom services were opened to the private sector in 1994, the Tata Group was among the first to enter. Today, Tata Teleservices offers a full suite of nation-wide voice and data services in the basic and mobile forms based on both CDMA and GSM technology, the latter in a partnership with Japan's NTT DoCoMo.

In 1998, Tata Motors developed and produced the Indica, the country's first indigenously produced passenger car, which marked India's entry into the club of developed nations with the capability of creating a car from the ground up. Indica's success emboldened Tata Motors' young engineers to take on the challenge of producing a car under the threshold cost of Rs 1 lakh (around $2,000), even when there was a long list of sceptics who doubted that such a feat could be achieved. But, as is widely known now, the Nano was launched in 2008 to unprecedented international interest, and went into production a year later. The company is now working towards adapting the car not just for economies similar to India but also advanced markets like Europe and the US.

The Nano is perhaps the best known of products launched by Tata companies as a conscious strategy to expand their addressable market by targeting the under-served larger base of India's social pyramid. The Nano itself was preceded by the Ace, India's first four-wheeler 'small truck' for last mile connectivity, at a price of less than $5,000. In six years, the Ace has sold more than 600,000 units and fuelled the entrepreneurial drive of its owners. Other similar notable products and services from Tata companies include IHCL's (Indian Hotels Company Limited) Ginger chain of 'Smart Basics Hotels' for rooms at a median price of $50 per night and Tata Chemicals' 'Swach' (Hindi for 'pure') water purifier for $12, which combines the use of an indigenous material, rice husk, with nano-silver particles as a filter to deliver clean drinking water to a family of five for less than $1 per month. What is common to these innovative offerings is the use of hi-tech to provide quality products that not only expand the market for the product category but also trigger a significant improvement in the quality of life of the users.

The other significant driver of growth among Tata companies in the last decade has been internationalization. India's economy underwent a prolonged slowdown in the latter half of the 1990s, affecting the Tata Group more than others because its major companies are in the basic industries. The experience underlined the importance for Tata companies to diversify their growth options and create a meaningful presence in select overseas geographies. Critically, however, it was also underlined that growth was not to be pursued for its own sake, but only when it was integral to the companies' strategy for growth. Of course, TCS, India's largest software exports, had been international in its reach for much longer, but in recent times it has endeavoured to extend its reach to many non-English-speaking geographies, even as it has been shaping itself into being a full solutions provider, inclusive of a substantial BPO (business process outsourcing) operation.

Tata Tea began its journey into internationalization in 2000 by its brave takeover of Tetley, the UK-based iconic tea company, then twice its size, as it sought to transform itself from being a plantation company to a marketing one. Today, the combined entity has been renamed Tata Global Beverages, mirroring its vision to further expand into beverages as a class, with a focus on the growing global market for wellness drinks.

Tata Steel, among the world's lowest-cost steel producers, began its strategic overseas growth thrust by acquiring finishing facilities in growth markets (NatSteel in Singapore, Millennium Steel in Thailand). But it moved into the Global Top Ten league only in 2007 when it acquired Europe's second largest steel maker, Corus, then more than three times its size. The acquisition not only gave it the much required size in a sector that was rapidly consolidating globally but also access to technologies for superior quality steel. Consequent to the acquisition of Corus, which has since been renamed Tata Steel Europe, the company's priority has been to create a global mining portfolio so as to improve its access to captive sources of raw material for steel making—primarily iron ore and coking coal—by acquiring assets in Canada, Australia, South Africa, Ivory Coast, and Mozambique.

Similarly, Tata Motors, with strengths in the light and medium range of commercial vehicles, saw a strategic fit in Daewoo Commercial Vehicles, with its range of heavy commercial vehicles, and acquired it in 2004. Four years later, it saw a similar strategic fit in Land Rover, an iconic high-end SUV which could complement its range of indigenous SUVs. But Ford bundled the sale of Land Rover along with Jaguar, so both the global brands came to be acquired by Tata Motors, to give the company an international salience in another sector seeing consolidation globally.

With the benefit of hindsight, the Corus and Jaguar/Land Rover acquisitions were later criticized as being overpriced when the global economy went into a slump soon after their takeover. But three years down the road, Jaguar/Land Rover sales have seen a strong rebound and the worst is over for Corus. Other major Group companies like Tata Chemicals, Tata Communications, Voltas, and Tata Power have pursued similarly aggressive strategy-driven overseas growth with notable success.

As I look ahead, I am optimistic for Indian industry and for the Tata Group. Indian industry has already demonstrated its ability to leverage the country's scientific and engineering talent pool to create value in a growing range of knowledge sectors. In recent times, the country's manufacturing sector too has begun to demonstrate its global competitiveness. The Tata Group, for one, intends to try and realize the full international potential for Indian industry in both the services and manufacturing sectors in a manner that would earn for it the same trust it enjoys in India.

RATAN TATA

Tax System and Reform

India's tax system is based on the assignment of separate taxation rights to the Parliament (at the Centre) and state legislatures (in the states). These taxation powers are contained in List I (Union List) and List II (State List) of the Seventh Schedule to the Constitution of India which have to be read with the relevant articles that provide the substantive power to levy and collect taxes. The evolution of the tax system over the last 60 years reflects the changes in India's development strategy, tax legislation, the institutional structure of tax administration, and the role of information technology (IT). This entry traces the evolution of the tax system over the last decade and the ongoing initiatives for tax reforms.

Central Taxes

The major direct taxes levied by the Centre are income tax (excluding tax on agricultural income) and wealth tax. The indirect taxes levied and collected by the Centre are central excise duty, customs duty, and service tax. A fixed proportion of all taxes collected by the Centre devolves to the states based on the recommendations of the Central Finance Commission which is set up every five years to review this sharing mechanism. Based on the recommendations of the Thirteenth Finance Commission, 32 per cent of the revenue collected from these taxes are currently being transferred to the states through devolution. The inter se share of different states is also determined on the basis of the recommendations of the Finance Commission. Some indirect taxes are levied by the Centre but collected by the states. Examples of this are the central sales tax and excise duty on medicinal and toilet preparations (containing alcohol). The revenues from these taxes are retained by the states.

State Taxes

Although the tax base of the states is variegated, the mainstay of tax revenues for state governments is the state value-added tax (VAT) which is applicable to intra-state sale of goods. Sales tax is levied on some special category goods, such as petroleum and tobacco. The other important taxes levied by the states are the state excise tax on the production, distribution, and import (into the state) of alcohol and alcoholic liquor for human consumption, of opium and of Indian hemp; luxury tax; entry tax; taxes on the transportation of goods and passengers; electricity duty; and entertainment tax. Stamp duty, taxes on land and buildings, tax on agricultural income, and profession/employment tax are the other taxes that the states are empowered to levy.

Tax Policy of the Central Government

Taxation has been an important component of the central government's policy on macroeconomic management, especially economic growth and its distribution. Tax policy has also been reviewed and guided by reports of expert committees on tax reforms instituted by the government at different stages. The reports of these committees are a useful guide to the challenges faced by the country's tax system and the responses to these challenges over the last 60 years. Another important source for analysis is the revenue foregone statement in the receipts Budget which is being tabled as part of the Budget documents since 2005–6.

Direct Taxes

Over the years, direct tax policy has been used to encourage savings and investment, reducing inequalities of income and wealth, and promoting investment in underdeveloped regions and in specific priority sectors. These objectives have been tempered by the need to enhance the ability of the tax system to raise revenues with minimum distortion in the economic decisions of taxpayers. Over the last decade, the emphasis has been on tax rates being lowered and maintained at a moderate level while simultaneously broadening the tax base by weeding out tax exemptions and by using IT to ensure compliance in reporting of financial transactions. A broad base with lower rates is desirable from a public policy perspective because elimination of exemptions and concessions reduces administrative and compliance costs as well as expectations of special treatment by different sectors in the economy. It also allows the tax administration to concentrate its resources in areas which need a higher level of enforcement rather than on monitoring and litigating complicated tax preferences. This provides stability and simplicity to the tax system in a developing, high growth economy like India.

India's development strategy in the first three decades after Independence was based on rapid industrialization through centrally planned and import substituting growth in heavy industry owned by the public sector. Scarce resources were to be channelled for this purpose and the belief was that the manufacturing capacity needed to be regulated and licensed to avoid wastage of resources. The tax system was, therefore, tasked with raising resources for the large and increasing requirements of public consumption and investment and also for achieving redistribution of incomes.

This resulted in very high rates for both personal income tax and corporation tax. In 1973–4, the personal income tax had 11 tax brackets with rates increasing from 10 to 97.5 per cent (including surcharge). In the case of corporates a distinction was made between widely held companies and different types of closely held companies, and the tax rate varied from 45 to 65 per cent.

The pursuit of a multiplicity of objectives complicated the tax system with adverse consequences on its efficiency and equity. Central planning priorities dictated and legitimized selectivity and discretion in tax policy and administration. Lack of an adequate information system hampered the implementation, monitoring, review, and evaluation of the discretionary elements of the tax system. Consequently, the tax system was faced with the challenges of increased incentives to both avoid and evade taxes, low probability of detection, and an ineffective implementation regime that failed to impose penalties within a reasonable time period.

It was in this scenario that in 1971 the Direct Taxes Enquiry Committee recommended a significant reduction in marginal tax rates. This was partially implemented in 1974–5 when the highest personal income tax rate (including surcharge) was brought down to 77 per cent. In 1976–7, this was further reduced to 66 per cent, while in 1985–6, the number of tax brackets was reduced from 8 to 4 and the highest tax rate was brought down to 50 per cent. In 1985–6, the basic corporate tax rate was reduced to 50 per cent, and rates applicable to different categories of closely held companies were unified at 55 per cent.

Further rationalization and simplification in direct taxes was initiated on the basis of the recommendations of the Tax Reforms Committee (1991 and 1993). In 1992–3,

Table 1 Personal Income Tax

Financial year	Exemption limit (Rs in lakh)	Lowest rate (inclusive of surcharge and cess) (%)	Highest rate (inclusive of surcharge and cess) (%)
2004–5	50,000	10.2	33.66
2005–6	1,00,000	10.2	33.66
2006–7	1,00,000	10.2	33.66
2007–8	1,10,000	10.3	33.99
2008–9	1,50,000	10.3	33.99
2009–10	1,60,000	10.3	30.9
2010–11	1,60,000	10.3	30.9
2011–12	1,80,000	10.3	30.9
2012–13*	2,00,000	10	30

Note: *Proposed in the Direct Taxes Code Bill (2010).

personal income tax slabs were down to three—20, 30, and 40 per cent. In 1997–8, these rates were brought down further to 10, 20, and 30 per cent. Though, in subsequent years, the need for revenue has led to a levy of surcharge and cess on these rates, the three rates have continued till date (see Table 1).

In the case of corporates, the distinction between closely held and widely held companies was scrapped in 1994–5 and the corporate tax rates were unified at 40 per cent. In 1997–8, the corporate tax rate was further reduced to 35 per cent. Subsequently, owing to revenue considerations surcharges were levied on the base rate of 35 per cent thus raising the overall tax rate. In 2005–6 the base rate was reduced from 35 to 30 per cent, and this has been retained till date though surcharge and cess continue to be levied on this base rate. Since 2010–11, the surcharge and cess is being gradually eliminated so that the base rate and the overall rate coincide at 30 per cent. To this end, the surcharge has been reduced to achieve an overall rate of 33.4 per cent in 2010–11 and of 32.4 per cent in 2011–12.

While moderating the rates, the challenge has been to also moderate tax incentives. The Advisory Group on Tax Policy and Tax Administration in 2001 and the Task Force on Tax Policy and Tax Administration in 2002 made a detailed list of these concessions. These included, in the case of personal income tax, tax preferences and concessions for savings, housing, retirement benefits, investment in and returns from certain types of financial assets, investments in retirement schemes, and income of charitable trusts. While serving to encourage and channelize savings or subsidizing pension incomes in old age in the absence of social security benefits, these incentives do nevertheless create a tax bias in the choice of saving instruments and also erode the tax base. A significant move towards moderating tax preferences in personal income tax was made in 2005–6 with the phasing out of the tax rebate on these investments and allowing them instead as a deduction from taxable income subject to a cap. Major tax incentives in the case of corporates are profit linked deductions for specified sectors and for businesses locating in underdeveloped areas. To broaden the tax base for corporates by moderating the effect of tax incentives, a minimum alternative tax (MAT) was introduced in 1996–7. MAT is levied if the tax liability, after availing tax incentives under the Income Tax Act, is less than the tax liability (at the MAT rate) on book profit, that is, the profit reported by a company to its shareholders. In subsequent years, a provision was incorporated allowing those companies paying MAT to take partial credit against their income tax liabilities in the following years. The overall rate of the MAT levy was enhanced from 11.33 in 2005–6 to 20 per cent in 2011–12 thus ensuring a threshold level of tax payment by all corporates, irrespective of tax incentives.

These measures led to an increase in the corporate taxes paid as a percentage of the total profits before tax for corporates from 19.26 per cent in 2005–6 to 23.53 per cent in 2009–10. The success of the strategy to moderate tax rates and limit tax preferences by levying MAT and phasing out profit linked deductions is reflected in the increase in the effective tax rate on corporates from 19.26 per cent in 2005–6 to 23.53 per cent in 2010–11 (see Table 2).

As India increasingly looks to attracting funds for developing its capital market, capital gains from sale of listed equities (held for more than a year by an investor) have been exempted from tax, both for domestic and

Table 2 Corporate Taxes

Financial year	Nominal corporate tax rate (inclusive of surcharge and cess)	MAT rate	Effective rate# (Total taxes paid to total profits before taxes, %)
2004–5	36.59	7.84	–
2005–6	33.66	8.42	19.26
2006–7	33.66	11.22	20.55
2007–8	33.99*	11.33	22.24
2008–9	33.99*	11.33	22.78
2009–10	33.99*	17	23.53
2010–11	33.22*	19.93	Not available
2011–12	32.44*	20	Not available
2012–13**	30	20	Not available

Source: # Revenue foregone statement in the Receipts Budgets for 2005–6 to 2009–10.

Note: * If net income exceeds Rs10 million.

**Proposed in the Direct Taxes Code Bill (2010).

international investors. A separate securities transaction tax (STT) at the rate of 0.125 per cent both on purchase and sale of equities on stock exchanges is, however, being levied since October 2004, a measure which ensures a steady and administratively simple means of collecting a minimum level of tax through the stock exchanges.

The increased use of information technology has enhanced the efficiency of the tax administration in providing taxpayer services as well as in monitoring and reporting financial transactions in order to bring them to tax. The use of a unique taxpayer identity number, extensive use of tax deduction at source, electronic reporting by registering authorities of transactions in real estate, banking and other transactions, electronic payment of taxes and electronic filing of returns, and the building up of a tax information network (TIN) has strengthened both voluntary compliance as well as the enforcement mechanism. Electronic filing of tax returns by companies has ensured a much higher level of monitoring and compliance and has, since 2005–6, also resulted in a detailed analysis of revenue foregone on account of direct tax incentives which is presented in the annual Budget documents. These measures, along with rapid growth in GDP, have resulted in a rapid rise in the direct tax to GDP ratio. In 2007–8, the central government's direct tax collections exceeded indirect tax collections which indicates a structural change towards a more progressive tax structure (see Table 3).

Table 3 Tax–GDP Ratio

Financial year	Centre			State	Total
	Direct	Indirect	Total		
2000–1	3.25	5.72	8.97	5.55	14.52
2004–5	4.08	5.33	9.41	5.85	15.26
2005–6	4.38	5.50	9.88	5.98	15.86
2006–7	5.25	5.80	11.05	6.15	17.20
2007–8	6.31	5.68	11.99	5.60	17.59
2008–9	6.08	5.19	11.26	5.74	17.00
2009–10	5.84	4.45	10.29	5.71	16.00
2010–11	6.08	4.29	10.37	N.A.	N.A

Direct Tax Legislation

The Income Tax Act, 1961, which replaced the pre-Independence Act of 1922, has been in effect for almost 50 years and has been subjected to numerous amendments by several Amendment Acts besides the amendments carried out through the annual Finance Acts. These were necessitated by policy changes due to the changing economic environment, increasing sophistication of commerce, increase in international transactions as a result of globalization, development of IT, attempts to minimize tax avoidance, and to clarify the statute in relation to judicial decisions. As a result of all these amendments, the basic structure of the Act has been overburdened and its language has become complex.

In order to revise, consolidate, and simplify the language and structure of direct tax laws, the draft Direct Taxes Code Bill, 2010, along with a discussion paper was released in August 2009 for public comments. It proposed to replace the Income Tax Act, 1961, and the Wealth Tax Act, 1957, by a single Code. After public and stakeholder feedback on the proposals, a revised discussion paper was released in June 2010. The Direct Taxes Code Bill, 2010, (DTC) was introduced in Parliament in August 2010, and is currently being examined by it.

DTC attempts to consolidate and integrate all direct tax laws by replacing both the Income Tax Act, 1961, and the Wealth Tax Act, 1957, with a single legislation; simplifying the language by using direct, active speech; indicating stability in direct tax rates by proposing the rates of taxes in a Schedule to the Code and not through annual legislation; strengthening taxation provisions for international transactions; and phasing out profit linked tax incentives and replacing them with investment linked incentives for priority sectors.

The ongoing challenges in building a strong direct tax policy regime primarily relate to strengthening the tax administration, integrating IT in the functioning of the tax administration, and reducing tax litigation.

Indirect Taxes

The year 1991 marks a watershed in the history of indirect taxes in India. Triggered by a serious balance-of-payments and consequent fiscal crisis, a process of far-reaching reforms guided by the recommendations of the Tax Reforms Committee was initiated. Until then, the efficiency of the indirect tax system and compliance levels were severely compromised by very high rates of duty coupled with a large number of exemptions for meeting a variety of socio-economic objectives—the most important one being the need to mitigate its regressive nature. Unduly high dependence on import duties as a source of revenue was also a characteristic of the system. Such a tax structure was not conducive to high growth as it engendered a high-cost economy riddled with tax cascading. It also did not raise adequate revenues commensurate with the tax rates and efforts, thus having a deleterious impact on the health of public finances.

With the inception of reforms, the effort has been of broadening the base and lowering the rates, an approach commonly known as the BBLR approach. Among the achievements of the reform process, the most critical has been the shift in the respective shares of direct and indirect tax collections in gross tax revenues of the Government of India.

Within indirect taxes, the contribution of border taxes, that is, customs duties, has fallen considerably compared to domestic taxes, that is, central excise duties and service tax. Reduction in the share of customs duties is even more pronounced if revenues from additional customs duties (commonly known as CVD and special CVD) which are meant to counterbalance excise duty, state VAT, central sales tax, and other local taxes and charges are included in the revenue collection from domestic taxes. This is due to the opening up of the economy and a dramatic reduction in customs tariffs with a view to improving the competitiveness of domestic manufacturing.

Remarkably, this shift in the composition of tax revenues towards direct taxes, on the one hand, and domestic taxes, on the other, has occurred despite a steep moderation in the rates of these taxes. It is evident that there has been considerable improvement in tax compliance over this period both as a consequence of rate reduction as well as the efforts made at strengthening the tax administration. Information technology has been deployed extensively to reduce physical interface between the taxpayer and the department. With the automation of all major locations, customs administration works almost entirely on the electronic data interchange (EDI) system now. Filing of import and export documents, and their processing and tracking is conducted electronically. The adoption of ACES (Automated Central Excise and Service Tax) for the other two taxes has simplified the processes of registration, return filing, and tax payments all of which can be transacted electronically. Self-assessment of tax liability by a taxpayer followed by risk-based selection for scrutiny or audit is the mode of tax collection for all these taxes. Internal work processes have also been revamped to impart greater efficiency in key processes, such as scrutiny and audit.

The other achievements of the reform process include: (i) imposition of service tax and the widening of its coverage; (ii) inclusion of capital goods within the ambit of the input credit scheme; and (iii) more effective tax neutralization so that duties paid on inputs may be neutralized by a service provider and tax paid on input services by a manufacturer of goods.

State taxes have also been a focus of attention in the reforms programme. Prior to 2005, the states were dependent primarily on sales taxes for raising revenues. Sales tax was applicable to intra-state sales. Central sales tax (CST) applies to inter-state sales. This tax is levied by the Centre but collected and appropriated by the states. The process of replacement of sales tax with state VAT began in 2005 with 22 states opting for this transition. By December 2008, all the states had completed this transition. The adoption of VAT, which applies to the entire value chain for goods starting from pre-manufacturing to retail, has had a very positive impact in mitigating double taxation and cascading. Rate wars among the states witnessed under the sales tax regime have ended and dispersion in rates has been reduced with dual rates. The rate of the central sales tax has been brought down from 4 to 2 per cent. Coupled with administrative re-engineering in many states, this reform has generated considerable revenue efficiency with almost all participating states registering double-digit growth in revenue collections.

Although far-reaching, these reforms have not completely eliminated the deficiencies or inefficiencies in the Indian tax system. There is still a large number and variety of indirect taxes, especially among those levied by the states. Examples of these include sales tax on crude petroleum and petroleum products, state excise on alcoholic liquor for human consumption, entry tax, octroi, entertainment tax, taxes on lotteries and gambling, luxury tax, electricity duty, and taxes on the transportation of goods and passengers. In addition, both the Centre and the states levy cesses and surcharges that are meant to generate resources for a particular purpose. Most of these apply to a narrow tax base and are non-VAT type of taxes. So input tax credit is not permitted. This generates cascading and double taxation at many points in the value chain for the production and distribution of goods and services.

Some instances of cascading are: (i) CENVAT or central excise duty is collected at the manufacturing stage and is not allowed for set-off against state VAT in the distribution chain; (ii) service tax paid on input services can be offset against CENVAT paid by manufacturers but not by dealers and traders in the distribution chain; (iii) state VAT paid on inputs purchased by manufacturers from dealers or traders cannot be set off against CENVAT; and (iv) central sales tax applicable to inter-state sales normally cannot be set off against any other taxes. Such a wide variety of taxes places domestic goods (and services) at a disadvantage vis-à-vis imports owing to the inability to counterbalance them fully through appropriate customs duties at the border. It has an adverse implication for export of goods and services in as much as it does not allow a full zero-rating of exports. The upshot is that the tax system creates distortions and anomalies for domestic manufacturing and trade. Moreover, it is also wasteful of administrative resources. A separate administrative mechanism is required for the collection of many of these taxes. Such an administrative structure has made it near impossible to optimize tax compliance through exchange of information about a taxpayer across tax jurisdictions. For a taxpayer, the compliance cost is high as he has to deal with multiple tax authorities.

The goods and services tax (GST) will mark a very significant improvement over the existing system because it will integrate the tax base across the value chain of supply of both goods and services in the economy. Not only will this enable the taxation of each stage of the value chain at a uniform rate, it will also enable the seamless pass through of input tax credit so that the incidence is effectively borne by final consumption of goods and services. It is well-accepted that such a tax system minimizes distortions in economic choice.

The Empowered Committee of State Finance Ministers released its 'First Discussion Paper on the Goods and Services Tax' in November 2009. This spells out the features of the proposed GST and has formed the basis for discussion between the Centre and the states so far. The paper envisages a destination-based, dual GST with the Centre and the states simultaneously levying it on a common base. It will replace several indirect taxes currently levied by the Centre and the states, respectively, including central excise duty, service tax, state VAT, and central sales tax. Input credit will flow seamlessly across the value chain in both CGST and SGST but not across these two taxes. Exports will be zero-rated. GST will apply to all goods other than crude petroleum, motor spirit, diesel, aviation turbine fuel, and natural gas. It will apply to all services barring a few to be specified. A common threshold exemption will apply to both CGST and SGST and dealers with a turnover below it would be exempt from tax. An Integrated GST (IGST) will be levied on inter-state supply of goods and services. This will be collected by the Centre so that the credit chain is not disrupted. Accounts will be settled periodically between the Centre and the state to ensure that the state GST component is transferred to the destination state where the goods or services are eventually consumed.

As pointed out earlier, the distribution of fiscal powers between the Centre and the states is enshrined in the Constitution of India. For GST to be introduced, this distribution needs redefinition so that both the Centre and the states may concurrently levy this tax. Based on the status of discussions so far, the Centre and the states have jointly prepared a draft Constitutional Amendment Bill for this purpose. This Bill was introduced in the Lok Sabha in March 2011. It needs to be passed by a two-thirds majority in both Houses of Parliament and subsequent ratification by at least half of the state legislatures. It is only after the Bill is enacted that suitable legislation for the actual levy of GST can be introduced either in Parliament or in the state legislatures.

Apart from forging a consensus on the Constitutional Amendment that will create the legal framework for the levy of GST, the administrative challenges in its implementation are quite formidable. The central and state governments will be required to collaborate (and not compete) closely for the first time, not only in raising tax revenues but also in formulating a tax policy in a harmonized way through the agency of the GST Council. There is likely to be a significant increase both in the number of taxpayers as well as their size and complexity. The expectation of the taxpayer community will be of high-quality service by the respective tax departments so that the compliance burden may be minimized. Above all, they will look for a similar experience (and treatment) at the Centre and across states. For this to happen, business processes across the two have to be completely harmonized and a single point of contact has to be made available to a taxpayer. The Centre and the states are agreed that this would, in turn, require a very strong IT infrastructure and have already set in motion the process of designing and implementing the GST network (GSTN) through a special purpose vehicle owned jointly by the Centre and the states and assisted by a technology partner. In addition, key business processes for the two tax administrations will have to be designed jointly. Finally, the efficient roll-out and implementation of GST will require the pooling of intellectual and human capital by the Centre and the states and a very robust coordination mechanism for conducting their day to day activities.

Conclusion

Apart from taking the reform process further, the two initiatives of introducing the Direct Taxes Code and the Goods and Services Tax present a great opportunity for synergizing the tax efforts of the central and state governments. In terms of timing they are almost synchronized. Besides, they are being launched at a juncture when the IT component of the tax administration at the Centre as well as in many of the states has already been substantially strengthened. In the remaining states, work for putting in place or upgrading IT infrastructure under the mission mode project has already started. Finally, the GST network will bring the Centre and all the states on a common electronic platform with regard to registration, return filing, and tax payments and host a wealth of data on taxpayer activity and behaviour. With the permanent account number (PAN) being a common business identifier, exchange of information across tax jurisdictions will enable much more effective compliance management than is feasible today.

SUNIL MITRA, ASHUTOSH DIKSHIT, AND VIVEK JOHRI

References

Government of India. 1953. *Report of the Taxation Enquiry Commission,* New Delhi, Ministry of Finance, Government of India.

——. 1956. *Indian Tax Reform,* New Delhi, Ministry of Finance, Government of India.

——. 1971. *Direct Taxes Enquiry Committee: Final Report,* New Delhi, Ministry of Finance, Government of India.

——. 1977. *Report of the Indirect Taxation Enquiry Committee,* New Delhi, Ministry of Finance, Government of India.

——. 1985. 'Long Term Fiscal Policy', New Delhi, Ministry of Finance, Government of India.

——. 1991. 'Tax Reforms Committee, Interim Report', New Delhi, Ministry of Finance, Government of India.

——. 1993. *Report of the Tax Reforms Committee,* New Delhi, Ministry of Finance, Government of India.

——. 2001a. 'Report of the Advisory Group on Tax Policy and Tax Administration for the Tenth Plan', New Delhi, Planning Commission.

——. 2001b. *Report of the Expert Group on Taxation of Services,* New Delhi, Ministry of Finance, Government of India.

——. 2002a. *Report of the Taskforce on Direct Taxes,* New Delhi, Ministry of Finance, Government of India.

——. 2002b. *Report of the Taskforce on Indirect Taxes,* New Delhi, Ministry of Finance, Government of India.

——. 2003. Report of the Task Force on Implementation of the Fiscal Responsibility and Budget Management Act, New Delhi, Ministry of Finance, Government of India.

——. 2004a. 'Indian Public Finance Statistics', New Delhi, Ministry of Finance, Government of India.

——. 2004b. *Report of the Taskforce on Indirect Taxes,* New Delhi, Ministry of Finance, Government of India.

——. Various Issues. 'Revenue Foregone Statements in the Receipt Budget (Annexure 15)', New Delhi, Ministry of Finance, Government of India, (2005–6 to 2010–11).

■ Teacher Absenteeism

Teacher absenteeism is a major problem for the education system in many developing countries. In India, the problem is acute. A study by Chaudhury and others (2004), reveals that one in four teachers is absent from government-run primary schools in India at any given time. Similar studies have been conducted in eight other developing countries and comparison shows that India has the second highest average absence rate among primary school teachers. For example, Peru has an average teacher absence rate of 11 per cent, Papua New Guinea 15 per cent, Bangladesh 16 per cent, and Zambia 17 per cent. Of all the countries studied, only Uganda had a poorer record of teacher absenteeism.

Why is teacher absenteeism a serious issue? On the face of it, the immediate concern is the waste of scarce resources. If 25 per cent of the teachers in government-run primary schools are absent on a given day, it means that a considerable portion of the government's limited education budget is going waste. More importantly, a growing concern is that India's rural mass has been cut off from the fruits of the country's growing prosperity. One reason is India's literacy rate which stands at a poor 65 per cent. If economic well-being, resulting from India's growing prosperity, is to spread to the masses, improvement of the literacy rate is imperative. And one crucial step in getting children to school is to get the teachers to school.

Absent Teachers

The study by Chaudhury et al. (2004) was conducted on 3,700 schools spread across 20 Indian states. Three unannounced visits were made on random days to each of these schools. A teacher was considered absent if the investigator could not find him/her in the school during regular working hours. Apart from a 25 per cent absence rate, the study found that only 45 per cent of teachers were actively engaged in teaching at the time of the visits. Within India, there is a wide variance in absence rates ranging from 15 per cent in Maharashtra to 42 per cent in the state of Jharkhand. Higher-income states like Maharashtra and Gujarat have lower absence rates than lower-income states like Jharkhand and Bihar. The study also reveals interesting correlates of teacher absence. First, higher teacher salaries do not make a significant difference to teacher absence. Head-teachers are more likely to be absent than ordinary teachers. Teacher absence is considerably lower in schools with better infrastructure (for example, in schools with better accessibility, toilet facilities for teachers, and all-weather school rooms). This last point is important as many government-run primary schools in rural India lack basic amenities such as drinking water facility or toilets.

The study by Chaudhury et al. (2004) is not the only one to provide a snapshot of the alarming rate of teacher absence in India. One of the first studies to examine the problem of teacher absenteeism is the PROBE Report (1999). The Pratichi Trust Report

(2002) also analyses the problem of teacher absence in primary schools. A recent independent study by Duflo and Hanna (2005) conducted over sixty schools in the district of Udaipur in Rajasthan revealed a 36 per cent absence rate among teachers.

The grim picture painted by these studies calls for serious effort on the part of the government to improve attendance. The various approaches to reduce absence rates among teachers mainly involve design of incentive schemes (both rewards and punishments) to improve attendance. Given the complex nature of the problem it is seldom clear whether the initiatives to fight absence are having the desired effect. In the rest of the entry, I will focus on issues related to some of these approaches to reduce absenteeism among teachers.

Incentive Schemes

Any design of an incentive scheme to punish shirkers and/or reward performers must have a monitoring authority in place to keep an eye on absence. The most common type of monitoring is one where someone in the institutional hierarchy (say the headmaster of a school or a government-appointed inspector) is given the task of keeping an eye on teachers and penalizing absence. Given the evidence that head-teachers have a higher absence rate, according them the task of monitoring may not be a good idea. In general, making a person in the institutional hierarchy the monitoring agent may give rise the problem of having to monitor the monitoring authority. The person may be too lazy to monitor, or for reasons external to the problem may not perform the task properly. For example, in order to avoid unpleasantness with his colleagues, the head-teacher may choose to simply ignore absence.

An alternative scheme would be to give monitoring control to potential beneficiaries. For example, one of the parents of the children sent to school could be given the task of keeping an eye on the teachers. Since beneficiaries are directly affected by delinquent behaviour, it is more likely they care more about it than others and are also better informed. So beneficiary control is likely to be an effective way to monitor absence among teachers. However, beneficiary control can only be effective if the reward or punishment schemes for the teachers are based on the monitoring undertaken by the beneficiaries. In India, beneficiaries of government schools have no say either in the decisions to hire or fire teachers or in determining the salaries paid. Moreover, while coming up with an incentive scheme, one cannot ignore the hierarchical nature of society in rural India. In many a case, the beneficiaries of public education are socially inferior to the teacher. Thus, even if beneficiaries have some say in hiring and firing decisions, they may choose not to exercise that option fearing retaliation from the socially more powerful government employee.

A third alternative would be to use some impersonal monitoring device, such as a camera, for recording absence. Banerjee and Duflo (2005) discuss the results of a randomized experiment using monitoring by camera conducted in sixty school in Udaipur, Rajasthan. In the experiment, the teacher was given a camera with tamper-proof date-time function, and was instructed to take pictures of himself/herself and the students everyday at opening and closing time. Teachers received a bonus for the number of valid days they actually attended. The experiment showed immediate result in improvement in teacher attendance. Although such impersonal monitoring devices are simple, easy to implement, and effective, they are yet to become normal practice in India.

Teacher absenteeism is part of a general problem of attendance by employees involved in public services, especially in rural India. If public services are to play their designated role in the lives of the poor, serious efforts need to be made to improve attendance. The foregoing discussion tried to focus on some of the possible ways to fight absence. It seems that a simple incentive scheme, mechanically monitored, like the camera programme, is an effective way to reduce absence in schools. Unfortunately, most incentive schemes in India are not implemented in this manner, but are mediated by people in the hierarchy such as school inspectors. The problem is that such mediated schemes involve human judgement, and in a system where rules are often bent, incentives may easily be distorted. Mechanically implemented systems, like the camera one, are immune to these problems. The only requirement in such cases is the willingness of the authorities to put such a system in place.

DIPJYOTI MAJUMDAR

References

Banerjee. A. and E. Duflo. 2005. 'Addressing Absence', mimeo, MIT.

Chaudhury, N., J. Hammer, M. Kremer, K. Muralidharan, and F.H. Rogers. 2004. 'Teacher and Health Care Provider Absenteeism: A Multi-country Study,' World Bank.

Duflo, E. and R. Hanna. 2005. 'Monitoring Works: Getting Teachers to Come to School,' mimeo, MIT.

Pratichi Trust. 2002. Pratichi Education Report.

PROBE Team. 1999. *Public Report on Basic Education in India*, New Delhi, Oxford University Press.

Teacher and Medical Worker Incentives

Education and health policy in developing countries such as India has largely centred on increasing the resource base and the number of government-run schools and clinics, while much less attention has been paid to the question of efficient spending of the allocated resources. However, given the extent of the leakages in government spending, it is essential for policy discussions (especially involving large outlays of public funds) to be accompanied by a thorough examination of the incentive structures for each agent in the chain from policy formation to actual implementation. Since salaries account for the largest fraction of most government spending, it could be argued that getting the incentives right for government personnel is the single most important[1] requirement to increase the effectiveness of government, especially in service provision to the poor.[2]

The Magnitude of the Problem

The scale of the incentive problem for teachers and medical workers can be gauged from the extent to which they are simply absent from work. Recent research, we find—using representative data from the 19 largest states[3] accounting for 98 per cent of India's population, has found that on any given day, 25 per cent of teachers in government schools, and 40 per cent of medical workers in government health clinics cannot be found at work. These estimates are based on direct physical verification[4] of the presence of staff assigned to the facility and exclude staff on deputation, on another shift, or not supposed to be based at the facility for any other reason. There is wide variation in provider absence levels across states with teacher absence ranging from 15 per cent (Maharashtra) to 42 per cent (Jharkhand) and doctor absence ranging from 30 per cent (Madhya Pradesh) to 71 per cent (Bihar).

[1]This is a point that is well understood in the private sector, where, for instance, Jack Welch (the former CEO of GE) said that he used to spend 70 per cent of his time on people development and management and creating the environment and motivation for them to perform at consistently high levels.

[2]The World Development Report (World Bank 2003) with the theme of 'Making Services Work for Poor People' has served to focus attention on this issue.

[3]See Chaudhury et al. (2006) for details of the cross-country project that this research was a part of, and Kremer et al. (2005) for detailed results on teacher absence. All results discussed in this essay are based on these two papers unless stated otherwise.

[4]The importance of direct physical verification of provider presence is borne out by the fact that in Andhra Pradesh (where I have more data from currently ongoing research) the teacher absence rate based on direct observation is 25 per cent, while the absence rate on the previous day as measured by the official attendance record is only 15 per cent.

Of course, while provider presence is a necessary condition for the delivery of quality outcomes in health and education, presence is by no means sufficient. The absence figures in the previous paragraph are a bare minimum estimate of the problem, because in many cases providers are present but not actively working. For instance, while 25 per cent of teachers were absent, another 25–30 per cent were in school but not teaching and so less than half of the teachers were engaged in teaching activity. The state-level variation in teachers who were found not engaged in teaching activity ranged from 41 per cent in Maharashtra to 81 per cent in Chhattisgarh.

Salary Level and Structure

An often-heard reason for poor performance by government employees is that they are not paid enough. But we (Chaudhury et al. 2006) didn't find any evidence to suggest that this is the case. If anything we found that more highly paid teachers in government schools—that is, more educated teachers, older teachers, and teachers holding higher ranks—are in fact *more* likely to be absent. On the other hand, private school teachers—who are on average paid *much lower* salaries (as low as *one-tenth* of regular government school teachers in many rural areas)—are less absent and more likely to be teaching when they are present.

The main theoretical reason for expecting a high wage 'level' to induce high effort is if we believe that this is an 'efficiency wage' situation. Under this scenario, employees are afraid of getting fired if caught shirking, and the consequent loss of the 'premium' over the market-clearing wage provides an incentive to work hard. We can see that this model does not apply here because only one head teacher in our sample of nearly 3,000 government primary schools had *ever* dismissed a teacher for repeated absence, even though the absence rates are so high. Compare this with the 35 head teachers out of the 600 rural private schools in our sample who had done so, which implies that delinquent teachers in private schools are 175 times more likely to have action taken against them, though their salary levels are much lower!

This discussion highlights an important distinction that is often forgotten, which is that that while the 'level' of salary is an important component of determining who gets attracted to a profession, it is the 'structure' of pay (in terms of the relation between performance and pay) that determines how hard people work once they are in a job. Studying the compensation structures in one of India's leading IIT-JEE coaching centres is highly illustrative. Teachers here are paid between Rs 2 lakh per year to Rs 20 lakh per year with only the very best teachers making the top end of that range. The institute bases the rating and compensation on a combination of hours of teaching, student feedback, creation of new pedagogical content, and a carefully constructed metric of 'Rank Potential Improvement' that uses internal tests to measure the extent to which faculty has *improved* the potential of a student. The salient point here is not the higher average pay as much as its *range*, which is what makes it possible to reward good performance without the unfeasible financial burden of increasing salaries across the board.

Preliminary results from ongoing research in Andhra Pradesh (with Venkatesh Sundararaman) suggest that even providing small monetary bonus payments (with an average annual bonus typically less than half a month's salary) to teachers on the basis of average *improvement* in student performance on independently administered tests led to large gains in student learning outcomes. Students in schools that (randomly) received the incentive programmes outperformed those in control schools by nearly 0.25 standard deviations in mathematics and 0.17 standard deviations in language, which are very substantial effects (another way of describing the results is that a median student in an incentive school would perform at around the 58th percentile in a control school). The fact that this study was carried out in a representative sample of government schools in Andhra Pradesh provides external validity to the experimental results and also shows that it is possible to implement performance pay measures in government schools, if the metrics are thoughtfully designed and transparently implemented.

Working Conditions

While we don't find any relation between higher salaries and teacher absence, we do find that better working conditions are associated with lower rates of teacher absence. Teacher absence is considerably lower in schools with better infrastructure, a potentially important element of working conditions. We compute an infrastructure index that assigns one point each for the existence of toilets for the teachers, an electricity connection, a library, covered classrooms, and *pucca* floors. Under this specification, each point on the index is associated with a 1.0–1.5 percentage point reduction in the probability of absence—so that moving from 0 to 5 on the index reduces the predicted absence rate by 5.0 to 7.5 points. Our data also show that teachers in schools that are far from a paved road are nearly 4 percentage points less likely to be in school than those closest to a road.

Monitoring and Supervision

Although school inspectors do not have much power, teachers in schools that had been inspected in the three months prior to the visit were about two percentage points less likely to be absent, suggesting that the role of formal monitoring and supervision may be important. One problem with simply having more inspectors (and with more power) is that they might be able to extract bribes from teachers in return for inaction when faced with shirking teachers. A clever solution is proposed by Duflo and Hanna (2005), who study the effects of basing teacher salary payments (in a sample of NGO-run schools in Udaipur district) on photographic evidence of teacher presence in the school (schools were given a camera with a time-date stamp and teachers were supposed to take pictures of themselves with the class at the beginning and end of each working day). They found that teacher absence in the (randomly chosen) camera schools was 18 per cent compared to 36 per cent in the control schools and that student performance went up by 0.17 standard deviations relative to control schools. The main lesson to be learnt from this experiment is not only that monitoring works, but also that creative use of technology can solve the verifiability problem of ensuring provider attendance in remote areas.

The evidence on teacher and medical worker absence suggests that a substantial portion of public resources spent in health and education is being wasted. Given the deadweight loss of raising tax revenue, the true social cost of inefficient spending is even higher than just the financial cost of absent providers. If we want additional spending on education and health to result in superior outcomes as opposed to inefficiently bloated salary bills, we need to think hard about how compensation and incentive structures can be designed to elicit continuous high performance. A unifying theme that emerges from the discussion of pay, working conditions, and monitoring is that what matters most is not lump-sum incentives such as the 'level' of pay as much as the *marginal* incentives (pay for performance, working conditions, and monitoring) since these are what determine the level of effort exerted on the job.

There are, of course, well-known difficulties with providing incentives in contexts where agents have to perform on multiple dimensions with differential ease of measurement (the multi-task moral hazard problem), and report to multiple principals with potentially different objectives—aspects that are especially true in the context of publicly provided goods.[5] But the difficulty of designing universally applicable incentive systems should not prevent us from thinking about the appropriate set

[5]See Dixit (2002) for an excellent overview of the literature on incentives in organizations in general and in the public sector in particular.

of monetary and non-monetary incentives in specific contexts, to ensure the efficiency of service delivery. Improving incentives for provider attendance[6] at work would be a good start.

KARTHIK MURALIDHARAN

References

Banerjee, Abhijit and Esther Duflo. 2006. 'Addressing Absence', *Journal of Economic Perspectives*, 20(1): 117–32.

Chaudhury, Nazmul, Jeffrey Hammer, Michael Kremer, Karthik Muralidharan, and F. Halsey Rogers. 2006. 'Missing in Action: Teacher and Health Worker Absence in Developing Countries', *Journal of Economic Perspectives*, 20(1): 91–116.

Dixit, Avinash. 2002. 'Incentives and Organizations in the Public Sector: An Interpretative Review', *Journal of Human Resources*, 37(4): 696–727.

Duflo, Esther and Rema Hanna. 2005. 'Monitoring Works: Getting Teachers to Come to School', National Bureau of Economic Research Inc NBER Working Papers, 11880.

Kremer, Michael, Nazmul Chaudhury, F. Halsey Rogers, Karthik Muralidharan, and Jeffrey Hammer. 2005. 'Teacher Absence in India: A Snapshot', *Journal of the European Economic Association*, 3(2–3): 658–67.

Muralidharan, Karthik and Venkatesh Sundararaman. Forthcoming. 'Teacher Incentives in Developing Countries: Experimental Evidence from India', mimeo, Harvard University.

World Bank. 2003. *World Development Report 2004: Making Services Work for Poor People*, Washington DC, Oxford University Press for the World Bank.

Technology Diffusion

Among the many technological innovations of the 20th century few have had the impact of the agricultural green revolution. The green revolution is associated with the introduction of high-yielding varieties (HYVs) of wheat and rice in the late 1960s, which was followed by their widespread adoption, dramatically increasing farm productivity and rural incomes throughout the developing world. Wheat and rice are staple cereals in the Indian diet and these crops typically dominate the Indian farmer's investment (acreage) portfolio. HYVs suited to local growing conditions were successfully developed for both these crops and so the Indian economy benefited disproportionately from this new technology. The tremendous accumulation of rural wealth in the decades following the green revolution set the stage for a balanced and sustained pattern of growth that distinguishes India from other developing countries.

Despite the promise of the new technology, the diffusion of the HYVs was not entirely smooth. Two of the original wheat varieties imported from Mexico, Sonora 64 and Lerma Rojo 64A, were found to be particularly suited to Indian conditions. They were crossed with local varieties to yield the first generation of HYVs released for mass distribution in 1967. Four of the five varieties released in 1967 were very robust to growing conditions and were adopted throughout the Northern Plains where wheat was traditionally cultivated. Two of these varieties—Kalyan Sona and Sonalika—completely dominated in terms of overall coverage and even spread to areas that had traditionally grown rice, such as eastern Uttar Pradesh and other states in eastern India. Sonalika accounted for 65 per cent and Kalyan Sona another 25 per cent of the total supply of government-certified HYV seed in 1977–8. No other variety accounted for more than 2.5 per cent of seed supply in that year (ICAR 1978).

In sharp contrast with the smooth diffusion of HYV wheat, the story for HYV rice is one of setbacks and disappointments. The original semi-dwarf varieties, Taichung Native 1 and IR8, were imported from the International Rice Research Institute (IRRI) in the Philippines. The first cross-bred HYVs released for mass distribution, Padma and Jaya, were found to be unsuitable in a variety of stress conditions such as water logging, salinity, and drought. They were also found to be susceptible to pests and diseases. Indian agricultural scientists realized very early that the wheat experience would not be replicated with rice. Over the subsequent decades, the thrust of the research effort was to develop HYVs that were suited to specific local conditions. Despite these efforts, the diffusion of HYV rice was a slow process, extending well into the 1980s (ICAR 1985).

Why did adoption patterns for wheat and rice differ so widely? HYV wheat provided a much higher return than the traditional technology that it replaced. It was also a relatively stable technology, associated with fairly certain yields. It is well known that an innovation with these characteristics will diffuse more rapidly. My research on the Indian green revolution has explored an alternative—learning—dimension along which the diffusion patterns for wheat and rice might have differed. When a farmer is faced with the choice between a traditional variety and a new variety, he will only adopt the new technology if he is sufficiently certain that it provides higher profits than the technology it is replacing. The farmer can learn about the performance of the new technology from the local agricultural extension agent. Perhaps more importantly, the farmer can learn from his neighbours'

[6]See Banerjee and Duflo (2006) for a discussion on strategies for improving provider attendance in health and education.

experiences—their acreage allocation decisions and subsequent yield realizations—about the new technology. A neighbour's (unexpected) decision to adopt the new technology indicates that he must have received a positive signal about its performance. His subsequent yield outcomes serve as an additional source of information. Such information received from neighbours' experiences is more credible than information provided by the local extension agent, since the neighbours have more to lose when they make a mistake, and social learning has been seen to have played an important role in the diffusion of agricultural technology, both during the green revolution and historically in US agriculture. Social learning generates natural lags in adoption because the set of neighbours the grower can learn from is restricted and because new information from them only appears each period. The point that I have tried to make in my previous research is that these learning lags may have been substantially greater for rice than for wheat, explaining in part the distinct adoption trajectories that were observed for the two crops.

Social learning is evidently weak, and diffusion rates will be slow, if the individual is unable to observe his neighbours' experiences perfectly. But this does not explain why some innovations diffuse faster than others, even when social information is readily available. It also does not explain why individuals or communities sometimes appear to persistently ignore their neighbours' (positive) experiences. For example, Ryan and Gross (1943), in an influential study that spawned an enormous diffusion literature in rural sociology, estimated that it took fourteen years before hybrid seed corn was completely adopted in two Iowa communities. I argue that such delays might arise because it is not enough to observe your neighbours' decisions and their subsequent outcomes when learning from them. The fact that a new technology worked well for a neighbour does not imply that it will work well for the farmer if characteristics that determine its performance vary in the population. The individual could control for differences between his own and his neighbours' characteristics when learning from their experiences, but only to the extent that these characteristics are observed. Social learning breaks down if unobserved, or imperfectly observed; individual characteristics are important determinants of neighbours' outcomes.

The rice-growing areas of Peninsular India are characterized by wide variation in soil characteristics, whereas conditions are fairly uniform in the Northern Plains where wheat is traditionally grown. The technological differences between the wheat and rice HYVs described earlier would have accentuated the differences between crops. The early rice HYVs were quite sensitive to soil characteristics such as salinity, as well as to managerial inputs, that are difficult to observe. The rice grower would thus have found it difficult to control for differences between his own and his neighbours' characteristics when learning from their experiences. The relatively stable HYV wheat technology, together with the uniform conditions in the wheat-growing areas of the country, would have resulted in conditions that were ideal for social learning. As we would expect, while slow diffusion rates were initially observed in the rice-growing areas of the country, the wheat HYVs spread rapidly and were ultimately adopted in areas that did not even traditionally grow wheat.

I have (Munshi 2004) statistically tested the link between unobserved heterogeneity and social learning by estimating the grower's response to his neighbours' decisions and outcomes, separately by crop. Wheat growers would have allotted relatively more weight to their neighbours' past acreage allocations and yield realizations, and relatively less weight to their own past decisions, if social learning was stronger for that crop. Although this would seem to be a simple test to implement, identifying social learning statistically is an extremely challenging problem. To understand the difficulties that could arise, suppose that each grower bases his acreage decision in part on an (unobserved) information signal that he receives in each period. If these information signals are correlated across growers in the village and over time, then neighbours' past decisions could simply proxy for the unobserved information signals. Manski (1993) points out more generally that a spurious correlation between the growers' current acreage decision and neighbours' past acreage decisions could be obtained if any unobserved determinant of acreage is correlated across neighbours and over time.

The prospects for identification of social learning improve considerably when we focus on the growers' response to lagged yield realizations in the village. Using data from a nationally representative sample of farm households over a three-year period at the onset of the green revolution, from 1968 to 1970, Munshi (2004) found that HYV wheat acreage responds strongly to lagged yield *shocks* in the village, whereas HYV rice acreage allocations do not. Consistent with the view that social learning was smoother for wheat, wheat growers also place relatively more weight on their neighbours' past acreage allocations and relatively less weight on their own past decisions, although as discussed earlier, the acreage effects are less easy to interpret.

I do not claim that the distinct diffusion patterns for HYV wheat and rice were driven entirely by differences along a single learning dimension. Nevertheless, the importance of social learning in generating variation in diffusion rates across these crops should not be minimized. If the view that rice growers are informationally disadvantaged is correct, then we would expect such growers to compensate for their lack of social information by experimenting on their own land. Agricultural production is divisible and so the grower can choose the precise level of HYV acreage that is optimal for him. Munshi's analysis concludes with the observation that rice growers who did adopt HYV allocated more land to the new technology than comparable wheat growers, despite the fact that average landholdings were smaller for rice growers than wheat growers and despite the fact that the likelihood of HYV adoption was significantly higher for wheat growers. Munshi shows formally that these empirical patterns are consistent with increased experimentation among rice growers to compensate for their lack of social information. In contrast, if diffusion rates were faster for wheat only because the new technology provided a higher relative return for that crop, or was more certain, then wheat adopters would have allocated more land to HYV as well. The fact that they did not, suggests that access to information significantly affected investment patterns across crops in this environment.

The Indian green revolution is now complete, but the lessons from that important historical episode could be applied in other settings in the future. Rice HYVs took at least a decade more than wheat HYVs to diffuse completely. This lag could perhaps have been shortened if information programmes that were responsive to the nature of the underlying social learning process had been adopted. Information was provided to growers in India through what is known as the Training and Visit (T&V) system of agricultural extension. Under the T&V system, extension workers focus their attention on a small group of contact farmers in each village. The implicit assumption here is that information will propagate from these farmers through the rest of the village. This system evidently worked very well with wheat. For rice, we would expect that the few contact farmers in each village had little impact on HYV adoption. In general, it may be necessary to invest in more concentrated external information programmes when the flow of social information is restricted.

KAIVAN MUNSHI

References

Indian Council of Agricultural Research (ICAR). 1978. *Wheat Research in India*, New Delhi.

——. 1985. *Rice Research in India*, New Delhi.

Manski, Charles F. 1993. 'Identification of Endogenous Social Effects: The Reflection Problem', *Review of Economic Studies*, 60(3): 531–42.

Munshi, Kaivan. 2004. 'Social Learning in a Heterogeneous Population: Technology Diffusion in the Indian Green Revolution', *Journal of Development Economics*, 73(1): 185–215.

Ryan, Bryce and Neal C. Gross. 1943. 'The Diffusion of Hybrid Seed Corn in Two Iowa Communities', *Rural Sociology*, 8.

Technology Transfer

Economic growth is aided, stimulated, and catalysed by technology. Developing economies can exploit technological changes generated by spillovers from inventions and innovations at international level along with options like buying technology. Technology transfer is the process of acquiring technology from a country that has substantially superior technological knowledge. Two principal ways of utilizing technology transfer are gradual learning and leapfrogging. In comparison to leapfrogging, gradual learning is incremental, painstaking, long term, and cumulative.

The role and contributions of multinational companies (MNCs) in technology transfer through original equipment manufacturing (OEM) have generated considerable interest in the recent economic literature. The symbiotic relationship between local suppliers and their MNC OEMs has enhanced local suppliers' ability to adopt and assimilate foreign technology (Ernst et al. 1998, Lall 2000). This is particularly important for large economies like India, where it is possible for firms to survive and grow catering just to the domestic market. But the exposure to the international market, particularly selling to MNCs, helps them speedily upgrade their technology.

Technology Transfer

International technology transfer has become a major source of technology for developing economies. Even so, there are two areas of concern: one, the capacity of firms and countries to absorb and then to innovate; and two, to disperse the technological competence so acquired within the firm or country (Narula and Dunning 2000). Two alternate sets of observations have been made in this context. The predominant neoclassical 'accumulation theories' emphasize the role of physical and capital investments in moving these economies along their production functions. According to these, higher investments will increase the capital per worker and drive the upgradation of technology. The 'assimilation theories', on the other hand, focus on learning in identifying, adapting, and operating imported technologies. Put in a different way, these stress that learning is a key prerequisite to making such investment (Ivarsson and Alvstam 2005, Javorcik 2004).

Acquiring new technology may not be considered a one-time task. The process is continuous in the context of the dynamic status of knowledge development, human labour condition, market, institutions, and the role of government. A competitive firm may lose in the long run due to a competitor's upgradation of technology. It is thus argued that countries or firms must move into more advanced technologies in order to remain competitive. Herein lies the importance of the government's role that it can indirectly support the firms by providing infrastructure, institutions, and incentives.

In the Indian context, Lall (1983) found that Indian research and development (R&D) was basically adaptive and consequently import of technology would encourage in-house R&D. A number of empirical exercises including Katrak (1989) and Siddharthan (1992) have confirmed the complementary relationship between imported technology and local R&D. In view of these findings, it may be concluded that India's closed technology policies with respect to foreign direct investment and technology licensing had the desired effect of promoting indigenous R&D. We present a few case studies in an attempt to capture the Indian experience with technology transfer.

Three Case Studies

Case 1: Sundaram Fasteners Limited

Sundaram Fasteners Limited (SFL) is the largest manufacturer and exporter of high-tensile fasteners in India. Its wide product range caters to almost all the vehicle manufacturers in India and many from outside the country. The company set up its first manufacturing plant in Padi, Madras, in 1965 and followed it up with a second fastener plant in Aviyur, a backward village of Ramnad district in Tamil Nadu in 1981. SFL commenced its first diversification venture in 1979 by setting up a unit for the manufacture of cold extruded components in Hosur, another backward district of Tamil Nadu, in technical collaboration with M/S Neumeyer Filespressen GmbH of Germany. In 1983, the company further diversified into powder metal (sintered) products in technical collaboration with Sintermetallwerke Krebsoege GmbH, also in Hosur.

An export-oriented unit to manufacture radiator caps, oil filler caps, and petrol filler caps was set up in 1992. Interestingly, this product category was a chance addition for SFL. SFL was exporting fasteners to the Opel plant of General Motors (GM) in Germany and during one of their visits, the GM technical auditors mentioned that GM was planning to close and sell a radiator caps plant in Britain. They enquired if SFL would be interested in making radiator caps for GM. Confident of its engineering and production capabilities and taking advantage of the liberalized economic environment in India, SFL bought the machinery from the plant in Britain, shipped it to Madras, and soon became a 100 per cent supplier of radiator caps to GM. SFL won the 'Supplier of the Year' award from GM five years in a row—from 1996 through 2000—and now supplies radiator caps to twenty-seven GM plants located across the globe.

SFL acquired Autolec, a leading manufacturer of oil pumps, fuel pumps, water pumps, and other automotive components in 1999 and the Cramlington precision forging unit of Dana Spicer Europe in 2003. Later in May 2004, SFL inaugurated its China plant to manufacture fasteners, both standard and special. This plant would be used to meet the domestic demand for fasteners in China as well as to export to other countries.

SFL has built a reputation of being a low-cost high-quality supplier. It has not only increased its business with GM but also broken into other international markets like the German market where it secured a sizable contract from Daimler Benz AG and the Japanese market where it secured orders from Japanese engineering giant Komatsu for track shoe bolts and nuts. It has also secured orders from Cummins US for supply of fasteners. SFL continues as a 100 per cent Indian company with no foreign direct investment (FDI), although it has benefited from technology collaborations as described earlier.

Case 2: Moser Baer India Limited[1]

Moser Baer India Limited (MBIL) is the third largest producer of recordable optical media in the world with an 11 per cent share of the global market. It was established as a modest joint venture in collaboration with Moser Baer AG of Switzerland in 1983 to manufacture time-recording devices in India. As this product did not do very well in the market, the company entered the magnetic

[1]This case is based on company Annual Reports and write-ups in *Business India* (14–27 October 2002) and *Economic Times* (14 January 2004).

removable storage media industry and started the production of 8" and later 5.25" floppy disks in 1985.

With the government initiating economic reforms in 1991, MBIL sensed the need to be globally competitive by scaling up volumes and capacities and by cultivating a strong R&D team. Consequently, 5.25" floppy disk capacity was expanded in 1991 and 3.5" disk capacity in 1994. From 5 million diskettes per year in the 1980s, production capacity increased to 120 million units by 1996.

Further expansion of production capacity was planned in 1996 but this was not implemented as the company realized that newer technologies were likely to affect the future growth of the magnetic media industry. Optical storage and retrieval technology was proving to be commercially viable and by 1997, the company decided to establish capacity for manufacturing CDs. The production of CDs actually started in 1999 and with this MBIL moved to another growth trajectory; it also signified a major strategic shift for the company.

With economic reforms gathering momentum, MBIL also slowly started developing the vision of being a world-class player in all the products it was manufacturing. The decision to quit the production of time-recording system was part of this vision as was the decision to expand capacities of 5.25" and 3.5" floppy disks. It already had a reputation for quality and it focused on achieving 'zero defect' manufacturing. MBIL also committed significant resources to its R&D which had the mandate of developing product and process technologies useful for the company.

R&D has emerged as one of the most important drivers of MBIL's success. Development of the company's PC12D process and its subsequent versions has helped the company's products achieve broad compatibility across a wide spectrum of drives with writing speeds from 1X to 52X along with significant cost reductions. The company developed the fastest CD-R line in the world in cooperation with a major German company in 2002–3. Its strength in R&D has helped it to develop the ability to design manufacturing facilities and fabrication equipment—as well as the ability to develop highly flexible processes—thereby enabling the company to move quickly between different optical disk formats including customized disks.

MBIL is now setting up a manufacturing unit in Germany that will produce up to 17 per cent of its expanded capacity of two billion discs a year. This is a pointer to the fact that MBIL has graduated to a stage where it is not dependent on low labour cost processes to gain competitive advantages. In fact, it is confident of competing effectively with other global producers even with the discs being produced in Germany.

MBIL is an Indian company managed by Indian promoters and it has not benefited from any direct investment by another foreign optical media producer, although many foreign institutional investors and private equity firms like the International Finance Corporation (IFC), Warburg Pincus, and Electra Partners, have invested in the company.

Case 3: Sona Koyo Steering Systems Limited[2]

Sona Koyo Steering Systems Limited is the largest manufacturer of steering gears in India with a market share of 50 per cent. Its product range includes manual and power steering systems, rigid, tilt and collapsible steering columns, axle assemblies, and propeller shafts for the automobile industry. Besides being a large domestic player, it has entered the export market in a big way after setting up its 100 per cent export-oriented unit (EOU) in 2004. In a way, the progress of Sona Koyo represents that of the Indian automobile industry in recent times.

With the entry of Maruti Udyog Limited in 1983 the automobile industry in India experienced a severe jolt from the low-volume, low-innovation, low-competition equilibrium it had settled into over the years. Set up as a joint venture between the Government of India and Suzuki Motors of Japan, Maruti was initially importing all its critical parts and components from its Japanese technical partner but it had massive indigenization plans. Sona Steering Systems Ltd. was set up in 1985 during this phase of indigenization to manufacture manual steering gear assemblies and steering column assemblies in technical collaboration with Koyo Seiko Co. Ltd. of Osaka, Japan. Sona Steering established its manufacturing plant in Gurgaon, in close proximity to the Maruti plant while Maruti also picked up a 10 per cent stake in its equity.

With a strong technical collaborator like Koyo Seiko, Sona Steering thrived in its initial years riding piggyback on the success of Maruti. As Maruti increased its market share in the growing but protected Indian automobile market, Sona Steering's sales also rose. However, Maruti continued to be its only large customer. For each steering assembly, Maruti paid Sona the unit cost plus a nominal profit. After the Indian government announced its policy of economic liberalization in 1991 and the automobile

[2]This case is based on company website and Annual Reports and write-ups in *Outlook Money* (17 July 2004), *Deccan Herald* (7 September 2004), *Financial Express* (18 August 1998), and *Economic Times* (29 October and 23 November 2004).

sector was opened up in the mid-1990s, Sona also had to upgrade its product mix and look beyond Maruti. In 1998, the company established its second plant in Chennai to cater to the requirements of car makers in southern India.

Sona Steering had established itself as a quality producer right from its early days. This reputation helped it increase its production and sales year after year. With rising demand, it increased its capacity in both the Gurgaon and Chennai plants, and in October 2004 it established a 100 per cent EOU in Sriperumbudur near Chennai to cater to the demand from its overseas customer, namely Koyo Seiko who is also its technical collaborator and financial partner.

As it caters to the OEM market, Sona Koyo realized that growth in volumes would be the key driver of earnings as there is limited scope for improvement in profitability. In fact, like others in the auto ancillary industry it finds itself unable to revise its price to completely offset any increase in input cost. Therefore, it had to learn the skills required to continuously improve its business and manufacturing processes to simultaneously achieve lower costs and better quality. Even now Sona Koyo largely depends on its technical collaborator Koyo Seiko for its product and process technology but it has gone a long way in not only absorbing and assimilating that technology but also in improving it—particularly the shop-floor implementation—through continuous improvement.

Sona Koyo identified its core competency areas and decided to do away with the non-core activities. Outbound logistics was outsourced as was management and control of the receiving, storage, and issue functions. Sona Koyo has also outsourced several activities such as milk-run collections of parts from local suppliers and pick up, transport, storage, and delivery of parts to its Chennai plants on a Just-in-Time basis to its 3PL service providers. Operations at Sona Koyo also had strong support from TPM and TQM techniques, resulting in drastic improvement in profitability and quality of its products. Involvement of all the employees in these techniques contributed to lasting operating results. Subsequently, in 2003, Sona Koyo emerged as the first steering systems making company in the world to win the coveted Deming Application Prize. The prize acted as a shot in the arm for everyone at Sona Koyo and strengthened its brand equity.

The company no longer felt the need to establish its credentials with global auto majors looking out for low-cost world-class suppliers. It thought it could leverage the Deming Prize to scale up its export plans. Accordingly, it had to revise its investment and product development plans and established its 100 per cent EOU. The GM certification also helped as did the new production network concept of Koyo Seiko around the same time, utilizing cost-competitive units elsewhere as production hubs. The company, through Koyo Seiko, has already secured export orders worth US$ 35 million for manual steering gears to be executed over a five-year period. It has also been identified as the sole supplier of manual steering gear for Toyota's new vehicle to be launched globally. Sona Koyo also established a toehold in Europe through its 21 per cent equity stake in Fuji Autotech France Sas acquired in October 2004.

R&D expenses are only 0.8 per cent of net sales at Sona Koyo. This is low by international standards but Sona Koyo has the advantage of technical assistance from its partner Koyo Seiko. Sales of new products developed not more than three years ago accounted for about one-third of total sales at Sona Koyo.

The three case study firms reveal some characteristics of Indian manufacturing companies and their different approaches to technology acquisition, development, and assimilation. Most of them developed their technical skills in the domestic market and then included the export markets on their radar screens. MBIL represents a handful of Indian firms that developed global ambitions with the launch of its optical storage media and followed them up with domestic sales at a later date. However, the role of economic liberalization can be seen in all the three cases.

The evidence suggests that there is no easy or automatic transition from latecomer to leader or follower status. Indeed, products are grown extremely rapidly and successfully on the basis of subcontracting, OEM, and ODM. Once some basic capabilities are developed, it is relatively easy for such a firm to shift to new products based on those capabilities. This could be seen in the case of SFL when it entered the production of radiator caps, which was an entirely new line of products. Similarly, once it developed the capability to produce manual steering assemblies, Sona Koyo did not find it very difficult to produce power steering assemblies given the technological support of its technical collaborator.

A transition to leadership and followership on a broad front would require radical changes not only in the way latecomer firms operate but also in the environment in which they compete. For example, firms would have to develop strong marketing capabilities and invest heavily in creating brand images acceptable to worldwide consumers. Similarly, they would have to create a strong research culture within their companies and considerably increase their investments in basic and applied research to generate significant new innovations.

ARINDAM BANIK AND PRADIP K. BHAUMIK

References

Ernst, D., T. Ganiatsos, and L. Mytelka. 1998. *Technological Capabilities and Export Success in Asia,* London, Routledge.

Ivarsson, Inge and Claes Goran Alvstam. 2005. 'Technology Transfer from TNCs to Local Suppliers in Developing Countries: A Study of AB Volvo's Truck and Bus Plants in Brazil, China, India and Mexico', *World Development,* 33: 1325–44.

Javorcik, Beata Smarzynska. 2004. 'Does Foreign Investment Increase the Productivity of Domestic Firms? In Search of Spillovers through Backward Linkages', *American Economic Review,* 94: 605–27.

Katrak, Homi. 1989. 'Imported Technology and R&D in a Newly Industrialising Country: The Experience of Indian Enterprises', *Journal of Development Economics,* 31: 123–39.

Lall, S. 1983. 'Determinants of R&D in a LDC: The Indian Engineering Industry', *Economic Letters,* 13: 379–83.

——. 2000. 'Technological Change and Industrialisation in the Asian Newly Industrializing Economies: Achievements and Challenges', in L. Kim and R.R. Nelson (eds), *Technology, Learning & Innovation, Experiences of Newly Industrialising Economies,* Cambridge, Cambridge University Press.

Narula, R. and J.H. Dunning. 2000. 'Industrial Development, Globalization and Multinational Enterprises: New Realities for Developing Countries', *Oxford Development Studies,* 28: 141–67.

Siddharthan, N.S. 1992. 'Transaction Costs, Technology Transfer, and In-house R&D: A Study of Indian Private Corporate Sector', *Journal of Economic Behaviour and Organisation,* 18: 265–71.

■ Telecommunications

Background

Spurred by rapid innovations in digital technology, the telecommunications (telecom) sector has been one of the most dynamic areas of the Indian economy. Development of this sector has also been aided by policy reforms, although the reform process, involving opening up the sector to private participation, has not been a smooth one. Challenges have arisen in initial allocations of resources, as well as regulation of ongoing operations of the private sector. Challenges as well as progress have been the most marked in the provision of wireless or mobile telephone services.

In 2002, teledensity (numbers per 100 people) in India was still very low, at 4.28, of which fixed lines comprised 3.66 and mobiles only 0.62.[1] By 2005, India had teledensities of 4.4 wired and 11.3 mobile subscribers, well behind China's corresponding figures of 26.6 and 56.5, respectively. In both the countries, wired line teledensities started declining gradually, while mobile line numbers took off. The 2008 figures for wireless lines were 29.4 and 47.9 for India and China, respectively, and by August 2010, India's number had reached 56.6 for wireless teledensity.

In other aspects of telecom, however, India has continued to lag. In 2008, the percentage of households with a computer was only 4.4, and of those with internet access was 3.4, well behind China's 31.8 and 18.3 per cent, respectively. Similarly, China's internet bandwidth was 280 bits per person in 2007, many times India's figure of 32. Particular interest in the telecom sector, including internet as well as traditional voice calling, arises from its role in reducing transaction costs in the economy, democratizing access to information, and providing spillover benefits to the rest of the economy. Modern telecommunications are a prime example of the power of digital technologies, simultaneously increasing the richness and reducing the cost of long distance information exchange.

Policy Reforms

The historical case for regulation or for nationalized provision in telecom was based on economies of scale, implying that competition would be unstable or inefficient. India, like most countries, chose the latter route, with provision of telephones under a department of a central ministry. Telephones were treated as a luxury good, their availability was severely rationed, and equipment and service quality were typically quite poor. Technological changes removed the justification for monopoly in significant portions of the telecom value chain, by lowering fixed costs and adding new technological options, allowing competition to become feasible. New technologies include satellites, wireless, and fibre optics. Since market power may persist in portions of the value chain, in particular with respect to ownership of large networks (where economies of scale can still matter), regulation of interconnection charges is still required to maintain

[1]All data are from Telecom Regulatory Authority of India and/or International Telecommunications Union.

a level playing field. However, it is difficult to justify directly managing technology choices and competition on any grounds, economic or otherwise. The main policy objective should be to promote competition, and possibly innovation as well, though the former may well be sufficient to drive the latter. Indian regulatory practices have struggled with defining clear objectives as well as with regulatory implementation.

India's systematic telecom reforms were pre-dated by successful efforts in the 1980s to expand rural access, and that of less-well-off urban residents, by allowing private operators of phone booths to go in for local and long-distance calling. However, ownership of the network and provision of services remained a government monopoly. Telecom connections with the rest of the world were particularly limited. Beginning in 1991, a general reorientation of government policy towards allowing more market-based allocation of goods was an important backdrop for telecom reforms. At the same time, the meteoric rise of the export-oriented Indian information technology (IT) services industry in the 1990s created pressure for improving telecom infrastructure, in particular of external access.

The IT industry uses international data links for accessing clients' hardware, communicating by e-mail, exchanging files among joint development teams, and carrying out remote diagnosis and maintenance work. IT-enabled services use voice lines for call centres and data lines for transmitting electronic files back and forth. Internet-based media companies also require data links. While all economic activity requires good communications infrastructure, the rapid rise of the internet has increased such needs. Some physical infrastructure investments were made to serve the needs of the IT industry, beginning in the 1990s. More important, two successive attempts were made, in 1994 and 1999, to reshape the telecom policy in a world where technological change in that sector was accelerating. Private firms were allowed into the nascent wireless/mobile telecom sector through auctions of licences. Despite corruption and mistakes in the process of allocating licences and in the design of licensing agreements, on the whole, this was a successful and significant change in improving telecom access for India's population. Liberalization and reforms were extended to other aspects of the telecom infrastructure, such as new fibre optic networks. The external gateway provider Videsh Sanchar Nigam Limited (VSNL) was also eventually privatized.

As part of the reform process, India created a new regulatory institution for telecom, the Telecom Regulatory Authority of India (TRAI). TRAI was constituted in 1997, but initially was relatively ineffective, due to lack of authority and interference by the Department of Telecommunications. TRAI was given greater and clearer authority in 2000 (Dossani 2002), and has evolved into a somewhat effective regulatory body, though still constrained by political interference. TRAI's scope includes establishing the quality of service parameters, monitoring compliance, examining technology choices, and so on. It is supposed to establish a level playing field and encourage competition, but it still lacks authority precisely where it needs it the most, in setting entry fees and some interconnection charges. Unfortunately, bringing quality of service, technology choice, and universal service obligations (USOs) into the regulatory mix has only served to muddy the waters, and diverted attention from what should be the core regulatory task of enabling and maintaining effective competition. TRAI has also continued to struggle with political pressure that comes from the needs of the government-owned former monopoly provider of telephone services, now a state-owned enterprise christened Bharat Sanchar Nigam Limited (BSNL). There have been continued concerns about a favourable treatment of this strong incumbent vis-à-vis private entrants. A similar privileged position has been held by Mahanagar Telephone Nigam Limited (MTNL), also a government corporation, which serves the lucrative Delhi and Mumbai markets.

The allocation of the wireless spectrum, which has a heavy influence on the functioning of the telecom industry, has also remained outside TRAI's control. Initial Indian auctions for wireless spectrum were held in 1995; these were affected by corruption, which led to inefficient allocations and unequal treatment of potential entrants. Subsequently, there was continual tinkering with licence conditions, including service obligations and revenue sharing requirements. The political power of the government-controlled incumbent, and its attempts to ensure it would not be marginalized by new entrants, also played a role in this process. In 2001, another significant allocation of licences was made. At that time, telecom penetration, both wired and wireless, was still relatively low, but growth accelerated shortly thereafter, fueled by increased investment (domestic and foreign), greater competition, overall economic growth, and continued innovation that brought down costs of infrastructure and mobile handsets.

In 2007, another significant allocation of spectrum was made, this time for 2G ('second generation'—shorthand for a newer set of wireless technologies and standards) telecom. However, the process this time appeared to be completely subverted by the telecom minister, replacing an auction with a highly discretionary and arbitrary procedure. The ostensible justification for not using an auction was to increase competition and allow entrants scope for initial investment and lower pricing by avoiding bidding up the price of spectrum. Indeed, the result of the new allocation was 'hypercompetition', with price wars and rapid expansion of the number of subscribers. However, it is clear that some firms which were allocated spectrum did not meet basic requirements to build businesses, and merely resold their stakes to realize quick windfall profits. Concerns raised by senior bureaucrats and by TRAI were ignored in the entire process. As of 2010, the 2G spectrum allocation stands out as India's most significant and single most costly example of corruption. In contrast, in 2010, licences for spectrum for 3G wireless services (which allow for true integration of data and voice, or internet and mobile telephony) were successfully and transparently auctioned, raising significant revenue for the government. It may be noted that BSNL and MTNL were both given significant head starts over private providers in providing 3G services.

Rural Access

The process of opening up the telecom sector to private participants has been accompanied by political rhetoric favouring goals of universal access. BSNL's special treatment has been justified by its extensive penetration in rural India, and its obligations to provide broader telecom access. As noted, USOs were also built into licensing deals for the new private service providers. These have taken the form of: (i) quantitative targets for installing rural telephones and (ii) funds created through a form of tax on basic services, to be used for proposed subsidies for rural users. However, in a situation where licensing and interconnection fees have made it uneconomical for local access providers with lower-cost technology to enter, it is not clear that the numerical targets have been of any use. The distinction between serving rural users in general (including the well-off) and providing shared telecoms access for the less well-off (through, for example, public call offices or internet kiosks) is crucial, and was made clear in a dissenting comment by committee member Rakesh Mohan, but this was not accepted by a majority of the TRAI committee that reported on the USOs (TRAI 2001).

In fact, rural telecom penetration has increased significantly, but it may be driven more by falling costs through innovation and competition, and by rising incomes, rather than numerical targets or USOs in general. The gap between urban and rural telecom penetration remains much greater than rural-urban income differentials. In June 2010, for example, wireless teledensities were 25.3 and 120.6 for rural and urban residents, respectively. Since overall internet penetration is very low in India, with an estimate of only 81 million users, the disparity between rural and urban internet access is almost certainly much greater than for basic wireless telecom.

Prior to mobile telephony taking off, there were several private not-for-profit attempts to provide rural internet access, or integrated voice and internet access through rural internet kiosks (Singh 2006). These efforts sought to scale up by creating an entrepreneurial model for local kiosk operators, but none of them were successful in achieving adequate scale or economic viability. The only exception has been the *e-choupals* set up by ITC, an Indian agribusiness conglomerate, where substantial gains are claimed in more efficient procurement of wheat and soybeans through the e-choupal networks. The greatest barrier to financial sustainability turned out to be the lack of access to low-cost, reliable connectivity to the network. ITC has used VSAT (very small aperture terminal) satellite connectivity, but that is not a cost effective solution. Unnecessary restrictions and high fees, including interconnect charges, licensing fees and deposit requirements for entry, restrictions on franchising, and limited bandwidth allocations all work to raise costs of rural telecom access. These problems were faced when the government was the monopoly telecom network provider, and may remain even with the entry of private providers, who will be seeking adequate rates of return. The spread of mobile telephony in rural areas also undermined attempts to bundle voice and internet services in rural kiosks, since those lost one important revenue stream.

In the context of promoting rural telecom access, an alternative to quotas, which are difficult to monitor and enforce, may be a narrowly targeted subsidy for enabling reliable rural telecom access. In particular, 3G (and ultimately 4G) services, which offer the use of the same networks for voice and data, will require new investments in infrastructure. Closed-ended subsidies (so that there is no incentive distortion at the margin) to deploy these new technologies and associated infrastructure may be justifiable in terms of social returns. One way to implement such a subsidy (see, for example, Dossani et al. 2005) would be to use USO funds collected from telecommunication providers to finance improved rural ICT access.

Rather than leverage previous private efforts or subsidize private telecom providers, the government has preferred to pursue rural internet access through a new nationwide network of common service centres (CSCs), although in a public private partnership. A scheme to have one CSC for every six villages was launched in 2006. As with earlier private efforts, the goal was to facilitate e-governance, education, health, and other services. The goal is to contract out CSC operations to various private service centre agencies (SCAs), which will create cadres of entrepreneurs to run them. In practice, while government statistics indicate significant progress in meeting numerical targets for setting up CSCs, in many cases, the SCAs and the CSCs under their control may not be functional in practice (Indicus Analytics 2010). While the government seeks to preserve incentives for service provision at the village level through this model, it is not clear whether it will be able to avoid the inefficiencies that plague government efforts in many spheres. There are also challenges of creating content and applications in local languages to attract rural users.

Earlier arguments for a focus on mobile phone access rather than internet kiosks in developing countries (*The Economist* 2005) neglected the convergence in technologies as well as the different functions served by the two access modes. Digital convergence means that separating voice from data in formulating policies for rural access no longer makes sense. Shared mobile phones are very effective for certain types of communication and their capabilities keep increasing, including internet access in 3G networks. Hence, they represent an important component of rural telecom access. However, for many types of information access, where quantity and ease of reading and processing matter more than mobility, the use of desktop or laptop computers is more cost-effective, or efficient more generally. In addition, a computer with a printer is able to provide a wide range of services that are not communication-related, but just involve processing of information. Ultimately, in the next stage of technological evolution, all access devices will share the same telecom networks, providing further economies.

Conclusion

Combining data and voice access in an economical manner through shared devices increases the value of connecting to the network. The benefits would accrue not just to the poor, but also to the tens of millions of lower middle-class households who are currently outside the affordability radius. Social returns can include better governance, as well as knowledge, which is an important enabler of 'empowerment', or 'development as freedom' (Sen 1999), as well as a potential input into basic services such as health and education. A denser domestic network can also increase the value of the network and of international links to it. Hence, there is a possible case for investing more heavily in India's telecom sector.

Telecom has changed dramatically over the last two decades, due to rapid innovation centred on digital technologies. In addition to traditional voice communications, all kinds of data and information can now be exchanged through modern telecom networks. In India, some of the benefits of these developments have been realized through policy reforms that have permitted more competition and private entry, leading to greater investment and cost savings that are passed on to consumers. Nevertheless, telecom regulation in India has not been ideal, and government policy has not focused adequately on ways to stimulate a cost-effective provision of telecom access to rural India, where a majority of the country's population still resides.

NIRVIKAR SINGH

References

Dossani, Rafiq. 2002. *Telecommunications Reform in India*, Westport, CT, Quorum Books.

Dossani, Rafiq, D.C. Mishra, and Roma Jhaveri. 2005. 'Enabling ICT for Rural India', Project Report, Stanford University and National Informatics Centre, India.

The Economist. 2005. 'The Real Digital Divide, Technology and Development Survey', 10 March.

Indicus Analytics. 2010. 'Ringing in a Revolution', *Business Standard*, 28 October, p. 14.

Sen, Amartya K. 1999. *Development as Freedom*, Oxford, Oxford University Press.

Singh, Nirvikar. 2006. 'ICTs and Rural Development in India', Project Report to the Rajiv Gandhi Institute for Contemporary Studies, New Delhi.

TRAI. 2001. *TRAI Recommendations on Universal Service Obligation (USO)*, 3 October, available at http://www.trai.gov.in/Recommendations_content.asp?id=61.

Textile and Apparel Industry

The Multi-Fibre Agreement (MFA), that had governed the extent of textile trade between nations since 1962, expired on 1 January 2005. It is expected that, post-MFA, most tariff distortions will gradually disappear and firms with robust capabilities will gain in the global trade of textile and apparel. The prize is the $360 billion market which is expected to grow to about $600 billion by the year 2010—barely five years after the expiry of the MFA. An important question facing Indian firms is whether their capabilities and their diverse supply chain are aligned to benefit from the opening up of the global textile market?

The history of textiles in India dates back to the use of mordant dyes and printing blocks around 3000 BC. The diversity of fibres found in India, intricate weaving on its state-of-the-art manual looms, and its organic dyes attracted buyers from all over the world for centuries. The British colonization of India and its industrial policies destroyed the innovative sector and left it technologically impoverished. Independent India saw the building up of textile capabilities, diversification of its product base, and its emergence, once again, as an important global player. Today, the textile and apparel sector in India employs 35 million people (and is the second largest employer), generates one-fifth of the total export earnings, and contributes 4 per cent to the gross domestic product thereby making it the largest industrial sector of the country. This textile economy is worth US$ 37 billion and its share of the global market is about 5.90 per cent. The sector aspires to increase its revenue to US$ 85 billion, its export value to US$ 50 billion, and employment to 12 million by the year 2010 (Texmin 2005).

The Textile and Apparel Supply Chain

The textile and apparel supply chain comprises diverse raw material sectors, ginning facilities, spinning and extrusion processes, the processing sector, weaving and knitting factories, and garment (and other stitched and non-stitched) manufacturing that supply an extensive distribution channel (see Figure 1). This supply chain is perhaps one of the most diverse in terms of the raw materials used, technologies deployed, and goods produced.

This supply chain supplies about 70 per cent by value of its production to the domestic market. The distribution channel comprises wholesalers, distributors, and a large number of small retailers selling garments and textiles. It is only recently that large retail formats are emerging, thereby increasing variety as well as volume on display at a single location. Another feature of the distribution channel is the strong presence of 'agents' who secure and consolidate orders for producers. Exports are traditionally executed through export houses or procurement/commissioning offices of large global apparel retailers.

It is estimated that there exist 65,000 garment units in the organized sector, of which about 88 per cent are for woven cloth while the remaining are for knits. However, only 30–40 units are large in size (as a result of long years of reservation of non-exporting garment units for the small-scale sectors—a regulation that was recently removed). While these firms are spread all over the country, there are clusters emerging in the National Capital Region (NCR), Mumbai, Bangalore, Tirupur/Coimbatore, and Ludhiana employing about 3.5 million people. According to my estimate, the total value of production in the garment sector is around

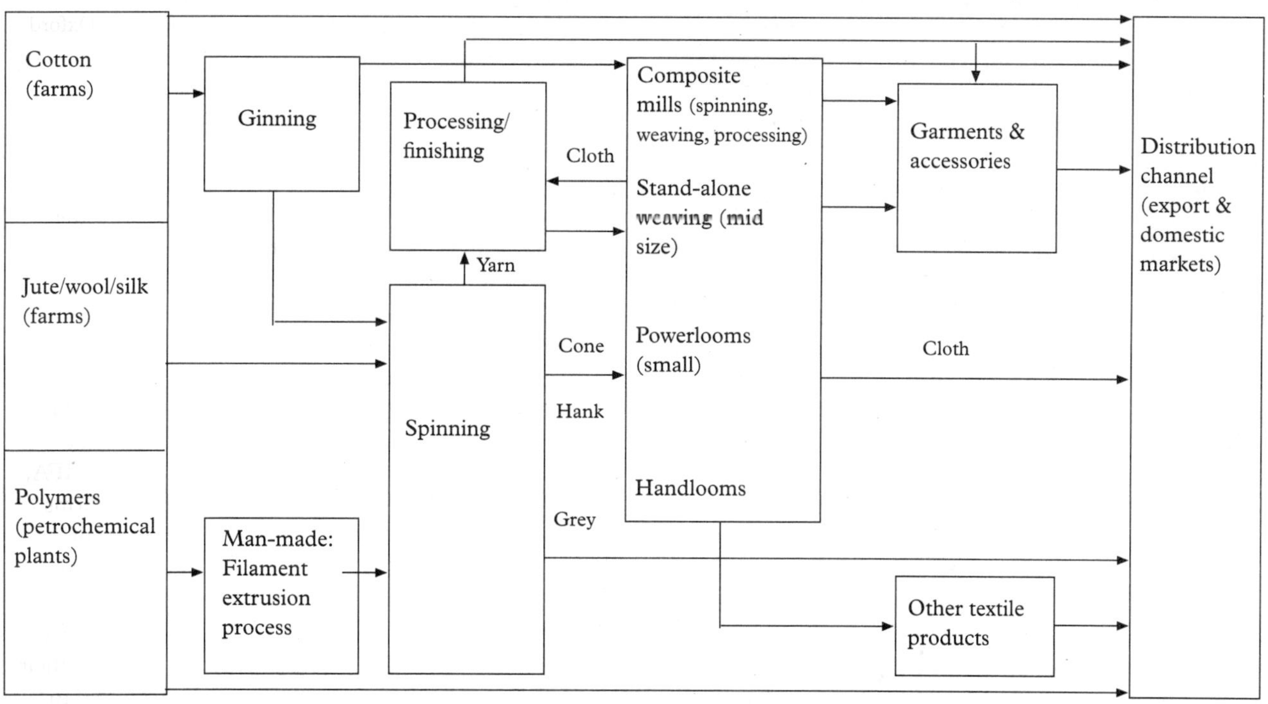

Figure 1 The Textile and Apparel Supply Chain

Rs 1050–1100 billion, of which about 81 per cent comes from the domestic market. The value of Indian garments (for example saree, dhoti, and salwar kurta) is around Rs 200–50 billion. About 40 per cent of fabric for garment production is imported—a figure that is expected to rise in coming years.

The weaving and knits sector lies at the heart of the industry. In 2004–5, of the total production from the weaving sector, about 46 per cent was cotton cloth, 41 per cent was 100 per cent non-cotton including khadi, wool and silk, and 13 per cent was blended cloth. Three distinctive technologies are used in the sector—handlooms, powerlooms, and knitting machines. They also represent very distinctive supply chains. The handloom sector (including khadi, silk, and some wool) serves the low and high ends of the value chain—both mass consumption products for use in rural India as well as niche products for urban and exports markets. It chiefly produces textiles with geographical characterization (for example, cotton and silk sarees in Pochampally or Varanasi) and in small batches. Handloom production in 2003–4 was around 5493 million sq. m, of which about 82 per cent was using cotton fibre. Handloom production is mostly rural (employing about 10 million, mostly, household weavers) and revolves around master weavers who provide designs, raw material, and often the loom.

Weaving, using powerlooms, was traditionally done by composite mills that combined it with spinning and processing operations. Over the years, government incentives and demand for low-cost, high-volume, standard products (especially sarees and grey cloth) moved the production towards powerloom factories and away from composite mills (that were essentially full-line variety producers). While some like Arvind Mills or Ashima transformed themselves into competitive units, others gradually closed down. In 2003–4, there remained 223 composite mills that produced 1,434 million sq. m of cloth. Most of these mills are located in Gujarat and Maharashtra. Most of the woven cloth comes from the powerlooms (chiefly at Surat, Bhiwandi, the NCR, and Chennai). In 2005, there were 425,792 registered powerloom units that produced 26,947 million sq. m of cloth and employed about 4,757,383 workers. The weaving sector is predominantly small scale, has on average 4.5 powerlooms per unit, suffers from outdated technology, and incurs high coordination costs. Knits have been more successful, especially in export channels. Strong production clusters like Tirupur and Ludhiana have led to growth of an accessories sector as well, albeit slowly. The hosiery sector, on the other hand, has largely a domestic focus and is growing rapidly.

The spinning sector is perhaps most competitive globally in terms of variety, unit prices, and production quantity. Though cotton is the fibre of preference, man-made fibre (polyster fibre and polyster filament yarn) is also produced by about 100 large- and medium-size producers.

Spinning is done by 1,566 mills and 1,170 small and medium enterprises (SME). Mills, chiefly located in north India, deploy 34.24 million spindles and 0.385 million rotors while the SME units produce their yarn on 3.29 million spindles and 0.119 million rotors producing 2,270 million kg of cotton yarn, 950 million kg of blended yarn, and about 1,106 million kg of man-made filament yarn every year. Worsted and non-worsted spindles (producing woollen yarn) have also progressively grown to 0.604 million and 0.437 million, respectively. The spinning sector is technology intensive and productivity is affected by the quality of cotton and the cleaning process used during ginning.

The processing sector, that is, dyeing, finishing, and printing, is mostly small in scale. The largest amongst these would dye and finish about 5,000 m of cloth per day. The remaining are independent process houses (or part of composite mills) that use automated large batch or continuous processing and have an average scale of about 20,000 m of cloth daily. About 82.5 per cent or 10,397 units are hand processors who dye cloth or yarn manually and dry in open sunshine. Of the remaining (and these use automated and semi-automated equipment), 2,076 are independent process houses.

Cotton remains the most significant raw material for the Indian textile industry. In 2003–4, 3,009 million kg of cotton was grown over 7.785 million acres. Other fibres produced are silk (15,742 tonnes), jute (10,985,000 bales), wool (50.7 million kg), and man-made fibres (1,100.65 million kg). Cotton grows mostly in western and central India, silk in southern India, and jute in eastern India; wool comes mostly from northern India. Significant quantities of cotton, silk, and wool fibres are also imported by the spinning and knitting sectors.[1]

Managing such a complex supply chain requires coordination through excellent managerial practices, technology, and facilitating policies.

Competitiveness of Indian Textile and Apparel Industry

India is one of the few countries that owns the complete supply chain in close proximity from diverse fibres to

[1]Except for garments, all data in this section were obtained from OTC 2004 and Texmin 2005.

a large market. It is capable of delivering packaged products to customers comprising a variety of fibres, diverse count sizes, cloths of different weight and weave, and a panoply of finishes. This permits the supply chain to mix and match variety in different segments to deliver new products and applications. This advantage is further accentuated by cost-based advantages and diverse traditions in textiles.

Indian strength in spinning is now well established—on unit costs on ring yarn, open-ended (OE) yarn, as well as textured yarn, Indian firms are ahead of their global competitors including China. The same is true of some woven OE-yarn fabric categories (especially grey fabrics) but is not true for other woven segments. India contributes about 23 per cent of world spindles and 6 per cent of world rotors (second highest in the world after China). In the last decade, 55 per cent of total investment in technology has been made in the spinning sector. Its share in global shuttleless looms, however, is only about 2.8 per cent (and it is ranked ninth in the world). The competitiveness in the weaving sector is adversely affected by low penetration of shuttleless looms (that is, 1.69 per cent of Indian looms), the unorganized nature of the sector (that is, fragmented, small, and, often, unregistered units and low investment in technology and practices especially in powerloom, processing, handloom, and knits), and higher power tariffs. There is, however, a recent trend of investment in setting up hi-tech, stand-alone mid-size weaving companies focusing on export markets. India also has the highest deployment of handlooms in the world (handlooms are low on productivity but produce specialized fabric). While production and export of man-made fibre (and filament yarn) has increased over the years, Indian industry still lags significantly behind the US, China, Europe, Taiwan, among others (Texmin 2005).

Indian textile industry has suffered in the past from low productivity at both ends of the supply chain—low farm yields affecting cotton production and inefficiency in garment sector due to restriction of size and reservation. Add to this, contamination of cotton with consequent increase in cost (as it affects quality and requires installation of additional process to clean and open cotton fibres before carding operations), poor ginning (most equipment dates back to the 1940s), high average defect rates in the production process (which also lead to increase in effective labour and power costs), hank yarn requirement, and its competitiveness gets severely compromised. Similarly, processing technology is primarily manual and small-batch oriented with visual colour matching and sun drying. This leads to inconsistency in conformance quality. Lead times across the sector continue to be affected by variability in the supply chain—defect rates average over 5 per cent, average of orders on time is about 80 per cent, variance in order size across firms is high (for example, the coefficient of variability of average order size for spinning firms is about 2.6)—and on an average sixteen days of sales as work-in-process (WIP) inventory (the highest for garment firms) and an average of 30 days of sales in raw material inventory (the highest for spinning firms) (Chandra 2004). Some of the hurdles (for example, reservation in the garment sectors) including tariff distortions between the organized and unorganized sectors have now been systematically removed by policy initiatives of the Government of India and this has opened avenues for firms to compete on the basis of their capabilities.

Trade data of post-MFA performance reveal some interesting trends—Indian firms registered a 27 per cent growth in exports to the US (against China's 52 per cent) during the January–April 2005 time period. Most of this growth has been in textiles while apparels show marginal gains. Apparels and accessories constituted 78 per cent of global exports to the US (FICCI 2005). (India is still a relatively small yet growing player in the global apparel market.) It is expected that India will soon replace Mexico as the second largest apparel supplier to the US.

Challenges Facing Indian Textile and Apparel Industry

Textile supply chains compete on low cost, high quality, accurate delivery, and flexibility in variety and volume. Several challenges stand in the way of Indian firms before they can command a larger share of the global market.

Scale

Except for spinning, all other sectors suffer from the problem of scale. Indian firms are typically smaller than their Chinese or Thai counterparts and there are fewer large firms in India. Some of the Chinese large firms have 1.5 times higher spinning capacity, 1.25 times denim (and 2 times grey fabric) capacity, and about 6 times more revenue in garments than their counterparts in India, thereby affecting the cost structure as well as ability to attract customers with large orders. The central tendency is to add capacity once the order has been won rather than ahead of the demand. Customers go where they see both capacity and capabilities. Large capacity typically goes with standardized products. These firms need to develop the managerial capabilities required to manage a large workforce and design an appropriate supply chain. For the size of the Indian economy, it will have to have bigger firms producing standard products in large volumes as well as small- and mid-size firms producing large variety in small- to mid-size batches (the tension between the organized and unorganized sectors will have to be addressed first, though). Then, there is the need for emergence of specialist firms that will consolidate orders, book capacities, and manage warehouses and the logistics of order delivery.

Skills

Three issues must be mentioned here: (i) there is paucity of technical manpower—there exist barely 30 programmes at graduate engineering (including diploma) level, graduating about 1,000 students—this is insufficient for bringing about technological change in the sector; (ii) Indian firms invest very little in training their existing workforce and the skills are limited to existing processes (Chandra 1998); and (iii) there is an acute shortage of trained operators and supervisors in India. It is expected that Indian firms will have to invest close to Rs 1,400 billion by the year 2010 to increase their global trade to $50 billion. This kind of investment would require, by my calculations, about 70,000 supervisors and 1.05 million operators in the textiles sector and at least 112,000 supervisors and 2.8 million operators in the apparel sector (assuming a 80:20 ratio of investment between textiles and apparel). The real bottleneck to growth is going to be availability of skilled manpower.

Cycle Time

Cycle time is the key to competitiveness of a firm as it affects both price and delivery schedule. Cycle-time reduction is strongly correlated with high first-pass yield, high throughput times, low variability in process times, and low WIP and consequently cost. Indian firms have to dramatically reduce cycle times that are currently quite high across the entire supply chain (Chandra 2004). Customs must provide a turnaround time of half a day for an order before Indian firms can expect to become part of larger global supply chains. Indian firms need a strong deployment of industrial engineering with particular emphasis on cellular manufacturing, JIT, and statistical process control to reduce lead times on shop floors. Penetration of information technology for improving productivity is particularly low in this sector.

Innovation and Technology

A review of the products imported from China to the USA during January–April 2005 reveals that the top three products in terms of percentage increase in imports were tire cords and tire fabrics (843.4 per cent increase over the previous year), non-woven fabrics (284.1 per cent increase), and textile/fabric finishing mill products (197.2 per cent increase) (FICCI 2005). None of these items, however, figures in the list of imports from India that have gained in these early post-MFA days. Entry into newer application domains of industrial textiles, nano-textiles, home furnishings, and so on, becomes imperative if we are to grow beyond 5–6 per cent of global market share as these are areas that are projected to grow significantly. Synthetic textiles comprise about 50 per cent of the global textile market. The Indian synthetic industry, however, is not well entrenched. The Technology Upgradation Fund of the government is being used to stimulate investment in new processes. However, there is little evidence that this deployment in technology has accompanied changes in the managerial regimes—a necessary condition for increasing productivity and order-winning ability.

Domestic Market

The Indian domestic market for all textile and apparel products is estimated at $26 billion and growing. While the market is very competitive at the low end of the value chain, the mid or higher ranges are overpriced (that is, 'dollar pricing'). Firms are not taking advantage of the large domestic market in generating economies of scale to deliver cost advantage in export markets. The Free Trade Agreement with Singapore and Thailand will allow overseas producers to meet the aspirations of domestic buyers with quality and prices that are competitive in the domestic market. Ignoring the domestic market, in the long run, will imperil the export markets for domestic producers. In addition, high retail property prices and high channel margins in India will restrict growth of this market. Firms need to make their supply chain leaner in order to overcome these disadvantages.

Institutional Support

Textile policy has gone a long way towards reducing impediments for the industry—sometimes driven by global competition and, at other times, by international trade regulations. However, few areas of policy weakness stand out—labour reforms (which is hindering movement towards higher scale of operations by Indian firms), power availability and quality, customs clearance and shipment operations from ports, credit for large-scale investments that are needed for upgradation of technology, and development of manpower for the industry. These are problems facing several sectors of industry in India and not this sector alone.

In conclusion, competitive strategies are developed by sector-level firms and it is their individual and collective initiatives that secure a higher market share in global trade. While one has to be ever vigilant regarding non-tariff barriers in the post-MFA world, the new market will be won on the basis of capabilities across the supply chain. Policy will need to facilitate this building of capabilities at firm level and the flexible strategies that firms will need to devise periodically.

PANKAJ CHANDRA

References

Chandra, P. (ed.). 1998. *Technology, Practices, and Competitiveness: The Primary Textiles Industry in Canada, China, and India*, Mumbai, Himalaya Publishing House.

——. 2004. 'Competitiveness of Indian Textiles & Garment Industry: Some Perspectives', a presentation, Ahmedabad, Indian Institute of Management, December.

Federation of Indian Chambers of Commerce and Industry (FICCI). 2005. 'Trends Analysis of India & China's Textiles and Apparel Exports to USA Post MFA', New Delhi, FICCI, July.

Office of the Textile Commissioner (OTC). 2004. 'Compendium of Textile Statistics', Mumbai, OTC, Ministry of Textiles, Government of India.

Texmin, Official website of Ministry of Textiles, Government of India. 2005. http://texmin.nic.in

Tourism

Tourism has come a long way from the luxury good it was perceived to be in the centrally planned Indian economy of the post-Independence era. It received little attention from the government until the 1960s, after which its foreign-exchange-generating potential was recognized in a closed economy severely short of foreign exchange. At the time, tourism infrastructure and services were limited and only the government had the resources, or indeed the incentive, to invest in these. But committing resources to tourism meant diverting them from areas such as agriculture and infrastructure, which were in dire need of investment. This called for very focused development of tourism, aimed mainly at generating foreign exchange, and an implicit decision was taken to attract high-end foreign tourists by investing in air capacity and luxury accommodation like the Ashok Hotel in New Delhi. In 1966, the government set up the India Tourism Development Corporation (ITDC) to promote the country as a tourist destination abroad, and to develop a hotel network for these tourists.

Domestic tourism at the time consisted mainly of pilgrimages and visits to relatives, with some of the wealthier people travelling to hill stations during summer to stay in circuit houses, summer rentals, or second homes. The government did little to actively encourage domestic travel, but took the more passive stance of setting up State Tourism Development Corporations and tourist offices, building some low-cost accommodation, and providing rail and bus services to the more popular destinations, mainly catering to lower-end travellers. It was the expansion of the leave travel concession (LTC) schemes—where government employees were encouraged to travel once a year with their families—which gave the initial boost to non-pilgrimage-based domestic tourism in the country.

Since then, the domestic tourism market has grown rapidly from an estimated 14 million in 1981 to 135 million in 1995, 220 million in 2000, and 309 million in 2003 (Ministry of Tourism 2004). (Domestic travel statistics are not as reliable as international arrivals data, as they are based on information collected by state departments of tourism, but they show a clear upward trend.) 'Attending social functions' has replaced 'pilgrimage visits' as the most common reason for travel, but this is followed closely by leisure and business travel (ibid.). The more recent rapid rise in domestic travel has been fuelled by the growing middle class, expansion in privately funded accommodation across all price ranges from *dharamshala*s to heritage palaces, and declining airfares in the wake of airline deregulation and competition.

International travel to India, in contrast, despite being the focus of tourism policy and programmes for the last forty years, has remained at almost the same level for the last decade. While domestic tourism within the country now accounts for a 4.6 per cent share of domestic tourism worldwide (2004), India's share of the world market has remained almost stagnant at 0.38 per cent since 1995 (Ministry of Tourism 2004). Between 1998 and 2003, international arrivals have hovered around 2.4 million to 2.7 million (of approximately 700 million total global arrivals), a large proportion of whom were non-resident Indians (NRIs) (ibid.).[1]

Thus, despite its tremendous richness as a cultural, historical, and adventure tourist destination, India lags behind its neighbours such as Indonesia, which

[1]International arrivals are used as a proxy for international tourism, but the data are an overestimate as they include all foreign visitors, both leisure and business, and refer to the actual number of arrivals into the country even if they are multiple trips made by one individual. The World Travel and Tourism Council (WTTC) estimates that around 8 per cent of international visitors come to India for business (WTTC 2004). However, Ministry of Tourism figures estimate that around 4 per cent visit for business.

received around 4.5 to 5 million tourists between 1998 and 2003, Thailand, which received 7.8 to 10 million tourists, and Malaysia, which received between 5.5 and 13 million in the same period (World Tourism Organization website). Interestingly, for every foreign visitor to the country, more than twice as many Indians travel abroad. With the easing of travel permits and foreign exchange restrictions, the number of Indians going abroad has grown from 1.9 million in 1991 to 4.9 million in 2002 (ibid.).

Till recently, tourism was considered an elitist activity conducted primarily to earn foreign exchange. It is only recently, in the National Tourism Policy of 2002, that the industry's potential as a catalyst for growth and employment generation has been recognized. Strong linkages between tourism and almost all sectors imply that the multiplier effect of tourism-related expenditure is very high, especially till the mid-1990s when the leakage rate (through tourism-related imports) was one of the lowest in the world, as strict foreign exchange controls meant that almost all inputs were sourced domestically. Tourism-related services today (2004) directly and indirectly employ 25 million people (WTTC 2004).

India's low share in the world tourism market and its poor performance compared to other developing countries have largely been a result of infrastructural constraints. Most foreign tourists (more than 30 per cent in 2003) (Ministry of Tourism 2003) originate from the UK or US, and high airfares, relative to comparable Asian destinations are a major deterrent to travellers. Travel within the country is hampered by the poor road network linking many tourist circuits, overcrowded trains, and expensive air travel. Most large Indian cities have very little by way of budget accommodation, unlike Asian competitors such as Jakarta, Bangkok, and Kuala Lumpur, because of the high cost of commercial real estate and cumbersome land acquisition process. In Mumbai, for example, procuring a licence to build a hotel involves more than a hundred applications.

Many of these problems arise from the shared responsibility for basic tourism infrastructure between the central and state governments which has worked against the integrated development of the industry. Also, state governments control many areas crucial to tourism—local infrastructure, transport systems, municipal taxation, sanitation, law and order, and the preservation of local monuments—and their commitment has varied over time and across states. This lack of planning is most evident in the popular hill resorts of the past, many of which have lost their intrinsic tourist appeal by becoming sprawling urban clusters, facing major environmental problems. While private investment has increased in many parts of the industry such as hotels, airlines, and road transport, and in areas that impinge on tourism services such as sanitation and telecommunications, bureaucratic red-tape and convoluted administrative procedures are still a strong deterrent.

Despite these drawbacks tourism continues to be an evolving, dynamic industry with new initiatives that have captured the interest of travellers. These include rural homestays combined with village tourism, which originated in Kerala but have been successfully replicated in Sikkim and other parts of the north-east; heritage tourism which has encouraged the restoration of *haveli*s, forts, and palaces, especially in Rajasthan and Madhya Pradesh; and mountain and adventure sports, such as river rafting, trekking, and rappelling. A 'Buddhist circuit' spanning several states is still evolving, but is becoming popular among visitors from the region, especially from East Asia. An emerging area that has received a boost through the new super-specialty hospitals is 'medical tourism', where patients visit the country for surgery and then recuperate in a resort of their choice. An estimated 150,000 medical tourists visited India in 2003. Changing demographics and widening price differentials in medical care between the US/Europe and India are expected to boost the Indian medical tourism industry to a $ 1 billion business by 2012 (CII–McKinsey Study on Healthcare 2004).

If managed well, these new ventures should lead to a more environmentally and culturally sustainable development of tourism than the random, unplanned path taken earlier, which has drastically affected the environment of the popular hill stations of the past.

ANURADHA BHASIN

References

CII-McKinsey Study on Healthcare. 2004. Quoted in www.embassyofindia.com/IndiaNewsMay2004.

Ministry of Tourism. Various years. Tourism Statistics. Market Research Division, Government of India.

World Travel and Tourism website (wttc.org).

World Tourism Organization website (world-tourism.org).

World Tourism Organization. 2004. Compendium of Tourism Statistics 2004.

World Travel and Tourism Council (WTTC). 2004. *India Travel and Tourism: Forging Ahead 2004*, Travel and Tourism Economic Research.

Trade Barriers in Manufacturing

The Nehru–Mahalanobis framework for Indian industrialization based on an import-substituting trade regime led to the emergence of trade barriers vis-à-vis Indian manufacturing. This regime of restrictions in trade continued for almost four decades after the initiation of planned development efforts in India in 1947. There have been several studies documenting the level of trade barriers in India's manufacturing sector. Evidence from these studies states that despite the prevalence of high import barriers, there have been conscious attempts since the mid-1970s to dismantle the complicated trade structure encompassing high and prohibitive levels of tariffs as well as a complicated licensing system for imports. In the 1990s, trade policies underwent major reforms. It was perceived that through widespread changes in rules and regulations that govern the trading of commodities and raw materials, Indian industries would be made competitive in global markets through better import conditions and easy export avenues. At the end of the 1990s, do we observe that the level of trade barriers for Indian manufacturing has declined substantially?

But first, what do we understand by trade barriers? In India, in the name of import-substitution-based trade strategy of industrialization, there were barriers to free trade (read imports) in the form of tariff and non-tariff measures. In simple terminology, an import tariff is a duty/tax on an ad valorem or specific basis levied on a product when it is imported into the country, whereas non-tariff barriers mean that there are various forms of restrictions on the import of a commodity. In India, for the period before the 1991 trade policy reforms, not only were the peak tariff rates high but there were multiple tariff rates. Further, for a single commodity we could find several rates of tariff if we include the exemptions that were prevalent. The government levied three types of indirect taxes on goods imported into India—basic customs duty, auxiliary duty, and additional duty. After the 1991 reforms, the auxiliary duty was merged with the basic customs duty and there were considerable reductions in the number of notifications issued. The actual rate often called the effective rate was determined by the various exemption notifications announced by the Government of India. The range of tariff rates extended from zero to almost 300 per cent in the pre-reform era and presently they are in the region of 15–20 per cent.

The second kind of trade barrier prevalent in the Indian economy was called the non-tariff barrier, which operated through the import licensing system put in place to regulate flow of imports to protect the domestic industries. This is a kind of quota that restricts the amount of commodity that can be imported into the country. The import licensing system divided imports into three broad categories: (i) intermediate goods raw materials, components, spare parts, and supplies; (ii) capital goods, and (iii) consumer goods. In India, there were four different types of restrictions on imports—banned, restricted, limited permissible, and canalized. Any item of import not covered by any of these four restrictions was categorized as open general licence (OGL) and was available for import without a licence and against payment of customs duties. Prior permission in the form of an import licence was required to import items that were classified under any one of the four categories listed earlier, subject to the importer satisfying some clauses, important amongst which were 'essentiality' and 'indigenous angle clearance' which meant that a product was an essential input and satisfactory specification and quality could not be supplied in a reasonable time by an Indian firm. Today, except for a small negative list consisting of items not allowed for import on account of health, environment, and social considerations, everything is available to industry against payment of restructured and low rates of tariffs inclusive of some items of consumer goods against special import licences.

Trade Barriers

Trade barriers constituted an important impediment for the Indian manufacturing sector. It is held that due to trade restrictions in the form of high tariff rates and a complex import licensing regime, Indian firms were unable to develop into competitive and global units. In the following paragraphs I assess the extent of trade barriers in Indian manufacturing by looking at three well-known measures—effective rate of protection, import coverage ratio, and import penetration rate. The effective rate of protection captures the distortion introduced in domestic value-added vis-à-vis world value-added due to tariffs on input as well as output. Import coverage ratios are calculated by determining the value of imports of each commodity subject to non-tariff barriers, aggregating by applicable commodity groups and expressing the value of imports covered as a percentage of total imports in the commodity group. The import penetration rate captures the impact of both tariff as well as non-tariff measures of protection and is calculated as the ratio of imports to domestic sales, with domestic sales defined as output of domestic industries minus exports plus imports.

The major sources of data for trade barriers are: (i) Monthly Statistics of Foreign Trade Volume I and II, Directorate General of Commercial Intelligence and Statistics, Ministry of Commerce, Government of India, (ii) Customs Tariff Working Schedule, Directorate of Publication, Customs and Central Excise, Government of India, and (iii) Export–Import Policy Documents, Ministry of Commerce, Government of India.

The assessment is over four five-year phases of trade reforms—Phase 1, which signifies ad hoc attempts at trade reforms; Phase 2, which signals the start of the process of trade reforms at moderate pace; Phase 3, which shows the major attempt at trade reforms in terms of tariff changes and abolishing of import licensing regime; and finally Phase 4, which shows the consolidation of the trade policy changes of 1991–2. The impact is documented on the use-based sectors to understand and appreciate the developments in line with the focus of policy in the Indian industrialization strategy, which gave priority to capital and intermediate goods sectors and sidelined the question of efficiency and competitiveness for consumer goods industries.

Table 1 Trade Barriers in Indian Manufacturing: Effective Rates of Protection

Industry group	Phase 1 1980–5	Phase 2 1986–90	Phase 3 1991–5	Phase 4 1996–2000	All phases 1980–2000
	Effective rate of protection (per cent)				
Intermediate goods					
Average	147.03	149.18	87.58	40.13	112.36
SD	75.79	64.85	24.15	9.11	44.27
CV	52	43	28	23	39
Capital goods					
Average	62.77	78.45	54.23	33.30	61.87
SD	29.02	30.18	18.49	12.03	22.64
CV	46	38	34	36	37
Consumer goods					
Average	101.51	111.55	80.55	48.28	87.47
SD	19.87	33.77	10.50	5.53	16.60
CV	20	30	13	11	19
All industries					
Average	115.11	125.93	80.18	40.43	95.19
SD	67.62	63.48	23.77	10.71	40.96
CV	59	50	30	26	43

Source: Author's calculations based on the (i) Customs Tariff Working Schedule, Central Excise and Customs, Government of India, (ii) The Monthly Statistics of Foreign Trade, Ministry of Commerce, Government of India, and (iii) Export–Import Policy Documents, Ministry of Commerce, Government of India.

Notes: 1. Period averages are computed as a value-added share weighted average of the yearly figures.

2. For all industries, the ERP is averaged over 72 three-digit industries.

3. SD stands for standard deviation and CV for coefficient of variation.

Effective Rate of Protection

A sharp fall in the level of protection across most industry groups can be observed in the 1990s as compared to the 1980s. The majority of industries belonging to the capital goods sector showed the maximum decline; for the intermediate goods industries, a decline could be observed from high levels of protection in the early 1980s to levels of around 40 per cent. A decline in the level of protection is noticeable even in the consumer goods sector. Thus protection by and large declined in the period after reforms, yet the degree of decline was uneven across different use-based sectors—capital, intermediate, and consumer as well as within each group. A glance at Table 1 shows the levels of effective rate of protection vis-à-vis Indian manufacturing industries.

Import Coverage Ratio

India had a complicated system of non-tariff barriers operating in the industrial sector of the economy till the overhauling of the trade regime in 1991, making it very difficult to quantify and assess the significance of non-tariff barriers. Using the import coverage ratio, I will assess the impact of non-tariff barriers on Indian manufacturing industries in the 1980s and 1990s. The percentage of imports subjected to non-tariff barriers remained close to 100 per cent in the early phases of trade reforms across all sectors—intermediate, capital as well as consumer goods industries. It was only in the first half of the 1990s that changes began to take place in terms of removal of import restrictions on products—that is, freeing certain items of capital and intermediate goods industries from import licence requirements. It was, however, the second half of the 1990s that finally saw substantial decline in import coverage ratio across most manufacturing industries, be it capital or intermediate items of production. The last five years of the 1990s saw a marked decline in the percentage of imports covered by non-tariff barriers for consumer goods items—banned for most part of the 1980s and 1990s. Table 2 gives an idea of the extent of non-tariff barriers across different use-based industry groups.

Import Penetration Rates

Table 3 provides data on the import penetration rates in different periods across industries; these data reveal that import penetration rates have improved only in the second phase of the 1990s, that is, the 1996–2000 period. The trade policy changes of the first three phases are not reflected in an increase in the import penetration rates. Only in the case of the intermediate goods industries, do we find an improvement, albeit

Table 2 Trade Barriers in Indian Manufacturing: Import Coverage Ratio

Industry group 1980–2000	Phase 1 1980–5	Phase 2 1986–90	Phase 3 1991–5	Phase 4 1996–2000	All phases
	Import coverage ratio (per cent)				
Intermediate goods					
Average	98.31	98.26	41.77	27.60	71.47
SD	12.89	12.65	42.63	37.88	20.43
CV	13	13	102	137	29
Capital goods					
Average	95.11	77.21	20.47	8.15	54.37
SD	21.56	26.94	25.36	16.96	16.69
CV	23	35	124	208	31
Consumer goods					
Average	98.69	87.85	45.69	33.43	68.77
SD	11.35	21.64	39.23	38.53	20.89
CV	12	25	86	115	30
All industries					
Average	97.59	91.64	37.97	24.82	67.11
SD	15.33	20.45	39.88	35.84	20.93
CV	16	22	105	144	31

Source: Author's calculations based on the (1) Customs Tariff Working Schedule, Central Excise and Customs, Government of India, (2) The Monthly Statistics of Foreign Trade, Ministry of Commerce, Government of India, and (3) Export–Import Policy Documents, Ministry of Commerce, Government of India.
Notes: 1. Period averages are computed as a value-added share weighted average of the yearly figures.
2. For all industries, the MCR is averaged over 72 three-digit industries.
3. SD stands for standard deviation and CV for coefficient of variation.

Table 3 Trade Barriers in Indian Manufacturing: Import Penetration Rates

Industry group 1980–2000	Phase 1 1980–5	Phase 2 1986–90	Phase 3 1991–5	Phase 4 1996–2000	All phases
	Import penetration rates (per cent)				
Intermediate goods					
Average	0.11	0.13	0.15	0.18	0.14
SD	0.12	0.11	0.15	0.15	0.12
CV	105	84	100	87	87
Capital goods					
Average	0.12	0.12	0.12	0.19	0.14
SD	0.15	0.12	0.11	0.15	0.13
CV	143	64	69	170	97
Consumer goods					
Average	0.04	0.04	0.04	0.10	0.05
SD	0.06	0.03	0.03	0.10	0.04
CV	143	64	69	170	74
All industries					
Average	0.10	0.11	0.12	0.16	0.12
SD	0.12	0.11	0.13	0.16	0.12
CV	119	97	112	98	98

Source: Author's calculations based on the (i) Customs Tariff Working Schedule, Central Excise and Customs, Government of India, (ii) The Monthly Statistics of Foreign Trade, Ministry of Commerce, Government of India, and (iii) Export–Import Policy Documents, Ministry of Commerce, Government of India.
Notes: 1. Period averages are computed as a value-added share weighted average of the yearly figures.
2. For all industries, the MPR, it is averaged over 60 three-digit industries.
3. SD stands for standard deviation and CV for coefficient of variation.

slow, in import penetration rates in Phases 2 and 3. This is not difficult to comprehend as the 1980s saw some movement in products like industrial raw materials, and components and parts from banned, restricted lists to OGL lists. Another important finding is that across different industry groups import penetration rates are the lowest for consumer goods industries, which is in line with the trade stance towards that sector. The reason that import penetration did not increase despite lowering of tariffs and removal of non-tariff barriers is that tariff and non-tariff barriers are not equivalent when perfect competition does not characterize the domestic market, an argument put forward by economist Jagdish Bhagwati, which holds true for Indian industries that operate by and large in imperfectly competitive markets.

Trade reforms attempt to relax the restrictions imposed on international trade. The data on trade barriers, however, show that only in the 1990s and after can we actually see changes taking place in the measures of the trade barriers discussed here. This holds across all use-based sectors and the direction of changes highlighted for each of the three measures reflects that there is perhaps a lagged impact of trade policy changes on the manufacturing sector, an issue that needs further investigation.

DEB KUSUM DAS

References

Das, D.K. 2001. 'Some Aspects of Productivity Growth and Trade in Indian Industry', unpublished PhD thesis, Department of Economics, Delhi School of Economics, University of Delhi, November.

——. 2003. 'Quantifying Trade Barriers: Has Protection Declined Substantially in Indian Manufacturing?', Working Paper #105, New Delhi, ICRIER, July.

Trade Unions

In the year 2000, there were about 65,000 registered trade unions with 5.4 million members—constituting 19 per cent of organized-sector employment, and less than

2 per cent of the workforce.[1] Unions are mostly functional in large factories and offices; over one-half of the union members work in utilities and in the tertiary sector, mainly in government and publicly owned entities. The unorganized sector remains largely outside the purview of trade unions, except perhaps in Kerala. As unionized workers largely represent educated and skilled workforce employed in capital- and knowledge-intensive sectors, their conduct usually has economy-wide effects.

The Trade Unions Act, 1926, permits registration of a union with seven members of a factory, firm, or trade, granting them immunity against civil and criminal proceedings to pursue their collective interest; in return, unions are required to submit annual reports of their membership and audited accounts. But the registration does not confer recognition as a bargaining agent in bilateral negotiations with management. Industrial relations in India rest on this law, along with the Industrial Disputes Act, 1947, and the Industrial Employment (Standing Orders) Acts, 1946. However, as labour is a concurrent subject under the Constitution, state governments can modify these laws, subject to Presidential approval.

Introduction of modern factory manufacturing during the second half of the 19th century, mainly in cotton and jute textiles, forms the genesis of the Trade Union Act. In a short time the cotton and jute mills became competitive in the domestic market and posed a challenge to the supremacy of the British textile industry, partly based on the wage differential between the two countries. Rapid growth of these industries in an unregulated environment also brought in concerns about workers' welfare and sporadic protests against long working hours and inhuman working conditions in these mills—especially for women and children. The British textile interests endorsed a similar view, as they were losing markets to upcoming Indian mills. Thus, in response to the growing concerns about labour welfare as well as the British textile interests, colonial government enacted many labour laws in the late 19th century, the Trade Union Act of 1886 being the prominent one; amended in 1926, the law continues to be in force to this day.

Historically, middle-class philanthropists, social workers, politicians, and freedom fighters led trade unions—often justified on the grounds that uneducated workers are usually unaware of legal and technical matters for negotiating with employers. While such a leadership may have been advantageous initially, such leaders have less appreciation of workers' grievances arising on the shop floor, and issues arising out of technical change, work intensification and economic incentives. Unions are invariably affiliated to political parties and claim to leverage their political strength to bargain with the employers, in return for workers' loyalty and votes. The Indian National Trade Union Congress (INTUC), the federation of unions affiliated to the Congress party, is probably the largest 'umbrella' of trade unions in recent times.

In the pre-Independence period, union leaders were drawn into the freedom movement with the motive not only of improving the conditions of factory workers but also of involving the emerging working class in the struggle for national independence, and (as with some unions) struggle against colonialism and British imperialism. Therefore, the evolution of the trade union movement is closely intertwined with national politics—a link that still persists (as in many countries).

Trends in Trade Unions

While the number of the registered trade unions rose over the four decades since 1960–1, their membership declined by about 0.6 million in the 1990s. More seriously, the proportion of workers unionized declined from 33 per cent of the organized workforce in 1960–1 to less than 20 per cent four decades later; the average size of the union has fallen from about 354 members to 83 (see Figure 1) in this period. Though the declining trend is indisputable, these numbers need to be treated with caution. They are based on the returns submitted by the unions, an exercise which has fallen precipitously to 11 per cent of the total number of unions. However, there is more to these numbers, as will be discussed in the following pages.

Proliferation of trade unions in the existing organizations and their divisions along political lines are distinctive features of the trade union movement. Unlike in the advanced countries, there seems to be no institutionalized system of collection of dues, statutory audit of unions' accounts, and filing of the returns.

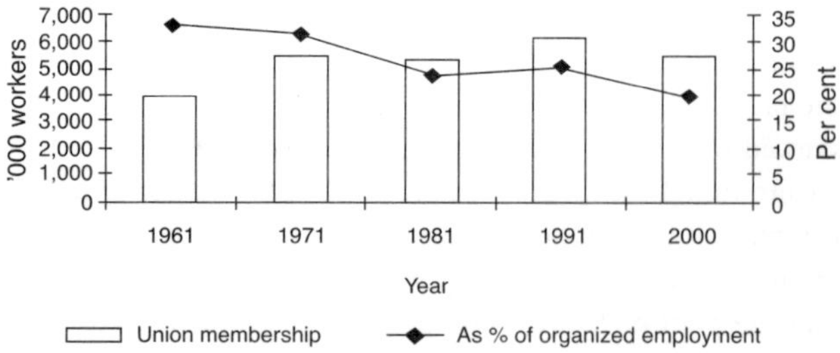

Figure 1 Trade Union Membership in India

[1]The organized sector consists of public sector, private corporate sector and cooperatives, manufacturing units registered under the Factories Act, 1948, or Bidi and Cigar Workers Act, 1966, and recognized educational institutions.

Therefore, information on the registered unions and their strength is largely notional. While registering a union may be easy, it is hard to find effective trade unions in smaller establishments with, say, up to hundred workers, as employers can easily victimize the unionized workers and their potential leaders. In a situation of excess supply of labour in a heterogeneous society, employers can easily replace the 'troublemakers' with docile workers, effectively divided along caste, communal, and linguistic lines.

What explains the decline in trade unionism? Partly, it represents a worldwide trend in the second half of the 20th century. However, there could be some specific factors relating to evolution of the Indian economy and its institutions that may also have contributed to the observed decline.

Despite being a large labour surplus economy (in contrast to many East Asian economies), the industrial sector in India was dominated by large factories, where it is easy to unionize the workers. But during the last half century, in response to a variety of policy initiatives and the development of capital market, spread of electricity and modern infrastructure, and growing inter-firm relations, industrial employment in India has moved into smaller-sized factories within the organized sector, and into the unorganized sector (employing 10 or less workers per establishment), where employers exercise greater control over the workplace and employment contracts tend to be flexible and often personalized; hence it is difficult to unionize workers. However, the evolution of industrial relations may also have contributed to the fall in trade union strength.

Industrial Relations in India

India follows a tripartite industrial relations system wherein the state, in principle, mediates in all disputes between workers and employers. The law forbids workers or employers from going on strike or declaring lockout without giving a notice of 14 days. When a strike or lockout notice is served, even if the labour department gets an inkling of a dispute, it initiates a conciliation process. If it fails, the dispute has to be referred for arbitration and finally for compulsory adjudication. On the face of it, the mechanism is highly interventionist, skewed towards labour to protect the weaker party, to ensure uninterrupted production and industrial harmony. But the reality seems different. The decision arrived at by the conciliation mechanism is not binding on the management or labour. The state does not have judicial powers to enforce its decision on the parties in dispute. Evidence suggests that these state-mediated settlement efforts can drag on for years, often hurting the interests of labour as it cannot sustain a struggle with loss of income.

In the event of a dispute, the employer and all the registered unions are invited to the conciliation process. This procedure, by design, invites competition among unions, divided along political lines, and there can be as many unions as political parties in the region. Competition often leads to spurious membership claims and counterclaims, an added reason for the overestimation of trade union membership discussed earlier.

Such competition, expectedly, gives the management an edge. The employer need not necessarily negotiate with the union (or group of unions) claiming to represent the majority of workers, but is free to negotiate with any combination of unions. Quite conceivably, if the demand arises, employers can (and do) prop up a dummy union of loyal workers and choose to negotiate with it, to break the other unions. For instance, history suggests, the rise of the Shiv Sena, a militant regional party in Maharashtra, in Mumbai is attributed to such a tendency among employers, to break the stronghold of left-leaning unions in the 1960s. A minority union affiliated to a political party in power in the state can use its political links to compel the labour department to decisively intervene to persuade the management to negotiate with that union, ignoring the other unions. In such an event other unions would get discredited, causing workers to shift their allegiance to the minority union. Such inter-union rivalry and competition for membership with political objectives often leads to fluidity of union membership. In another instance, a recognized union (as per the Bombay Industrial Relation Act in Maharashtra), favoured by the management, that may have lost the support of the majority of workers could not be ousted as the sole bargaining agent, since there is no system of secret ballot to ascertain the strength of the incumbent union. If, for some reason, the employer persists with the incumbent union, then there is no mechanism available for a rival union to prove its majority except appeal in courts (as was the case in the famous Dutta Samant-led Bombay Textile strike in 1982).

Thus competitive politics of parliamentary democracy seems to be inhibiting evolution of healthy industrial relations practices. Many political parties, for fear of losing their labour constituency—perhaps the Congress party more than most—have opposed changes in labour laws to promote shop-floor democracy, union recognition, and an institutionalized mechanism for collection of membership fees to put the unions on sound financial footing.

In such a situation, workers' interests often seem to get reduced to wage demands; ignoring many issues like disputes on the shop floor, problem of work intensification, and sharing of productivity gains. Though employers gain an upper hand in such situations in dealing with labour, they bring in uncertainty and the need to 'manage' politics at local and state levels.

Emerging Tendencies

Admittedly, trade unionism has not remained static in the shadow of competitive politics.

- Workers are increasingly economistic in their demands, shifting their allegiances to maximize their private gains, with decreasing interest in a political agenda.
- There has been a rise of factory- or company-based 'independent' unions not affiliated to political parties, though numbers are hard to come by. Such unions are often led by educated and experienced rank-and-file workers with a better grasp of the shop-floor issues, and are often open to negotiations with managements on issues like automation and productivity-linked incentive systems.
- There has been decline of industry- and region-wide wage settlements, as productivity and manning levels have changed across factories in response to technological changes and market conditions.
- Although labour market reforms have not been initiated to any significant extent for lack of political consensus, the state has gradually withdrawn from getting involved in industrial disputes or has chosen to look the other way when the laws are violated. If we concede that the state was, contrary to the stated principle, dysfunctional and not in favour of the weaker agent—labour—then it can be considered a favourable development. However, such a decline in the absence of shop-floor democracy and a healthy bipartite bargaining mechanism would perhaps only weaken the bargaining position of the workers. This is perhaps well reflected in the sharp fall in employment in organized manufacturing since the second half of the 1990s without a murmur of protest from the trade unions which are perhaps not in a position to protect the interests of their workers.

What is the future of trade unions? Apparently, not bright. With intensification of competitive politics, prospects for genuine reform of labour laws that enhance collective bargaining and shop-floor democracy seem weak. Simultaneously, political parties have discovered that organized labour forms a numerically minor fraction of the total voters, and have, therefore, lost interest in organized labour. However, as collective bargaining is likely to grow in a decentralized manner with gradual withdrawal of the state, employers would get an upper hand. With deregulation and increased international competition even in many service industries, the role of trade unions could decline in these areas as well, as has happened in manufacturing during the last two decades.

If one agrees that trade unions have a positive role in countering oligopolistic power of employers in the workplace and in favourably influencing public opinion in a democracy, then the prospect of declining trade unions does not augur well for the economy and society in the long run.

R. NAGARAJ

References

Bhaumik, Sharit K. 2004. 'The Working Class Movement in India: Trade Unions and the State', in Manoranjan Mohanty (ed.), *Class, Caste and Gender*, New Delhi, Sage.

Nagaraj R. 1994. 'Employment and Wages in Manufacturing Industries: Trends, Hypothesis and Evidence', *Economic and Political Weekly*, 22 January, 29(4).

——. 2004. 'Fall in Organised Manufacturing Employment: A Brief Note', *Economic and Political Weekly*, 24 July, 39(30): 3387–90.

Ramaswamy, E.A. and Uma Ramaswamy. 1981. *Industry and Labour: An Introduction*, New Delhi, Oxford University Press.

Seth, N.R. 1993. 'Our Trade Unions: An Overview', *Economic and Political Weekly*, 6 February, 28(6): 231–6.

■ Tribal Development

India has one of the largest concentrations of tribal people in the world. According to the 2001 Census, about 84.3 million Indians, or 8.2 per cent of its total population, were classified as tribal. Over 90 per cent of the tribal population was classified as living in rural areas. Although tribes live in all states and union territories of India except Delhi, Punjab, Haryana, Puducherry, and Chandigarh, the tribal population is concentrated in the north-east, central, and western states. More than half of the tribal population lives in the central and western states of Madhya Pradesh, Chhattisgarh, Orissa, Jharkhand, Maharashtra, and Gujarat. In addition, tribes form a majority of the population in the north-eastern states of Meghalaya, Tripura, Arunachal Pradesh, Mizoram, and Nagaland, and the union territories of Lakshadweep and Dadra and Nagar Haveli. Across India, tribal settlements comprise about 15 per cent of the total geographical area and span a wide range of ecological and climatic regions.

The tribes of India are often referred to as aboriginal, autochthonous, or *adivasi* ('first settlers'), but they are not a racially homogenous population, as there is considerable racial diversity among the different tribal groups. There is also no distinct separation in racial or physical traits between tribal and non-tribal populations, probably due to the coexistence and intermixing between the two groups over several centuries (Beteille 1998). In some cases, the passage of time and the impact of modern media and communication facilities has also changed the character of the tribal population from isolated, economically and socially self-contained communities to those more integrated into the mainstream, non-tribal population (Beteille 2008). To a large extent, however, tribes can be distinguished from the non-tribal population based on their habitats (mostly forest and hilly areas and peripheries of the subcontinent, including the islands), language, and level of social, economic, and political marginalization.

The size of the recorded tribal population has been on the increase since the 1951 Census (when it numbered about 19 million, or 5 per cent, of the total population). The population growth rate (24.5 per cent between 1991–2001) of the tribal community has also consistently outpaced that of the general population. To some extent, these numbers may be affected by the complex classification and rules defining a tribe, since for practical and legal purposes, tribal identity is derived from the Indian Constitution and brings with it certain privileges. The Fifth Schedule of the Constitution defines tribal populations as scheduled tribes (STs), and various Constitutional Articles, such as Article 342 and Article 46, recognize ST communities (as well as scheduled caste and other minority groups) as the weaker sections of society, calling for the promotion of their educational and economic interests, which have resulted in the implementation of affirmative action programmes, offering them political and economic advantages. In some cases these may also have provided incentives to 'non-tribal' communities to try and secure ST status. Notwithstanding, over 700 communities are recognized by the Indian government as STs (Ministry of Tribal Affairs 2010). Of these, 75 groups, characterized by extreme economic underdevelopment and geographical isolation, are classified by the government as Particularly Vulnerable Tribal Groups (PTGs) (Planning Commission 2008).

Since Independence, the government's tribal development policy has followed Jawaharlal Nehru's *panchsheel* (five principles) of tribal development. Nehru called for integrating tribes with mainstream India and bringing them to an equal footing economically while, at the same time, maintaining their cultural distinctness. Since the Fifth Five Year Plan (1974–5 to 1978–9), distinct policies for tribal development, called Tribal Sub-Plans (TSPs), have earmarked resources from state and central budgets specifically for tribal areas to reduce poverty and improve the physical and social infrastructure in these areas. In the last decade, there has been a shift from a welfarist approach in tribal development to an approach of empowerment (Planning Commission 2008). Specifically, Constitutional Amendments and the Panchayats (Extension to the Scheduled Areas) (PESA) Act, 1996, have enabled tribal populations to participate in local governance bodies such as gram sabhas and Panchayati Raj Institutions (PRIs). In addition, a separate ministry for tribal development (the Ministry of Tribal Affairs) and a national institution providing financial assistance to schemes dedicated to the economic development of the tribal population (the National Scheduled Tribes Finance and Development Corporation) were established in 1999 and 2001, respectively, to oversee policies and programmes that focused on tribal development. In 2006, the historic Scheduled Tribes and Other Traditional Forest Dwellers (Recognition of Forest Rights) Act (RFRA) was established by the government in order to protect the traditional dwellings and livelihoods of many tribal communities. Programmes aimed at improving the educational status of ST communities, such as Post-matric Scholarship Scheme, which has been in place since 1944–5, have been implemented. Similarly, programmes aimed at improving ST women's status, such as the Adivasi Mahila Sashaktikaran Yojana, which facilitate income-generating activities through women's self-help groups (SHGs) have been established. A Central Sector Scheme targeted specifically at the development of PTGs has been in place since 1998–9.

In spite of these steps, tribal communities continue to suffer from very low levels of economic development. The poverty rate is considerably higher for the ST population than for the all-India population. While the poverty level for the ST population has declined in the last decade, the rate of decline is much lower than compared to the decline in the all-India population (Planning Commission 2008). For example, while the poverty levels for the all-India rural population fell from 37.3 per cent in 1993–4 to 32.4 per cent in 2004–5, the poverty level for the rural ST population fell from 51.9 per cent in 1993–4 to 47.3 per cent in 2004–5. According to the 2001 Census, a vast majority—about 82 per cent—of main workers in ST households are primary-sector workers, such as cultivators or agricultural labourers, indicating the low level of livelihood diversification in the ST population. For the all-India population, the corresponding figure is only about 58 per cent.

In terms of human development, the ST population, also fares poorly. For example, in 2001, the literacy rate for the all-India ST population was 47.1 per cent, compared to 64.8 per cent nationally (Planning Commission 2008). While there has been an upward trend in literacy rates among the ST population since the 1960s and the gap between their literacy rates and that of the all-India population decreased between 1991 and 2001, the absolute literacy rate of the ST population continues to be abysmally low. The literacy rate for the ST female population was still lower, at 34.8 per cent in 2001 (Planning Commission 2008). The under-five mortality rate per 1,000 live births was 95.7 for the ST population compared to 74.3 for the all-India population (IIPS and Macro International 2007). While the sex ratio of 977/1,000 in ST communities is favourable when compared to the ratio in the general population of 933/1,000, the sex ratio in the ST population is on the decline (Census, various years).

Similarly, in terms of indicators of social and physical infrastructure, villages with a majority ST population lag behind villages with a majority non-ST population. In particular, since most tribal settlements tend to be in geographically isolated regions characterized by forest areas and/or rocky terrains, tribal villages have limited access to roads, communication, health, education, electricity, drinking water, and other essential infrastructure.

While affirmative action programmes have increased tribal participation in the political process, the share of the ST population in central government services that are responsible for decision making continues to be low. For example, the share of ST individuals in Group A of the central government services increased from 2.9 per cent in 1994 to only 4.1 per cent in 2004 (Planning Commission 2008).

The struggles of tribal communities in Orissa against large corporations like Vedanta and Pohang Iron and Steel Company (POSCO) have also brought to the forefront the urgent need to rationalize forest, tribal, environmental, and industrialization policies. More alarmingly, growing Maoist-inspired violence in the so-called Red Corridor in eastern and central India, which overlaps with some of the poorest districts, most of which have a large tribal population, poses a serious internal security and economic threat (Thottam 2010).

In light of these facts, and given the Byzantine programmes and policies aimed at tribal development, the Ministry of Tribal Affairs is currently formulating a more cogent National Tribal Policy, based on constitutional principles, PESA, as well as the strengths of tribal traditions and cultures (Ministry of Tribal Affairs 2010). In addition, the Eleventh Five Year Plan professes a desire to make a 'paradigm shift with respect to the empowerment of the tribal policy' by operationalizing the Fifth Schedule, TSP, PESA, and RFRA and enabling 'a tribal-centric, tribal-participative and tribal-managed development process; and the need for a conscious departure from dependence on a largely under-effective official delivery system' (Planning Commission 2008: 115). In particular, the Plan addresses the interconnections between tribal development, forest management, and increasing agitation in tribal areas, and delineates the role of socio-economic underdevelopment, physical and economic exploitation, land alienation, and other problems in tribal areas as being root causes of tribal unrest. In order to ameliorate the situation, it calls for preventing exploitation by the non-tribal population; implementing the 1989 SC/ST (Prevention of Atrocities) Act; making tribal livelihoods more productive and sustainable; amending various, sometimes archaic, Acts, such as the Land Acquisition Act (1894), Forest Act (1927), Forest (Conservation) Act (1980), Coal Bearing Areas (Acquisition and Development) Act (1957), and the National Mineral Policy (1993), in order to enable better protection of tribal communities in today's rapidly changing economic and industrial landscape, avoiding displacement where possible and formulating an effective rehabilitation policy for tribal communities displaced by development and industrial projects. In particular, it calls for effective implementation of RFRA. The Plan also aims to strengthen local democratic institutions and enable self-governance in scheduled areas, improving the socio-economic status of the tribal population by providing, among other things, basic infrastructure in tribal villages, relevant education, food security, drinking water, and basic healthcare services. Disconcertingly, many of these aims are similar to those professed in earlier Five Year Plans. If agitation in tribal areas is to be abated, then the government has to enact its plans for tribal development effectively. In doing so, while it is essential to recognize the distinctness of tribal communities, it is also important to keep in mind that the tribal population is no different from any other in wanting, among other things, economic betterment, food security, housing, education for its children, accessible healthcare facilities, and the use of modern conveniences, such as electrical lighting and fans, mobile phones, and motorized vehicles (Bhattamishra 2008; Dreze 2006).

RUCHIRA BHATTAMISHRA

References

Beteille, A. 1998. 'The Idea of Indigenous People', *Current Anthropology*, 39(2): 187–91.

——. 2008. 'Tribes and Castes—Politics is Being Driven by the Competition of Backwardness', *The Telegraph*, 24 June.

Bhattamishra, R. 2008. 'Field Notes (Kashipur, Orissa)', 'Grain Banks: An Institutional and Impact Analysis', PhD Dissertation, Department of Economics, Cornell University.

Census of India. Various Years. New Delhi, Government of India.

Dreze, J. 2006. 'Foreword', in G.C. Rath (ed.), *Tribal Development in India: The Contemporary Debate*, New Delhi, Sage Publications.

International Institute for Population Sciences (IIPS) and Macro International. 2007. *National Family Health Survey (NFHS-3), 2005–06: India*, Vol.1, Mumbai, IIPS.

Ministry of Tribal Affairs. 2010. *Annual Report 2009–10*, New Delhi, Ministry of Tribal Affairs.

Planning Commission. 2008. 'Social Justice: Scheduled Castes, Scheduled Tribes, Other Backward Classes, Minorities and Other Vulnerable Groups', in *Eleventh Five Year Plan 2007–2012, Vol. 1: Inclusive Growth*, Planning Commission, Government of India; New Delhi, Oxford University Press.

Thottam, J. 2010. 'India's Scourge', *Time Asia*, 24 October, available at http://www.time.com/time/magazine/article/0,9171,2026792,00.html#ixzz1LJzXci1v, accessed on 1 May 2011.

U

Undernutrition

The Magnitude of the Problem and Its Consequences

Despite the progress made on poverty reduction, the magnitude of undernutrition remains high in India. The latest nationwide National Family Health Survey (NFHS-3), conducted in 2005–6, indicates that the progress in reducing undernutrition has not been commensurate with the progress in income growth.[1] As indicated in Table 1, between 1998–9 and 2005–6, the percentage of young children under three years who were moderately stunted hardly changed: from 23.3 to 22.9 per cent and the prevalence of severely stunted children declined by a mere 6 percentage points from nearly 28 to 22 per cent (Table 1).[2] India also fares dismally in another key indicator: birth weights. The NFHS-3 data suggest that one-fifth of all children in the country are born with low birth weight while another estimate puts the figure at 30 per cent (Black et al. 2008: webtable 5). All these figures are among the highest in the world.

It may be tempting to dismiss these numbers—or at least not view them as a matter of concern—as a demonstration of the 'small but healthy' hypothesis: that

Table 1 Selected Indicators of Undernutrition, 1998–9 and 2005–6 (per cent)

	1998–9	2005–6
% of children under three years moderately (not severely) stunted	23.3	22.9
% of children under three years severely stunted	27.7	22.0
% of children under three years moderately (not severely) underweight	25.1	24.6
% of children under three years severely underweight	17.6	15.8
% of children 6 to 35 months with mild anaemia	22.9	25.7
% of children 6 to 35 months with moderate anaemia	45.9	49.4
% of children 6 to 35 months with severe anaemia	5.4	3.7
% of children 6 to 35 months with any anaemia	74.3	78.9
% of ever married women with heights less than 145 cm*	13	12
% of ever married women who are thin, with body mass index <18.5*	36	33

Source: International Institute for Population Sciences and Macro International (2007: chapter 10).
Note: *Figures on women's indicators refer to ever married women to ensure comparability across the two surveys.

[1]The entry by Indrani Gupta in this volume addresses issues relating to mortality outcomes and hence these are not dealt with directly here.

[2]Moderate stunting is defined as the percentage of children whose height-for-age is between –2 and –3 standard deviations below the International Reference Population (IRP) median, while severe stunting refers to the percentage of children below –3 standard deviations of the IRP median. Another indicator—weight-for-age—also does not show much change, with a quarter of the country's children being moderately underweight, and 16 per cent being severely so. The definition of moderate and severe underweight is analogous.

Indians are shorter in stature than other (international) populations used in defining growth and weight standards because of their distinct genetic endowments. Unfortunately, there is no substance to this hypothesis. Children of Indian families settled in the UK follow international growth standards; had there been a genetic component, such children should have been smaller than the international norms (Tarozzi 2008).

There also appears to be a marked gender component to the relatively modest improvements in children's heights. Tarozzi and Mahajan (2007) suggest that earlier improvements in stunting were far more visible for boys than for girls.

Another important indicator of undernutrition is anaemia. Nearly 80 per cent of the children under the age of three were anaemic in 2005–6, a figure that has not changed—indeed increased slightly—since the previous survey in 1998–9 (Table 1). Both inadequate dietary intakes of iron and parasitic infections such as hookworms contribute to the high magnitudes of anaemia.

The consequences of such large numbers of undernourished children are varied and significant. For example, children who are moderately stunted are 1.6 times at greater odds of dying than children who are not, while the odds for children who are severely stunted are four times as much. The corresponding mortality odds ratios for moderately and severely underweight children are 2.5 and 9.7, respectively (Black et al. 2008).[3] Low birth weight similarly translates into considerably higher mortality risks. According to one estimate, nearly half of all the mortality of children under five years of age can be attributed to malnutrition; also, because of the relatively large magnitude of mildly and moderately undernourished children, more deaths can be attributed to these categories, than to severe malnutrition (Arnold et al. 2009).

Apart from mortality, there are other significant consequences. Low birth weight increases the risk of learning disabilities, lower IQ, and visual and hearing impairment. All these have an impact on education and, therefore, on income outcomes. It also increases the risk of non-communicable diseases, such as hypertension and diabetes in adulthood. Stunting is an indirect indicator of the risk of zinc deficiency; inadequate zinc status is associated with increased risk of diarrhoea and pneumonia (Bhutta et al. 1999). Stunting during childhood is often irreversible and, therefore translates into short stature as adults. This in turn has lifelong economic consequences, as numerous studies have demonstrated a positive correlation between adult heights and wages (see Steckel 1995 for a review) with the causality running both ways. While the consequences of anaemia do not manifest themselves in terms of higher mortality outcomes (except in the case maternal mortality), they are manifest both in cognitive and physical impairments (see discussion in Stein et al. 2008). Once again, these have implications for adults' income-earning potential.

Although much of the focus thus far has been nutritional outcomes for children, undernutrition among adult women is also important: 12 per cent of Indian women have heights below 145 cm, and one-third have low body mass index (Table 1).[4] Both increase the risk of intrauterine growth retardation and low birth weight babies, thereby perpetuating the cycle of undernutrition (Black et al. 2008).

In order to quantify the economic burden of undernutrition, a useful metric is the Disability-Adjusted Life Year (DALY), which presents an annual measure of the burden of disease. Diseases/functional outcomes are assigned disability weights, with a higher weight representing a greater disability—mortality outcomes receive a weight of unity. In this way, it is possible to 'add' disease and mortality. The measure also takes into account the duration of disease (with mortality, the duration is taken as the remaining life expectancy) and is expressed after discounting as the sum of the number of years lost due to mortality and illness. That is, each DALY represents a year spent in ill-health, with the concomitant loss in income and quality of life. In 2004, it was estimated that one-fifth of the global DALY burden among children under five years of age could be attributed to poor nutritional status (Black et al. 2008). The figures for India are no different, with a total of 24.6 million DALYs attributed to stunting, severe wasting, and low birth weight. Similarly, iron deficiency anaemia—representing about 60 per cent of overall anaemia—is estimated to result in nearly 4 million DALYs lost each year (Stein et al. 2008).

The Causes of Undernutrition

Figure 1 sets out a simplified framework for analysing the complex causes of undernutrition, distinguishing between proximate and underlying causes. The set of underlying causes may be categorized into three groups: household resources (including inadequate family

[3]The odds ratio is defined as the odds for stunted children relative to the odds for non-stunted children, where the odds in turn are defined as the probability of the event (death) divided by the probability of the non-event (being alive).

[4]This refers to women whose body mass index, defined as height in metres divided by weight in kilograms squared, is below 18.5.

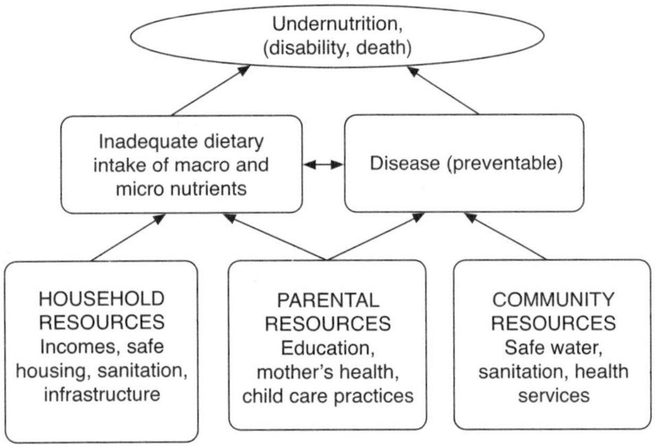

Figure 1 Framework for Analysing the Causes of Undernutrition

incomes); parental resources (for example, mothers with poor education and/or health); and community resources (lack of access to health services and immunization, lack of clean drinking water supplies). These factors work through the proximate causes of malnutrition: at the household level, low household incomes may translate into inadequate diets both in terms of quantity and quality; similarly, a better-nourished mother is likely to be better able to take care of her child so that s/he is better nourished. Poor sanitation, with no access to safe drinking water (whether at the community or household level), for example, may lead to an environment where preventable diseases such as diarrhoea occur. While inadequate intake of nutritious food renders children more susceptible to infection, infectious diseases may in turn cause sick children to lose appetite and not eat adequately, or not be able to absorb the nutrients that are consumed. This interaction between inadequate intakes and the disease environment leads to undernutrition and associated disabilities and mortality.

Determining which of these pathways is most critical clearly has implications for designing the most effective policy response; unfortunately it is difficult to provide an unambiguous answer. Recent literature has focused on the relationship between incomes and energy intakes (Deaton and Dreze 2009). For a population that is considered to be food-insufficient, the apparent lack of a relationship—as expressed by a low-income elasticity of demand for calories—appears surprising. The issues related to this paradox have been examined by Dreze in this volume and are, therefore, not dealt with here.

Another paradox has to do with the apparent lack of a clear relationship between food intakes, on the one hand, and nutritional and health outcomes, on the other. As indicated in Figure 2, states such as Uttar Pradesh have high energy intakes, and yet perform poorly on nutritional outcomes. At the other end of the spectrum, energy intakes in southern states such as Kerala and Tamil Nadu remain among the lowest, and yet these states perform much better on all these indicators.[5] It is only when these states (and Goa and Tripura) are excluded as outliers, that the relationship between the prevalence of stunting and energy intake becomes statistically significant, although the coefficient is quite small.

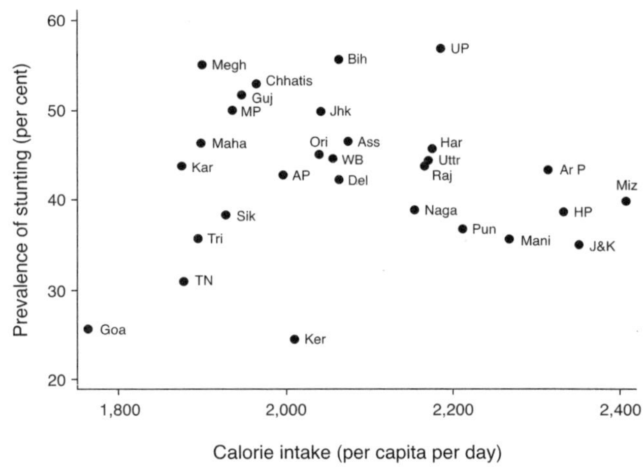

Figure 2 Relationship between the Prevalence of Stunting and Energy Intakes

Source: Stunting prevalence data is from International Institute for Population Sciences and Macro International (2007). Energy intake data are calculated from National Sample Survey Organisation (2007).

Apart from the quantity of energy, the *quality* of food intakes is important: improved quality diets imply higher intakes of key micronutrients, such as zinc and iron. Bennett's Law states that the percentage of calories that are derived from starchy staples declines rapidly with income growth, as people begin substituting into more expensive—higher quality—calories. Thus overall energy intakes may remain unchanged or even decline. This certainly appears to be the case in India; the data clearly indicate a switch to more expensive foods, such as milk and vegetables (Deaton and Dreze 2009), albeit at a rate slower than might be expected. Such diet diversification and the implied

[5]Some have argued that it is the secular decline in energy intakes that is responsible for the lack of improvement in nutritional outcomes, but this argument is hard to justify on behavioural grounds.

improvement in micronutrient intakes are more likely to be associated with improvements in nutritional status, than the quantity of energy intakes per se.

For India, there are unfortunately few data sets that combine information on nutritional outcomes, nutrient (especially micronutrient) intakes, and socio-economic indicators. Most studies that use the National Family Health Survey use food frequency as a proxy for dietary intakes. Radhakrishna and Ravi (2004) model the risk of being underweight or stunted using 1998–9 data from NFHS. They find that birth order, frequency of intake of micronutrient-rich foods, mother's education and health status, and household wealth status, all significantly influence the probability of a child being undernourished. Community-level variables, such as access to an *anganwadi* were insignificant, while village drainage was significant. Using the same data set, but using weight-for-age as the dependant variable, Sharma et al. (forthcoming) find similar results for rural India, although mother's education is insignificant in their specification. Also, at the community level, while access to a health facility was a significant determinant of nutritional outcomes, the availability of an anganwadi centre was not. Bhargava et al. (2011), using the more recent NFHS-3 data and a more comprehensive empirical strategy, find that vaccinations, food intakes, and maternal health, among other factors, are important determinants of child nutritional outcomes (including anaemia).

Policy Interventions

This suggests that a multi-factoral approach to addressing undernutrition is necessary. Although anti-poverty and food subsidy programmes[6] will continue to be important, interventions that do not focus exclusively on protection/generation of income have come to assume importance in tackling undernutrition. Alderman (2005: 4837) notes that 'Governments which focus on growth as a means to address nutrition will require an *extra generation* to make substantial inroads compared to governments which successfully implement nutritional programmes' (emphasis added).

One such programme is the Integrated Child Development Services (ICDS), which provides supplemental nutrition, access to vaccinations, deworming, and so on. In light of the potential importance of this intervention, the Supreme Court mandated universal coverage of the programme within a narrow time frame in 2001. How effective is ICDS? The oft-cited study by Lokshin et al. (2005), using 1998–9 data, found no difference in underweight or stunting prevalence between children with access to an anganwadi centre, and comparable children that did not. Ongoing research based on the more recent survey in 2005–6 paints a more promising picture, with utilization of ICDS services translating into improvements in child nutritional outcomes (Jain 2011).[7]

Given the nutritional burden imposed by water-borne diseases, interventions relating to water supply and sanitation are also key. While literature on India does not explicitly look at the impact of these interventions on child nutritional outcomes, two studies that focus on diarrhoeal outcomes merit attention. Jalan and Ravallion (2003) find that the provision of piped drinking water makes a significant difference to the prevalence of diarrhoeal episodes, especially in wealthier households; education is also important. Khanna (2008), on the other hand, finds that piped water per se is not associated with lower incidence of diarrhoea; rather she suggests that there is a need to pay attention to the quality of water that is thus delivered, and in identifying sources of contamination. Her analysis also points to the role played by awareness (that can be enhanced by public health campaigns) in reducing morbidity from diarrhoea. To the extent that frequent exposure to diarrhoea contributes to stunting, these results are indicative of important pathways to improved nutritional outcomes.

These studies suggest that stand-alone interventions are unlikely to produce results; food-based interventions without a focus on diet quality alone are unlikely to make an impact on child nutritional outcomes. A concerted effort not only involving a multiplicity of interventions but also a coherence and convergence in their implementation is clearly necessary. Unfortunately, such convergence is lacking: even within the government, a multiplicity of ministries, that may not necessarily communicate with one another, are involved. For example, water supply and sanitation interventions are housed in the Ministry of Rural Development; ICDS is housed within the Ministry of Women and Child Development; food subsidies are managed by the Ministry of Consumer Affairs Food and Public Distribution; and other programmes are implemented by the Ministry of Health and Family Welfare. Ensuring that these interventions are delivered effectively and in a concerted form—perhaps through

[6] Interventions such as the Public Distribution System have been reviewed elsewhere in this volume and hence are not included in this discussion.

[7] The 2005–6 survey asked a direct question on the respondent's utilization of ICDS, the earlier survey in 1998–9 pertained merely to whether there was an ICDS centre in the village.

the creation of a separate Directorate of Public Health as Tamil Nadu has done, or through the National Rural Health Mission—may hasten the decline in the prevalence of undernutrition.

J.V. Meenakshi

References

Alderman, Harold. 2005. 'Linkages between Poverty Reduction Strategies and Child Nutrition: An Asian Perspective', *Economic and Political Weekly*, 12 November, 40(46): 4837–42.

Arnold, Fred, Sulabha Parasuraman, P. Arokiasamy, and Monica Kothari. 2009. *Nutrition in India: National Family Health Survey (NFHS-3), India, 2005–06*, Mumbai, International Institute for Population Sciences.

Bhargava, Alok, Aravinda Guntupalli, and Michael Lokshin. 2011. 'Healthcare Utilization, Socio-economic Factors and Child Health in India', *Journal of Biosocial Science*, June, DOI:1017/S002193201100241.

Bhutta, Z., R. Black, K. Brown, J.M. Gardner, S. Gore, A. Hidayat, F. Khatun, R. Martorell, N.X. Ninh, M.E. Penny, J.L. Rosado, S.K. Roy, M. Ruel, S. Sazawal, and A. Shankar. 1999. 'Prevention of Diarrhea and Pneumonia by Zinc Supplementation in Children in Developing Countries: Pooled Analysis of Randomized Controlled Trials', *Journal of Pediatrics*, 135: 689–97.

Black, Robert E., Lindsay H. Allen, Zulfiqar A. Bhutta, Laura E. Caulfield, Mercedes de Onis, Majid Ezzati, Colin Mathers, and Juan Rivera. 2008. 'Maternal and Child Undernutrition: Global and Regional Exposures and Health Consequences', *The Lancet*, doi:10.1016/S0140-6736(07)61690-0.

Deaton, Angus and Jean Dreze. 2009. 'Food and Nutrition in India: Facts and Interpretations', *Economic and Political Weekly*, XLIV(7): 42–65.

International Institute for Population Sciences and Macro International. 2007. *National Family Health Survey (NFHS-3) 2005–6: India*, Vol. 1, Mumbai, IIPS.

Jain, Monica. 2011. 'India's Struggle against Malnutrition: Is the ICDS Program the Answer?', mimeo.

Jalan, Jyotsna and Martin Ravallion. 2003. 'Does Piped Water Reduce Diarrhea for Children in Rural India?', *Journal of Econometrics*, 112: 153–73.

Khanna, Gauri. 2008. 'The Impact on Child Health from Access to Water and Sanitation and Other Socioeconomic Factors', Geneva, Graduate Institute of International Studies, HEI Working Paper No: 02/2008.

Lokshin, Michael, Monica Das Gupta, Michele Gragnolati, and Oleksiy Ivaschenko. 2005. 'Improving Child Nutrition? The Integrated Child Development Services in India', *Development and Change*, 36(4): 613–40.

National Sample Survey Organisation. 2007. *Nutritional Intakes in India, 2004–2005*, NSS 61st Round, July 2004–June 2005, Report No. 513, New Delhi, Ministry of Statistics and Programme Implementation.

Radhakrishna, R. and C. Ravi. 2004. 'Malnutrition in India: Trends and Determinants', *Economic and Political Weekly*, 14 February, 39(7): 671–76.

Sharma, Rekha, J.V. Meenakshi, and Sanghamitra Das. Forthcoming. 'Understanding the Drivers of Nutritional Status of Children in Rural India', in K. Puspangadan and V.N. Balasubramanyam (eds), *Growth, Development and Diversity: India's Record since Liberalization*, Oxford University Press.

Steckel, Richard. 1995. 'Stature and the Standard of Living', *Journal of Economic Literature*, 33(4): 1903–40.

Stein, Alexander, J.V. Meenakshi, Matin Qaim, Penelope Nestel, H.P.S. Sachdev, and Zulfiqar A. Bhutta. 2008. 'Potential Impacts of Iron Biofortification in India', *Social Science and Medicine*, 66: 1797–1808.

Tarozzi, Alessandro. 2008. 'Growth Reference Charts and Nutritional Status of Indian Children', *Economics and Human Biology*, 6: 455–68.

Tarozzi, Alessandro and Aprajit Mahajan. 2007. 'Child Nutrition in India in the Nineties', in *Economic Development and Cultural Change*, pp. 441–86.

Unemployment, The Measurement of

The unemployed are those who are looking for work or are willing to work but cannot find it at the going wage. This notion of unemployment is motivated by the neoclassical conception of the labour market where wages clear the market and the failure to get work is voluntary. Deviations from this ideal are measured by the above definition of involuntary unemployment. Other definitions have also been used. The influential two-sector development models (Lewis 1954, Fei and Rannis 1964) theorized non-neoclassical labour markets in sectors dominated by subsistence family enterprise (such as agriculture). As output was shared among family members, the family enterprise aimed to produce as much as possible without regard to the marginal productivity of labour. This led to the concepts of 'labour surplus' and 'disguised unemployment' both of which referred to people who were employed with low productivity in the subsistence sector and could, therefore, be transferred to the modern high-productivity sector without output loss in the subsistence sector. The early literature on unemployment in India attempted to measure such unemployment through measures that were defined with respect to low productivity or low incomes. However, they suffered from inconsistencies and were hard to implement operationally as well (Krishna 1976).

Unemployment is measured through labour force surveys that elicit the 'activity' status of the respondent for a given reference period. First, the respondent is identified as not working. Second, for those not working, the typical question is of the form: are you available for work, and have you made some effort to find work during the last *x* days? Those who answer in the affirmative are the unemployed while those who answer in the negative are the people who have opted out of the labour force. The labour force is the sum of the employed and the unemployed and the rate of unemployment is the proportion of labour force that is unemployed. The reference period could vary from a week to four weeks to a year. Such an approach works well when the activity status is invariant within the reference period, that is, the person is either employed, unemployed, or out of the labour force. But what if an individual is unemployed for part of the reference period and is either employed or out of the labour force for the remainder? Should this person be counted as unemployed?

In India, employment–unemployment surveys are conducted by the National Sample Survey Organisation (NSSO). Beginning with the 27th round in 1972–3, labour force surveys have been conducted every five years using standardized concepts and procedures based on the recommendations of the Committee of Experts (Planning Commission 1970). The 'usual' status unemployment measure is defined with respect to a reference period of a year. The multiple activity status issue, which is more acute the longer the reference period, is resolved on the basis of majority time. This criterion is used first to classify a person as either belonging to the labour force (that is, employed or unemployed) or not belonging to the labour force. If the person belongs to the labour force, then whether the person is to be classified as employed or unemployed is decided once again on majority time. The survey also uses a reference period of a week to compute a 'weekly' status unemployment measure. Here a person is regarded as employed if she or he worked for at least one hour during the reference week. It follows that a person is unemployed if she or he did not work for even one hour during the reference week and sought work or was available for work during the reference week.

Clearly, the usual status measure reflects only long unemployment spells. For instance, a male in the working-age group (who is never out of the labour force) would be unemployed on the usual status measure only if the unemployed spell during the year is longer than the employed period. While the weekly status measure captures short unemployment periods, it ignores unemployment for less than a week.

A third approach is to abandon the effort to assign every individual a unique activity status over the reference period. The NSS employment survey elicits an individual's time disposition during each day of the reference week. A day is split into two half units and an individual is assigned a unique activity status for that period (rather than the reference week). This information can be used to compute person days of unemployment in the economy. As households are surveyed uniformly throughout the year, the aggregates derived from weekly data are representative of annual aggregates. The 'daily' status rate of unemployment is the proportion of labour force (measured in person days) that is unemployed (also in person days).

Individuals with regular wage employment constitute only 14 per cent of the workforce. More than half of the workforce is self-employed (53 per cent), the great majority in agriculture and about one-third as casual wage workers (Papola 2006). Furthermore, over 80 per cent of female workers in unorganized manufacturing work out of their homes mostly in subcontracting relationships where the intermediary supplies raw material and buys back their output (Unni and Rani 2005). For most of the labour force, therefore, work is seasonal, short-term, and without tenure. Consequently, an individual's activity status can vary even within as short a reference period as a week. The daily status unemployment rate would, therefore, seem the appropriate measure for capturing their unemployment.

The data show a clear and stable ordering among these unemployment rates (Papola 2006). Between 1972–3 and 1999–2000, daily status unemployment rates are the highest (between 6 and 8 per cent), usual status rates are lowest (3–4 per cent), and weekly rates are in between (4–5 per cent). The data imply that while few are unemployed all through the year, unemployment spells are not uncommon. As the daily status measure is the only one that is immune to multiple activity status, it is widely agreed to be the most accurate measure of unemployment (Planning Commission 2001, 2002).

For instance, in the rural sector, among those who reported some unemployment during the reference week, 67 per cent reported a spell of less than a whole week and 50 per cent a spell of less than half a week (Table 1).

Table 1 Multiple Activities in the Rural Sector, 1999–2000

Unemployment spell of households	% of individuals who had some unemployment	
	All rural	Rural labour
≤ half week	50	55
< full week	67	73
= full week	33	27

Table 2 All-India Unemployment Rate (%)

	1999–2000		1993–4		1983	
All	7.24		6.03		8.28	
	Rural	Urban	Rural	Urban	Rural	Urban
All	7.08	7.79	5.61	7.43	7.93	9.53
Males	7.09	7.45	5.64	6.72	7.51	9.22
Females	7.03	9.42	5.55	10.52	8.98	11.01

Among rural labour households, 73 per cent of those who experienced some unemployment reported spells of less than a whole week and 55 per cent reported spells of less than half a week. None of these would be counted as unemployed even under the weekly status. Therefore, from the point of view of designing poverty-alleviation programmes that target the unemployed, the daily status measure would seem to provide the best estimate of unemployment, since it is the poor who are likely to experience short spells of unemployment rather than the non-poor who can afford to stay unemployed longer. The rest of this entry will be restricted to daily status rates.

Table 2 presents the all-India unemployment rates for 1983, 1993–4, and 1999–2000.[1] The data are also broken down by gender and by location (rural/urban). Two robust facts emerge from the tabulation. Unemployment rates in the urban sector are higher than those in the rural sector. While urban rates are in the range 8–9.5 per cent, rural rates are about 1 percentage point lower, fluctuating in the 7–8 per cent range. The second feature is that female unemployment rates are markedly higher than those for males in urban areas while they match those for males in the rural sector. Urban female unemployment rates have ranged between 9.5 and 11 per cent as compared to the 7–9 per cent range for males. In the rural sector, while the unemployment rate for women in 1983 was higher than that of males by more than one percentage point, the rates became similar in later years.

[1]The NSS surveys in 1999–2000 and 1993–4 were conducted during the agricultural year—July through June. In 1983, the survey was conducted during the calendar year—January through December.

While there is not much variation in the unemployment rate across sectors in 1999–2000, there is considerable variation across states. Gujarat, Haryana, Karnataka, Madhya Pradesh, Punjab, Rajasthan, and Uttar Pradesh have unemployment rates much lower than the national average, ranging between 4 and 6 per cent. Andhra Pradesh, Assam, Bihar, Maharashtra, and Orissa have unemployment that is close to the national average. Finally, Kerala, Tamil Nadu, and West Bengal have rates far in excess of the national average, with unemployment in Kerala being greater than 20 per cent. These high unemployment rates pose a challenge to the understanding of labour markets. Why do wages not fall in the face of such unemployment? A generic explanation is the efficiency wage theory according to which wages higher than market clearing levels can be sustained if they elicit more effort from the employed. Other explanations have been offered in terms of societal norms and the workings of particular institutions such as trade unions and government laws on minimum wages. The latter set of factors would seem to be relevant for employment in the organized sector. But what of the labour force that does not have these protections? Would it have low unemployment rates?

It is often asserted that the poor cannot afford to remain unemployed. This is not borne out by the data, however. Table 3 presents the daily status unemployment rates in 1999–2000 for poor households and for labour households. Poor households are those with monthly per capita expenditures less than the official poverty line. Labour households are those whose major source of income is agricultural labour and other manual work in rural areas and casual labour activities in urban areas. There is a large overlap between poor and labour households. While 55 per cent of poor households are rural labour households, only about 39 per cent of rural labour households are poor. However, if we look at the average consumption expenditure of rural labour households, 75 per cent have expenditures less than 1.5 times the rural poverty line and 90 per cent have per capita expenditures less than twice the poverty line. The figures are similar for casual labour households in the urban sector.

Table 3 shows significant unemployment among poor and labour households with rates approaching 12 per cent for labour households in both urban and rural areas. These rates are higher than those for the overall population (in Table 2). As the NSS surveys households throughout the year, we can also compute the distribution of the unemployment rate across different quarters for

Table 3 Unemployment among the Poor, 1999–2000

	Rural	Urban
Poor households	9.19	9.38
Labour households	11.74	11.61

Table 4 Seasonality in Unemployment, 1999–2000

Quarter	Rural*	Urban**
July–September	14.95	12.10
October–December	10.10	10.70
January–March	10.64	10.79
April–June	11.20	13.02

Notes: * Rural labour households; ** Urban casual labour households.

rural and casual labour households (Table 4). As one might expect, there is no particular seasonal pattern in the urban sector, while rural unemployment displays clear seasonality. The unemployment rate at 15 per cent is highest in the monsoon months from July to September when not much work can be done in the fields. Thus while agriculture-driven seasonality is part of the explanation for high unemployment rates among rural labour households, it cannot be the complete story as the unemployment in the busy *kharif* period (October to December) is as high as 10 per cent.

The overall all-India picture masks significant inter-state variation in the incidence of unemployment among labour households. Kerala, Tamil Nadu, and West Bengal are striking for unemployment rates of 20 per cent and more. Bivariate associations (not reported here) do not suggest any systematic relationship between real wages and the level of unemployment. A satisfactory theory of labour markets in India will have to reckon with persistent short-term unemployment among the poor.

WILIMA WADHWA AND BHARAT RAMASWAMI

References

Fei, John C.H. and Gustav Ranis. 1964. *Development of the Labor Surplus Economy: Theory and Policy*, Homewood, IL, Richard A. Irwin, Inc.

Krishna, Raj. 1976. 'Rural Unemployment—A Survey of Concepts and Estimates for India', Trivandrum, Centre of Development Studies, Reprinted in V. Krishna (ed.), *Raj Krishna: Selected Writings*, New Delhi, Oxford University Press, 1995.

Lewis, W. Arthur. 1954. 'Economic Development with Unlimited Supplies of Labor', *Manchester School of Economic and Social Studies*, 22: 139–91.

Papola, T.S. 2006. 'Employment Trends', this volume.

Planning Commission. 1970. *Report of the Committee of Experts on Unemployment Estimates*, New Delhi, Government of India.

———. 2001. *Report of the Task Force on Employment Opportunities*, New Delhi, Government of India.

———. 2002. *Report of the Special Group on Targeting Ten Million Employment Opportunities per year over the Tenth Plan Period*, New Delhi, Government of India.

Unni, Jeemol and Uma Rani. 2005. 'Home Based Work in India: A Disappearing Continuum of Dependence?' Working Paper No. 160, Gujarat Institute of Development Research.

Unique Identification

When I talk about the unique identification initiative, one aspect that often comes up is the migrant experience. For Indians, this experience is instantly relatable. Our population has a large segment of migrants—conservative estimates peg the number at around 300 million—and this includes the educated and the middle class. Many of us have settled in places far from what we used to call home. We have done this for education opportunities, to find better jobs, and for marriage.

However, the migrant experience in India is not a uniform one, and it varies most of all with income and education. When middle-class Indians travel across the country, they rely on the same service providers that they always use: they use the same bank, they make phone calls on their mobiles, and they find jobs based on past credentials and experience, all of which are documented.

For the poor, however, migration entails an entirely different experience. When low-income migrants leave their village, they find that the systems they relied on, including the local moneylenders, their subsidized ration, their local community networks which are aware of their reliability at work, are no longer available to them. Instead, outside their village, they find that they are without identification and unrecognized, and with few ways to redress their situation. The documents they have, such as a ration card and NREGA job card, are unlike that of middle-class residents, and are valid only in their village. They have no means to access a bank or an insurance company, and lack the paperwork to establish their financial history, or past employment. In the absence of effective means to verify the identity of potential migrant workers, employers in sectors such as construction and manufacturing depend on sub-contractors to guarantee the migrants' identity and dependability. The migrants depend on the sub-contractor's brokers and networks not just for employment, but even to buy their food and basic necessities. In every real sense, they are anonymous, largely invisible to service providers.

While the above illustrates the challenges of anonymity and identification migrant workers face, these problems are not limited to them. The problems of identification bog down millions of people in India across communities and in different situations. Rural women, for example, face difficulties in accessing social benefits and employment, especially if they are not part of a household—most local benefits and programmes, as well as identity mechanisms are linked to households, and as a result single women and widows are excluded. Backward communities and tribal groups similarly find themselves caught in a cycle of exclusion, where the lack of one service cuts off identification documents and consequently access to other services, such as when the inability to get a ration card also means difficulty in opening a bank account.

The Urgency of the Challenge

Addressing these fundamental problems of exclusion has become especially urgent for us today. India is experiencing a period of high growth, with millions of Indians getting a realistic shot at improving their incomes, and having a life much better than their parents did. But the country's rapid growth also makes inclusion our defining challenge.

Access to economic opportunity in India so far has been highly inequitable—India's urban, middle class, and elite residents have seen the most significant gains from growth, thanks to the easy access that they have to infrastructure and institutions, such as in education, health, and finance. For these residents, the fruits of growth have been tangible: employment opportunities on completion of college, or from training in IT skills and English; access to finance instruments that enable entrepreneurship, savings, and investment; and access to infrastructure, such as telecom, internet, roads, rail, and air connectivity that have helped improve productivity and incomes. On the other hand, such opportunity has been harder to come by for the poor in rural India and in our cities and towns.

The objective of the Unique Identification Authority of India (UIDAI) to issue a unique identity number for every resident in the country goes to the heart of ensuring greater opportunity. The role of the Aadhaar number is that of an enabler—a number that helps governments design better welfare programmes, enables residents in both urban and rural India to access resources more easily, and allows agencies to deliver services more effectively and transparently.

An Individual, Recognized Identity

In India we have made substantial progress over the last few years in how we approach and tackle poverty. For one, we view poverty less as a monolithic experience. We have acknowledged that disadvantaged individuals face different kinds of shortages, and need varied interventions at different points in their lives to move out of poverty, and access the opportunities that India's growth offers. Children of below poverty line (BPL) families, for instance, require effective investments in school education and immunizations, which will give them the skills and ability to be employable as adults. Adults who are in the BPL category need investments in re-skilling programmes, safety nets to protect them during periods of unemployment, and financial access that will enable them to save and invest. And finally, the impoverished elderly require protections, such as a regular, reliable pension.

This recognition means that the individual is the real target of social programmes, and not the household. The government has accordingly launched a gamut of programmes aimed at addressing the varied requirements of people in poverty: the Janani Suraksha Yojana effort is targeted at the health of pregnant women and their infants; the Sarva Shiksha Abhiyan programme focuses strongly on keeping children in school; the Rashtriya Swasta Bima Yojana provides health insurance for adults and children; and the National Rural Employment Guarantee Scheme guarantees 100 days of work for the rural unemployed, and is a cushion for lean, hard times.

However, even as we tailor our approach to welfare and social protection, fundamental issues of identification remain. Our programmes, for instance, have remained focused on household-based identification and the coverage of such identification is programme-based and not universal.

The Aadhaar number is a powerful tool as governments move to more individual-oriented programmes. It is an identification infrastructure that is available to every resident in India, including infants—the youngest person to receive an Aadhaar number so far has been a 13-day-old baby.

A Technology-based Infrastructure

The Aadhaar number represents a sharp transition from paper-based to IT-enabled identity systems. These numbers, which will be linked to biometric and demographic information to ensure their uniqueness, will be stored in a secure central database. The database can be contacted for identity authentication from anywhere in the country. Residents can verify their identities online and in real-time by providing their demographic or biometric information. Such an IT-enabled infrastructure would also support the remote verification of identity, creating possibilities for the remote delivery of services across the country.

Technology-enabled identity systems like the Aadhaar number are critical when the country's banking systems, trading markets, and service delivery are ramping up their technology capabilities and enabling remote delivery of services. Public investment in the Aadhaar infrastructure is necessary to ensure that impoverished and disadvantaged groups in the population are not excluded from such technology infrastructure, and are able to access and leverage them for their benefit. For example, while mobile telephony has become widely available, only a small segment of the population can use such phones to buy products and services remotely, due to the difficulties in remote identity authentication. Aadhaar-linked remote authentication would enable poor residents to access such services easily.

Accountability through Clear Identification

In my view, the biometric aspect of Aadhaar is a particularly powerful feature of the number, and will play a significant role in increasing accountability for service providers and in broadening access. Biometric-linked authentication to access benefits would make it easy for service providers to limit leakages of resources and benefits to those who are not entitled to them. An Aadhaar-linked system at a NREGS worksite, for example, would require workers to verify their presence through biometrics. The wages that are due to them could then be transferred directly to an Aadhaar-linked bank account, from where money can be withdrawn only through Aadhaar authentication.

Biometric authentication also makes it easier to deliver public resources and services through a variety of agencies—public, private, and non-profit. The two-way approach in delivering entitlements and services—delivery followed by confirmation through biometric authentication—increases the accountability of public and private service providers to the resident, since the resident's relationship with the agency is far more direct, and confirmation bypasses all intermediaries.

Seamlessness in Service Delivery

In India, a narrative has long existed on the divide between urban and rural India—while urban India survived and even prospered, the rural country, 'Bharat', was left behind, and its inhabitants became history's victims, to be provided for and rescued from their circumstances. The divide was not merely one of perception, but there were real, vast economic distances between the urban and rural country in the absence of effective infrastructure linkages, clear occupational divides, and markets largely limited to urban cities and towns. Services in rural India were difficult to access for residents because of these limitations. In governance as well, we approached these regions differently, with separate ministries for urban and rural development, and separate regulatory institutions in banking, insurance, and other services. Welfare programmes have also been tailored individually. The National Rural Health Mission, for example, targets health services in rural India while the Urban Health Mission was planned for India's cities and towns; JNNURM is focused specifically on urban renewal, while BRGF funds infrastructure in backward, rural regions.

However, over the last two decades, Indian residents have attempted to bridge this divide in their millions, as workers migrate in search of jobs, entrepreneurs venture into villages in search of opportunity, and as infrastructure investments and urban growth blur the boundaries between the village and the city.

Aadhaar would enable us to incorporate these changes into our policies and our economic approach, by powering up applications that address infrastructure challenges in rural regions, and deliver services seamlessly to both urban and rural India. Service providers can, for example, verify identity remotely through Aadhaar-linked technology systems and then deliver services, reducing the investments required to provide services in rural and sparsely populated regions, increasing competition, and providing choice to the consumer.

For instance, today urban residents are able to use ATMs to access their bank accounts and withdraw money, such access is rarely more than a short distance away. For the rural community, however, banking services are difficult to access; bank branches are at some distance away and are understaffed. The costs of these shortages are borne by residents. Micro-finance companies which work in hard-to-service areas, typically charge rural residents an interest rate of 25 per cent or more per annum on a loan currently, compared to 12 per cent per annum in the urban, non-poor market. The higher rate comes not just from the higher costs of reaching out to these groups, but also due to the perception that it is riskier to provide services to these residents in the absence of a financial history or a clear, mobile identity.

An Aadhaar-linked banking solution, however, could create local networks of business correspondents who enable residents in both rural and urban India to verify themselves using the Aadhaar number, and make transactions, remotely, through a mobile device. This would pave the way for the equalization of access, and cheaper services.

It would also give rural India the opportunity of self-service. Just as remote connectivity to markets through mobile phones has helped eliminate middlemen and allowed farmers in some areas to negotiate crop prices directly with the *mandi*s, remote Aadhaar authentication allows rural customers to employ the same self-service models that urban residents now access, in not just banking transactions but also in buying stocks, retail goods, and accessing a multitude of information services through their mobile phones.

A reliable identity infrastructure like the Aadhaar number can help establish widespread trust relationships with poor residents since credit and the other history of residents become mobile. Agencies would no longer have to carry out their own KYC (Know Your Customer) procedures before they service customers—Aadhaar KYR (Know Your Resident) could be used before an insurance company issues a new policy, or before a bank opens a new account.

This clarity and ease in verifying identity represents a significant growth opportunity for public and private agencies in India. It would lower organizational risks and empower agencies in banking, insurance, and other consumer industries to offer more services, expand their modes of delivery, and include larger numbers of impoverished residents within their ambit.

Such seamlessness in service delivery will become possible not only between urban and rural India, but also within markets. A resident will also be able to switch service providers with less information loss—for example, mobile financial records linked to the Aadhaar number would allow residents to easily establish their credit worthiness to any financial service provider, in any part of the country.

The Uniqueness of the Aadhaar Effort

The Aadhaar number is the first time that the government is implementing an infrastructure solely for establishing the identity of an individual. We should not underestimate how significant an effect such identity recognition by the state can have. Identities of people are inevitably in part social and political constructions, which respond to how public programmes are shaped, and how governments enumerate their populations. A living example of this is how the census classification and enumeration, which first began towards the end of the 19th century, has shaped Indian politics.

The groups enumerated in the Indian Census discovered their influence in two ways: the first was the impact of the state formally recognizing the existence of the group. As social scientists, such as Andre Beteille point out, 'Before the Census took hold, caste was more of an identity marker in the eyes of the British than among Indians.' Within Indian communities, caste was hardly monolithic or unified—in rural India, people segregated themselves into complex, locally defined occupational and social sub-groups; in cities and towns, people tended to segment themselves by income and occupation.

However, caste was central to the colonial census, and as this exercise became well-established in British India, the population responded accordingly in how they identified themselves and negotiated with the state. By the time of the 1931 Census, some communities had organized themselves to respond to census questions in specific ways. A flyer that was distributed by one organization in that year stated, 'Remember! Census operations have begun' and suggested specific answers for respondents to questions on ethnicity, religion, and caste.

The second source of influence for census groups came from empowerment through self-awareness, as linguistic-based, gender, age, religious, and other communities realized how significant their numbers were in the country. It paved the way for later debates on linguistic boundaries for states in the 1950s and 1960s, and on special minority rights for backward communities.

The census is an instance of how identity recognition empowered weaker social and economic groups to access resources, and negotiate more effectively with the state. The Aadhaar number has the potential to do for individuals in the 21st century what the census did for groups in the 20th century. The recognition of individual identity will enable residents to claim benefits and services that are owed to them. This would be of greatest benefit to marginal and disadvantaged groups—the act of registering these groups for the Aadhaar number makes them more visible, and it would become more difficult to deny benefits to these groups, and to civil society organizations and rights groups seeking access to resources on their behalf.

Capturing the Spirit

In the last few years, we have witnessed a widespread rethinking on how we view the mechanisms through which people can access development and opportunities for growth. From thinking purely in terms of our interventions—the funding of welfare schemes and public services—we have started considering how these efforts can empower and provide individuals with effective tools to come out of poverty. This language of empowerment is now being championed by our most prominent leaders and policymakers. Prime Minister Dr Manmohan Singh speaks of the importance to 'empower the poor to help them confront the challenges of development'; President Pratibha Patil highlighted the need to 'empower the disadvantaged, enabling them to move up the economic ladder and join the ranks of the prosperous'.

The Aadhaar number strengthens our ability to respond to this call, and imbue our policies with the principles of greater economic and social power for the poor. We have the opportunity to move to an environment where the residents of the country are given choice and power in exercising their benefits, and interacting with responsive, accessible governments and service providers. These gains would go down to the last person in the line: to the most impoverished, the marginalized, and the destitute.

Many commentators on India have remarked on the country's emerging 'can do' spirit, the momentum for change in that is evident in our burgeoning entrepreneurship, the mushrooming of our civil society organizations, and the millions of young people coming to our cities in search of bright lights and a brighter future. We have to act now to implement policies that respond to this spirit and the country's promise, and ensure long-term, sustainable, and participatory growth.

NANDAN NILEKANI

Urbanization and Its Management

In 2008 the world passed a demographic watershed, as for the first time more than 50 per cent of the world population was residing in urban areas. Today, roughly 51 per cent of the global population—or 3.4 billion people—reside in urban areas (Figure 1), a number that is projected to increase to roughly 6.3 billion people by 2050 (Figure 1).[1]

There are three main drivers of urban population growth: natural population growth of the urban sector, reclassification of non-urban areas as urban, and migration to urban areas from non-urban settings. Natural growth derives from the births and deaths in a country's population and does not take into account migration; for natural growth to occur, crude birth rates must be higher than crude death rates. Non-urban areas may also experience population growth, and if these areas surpass the 'urban threshold' they are reclassified as urban. Reclassification can also occur if non-urban areas become absorbed into the urban landscape as cities expand into surrounding non-urban areas. Lastly, rural-to-urban migration also increases the size of the urban population, as individuals seek out new opportunities in growing cities.

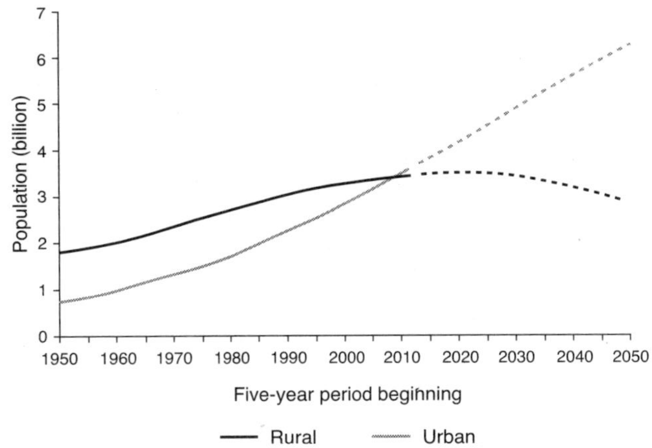

Figure 1 World Population Growth, by Sector, 1950–2050

Source: UN (2010).

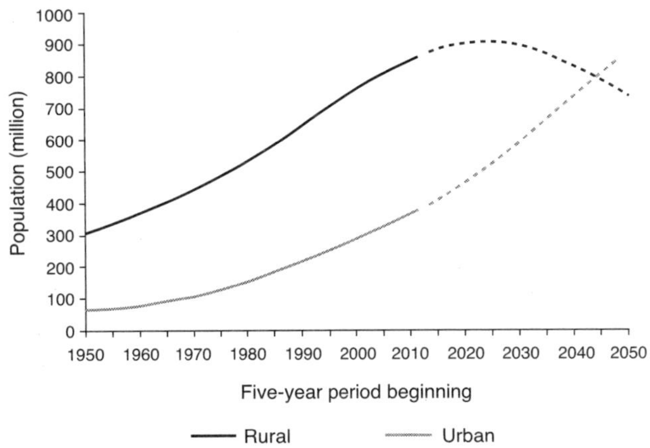

Figure 2 Population Growth in India, by Sector, 1950–2050

Source: UN (2010).

All three drivers of urban growth have led to a rise in the number of city dwellers in India, the second most populous country in the world. In 1950, 80 million people, or 17 per cent of India's population at that time, resided in an area classified as urban (Figure 2).[2] Today,

[1]The definition of 'urban' varies by country and depends on features such as population size and density.

[2]The definition of urban area used by India since 1971 is: '(a) All statutory places with a municipality, corporation, cantonment board, or notified town area committee, etc. (b) A place satisfying the following three criteria simultaneously: (i) a minimum

some 364 million people, or 30 per cent of the current population, reside in urban areas. And in 2045, India's population will mark its own demographic milestone, as 50 per cent of its projected population—or roughly 806 million people—will reside in urban areas.

Urban growth in India has produced some of the world's largest cities, including both megacities, whose populations number 10+ million, and metacities, whose populations number 20+ million. As Figure 3 shows, Delhi, Mumbai, and Kolkata are all classified as megacities, while Delhi (and soon Mumbai) also satisfies the metacity threshold. Interestingly, Delhi initially trailed Mumbai and Kolkata in growth, but following significant inward migration and natural population growth beginning in the 1990s, it soared to become the largest city in India by 2005. In addition to these three megacities, seven other cities will grow considerably through 2025, rounding out the 10 largest cities in India since 2005. These include Chennai, Bangalore, Hyderabad, Ahmedabad, Pune, Surat, and Kanpur.

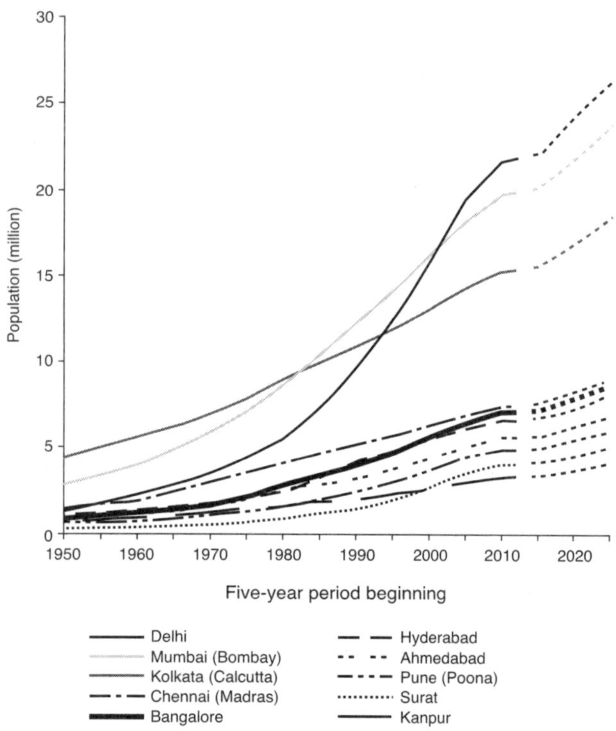

Figure 3 Urban Growth in India's Cities, 1950–2025

Source: UN (2010).

population of 5,000; (ii) at least 75 per cent of male working population engaged in non-agricultural pursuits; and (iii) a density of population of at least 400 per sq. km. (1,000 per sq. mile)' UN (2010).

Urbanization has had a variety of positive implications for India's economy, as cities are generally considered engines of economic activity and growth. Urban areas, for example, help to cluster businesses, universities, and skilled workers, all of which can promote learning and innovation synergies, new business models and partners, and economies of scale. This clustering effect is already apparent in many of India's urban areas: Mumbai is home to a host of financial firms; Bangalore and Hyderabad are known for their strong IT sectors and; Gurgaon, situated just outside Delhi, boasts a vibrant auto industry. Overall, India's cities, which house just 30 per cent of the total population, already contribute roughly 63 per cent to GDP, a number that is expected to increase to 75 per cent by 2021.

Despite these economic benefits, urbanization also has a series of negative implications for urban residents and businesses. In many cities, including Mumbai, urbanization has been rapid and largely unplanned, which has placed considerable strain on municipal services that are critical to growing economies. For example, cities like Chennai schedule daily rolling blackouts (also known as 'load shedding') to alleviate energy strains, negatively impacting the activities of homes and businesses. Limited and slow investment in public transportation systems has resulted in overcrowded railway systems; it is estimated that in 2008 roughly 850 people died after falling from overcrowded trains in Mumbai alone. Antiquated land use policies have contributed to rising land prices and a lack of affordable property, placing considerable strain on businesses and the middle- and lower-class populations of India's cities. The shortage of affordable housing has contributed to settlements in urban slums, areas characterized by further municipal challenges, crime, poverty, and disease. Insofar as reliable and high-quality municipal services are essential to recruiting firms and skilled residents, the Government of India (GoI) has a key incentive to better manage its urban growth so as to ensure that the economic benefits of urbanization do not wane going forward.

To tackle current urban challenges and to better manage future urbanization, the GoI has proposed and adopted a variety of policy measures. Many of these strategies feature prominently in India's 'Five Year Plan' series, which describe planning initiatives to guide development and growth. Specifically, the GoI has proposed investments in small- and medium-size cities, so-called 'second-tier' cities, to mitigate the strain placed on large megalopolises like Delhi, Mumbai, and Kolkata. Second-tier cities feature incentives designed to encourage settlements by residents and businesses, including improved transportation links, lower and regulated land prices, and 'special economic zone' (SEZ) privileges. SEZs are areas that are designed to accelerate economic growth by providing companies with significant tax breaks and well-planned municipal services. During 2007–14, the GoI plans to invest $29 billion to upgrade urban infrastructure and municipal services in 63 second-tier cities.

Nagpur, a long-standing coal mining city located in central India, is one such second-tier city currently undergoing upgrades. The GoI has aspirations of transforming this city into both a technology and air cargo hub, and has already allocated $280 million for new roadways, eco-friendly mass-transit systems, and new airport runways capable of receiving large jumbo jets. In addition to sizeable tax breaks, the city also offers residents and companies ready-to-use water, electricity, and fibre optic cable for connectivity purposes. Boeing, a leading American aerospace and defence company, has already purchased land to serve as a maintenance hub for its aircraft, while outsourcing companies like HCL Technologies have also established centres in Nagpur. The GoI remains hopeful that second-tier cities like Nagpur will also help in connecting local industries to new markets and encouraging the rise of home-grown entrepreneurs, all while mitigating the growth of mega and metacities.

The GoI has also proposed another strategy to curtail growth in India's megalopolises: the development of satellite cities. Under this proposal, local governments would guide responsible horizontal expansion of existing large cities by investing in well-planned townships and the suburbs around them. These new 'bedroom communities' will in theory service the residential needs of those who commute to the larger city for work. In Hyderabad, an IT hub and one of the 10 largest cities in India, construction has already started on several of its 22 proposed satellite cities. Developers aim to price homes in the satellite townships at affordable rates both to encourage newcomers to settle outside the city and to entice current residents of Hyderabad to relocate outside the city proper. The local government is also investing in strong and reliable transportation and communication systems to ensure connectivity between Hyderabad and its many satellites.

Conclusions

Urbanization has undoubtedly been instrumental to India's development and economic success. Demographic projections suggest that India's population will become increasingly urban over the next 40 years, signaling potential future economic gains. However, recent urban trends and observations also suggest that India could continue to face challenges resulting from poor urban planning and design, such as inadequate municipal services and sprawling urban slums, obstacles that could deter interest and investment in India. To mitigate prospective tensions between urbanization and economic development, the GoI has turned to policy to steer urban growth in a direction that encourages inclusive economic development. To this end, the GoI has invested in second-tier cities to stir new and planned growth in small- and medium-scale cities throughout the country, by providing incentives for industry to settle in new areas. While some economists argue against this form of industrial policy, believing instead that the market should ultimately determine how to best allocate resources, India seems less inclined to risk additional unplanned urban growth. Likewise, investment in satellite cities ensures that megalopolises can continue to thrive responsibly without compromising the living standards of their residents and workforces. The second-tier plan, SEZs, and satellite cities demonstrate that GoI is invested in urban reforms and is committed to ensuring that inclusive economic growth continues because of urbanization, not despite it.

David E. Bloom, Jennifer O'Brien, and Marija Ozolins

References

Batty, M. 2008. 'The Size, Scale, and Shape of Cities', *Science*, 319(5864): 769–71.

Bloom, D.E., D. Canning, and G. Fink. 2008. 'Urbanization and the Wealth of Nations', *Science*, 319(5864): 772–75.

Dye, C. 2008. 'Health and Urban Living', *Science*, 319(5864): 766–69.

Giridharadas, A. 2007. '"Second Tier" City to Rise Fast Under India's Urban Plan', *New York Times*.

Government of India (GoI). 2011. *Special Economic Zones in India*, New Delhi, Ministry of Commerce & Industry, GoI.

Grimm, N.B., S.H. Faeth, N.E. Golubiewski, C.L. Redman, J.Wu, X. Bai, and J.M. Briggs. 2008. 'Global Change and the Ecology of Cities', *Science*, 319(5864): 756–60.

Montgomery, M.R. 2008. 'The Urban Transformation of the Developing World', *Science*, 319(5864): 761–64.

Planning Commission. 2011. *Eleventh Five Year Plan*, New Delhi, Government of India.

United Nations 2010. *World Urbanization Prospects: The 2009 Revision*, New York, United Nations, Department of Economic and Social Affairs.

World Bank. 2011. *World Development Indicators Online (WDI) Database*, World Bank.

V

■ Value-added Tax in the States

One of the most important developments in the taxation scenario in India has been the recent introduction of value-added tax (VAT) in the states. After a period of preparation, 22 states out of a total of 29 have started implementing VAT in 2005–6. The remaining are expected to follow soon. There is a natural concern about this new system of taxation. In this short entry, I therefore begin by raising and answering the basic question: Why is VAT introduced in place of sales tax? After giving the justification for VAT, the background of its introduction is traced. The design of state-level VAT is then presented. The results of its introduction in the states are analysed next, and finally, possible future courses of action are outlined.

Justification for VAT

In the sales tax structure, there are genuine problems of double taxation of commodities and multiplicity of taxes, resulting in a cascading of the tax burden. For instance, inputs are first taxed, and then after a commodity is produced with input tax load, output is again taxed. This causes an unfair double taxation with cascading effects. In VAT, a set-off is given for input tax as well as tax paid on previous purchases, and the cascading effects are removed.

Moreover, in the sales tax structure, there is often a multiplicity of taxes, such as turnover tax, surcharge on sales tax, and additional surcharge. With the introduction of VAT, these other taxes are abolished. In addition, central sales tax on inter-state sales tax is phased out. As a result, under the VAT system, the average tax burden is rationalized, and the tax component in prices of a significant majority of commodities falls.

A distinctive feature of VAT is that it replaces the existing system of inspection by a system of built-in self-assessment by the dealers (that is, manufacturers and traders) and then transparent auditing. As a result, tax assessment and collection become more transparent and simple. At the same time, since both these advantages of 'set-off' and 'self-assessment' are based on documentation of tax payment, tax evasion is extremely difficult under a comprehensive VAT system. That improves tax compliance and also causes a significant growth in revenue. The VAT can thus help common people, traders, manufacturers, and also the government. It can, indeed, be a positive-sum game.

Background of Introduction of VAT

The VAT system was first introduced in Brazil in the mid-1960s, then in European countries in the 1970s, and subsequently in about 140 countries. In Asia, it has been introduced by a large number of countries from China to Sri Lanka. Even in India, a VAT system has been in place for about the last 10 years with respect to central excise duties only.

For the introduction of VAT in place of sales tax in the states, preliminary discussions took place in a meeting of Chief Ministers convened in 1995 by Dr Manmohan Singh, the then Union Finance Minister. At this meeting, the basic issues of VAT were discussed in general terms, and this was followed by periodic interactions of state Finance Ministers. Thereafter, in a significant meeting of all Chief Ministers, convened on 16 November 1999 by Yashwant Sinha, then Union Finance Minister, an important decision was taken. The decision was that before the introduction of state-level VAT, the self-defeating and unhealthy sales tax rate 'war' among states would have to end and that sales tax rates would need to be harmonized by implementing uniform floor rates for different categories of commodities with effect from 1 January 2000. On the basis of fulfilment of this objective, steps were to be taken by the states for the introduction of a state-level VAT after adequate preparation. For implementing this decision, it was resolved that an Empowered Committee of State Finance Ministers would be set up.

Thereafter, this Empowered Committee has met regularly, attended by the state Finance Ministers, and also by the Finance Secretaries and Commissioners of Commercial Taxes of the state governments as well as senior officials of the Revenue Department of the Ministry of Finance, Government of India. Through repeated discussions and collective efforts, it was possible within a period of about a year and a half to achieve nearly 98 per cent success in the objective of harmonization of sales tax structure through implementation of uniform floor rates. As a part of regular monitoring, whenever any deviation was reported from the uniform floor rates of sales tax, the Empowered Committee would take the matter up with the concerned state government for necessary rectification.

After reaching this stage, steps were then initiated for systematic preparation for the introduction of state-level VAT in terms of Entry 54 of the State List of the Constitution. Once again, to avoid any unhealthy competition among states that may lead to distortions in manufacturing and trade, attempts were made from the very beginning to harmonize the VAT design in the states, while at the same time keeping in view the distinctive features of each state and the need for federal flexibility. This has been done by the states collectively agreeing, through discussions in the Empowered Committee, to certain common points of convergence regarding VAT, and allowing at the same time certain flexibility for the local characteristics of the states. The Empowered Committee of State Finance Ministers has held nearly 90 meetings for frank exchange of views in arriving at this balanced convergence, upholding the spirit of federalism and democracy.

Along with these measures to ensure convergence on the basic issues on VAT, steps have also been taken for necessary training, computerization, and interaction with trade and industry, particularly at state level. This entire exercise initially faced obstacles. There were nationwide strikes called by organizations of traders. The Empowered Committee patiently discussed the issues with the trade organizations, listened to their problems at ground level and tried to address these, and, at the same time, convinced them of the beneficial effects of VAT on trade. The end result of this entire exercise has been rewarding. As mentioned earlier, 22 states started implementing VAT in 2005–6 with quite positive results in the first year of its implementation. The remaining states are expected to adopt VAT in the next year (2006–7). A national-level Consultative Committee has been formed with representatives of the Empowered Committee and organizations of trade and industry, with similar interactive bodies in the states, to sort out problems in the course of implementation of VAT.

It also needs to be mentioned that although VAT leads to substantial revenue growth within a few years, there might be inadequate revenue growth for some states in the initial years of transition. For this reason, the Empowered Committee of State Finance Ministers had strongly urged the Centre for appropriate budgetary compensation. All the Union Finance Ministers since 1999 had, in principle, agreed to provide this compensation, and Shri P. Chidambaram, present Union Finance Minister, played a helpful role in interacting with the Empowered Committee in this regard. A formula was worked out for 100 per cent compensation of the loss in the first year, 75 per cent in the second year, and 50 per cent in the third year of implementation of VAT.

Design of State-level VAT

As already mentioned, the design of the state-level VAT has been formulated by the Empowered Committee by striking a federal balance between the common points of convergence regarding VAT and flexibility for the local characteristics of the states. Since the state-level VAT is centred on the basic concept of 'set-off' for the tax paid earlier, the needed common points of convergence also relate to this concept of set-off/input tax credit, its coverage, and related issues.

Concept of VAT and Set-off/Input Tax Credit

The essence of VAT lies in providing set-off for the tax paid earlier, and this is given effect through the concept of input tax credit. This input tax credit in relation to any period means setting-off the amount of input tax by a registered dealer against the amount of his output tax. The value-added tax (VAT) is based on the value addition to the goods, and the related VAT liability of the dealer is calculated by deducting input tax credit from tax collected on sales during the payment period (say a month).

If, for example, input worth Rs 1,00,000 is purchased and sales are worth Rs 2,00,000 in a month, and input tax rate and output tax rate are 4 per cent and 10 per cent, respectively, then input tax credit/set-off and calculation of VAT are as shown in Table 1.

Table 1 Set-off under VAT System

(a)	Input purchased within the month	Rs 1,00,000
(b)	Output sold in the month	Rs 2,00,000
(c)	Input tax paid	Rs 4000
(d)	Output tax payable	Rs 20,000
(e)	VAT payable during the month after set-off/input tax credit [(d)–(c)]	Rs 16,000

Coverage of Set-off/Input Tax Credit

This input tax credit is given for both manufacturers and traders for purchase of inputs/supplies meant for both sale within the state as well as to other states, irrespective of when these will be utilized/sold. This also reduces immediate tax liability.

Even for stock transfer/consignment sale of goods out of the state, input tax paid in excess of 4 per cent is eligible for tax credit.

Carrying over of Tax Credit

If the tax credit exceeds the tax payable on sales in a month, the excess credit may be carried over to the end of the next financial year. If there is any excess unadjusted input tax credit at the end of the second year, then the same is eligible for refund. In fact, however, several states have started completing this refund for specified cases even within the first year.

Input tax credit on capital goods is also available for traders and manufacturers. Tax credit on capital goods may be adjusted over a maximum of 36 equal monthly instalments. The states may, at their option, reduce this number of instalments. Here, again, many of the states have, in fact, started completing this adjustment within the first year.

Treatment of Exports

For all exports made out of the country, taxes paid within the state are refunded in full, and this refund is to be made within three months. Units located in SEZs (special economic zones) and export-oriented units (EOUs) are granted either exemption from payment of input tax or refund of the input tax paid within three months.

Inputs Procured from Other States

Tax paid on inputs procured from other states through inter-state sale and stock transfer is not eligible for credit. However, a decision has been taken for duly phasing out of inter-state sales tax or central sales tax on the basis of adequate compensation. This issue is discussed later.

Treatment of Opening Stock

All tax-paid goods purchased on or after 1 April 2004 and still in stock as on 1 April 2005 are eligible to receive input tax credit, subject to submission of requisite documents. Resellers holding tax-paid goods on 1 April 2005 are also eligible. It may be noted that all the VAT-implementing states have already completed this process of refund of input tax credit on the opening stock of goods.

Compulsory Issue of Tax Invoice, Cash Memo, or Bill

This design of VAT with input tax credit is crucially based on documentation of tax invoice, cash memo, or bill. Every registered dealer having turnover of sales above an amount specified shall issue to the purchaser serially numbered tax invoice with the prescribed particulars. The dealer shall keep a counterfoil or duplicate of such tax invoice duly signed and dated, for purposes of audit.

Registration, Small Dealers, and Composition Scheme

Registration of dealers with a gross annual turnover above Rs 5 lakh is compulsory, but small dealers with gross annual turnover not exceeding Rs 5 lakh are not liable to pay VAT. States have flexibility to fix the threshold limit within Rs 5 lakh. Small dealers with annual gross turnover not exceeding Rs 50 lakh who are otherwise liable to pay VAT, again have the option of a composition scheme with payment of tax at a small percentage of gross turnover. The dealers opting for this composition scheme are, however, not entitled to input tax credit.

Return

Under VAT, a simplified form of returns is notified. Returns are to be filed monthly/quarterly as specified in the State Acts/Rules, and are accompanied by payment *challans*. Some initial difficulties were reported by traders regarding the return forms. Steps have since been taken by the states to ensure simplicity of these return forms.

Procedure of Self-assessment of VAT Liability

The basic simplification under VAT is that VAT liability is self-assessed by the dealers themselves in terms of submission of returns upon setting-off the tax credit. There is no longer any compulsory assessment at the end of each year. If no specific notice is issued proposing departmental audit of the books of accounts of the dealer within the time limit specified in the Act, the dealer will be deemed to have been self-assessed on the basis of returns submitted by him.

Audit

The self-assessment will be checked through a system of departmental audit. A certain percentage of the dealers will be taken up for audit every year on a scientific basis. If, however, evasion is detected on audit, the concerned dealer will be taken up for audit for previous periods. The audit team will conduct its work in a time-bound manner and the audit will be completed within six months. The audit report will be transparently sent to the dealer also.

Incentives

Under the VAT system, the existing incentive schemes may continue up to their previously announced time limits in the manner deemed appropriate by the states after ensuring that the VAT chain is not affected.

Other Taxes

As mentioned earlier, all other existing taxes such as turnover tax, surcharge, additional surcharge, and Special Additional Tax (SAT) have already been abolished by the VAT-implementing states.

Coverage of Goods under VAT

In general, all goods, including declared goods, are covered under VAT and will get the benefit of input tax credit.

The only few goods that are outside VAT are liquor, lottery tickets, petrol, diesel, aviation turbine fuel, and other motor spirits since their prices are not fully market-determined. These will continue to be taxed under the Sales Tax Act.

As decided by the Empowered Committee, VAT on Additional Excise Duty items (namely, sugar, textile, and tobacco) will not be imposed for one year after the introduction of VAT because of initial organizational difficulties, and till then the existing arrangement will continue. The position will be reviewed after one year.

VAT Rates and Classification of Commodities

Under the VAT system, covering about 700 broad categories of goods, there will be only two basic VAT rates of 4 per cent and 12.5 per cent, plus a specific category of tax-exempted goods and a special VAT rate of 1 per cent only for gold and silver ornaments, and so on. Thus the multiplicity of rates in the existing structure is done away with under the VAT system.

Under the exempted category, there are about 60 commodities comprising natural and unprocessed products in the unorganized sector, items which are legally barred from taxation, and items which have social implications. Included in this exempted category is a set of a maximum of 10 commodities flexibly chosen by individual states from a list of goods (finalized by the Empowered Committee) which are of local social importance for the individual states without having any inter-state implication. The rest of the commodities in the list are common for all the states. Under the 4 per cent VAT rate category are included the largest number of goods, common for all the states, comprising basic necessities such as medicines and drugs, all agricultural and industrial inputs, capital goods, and declared goods. The goods in the exempted category and in the 4 per cent VAT rate category together constitute nearly two-thirds of all the goods. The remaining commodities, common for all the states, fall under the general VAT rate of 12.5 per cent. The schedule of commodities with VAT rates is attached to the VAT Act of every state.

Effects of the VAT System

With reference to the objectives of VAT, as mentioned earlier, it is useful to study the effects of VAT in terms of (i) growth of revenue, (ii) acceptance by the dealers, and (iii) tax component in the prices of commodities, from the data available for the VAT-implementing states for the first three-quarters (1 April to 31 December) of the current year (2005–6).

Revenue Growth

The overall growth of tax revenue of the VAT-implementing states in the first three-quarters of the current year has been 15.6 per cent, which is significantly higher than the average rate of growth of sales tax of 12.3 per cent in the states for the last five years (2000–5). Of the total central budgetary provision of Rs 5,000 crore for 100 per cent compensation for possible revenue loss in the VAT-implementing states in the first year, it is now estimated that not more than Rs 3,000 crore will be required, and there will be savings. It may be noted that for several of the VAT-implementing states, the growth of revenue in the first nine months has exceeded 30 per cent. At the same time, for some of the states where the previous sales tax structure had high rates, the rate of growth of revenue under the VAT regime has been below the all-state average. It may be particularly noted that these rates of growth have been achieved in the first year when set-off had to be given to the opening stock (which will not be needed from the next year) and there have been initial difficulties in penetrating layers of trade for capturing full tax on value addition. It is expected that from the next year, without any need for set-off for closing stock and more penetration, there may be a very significant growth of revenue in all the VAT-implementing states.

Acceptance of VAT by Dealers

Even in the first nine months of the initial year, the rate of growth of registration of new dealers has exceeded 20 per cent for several states. This is a very significant development, indicating the beginning of the process of trade-layer penetration. If this process is deepened, combined with the discipline of issue of cash memo (not strictly enforced in the first nine months to allow for some spontaneity in the response of dealers), then the full beneficial effects of VAT will be increasingly felt.

Effect on Tax Component under VAT

A study conducted for the state of West Bengal for about 700 commodity groups indicates that in comparison with previous sales tax rates, tax rates under the VAT system have gone down for 487 commodities, remained the same for 39 commodities, and increased for 181 commodities. Thus the tax component has fallen for a significant majority of commodities as mentioned in the objectives of VAT.

Tax component under VAT has been compared with that under sales tax in Table 2 where the same rates of input tax (4 per cent) and output tax (10 per cent) have been applied for both VAT and sales tax under the supposition that manufacturer's cost (including profit) is Rs 100, input and wage component are in the proportion of 75:25, and total value addition is 10 per cent.

It is seen that the tax component in the sale price of the commodity, in general, will fall under VAT in comparison with sales tax. This comparative position, it can be checked, remains unchanged even if value addition is as high as 30 per cent. This position can only change if the VAT rate is significantly higher than sales tax rate for certain commodities—a situation which again is less likely due to the overall downward trend in the VAT rate as mentioned earlier.

Data available for the first three quarters of the current fiscal year thus indicate that the effects of VAT on revenue growth, acceptance of traders, and tax compliance are in the direction outlined in the objectives of VAT.

Future Courses of Action

In order to lessen distortions, there is a need, after the introduction of VAT, for phasing out of Central Sales Tax (CST). However, the states are now collecting nearly Rs 18,000 crore every year from the CST. Accordingly, there is a requirement for compensation from the Government of India for this loss of revenue. Simultaneously, the states have a justified need for a larger share of devolution from the central collection of service taxes as well as greater powers of collection and retention of proceeds of such collection. Moreover, after the introduction of VAT, the states should also be given the power to impose of VAT on imports, which may be collected centrally and then distributed among the states on the basis of destination. If these steps are taken, then phasing out of the CST can be implemented. The Empowered Committee is in the midst of discussions with the Union Finance Ministry for resolving these issues.

For phasing out the CST, there is also a critical need for putting in place a regulatory framework in terms of a

Table 2 Tax Component under Sales Tax and VAT

Sales tax (in rupees)		VAT (in rupees)	
1. Manufacturer's cost including profit	100.00	1. Manufacturer's cost including profit	100.00
(a) Wages and profit	25.00	(a) Wages and profit	25.00
(b) Input	75.00	(b) Input	75.00
2. Sales tax on input	3.00	2. Input tax (with set-off)	0.00
3. Selling price before output tax	103.00	3. Selling price before VAT liability	100.00
4. Sales tax on output	10.30	4. VAT liability on output	10.00
5. Selling price including sales tax	113.00	5. Selling price with VAT liability	110.00
6. Value addition	10.00	6. (a) Value addition	10.00
		(b) VAT at distribution level	1.00
7. Retail sale price	123.00	7. Retail sale price	121.00
8. Total sales tax component (2) + (4)	13.30	8. Total VAT component (4) + (6 (b))	11.00

Computerized Taxation Information Exchange System to comprehensively, and on a regular basis, track down inter-state trade of all commodities. After discussion in the Empowered Committee, this Taxation Information Exchange System has already been launched, and the states are preparing to make it fully operational in the next year. Simultaneously, the states have started combining this measure with penetration of all layers of trade, and computerization for tracing of all records of input and output taxation within each state, so as to capture the taxation of the entire chain of value addition. The revenue growth from VAT should show a very significant increase from the next year as these two types of measures are put into synchronized operation.

The experience of implementation of VAT across countries has often indicated serious problems of acceptance by traders, and also problems of overall revenue growth in the initial year, with an upward trend of acceptance and revenue growth from the second year. Judging by that experience, the results of introduction of state-level VAT in the complex federal structure of India, with traders eventually accepting VAT and the overall rate of growth of revenue being higher than the past trend even in the first year, have indeed been encouraging. There is, for reasons mentioned earlier, also a strong basis for much stronger improvement from the next year.

Along with the introduction of VAT in the states, the next step should be to put into operation a computerized system of continuous cross-checking of documents of set-off and tax returns of state-level VAT with those of central excise and income tax on the basis of coordination between the tax authorities of the state governments and the central government. This will mean an important breakthrough in preventing tax evasion and the important beginning of a systematic unearthing of tax-evaded 'black money' in the country, and will lead to a further mighty increase in revenue from VAT in the states as well as from central excise and income tax.

Under the pre-existing tax system in India, there has been a situation of unequal competition, with one group of dealers complying with tax payment and another group evading it. The VAT system basically makes this tax evasion extremely difficult and helps a move towards more equal competition. If this VAT initiative is also supported by other tax and non-tax measures towards more equal access to important facilities (such as credit, infrastructure, and R&D) for common manufacturers, farmers, traders, and service providers, then this move towards equal competition will be further strengthened for release of forces of production.

ASIM K. DASGUPTA

Voluntary Retirement Schemes

Voluntary Retirement Schemes (VRS) have become popular in India with companies in the private and public sector alike with the launch of economic reforms in June 1991. Shedding manpower deemed as surplus through promises of monetary compensation emerged as an attractive strategic option in an increasingly competitive business environment where employers needed to cut costs and achieve flexibility but were constrained by labour regulations. State governments rarely authorized firms with workforces of 100 or more people to dismiss or lay off personnel, something that was understandable given both endemic unemployment and the absence of a social security net. In the current context of deregulation, employers can, therefore, circumvent the law by persuading employees to 'voluntarily' surrender their jobs in return for material incentives and other forms of assistance. For the government as well, VRS presents the advantage of functioning as an unofficial exit policy, at a time when it faces pressure from various quarters to change the existing legislation.

No reliable statistics exist indicating the total number of employees who have opted for voluntary retirement. In central government-owned industrial undertakings, job buyout plans have resulted in the departure of 4.87 lakh officers and non-officers between 1988 and March 2003. Close to 1 lakh employees of public banks are said to have availed of this scheme up to March 2001. Most big private houses, including Birlas, Bajaj, Hindustan Lever, Reliance, and Tatas, have also implemented VRS—a strategy greatly facilitated by the creation of extensive outsourcing networks from the 1980s onwards—but aggregate figures are unavailable.

Financing for VRS has come essentially from the companies' own coffers or through public issues, but relaxations in income tax and accounting rules have helped to soften the blow on profit margins caused by the huge cash outflows. In the case of the public sector, the government established a National Renewal Fund (NRF) in 1992 to pay for and manage various aspects of the voluntary retirement programme. Disbanded eight years later, the fund was able to extend no more than limited monetary support, and that too only to companies controlled by the central government, because of inadequate resources. Nor did it meet with greater success in fulfilling its other mission of counselling, retraining, and redeploying retrenched employees.

Significant variations can be found in the size of the separation package paid to employees. In the Durgapur area, workers in private firms received on average Rs 40,000, compared to the Rs 1.44 lakh paid out to their counterparts in the public sector. The average compensation earned by central public-sector industrial employees up to the end of the 1990s is estimated to be Rs 1.3 lakh, but the lacklustre response to VRS in some public enterprises is prompting managements to raise severance payments. In the nationalized banks the size of the golden handshake is expected to hover around Rs 8 to 10 lakh per employee, an amount equivalent to that distributed by certain private corporations. Rhone Poulenc, for instance, handed out a package of Rs 7 to 8 lakh plus up to 100 grams of gold.

Even though VRS is normally introduced with the tacit accord of the union at least, notwithstanding the negative effects this would have on its strength, in several companies these schemes are voluntary only in name. Employees often quit either because repeated management propaganda has created fear that the company will close down or declare a lockout, depriving them of all but minimal compensation, or because they are subjected to various forms of coercion, including physical violence. 'Non-performers', a category that includes unskilled, chronically indebted, or medically unfit employees, who refuse to accept the buyout are separated from the rest of the workforce, kept idle, or even asked to stay at home while continuing to be paid. Inversely, in those companies where workers neither believe their jobs and salaries are at threat nor face overt harassment, VRS has proved to be relatively unsuccessful. With unemployment and casualization on the upswing, younger and less qualified workers, particularly in the public sector, are clearly reluctant to trade away the long-term advantages of job security for short-term monetary benefits.

However, large numbers of employees have also chosen voluntary retirement of their own accord. Despite the union's steadfast opposition, the entire workforce at Sriram Mills, for example, approved the company's separation package. The prospect of obtaining a substantial sum of money, quite often upfront, is an extremely attractive one for cash-strapped workers as it offers them a chance to finalize their childrens' marriages or finance their education, clear long-standing debts, build or renovate a house, retire to their home towns, or even go into self-employment. But employers defaulting on compensation payments, a not infrequent occurrence, means that these projects sometimes never materialize. Failures have also invariably marked entrepreneurial forays since employees rarely possess the required expertise and networks, while many of those seeking to re-enter the labour market either cannot find work or end up in poorly paid contract or casual jobs. Boredom and loss of self-esteem, lack of consideration from family members, and losing compensation benefits in swindles or imprudent business ventures are among the other problems buyout takers have to commonly contend with, the awareness of all of which also dissuades quite a few employees from opting for early retirement.

For employers too, VRS has not been without unintended consequences. Companies have suffered from a talent flight as better-qualified and more useful sections of the workforce capitalized on the scheme to leave. At the State Bank of India, services have been badly affected following the exodus of officers, a number of them joining private banks, whereas very few clerical staff and lower-ranking employees, the two main categories targeted by VRS, gave up their jobs. Similarly, at ITI, production flows were interrupted consequent to the en masse departure of shopfloor operatives. A survey of 30 companies having introduced VRS also revealed that it had resulted in improved performances (measured in terms of the ratio of profit after taxes to total assets) in just seven cases. Moreover, only a small proportion of these companies succeeded in achieving their stated objectives of reducing surplus manpower and overhead costs, and improving competitivity.

DILIP SUBRAMANIAN

References

Barse, Myrtle A. 2001. 'Social Implications of Voluntary Retirement Scheme: A Study of Mumbai', *Economic and Political Weekly*, December, 36(52): 4828–35.

Maheshwari, Sunil Kumar and Vilas Kulkarni. 2002. 'Implementation of VRS Schemes in India', *Vikalpa*, 28(2): 75–82.

Maniben Kara Institute. 1994. 'Voluntary Retirement Schemes & Workers Response: An Analysis of a Study on Voluntary Retirement Schemes and Their Impact on the Acceptors of Retrenchment Benefits in Bombay—Thane Region of Maharashtra State', April.

W

■ Wage Inequality

Since 1991, India has undertaken a major economic reforms programme under which significant and far-reaching changes have been made in industrial and trade policy to encourage foreign direct investment (FDI) flows and trade. Incentives have also been given to encourage higher imports of technology. With the change in the policy environment, the post-reforms period has witnessed a marked acceleration in the growth of both FDI and trade flows. Net FDI inflows as a percentage of gross capital formation increased from 0.23 per cent in 1980 to 3.4 per cent in 2004, while total trade as a percentage of GDP increased from around 15 per cent to almost 35 per cent.

Increased liberalization is generally found to be accompanied by increase in labour productivity in the manufacturing sector. However, there is some evidence that increasing openness of an economy is accompanied not only by increasing labour productivity but also by rising wage inequality among skilled and unskilled workers, particularly in the organized manufacturing sector. Several studies have documented rising wage inequality between skilled and unskilled workers in developed countries, particularly the United States and United Kingdom since the 1980s. However, not many studies exist for developing countries.

In this context, this entry examines the impact of liberalization, in particular the rise in FDI, trade and technological advancement, and wage inequality between skilled and unskilled workers in the Indian manufacturing sector. It is structured as follows: The first section examines the theoretical framework that explains the impact of FDI and trade on wage inequality; the second section discusses the data sources, methodology, and the empirical results estimated. Finally, the last section concludes the study and derives policy implications.

Impact of FDI and Trade on Wage Inequality: Theoretical Framework

Theoretical models show that FDI increases relative demand (and, therefore, wages) for skilled workers in both the North and the South. The North produces high-quality goods reducing demand for unskilled workers and since from the South's perspective these activities are relatively skilled, the demand for skilled labour rises as firms relocate their activities from North to South.

Further, it has been argued that FDI, along with introducing better technology and leading to improvement of overall labour productivity in the host country's industry, also introduces technologies that are skill-biased and are associated with skill upgrading. This brings out a more general point that foreign ownership is often associated with skill-biased technical progress leading to an improvement in the relative position of skilled workers.

Barry et al. (2001) formulated a theoretical model and showed that increase in foreign capital raises economy-wide demand for skilled labour and drives up skilled wages as skilled labour is fully employed. This crowds out domestic exporters from the skilled labour market and leads to substitution of unskilled labour. What happens to the wages of unskilled labour will depend on the process by which unskilled wages are set. It is also argued that in developing countries unskilled labour is either unemployed or underemployed. Foreign firms pay relatively higher wages (that is, wages over and above opportunity cost of labour) to unskilled workers and, therefore, reduce the wage gap.

Alternatively, Figini and Gorg (1999) have developed a theoretical model based on endogenous growth models. They show that the impact of FDI on wage inequality between skilled and unskilled workers is an inverted U shape, that is, with increasing presence of multinationals, wage inequality first increases, reaches a maximum, and then eventually decreases, ceteris paribus. The main idea is related to the Kuznets hypothesis that the development process implies first an increase and then a decrease in inequality. They use data from the Irish manufacturing sector and find that FDI first increases the wage gap due to introduction of new technologies which increase demand for skilled labour, but over time domestic firms learn new technology and previously unskilled workers become skilled by working with the new technology. This reduces the wage gap.

With respect to the impact of trade on wage inequality, standard trade theory, based on the Heckscher–Ohlin model, suggests that in developing countries trade will have a favourable effect on manufacturing employment since most of the exports are expected to originate from labour-intensive industries and higher exports may lead to higher employment. Under the H-O-S (Heckschor–Ohlin–Samuelson) framework, globalization suggests a redistribution of employment from the import sector towards the export sector; thus increased imports reduce employment and increased exports increase employment. The theory predicts that in their trade with developed countries, developing countries would export unskilled-labour-intensive goods and services and import skilled-labour-intensive goods and services.

According to the theory, therefore, trade would tend to increase demand for unskilled labour as it moves towards specialization of unskilled-labour-intensive products and, therefore, would reduce wage inequality, ceteris paribus. For example, a labour-abundant country specializes in the production of labour-intensive goods. Trade for this country will induce a rise in the wage rental ratio as the labour-intensive sector expands (the Stolper–Samuelson theorem). Thus the real reward of the country's abundant factor rises. In turn, this leads to factor price convergence for the two countries. However, the magnitude of the impact on relative wages would depend on their responsiveness to changes in demand.

The ambiguity in the direction and magnitude of the results with respect to impact of trade and FDI on wage inequality has made the issue an increasingly empirical one.

Impact of FDI and Trade on Wage Inequality in India: Empirical Results

Data Sources

No single source of data exists for the Indian economy that provides data on wages, FDI, and exports in an industry, which are required by this study. I, therefore, draw upon data from two different sources, that is, the *Annual Survey of Industries* (ASI), which is published by the Central Statistical Organisation, Government of India, and *Prowess*, published by the Centre for Monitoring Indian Economy Pvt Ltd (CMIE). The ASI provides reasonably comprehensive and reliable disaggregated estimates for the manufacturing industries. The data used in the study are constructed for 78 industries at the three-digit level of industrial classification (National Industrial Classification) for the period 1991–2 to 1997–8.[1] Data for most of the variables are drawn from the ASI while data on FDI, exports, and technology for the matched industries are obtained from *Prowess*.

The share of foreign companies in total sales of the industries has been taken as indicator of the level of FDI. Export intensity is measured by the ratio of exports to sales. To estimate the impact of imports, I use effective rate of protection (ERP) at industry level. The ERP series used has been taken from a study by the National Council of Applied Economic Research (NCAER).

The impact of trade and liberalization on wage inequality is estimated after controlling for extent of technology acquisition in the industry. To measure the impact of technology, an index of technology acquisition has been constructed using data on R&D expenditure, payment of royalty and technical fees for technology imports, and capital goods imports. The construction of the index has been done in two steps. First, the relevant ratios (for example, R&D expenditure to sales) have been constructed for the 78 major industry groups from firm-level data taken from the *Prowess* database of the CMIE. Next, applying the principal component analysis and taking the first principal component, the index has been drawn. The index combines the three technology-related variables using factor loadings as weights. All data are converted into natural logarithms.

[1]The period chosen has been constrained by the non-availability of comparable data since 1998. The reason being that the ASI has changed its industrial classification from 1998–9.

There are considerable problems in obtaining good-quality time-series data on wages by skill level. For my purposes, I use the available information on wages contained in the ASI database. This source provides the average number of full-time production process 'workers' and 'employees' (which includes in addition to 'workers', non-production workers like supervisors and clerks) employed per day after taking account of reported multiple-shift working. Wages of production workers are taken as wages of unskilled workers and these are subtracted from wages and salaries of employees to arrive at wages of skilled labour.

Methodology

To analyse the effect of FDI on the market for skills, I use a demand and supply framework. I estimate a two-factor constant elasticity of substitution (CES) production function with low-skilled labour (U) and skilled labour (S) (following Katz and Murphy 1992). I use different methodologies to estimate the impact of FDI and trade on wage inequality, which are ordinary least squares (OLS), fixed effects, random effects, and generalized least squares (GLS) estimations.

Empirical Results

With respect to the Indian manufacturing industry an important result that emerges from the analysis is that there has been an exogenous increase in wage inequality between skilled and unskilled workers over time.

To explain this increase, I focus on some of the determinants of skill-specific wages. The results show that, as expected, the higher the proportion of skilled labour to unskilled labour in an industry, the lower is the wage disparity. In other words, in industries that have more skilled labour, the difference between the wages of skilled and unskilled labour is less than in industries where the proportion of skilled labour is low.

The results with respect to impact of FDI show that it has a significant positive impact on wage inequality, once we control for other variables like trade and technology. *FDI has, therefore, contributed to the rising wage inequality in Indian industries*. This is in line with the findings of many studies for developing countries (for example, Zhao 2001, for China). The inference here is that FDI impacts positively on labour productivity, and in turn demands high-quality labour and, therefore, raises the wages of skilled labour. This may lead to wage-spillover effects whereby domestic firms are also forced to pay more to skilled workers in order to retain them.

I test the hypothesis put forward by Figini and Gorg (1999), that is, FDI may have an impact on wage inequality which is essentially inverted U-shaped. Thus, after a period of time, as overall skill levels in the industry increase, FDI may eventually reduce the wage gap. But I do not find it to be true for India. Perhaps it may take a long time, that is, it may take more than a decade for foreign firms to reduce wage inequality.

However, the results show that export intensity of an industry has a negative impact on wage inequality in an industry after controlling for supply effects. Higher exports are, therefore, found to reduce wage inequality. One reason for this could be that it is mainly low-skilled labour-intensive industries that export in India and, therefore, higher exports raise the demand for low-skilled labour, reducing the wage gap.

Apart from FDI and trade, the results show that rise in wage inequality over time may be attributed to technological progress. Import of capital goods is found to have a positive impact on wage inequality and the technological acquisition index is also found to have a significant impact on wage inequality. This indicates that in Indian manufacturing industries technological progress has probably been skill-biased. The impact of technological progress is stronger than the impact of trade, since over time wage inequality has been found to have increased.

Policy Implications

This entry estimates the impact of liberalization, that is, FDI and trade, after controlling for technology acquisition, on wage inequality between skilled and unskilled labour in the post-reforms period.

The results show that wage inequality between skilled and unskilled workers has increased in the liberalized regime and FDI, trade, and technology acquisition have differential impact on wage inequality. Higher FDI in an industry has worsened wage inequality, while higher export intensity of an industry has lowered wage inequality. Further, technological progress is found to be skilled-biased in the post-reforms period, and higher extent of technology acquisition in an industry has led to higher wage inequality.

One of the direct implications for policy that can be derived from the above results is that it is important to attract FDI in the export-oriented sector in India. I found that FDI has not yet entered export-intensive industries in India that are characterized by low-skilled labour. Entry of foreign firms in export-oriented industries will negate the adverse effects of FDI on wage inequality, as foreign firms will drive up the demand for unskilled labour in these industries. This will also help in improving the skills of the workers in this low-skilled sector.

One of the ways of encouraging FDI in the export-oriented sector is by reducing the relative cost of production and operation of foreign firms in this sector. With relaxed labour laws and higher education and training of labour in India, higher FDI is expected to flow into the export sector. Further, efforts should be undertaken in selected industries, especially import-competing industries, to improve the skills of the employed labour. Imparting training programmes by the state and increasing overall investments in education, health, training, and industrial relations can do this.

Rashmi Banga

References

Barry, Frank, Holger Gorg, and Eric Strobl. 2001. 'Foreign Direct Investment and Wages in Domestic Firms: Productivity Spillovers vs Labour Market Crowding Out', Nottingham NG7 2RD, UK.

Figini, P. and H. Gorg. 1999. 'Multinational Companies and Wage Inequality in the Host Country: The Case of Ireland', *Weltwirtshaftliches Archives*, 135: 594–612.

Katz, L.F. and K.M. Murphy. 1992. 'Changes in Relative Wages, 1963–1987: Supply and Demand Factors', *Quarterly Journal of Economics*, 107: 35–78.

Zhao, Yaohui. 2001. 'Foreign Direct Investment and Relative Wages: The Case of China', *China Economic Review*, 12: 40–57.

■ Water

Magnitude of Water Resources

As everywhere else, the magnitude and characteristics of India's water resources are determined by topography, geology, and, most important, the quantum and seasonal distribution of rainfall. The average annual rainfall for the country as a whole is estimated at around 600 mm, ranging from less than 100 mm in the Thar desert to over 11,000 mm in parts of the north-east. On an average, the total quantum of rainfall over the country (including snowfall in the Himalayas) is estimated at some 4,000 bcm.[1] Most parts of the country get the bulk of rainfall between June and October, the period of the south-west monsoon. The dates of onset and retreat of the monsoon, the quantum of rainfall during the season, and its contribution to annual rainfall vary across regions.

A part of the rainfall is absorbed and retained in the topsoil; a part seeps into the lower strata and recharges groundwater; and a third part constitutes surface run-off in streams and rivers. The Central Water Commission estimates the average annual surface flow at 1953 bcm; the Central Groundwater Board (CGWB) estimates average annual groundwater recharge from rainfall at around 430 bcm. The balance (around 1,600 bcm) gives a measure of what is absorbed and retained in the topsoil. The balance is accounted for by evaporation from exposed water bodies (including natural streams and rivers) and wet surfaces, and by evapo-transpiration by forests, grasses, shrubs and other vegetation on uncultivated land, and crops grown on cultivated land. On a rough estimate the quantum of evapo-transpiration by cultivated crops from soil moisture derived from rainfall is estimated at around 460 bcm.

Rainfall is the ultimate source of replenishable water resources. In addition, there are stores of underground water accumulated in deeper strata over a long period in the past. Some estimates of its magnitude have been made by the CGWB based on the area and depth of different geological formations and their water-holding capacity. This so-called 'static reserve' is currently estimated at some 10,800 bcm.

These estimates, it must be noted, are only indicative. Surface flow estimates are based on measurements at selected observation sites in all major rivers. But not all rivers are covered and even in major rivers the measurement sites are too few and devices not sophisticated enough to give reliable estimates. No allowance is made for changes in the surface flow regimes due to changes in land-use pattern and, in particular, the reduction in the extent and quality of forest cover, soil erosion due to expansion of cultivation to marginal and fragile soils, and interruption of natural drainage networks due to urbanization and expansion of road and rail networks. Crop evapo-transpiration in different agro-climatic regions is computed on metereological observations of temperature, rainfall, and other climatic variables based on certain empirical formulae relating to evaporation rates under different climatic regimes. However, the low density of observation sites and the instruments and methods of recording do not make for reliable and representative data. Groundwater recharge estimates are based on infiltration rates under different soil and subsoil characteristics, rainfall levels, and intensities. No estimates of non-crop evaporation are available.

The volume of rainfall, magnitude of surface flow natural groundwater recharge, and static groundwater reserves for the country as a whole and for different river basins are given in Table 1.

Utilizable Resources

Diversion and impoundment of surface flow and exploitation of groundwater add to the quantum of

[1] 1bcm = 1cu.km

Table 1 Water Resources Potential of River Basins in India

(bcm)

		Surface water			Groundwater				
Basin	Precipitation	Surface flow	Utilizable flow	Utilized flow	Stock total	Replenishable	Canal	Natural	Estimated utilization
1 Indus	560	73.3	46	44	1338	26.5	12.2	14.3	18.2
2 Ganges	1160	525	250	145	7834	172	35	136	49.6
3 Brahmaputra–Barak	4080	677	24	1	1018	35	0.8	34	1
4 Basins between Ganges and Mahanadi	1470	41	25		54	5.8	0.8	5	0.5
5 Mahanadi, Godavari Krishna, Pennar	3370	254	191	156	226	88.4	17.4	71	14.6
6 Basins between Mahanadi and Pennar	1110	23	13		41	18.8	6	12.8	
7 Cauvery	990	21	19	18	42	12.3	3.5	8.8	5.8
8 Basins between Pennar and Kanyakumari	820	25	17	22	66	18.2	5.5	12.7	10.5
9 Tapi, Narmada, Mahi, Sabarmati	3580	75.3	54	25.5	59	26.7	3.8	22.9	6.6
10 Luni, Saurashtra–Kutch	380	15	15	2.5	113	11.2	2.1	9.1	11.4
11 All others	3700	231	36	11.4	11	17.7	2.1	15.5	3.3
12 Total	21,220	1953	690	425.4	10,812	432	89.2	342.1	121.5

Sources: GoI. 1998. Central Water Commission, Water Related Statistics. GoI. 1999. Ministry of Water Resources, Report of the National Commission on Integrated Water Resources Development.

water available for agricultural and non-agricultural uses (including domestic consumption). But it is neither possible nor desirable to use the entire surface flow for these purposes. Most of the surface flow in Indian rivers (90 per cent in the Himalayan rivers and 80 per cent in peninsular rivers) is concentrated during June to September. The peak monsoon flow can be used to augment supplies in the rest of the year only by storing it. The extent to which this is possible is constrained by the availability of suitable storage sites, the capacity of reservoirs that can be built at these sites, geological conditions that determine the technical feasibility of constructing dams of acceptable safety standards, and of course the costs involved relative to the likely benefits that augmented supplies in the dry season can bring. According to the Central Water Commission, taking all these considerations into account, only about a third of surface flow is potentially utilizable. This assessment is necessarily tentative subject to the results of detailed site surveys and geological investigations. Some of the identified sites with huge storage capacities are in the seismically active sub-Himalayan regions. There are questions about the availability of cost-effective technology for exploiting these sites and ensuring that they can withstand high-intensity earthquakes.

Utilizable groundwater is taken to be equal to the annual recharge mostly from rainfall with an additional small quantity derived from recharge from seepage of water in canal-irrigated areas. This defines the level of use that is sustainable over time. Exploitation exceeding this level would mean dipping into the static reserve. And if it persists the reserve will get progressively depleted and eventually exhausted.

Levels and Pattern of Utilization

The last five decades have witnessed a concerted effort to increase the utilization of both surface water and groundwater resources. Surface water utilization has increased from 94 bcm in the early 1950s to 425 bcm in the late 1990s. Most of this increase has come from large, and some very large, irrigation and multipurpose reservoirs. Groundwater usage has gone up from 40 bcm to 120 bcm as a result of increase in the number of shallow wells (which has grown some two and half times) and the rapid spread of energized pumps to cover some three-fourths of wells. The major part of the growth is due to the advent of tube wells in the 1950s and their phenomenal growth to 4 million in the 1990s.

At present about two-thirds of utilizable surface water potential is being used. With the completion of the large number of projects under construction, utilization may go up to 600 bcm, or nearly 85 per cent of the assessed potential. Further expansion would be both technically and economically more difficult. In the case of groundwater, official estimates shown in Table 1 would suggest that taking the country as a whole, current utilization is barely 30 per cent of the potential. This is, however, at odds with CGWB data, compiled from a sizeable number of observation wells all over the country, showing a progressive and substantial fall in groundwater levels in nearly 60 per cent of the country's districts over the past 20 years. Sample surveys of some areas (Tamil Nadu, Gujarat, and Punjab) point to a much steeper decline in the depth of wells.

Available estimates of water utilization by use are given in Table 2. Being based on sketchy data and arbitrary assumptions, they are gross approximations. What they point to is the predominance of agriculture and livestock as users of water mobilized by human intervention. While other uses are growing much faster—more than threefold for domestic use, more than ten times for industry in absolute terms—and their combined share has more than doubled, the bulk—close to 90 per cent—of water is used by agriculture and livestock.

Table 2 Gross Utilization by End Uses of Water

bcm

	1968–9*		1997–8**	
	Total	%	Total	%
Domestic	9.1	2.9	30	5
Industrial	2.7	.7	30	5
Thermal power	6.9	1.8	9	1.5
Agriculture & livestock	356.8	95.0	524	88.5
	375.5	100	593	100

Sources: *Chaturvedi, M.C. 1976. *Second India Series: Water*, Delhi, Macmillan. **GoI, Ministry of Irrigation and Power. 1999. *Integrated Water Resource Development: A Plan for Action Report of the National Commission for Integrated Water Resources Development*, Vol. 1, New Delhi, September.

Emerging Problems and Responses

Agricultural demand for water has been increasing because of a large and growing differential between the productivity of irrigated and unirrigated land. Non-agricultural demand has grown even faster because of population growth, urbanization, and industrialization. There is ample evidence that the expansion in supplies, though large and historically unprecedented, has not kept pace with demand. Growing competition among farmers is reflected in (i) extensive violations of rules of allocation and use (including unauthorized tapping of canal water by farmers within and outside the command); (ii) the proliferation of wells and tube wells and competitive deepening in the face of falling water tables; (iii) growing complaints of water shortage in urban areas; and (iv) the social and political tensions generated by attempts to meet non-agricultural demands by diverting supplies from irrigation.

Public policy response to the growth of demand has focused primarily on augmentation of supplies. Falling groundwater levels imply mining of static reserves and this is unsustainable. Groundwater policy is yet to recognize this and take measures to even arrest, let alone reverse, the trend. The notion that the utilizable surface flow can be substantially augmented, and the country's water problems solved, by diverting the monsoon floods of Himalayan rivers to the relatively drier regions of the south and the west was mooted several decades back by Visvesarayya and subsequently by K.L. Rao. It was not pursued in the face of strong criticism on technical basis, economic viability, and environmental consequences. But the idea has recently been revived and has become a live issue thanks to a directive from the Supreme Court that it be implemented within a period of 15 years.

The latest project (estimated to cost Rs 5,000 billion at late 1990s prices) has two components: one for harnessing the waters of the Ganges and Brahmaputra for hydropower generation and for diverting surpluses to the south; and the other for interlinking of (mostly east-flowing) peninsular rivers. The former, which involves international rivers and requires construction of huge storages in seismically active regions, is not being actively pursued. Following the Supreme Court directive, the Government of India set up a special task force to implement the peninsular component.

Almost every aspect of the project—the estimated magnitude of surpluses, the proposed modes and locations of transfer, the extent to which transferred water can be used to solve the domestic water problem and extend irrigation in water-short areas, the technical problems of transporting water over long distances in difficult terrain, the likely adverse impact by way of ecological disruption, forest submergence and human displacement, and the magnitude of investment relative to net additional supplies—has attracted criticism. So have the necessity for and wisdom of pursuing such a massive project without proper feasibility studies and assessment of its environmental and social consequences, and without semblance of open public scrutiny of all its aspects.

Partly because of this criticism, the taskforce has since been disbanded without abandoning the project. The government, evidently reluctant to confront the judiciary, has chosen to adopt a rather cautious and ambivalent posture on the matter. In the process attention and resources are being distracted, if not diverted, from urgently needed measures to complete the huge overhang of half complete projects and for improving the efficiency of existing irrigation systems.

Corrective Measures

The situation in all these respects is worsening. Corrective measures are thus imperative. These measures must recognize that, unlike other resources, water is in the nature of a common pool serving multiple uses and users. They must be such as to address the need to ensure that the distribution of access to and use of this limited resource among competing uses and users is seen to be fair and equitable and that the supply of water for future generations is not jeopardized. The neo-liberal prescription of privatization and market-mediated allocation is no solution. Property rights in a fluid common-pool resource prone to pervasive interference by users are difficult to define and impossible to enforce through markets. Private enterprises are primarily concerned with returns to their financial investment. Issues of overall productivity of water, fair distribution of cost and benefits, and long-term sustainability hardly enter their calculations. Public intervention is essential to address these concerns. Government, therefore, necessarily has a key role in water governance.

However, the present system of governance leaves much to be desired. Public irrigation and water supply systems are designed, constructed, and managed entirely by the government. Users have no stake or say in any of these functions. The various functions involved in the development and efficient management of water resources—such as defining the nature and basis of entitlements, laying down broad principles and institutional mechanisms for deciding and implementing projects, for regulatory functions and dispute settlement—are all conflated in the executive arm of government.

Rules are made and enforced by government fiat, guided more by considerations of political expediency than any serious concern for efficient use and equitable distribution of water. Extensive violations of rules of entitlement for access and use have not only been tolerated but in fact encouraged by the policy of providing water at far below cost. Water charges are so low and collections so lax that users have hardly any incentive to avoid waste and make prudent use of available water. Conflict resolution mechanisms do not exist or have become defunct or ineffective. In such a situation, there is no transparency, due process, or accountability in the discharge of these functions. The interests of the political executive and their parties and the bureaucracy, rather than the larger and longer-term public interest, dominate the whole process.

These trends cannot be arrested, much less reversed, without drastic changes in policies and institutional arrangements for water resource management. A shift in policy focus from supply augmentation to measures for conserving water and improving the efficiency of its use is imperative and urgent. This calls for (i) a change in investment priorities from construction of new projects to improvements in physical facilities and engineering structures needed for better control over quantum and timing of water deliveries in surface systems and (ii) a change in the current policy of financing investments and pricing of canal water and energy inputs for pumping groundwater to create strong incentives for users to make prudent and efficient use of water. For this purpose users' stake in better management needs to be strengthened by requiring them to contribute at least a part of the cost of construction. Water and energy pricing policies should be geared to achieving full cost recovery with a rate structure that reflects the volume consumed for various purposes.

These measures have to be combined with a major restructuring of governance structure for water. There is clearly a great deal of room for improving the quality of project design, more economical and speedier construction of projects, and better coordination of programmes and policies relating to different sources and uses of water. These tend to be viewed primarily in terms of reorganizing government agencies concerned with water resource development. The creation of unified water resource organizations in some states, enactment of laws enabling user participation in management of irrigation systems, and integrated watershed development programmes reflect this approach. While these mark a significant and welcome change of approach, the 'reforms' are limited and piecemeal in both concept and implementation. They do not address the much wider and deeper weaknesses in water institutions and the way they are managed.

The following are some of the essential changes required: (i) limiting the government's role to laying down the broad principles regarding the nature and content of entitlements for water, the basis for determining entitlements of different uses and users within a basin and within individual systems, and intervention under specified contingent circumstances; (ii) creation of autonomous and financially self-reliant organizations for integrated planning and management of water resource for different uses and different sources in individual systems and for river basins with effective participation of users' representatives; (iii) these organizations should levy and collect water charges to cover costs (including capital costs) without any state subsidy or subject to explicitly defined limits of budgetary subsidies and they should be empowered to decide and enforce rules of entitlement, access, and use as well as rates within their domains; and (iv) redefining the law relating to private rights over groundwater towards community control and regulation.

Reforms of such far-reaching scope, however, figure nowhere as yet in the reform agenda. There is growing interest in integrated watershed development for rain-fed areas and creating water users associations and giving them a greater role in water management at the tertiary levels of public irrigation systems. Substantial investments for watershed development are being allocated under the public-sector plans. The idea of users' participation and turnover of management to water users associations has acquired wide currency. A few states have enacted and implemented legislation for this purpose. But the scope of these reforms is limited to tertiary levels of public canal systems. Water users associations are entrusted with limited functions (maintenance and, in some cases, recovery of water charges). They do not envisage empowering user-managed organizations to make, change, and enforce rules at the upper tiers and the system level. They have neither the freedom to decide water rates nor the compulsion to meet specified standards of cost recovery. There is little interest in pricing reform or in taking urgently needed but unpopular steps to check the depletion of groundwater. How to generate stronger pressures for reform and how to engineer them through the political process remains a challenge.

A. VAIDYANATHAN

Women in the Labour Force

Measuring participation of women in economically productive work is an area fraught with huge estimation problems. This is true not only for India but for the entire developing world. Women are involved in all kinds of productive work both inside and outside the home, but tend to underestimate and deny their involvement. Women's evaluation of their own work is shaped by the low social evaluation of their work. Thus official and non-official statistics show low participation rates for women, but day-to-day observation, case studies, and simple common sense indicate otherwise. Given high levels of poverty in most of the developing world, sheer economic compulsion would drive women to work. However, especially in India, an admission of working for wages is seen as a mark of low status. Additionally, women's underestimation of their work stems from the fact that it is often unpaid, and when it is paid, women have very little control over their earnings.

Since women are engaged simultaneously in multiple activities, the main problem in documenting participation rates arises when defining what constitutes 'work' (as in economically productive work). For India, most survey questionnaires ask: 'In addition to your regular work, what activities have you been engaged in?' Often, women do not understand which of their activities constitute 'regular work' and which additional work. For example, most women in rural areas tend to view their unpaid agricultural work as a part of their regular household chores and do not realize that if the work had been done by someone outside the family, he would have been paid for the job.

Trends in Female Labour Force Participation Rates

The major sources of data on labour force participation rates (LFPRs) for India are the decennial population censuses (Census of India) and surveys of the National Sample Survey (NSS) Organisation, the largest, non-census sample of the Indian population. For comparable definitions of work, census figures give a lower estimate of workforce participation than the NSS. For instance, using the principal status definition of the NSS, the workforce participation rate of rural women was 23.4 per cent for 1993–4, whereas according to the census, for main workers (comparable to the NSS principal status) it was 18.8 per cent in 1991. As the preceding discussion suggests, the NSS figure is an underestimate of the actual involvement of women in productive work—the census underestimates it even further.

Table 1 shows the LFPRs for men and women according to the various rounds of the NSS. Predictably, female LFPRs are lower than male LFPRs for all the years. However, female LFPRs have fallen marginally since the late 1970s. For instance, the rural female principal status LFPR has fallen from 24.8 in 1977–8 to 23.[1] in 1999–2000. This decline, for both rural and urban women, basically started in the late 1980s—the period that saw the introduction of the 'New Economic Policy'. The corresponding trends for males indicate that for rural areas, over the whole period, LFPRs have fallen by roughly similar percentage points. Male LFPRs show slightly greater fluctuation compared to female rates. This could reflect either a shrinking of employment opportunities in rural areas, or migration from urban to rural areas, or both. For urban areas, male LFPRs rose slightly over the whole period, but they stagnated over the 1990s. Looking at the figures by marginal/subsidiary status, the decline is similar for both men and women.

Table 1 also indicates consistently lower urban female LFPRs compared to rural rates, whereas the rural–urban LFPRs for males are comparable. This could

[1]Principal status is defined as the activity in which the person spent a relatively longer time (that is, major time criterion) during the 365 days preceding the survey. Subsidiary status is one in which the person spent a relatively shorter time (minor time) during the reference period of 365 days preceding the survey. Prior to determining the usual/principal status, and so on, it has to be first determined that the person belongs to the labour force.

Table 1 Labour Force Participation Rates, Various Years (%)

	Years				
	1977–8	1983	1987–8	1993–4	1999–2000
Rural					
Female					
main/principal status	24.8	24.8	24.5	23.4	23.1
marginal/subsidiary status	8.3	9.2	7.8	9.4	6.8
Male					
main/principal status	53.7	52.8	51.7	53.8	52.2
marginal/subsidiary status	1.5	1.9	2.2	1.5	0.9
Urban					
Female					
main/principal status	12.3	12	11.8	12.1	11.7
marginal/subsidiary status	3.3	3.1	3.4	3.4	2.2
Male					
main/principal status	49.7	50	49.6	51.3	51.3
marginal/subsidiary status	1.1	1.2	1	0.8	0.5

Source: NSSO. 2001. NSS 55th Round, July 1999–June 2000, National Sample Survey Organisation, Ministry of Statistics and Programme Implementation, Government of India, May.

be because labour relations in urban areas are marked by competition between individual units of labour rather than complementarity that is the hallmark of the traditional division of labour in rural areas. Thus women may be less able to compete because the technologically advanced urban settings require the acquisition of new skills that women possess to a lesser degree. Also, a large part of the work is outside wage jobs and there are fewer opportunities for working on family enterprises in or near one's own household compared to rural areas. Further, women need to combine household responsibilities with productive work, and that is easier to do in rural rather than urban settings.

The NSS has alternative definitions of work: usual status, daily status, and weekly status.[2] In view of the problems inherent in defining women's work, it is believed that definitions of work based on a shorter time span are better able to capture the workforce participation of women. For women, LFPRs with principal and subsidiary status combined are higher than those based on principal status alone, but the decline from the late 1980s is sharper for rural women based on principal status alone. Current weekly and daily status LFPRs are not higher than rates where principal and subsidiary status are combined, but they show an increase until 1993–4 and a decline thereafter for both urban and rural women. On the other hand, the male LFPRs show a near stagnation in rural areas and a slight increase in urban areas.

The age-decomposed LFPRs for men and women suggest that for both rural and urban women, the highest LFPRs occur between ages 30 and 45. In the productive years (roughly 30 to 50), the sex difference in the LFPRs is the sharpest, particularly for urban men and women. Over the entire period, there is a perceptible decline in female LFPRs in the age group 5–15. It has been argued that this reflects greater school enrolment of girls. However, there is a similar decline for boys as well, which leads us to think that there is greater school enrolment of both boys and girls. A similar trend is seen in the next age group, 15–19 years, but participation rates are much higher for this age group as compared to the younger girls, such that even in 1999–2000 the rural female LFPR in this group was about 30 per cent. Given that underestimation of total numbers would equally apply to this age group, this reveals the problem of high drop-out of girls in the secondary and higher secondary school levels.

It needs to be noted that there is considerable regional variation in both levels and trends of LFPRs. Abysmally low LFPRs are recorded for rural women, especially in the northern part of the country: Punjab, Haryana, Delhi, Jammu and Kashmir, Bihar, and Uttar Pradesh. These rates are particularly low in comparison with the western states (Maharashtra, Rajasthan) or the southern states (Tamil Nadu, Andhra Pradesh, or Karnataka). The only exception to the northern trend of low female LFPRs is Himachal Pradesh, a state that has shown exceptional advances in female literacy and total literacy in recent years. The same picture of regional variation is applicable to urban areas.

There are several factors that explain levels of female LFPRs. However, the existence of the underestimation phenomenon in the first place complicates the issue. Also, it must be noted that the explanatory power of most of the empirical work varies widely, calling for caution in formulating generalizations. However, some conclusions can be drawn:

(i) The impact of poverty on labour force participation is striking.
(ii) Studies suggest that education seems to delay participation in the labour market, but subsequently increases LFPRs.
(iii) On the whole, studies that include socio-cultural factors such as caste and religion seem to indicate

[2]Usual status is defined in footnote 1 (principal status). Current weekly activity status of a person is the activity status obtaining for a person during a reference period of seven days preceding the date of survey. It is decided on the basis of a certain priority-cum-major time criterion. Current daily activity status for a person is determined on the basis of his/her activity status on each day of the reference week using a priority-cum-major time criterion (day-to-day labour time disposition).

that these are relatively weak in explaining female LFPRs.

Occupational Distribution of Women

For rural women, by principal status, there was a 4 percentage point decline in the self-employed category between 1983 and 1999–2000 and a similar rise in the casual labour category over the same period, which is a clear indication of 'casualization' of female labour. The same trend is seen when we look at principal and subsidiary status together. Again, the same trend is evident for men in rural areas, so there is evidence of casualization of the overall rural labour force for both men and women.

For urban women, the category of regular employees shows an increase, and there is a decline in both self-employed and casual labour. However, urban men do not share this trend in that the category of regular employees shows a decline by both activity status categories and there is a marginal increase in the other two employment categories.

Looking at occupational distribution by broad industrial categories, for rural areas, agriculture continues to be the sector providing employment to the majority of workers—both men and women. However, since 1983 the share of agriculture has declined more for men than for women. But in 1999–2000, agriculture continued to employ 85 per cent of rural women. For both men and women, rural manufacturing is the next largest employer. It has been argued that men are concentrated mostly in non-household manufacturing and women in household manufacturing. This is indicative of the fact that as industries are shifting from cities to nearby rural areas, more men than women tend to get absorbed in the new employment opportunities.

Agriculture is a significant employer of both men and women in urban areas too, but more for women than men. For urban women, the next most significant category that shows a rising trend until 1993–4 is public administration. However, in the 1990s this category has seen a decline. This could be due to the reduction in public-sector jobs as a part of the overall strategy to reduce the role of the government in the economy. If this trend continues, and it is likely to, it means that the only avenue open to urban women is the 'trade, hotel, and restaurant' sector since that is the only sector in which the percentage of women employees is rising. Urban manufacturing is the other significant sector of employment for women, but here again the employment trend is declining. The share of women in finance and business remains abysmally low, and is only marginally better in urban than in rural areas. The occupational distribution seems to follow stereotypical lines: that is the share of women in mining and quarrying, electricity, water, transport, and so forth, in other words, in the 'male' occupations, continues to be insignificant over the period. Liberalization and the strategy of neo-liberal globalization do not appear to be reversing this trend.

Underemployment

The proportion of person days of the usually employed utilized for work was quite low for women compared to men throughout the period 1987–8 to 1999–2000. During 1999–2000 this proportion was estimated at about 68 per cent and 79 per cent for women in rural and urban India, respectively, versus 90 per cent and 94 per cent for men. In other words, women are underemployed in far greater measure than men. Also, when work is not available, large proportions of women simply withdraw from the labour force rather than report themselves as unemployed.

Wage Differentials

There is evidence of male–female wage differentials across broad occupational categories based on NSS data. Differences in human capital characteristics are often cited as the reason for the existence of these differentials. However, this differential is seen to exist within each educational category; in other words, men and women in similar occupational and educational categories earn disparate average salaries. This constitutes, prima facie, evidence of gender discrimination at the workplace. The picture holds true for both rural as well as urban areas, where the gap in the average wage for men and women increased from Rs 7 in 1987–8 to Rs 30 in 1999–2000. In addition to wage discrimination, the more important problem is that women are relegated to dead-end jobs and tasks with little scope for upward mobility.

ASHWINI DESHPANDE

■ Worker Benefits*

Statutory worker benefits for the private sector in India are provided primarily through seven schemes. These schemes can be categorized into two types based on their mode of financing: contributory and non-contributory. The contributory schemes are the Employees' Provident Fund (EPF), Employees' Deposit Linked Insurance

*The views expressed in this entry are entirely those of the author. They do not necessarily represent the views of the World Bank, its Executive Directors, or the countries they represent.

(EDLI), Employees' Pension (EP), and Employees' State Insurance (ESI) schemes, while the non-contributory, employer-liability schemes are the Workmen's Compensation (WC), Payment of Gratuity (PG), and Maternity Benefit (MB) schemes. Together, these schemes currently cover at most 10–15 per cent of the labour force in the private sector, and are basically limited to a small segment of the organized private sector. This situation represents one of the more critical shortcomings of these schemes, which the government hopes to address by expanding the coverage of these and other existing schemes as well as by introducing new schemes targeted at the unorganized sector (Planning Commission 2001). The main aim of this entry, however, is to provide a brief overview of the salient design features of the seven aforementioned schemes. It also touches on a few selected issues related to their implementation and performance.

Starting first with the contributory schemes, the EPF, EDLI, and EP schemes are administered by the Employees' Provident Fund Organization (EPFO), an autonomous body composed of representatives from the government, employers, and employees, under the aegis of the Ministry of Labour and Employment. By design, the coverage of all three schemes overlap—they apply to workers earning Rs 6,500 or less per month employed at worksites or in establishments with 20 or more employees in certain specified industries and classes of establishments. In early 2003, these three schemes covered about 39.5 million workers in 344,508 establishments across 180 industries and classes of establishments (EPFO).

The schemes are mainly financed by regular contributions from employers (EPF: 3.67 per cent of the covered wage bill; EDLI: 0.50 per cent; EP: 8.33 per cent) and employees (EPF: 12 per cent of wages).[1] These contribution rates are comparatively high by international standards, only exceeded by the transition economies of Central and Eastern Europe in general. The contributions to the EPF scheme are deposited into individual worker accounts. The funds in these accounts are invested largely in public-sector securities and earn returns at prescribed rates. The prescribed nominal rate of return on EPF accounts in 2002–3 was 9.5 per cent (EPFO). Historically, these rates have been very low in real terms. For example, from 1959 to 1999 the average real rate of return was less than 1 per cent (World Bank 2001).

The EPF scheme is a defined contribution scheme. Upon discontinuation of employment due to retirement (upon attaining age 55), resignation, termination, or permanent and total disablement, the worker is entitled to withdraw the full balance in his EPF account. The vast majority of full withdrawals have been due to resignation, running counter to the scheme's original raison d'être, namely, providing old-age income security. The worker is also entitled to partial withdrawals from his EPF account while employed for a wide range of stipulated reasons.[2] Depending on the specific reason for early withdrawal, different eligibility conditions and withdrawal limits apply. In 2002–3, the average amount of full withdrawal was about Rs 36,200 (EPFO). Concerns regarding the prevailing rates of partial withdrawals as well as full withdrawals due to resignation have prompted the Second National Commission of Labour to call for a tightening of withdrawal rules.

The EDLI is essentially a defined contribution scheme that provides survivor benefits. If the worker dies while employed, the designated survivor is entitled to receive a lump-sum benefit equal to the average balance of the deceased worker's EPF account over the 12-month period preceding the worker's death. If the average balance exceeds Rs 35,000, the withdrawal amount is based on a more complicated formula, subject to a maximum of Rs 60,000. In 2002–3, the average benefit amount was around Rs 25,800 (EPFO).

The EP scheme is a defined benefit scheme. It provides retirement, survivor, and disability benefits mainly in the form of an annuity. Under the scheme, the worker is entitled to regular retirement benefits upon attaining 58 years of age and reduced early retirement benefits upon attaining the age of 50. Eligibility for standard retirement benefits requires 10 or more years of contributory service. The monthly retirement benefit is calculated based on the worker's years of contributory service and monthly salary over the last year of contributory service. The worker is also entitled to disability benefits in the case of permanent and total disablement due to a work-related injury. The monthly benefit is based on the same formula as that for retirement benefits. In the case of the death of the worker occurring before or after retirement, the worker's family is entitled to survivor benefits equal to a specified percentage of the deceased worker's retirement benefit.[3] This percentage varies based on the recipient's relationship

[1]The government also makes regular contributions (1.16 per cent of the covered wage bill) to the EP scheme. In addition, employers bear the costs of administering the EPF and EDLI schemes, while the central government bears the costs of administering the EP scheme.

[2]The reasons include financing the purchase or construction of a home, children's education, worker's or children's wedding expenses, and worker's hospitalization expenses.

[3]If the worker dies while employed, the worker's retirement benefit is calculated based on the years of contributory service until death.

to the deceased worker, among other things. Eligibility for disability and survivor benefits requires at least one month of contributory service by the worker.

Although the EP scheme provides longevity insurance (unlike the EPF and EDLI schemes), the annuity benefits are not indexed to inflation. Consequently, benefit recipients are not insured against price increases.[4] There are also concerns that the benefits are not calculated in an actuarially fair manner and that the long-run financial viability of the scheme is exposed to risk due to the fact that the scheme is not fully funded (World Bank 2001).

The ESI scheme is a defined benefit scheme that provides a broad range of social security benefits to workers. It is administered by the Employees' State Insurance Corporation (ESIC), an autonomous body composed of representatives from government, employers, employees, and the medical establishment, under the aegis of the Ministry of Labour and Employment. The ESI scheme covers specified non-seasonal manufacturing- and service-sector establishments above a certain size. Within these establishments, the scheme covers workers earning Rs 7,500 or less per month. The ESI scheme is currently implemented in 687 localized areas across 25 states and union territories, and covers about 7.9 million workers in 254,000 establishments. The scheme is mainly financed by regular contributions from employers (4.75 per cent of the covered wage bill) and employees (1.75 per cent of wages).[5] In addition, state governments assume a stipulated share of the costs of medical care provided to covered workers.[6]

In terms of benefits, the worker and his dependents are entitled to free medical care through the ESIC or ESIC-approved medical facilities from the start of covered employment. The worker is also entitled to cash benefits for various contingencies such as sickness (roughly 50 per cent of wages for a maximum period of 91 days),[7] temporary disablement due to a work-related injury (roughly 85 per cent of wages for the period away from work due to the disability), permanent disablement due to a work-related injury (an annuity benefit proportionate to the medically assessed loss in earnings capacity), and maternity (roughly 100 per cent of wages for a maximum period of 12 weeks). In April 2005, the ESI scheme introduced unemployment benefits. The worker is now entitled to roughly 50 per cent of wages for a maximum period of six months over his lifetime in the case of involuntary lay-off due to establishment closure or workforce retrenchment.[8] Depending on the type of cash benefit, different eligibility conditions apply (ESIC).

Several official recommendations have been made to improve the performance of the ESI scheme, the most important of which are to extend coverage of the scheme to new areas and smaller establishments, to raise and ultimately remove the wage ceiling for benefit qualification, and to improve the quality of medical services provided by ESI medical facilities from its widely perceived low levels (Planning Commission 2001).

Turning next to non-contributory employer-liability schemes, the Workmen's Compensation (WC) scheme presently covers workers in 50 hazardous occupations and requires employers to compensate the worker in the event of death or disablement due to a work-related injury or illness.[9] More specifically, in the case of permanent total disablement or death, the employer is required to provide a lump-sum benefit calculated on the basis of the worker's wage and age at the time of the event, while in the case of permanent partial disablement, the benefit is proportionate to the medically assessed loss in the worker's earnings capacity, subject to minimum and maximum amounts. In 2001, the average benefit payout for death and permanent disability was around Rs 160,000 and Rs 83,000, respectively (Labour Bureau 2004). Employers are also required to pay a benefit in the case of temporary disablement equal to 50 per cent of the worker's wages for the period away from work due to the disability, subject to a maximum period of five years. Administrative responsibility for the WC scheme lies with the state governments.

The Payment of Gratuity (PG) scheme covers worksites and establishments with 10 or more employees, and requires employers to provide workers with a lump-sum benefit upon discontinuation of employment due to retirement, resignation, termination, disablement, or death. Under the scheme, the employer is required to pay 15 days of the worker's final salary per year of continuous service subject to a current maximum of Rs 350,000.[10] Eligibility for benefits requires a minimum of five years of continuous service. This condition does not apply in

[4]The average annual CPI-based inflation rate was around 9.5 per cent during the 1990s, and 4 per cent over the 2000–4 period.
[5]Workers earning Rs 50 or less per day are exempt from making contributions.
[6]State governments assume 12.5 per cent of the costs of ESI-provided medical care up to a ceiling of Rs 750 per covered patient per year and 100 per cent of the costs above this ceiling.
[7]In the case of certain specified chronic illnesses, the worker is entitled to sickness benefits for up to two years.

[8]The worker is also entitled to unemployment benefits in the case of permanent disablement due to a non-work-related injury.
[9]Workers who are covered by the ESI scheme are not eligible for benefits under the WC scheme.
[10]Seasonal workers are entitled to seven days' wages for each year of service.

the case of disablement or death, however. Administrative responsibility for the PG scheme is divided between the central and state governments according to establishment type and location (GoI, Payment of Gratuity Act, 1972).

The Maternity Benefit (MB) scheme covers worksites and establishments with 10 or more employees and requires employers to provide maternity benefits to all female workers.[11] Under this scheme, the employer is required to pay a benefit equal to the worker's wage for a maximum period of 12 weeks. Eligibility for benefits requires a minimum of 80 days of employment in the 12-month period preceding the expected delivery date. In 2001, the average benefit payout in factories and plantations was around Rs 13,000 and Rs 2,900, respectively (Labour Bureau 2004). Like the PG scheme, administrative responsibility for the MB scheme is divided between the central and state governments according to establishment type and location (GoI, Maternity Benefit Act, 1961).

In terms of operational performance, all three schemes have suffered greatly from weak enforcement by the responsible government authorities. Implementation has mostly relied on self-compliance by employers, which, needless to say, has been far from widespread. Notwithstanding, employer compliance appears to be generally higher in establishments where trade unions are present. The poor overall record of compliance is also largely attributable to the inability of employers to meet their liabilities under these schemes. This has been a problem especially with smaller employers (Planning Commission 2001). The government has attempted to deal with this problem in the PG scheme by requiring employers to insure their benefit liabilities. To further address this and other concerns, the Second National Commission of Labour has recommended converting the MB and PG schemes into contributory schemes and integrating them into the ESI and EPF schemes, respectively.

DHUSHYANTH RAJU

References

Employees' Provident Fund Organization, India. Website: www.epfindia.com, accessed on 3 November 2005.

Employees' State Insurance Corporation, India. Website: http://esic.nic.in, accessed on 3 November 2005.

Government of India. 'Maternity Benefit Act 1961', IndiaLawInfo.com website, http://www.indialawinfo.com/bareacts/maternity.html, accessed on 3 November 2005.

[11]Workers who are covered by the ESI scheme are not eligible for benefits under the MB scheme.

———. 'Payment of Gratuity Act 1972', IndiaLawInfo.com website, http://www.indialawinfo.com/bareacts/gratuityact.html, accessed on 3 November 2005.

Labour Bureau, Ministry of Labour and Employment, Government of India. 2004. *Pocket Book of Labour Statistics, Year 2003 & 2004.*

Ministry of Labour and Employment, Government of India, '2nd National Labour Commission Report', Ministry of Labour and Employment, Government of India, http://www.labour.nic.in/lcomm2/nlc_report.html, accessed on 3 November 2005.

Planning Commission, Government of India. 2001. 'Report of the Working Group on Social Security for the 10th Five Year Plan 2002–2007', Planning Commission, Government of India, October, http://planningcommission.nic.in/aboutus/committee/wrkgrp/wg_soclscty.pdf, accessed on 3 November 2005.

World Bank. 2001. *India: The Challenge of Old Age Income Security*, Washington DC, 5 April.

World Trade Organization

The World Trade Organization (WTO) came into existence on 1 January 1995. It has 148 members currently and membership has been steadily growing. Its main functions are serving as a forum for negotiations among members on issues relating to international trade, administering those agreements that result from the negotiations, and serving as a clearing house for dispute settlement among member nations. The existing WTO agreements cover three main areas: trade in goods; trade in services; and intellectual property. The main agreements covering these areas, respectively, are the General Agreement on Tariffs and Trade (GATT); General Agreement on Trade in Services (GATS); and Agreement on Trade-related Aspects of Intellectual Property Rights (TRIPS). In addition, there are several other agreements that clarify or build upon these three central agreements. The WTO also has a strong dispute settlement system to address complaints by member country governments of the violation of their WTO-sanctioned rights by other members.

Prior to the WTO, only trade in goods had been subject to genuine multilateral discipline. This discipline was contained in the GATT, which was signed in late 1947 and came into force on 1 January 1948. GATT was a treaty but the secretariat administering it effectively also served as an informal international organization. Thus the acronym GATT is sometimes used to refer to both the treaty and the organization. When the WTO was formed, GATT as an organization ceased to exist while the GATT treaty became a part of the WTO agreements governing international trade in goods. The WTO also took over the GATT secretariat's various functions including the conduct of future negotiations, administration of past agreements, and dispute settlement.

During the approximately forty-five years of its independent existence, GATT conducted eight rounds of negotiations among its members. These rounds resulted in progressive liberalization of world trade. The last three of these rounds—Kennedy, Tokyo, and Uruguay—were more comprehensive than the first five in that they went beyond tariff reductions. The Uruguay Round, in particular, transformed GATT into a formal international organization called the WTO and brought trade in services and intellectual property rights under multilateral disciplines.

India was one of the 23 founding members of GATT and is also a founding member of the WTO. Along with Brazil, it has been at the forefront of GATT and the WTO as the advocate of developing country interests that it has often seen as being in conflict with those of developed countries. Following the end of the Second World War, the United States had led an effort to create an International Trade Organization (ITO) to lay down global rules of international trade. In the end, the ITO was stillborn but GATT, which had been initially signed as a stopgap treaty to be replaced by the ITO, filled the void. At the meetings for the ITO, India, Brazil, and Cuba had been very critical of the US proposals and argued that the ITO was contrary to the interests of developing countries and was intended to ensure that they remained dependent on developed countries.[1]

Later, when Part IV entitled 'Trade and Development' was added to GATT in 1965, India played an important role in pushing for it. A key substantive provision of Part IV of GATT was that developed countries agreed not to insist on reciprocity in tariff concessions from developing countries. This effectively turned developing countries into non-participants in trade-liberalization negotiations until the Uruguay Round when developed countries once again started to demand liberalization from developing countries. In my judgement, though developing countries had pushed for the non-reciprocity provision, it hurt their interests. The provision made it easier for developed countries to maintain high tariffs and even quantitative restrictions on products of interest to developing countries. In particular, little liberalization took place in agriculture. Likewise, textiles and clothing remained subject to bilateral quotas for the following 40 years.

[1]For the history of GATT, see Wilcox (1949), Dam (1970), and Jackson (1997).

The main 'accomplishment' of developing countries between the end of the Kennedy (1962–7) and Tokyo (1973–9) Rounds was the negotiation of a set of exceptions for them to the rules of GATT. These exceptions were initially granted through a 10-year waiver in 1971, which was superseded in 1979 by a decision entitled 'Differential and More Favorable Treatment, Reciprocity and Fuller Participation of Developing Countries', popularly called the Enabling Clause. The latter provided the legal basis for the grant of one-way trade preferences by developed to developing countries, which had been pushed in parallel by the United Nations Conference on Trade and Development (UNCTAD) under the rubric of the so-called 'Generalized System of Preferences' (GSP). The Enabling Clause also gave developing countries the right to exchange trade preferences among themselves, effectively exempting them from adhering to the central Most Favoured Nation (MFN) principle of GATT, which forbids member countries from discriminating among trading partners in their trade policy. GATT allowed member countries discrimination only if they formed full Free Trade Areas (FTA) or Customs Unions (CU). The Enabling Clause gave developing countries the right to exchange all kind of trade preferences among themselves regardless of whether or not the intent was to form an FTA or CU.

From the beginning, India had chosen the path of import-substituting industrialization (ISI) and adopted progressively protectionist policies. Article XVIII of GATT allows developing countries to maintain quantitative barriers indefinitely on the grounds of a threat to the balance of payments. Taking advantage of this provision, India created a regime of strict import licensing across all products, complementing it by equally strict foreign exchange controls. With some modifications, this regime remained in place until the systematic liberalization that began in 1991. India freed capital goods and intermediate inputs from licensing in 1992. But the virtual prohibition on imports of consumer goods was not withdrawn until a challenge by the United States in the WTO dispute settlement body forced the government's hand on 1 April 2001. Given that by now India had adopted a flexible exchange rate and had accumulated a very large stock of foreign exchange reserves, the argument that it faced a threat to the balance of payments if it allowed consumer goods imports became indefensible.

When negotiations for the Uruguay Round were being launched in 1986, India and Brazil led the opposition to the inclusion of services in the agenda. India feared that an agreement on services would automatically open the door to foreign investment for which it was not yet ready.

Indeed, at the time, India had very tough laws against foreign investment. The opposition was sufficiently strong that services ended up on a separate negotiating track on the Uruguay Round agenda with the possibility that countries would be allowed to opt out of signing the agreement on them.

The remaining agenda of the Uruguay Round was on a separate track and any agreement on it was to be a 'single undertaking' meaning that countries would have to sign it in total or stay out of it entirely. They would not be allowed to sign some parts and not others. Included in this 'single undertaking' were two short paragraphs on intellectual property rights (IPRs). The wording of these paragraphs gave no hint of the real intentions of developed countries to use them as a basis for their demand for a wide-ranging agreement on the norms and standards in all areas of intellectual property (Ricupero 1998, Zutshi 1998, Panagariya 2000). Once those intentions became clear, India and other developing countries became fierce opponents of such an agreement. As negotiations progressed, India led the developing country demands for building various flexibilities into the draft Agreement on TRIPS but remained opposed to the evolving Uruguay Round (UR) Agreement. Dissatisfaction with the offers in the area of agriculture also made developing country members of the Cairns Group, which included developed and developing countries with comparative advantage in agriculture seeking significant liberalization in agriculture, unwilling to sign an agreement.

As it turned out, in the course of the negotiations, developed countries decided to create the new institution called the WTO that would supersede GATT with the negotiating member countries having the option to either join this new institution and agree to all its discipline or be out of the multilateral trading system altogether — in effect, a Hobson's choice. India remained opposed to the agreement till the end but acquiesced because its only other alternative was to stay out of the multilateral trading system and risk trade sanctions by other countries.

Under the UR Agreement, India committed to replacing all border barriers on agricultural products by tariffs and binding the latter.[2] It also undertook obligations for tariff reductions and binding them in both industry and agriculture. Other areas of commitment included liberalization in services and improved IPR standards as laid out in the Agreement on TRIPS. The implementation period for the UR Agreement having ended on 1 January 2005, India has fully complied with its obligations. The last important and controversial step was a new patent Act for pharmaceuticals that provides both product and process patent for 20 years.

A simplistic but broadly correct characterization of the approach India has taken towards the WTO negotiations since the Uruguay Round is that it has worked towards slowing down the negotiations for further agreements. In the case of many of the new demands put on the table by the developed countries, especially the United States and European Union (EU), this is a justifiable approach. But in so far as India has also been nearly unequivocally opposed to trade liberalization, the approach has been counterproductive and against its own interest.

Thus, soon after the conclusion of the UR Agreement, the US had begun to push for the inclusion of labour standards in the WTO agenda. India lobbied against the inclusion with other developing countries and was successful at the first WTO Ministerial Conference at Singapore in 1996. The Singapore Ministerial Declaration explicitly delegated the issue of labour standards to the International Labour Organization (ILO). The issue did not disappear from the WTO agenda, however, and countries such as India and Brazil have had to continuously fight against it at subsequent ministerial meetings, especially at Seattle in 1999.

Developed countries were, however, successful in introducing four new issues into the WTO agenda at Singapore: investment, competition policy, government procurement, and trade facilitation. India had opposed the inclusion of these issues, which subsequently came to be called the Singapore issues. Even though the issues entered the agenda only as 'study' issues, by this time, developing countries had understood the strategy and knew that the study would be followed by demands for negotiations.

Therefore, when the Singapore issues (along with agricultural liberalization) became central to talks on the launch of what is now known as the Doha Round, India's Commerce Minister Murasoli Maran was prepared to fight to the end and so he did. He successfully negotiated a statement on the inclusion of these issues that was subject to two interpretations: one that an agreement to launch negotiations on the issues had been reached and the other that any country not wishing for the negotiations could veto them. Maran was widely criticized in the Western press for being obstructionist and even took some heat in the domestic press (Panagariya 2001). But in the end he prevailed: at the WTO Ministerial in Cancun in 2003, the EU effectively agreed to take its demand for negotiations on the Singapore issues off the table. Subsequently, apart from trade facilitation, which

[2]In WTO parlance, binding a tariff implies that the country cannot raise the custom duty above its bound rate without renegotiation with its trading partners who would be adversely impacted by the increase in the tariff.

India did not oppose as vigorously as the other issues, all the Singapore issues have been dropped from the negotiating agenda.

Nevertheless, Maran and his successors can be legitimately criticized for extending their opposition to liberalization even in the area of industrial goods. At a time when India had been rightly lowering its trade barriers and was also seeking reductions in tariffs on labour-intensive goods by developed countries, its stance at Doha that there be no negotiations on industrial goods liberalization was indefensible. As I have argued elsewhere (Panagariya 2002), by taking a negative stand on even the launch of a new round, India unduly lost goodwill and provided the Western press free ammunition.

At Doha, the People's Republic of China was formally entered into the WTO. China gave very substantial concessions to the existing members, especially the United States and European Union, to obtain entry but successfully insisted on developing country status. Given the substantial weight China carries both as the world's most populous country and on account of a more than 5 per cent share in world exports, its entry has strengthened the developing country bargaining position. India has sought to forge common negotiating positions with China, which is highly desirable. China also joined hands with G-20, a group of major developing countries formed to represent the joint interests of the member countries during the negotiations at the WTO Ministerial Meeting in Cancun in September 2003. The interests of India and China will not always coincide but when they do, they will greatly enhance their bargaining power by negotiating jointly.

At the time of writing, preparations are under way for the 2005 WTO Ministerial in Hong Kong to conclude the Doha negotiations. Prospects for closing the round at this Ministerial are dim, however, which is not surprising since the negotiations in recent history have rarely been closed in four years. Liberalization in agriculture has been and remains the key contentious issue in this round. Once again, India has taken the stand that it wants developed countries to liberalize their agriculture but should not be asked to reciprocate. The argument it has been making is that 650 million people in India survive on agriculture, making agricultural liberalization a major risk. But for a country with very limited negotiating power due to its low share in world trade, such a stance is preposterous. If India is not prepared to give access to its markets, it is not going to get market access in return. The fear that Indian farmers cannot compete in the world marketplace is also exaggerated. In a world without export subsidies and low protection in the developed countries, Indian farmers stand to benefit from liberalization by India. Such liberalization will require specialization in fewer crops and, therefore, some adjustment, but it will be to the eventual overall good.

In India and many other developing countries, actual tariffs on industrial products are much higher than applied tariffs. Recently, this has led the developed countries to demand that negotiations be on the actual rather than bound tariff rates. This is a dangerous demand and India has rightly opposed it. If developing countries find that future negotiations will be on the actual tariffs, their unilateral tariff liberalization programmes will come to a standstill. Indeed, they will even be tempted to roll back liberalized tariffs to bring them to the existing bound levels.

To conclude, it is important for India to take a more pro-liberalization stance in so far as trade is concerned. A country's own liberalization brings benefits to it as India has learned from its liberalization experience over the last 15 years. Through multilateral negotiations, it can multiply this benefit by getting its partners to liberalize as well. It is for this reason that I have argued that India should push for complete free trade in industrial products by 2015 for developed and by 2020 for developing countries. Such liberalization will also help end the discrimination that already exists against its products in North America and Europe due to the existence of trade blocs in those regions.

Arvind Panagariya

References

Dam, K. 1970. *The GATT: Law and International Economic Organization*, Chicago, University of Chicago Press.

Jackson, John. 1997. *The World Trading System*, Cambridge, Massachusetts, MIT Press.

Panagariya, Arvind. 2000. 'The Millennium Round and Developing Countries: Negotiating Strategies and Areas of Benefits', UNCTAD and Center for International Development, G-24 Discussion Papers Series, No. 1, March.

——. 2001. 'India Arrives at the WTO', *Economic Times*, 21 November.

——. 2002. 'India at Doha: Retrospect and Prospect', *Economic and Political Weekly*, 26 January, 37(4): 279–84.

Ricupero, Rubens. 1998. 'Integration of Developing Countries into the Multilateral Trading System', in J. Bhagwati and M. Hirsch (eds), *The Uruguay Round and Beyond: Essays in Honour of Arthur Dunkel*, Berlin, Springer-Verlag.

Wilcox, Clair. 1949. *A Charter for World Trade*, New York, The Macmillan Company.

Zutshi, B.K. 1998. 'Bringing TRIPS into the Multilateral Trading System', in J. Bhagwati and M. Hirsch (eds), *The Uruguay Round and Beyond. Essays in Honour of Arthur Dunkel*, Berlin, Springer-Verlag.

Contributors
(with Entries)

Bina Agarwal (*Gender Inequality*)
Director and Professor of Economics, Institute of Economic Growth, Delhi, India

Isher Judge Ahluwalia (*Industry*)
Chairperson, Board of Governors, Indian Council for Research on International Economic Relations (ICRIER), New Delhi, and Vice Chairperson, Global Development Network, New Delhi, India

Montek S. Ahluwalia (*Planning*)
Deputy Chairman, Planning Commission, Government of India

Yoginder K. Alagh (*Green Revolution*)
Chancellor, Nagaland University; Chairman, Institute of Rural Management Anand (IRMA); and Vice-Chairman, Sardar Patel Institute of Economics & Social Research, Ahmedabad, India

Mukesh Anand (*Pensions*)
Assistant Professor, National Institute of Public Finance and Policy (NIPFP), New Delhi, India

Ritu Anand (*External Debt*)
Group Head—Policy and Chief Economist, Infrastructure Development Finance Company Ltd. (IDFC), Mumbai, India

T.C.A. Anant (*Environment and Law*)
Chief Statistician of India, Ministry of Statistics and Programme Implementation, Government of India, and Professor of Economics, Delhi School of Economics, University of Delhi, Delhi, India

Reena Badiani (*Data Sets, co-authors Siddharth Sharma and Himanshu*)
PhD Student, Economic Growth Centre, Yale University, USA

Amiya Kumar Bagchi (*State Bank of India*)
Director, Institute of Development Studies Kolkata, India

Jugnu Bagga (*Rent Control Acts, co-author Shubhashis Gangopadhyay*)
Formerly with India Development Foundation, Gurgaon, India

Kanti Bajpai (*Defence Strategy*)
Professor, Department of Politics and International Relations, School of Interdisciplinary Area Studies, University of Oxford, UK

G. Balachandran (*Reserve Bank of India, co-author T.C.A. Srinivasa-Raghavan*)
Professor of International History and Politics, Graduate Institute of International Studies, Geneva, Switzerland

Kaushik Ranjan Bandyopadhyay (*Human Rights, co-author Arjun K. Sengupta*)
Associate Professor, Department of Policy Studies, TERI University, New Delhi, India

Tamal Bandyopadhyay (*Interest Rates; Repo Market*)
Deputy Managing Editor, *Mint*, HT Media Business Paper, India

Abhijit V. Banerjee (*Public Goods*)
Professor, Department of Economics, Massachusetts Institute of Technology, Cambridge, USA

Anirvan Banerji (*Business and Growth Rate Cycles, co-author Pami Dua*)
Co-founder and Chief Research Officer, Economic Cycle Research Institute (ECRI), New York, USA

Sanjay Banerji (*Finance and Law*)
Reader in Finance, Essex Business School, University of Essex, UK

Rashmi Banga (*Wage Inequality*)
Senior Economist, United Nations Conference on Trade and Development (UNCTAD)—India Program, New Delhi, India

Arindam Banik (*Technology Transfer, co-author Pradip K. Bhaumik*)
Professor of Economics, International Management Institute, New Delhi, India

Pranab Bardhan (*Political Economy*)
Professor of Economics, University of California, Berkeley, USA

Alaka Malwade Basu (*Infant and Child Mortality; Population Policy*)
Professor of Demography, Department of Sociology, Cornell University, New York, USA

Arnab Basu (*National Rural Employment Guarantee Act, co-authors Nancy H. Chau and Ravi Kanbur*)
Professor, Asian and Middle Eastern Studies, Global Studies, College of William and Mary, Williamsburg, VA, USA

Kaushik Basu (*Inflation: Experience and Policy*)
Chief Economic Adviser, Ministry of Finance, Government of India, and C. Marks Professor, Department of Economics, Cornell University, New York, USA

Suman Bery (*NCAER's Household Survey*)
Director-General, National Council of Applied Economic Research (NCAER), New Delhi, India

Laveesh Bhandari (*Home-based Work*)
Director, Indicus Analytics, New Delhi, India

Vinay Bharat-Ram (*Manufacturing Hub*)
Chairman and Managing Director, DCM Group, India

Anuradha Bhasin (*Tourism*)
Consultant, National Council of Applied Economic Research (NCAER), New Delhi, India

Aditya Bhattacharjea (*Antitrust Law*)
Professor, Department of Economics, Delhi School of Economics, University of Delhi, Delhi, India

Ruchira Bhattamishra (*Tribal Development*)
PhD Student, Department of Economics, Cornell University, New York, USA

Pradip K. Bhaumik (*Technology Transfer, co-author Arindam Banik*)
Professor of Quantitative Techniques & Operations Management, International Management Institute, New Delhi, India

Sharit K. Bhowmik (*Street Vendors*)
Dean and Professor, School of Management and Labour Studies, Tata Institute of Social Sciences (TISS), Mumbai, India

David E. Bloom (*HIV/AIDS, Economics of, co-authors Bhargavi Rao, Ajay Mahal, and Kavita Sivaramakrishnan; Urbanization and Its Management, co-authors Jennifer O'Brien and Marija Ozolins*)
Clarence James Gamble Professor of Economics and Demography, Department of Global Health and Population, Harvard School of Public Health, Boston, Massachusetts, USA

Vani K. Borooah (*Religion and Economic Well-being*)
Professor of Applied Economics, University of Ulster, Jordanstown, Northern Ireland, UK

Amitava Bose (*Employment*)
Professor of Economics, Indian Institute of Management Calcutta, Kolkata, India

Sumit Bose (*Public-sector Enterprises, co-author Sharat Kumar*)
Secretary, Department of Expenditure, Ministry of Finance, Government of India

Rajesh Chakrabarti (*Foreign Exchange Markets; Foreign Institutional Investment*)
Assistant Professor of Finance, Indian School of Business, Hyderabad, India

RUPA CHANDA (*Services-led Growth*)
Professor of Economics and Social Sciences, Indian Institute of Management Bangalore, India

PANKAJ CHANDRA (*Textile and Apparel Industry*)
Director and Professor of Operations and Technology Management, Indian Institute of Management Bangalore, India

C.P. CHANDRASEKHAR (*Financial Crisis*)
Professor, Centre for Economic Studies and Planning, School of Social Sciences, Jawaharlal Nehru University, New Delhi, India

A.V. CHARI (*Licensing*)
Associate Economist at RAND, USA

ARKADEV CHATTERJEA (*Academic Research, co-author Satya Priya Moulik; Doctoral Education*)
Research Fellow, Center for Excellence in Investment Management, Kenan-Flagler Business School, University of North Carolina at Chapel Hill, and Affiliated Faculty, Cornell Higher Education Research Institute (CHERI), Cornell University, USA

MIRAI CHATTERJEE (*Social Protection for Informal-sector Workers*)
Director, Social Security, Self-Employed Women's Association (SEWA), Ahmedabad, India

NANCY H. CHAU (*National Rural Employment Guarantee Act, co-authors Arnab Basu and Ravi Kanbur*)
Professor, Charles H. Dyson School of Applied Economics and Management, Cornell University, New York, USA

BASUDEB CHAUDHURI (*Regional Disparities, co-author Velayoudom Marimoutou*)
Director, Centre de Sciences Humaines, New Delhi, India, and Associate Professor of Economics, CREM, University of Caen, Caen, France

MRINAL DATTA CHAUDHURI (*V.K. Ramaswami*)
Former Professor, Delhi School of Economics, University of Delhi, Delhi, India

SAUMITRA CHAUDHURI (*Housing Finance*)
Member, Economic Advisory Council to the Prime Minister; and Member, Planning Commission, New Delhi, India

SUDIP CHAUDHURI (*Pharmaceutical Industry*)
Professor of Economics, Indian Institute of Management Calcutta, Kolkata, India

P. CHIDAMBARAM (*Fiscal Policy Reforms since 1991*)
Union Minister of Home Affairs, Government of India

IGNATIUS CHITHELEN (*Entrepreneurs in India and Abroad, co-author Shankar Parameshwaran*)
Managing Partner, Banyan Tree Capital Management, New York, USA

DEB KUSUM DAS (*Trade Barriers in Manufacturing*)
Reader, Department of Economics, Ramjas College, University of Delhi, Delhi, India

GURCHARAN DAS (*Entrepreneurship*)
Author, Commentator, and Public Intellectual, and former CEO, Procter & Gamble India

JISHNU DAS (*Chronic Illnesses, co-author Jeffrey S. Hammer; Medical Care, Quality of, co-author Jeffrey S. Hammer*)
Senior Economist, Development Economics Research Group, World Bank, Washington DC, USA, and Visiting Scholar at Center for Policy Research, New Delhi, India

MAUSUMI DAS (*Prashanta Chandra Mahalanobis*)
Reader, Department of Economics, Delhi School of Economics, University of Delhi, Delhi, India

MONICA DAS GUPTA (*Public Health*)
Senior Demographer, Development Research Group, World Bank, Washington DC, USA

ARINDAM DAS-GUPTA (*Corruption*)
Professor, Goa Institute of Management, India

ASIM K. DASGUPTA (*Value-added Tax in the States*)
Former Finance Minister, West Bengal, India

DIPAK DASGUPTA (*Fiscal Deficit, co-author Supriyo De*)
Principal Economic Adviser, Ministry of Finance, Government of India

SUGATO DASGUPTA (*Elections and Political Business Cycles*)
Professor, Centre for Economic Studies and Planning, Jawaharlal Nehru University, New Delhi, India

SUPRIYO DE (*Fiscal Deficit, co-author Dipak Dasgupta*)
Officer on Special Duty to the Chief Economic Adviser, Ministry of Finance, Government of India

BIBEK DEBROY (*Higher Education: Regulation and Control; Law and Legal System in India*)
Professor, Center for Policy Research, New Delhi, India

ASHOK V. DESAI (*Convertibility*)
Consultant Editor, *Business World*, New Delhi, India

NITIN DESAI (*Sustainable Development*)
Honorary Professor, Indian Council for Research in International Economic Relations (ICRIER), New Delhi, India

SONALDE DESAI (*Middle Class*)
Professor of Sociology, University of Maryland, USA

ASHWINI DESHPANDE (*Affirmative Action; Caste; Women in the Labour Force; Caste*)
Professor, Department of Economics, Delhi School of Economics, University of Delhi, Delhi, India

R.S. DESHPANDE (*Farmers' Distress and Suicides*)
Director, Institute for Social and Economic Change (ISEC), Bangalore, India

S. MAHENDRA DEV (*Agriculture Development*)
Director (Vice Chancellor), Indira Gandhi Institute of Development Research (IGIDR), Mumbai, India

AMRITA DHILLON (*V.M. Dandekar; Fiscal Federalism*)
Professor, Department of Economics, University of Warwick, UK

ASHUTOSH DIKSHIT (*Tax System and Reform, co-authors Sunil Mitra and Vivek Johri*)
Joint Secretary (TPL-I), Central Board of Direct Taxes, Department of Revenue, Ministry of Finance, Government of India

RAFIQ DOSSANI (*IT-enabled Sectors*)
Senior Research Scholar and Director, Center for South Asia, Stanford University, Stanford, California, USA

JEAN DRÈZE (*Food and Nutrition; Ashok Rudra, co-author Suman Sarkar*)
Visiting Professor, Department of Economics, University of Allahabad, Allahabad, India

PAMI DUA (*Business and Growth Rate Cycles, co-author Anirvan Banerji*)
Professor and Head, Department of Economics, Delhi School of Economics, University of Delhi, Delhi, India, and Senior Research Scholar, Economic Cycle Research Institute, New York, USA

ESTHER DUFLO (*Dams, co-author Rohini Pande*)
Abdul Latif Jameel Professor of Development Economics and Poverty Alleviation, Massachusetts Institute of Technology, Cambridge, Massachusetts, USA

BHASKAR DUTTA (*Discretionary Centre–State Transfers; Disinvestment, The Economics of*)
Professor of Economics, Department of Economics, University of Warwick, UK

INDRANIL DUTTA (*Inequality; co-author Ajit Mishra*)
Research Associate, Brooks World Poverty Institute, The University of Manchester, UK

MUKESH ESWARAN (*Gender and Empowerment*)
Professor of Economics, Department of Economics, University of British Columbia, Canada

TATIANA FIC (*India's Growth Turnaround, co-authors Chetan Ghate and Stephen Wright*)
Senior Research Officer, National Institute of Economic and Social Research, London, UK

GARY S. FIELDS (*Income Mobility*)
Professor of Labor Economics and and the John P. Windmuller Chair of International and Comparative Labor, Cornell University, New York, USA

RAGHAV GAIHA (*Employment Guarantee Scheme*)
Professor, Faculty of Management Studies, University of Delhi, Delhi, India

IRA N. GANG (*Small-scale Industries, co-author Mihir Pandey*)
Professor, Department of Economics, Rutgers University, USA

SHUBHASHIS GANGOPADHYAY (*Rent Control Acts, co-author Jugnu Bagga*)
Director, India Development Foundation, Gurgaon, India

MAITREESH GHATAK (*Land Reform*)
Professor, Department of Economics, London School of Economics, UK

CHETAN GHATE (*India's Growth Turnaround, co-authors Stephen Wright and Tatiana Fic*)
Associate Professor, Planning Unit, Indian Statistical Institute, Delhi Centre, New Delhi, India

AJIT K. GHOSE (*Informal Labour*)
Senior Economist, Economic and Labour Market Analysis Department, International Labour Organization, Geneva, Switzerland

SAIBAL GHOSH (*Banking, co-authors Dilip M. Nachane and Partha Ray*)
Assistant Adviser, Department of Economic Analysis and Policy, Reserve Bank of India, Mumbai, India

SUBIR GOKARN (*Railways*)
Deputy Governor, Reserve Bank of India, Mumbai, India

OMKAR GOSWAMI (*Corporate Governance*)
Chairman, CERG Advisory Pvt. Ltd, New Delhi

ASHIMA GOYAL (*International Finance*)
Professor of Economics, Indira Gandhi Institute of Development Research (IGIDR), Mumbai, India

ASHOK GUHA (*International Trade*)
Professor, School of International Studies, Jawaharlal Nehru University, New Delhi, India

ASHOK GULATI (*Agribusiness*)
Director, International Food Policy Research Institute (IFPRI), New Delhi, India

MUKESH GULATI (*Industrial Clusters, co-author Amar Singh*)
Executive Director, Foundation for MSME (micro, small and medium enterprises) Clusters, New Delhi.

INDRANI GUPTA (*Health Indicators*)
Professor and Head, Health Policy Research Unit, Institute of Economic Growth, Delhi

JEFFREY S. HAMMER (*Chronic Illnesses, co-author Jishnu Das; Medical Care, Quality of, co-author Jishnu Das*)
Charles and Marie Robertson Visiting Professor in Economic Development, Woodrow Wilson School of Public and International Affairs, Princeton University, USA

RONALD J. HERRING (*Genetically Modified Crops*)
Professor, Department of Government, Cornell University, New York, USA

HIMANSHU (*Data Sets, co-authors Reena Badiani and Siddharth Sharma*)
Assistant Professor, Centre for the Study of Regional Development, School of Social Sciences, Jawaharlal Nehru University, New Delhi, India

NARENDRA JADHAV (*B.R. Ambedkar*)
Member, Planning Commission, Government of India

BIMAL JALAN (*Indira Gandhi*)
Former Governor, Reserve Bank of India

ROGER JEFFERY (*Education and Religious Minorities*)
Professor of Sociology of South Asia, School of Social and Political Studies, University of Edinburgh, Edinburgh, Scotland, UK

SHIKHA JHA (*Food Procurement Policy*)
Principal Economist, Economics and Research Department, Asian Development Bank

RENANA JHABVALA (*Globalization and the Poor, co-author Ravi Kanbur*)
National Coordinator, Self-Employed Women's Association (SEWA), Ahmedabad, India

VIVEK JOHRI (*Tax System and Reform, co-authors Sunil Mitra and Ashutosh Dikshit*)
Joint Secretary (TRU-I), Central Board of Excise and Customs, Department of Revenue, Ministry of Finance, Government of India

PRITAL SAILESH KADAKIA (*Roads*)
Department of Economics, Harvard University, Cambridge, Massachusetts, USA

RAVI KANBUR (*Globalization and the Poor, co-author Renana Jhabvala; National Rural Employment Guarantee Act, co-authors Arnab Basu and Nancy H. Chau*)
T.H. Lee Professor of World Affairs and Economics, Cornell University, New York, USA

MILIND KANDLIKAR (*Outsourcing, co-author Ashok Kotwal*)
Assistant Professor, Centre for India and South Asia Research (Institute of Asian Research) and Liu Institute for Global Studies, University of British Columbia, Vancouver, Canada

DEVESH KAPUR (*Higher Education, co-author Pratap Bhanu Mehta; International Migration from India: Economic Impact*)
Director, Center for the Advanced Study of India, University of Pennsylvania, USA

SANDEEP KAPUR (*Literacy, co-author Mamta Murthi*)
Professor of Economics, Department of Economics, Mathematics and Statistics, Birkbeck, University of London, UK

RUTH KATTUMURI (*Low-carbon Growth and Development, co-authors Nicholas Stern and James Rydge*)
Co-Director, India Observatory, London School of Economics (LSE), UK

P.C. KESAVAN (*Disaster Management, co-author M.S. Swaminathan*)
Emeritus Professor, Indira Gandhi National Open University (IGNOU), New Delhi, and Distinguished Fellow, M.S. Swaminathan Research Foundation, Chennai, India

DEENA KHATKHATE (*I.G. Patel*)
Former Assistant Director, International Monetary Fund and Managing Editor, *World Development*

SUNIL KHILNANI (*Jawaharlal Nehru*)
Director and Professor of Politics, India Institute, King's College, London, UK

GEETA KINGDON (*Secondary Education*)
Chair, Education Economics and International Development, Institute of Education, University of London, UK

STEFAN KLONNER (*Non-banking Financial Companies*)
Professor of Development Economics, South Asia, Südasien Institut, Ruprecht Karls Universität Heidelberg, Germany

ANJINI KOCHAR (*Primary Education*)
Director, India Program, and Senior Research Scholar, Stanford Center for International Development (SCID), Stanford Institute for Economic Policy Research (SIEPR), Stanford University, Stanford, California, USA

ASHOK KOTWAL (*Employment and Poverty; Outsourcing, co-author Milind Kandlikar*)
Professor of Economics and Director, Centre for India and South Asia Research, Institute of Asian Research, University of British Columbia, Vancouver, Canada

K.L. KRISHNA (*National Income*)
Chairman, Centre for Economic and Social Studies (CESS), Hyderabad, India

VIJAY KRISHNA (*Raj Krishna*)
Professor of Economics, Penn State University, University Park, Pennsylvania, USA

K.P. KRISHNAN (*Financial-sector Reforms*)
Secretary, Prime Minister's Economic Advisory Council, Government of India

K.S. KRISHNASWAMY (*Krishna Raj*)
Former Deputy Governor, Reserve Bank of India

MEDHA MALIK KUDAISYA (*G.D. Birla*)
Associate Professor, Department of History, National University of Singapore, Singapore

A.K. SHIVA KUMAR (*Millennium Development Goals*)
Visiting Professor, Institute for Human Development, New Delhi, India, and Adviser to UNICEF India

NAGESH KUMAR (*Foreign Direct Investment*)
Chief Economist and Director, Macroeconomic Policy and Development Division (MPDD), United Nations Economic and Social Commission for Asia and the Pacific (UN-ESCAP)

RAJIV KUMAR (*Foreign Exchange Reserves*)
Secretary General of the Federation of Indian Chambers of Commerce and Industry (FICCI), New Delhi, India

SHARAT KUMAR (*Public-sector Enterprises, co-author Sumit Bose*)
Economic Adviser, Department of Public Enterprises, Government of India

AMITABH KUNDU (*Mobility of Population*)
Professor of Economics, Centre for the Study of Regional Development and Dean, School of Social Sciences, Jawaharlal Nehru University, New Delhi, India

ASHOK K. LAHIRI (*Monsoon*)
Former Chief Economic Adviser, Ministry of Finance, Government of India

SAJAL LAHIRI (*Exogamy and Endogamy, co-author Sharmistha Self*)
Vandeveer Professor of Economics, Department of Economics, Southern Illinois University Carbondale, Carbondale, Illinois, USA

DEEPTI MAHAJAN (*Energy, co-author R.K. Pachauri*)
Area Convenor, Centre for Research on Energy Security, The Energy Research Institute (TERI), New Delhi, India

AJAY MAHAL (*HIV/AIDS, Economics of, co-author Bhargavi Rao, Kavita Sivaramakrishnan, and David E. Bloom*)
Adjunct Associate Professor of International Health Economics, Department of Global Health and Population, Harvard School of Public Health, Boston, Massachusetts, USA

DIPJYOTI MAJUMDAR (*Teacher Absenteeism*)
Professor, Department of Economics, Concordia University, Montréal (Québec), Canada

PAYAL MALIK (*Power Sector and Regulation*)
Associate Professor of Economics, University of Delhi, Delhi, India

VELAYOUDOM MARIMOUTOU (*Regional Disparities, co-author Basudeb Chaudhuri*)
Director and Professor, Institut Français de Pondicherry, Pondicherry, India

SUGATA MARJIT (*Exports and Export Policy*)
Director and Reserve Bank of India Professor of Industrial Economics, Centre for Studies in Social Sciences, Kolkata, India

R.A. MASHELKAR (*Intellectual Property Rights*)
National Research Professor, CSIR Bhatnagar Fellow and President, Global Research Alliance, Pune, India

J.V. MEENAKSHI (*Undernutrition*)
Professor, Department of Economics, Delhi School of Economics, University of Delhi, Delhi, India

RAJNISH MEHRA (*Equity Premium*)
E.N. Basha Arizona Heritage Chair, Professor of Finance and Economics, W.P. Carey School of Business, Arizona State University, USA

PRATAP BHANU MEHTA (*Higher Education, co-author Devesh Kapur*)
President, Centre for Policy Research, New Delhi

GAYATRI AMBIKA MENON (*Slums*)
Visiting Assistant Professor of Sociology, Department of Sociology, Franklin & Marshall College, Lancaster, PA, USA

DIVYA MINISANDRAM (*Brain Drain*)
Graduate, Harvard University, Cambridge, Massachusetts, USA

AJIT MISHRA (*Inequality, co-author Indranil Dutta*)
Senior Lecturer, Economics and International Development, University of Bath, Bath, UK

ASHOK MITRA (*Sachin Chaudhuri*)
Former Minister of Finance, West Bengal, India

SUNIL MITRA (*Tax System and Reform, co-authors Ashutosh Dikshit and Vivek Johri*)
Former Union Finance Secretary and Revenue Secretary, Government of India

PURAN MONGIA (*Environment Policy; Forest Policy; Global Warming*)
Former Professor of Economics, Centre for Development Economics, Delhi School of Economics, University of Delhi, Delhi, India

DILIP MOOKHERJEE (*Panchayats*)
Professor of Economics and Director, Institute for Economic Development, Boston University, Massachusetts, USA

SEBASTIAN MORRIS (*Infrastructure*)
Professor of Economics, Indian Institute of Management Ahmedabad, India

SATYA PRIYA MOULIK (*Academic Research, co-author Arkadev Chatterjea*)
Fellow of the Indian National Science Academy and UGC Emeritus Scientist

PRANAB MUKHERJEE (*Budget Making*)
Union Minister of Finance, Government of India

HIRANYA MUKHOPADHYAY (*Government Subsidies, co-author Sudipto Mundle*)
Public Management Economist, Asian Development Bank, Manila, Philippines

SUDIPTO MUNDLE (*Government Subsidies, co-author Hiranya Mukhopadhyay*)
Emeritus Professor, National Institute of Public Finance and Policy (NIPFP), New Delhi, India

KAIVAN MUNSHI (*Technology Diffusion*)
Professor of Economics, Department of Economics, Brown University, Rhode Island, USA

KARTHIK MURALIDHARAN (*Teacher and Medical Worker Incentives*)
Assistant Professor of Economics, University of California, USA

MAMTA MURTHI (*Literacy, co-author Sandeep Kapur*)
Sector Manager, Education, Europe and Central Asia Region, World Bank, Washington DC, USA

N.R. NARAYANA MURTHY (*Software and Services Exports*)
Founder-Chairman, Infosys, Bangalore, India

DILIP M. NACHANE (*Amiya Dasgupta; Banking, co-authors Saibal Ghosh and Partha Ray*)
Professor Emeritus, Indira Gandhi Institute of Development Research (IGIDR), Mumbai, India

R. NAGARAJ (*Industrial Growth; Trade Unions*)
Professor, Indira Gandhi Institute of Development Research, Mumbai, India

REEMA NANAVATY (*Self-Employed Women, The Organization of*)
Director, Economic and Rural Development, Self-Employed Women's Association (SEWA), Ahmedabad, India

D. NARAYANA (*Self-help Groups*)
Reserve Bank of India Chair Professor, Centre for Development Studies, Thiruvananthapuram, India

SUDHA NARAYANAN (*Contract Farming*)
PhD Student, Department of Applied Economics and Management, College of Agriculture and Life Sciences, Cornell University, New York, USA

K. NAVANEETHAM (*Demographic Dividend*)
Professor, Centre for Development Studies, Thiruvananthapuram, India

PULIN B. NAYAK (*Sukhamoy Chakravarty; Privatization*)
Professor of Economics, Delhi School of Economics, University of Delhi, Delhi, India

DEEPAK NAYYAR (*International Migration*)
Professor of Economics, Jawaharlal Nehru University, New Delhi, India, and Distinguished University Professor of Economics at the New School for Social Research, New York, USA

S. NEELAKANTAN (*Land Rights and Acquisition*)
Professor of Economics, Madras Institute of Development Studies, Chennai, India

NANDAN NILEKANI (*Unique Identification*)
Chairman, Unique Identification Authority of India (UIDAI)

T.N. NINAN (*Dhirubhai Ambani and Reliance Industries*)
Editorial Director and Chairman of Business Standard Ltd, India

MANDAR P. OAK (*Credit Market Regulation, Evolution of*)
Assistant Professor of Economics, Department of Economics, Williams College, Williamstown, Massachusetts, USA

JENNIFER O'BRIEN (*Urbanization and Its Management, co-authors David E. Bloom and Marija Ozolins)*
Harvard School of Public Health, Boston, Massachusetts, USA

S.R. OSMANI (*Famines*)
Professor of Developmental Economics, School of Economics and Politics, University of Ulster, Jordanstown Campus, UK

MARIJA OZOLINS (*Urbanization and Its Management, co-authors David E. Bloom and Jennifer O'Brien)*
Harvard School of Public Health, Boston, Massachusetts, USA

R.K. PACHAURI (*Energy, co-author Deepti Mahajan*)
Director-General, The Energy Research Institute (TERI), New Delhi

ARVIND PANAGARIYA (*World Trade Organization*)
Professor of Economics and Jagdish Bhagwati Professor of Indian Political Economy, Columbia University, New York, USA

ROHINI PANDE (*Dams, co-author Esther Duflo; Rural Credit*)
Mohammed Kamal Professor of Public Policy, Harvard Kennedy School, Harvard University, Cambridge, Massachusetts, USA

MIHIR PANDEY (*Small-scale Industries, co-author Ira N. Gang*)
Associate Professor in Economics, Ramjas College, University of Delhi, Delhi

T.S. PAPOLA (*Employment Trends*)
Honorary Professor, Institute for Studies in Industrial Development, New Delhi, India

SHANKAR PARAMESHWARAN (*Entrepreneurs in India and Abroad, co-author Ignatius Chithelen*)
Associate Editor of India Knowledge@Wharton

KIRIT S. PARIKH (*Petroleum Product Pricing*)
Former Member, Planning Commission, and Chairman, Integrated Research and Action for Development (IRADe), New Delhi, India

ILA PATNAIK (*Tariffs*)
Professor, National Institute of Public Finance and Policy (NIPFP), New Delhi, India

PRABHAT PATNAIK (*Krishna Bharadwaj; Inflation*)
Retired Professor, Centre for Economic Studies and Planning, Jawaharlal Nehru University, New Delhi, India

UTSA PATNAIK (*Bonded Labour*)
Retired Professor, Centre for Economic Studies and Planning, Jawaharlal Nehru University, New Delhi, India

PRASANTA K. PATTANAIK (*Mahatma Gandhi*)
Emeritus Professor, Department of Economics, University of California, Riverside, USA

ANANDITA PHILIPOSE (*Child Malnutrition and Feeding Practices*)
Cornell Institute of Public Affairs, Cornell University, New York, USA

K. SEETA PRABHU (*Human Development Index*)
Senior Assistant Country Director, United Nations Development Programme, New Delhi, India

ANINDITA PUJARI (*Constitution and Economic Reforms*)
Advocate, Supreme Court of India

DHUSHYANTH RAJU (*Worker Benefits*)
Senior Economist, South Asia Education Department, World Bank, Washington DC, USA

MIHIR RAKSHIT (*Oil Price Shocks*)
Director, Monetary Research Project, Information and Credit Rating Agency (ICRA), Kolkata, India

BHARAT RAMASWAMI (*Public Distribution System; Unemployment, The Measurement of, co-author Wilima Wadhwa*)
Professor, Planning Unit, Indian Statistical Institute, Delhi, India

C. RANGARAJAN (*Food Security*)
Chairman, Economic Advisory Council to the Prime Minister, India

BHARGAVI RAO (*HIV/AIDS, Economics of, co-author Ajay Mahal, Kavita Sivaramakrishnan, and David E. Bloom*)
Clinical Specialist, Harvard Medical School (Division of AIDS), Boston, Massachusetts

C.N.R. RAO (*Scientific Research*)
National Research Professor and Honorary President & Linus Pauling Research Professor, Jawaharlal Nehru Centre for Advanced Scientific Research, Bangalore, India

S.L. RAO (*V.K.R.V. Rao*)
Former Chairman, Institute for Social and Economic Change (ISEC), Bangalore, India

U.R. RAO (*Space Satellites*)
Chairman, Governing Council, Department of Space, Physical Research Laboratory, Ahmedabad, India

VIJAYENDRA RAO (*Dowries; Sex Work, co-author Manisha Shah*)
Lead Economist, Development Research Group, World Bank, Washington DC, USA

PARTHA RAY (*Banking, co-authors Dilip M. Nachane and Saibal Ghosh*)
Adviser to Executive Director (India), International Monetary Fund (IMF), Washington DC, USA

RANJAN RAY (*Household Welfare and Decision Making*)
Professor of Economics, School of Economics and Finance, University of Tasmania, Australia

C. RAMMANOHAR REDDY (*Defence Expenditure, co-author Tanya Sethi*)
Editor, *Economic and Political Weekly*, Mumbai

Y.V. REDDY (*Monetary Policy*)
Former Governor, Reserve Bank of India

TIRTHANKAR ROY (*Handicrafts; Industrialization*)
Reader in Economic History, London School of Economics and Political Science, UK

JAMES RYDGE (*Low-carbon Growth and Development, co-authors Nicholas Stern and Ruth Kattumuri*)
Research Officer, Grantham Research Institute on Climate Change and the Environment, London School of Economics (LSE), UK

ABHIRUP SARKAR (*Monsoon and Economic Activity; Special Economic Zones*)
Professor of Economics, Economic Research Unit, Indian Statistical Institute, Kolkata, India

ASANI SARKAR (*Derivatives*)
Research Officer, Federal Reserve Bank of New York, New York, USA

JAYATI SARKAR (*Corporate Ownership and Performance, co-author Subrata Sarkar*)
Associate Professor, Indira Gandhi Institute of Development Research (IGIDR), Mumbai

SUBRATA SARKAR (*Corporate Ownership and Performance, co-author Jayati Sarkar*)
Professor, Indira Gandhi Institute of Development Research (IGIDR), Mumbai

SUMAN SARKAR (*Ashok Rudra, co-author Jean Drèze*)
Professor, Visva-Bharati University, Santiniketan, India

N.C. SAXENA (*Land Acquisition for Industry*)
Member, National Advisory Council, Government of India

SHARMISTHA SELF (*Exogamy and Endogamy, co-author Sajal Lahiri*)
Associate Professor, Department of Economics, Missouri State University, Springfield, MO, USA

AMARTYA SEN (*Democracy and Social Welfare*)
Thomas W. Lamont University Professor and Professor of Economics and Philosophy, Harvard University, USA

ANINDYA SEN (*Business Policy*)
Professor of Economics, Indian Institute of Management Calcutta (IIMC), Kolkata, India

LATE ARJUN K. SENGUPTA (*Human Rights, co-author Kaushik Ranjan Bandyopadhyay*)
Member of Parliament (Rajya Sabha), India

RAMPRASAD SENGUPTA (*Power Industry; Steel Industry*)
Professor of Economics at Centre for Economic Studies and Planning, Jawaharlal Nehru University, New Delhi, India

TANYA SETHI (*Defence Expenditure, co-author C. Rammanohar Reddy*)
Assistant Editor, *Economic and Political Weekly*

AJAY SHAH (*Securities Markets; Stock Market Indexes, co-author Susan Thomas*)
Professor, National Institute of Public Finance and Policy (NIPFP), New Delhi, India

MANISHA SHAH (*Sex Work, co-author Vijayendra Rao*)
Assistant Professor of Economics, Department of Economics, University of California-Irvine, USA

KAMESHWARI SHANKAR (*Labour Turnover in the High-technology Sector*)
Assistant Professor of Economics, City College of New York, USA

SIDDHARTH SHARMA (*Data Sets, co-authors Reena Badiani and Himanshu*)
Research Analyst, Middle East and North Africa Region, World Bank, Washington DC, USA

SUNIL SHARMA (*Exchange Rates; IMF Conditionality*)
Director, IMF–Singapore Regional Training Institute, Singapore

ALOK SHEEL (*G-20 and Multilateral Economic Cooperation*)
Joint Secretary, Department of Economic Affairs, Government of India

PARTHASARATHI SHOME (*Savings and Investment*)
Director and Chief Executive, Indian Council for Research on International Economic Relations (ICRIER), New Delhi, India

AMAR SINGH (*Industrial Clusters, co-author Mukesh Gulati*)
Deputy General Manager, Foundation for MSME (micro, small and medium enterprises) Clusters, New Delhi

JAIVIR SINGH (*Labour Laws*)
Associate Professor, Centre for the Study of Law and Governance, Jawaharlal Nehru University, New Delhi, India

KANHAIYA SINGH (*Oil*)
Senior Fellow, National Council of Applied Economic Research (NCAER), New Delhi, India

NIRVIKAR SINGH (*Call Centres; Telecommunications*)
Professor, University of California, Santa Cruz, USA

RAM SINGH (*Liability Rules*)
Associate Professor, Department of Economics, Delhi School of Economics, University of Delhi, Delhi, India

ANUP KUMAR SINHA (*Corporate Ethics*)
Professor, Management Information Systems, Indian Institute of Management Calcutta (IIMC), Kolkata, India

U.K. SINHA (*Stock Exchange*)
Chairman, Securities and Exchange Board of India (SEBI)

KAVITA SIVARAMAKRISHNAN (*HIV/AIDS, Economics of, co-author Bhargavi Rao, Ajay Mahal, and David E. Bloom*)
Research Fellow, Harvard Center for Population and Development Studies, Harvard School of Public Health, Boston, Massachusetts, USA

E. SOMANATHAN (*Biodiversity*)
Professor, Planning Unit, Indian Statistical Institute, Delhi, India

ROHINI SOMANATHAN (*Poverty and Exclusion*)
Professor, Department of Economics, Delhi School of Economics, Delhi University, Delhi, India

KALA SEETHARAM SRIDHAR (*Cities*)
Head, Public Affairs Centre (PAC), Bangalore, India

T.C.A. Srinivasa-Raghavan (*Aviation; Ports and Shipping; Reserve Bank of India, co-author G. Balachandran*)
Associate Editor, *Business Line*, India

Nicholas Stern (*Low-carbon Growth and Development, co-authors Ruth Kattumuri and James Rydge*)
IG Patel Chair and Director, London School of Economics (LSE) Asia Research Centre, UK

D. Subbarao (*Financial Inclusion*)
Governor, Reserve Bank of India (RBI)

Arvind Subramanian (*Growth Experience*)
Senior Fellow jointly at the Peterson Institute for International Economics and the Center for Global Development, Washington DC, USA

Dilip Subramanian (*Voluntary Retirement Schemes*)
Professor, Reims Management School, Reims, France

S. Subramanian (*Poverty*)
Professor, Madras Institute of Development Studies, Chennai, India

M.S. Swaminathan (*Disaster Management, co-author P.C. Kesavan*)
Chairman, M.S. Swaminathan Research Foundation, Chennai, India

Madhura Swaminathan (*Child Labour*)
Professor, Indian Statistical Institute, Kolkata, India

Ratan Tata (*Tata, The House of*)
Chairman, Tata Group, Mumbai, India

Suresh D. Tendulkar (*National Sample Surveys*)
Former Professor of Economics, Delhi School of Economics, University of Delhi, Delhi, India and Chairman, National Statistical Commission, Government of India

Susan Thomas (*Stock Market Indexes, co-author Ajay Shah*)
Assistant Professor, Indira Gandhi Institute of Development Research (IGIDR), Mumbai, India

Jeemol Unni (*Agricultural Labour*)
RBI Chair Professor in Rural Economics, Institute of Rural Management Anand (IRMA), India

A. Vaidyanathan (*Irrigation; Water*)
Honorary Fellow of the Centre for Development Studies, Thiruvananthapuram, India, and a member of the Central Board of Directors, Reserve Bank of India

Arvind Virmani (*Balance of Payments; Foreign Direct Investment for Media*)
Executive Director, International Monetary Fund (IMF)

B.P.R. Vithal (*Finance Commissions*)
IAS (Retired); Member, Tenth Finance Commission, India

V.S. Vyas (*M.L. Dantwala*)
Professor Emeritus, Institute of Development Studies, Jaipur, India

Wilima Wadhwa (*Unemployment, The Measurement of, co-author Bharat Ramaswami*)
Director, Statistics, Assessment Survey Evaluation Research Centre, New Delhi, India

Jayashree Watal (*Patents*)
Adjunct Professor of Law; Counsellor, Intellectual Property Division, World Trade Organization, Geneva, Switzerland

Stephen Wright (*India's Growth Turnaround, co-authors Chetan Ghate and Tatiana Fic*)
Professor of Economics, Department of Economics, Mathematics and Statistics, Birkbeck College, University of London, UK

Name Index

(Note: Page numbers in bold type indicate authors' entries or biographical entries)

Subject Index

(Note: Page numbers in bold type indicate entries)

'For years to come, this book
anyone seeking to understand
and political economy

'Kaushik Basu has done a g
broader scope and assembling a
accessible style.' —*b*

'...a unique and important
economy, and also a collectio
of the world's true exp

'...an indispensable and inno
economics, not only for econo
are affected by eco

'The volume is a unique exp
a variety of themes penned b
A must-buy for each and ever
libr
—*Busi*

'This is a dictionary that expl
leaves it for readers to expl
engaging and useful res

'Too many economists may s
can certainly produce a good e
Ou

'India's first companion to e
the more impressive additio
encyclopedias.' —

'For years to come, this book will be an essential reading for anyone seeking to understand India's economic development and political economy.'
—Ashutosh Varshney

'Kaushik Basu has done a great job in giving economics a broader scope and assembling authors who write expertly but in accessible style.'
—Lord Meghnad Desai

'... a unique and important guide to the dynamic Indian economy, and also a collection of penetrating essays by many of the world's true experts.'
—Stephen P. Cohen

'... an indispensable and innovative addition to the library of economics, not only for economists but also those whose lives are affected by economics.'
—*India Today*

'The volume is a unique experience as it exposes readers to a variety of themes penned by the distinguished writers ... A must-buy for each and every college, university and public library ...'
—*Business India*

'This is a dictionary that explains fundamental concepts and leaves it for readers to explore on their own ... [A] clear, engaging and useful resource.'
—*Business Standard*

'Too many economists may spoil the policy broth, but they can certainly produce a good encyclopedia on the economy!'
—*Outlook*

'India's first companion to economics is certainly among the more impressive additions to the catalogue of Indian encyclopedias.'
—*The Financial Express*

THE NEW OXFORD COMPANION TO ECONOMICS IN INDIA

THE NEW OXFORD COMPANION TO ECONOMICS IN INDIA

Volume I A–H

EDITED BY
KAUSHIK BASU
ANNEMIE MAERTENS

OXFORD
UNIVERSITY PRESS

OXFORD
UNIVERSITY PRESS

Oxford University Press is a department of the University of Oxford.
It furthers the University's objective of excellence in research, scholarship,
and education by publishing worldwide. Oxford is a registered trademark of
Oxford University Press in the UK and in certain other countries

Published in India by
Oxford University Press
YMCA Library Building, 1 Jai Singh Road, New Delhi 110 001, India

First Edition 2007
Revised Edition 2008
This Edition 2012

ISBN-13: 978-0-19-807855-5
ISBN-10: 0-19-807855-2

Typeset in Plantin 9.5/12
by Eleven Arts, Keshav Puram, Delhi 110 035
Printed in India at Thomson Press (India) Ltd., New Delhi 110 020

Contents

Entries A–Z

Volume I (A–H)

Volume II (I–Z)

Preface to the New Edition

The Oxford Companion to Economics in India (OCEI), published in 2007, was conceived in recognition of the fact that the Indian economy is complex beyond any single person's comprehension. The editor of *OCEI* (Kaushik Basu) and the publisher (Oxford University Press, OUP) felt that there would be a large demand for a book that brought between two covers the entire swathe of important topics pertaining to the Indian economy, and also the opinions of prominent economists, policymakers, and politicians on various issues related to India. In the event, they underestimated the largeness of the large demand. The first print run was sold out in the same year, and a revised edition (with updates and a few fresh entries) was out in the market in early 2008. The *OCEI* turned out to be a landmark both in publishing as well as the economics discipline in India, being the first A–Z reference book on 'economics in India'. It received an overwhelming response and has been widely reviewed, read, referenced and, on occasion, reviled. It has been used by students, teachers, scholars, and practitioners not just in India but also abroad, reflecting the expanding interest in the Indian economy. This was gratifying but also somewhat daunting in terms of the responsibility it implicitly placed on us.

Keeping in mind the requirements of students of economics and business, OUP went on to bring out a student-friendly, concise version of the same book—*The Concise Oxford Companion to Economics in India* (eds Kaushik Basu and Annemie Maertens)—in early 2010. This had a selection of entries from the original, which were arranged sectorally, and catered to economics courses throughout the country. It also included new entries on topics that had gained salience since the publication of the *Companion* (for instance, the financial crisis of 2007–9 and the accompanying recession), in addition to an appendix with a selection of statistics pertaining to the Indian economy and society. The concise edition has also been extremely well-received and has gone through two reprints already.

The downside of the good reception has been a demand for more—both in terms of topics and topicality. With a little arm twisting from our editors at OUP, last year in September, we started working on updating the concise edition. This process, however, got all of us thinking about doing a revised edition of the original *Companion*. We realized that there continued to be a large demand for the original *Companion*, given its broader scope. OUP had also been receiving regular queries on an updated edition from several universities and institutions.

Also, much water had flown between 2007 and now: the great global recession, arguably the most traumatic global downturn since the Great Depression of the 1930s; the sub-prime crisis, bringing to the fore concerns about financial markets and how to regulate them; and the revival of G-20 and the effort to engage heads of states of multiple nations in coordinating global policy, in which India has found itself taking an active role. We decided that the time had come to read through all entries, revise and update many of them, and commission new essays, paying special attention to the growing complexity of financial and fiscal policies, and the role of India in international collective action. The *New Oxford Companion to Economics in India* is the outcome. The *New OCEI* includes a total of 232 entries, more than 80 substantially revised and updated entries, and 24 new entries on issues of current and ongoing relevance. The expansion in size has meant that what originally appeared between two covers, now needed four. The *New OCEI* thus appears in two volumes in a boxed set.

Between the time when the original *OCEI* was published and now, one of the editors, Kaushik Basu, had moved from academe to policymaking. With the other editor, Annemie Maertens, in academe, we had a team that could appreciate the needs of researchers and students in the university grappling with and trying to create new theory and researching into statistical regularities and micro realities, and also of the policymaker, grappling with inflation, macro-prudential risk, currency unions, and more. Taking advantage of this dual perspective we decided to draw on both kinds of contributors for the *New OCEI.*

In editing this book we had to keep in mind the fact that India is growing, and growing complex in leaps and bounds. Managing and making policy for this behemoth is truly a challenge. No one can understand it all. We have to rely on the decentralization of knowledge and the availability of compendia written by multiple authors, each with expertise in some slender aspect of the economy. The best that the student of India and the policymaker for India can do is to study and ingest these broad brush accounts of the multifarious aspects of the Indian economy and then develop specialization as and when he or she needs to. We hope that this *New OCEI* will go some distance in fulfilling this need.

The key criteria for selecting entries for revision were areas in which there have been new developments, more recent data is available, and there have been important changes in policy. We got an extremely good response from contributors. However, we were unable to contact certain contributors and some were not able to meet our deadline. Most of these entries we have carried in their original form because, we feel, they highlight issues and concepts that continue to be relevant for understanding the issues of today. For a few others, where the author was unavailable, we got fresh entries on the same subject by new contributors (for instance, 'Fiscal Deficit' by Supriyo De and Dipak Dasgupta [original entry by Amaresh Bagchi]; 'Financial-sector Reforms' by K.P. Krishnan [original entry by Charan Singh]).

Keeping with the tradition of the original *Companion*, the new entries were invited from experts in varied fields (academics and practitioners at the highest levels), and these further enrich the diversity of perspectives included. They are a testament to not just the dynamism of the Indian economy but also of the discipline of economics. We have included some new entries on areas already covered in the original *Companion*—but these compliment the existing entries with fresh ideas and new areas of focus. Thus we have an entry on 'Inflation' by Prabhat Patnaik, which is a theoretical piece and was part the original *Companion*, and now we have a new entry (by Kaushik Basu) on virtually the same topic, which focuses on policy and experience, and comments on India's travails with inflation over the last few months and years.

In closing we may remind the reader that the *New OCEI,* like the original *Companion,* is conceptualized as an encyclopaedia. Thus there were limitations on the length of the entry as well as the number of references that could go with each entry. Each entry, therefore, provides an overview of the topic and is not meant to cover all its aspects in detail. There are various ways in which readers can browse through the *Companion*—alphabetically (A–Z), by topic through the comprehensive index, or by contributor (the 'list of contributors' has cross-references to the entries). Above all, this is a reference volume, meant to sit on the shelf to be pulled out as and when it is needed. The detailed index at the end as well as the accompanying CD is meant to make it friendly for those using it as a reference encyclopedia.

Producing a mammoth work like this invariably means a mountain of debt. One has to depend not just on the authors for taking the task seriously and delivering their entries but there is a whole host of other players—copyeditors, proof-readers, designers, and the marketing team—that may not be as visible but is, nevertheless, critical. Oxford University Press provided us with unstinting managerial and intellectual support and chased with deadlines not just the authors but, on some occasions, even one of the editors, whose identity will remain undisclosed. As editors we are acutely aware of the help that we received from this large cast of characters and thank them all. The list is too long to name them individually but it would be amiss if we did not mention Supriyo De and Shweta in the Ministry of Finance, who both assisted Kaushik Basu in numerous ways.

KAUSHIK BASU AND ANNEMIE MAERTENS
November 2011

Introduction

Experts on the Indian economy are a vanishing tribe, and for good reason. The complexity of the economy has grown to such enormous proportions that its full comprehension is beyond the capacity of any single human mind. And the complexity continues to grow as the economy gathers steam. But, of course, policies have to be crafted, taxes designed, subsidies doled out or rolled in, exchange rates propped up or allowed to flag, and laws pertaining to the economy enacted, amended, or repealed. Given the multifarious tasks that Indian policymakers have to contend with, there is a growing need to collate and coordinate information and wisdom that is scattered across a large number of institutions and individuals. Then there are the students of economics and commerce—a growing tribe in India, who need information and analysis on contemporary themes, which are deeper than what is to be found in newspapers and magazines and for which they cannot be expected each time to go to the original source or data archive. This companion is meant to be a response to these pressing needs of our times.

As often happens with such ventures, this one began with the editor's own felt need. I take active research interest in the policies that guide this huge organism called the Indian economy and I consider myself an expert on some aspects of it. Yet I am acutely aware of large swathes about which I know next to nothing. When in 1992 India's most famous stock market scam—the Harshad Mehta scandal—broke, an economist and a top official of the Government of India admitted that he (or she, let me add, in the interests of anonymity) did not even know the meaning of the many things that the evil genius of Harshad Mehta had manipulated. No one can blame him (or her). Anybody interested in the Indian economy, whether a student, researcher, policymaker, corporate manager, or ground-level activist, will appreciate the need for a reference source, where one can find most of the basic information and ideas concerning the Indian economy and the best of contemporary thinking on the subject. As befits a reference, the entries are organized alphabetically. The titles were selected carefully, with help from the editorial advisory board, to cover the essentials of the Indian economy. It should be mentioned here that the editorial board consists of people who cover a diverse range of expertise—from fiscal policy, globalization, and governance to agriculture and basic needs programmes. In addition to the alphabetical search, the reader can use the book's elaborate index of subjects and names or the CD-ROM version to search for topics thematically and by the names of contributors and prepare their own reading lists.

In his essay, 'Economic Possibilities for our Grandchildren', John Maynard Keynes, no doubt slightly dizzy from the then-recent rapid advances in economics, had predicted that within the next few decades all the major problems of the economy would be solved, and economics would cease to be an important subject. For once, the self-assured Maynard Keynes was completely wrong. Implicit in his observation was a view of the economy as a static object, waiting to be dissected and diagnosed. In reality, the complexity of the economy grows in step with our understanding of it. As we have a scientific breakthrough and begin to fathom some of this complexity, that very understanding enables our entrepreneurs, managers, consumers, and workers to discover new strategies and actions; and that, in turn, gives rise to newer complexities in the economy. Hence, like Sukumar Ray's famous character, Chandidas's uncle, who when setting out on long journeys dangled his favourite foods in front of him, from a mast anchored to his shoulders, in economics, unlike in the natural sciences, our investigation and the object of our investigation have a tendency to move in tandem.

Even as this volume is being compiled and edited, the economy of India is evolving into an evermore intricate organism. An interesting testimony to the dynamism of the economy concerns the entry on 'software exports'. As we were finalizing the proofs, it struck me that India's 'current' software exports figure may need to be updated, since the entry had been received a while ago. On checking back with the author, it turned out that in that short time interval, India's software exports (per unit of time) had not just risen but done so by over 30 per cent. While software in India is no doubt special, change is a perennial feature of any economy. Hence, a project like this volume, while it has its intellectual excitement, also has its preordained frustrations, because one knows that it can never be comprehensive and be able to totally live up to the task.

In taking on this large project—though its enormity dawned on me only after I had waded into it beyond the point of no return (otherwise there may not have been this book)—I decided that the book had to achieve two tasks. It had to be a reasonably comprehensive reference volume on basic facts and uniformities that gird the contemporary Indian economy, and also be a record of the best contemporary thinking on the subject. I must admit I had in mind the *Palgrave Dictionary of Economics*, which has been a lasting source of reference and an intellectual treasure house for economists and related social scientists. Hence, I invited some of the leading economists, scribes, industrialists, policymakers, and politicians of or connected to India to write. And the response (close to a 100 per cent, though not without repeat phone calls, cajoling, and threats) has been overwhelming, as the list of authors who figure in the pages that follow must make amply clear. The reader will find in this companion the thoughts and reflections of individuals who have been directly involved in shaping the economy of contemporary India, through their pioneering entrepreneurship, by their stewardship of the country's monetary and fiscal policy, and through the publication of their scientific ideas. What I hope will give this volume an added edge is that the list of authors includes not just the éminence grise but also a small number of students of economics—from Cornell, Delhi, and Harvard.

Since the mid-1990s not only has the overall economy of India surged, with growth rates frequently crossing the 7 per cent per annum mark and occasionally rising above 8 per cent, there is also a clear and evident increase in the sophistication of our scholars and researchers. The old polarization of 'left' and 'right', where people took up positions not from facts and deductive reasoning, but from their chosen texts and pre-committed opinions, is less evident today. Barring a few diehards at both ends, most analysts approach the subject much more scientifically. We wanted the best of this new opinion, irrespective of ideology, to be represented in this volume. And to that extent the book is aimed at those interested in not just policy but also in the conundrums of the economy as an intellectual challenge per se. Moreover, while this companion is meant to span the recent cover stories of India's high growth, leadership role in software and information technology, and outsourcing success, it also acknowledges the gloomy backwaters—the widespread poverty, farmer suicides, child labour, and the large and impoverished informal sector where a vast majority of India's labourers work.

There is virtual consensus that while India has grown rapidly over the last decade and poverty, as measured by the percentage of population living below the poverty line, has declined, inequality—whether it be regional or personal—has worsened and employment has not grown in step with the growth of the labour force. Understanding the basis of these seeming anomalies is extremely important. A huge rise in inequality can create political upheavals, which can in turn spell doom for growth. Moreover, there are many (the present author included) who consider such huge inequalities to be innately unconscionable even if the disadvantaged are too weak to protest and destabilize the economy.

But even if one were not trying to think of policies to avoid such a predicament, understanding the diverse changes in India is an intellectual challenge of no mean proportion. Is the growth in inequality a consequence of economic liberalization or a necessary concomitant of global changes, and, hence largely beyond the reach of national governments? Are movements in stock prices reflections of underlying strengths and weaknesses of the economy or the moods and machinations of investors and speculators? This companion is aimed at providing readers with the basic facts and ideas that will help them form their own opinion about these difficult questions. Hence, my hope is that this companion will be of value to both policymakers and professional economists as well as to students—graduate and undergraduate—interested in the Indian economy, and development economics in general.

Reference companions like this, by their sheer weight in the hands of the reader, raise expectations that are virtually impossible to fulfill. There are invariably topics and entries that disappoint by their omission. The decision of what to omit can actually be very challenging. I thought hard, for instance, about biographical entries—whether to include them or not. Some members of the editorial board were against such entries, some in favour, and others non-committal, which meant that the decision was finally mine. It was evident that any list would draw criticism about why, if x was there, was y not? Quite early in the project it was decided to confine biographical entries to only the dead, thereby silencing the potentially most vociferous objectors—those among the living who might not have appeared in the book but believed that they should have. In choosing names from history there is first the advantage that, with the passage of time and the advantage of hindsight, we have better idea about who deserves to be in and who out; and the added advantage that even when we are wrong there is no worry about having to contend directly with offended parties.

While most choices and omissions are by design, some are inadvertent as in cases of missed deadlines that became evident too late to make replacements possible. Indeed, the final stages of a work like this, involving close to 200 authors and over 200 entries, are spent mainly in chasing truant authors and getting them to turn in their pieces. And this, in turn, means that the editor has to get used to the magic reality of finding economists he sees at a distance (for instance while walking up to a group at a dinner party) vanish by the time he gets there.

But all said and done, the pleasures of a task like this outweigh the costs. For one, there is an enormous amount of learning-by-doing and this happens effortlessly as one reads and edits the manuscript. Then there is the pleasure of human interaction, since one has to work not just with the authors numbering in hundreds, but with teams of editors, editorial assistants, copyeditors, proofreaders, and research assistants. What now remains is only the 'interaction' with the reviewers and readers and, for that, I fortunately have to do nothing but keep my fingers crossed.

My foremost thanks to the editorial team at Oxford University Press whose unstinting support helped move this mammoth project smoothly along the conveyor belt. During the approximately two years of work on this book I moved frequently between India and the US. Though I tried to do the bulk of my work on this project when in India, I invariably had to carry parts of it to Cornell University. There I was aided by a talented group of research assistants—Amanda Felkey, Hyejin Ku, and Anandita Mariam Philipose—and had remarkably smart secretarial assistance from Amy Moesch. Finally, I owe a special thanks to a most outstanding Board of Editors—T.C.A. Anant, Pranab Bardhan, Jean Drèze, Dilip Mookherjee, and M. Govinda Rao. These are individuals of outstanding intellectual strengths and I called on them liberally at several stages—about what kinds of entries to include and what to omit, about possible authors, and also to have them read and comment on several of the entries. But, in the end, the final decisions were mine; and, as the overall in-charge of this project, I am reconciled that the brickbats, no matter how much I would like to deflect them elsewhere, must perforce end up at my doorstep.

KAUSHIK BASU
January 2007

Postscript

While it may not speak well of one as a forecaster, there are few things as gratifying to an editor as that of stocks of the book running out quickly. The *Oxford Companion to Economics in India* was released in February 2007. The reception was overwhelming. My apprehension that journals and newspapers would either not find reviewers since virtually all potential ones were authors or would get bad reviews from the ones who were not authors for that very reason, fortunately turned out to be misplaced. The book was widely reviewed and, more often than not, praised. It was viewed as a much-needed guide to a newly vibrant and increasingly complex India. The demand for the book from readers, in India and abroad, matched this evaluation. Within months it was evident that stocks would run out before the year's end, and in June we took a decision to go for another print run.

This turned out to be a blessing in disguise. While this did not give us the time to do a full overhaul, as would be the case with a completely new edition, it provided a window of opportunity to make some essential changes. First, there were some topics that had grown in significance since the time that the original volume was planned and produced and which did not have an entry. *Special Economic Zones* and *Land Rights and Acquisition* are two such examples. From being themes on the fringes of economic discourse in India, they had moved to centre space, with strong voices of support for and equally strong ones of dissent against the policy of acquiring land to set up new industries and special economic zones. A few such new entries have now been included in this reprint version. Second, a book of this kind invariably has some entries that are especially prone to getting dated. In the case of today's India this is true of, for instance, information technology and foreign direct investment. We asked the authors of several such pieces to revise their entries taking account of any important new information that may have come to light since the entries were originally written. Finally, we took this opportunity to make large improvements to the subject index, which should make the book more reader-friendly. The book is meant to be used not just by students of economics but journalists writing on India, grass-roots activists preparing a plan, policymakers crafting an intervention, and managers of corporations trying to enhance their understanding of the Indian economy. The two indexes were prepared carefully to help all these diverse readers navigate through the multifarious entries and topics that form this companion.

KAUSHIK BASU
January 2008

A

■ Academic Research

The New Oxford Dictionary of English (1998) defines 'research' as 'the systematic investigation into and study of materials and sources in order to establish facts and reach new conclusions'. A key to creating the wealth of a nation is applied research, which, in turn, traces back to academic research. Academic research is typically conducted in *universities* (which offer advanced studies in a large number of disciplines) and *research institutes* (which have a narrower interest and focus). Advanced nations have powerhouse universities and institutes that developing countries aspire to emulate.

Academic Research in India (Pre-1947)

Modern academic research in India goes back to 1784 when the distinguished orientalist and jurist Sir William Jones established the Asiatic Society of Bengal in Calcutta for promoting oriental studies. The English rulers primarily set up teaching institutions. They were also interested in applied areas and field sciences like archaeology, botany, geology, trigonometrical survey, and zoology. The greatest academic recognition for such endeavours came in 1902 when Sir Ronald Ross won the Nobel Prize for his work done in India on the life cycle of malarial parasites.

These efforts spawned the formation of many learned and scientific bodies in India and paved the way for academic research. A significant advancement manifested in the establishment of the Indian Association for the Cultivation of Science (IACS) in Calcutta in 1876, whose founder Dr Mahendra Lal Sircar envisioned an institution for 'pure-science learning and science-teaching' (see Ghatak et al. 1976). Supported by private and government funds, IACS established a library, offered scholarships, created endowed professorships, and set up a laboratory where physicist Sir Chandrasekhara Venkata Raman discovered the 'Raman Effect' which won him Asia's first science Nobel Prize in 1930. Beginning in the late 19th century, physicist/botanist Sir Jagadis Chunder Bose and chemist Sir Prafulla Chandra Ray, both professors at Calcutta's Presidency College, conducted pioneering research that was published in some of the world's finest academic journals.

In the early 20th century, Indian universities started playing an active role in fostering advanced teaching and academic research. This was initiated by the legendary vice chancellor of the University of Calcutta, Sir Asutosh Mookerjee, who hired outstanding professors in diverse fields of study, including Sir C.V. Raman and philosopher Sir Sarvepalli Radhakrishnan whose writings interpreted Indian thought for the Western world. Graduates of the university at this time included Professor Satyendra Nath Bose of the Bose–Einstein Statistics fame (after whom fundamental particles 'bosons' are named), Dr Meghnad Saha who developed the 'Saha Ionization Equation', and renowned radio physicist Dr Sisir Mitra. All of them became Fellows of the Royal Society (FRS) of England.

Many other distinguished European and Indian scientists working in India were elected FRS. The list includes Professor H.J. Bhabha (physicist, Indian Institute of Science [IISc] Bangalore; later co-founded the Tata

Institute of Fundamental Research in Bombay and became Chairman of the Indian Atomic Energy Commission), Sir S.S. Bhatnagar (chemist, University of Punjab; later became Director of the Council of Scientific and Industrial Research), Sir J.C. Bose (later founded the Bose Institute in Calcutta), Sir A.G. Bourne (zoologist, University of Madras, IISc Bangalore), Sir K.S. Krishnan (physicist, IACS, University of Dacca; later became Director of the National Physical Laboratory), Professor P.C. Mahalanobis (statistician, Presidency College Calcutta; later founded the Indian Statistical Institute), Professor P. Maheshwari (botanist, Universities of Dacca and Delhi), Professor B. Sahni (botanist, University of Lucknow), Professor T.R. Seshadri (chemist, Universities of Andhra and Delhi), Sir J.L. Simonsen (chemistry, Presidency College Madras), and Professor D.N. Wadia (geologist, Prince of Wales College, Jammu; Geological Survey of India). Professor Simonsen and Professor P.S. MacMahon founded the Indian Science Congress Association in 1914).[1] Many talented academicians, including classical scholars, social scientists, geographers, historians, linguists, musicologists, and philosophers, attained name and fame for their scholarly works. They were helped by kings, zamindars, industrialists, and successful professionals who gave generously to support academic causes.

This was a great start. An active group of academics got assembled in colonial India who did cutting-edge research and published articles in the world's leading academic journals. They attracted and trained doctoral students and founded and nurtured institutions to elevate them to reputed centres of advanced research. Some of them oriented themselves to applied research and gave leadership to the government's research laboratories. With the devotion of teachers, motivation of students, vision of institution builders, foresight of creators of learned bodies, emerging culture of donating money towards education, and an evolving tradition of quality research work, India established a huge lead in academic research and doctoral education over other Asian nations except Japan. Yet, India got lost in a quagmire during the period that followed.

Academic Research in India (Post-1947)

Independent India achieved significant success in diverse areas like crop development, space programme, and nuclear research. It boasts of a large number of research laboratories and educational institutions and one of the world's largest academic and scientific communities. Yet India fares poorly in terms of quality of academic research. A proper understanding of this would require an examination of publications in top-ranked journals and an evaluation of books and monographs written by every India-based academic in all fields of study. Due to lack of time and resources for such a study, we rely heavily on the highly influential AWRU rankings.

Consider the first global league table of universities, the highly influential 'Academic Ranking of World Universities' produced since 2003 by China's Shanghai Jiao Tong University.[2] ARWU ranks institutions in terms of a composite index based on six objective research indicators—the number of alumni and staff winning Nobel Prizes and Fields Medals, number of highly cited researchers selected by Thomson Scientific, number of articles published in the journal *Nature and Science*, number of articles indexed in Science Citation Index—Expanded and Social Sciences Citation Index, and per capita performance with respect to the size of an institution. Like any ranking system, ARWU has weaknesses in terms of what is included and what gets

Table 1 Selective Country-wise Statistics of Number of Universities Ranked among Globally High-ranked Universities

Rank	Country	Top 20	Top 100	Top 200	Top 300	Top 400	Top 500
1	USA	17	54	89	111	137	154
2	UK	2	11	19	30	35	38
3	Japan	1	5	9	10	17	25
4	Germany		5	14	23	33	39
5	Canada		4	8	18	18	23
6	France		3	7	13	18	22
7	Australia		3	7	9	13	17
8	Switzerland		3	6	7	7	7
9	Sweden		3	4	9	10	11
10	Netherlands		2	9	9	11	12
12	Israel		1	4	4	6	7
15	Russia		1	1	1	2	2
18	China			4	13	19	34
20	South Korea			1	4	7	10
23	Singapore			1	1	2	2
33	India					1	2
37	Saudi Arabia					1	2

Source: ARWU 2010, Shanghai Jiao Tong University, available at http://www.arwu.org/ARWUStatistics2010.jsp.

[1]This list focuses on scientists in India and excludes Indian scientists who spent their academic careers abroad such as the great mathematician Srinivasa Ramanujan and Nobel Laureates physicist Professor S. Chandrasekhar and chemist/biologist Professor H.G. Khorana.

[2]See http://www.arwu.org/aboutARWU.jsp for the rankings and a discussion of the methodology.

left out.[3] It has been criticized for neglecting teaching and focusing solely on research (which wonderfully suits our purpose!) and a heavy bias towards the sciences and an inadequate representation of many areas of humanities where book writing is an indication of academic scholarship. Still, it is preferred over the two other major global tables—UK-based 'Times Higher Education World University Rankings' and 'QS World University Rankings' (which, till 2009, used to provide the Times rankings). These rankings are produced by commercial organizations, which frequently tinker with their methodologies so that the top rankings rotate, creating headlines and stories to sell (see Goodall 2009). Moreover, these rankings use subjective criteria like reputational surveys by anonymous academics, which diminish their attractiveness in the eyes of many experts.

Table 1 gives the performance of some countries in terms of ARWU rankings for 2010. Tables 2 and 3 show how China and India, which often get compared with one another, have fared over the years in these annual rankings. Our findings and some related issues are as follows:

- In 2010, no Indian university or institute was ranked among the world's top 300 universities; IISc Bangalore was ranked between 301 and 400 and the Indian Institute of Technology (IIT) Kharagpur was ranked between 401 and 500. India's top research institution IISc, which was ranked between 201 and 300 in 2003 and 2004, has since moved down. The number of Indian universities in this top 500 list fell from 3 to 2 and India's overall rank declined from 27 to 33.[4]
- India takes pride in the IITs, which are frequently cited as peerless institutions in the world. ARWU has also created similar league tables for several subject areas. In the ARWU in Engineering/Technology and Computer Sciences (2010), no Indian institution ranks among the top 75 (IISc and IIT Kharagpur were placed among 76–100) but 11 Chinese universities (which comprise of institutions from People's Republic of China, Hong Kong, and Taiwan) rank among the top 75. Recent expansion (2008–10) in the number of IITs (and Indian Institutes of Management) with no concomitant quality control is extremely unlikely to improve academic research output from these institutions.
- It is hardly surprising that no Indian institution appears in the ARWU in the Economics/Business (2010) list (China has two in this list). Indian School of Business (Hyderabad), which boasts of a star-studded list of visiting professors and has resident faculty who were trained at some of the world's best universities, is yet to make its mark in academic research. Indian Institutes of Management (IIMs), where a vast number of professors have very weak and sometimes zero academic research record, have emerged as centres of teaching and consulting. The recent governmental policy of granting autonomy to the IIMs (in their current setting) is very likely to do long-lasting damage to academic research in management areas; mediocrity will be perpetuated because weak professors have no incentive to hire talented researchers.
- India is viewed as a global powerhouse in computer science and information technology. But ARWU in Computer Science (2010) does not list any Indian institution in the top 100 but places 13 universities from China. Top academic researchers in computer science are unlikely to be found in India.
- ARWU rankings were originally created to find out 'the gap between Chinese universities and world class universities, particularly in aspects of academic or research performance'. Over the years, China has moved up in the rankings while Indian performance, already miserable, has further declined (the ARWU website notes that China and India, respectively, have 19.8 and 17.1 per cent of the world population but 6.8 and a mere 0.4 per cent of the world's top 500 universities). Enserink (2007) noted that France's poor showing in the ARWU rankings (just two universities among the top 100) led to 'a national debate about higher education that resulted in a new law ... giving universities more freedom.' No debate or attempt for improvement has taken place in India.

Table 2 Performance of Chinese Universities in ARWU, 2003–10

Year	Rank among nations	Top 200	Top 300	Top 400	Top 500
2003	21	1	5	12	19
2004	19	1	6	13	16
2005	19	2	6	15	18
2006	18	3	9	15	19
2007	18	2	11	16	25
2008	18	1	10	16	30
2009	18	1	12	17	30
2010	18	4	13	19	34

Source: ARWU 2003–10, available at http://www.arwu.org/.
Note: Chinese universities include universities and institutes in People's Republic of China, Hong Kong, and Taiwan.

[3]See Enserink (2007) and Goodall (2009) for a discussion of these issues.
[4]Times 2005 rankings placed the Indian Institute of Technology as 50th, Indian Institute of Management as 84th, and Jawaharlal Nehru University as 192nd. But no Indian institution appears among the world's top 200 in the Times 2010 rankings.

Table 3 Performance of Indian Universities in ARWU, 2003–10

Year	Rank among nations	Top 200	Top 300	Top 400	Top 500
2003	27	0	1	1	3
2004	29	0	1	1	3
2005	33	0	0	1	3
2006	33	0	0	1	2
2007	33	0	0	2	2
2008	32	0	0	2	2
2009	33	0	0	1	2
2010	33	0	0	1	2

Source: ARWU 2003–10, available at http://www.arwu.org/.

What caused this decline (or failure to take-off) in the ability of Indian institutions?

Probable Causes of Poor Performance

Developing and leading top-flight universities is a highly complex activity that eludes simple descriptions and easy generalizations. Hence, we begin with a cautious discussion of several important factors that are preventing Indian universities and institutes from excelling in academic research and suggest some possible remedies.

1. *The faculty*. Before 1947, almost all Indian academics were employed in India. In 2011, by contrast, an overwhelming majority of top- and medium-level Indian academics worked in foreign universities. Of course, many distinguished academics studied abroad, came back, and built successful careers in independent India. But many more could have returned.

The reasons behind this migration are complex and multifarious. Commonly cited causes like poor academic environment, dearth of academic resources, low salary (compared to a person's potential global salary after purchasing power adjustments; stagnation vis-à-vis industry salaries), same salary regardless of academic merit, and dearth of potential collaborators and doctoral students of high academic calibre need to be carefully examined and appropriately remedied.

There are no plans for luring the faculty back. Instead, it has become progressively harder for expatriates to return:[5]

- Since the late 1970s, India does not recognize medical qualifications acquired in the UK or the USA because they do not recognize Indian qualifications; this 'patriotism' argument raises hurdles for talented doctors and medical school professors contemplating return.
- Only Indian citizens can work for the government (exceptions are rare), which makes it difficult for expatriates who have adopted other citizenships to come back and work at premier universities and institutes, a majority of which are government owned.
- Returnees used to be exempt from paying Indian taxes on foreign-sourced income for nine years. Since 2003, the Indian government suddenly reduced this period to two years, making it expensive for potential returnees who have accumulated a nest egg abroad or would like to supplement a relatively meagre Indian salary by teaching, doing research, or consulting elsewhere. Moreover, this jeopardizes tax planning—investors now have to pay 30 per cent Indian tax.[6]

Thus, a typical US-based medical/business/law/engineering school professor will make less than 15 per cent of his or her existing salary in India and will surrender lifetime employment for a job that requires retirement at the age of 62 years. Extensions are ad-hoc: a governmental policy of granting extensions on the basis of academic research talent is yet to evolve.

Let us look at the experience of some other Asian nations. Japan has long focused on applied as well as academic research. Although a majority of the students enrol in private universities, Japan's public national universities (now partially privatized) are its strongest institutions. At the apex of the system are seven major research universities (formerly, imperial universities), which ARWU ranks among the top 200 in the world; Japanese professors rarely settle abroad these days. Overall, Japan is ranked third in the ARWU list.

Paradoxically, India is tightening the noose at a time when other Asian countries are reaching out and taking active steps to build great universities:

- Realizing that they cannot pay professors their 'world market' salaries, Israel grants them generous leaves of absence to spend time abroad and even hold concurrent positions at American and European universities. Israeli doctoral students get less actual hours but spend more 'quality time' with their professors and greatly benefit from academic networks that their mentors maintain with overseas support. This is intelligent policymaking—basically, others are subsidizing Israeli universities and helping them to excel. Israel is ranked 2nd in Asia and 12th in the overall ARWU list.

[5]See Chatterjea (2004) for a discussion of these issues.

[6]Enacted in 2003, the Overseas Citizen of India programme grants certain benefits to people of Indian origin (and their offsprings) who have become citizens of other nations. However, it is a 'citizenship' without the rights to vote, run for constitutional office, and hold government jobs.

- Top-ranked Asian universities seriously encourage high-quality research publications and even offer cash rewards for papers accepted in world class journals. Some Indian institutions have started doing this.[7] Such incentives can help scholars turn away from chasing consulting money and lucrative teaching assignments and focus on high-quality academic research.
- *The New York Times* reported that China wants to transform 'its top universities into the world's best within a decade' (28 October 2005). The model is simple: 'Recruit top foreign-trained Chinese and Chinese-American specialists, set them up in well-equipped labs, surround them with the brightest students and give them tremendous leeway. In a minority of cases, they receive American-style pay; in others, they are lured by the cost of living, generous housing and the laboratories. How many have come is unclear.'

Singapore and South Korea are strengthening their universities by making similar efforts.

2. *Doctoral students.* A majority of high-quality Indian students go abroad for their PhDs. The problems with doctoral education are discussed in a separate entry in this volume (see 'Doctoral Education' by Chatterjea).

3. *Financial resources and research support.* It is expensive to attract, retain, and nurture scholars.[8] In the United States, it typically costs half a million dollars to support an assistant professor and a million dollars to support a full professor in laboratory sciences—the costs include faculty salary, PhD student and postdoctoral researcher stipends, price of chemicals and samples, cost of machines and equipments, cost of laboratory space, expenditures for conference attendance, and journal subscriptions. It is costly to add buildings, research labs, lecture halls, and campus facilities for academic work.[9] *The New York Times* story reports that China sharply increased expenditure on higher education and spent more than Rs 46,000 crore ($10,222 million) on it in 2003.

By contrast, India spent a paltry Rs 1,748.37 crore ($388.5 million) on higher education during 2002–3, which is less than 5 per cent of the Chinese amount.[10] Resource-starved Indian institutions need more money. In the 2009–10 Union Budget, Rs 7,952 crore was allocated under the heading of Department of Higher Education, a fraction of which went to directly support academic research.

A series of stories in a 2006 volume titled *Indian Science Rising: Chemical & Engineering News* report that the government and the private sector have reached a consensus about strengthening India's research and development (R&D) potential by harnessing the talent of Indian scientists, living in India and abroad, by providing them with lucrative employment and necessary infrastructural and other facilities (see Yarnell 2006). Research institutions and pharmaceutical industries had shown interest in participating. The central government had proposed the setting up of a fully autonomous agency, the National Scientific and Engineering Research Foundation (NSERF, fashioned after the National Science Foundation of the US), for providing financial support and other help to such ventures. This is a ray of hope—if these plans materialize, they would spawn applied research, and, hopefully, academic research in the future.

4. *Academic administrative leadership.* Selected through a rigorous screening process, heads of top-ranked US universities are extraordinarily talented individuals who typically possess high academic distinctions, leadership skills, pleasing personalities, fund-raising abilities, strong prior administrative records, and a long list of other accomplishments; political appointees are rare. These qualities are increasingly being sought among the heads of high-ranked universities in other nations (see Goodall 2009).

By contrast, most leaders of Indian institutions lack academic leadership talent, are exempt from extensive scrutiny, and often end up being political appointments. Consequently, academic leaders in leading universities abroad are much more successful in raising money, and far more likely to support academic research and seek and retain good scholars, than their Indian counterparts.

5. *Governing bodies.* If one looks at the history of Harvard University, it began under church sponsorship in 1636, came under political control over the next two centuries, and finally in 1865, the university alumni began electing members of the governing board (see Harvard University 2011). Eventually, governing bodies of US universities came to have an overwhelming representation of alumni members who would like to see their alma maters flourish because then 'the value of their degrees will go up'. Because they have respect for 'the place and the people', they are unlikely to indulge in activities that would hurt the institutions. Some alumni trustees are nominated while others are voted into office by alumni

[7]For example, IIM Ahmedabad pays 'Rs 5 lakh for research papers published in frontranking journals' (see 'The Cutting Edge' in *Business Today*, 9 October 2010).

[8]See Cornell University professor Ronald G. Ehrenberg's work (2002) for a discussion of different factors that contribute to rising costs of higher education.

[9]India spends significant amounts on building faculty and staff quarters. Such expenses are either absent or form an insignificant part of the total expenditure of US universities.

[10]Available at http://indiabudget.nic.in/ub2003–04/eb/sbe57.pdf (accessed on 26 January 2006).

members. This is a wonderful combination of democracy and enlightened self-interest.

By contrast, the boards of trustees in Indian universities and institutes are often selected in an ad-hoc manner with little consideration of trustees' stake in the institution (for example, Ministry of Human Resource Development appointed one of India's most distinguished business leaders, chairman of ITC Limited Mr Y.C. Deveshwar, as chairman of the Board of Governors of IIM Calcutta; a better decision would have been to request him to chair the board of a much larger institution, IIT Delhi, his alma mater). Moreover, heavy interference by politicians tends to blunt a trustee's incentives to govern independently and effectively. As a result, academic research and reputation of the institution take a beating.

Recent Changes and Some Policy Recommendations

Since the first version of this article was published in 2007, there have been some positive developments. The Honourable Prime Minister Dr Manmohan Singh has announced that foreigners can work in Indian educational institutions. The government is granting funds to many researchers. A panel headed by Professor N.R. Madhava Menon has explored ways of granting more autonomy to higher-education institutions and recommended to the Ministry of Human Resource Development that the vice chancellor, who is a university's executive head, should be 'a person of academic excellence' (see report in *The Telegraph*, Kolkata, dated 10 May 2011).

However, deep problems, as documented in this article, remain. For a start, we provide the following recommendations:

- Indian universities have a tremendous shortage of talented researchers—the nation needs to nurture existing researchers and attract researchers from elsewhere.
- Faculty members should be hired on the basis of academic merit and no other criteria.
- In particular, institutions should not be breeding grounds and resting places for political supporters. Whenever that happens, costs and benefits get misaligned—a political party reaps small benefits but damage to the society is enormous. And, efforts to redress past social injustices through these institutions need to be minimized.
- The power in superior universities rests with faculty members who have distinguished themselves in research—this needs to be instituted in India.
- India needs to rethink how the boards and governance structures of Indian universities and institutes need to be optimally structured. As the world's best universities have shown, alumni members, if properly engaged, can do an excellent job taking their alma mater forward. Most of the education bureaucrats that serve on Indian boards need to go. So should businessmen and industrialists who serve on boards but have no real ties to the institution.
- Academic leaders such as vice chancellors and directors need to be selected from ranks of proven scholars who would dedicate themselves to taking the institutions forward in terms of academic research. Their task is simple: 'Hire scholars who would raise the average quality.' But, it is hard to implement this in practice.
- Creation of great universities takes much more than salary increases. For example, ISB Hyderabad's resident faculty members enjoy some of the world's highest salaries among business school professors on a purchasing power adjusted basis—but, their research output trails far behind that of professors in the world's top 20 business schools. Currently, Indian professors are paid good salaries, but where is the research and academic output?
- Accountability is needed for money that is currently given by the government to support research. It must be ensured that the research is of excellent quality and wastages and slippages are minimized.
- India has over 50 billionaires and many more wealthy people. The government can play a broker's role and help engage them with academic institutions where they would provide patronage.

What would it take to change the Indian academic waste land? Our tables and text illustrate that the existing model has failed to deliver and complete rethinking is needed. There are people who have good understanding of Indian higher education but do not know how to build great multi-product research universities. There are people who know how great universities function but do not know the Indian situation. There is an urgent need for leadership that would combine both to build superb research universities and create a culture of academic excellence as Sir Asutosh Mookerjee managed to do, under extremely strained circumstances, a century back.

ARKADEV CHATTERJEA AND SATYA PRIYA MOULIK

References

Chatterjea, Arkadev. 2004. 'Two Roots, and Little Else', Op-ed article, *The Telegraph*, 14 January, Kolkata.

Ehrenberg, Ronald G. 2002. *Tuition Rising: Why College Costs So Much*, Cambridge, Massachusetts, Harvard University Press.

Enserink, Martin. 2007. 'Who Ranks the University Rankers?' *Science*, 317: 1026–8.

Ghatak, U.R., S.C. Mukherjee, A.K. Chaudhuri, S.B. Banerjee, S.N. Bhattacharya, S.P. Ghosh, and M.N. Bagchi. 1976.

Indian Association for the Cultivation of Science: A Century, Calcutta, Indian Association for the Cultivation of Science.

Goodall, Amanda H. 2009. *Socrates in the Boardroom: Why Research Universities Should be Led by Top Scholars*, Princeton, New Jersey, Princeton University Press.

Harvard University. 2011. In *Encyclopaedia Britannica*, available at http://www.britannica.com/EBchecked/topic/256300/Harvard-University (accessed on 13 June 2011).

The New Oxford Dictionary of English. 1998. New York, Oxford University Press.

Yarnell, Amanda. 2006. Articles in the series *Indian Science Rising: Chemical & Engineering News* (*USA*), 84(12): 12–20.

Affirmative Action

The affirmative action (AA) programme in India is primarily caste based (there is now some affirmative action for women in local self-governments). The caste system in India is believed to be over 2500 years old. The ancient manifestation of the system, the varna system, divided the population into first four, and later five, hereditary, endogamous, mutually exclusive, and occupation-specific groups: Brahmins, Kshatriyas, Vaisyas, Sudras, and later Ati-Sudras. The latter did the most menial jobs, were subjected to complete untouchability, in that even sight of them was considered polluting, and thus were victims of highly degrading segregation, discrimination, and exclusion. Over the years, this system metamorphosed into the contemporary jati system (also translated into English as caste), which has the same basic characteristics as the varna system. However, jatis (estimated to number between 2,000 and 3,000) are regional categories and are not clear subsets of the varnas, thus leading to claims and counterclaims of varna affiliation and the attendant status. In addition to the caste system, India is home to more than 50 million adivasis (indigenous tribes) who are subjected to extreme deprivation and discrimination.

Even before Independence, the British administration introduced a policy of AA for the untouchable castes and adivasis (called the 'depressed classes'). After Independence in 1947, the policy of reserving 22.5 per cent of seats in educational institutions, government jobs, and electoral seats at all levels was enshrined into the Indian Constitution. The jatis and tribes entitled to these quotas were listed in a government schedule and are, therefore, called scheduled castes (SCs) and scheduled tribes (STs). These are official terms; the term dalit (meaning oppressed) is often used as a term of pride for these groups. The reservation programme for SCs–STs is comparatively less controversial and, being constitutionally guaranteed, cannot be challenged completely.

Since 1991, a further 27 per cent quota has been introduced for other low castes (called other backward classes or OBCs) that, however, is not constitutionally guaranteed. The assignment of OBC status to jatis is fraught with difficulty, given the fluidity of the jati–varna link. The position of the OBCs in the caste hierarchy represents a situation of 'graded inequality', rather than a sharp distinction vis-à-vis upper-caste Hindus. Both the extension of the reservation system to the OBCs as well as the designation of jatis as OBC have been moves that are politically highly contentious. OBC lists typically comprise a range of jatis: some that are very close to SCs–STs in social and economic position, but also some jatis that are believed to be much more prosperous. Despite this mixed composition, latest national data (for instance, consumption expenditure surveys from the National Sample Survey [NSS]) reveal clear disparities between the OBCs and upper-caste Hindus in 1999–2000. Also, since 1993, 33 per cent of seats in local self-governments have been reserved for women. In addition to the reservation policy, AA in India also takes the form of a provision for preferential treatment of SC–ST groups in other government schemes that are meant for the general population.

The case for a caste-based AA (particularly for SC–ST groups) is based on the following set of factors. One, continuing inter-caste disparities in all spheres: monthly per capita expenditure, educational attainment, occupational distribution, landownership, asset ownership, and health indicators. There is evidence to suggest that this is not simply a hangover from the past, but that inequalities are being perpetuated in contemporary India. The evidence on trends in monthly per capita expenditure over the last 20 years (from the NSS) indicates that the gap between SCs–STs and the 'others' is *not* closing. Two, dalits continue to suffer from a 'stigmatized ethnic identity' due to their untouchable past and there is corresponding social backwardness. Three, given the objective of equality of opportunity between castes, AA is needed to provide a 'level playing field'. Four, AA is needed to compensate for the historical wrongs of a system that generated systematic disparity between caste groups and actively discriminated against certain castes. It should be noted that unlike the much more radical Malaysian AA programme, AA in India does not really aim to rectify the disparities in wealth ownership that are directly the outcome of the caste system that prevented the untouchables from acquiring property. Thus it is a much weaker programme of compensation than what would be construed fair, given the magnitude of wealth disparities. Five, there is evidence to suggest that caste-based discrimination in labour markets continues in both urban and rural areas, in the formal and informal sectors, and is manifested both as wage and job discrimination. There is evidence that points to a discriminatory gap in earnings between SCs–STs and others.

Political reservations have an added, independent justification that is distinct from those for job and educational reservations. In the absence of proportional representation and the predominance of a first-past-the-post electoral system, there are special handicaps that minority groups face in terms of being guaranteed equality of political opportunity, even if theoretically they were not historically discriminated against. Another argument in favour of job and educational reservations is that individuals who manage to get better education and jobs could serve as role models and provide dynamic motivation to the rest of the community. On the other hand, critics of reservation argue that there might be more efficient ways of helping disadvantaged groups like special scholarships, credit subsidies, and job training. It is also argued that ideally these programmes should be time bound, as was provided for by the Constitution, but vested interests in the beneficiary communities would like the system to be perpetuated.

An assessment of these programmes suggests that their impact has been mixed. Quotas have been fully implemented in the electoral sphere but their implementation in education and jobs has been less than optimal. Moreover, reservations are often seen as the end and not the beginning of the AA programme. SC–ST quotas are constitutionally mandatory, but are often circumvented using loopholes in the system. Additionally, private-sector jobs are free from quotas, and with increasing liberalization of the economy, confining AA to the government sector is gradually making it redundant. Despite all these weaknesses, the AA programme has led to the creation of a dalit middle class and many more dalit families are freed from their traditional subservient roles. However, the case for AA continues to be strong for all the reasons listed here. Preliminary studies indicate that liberalization of the economy does not seem to be reducing inter-group disparities.

There are other countries, such as the USA, where the AA programme is not quota based. Comparative assessments of these programmes suggest that the key to the success of an AA policy may not lie in whether or not the programme is quota based. A successful programme would be one that is backed by the requisite political will. The Indian experience suggests that political reservations would be a crucial element to build that reservoir of political will.

ASHWINI DESHPANDE

■ Agribusiness

Indians spend around 55 per cent of their household budget on food, which implies that the Indian economy, to a large extent, still revolves around food and food habits. Although the growth in per capita income has decreased the share of food in household budgets, it has also changed the complexion of Indian agriculture, giving a boost to agro-industry and agribusiness.

The Push and Pull for Indian Agribusiness

The pull for agribusiness has come from the change in consumption patterns, increase in rural incomes, and emerging export opportunities. Increasing per capita income and urbanization have changed the composition of domestic food demand, on the one hand, reducing the share of food in household budgets and, on the other hand, increasing the share of the food budget allocated to high-value commodities like fruits and vegetables, livestock, and fishery. Per capita cereal consumption registered a decline in annual growth by 0.4 per cent from 1990 to 2000, while it increased for fruits (2.9 per cent), vegetables (2.1 per cent), milk (1.9 per cent), meat (0.9 per cent), eggs (1.9 per cent), and fish (2 per cent) (Gulati et al. 2005).

Growth in export demand for high-value and processed food has given a further boost to agribusiness. High-value agricultural exports as a percentage of total agricultural exports increased from 21 per cent in 1990 to 36 per cent in 2000 (Gulati et al. 2005). Processed food also registered an annual export growth of 8.4 per cent from 1980 to 1999, higher than agricultural exports of 7.3 per cent during the same period (Athukorala and Jayasuriya 2003).

External factors like new tax incentives for exports are also providing the much-needed push for agribusiness. For example, in order to promote agro-processing industries, a deduction of 100 per cent of profits for five years and 25 per cent of profits for the next five years has been made under the Income Tax Act for new industries involved in processing, preserving, and packaging of fruits and vegetables. As many of these come under the definition of small-scale industry, that is, within Rs 4 crore turnovers, they are not required to pay excise duties either.

The Structure of Agro-industry in India

All these factors have given a boost to the agro-processing sector in India. However, three important factors have to be taken into consideration. First, a substantial part of the agro-output in India is still not processed. India produces the highest amount of milk and livestock in the world, is the second largest producer of fruits and vegetables, and comes third in food grain production, fifth in egg production, and seventh in fish production. However, conservative estimates put processing levels in the fruits and vegetables sector at 2 per cent, in meat and poultry at 2 per cent, in milk by way of modern dairies at 14 per cent, in fish at 4 per cent, and in bulk meat deboning at 21 per cent. Further, the value addition to raw produce by processing is 7 per cent in India, compared to as much as 45 per cent in the Philippines and 23 per cent in China (GoI 2005).

Second, most of Indian agro-processing is concentrated in the unorganized sector. More than 99 per cent of production units and 86 per cent of manufacturing employment are concentrated in the unorganized sector but it contributes only 25 per cent of gross value added in manufacturing, whereas organized manufacturing with a mere 14 per cent of employment contributes 75 per cent of gross value added. Within manufacturing, agro-industry employs around 73 per cent of workers and contributes 40 per cent to gross value added, and food processing is an important component of agro-industry with 38 per cent employment and 53 per cent of gross value added, although this is predominantly concentrated in the organized sector (Chadha and Gulati 2007).

Third, since Indian agriculture is dominated by smallholders, agribusiness has to take into consideration the issues and integration of smallholders in agro-industry. Around 81 per cent of Indian farms are less than 2 ha, operating only 36 per cent of total farm area. Small farmers have great opportunity in high-value agriculture due to the high labour intensity of products but are constrained due to high transactions costs, market risks, and lack of capital.

Entry of Private Players in Agro-industry

In this new environment, the scope for agribusiness—from cultivation to processing and retail—is immense. However, India has relatively tight regulations on foreign investment in the retail food sector and corporate farming is still prohibited. The biggest chunk of private investment, whether domestic or foreign, has thus been directed towards agro-processing.

The entry of private investment in agro-processing and the emerging new vertical linkages have transferred technological innovations in the farm sector, leading to global market access for smallholders. For example, Pepsi set up the biggest tomato-processing plant in Asia in 1989 and introduced new technology and seed varieties which more than doubled tomato yield within three years of operation. Private investment is also leading to infrastructural development and agricultural extension services. Indian telecom giant Bharti Enterprise's joint venture with de Rothschilds will lead to infrastructural development in the entire supply chain through the creation of storage facilities, processing plants, and cold transportation capabilities, besides plans to establish a research centre and model farm.

High market risks for smallholders are also being countered by improving information sharing through a vertically coordinated framework. One such initiative is the ITC's *e-choupal* initiative in India, which connects 3.1 million farmers through 'e-chain', which reduced transactions costs for a typical soyabean farmer from Rs 705 to Rs 335 per metric tonne (Sivakumar 2004).

Role of Public Policy in Encouraging Agribusiness

While private business can invigorate the agro-industrial sector by providing much-needed investment, public policy is as important in creating an enabling environment. Public investments in infrastructure and institutions especially are essential due to the perishable nature of high-value commodities. Government initiative is necessary to support and develop institutions to address food safety and food quality issues, for better channelling of credit, and to address issues of environmental degradation, deforestation, and water scarcity.

ASHOK GULATI

References

Athukorala P. and S. Jayasuriya. 2003. 'Food Safety Issues, Trade and WTO Rules: A Developing Country Perspective', *World Economy*, 26(9): 1395–416.

Chadha, G.K.and A. Gulati. 2007. 'Performance of Agro-industry in India: Emerging Issues and Prospects', in P.K. Joshi, A. Gulati, and R. Cummings Jr. (eds), *Agricultural Diversification and Smallholders in South Asia*, New Delhi, Academic Foundation.

Government of India (GoI). 2005. 'Food Processing Policy 2005', Ministry of Food Processing Industries, New Delhi.

Gulati, A., N. Minot, C. Delgado, and S. Bora. 2005. 'Growth in High-value Agriculture in Asia and the Emergence of Vertical Links with Farmers', paper presented at the Symposium 'Toward High-value Agriculture and Vertical Coordination: Implications for Agribusiness and Smallholders', New Delhi, International Food Policy Research Institute.

Sivakumar, S. 2004. *Indian Agribusiness and ITC e-choupal*, DuPont NSM.

■ Agricultural Labour

Agricultural labourers constitute a large section of the rural population in India (26 per cent in 2001). A sizeable proportion of the female workers in rural areas are agricultural labourers (about 36 per cent in 2001). The proportion of agricultural labourers in the rural workforce, however, declined from 50 per cent in 1991 to 30 per cent in the 2001 Population Census due to reasons discussed later. These labourers are drawn from the most socially and economically deprived sections of the rural hierarchy and are hence doubly disadvantaged and vulnerable. About 40 per cent of the scheduled caste households were agricultural labour households in 2004–5, though this proportion had declined from 52 per cent in 1983 to 49 per cent in 1999–2000. The proportion of agricultural labour households among the scheduled tribes, however, increased from 33 to 38 per cent during 1983 to 1999–2000, but declined to 34 per cent in 2004–5.

'Attached' versus 'Free' Labour

An agricultural labourer may enter into a contract with an employer on his own free will in which case he is a 'free' casual labourer. He may, however, enter into a contract due to a pre-existing obligation arising from customary social relations or on account of credit and/or land relations. This form of 'attached' or 'bonded' labour has its role in the functioning of the overall market for agricultural labourers. Several historical studies have shown that as agriculture developed and became commercial there was a general tendency to move from labour contracts signifying relatively little freedom for the workers to freer, more impersonal forms of contract. Inter-generational bondage characterized by extra-economic coercions also tended to decline.

In recent times, however, other types of attachments, not necessarily of an unfree nature, arose due to the exigencies of the production process. Modernization of agricultural technology increased the demand for a form of attached labour as it was seen as useful in overseeing the work of casual labourers (Bardhan 1984). The interlinking of labour and land markets through various forms of tenancy and sharecropping arrangements has been common in India. One of the most common sharecropping contractual arrangement was that output was shared equally between the tenant and the landlord, and so were input costs, but labour and seeds were provided by the tenant. This is, therefore, in some sense a form of disguised 'attached' labour contract. Leasing out of small pieces of land to tenants on 'fixed' rent also exists, but is perhaps less common. A form of reverse tenancy has also been observed in some parts of India, where the small landholders, unable to cultivate their land, lease out to the large holders. Operation Barga successfully conducted in West Bengal was a form of legally recognizing various forms of tenancy arrangements and this has proved useful in increasing productivity on the farms.

Land Distribution and Diversification

The decennial landholding surveys indicate an increase in semi-landlessness, less than 0.2 hectares (ha), from 37 to 42 per cent of rural households, and marginal land holdings of 0.002 to 1.01 ha, from 62 to 72 per cent during 1972 to 1992. In 2004–5 about 6.6 per cent of rural households were landless and 73 per cent owned less than 1 ha land (NSSO, 61st Round, Report No. 515). Even though the proportion of completely landless households has not increased much in the last decade, a large proportion of the semi-landless and marginal landholders would be working as casual agricultural labourers. The Rural Labour Enquiry data also shows that the proportion of labour households with cultivated land had increased over the period. This corroborates the earlier observation that these are actually semi-landless and marginal landholders who are forced to enter the wage labour market often due to failure of the monsoon or because their small plots of poor quality land are not able to yield enough to sustain the household (Unni 1997).

There was an increasing casualization of the total workforce in rural areas till 1999–2000, but there was a decline in 2004–5. We observed a decline in the proportion of agricultural labourers. An interesting feature observed in the labour households in the Rural Labour Enquiry was the decreasing proportion of wage earners despite casualization. This trend reflects an increasing diversification of economic activities among labour households. This diversification into non-wage activities is partly due to the increase in labour households with cultivated land. The avenues open for self-employment are obviously greater in such households. The diversification of economic activities in labour households over time was also reflected in the declining percentage of days in a year spent in wage employment (Unni 1997).

Overall, this implies that the character of the recent entrants to the agricultural labour force had changed. The proportion of scheduled caste households in agricultural labour declined while that of scheduled tribes remained the same. The agricultural labourers now also increasingly belonged to broader caste groups and were households with small landholdings and a diversified portfolio of economic activities.

Migration: A Symptom of Poor Agricultural Performance

That all is not well with the agricultural sector in large parts of India is reflected in the shrinking share of the rural gross domestic product (GDP), particularly rural GDP including agriculture during the decade 1980 to 1993 (Unni and Rani 2005). The emphasis on economic reforms has tended to concentrate on the secondary and tertiary sectors with less importance being given to agriculture. Massive public investments in agriculture occurred in the 1970s that supported the agricultural system, such as large irrigation projects. Such investments have declined considerably in the last decade. Lack of water for irrigation and casual development of the semi-arid regions has led to increase in migration from rural to rural and urban areas.

Lack of irrigation facilities, low productivity of the land, and an uncertain monsoon, leads to single crop cultivation and strengthens the pressure to migrate. A circular mobility of labourers occurs as a consequence of unbalanced resource endowments and regional development. This is in the nature of distress migration. On the one hand, there is a net transfer of slack labour from the backward areas to relatively developed areas in the form of seasonal migration. In some areas the demand for labour in the peak season cannot be met by the local supply of labour and these areas attract agricultural labourers from outside. Such circular migration can also be to urban areas where rural migrants do not settle permanently in cities and continue to maintain their links with the area of origin, where they return regularly. Another form of migration to urban areas is of a more permanent nature that leads to the settlement of migrants in urban areas.

Poverty Debate

Debate on the changing economic conditions of agricultural labourers has raged since the 1970s and it continues till today. While no one can deny that the agricultural labourers form the lowest deciles of the poor, it is debated whether their conditions have improved over time. In the 1970s the discussion was on whether the conditions of agricultural workers had improved since the advent of the Green Revolution. More recently, the debate has been on whether the economic reforms of the 1990s have benefited rural labourers.

Attempts at theorizing about rural labour markets have focused on the process of wage determination. In attempting to empirically determine whether the status of agricultural labourers has improved, the arguments have focused on real wage rates. While many have argued that the trickle-down effects of the Green Revolution were beginning to reach the agricultural labourers as reflected in a rise in real wage rates, others have argued that this was restricted to a few states where organization of the workers was strong. However, much of this debate has been based on male wages alone. Jose (1978) argues that real wages alone did not tell us the real story and the quantum of employment available in terms of days of work was important in determining the real incomes received by these workers. Further, the increase in real wage rates in the 1980s has been attributed to the massive public expenditures on public works (Sen 1996).

A similar argument showing that the economic reforms had improved the economic condition of casual workers in the 1990s was also based on the real wage rates (Sundaram 2001). Recently, a strange phenomenon of decline in real earnings of urban and rural non-agricultural regular workers was observed in 2004–5. While urban casual workers also recorded a decline in real wages, those in rural areas retained their low levels of real earnings (Unni and Raveendran 2007). There have been only a few attempts to look behind these aggregate figures towards the declining capacity of the poor to obtain adequate nutrition or the lack of association between economic growth and poverty reduction and the declining employment elasticity of output.

Organization of Labour

The traditional organization of agricultural labourers in India was by trade unions, most of which were under a political party. This strategy mainly concentrated on economic demands, such as increase in wage rates and implementation of statutory minimum wages. The strategy, however, yielded positive results only in some regions, such as Kerala, Andhra Pradesh, and Punjab. Mobilization of labour by the leftist political parties was based on class lines. Agricultural labourers are deprived of land and resources; organization helped them resist the oppression of the dominant classes. The Bahujan Samaj Party mobilized labourers on the understanding that caste-based oppression of the lower castes (dalits) is the root cause of exploitation of the poor. The traditional high castes deprived the lower castes of means of production and used the caste system to force them into adopting this occupation (Gill 1998).

A more recent form of organization has been through non-governmental organizations (NGOs) and voluntary groups. These organizations take up more broad-based issues pertaining to agricultural labourers and other groups at the grass-roots level. Here the focus is on economic issues, such as minimum wages and acquisition of cultivable wastelands and forests for cultivation, supply of food grains, legal aid, healthcare, and social security issues. Only a few of these NGOs have taken up an anti-state position, while many of them have acted as agents for the government taking up implementation of the official programmes (Gill 1998). The limitation of NGOs and voluntary organizations is that they remain limited to local areas and are unable to mobilize a mass base at the national level, unlike political parties, and hence rarely have much bargaining power.

A recent terminology used to distinguish organizations that elect their leaders and operate on democratic principles is of membership-based organizations (MBOs) (Chen et al. 2007). Unlike NGOs, these organizations have registered members mainly from a particular trade, which make them accountable to that particular constituency.

A new strategy that has been adopted in recent years is that MBOs and NGOs often join together in loose networks of grass-roots organizations linking local communities to one another (Fisher 2003). They join together to work on certain specific issues or a clearly drawn up agenda. This is done to improve their powers of negotiation. Networks are formed through alliances between NGOs, MBOs, federations of trade unions, cooperatives, and savings and credit groups.

State Response to Issues of Agricultural Labourers

The Minimum Wages Act was adopted in India as early as 1948. The Act requires the appropriate government to fix minimum rates of wages in respect of employment specified in a Schedule, including agricultural labour. While the implementation of this Act is not monitored, it provides trade unions and NGOs with a legal weapon to fight for the cause of agricultural labourers.

The issue of lack of demand for agricultural labour and consequent seasonal migration is addressed by the government through rural public works programmes. The government sponsors these public works as a form of insurance against the shock of a drought. In theory, public works programmes can play multiple roles, such as alleviation of poverty, construction of infrastructure, and environmental protection. All these together can help mitigate the problem of lack of demand for agricultural labour. However, in reality all these goals are rarely achieved.

In Maharashtra, the Employment Guarantee Scheme has initiated the public works programme on a more permanent basis. It has been lauded as a successful programme where it works almost as a right to work model. The workers are entitled to paid work and they can demand public employment on rural works.

The Mahatma Gandhi National Rural Employment Guarantee Scheme (MNREGS) under the 2005 Act is an effort by the Government of India to universalize this programme for the country. Evaluations of the programme are ongoing and there are issues of corruption and misuse, which need to be looked into. Overall, the programme has been well received by people in need of employment, labourers, and also state governments. Efforts are also on to make wage payments through smart card transactions to minimize transaction costs and time taken for remunerations to reach the poor.

JEEMOL UNNI

References

Bardhan, P. 1984. *Land, Labour and Rural Poverty: Essays in Development Economics*, New Delhi, Oxford University Press.

Chen, M., R. Jhabvala, R. Kanbur, and C. Richards. 2007. *Membership Organizations of the Poor*, New Delhi, Routledge.

Fisher, Julie. 2003. *Non-governments: NGOs and the Political Development of the Third World*, Jaipur, Rawat Publications.

Gill, S.S. 1998. 'Unionising Agricultural Labour: Some Issues', in R. Radhakrishna and A.N. Sharma (eds), *Empowering Rural Labour in India: Market, State and Mobilisation*, New Delhi, Institute for Human Development.

Jose, A.V. 1978. 'Real Wages, Employment and Income of Agricultural Labourers', *Economic and Political Weekly*, 13(12): A16–A20.

Sen, A. 1996. 'Economic Reforms, Employment and Poverty', *Economic and Political Weekly*, 31(35–37): 2459–77.

Sundaram, K. 2001. 'Employment and Poverty in India in the 1990s: Further Results from NSS 55th Round Employment–Unemployment Survey, 1999–2000', *Economic and Political Weekly*, 36(32): 3039–49.

Unni, J. 1997. 'Employment and Wages among Rural Labourers: Some Recent Trends', *Indian Journal of Agricultural Economics*, 52(1): 59–72.

Unni, J. and U. Rani. 2005. 'Gender and Non-farm Employment', in R. Nayyar and A.N. Sharma (eds), *Rural Transformation in India: The Role of the Non-farm Sector*, New Delhi, Institute of Human Development.

Unni, J. and G. Raveendran. 2007. 'Growth of Employment at the Turn of the Century: Illusion of Inclusiveness?', *Economic and Political Weekly*, 42(3): 196–9.

■ Agriculture Development

Agriculture plays a pivotal role in the Indian economy. Although its contribution to gross domestic product (GDP) is now around one-sixth of the total, it provides employment to 56 per cent of the Indian workforce. Also, the forward and backward linkage effects of agriculture growth increase incomes in the non-agriculture sector. The growth of some commercial crops has significant potential for promoting exports of agricultural commodities and bringing about faster development of agro-based industries.

Thus agriculture not only contributes to the overall growth of the economy, but also reduces poverty by providing employment and food security to a majority of the population in the country, and is thus among the most inclusive growth sectors of the Indian economy.

The objective of this entry is to examine the performance and policy issues in Indian agriculture since Independence, with an emphasis on the last two decades. It is divided into four sections. The next section deals with performance while the following section briefly examines the policies since Independence. The last section is devoted to a discussion of the policy changes that are needed for higher growth in agriculture.

Performance of Agriculture

One of the paradoxes of the Indian economy is that the decline in the share of agricultural workers in total workers has been slower than the decline in the share of agriculture in GDP. For example, the share of agriculture and allied activities in GDP declined from 57.7 per cent in 1950–1 to 15.7 per cent in 2008–9 (Table 1). The share of agriculture in total workers, however, declined slowly from 75.9 per cent in 1961 to 56.4 per cent in 2004–5 (Table 1).

Between 1961 and 2004–5, there was a decline of 34 percentage points in the share of agriculture in GDP while the decline in share of agriculture in employment was of only 19.5 percentage points. As a result, the gap between labour productivity in agriculture and non-agriculture increased rapidly.

Table 1 Share of Agriculture in GDP and Employment: All-India

Year	Share in GDP (%)		Share in employment (%)
	Agriculture, forestry, and fishing	Agriculture*	
1950–1	57.7	50.2	–
1960–1	53.0	47.3	75.9
1980–1	39.7	35.8	–
2004–5	18.9	15.9	56.4
2008–9	15.7	13.3	–

Source: 'National Accounts Statistics of India: 1950–51 to 2002–03', Economic and Political Weekly Research Foundation, December 2004, Mumbai; Brochure on the New Series of National Accounts, Base Year 2005; K. Sundaram (2001, 2007).

In terms of growth, the performance of agriculture in the post-Independence era has been impressive as compared to the pre-Independence period. The all-crop output growth of around 2.57 per cent per annum in the post-Independence period (during 1949–50 to 2007–8) was much higher than the negligible growth rate of around 0.4 per cent per annum in the first half of the last century. As a result, India achieved significant gains in food grains and non-food grain crops.

The highest growth rate of GDP from agriculture and allied activities of 3.9 per cent per annum in recent years was recorded during 1992–3 to 1996–7 (Table 2). If we look at the decadal average, the 1980s recorded the highest growth rate of more than 3 per cent per annum. In the post-reform period, this declined to 2.76 per cent per annum. The deceleration in the GDP growth rate from agriculture between the first half of the 1990s and the later period is glaring. It is disquieting to note that during 1997–8 to 2004–5, agriculture growth was only 1.6 per cent per annum (Table 2). Fortunately, it recorded a growth of 3.5 per cent per annum during 2004–5 to 2010–11. Significant fluctuations in agriculture growth are a matter of concern.

Extensive cultivation has characterized Indian agriculture during the pre-1965 era, and in the post-Green Revolution period. There has been significant increase in the use of modern inputs in Indian agriculture. During 1950–1 to 2003–4, the percentage of net irrigated area to net cultivated area increased from around 17 to 41 per cent. During the same period, fertilizer consumption showed a significant rise from less than 1 kg/ha to 90 kg/ha. Similarly, the percentage area under high yielding varieties (HYVs) to cereals cropped area increased from 15 in 1970–1 to 75 per cent in the late 1990s. The share of agriculture in electricity consumption also increased from 4 per cent in 1950–1 to nearly 30 per cent in recent

Table 2 Growth Rates in Agriculture GDP: All-India

Period	Growth rate (per cent per annum)
1950–1 to 1964–5	2.51
1867–8 to 1980–1	2.20
1980–1 to 1990–1	3.07
1992–3 to 1996–7	3.85
1992–3 to 2001–2	2.76
1997–8 to 2004–5	1.60
2004–5 to 2010–11	3.47

Source: National Accounts Statistics (various years), Central Statistical Organisation, Government of India.
Note: GDP is in 1980–1 constant prices from 1950–1 to 1980–1; in 1993–4 constant prices for 1980–1 to 2004–5; in 2004–5 constant prices for 2004–5 to 2010–11. Quick estimates for 2009–10 and advanced estimates for 2010–11.

Table 3 Compound Growth Rates of Area, Output, and Yield: All-India

Period	All crops			Food grains			Non-food grains		
	Area	Output	Yield	Area	Output	Yield	Area	Output	Yield
1949–50 to 1964–5	1.58	3.15	1.21	1.35	2.82	1.36	2.44	3.74	0.89
1967–8 to 1980–1	0.51	2.19	1.28	0.38	2.15	1.33	0.94	2.26	1.19
1980–1 to 1989–90	0.10	3.19	2.56	–0.23	2.85	2.74	1.12	3.77	2.31
1990–1 to 1999–2000	0.25	2.28	1.34	0.17	1.94	1.52	1.37	2.78	1.04
1994–5 to 2009–10	0.26	2.30	2.23	–0.02	1.70	1.57	0.95	2.69	1.77
1949–50 to 2007–8	0.51	2.57	1.64	0.27	2.35	1.77	1.22	2.92	1.40

Source: *Agriculture at a Glance* (various issues), Department of Agriculture & Co-operation, Ministry of Agriculture, Government of India.

years. All this led to a significant increase in agricultural output over time.

Output of all crops increased at a compound growth rate of 3.15 per cent per annum during 1949–50 to 1964–5, significantly led by area expansion (Table 3). There has not been any significant increase in agricultural growth in the post-Green Revolution period. However, the sources of growth have changed from area expansion in the pre-Green Revolution period to yield growth in the later periods. Yield growth at 2.56 per cent per annum was the highest in the 1980s. However, it declined significantly to 1.31 per cent in the 1990s. In the last one and half decades (1994–5 to 2009–10), yield growth has increased as compared to the decade of the 1990s. In general, output and yield growth for non-food grains is higher than those for food grains.

The aggregate output growth at the national level hides a great deal of variation in the performance of different crops and regions. While wheat has recorded high and accelerated rates of yield increases, others like coarse cereals and pulses have not. Food grains and non-food grains recorded the highest growth rates in output as well as yields in the 1980s. In the 1990s, growth rate decelerated for both food grains and non-food grains. Increasing commercialization of agriculture started in a significant way in the 1980s. There were two revolutions in the last decade in the form of BT cotton and hybrid maize. Production increased significantly in these two crops.

There are large regional disparities in output across regions (see Vaidyanathan 1994). Certain regions, such as Punjab, Haryana, western Uttar Pradesh, parts of Andhra Pradesh, and Tamil Nadu benefited more than the other states during the initial phase of the Green Revolution. This had accentuated regional disparities in the immediate post-Green Revolution period. An important feature of the 1980s and the early 1990s, however, is that there was much more equitable spread of agricultural growth. According to Bhalla and Singh (1997), the period 1980–3 to 1990–3 marks a turning point (in terms of growth) in India's agricultural development. After performing poorly during the early years of the Green Revolution, many of the states where poverty is widespread—Assam, Bihar, Orissa, Madhya Pradesh, and West Bengal—showed significant growth in the 1980s. Oilseeds also gained in the dry belt of Rajasthan, Madhya Pradesh, Karnataka, and Maharashtra.

During the post-reform period, in response to growing domestic and export demand for non-cereal food items, there has been a discernible shift in the allocation of resources in Indian agriculture in the recent period away from cereals, particularly coarse cereals, to dairy farming, poultry, edible oils, meat, fish, vegetables, and fruits. These enterprises, being labour intensive, are suited to smallholders and lead to an increase in wage employment. Besides, they are environment friendly, as they are generally less land and water intensive, and they result in an increase in the incomes of farmers growing high-value products.

The deceleration in agricultural growth during the period 1997–8 and 2004–5, although most marked in rainfed areas, occurred in almost all the states and covered almost all the sub-sectors, including horticulture, livestock, and fisheries where growth was expected to be high (GoI 2007). However, there have been some positive developments in the last decade. Apart from revolutions in BT cotton and hybrid maize, there has been some increase in high-value agriculture. Some of the lagging regions like Bihar have shown relatively high growth in recent years. Similarly, Gujarat recorded a high growth of 9 per cent per annum during 2001–2 to 2007–8.

Policies since Independence

At the outset it may be mentioned that agriculture is a 'state subject' under the Constitution of India. However, the central government plays a crucial role in shaping agricultural policies. Although Indian agriculture is in private hands, government policies have greatly influenced its pace and character.

Broadly, agricultural development policies over time can be divided into four sets of policy packages:

(i) institutional reforms; (ii) public investment policies; (iii) incentive policies; and (iv) reforms and globalization policies. The relative importance of the first three sets has varied over time.

Thus, during the first three Five Year Plans (1950–65), institutional reforms and public investment packages dominated. The central and state governments enacted a number of laws regarding land reforms. These laws mainly related to three aspects: abolition of the zamindari system, land ceiling and redistribution of land, and tenancy reforms. The government was successful in abolishing the zamindari or intermediary system after paying compensation to the zamindars. The land ceiling laws were not effective although there was redistribution of some land to the beneficiaries. The tenancy reforms were more successful in two states—West Bengal in the east and Kerala in the south—than in others. West Bengal succeeded in giving ownership rights to tenants, particularly sharecroppers (*bargardars*). Since Independence some efforts have been made to consolidate fragmented holdings. These efforts have been relatively successful in some parts of north and north-west India.

There was significant public investment in agriculture during 1950–65. To achieve the objective of self-sufficiency in food grains, there was massive investment particularly in constructing irrigation reservoirs and distribution systems. Another important policy during this period was the expansion of institutional credit which helped reduce informal sources that had been exploitative with respect to interest rates and terms and conditions.

During 1967–90, incentive policies for adoption of new technology and public investment policies dominated government strategy in agriculture. After the humiliating experience with the import of food grains in the mid-1960s, there was a vigorous drive for achieving self-sufficiency by stepping up public investment in irrigation and introducing new technology through incentives. There was a need to increase domestic food production at a faster rate by much higher productivity without upsetting the agrarian structure. Luckily at that time new high-yielding dwarf varieties of wheat and rice were available in Mexico and the Philippines, respectively. Yields increased significantly for wheat initially and later for rice. This breakthrough is popularly known as the 'Green Revolution'. The productivity improvement associated with the Green Revolution is best described as forest- or land-saving agriculture. It may be noted that without the Green Revolution it would not have been possible to lift the production potential of Indian agriculture.

As mentioned earlier, inter-regional variations increased in the initial phase of the Green Revolution as it was limited to a few states like Punjab, Haryana, and Uttar Pradesh. However, unlike in the first decade of the Green Revolution, the experience in the 1980s indicates that the Green Revolution is spreading to new areas, particularly to the eastern and western regions; the new technology is being increasingly adopted by small farmers; there is a decline in the relative prices of food grains; and the real wages in agriculture have started increasing, especially in the less developed regions (Rao 1994: 63).

Incentive policies focused on both inputs and output. Subsidies for inputs like irrigation, credit, fertilizers, and power increased significantly in the 1970s and 1980s. The objective of the subsidies is to provide inputs at low prices to protect farmer interests and encourage diffusion of new technology. Similarly, on the output side, there has been a comprehensive long-term procurement-cum-distribution policy in the post-Green Revolution period. The government announces the support prices at sowing time and agrees to buy all the grains offered for sale at this price. To support these operations, institutions like the Food Corporation of India (FCI) and the Agricultural Prices Commission (APC) were established in the mid-1960s.

Post-1991, economic reforms in India have improved the incentive framework and agriculture has benefited from reduction in protection to industry. The terms of trade for agriculture have improved and private investment has increased. Export of commodities, particularly cereals, has risen and there has been some progress on market reforms in terms of removing domestic and external controls. However, there were also concerns about agriculture and food security in the 1990s. There has been emphasis on price factors at the cost of non-price factors like research and extension, irrigation, and credit. Economic reforms largely neglected the agricultural sector and it is only in the last few years that domestic and external trade reforms in the sector have started.

Trade policies in India during the last five decades have been highly interventionist and discriminating against agriculture. There has been pessimism regarding international trade in agriculture.

Trade liberalization in agriculture was faster towards the end of the 1990s in tune with WTO agreements. There has been considerable progress in the liberalization of export controls, and quantitative controls on imports and on decontrol of domestic trade. The Eleventh Five Year Plan focuses on 'faster and inclusive growth'. An important aspect of 'inclusive growth' in the Eleventh Plan is its target of 4 per cent per annum growth in GDP from agriculture and allied sectors. A detailed agenda for action is spelt out in the Mid-Term Appraisal of Eleventh Five Year Plan covering improved access to water, improvement in the supply of good quality seeds, replenishment of soil nutrients, improvements in agricultural research and extension, reforms in land tenancy, and improvements in agricultural marketing which is particularly important for perishable produce. The Twelfth Five Year Plan will focus on small and marginal farmers and resource poor regions.

Policy Changes Needed for Higher Growth

The slowing of agriculture growth occurred at a time when economic reforms were undertaken in the country. Some have concluded that this slowing is linked directly to structural macro reforms in the country and globalization. This view is limited and the slowing in agriculture is not due to industrial and trade reforms, including joining of WTO. Slowing down of agriculture growth could be attributed to structural factors on the supply side, such as decline in public investment, credit, and technology, rather than trade and industrial reforms.

The agriculture sector has many problems. Growth decelerated from 3.5 per cent during 1981–97 to 2 per cent during 1997–2005. Further scope for increase in net sown area is limited. Land degradation in the form of depletion of soil fertility, erosion, and water logging has increased. There has been a decline in the expansion rate of surface irrigation and reduction in the groundwater table. Risk and vulnerability too has increased. Disparities in productivity across regions and crops are persistent. Long-term factors like steeper decline in per capita land availability and shrinking of farm size are also responsible for the slow performance of agriculture.

The Steering Committee report on agriculture for the Eleventh Plan (GoI 2007) has identified the possible reasons for deceleration in agriculture since the mid-1990s. According to the report, the major sources of agricultural growth are: public and private investment in agriculture and rural infrastructure, including irrigation, technological change, diversification of agriculture, and fertilizers. The progress on all these sources slowed down in the 1990s particularly since the mid-1990s. Expansion was noticed in the case of agricultural credit.

There are three goals of agricultural development: (i) achieving 4 per cent growth in agriculture and raising incomes by increasing productivity (land, labour), diversification to high-value agriculture and rural non-farm by maintaining food security; (ii) sharing growth (equity) by focusing on small and marginal farmers, lagging regions, women, and other marginalized groups; and (iii) maintaining sustainability of agriculture by focusing on environmental concerns (see Dev 2008).

What are the policy reforms needed to achieve these goals? There are basically seven factors which need focused reforms in the short and medium terms. These are: (i) price policy; (ii) subsidies and investments; (iii) land issues; (d) irrigation and water management; (iv) research and extension; (v) credit; and (vi) domestic market reforms and diversification. Institutions have to be developed in all these aspects.

Investment in irrigation and rural infrastructure is important for agricultural growth. It is known that public investment in agriculture is lower than what is required for achieving 4 per cent growth. The Bharat Nirman Programme is in the right direction but the progress has to be much faster.

The decline in productivity growth is attributed, among other things, to deterioration in soil quality and water shortages, including groundwater depletion. Therefore, land and water management should be given number one priority. Both investment and efficiency in use of water are needed. Investment in irrigation, watershed development, and water conservation by the community are needed under water management. The pros and cons of the government's recent proposal of direct delivery of fertilizers to farmers are not known yet. However, in order to improve soil quality, the government can restructure fertilizer subsidies in such a way that it reduces the consumption of nitrogen (N) and encourages phosphatic (P) and potassic fertilizers.

As the National Commission on Farmers mentions, there is a knowledge gap in the existing technology. Therefore, extension becomes crucial for improving agricultural productivity. In view of high variability in agro-climatic conditions, particularly in unfavourable areas, research has to become increasingly location-specific.

It is true that in recent years there have been some improvements in the flow of farm credit. However, the government has to be sensitive to the four distributional aspects of agricultural credit: (i) not much improvement in the share of small and marginal farmers; (ii) decline in credit–deposit (CD) ratios of rural and semi-urban branches; (iii) increase in the share of indirect credit in total agricultural credit; and (iv) significant regional inequalities in credit.

The most significant problem for the farmers is output price fluctuations. There is a big gap between producer and consumer prices. For example, sometimes farmers get 50 paise per kg of tomatoes while the consumers pay Rs 20 to Rs 30 per kg in urban areas. In order to protect farmers from national and international price volatility, a price stabilization fund is needed. There are different models for marketing collectively by small and marginal farmers: the self-help group model, the cooperative model, small producer cooperatives, and contract farming. The real challenge lies in organizing small and marginal farmers for marketing and linking them to high-value agriculture. Thus, a group approach is needed for getting benefits from marketing.

There has been diversification in the Indian diet away from food grains to high-value products like milk and meat products, vegetables, and fruits. Since diversification involves a high risk, necessary support in infrastructure and marketing is needed. The price policy should also encourage diversification. The government wants to have a second 'Green Revolution' by diversifying agriculture to the crop sector and allied activities. To promote holistic growth of the horticulture sector through area-based regionally differentiated strategies, the National Horticulture Mission (NHM) was launched in the country during the Tenth Plan. The impact of this mission has to be strengthened further to improve productivity in the horticulture sector. The crop sector may not be able to grow at 4 per cent per annum. But horticulture and allied activities like dairying, poultry, and fisheries have to grow at a rate of 6 to 7 per cent to achieve 4 per cent growth in agriculture.

Climate change is a reality. India has reasons to be concerned about climate change. A vast majority of its population depends on climatic sensitive sectors like agriculture, forestry, and fishery for livelihood. The adverse impact of climate change in the form of declining rainfall and rising temperatures, and thus the increased severity of drought and flooding, would threaten food security and livelihood in the economy. India has to take measures for adaptability and mitigation to reduce the adverse impact of climate change.

It is known that more than 80 per cent of India's farmers belong to the categories of small and marginal farmers; they have an area share of more than 40 per cent. Support systems and policy changes have to support increasing productivity and incomes of the small and marginal farmers. The National Commission for Enterprises in the Unorganized Sector (NCEUS 2008) suggests special programmes for small and marginal farmers. The principal activities proposed under this include promotion of marginal and small farmers' groups, enabling greater access to institutional credit, training and capacity building, support for strengthening non-farm activities, gender-focused activities, and planning for development of marginal and small farmers.

There are six deficits in Indian agriculture: (i) investment, credit, and infrastructure deficit; (ii) land and water management deficit; (iii) research and extension (technology) deficit; (iv) market deficit; (v) diversification deficit; and (vi) institutions deficit. Focus has to be on small and marginal farmers and resource poor regions.

Finally, reforms should be undertaken for the growth of the rural non-farm sector. The rigidities in rural non-farm employment have to be removed in order to bring about rural transformation. The very low educational levels in rural areas limit access to better-paid employment, leaving rural workers with low skills, low productivity, and, therefore, probably low wage jobs. Education, infrastructure, and credit have to be improved in order to raise the productivity of rural non-farm employment. Policy changes in the food and agricultural sector and in the rural non-farm sector are expected to reduce rural poverty through rural transformation.

S. MAHENDRA DEV

References

Bhalla, G.S. and Gurmail Singh. 1997. 'Recent Developments in Indian Agriculture: A State Level Analysis', *Economic and Political Weekly*, 29 March–4 April, 32(13).

Dev, S. Mahendra. 2008. *Inclusive Growth in India: Agriculture, Poverty and Human Development*, New Delhi, Oxford University Press.

Government of India (GoI). 2007. *Report of the Steering Committee on Agriculture for 11th Five Year Plan*, New Delhi, Planning Commission.

——. 2008. *Eleventh Five Year Plan 2007–2012*, New Delhi, Oxford University Press.

——. 2011. *Mid-Term Appraisal, Eleventh Five Year Plan 2007–2012*, New Delhi, Oxford University Press.

NCEUS. 2008. *The Challenge of Employment in India*, New Delhi, NCEUS, Government of India.

Rao, C.H.H. 1994. *Agricultural Growth, Rural Poverty and Environmental Degradation in India*, New Delhi, Oxford University Press.

Sundaram, K. 2001. 'Employment and Poverty in 1990s, Further Results from NSS 55th Round, Employment-Unemployment Survey, 1999–2000', *Economic and Political Weekly*, 11 August, 36(34): 3039–49.

——. 2007. 'Employment and Poverty in India, 2000–2005', *Economic and Political Weekly*, 28 July, pp. 3121–31.

Vaidyanathan, A. 1994. 'Performance of Indian Agriculture since Independence', in Kaushik Basu (ed.), *Agrarian Questions*, New Delhi, Oxford University Press.

■ Dhirubhai Ambani and Reliance Industries

If the story about Dhirubhai Ambani and Reliance Industries were told as fiction, it would appear too far-fetched to work as a credible plot. For a village schoolteacher's son, who started life as a gas station attendant in Yemen, to lead a company that runs the world's largest grass-roots oil refinery, would require many leaps of financial logic and a Bradman-esque tale set in the corporate world. And yet it is true that the company that Dhirubhai founded became the largest in India in terms of assets, sales, and profits within a quarter century of going public in 1977, and is now among the top 200 in the world when ranked on profits.

That is only the bare bones of the blood and thunder story of a man who created opportunity out of obstacles, started a love affair with the stock market (at one stage the company boasted of the world's second largest retail investor base), thought global scale and vertical integration before his contemporaries, and who innovated in financial structuring and made speedy project execution a trade mark, both designed to keep capital costs low in a capital-intensive business.

Along the way, he redefined his business every decade: it was pure trading in the 1960s and then textile manufacture in the 1970s before the principal business became petrochemicals in the 1980s and energy in the 1990s. The new century has belonged to diversification: first into telecom and then (after Dhirubhai's sons Mukesh and Anil split the business in 2005) into retailing, power, finance, and infrastructure management.

When Dhirubhai was at the helm, outsize vision was almost always matched by project execution. The record has dimmed since the brothers split in 2005. Anil Ambani has expanded the telecom business rapidly, but at the cost of acquiring enormous debt. Mukesh's gas exploration and production business, in the Krishna–Godavari basin, has made slow progress in reaching the promised level of output. Anil's power projects have been even slower to get off the ground. And while Mukesh's retail business has had its hiccups, and little is heard of the life sciences foray, some of Anil's infrastructure management projects have been dogged by delays or underperformance.

When they split, Mukesh got the cash-spewing businesses while Anil got the ones with immediate growth potential. As things have turned out, Anil has shown faster growth, and rapidly ramped up the number of telecom customers while grabbing some big power projects, but project execution for him remains a weak area. Mukesh is now better positioned for grabbing future opportunities because he has the financial muscle while Anil has to downsize his debt.

From the beginning, business performance was only half the story. Dhirubhai Ambani and Reliance have been inseparable from controversy, it would seem. The charges have ranged from violating import rules to dealing in duplicate shares, from physically attacking a business rival to forgery, and from upending the rules to gain delayed entry into the telecom market to misusing funds raised overseas. Not long after the brothers went their separate ways, they were at war with each other over a gas pricing agreement, the matter going to the Supreme Court. Mukesh also stymied Anil's bid to acquire a telecom company in South Africa that eventually went to Sunil Mittal's Bharti Group.

In the late 1980s, the controversies swirling around Reliance became the subject of an intense media war that sucked in the government as well (not the last time this was to happen). The twists and turns in the plot would beat most thrillers, and figures extensively in a book on the Ambanis (*Ambani & Sons* by Australian journalist Hamish MacDonald). It is interesting that both brothers have recently been investing in media companies. The media, meanwhile, has become more circumspect about digging too deep into the Ambani affairs.

Most of the allegations against Reliance have never been proven, with the exception of one adverse court judgement on some small imports using back-dated bank letters of credit in the 1980s. The company paid compounding fees in the duplicate shares case in the 1990s in order to buy peace without admitting guilt. Most recently, Anil and his director-colleagues agreed to a consent order in the matter of misusing overseas funds, paying Rs 50 crore and agreeing to accept limited access to the stock market. But these have had no more effect than parking tickets would. Still, the revelations that surfaced before the brothers parted ways, did not speak of high governance standards.

Yet, as if to answer critics who have argued that the company owed its stand-out success to its ability to exploit the 'licence-permit raj' era of controls on business, Reliance has done even better in the reforms period, post-1991, and has been repeatedly voted among the country's most admired industrial houses. When the government began selling state-owned enterprises, Reliance picked up Indian Petrochemicals Corporation (seen as a public-sector success story) and promptly improved its operating parameters.

Those who argued that the company would not be able to maintain its growth record after Dhirubhai passed on in 2002, saw the company trebling its value on the stock market in 2002–5 to cross Rs 100,000 crore (Rs 22 billion)—reflecting rapid growth despite having reached a global scale. Growth has continued in recent years, but the pace has slowed and quite a few groups have outdone the Ambani brothers when it comes to overall performance. Certainly, Ratan Tata has blazed a trail in going global, which neither Ambani has been able to do despite trying.

Still, the profit margins that the company reports are better than normal in 'commodity' businesses like petrochemicals and oil refining. Credit Dhirubhai and Mukesh with focusing on value-added products that get better margins, for designing a refinery to maximize margins by having flexibility on crude quality, and for making sure that the company enjoys a significant sales tax concession in Gujarat apart from customs duty protection when it mattered.

Dhirubhai Ambani was unarguably the greatest Indian businessman of the last one-third of the 20th century, adding his name to the league of the Tatas and Birlas who dominated the earlier two-thirds of the century. At the end of the first decade of the 21st century, his sons continue to believe that their stage should be India, more than the world, and that single-industry focus is for the management pundits; in a world full of diverse opportunities, they will grab everything that comes their way.

T.N. Ninan

■ B.R. Ambedkar

Dr B.R. Ambedkar, affectionately known as Babasaheb, was one of the most illustrious sons of India. He appeared on the Indian socio-political scene in the early 1920s and remained in the forefront of all social, economic, political, and religious efforts for upliftment of the lowest stratum of Indian society, known as untouchables. Babasaheb was a great scholar who made outstanding contributions as an economist, sociologist, legal luminary, educationalist, journalist, Parliamentarian, and above all a social reformer and champion of human rights. Babasaheb organized, united, and inspired the untouchables in India to effectively use political means towards their goal of social equality.

Born in 1891 to an untouchable schoolteacher in the British Army, he was highly educated—PhD from Columbia University (1917), D.Sc. from London School of Economics, and Bar-at-Law from Gray's Inn in London (1923). These achievements, spectacular by any standard, were truly incredible for an untouchable.

Dr Ambedkar was an economist by his basic training. Two distinct phases can be distinguished in his career: first, up to 1921 as a professional economist contributing scholarly books and, second, as a political leader thereafter until his demise in 1956, during which he made path-breaking contributions as a champion of human rights for the untouchables.

Dr Ambedkar wrote three scholarly books on economics:
(i) *Administration and Finance of the East India Company*,
(ii) *The Evolution of Provincial Finance in British India*, and
(iii) *The Problem of the Rupee: Its Origin and Its Solution*.

The first two represent his contribution in the field of public finance: the first one evaluated finances of the East India Company during the period 1792 through 1858, and the second one analysed the evolution of Centre–state financial relations in British India during the period 1833 through 1921. The third book, his magnum opus in economics, is a seminal contribution to the field of monetary economics. In this book Dr Ambedkar examined the evolution of Indian currency as a medium of exchange, covering the period 1800 to 1893, and discussed the problem of choice of an appropriate currency system for India in the early 1920s. On his return to India, Dr Ambedkar did not write any book on economics per se, though several of his other contributions during that period carry a distinctive imprint of the economist in him.

As a member of the Bombay Legislative Assembly (since 1926), Ambedkar gave effective expression to the grievances of the rural poor through his mass movements. His successful struggle against the prevailing land tenure system called *khoti* liberated a vast majority of rural poor from an extreme form of economic exploitation. His successful agitation against *Mahar vatan* emancipated a large section of rural poor from virtual serfdom. He presented a Bill in the State Assembly to protect the poor from the malpractices of moneylenders. On the industrial front, Dr Ambedkar founded the Independent Labour Party in 1936. While the prevailing trade unions fought for the rights of workers, they were indifferent to the human rights of untouchable workers. The new political party took up their cause. Subsequently, as Labour Member of the Viceroy's Executive Council from 1942 to 1946, Dr Ambedkar was instrumental in bringing about several labour reforms including establishment of employment exchanges, generally laying the foundations of industrial relations in independent India. His ministry also included irrigation, power, and other public works. He played an important role in shaping the irrigation policy, especially the Damodar Valley Project.

A distinctive feature of Dr Ambedkar's scholarly contribution is his perceptive analysis of the economic dimension of social maladies such as the caste system and untouchability. While Mahatma Gandhi had defended the caste system on the basis of division of labour, Ambedkar came out with a hard-hitting critique in his book *Annihilation of Castes* (1936), pointing out that what was implicit in the caste system was *not* merely division of labour but *also* a division of labourers. Dr Ambedkar's attack on the caste system was not merely aimed at challenging the hegemony of the upper castes but had broader connotations of economic growth and development. He argued that the caste system had reduced the mobility of labour and capital which, in turn, impeded economic growth and development in India.

In his memorandum submitted to the British government titled 'States and Minorities' in 1947, Dr Ambedkar laid down a strategy for India's economic development. The strategy placed 'an obligation on the State to plan the economic life of the people on lines which would lead to highest point of productivity without closing every avenue to private enterprise and also provide for the equitable distribution of wealth'.

After Independence, Dr Ambedkar became the first Law Minister of India. Even while drafting the Indian Constitution (as Chairman, Drafting Committee) in 1948–9, the economist in Dr Ambedkar was very much alive. He strongly recommended democracy as the 'governing principle of human relationship' but emphasized that the principles of equality, liberty, and fraternity, which are the cornerstones of democracy, should not be interpreted narrowly in terms of political rights alone. He highlighted the social and economic dimensions of democracy and warned that political democracy cannot succeed when there is no social and economic democracy. He gave expression to the objective of economic democracy by incorporating the Directive Principles of State Policy in the Indian Constitution.

As Law Minister, Dr Ambedkar fought vigorously for the passage of the Hindu Code Bill, the most significant reform for women's rights in respect of marriage and inheritance. He resigned in September 1951 when the Bill was not passed by Parliament.

There is a unified theme running through Ambedkar's multifaceted and diverse contributions. The economic philosophy underlying it is best captured in his own phrase: *Bahujan Hitaya Bahujan Sukhay* (that is, greatest good to the largest number of people). Ambedkar's philosophy is suffused with social, religious, and moral considerations. The focal points of the philosophy are the oppressed and the depressed. The philosophy aims at giving life to those who are disowned, elevating those who are suppressed, ennobling those who are downtrodden, and granting liberty, equality, and justice to all irrespective of caste. Before his death in 1956, Dr Ambedkar converted nearly three-quarters of a million untouchables to Buddhism.

NARENDRA JADHAV

■ Antitrust Law

What is Antitrust Law?

Antitrust law (also known as competition law) is primarily concerned with the prohibition or regulation of practices undertaken by firms in order to limit competition. The most common practices include the following.

- 'Horizontal' agreements between competitors selling the same or similar products to restrict competition between themselves. The most egregious are agreements to fix prices, restrict output, divide up markets, or make collusive bids in an auction or procurement process. Groups of firms that enter into such agreements are commonly known as 'hard-core cartels'.
- 'Vertical' agreements between firms at different stages in the production and distribution chain that would limit competition. For example, agreements in which producers require distributors not to sell a competitor's product, not to sell outside a particular territory, or to maintain recommended retail prices.
- Actions taken by a dominant firm to drive out rivals or prevent entry by potential competitors. This may involve temporarily charging prices below costs ('predatory pricing'), or denying rivals access to crucial raw materials or essential facilities, such as a wire network (for telecommunications) that are owned by the dominant firm.

Apart from controlling such anti-competitive practices, many countries regulate corporate mergers and acquisitions (M&As) that might have an adverse effect on competition. In most countries, only hard-core cartels are held to be illegal per se (with some clearly-defined exceptions), while M&As and the other practices described above may be approved under a 'rule of reason' on a case-by-case basis if they provide efficiency gains that offset any adverse effect on competition. However, firms may enter into restrictive agreements informally, so effective enforcement of an antitrust law requires the creation of an agency with investigative powers. It also requires economic and statistical expertise to determine the effects of a particular practice on competition, including potential competition, in the relevant market.

The legal situation in India has recently undergone a major change. In 2009, the 1969 Monopolies and Restrictive Trade Practices (MRTP) Act was repealed, and sections of the 2002 Competition Act were brought into force. A brief review of the old Act is necessary in order to appreciate the strengths and weaknesses of the new one.

The MRTP Act, 1969–2009

The MRTP Act was passed in response to growing evidence of concentration of economic power in Indian industry. It originally required firms that were either 'large' (controlling, along with their 'interconnected undertakings', assets above a certain threshold) or 'dominant' (having assets above a lower threshold as well as a minimum market share) to register themselves with the central government, and to obtain its approval for substantial expansion, establishment of new undertakings, M&As, and appointment of their directors in other undertakings. The government could refer M&A applications to the MRTP Commission, but did not do so in most cases, and was not bound by the Commission's advice. All these sections of the Act were repealed by a 1991 amendment on the grounds that they had hindered industrial growth. A section giving the government the power, after a referral to the Commission, to divide undertakings or to order severance of interconnections between them was retained, but was never used.

Although the MRTP Act also had sections on 'monopolistic' and 'restrictive' trade practices that covered the standard anti-competitive practices described earlier, the limited investigative resources of the Commission impaired its ability to deal with them. Also, its powers were confined to issuing 'cease and desist' orders; trivial fines could only be imposed for non-compliance with these orders. Most of its orders under these sections pertained to vertical arrangements, and cartels were rarely brought to book. In many cases, the Commission entertained complaints of unfair or discriminatory pricing or delayed delivery, which were essentially contractual disputes that had no competition dimension. Overarching considerations of 'fairness' or 'the public interest', rather than a balancing of effects on competition and efficiency, were decisive in a large number of cases. From 1999 onwards, a series of Supreme Court orders overturned many of these decisions and directed the Commission to focus on the effects on competition. The Commission then dismissed many of the irrelevant complaints, but limited resources and a huge backlog of cases did not allow it to develop the skills to conduct competition analysis of more relevant cases.

The Act was amended in 1984 to include a new category of 'unfair trade practices' (UTPs), dealing with misleading advertising and prize schemes. The same amendment gave the Commission the power to issue injunctions and compensation orders. Despite the enactment of a Consumer Protection Act (COPRA) in 1986 with almost identical provisions, several advantages ensured that the MRTP Commission remained a favourite forum for such complaints. By the 1990s, the vast majority of cases pending before the Commission concerned such matters, further stretching its resources and weakening its ability to deal with anti-competitive practices that are usually the focus of antitrust law.

The Competition Act

In December 2002, Parliament passed a new Competition Act. However, its implementation was held up by a legal challenge to the constitutional validity of its provisions relating to the composition and selection procedure for the proposed Competition Commission of India (CCI). An amending Act was passed in 2007 to get around this problem, but it was not until May 2009 that the CCI was fully constituted and sections of the Act pertaining to anti-competitive agreements and abuse of dominance were brought into force. The MRTP Act was repealed in September 2009, and the MRTP Commission was abolished the following month.

Unlike the original MRTP Act, the new Act does not attempt to control the size or dominance of firms. Instead of monopolistic, restrictive, and unfair trade practices, it follows a modern classification in terms of anti-competitive agreements, abuse of dominance, and 'combinations' (M&As). It does not have any counterpart to the UTP section of the MRTP Act, which diverted the resources of the MRTP Commission. Its other novel features, from the perspective of economics, are: mandatory notification and review (by the CCI, not the government) of combinations for firms above specified asset or turnover thresholds, with the authority to prevent, undo, or modify those having an 'appreciable adverse effect on competition' (AAEC); long lists of economic factors that the CCI should have 'due regard to' in deciding a case; and provision for substantial monetary penalties, which can be reduced for any party to a cartel agreement who discloses vital information about its functioning. Unlike the MRTP Commission, the CCI can employ outside experts, take action against conduct by firms based abroad that might have an AAEC in India, and enter into cooperation agreements with foreign antitrust authorities. It has also been entrusted with competition advocacy, and may advise the government or any statutory body on matters that come under the Act.

However, concerns have been expressed about potential conflicts between the CCI and sectoral regulators which have been regulating competition in areas such as telecommunications, financial markets, and electricity. Concerns also arise regarding specific clauses in the Act that empower the government to issue binding policy directives to the Commission, or to supersede it entirely, thus threatening its autonomy. Several other clauses are ambiguous and may defeat the intention of protecting competition. For example, the Act allows the CCI to take into account the 'contribution to economic development' of a combination or an enterprise in a dominant position, and 'development' may be idiosyncratically interpreted to justify abuse of dominance or an anti-competitive merger. Further, instead of regarding hard-core cartels as illegal per se without investigating their effects, the Act only states that they are *presumed* to have an AAEC. But a presumption is legally rebuttable, so this may allow for an efficiency defence of cartels, which is contrary to international practice. On the other hand, the Act does not require an AAEC to establish abuse of dominance. This may invite contractual disputes and complaints about unfair or discriminatory pricing, of the kind that deluged the MRTP Commission. Most of the cases taken up by the CCI in the first two years of its functioning were in fact of this kind, and the CCI routinely dismissed them. Further comment on the enforcement of the Act is not possible, because as of April 2011 when this entry was revised, the CCI had not issued any final orders finding contraventions of the Act, and the sections of the Act on merger review (which have been strenuously opposed by business interests) were yet to be brought into force by the government.

ADITYA BHATTACHARJEA

References

Bhattacharjea, Aditya. 2008. 'India's New Competition Law: A Comparative Assessment', *Journal of Competition Law and Economics*, Oxford University Press, 4(3): 609–38. Reprinted in Eleanor Fox and Abel Mateus (eds), *Economic Development: The Critical Role of Competition Law and Politics*, Vol. II, Cheltenham, Edward Elgar, 2011.

———. 2010. 'Of Omissions and Commissions: India's Competition Laws', *Economic and Political Weekly*, 45(35): 31–7.

———. Forthcoming. 'India's New Antitrust Regime: The First Two Years of Enforcement', *The Antitrust Bulletin*.

Competition Commission of India website (for the text of the Competition Act and the CCI's implementing regulations, orders, organizational structure, advocacy, and other materials), available at www.cci.gov.in.

Mehta, Pradeep (ed.). 2005. *Towards a Functional Competition Policy for India*, New Delhi, Academic Foundation.

■ Aviation

Airlines

Until a decade ago, aviation in India was a government monopoly. The Directorate General of Civil Aviation controlled every aspect of flying. The Airports Authority of India ran the airports and still does. The result was that for a country its size, India has a relatively poorly developed aviation industry. By international standards, the airports are primitive and the overall fleet, public and private sectors combined, is around 150 aircraft, largely medium-haul jets with around 200 seats. In fact, until 1993, when private operators were allowed, there were just around 50 aircraft in the domestic fleet. The reason was that from the mid-1970s air travel was regarded as an elitist indulgence and, therefore, starved of investment. The business had been nationalized in 1953 and only a public-sector monopoly, Indian Airlines (IA) for the domestic sector, existed. The foreign routes were served by another public-sector monopoly, Air India, which even now has only around 30 aircraft. Neither received much attention by way of investment and by the mid-1980s, both had become typical public-sector firms—inefficient, corrupt, and overmanned. To make matters worse, IA was required to service politically convenient routes on the pretext that this served the cause of social justice, whereas in fact it only helped the ministers and members of Parliament please their rich constituents. The volume of traffic was not at all a factor in the decision to ply on several routes, called category C routes.

In recent years, however, all this has changed. The government monopoly was dismantled in 1993 when the Air Corporations Act was repealed. Aviation is now seen as a major infrastructure requirement of travel and trade. The Airports Authority of India Act has also been amended to permit the privatization of the airports of Delhi and Mumbai. However, while foreign investment in airlines is allowed, incomprehensibly, foreign airlines are not allowed to invest beyond 49 per cent in an airline firm registered in India. They are also not allowed to fly on domestic routes.

On balance, however, it would be correct to say that India has now solved the airlines, fleet, and competition problems. At present there are nearly a dozen airlines that operate the domestic routes, several of them being low-cost, no-frills airlines. As a result of this competition, fares have fallen drastically without—so far at least—any major adverse impact on airline profits. This is largely due to efficiency gains and growing demand. The fact that the railways, another government monopoly, are no longer competitive for the business traveller has helped as well. One noteworthy feature of the recent developments is that the new airlines are focusing on the short-haul markets, rather than the more crowded medium-haul ones. This is serving the same purpose as the old policy of Category C routes. Competition is achieving what the old monopoly could not, namely, better air connectivity. An important factor that has contributed to this development is the reduction of government control on fleet acquisition. Unlike in the old days, airlines are now free to import whatever type of aircraft they need.

Even so, certain problems remain to be addressed, mostly in respect of operating costs. Landing charges, ground overheads, and government taxation are still very high, as is the cost of finance. Taxes on aviation fuel are especially high. More than 50 per cent of the revenue collected on airline operations goes to the government. This has raised the break-even point to a load factor of over 60 per cent. The international norm for comparable fleets is 45 per cent. In short, the policy focus has now shifted from aviation to tax policy.

Where the international aspect is concerned, flights into and out of India are governed by the internationally mandated system of bilateral agreements between countries. These bilaterals limit the flights to and from two pairs of countries to designated national carriers. The number of flights and destinations within a country are negotiated periodically. The system favours bigger airlines that have larger fleets. As a result, Air India, throughout the 1990s, because its fleet size did not increase, was forced to not only give up existing gateways, but also concede its rights under the bilaterals to foreign airlines that increased their market share into and from India. This led to a demand from the private sector that it be allowed to take up the investment slack. This was recently permitted and it is expected that Indian carriers will now win back the market shares lost by Air India.

Airports

India has nearly a hundred airports. None of them is modern or large enough yet to accommodate the growing air traffic. But the airports in Delhi and Mumbai have been privatized and by 2010 will acquire additional capacity. To put it in perspective, Mumbai still handles less than a fourth of the air traffic that Heathrow does and Delhi just around 18 per cent. Delhi and Mumbai (and these are the best in the country) simply do not have the capacity to handle more traffic today. While terminal 1B at Delhi has the capacity to handle only 800 passengers an hour, it handles over 2000 now. Delhi also has additional problems caused by security needs after the attack on Parliament in December 2001. Planes have to hold themselves at least 25 nautical miles away if they do not get landing permission. Overall, while the international norm for aircraft handling is 50–60 per hour, even if everything goes smoothly Delhi and Mumbai will not be able to handle more than 35 until the fresh capacity is added. They currently handle around 30 per hour. A second runway could be a solution but Mumbai does not have the space for it. The conservative approach of the air traffic controllers is also a problem because they have so far (June 2007) refused to accept a time separation of less than four minutes between aircraft that land or take off. This has had the effect of reducing runway capacity.

No wonder that the International Air Transport Association's (IATA) last airport survey of 57 big international airports ranked Mumbai and Delhi as 56th and 57th, respectively. China has seven airports in the world's top 150 while India has just two. The situation is especially bad at the metros of Mumbai and Delhi. However, the good news is that the idea that airports need not be a state monopoly has caught on and several states are now starting to privatize the smaller, feeder airports. It is only a matter of time before the major non-metro airports are also privatized.

Airports are expected to remain as they are for the next few years. A National Policy on Airports was enunciated in 2002, which said that 'no greenfield airport will normally be allowed within an aerial distance of 150 kilometres of an existing airport'. The expert committee has endorsed this. It is expected that by the end of 2007, aircraft may have to circle for as much as 45 minutes at peak hours and about half that at off-peak hours because apron space and gates will continue to remain inadequate in spite of the additions to capacity in all major airports. A part of the problem is the poor management of existing facilities, as they are operated by the public-sector Airports Authority of India. Its strong unions have been preventing modernization.

T.C.A. SRINIVASA RAGHAVAN

B

Balance of Payments

This entry describes the position of balance of payments (BOP) in India starting from the second oil shock of 1979 to the present. It is divided into two parts: before and after the BOP crisis of 1990–1.

BOP Crisis

A rise in the gross domestic product (GDP) growth rate in the 1980s (relative to the 1970s) was accompanied by higher fiscal deficits, rising current account deficits, and larger external debt. The worsening fiscal situation, in the presence of inadequate flexibility of the exchange rate, led to a rising current account deficit. With foreign direct investment (FDI) and foreign portfolio inflows restricted, the higher current account deficit translated into rising levels of external debt. The low productivity of government expenditure contributed to external vulnerability by lowering the rate of return on the borrowed funds. The declining trend in concessional aid and the consequential recourse to private sources of external borrowing led to rise in the interest costs. The cost of servicing external debt was, therefore, rising faster than the return on its use.

As the perceived risk in international lending traditionally rises with outstanding external debt, this along with the increasing private sourcing of external borrowing made capital flows vulnerable and open to politically related perceptions. The proportion of long-term public and publicly guaranteed external debt sourced from private creditors rose sharply from 9.1 per cent of total long-term debt in 1980 to 31.2 per cent in 1990. From the user side, private non-guaranteed long-term debt more than doubled from 10.4 per cent of GDP in 1980 to 24.2 per cent of GDP in 1990. A substantial part of this debt was channelled to the central government, public-sector units, and public financial institutions during the 1980s. Thus, if the fixity of the exchange rate contributed to excessive external borrowing, the main borrowers so affected were the central government and public institutions.

There is evidence of growing overvaluation of the exchange rate in the late 1980s. During 1990–1, the BOP gap opened significantly and the need for devaluation was quite clear. The overvaluation manifested itself through the invisibles account and the capital account. The highly controlled external payments regime and the public banking oligopoly meant that the transaction costs of remitting money through the official markets were high. The ban on import of gold meant that the large domestic demand for gold could only be met through gold smuggling into India financed by underground ('*hawala*') markets for foreign exchange. Increased overvaluation of the exchange rate made the incentive for diversion greater and slowed the flow of remittances (private transfers) and service earnings through the official foreign-exchange market.

An unusual combination of external and domestic political developments between end 1989 and early 1991 accentuated all these vulnerabilities to produce the BOP crisis in India. This BOP crisis was more akin to the earlier (1980s) debt crises in Latin America than the subsequent Asian crisis as it had its origins in government finances and functioning rather than in the private sector.

The crisis cannot be attributed to trade imbalances as many left-oriented economists did at that time. Though imports increased by 2.3 per cent of GDP (to 7.9 per cent of GDP), about one-third of this increase was due to the second oil shock (1979) which doubled the value (US$) of oil imports. Non-oil, non-customs imports that were the focus of import liberalization during the 1980s contributed about half the total increase in the import–GDP ratio. As exports increased by only 0.3 percentage point of GDP, the trade deficit increased from an average of 1.2 per cent of GDP in the 1970s to an average of 3.2 per cent of GDP in the 1980s. The current account deficit, therefore, rose sharply from an average of 0.1 per cent of GDP during the 1970s to an average of 1.8 per cent of GDP during the 1980s.

Both the sharp rise in trade deficit in the early 1980s and the declining trend thereafter were largely due to the second oil shock in 1979. The import–GDP ratio fell from an average of 8.2 per cent in the first half to 7.7 per cent during the second half of the 1980s, even though non-oil imports increased by 0.6 per cent of GDP between the two periods. The trade deficit, therefore, declined from 3.5 per cent of GDP in the first half of the 1980s to an average of 3 per cent of GDP in the second half.

The current account deficit, which shot up to 1.5 per cent of GDP during 1980–4, increased further to 2.1 per cent of GDP during 1985–9, because of a shrinking surplus on the invisibles account, which followed an inverted U pattern during the 1980s. After rising from 1.1 per cent of GDP in the 1970s to an average of 2 per cent of GDP in 1980–4, it fell to an average of 0.8 per cent of GDP during 1985–9. Underlying the long-term deterioration in the invisibles balance were all three major sub-components. The non-factor service surplus increased from an average of 0.3 per cent of GDP in the 1970s to 0.6 per cent of GDP during 1980–4 and then declined again to 0.3 per cent of GDP during 1985–9. Similarly, private transfers rose from 0.6 per cent of GDP to 1.3 per cent of GDP and then declined to 0.9 per cent of GDP over the same periods. Finally, income deficit went from an average of 0.3 per cent of GDP (1970s) to 0.1 per cent of GDP (1980–4) and then to 0.6 per cent of GDP (1985–9). Thus in a medium-term perspective the invisibles balance was a much more significant element in the BOP crisis of 1990–1 than the trade deficit.

The declining invisibles surplus was driven by the income deficit, which was rising up to the crisis year. A fall in concessional (International Development Association [IDA]) lending from the multilateral development banks led to rising average interest rates, and this coupled with a rising debt–GDP ratio led to rising interest payments.

BOP Post-reform

The comprehensive import control (quantitative restriction [QR]) regime was gradually dismantled, starting with capital and intermediate goods and moving, after a period of slowdown, to consumer goods. Tariff rates were brought down over a decade from a peak rate of about 300 per cent to a peak rate of 35 per cent. The problem of overdependence on debt and the high proportion of short-term debt was addressed by liberalizing FDI and foreign equity inflows while keeping a very tight lid on short-term debt obligations and maintaining the control regime for external commercial borrowing. A comprehensive reform of the exchange control regime was undertaken based on thorough intellectual and administrative preparation. The illegal foreign exchange market and its link with smuggling and invisibles transactions were addressed by a comprehensive liberalization of gold imports.

The macroeconomic response to the BOP crisis as it existed at the start of 1991–2 was the classic textbook one of expenditure compression through a sharp fiscal correction and expenditure switching through devaluation. The fiscal deficit of the Centre was reduced from 7.8 per cent of GDP in 1990–1 to 5.6 per cent of GDP in 1991–2. The nominal effective exchange rate (NEER) was depreciated by 18 per cent in 1991, resulting in a real effective depreciation of 12.4 per cent. The fiscal squeeze and the real depreciation reduced the current account deficit by 1.03 per cent of GDP and 0.97 per cent of GDP, respectively. The total effect of these two measures was, therefore, to reduce the current account deficit by 2 per cent of GDP out of the total actual decline of 2.8 per cent of GDP. The decline of 1.6 percentage points in the private investment rate contributed about 0.5 per cent to the reduction. The remaining decline of 0.3 per cent of GDP can perhaps be attributed to the overall increase in private confidence arising from the major economic reforms initiated in 1991–2.

The trade policy of April 1992 freed imports of almost all intermediate and capital goods. Only 71 items remained restricted/licensed (3 banned, 7 canalized), most of which were either dual-use goods like office equipment or consumer goods. After this initial major step, further liberalization was slow, because the potential beneficiaries were fragmented and unorganized while the losers were few and organized. It was only the loss of the World Trade Organization (WTO) case against India that finally led to the complete elimination of QRs on consumer goods, previously justified on BOP grounds, on 1 April 2000.

The decontrol of FDI took the form of an 'automatic route'. FDI with up to 51 per cent (from 40 per cent) foreign equity was freed for a list of 34 'priority' (intermediate and capital goods) industries and international trading companies (dividend-balancing condition remained). The 51 per cent level was chosen as this allowed foreign companies to amalgamate profits and losses from such a company into those of the parent company for tax purposes. Technology import was also put under the automatic route subject to conditions on royalty (< 5 per cent domestic, < 8 per cent export) and lump-sum payment (< Rs 1 crore). Any FDI or technology import outside these limits had to be approved by a newly created Foreign Investment Promotion Board (FIPB).

India was among the early openers of the equity market to foreign portfolio investment, with direct portfolio investment by foreign institutional investors (FIIs) allowed in 1992–3. At this time the degree of openness was greater than in almost all East and Southeast Asian emerging economies. Only Mexico started a country fund for foreign equity investment about six years prior to India, while the South Korean fund was set up only one year before India's. Both FDI and portfolio flows increased rapidly through the mid-1990s.

India introduced a 'dual exchange rate' system to ease the transition from a heavily controlled trade regime to a free market system encompassing both trade and payments. According to the 'Liberalized Exchange Rate Management System', exporters and remittances would surrender 40 per cent of exchange at the official rate (which was left unchanged at Rs 25.89 per US$), while the rest would be converted at the free-market rates. This effectively meant that export proceeds were taxed at 0.4 times the difference between the market and official exchange rates. Hundred per cent export-oriented units and export-processing zones could sell the entire amount at market rate and were thus not taxed in this way. All capital account transactions (except International Monetary Fund [IMF] multilateral flow against rupee expenditure) would also be at the market rate. Exporters could retain up to 15 per cent of earning in a foreign currency account with an authorized bank. The exchange surrendered at the official rate was to be used by the government for official transactions, thus effectively subsidizing these uses by the difference between the market and official rates. This represented a cross tax-subsidy scheme in which exporters subsidized certain types of government-related imports. This minimized the direct fiscal impact reducing the risk to macroeconomic balance.

The dual exchange rate mechanism was so successful that the official channel was abolished in 1993–4 leaving only a single market channel. On integration in February 1993, the exchange rate depreciated to Rs 32.43 per US$, but appreciated thereafter. Till August 1995 it remained below the peak reached in February 1993. Only in September 1995 did it depreciate to Rs 33.58 per US$. As the Reserve Bank of India (RBI) retains the right to intervene (and does intervene) to even out excessive volatility in the exchange rate, the system is classified as a 'managed float'.

Current account liberalization was initiated with an easing of rules for foreign exchange allocation to business travellers. This was followed in 1994 with indicative limits for travel, etc., on the basis of which foreign exchange could be bought by citizens directly from authorized foreign exchange dealers. In August 1994 India accepted the IMF Article VIII and thus the rupee officially became convertible on the current account.

A new Foreign Exchange Act was introduced in 1999–2000, based on a conceptual approach that current account convertibility must be codified in the new law and capital controls minimized and based on a regulatory rather than control approach.

Capital-flow liberalization led to an unprecedented surge in equity inflows between October 1993 and November 1994. Based on analysis and internal discussions, India developed a macro-management strategy for this 'Dutch Disease' problem that was quite different from the standard one proposed by the IMF. Though other countries in other time periods have undoubtedly used variants of the same policy, India's experience in this regard may also have useful lessons for others.

The invisibles account improved significantly in the post-crisis period, with inflows rising to 2.0 per cent of GDP compared to 1.4 per cent of GDP in the 1980s. Thus these invisible flows are back to the high levels seen during 1980–4. Part of the improvement was due to the reform of gold policy, which led to a big jump in remittances through official channels. Private transfers, which had averaged 1.1 per cent of GDP in the pre-crisis period, more than doubled to 2.5 per cent of GDP in the post-crisis period. The investment and other income outflows after rising to a peak of 1.4 per cent of GDP in 1991–2 and 1992–3 declined progressively to 0.8 per cent of GDP by 2000–1. In the earlier years external debt was the driving factor while in the latter years FDI and portfolio flows have also started playing a role.

Contrary to popular perception non-factor services, which include software exports, have not played a role in this improvement. This is primarily because software exports have offset declines in other non-factor services. The sharp increase in software exports is reflected in miscellaneous receipts (not net) from 0.6 per cent of GDP in the 1980s and in 1990–4 to 1.3 per cent of GDP during 1995–9.

As a result of the strengthening of the invisibles account, the current account deficit averaged 1.1 per cent of GDP in the post-crisis period. There is no evidence of deterioration in the current account over the decade, with the current account deficit being marginally lower (1.2 per cent) during 1995–9 compared to 1990–4 (1.3 per cent). The current account deficit is lower than the pre-crisis average of 1.8 per cent of GDP and the 1.5 per cent average of 1980–4. The position was even better (0.5 per cent) in 2000–1. The external reforms have, therefore, been successful in putting the current account balance on a sustainable path.

The capital account of the BOP has also shown corresponding improvement. Capital inflows (excluding 'other capital') increased from an average of 1.6 per cent of GDP in the pre-crisis decade to an average of 2.2 per cent of GDP in the post-crisis period. Foreign investment inflows averaged 1.1 per cent of GDP in the post-crisis period (nil earlier). The contribution of external assistance and rupee debt declined by 0.2 per cent of GDP (each), while that of external commercial borrowing increased by 0.1 per cent of GDP. Thus the objective of raising the equity–debt ratio of external liabilities was achieved.

The total fiscal deficit during the five years to 2001–2 is comparable to the fiscal deficit in the first half of the 1980s, while the current account deficit has declined dramatically. The difference in impact is due to the external sector (including the managed floating exchange rate) and other reforms that have improved the flexibility of the economy. They have reduced the external spillover effect of the fiscal deficit on the current account deficit as well as its effect on inflation (more open economy). The high fiscal deficit may in future, however, act as a drag on economic growth. Regression equations using a slope dummy for the post-crisis period suggest that the impact of the central fiscal deficit on the current account is a fraction of what it was till 1991–2.

Contrary to the perception of many outside observers, the Indian economy has become more open relative to other emerging economies. India's ranking with respect to trade, FDI, and portfolio flows has improved noticeably over the 1980s. In the case of tariffs, India was a complete outlier and only in 2005–6 is the peak non-agricultural tariff rate of 15 per cent beginning to move us up in the rankings. India's economy is, however, still relatively closed compared to its 'peer competitors' and there is a long way to go to attain a ranking in trade and FDI that is commensurate with the size of the economy. Further reduction of tariff protection and liberalization of capital flows will enhance the efficiency of the Indian economy and, along with reform of domestic policies, will stimulate investment and growth.

External-sector reforms have been the most successful of all the reforms that were undertaken in the 1990s, proving that a well-regulated market-based foreign trade and payments system would be more efficient and equally stable. Both the trade and invisibles accounts are now much more resilient than they were in the 1980s. Capital inflows are now much more diversified and, therefore, much less risky for the country. The strength of the external account rests substantially on the flexibility of the 'managed float' in responding to changes in demand–supply conditions in the exchange market.

The primary lesson of the 1990s is that liberalization of the current and capital accounts increases the flexibility and resilience of the BOP. This applies to trade, invisibles, equity capital, medium- and long-term debt flows, and the exchange market. A corollary lesson is that even though the balance of trade may not be the cause of BOP problems (excess demand for foreign currency), an exchange rate depreciation by improving the balance of trade and the invisibles account can help minimize the probability of a crisis. The analysis here confirmed that in India the exchange rate is a powerful instrument of adjustment in the current account deficit. It also confirms that equity outflows are very unlikely to be a major cause of BOP problems (unlike short-term debt).

ARVIND VIRMANI

References

Virmani, Arvind. 1991. 'Demand and Supply Factors in India's Trade', *Economic and Political Weekly*, 9 February, 26(6): 309–14.

———. 1992a. 'Trends in Current Account Deficit and the Balance of Trade: Separating Facts from Prejudices', *Journal of Foreign Exchange and International Finance*, April–June, 6(1): 72–8.

———. 1992b. 'Partial Convertibility of the Rupee (PCR) Implications for Exporters', *RBI Bulletin*, August, pp. 1300–2.

———. 2001. 'India's 1990–91 Crisis: Reforms, Myths and Paradoxes', Planning Commission Working Paper No. 4/2001-PC, December, available at http://www.planningcommission.nic.in/reports/wrkpapers/wp_cris9091.pdf.

———. 2003. 'India's External Reforms: Modest Globalisation Significant Gains', *Economic and Political Weekly*, 9–15 August, 37(32): 3373–90.

Banking*

Introduction

The banking structure that India inherited at the time of Independence suffered from three major drawbacks: (i) interlocking of directorship of industry houses and banks, (ii) paucity of credit to socially and economically important sectors of the economy, and (iii) low capitalization. The numerous problems arising in the wake of these drawbacks provided the economic rationale for the momentous decision to nationalize 14 private banks in 1969, as well as for the subsequent nationalization of six more banks in 1980. The post-nationalization phase was characterized by a strategy of massive expansion of the banking network coupled with stipulations on sectoral lending (see, for instance, Burgess and Pande 2005 for the beneficial effects of social banking on poverty reduction). Even today, when the euphoria over nationalization has given way to considerable scepticism, it cannot be denied that the liberal branch licensing norms, coupled with a system of directed credit stipulations, made a significant dent on rural and (to some extent) urban poverty and mitigated the dependence of the socially and economically disadvantaged groups on indigenous moneylenders. Additionally, many would agree that the system did contribute to rapid growth by providing timely and concessional credit to several industrial sectors.

However, the strict regulation over banks' lending, combined with extensive regulation of interest rates across the entire maturity spectrum, also paved the way for the banking sector to be increasingly cast in the role of a 'handmaiden' to government policies. The high cash reserve ratios (CRRs) and statutory liquidity ratios (SLRs), though ostensibly serving the purposes of credit regulation, financial stability, and inflation control, adversely impacted the profitability of banks and represented a substantial (about 63.5 per cent) pre-emption of bank resources. Additionally, the administered interest structure, assumed over time, an extremely complex character, with rates being distinguished according to bank size, maturity profile, and economic conditions, which permitted only a limited role for market forces in the pricing and allocation of credit. It was inevitable that such a highly regulated banking system should get riddled with administrative inefficiencies and red tape. The constellation of economic features resulting from these developments is usually subsumed under the rubric of 'financial repression'.

A process of liberalization of the economy was initiated in India in 1991–2, aimed at raising the allocative efficiency of available savings, improving the return on investments, and promoting accelerated and equitable growth of the real sector. Towards this end, a multi-pronged reform strategy was initiated encompassing all areas of economic activity. In the financial sector specifically, the thrust of the reforms was to promote a diversified, efficient, and competitive financial system. While these reforms were underway, the world economy also witnessed significant changes, coinciding with the movement towards global integration of financial services.

Before turning to an appraisal of banking reforms in India, it may be helpful to have a *helicopter overview* of the financial intermediaries in India, in general, and of the Indian banking sector, in particular. Conventionally, the banking sector is classified into two broad categories: commercial banks and cooperative banks. The various sub-components of these two categories, together with two broad indicators of their relative significance (that is, number of institutions and asset size), are presented in Table 1.[1] The exclusive focus of this entry is on the commercial banking system which currently accounts for over 75 per cent of the assets of the banking sector.

Table 1 Financial Intermediaries in India: Number of Institutions and Aggregate Assets

(as on March 2007)

Institution	Number of institutions	Per cent to total asset
1. Commercial banks (a + b)	182	75.2
(a) Scheduled commercial banks (excluding RRBs)	82	72.9
Public sector banks	28	51.4
Private-sector banks	25	15.7
Foreign banks	29	5.9
(b) Regional rural banks	96	2.2
(a) Local area banks		0.0
2. Cooperative banks (a + b)	1,09,310	12.8
(a) Rural cooperative banks	1,07,497	3.4
(b) Urban cooperative banks	1,813	9.5
3. Non-banking financial institutions	591	12.0

Source: Reserve Bank of India (2008).

*The views expressed in this entry are strictly personal.

[1]Cooperative banks belong to different genres with different institutional set-ups and governance characteristics, and hence are not explicitly dealt with in the analysis.

Banking Reforms: Some General Considerations

The first phase of financial sector reforms in India was guided by the recommendations of the Committee on the Financial System (Chairman: M. Narasimham). Several features of the reform process deserve mention (Reddy 2004). First, financial sector reforms were undertaken early in the economic reform cycle. Second, reforms in the financial sector were initiated autonomously in a well-structured, sequenced, and phased manner and were not induced by a crisis, although the balance-of-payments problems in 1991 did provide the wake-up call. Third, a consultative approach towards policy formulation was adopted, which not only enabled benchmarking the financial services against international best standards in a transparent manner, but also provided useful lead time to market players for smooth adjustment to regulatory changes. Importantly, unlike the 'stop-go' approach adopted in several Latin American and Asian economies, the Indian approach to financial sector reforms has been marked by 'gradualism' so as to ensure a gradual, non-disruptive, and transparent approach to the process (Ahluwalia 2002).

It seems useful to classify the liberalization process of Indian banking as the confluence of three distinct but mutually reinforcing sets of factors: (i) liberalization imperatives, (ii) stimuli from domestic forces, and (iii) stimuli from external forces. This compartmentalization is, however, not watertight and, more often than not, might reflect overlapping considerations. The details of banking reforms in India are detailed in Box 1.

Box 1 Banking Reforms in India

Liberalization Imperatives

- Sharp reduction in CRR and SLR.
- Dismantling of administered interest rates with a few exceptions (for example, interest rates on savings deposits).
- Auction-based pricing for government securities.
- Measures to strengthen risk management through recognition of different components of risk, assignment of risk-weights to various asset classes, norms on connected lending, risk concentration, application of marked-to-market principle for investment portfolios, and limits on deployment of funds in sensitive activities.

Stimuli from Domestic Forces

- Granting of operational autonomy and broad-basing ownership in public sector banks by allowing them to raise capital up to 49 per cent of equity.
- Enhanced transparency and disclosure norms to facilitate market discipline.
- Introduction of pure inter-bank call money market, auction-based repos/reverse repos for short-term liquidity management, and facilitation of an improved payments and settlement mechanism.
- Focused efforts towards financial inclusion and improvement of the credit delivery mechanism.

Stimuli from External Forces

- Introduction of norms on risk-based capital standards (broadly in line with Basel I and later Basel II accords), accounting, income recognition, asset classification, provisioning, and exposure norms.
- Transparent norms for entry of new private sector, liberalized entry for foreign banks and insurance companies, permission for foreign investment through foreign direct investment/portfolio investment, and permission to banks to diversify product portfolios and business activities.
- Settling up of Lok Adalats (people's courts), debt recovery tribunals, asset reconstruction companies, settlement advisory committees, corporate debt restructuring mechanisms, and so on, for quicker recovery/restructuring of loans. Promulgation of Securitization and Reconstruction of Financial Assets and Enforcement of Securities Interest (SARFAESI) Act and its subsequent amendment to ensure creditor rights.
- Introduction of the CAMELS supervisory rating system, move towards risk-based supervision, consolidated supervision of financial conglomerates, strengthening off-site surveillance through technology-driven control returns, and so on.

- Strengthening corporate governance, enhanced 'due diligence' on important shareholders, 'fit and proper' tests for directors, etc.
- Institution of Credit Information Bureau for information sharing on defaulters as also other borrowers.
- Establishing the Clearing Corporation of India Limited to act as a central counter party for facilitating payments and a settlement system relating to fixed income securities and money market instruments.
- Setting up of INFINET as the communication backbone for the financial sector, introduction of the Negotiated Dealing System for screen-based trading in government securities and the Real Time Gross Settlement System.

Source: Mohan (2005); Reserve Bank of India (2008).

The net impact of these policy changes is gradually getting reflected in the financial performance of banks. That banks have been able to cope successfully with the new liberalized environment is evident from the marked improvement in their standard performance indicators, as reflected in Table 2.

Spurred by the gradual tightening of prudential norms over the years (reflecting an increasing convergence towards international best practices as detailed in Basel II), there has been considerable improvement in two other traditional areas of concern. The overall capital adequacy ratio of commercial banks, which was 10.40 per cent in 1996–7 trended upwards to cross 13 per cent in 2009–10. Likewise, improved recovery management and better risk assessment resulted in a steady decline in the non-performing loans of banks.

Emerging Issues

Most analysts foretell a fundamental structural transformation for the Indian banking industry over the coming years. The reasons for such a prognosis are manifold but could be encapsulated in four basic set of factors: (i) liberalization of trade in financial services under WTO auspices, (ii) autonomous diffusion of information technology, (iii) international harmonization of financial standards involving improved levels of transparency and disclosure standards, and (iv) greater emphasis on governance through shareholder value creation. These four basic factors, acting singly and in combination, are the major drivers of the various changes that are being envisaged for the Indian banking sector in the future. We briefly survey some of these emerging issues and also draw attention to the relatively seamless adjustment of the Indian financial system to the recent global crisis.

Table 2 Performance Indicators of Indian Commercial Banks

(as % of total assets)

Bank group	1980–91	1992–6	1997–2001	2001–2	2002–3	2003–4	2006–7
Operating expense	2.53	2.74	2.64	2.19	2.24	2.20	1.84
Spread	1.90	2.94	2.87	2.57	2.77	2.86	2.60
Net profit	0.15	-0.16	0.61	0.75	1.01	1.13	0.84

Source: Reserve Bank of India (2008).

Consolidation

The liberalization under way has as yet not impinged significantly on the structure of the Indian banking system. The consolidation process witnessed within the industry in recent years has primarily been confined to a few mergers in the private sector (often a response to localized bank failures). However, the rapid growth in global trade and investment flows has opened up avenues for cross-border financing of economic activities, propelling the inducement for cross-border mergers of banks, to avail of mutual location and business-specific complementarities. Technology developments have facilitated the integration of global transactions and in the process introduced substantial economies of scale. Recognizing the imperatives of consolidation, efforts have been initiated by the government and RBI to iron out the various legal impediments inherent in the process.

Competition and FDI in the Banking Sector

The post-liberalization phase has also seen the emergence of newer competitive forces in the largely public sector dominated Indian banking scenario. So far these forces have been confined to a highly modernized and efficient domestic private banking, but in the wake of India's commitment to the GATS section of WTO on liberalization of financial services, foreign banks are very likely to exhibit a dramatic growth in their presence in India (going by the experience of other emerging market economies, which had relaxed restrictions on foreign banking presence in the early 1990s).

A related issue bears on the rules governing FDI in Indian banks, which have also been considerably liberalized in the last few years. Until recently, minority foreign participation by foreign banking companies as technical collaborators or co-promoters, through the FIPB route in private-sector Indian banks was restricted to 20 per cent. The limit was raised to 49 per cent in May 2001 (and subsequently to 74 per cent in 2004). Foreign banks having branch presence in India are also eligible for FDI in private-sector banks subject to an overall cap of 49 per cent. One of the major demands of foreign investors has been the removal of the 10 per cent cap on their voting rights in the management of banks and available indications point to the amendment of this limitation in the near future.

However, several concerns attend the issue of liberalizing the entry norms for foreign banks (and FDI in the banking sector). First, in view of the well-known tendency of foreign banks to 'cherry-pick' the loans market, a large foreign presence could leave domestic banks saddled with less creditworthy customers, increasing the overall risk of domestic bank portfolios. Second, the supervision of the more sophisticated activities of foreign banks and monitoring of new products usually introduced by them entails a continuous challenge for regulatory authorities. Another important supervisory issue is whether depositors in foreign banks would be entitled to receive the same degree of protection as depositors in domestic banks and whether the central bank of the host country should extend the 'lender of last resort' umbrella to foreign banks facing illiquidity crises. There is also the possible threat of excessive concentration, since foreign subsidiaries backed by their parent corporations (often 'banking behemoths') could exert substantive market power and extract higher interest margins in the domestic market. Finally, it should be highlighted that the admission of foreign subsidiaries should be accompanied by the removal of all discriminatory practices vis-à-vis domestic banks.[2]

Credit Delivery

It is being increasingly recognized in recent years that large segments of the rural population face 'financial exclusion' from the formal banking sector, and continue their traditional dependence on the informal sector. Two areas in particular have been of concern to policymakers: priority sector lending and timely flow of credit to the needy and deserving.

With regard to the first, the definition of priority sector has been gradually enlarged, interest rates on priority sector lending left to market forces (except for a cap on small loans), and alternativee avenues of investment permitted, thus making priority lending far more flexible than before, in line with the major recommendations of the Advisory Committee on Flow of Credit to Agriculture and Related Activities from the Banking System (Chairman: V.S. Vyas; see Reserve Bank of India 2004).

With regard to the issue of credit delivery, the 'lending inertia' on the part of a mid-sized commercial bank has been well-documented in an influential study (Banerjee et al. 2004). In recognition of this fact, recent policies have placed explicit emphasis on streamlining credit delivery through a gamut of measures, including, inter alia, (i) widening the scope of infrastructure lending, (ii) revamping the rural credit delivery system by envisaged restructuring of the rural banking segment, (iii) widening the scope of priority sector lending, (iv) introduction of innovative instruments on the lines of *kisan* credit cards buttressed with various value-added features, and (v) according all possible encouragement for forging appropriate public–private partnerships in the field of micro-finance activities.[3]

Finally, there is the long-felt imperative to streamline and coordinate the activities of the four major institutions involved in the rural credit structure: (i) commercial banks, (ii) a three-tier federal cooperative banking system (with the state cooperative banks at the state level, district cooperative central banks at the district level, and the primary agricultural credit societies at the village level), (iii) the state cooperative agriculture and rural development banks with primary cooperative agriculture and rural development banks affiliated to them, and finally (iv) regional rural banks (RRBs). Action on this front by the authorities is presently underway.

Corporate Governance

The issue of corporate governance has come to the fore in the current liberalized environment where banks are expected to function as commercial entities with explicit emphasis on shareholder value creation (Caprio and Levine 2002). The commercial character of banks is getting increasing emphasis with more and more banks

[2]Some of the current discriminatory practices operate against foreign banks (for example, ban on accepting public sector company deposits, and higher tax rates), others operate in their favour (lower priority sector lending requirements and exemption from rural branching stipulation).

[3]Self-help groups (SHGs) formed by non-governmental organizations and financed by banks represent an important pillar of this development process.

getting listed on the stock exchange, and the proposed lowering of government stock holdings in banks to a minimum of 33 per cent (first envisaged in the Union Budget 2000–1) would reinforce this character apart from providing bank boards with greater flexibility. The quality of corporate governance in banks in the emerging scenario, would be crucially guided by their ability to find suitable, qualified, and independent professionals to serve on their boards.

Risk Management

In the highly regulated and protected financial system of the pre-reform era, risk management was a secondary issue for the public sector dominated banking system. The picture has changed drastically with the deregulation and liberalization of the financial system.

So far as 'credit risk' is concerned, the envisaged introduction of 'core banking' solutions would enable banks to segregate credit sourcing (front office) and appraisal (back office) functions, which can, over time, build up expertise and monitor credit migrations on a bank-wide basis, a key factor behind the application of the Basel II approach (Nachane et al. 2005). The use of dynamic credit scoring models coupled with the full-fledged operationalization of the credit bureau would enable banks to switch from traditional proprietary models to newer methods of credit evaluation to reflect repayment and recovery experiences across a spectrum of asset classes and spatial locations.

The recent reversal of the soft interest rate regime has also raised concerns about the interest rate risks in banks' portfolio, in view of their large holdings of government securities. It appears very likely that banks will be exposed to increasing market risk on their debt investment portfolios. Additionally, in view of the increased regulatory capital allocation for market risk in the future, most banks would need to bolster their capital position. All these considerations underline the fact that banks need to put in place appropriate risk management processes (such as value-at-risk models) to not only identify the risks, but also to effectively measure, monitor, and manage them.

Technology and Human Resources

The success of Indian banks in capitalizing on future opportunities will critically depend on how well they are able to harness emerging trends in global technology to their advantage. The increasing sophistication, flexibility, and complexity of products and services makes the effective use of technology critical for managing the risks associated with the banking business. Additionally, technology becomes the key factor in servicing almost all customer segments. Of course the rate of technology adoption is crucially constrained by the availability of trained personnel, so that investment in human resources by banks may be viewed as largely complementary to investment in technology.

Impact of the Financial Crisis on the Banking Sector

The fact that the Indian banking system has emerged largely unscathed from the recent global crisis has attracted a certain amount of attention (and qualified praise) from international academic and policymaking circles. The Indian banking system had no direct exposure to the toxic financial assets and had non-significant exposure to off-balance sheet activities or securitized assets. While direct impact on account of *direct exposure* to the sub-prime market was almost non-existent, a few banks did suffer some losses on account of the mark-to-market losses due to the widening of the credit spreads arising from the sub-prime episode on term liquidity in the market. While the banking sector, by and large, remained unaffected, some segments of the financial market bore the brunt, reflecting increasing globalization of the Indian economy via trade, investment, and financial channels (Subbarao 2009).

Concluding Remarks

The Indian financial system has exhibited a fair degree of resilience in responding to structural adjustments; nevertheless, some tendency towards slippages has also been evident with even slight relaxations of the regulatory leash. A 'bang-bang' approach to financial sector liberalization, in spite of being advocated by influential sections of domestic and global opinion could well prove counter-productive and impose irreversible costs on the Indian system. As in other areas of reforms, 'gradualism' seems to be the ideal prescription. In retrospect, thus, it seems that the resilience of the Indian banking sector stood the stress test of the tail risks arising out of the global financial crisis.

D.M. NACHANE, SAIBAL GHOSH, AND PARTHA RAY

References

Ahluwalia, M.S. 2002. 'Economic Reforms in India Since 1991: Has Gradualism Worked?', *Journal of Economic Perspectives*, 16: 67–88.

Banerjee, A., S. Cole, and E. Duflo. 2004. 'Banking Reform in India', *Brookings Papers on Economic Activity, Economic Studies Program*, The Brookings Institution, 1(1): 277–332.

Burgess, Robin and Rohini Pande. 2005. 'Can Rural Banks Reduce Poverty? Evidence from the Indian Social Banking Experiment', *American Economic Review*, 95(3): 780–95.

Caprio, G. and R. Levine. 2002. 'Corporate Governance in Banks: Concepts and International Observations', paper presented at the Global Corporate Governance Research Forum, April.

Mohan, R. 2005. 'Financial Sector Reforms in India: Policies and Performance Analysis', *Economic and Political Weekly*, XL(12): 1106–21.

Nachane, D.M., P. Ray, and S. Ghosh. 2005. 'The New Basel Capital Accord: Rationale, Design and Tentative Implications for India', in K. Parikh and R. Radhakrishna (eds), *India Development Report 2004–05*, New Delhi, Oxford University Press, pp. 171–90.

Reddy, Y.V. 2004. 'Monetary and Financial Sector Reforms in India: A Practitioner's Perspectives', in Kaushik Basu (ed.), *India's Emerging Economy*, Cambridge, Massachusetts, MIT Press.

Reserve Bank of India. 2008. *Report on Currency and Finance (2003–08)*, Vol. IV (Banking Sector in India: Emerging Issues and Challenges), Mumbai, Reserve Bank of India.

Subbarao, Duvvuri. 2009. 'Impact of the Global Financial Crisis on India—Collateral Damage and Response', speech at the symposium on 'The Global Economic Crisis and Challenges for the Asian Economy in a Changing World', organized by the Institute for International Monetary Affairs, Tokyo, 18 February.

Krishna Bharadwaj

Krishna Bharadwaj was born in 1935 in a lower middle class family in Karwar, a small town in the Konkan, the youngest of six children. Her father was a schoolteacher who inculcated in the children a commitment to simplicity, dedication, and justice. The political ambience in the family was one of anti-colonial nationalism, support for the progressive social reform movement, and a loose commitment to socialism derived from exposure to the activities of the Socialist Party which was quite strong in the Konkan region. After early education in Belgaum where the family had moved when Krishna was two years old, she joined Bombay University for an Honours degree in economics. A brilliant student, she won numerous academic laurels and went on to do research work in economics at the same university, the first woman ever to have done so. After a stint of postdoctoral work at the MIT (Massachusetts Institute of Technology) in the company of her husband Ranganath Bharadwaj, she returned to join the faculty of Bombay University as a young lecturer. Sachin Chaudhury of the *Economic Weekly* used to get young faculty members to write notes, editorials, and book reviews for the journal, and once asked Krishna to review Piero Sraffa's newly published *Production of Commodities by Means of Commodities.* When the review appeared in 1964, both Joan Robinson and Piero Sraffa were struck by the depth of Krishna's understanding of the core argument of the book, an understanding that had eluded even such profound reviewers of the book as Roy Harrod.

The book changed Krishna's intellectual outlook as well as personal life. Intellectually her rupture with neoclassical economics, or what she was later to call 'demand-and-supply' theory, became complete, even as it acquired a new depth. As for her personal life, she moved for several years to Cambridge, where she interacted closely with its galaxy of outstanding economists at that time. When she finally returned to India, she located herself in Delhi where she founded the Centre for Economic Studies and Planning at Jawaharlal Nehru University. She continued to guide and nurture this Centre till her untimely death in 1992.

While Krishna's applied work was substantial and trend setting (on this more later), it is her contribution as a theorist and exponent of the Sraffian tradition that has attracted worldwide attention. This tradition differed from the mainstream neoclassical one in several fundamental ways. First, it saw production not in terms of the coming together of a scarce set of 'factors of production', but essentially as the application of labour to a set of means of production that were themselves produced and whose supplies, therefore, were augmentable. True, there might be certain non-augmentable inputs like land, but their presence did not create any analytical difficulties for a theory that saw production in this manner (as Ricardo had demonstrated with land); post-Jevonian theory by contrast, by lumping together produced means of production under a catch-all and supposedly scarce 'factor of production' called 'capital' had tied itself in logical knots. Second, as a consequence, distribution of output could not be determined by the so-called 'scarcity prices' (in equilibrium) of these 'factors of production', but had to be socially determined in a realm outside that of demand and supply. (Krishna's original review article on Sraffa was aptly called 'Value through Exogenous Distribution'.) Equilibrium-relative prices between commodities in other words could be determined only if a distributional parameter was already specified, which was in complete contrast to the neoclassical proposition that equilibrium product and 'factor' prices were simultaneously determined. Third, since the price system did not determine distribution but was itself determined only on the basis of a prior specification of distribution (such as the specification of a 'subsistence wage' in the

Classical system), the role of prices, it followed, was not to allocate 'scarce means among alternative uses'. Rather, the role of prices was to distribute profits among different capitalists. Competition ensured, through the mobility of labour and 'capital', equal wages for (homogeneous) labour in all spheres and an equal rate of profit on 'capital' (seen as a value sum evaluated at equilibrium prices) in all spheres; once either the wage rate or the rate of profit was given (from outside the realm of demand and supply), the equilibrium prices were set, whose role ipso facto was to allocate profits among the different capitalists.

All this meant a return to the Classical tradition and a fundamental break with the post-Jevonian one. But the point was not just to suggest an alternative approach. Sraffa's work, carried forward by Krishna and others, demonstrated, through the famous example of the 'reswitching of techniques', the logical fallacy of using any aggregate notion of 'capital' as a factor of production. Capital was a value sum whose magnitude could be known only when equilibrium prices were known, that is, only when the rate of profit was already specified (or already determined together with prices on the basis of a specification of the wage rate). The rate of profit, it followed, could not be determined by anything called a 'marginal product of capital'. Indeed the very concept of a 'marginal product of capital', or for that matter the 'marginal product' of any 'factor' used together with 'capital' in a production function, was meaningless.

Mainstream economics of yore was never to recover from this body blow. Its response was to withdraw increasingly to a Walrasian short-period setting, where scarce inputs earned quasi-rents but there was no question of any overall category called a 'rate of profit'. While this was formally immune, unlike the aggregate production function approach of the Austrians, to the charge of being logically fallacious, its limited ability to explain social phenomena, in contrast to the 'surplus approach' of Classical political economy which Sraffa had revived and, in a way, revalidated, was highlighted by Krishna in a number of her writings.[1]

It would be unfair to Krishna, however, to confine her criticism of mainstream economics to this level alone (where anyone with a knowledge of the 'non-substitution theorem' would keep her company). Her criticism went much deeper. It was a methodological rejection of any theory based on the notion of hypothetical change. On a production function we observe only one point. All other points acquire meaning only in the context of a hypothetical change. Explaining the observed state on the basis of what might have happened had there been a hypothetical change away from the observed state, was a method she rejected. This was in keeping with the position of Sraffa himself, who did not, contrary to popular interpretation, postulate a 'non-substitution theorem', because he did not assume constant returns to scale, which would have entailed the notion of a hypothetical change.

Krishna's approach may be seen as something like this. There is in any period an observed production structure with an output vector. With (say) given wages, there is embedded in this structure a set of equilibrium prices, from which the market prices would normally diverge. But as movements of capital and labour across sectors push market prices towards equilibrium prices, basic changes occur in the technology of production and in the pattern of demand as a result of capital accumulation. This leads to a new output vector with a new set of equilibrium prices embedded in it. It is far more important from the point of view of social analysis to inquire into the mode of deployment of surplus, the change in distributional parameter over time, the nature and pace of technological progress, and the changing structure of demand with its effect on the output vector, than to look at the transition from market prices to equilibrium prices in the initial situation. It follows then that the equilibrium prices embedded in a given output vector can be used as the benchmark for analysis even though these prices would not actually be ruling at any time. On the other hand, starting from the demand and supply prices one cannot get to the concept of surplus, and hence any meaningful social analysis gets foreclosed.

Krishna's theoretical research did not prevent her from being actively engaged in development economics. On the contrary, she used the Classical and Marxian perspectives to make remarkable contributions, both analytical and applied, to the development literature. Two areas in particular saw major contributions from her. One was the so-called 'dual economy' literature. In a paper in 1972 she had already argued that even if labour was available at a given subsistence wage rate, as assumed by W.A. Lewis, and even if there was no constraint on the availability of wage goods, industrialization in an economy like India with its multiplicity of structures would still run into a dead end. She carried this work forward in a later paper (Bharadwaj 1979) to argue that the Indian situation was characterized neither by 'dualism' as often claimed, nor by a dynamic capitalist industrial sector as in the

[1]These are collected together in Bharadwaj (1989).

case of classical industrializers, but by a set of variegated structures that were highly durable.

Another area where she made remarkable contribution was the study of Indian agriculture (Bharadwaj 1974) where she was the first to suggest the idea of 'interlinked markets', which later acquired much currency in the literature. The idea was to capture the coexistence of different and intertwined modes of exploitation in the agricultural sector. An illustration of this is the fact that the landlord who receives rent from a tenant also acts as a moneylender who extracts usurious income from the same tenant appearing before him once again in the guise of a borrower: the land market and the loan market are thus interlinked. This idea of Krishna's saw much employment of game-theoretic methods by researchers who were fascinated by it. But Krishna always distanced herself from such game-theoretic exercises. Her concern, she emphasized, was not with the analysis of static equilibrium situations in the context of interlinked markets but with the nature of the macrodynamic trajectories, including the divergent paths for the different sectors, which such interlinking gave rise to. As in the case of the so-called 'dual economy' framework, she was sensitive to the importance of variegated structures and divergent movements.

No account of Krishna's life would be complete without a reference to her great contribution as an institution builder. It is testimony to her vision that the Centre for Economic Studies and Planning at the Jawaharlal Nehru University which she founded has developed into a major centre for teaching and research in economics in the country today. Apart from being remarkably broad-minded in her outlook, and totally devoted to the welfare of her colleagues and students (an attitude inherited perhaps from her school teacher father), Krishna imprinted upon the Centre three basic ideas: the necessity for combining teaching with research; the necessity for combining theoretical, statistical, and historical researches within the Centre; and the necessity for exposing the students to the many alternative perspectives in economics, notably the Classical, the Keynesian, and the Walrasian. A product of the Mahalanobis period of Indian planning, her commitment to institution building was a reflection inter alia of her nationalism. She was convinced that we could have institutions here as good as any in the world, provided these did not just ape metropolitan institutions but were informed with a sense of national purpose.

PRABHAT PATNAIK

References

Bharadwaj, K. 1964. 'Value through Exogenous Distribution', *The Economic Weekly*, August, pp. 1450–3. Reprinted in G.C. Harcourt and N.F. Laing (eds). 1977. *Capital and Growth*, Harmondsworth, Penguin Books (1977).

——. 1974. *Production Conditions in Indian Agriculture*, Cambridge, Cambridge University Press.

——. 1979. 'Towards a Macroeconomic Framework for a Developing Economy: The Indian Case', *Manchester School Journal*, 47: 270–302.

——. 1989. *Themes in Value and Distribution: Classical Theory Reappraised*, London, Unwin Hyman.

■ Biodiversity

Biodiversity is under threat worldwide.[1] For example, the global mammalian extinction rate of 0.35 per cent of species per century since 1600 is calculated to be between 17 and 377 times the mammalian background extinction rate during the past 65 million years, that is, since the mass extinction that removed the dinosaurs. India has considerable biodiversity that is under threat as Table 1 (which deals only with animals) indicates.

Biodiversity, as measured by the numbers of plant and vertebrate species, is greatest in the Western Ghats and the north-east. This is because of the presence of tropical rainforests that are typically the richest habitats for species diversity. Both these areas are included in the list of world

Table 1 Summary of Animal Biodiversity Threats

	Number of Indian species (per cent of world total)	Per cent of Indian species evaluated	Species threatened in India as per cent of those evaluated	Number extinct (per cent of those evaluated)
Mammals	386 (7)	59	41	4 (1.8)
Birds	1219 (12)		7	unknown
Reptiles	495	73	46	unknown
Amphibians	207 (4)	79	57	unknown
Freshwater fish	700	46	70	unknown

Source: Based on Kumar et al. (2000).
Note: For birds, unlike for other animals, the threat refers to worldwide extinction rather than extinction in India. Threatened species are those defined as critically endangered, or vulnerable according to the International Union for Conservation of Nature (IUCN 2004) definitions.

[1]This entry confines itself to discussing wild-species diversity. Genetic and consequent morphological diversity within species is also of interest, particularly for domesticated plants and animals.

hotspots of biodiversity—small geographic areas with high species diversity. Of the two, the Western Ghats have more endemic species, those that are found nowhere else.

Threats to species are principally due to a decline in the areas of their habitats, fragmentation of habitats and declines in habitat quality, and, in the case of some mammals, hunting (Kumar et al. 2000). Fragmentation raises the extinction risk because isolated sub-populations can go extinct one by one without being repopulated. Stochastic declines in small sub-populations make it more likely that they will go extinct, and this is further exacerbated by the reduction of genetic variability in sub-populations resulting from isolation. Species with already restricted ranges are particularly vulnerable to these threats.

For the terrestrial species, the declines in habitat quality and quantity arise from conversion of forests and grasslands to agriculture and natural forests to monoculture plantations, and from grazing and woodcutting pressures. In some areas, invasion by exotic species of plants also results in habitat degradation. Prominent examples are the spread of the Peruvian thorny tree *Prosopis juliflora* in the dry parts of northern India where it replaces native species such as *Acacia nilotica* (babool), and the spread of the South American flowering bush *Lantana camara* in the sub-Himalayan belt.

For aquatic and semi-aquatic species, the declines in habitat quality are due to diversion of ground and surface water, resulting in the drying up of streams and other water bodies, siltation, and pollution from pesticides and other chemicals. Freshwater fish are also threatened by the introduction of exotic species which may be predators or competitors.

Why is biodiversity loss an economic concern? There are several reasons why biodiversity has economic value. Pharmaceutical value is one. Recent work suggests that earlier work claiming that the pharmaceutical value of biodiversity is negligible was mistaken. It remains unclear, however, how generally poor populations living in biodiverse environments and having the means to affect extinction prospects could capture these values.

A second source of value is ecosystem. Loss of biodiversity may trigger large unpredictable changes in an ecosystem stability and some of these may adversely impact agriculture or human health, perhaps through induced changes in hydrology or pest populations. Again, there is no directly useable information on the magnitude of such risks.

A third source of value is tourism. The principal attraction for tourists in areas such as the Silent Valley National Park in Kerala is biodiversity. While biodiversity per se may not be the attraction for most tourists visiting areas with high biodiversity, their willingness to pay for the preservation of such areas in their 'natural' state or for the survival of some charismatic species of birds and animals means that habitat protection for these species has a market demand and biodiversity conservation thus finds a source of finance.

Finally, there is the existence value of biodiversity. This may be negligible for the bulk of the Indian population but may be quite significant for a minority among the relatively wealthy as well as for a minority in developed countries. It may be very large if future generations' likely preferences are taken into account.

It is the last source of value, the preference of an elite minority, that has been the principal driver of policies to conserve biodiversity in India. These have taken the form of legislation such as the Wildlife Protection Act of 1972 and its various amendments and the Forest Conservation Act of 1980 that extended the colonial Forest Acts of 1878 and 1927 to evict inhabitants of forests and other wild areas by declaring large areas of forest or other wild areas 'Reserved', 'Protected', 'Wildlife Sanctuaries', or 'National Parks', and stripping them of their rights to exploit these natural resources (Saberwal et al. 2001; Vasan 2005). This was possible when political power was centralized in the Congress party, with a prime minister (Indira Gandhi) who was sympathetic to the cause of conservation.

The capacity of the Forest Department and other departments of state governments to enforce legislation protecting wild habitats deteriorated with the general decline in administrative capacity occasioned by the spread of a system of electoral fund-raising that depended on corrupting the civil services to raise money for the party in power. By the 1990s it had become clear to almost all observers that the system could not be relied upon to resist encroachment on forest habitats by politically powerful industrial and agricultural interests. Meanwhile the system of restrictions on the user rights of poor, largely tribal, forest dwellers has become, in the absence of political commitment to protect wild habitat, an extortion mechanism (Vasan 2005). As an illustration of the by now almost surreal nature of the system, consider the following line from an advertisement by the Government of Chhattisgarh touting its achievements in development in *The Hindu* of 29 October 2005: 'Amnesty for more than 250,000 ST/SC and below poverty line people for petty forest crimes.' Having sown the wind of dispossession, elite conservationists are now seeing the first signs of the resulting populist whirlwind.

In response to the realization that conservation by fiat was failing, Joint Forest Management and eco-development schemes were initiated in the 1980s and 1990s. While the former assign a share of cash flow (including in-kind) rights to local communities, tenure is insecure. The latter are based on the premise that investments in non-forest-related activities financed by governments will lower the relative returns to natural resource exploitation. It may well be the case, however, that this may induce a subset of the relevant population to desist from natural resource exploitation and also cause them to lose any interest in protecting the natural asset, which may then be degraded by another subset of the population.

Local communities exercise influence over the exploitation of the natural assets in question. They can preserve them and prevent others from degrading them if they were motivated to do so. The best chance of preserving the assets, therefore, seems to be to assign the full rights to revenue flows from *non-extractive uses* such as tourism to these communities together with a democratic and transparent institution that allows them to resolve internal common-pool problems. In addition, rights to extractive uses, at least within limits that would not degrade the resource,[2] together with tenure security should be granted (or restored). This would give local communities the incentive to both maintain the resource and to exclude outside appropriators. Local democracy restricted to such a limited set of issues is likely to be more successful at resolving common-pool problems of over-extraction than the political system has been at state and national levels.

In many cases this may be enough to induce communities to preserve biodiversity while continuing to use the areas for grazing, firewood collection, timber, and collection of other forest produce.[3] In and around existing 'Protected Areas' (Wildlife Sanctuaries and National Parks), tourism values may be high enough for this to be the profit-maximizing option. Fees are presently much lower than profit-maximizing levels (Chopra 2000) and policing costs inefficiently high (Somanathan et al. 2005). When a community has full ownership of tourism revenues, the right to set fees, and manage policing, we may expect much higher revenue streams together with much reduced costs of protection from most Indian Protected Areas. This could bring unprecedented prosperity to some of the poorest areas of the country.

In cases where there are no easily seen charismatic species or scenery, direct payment for biodiversity conservation may be necessary in addition to tourism and revenues from extractive use in order to give local managers sufficient incentives to prevent biodiversity reduction or habitat conversion. If reputed NGOs were to create trust funds to be used for the preservation of specific areas, they may well be able to raise enough contributions domestically and abroad to give local communities that extra incentive to protect many threatened areas. It helps that biodiversity has a highly uneven distribution so that protecting small areas can have very high pay-offs in terms of biodiversity conservation.

Current debates over the Tribal Rights Bill suggest that neither conservationists nor tribal-rights activists have seriously considered a solution involving the transfer of tourist revenues to local communities, although some (Saberwal et al. 2001) have called for much more meaningful local involvement in conservation management. Conservation NGOs, despite their belated realization that alienating local people increases the risk of a populist open season on natural assets, have not recognized the importance of granting them security of tenure and rights to and control over tourist and other revenues. Nor have they taken actions to promote locally run tourist parks on the peripheries of the officially Protected Areas. Trust funds for direct payments to private landowners and communities have not yet begun even though this may be the only way to protect certain habitats housing less conspicuous endangered animals such as amphibians which are often not in Protected Areas (Bawa et al. 2004).

Tribal-rights activists have campaigned for a restoration of tribals' expropriated land and user rights. They have not demanded full rights to all revenue flows, whether in cash or in kind, tenure security over commonly held forest areas, and control rights for setting access fees and regulating use. By couching their arguments in terms of justice and equity alone, they have failed to make the case for a larger transfer of assets that would promote efficiency by preventing resource dissipation and reducing monitoring costs, and make for a more genuinely equitable distribution of resources.

The principal obstacle to such a development is the interest of politicians in maintaining a degree of state control over natural resources so as to continue to generate

[2]If such limits violate prior patterns of use, then compensation would have to be provided. In many cases, rights to profits from tourism would be sufficient to cover these losses. Enforcement of such limits would, however, remain problematic so long as local communities did not feel the limits would be in their own interest. Incentive payments, rather than coercive regulation, would probably be the best option in such cases.

[3]Saberwal et al. (2001) show that it is a misconception that extractive human use is incompatible with biodiversity conservation. In some cases, as in the famous bird refuge at Keola Deo Ghana, biodiversity depends on certain human uses such as grazing. The ban on grazing there resulted in water-bird habitat being choked by vegetation.

illegal revenues for campaigning and private consumption. It is significant that both the Joint Forest Management and eco-development schemes fall far short of true community ownership despite the provision made for 'village forests' in the Forest Act of 1927, and also despite the success of van panchayats in eastern Uttaranchal—an organizational form established by the colonial government in 1930. Somanathan et al. (2005) show that the van panchayats have been just as good, if not better, at forest conservation than the state forest department and at less than a tenth of the cost per hectare.

An alliance of conservationists and tribal-rights activists may, however, succeed in initiating genuine reform in a political climate in which tribals are becoming ever more active. In this case, considerable government resources could be freed up when forest departments are gradually downsized and redirected to a mainly scientific and advisory rather than policing role.

An important exception to the pattern of dispossession and alienation of forest communities and failed state regulation is seen in the north-eastern states other than Assam and Tripura. They are demographically different from the rest of India in that scheduled tribes constitute a majority of the population and this meant that the Forest Acts were never applied in a way that resulted in the loss of tribal control over forest land. To the best of my knowledge there are no systematic comparisons of the performance of these states in forest conservation with the rest of India. However, there does not seem to be any evidence that they have performed more poorly. It is probably true that with the spread of firearms, hunting has greatly reduced wild animal populations. It is notable that there has been no serious attempt to apply the provisions of the Wildlife Protection Act restricting hunting in these areas. It would be politically impossible to do so. These areas constitute a promising region for experiments by conservation NGOs in starting locally run tourist parks.

E. SOMANATHAN

References

Bawa, K.S., A. Das, U. Karanth, J. Krishnaswamy, and M. Rao. 2004. 'Ecosystem Profile: Western Ghats and Sri Lanka Hotspot, Western Ghats Region', Critical Ecosystem Partnership Fund.

Chopra, K. 2000. 'Economic Aspects of Biodiversity Conservation: Micro and Macro Strategies for Intervention', in S. Singh, A.R.K. Sastry, R. Mehta, and V. Uppal (eds), *Setting Biodiversity Conservation Priorities for India*, Vol. 2, New Delhi, WWF-India, pp. 571–9.

IUCN. 2004. The 2004 IUCN Red List of Threatened Species, IUCN.

Kumar, A., S. Walker, and S. Molur. 2000. 'Prioritisation of Endangered Species', in S. Singh, A.R.K. Sastry, R. Mehta, and V. Uppal (eds), *Setting Biodiversity Conservation Priorities for India*, Vol. 2, New Delhi, WWF-India, pp. 341–425.

Saberwal, V., M. Rangarajan, and A. Kothari. 2001. *People, Parks and Wildlife: Towards Coexistence*, New Delhi, Orient Longman.

Somanathan, E., R. Prabhakar, and B.S. Mehta. 2005. *Does Decentralization Work? Forest Conservation in the Himalayas*, Delhi, Indian Statistical Institute.

Vasan, S. 2005. 'In the Name of Law: Legality, Illegality and Practice in Jharkhand Forests', *Economic and Political Weekly*, 40(41): 4447–50.

G.D. Birla

Ghanshyamdas Birla (1894–1983) was an industrial pioneer, a generous financier of Mahatma Gandhi, and a key spokesperson and strategist of Indian big business. Born on 14 April 1894 in Pilani in the northern Indian state of Rajasthan, Birla belonged to the Maheshwari sub-caste of the trading community of Marwaris. His grandfather had migrated to Bombay in 1858 in search of fortune and by the time of G.D.'s birth, the family business of trading and speculation was based in both Bombay and Calcutta. The Birla family firm engaged in opium *satta*, carried out forward trading in several commodities such as cotton, piece-goods, wheat, rapeseed, and silver, and acted as brokers in the jute and gunny trade. Birla started his business career at the age of 12 after a traditional trader's and rudimentary English education. Within a few years, through astute leadership, he stood at the helm of the expanding family firm that made windfall profits during World War I from export of jute products, hedge transactions in raw jute and gunny, and speculative operations in silver and jute stocks. These profits led Birla to boldly venture into European-dominated jute manufacturing by establishing the Birla Jute Manufacturing Company Limited in 1919. G.D. Birla, with the support of his brothers Jugalkishore, Rameshwar Das, and Braj Mohan, led the transition of the family business from old-style trading to modern industry. Birla firms diversified into cotton textiles, sugar mills, publishing, paper, and insurance. By the mid-1930s the Birlas owned four textile mills, five sugar mills, and one jute mill. In the 1940s, expansion followed in banking, textile machinery, automobiles, engineering, and plastics. Following Independence, Birla oversaw the family business move into challenging areas like chemicals, rayon fibre, engineering goods, aluminium, and fertilizers. These years saw enormous growth of the Birla business empire with a doubling of gross capital stock of the Birla public companies from Rs 65.26 crore in 1951 to Rs 152.14 crore by 1958, and a jump in the number of private companies controlled by the Group from 61 in 1951 to 105 by 1958. In the 1960s and 1970s, Birla encouraged the younger generation of his family to venture overseas and they set up factories in Nigeria, Kenya, Thailand, the Philippines, Indonesia, Malaysia, and Egypt to emerge as India's first multinational business house.

Alongside business, Birla always took keen interest in politics. A staunch nationalist, he became a strong financial supporter of leaders such as Madan Mohan Malaviya, Lala Lajpat Rai, and Mahatma Gandhi. Birla came to regard Gandhi as a guru and financed causes that the Mahatma espoused. From the 1920s onwards Birla also increasingly played the role of spokesperson of Indian big business. A propagator of solidarity among Indian business, he helped establish the Indian Chamber of Commerce in Calcutta in 1925. He also played a leading role in the formation in 1927 of the Federation of Indian Chambers of Commerce and Industry (FICCI), the first apex association of Indian business that brought together regional chambers of commerce. He was responsible for forging much of the solidarity that Indian capital displayed against the British colonial state before 1947. FICCI became a vehicle for the struggle of Indian big business against European domination of the Indian economy. For over three decades between 1927 and the 1960s Birla remained a powerful voice within FICCI as its chief strategist.

In the years following Independence, Birla continued to provide visionary leadership to private enterprise. His abiding concern was that economic policies in free India must create an enabling environment for private enterprise so that it could contribute meaningfully to national development. However, Birla had lukewarm relations with Jawaharlal Nehru whose economic philosophy emphasized a predominant role for the state in economic life. While distancing himself from Nehru's economic philosophy, Birla was astute enough not to waver in his support of the Congress Party as he was convinced that the interests of private enterprise could best be served through centrist parties. Notwithstanding his differences with Nehru, Birla was able to maintain his relationship with a range of Congress leaders. In 1957, at the height of Nehru's socialist rhetoric, he was awarded the Padma Vibhushan, one of the country's highest awards.

To his fellow industrialists, Birla advocated a flexible approach to accommodate diverse political interests, including that of the Communists. Thus, when a Communist government came to power in Kerala in 1957, he was the first businessman to invest in the state. Birla's vision was somewhat circumscribed under Nehru and the turbulent years of Mrs Gandhi's premiership, when big business faced political challenges and felt disadvantaged, but the astute political sense of his generation of business leaders enabled it to survive these years to re-emerge as an important player when conditions became favourable.

By the time Birla died in 1983 at the age of 89, despite the restrictive economic regime of his later years, his business empire had grown to be the largest family business in India. It consisted of over 200 companies under direct control and 70 under indirect control. The Birla group owned the country's biggest jute mills, the largest tea gardens, the second largest paper mill, the biggest car manufacturing unit, and produced 45 per cent of the country's aluminum and 3 per cent of its sugar. Its overseas business operations extended to a dozen countries. It also ran a large number of educational charities, one of the country's best regarded institutes of technology, charitable trusts, hospitals, more than 40 temples, *dharamshalas,* and a planetarium. The business had passed into the hands of the fifth generation which had been ably trained to continue the tradition. Yet Birla failed to work out clear lines of succession within the family and his passing away left behind disputes over the division of assets and responsibilities that could never fully be resolved.

As India emerges as an economic power, Birla's vision is being realized. This vision of an independent 'Hindustan' and a capitalist one is best epitomized in the names of two of the newspapers that he owned—the *Hindustan Times* and the *Eastern Economist.* Throughout his later public career, he had stressed the need for economic reforms, greater reliance on private enterprise, and a deeper integration with the world economy. It appears that Birla's vision has, at last, been embraced by the Indian political leadership. In a sense the India of the 21st century, as it emerges as an economic power, represents a vision that was closer to Birla's than to Mahatma Gandhi's or Jawaharlal Nehru's.

MEDHA MALIK KUDAISYA

References

Birla, G.D. 1953. *In the Shadow of the Mahatma: A Personal Memoir,* with a foreword by Dr Rajendra Prasad, Bombay, Orient Longman.

Kudaisya, Medha M. 2003. *The Life and Times of G.D. Birla,* New Delhi, Oxford University Press.

Bonded Labour

The concept of 'bonded labour' can encompass the entire gamut of servitude of the worker to the employer, ranging from non-market direct coercive relations for extracting unpaid labour services against food alone, to more mediated forms of bondedness, as owing to debt which is to be repaid through work but which, owing to the low valuation of labour or high interest rates, is deemed never to be repaid and is handed down to succeeding generations. Bonded labour of both types has long been a feature of relations of production in India, particularly in agriculture, but it is found in labour-intensive small-scale mining and industry as well. This entry will consider the modern phenomenon of bonded labour in India with respect to the conditions under which it arises, persists, and may become more prevalent.

The state of bondedness may be defined as one in which the labourer becomes tied to a particular employer under adverse conditions of work and living, which can include one or more of the following features: physical confinement and work extracted against food alone; partial or entire loss of freedom to work for another employer; long and unregulated working hours; lower-than-market wage rate used for valuing work; hereditary nature of the relationship with the employer; an advance from the employer on which a usurious interest is charged and which is to be repaid by work with little chance of discharging the initial debt. Some of these features can give rise to others: for example, advances are used to tie the destitute worker, and a combination of low wage and high interest deduction applied to calculate net payment to the worker keeps the worker and family members perpetually and hereditarily indebted. In some cases the workers can change employers under a system where the new employer discharges the worker's debt to the previous employer and reimposes the arrear of debt on the worker.

What are the origins of bonded labour? Historically there has been a strong link between caste and bonded status in the agrarian sphere. Landless households of particular castes, lowest in the caste hierarchy in the Tamil- and Malayalam-speaking regions, were held as servile tied households by the entire community of high-caste landowners in the pre-colonial period and their labour was used for agricultural fieldwork and livestock maintenance. By the late 18th century the community character of such agrestic servitude was modified to individual relations of servility with high-caste households. While the systematic use of servile bonded labour for agricultural production on the southern model seems to have been absent in western and northern India, the landless and land-poor lower-caste households were required to provide *begar* or free labour in many other forms (porterage, serving, and performing during life-cycle ceremonies; maintaining water distribution systems) to the dominant landholding zamindar households. Bonded labour for domestic services and for artisan production for the class of feudal aristocrats, was extremely widespread up to the early colonial period. The legal abolition of 'slavery' in India in 1843 and new employment avenues in plantations both in the country and abroad, loosened these traditional caste-based customary relations but substituted a modern form of bondage under the indenture system. The destruction of artisan production, with the inflow of foreign goods, pauperized many higher-caste rural workers and drove them too into perpetual debt bondage.

Who becomes a bonded worker, and under what circumstances are free persons likely to become bonded? With modern economic development the relations of bondage were widely expected to be replaced by 'free' contracts, but many specific factors militate against this to preserve and, in some spheres, even to increase bondage. First, asset distribution in rural India remains one of the most unequal in the world owing to ineffective land reforms. Forty per cent of the rural population operates only 6 per cent of the cultivated area, and these landless and land-poor still belong in the main to the 'scheduled' castes and tribes. The fruits of economic growth are unequally distributed, since landlords and rich farmers going in for multiple cropping find it profitable to mechanize their operations despite low wages of labour, leading to declining labour demand per unit of output. Bad harvests and price declines today, as in the past, drive free small and poor peasant families into debt, and the creditor can demand that the debt be paid off through labour. Since this labour is valued well below market rates by the creditor and interest rates are usurious, charged by the month and ranging from at least 36 to 60 per cent annually, the debt is never deemed to be repaid, leading to perpetual bonded status.

The increasing landlessness and destitution of the poorest agricultural workers, who to this day mainly belong to the 'scheduled' castes and tribes, obliges many to accept long-term work contracts against food or cash advance. Under such contracts working hours are long, wages per day work out to well below market wage rates, and, with no scope for upward mobility, the children of such households also remain bonded. The incidence of trauma among labourers and loss of limbs from operating unsafe machinery owned by the employer was found to be high. Migrant labour from low-wage areas in eastern India is recruited by labour contractors to work for large-scale farmers in Punjab and, in many cases though not all, the conditions of work included physical confinement, physical chastisement, and prohibition on working for other employers.

The migrant land-poor and landless rural workers and their families also provide hands for stone quarrying, and small-scale labour-intensive processing and manufacturing enterprises in rural and urban areas which range from brick kilns and the weaving of textiles and carpets, to the manufacture of glass, matches, and fireworks. The last three are particularly hazardous occupations in which children are extensively employed. The loans taken by their parents oblige them to work under conditions in small-scale enterprises that in most cases amount to bondage. The employer gives a wage advance to meet immediate consumption needs of the worker but values the labour performed at a low rate, or charges explicit interest so that the advance can never be repaid and debt bondage results.

Second, whether bonded status is tending to get reduced or reinforced over time also depends crucially on whether the policies followed at the macroeconomic level are expansionary, tending to increase employment opportunities, or are deflationary and tend to reduce employment. Up to the end of the 1980s the share of rural development spending in total plan spending was maintained, and the growth rate of employment in rural India kept pace with the growth of the workforce. In the 1990s to date, however, the development-spending share in rural India has dropped sharply, employment growth has declined below workforce growth, and open unemployment has been growing fast. Under such adverse conditions the unemployed will tend to enter into work contracts on extremely unfavourable terms and the incidence of debt-bonded labour may be expected to increase.

The Bonded Labour System Abolition Act was passed in 1976. Legal recognition of the unacceptability of bonded status is important, but given the strong connection between lack of assets, poverty, and unemployment, on the one hand, and bondage including debt bondage, on the other, legal and political efforts alone will not end the system. Implementing existing land-reform laws for redistributing land to the landless and land-poor, combined with cheap credit and increased development spending in rural areas, would go a long way both in undermining caste-based discrimination in labour relations and eliminating the economic reasons for the persistence of bonded labour.

UTSA PATNAIK

References

Breman, Jan. 1985. *Of Peasants, Migrants and Paupers: Rural Labour and Capitalist Production in Western India*, New Delhi, Oxford University Press.

International Labour Organization. 2002. *Annotated Bibliography of Forced/Bonded Labour in India*, L. Mishra, Geneva, ILO.

National Commission on Rural Labour. 1991. *Report of the National Commission on Rural Labour*, vol. 1, ch. 8 and vol. 2 (Study Group on Bonded Labour), New Delhi, Ministry of Labour, Government of India.

Patnaik, Utsa and Manjari Dingwaney (eds). 1985. *Chains of Servitude: Bondage and Slavery in India*, New Delhi, Sangam Books, Orient Longman.

Sarma, Marla. 1981. *Bonded Labour in India—National Survey on the Incidence of Bonded Labour, Final Report.*

Brain Drain

The costs and benefits of brain drain from India have been heavily debated with Indians having emigrated to a variety of countries, including the US, UK, Australia, and countries in the Middle East and Africa. The magnitude of brain drain has significantly increased from the 1970s onwards. As the trend of skilled Indian professionals emigrating to the US grew, research on brain drain from India revolved largely around the US and educated workers. Reflecting the research, this overview of the brain drain focuses on this US–India dimension. In the 1990s, along with India's liberalization, the emigration of Indians to developed countries, particularly the US, steadily increased. Prior to 1990, the US issued only H-1 visas, aiding domestic employers in finding temporary workers. This visa required an expression of intent by the recipient to return. However, with the Immigration Act of 1990, this provision was replaced by the H-1B visa which allowed the recruitment of foreign workers by employers in the US for a six-year period (Desai et al. 2004).

In 1989, healthcare professionals accounted for a larger share of professional visas (28 per cent) compared to information technology (IT) professionals (11 per cent). A decade later, 60 per cent of the H-1B visa recipients were in the IT sector. Following the rise of the IT sector in the US, in 1999, Indians received 48 per cent of the H-1B visas and comprised three-fourths of the IT sector with H-1B visas that year, according to the US General Accounting Office in 2000 (Desai et al. 2004). This trend of high Indian emigration has continued steadily. In 2009, professionals of Indian origin accounted for 103,059 (48 per cent) of all approved H-1B petitions. Of these 103,059 H-1B visas, 33 per cent were given for initial employment and 67 per cent for continuing employment, indicating the strong base of Indian professionals continuing their employment in the US (United States Citizenship and Immigration Services 2010).

As the trend of Indian emigration persists, the net impact of brain drain on India is a subject of great debate. From a cost perspective, Indian brain drain accounts for a significant loss of Indian professionals and educated labour within India. This disproportionate loss of educated people, it is argued, is a big cost for India. Others argue that brain drain actually results in brain gain because of the remittances and information networks that the emigrant Indians provide to those in India along with the increased incentive to invest in education due to attractive employment opportunities in countries like the US. Discussions of how to offset the costs of brain drain often include a version of the 'Bhagwati Tax', which entails the taxation of all Indian nationals regardless of their location of residence. At the same time, with economic growth in India, one is also seeing the emergence of reverse brain drain, with the entrance of Indians and foreign nationals into India.

Over the past decade, the costs of brain drain from India have been significant. In the United Nations *Human Development Report 2001*, the cost of brain drain to India was estimated to reach $2 billion in lost resources annually (United Nations 2001). The cost of emigration of professionals is particularly high in India due to the relatively low percentage of qualified professionals, particularly in the fields of medicine, computers, and education. Emigration is skewed towards graduates of the top educational institutions in India, including the All India Institute of Medical Sciences and the Indian Institute of Technology (IIT). In 1980, only 3 per cent of Indian doctors emigrated to the US. However, India's loss is worse than it seems as a disproportionate share of these emigrated doctors were from the top medical institution, the All India Institute of Medical Sciences, with 56 per cent of graduates emigrating from 1956 to 1980. There was a slight decline to 49 per cent emigrating in the 1990s (*The Economist* 2002). Looking at one of the IITs (Madras), in 2004, while the total number of degrees offered by the institution throughout its history was only 27,613, the US accounted for 6,000 of its registered alumni, which is close to 25 per cent of the registered alumni base (Kapur 2010: 69). Further, as the government subsidizes the tuitions of the IITs and other government funded schools, it loses the $15,000 to $20,000 it spends on every university student (United Nations 2001).

In addition, there is an increase in the financial cost because of the loss of income stream of educated people who emigrate, which leads to a decrease in the Indian tax base and a loss of direct taxes on the high incomes of skilled workers who emigrate (United Nations 2001). This loss was estimated to account for about 12 per cent of India's tax base (Desai et al. 2004). There are many ways in which the Indian government could potentially attempt to tax Indian emigrants. One way could be for it to charge an exit fee, which serves as a flat tax and is paid when the visa is granted. The value of this exit fee could be equal to the charges of headhunters (two months' salary), which are estimated to be approximately $10,000. This fee could either be paid by the employee emigrating or the firm in the host country. Revenues from such a flat tax, which could add up to $1 billion annually, could be used towards more investment in higher education by the government to increase the skill base within India. In addition, the Indian government could potentially balance the costs of brain drain by following the US model of taxing by citizenship. Executing this would entail the negotiation of bilateral tax treaties. These tax revenues could be used to redistribute income and subsidize education for the lower classes. Another approach could be to have a requirement for university students to take loans, equal in value to the subsidy that the state provides, to be repaid if a student leaves the country. In addition, countries such as South Korea are launching programmes with competitive incentives like attractive wages and provisions for skilled and educated workers to return. Hence, these emigrants will return with skills that they have acquired abroad (United Nations 2001). India could also consider similar policies.

Even without such policies, there are benefits that help offset, at least partially, the financial costs of brain drain, primarily through the channels of remittances and network effects. Remittances are important in India because of credit and liquidity constraints due to imperfect local capital markets, particularly in rural areas. Hence, remittances from Indians working abroad are a steady stream of financial resources which impact the education, investment, and consumption decisions made by those living in India (Docquier and Rapoport 2004). In absolute dollar terms, remittances to India have risen rapidly in the past decades from $2 billion in 1990, to $13 billion in 2000, and $52 billion in 2008. As a percentage of GDP, remittances have more than doubled to 3 per cent of GDP in the 2000s as compared to 1.2 per cent in 1990 (Kapur 2010: 112). Due to the increase in remittances as well as local expenditures of non-resident Indians (NRIs) in India, NRI deposits have significantly increased. In 2003, NRIs accounted for more than 16 per cent of the total deposits held in commercial banks among Indian residents (Kapur 2010: 109). In addition, NRIs channel their income back to India through various investments in the country. For example, NRI foreign direct investment (FDI) in India was Rs 95 billion between 1991 and 2004. Though this is only 7 per cent of the Rs 1,368 billion of the total FDI that came into the country, the amount is by no means insignificant (Kapur 2010: 105).

In addition to direct financial contributions by Indian emigrants, the network effects of brain drain from India have been significant due to India's openness to innovation and rapid growth in the 1990s. They include increased trade between India and the host country, investments, and spread of technology. This impact has been referred to as 'brain circulation' and 'brain exchange' (United Nations 2001). For example, Indians from the Silicon Valley played an important role in the development of the IT sector in Bangalore and Indians from the Silicon Valley and other technology hubs make contributions to Indian universities, increasing their endowments. In addition, the success of Indians, particularly in the IT sector and in Silicon Valley, has created a worldwide image of Indian success in the sector, helping its growth in India. Further, Indians in the US play a significant role in the hiring of Indian nationals with 10 of the top 25 employers of foreign workers being Indian companies or companies run by Indian nationals. In addition, Indians running 'front offices' in the US have started manufacturing plants in India, providing valuable training in technology (Desai et al. 2004). Hence, there is an increase in the exchange between India and the US and other host countries through such network effects which is beneficial for India.

In addition to the financial costs and benefits of brain drain, there is a looming impact of emigration on the human capital base in India. As mentioned earlier, a significant share of graduates from India's top educational institutions work outside India. Some say that this emigration is a benefit to the human capital base in India as the opportunity to emigrate increases the incentives for Indians to invest more in education. As the wage premium ranges from two to five times higher, adjusting for purchasing power parity, for medical (2–4) and IT professionals (3–5), the prospect of emigration largely increases returns to education (Docquier and Rapoport 2004). Indians in the US account for 0.1 per cent of the population of India but earn 10 per cent of the national income of India. Due to these increased returns to education abroad, it is argued that there is an increased incentive to invest in education in India, which increases the human capital base in the country. However, despite this increase, India is not able to reap the primary benefits of this educated population as these skilled workers represent a disproportionate percentage of the population that leaves. While technical graduate and postgraduate degree holders were only 0.5 per cent of the population in 2001, they accounted for more than 50 per cent of those who emigrated (Kapur 2010: 120). Hence, though the education level had increased among Indian nationals, once we account for emigration, the education level of the remaining population actually decreases as the most educated leave. In addition to impacting the current education base of India, brain drain also threatens the future quality of human capital in the country. The trend of tertiary education professors, particularly in technological fields, and of teachers from grades kindergarten to Class XII emigrating to the US and UK threatens the educational base of India and its future quality. As the number of postgraduates in India is very low, particularly in the technology sectors, this will exacerbate the issue of widely prevalent teacher vacancies, particularly in postgraduate schools (Desai et al. 2004). Therefore, there is strong reason to believe that India is not the primary beneficiary of this increased investment in education as the best qualified graduates emigrate.

However, there are two ways in which India can benefit from this increased investment in education. One, if an individual invests in education under the assumption of going abroad, but for some reason s/he does not go, this would increase the Indian educational base. This scenario's likelihood is increasing over time given the caps on new visas to countries like the US as well as the growing opportunities within India. Two, if more temporary visas were issued then there would be a lower threat of India permanently losing the most-educated population. Though the use of temporary visas could decrease the incentive to invest in education, it could also guarantee the return of emigrants, who bring back the skills they have learned working in foreign countries with higher technology (Docquier and Rapoport 2004).

Due to the steady economic growth in India, there is increased discussion and reference to reverse brain drain, with Indians and foreign nationals coming to India. However, given the large number of immigrant visas currently issued, this reverse brain drain is not yet sufficient to offset the brain drain. While in places like Taipei many domestic companies have been started by returned emigrants, in the IT sector in Bangalore, the number of companies started by returned emigrants is limited reflecting the low return rate of emigrants. The return of emigrants has largely been the *result* of increased growth of the sector rather than the *cause* of it.

However, this does not mean that Indian professionals living in developed countries, such as the US, do not play a role in the growth of the sector. Their role is primarily through network effects, as Indian nationals in developed countries provide contacts for companies starting in India as well as the exchange of ideas within the IT sector. In addition, 30–40 per cent of the higher-level employees in the Indian IT sector are returned emigrants (Docquier and Rapoport 2004). As economic opportunities continue to grow in India, reverse brain drain will become an increasingly important factor.

In conclusion, in India's context, the brain drain issue has many diverse facets. One issue of focus has been a cost–benefit analysis of the phenomenon. On the cost side, India is losing the returns on its investment in education and its base of skilled workers. The negative repercussions of this loss of the educated labour force are even greater as they threaten the education system in India, from primary to tertiary education, with the outflow of educational professionals. On the benefit side, the outflow of Indians leads to network effects, which provide greater linkages with the host country, and remittances, which lead to greater financial resources within India. Another potential benefit is the increase in the investment in education due to the opportunity to emigrate. However, the extent of its benefit to India is questionable as the most-educated population is lost to emigration. There are policies that could be used to mitigate the costs of brain drain, such as taxation, whether it is a flat fee upon exit or a taxation system based on Indian nationality. This would increase tax revenues in India, which could fuel government expenditure and access to education. Though the number of visas issued is still high, with the growth in sectors such as IT in India, there has been an increase in the return of Indians and the immigration of foreign nationals into India. To further encourage this reverse brain drain, there could be more emphasis on temporary emigration, which could decrease incentives to invest in education, on the one hand, and lead to the increased retention of skilled workers along with the spillover of skills that emigrants learn in foreign countries, on the other. The focus of research is primarily on skilled-labour emigration. Though educated workers are a relatively small percentage of the population of India, they represent a disproportionate amount of the emigration and drain of Indian talent, particularly from leading institutions in the country. However, there are significant outflows of relatively unskilled labourers as well. With over 2.8 billion Indian-born individuals in the US in 2007 and an Indian diaspora of over 20 million people across 110 countries (Kapur 2010: 53), there is little reason to believe that brain drain from India and its impact will decrease any time soon despite legislative moves in various host countries, like the US, to restrain future immigration. Therefore, the debates regarding the costs and benefits of brain drain will continue and lead to future legislative policy implications in both India and the host countries.

Divya Minisandram

References

Desai, Mihir A., Devesh Kapur, and John McHale. 2004. 'Sharing the Spoils: Taxing International Flows of Human Capital', *International Tax and Public Finance*, 11(5): 663–93.

Docquier, Frederic and Hillel Rapoport. 2004. 'Skilled Migration and Human Capital Formation in Developing Countries—A Survey', December.

The Economist. 2002. 'Outward Bound', 26 September.

Kapur, Devesh. 2010. *Diaspora Development and Democracy: The Domestic Impact of International Migration from India*, Princeton, Princeton University Press.

United States Citizenship and Immigration Services. 2010. *Characteristics of H-1B Specialty Occupation Workers*, Washington DC, Department of Homeland Security.

United Nations. 2001. *Human Development Report 2001*, New York, United Nations.

Budget Making

Budget making in India is a complex and interesting exercise. Since the process of budget making occurs under great secrecy, common people have a lot of interest and curiosity regarding the budgetary exercise and the persons involved in the process of budget making. Interestingly, though the word 'Budget' is so widely used in government policymaking, in the whole text of the Constitution there is no mention of this word. Article 112 (1) of the Indian Constitution provides that every year the President shall in respect of every financial year cause to be laid before both the Houses of Parliament a statement of estimated receipts and expenditures of the Government of India for that year. This 'annual financial statement' is referred to as the Budget. This relates to the federal Parliament. There are similar provisions for the states.

The Budget can be presented only in the directly elected House, that is, the Lok Sabha and Legislative Assembly. It cannot be presented in an indirectly elected House like the Rajya Sabha or the Legislative Councils because on all money matters, elected representatives of the people are entrusted with the authority. Parliament has total control over money and finance in three ways. First, Parliament has to approve all expenditure proposals of the Government of India. Second, Parliament has to allow the executive to withdraw money from the Consolidated Fund of India by passing the Appropriation Bill. And third, no tax can be levied except by the authority of law passed by Parliament.

Regarding the discharge of this function, according to the Allocation of Business Rules of the Government of India (1961), preparation and presentation of the Budget is the responsibility of the Finance Minister. The Finance Minister, along with the Finance Secretary, and other secretaries of the departments of the Ministry of Finance, the Chief Economic Adviser, the chairpersons of the two boards (Central Board of Direct Taxes [CBDT] and Central Board of Excise and Customs [CBEC]), and the Finance Minister's adviser participate in the making of the Budget. All participants do not take part in all the meetings. For instance, when direct taxes are discussed, only the Chairman, CBDT, is involved. Similarly, when indirect taxes are discussed, only the Chairman, CBEC, is involved. But a larger group participates in discussing the general Budget.

Earlier, there was a system of one officer representing the Prime Minister's Office (PMO) being present in the budgetary exercise. When I was the Finance Minister, between 1982 and 1985, Dr Arjun Sengupta, the Secretary to the Prime Minister on Economic Affairs, would be present. While this practice has been discontinued, as discussed subsequently, the Finance Minister does consult the Prime Minister and keeps him apprised of the budgetary process.

For preparing the Budget, the Finance Minister takes into account the projected revenue, the estimated expenditure, the means to raise revenue, the allocation of expenditure, and the amount to be borrowed. All these figures are analysed in the context of the overall economic situation in consultation with advisers and experts.

The Budget document includes a Plan Budget and a Non-Plan Budget. Such a classification did not exist before 1951, when we began our planning process. In the Budget of 1951–2, it was mentioned for the first time that there would be a Plan Budget and a Non-Plan Budget.

The Budget is generally presented on the last working day of February, that is, typically on 28 February if it is a working day. If it is a Sunday, then the Budget has to be presented a day before that. If it is a leap year, then the Budget is presented on 29 February, provided it is a working day. But the first Budget of independent India was not presented on the last working day of February. Before the country became independent in August 1947, the 1946–7 Budget was placed by the then Finance Minister Mr Liaquat Ali Khan (who later became Prime Minister of Pakistan), before the Central Assembly. Then the country became independent and resources were distributed between India and Pakistan. But there was a desire among the people for a new Budget for independent India. Therefore, Mr R.K. Shanmukham Chetty, who was the first Finance Minister of independent India, presented the Budget on 26 November 1947. The total volume of the Budget was miniscule by today's standards. For the year 2010–11, a Budget of more than Rs 11 lakh crore was presented. The total amount of the Budget for independent India in 1947–8 was Rs 197 crore.

In terms of allocations, there was no Plan and Non-Plan expenditure, so the division was very simple: Civil Budget and Military Budget. The Military Budget was Rs 92 crore and the Civil Budget was Rs 105 crore. For raising the amount of Rs 197 crore, there were two important taxes—income tax and the customs duty. Income tax realization for that year was roughly Rs 118 crore and customs duty was around Rs 50 crore, bringing the total to about Rs 168 crore. Further, there was a tax on imported alcohol, which contributed to around Rs 2.5 crore. So the deficit was only around Rs 26 crore. That was the composition of the first Budget of independent India.

In the current context, the budget making process not only deals with larger resources but is also more comprehensive and consultative. Before the Budget is presented, the Finance Minister elicits the views of various stakeholders through group meetings and consultations. Consultations are held with various groups, including agriculturists, economists, industrialists, trade unions, exporters, construction industry representatives, non-governmental organizations, and financial regulators.

In addition, in my present tenure as Finance Minister, a system of discussions with the state finance ministers has been started. To facilitate this process, a note explaining the state of the economy, the trends in revenue and expenditure, and the Plan and Non-Plan expenditure is circulated. Broad economic parameters, GDP growth, sectoral growth, trade performance, and inflation are also mentioned. The Finance Minister requests the participants to give their views and suggestions for the ensuing Budget. The secretaries, the Chief Economic Adviser, and other important officials take note of the suggestions received. When subsequent deliberations are held for finalizing the Budget, these suggestions are considered. Their viability in terms of implementation and financing are examined carefully.

In preparing the Budget, the Finance Minister also takes into account the relevant Five Year Plan document. From 1951 onwards, India has followed a system of planning wherein an overall assessment is made of the availability of resources for a period of five years. This takes into account the rate of savings, its sectoral compositions, including public sector, private sector, and household savings. It also takes into consideration investment requirements and priority areas for investment, like infrastructure, agriculture, industry, and the social sectors. The Planning Commission makes an assessment of the total resources which would be available for a period of five years, including borrowings and how these resources would be utilized. The Plan document is prepared by the Planning Commission and approved by the National Development Council (NDC). The NDC consists of cabinet ministers of the central government and all state chief ministers. Currently, the Eleventh Five Year Plan is being implemented. The Five Year Plans apply to both the central government and the various state governments. Though the plans are for a period of five years they are implemented annually. For this process, around December or January, the Deputy Chairman of the Planning Commission informs the Finance Minister of the budgetary requirements. Given the nature of the budgetary process, the Deputy Chairman usually asks for an enhanced outlay while the Finance Minister tries to balance this demand keeping in view the overall fiscal considerations. Sometimes, the Prime Minister has to intervene, and eventually a figure is arrived at. For instance, for fiscal 2010–11, I informed the Deputy Chairman, Planning Commission that the year's plan allocation was Rs 3,73,000 crore. Once the budgetary support for the plan is fixed, it is Planning Commission's task to allocate it between the states and among the various departments of the central government. The Deputy Chairman provides a consolidated statement of the detailed allocation by early February for incorporation in Budget documents.

The Parliament exercises its control on the Budget, but the cabinet also has a vital role in its approval. The Budget is the only document which is approved by the cabinet just one hour prior to its presentation before Parliament. This is because strict secrecy of the Budget has to be maintained. If the taxation proposals of the Budget are leaked there is a possibility that this information may be misused in the equity and other markets. Therefore, on the day the Budget is presented, a cabinet meeting takes place about an hour in advance. Here again, there is a deviation from the usual norm followed for cabinet meetings. Normally in cabinet meetings, cabinet notes are circulated in advance by the Cabinet Secretary. In the cabinet meeting to consider the Budget proposal, the note is circulated by the Finance Secretary who coordinates the preparation of the Budget. Each copy is numbered and circulated to the members in the meeting. They are given some time, say 15 to 20 minutes, to study the proposals and then the Finance Minister explains the salient features of the Budget. The cabinet ministers may have some queries which the Finance Minister clarifies. Then the Prime Minister allows the Finance Minister to proceed to the Lok Sabha, while the other cabinet ministers remain behind. The Finance Minister, accompanied by the Parliamentary Affairs Minister, proceeds to the Lok Sabha with a briefcase containing the Budget documents. Before he arrives at the Lok Sabha a short photo session is held. The Prime Minister, accompanied by the rest of the cabinet, arrives a little earlier and at 11am, the Finance Minister starts presenting the Budget.

In the past, the Budget was presented at 5 pm. This was a colonial tradition that was followed keeping in mind the time difference between London and India. Moreover, the stock market remained closed at the time when the Budget was presented. This prevented speculative trading and excessive volatility. This practice has now been discontinued to allow smooth and real time flow of information on Budget proposals to the markets.

Though the Parliament has to approve all expenditures, when the Finance Minister presents the Budget, the proposals on indirect taxation contained in the Finance Bill become operational immediately. The moment the Finance Minister utters, 'I introduce the Finance Bill', all the indirect taxes come into effect. The question then arises: Where is parliamentary control? After all, parliamentarians have not yet seen the Budget in totality. They have just listened to some proposals from the Finance Minister's speech. Hence, a provision has been made in the Constitution that within 75 days from the day that the Budget is presented, the Finance Bill has to be approved by the Lok Sabha. If it is not approved, then all the taxes collected from 28 February till that date will have to be refunded. If this happens it would be very disruptive, so the Parliament generally approves the Budget even if the government changes. This happened when Mr Deve Gowda's government collapsed in 1997. The Budget had been presented by Mr P. Chidambaram who was the Finance Minister then. The Prime Minister decided that he would resign but the 1997–8 Budget was passed by Parliament. After that the new government came into power. This reveals that despite political differences, Indian parliamentarians have been responsible enough to ensure that a financial crisis is not created.

Another interesting issue with regard to the approval of the Budget arises as a consequence of our financial year extending from 1 April to 31 March. The Budget presented on the last day of February is too voluminous to read, comprehend, discuss, debate, and pass before 31 March. The sums involved, like the total amount of over Rs 11 lakh crore spent by the Government of India in 2010–11, are very large and merit detailed consideration. There are also over 14 to 15 documents, including the *Economic Survey* to read and analyse. The *Economic Survey* is a vital document prepared by a team led by the Chief Economic Adviser and tabled in Parliament by the Finance Minister about two or three days before the Budget. This comprehensive document takes an overall view of the country's economy in the context of the global situation, the macroeconomic outlook, policy priorities, and socio-economic factors. The members need time to study this. The expenditure proposals with about 160 demands are also voluminous and need time for appraisal. Hence, a system has been evolved whereby the Finance Minister proposes a 'Vote on Account' asking for approval of the expenditure and taxation proposals, and other related proposals for one quarter till the Budget is passed. So the Parliament passes the Vote on Account to meet the immediate revenue and expenditure needs. Since every demand is to be approved by Parliament, if during the discussions it is found that time is running out while a large number of demands are yet to be voted on, then the Speaker puts all the demands together to vote in the House at an appointed time on a predetermined date. This is called putting the demands under guillotine. The Finance Minister also seeks approval of the Appropriation Bill so that the government can withdraw money to meet necessary expenditures.

The Finance Minster presents the Budget on behalf of all the departments and ministries except Railways (the Railway Budget is separate and is discussed later). He/she presents the demands of all the ministries. Thereafter, when a respective ministry's demands are discussed and debated, it is the minister of the respective department/ministry who responds and not the Finance Minister. The Finance Minister presents the Budget, responds to the general discussion on the Budget, replies to the Appropriation Bill if there is a debate, and steers the demands when they are being voted and passed. Thereafter, the Finance Bill (containing taxation proposals) is taken up for consideration. After the Finance Bill is approved, the budgetary exercise is complete.

It may be recalled that the cabinet gets just about one hour to discuss the Budget. If there is a difference of views on any particular item in the cabinet, how is it resolved? In the cabinet system, the Prime Minister is apprised of the Budget. The Finance Minister meets the Prime Minister four or five times while formulating the Budget proposals. The Finance Minister informs the Prime Minister regarding how he intends to address the problems which the economy may be facing, like fiscal deficit, inflation, industrial stagnation, and lack of growth. The overall strategy, major aspects, and broad taxation proposals are also discussed with the Prime Minister and his general approval is sought (though not on individual files). Then about a day before the presentation of the Budget, or on the day of presentation, the Finance Secretary brings the original Budget document to the Finance Minister and signs it in the presence of the Finance Minister. Then the Finance Minister signs, and together with the other secretaries they take it to the Prime Minister for his/her signature. Subsequently, the Budget document is taken by the Finance Minister and other important officials to the President for his/her signature. Generally the appointment with the President is fixed for 9.30 am on the day of the Budget. The President may have queries which are responded to. Sometimes, the Prime Minister also asks the Finance Minister certain questions. For instance, when Mrs Indira Gandhi was Prime Minister, she would be interested in stepping up the plan expenditure. When I became Finance Minister, during the Sixth Plan period, the Plan outlay was Rs 97,500 crore. I did not join the Finance Ministry immediately after the elections in 1980. The Plan started from 1980 and Mr R. Venkataraman who was the Finance Minister for the first two years compressed the Plan expenditure in order to contain inflation. Thereafter, Mr Venkataraman went to the Ministry of Defence, while I came to Finance from Commerce. For each Budget, Mrs Indira Gandhi would ask about an increase in Plan allocation. In that period of three years, every year I had to step up the Plan expenditure to the extent of 26 per cent, since in the first two years, the total Plan expenditure was only 14 per cent. So certain priorities are set by the Prime Minister. When Mr Morarji Desai was Prime Minister and Mr H.M. Patel was the Finance Minister, Mr Morarji Desai would raise queries about the deficit because he was against deficit financing. Our present Prime Minister, Dr Manmohan Singh, is an eminent economist and has extensive knowledge and experience since he has presented five Budgets. So he takes a comprehensive view and has most economic issues on his fingertips. However, all Prime Ministers have not been Finance Ministers or economic experts. But they have specific priorities and focus areas taking into account the overall situation.

In our country, three prime ministers, Pandit Jawaharlal Nehru, Mrs Indira Gandhi, and Mr Rajiv Gandhi had presented one Budget each as Prime Minister. Pandit Nehru presented the 1958–9 Budget when Mr T.T. Krishnamachari resigned. Pandit Nehru presented the Budget and commented that this was not his area. He observed that he was a bird of passage who for a short while had stopped on this leaf. Mrs Gandhi presented the 1970 Budget when Mr Morarji Desai was dropped from the government and the Finance portfolio was taken from him. Mr V.P. Singh presented two Budgets—1985–6 and 1986–7. Mr Rajiv Gandhi presented the 1987–8 Budget when Mr V.P. Singh was moved to Defence from Finance. The rest of the Budgets have been presented by finance ministers. And there was one Finance Minister, Mr H.N. Bahuguna, who could not present the Budget. He was appointed Finance Minister sometime in July 1979, when the budgetary exercise was over, and then before the next Budget Mr Charan Singh's government fell.

Till date, the largest number of Budgets have been presented by Mr Morarji Desai (eight main Budgets for 1959–60, 1960–1, 1961–2, 1962–3, 1963–4, 1967–8, 1968–9, and 1969–70, and two interim Budgets for 1962–3 and 1967–8). Mr P. Chidambaram presented two Budgets during Mr Deve Gowda's government (1996–7 and 1997–8) and five Budgets under Dr Manmohan Singh (2004–5, 2005–6, 2006–7, 2007–8, and 2008–9) totaling seven. The 2011–12 Budget is my seventh Budget including the interim Budget of February 2009.

Generally, except the four to five secretaries, the Chief Economic Adviser, and the chairmen of the two Boards, nobody, not even junior ministers, are involved in the Budget. However, once in 1976, as a Minister of State, I participated in the Budget process. At that time, the Ministry of Finance charges were divided into: (i) revenue and banking and (ii) expenditure and economic affairs. Mr C. Subramaniam, as senior minister, was in charge of economic affairs and expenditure and I, as Minister of State, was in charge of revenue and banking. Since the Budget could not be formalized without involving the revenue function, the Prime Minister passed a special order that as Minister of Revenue and Banking, I should be involved in the budget making process. This is the only instance when a junior minister was involved in the formulation of the Budget. Otherwise, though some files come through junior ministers, they do not have any involvement in budget making.

For taxation proposals, we have a system where the concerned joint secretaries bring the files, have them signed by the Finance Minister and then take them back, so that the papers are not misplaced and secrecy is protected.

Finally, let me elaborate on the only ministry that has a separate budget presentation—the Ministry of Railways. The Railway Budget was separated from the main Budget in 1924. In 1919 there were major reforms in the government known as the Montagu–Chelmsford Reforms. At that point of time, railways were owned by different companies, like East India Railways (EIR), Bengal–Nagpur Railways (BNR), Western Railways, and Deccan Railways. They paid dividends to the central government. Apart from that, territory-wise, only about 65 per cent of India was directly administered by the British. The remaining territories were administered by princely rulers. Some of them had separate railway systems. After the Montagu–Chelmsford Reforms of 1919, the office of the finance member was created in the Government of India. But it was decided that the transport member would present the Railway Budget to the Central Assembly while the finance member would present the general Budget. This was probably because the British did not like the vital finance member post to go to an Indian. At the same time, the transport member's post was allowed to be held by an Indian member with some devolution of financial powers by having a separate Railway Budget. An important aspect is that while the general Budget is approved by the cabinet, the Railway Budget is approved by the Finance Minister and not by the cabinet.

PRANAB MUKHERJEE

■ Business and Growth Rate Cycles

This entry describes business and growth rate cycles with special reference to the Indian economy. It uses the classical NBER (National Bureau of Economic Research) approach to determine the timing of recessions and expansions in the Indian economy, as well as the chronology of growth rate cycles, namely, the timing of speed-ups and slowdowns in economic growth. The reference chronology for business as well as growth rate cycles is determined on the basis of the consensus of key coincident indicators of the Indian economy, along with a composite coincident index comprised of those indicators, which tracks fluctuations in current economic activity. Finally, it describes the performance of the leading index—a composite index of leading economic indicators, designed to anticipate business cycle and growth rate cycle upturns and downturns.

Business Cycles, Growth Cycles, Growth Rate Cycles

Economic cycles are characteristic features of market-oriented economies—whether in the form of the alternating expansions and contractions that characterize a classical business cycle, or the alternating speed-ups and slowdowns that mark cycles in growth. With the progress of the liberalization process, which has transformed the Indian economy into more of a market-driven one, such cycles are destined to become prominent features of the economic landscape.

The NBER, founded in New York in 1920, pioneered research into understanding the repetitive sequences that underlie business cycles. Wesley C. Mitchell, one of its founders, first established a working definition of the business cycle that he, along with Arthur F. Burns (1946), later characterized as follows:

> Business cycles are a type of fluctuation found in the aggregate economic activity of nations that organize their work mainly in business enterprises: a cycle consists of expansions occurring at about the same time in many economic activities, followed by similarly general recessions, contractions and revivals which merge into the expansion phase of the next cycle; this sequence of changes is recurrent but not periodic; in duration business cycles vary from more than one year to ten or twelve years; they are not divisible into shorter cycles of similar character with amplitudes approximating their own.

This definition of the business cycle does not make explicit the notion of 'aggregate economic activity', leading some to argue in recent years that a satisfactory proxy for this concept is a country's GDP, which is, after all, about as aggregate a measure of output as possible. On this narrow, output-based view, if one had available a monthly estimate of GDP, then its peaks and troughs would be all that would be needed to determine the peak and trough dates for the business cycle.

But Geoffrey H. Moore, who worked closely with Mitchell and Burns at the NBER, noted (1982) that:

> No single measure of aggregate economic activity is called for in the definition because several such measures appear relevant to the problem, including output, employment, income and [wholesale and retail] trade ... Virtually all economic statistics are subject to error, and hence are often revised. Use of several measures necessitates an effort to determine the consensus among them, but it avoids some of the arbitrariness of deciding upon a single measure that perforce could be used only for a limited time with results that would be subject to revision every time the measure was revised.

Basically, both on the basis of the meaning of aggregate economic activity and issues of revision and measurement error, Moore advocated the determination of business cycle dates based on multiple measures. This approach is, in fact, the basis of the determination of the official US business cycle dates by the NBER, and of international business cycle dates by the Economic Cycle Research Institute (ECRI), founded by Moore.

What is a Recession?

In this context, it is important to understand something of the mechanism that drives a business cycle. A recession occurs when a decline—however initiated or instigated—occurs in some measure of aggregate economic activity and causes cascading declines in the other key measures of activity. Thus, when a dip in sales causes a drop in production, triggering declines in employment and income, which in turn feed back into a further fall in sales, a vicious cycle results and a recession ensues. This domino effect of the transmission of economic weakness from sales to output to employment to income, feeding back into further weakness in all of these measures in turn, is what characterizes a recessionary downturn.

At some point, the vicious cycle is broken and an analogous self-reinforcing virtuous cycle begins, with increases in output, employment, income, and sales feeding into each other. That is the hallmark of a business cycle recovery. The transition points between the vicious and virtuous cycles mark the start and end dates of recessions.

Under the circumstances, it is logical to base the choice of recession start and end dates not on output or employment in isolation, but on the consensus of the dates when output, income, employment, and sales reach their respective turning points. To do any less is to do scant justice to the complexity of the phenomenon known as the business cycle (Layton and Banerji 2004).

That is also why a decline in GDP alone—when it does not trigger the characteristic vicious cycle of falling employment, income, and sales—does not constitute a recession. Similarly, that is why a transient rise in GDP, which does not ignite a self-reinforcing recovery in employment, income, and sales, may be part of a 'double-dip recession', but does not qualify as a new expansion.

However, because of its simplicity, two consecutive quarterly declines in GDP has become perhaps the most popular rule for determining the onset of recession. Yet, the use of such a rule may produce quite a nonsensical set of business cycle dates. One could well imagine a period of depressed economic activity associated with falling output and employment and with unemployment climbing, but with two clear quarterly declines in GDP happening to have a modestly positive intervening quarter. Similarly, to automatically conclude that a country was in recession simply because of two minutely negative quarterly growth rates in GDP—particularly if they occurred simply because they followed on from one or two quarters of unusually strong quarterly growth—seems just as misguided. In the Indian case, quarterly GDP data were not available until the late 1990s, so it would be difficult in any case to base the historical business cycle dates on such a rule.

The preceding discussion describes classical business cycles that measure the ups and downs of the economy in terms of the absolute levels of the coincident indicators, that is, indicators that gauge current economic activity. However, in the decades that followed the end of World War II, many economies like Japan and Germany saw long periods of rapid revival from wartime devastation, so that classical business cycle recessions seemed to have lost their relevance. Rather, what was considered increasingly germane was a second NBER definition of fluctuations in economic activity, termed 'growth cycle'. A growth cycle traces the ups and downs through deviations of the actual growth rate of the economy from its long-run trend rate of growth. In other words, a growth cycle upturn (downturn) is marked by growth higher (lower) than the long-run trend rate.

Economic slowdowns begin with reduced but still positive growth rates and can eventually develop into recessions. The high-growth phase typically coincides with the business cycle recovery, while the low-growth phase may correspond to the later stages leading to recession. Some slowdowns, however, continue to exhibit positive growth rates and are followed by renewed upturns in growth, not recessions. As a result, all classical business cycles associate with growth cycles, but not all growth cycles associate with classical cycles.

Of course, growth cycles, measured in terms of deviations from trend, necessitated the determination of the trend of the time series being analysed. However, while growth cycles are not hard to identify in a historical time series, they are difficult to measure accurately on a real-time basis (Boschan and Banerji 1990). This is because any measure of the most recent trend is necessarily an estimate and subject to revisions, so it is difficult to come to a precise determination of growth cycle dates, at least in real time.

This difficulty makes growth cycle analysis less than ideal as a tool for monitoring and forecasting economic cycles in real time, even though it may be useful for the purposes of historical analysis. This is one reason that by the late 1980s, Moore had started moving towards the use of *growth rate cycles* for the measurement of the series that manifested few actual cyclical declines, but did show cyclical slowdowns.

Growth rate cycles are simply the cyclical upswings and downswings in the *growth rate* of economic activity. The growth rate used is the 'six-month smoothed growth rate' concept, initiated by Moore to eliminate the need for the sort of extrapolation of the past trend needed in growth cycle analysis. This smoothed growth rate is based on the ratio of the latest month's figure to its average over the preceding 12 months (and, therefore, centred about six months before the latest month). Unlike the more commonly used 12-month change, it is not very sensitive to any idiosyncratic occurrences 12 months earlier. A number of such advantages make the six-month smoothed growth rate a useful concept in cyclical analysis. Cyclical turns in this growth rate define the growth rate cycle.

At ECRI, growth rate cycles rather than growth cycles are used along with business cycles as the primary tool to monitor international economies in real time. The growth rate cycle is, in effect, a second way to monitor slowdowns in contrast to contractions. Because of the difference in definition, growth rate cycles are different from growth cycles. Thus, what has emerged in recent years is the recognition that business cycles, growth cycles, and growth rate cycles all need to be monitored in a complementary fashion. However, of the three, business cycles and growth rate cycles are more suitable for real-time monitoring and forecasting, while growth cycles are suited primarily for historical analysis.

Dating of Business Cycles and Growth Rate Cycles in the Indian Economy

For India, Chitre (1982) had initially determined a set of growth cycle dates. Following the classical NBER procedure, Dua and Banerji (1999) later determined business cycle and growth rate cycle dates for the Indian economy. These dates were further revised and reported in Dua and Banerji (2004a).[1]

Coincident Index and Reference Chronology

The timing of recessions and expansions of Indian business cycles is determined on the basis of a careful consideration of the consensus of cyclical co-movements

[1]The latest updates to the chronologies are available at http://www.businesscycle.com/internationalcycledates.php.

in the broad measures of output, income, employment, and domestic trade that define the cycle. A summary combination of these coincident indicators, that is, variables that move in tandem with aggregate economic activity, is called the *Coincident Index*, whose cyclical upswings and downswings generally correspond to periods of expansion and recession, respectively.

Table 1 reports the business cycle chronology for the Indian economy since the 1960s and gives the dating of peaks and troughs as well as the duration of recessions and expansions. This shows that during the 1990s, the Indian economy experienced two short recessions—the first from March 1991 to September 1991 and the second from May 1996 to November 1996. Prior to these recessions, it experienced a very long expansion from March 1980 to March 1991.

Likewise, the reference cycle, derived from the central tendency of the individual turning points in the growth rates of the coincident indicators that comprise the coincident index, gives the highs and lows of the growth rate cycle. This dates the slowdowns and speed-ups in economic activity. Table 2 gives the reference chronology of the growth rate cycle along with the duration of slowdowns and speed-ups in the Indian economy since the 1960s. While the economy experienced only two short recessions in the 1990s, it exhibited four slowdowns—March 1990 to September 1991, April 1992 to April 1993, April 1995 to November 1996, and September 1997 to October 1998. Thus, the growth rate cycle peaks led their comparable business cycle peaks, highlighting the distinction between a slowdown and a full-fledged recession. In the first decade of the 21st century, while there have been no recessions, the economy experienced four slowdowns—March 2000 to July 2001, April 2004 to October 2004, October 2005 to March 2006, and January 2007 to January 2009.

Table 1 Business Cycle Chronology for India

Dates of peaks and troughs		Duration (in months)	
Trough	Peak	Contraction (peak to trough)	Expansion (trough to peak)
	November 1964		
November 1965	April 1966	12	5
April 1967	June 1972	12	62
May 1973	November 1973	11	6
February 1975	April 1979	15	50
March 1980	March 1991	11	132
September 1991	May 1996	6	56
November 1996		6	
Average (months)		10.4	51.8
Median (months)		11	53
Standard deviation (months)		3.3	46.6

Table 2 Growth Rate Cycle Chronology for India

Dates of peaks and troughs		Duration (in months)	
Trough	Peak	Slowdowns (peak to trough)	Speed-ups (trough to peak)
	September 1960		
July 1961	February 1962	10	7
November 1962	May 1964	9	18
November 1965	April 1966	18	5
March 1967	April 1969	11	25
February 1974	February 1976	58	24
September 1977	May 1978	19	8
December 1979	October 1980	19	10
February 1983	August 1984	28	18
September 1985	October 1986	13	13
December 1987	June 1988	14	6
May 1989	March 1990	11	10
September 1991	April 1992	18	7
April 1993	April 1995	12	24
November 1996	September 1997	19	10
October 1998	March 2000	13	17
July 2001	April 2004	16	33
October 2004	October 2005	6	12
March 2006	January 2007	5	10
January 2009	July 2010	24	18
Average (months)		17.0	14.5
Median (months)		14.0	12.0
Standard deviation (months)		11.5	7.8

The historical chronology of business and growth rate cycles helps design a system for the prediction of recessions and recoveries as well as slowdowns and pick-ups. In fact, the reference chronology provides a test of the performance of leading indicators in anticipating turning points of the cycles.

Leading Index: The Indian Experience

Leading indicators are designed to anticipate the timing of the ups and downs in the business cycle. They are related to the drivers of business cycles in market economies, which include swings in investment in inventory and fixed capital that both determine and are determined by movements in final demand. They also include the supply of money or credit, government spending and tax policies, and relations among prices, costs, and profits. An understanding of these drivers can help identify the predictors of the downturns and upturns. Remarkably, decades of experience of the researchers at ECRI have shown that in a wide variety of market economies, both developed and developing, similar leading indicators consistently anticipate business cycles, underscoring the fundamental similarity of market economies. Such robust leading indicators can be used as the foundation for reliable cyclical forecasts.

A composite of the leading indicators yields the *leading index* peaks and troughs, which anticipate or 'lead' peaks and troughs in the business cycle. Also, peaks and troughs in the leading index growth rate anticipate peaks and troughs in the growth rate cycle, that is, slowdowns and speed-ups in economic growth, respectively. The leading index for the Indian economy is described in Dua and Banerji (2004a).

The performance of the leading index for the Indian economy vis-à-vis the business cycle reference chronology is shown in Figure 1 while the performance of the leading index growth rate is shown in Figure 2. Leads are shown with a negative sign. Both charts show that the emergence of fairly consistent leads (especially with respect to troughs) started only in the post-liberalization period that began in earnest in 1991.

Before that, the government long dominated the 'commanding heights of the economy', and the assumption of a free-market economy was questionable. For the first four decades after India's Independence, the government owned roughly half of the economy's productive capacity. Even the private sector was hemmed in by myriad regulations and rampant distortions of the free market, such as controls on prices and interest rates and extensive licensing procedures for the establishment of new factories or expansion of existing capacity. Generally, there were major barriers to entry and exit in most industries, including the difficulty of laying off any part of the labour force regardless of the profitability.

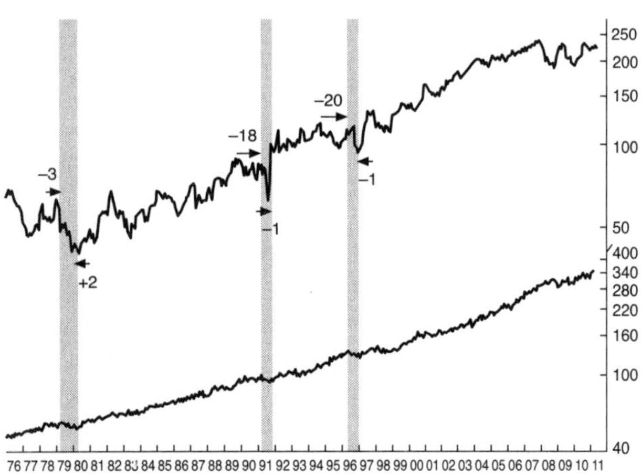

Figure 1 Indian Leading and Coincident Indexes (1992 = 100)

Note: Shaded areas represent Indian business cycle recessions. A minus symbol denotes leads while a plus shows lags.

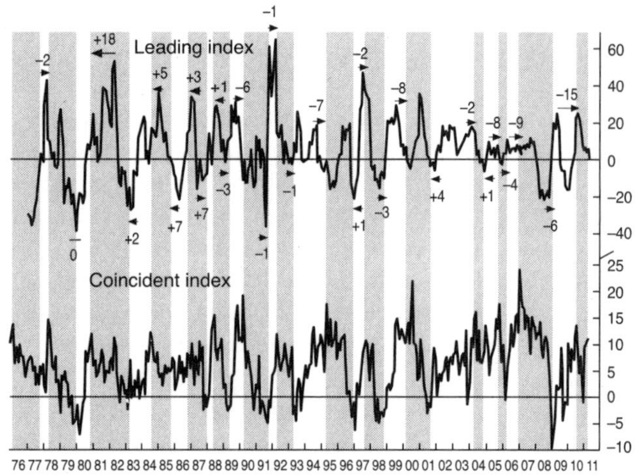

Figure 2 Indian Leading and Coincident Indexes, Growth Rates (%)

Note: Shaded areas represent Indian growth rate cycle downturns. A minus symbol denotes leads while a plus shows lags.

Under such circumstances, endogenous cyclical forces do not necessarily drive business cycles. It is thus understandable that the leading indicators that typically anticipate business cycles in market economies did not lead in a systematic manner. In fact, Indian recessions before the 1990s were mainly triggered by bad monsoons, which cannot be predicted by leading indicators. In a sense, the emergence of the leads since the early 1990s is evidence that the free market is starting to dominate the economy.

Another aspect of the liberalization of India's economy is the growing importance of exports, which have become increasingly important to its overall growth prospects. Like domestic growth, export growth is also cyclical, but is driven by business cycles in the main export markets. Thus, in order to predict the timing of peaks and troughs in exports growth, it is logical to combine ECRI's leading indexes for those foreign economies with a real effective exchange rate, which determines the price competitiveness of Indian exports, to arrive at a leading index for India's exports (Dua and Banerji 2004b, 2007), which leads turning points in Indian exports growth by an average of nine months. This leading exports index complements the leading index for the Indian economy, to provide the means to monitor cycles in domestic cycles and well as exports cycles.

Pami Dua and Anirvan Banerji

References

Boschan, C. and A. Banerji. 1990. 'A Reassessment of Composite Indexes', in A. Klein (ed), *Analyzing Modern Business Cycles*, New York, M.E. Sharpe.

Burns, Arthur F. and Wesley C. Mitchell. 1946. *Measuring Business Cycles*, National Bureau of Economic Research, New York.

Chitre, V.S. 1982 'Growth Cycles in the Indian Economy', *Artha Vijnana*, 24: 293–450.

Dua, P. and A. Banerji. 1999. 'An Index of Coincident Economic Indicators for the Indian Economy', *Journal of Quantitative Economics*, 15: 177–201.

———. 2004a. 'Monitoring and Predicting Business and Growth Rate Cycles in the Indian Economy', in P. Dua (ed.), *Business Cycles and Economic Growth: An Analysis Using Leading Indicators,* New Delhi, Oxford University Press.

———. 2004b. 'Economic Indicator Approach and Sectoral Analysis: Predicting Cycles in Growth of Indian Exports', in P. Dua (ed.), *Business Cycles and Economic Growth: An Analysis Using Leading Indicators,* New Delhi, Oxford University Press.

———. 2007. 'Predicting Indian Business Cycles: Leading Indices for External and Domestic Sectors', *Margin: The Journal of Applied Economic Research*, 1: 249–65.

Layton, A.P. and A. Banerji. 2004. 'Dating Business Cycles: Why Output Alone is Not Enough', in P. Dua (ed.), *Business Cycles and Economic Growth: An Analysis Using Leading Indicators,* New Delhi, Oxford University Press.

Moore, Geoffrey H. 1982. 'Business Cycles', in *Encyclopaedia of Economics*, D. Greenwald, Editor in Chief, McGraw Hill Book Company, New York.

■ Business Policy

Business policy is concerned with specifying and achieving an organization's objectives. It, therefore, involves (i) setting out the long-term goals for a firm in line with the expectations of its stakeholders, (ii) formulating an action plan for meeting these goals, (iii) allocating resources for meeting the goals, (iv) implementing the action plan by modifying/building an appropriate structure within the organization, and (v) evaluating the end-results through a review of results and future possibilities. Business policy is, therefore, dynamic and forward looking. It is the highest level of activity in a firm and usually falls in the domain of decision making by the chief executive officer and the senior management team.

Two of the most important decisions facing a firm relate to scale and scope, that is, the size and range of activities. Size is in turn driven by growth. The famous PIMS study carried out over 19 years had seemed to yield the conclusion that the greater a firm's market share, the greater its rate of profit.[1] High market share enables a firm to gain from economies of scale through large volumes, and over time provides experience and learning curve advantages. The task of building up market share in turn forces a consideration of growth strategies. Should growth occur via diversification (related or unrelated), horizontal or vertical integration, mergers and acquisitions, strategic alliances and joint ventures, or franchises?

However, some research also indicated that a low market share strategy focusing on niche segments could also be highly profitable, in other words, that 'small is beautiful'.

The optimal range of activities, markets, and products was the second question that needed to be addressed. The theory of financial portfolios was extended to product portfolio decisions and operating division portfolios. As companies expanded their scope of operations, their organizations witnessed a transformation from U-form (unitary form) structures organized along functional lines to M-form (multidivisional form) structures organized along semi-independent profit centres called 'strategic business units' (SBUs). Each of these SBUs was viewed as an element in the corporate portfolio. In deciding on the optimal portfolio, considerations of risk reduction had to be combined with considerations of market penetration and growth.

By the late 1970s, Japanese companies had started posing increasingly severe challenges to American companies. What was the secret of the Japanese success? In 1981, Pascale and Athos claimed that the Japanese success rested on the bedrock of superior management techniques. Rather than strategy, structure, and systems, the Japanese placed emphasis on corporate culture, shared values and beliefs, and social cohesion in the marketplace. The end-result was higher productivity. Moreover, the Japanese companies had a longer term vision. Ohmae (1982) went further in claiming that strategy making in America was too analytical and had forgotten to be a creative art. These ideas were complemented later by authors who pointed out that successful companies often manage to develop a core ideology shared by all the employees. One can trace this line of thinking to Peter

[1]The PIMS (Profit Impact of Market Strategy) of the Strategic Planning Institute is a large-scale study designed to measure the relationship between business actions and business results. The project was initiated and developed at the General Electric Co. from the mid-1960s and expanded upon at the Management Science Institute at Harvard in the early 1970s; since 1975, the Strategic Planning Institute has continued the development and application of PIMS research.

Drucker's (1973) belief that workers should be treated as resources rather than just as costs.

Michael Porter's (1980) work identified clearly the five forces that shape a firm's strategic environment. Analysis along Porterian lines enables a clearer articulation of a SWOT (strengths, weaknesses, opportunities, threats) analysis. Porter also identified the three generic strategies of cost leadership, product differentiation, and focus. Porter's highlighting of industry factors for a firm's success was countered by a number of authors who developed the resource-based view of a firm, arguing that it is only the possession of certain superior, scarce, and non-imitable intangible resources that can confer a sustainable competitive advantage on the firm. Prahalad and Hamel (1994) saw a company as a portfolio of resources and competencies and focused on the need for a company to identify its core competencies.

In recent years, several new forces have shaped thinking on business policy. First, attention is turning to management in non-profit enterprises and government, as well as state-owned enterprises. Within the former category, civil society organizations are now the subjects of debate and research. Second, in the context of a more volatile environment, as organizations have to frequently reconfigure themselves to cope with the demands of the changing environment, change management has acquired a critical role. Third, for-profit organizations are increasingly subject to scrutiny with respect to their societal roles. Therefore, while deciding how to achieve organizational goals, CEOs have to worry about marrying usual business practices with ethical concerns. Moreover, a greater focus on the environmental effects of the production process means that profitable adoption of greener technology poses new challenges for managers.

In earlier years, much of the business policy was conditioned by the context of industrialized countries. As growths in these markets tapered off and MNCs had no choice but to turn increasingly to emerging markets exhibiting faster rates of growth, a new strand of the literature developed based on the experience of these emerging economies. Several issues were highlighted by this literature. First, could lessons learnt from the developed countries be transplanted wholesale to these emerging economies? For example, going against the prescription of core competence, Khanna and Palepu (1997) have argued that conglomerates engaging in unrelated diversification in the emerging economies are helping to fill up institutional voids. Their reputation and internal capital and labour markets enable them to introduce new products and processes much more easily than stand-alone companies.

Second, can businesses be successful in these countries with the same practices and policies as in developed economies? Thus, researchers have pointed to the lack of brand loyalty and price sensitivity of consumers in the emerging economies that make it difficult for MNCs to quickly grab market shares. Prahalad (2005) has been influential in drawing attention to the 'fortune at the bottom of the pyramid', that is, the purchasing power in the hands of the lower-income groups who are usually neglected by the MNCs. Targeting this segment of the population requires paying close attention to their needs and finding innovative solutions. These innovative solutions can range from introduction of low-cost solutions to transformation of business models. In learning the new rules of the game, MNCs might themselves be transformed by their exposure to new ways of doing business.

Third, the growing internationalization of business has important implications for the field of business policy. Increasing competition has forced firms in developed countries to try to achieve lower costs through outsourcing. At first outsourcing took place in the lower rungs of the value chain and these firms felt no threat to their existence. But as firms in emerging markets learnt new skills and moved up the value chain, the outsourcing firms were faced with the critical question of identifying their core capabilities. Further, as the firms from the emerging economies grew larger and grew in self-confidence, they started competing on the home turfs of the developed country MNCs. For example, Lenovo Group Limited, acquired the former IBM PC Company Division in 2005 and by 2009 was the fourth largest vendor of personal computers in the world.

The Indian Context

For 40 years after Independence, strategies of Indian companies were largely shaped by the industrial policy regime resting on the planks of industrial and import licensing, high tariffs, and tight regulation of technology imports. In an era of policy induced entry barriers and low level of competition, Indian firms were not forced to develop capabilities for sustainable competitive strategies. Corporate growth and diversification strategies were shaped by licencing policy and the ability of top management to lobby for licences and procure scarce foreign exchange and bank finance. Unrelated diversification was the norm rather than the exception. Even where entry was permitted through grant of an industrial licence, the government specified the size and the location of the plant. Planners were guided by the concept of 'economic size' of plants and prevention of dominance through pre-empting of capacity. As a result, targeted capacity was fragmented between several medium size units, unable to exploit scale economies.

The 1991 reforms combined macro-level changes with micro-level changes that lowered entry barriers for both domestic and foreign producers. Therefore, from the early 1990s Indian firms suddenly found themselves in a situation in which they were free to make investment, production, and pricing decisions. As a result, business policy formulation came to occupy centre stage. Even public-sector units that were earlier monopolies had to rethink their strategies in an era of greater competition and withering support from the government. For example, when the insurance sector was opened up, employees of the Life Insurance Corporation, a former public-sector monopoly, came up with concrete proposals to improve customer service.

The growth and success of different firms under the new regime rested on different strategies. Thus Reliance Industries Limited became a giant in the petrochemicals industry by following the strategy of growth through backward integration and building up 'world scale' capacities that enabled it to reap economies of scale and achieve cost leadership. The Ispat International Group's growth was largely driven by a series of acquisitions in different countries.

In contrast to companies like Reliance and Ispat International which have a relatively narrower range of product portfolios, one can cite Hindustan Unilever Limited, the Indian subsidiary of Unilever, whose businesses were divisionalized in 1991 into chemicals, detergents, agri-products, personal products, and exports. Again, while today we identify Wipro with its IT division, in 1994, Wipro Corporation's activities spanned vanaspati, toilet soaps, toiletries, hydraulic cylinders, computer hardware and software, lighting, financial services, medical systems, diagnostic systems, and leather exports. Azim Premji described Wipro as a 'diversified integrated corporation', the integration being achieved through 'a set of shared beliefs and leadership values, and through people and through management processes' (Ghoshal et al. 2002: 421–2).

Indian companies are also devoting attention to the softer set of issues of managing people in the workplace and revitalizing their organizations. It is now recognized that the 'internal behavioural context' determines whether employees can be motivated to do their best. Ispat's success in being the lowest cost producer of steel in country after country depends on motivating its employees to drive costs down. HDFC has tried to foster a more open, entrepreneurial orientation, where shared responsibilities and a sense of ownership are married to customer orientation.

The international ventures of some Indian companies, like Tata Motors' acquisition of Jaguar and Land Rover brands, have attracted global attention. Such international acquisitions testify to the growing confidence of Indian companies in operating abroad. Indian companies have also innovated to reach consumers at the bottom of the pyramid. A much analysed programme is e-Choupal introduced by ITC Limited, which involves the installation of computers with internet access in rural areas to offer farmers up-to-date marketing and agricultural information. The programme allows ITC to establish direct links with farmers for procurement of agricultural and aquaculture products.

MNCs in Indian markets are learning from their experience with local markets and consumers. Some multinationals, such as PepsiCo and General Electric, are even using emerging markets to try out disruptive business models. In March 2010, PepsiCo Chief Executive Officer Indra Nooyi announced her vision of transforming the company from a traditional food and drink supplier to a wellness-solution provider. She is using emerging markets, especially India, to try out this new business model. MNCs like PepsiCo are seeking out Indian partners to help implement such visions. Thus PepsiCo has forged an alliance with Tata Tea to co-develop a range of healthy food and beverage products.

ANINDYA SEN

References

Drucker, Peter. 1973. *Management*, New York, Harper and Row (paperback edition 1983).

Ghoshal, Sumantra, Gita Piramal, and Sudeep Budhiraja (eds). 2002. *World Class in India*, New Delhi, Penguin Books.

Khanna, Tarun and Krishna Palepu. 1997. 'Why Focused Strategies May Be Wrong for Emerging Markets', *Harvard Business Review*, July–August, 75(4): 41–51.

Ohmae, Kenichi. 1982. *The Mind of the Strategist*, New York, McGraw-Hill.

Pascale, Richard and Anthony Athos. 1981. *The Art of Japanese Management*, New York, Penguin Books.

Porter, Michael. 1980. *Competitive Strategy*, New York, Free Press.

Prahalad, C.K. 2005. *The Fortune at the Bottom of the Pyramid*, Delhi, Pearson Education (Singapore) Pte. Ltd.

Prahalad, C.K. and G. Hamel. 1994. *Competing for the Future*, Boston, Harvard Business School Press.

C

Call Centres

Call centres are facilities that handle a range of business communications, involving one-on-one voice interaction between customers and employees of business firms. The most common form of interaction is customer service, which is initiated by a customer typically after a sale, including technical support, billing questions, warranty issues, and delivery queries. Customers may also initiate queries before a transaction. Business-initiated interactions include follow-up customer service calls, those related to payments and billing, and a wide range of marketing-related efforts. An encompassing term that has come to be used for call centre services is 'customer interaction and support'.

A call centre is a specialized facility that may be owned by a firm that provides the relevant products or services, or be owned by a different firm, which provides call centre services to its client. In the latter case, the call centre services are an example of outsourcing. In either case, if the facility is located in a country different from the main location of the firm's customers who rely on the services of the call centre, this is termed offshoring. Thus, the two terms are conceptually distinct, and neither one necessarily implies the other, though they are often implemented together. Outsourced call centres are a special case of business process outsourcing (BPO), and somewhat synonymously, information technology enabled services (ITES). BPO is a broad term, including accounting, research and analysis, human resource management, and information technology (IT) infrastructure management (Singh 2004). Call centres are an important sub-category of BPO, and often the most controversial, because of their unique demands on employees. They may handle other BPO tasks, but are more likely to specialize in voice interactions, and even handle only certain kinds of these (for example, just technical support, or just credit card-related issues).

Call centres in India may serve domestic firms, but their greatest prominence arises in cases where their clients or owners are developed country firms, chiefly those in the United States. The main motivation for offshoring call centres to countries like India has been cost savings. These savings may also be coupled with factors such as workforce availability and quality, expanded response availability due to differences in time zones, and diversification motives. In India, the growth of the software and IT services industry was crucial in paving the way for offshored call centres. The success of Indian firms in IT services accelerated the development of digital communications infrastructure linking India with the United States and Europe, developed and demonstrated the managerial competence of Indians, and proved the workability of providing global quality services from India.

Statistics for Indian call centres are typically not broken out from overall ITES–BPO data. India's National Association of Software and Services Companies (NASSCOM) reported ITES–BPO export revenue of about US$12 billion (over half of which was from the US) in 2009, domestic revenue of almost US$ 2 billion, and direct employment of close to 1,000,000

(Italian Trade Commission 2010). Of these totals, the figures for customer interaction and support (across all industries or verticals) were US$ 5 billion from exports and US$ 1.4 billion from domestic sources, with employment figures of perhaps 400,000, if assumed proportional. The overall numbers are small relative to the Indian economy, but growth rates have been high, with the 2009 numbers representing more than a tripling over the previous six years.

Call centres in India are run by independent domestic firms as well as subsidiary operations of major global firms. In some cases, such as Daksh by IBM, an independent Indian firm has been acquired by a multinational. In other cases, such as Spectramind by Wipro, the acquirer has been a larger Indian firm. Other examples of large Indian firms in ITES include the WNS Group, Convergys and Zenta, as well as subsidiaries of ICICI, HCL, and Hindujas. There are numerous smaller firms as well, despite continuing consolidation and an ongoing shakeout of poor performers. Multinationals with call centre operations in India include firms such as AOL, Accenture, Dell, EDS, GE, and several financial sector firms. Again, data on call centre components of overall ITES are not available for individual firms.

Call centres, and ITES–BPO in general, are seen as contributing to the growth of the Indian economy, and providing employment for educated urban youth who have otherwise found limited job opportunities, even after economic reforms. Some studies find significant local effects of call centres on educational enrollments (Jensen 2010; Oster and Millett 2010). The overall impact of this sector on the Indian economy is hard to quantify, but, in combination with the IT sector, may have contributed a percentage point or so to the economy's growth rate. There are also positives to be found in the training, skill formation, and workforce entry opportunities that call centres and ITES–BPO in general provide. Call centre employees may welcome the freedom and new opportunities that come with their jobs. Women, in particular, may find call centres a significant addition to options for white collar work. Call centres have clearly become part of India's popular culture (for example, Bhagat 2005).

On the other hand, call centres are singled out for criticism because of the relatively low level of skills required (versus some other BPO segments), and for their negative impacts on young people's lives. The latter, according to critics, include high pressure and stress; night work and associated safety issues; distortion of values, language, and culture; and possibly other forms of exploitation. These criticisms can be tempered by noting that employment is voluntary, that working conditions are subject to regulation, and that employers themselves have a strong incentive to make these jobs attractive to reduce the high turnover rates (as high as 40 per cent a year) that do characterize the industry. Turnover imposes high training costs on employers, and may also have negative spillover effects on morale and productivity of those who remain. One can conjecture that successful, growing Indian call centre firms will adjust their working conditions to overcome these problems. In some cases, NASSCOM may serve as a guiding force and as an industry self-regulator.

Recent trends have seen some US firms move customer interaction services back home, using home-based workers rather than foreign call centres to keep costs down. The slack US job market and customer dissatisfaction with foreign-sounding support staff have helped drive this trend. Even more significantly, the Philippines has emerged as a major competitor for India in customer interaction services, overtaking India in revenues in 2010. The Philippines government studied the operations of Indian call centres, and invested in workforce training. While costs in the Philippines are marginally higher, greater cultural and linguistic affinities have made it a strong competitor (Srivastava 2010). On the other side of the coin, Indian firms are exploring setting up call centres in Africa to compete more effectively worldwide (India Brand Equity Foundation 2010). Overall, though, Indian firms probably see other BPO segments as more lucrative and sustainable in the long run.

In conclusion, call centres in India and elsewhere are part of growing globalization and disaggregation of work, enabled by the falling cost of using information technology for communication and collaboration. They present challenges to existing industrial models, as well as to their host societies; they also provide substantial benefits by contributing to investment and employment. They are likely to be increasingly important over time, but represent just one aspect of globalization and economic change in India.

NIRVIKAR SINGH

References

Bhagat, Chetan. 2005. *One Night at the Call Centre*, New Delhi, Rupa and Co.

Indian Brand Equity Foundation. 2010. 'IT-enabled Services (ITeS)', available at http://www.ibef.org/artdispview.aspx?art_id=26437&cat_id=122&in=41, accessed on 15 December 2010.

Italian Trade Commission. 2010. *India: Information Technology & Information Technology Enabled Services, Profile 2010*, available at http://www.ice.gov.it/paesi/asia/india/, accessed on 15 December 2010.

Jensen, Robert. 2010. 'Economic Opportunities and Gender Differences in Human Capital: An Experimental Test for India', Working Paper, UCLA.

Oster, Emily and Bryce Millett. 2010. 'Do Call Centers Promote School Enrollment? Evidence from India', Working Paper, University of Chicago Booth School of Business.

Singh, Nirvikar. 2004. 'Information Technology and India's Economic Development', in K. Basu (ed.), *India's Emerging Economy: Performance and Prospects in the 1990's and Beyond*, MIT Press, pp. 223–61.

Srivastava, Mahul. 2010. 'Manila's Banter Beats Bangalore in $21 Billion Call-Center Race', Bloomberg, 2 December, available at http://www.bloomberg.com/news/2010-12-02/manila-s-night-banter-beats-bangalore-in-21-billion-call-center-industry.html, accessed on 15 December 2010.

■ Caste

Estimated to be over 2500 years old, the caste system has undergone many transformations, from the ancient *varna* system to the contemporary *jati* system.[1] The varna system divided the population initially into four and later into five mutually exclusive, endogamous, hereditary, and occupation-specific groups: Brahmins (priests, teachers), Kshatriyas (warriors, part of royalty), Vaisyas (traders, retailers, moneylenders, other businessmen), and Sudras (all manual work, menial jobs). The latter split into two over the years, adding another category: the Ati-Sudras.[2] The last two comprised all castes doing menial jobs with the latter being considered 'untouchables' in that even their presence was considered polluting and thus to be avoided.[3] The three higher varnas are often referred to as 'caste Hindus' (upper caste Hindus) or as 'twice born', since (the men of) these castes enter an initiation ceremony (the second birth) and are allowed to wear the sacred thread. Together, the upper castes constitute 17–18 per cent of the population. The Ati-Sudras are roughly 16 per cent of the population. Numerically, the largest varna is Sudra, constituting nearly half of the population.

Clearly, this division of castes corresponded to a rudimentary economy. Over the years as economy and society grew more complex, this system metamorphosed into the jati system with features similar to the varna system, but with some differences. First, the exact number of jatis is not known with certainty; they are estimated to be over 3,000. Second, jatis are regional categories, making inter-regional comparisons of jatis less than straightforward. Third, the jati–occupation link is not as straightforward as the varna–occupation link. Jatis are not clear subsets of the varnas, thus making the ranking of jatis an enormously complicated task, if not an impossible one. It is useful to think of varnas as a scale on which the jatis try and align themselves. Thus claims and counter-claims by jatis of a certain (coveted) varna status are common, the validity of which is often impossible to establish. However, the association between jati and varna at the topmost level (Brahmin jatis, most Kshatriya jatis) and at the bottom (Ati-Sudra or former untouchables) is clearer than it is in the middle ranks.

Being at the bottom of the caste hierarchy, the former untouchables are not only poorer, but also continue to be targets of discrimination, oppression, violence, and exclusion. Thus the affirmative action programme in India is targeted at these jatis, designed both to bring these groups into the mainstream and to compensate them for centuries of discrimination. The names of these jatis are listed in a government schedule and thus in official literature these castes are referred to as scheduled castes, or simply as SCs. Mahatma Gandhi referred to them as Harijans, literally as people of (close to) God, but some view this as a patronizing term. Most prefer to use the originally Sanskrit, but now Marathi, 'dalit' meaning the oppressed, which is seen as a term of pride. It should be noted that in independent India, untouchability is abolished by law, and caste-based discrimination in principle is punishable by law. Also, in keeping with the ideal of a casteless society, an individual is not obliged to disclose his/her caste (jati) anywhere. The last jati-based census was in 1931. Subsequent cenuses did not collect information on caste. In a controversial move, the 2011 Census will undertake a separate exercise of enumerating castes, the exact mechanics of which are not clear at the time of writing. Since caste is not ascriptive in the same way as

[1]Unfortunately, these are translated into a single English term, the caste system, which does not enable us to distinguish between these manifestations.

[2]The Ati-Sudras were stigmatized because of their low position in the caste hierarchy. They are thus referred to also as 'avarnas' (literally those without a varna), so low that they are beyond the pale of the caste system in that they are not considered worthy even of being assigned a varna.

[3]The Ati-Sudras were considered untouchables because almost the entire range of social interaction with them was to be avoided by other castes. However, between the other jatis, traditional rules of interaction are complex in that certain interactions (sharing food, for instance) are permitted between certain jatis but not others and these rules vary widely between regions.

race, it is not always possible to ascertain the caste status of an individual if he/she chooses not to reveal it, especially in urban areas.[4] However, overt and covert instances of untouchability continue and caste is used as a basis of both social and economic discrimination.

While the caste system is conventionally associated with Hinduism, all religions in India, including Christianity and Islam, display inter-group disparity akin to a caste system leading to the hypothesis that perhaps caste was a system of social stratification in pre-modern India. This is also true for the so-called egalitarian religions such as Buddhism. 'The term "Brahmana" of the Vedas is accepted by the Buddhists as a term for a saint, one who has attained final sanctification' (Radhakrishnan 2004).[5] Thus Buddhism makes a distinction between Brahmins and others. This is ironic, since Buddhism has been embraced by low castes in large numbers in the belief that it will provide them with the equality that Hinduism denies them. Often, those with a stigmatized ethnic identity, the 'untouchables', have converted to other religions, including Christianity and Islam, as an escape from discrimination and exclusion. However, such conversions do not necessarily guarantee social equality; for instance, the census label 'neo-Buddhist' indicates an ex-untouchable who has converted to Buddhism.

In addition to the caste system, more than 50 million Indians belong to tribal communities that are often distinct from the Hindu religious fold. These are the *adivasis* (literally original inhabitants) who have origins that precede the Aryans and even the Dravidians of the south. Many have lifestyles and religious practices that are distinct from any of the known religions in India and languages distinct from the official languages of India and their dialects. Most live on the margins of existence, excluded from the mainstream development process. These tribes are also targets of affirmative action, similarly notified in a government schedule and hence referred to as scheduled tribes or STs.

Very close to the social and economic position of the dalits are several of the erstwhile Sudra jatis that, however, have *not* been targets of untouchability. The blanket term 'Other Backward Classes' (OBCs) is supposed to capture these jatis that have been described in the Constitution as 'socially and educationally backward classes'. The demand for extending affirmative action to these jatis was finally conceded in 1991 when the Government of India accepted the recommendations of the Mandal Commission report.

The implication of these categories on data availability is the reduction from an extremely high indeterminate number to either three or four categories, making comparisons easier. Up to the early 1990s, government data were available for three categories: SC, ST, 'Others' (everyone who is neither SC nor ST: the residual category). From the mid-1990s, 'Others' got divided into OBCs and 'Others' (non-SC/ST/OBC residual). While the narrowing of the number of categories definitely eases analysis, the non-availability of data by jati does not enable us to isolate the status of the upper castes. However, it should be apparent that any estimate of inter-group disparity, based on this three- or four-way division, will *underestimate* the gap between the top and the bottom end of the caste hierarchy. This is because 'Others' is a residual term that includes 'everyone else' and it thus includes jatis that are very close to SCs in economic and social position.

ASHWINI DESHPANDE

References

Darity Jr, William and Ashwini Deshpande (eds). 2003. *Boundaries of Clan and Colour: Cross National Comparison of Inter-group Inequality*, London, Routledge.

Radhakrishnan, S. 2004. 'The Dhammapada', ch. XXVI, 'Brahmanavaggo', in *The Buddhism Omnibus*, New Delhi, Oxford University Press.

Sukhamoy Chakravarty

Sukhamoy Chakravarty (1934–90) was one of the foremost economists of post-Independence India. He was of course a theorist of the first rank but by his contemporaries as well as generations of his students at the Delhi School of Economics, where he was Professor of mathematical economics from 1964 till his death in 1990, he would be remembered as a scholar of formidable intellect and extraordinary erudition. He combined his professorial commitments with practical policymaking at the highest levels of government from the relatively early age of 37, when he was inducted as member of the central government's Planning Commission. With his untimely death at the age of 56, the profession lost one of the most gifted analysts of development economics as well as the Indian growth

[4]For the differences between race and caste as categories, see 'Introduction' to Darity and Deshpande (2003).

[5]Radhakrishnan (2004: 177) quotes J.G. Jennings: 'It should never be forgotten that Buddhism is a reformed Brahmanism, as is evidenced by the invariably honorific use which Gautama makes of the title "Brahmin" and it therefore takes for granted certain Vedic or Vedantic postulates.'

process from whom many more insightful contributions could have been expected.

Sukhamoy was born on 26 July 1934 in Mymensingh, Bangladesh, in an intellectually distinguished family, the third child among five brothers and two sisters. His father Somnath Chakravarty was a lawyer who retired as a judge of Dhaka High Court. Sukhamoy's paternal grandfather was also a lawyer, but he had only a brief stint at the District Court in Mymensingh, and his real interest was Indian philosophy. Sukhamoy's mother was Bindubasini, a simple and upright person, whose father had studied at Calcutta's Sanskrit College and ran his own Sanskrit school in a village in northern Mymensingh.

Sukhamoy performed brilliantly at Ballygunge Government School and then Presidency College, Calcutta, from where he completed his bachelor's in economics in 1953. After finishing his master's in 1955 he began working at the Indian Statistical Institute in Calcutta where he worked with the physicist–statistician Prasanta Mahalanobis. He worked out a generalization of the 'Mahalanobis model' which formed the core of India's Second Five Year Plan. He then proceeded to the Netherlands School of Economics to work on his PhD under Jan Tinbergen, who was later to be one of the first two to receive the Nobel prize in Economics. After completing his doctorate in 1958, which was later published as *The Logic of Investment Planning* by North-Holland, Sukhamoy went to the Massachusetts Institute of Technology (MIT) as Assistant Professor and came to know Paul Samuelson, Robert Solow, and Paul Rosenstein-Rodan. Paul Samuelson was to remain among Sukhamoy's lifelong band of admirers.

After a brief spell of teaching at Presidency College and then again at MIT in the early 1960s, Sukhamoy came to the Delhi School of Economics in 1964 to take up the chair Professorship in mathematical economics. From here on it was to be a lifelong association with the Delhi School, barring a few spells in government and some universities abroad.

To say that Sukhamoy made a strong impact among students and faculty with his formidable learning would be a gross understatement. Amartya Sen and Jagdish Bhagwati had joined the Delhi School around the same time. Around the mid-1960s the Delhi School was a major centre of learning with many prominent scholars working there who included K.N. Raj, Tapan Raychaudhuri, A.L. Nagar, Dharma Kumar, and Mrinal Datta Chaudhuri. It was still the early stage of post-Independence India and the intellectual climate was redolent with possibilities for a country that was still mired in abysmal poverty, illiteracy, and ill health. Sukhamoy stood out amongst his eminent colleagues with his acute scholarship and his fundamental belief that cerebral intellectual pursuits could be brought to bear upon the vast tasks that lay before a young and resurgent nation.

The earliest academic concerns of Sukhamoy centred on the question of investment planning. His PhD thesis was a dynamic generalization of Mahalanobis's four-sector model, and the exercise was formulated in terms of Tinbergen's fixed targets framework. Sukhamoy was careful to emphasize the structural features of underdevelopment and he paid particular attention to gestation lags in the production process. He soon turned his attention to the question of optimum savings and using techniques of control theory, and dynamic programming was able to characterize the optimum path of saving and growth over an infinite time horizon. This was precisely the agenda that was laid out in the late 1920s by the work of the brilliant Cambridge economist Frank Ramsey who had an untimely death at the age of 26. Sukhamoy later considered the optimum saving question with a finite planning horizon, with well-specified terminal capital requirements at the end of the time horizon. This work was very similar to the explorations of another Cambridge economist, Richard Goodwin, who independently arrived at similar conclusions around the same time.

Sukhamoy's seminal contributions on mainstream growth and development theory are contained in his classic monograph, *Capital and Development Planning*, published in 1969 by MIT Press. In the foreword to this book, Paul Samuelson described Sukhamoy as 'that rare specimen of an almost empty set—namely, the logical intersection of C.P. Snow's two cultures'.

In an autobiographical essay about his own career Sukhamoy writes that towards the end of the 1960s he began to feel that he required a closer exposure to real-life situations if some relevance was to be breathed into the abstract planning models he was engaged in exploring. He was appointed member of the Indian Planning Commission in 1971, and was assigned wide-ranging responsibilities starting with perspective planning and ending with the preparation of annual budgets. From here on Sukhamoy's intellectual concerns decidedly turned towards the Indian planning and development process. His most notable work in this area is his book entitled *Development Planning: The Indian Experience*, published in 1987 by Clarendon Press, which was based on his highly successful Radhakrishnan Memorial Lectures delivered at Oxford University. In this he offers what may be called an insider's, but at the same time a critical and nuanced, view of the various policy strategies that were adopted by the Indian planners.

Sukhamoy was a voracious reader and even though he has described himself primarily as a development economist, there was hardly any branch of economics on which he had not read widely as well as deeply. He was particularly well read in the history of economic thought. Towards the latter part of his career Sukhamoy distanced himself from the formal strands in Anglo-American mainstream economics and found himself intellectually closer to the thought of, among others, Allyn Young, Adolph Lowe, and, especially, Joseph Schumpeter. In 1980 he published a brief monograph entitled *Alternative Approaches to a Theory of Economic Growth: Marx, Marshall and Schumpeter*, based on his R.C. Dutt Memorial Lectures delivered in Kolkata. His contention here was that after the original formulations of growth and development contained in the works of Smith and Ricardo, two strands, or branches, may be discerned. The first he calls the Mill–Marshall approach, which eventually gave rise to the modern neoclassical growth theory, very much in the mainstream tradition. Sukhamoy identifies the other strand, also emerging from Smith–Ricardo, to be discerned in the writings of Marx and then Schumpeter, which, to his mind, had not been adequately explored, and which carry, in his words, 'indispensable ingredients for gaining deeper insights into a revolutionary process in economics'.

Several honours came Sukhamoy's way. Only a few need be mentioned here. He was President of the Indian Econometric Society during 1983–5 and President of the Indian Economic Association for 1985–6. He was a recipient of the Mahalanobis Memorial Gold Medal in 1974 and the first recipient of the V.K.R.V. Rao Prize in the Social Sciences in 1978. From 1983 till his death he was Chairman of the Economic Advisory Council of the Prime Minister. From 1987 onwards he was also Chairman of the Indian Council of Social Science Research.

Despite his various public commitments, Sukhamoy's passion for ideas never waned. He was a polymath, and other than economics he was prodigiously well read in philosophy, history, mathematics, and physics. And he never wavered in his fundamental belief in the power of well-intentioned intellectual pursuits to ultimately improve the human condition.

PULIN B. NAYAK

■ Sachin Chaudhuri

Two individuals, neither a professional economist per se, are responsible for the distinguished stature economics has reached in India today. One of them is P.C. Mahalanobis, the statistician; the other is Sachin Chaudhuri (1904–66) founder–editor of the *Economic Weekly* and, later, the *Economic and Political Weekly* (*EPW*). Chaudhuri did courses in economics at the University of Dacca in the early 1920s but, unlike the single-minded devotion to the discipline exemplified by his friend and contemporary A.K. Dasgupta, Chaudhuri's interests had a far broader sweep. He was enamoured of the classics and loved to flaunt his easy acquaintance with Sanskrit literature and grammar. He was equally interested in history, music, philosophy, and political activism: in other words, a dilettante par excellence. For more than two decades following his graduation from Dacca, he would occupy himself in fleeting diverse roles: an occasional participant in the nation's freedom struggle, an off-and-on private tutor for wayward children of rich families, a wandering journalist, a stock market analyst, and an errant PhD scholar at the School of Economics and Sociology of the University of Bombay. The Second World War saw him transformed into a scriptwriter for War documentaries. For a time he was also general manager of the country's leading film-producing concern. His curiosity concerning both economic theory and national and international economic affairs was, however, of an abiding nature. Stories vary about what provoked him into floating the *Economic Weekly* in 1949, but he finally got trapped in a mission. Finances were arranged by a younger brother, but the idiosyncrasy the journal displayed from the very beginning bore the stamp of Chaudhuri's persona. Barring perhaps the fare served by the *Ekonomist* of the Netherlands, the mix of the *Economic Weekly*'s contents was quite unique: semi-journalistic, semi-scholarly patter on economic issues, tongue-in-cheek discourses on high and low political events, stock market notes, interspersed with serious papers and articles on problems belonging to the arcane world of economic theory. Such juxtaposition amused Chaudhuri even as it attracted a growing crowd of admirers from far and near. The admirers soon turned into acolytes. The rich spread the *Economic Weekly* provided went far beyond economics. Every week there would be some interesting articles or comments on issues of domestic politics, international affairs, international law, history, sociology, anthropology, and so on. The emphasis on the heterogeneity of themes was accompanied by an obsession with readability. While the general stance was one of responsible-sounding pontification, the journal never ceased to be either irreverent or cheeky. It would obstinately carry doggerel—and cartoons too—lampooning characters in current economic and political fracases. It pioneered psephological research in India; it pioneered no-holds-barred debates on the gender problem; it also featured a regular column on corporate affairs. The *Economic Weekly* started as a tour de force and came to endure as an institution.

The success the journal achieved is largely attributable to two factors. The first of course is Chaudhuri's charm, which attracted into his parlour an unending flock of young academic aspirants. They discovered in the journal a haven that offered them shelter and encouraged them to try out, in an open forum, their ideas, howsoever wayward and irresponsible they might seem. It would be difficult to spot even a single Indian academic with recognized contribution in any of the social sciences who did not have his early grooming in the pages of the *Economic Weekly*. The journal taught them to think, and to chisel their thoughts. In the process, the *Economic Weekly* played host to some remarkable debates on several economic and political issues of contemporary relevance: plan models and planning techniques, the relationship between farm size and productivity or between growth and income distribution, facets of rural and urban poverty, the choice of technology, monetory, fiscal and trade policies, problems of education and literacy, agrarian structure and tenurial reforms, population growth and demographic matters, law and civil society, and so on.

What equally explains the journal's rapidly growing influence was the intense care Chaudhuri took to put into shape manuscripts submitted by academic greenhorns. Such magnanimity on his part sprouted many exciting scholarly careers. He did not stand for rank or reputation and treated with equal respect persons from different social strata; a modest fund of imagination and some originality of thought were the passwords for entry into Chaudhuri's benign circle. His fierce independence of outlook was at the same time instrumental in attracting the respect of politicians, civil servants, and corporate kinds.

Chaudhuri's personal beliefs leaned to the left-liberal direction. He had faith in the pivotal role of the public sector as the centrepiece of creativity in post-Independence India. He was in that sense a political romantic with strong moorings in the ideology of egalitarianism garnished by tolerance. The focus of his adoration was equally on the heritage of Gandhi and Nehru. This was somewhat surprising for a Bengali intellectual of the times, but there it was.

Because he preferred freedom from entanglement of all species—he was a confirmed bachelor given to chaotic living—he also had a genuine contempt for regularity and organization. He took pride in running the *Economic Weekly* as a cottage industry, and on a shoestring basis. This was fine as a personal philosophy, but it jeopardized the financial viability of the journal. A crisis reached its head in early 1966, when the weekly had to close down. Friends intervened and the journal was revived as the *Economic and Political Weekly* from August of that year. The *EPW* started on a firmer financial footing under the monitorship of the Sameeksha Trust, of which Sachin Chaudhuri was named managing trustee. But his heart, one suspects, was not in attachment to a structured organism. He died of a massive cardiac arrest in the final week of the year. The *EPW* has since emerged as Asia's leading journal in social sciences. Its present state of financial health would have scandalized Sachin Chaudhuri.

Ashok Mitra

■ Child Labour

Although scholarship and public policy have made it possible to clearly analyse the causes of and solutions to the problem of child labour, the lessons of such analysis have thus far been lost on the Indian state. There are more child workers in India than in any other country in the world. While the policy of modern states is based on a sociological view of 'childhood being, *inter alia*, a period of learning through school, recreation, and other activity, not essentially a period of working at income-bearing tasks', policy in India is not based on such an understanding. As Myron Weiner points out in his landmark study *The Child and the State in India*, in India, neither is child labour illegal nor school education compulsory.

Definition of Child Labour

There are two immediate determinants of the definition of child labour: first, the age until which a person is to be considered a 'child' and second, the definition of 'work' itself.

The resolution of the International Labour Organization (ILO) 'Concerning Minimum Age for Admission to Employment' (Convention No. 138), passed in 1973, recommends that no person below 15 years be considered suitable for employment. For this reason, most scholars in the field take child labour to refer to workers below the age of 15. The UN Convention on the Rights of the Child (1989), however, refers to children as persons below the age of 18. The two major sources of data on the labour force in India, namely, the Census of India and the National Sample Survey (NSS), define 'work' as participation in any economically productive activity.

The Census of India and the NSS tend to undercount the number of child workers for three main reasons. First, children working in factories and other urban locations may be hidden from enumerators and simply not be counted when data are collected. Second, it is difficult to identify child workers in an economy where subsistence production still occurs on a large scale and where many children work in homes or in the informal economy. Third, a substantial part of the child labour force is likely to be employed at housework and family-based work that lie outside the system of national accounts (and consequently outside the definition of 'work').

Thirty-one per cent of children in the age group 5 to 14 years in 2001 comprised children who were neither attending school nor participating in work. Such children numbered 92 million. A large proportion of such children may be employed in household and family-based work; those who are not, constitute potential child labour.

Estimates of Child Labour

According to the Census of India, there were 12.6 million workers in the age group 5 to 14 years in India in 2001. According to the NSS, there were 10.3 million workers in the same age group in 1999–2000 (5.5 million boys and 4.8 million girls), down from 13.1 million in 1993–4.

The ratio of child workers to all children aged 5 to14 years in 2001 was 5.1 per cent among boys and 4.8 per cent among girls. These ratios were higher in 1991: 5.7 per cent among boys and 5.1 per cent among girls. Estimates of work participation rates among children in the same age group from the NSS also show a decline over time. In rural areas, for example, work participation rates fell from 7.1 per cent in 1993–4 to 4.7 per cent in 1999–2000 for boys and from 7.2 to 4.9 per cent for girls during the same period. The rate was lower in urban areas and the decline was also smaller (from 3.6 to 2.7 per cent for boys and from 2.5 to 1.9 per cent for girls between 1993–4 and 1999–2000).

The all-India average hides large variations across states. In 2001, the rural work participation rate for children in the age group 5 to 14 years was 7.7 per cent in Andhra Pradesh and 0.5 per cent in Kerala. Some other states with a higher-than-average child work participation rate were Karnataka, Madhya Pradesh, Jharkhand, Chhattisgarh, and Rajasthan. The rural child work participation rate in states considered to be relatively backward such as Bihar and Uttar Pradesh was, in fact, lower (4.7 per cent and 4.1 per cent respectively). However, in terms of absolute size, 53 per cent of all child workers in 2001 were concentrated in the five states of Andhra Pradesh, Bihar, Madhya Pradesh, Rajasthan, and Uttar Pradesh.

Child labour is predominantly a rural phenomenon: rural areas account for 85 per cent of child workers and the incidence of child labour is higher in rural areas than in urban areas. Almost 80 per cent of estimated child workers are employed in agriculture. Nevertheless, there are some urban pockets with a high incidence and visible concentration of child labour in specific industries. These include gem polishing in Jaipur, fireworks in Sivakasi, diamond cutting in Surat, slate making in Markapur, and silk weaving in Varanasi.

Conditions of Work, Hazardous Work, and Legislation

Child work in India is characterized by exploitative work contracts and abysmal conditions of work. Children work long hours (12–14 hours a day in the lock-making industry of Aligarh) for low wages (a child's wage was one-tenth an adult's in gem polishing in Jaipur), and in dangerous work environments (close to hot furnaces in the glass factories of Firozabad) (Burra 1995). Literacy among child workers is very low, they suffer ailments at an early age, and their life expectancy is unlikely to be high. There is also a sexual division of labour, with girls generally employed at lower wages than boys.

Current legislation in India does not ban all forms of child labour. The Child Labour (Prohibition and Regulation) Act, 1986, is concerned only with 'the engagement of children in certain employments' and accordingly lists specific occupations and processes in which the employment of children is banned or is to be regulated. The occupations specified in the Act include work in the railways, ports and the sale of fireworks, and the processes specified include, for example, *bidi* making, carpet weaving, and the manufacture of soaps, matches and cement. Recently, work as domestic servants and in hotels and teashops has been added to the list of hazardous occupations.

The ILO Convention (No. 182) on the Worst Forms of Child Labour, 1999, seeks the immediate elimination of certain types of child labour including slavery (sale of children, debt bondage, etc.), prostitution, drug trafficking, and other hazardous activity (or 'work which is likely to harm the health, safety, or morals of children'). While the objective of legislation and policy must be to illegalize *all* forms of child labour immediately, there is no doubt that bonded labour and other extremely exploitative forms of chid labour require specific and priority attention. It may be noted here that quite apart from the fact that all working children are exposed to a variety of hazards, only some of which are intrinsic to the work process, many 'dangerous processes' are actually excluded from the purview of the 1986 Indian Act (Burra 1995). Hazards arise from the work environment and conditions of work and the vulnerability of children (ibid.). Work in a carpenter's workshop or as field labour is not considered hazardous in India but can be dangerous for young children.

Causes for the Persistence of Child Labour

Why does child labour persist? Undoubtedly, income poverty is the seed-bed for child labour. It is the children of the poor, and of the socially and economically deprived sections of the population, who work. However, while 'poverty provides conditions for the supply of child labour it is not a sufficient explanation' for the prevalence of child labour in India today (Chandrasekhar 1997; Basu and Van 1998). There is no simple correlation between the incidence of child labour and that of income poverty across states. Surveys have also shown that the overwhelming majority of income-poor parents desire their children to go to school and not to work (PROBE 1999).

A central factor in the persistence of child labour is the *demand* for child labour. The demand for child labour is broadly of two types: first, from employers who attempt to make larger profits by employing cheap workers and, second, from small employers or household enterprises attempting to survive in low-productivity activities (Chandrasekhar 1997).

A detailed study of the match-making industry in the Sivakasi–Sattur belt of Tamil Nadu found that the handmade match sector survived mainly because of cheap female and child labour (Chandrasekhar 1997). If child workers withdraw from the industry, adult wages would rise (thus increasing the earnings of worker households) but the costs of production would also rise. The latter costs, however, could be transferred to consumers (through price increases) or be taken from profit mark-ups and trader margins through a reorganization of the industry. The study showed that costs to employers of abolishing child labour are not excessive and can be met through technological and organizational change.

Two arguments are used to justify the continuation of at least some forms of child labour. The first argument is that children have certain special skills, for example, 'nimble fingers', which help them perform certain activities and processes better than adult workers. This argument has been proved to be wrong. No occupation in India is wholly child-specific: in every activity that children are employed in, adults are also employed. There is no process where the labour power of children cannot be replaced by the labour power of adults, and no technological reason for the continuation of child labour (Chandrasekhar 1997). The 'nimble fingers' argument is in fact a mask for the demand for a low-cost and obedient workforce.

The second argument pertains to skill formation. It is argued that some traditional skills are acquired over time through the process of work itself. Early training, it is argued, leads to better skills and improved incomes and job mobility. This argument is also incorrect. There is evidence that starting work at an early age does not bring any additional economic benefits. A study of teenage workers in Bhavnagar, Gujarat, separated those who began work before the age of 14, the early starters, from those who started working at the age of 15 or later, and found that among boys, the early starters earned less and put in longer hours of work than the late starters (Swaminathan 1997). The primary determinant of wage differentials was not how early in his childhood a worker had begun to work, but the level of education of the individual worker.

What Needs to be Done

It is time to recognize in practice that all children have a right to education and leisure and other means to develop their physical and mental capabilities during childhood, and consequently, to end all forms of child labour.

Some argue that child labour cannot be stopped (and even that it is harmful to stop child labour) until income poverty is eradicated. Their grounds are usually two: first, a concern for the household that depends on the earnings of the child worker and, second, the alleged impossibility of enforcing a ban on child labour in a situation of poverty.

History and comparative development experience clearly demonstrate that the achievement of universal school education and the abolition of child labour are not dependent on the level of per capita income or the level of industrialization or the socio-economic status of families (Weiner 1991). Even in India, the experience of Kerala shows that near-universal schooling and a very low incidence of child labour can be achieved at a relatively low level of per capita income. In almost all countries of the world, the spread of mass education and accompanying reduction in child labour *preceded* economic growth (and was, in fact, a *precondition* for economic development). The abolition of child labour does not have to wait for the end of income poverty.

With regard to enforcement, it is easier to ensure that children go to school than to enforce a ban on child labour by inspecting workplaces. The only way to ensure an end to child labour is to make schooling universal and compulsory. The task of ensuring universal compulsory schooling in a poor country is by no means easy. The state must commit itself to providing adequate school infrastructure and make primary and secondary education of good quality accessible to all children. Schools need trained teachers, teaching material, sports equipment, and other basic infrastructure. The majority of children need not just free tuition but also books and uniforms as well as special incentives such as hot school meals.

It is also important to influence parents and their decision to send children to work, and while reducing poverty is essential, a direct impact on child labour participation can be expected from a rise in adult wages. To improve wages and working conditions, adult workers—and not child workers (as some would have it)—need to be organized.

On the demand side, governments must enforce a legal ban on all forms of child labour and punitive measures against employers of child labour. Trade sanctions are product- or sector-specific measures, and as such of limited relevance, besides often being disguised protectionism by advanced capitalist countries.

MADHURA SWAMINATHAN

References

Basu, K. and P.H. Van. 1998. 'Economics of Child Labour', *American Economic Review*, 88(3): 412–27.

Burra, Neera. 1995. *Born to Work: Child Labour in India*, New Delhi, Oxford University Press.

Chandrasekhar, C.P. 1997. 'The Economic Consequences of the Abolition of Child Labour: An Indian Case Study', *Journal of Peasant Studies*, April, 24(3): 137–79.

PROBE Team. 1999. *Public Report on Basic Education in India*, New Delhi, Oxford University Press.

Swaminathan, Madhura. 1997. 'Do Child Workers Acquire Specialised Skills? A Case Study of Teenage Workers in Bhavnagar', *Indian Journal of Labour Economics*, 40(4). 829–39.

Weiner, Myron. 1991. *The Child and the State in India: Child Labour and Education Policy in Comparative Perspective*, Princeton, Princeton University Press.

■ Child Malnutrition and Feeding Practices

With one in every three malnourished children in the world living in India, malnutrition is one of India's largest development problems. Around 46 per cent of all children below the age of 3 are too small for their age, 47 per cent are underweight, and at least 16 per cent are wasted (UNICEF website on Nutrition in India). More than half of all child deaths are associated with malnutrition. The prevalence of malnutrition varies across states, with Madhya Pradesh recording the highest rate (55 per cent) and Kerala among the lowest (27 per cent).

Malnutrition that sets in during the first three years of a child's life has effects on the child such as stunted growth, weakened immune systems, and lower IQ rates that persist long after infancy and into adulthood. The effects of malnutrition that sets in during this young period in a child's life are often irreversible and lead to severe health problems in adulthood as well. Malnourished children are less likely to perform well in school and more likely to grow into malnourished adults, at greater risk of disease and early death. 'Though quieter than famine, it (persistent undernutrition) kills many more people slowly in the long run than famines do' (Drèze and Sen 1989).

The Causes of Malnutrition in India

The reasons for the high rates of malnutrition in India are manifold. Some of the most common are: low birth weight that is attributed to the poor nutritional status of the mother, both in terms of food intake as well as high levels of anaemia (iron deficiency), high levels of disease often caused by poor hygienic conditions and poor water, lack of availability or adequate use of medical facilities to promote child's health and growth, and, finally, improper feeding practices including lack of exclusive breastfeeding and lack of proper supplementary feeding.

This entry focuses on the last aspect, namely, how proper feeding practices can help prevent malnutrition. Practices that constitute 'proper' or 'best' feeding are defined in *Facts for Life*, a guide to proper nutrition and healthcare published by UNICEF, UNAIDS, UNDP, UNFPA, WHO, UNESCO, WFP, and the World Bank. These are:

1. The infant must be breastfed within 30 minutes of birth with the mother's colostrum. Colostrum is the thick, yellow breastmilk produced in the first three or four days of the baby's life, which is rich in vitamins and helps build the child's immunity.
2. The child should be exclusively breastfed at least five times a day for six months. This means that the baby should not be fed anything but breastmilk as water, other beverages, and solid foods are not easily digestible and may not be hygienically prepared. Breastmilk is superior to all other foods and breastmilk substitutes since it provides essential fatty acids and nutrients that assist the child's development and protect him/her from infection.

3. Supplementary foods must be introduced when the child is approximately six months old. *Dal*, rice, gruel, and *idly* are examples of nutritious Indian foods that are shown to facilitate normal growth of the infant.
4. The child should continue to breastfeed until it is about 24 months, gradually decreasing breastmilk intake until completely transitioned into solid foods.

There is some debate on the viability of the six-month exclusive breastfeeding period mainly due to the fact that many malnourished mothers are often deficient in breastmilk and, therefore, unable to breastfeed the baby as often as it should be during that six-month period (Anandaiah and Choe 2000). However, it is acknowledged that the above guidelines can help prevent child malnutrition. Moreover, these guidelines are relatively simple to follow and need no external agencies to implement.

Policy in India: Integrated Child Development Services

The Integrated Child Development Services (ICDS) scheme, a Government of India programme, is the largest programme for promotion of maternal and child health and nutrition in the world (ICDS website). UNICEF and the World Bank helped launch the ICDS in collaboration with the Government of India in 1975 and have provided it with technical and financial assistance. The ICDS has now expanded to cover 4.8 million expectant and nursing mothers and over 23 million children under the age of 6 (UNICEF website on ICDS). It is an integrated early childhood programme aimed at improving the development, nutrition, and education of children and comprises the following components: healthcare counselling for mothers, non-formal schooling for pre-school children, supplementary feeding for all children, pregnant and nursing mothers, growth monitoring and promotion, and links to primary healthcare services such as immunization and Vitamin A supplements.

The ICDS, at the local level, operates through the *anganwadi* worker, a local woman resident of the village with at least seven years of education. She and one other female helper are trained by the government for seven months to perform the duties of the ICDS at village level. As part of the ICDS nutritional component, the anganwadi worker is supposed to distribute nutritional packages to mothers of young children and conduct house visits to give personal counselling and healthcare education to pregnant and lactating mothers and encourage them to go to the hospital for delivery and health check-ups. Encouraging mothers to adopt the 'proper' feeding practices is supposed to be an essential part of the outreach, in-home counselling done by the anganwadi worker. Even though the successes of the ICDS have been rather uneven and heavily dependent on the character of each individual anganwadi worker, there have been moderate improvements in the nutritional status of children and a more widely adopted usage of the feeding practices. However, customs such as feeding the baby sugar water, animal's milk, or infant baby formula are still prevalent and are often more heavily influenced by other factors than the ICDS programme and, therefore, need to be accounted for in policymaking.

Policy Considerations

It is widely acknowledged that an increase in the mother's status—her education, role in family decision-making, and income-holding abilities—increases the health, nutrition, and educational levels of her children. Also, the mother's well-being determines the nutritional status of her children. Therefore, it is crucial that policies meant to address malnutrition go hand in hand with measures to improve women's status and nutritional health. Only then is a mother 'capable' (Sen 1999) of providing her child adequate care and nutrition.

The mother's exposure to mass media can also influence the child's nutritional status. Mass media is an important means of information dissemination. It can function as an educational medium enabling messages on child-care techniques to reach a much larger, more receptive audience. Therefore, alternative means of communication and information dissemination, such as advertising, messages through popular media, and public-service announcements, need to be further developed and utilized to increase awareness of proper feeding practices and child care.

Finally, many pregnant and lactating mothers take advice from family members on how to raise their children. Yet many counselling services and outreach programmes fail to include the larger family in educating them about the feeding practices and other child-care techniques. Policies that aim at educating the mother must also educate the larger family as it forms the largest source of support, information, and advice for the new mothers.

ANANDITA PHILIPOSE

References

Anandaiah, Ravilla and Minja Kim Choe. 2000. 'Are the WHO Guidelines on Breastfeeding Appropriate for India?', *National Family Health Survey Bulletin*, No.16, May, Mumbai, International Institute for Population Sciences and Honolulu, East–West Center.

Drèze, J. and A.K. Sen. 1989. *Hunger and Public Action*, Oxford, Clarendon Press; New Delhi, Oxford University Press, 1998.
Facts for Life, Third Edition. 2002. Published by UNICEF, WHO, UNESCO, UNFPA, UNDP, UNAIDS, WFP, and the World Bank.
Integrated Child Development Services website. http:/www.indianembassy.org/policy/Children_Women/icds.html:Integrated Child Development Services.
Mishra, Vinod and Robert D. Retherford. 2000. 'Women's Education can Improve Child Nutrition in India', *National Family Health Survey Bulletin*, No.15, February, Mumbai, International Institute for Population Sciences and Honolulu, East–West Center.
Sen, Amartya. 1999. *Development as Freedom*, Oxford, Oxford University Press; New Delhi, Oxford University Press, 2000.
UNICEF website on Nutrition in India. http://www.unicef.org/india/nutrition.html.
UNICEF website on the ICDS. http://www.unicef.org/earlychildhood/files/india_icds.pdf.

■ Chronic Illnesses

India is in the midst of an 'epidemiological transition' whereby, as the population grows richer and older, the burden of illness shifts from infectious diseases to chronic illnesses like diabetes or hypertension. Chronic illnesses pose unique problems in health policy for two reasons: (1) chronic illnesses can only be *managed*, not cured and (2) chronic illnesses are harder to diagnose and patients can remain asymptomatic for a long time. Delays in diagnosis are costly: caught in time, diabetes can be managed without significant losses; left to linger, it can lead to amputated limbs, blindness, and death.

That the same symptoms (tingling in the fingers, occasional fainting) can represent an acute illness or an underlying chronic condition (diabetes) implies that the treatment of such an illness has to be preceded by *search* for a diagnosis. Better diagnosis of chronic illness among higher-income people seems to be one good explanation of the puzzling but consistent relation, across and within countries, that richer people self-report being ill more often than the poor.

The search for accurate diagnoses also raises important questions of incentives in the medical market and equity between rich and poor. Systematic and pervasive failures in the market for diagnostic information lead to underprovision in the private sector. This suggests a role for the government in disseminating information, encouraging preventive behaviour, and improving the accuracy and timeliness of diagnoses.

Whether the government should also subsidize the *treatment* of chronic illnesses is an empirical question that trades off the losses arising from the inadequate management of such illnesses against the opportunity cost of using the same resources for other illnesses. Given the current morbidity profile in India and the low cost of drugs, spending on the treatment of infectious diseases remains a priority that likely leads to a more progressive distribution of government subsidies than subsidizing the treatment of chronic diseases.

What Do We Know about Chronic Illnesses in India?

Most of what we know about chronic illnesses in India is based on small-scale clinical studies of prevalence. These studies show that chronic illnesses differ from acute illnesses in important ways: unlike acute and vaccine-preventable illnesses, chronic illnesses are more common in urban than in rural regions. Furthermore, there has been an increase in chronic and a decline in acute illnesses over time, more so for urban compared to rural regions (Gupta 1997). While changes in life expectancy and selective mortality partially explain this increase, factors consistent with the epidemiological transition clearly play a role.

Patterns of prevalence also differ across income groups. Acute illnesses affect the poor more than the rich—individuals in the poorest quintile are 4.5 times more likely to report tuberculosis, 3.2 times more likely to report malaria, and 2.8 times more likely to report leprosy than those in the richest quintile. The gradient of chronic illnesses with income is less clear. Clinical studies of some chronic illnesses such as hypertension and diabetes suggest a mildly positive relationship with wealth; for other cases, such as anaemia, prevalence rates are higher among the poor. For some chronic illnesses (notably 'life-style' illnesses) the protective effects of income are offset by worse dietary and exercise regimes.

Data on *self-reported* illness paint a different picture. Figure 1 relates self-reports of chronic and acute illnesses to age for a sample of 1,600 individuals in Delhi. Rich households are 9 percentage points, or 72 per cent, more likely to self-report a chronic illness; the effect is equal and opposite for acute illnesses. This difference is seven times larger than the modest rich–poor differences found in clinical studies (typically of the order of 10 per cent). Combining acute and chronic illnesses, the rich self-report *higher* morbidity than the poor, replicating a relationship widely documented in India and other countries.

One explanation is that the rich report more chronic illnesses because they receive accurate diagnoses earlier. In contrast, the high burden of acute illnesses among the

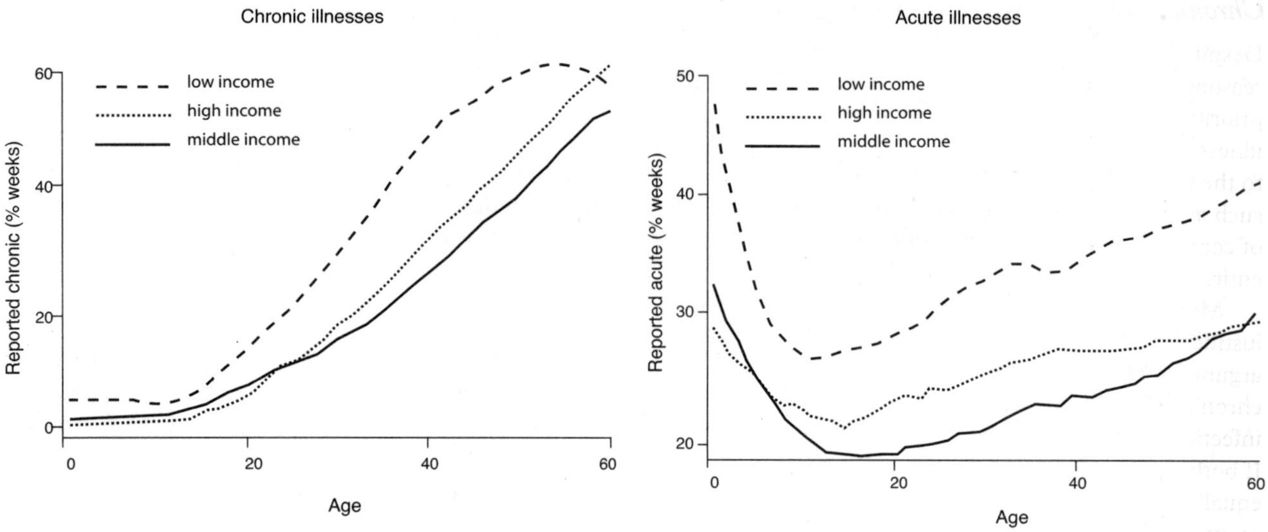

Figure 1 Chronic and Acute Illnesses

Source: Das and Hammer (2005a).
Note: Both figures show the percentage of weeks reported with an illness (chronic or acute) for three income groups plotted non-parametrically against the age of the respondent. Respondents were observed over two years for a total of thirty-five weeks.

poor could (partially) reflect underlying and undiagnosed chronic illnesses—a rich person with high blood pressure medicates regularly and reports hypertension; a poor person reports sporadic headaches and fainting episodes. This phenomenon, known as 'acute-reactive' disorders, imposes significant costs—both because the poor spend frequently (and unproductively) on headaches instead of blood pressure control and because the longer-term consequences of undiagnosed hypertension are severe. The lack of information regarding chronic illnesses plays a substantial role in explaining the positive morbidity–income gradient.

Consumer and Producer Responses to Chronic Illness and Information

New information regarding whether one is suffering from a chronic condition *does* change behaviour regarding healthcare. A longitudinal study in Delhi finds that when people were diagnosed with a chronic illness both the rich and the poor sharply increased their use of medication and maintained this higher use over time. Acute illnesses declined dramatically confirming the hypothesis of 'acute-reactive' disorders. And the labour supply of these individuals, which was on a declining trend prior to the diagnosis, stabilized, leading to substantial productivity gains within a six-month period. Indeed, health expenditures for the poor did not increase, but were reallocated from spending on acute-reactive disorders to spending on the underlying chronic condition (Das and Hammer 2005b). An important factor that allowed the poor to maintain treatment over time could be low drug prices: drug prices in India are the lowest in the international market, sometimes by an order or magnitude (Bala and Sagoo 2000). A week's supply of hypertensive drugs, for instance, costs 50 cents in India compared to $9 in Cameroon.

Timely diagnosis of chronic illnesses thus results in economic and health gains. Nonetheless, *both* the private and public sectors are unlikely to provide economically efficient levels of diagnoses. Doctors in the private sector are not perfect 'agents' and depend on fees. Repeat visits for acute-reactive disorders increase future earnings more than self-medication by patients, tilting the balance in favour of regular treatments over diagnoses and self-medication. Doctors in the public sector who are on a fixed salary are less likely to favour treatment over diagnoses and much less likely to prescribe unnecessary medicines (Phadke 1998; Das and Hammer 2005b). But unfortunately, they also have little incentive to provide *any* effort at all—doctor–patient interactions in the public sector last an average of two minutes. Consequently, for the poor, it is *better* to visit a less qualified provider in the private sector than a more qualified one in the public sector (Das and Hammer 2005b). This problem is not specific to India—poor patients in the US face similar problems with large estimated losses from delays in diagnosis.

Chronic Illness and Policy

Despite increasing chronic illnesses, there are compelling reasons why subsidized *treatment* may not be a high priority for public expenditure. The treatment of chronic illnesses is a private good and the benefits accrue only to the patient. In contrast, treating infectious diseases such as tuberculosis or malaria decreases the likelihood of contagion, extending the benefits of treatment to the entire population.

Moreover, promoting *equity* in health is an oft-stated justification for public health systems. Here, again, the argument favours attacking infectious disease more than chronic. The odds for a poor person suffering from an infectious illness are much higher than for a rich person. If both the poor and the rich use public health systems equally, of every rupee spent on tuberculosis, 80 paise are spent on the poor and 20 on the rich; of every rupee spent on diabetes, the proportion spent on the rich and poor are roughly 50 paise each.

Health policy towards chronic illnesses should focus on improving diagnostic capabilities and the detection of chronic illnesses. The problem is how to balance the opposing incentives for treatment in the public and private sectors—public-sector providers have no incentive to exert effort and the private-sector providers favour treatments that encourage repeat visits. Health Maintenance Organizations in the US with similar problems have introduced payments to doctors based on the illness indicator (blood pressure and insulin levels) for patients under the doctor's care rather than a fixed salary or a fee for service. Recent evaluations show large benefits from such schemes.

Redesigning incentives in the public sector is a long-term proposition. One alternative is to concentrate on the prevention of chronic illnesses by encouraging life-style changes through better information. Information to the public on how to prevent or what to expect from treatment for anaemia, hypertension, and diabetes is a relatively cheap intervention that could yield substantial benefits.

JISHNU DAS AND JEFFREY S. HAMMER

References

Bala, K. and Kiran Sagoo. 2000. 'Patents and Prices', *HAINEWS*, 112, available at http://www.haiweb.org/pubs/hainews Patents%20 and% 20Prices.html.

Das, Jishnu and Jeffrey Hammer. 2005a. 'Chronically Misinformed: Chronic Illnesses, Information and Behavioral Change in Delhi, India', World Bank, Processed.

——. 2005b. 'Money for Nothing: The Dire Straits of Medical Practice in Delhi, India', Policy Research Working Paper No. 3669.

Gupta, R. 1997. 'Meta-analysis of Prevalence of Hypertension in India', *Indian Heart Journal*, 49(1): 43–8.

Phadke, A. 1998. *Drug Supply and Use: Towards a Rational Policy in India*, New Delhi, Sage Publications.

■ Cities

During 1960–2000, world output increased four times, whereas urban population tripled, from 33 per cent to 47 per cent (Mohan and Dasgupta 2005).[1] According to international experience, urbanization picks up faster growth after the proportion of urban population reaches 25 per cent. In India, in 2011, urbanization reached 31 per cent, which means that it is now going to pick up pace.[2] Further, economic reforms in India and globalization have made cities the primary engines of economic growth. As a result of the liberalization policies adopted by the Government of India, the share of the urban population is expected to increase to about 40 per cent of the total population by 2021. While as of 2005, it was expected that roughly half of India's GDP originated in its urban areas, it was estimated that by 2011, urban areas would contribute to about 65 per cent of the country's GDP, highlighting their importance in achieving national growth targets.

In this context, it may be useful to note that more urbanized states (such as Maharashtra, Tamil Nadu, and Gujarat) recorded more than 50 per cent growth in their per capita net state domestic product (at constant 2004–5 prices) during 2004–5 to 2009–10, which was much higher than the average growth for the country (40 per cent over the same period). Even in comparatively less urbanized eastern and northern states, such as Bihar, Orissa, and Uttar Pradesh, the population increase in Class I cities was higher than the growth of the urban population for these states (Lahiri-Dutt and Samanta 2001).[3] Further, cities such as Pune and Hyderabad have

[1]Worldwide, countries define urban areas typically by the number of residents, population density, proportion of people not dependent on agriculture, or the provision of public utilities and services, such as electricity and education. There are no universal standards, and different countries define them differently.

[2]The Census of India defines settlements having the following characteristics as urban areas:

(a) A population of 5,000 or more
(b) A minimum density of 1,000 people per square mile
(c) At least 75 per cent of the workforce outside agriculture

In India, a city is a more specific term referring to a town with a population of 100,000 or more.

[3]The Census of India's definition for various class size cities is:

grown rapidly. Pune's population grew at a whopping rate of 51 per cent over 1991–2001, compared to its growth of 45 per cent over 1981–91. Hyderabad's growth has also been rapid, at 27 per cent over 1991–2001, though it has been less spectacular than that of Pune, and less than half its own growth rate over 1981–91 (67 per cent).[4]

The economic reforms of the 1990s have accelerated the process of city growth. The number of urban agglomerations (UAs)[5] in India grew from 275 to 384 over 1991–2001, with 35 of them being million-plus UAs.[6] The number of cities with million-plus population was 35 in 2001, as compared to only 23 in 2001. The role of million-plus cities is quite significant since, according to the 2001 Census, they accommodated more than one-third of India's urban population.

While Anderson and Ge (2004) examine whether economic reforms in China accelerated urban growth, there are several reasons why we may expect economic reforms to affect city growth in the Indian context.[7] Several examples may be cited of the effect of reforms on cities. First, the Urban Land Ceiling and Regulation Act (ULCRA), which continued to thwart private holdings of vacant land above certain limits in urban areas, was repealed in 1999. With freedom from this control (in all states except West Bengal and Jharkhand as of 2011), urban land should be in a position to claim its market price. This will make housing more affordable and encourage city growth.

Second, with steady liberalization in various sectors, the government, in the 2005–6 Budget, permitted up to 100 per cent foreign direct investment (FDI) in construction and property development. Further, FDI was allowed in areas such as hotel development, resorts, hospitals, educational institutions, and housing projects. In the 2011–12 Budget, in order to give a boost to infrastructure development in railways, ports, housing, and highways development, the government allowed tax free bonds of Rs 30,000 crore to be issued by various government undertakings in 2011–12. Considering the importance of housing, the government also proposed investment linked deduction to businesses which develop affordable housing under a notified scheme along with a number of incentives for facilitating housing sector finance in 2011–12. These are other aspects of urban reforms that increase the supply of housing and other urban amenities that favourably affect city growth.

Third, with increasing liberalization in various sectors, various forms of public–private partnerships are actively being considered by several cities for many city-level infrastructure projects. This means that the private sector will now play a significant role in increasing city production capacity and increasing settlements of people, which is consistent with the standard theory which shows that economies of scale in production necessitate larger plants, requiring increasing numbers of people and resulting in city growth.

More generally, we should ask the question as to what are the factors that drive city growth in India. First, the city's economic base as reflected in the share of manufacturing vis-à-vis service employment is important in its growth. As Lahiri-Dutt and Samanta (2001) point out, the emergence of the powerloom industry in Surat has turned it into a city with million-plus population. In fact, if we examine the rate of growth of all million-plus cities during 1991–2001, Surat grew at the highest rate, with Nasik, Patna, Rajkot, Jaipur, Delhi, and Pune, occupying successive places. Alternatively, the recent rise of cities such as Pune and Hyderabad as hubs for information technology (IT) and IT-enabled services in India, does suggest that while manufacturing cities tend to grow in the early stages of industrialization, services could become important later.

Further, India's 74th Constitutional Amendment Act of 1992 formally recognized local bodies as the

---

Class I: Population >100,000
Class II: Population of 50,000–99,999
Class III: Population of 20,000–49,999
Class IV: Population of 10,000–19,999
Class V: Population of 5,000–9,999
Class VI: Population <5,000.

[4]Unfortunately, even at the time this entry was being revised in September 2011, Census 2011 had not yet released city-level populations.

[5]While, in general, urban agglomerations are areas of 1 million population or more, an UA, according to the Census of India, is:
(a) a city or town with continuous outgrowth(s), the outgrowth being outside the statutory limits, but located within the boundaries of the adjoining village or villages; or
(b) two or more adjoining towns with their outgrowth(s); or
(c) a city with one or more adjoining towns with their outgrowths all of which form a continuous spread.

An outgrowth refers to a conglomeration of houses outside the formal limits of a town (not constituting a settlement/village on their own), having a high degree of interdependence with the town.

An UA, as may be clear, reports data separately for the core city (roughly, the equivalent of the central city or Central Business District [CBD] in American Metropolitan Statistical Areas [MSAs]) and outside of the core city.

[6]As described earlier, the Census of India 2011 had not yet released information on the number of urban agglomerations in the country as of September 2011, when this entry was revised.

[7]Here city growth is defined as a trend that is closely related with industrial expansion and population growth, not merely a process that occurs due to redefinition of urban boundaries. See also Sridhar (2010) which makes a distinction between city *population* growth and city *economic* growth.

third tier of government, making them accountable to the public. This Act devolved new responsibilities, such as planning for social and economic development and poverty alleviation to local governments that were hitherto concerned only with basic services, such as water supply, sanitation, street lighting, and transportation infrastructure.

This constitutional amendment has clear implications for city growth. As the well-known Tiebout hypothesis demonstrates, cities with better levels and quality of public services, such as water, sanitation, sewerage, solid waste management, roads, public safety, and other amenities, may be expected to grow faster. Good public services attract residents and firms, while higher levels of poverty with their corresponding problems of poor sanitation and distress, repel residents and firms. If local revenues from property taxes were to be used to finance the provision of these services, as is done in the US, the public would have the choice between cities that offer varying combinations of tax-service packages. These could be high tax-high quality services, low tax-low quality services, low tax-high quality services, and high tax-low quality services, depending on their efficiency. Then city growth should occur with a combination of high tax-high services quality or, better, low tax-high quality of services offered by their governments. While we do not find evidence of competition to improve public services among city or local governments in India for residents yet, such competition should accelerate city growth.

Next, the instance of fast-growing cities such as Bangalore, Pune, and Hyderabad does suggest that accumulation of human capital causes city growth. This is especially the case if jobs were to follow people, as Mills and Price (1984) and Sridhar (2007) find with respect to the US and India, respectively. Sridhar (2007) finds that for a variety of employment sub-sectors in India, such as manufacturing, transport, communications, and trade and commerce, skills are important in determining the suburbanization of those jobs. So, if cities were to accumulate human capital or a skilled workforce, appropriately measured, firms follow them.

In the Becker–Mills–Williamson model, a computable general equilibrium model of the Indian economy, limits to city growth occur due to the inflation of urban site rents. Rents are aggravated in India's cities because of the existence of rent control (as in many cities worldwide) that diminishes the incentives of property owners to maintain their property, artificially restricts the supply of rental housing, and limits city growth.

Finally, city-specific characteristics, such as land area, and whether or not they are situated in the coastal regions of the country do influence their growth. Everything else remaining the same, cities in the coastal regions grow faster than their counterparts in the inland. This is because coastal cities are characterized by the fact that they are more connected to metropolitan areas abroad than to their own hinterlands. The cities in China's coastal special economic zones are an instance of this phenomenon. The growth of Mumbai as the financial capital of the country is directly attributable to this. The Government of India's attempt, as part of its Budget proposals for 2005–6, to make Mumbai, strategically located midway between London and Tokyo, a regional financial centre is an example of the trend to nurture such cities.

This discussion, while depicting essentially a partial equilibrium approach to city growth, presents a set of testable hypotheses, amenable to be tested with data, if they were to be available. Taking cues from this, Sridhar (2010) empirically examines the determinants of city population growth and economic output in India. In that paper, city growth and economic output regressions are estimated using several approaches. Since only growing areas are usually designated as towns, the urban population of districts that are larger geographical areas than cities is also estimated. The paper finds that at the district level, the proximity to large cities causes cities to grow at a lower rate, reflecting the fact that larger cities thwart the growth of smaller towns in their vicinity. Human capital as measured by the literacy rate has a significant impact on net output per capita. This shows that investment in primary education in cities has to be stepped up because of their favourable and positive impacts on non-agricultural output per capita. The results in Sridhar (2010) also imply that if incentives are provided to develop smaller towns, then their growth rate (rather than their size) may be expected to increase with distance from large cities.

In this manner, many of India's areas could benefit from increasing urbanization and better public services.

Kala Seetharam Sridhar

References

Anderson, G. and Y. Ge. 2004. 'Economic Reform and Urban Growth in China', *Urban Studies*, 41(11): 2197–210.

Lahiri-Dutt, K. and G. Samanta. 2001. 'Million Cities of India: A Review of 2001 Census Data', *Urban India*, 21(2): 97–110.

Mills, E.S. and R. Price. 1984. 'Metropolitan Suburbanisation and Central City Problems', *Journal of Urban Economics*, 15: 1–17.

Mohan, R. and S. Dasgupta. 2005. 'The 21st Century: Asia Becomes Urban', *Economic and Political Weekly*, 40(3): 213–23.

Sridhar, K.S. 2007. 'Density Gradients and Their Determinants: Evidence from India', *Regional Science and Urban Economics*, 37(3): 314–44.

——. 2010. 'Determinants of City Growth and Output in India', *Review of Urban and Regional Development Studies*, 22(1): 22–38.

Constitution and Economic Reforms

Economic reforms in India mark a new phase in the trajectory of India's economic policymaking. Among other things, the reforms represent changes in the role of the state in relation to policies, principles, procedures, institutions, institutional structures, and governance patterns marking a break from an earlier era that was characterized by state-centred economic planning—an era where a number of constitutional amendments were made to accommodate the economic policies of the time. Considering that the 'planning era' was accompanied by considerable constitutional changes through amendments backed by judicial pronouncements and many of the constitutional provisions having direct or indirect bearing on the economy—ranging over the gamut of the Preamble, Part III dealing with Fundamental Rights, Part IV dealing with Directive Principles of State Policy, Part XII dealing with finance, property, contracts, suits (which includes chapters on finance, borrowing, property, contracts, rights, liabilities, and obligations and suits), and Part XIII dealing with trade, commerce, and intercourse within the territory of India and the Seventh Schedule—economic reforms have been introduced without any apparent constitutional amendments coupled with seeming judicial restraints in economic policy matters. This minimally raises two concerns in relation to potential tensions emanating from the interface between the Constitution and economic reforms—one, the understanding as to what construes the state, and two, whether the Indian Constitution adequately serves the moves associated with economic reforms.

Expansive Definition of the State

It is important to raise the issue of what construes the 'state' from a constitutional perspective as it is directly associated with the protection of the fundamental rights of people and their enforcement besides requiring the 'state' to act in a fair, just, transparent, and accountable manner, guaranteeing a level playing field to all, and upholding principles of equality and justice as enshrined in the Constitution of India. In the pre-reforms era, an expanding state had prompted the judiciary to liberally interpret Article 12 of the Constitution and widen the meaning of the term 'state', whereby the initial judicial inhibition of defining the 'state' as a body having sovereign functions gave way to holding all agencies and instrumentalities of the state liable for the protection of Fundamental Rights, which had come to include within its ambit public enterprises, government companies, electricity boards, and universities (see *R.D. Shetty* vs *International Airport Authority* 1979). This expansion rested largely on exploring the nature of functions performed by various agencies, and the need for such agencies to become accountable and transparent in a democratic system of governance. Since the definition of the state has rested so intimately on 'functions', and Fundamental Rights have been defined in relation to these functions, changes in the role of the state and active involvement of various other agencies in carrying on activities that were earlier in the domain of the state is bound to lead to a strain on how Fundamental Rights are to be construed in the era of the changing 'state'. The Supreme Court has been somewhat hesitant in bringing private bodies under the purview of the 'state' but not entirely so as has been the case with environmental jurisprudence where writ petitions have been accepted against private parties (see *M.C. Mehta* vs *Kamal Nath* 1997). Notwithstanding the expanding role of the private sector, and the narrowing down of the activities of the state, including the mere regulatory functions in many a sphere, the Supreme Court has refrained from widely interpreting the 'state', which has had limiting impact on the protection of fundamental rights (see *Balco Employees Union* vs *Union of India*, AIR 2002 SC 350; *Zee Telefilms Ltd.* vs *Union of India*, AIR 2005 SC 2677; *All India ITDC Workers Union* vs *ITDC*, 2006 AIR 2007 SC 301; *Prasar Bharti* vs *Amarjit Singh*, AIR 2007 SC 1269; *Indian Airlines Officers Association* vs *Indian Airlines Ltd.*, AIR 2007 SC 2747; *BPCC Mazdoor Sangh* vs *NTPV*, Appeal (Civil) No. 678 of 2006). There are, however, exceptions to this judicial trend (*Flamingo Duty Free Shop Pvt. Ltd* vs *Union of India*, W.P. No. 617 of 2007 of the Bombay High Court). Besides the protection of Fundamental Rights, the definition of state also raises serious questions on transparency, accountability, and participation, especially when the first two decades of reforms witnessed the Supreme Court passing a number of judgements to unearth corruption and maintain probity in governance, ensuring fair play in granting state largesse and government contracts (see *Delhi Science Forum*, *Tata*

Cellular vs *Union of India*, (1996) 2 SCC 405; *Reliance Energy Ltd.* vs *MSRDC*, Appeal (Civil) No. 3526 of 2007; *Dr. Subramanian Swamy* vs *Dr. Manmohan Singh and Anr*, SLP (C) No. 27535 of 2010). The Court has fallen short of stretching the functionality test to an extent to include private bodies, thus minimally requiring the necessity of amending the Constitution to settle the tension between accountability and fairness, on the one hand, and the problem of interpretation, on the other, which includes adequately addressing public–private partnership models and widening the umbrella of right to information. One crucially problematic area is emerging forms of affirmative action, as is evident in the debate over private-sector reservations (see *Dalco Engineering Private Ltd.* vs *Satish Prabhakar Padhey*, AIR 2010 SC 1576) and quota-based government procurement norms.

Laying Down Constitutional Priorities

In attempting to think of constitutions in relation to economic activity, it is important to view them as being characterized by the generality and stability of their provisions and also as a source of legitimizing institutional structures (Cooter 2000). The era of planning and development considerably narrowed down the generality of the Indian Constitution. Some of the critical changes that have been introduced over the period associated with 'Planning Commission Jurisprudence' (see Dhavan 1989) include the addition of the term 'socialism' to the preamble to the Constitution, which, along with Articles 38 and 39 (b) and (c), has been used to justify 'nationalization' on 'doctrinaire grounds' (*Akadasi Pradhan* vs *State of Orissa* 1963); and changes in Part III of the Constitution that contains the Fundamental Rights, in particular the reduction of the 'right to property' to a constitutional right (see Singh 2005), and more generally subjection of individual liberties, such as the freedom to carry on trade and business to privilege 'reasonable restrictions in the public interest' and/or to further 'Directive Principles', sometimes selectively altered. This regime-specific orientation needs reconsideration, especially when the old planning method of resource allocation has been replaced with a market economy. The fiction of 'public interest' has repeatedly been used by the legislature to mask a variety of interests (see Buchanan and Tullock 1962) and 'public purpose' has been invoked to acquire natural resoures such as land. The judiciary has typically justified interventions by the state in the economy on the grounds that the legislature is the best purveyor of the interests of the people (see *Hamdard Dawakhana* vs *Union of India* 1960), often not even conceiving an impact assessment of judicial pronouncements, letting abstract constitutional aspirations overshadow economic considerations, which is gradually being reconsidered by the Supreme Court, not merely on the technical ground of institutional propriety, but also on the basis of judicial self-introspection on excessive judicial review (see *BSNL* vs *M/s Telephone Cables Ltd.*, AIR 2010 SC 2671). The Constitution can be made adaptable to the process of economic reforms by either replacing the existing set of specific rules with another set of constitutional rules or restoring the generality of provisions in the Constitution. However in the absence of both, there are occasions when the Supreme Court has stepped in and has invoked prembalular aspirations such as justice—social and economic—in a way that unshackles the confines of specificities of attaining it (see *Harjinder Singh* vs *Punjab State Warehousing Corporation*, AIR 2010 SC 1116). Such an approach would allow space for experiments in various models of economic development. In this context it needs to be noted that a constitution is not a static document—it does not necessarily contain absolute values. To the extent a constitution is an organic document, it has to undergo gradual evolution to meet the demands of time, when it outgrows its utility. Society has the right to dismantle constitutional structures to enunciate a new set of principles. In *Golaknath* vs *State of Punjab* (1967), the Supreme Court rightly observed that amendments are a constitutional alternative of revolution. The point, however, is that any change in the meta-rules must not only ensure rules that privilege substantive justice, but also ensure that the rules pass the triple procedural tests of justness, fairness, and non-arbitrariness. Thus, economic reforms have provided an opportunity to enquire into constitutional resilience, which can be addressed either by constitutional amendments or by judicial intervention and the constitutional tensions arising out of economic reforms can be mitigated.

ANINDITA PUJARI

Cases

R.D. Shetty vs *International Airport Authority*, AIR 1979 SC 1628.

M.C. Mehta vs *Kamal Nath* 1997 (1) SCC 388.

Akadasi Pradhan vs *State of Orissa*, AIR 1963 SC 1047.

Hamdard Dawakhana vs *Union of India*, AIR 1960 SC 554.

Golaknath vs *State of Punjab*, AIR 1967 SC 1643.

Balco Employees Union vs *Union of India*, AIR 2002 SC 350.

Zee Telefilms Ltd. vs *Union of India*, AIR 2005 SC 2677.

All India ITDC Workers Union vs *ITDC*, 2006 AIR 2007 SC 301.

Prasar Bharti vs *Amarjit Singh*, AIR 2007 SC 1269.

Indian Airlines Officers Association vs *Indian Airlines Ltd.*, AIR 2007 SC 2747.

BPCC Mazdoor Sangh vs *NTPV*, Appeal (Civil) No. 678 of 2006.

Flamingo Duty Free Shop Pvt. Ltd vs *Union of India*, W.P. No. 617 of 2007.

Delhi Science Forum vs *Union of India*, 1996 2 SCC 405.

Tata Cellular vs *Union of India*, 1996 2 SCC 405.

Reliance Energy Ltd. vs *MSRDC*, Appeal (Civil) No. 3526 of 2007.

Dr. Subramanian Swamy vs *Dr. Manmohan Singh and Anr*, SLP (C) No. 27535 of 2010.

Dalco Engineering Private Ltd. vs *Satish Prabhakar Padhey*, AIR 2010 SC 1576.

BSNL vs *M/s Telephone Cables Ltd*, AIR 2010 SC 2671.

Harjinder Singh vs *Punjab State Warehousing Corporation*, AIR 2010 SC 1116.

References

Buchanan, James M. and Gordon Tullock. 1962. *The Calculus of Consent: Logical Foundations of Constitution and Democracy*, Michigan, University of Michigan Press.

Cooter, Robert D. 2000. *The Strategic Constitution*, New Jersey, Princeton University Press.

Dhavan, Rajeev. 1989. 'Introduction', in Marc Gallanter (ed.), *Law and Society in Modern India*, New Delhi, Oxford University Press.

Singh, Jaivir. 2005. '(Un)constituting Property Rights: The Deconstruction of the Right to Property in India', CSLG Working Paper Series, CSLG/WP/04–05, New Delhi, Centre for the Study of Law and Governance.

■ Contract Farming

Contract farming can be described broadly as an institutional arrangement between farm and firm to produce and transact agricultural commodities on predetermined terms.

The core of contract farming arrangements is some form of commitment, oral or written, on the part of the farmer to provide a commodity of a particular quality and quantity, grown according to specified methods agreed upon before sowing, with a corresponding commitment on the part of the firm to buy that produce at a pre-fixed price. Such an agreement could also involve the firm providing production support through, for example, the supply of inputs and technical advice. This is not the typical arrangement in most developing countries, where farmers make production decisions independently and the produce then passes through many hands before reaching the final buyer.

In theory, contract farming offers farmers an opportunity to link up with a buyer and fix a price even before sowing, thus offering a kind of insurance—not only against price fluctuations, but also against the prospect of not finding a buyer. For firms, the attractiveness of contracting derives from being able to procure timely supplies of quality produce without having to take on the responsibility of managing cultivation on factory-owned farms. It offers an advantage over the spot market too, where supply is usually uncertain and produce might be of variable quality. Further, the direct link between firm and farm implies disintermediation or the elimination of trader–middlemen, saving on transaction costs. In principle, therefore, contract farming is regarded a win–win arrangement with both the farmer and firm standing to benefit.

Contract Farming in India: History and Policy

In India, contract farming goes back to the colonial era when indigo, opium, tobacco, and cotton were sourced from cultivators using forms of marketing contracts. In the post-Independence era, commercial seed production by seed companies that emerged in the 1960s, private and public, has invariably been organized around some kind of contract production. Seed potato and cotton stand out as examples where seed multiplication for firms is undertaken on a large scale by contract farmers. Milk production in the cooperative sector, too, has been along these lines, following Operation Flood in the 1970s. Private-sector milk processors have largely been content following this model. Sugarcane is often cited as a prominent example of contract farming, where the state mandates a command area around sugar mills for procurement on pre-specified terms.

Clearly, contract farming is not a new phenomenon. Yet, a recent wave of industrialization of agriculture in developing countries is precipitating a vigorous shift in favour of contract farming on a scale that is probably unprecedented. Changing tastes of consumers, higher demand for processed foods, and globalization of the agro-industry have, each in their own way, contributed to this redefining of producer–processor relationships in developing countries.

India is no exception. The years since the mid-1990s have seen dramatic change in the institutional landscape of Indian agriculture and could well signify a watershed. To understand why this ongoing transformation is noteworthy, it is useful to step back to look at the recent history of agricultural policy in India.

Ever since Independence, transactions in farm commodities have been regulated heavily, notably through the Essential Commodities Act (ECA) and the Agricultural Produce Marketing Committees Act (APMC Act). The ECA imposes restrictions on storage and movement of certain 'essential' commodities by private parties, mainly to protect consumers. The APMC Act, on the other hand, mandated that purchases of certain agricultural commodities be through government-regulated markets (*mandi*s) with the payment of designated commissions and marketing fees. Furthermore, the Land Ceiling Act proscribed firms from owning and operating large-scale factory-farms. Together, these severely circumscribed private-sector participation in agriculture.

Though the APMC Act was designed to protect farmers' interests, it perversely rendered farmers dependent on middlemen—who were financiers, information brokers, and traders, all rolled into one. This dependency often turned exploitative; farmers received but a fraction of the price paid by the final consumer, with middlemen cornering a large part of the rest. Over time, critics felt that APMC Act and the ECA had perhaps overextended their reach, compromising farmers and consumers in favour of trader–middlemen.

Since 1991, with economy-wide reforms, three broad trends began to put severe pressure on these policies that were perceived to be anachronistic, inefficient, and iniquitous. First, with the growth of private-sector participation and export orientation in the processing industries following delicensing, control over the source of feedstock to ensure quality and traceability became desirable. Second, the emergence of supermarkets and modern retail chains necessitated a steady supply of fresh produce of consistently good quality (Gulati 2007). Third, against a background of a silent collapse of state extension systems and rising input subsidies to agriculture, the state began to disengage from traditional forms of policy intervention seeking to create spaces for the private sector within agriculture. Contract farming began to feature prominently in this effort.

In 2000, as part of what was termed a 'Rainbow Revolution', the National Agricultural Policy stated: 'Private sector participation will be promoted through contract farming and land leasing arrangements to allow accelerated technology transfer, capital inflow, and assured market for crop production ...' Soon after, in 2003 a Model Act (The State Agricultural Produce Marketing Development & Regulation Act) outlined a framework for contract farming operations that would safeguard the interests of both firms and farmers equitably. It also paved the way for private market yards, direct buying and selling, among other things. This was later complemented by the creation of Agri-Export Zones (AEZ) across the country, where firms involved in agri-processing for exports would benefit from tax breaks and specific infrastructural facilities. Contract farming in high-value crops also became part of a larger strategy for diversification, weaning farmers away from the rice–wheat system that so dominated Indian agriculture.

In India, agriculture is a state subject so that substantive policy levers in the country work within individual states. Some states, like Tamil Nadu, had always permitted contract farming. Others were already providing space for such arrangements in select sectors such as horticulture. It was, however, Punjab that led the way, when it permitted PepsiCo to take up tomato contracting for its processing plant in 1989. Soon after, contracting in high-value commodities, such as *basmati*, spices, chillies, flowers, and fruits began in many states. By the late 1990s, the basket of contract crops already included 'exotic' commodities like baby corn and cut flowers.

Several states followed suit. According to the *Economic Survey* of 2009, barring a few states, most have reformed the APMC Act, albeit to different degrees. Some states have, however, desisted from deep reform. For example, in 2008 Metro Cash and Carry's APMC licence was renewed in West Bengal only under the condition that it would not pursue contract farming.

Extent and Spread

While the precise implications of these reforms for private marketing remain unclear, overall it has provided firms a broader space for operations than ever before. Contract farming schemes now embrace a wider range of crops and new geographies.

The true extent of contract farming in India is largely unknown since there is no formal recording system. It is clear, however, that a rich mosaic of corporate, civil society, and state actors has entered the fray, across the country (though less in the east and north-east), seeking to source produce for processing and retail. These arrangements are polymorphic, differing greatly in the nature of actors, relationship intensity, degree of formality, and specific terms and scale of operation. Some contract with as few as 50 farmers, others with so many farmers that they contract with agents or intermediaries, who then contract with farmers. The development of contract farming in India is still in flux. Mortality of contract schemes is high but rarely recorded and it is unclear how many initiatives survive beyond a few seasons.

Contract farming has endured best in high-value, niche commodities, especially for the export market, and where a well-functioning, competing, domestic market does not exist. Gherkins offer the best example. Introduced into peninsular India in the early 1990s by pickling plants in the region, gherkins are almost entirely sourced through contracts. By Triennium Ending 2008, India accounted for as much as 15 per cent of the world's exports of pickled gherkins. Similarly, large swathes of land, especially in Karnataka, are now under high-value medicinal plants and herbs, ashwagandha, aloe vera, coleus, stevia, and so on, for nutraceutical firms. Certified organic supply chains have emerged too for which a whole range of spices and horticultural produce are now contracted (for example, in Uttarakhand).

Contract farming finds least traction when it emerges against a strong alternate domestic market or when too many partners hold the arrangement together. Many rice and wheat contract farming efforts by private-sector banks and firms folded up after initial experiments. Cotton contract farming schemes in states such as Tamil Nadu are fast fading into Corporate Social Responsibility initiatives. In other instances, state-supported schemes for jatropha and oil palm did not take off. In many of these cases, production risks were high and disagreements over pricing led to disgruntled farmers shifting out of the crop.

Despite some commonalities, the relative success of a scheme depends ultimately on the particular relationship between the firm and farmers and factors in the external environment. There are numerous examples of successful schemes that have stabilized and are now over a decade old, despite having competing markets and competitors—wheat and soy contracts for flour making in Madhya Pradesh and Uttar Pradesh, sunflower and safflower for oil in western and central India, and marigold and papaya for extracts in Karnataka and Tamil Nadu.

The broiler industry in the states of Andhra Pradesh, Maharashtra, and Tamil Nadu is today almost entirely integrated through contract farming, led by Godrej Agrovet Ltd., Suguna Poultry, and Venkateshwara Hatcheries Pvt. Ltd. In fact, the industry's embrace of contract farming virtually rescued the poultry sector in Tamil Nadu, at a time when price volatility and poultry disease had dismantled the livelihoods of small poultry farmers.

More recently, a few firms have successfully acted as back-end integrators for retailers based in Europe and the USA, contracting for fresh produce in north-western India.

Apart from retailers and processors, many contract farming schemes have been initiated by input manufacturers, especially of fertilizers and pesticides (for example, Rallis), along with partners who take responsibility for buy-back. Banks, like ICICI and the State Bank of India, have partnered contracting firms in multi-partite arrangements to provide crop loans and working capital, with the contract itself as collateral.

Some state governments too have been proactive, engaging hands-on in tripartite contract farming ventures with agribusinesses and banks, acting sometimes as guarantors, sometimes as relationship managers. For example, the Punjab Agro-Industries Corporation founded in 1996 has partnered a number of agribusinesses in implementing projects. Tamil Nadu adopted a public–private tripartite model for cotton contract farming in 2004–5. Karnataka actively promoted gherkins and grape clusters in the state with great success. States such as Andhra Pradesh and Mizoram have attempted to replicate the sugarcane model for oil palm contract farming, mandating farmers to supply fresh fruit bunches to privately owned mills at administered prices.

Non-governmental organizations have been involved as well, mediating contractual relationships between groups of small farmers and agribusinesses as with BASIX (for chipping potato contracts with Frito Lays India Ltd. in Jharkhand) and PRADAN (also in Jharkhand).

Sometimes contracting is just one element of a broader and deeper relationship with the farmer. This model, now called 'open-source intermediation' involves establishing rural business hubs, where a multiplicity of farmers' needs is addressed under a single roof. ITC's Choupal Fresh and DCM Shriram Consolidated Ltd. (DSCL)'s Hariyali Kisan Bazaar are two such ventures, which offer to buy back produce from farmers without obligations to do so.

Impact: The Good and the Bad

A majority of studies on income gains from contracting in India suggest that contract farmers earn substantially higher profits than non-contract farmers (anywhere between 1.2 to 4 times depending on the commodity and scheme). These gains come partly from savings in transactions costs (estimated at 60–90 per cent for dairy, vegetables, and poultry) and sometimes through productivity gains. Often contracting firms introduce new methods of cultivation or technologies (drip irrigation, new cultivars, and so on) that reduce unit production costs, contributing to improved relative profit efficiency. There is some documented evidence of this for livestock and tomato contract farmers. Contract farming is also known to reduce certain risks. In poultry contracting, for instance, farmers transferred 88 per cent of production and marketing risks to the firm, implying that contracting reduces the volatility growers would have faced if they had produced for alternate markets (Birthal et al. 2005).

Despite these observed benefits, contract farming often brings attendant risks. The chief problem stems from enforcement issues. In the context of agriculture, it is virtually impossible to fashion a contract that provides for all possible contingencies in a way that is verifiable by a third party. Further, the very idea of a contract carries little meaning in a context where few farmers understand the document they are supposed to sign. This has allowed fly-by-night operators to dupe farmers of their lands (as is known to have happened in Orissa).

Even if it were possible to write out complete, verifiable contracts, the proverbially slow legal machinery in India implies huge costs, especially when firms contract with a large number of farmers. For the farmer, recourse to legal redress is practically out of reach. Interestingly, among agribusinesses in India, contract farming is referred to with many epithets—corporate-linked farming, relationship farming, even contact farming! Each of these terms negates the idea of formal contracts. Indeed, one written contract carries a clause that reads: 'This agreement is based on mutual trust and belief' (Singh and Ashokan 2005).

Weak enforcement then gives latitude to both farmers and firms to renege on the contract. Farmers typically divert contract produce to buyers who pay more, or use contract inputs for non-contract crops. Firms establish non-transparent quality standards, reject produce arbitrarily, and alter prices when the produce is delivered. On occasion, when they have enough supply, they do not turn up at all. In general, farmers are in a weaker position, relative to the firm, unless there is a viable alternate market and one where collusion among buyers is not possible.

There are also relevant questions about corporate commitment, or rather the lack of it, to long-term ecological and social consequences of these arrangements. Since most contract farming schemes tap into unpaid family labour, it often bids women and children from other activities into the contract farm in ways that might not be entirely desirable. Even where contract farms use hired labour, thus generating a positive employment effect, the conditions of work leave much to be desired (Singh 2003). For high-input use crops, farmers often report that it depletes soil quality, with lingering impacts on yields. Gherkin farmers in Tamil Nadu report that they often have to replace the topsoil for plots that have grown gherkins. Often, firms respond by moving on to contract from another region. There have also been documented instances of inappropriate advice extended to farmers by contracting firms, destroying standing crops. On the other hand, many farmers report that they benefit from technical advice from the firms, not just for the contract crops but for other crops as well.

The Future of Contract Farming

It is apparent that farm–firm relationships tend to be fragile and fraught with friction. Enduring partnerships between farm and firm are difficult to build and to maintain these requires exceptional effort by the firm. Many firms have had to absorb large losses in order to build trust and persuade the farmer of the firm's commitment. For the farmer, the relationship has to hold significantly greater rewards than alternatives they have and not expose them to a new set of risks.

Given the difficulties in sustaining contractual relationships, the equivocal impact of contract farming, and its selective success, contract farming cannot serve as a broad-based strategy for rural development (see also Minot 2007). Further, evidence on farmer participation in contract farming schemes suggests that small resource-poor farmers may not always participate. In most cases, selection is spatially skewed. It is time-variant as well, with high levels of farmer attrition. This suggests that the instrumentality of contract farming in delivering technology, access to markets and finance, or in enabling small farmers take advantage of opportunities in high-value agriculture is probably overstated.

Yet, the pressure to enable firms to contract for produce is likely to grow stronger in the near future. How should the state respond to this challenge?

On the one hand, weak enforcement mechanisms are prompting several firms to take their contract farming operations to other countries in Southeast Asia and Africa. Yet, establishing a single legal framework that provides for fair contracts and an effective redressal mechanism is unlikely to encourage formal contract farming. From a business standpoint, firms face an expensive system that does not offer predictable dispute resolution and one that is prone to supporting farmers. Indeed, indications are that mandating state overseeing of private contracts might further informalize contract farming where firms end up pole-vaulting the law.

In this scenario, public policy should focus on the context of contract farming rather than contract farming itself. While providing a recommendatory framework is important, states should ensure that farmers' titles to land are secure to guard against unscrupulous operators. Public policy should focus sharply on zones that are excluded by agribusinesses and in regions where they do operate, the state should work to expand farmers' choice set in terms of cropping options, marketing channels, and so on, so that they are not caught in a relationship that creates dependency. Part of this involves provision of public goods like irrigation, power, infrastructure, market information, and extension, so that farmers face fewer constraints while making decisions. This might be the best way to ensure that the benefits of contract farming filter through without its costs.

SUDHA NARAYANAN

References

Birthal, Pratap S., P.K. Joshi, and Ashok Gulati. 2005. 'Vertical Coordination in High-value Commodities: Implications for Smallholders', MTID Discussion Paper 85, International Food Policy Research Institute, Washington DC.

Gulati, Ashok. 2007. 'Agribusiness', in Kaushik Basu (ed.), *The Oxford Companion to Economics in India*, New Delhi, Oxford University Press.

Minot, Nicholas. 2007. 'Contract Farming in Developing Countries: Patterns, Impact, and Policy Implications', Case Study #6–3, in Per Pinstrup-Andersen and Fuzhi Cheng (eds), *Food Policy for Developing Countries: The Role of Government in the Global Food System*, Ithaca, NY, Cornell University Press.

Singh, Gurdev and S.R. Ashokan. 2005. *Contract Farming in India: Text and Cases*, New Delhi, Oxford & IBH Publishing Co. Pvt. Ltd.

Singh, Sukhpal. 2003. 'Contract Farming in India: Impacts on Women and Child Workers', Gatekeeper Series No.111, IIED, UK.

Convertibility

Before the development of modern banking, convertibility of a currency meant the willingness of a government to convert its currency into gold or silver at a fixed rate. Nowadays, convertibility is best defined negatively as absence of official restrictions on conversion of balances held in a home currency into foreign currencies. Table 1 lists thirteen major types of controls on transactions in foreign exchange levied by the number of member countries of the International Monetary Fund (IMF) (out of a total 184) that imposed such restrictions in 2004. Only 35 had independently floating currencies; the rest intervened in foreign exchange markets. Most of the latter controlled foreign exchange transactions to prevent financial flows that would overwhelm official influence or profit from predictable, officially engineered exchange rate movements. Aside from this overriding motive of curbing private competition in the foreign exchange market, many countries controlled foreign exchange to prevent foreigners from buying or controlling too much of industrial, landed, or financial property.

Table 1 Frequency of Occurrence of Types of Exchange Control across Countries in 2004

Controls on	Number of countries
Direct investment	143
Real estate transactions	136
Capital market securities	126
Financial credits	109
Money market instruments	105
Commercial credits	98
Collective investment securities	96
Personal capital transactions	95
Payments for invisible transactions	94
Guarantees, sureties, and financial back-ups	89
Derivatives and other instruments	79
Earnings surrender requirements	75

Source: International Monetary Fund. 2004. *Annual Report on Exchange Arrangements and Exchange Restrictions 2004*, Washington DC.

After the British defeated the Marathas in 1818, they made the rupee coin of 180 grains of standard silver (11/12 purity) legal tender in south India. In 1835, it was made legal tender over all of India. The government thereby introduced a silver standard: it was prepared to do all its transactions in silver rupees, and to mint silver brought to it into rupees at a nominal charge. The government also kept the value of the rupee close to 1s 4d (that is 16 pence: it implied an exchange rate of Rs 15 to a pound of 240 pence). The exchange rate against the pound was maintained through the issue of Council Bills—bills of exchange that the India Office of the British government sold in London. They could be taken to India and sold to the Indian government at the fixed exchange rate.

Britain made gold legal tender in 1821; after that the exchange rate of the rupee into sterling depended on the relative prices of gold and silver. They varied little till 1871; but in the next 20 years, the price of silver in terms of gold fell sharply. The Government of India used to make large payments in sterling to service loans and to pay civil service pensions. It continued to convert its liabilities into sterling at 1s 4d a rupee whereas the gold value of the rupee fell much lower; the losses on exchange were borne by the Government of India and severely strained its Budget.

Finally in 1892, the government refused to take in any more silver for minting. The stoppage of new supply led to a scarcity of the silver rupee, until its exchange value came to correspond to the relative price of gold and silver by 1898. In the years that followed, the value of the metal in the rupee continued to be much below its market value; the rupee was a token currency, just like currency notes. But out of its trade surplus with the rest of the world, India built up sterling reserves in London, and used them to make payments in sterling at an exchange rate of 1s 4d. Sterling in turn was tied to gold. This arrangement, known as gold exchange standard, continued till 1931.

In 1931, the gold reserves of the Bank of England declined sharply, it could no longer support the gold value of sterling, and allowed the sterling to depreciate. After this date, the Government of India only supported the value of the rupee at 1s 6d; in effect, it placed the rupee on a sterling exchange standard. It announced that it would buy and sell sterling only for normal trade- and investment-related transactions; this was the first introduction of exchange control. The ordinance was withdrawn in January 1932. But for this brief period, the rupee remained convertible till 1939. The management of foreign exchange was taken over by the Reserve Bank of India (RBI) after it was set up in 1934 (Mathew 1992).

Full exchange control was introduced on 3 September 1939 following the declaration of war between Britain and Germany. During World War II, imports as well as capital issues were controlled. Foreign trade was also constrained by the shortage of shipping space, which the government allocated. The release of any foreign exchange to a private entity had to be cleared by one or other department of the Government of India. The function of exchange control then was to ensure that all payments in foreign exchange were backed by a document proving government approval. On the receipts side, the rule was that exporters must convert their export proceeds into rupees within a specified period; private entities were not allowed to hold foreign exchange unless they were authorized dealers approved by the RBI. Residents could continue to hold assets in non-sterling areas acquired before 3 September 1939, but not those acquired later. The same prohibition was introduced for assets in sterling area as from 8 July 1947 when the powers taken under the Defence of India Rules were replaced by the Foreign Exchange (Regulation) Act.

The chief source of civilian as well as military supplies to Britain and its Indian colony during the War was the United States. So the British government pooled all US dollar receipts of Commonwealth countries; they were credited with sterling for the dollars they paid into Britain's dollar reserves. In this way, the Government of India built up large sterling reserves in London. Between September 1939 and March 1946, the British government credited the Government of India with 1.632 billion pounds for War supplies; another 813 million was earned from export proceeds. Net of payments, the Government of India received 2,026 million pounds, and was left with a balance of 2,554 million pounds (RBI 1946).

Even after the War, however, these balances could not be used to increase imports because the United Kingdom continued to be short of both productive capacity and US dollars, and controlled the release of sterling balances. Hence, exchange control was continued in India. But after the War, the purposes for which foreign exchange was released became more diverse; for each, an official authority was appointed whose approval was required to get foreign exchange. Thus businessmen needed approval from the Commerce Ministry to travel and students who wished to go abroad for study, from the Educational Adviser to the Government of India. Economic relations with countries that had been at war were restored, and the number of currencies in which there were dealings increased. The RBI kept its reserves in sterling; authorized dealers (holders of a licence to stock and trade in foreign exchange) were allowed to convert other currencies into sterling and to hedge them up to six months in the London market.

Despite Britain's restrictions on the spending of sterling reserves, sterling was less scarce and hence subject to less stringent exchange control than the US dollar. The rest of the world was divided into countries, chiefly of the Commonwealth, that maintained reserves and freely allowed transfers in sterling, and countries aligned to the US dollar. They came to be known as soft currency and hard currency areas; exchange control was more stringent vis-à-vis the latter. In 1958, Britain made the sterling held by non-nationals convertible; so did 12 European countries. The RBI then merged their accounts with those of the dollar account countries and termed them transferable accounts; the special concessions to sterling area in exchange control came to an end.

Beginning with Egypt in 1953, India made bilateral agreements with over 25 developing countries in the 1950s stipulating that proceeds of trade with each would go into non-convertible rupee accounts; the aim was to ensure that trade with those countries balanced. As an incentive, the countries were given rupee credits. In 1958, India made an agreement with the Soviet Union whereby their bilateral trade was conducted in rupees. Agreements with other communist countries followed; they came to be called rupee account countries.

A black market in the rupee account currency developed in the 1960s; a number of East European countries were offering the rupees they earned from their exports to India at a discount to importers in Western Europe (Batliwala 1998, Batliwala and Balachandran 1998). A major dispute erupted between India and East European countries about revaluation of contracts after India's devaluation in 1966. After it, the latter lost interest in rupee trade, their exports under rupee account agreements declined, and so did the black market.

Facing a severe payments crisis in 1961, the RBI permitted non-resident Indians (NRIs) to invest in government securities and to sell them and repatriate the proceeds without its permission. The outbreak of hostilities between India and Pakistan in April 1965 worsened the balance of payments (BOP); to augment foreign exchange reserves, NRIs were permitted to place deposits in special accounts with banks in India. In 1968 they were allowed to lend to private and government companies and to set up partnerships with residents. Approval was also extended to portfolio investment by them in and through government financial institutions.

These efforts to attract NRI money were largely a failure till after 1973. Then the emigration of Indian workers to the booming oil economies of the Middle East led to a flood of inward remittances. There had been an informal market in foreign exchange since 1958 when the RBI ceased to release foreign exchange for travel other than to businessmen and students; foreign exchange diverted by underinvoicing exports or overinvoicing imports was sold to travellers abroad. This market expanded considerably after the oil boom. Agents sprang up in the cities where Indian workers were concentrated, principally Dubai and Abu Dhabi. They bought local currencies from the workers on the promise that an equivalent sum in rupees, converted at a better than the official exchange rate, would be delivered to their relatives in India. Most of the foreign exchange thus intercepted was used to buy gold and silver which were then smuggled into India (bullion imports were banned in 1939); profits from the smuggling were partly used to give workers abroad who used the smugglers to send money home a premium that varied between 25 and 50 per cent. A substantial *hawala* trade, as the illegal market in foreign exchange was called, continued until gold imports were liberalized in 1997.

To attract the remittances into legal channels, the government allowed its own banks to open branches in the Middle East and allowed NRIs to keep money in savings as well as deposit accounts with Indian banks. The permission was then extended to equity investment and residential property, and to corporate bodies created by NRIs. The RBI bore the exchange risk. Since interest rates were considerably lower in the industrial countries and Middle Eastern countries where most NRIs were settled, the banks found it profitable to borrow from the NRIs at rates slightly above those in their home countries and lend the money in India. As a result, NRI deposits grew rapidly in the 1980s.

These deposits were freely convertible. When the BOP deteriorated in the late 1980s, the NRIs were the first to take warning and withdraw their money; the flight of these funds precipitated the payments crisis of 1991. That crisis also saw loss of foreign exchange from leads and lags—that is, from early payments for imports and delayed realization of export proceeds. It finally convinced the government of the ineffectiveness of controls for managing the BOP and began a process of slow relaxation.

In 1990–1, the government issued more than a million import licences and gave Rs 30 billion in export subsidies. The new government which was voted to power in May 1991 printed import licences in standard denominations like currency notes, issued them to exporters in proportion to their exports, allowed them to sell the licences in the market, and stopped issuing import licences for commercial imports. The licences were soon counterfeited; but otherwise the arrangement worked so well that the government gained the confidence to permit a market in foreign exchange in which exporters were allowed to sell a part of their earnings and from which commercial importers had to satisfy their requirements. The market rate was higher than the official exchange rate. There was thus an incentive to obtain exchange at the official rate and sell it in the market. The possibility of exchange diversion led the RBI to unify the exchange rate, widen the market, and free all current transactions from exchange control in March 1993; official purchases and sales of foreign exchange were used to control the market exchange rate. Following commitments made at the conclusion of the Uruguay Round of trade negotiations in 1995, import licensing was abolished in April 2001. Since then, exchange control has applied only to capital account transactions. Foreign exchange releases for current account transactions are still subject to quantitative limits, but they have been raised to comfortable levels.

On the removal of restrictions on capital account transactions, however, the government has dithered. The RBI appointed two committees in the 1990s—the Sodhani Committee in 1994 and the Tarapore Committee in 1997—to prepare for relaxation of exchange control (RBI 1995, 1997). The first confined itself to measures to increase the depth of foreign exchange markets and the range of products they traded in. The second explicitly addressed capital account convertibility, reviewed international experience, and proposed four preconditions: (1) the central and state governments should reduce their fiscal deficits and stop borrowing to repay old debt, and the central government must stop borrowing from the RBI; (2) the RBI should adopt explicit targets for the real effective exchange rate and for inflation; (3) banks' bad debts and the cash reserves they were required to hold must be brought down; (4) exchange reserves should exceed (a) six months' imports, (b) three months' imports plus half of annual debt service payments plus a month's commodity trade (sum of imports and exports), (c) two-third times the sum of short-term debt and portfolio investment, and (d) 40 per cent of M_1. Of these conditions, there was never any difficulty with the second, the fourth was fulfilled even in 1997, and the third has been fulfilled since. But the government is no closer to fulfilling the fiscal deficit condition than it was then.

Since the introduction of current account convertibility, India's foreign exchange reserves have been comfortable, and have at times increased so rapidly as to flood the economy with liquidity, forcing the government to borrow more than it needed (Patnaik 2004). The excessive accumulation of reserves implies that the RBI prevented the rupee from appreciating, being concerned to keep export prices down. Undervaluation of the exchange rate, however, also raised inflation; so the gain to the real economy is not unequivocal.

Convertibility makes foreign funds available to finance state deficits; but such financing is subject to exchange risk, and governments that were unable to control deficits have been landed in a combination of fiscal and payments crises. Hence the Tarapore Committee stressed fiscal consolidation. In theory, convertibility can discipline a government prone to deficits. But as Kenneth Kletzer has pointed out, governments in India have derived considerable although diminishing cross-subsidies from banks, which are mostly owned by the central government, in the form of differential interest rates (Kletzer 2004). Their inability or unwillingness to forgo these subsidies makes the central government unwilling to relax its controls on banks; and unless banks are freed to compete with funds from abroad, convertibility could lead to both a banking and a fiscal crisis. This may be the overriding reason for India's failure to advance towards capital account convertibility.

ASHOK V. DESAI

References

Batliwala, C.J. 1998. 'Administering Exchange Controls', Appendix E, in G. Balachandran (ed.), *The Reserve Bank of India 1951–1967*, New Delhi, Reserve Bank of India and Oxford University Press.

Batliwala, C.J. and G. Balachandran. 1998. 'Bilateral Rupee Payment Agreements', Appendix G, in G. Balachandran (ed.), *The Reserve Bank of India 1951–1967*, New Delhi, Oxford University Press.

Kletzer, Kenneth. 2004. 'Liberalizing Capital Flows in India: Financial Repression, Macroeconomic Policy and Gradinal Reforms', *India Policy Forum*, 1: 227–76.

Mathew, Joseph. 1992. *Exchange Rate Policy: Impact on Exports and the Balance of Payments*, Delhi, Deep Publications.

Patnaik, Ila. 2004. 'India's Experience with a Pegged Exchange Rate', *India Policy Forum*, 1: 189–226.

Reserve Bank of India (RBI). 1946. *Report on Currency and Finance for the Year 1945–46*, Bombay.

____. 1995. *Report of the Expert Group on Foreign Exchange Markets in India*, Bombay.

____. 1997. *Report of the Committee on Capital Account Convertibility*, Bombay.

Corporate Ethics

Moral Agency

Corporate ethics are a part of business ethics in the broad sense of applying moral standards to evaluate business decisions, transactions, and outcomes. This area of applied ethics addresses moral issues involving the acts of earning business profits and creating wealth. It is reasonably easy to apply principles of individual ethics when decisions are taken by a single person, for instance, an entrepreneur. The individual is supposed to possess moral agency. This implies that the person understands the moral reasons of right and wrong underlying the decision, and is accountable for specific consequences that may arise out of that decision. However, when it comes to a business corporation, the difficulty arises in treating a collective entity as a single individual possessing moral agency. Here decisions are, more often than not, taken at several stages where many individuals discuss and decide. Yet many important decisions are taken *on behalf* of the corporation. The law in most countries, including India, treats corporations as a legal individual. The corporation can sue and defend itself on legal matters. Does the corporation (treated as if it were an individual) possess moral agency?

The answer to this question is not merely a philosophical issue. It has enormous practical implications.

There are innumerable cases all over the world where a business corporation's decision has had widespread consequences in terms of incurring social costs. These costs could be borne by people who have nothing to do with the corporation. These costs could also be borne by customers, shareholders, or other stakeholders, such as suppliers and workers. The corporation can be penalized (if proven guilty of imposing the cost, such as adulterating a medicine) by imposing a monetary fine. The cost of the fine may well be ultimately borne by the shareholders. There may be too many individuals involved within the corporation for establishing managerial guilt or negligence. This could be a perverse effect of justice if the shareholders themselves turn out to be aggrieved parties.

Corporate Governance

India, like most nations, has laws and specific regulations governing corporations in terms of fiduciary responsibilities, financial disclosures, and directorial oversight. A corporation is also bound by the laws of the land, especially those pertaining to contracts, property, payment of remuneration, working conditions and safety, and tax compliance. Each corporation has a structure of governance too. Managers are accountable to the board of directors and the board ultimately to the shareholders whose wealth is being managed by the firm.

Despite these laws, there are frequent violations and non-compliance by corporations. One set of transgressions occurs when a corporation fails to comply with some law or regulation by fudging data or failing to disclose some critical information. For instance, a firm may gain by violating the law by not paying all taxes due. To take another example, a firm may 'create' fictitious profits where none exist. This could have a positive short-term effect on stock prices and hence for some individuals (such as senior managers and directors) in the corporation who could book personal profits by selling their stocks when prices are very high. The consequences for an ordinary shareholder could be heavy if the fraud was exposed and the stock market reduced the valuation of that stock. The brand equity of the corporation would also be seriously damaged.

This kind of violation pertaining to corporate governance can be deterred by enforcing the existing set of laws and by amending any ambiguities in a law. Having more alert directors, and holding them responsible, could enhance accountability to stakeholders. Here the ethical issue is quite straightforward. Wilfully, and in full knowledge, violating a regulation or law has its own consequences. It is tantamount to a criminal act. In the summer of 2002 a large number of highly reputed corporations in the US were involved in financial scandals that appeared to be blatant violations of the law and obvious accounting frauds. In India, where corruption is very high in business and public life such violations are common too, but they often go undetected through the help of bribes and other forms of opportunistic behaviour. Therefore, it is not surprising that even the best known companies (like Satyam) get involved in the worst kinds of fraud and unethical behaviour.

There could, however, be an adverse effect of too much regulation. If senior decision-makers feel afraid of being hauled up for financial impropriety, such as taking a decision that is perceived (ex post) to have been taken against the interests of the shareholders, it could affect risk-taking behaviour. Such perceptions can indicate the need for further regulations to protect the shareholders. The quantity as well as the quality of regulations is likely to deteriorate. Availing of market opportunities involves taking risks where outcomes are bound to be uncertain. Too much fear about the long-term consequences of taking a risk can adversely affect investments. It can be difficult to distinguish between genuine risk-taking motivations and other dishonest intentions.

Corporate Social Responsibility

A second kind of ethical problem occurs when there is no direct law or regulation that is being violated, but some principle of fairness is. It could be a nuance in how a product is advertised, claims about what the product can do, or in the implicit understanding of the attractiveness of a business project. Is the product being advertised by using children or women in a socially unacceptable way? Is the claim regarding the utility of the product based on incomplete or ambiguous research evidence? Is there a subtle understatement of the risks involved in a project? Is there a silence on the environmental impact of a business activity? Often these issues are taken up by stakeholders or by social activists for creating public opinion and inducing the corporation to rectify the lapse. In such instances corporations often respond and take quick corrective action. Fear that customers may boycott the product resulting in a loss of market share and revenues induces such a positive response. This is enlightened self-interest at work, and anticipating and taking corrective action on these counts are referred to as corporate social responsibility. Many big Indian business houses are beginning to appreciate the need to respect customers' ethical concerns. In a well-known example, a famous shoe company in the US did not violate any law when it outsourced its production to contractors in Asian countries where people worked in abysmal conditions and at extremely low wages. When public (customer) opinion went against the corporation, corrective action was swift.

Many of the strategic questions raised by issues of corporate ethics revolve round the primary duty of a corporation. Should it exclusively focus on maximizing the returns on shareholders' investments, subject to the rule of law? Or should it define an enlightened self-interest and trade off wealth making with a larger social responsibility? While the most important contract a corporation enters into is to enhance shareholder wealth, it is equally true that a corporation's charter to do business is granted legitimacy by society at large.

Ethics and Consensus in Decision Making

One complex, though interesting, aspect of corporate ethics is the process by which a decision with ethical implications is taken. Most corporate decisions are collective ones, made by a committee or a board of directors. As in any decision-making process, there could be problems of disagreement and differences of opinion. The complexity arising from the need to arrive at a decision is twofold. First, more likely than not, the individuals involved in the decision-making process may come from different cultural backgrounds and hence may take different positions on an issue. The cultural context of ethics is well-researched and accepted. Individuals coming from societies where a greater emphasis is put on individual performances and values are likely to take an ethical position on an issue quite different from those brought up in a society where collective or group outcomes are assigned greater value.

There could be a second source of difference. Even within the same cultural context, a plurality of ethical positions might be possible. For instance, in the context of 'Western ethics' a consequentialist (concerned more with the good than the right) may take a position completely contrary to a deontologist (concerned more with the right than with the good).

The decision-making process may well depend upon the distribution of ethical positions in a given collection of individuals. Hence, the same collective entity (the corporation) could take different decisions on the same ethical issue. The decision is contingent on the specific set of people involved in taking the decision on behalf of the corporation. Thus, the corporation, in itself, has no moral position.

The decision resolving the ethical problem (or dilemma) could in some cases be actually easier to arrive at than warranted by the two levels of complexities. The final decision could be arrived at through completely different ethical reasoning. For instance, if the issue is one of whether to give a sum of money as bribe to get a large contract for the corporation, the consensus decision could be a 'no'. The reasons behind this decision could be different for different people—someone could take a deontological position to argue that giving a bribe was not right, and hence unacceptable. Another person could argue that the long-run reputational costs to be incurred by the firm would be much more than the short-term gains and hence from the point of view of an undesirable consequence, the bribe should not be paid.

The really complex situations are where the collective decision-making process leads to an impasse. The process through which such problems are ultimately resolved could form fascinating case studies in corporate ethics. However, such processes are seldom documented. Even if they are, or can be recounted by a participant, they are seldom available in the public domain.

In India, corporate ethics is a growing area of research and teaching, and most business schools teach courses on the subject as part of their curricula. Corporate ethics has also gone beyond the academic setting. As part of a worldwide movement, there is increasing stakeholder activism to reveal unethical behaviour. Quite a few Indian corporations have started reporting triple bottom lines to show their social responsibility and environmental commitments beyond the traditional bottom line of business profits. Some firms are beginning to adopt their own codes of conduct or statements of values and beliefs. Some normative issues are becoming more complex too as markets and business operations become globally integrated. The corporate ethics movement is gaining momentum across the world. This trend is undoubtedly laudable but in a country where business corruption is high, ethical postures can be used as a mask to conceal amoral corporate behaviour.

ANUP KUMAR SINHA

References

Elster, Jon. 1989. *Nuts and Bolts for the Social Sciences,* Cambridge, Cambridge University Press.

Jackson, Terence. 2011. *International Management Ethics: A Critical, Cross-cultural Perspective,* Cambridge, Cambridge University Press.

Monks, Robert A.G. and Nell Minow. 2004. *Corporate Governance* (third edition), Oxford, Blackwell Publishing.

Reed, Darryl and Sanjoy Mukherjee. 2004. *Corporate Governance, Economic Reforms and Development: The Indian Experience,* New Delhi, Oxford University Press.

Shaw, William. 1999. *Business Ethics,* Toronto, Wadsworth Publishing Company.

Corporate Governance

It is strange but true that the first significant initiative to foster better corporate governance in India came neither from the government, nor the securities market regulator, nor even shareholder activists, but from where it is usually least expected—an industry association. In 1996, the Confederation of Indian Industry (CII) set up a task force of industrialists and CEOs under Rahul Bajaj of Bajaj Auto Limited to draft a voluntary code of corporate governance for listed companies. As a person who had worked on the subject, I was inducted in the task force to raise the key issues, challenge the members, and help draft the report.

A dozen years after the event, I still cannot fathom the proximate reasons for the CII to arrive at a progressive consensus that allowed the publication of a much appreciated, state-of-the-art report in April 1998 (CII 1998). There was neither an economy-wide crisis as in Southeast and East Asia in 1997–8 which forced a complete rethink on capital markets, banking, corporate governance, and the mechanics of corporate control; nor at that point of time were there any embarrassing corporate or stock market scandals, which could have induced an industry association to take a leadership role in cleaning the Augean stables. Notwithstanding occasional references by the financial press about the need for good corporate governance, there were no immediate reasons for a body representing industrial and corporate interests to advocate a series of enlightened, far-reaching proposals which could not have been gladly welcomed by its wider membership.

But it did. The time path was this: the CII code was soon followed by a report of a SEBI committee chaired by a young industrialist, Kumar Mangalam Birla, which incorporated almost *in toto* the provisions of the CII report; this, in turn, formed the basis for drafting Clause 49 of the Listing Agreement in February 2000, which defined the required corporate governance structure of listed companies. In 2003, the SEBI appointed a new committee under the chairmanship of N.R. Narayana Murthy of Infosys to suggest changes, if any, that may be needed to the existing Clause 49. Based on the Murthy Committee report, the SEBI amended the original Clause 49 in October 2004. The new Clause 49 is the document that currently defines the contours of corporate governance regarding listed companies vis-à-vis the stock market and securities regulator. At the time of writing, the Government of India was proposing to make changes in the Companies Act, 1956, to explicitly incorporate some other aspects of corporate governance in the 'mother' Act. But more of that later.

Let me begin the substantive part of this entry by stating some of the corporate governance criteria as reflected in Clause 49 of the Listing Agreement.[1]

Board of Directors and Committees of the Board

- At least half of the board of directors of any listed company must consist of non-executive directors. Moreover, if the chairman is a non-executive director, at least a third of the board should comprise independent directors; and if the chairman is an executive of the company, then independent directors must account for at least half of the board.
- Independent directors are a sub-set of non-executive directors, and must fulfil several criteria, such as:
  - apart from receiving a director's remuneration, not having any material pecuniary relationships or transactions with the company, its promoters, its directors, its senior management, or its holding company, its subsidiaries, and associates which may affect the independence of the director;
  - not being related to promoters or senior management;
  - not being an executive of the company in the immediately preceding three financial years;
  - not being a partner or an executive currently or during the preceding three years, of the statutory audit firm or the internal audit firm of the company, or any legal and consulting firm that has had a material association with the company;
  - not being a material significant supplier, service provider, customer, lessor, or lessee of the company; and
  - not being a substantial shareholder of the company, that is, owning 2 per cent or more of the block of voting shares.
- Boards must meet at least once every three months, or at least four times a year, with a gap of no more than four months between meetings.
- The attendance record of each director must be clearly stated in the company's annual report to its shareholders. So too must the remuneration of each director, including stock options. India is one of the very few countries that have these requirements. Moreover, directorial remuneration in any form has to be approved by the voting shareholders of the company in its annual general meeting.
- No director can sit on the board of more than 10 board-level committees of listed companies

[1]See SEBI, Clause 49 of the Listing Agreement, 29 October 2004, which came into effect from 1 April 2005.

(specifically, audit committees and shareholder grievance committees mandated by the SEBI), or serve as a chairman of more than five such committees.

- All listed companies must have an audit committee consisting of only non-executive and independent directors, with the majority as well as the chairman being independent. The audit committee must meet at least four times in a year, with no more than four months elapsing between two meetings. The chairman of the audit committee must be present at annual general meeting to answer shareholder queries. Among others, the tasks of the audit committee are:
  - oversight of the company's financial reporting processes and disclosures to ensure that the financial statements are correct and credible;
  - recommending to the board the appointment or replacement of the statutory auditor and fixing the audit fees, as well as the appointment, removal, and remuneration of the chief internal auditor;
  - approving payment to statutory auditors for any non-audit services;
  - reviewing the quarterly, half-yearly, and annual financial statements before submission to the board with the management;
  - reviewing the performance of both the statutory and the internal auditors as well as the adequacy of internal control systems with the management;
  - discussing with internal and statutory auditors their annual audit plans, as well as any significant findings that have implications on control systems and financial reporting processes; and
  - evaluating instances and nature of related party transactions.

Disclosures to Shareholders

- In addition to disclosures regarding the board of directors, listed companies must, in the annual report, have a chapter on management discussion and analysis, which is expected to deal with industry structure and developments, opportunities and threats, segment-wise performance, outlook, risks, internal control systems and their adequacy, financial and operational performance, and issues relating to human resources.
- There must also be a corporate governance report which, among others, must list the date, time, and venue of the company's annual general meeting, the financial calendar, date of book closure, and of dividend payment if any, listing on which stock exchanges, market price data both in terms of monthly highs and lows as well as comparison of stock price with broad-based indices, distribution of shareholdings at the close of the financial year, the company's share transfer system and the extent of dematerialization of shares, and whether there are outstanding warrants or any convertible instruments and their likely impact on equity.
- Any listed company must frame its code of conduct for director and employees, which must form a part of the annual report disclosure and be posted on the company's website.
- In a manner similar to the certification mandated in the US by the Securities and Exchange Commission (SEC) under Section 404 of the Sarbanes-Oxley Act (popularly called SOX 404), the chief executive officer (CEO) and the chief financial officer (CFO) of any listed Indian company are required to certify that:
  - they have reviewed financial statements for the year, and to the best of their knowledge and belief these do not contain any materially untrue or misleading statement or omit any material fact and, hence, present a true and fair view of the company's affairs for the period under consideration;
  - there are, to the best of their knowledge and belief, no transactions entered into by the company during the year which are fraudulent, illegal, or violating the company's code of conduct;
  - they accept responsibility for establishing and maintaining internal controls, have evaluated the effectiveness of such systems, and have disclosed to the auditors and the audit committee, deficiencies in design or operations, if any, of which they are aware and the steps they have taken or propose to take to rectify these, and
  - they have indicated to the auditors and the audit committee any significant change in internal controls during the year, significant changes in accounting policies which have also been disclosed in the notes to the financial statements, and any instance of significant fraud of which they have become aware, the involvement of the management or an employee in such an episode, and steps taken in this regard.

Accounting Disclosures

In addition to these mandated requirements, the Institute of Chartered Accountants of India (ICAI) has set fairly stringent accounting disclosure standards over the years. These have, in large measure, brought the financial statements of Indian companies prepared according to the Indian GAAP (Generally Agreed Accounting Practices) in line with best-in-class global accounting treatment. A few of these need to be stated.

- Over and above the balance sheet and profit and loss account with their schedules, listed Indian companies have to present a detailed cash flow statement.
- Segment reporting is now mandatory. Moreover, a company must disclose income, operating profits, as well as capital employed in each business segment for the year.[2]
- Very detailed disclosures are mandated for related party transactions.
- Consolidated balance sheets and profit and loss accounts are now mandatory. This gives shareholders a complete overall view of the reporting company as well as its subsidiaries.
- Deferred taxes now have to be accounted for.[3]

Why These Changes?

There is little doubt that India's mandated corporate governance standards and disclosures rank among the best in the world. By almost any canon, these are at least as good as the norms prescribed by the US and Australia; generally better than the UK; appreciably better than all the countries in continental Europe and Latin America; and, barring perhaps Singapore, significantly superior to any country in Asia. This is now recognized and acknowledged by corporate governance specialists throughout the world, which raises a question: Why has a nation with a per capita income of less than $1,000 created corporate governance standards that are superior to most OECD countries?

The answer has much to do with the enormous churning that has occurred in corporate India since the mid-1990s, and more so after 2000. Within a decade of the advent of economic reforms, India started witnessing a number of entrepreneurs who, unencumbered by protectionist baggage of their predecessors, wanted to prove their worth in a more competitive economy. They were the likes of Ratan Tata who wanted to create a more focused, cohesive conglomerate out of a loose confederation of independent satrapies; of Narayana Murthy and the people of Infosys, Azim Premji of Wipro, F.C. Kohli and S. Ramadorai of TCS who wanted to build internationally respected IT powerhouses; Parminder Singh and Davinder Brar of Ranbaxy and K. Anji Reddy of Dr Reddy's Laboratories, K.V. Kamath and his team at ICICI Bank, Deepak Parekh of HDFC, Sunil Mittal of Bharti, Baba Kalyani of Bharat Forge, and Kiran Mazumdar-Shaw of Biocon, to name but a few.

Facts bear this out over the last 15 years. Consider the losers. The top 50 companies in terms of market capitalization in January 1995 dropped their average ranking by over 60 notches in January 2010. For the top 100 companies, the average drop in rank was even more precipitous—a fall of over 105 points. And for the top 200, it was worse still—an average drop of 130 points. Here are some examples. Remember a blue chip called Bombay Dyeing? Or DCM? Or Century Enka? Or Escorts? Or E.I.D. Parry? None could deal with the power of competition.

The power of this churn was not only in throwing out losers but in spewing winners with even greater force. Here are some names that were either not listed in 1995, or were way below the pecking order as compared to the ancient *dirigiste* dinosaurs. TCS, Infosys, Cognizant, Wipro, and HCL in the IT space; Maruti Suzuki, Mahindra & Mahindra, and Hero Honda in automotives; ICICI Bank, HDFC Bank, Axis Bank, and Kotak Mahindra in banking; Ranbaxy (now sold to Daiichi Sankyo), Dr Reddy's Laboratories, Cipla, Sun Pharma, Lupin, and Biocon in pharmaceuticals; Bharti Airtel and Reliance Communication in telephony; Sterlite and Sesa Goa in mining; NIIT in software education; Cairn India in oil and gas; Powergrid Corporation in electricity transmission; Suzlon Energy in wind power; DLF in

[2]Incidentally, this is the most stringent segment reporting disclosure in the world because one cannot only calculate segment profitability per rupee of sale, but also return on capital employed. Some managers believe that in an increasingly globalized world, such a disclosure gives too much competitive information to non-Indian competitor companies, who do not have to give segment reports.

[3]This may be a bit abstruse for most economists and non-financial readers. But because it is a very important financial disclosure, let me explain it as simply as possible. In most countries, there are legally mandated differences in the treatment of depreciation between the accounts presented to the shareholders and those given to the tax authorities for the purpose of calculating corporate income tax. Invariably, the latter get higher depreciation allowances (that is, more tax breaks) than the former. India is no exception. Therefore, the profits presented to shareholders in the annual accounts are greater than those in the corporate income tax returns. From a purely disclosure point of view, the way of bridging the two over time is to account for deferred taxes. When this is done, a tax break under income tax laws (the difference between the two depreciation rates) will be treated as a deferred tax liability and provisioned for in the shareholders' balance sheet profit and loss account. It has no financial or cash flow implications, but it does help significantly in creating more transparent and better aligned accounts.

realty; Bharat Forge in automotive and specialized forgings; the list is huge.

What has this churn done to Indian business? At the bottom of the pack are companies that have become history. But the more exciting news is that corporations have re-engineered themselves to deal with a more competitive world. In the process, most of them have realized that fostering good corporate governance, having a strong board, and making the right kind of disclosures create powerful signals—and are valuable tools to accessing international capital, best-in-class human resources, and ultimately in increasing competitiveness.

Indeed, I would argue that the growth story of India coupled with credible corporate governance have delivered results in terms of an unprecedented inflow of foreign portfolio investment in Indian equity. Between November 1992 and end-2010, net cumulative foreign portfolio investment in corporate India was $120 billion, of which $102 billion was in equity alone.[4] Today, foreign portfolio investors average over 25 per cent of the shareholding of the top 100 listed companies, which account for 85 per cent of India's market capitalization. For many of these, the combined shareholding of foreign institutional investors exceeds 50 per cent.[5] Thus, foreign portfolio managers are comfortable investing in Indian risk capital. Some of that reassurance comes from India's corporate governance practices and quality of financial disclosures.

Then Came Satyam

Beyond the horizon, every blue sky hides a grey cloud. That cloud burst in early 2009 with the Satyam scam. Founded by an Andhra Pradesh entrepreneur, B. Ramalinga Raju, Satyam was the fourth largest IT company in India, and listed in India as well as in the US. It was a darling among the media and fund managers.

On 7 January 2009, Ramalinga Raju confessed to massive falsification of the books and resigned. According to him, the half yearly accounts of 30 September 2008 contained the following:

- Inflated cash and bank balances of Rs 5,040 crore (over $1.1 billion)
- Non-existent accrued interest of Rs 376 crore ($82 million)
- Understated liability of Rs 1,230 crore ($267 million)
- Overstated sundry debtors' position of Rs 490 crore ($106 million)

[4]Data are from the website of the Securities and Exchange Board of India (SEBI).
[5]Data are from *CapitalOnline*, an electronic database of listed companies.

All hell broke loose. It was soon clear that the board and independent directors had seriously failed in their fiduciary duties. So, too, had the statutory auditors. Indeed, the conduct of the board had come under severe criticism a few weeks before the scam was exposed, when it approved a very questionable party transaction between Satyam and a sister company Maytas (Satyam spelt backwards)—only to be forced to recant because of the sheer fury of institutional investors.

There were two positives and a negative arising out of the Satyam scandal. On the plus side, those who were presumed guilty based on prima facie evidence were placed in judicial custody, which included Raju, his brother, the CFO, and a partner from the statutory audit firm. As of end 2010, Raju and the CFO remain in custody—and that is saying a lot in a country where the rich and influential have an uncanny ability to escape incarceration. The other positive was the speed with which Satyam was sold off. Within weeks, the Ministry of Corporate Affairs (MoCA) appointed outside directors to take charge of the company; and by 13 April 2009, a stake of 46 per cent in Satyam was purchased by Tech Mahindra—a Mahindra & Mahindra company—through a formal public auction process. By July 2009, Satyam was restructured and rebranded under the new management as Mahindra Satyam.

The negative has been quite severe, to which we now turn.

Satyam's Aftermath

Given the long history of pervasive state control across most spheres of economic, commercial, and corporate activity, it is not surprising that in the heart of most bureaucrats and ministers lurks the desire to impose insidious controls if they can get away with them. That possibility arose with Satyam.

Two agencies regulate companies in India: the MoCA through the Companies Act, and the SEBI, whose writ covers all listed entities. Until January 2009, the SEBI was the winner. The companies that really mattered were listed and, therefore, under the SEBI's jurisdiction; the key clauses of the Listing Agreement clearly defined the norms for financial disclosure and corporate governance; most important, the SEBI was considered a more transparent and professional body compared to the MoCA.

Satyam changed that. As a stunned corporate world was figuring out how half a dozen felons led by Ramalinga Raju stole monstrous amounts of company money with neither the statutory auditors nor the non-executive directors having a clue, the MoCA assumed charge. It played the lead role with the investigators, the new Satyam board, the press, and the politicians. In the process, it consigned the SEBI to purgatory. Since then, the MoCA has been determined to define a new control raj and hold the aces.

That brings me to the Companies Bill, 2009, which is a particularly gross example of the MoCA calling the shots. The original Bill was significantly modified by the MoCA and the Parliamentary Standing Committee (PSC) chaired by Yashwant Sinha. The PSC report—including the altered Bill—was presented to the Lok Sabha on 31 August 2010. It will be debated in Parliament some time in 2011. Given how little parliamentary debate occurs in matters such as competition and corporate law, it will be almost certainly passed.

Regarding corporate governance, few will deny that the Companies Act, 1956, needed to be changed in line with Clause 49 of the Listing Agreement and to be brought to the 21st century. But in doing so, the MoCA displayed some terrible aspects of the old control raj, and excessive over-reach of law. Here is a small sample.

Board size. The Companies Bill, 2009, states that every public limited company must have a minimum of three and a maximum of 15 directors, excluding nominees from lending institutions. A company wishing to appoint more directors can only do so after obtaining prior approval of the central government and passing a special resolution. Every sensible country's corporate law prescribes the minimum, as it should. But why should it impose a maximum? Is that not a matter for a company's shareholders to decide? And if the shareholders agree to such a special resolution, why does a company need 'prior approval of central government' to increase its board size beyond 15?

An independent director's term. According to a new clause in the Bill: (i) no independent director shall have a tenure exceeding, in the aggregate, a period of 10 consecutive years (five plus five) on the board of a company; and (ii) three years must elapse before such a person is inducted in the same company in any capacity.

No corporate law in any country worth the name legislates the maximum number of years that a director can serve on a board. Not in the US, in the UK, in Australia, in Canada, in Singapore, in Hong Kong, and in many more. Such a ceiling, if it exists at all, is in the memorandum and articles of association of a company, or as a board practice. Legislation does not prescribe a ceiling.

Is there a law that states the maximum number of terms for a Lok Sabha MP? If political representatives have no ceiling on the number of terms that they can be elected, why is it imposed upon corporate fiduciaries? How can law decide the maximum tenure of an elected appointee of the shareholders? It is for a company's shareholders to choose and not for the state.

Such a clause seriously impairs the working of boards and corporate governance. Consider multi-product, multi-location, multi-service companies, or businesses with substantial regulatory interface, such as banks, mutual funds, and insurance companies. Even with serious training, it normally takes a new independent director a couple of years to properly understand the nuances of these businesses. What is proposed is that the effective tenure of being an informed and sensible fiduciary be a maximum of eight years. After that the nomination committee of the board will have to hunt for a replacement.

What great corporate governance is this? Where is the hard evidence that independence in judgement ends after serving 10 years on a board? None whatsoever. How then did it come to pass? Because the MoCA found it 'worthy' for legislative over-reach.

Number of directorships. A new clause inserted by the MoCA states that no person can be a director of more than 15 public companies, and within these, in no more than seven listed companies. That is probably fair. But PSC has tightened this further. The maximum number of public companies has been reduced to 10; and listed companies have been reduced to five. Capping it at five is extreme. A person can, with full diligence, serve on seven to nine listed boards, especially if these are not as meeting-intensive as those of banks. Limiting board positions to five will not improve governance, but it will certainly increase the stress of finding new directors. Here is the truth. Today, there are not even 250 to 300 people who are genuinely competent to be independent directors of major corporations. The law will not suddenly increase the supply to 500 or 1,000. This clause may change for better, but it is not clear which way at the time of writing this entry.

Ban on stock options. A proposed clause states that 'an independent director shall not be entitled to any remuneration, other than sitting fee, reimbursement of expenses for participation in the Board and other meetings and profit-related commission as may be approved by the members.'

Thus, stock options have been omitted in law 'to allow independent directors to remain independent in decision making' (PSC). Here are four questions:

- Which significant nation's (US's, UK's, Canada's, Australia's, Singapore's, and Hong Kong's to

name some) corporate law bans stock options for independent director?
Answer: None.

- Where is the quantified evidence that stock options given to independent directors systematically encourage corporate mis-governance and self-seeking behaviour at the cost of long-term shareholder value?
Answer: Few, if any.
- How can one expect to attract best-in-class independent directors on boards of start-ups without getting stock options?
Answer: Cannot.
- How can one attract good independent directors to sit on boards of financially distressed but sound companies without getting stock options?
Answer: Cannot.

One can impose constraints. For example, listing norms can state that stock options, even if converted to shares by an independent director, cannot be sold until six months after the director has exited from the board. Such restrictions are worth debating. But to ban stock options is counter-productive.

Statutory auditors. Big auditing firms have been the target of the MoCA's wrath. A clause states that no company shall appoint/re-appoint an individual or a firm as auditor for more than five consecutive years. Moreover, such a firm or individual auditor shall not be eligible for re-appointment as auditor in the same company for five or three years, respectively, thereafter. Besides, where a firm is appointed as an auditor, the auditing partner of the firm must be rotated after three consecutive years and shall not be eligible to be re-appointed as auditing partner of the same company for the next three years.

These are absurd. Only Italy has compulsory rotation of auditors by law—and Italy is hardly the model for corporate governance. No sensible common law or civil law country has these provisions. This clause is due to pressure from the ICAI. The large mass of the ICAI members want to audit large corporations, even if they do not have the requisite skill sets. They are hoping to change the law to get entry. It is almost certain that such short period rotation will harm the quality of audit. Worse still, even the small firms will lose their few marquee clients.

There are many more objectionable clauses in the Companies Bill, 2009. But here's the *piece de resistance.* PSC has recommended that the maximum percentage for political contributions per year be raised from 5 to 7.5 per cent of average net profits during the three immediately preceding financial years! That is brilliantly self-seeking corporate governance, isn't it?

Conclusion

It is difficult to tell whether the Companies Bill, 2009, will pass as it stands today or whether the MoCA will make sensible changes before introducing it for the final time to Parliament. I have critiqued the Bill sufficiently. Let me touch upon three other issues that have implications for the quality of corporate governance.

The first has to do with supply. Strange as it may seem for a country of over 1.1 billion people, corporate India has not found enough independent directors who have the requisite qualifications, experience, and time to discharge increasingly more demanding fiduciary responsibilities, especially those required for audit committees. Even if one were to forget about the 10,000-plus listed companies and, instead focus on the top 350, which account for over 95 per cent of India's market capitalization, and further assume an average board size of nine, there is still a need for 2,500 independent directors, two-thirds of whom have to serve on audit committees. This is where there are severe quality bottlenecks. For one, the number of people who have both financial acumen and the time to serve on audit committees is limited. For another, with significantly greater fiduciary responsibilities and liabilities, a median compensation of Rs 1,75,000 per annum for independent directors of the top 350 companies is not good enough to attract the competent, leave aside the best. This supply-side problem will only increase as fiduciary requirements become more burdensome.

The second issue has to do with form versus substance. With such a vast array of mandated norms—and possibly more to follow if the present Companies Bill becomes law—there is real fear of a laundry list form of corporate governance, where the company secretary ticks a large checklist, and where form overwhelmingly dominates substance. Not surprisingly, there is now developing a thriving market for so-called corporate governance 'consultants', who are hired by companies at the end of each financial year to ensure that the annual reports follow the letter, not the spirit, of Clause 49. Given a high degree of mandating, the law does nothing to separate the wheat from the chaff. Today, as before, a serious analyst has to go beyond the legislated disclosures to get the real picture of actual corporate governance.

The third problem is that of enforcement. Neither the SEBI nor the stock exchanges are equipped to carefully monitor the implementation of corporate governance and, therefore, cannot expeditiously enforce penalties for serious breaches. In fact, the extreme penalty is the threat of de-listing, which is hardly credible because if that were to happen it would only hurt the minority shareholders—

precisely the investors who good corporate governance seeks to protect.

Having said so, there is no doubt that India has made huge strides in corporate governance between 1998 and today. Credit for this goes not only to organizations like the CII, the SEBI, some economists and policymakers, a band far-thinking corporate chieftains, and even the MoCA. Credit also goes to a free and powerful financial press that has championed this cause. Somewhere, such accountability must spill over to public governance. Or so we hope.

OMKAR GOSWAMI

References

CapitalOnline, Database of Listed Companies.

Centre for Monitoring the Indian Economy (CMIE), Prowess.

Confederation of Indian Industry (CII). 1998. *Desirable Corporate Governance: A Code*, April.

Goswami, Omkar. 2003. 'The Tide Rises, Gradually: Corporate Governance in India', in Charles Oman (ed.), *Corporate Governance in Development: The Experiences of Brazil, Chile, India and South Africa*, Paris, OECD Development Centre, pp.105–60.

Government of India. 2002. *Report of the Committee on Corporate Audit and Governance* (Chair: Naresh Chandra), New Delhi, Department of Company Affairs, Government of India.

——. 2005. *Report of the Expert Committee on Company Law* (Chair: J.J. Irani), New Delhi, Department of Company Affairs, Government of India.

SEBI. 2000 and 2005. Clause 49 of the Listing Agreement.

——. 2003. *Report of the SEBI Committee on Corporate Governance* (Chair: N.R. Narayana Murthy).

——. SEBI website.

Corporate Ownership and Performance

Background

The question of whether ownership characteristics of firms are related to their performance has been extensively debated in the academic literature. Existing studies in this area can be broadly classified into two types. The first type focuses on public and private ownership forms at an aggregate level, while the second type is more micro-theoretic in nature and tries to link differences in performance of mainly private-sector firms to their underlying equity ownership structures.

The debate between pubic versus private ownership firms often highlights two extreme positions. At one end is the view that 'ownership always matters', which is subscribed to by property rights and public choice theorists who maintain that private firms would necessarily outperform public firms. According to property rights theorists, the reason for this is that shareholders of private firms can easily sell their shares in case of poor performance which is not the case for public firms. The potential for takeovers and the consequent loss in reputation and income forces private-sector managers to perform. Public choice theorists point to specific X-inefficiency factors like lack of well-defined and fixed objectives for managers, presence of special interest groups, and political rent seeking that cause public-sector firms to underperform vis-à-vis their private-sector counterparts. The other extreme position in this debate is the 'no difference in efficiency' view, where some argue that the link between the market for corporate control and superior private enterprise efficiency can be weak because of possible free-rider problems in takeover activity, given that private firms are often owned largely by small shareholders. Some others point to the 'primacy of competition over ownership', arguing that product market competition, by creating the necessary pressure on managers of public firms, can eliminate any performance differential between public and private firms.

Studies that look into the relation between ownership structures and performance of private-sector firms originate in corporate governance literature and are rooted in the observation that the distribution of ownership structure of private corporations matters in performance. Here, two types of corporations can be distinguished: one, the prototype Berle and Means corporations with dispersed ownership leading to separation of ownership and control and, two, corporations with concentrated ownership and control. In the former type, typically found in the US and the UK, where ownership of the corporation lies with dispersed shareholders (the principal) and the day-to-day control lies with the manager (the agent), managers are able to take self-serving actions (such as appropriating funds for over consumption of perquisites and empire building) that, while increasing their private returns, are inconsistent with shareholder value maximization. Given such costs, dubbed in literature as *Type I* agency costs, and arising due to asymmetric information and moral hazards, various internal and external mechanisms are recommended for aligning the interest of managers and shareholders. Equity ownership is one such crucial internal mechanism. For example, giving managers significant equity ownership may lead to the 'convergence' of managerial and shareholder objectives leading to maximization of firm value. Likewise, few large shareholders, as compared to dispersed ones, can have the power and incentives to monitor managers effectively.

While corporations with dispersed ownerships with separation of ownership and control have dominated the US and UK, cross-country studies have shown that there is significant concentration of ownership and control, particularly in Continental Europe, Latin America, and Asian economies. In such cases the nature of the agency problem changes from shareholder–manager conflicts to conflicts between two categories of principals—the controlling inside shareholders and minority outside dispersed shareholders. Controlling insiders, by virtue of substantial equity stakes, would have a strong incentive to monitor, thereby attenuating *Type I* agency problems. However, the presence of controlling shareholders can also lead to a conflict of interest between them and outside minority shareholders, dubbed as *Type II* agency costs, if the former seek to extract private benefits for themselves at the expense of the minority shareholders. Such expropriation can be accomplished through the use of structural devices like dual class shares and stock pyramids that create a divergence between control rights and cash flow rights. Such a wedge works as a vehicle for expropriation of minority shareholders by the controlling shareholders whereby the latter, through various means at their disposal (like transfer pricing), can transfer wealth from firms in which cash flow rights are lower to firms where their cash flow rights are higher. This phenomenon, *tunneling*, is one way in which expropriation of minority shareholders can take place.

Given the two distinct types of ownership structures, diffuse and concentrated, questions regarding ownership and performance take on conflicting dimensions, such as whether large shareholders necessarily increase firm value or instead use their controlling power to pursue objectives that benefit them at the expense of the minority shareholders. Existing empirical evidence on the ownership-performance issue, both with respect to developed and developing countries, closely mirrors the diversity in theoretical opinion, and is largely inconclusive. The diversity of findings across countries and over time has increasingly strengthened the viewpoint that 'institutions matter' in determining the relationship between ownership and performance. For instance, it is argued that the institutional specificities of developing countries, such as less active capital and takeover markets or the absence of a well-developed managerial market, can impact the costs and benefits of different types of ownership in unique ways. Thus, findings on ownership and performance in developed countries may not necessarily hold in the context of developing countries.

Empirical Evidence on Ownership and Performance in India

Literature on ownership and performance in India, as in the case of many developing countries, is relatively recent and can, in line with the background discussion, be split into two types. The first type consists of studies comparing the performance of the public sector vis-à-vis the private sector. Most of these studies use the 'dummy variable approach' under which the *average* performance of one ownership group is compared with that of the other, without considering their detailed ownership structures. The second type, focusing mainly on private-sector firms, links the structure of their equity ownership across different types of shareholders, to their performance.

Public versus Private Firms

The relative performance of public and private-sector firms in India for the 21-year period, 1989 to 2008, is shown in Figure 1. Private-sector firms are classified into (Indian) private firms and foreign firms operating in India. Their performance is measured in terms of mean return-on-assets (ROA) calculated as profits before depreciation, interest, and taxes divided by the total assets. This period witnessed the deregulation and liberalization of the Indian economy, starting in the mid-1980s and gathering momentum after the adoption of the structural reforms programme in July 1991. Additionally, while the blueprints of the industrial policy in post-Independence India had accorded 'commanding heights' to the public sector, India's economic transition since the 1990s has been marked by an increasingly level playing field between the private and public sector.

Trends in ROA in Figure 1 reveal that since the onset of liberalization, foreign firms have persistently

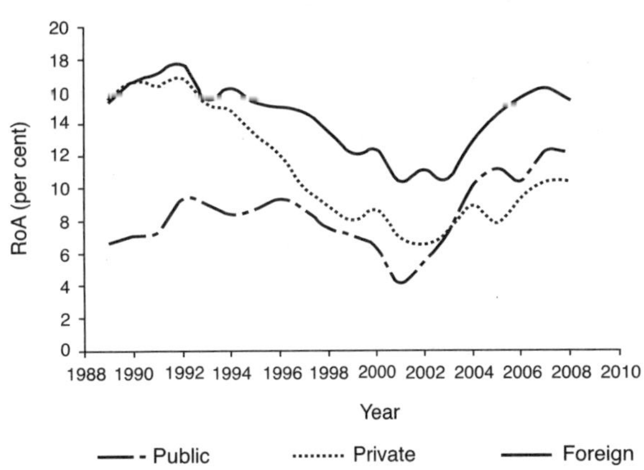

Figure 1 Trends in Return on Assets (Percentage)

Source: Prowess.

outperformed both private domestic firms and public-sector firms. Comparing the latter two, trends in ROA reveal a narrowing of profit differentials till 2004, implying that increased market competitiveness may have worked to erode ownership effects. However, since 2004, there seems to be a reversal of trends, albeit in a different direction, with public firms appearing to have done better compared to private firms. Such a reversal does not appear if one considers a sample of private and foreign firms with asset bases at least equal to the median asset base of public-sector firms.

Figure 1 displays only univariate trends in ROA among the major ownership groups. Ideally, empirical evidence on the question of whether ownership matters should be drawn from multivariate empirical analyses that control for other factors like size, industry affiliation, and age, which can also affect performance and use robust quantitative analyses to draw their conclusions. Most of the existing studies in this regard are with data till the late 1990s, and the general message from these studies seems to be that in a deregulating economy competition can be a significant driver of economic performance, with ownership becoming less important. Considering the pre-deregulation years 1973–89, characterized by little competition among the different ownership groups, and using industry level data, Majumdar (1998) finds that private and mixed-sector firms had higher efficiency compared to public-sector firms. However, support for primacy of competition over ownership is also found in the study—the gap between private and public firms is shown to narrow as the economy was being deregulated and measures to reform underperforming public-sector firms were being adopted.

While there is a dearth of firm-level evidence on the relative performance of public and private firms, evidence that private firms may not be unambiguously superior to public firms is found in a case study of the Indian banking industry (Sarkar et al. 1998) conducted for a cross-section of public, domestic private, and foreign banks around the initial reform years of 1993–4 and 1994–5. Consistent with the property rights hypothesis, this study found that the relative performance of different ownership groups is correlated with the extent of their links with the market for corporate control, with foreign banks performing better than traded private banks which outperformed non-traded private banks. Non-traded private banks, however, had no significant differences in performance, either with respect to profitability or efficiency vis-à-vis public-sector banks. A follow-up analysis by Bhaumik and Dimova (2004), examining whether ownership continues to matter in any way following further deregulation and entry of private-sector banks, was conducted for 1995–6 to 2000–1. Consistent with the role of competition envisaged in the 'no difference' in performance view, the study found that ownership was no longer a significant determinant of performance; instead, greater competition had caused public-sector banks to eliminate the performance/efficiency gap that existed vis-à-vis domestic private-sector and foreign banks.

An increasingly researched issue in recent years that has offered some insights on the relevance of ownership in performance in India is the analysis of partial privatization, that is, the divestiture of a part of the equity by the government without giving up management control. Between 1991, the inception year of the divestment programme, and December 2007, 40 central public-sector undertakings across different industries were partially privatized. While several studies have analysed the performance effects of such divestments, detailed statistical investigation of the ownership effects of partial privatization using firm-level data is found in Gupta (2005) and Sarkar and Sensarma (2010). In her analysis of partial privatization of public-sector enterprises for 1990–2000, Gupta (2005) argues that partial privatization helps to separate the agency cost determinants and the political determinants of public-sector performance since under partial privatization while agency costs are mitigated through the market for corporate control, political control still remains with the government. The study, after controlling for the fact that the better firms are more likely to be chosen for privatization, finds that partial privatization has a positive impact on profitability, productivity and investment. Similar results are found by Sarkar and Sensarma (2010) analysing partial privatization of Indian public-sector banks for 1986–2003. Using stochastic frontier analysis, the authors find that partial privatization resulted in a significant increase in total factor productivity of public-sector banks. The results from these studies suggest that faced with political opposition to full privatization, even if the government does not relinquish control, the exposure to market discipline through partial privatization may be an effective way of improving performance of state-owned enterprises.

Ownership Structures and Performance of Private-sector Firms

Empirical work linking ownership structure and performance of private-sector firms has been gaining currency in India following the increasing focus on corporate governance issues. With the adoption of the structural reforms programme in 1991, as India became more integrated with the world market and more companies started tapping external sources of finance from the debt and capital markets, public concerns started zeroing in on understanding how ownership structures of firms are organized and their implications on performance, how firms are governed by their shareholders, whether minority shareholders are protected from expropriation from the majority, and whether large blockholders like banks and institutional investors were active in governance. While published work analysing the link between ownership structures and performance in private-sector firms is relatively less in India as compared to the repository of such work in developed countries, these studies do provide some interesting insights.

An examination of the composition of ownership of listed private-sector companies in India based on data from ownership disclosures made under more transparent ownership disclosure regulations for listed companies since 2001 for the period 2001–8 is given in Table 1. As can be seen from the estimates, Indian listed firms are characterized by concentrated ownership in the hands of controlling insiders, referred to as 'promoters'. Among all ownership constituents, promoters on an average are the single largest type of blockholders, with more than 45 per cent controlling stakes with their relative position showing a marginal increase over the period. Holdings by other blockholders, namely, financial institutions and domestic and foreign institutional investors are relatively small at less than 5 per cent on an average. Further, while there is some increase in holdings by foreign institutional investors, there has been a noticeable fall in holdings by banks and financial institutions, as well as by mutual funds and insurance companies. Finally, substantial holdings by individuals in the range of 30–35 per cent signify the importance of outside dispersed shareholders. The ownership structures of private-sector firms as presented Table 1 suggest that the corporate governance system in India is by and large a hybrid of the 'outsider systems' of the US and the UK, and the 'insider systems' of Continental Europe and Japan (Sarkar and Sarkar 2000).

Like their counterparts in East Asia, Japan, and several European countries, concentrated ownership structure in India is the norm rather than the exception. Equity holdings by non-financial corporations, which are primarily inter-corporate cross-holdings, are much higher in India than that in the US and the UK and are more comparable to that found in Germany and Japan. However, the participation of the small investor in corporate equity is at comparable levels with the US, with India having the largest number of listed companies in the world. While different types of financial corporations in India separately hold much smaller blocks in comparison to those in other countries, given that nearly all of these corporations are government controlled, together they form a significant block in the equity ownership of Indian companies. The participation of institutional investors like mutual funds and insurance companies which are nearly fully owned by the government in India is comparable to the extent of their participation in Japan and Germany, but much less in scope than that in the US.

What implications does ownership composition have on firm performance? The first set of valuable insights on this issue is provided by a handful of studies using ownership data from the 1990s and postulating both linear and non-linear specifications of the relationship between ownership composition and firm performance (Chhibber and Majumdar 1999; Khanna and Palepu 2000; Sarkar and Sarkar 2000). While the study by Chhibber and Majumdar (1999) primarily analyses the relation between foreign ownership and company performance, the remaining two studies examine the effect of other blockholders like directors, institutional investors, domestic financial institutions, and foreign investors on company value. A general finding across these studies is that foreign equity ownership is beneficial for performance. While Khanna and Palepu (2000),

Table 1 Trends in Distribution of Equity Ownership of Listed Companies

Type of owners	Equity ownership (per cent)							
	2001	2002	2003	2004	2005	2006	2007	2008
Promoters	46.68	47.80	48.36	48.76	48.56	47.23	47.46	48.01
Mutual funds	2.11	1.70	1.49	1.28	1.21	1.53	1.40	1.44
Banks, financial institutions, and insurance companies	3.68	3.70	3.63	3.16	2.68	2.28	2.05	1.85
Foreign institutional investors	0.90	0.73	0.68	1.14	1.56	2.64	2.86	3.14
Non-financial corporations	12.25	11.95	11.40	11.47	11.99	12.19	10.43	10.69
Individuals	33.28	33.13	33.38	33.08	32.74	32.62	32.91	31.29
Others	1.11	0.99	1.06	1.11	1.23	1.51	2.55	3.13

Source: Prowess.

postulating a linear relationship between concentrated ownership and firm value, find no evidence of a beneficial impact of equity ownership by domestic financial institutions or directors on company value, Sarkar and Sarkar (2000) find evidence of a piece-wise linear relationship between the different equity owners. In the latter study, shareholding by directors, who are in many cases de facto owners of family-dominated companies, positively impacts company value once their holdings cross a threshold (25 per cent), a result that is consistent with that of some well-cited studies in the US. The study also finds effective monitoring by financial institutions once they have substantial equity holdings. Further, this monitoring is reinforced by the extent of debt holdings by these institutions. The overall evidence, confirmed by later studies using more recent data, points to the positive role that can be played by blockholders in mitigating managerial agency problems in developing countries like India that are characterized by weak legal protection.

While large shareholders are found to play a beneficial role in influencing firm performance across Indian firms in general, this picture somewhat changes when the role of such shareholders is considered specifically with respect to firms affiliated to business groups. One key governance issue in the case of such firms is whether controlling shareholders expropriate minority shareholders. Robust evidence to this effect is found in a study by Bertrand et al. (2002) with respect to pyramidal business groups in India. The study finds that group firms transfer unexpected increases in their profits following industry-specific shocks, to member firms, with the extent and direction of transfer consistent with the tunnelling hypothesis.

A common feature of existing ownership and performance studies in India, as with a majority of such studies elsewhere, is that ownership structures of firms are taken as exogenous, that is, as given, and then their effect on performance is examined. However, a growing body of research suggests that such structures may themselves evolve in response to differences in performance and other firm characteristics, and that in the end performance may not vary with ownership. Empirical studies using sophisticated econometric techniques that account for this simultaneous determination of ownership and performance should be able to corroborate these theoretical predictions. Findings of these studies, taken together with existing evidence, can throw valuable insights on the ongoing debate in India on whether privatization would matter in the first place, and if so, the type of ownership structure that will maximize post-privatization performance.

Jayati Sarkar and Subrata Sarkar

References

Bertrand, Marianne, Paras Mehta, and Sendhil Mullainathan. 2002. 'Ferreting Out Tunneling: An Application to Indian Business Groups', *The Quarterly Journal of Economics*, 117(1): 121–48.

Bhaumik, Sumon Kumar and Ralitza Dimova. 2004. 'How Important is Ownership in a Market with Level Playing Field? The Indian Banking Sector Revisited', *Journal of Comparative Economics*, 32(1): 165–80.

Chhibber, P.K. and S.K. Majumdar. 1999. 'Foreign Ownership and Profitability: Property Rights, Control, and the Performance of Firms in Indian Industry', *Journal of Law and Economics*, 42(1): 209–39.

Gupta, Nandini. 2005. 'Partial Privatization and Firm Performance', *The Journal of Finance*, 60(2): 987–1015.

Khanna, Tarun and Krishna Palepu. 2000. 'Emerging Market Business Groups, Foreign Investors and Corporate Governance', in Randall Morck (ed.), NBER volume on *Concentrated Ownership*, Chicago, University of Chicago Press.

Majumdar, Sumit K. 1998. 'Assessing Comparative Efficiency of the State-Owned, Mixed, and Private Sectors in Indian Industry', *Public Choice*, 96(1–2): 1–24.

Sarkar, Jayati and Subrata Sarkar. 2000. 'Large Shareholder Activism in Corporate Governance in Developing Countries: Evidence from India', *International Review of Finance*, 1(3): 161–94.

Sarkar, Jayati, Subrata Sarkar, and Sumon Bhaumik. 1998. 'Does Ownership Always Matter?—Evidence from the Indian Banking Industry', *Journal of Comparative Economics*, 26(2): 262–81.

Sarkar, Subrata and Rudra Sensarma. 2010. 'Partial Privatization and Bank Performance: Evidence from India', *Journal of Financial Economic Policy*, 2(4): 276–306.

Corruption

Types of Corruption

Corruption and its control were discussed in Kautilya's *Arthashastra* around 2,000 years ago. Recent Indian scholarly and policy discussion continue this tradition of contributing to the understanding of corruption and its remedies.

As is done here, corruption is usually defined as the misuse of public office for private gain. Common manifestations of corruption are bribes in cash or kind taken by politicians or bureaucrats either in return for illegal favours (referred to here as voluntary bribes) or for refraining to use official power to cause harm (coercive bribes). With voluntary bribes, both the bribe giver and the bribe taker benefit at the cost of the public. Coercive bribes benefit the bribe takers at the expense of the bribe givers. Threats of harassment generally provide the inducement for paying coercive bribes.

Besides bribes, nepotism and misuse or theft of public property by responsible officials are other common types of corruption. The *Arthashastra* lists 40 ways in which public officials can steal government money or harass citizens.

A 2002 Transparency International (TI) survey of individuals in South Asia who had recently used one of seven public services found various types of corruption-prone activities in different sectors. Types most often encountered by the 5,157 Indian respondents ranged from *hafta* or periodic bribe to the police by businesses to avoid harassment, to bribes for admissions or continued service in health, education, and power, and bribes to ensure low tax assessments. A 2007 TI survey of 23,000 randomly selected below poverty line (BPL) households in India covering 11 public services found that even the poor are not spared, with bribes being extracted for services varying from water connections, to bank loans and registration for employment under the National Rural Employment Guarantee Scheme (NREGS).

It is likely that the survey respondents would be less forthcoming about voluntary bribes compared to coercive bribes. Nevertheless these surveys suggests that bribes in India are largely coercive, except perhaps in the case of taxes. Even for taxes, other studies have found coercive bribes for getting refunds and clearances and for releasing goods at warehouses and check posts to be important.

The World Bank's World Business Environment Survey (WBES) in 2001–2 provides information about bribes by companies. According to respondents in India, about two-thirds of the time, bribe amounts are known to companies in advance, allowing bribe costs to be taken account of in business plans. On the other hand, payment of bribes only ensures that promised favours will be delivered a quarter of the time. According to Bardhan (1997) inability to deliver promised favours in centralized bureaucracies often results from the need to get approvals from multiple officials. Going by recent bribe scandals reported in the press, sectors where business bribes are the most prevalent are in relation to the award of government contracts (for example, in relation to the 2010 Commonwealth Games or for armament purchases), the award of licences ranging from mining leases to allocation of mobile phone spectrum, and land allotment.

Regarding stealing of public property, studies in India have focused on siphoning of public funds for infrastructure works such as irrigation and roads, for social and anti-poverty services, and from publicly funded loans to the poor. For example, Bhatia and Dreze (1998) document how heads of village administration (*sarpanch*es) collude with development officials to misappropriate around 20 per cent of the funds for village-level development works. The Central Vigilance Commission (CVC) regularly reports cases of misappropriation.

Some Indian policy writings have pointed to large-scale corruption in government recruitments and transfers to 'lucrative' positions, and in awarding public procurement contracts. These types of corruption involve both politicians and bureaucrats. While bribes for postings do not immediately affect ordinary citizens, officers who have paid for posts later indulge in bribe taking to make good their 'investment'.

Extent and Distribution of Corruption

The Corruption Perceptions Index (TI 2010), based on surveys of foreign business executives, ranks India as the 87th most corrupt out of 178 countries compared to a 2004 rank of 56th of the 146 countries covered. However, during this period, India's corruption index score improved from 2.8 to 3.3 on a scale of 0 to 10.

In its 2009 Global Corruption Barometer, TI found that 58 per cent of Indians polled (during October–November 2008) perceived politicians to be the most corrupt. Smaller proportions rated civil servants and public officials being most corrupt (13 per cent) followed by Parliament and law-making bodies (10 per cent), business and the private sector (9 per cent), media (8 per cent), and the judiciary (3 per cent).

In the 2002 TI survey mentioned earlier, corruption encountered by respondents was in (decreasing order) the police, judicial services, land administration, education, power, tax departments, and health services. Indian respondents to the survey who had used a service and encountered corruption ranged from 100 per cent for the police and courts to 15 per cent for tax and health services. TI's 2007 survey of BPL families found the incidence of bribes ranging from 48 per cent for the police to 3.4 per cent for secondary school officials. Other studies have found a much higher incidence of bribes among taxpayers, particularly business firms and companies. The WBES suggests that over 50 per cent of the companies commonly pay bribes.

A finding of both the 2002 and 2007 TI surveys is that most bribes are paid directly to officials rather than to middlemen or 'contacts'. Exceptions to this, as documented, for example, by Caseley (2004), are for property registration and obtaining driving licences. Furthermore, the 2002 TI survey found that bribes were paid directly to *officer-level* staff, like police officers, doctors, land revenue surveyors, tax officers, teachers, and school managements, rather than to subordinate staff. A partial exception was judicial services, where the incidence of bribes to judges and public prosecutors was much lower than to court officials.

On the willingness of citizens to pay voluntarily bribes, the surveys fail to adequately distinguish between coercive and voluntary bribes. Limited available evidence suggests two trends. First, other things being equal, the willingness to pay voluntary bribes has increased secularly since India's Independence. Second, however, given fewer government controls, increased private-sector alternatives, and reduced tax rates, the extent of corruption and quantum of bribes have both decreased, especially in the deregulated sectors.

On the size of bribes, the various surveys taken together suggest that bribes range from 10 to 20 per cent of the legal sums involved. This appears to be low compared to countries at similar levels of development. The average annual bribe payment in 2007 was around Rs 500 for bribe-paying BPL families. This is low given the monthly individual (urban cum rural) poverty line of around Rs 500. So though the incidence of corruption in India may be high, additional costs of corruption are probably not. Even so, recent news coverage of 'bribe scandals' suggests that they can be large in absolute terms if the benefits from purchased favours are themselves large. Bardhan (1997) refers to the tendency for voluntary bribes in some countries to be much lower than bribers' benefits as the 'Tullock Paradox'.

Causes of Corruption

An economic analysis of causes of corruption by Indian authors encompasses different approaches to understanding corruption. With some important exceptions, the research focuses on proximate institutional determinants, taking as given willingness to pay and receive bribes.

One major research concern is with the impact on corruption of incentives—reward and punishment structures—of corrupt officials dealing with dishonest citizens. This concern with incentives dates to the *Arthashastra*. Recent research has helped identify desirable practical design features of joint systems of performance-based rewards and corruption penalties.

Next consider extortionate bribes. In Mookherjee (1997) and Marjit et al. (2000), extortion arises if a government inspector over-reports the extent of violation, if any, by a citizen. In the tax game the latter paper studies, richer taxpayers are likely to pay bribes and evade taxes, while poorer taxpayers are likely to avoid facing tax officials by not filing tax returns. The importance of this research is that it illustrates how corruption can directly cause additional, seemingly unrelated, economic crimes in the case of poor taxpayers.

Partly informed by this research, some Indian policy analysts stress the corruption reducing impact of performance incentives and institutions to promote accountability, such as independent audits and vigilance. Related policy analysis suggests that higher collusion costs of bureaus like tax departments organized on functional lines make them less corruption prone than those where groups of taxpayers are assigned to a single tax inspector. On penalty design, one innovative recent proposal is to remove punishment for those paying extortionate bribes while retaining the payment for takers of such bribes. This gives the bribe payer the incentive to report the bribe to recover the amount, so deterring extortion.

Related research focuses on the impact of supervisory hierarchies, where supervisors are themselves corruptible, given different reward and punishment structures. One theoretical study looks at corruptible tax auditors employed to detect tax evasion by dishonest taxpayers. Given a properly designed set of rewards and fines for auditors, the study predicts that more supervisory levels in the hierarchy increase tax revenue, with the extent of increase depending on the size of rewards and intrinsic abilities of auditors and supervisors to detect tax evasion or bribe taking. The practical impact of this research is still limited.

On the willingness to tolerate or engage in corruption, Indian research has followed several lines of enquiry. The theoretical prediction of differential attitudes of rich and poor taxpayers to bribery has already been discussed. How high levels of prevailing corruption can evolve into a social norm is the subject of another theoretical enquiry. The Indian relevance of this theoretical prediction found experimental support in a study where tolerance for corruption of experimental subjects in India was higher than that of Australian subjects. Another theoretical prediction with some empirical support is that owner-managed firms have a lower propensity to bribe than professionally managed firms, though, when they do bribe, bribes tend to be relatively large. In an important empirical study, Shankar et al. (2010) examine targeting of the NREGS and show how, paradoxically, improved information can cause increased corruption. Information through television, social media, and public meetings disproportionately benefit the non-poor thus increasing the proportion of non-target beneficiaries of the NREGS.

Another area where major contributions have been made by Indian scholars is on the impact of institutions and their implications for political corruption. This area has been surveyed by Pande (2007), who critically reviews evidence for the hypothesis that political corruption and the willingness to tolerate corruption can be explained as a rational outcome of the political and economic environment. One theoretically and empirically supported proposition is that a political candidate's policy platform and corruptibility are both important in determining electoral outcomes. For example, a study reported by Pande (2007) finds that low socio-economic group candidates may simultaneously support redistributive policies and line their own pockets. This study also finds empirical support for its prediction that corruption increases among the candidates of the pro-majority party while reducing that of candidates from pro-minority parties, with the effect being more pronounced when the majority is larger.

A second set of factors surveyed by Pande (2007) is how political power and opportunities for corruption arise, particularly in developing countries. She reviews explanations that point to the close link between economic and political power, on the one hand, and gender-based and ethnic labour market distortions, on the other, as important factors explaining political participation and corruption. She also reviews (mixed) evidence of the impact of voter educational attainments on political corruption.

Overall though there have been insights into causes of corrupt behaviour by bureaucrats and politicians, both in theory and in Indian evidence, and also on the demand or tolerance for corruption, further insights can be expected in the future.

Consequences of Corruption

One clear economic consequence of corruption is reduced government revenue, adversely affecting its ability to deliver public services or, alternatively, accentuating macroeconomic instability when deficit financing is resorted to. The policy literature in India identifies a variety of direct and indirect revenue loss channels. To take some key examples, corruption facilitates direct tax evasion and can also lead to further unaccounted (bribe) income. As the widely reported recent (2010) 2G spectrum scandal shows, corruption through inappropriate licence allotment rules can also lead to a loss of non-tax revenue and cause further unaccounted bribe income. Unaccounted bribe income has been alleged to be a major source of unaccounted funds held outside the country, leading to further revenue loss.

A second, real cost of corruption is increasing business and individual regulatory compliance costs because of red tape either to prevent regulatory non-compliance or to facilitate the extraction of bribes as pointed out by Banerjee (1997).

The other side of the coin, the negative impact of corruption on the effectiveness of government services and their unit costs, can be inferred from this discussion. Evidence on the magnitude of these costs is available from the Comptroller and Auditor General of India (CAG) and also increasingly in recent surveys and studies. Banerjee's (1997) important insight is that corruption is also *indirectly* responsible for high delivery costs since corrupt bureaucrats have the incentive to generate excessive red tape which adds to costs. This theory is supported in the Indian context by a recent field experiment.

Corruption also makes anti-poverty services relatively inefficient due to poor targeting and leakages adversely affecting poverty alleviation. This has been documented in the case of the NREGS, the public distribution system and also, to a lesser extent, old age pensions. For the NREGS, the 2007 TI survey found that between 4 and 10 per cent of BPL households used 'contacts' to get services, the highest percentages being in connection with housing and land registration services. BPL households with no access to 'contacts' or who were unable to pay bribes (2 to 4 per cent) could not benefit from various public services, including electricity, housing, land registration, NREGS, PDS, police, and school education.

An implication of studies surveyed in Pande (2007) is that systematic differences in political preferences may interact with voting institutions and also result in misallocation of public resources. The theoretical prediction discussed above that extortion is regressive finds empirical support in the 2007 TI survey.

Examples of how corruption causes further corruption or other economic crimes include the non-filing of tax returns by poor taxpayers in Marjit et al. (2000), and in the context of government recruitments and postings. To take another example, businesses must evade taxes to generate unaccounted money for bribes. There is anecdotal evidence of entire departments set up to deal with government regulators in some prominent companies. So reduced hidden business costs are one important effect of deregulation.

The negative impact of corruption on business costs clearly also reduces international competitiveness. Bardhan's (1997) review of the negative impact of corruption on efficient resource allocation, investment, particularly foreign investment, and economic growth suggests that these costs are appreciable. As Bardhan points out, efficiency and growth costs are not limited to direct costs. Indirect cost channels include the reduced information transmitting efficiency of markets since corruption is necessarily secretive; business uncertainty since corrupt favours are not always delivered; and further uncertainty since corrupt courts cannot be relied upon to uphold property rights and enforce contracts. Another indirect channel identified in Indian writing is the two-way link between corruption and unaccounted wealth, including wealth held outside the country in secretive foreign jurisdictions. Conspicuous consumption from 'black' wealth and curtailed investment opportunities further reduce growth. The overhang of black wealth from the pre-liberalization period is also thought to reduce the growth benefits of liberalization since black money cannot always flow to sectors with the highest returns.

Continuing corruption eventually reduces respect for the rule of law and honesty in public life. Evidence from cross-country studies suggests that the rule of law is an important determinant of economic growth. Though this decline should have large economic costs, no estimate is yet available for India.

Combating Corruption in India

The only sure way to incorruptibility is changed individual values and social norms, making corruption unacceptable. Since how to achieve this is not well understood, a widely accepted second best strategy is improving institutions of governance. Important institutions include few, transparent regulations; transparency through institutions to effectively implement legislated rights to information about government activities; institutions promoting accountability, including independent audit of government bureaus; a free press and involvement of civil society in public education and government monitoring; effective citizens' grievance redressal channels; and performance incentives for government servants. Economic growth and also a reduced government role through privatization and deregulation can reduce corruption though, as a telling example in Bardhan (1997) makes clear, indiscriminate privatization of even corrupt government functions is not advisable.

However, 45 per cent of TI's 2009 Global Corruption Barometer Indian sample rated the government's efforts to curb corruption as ineffective, though the perception of government effectiveness in relation to addressing corruption had improved from 2007.

Governance reforms in India have focused on privatization and on automating government departments and procedures. Evidence on the limited impact of automation is in Caseley (2004) and Deininger and Goyal (2010). Concurrent institutional reforms to ensure that information and transparency advantages of automation actually result in improved performance and reduced corruption are present only in some cases. Regarding institutional reforms coupled with automation, one study comparing unsuccessful land registration reforms in Andhra Pradesh and Karnataka with the successful reforms in Maharashtra makes it clear that for reform implementation, 'the devil is in the details'. This point is also made with respect to Karnataka's successful 'Bhoomi' land record reforms in another study.

India's legal framework has important enabling laws, including the Prevention of Corruption Act and the Right to Information Act in several states. Though of relatively recent vintage, a significant impact in combating corruption has been found by recent research (for example, Right to Information India, 2007). Regarding courts, however, even in cases where court action is initiated, rulings take a long time and are often inconclusive. Existing anti-corruption agencies such as the CVC and, in part, the CAG have had limited success in curbing public corruption. The setting up of a key agency—the Lok Pal (the central ombudsman)—has been pending for decades.

There have been some successes in civil society monitoring to combat corruption. Prominent examples are institutionalized public hearings by the Mazdoor Kisan Shakti Sangathan in Rajasthan and the survey-based public service Report Cards of the Public Affairs Centre, Bangalore.

Evidence for other macroeconomic factors which have a negative impact on corruption is also to be found in Indian writing. This includes economic freedom, democracy, and economic growth.

Though the spate of major recent corruption scandals seem to suggest the contrary, as Bardhan suggests, corruption is likely to decline as India develops. The pace of decline could be speeded up with greater public will leading to more effective institutional reforms.

ARINDAM DAS-GUPTA

References

Banerjee, Abhijit V. 1997. 'A Theory of Misgovernance', *Quarterly Journal of Economics*, 112(4): 1289–332.

Bardhan, Pranab. 1997. 'Corruption and Development: A Review of Issues', *Journal of Economic Literature*, 35: 1320–46.

Bhatia, Bela and Jean Dreze. 1998. Campaign in Rural India,

Berlin, Transparency International, available at http://www.transparency.org/working_papers/bhatia-dreze/bhatia-dreze.html, accessed in February 2005.

Caseley, Jonathan. 2004. 'Public Sector Reform and Corruption: CARD Façade in Andhra Pradesh', *Economic and Political Weekly*, 39(11): 1151–6.

Deininger, Klaus and Aparajita Goyal. 2010. 'Going Digital: Credit Effects of Land Registry Computerization in India', World Bank Policy Research Working Paper 5244, Washington DC.

Marjit, S., V. Mukherjee, and A. Mukherjee. 2000. 'Harassment, Corruption and Tax Policy', *European Journal of Political Economy*, 16: 75–94.

Mookherjee, Dilip. 1997. 'Incentive Reform in Developing Country Bureaucracies: Lessons from Tax Administration', in B. Pleskovic and J. Stiglitz (eds), *Annual World Bank Conference on Development Economics*, Washington DC, World Bank.

Pande, Rohini. 2007. 'Understanding Political Corruption in Low Income Countries', in T. Paul Schultz and John A. Strauss (eds), *Handbook of Development Economics*, available at http://www.sciencedirect.com/science/article/B7P5D-4RWXCH1-C/2/37caab1ce47c5d4ee3d6397ea633bdc2. [Working Paper available at http://web.hks.harvard.edu/publications/workingpapers/citation.aspx?PubId=4806, accessed on 17 February 2011].

Right to Information India. 2007. 'RTI Brought Marked Decline in Corruption in India: Study', available at http://www.rtiindia.org/forum/389-right-information-brought-marked-decline-corruption-india-study.html, accessed on 17 February 2011.

Shankar, Shailashri, Raghav Gaiha, and Raghavendra Jha. 2010. Information and Corruption, ASARC Working Paper, available at http://www.crawford.anu.edu.au/acde/asarc/pdf/papers/2010/WP2010_02.pdf, accessed on 17 February 2011.

Transparency International. 2010. Corruption Perceptions Index 2010, available at www.transparency.org, accessed on 17 February 2011.

■ Credit Market Regulation, Evolution of

Development economists are well aware of several theoretical reasons why in an underdeveloped society the free hand of the market may fail to direct much-needed and scarce credit to its most productive use. Moreover, the asymmetry of power between the moneylender and borrower in such societies often results in the former enjoying excessive rents to the detriment of the latter. Hence, attempts to regulate usury[1] are pervasive in legal traditions around the world and India is no exception. In this entry I shall trace the origins and evolution of the legal framework under which the credit markets in India operate. The historical experience of credit market regulation is particularly instructive for the regulatory reforms currently underway. While the term 'credit market' can mean several things, I shall use it primarily to mean 'a market in which private persons (individuals and businesses) borrow money for consumption and investment'.

Pre-British Period

The traditional Hindu Law, whose textual sources can be traced back to the *smrti* documents written around AD 200, laid down several rules governing the rights and duties of lenders as well as borrowers. These texts mention restrictions on rates of interest, permissible means of debt recovery, and punitive consequences of defaulting on a debt (Kane 1946). For instance, the rule of pious obligation required that a man's debts be paid with interest by his sons even when no property was bequeathed to them. Another rule, the rule of Damdupat, required that the creditor cannot collect more than twice the original principal. Prescriptions laid out in the smrti texts supplemented by local customs formed the basis of the medieval law governing credit contracts in India. This practice continued even during the Mughal period notwithstanding Islam's summary ban on usury (Habib 1964). While there were important spatial and temporal variations in the functioning of credit markets, certain common features can be discerned. Indian society was predominantly an agricultural society and the demand for credit was occasioned by the investment and consumption needs arising out of the vagaries of monsoon-fed agriculture. In the pre-British period (and in some instances even afterwards) the enforcement of credit contracts was a local affair: the village councils often adjudicated disputes between the borrower and the moneylender; the state had a limited role in contract enforcement; and the informal forces of social custom and moral pressure, not to mention the moneylender's muscle power, often played a more important role. The mutual dependence between the moneylender and the village community helped, to some extent, in curbing the lender's rapacity. Even to this date, surveys of the informal credit sector in backward rural areas of India reveal a similar picture.

[1]In its original sense, the term 'usury' merely means the practice of lending at interest. It is only in subsequent usage that the term acquired the negative connotation of lending at exorbitant interest.

British Period

The advent of British rule brought about important changes to the legal system in India. Influenced by the classical liberal views of political economy, the British sought to establish a legal system that would secure property rights and enforce private contracts. Several innovations were introduced that resulted in a significant change in the legal framework under which credit contracts were enforced. For instance, the British introduced a system of civil courts that expedited the loan recovery process by granting ex parte decrees, that is, rulings in the absence of the defendant. Land titling converted communal land into private property and thus enabled the use of land as collateral. Moreover, overriding local customs, the British Law permitted seizure of land in lieu of loan repayment even if it had not been explicitly pledged as collateral. While these reforms succeeded in their goal of increasing competition among lenders, they destroyed the incentive of the lenders to insure farmers in times of adverse shocks. This in turn contributed to a dramatic increase in the incidence of rural indebtedness in the Bombay Deccan and Punjab provinces (Kranton and Swamy 1999). The point was brought home by the Deccan Riots of 1875. Following a period of growing indebtedness and loan defaults, villagers in the Poona and Ahmednagar districts of the Bombay Deccan rioted against the local moneylenders, seizing and destroying the bonds and decrees in the hands of their creditors. In some cases, shops and houses of moneylenders were targeted.

The Deccan Riots Commission of 1876 and its legislative sequel—the Deccan Agriculturists' Relief Act of 1879—mark an important juncture in the regulation of credit markets in India. In a decisive break from the laissez-faire approach of the earlier period, this Act gave the courts a right to go beyond the letter of the debt contract. The courts were given powers to determine and award only reasonable interest rates and to explicitly take into account the fairness of the contract in determining its validity. Among the specific provisions of this Act were the recognition of the traditional rule of Damdupat and a ban on seizure of land unless explicitly pledged. Other Acts imposing restrictions on the credit contracts that followed included the Punjab Alienation of Land Act, 1900; the Usurious Loans Act, 1918; and the Punjab Relief of Indebtedness Act, 1934. These efforts met with mixed success. While they succeeded in providing specific relief, the general problem of rural indebtedness and lack of a well-functioning rural credit market remained unaltered.

By the turn of the 19th century, banking companies began to emerge in the urban centres of Bombay, Delhi, and Calcutta. Moreover, recognizing the limited success in regulating rural moneylenders, the British encouraged formation of cooperative credit societies as a means of providing rural credit. There was a definite change in thinking regarding the strategy for credit market regulation.

The minimalist approach of the earlier era, of providing a legal framework and then relying on market forces to do the rest, was set aside and the government took proactive measures to establish a modern banking sector as the mainstay of the credit delivery system. The regulatory infrastructure for this project was established by enacting the Reserve Bank of India (RBI) Act, 1935, and the Indian Companies (Amendment) Act, 1936. The RBI Act established the RBI as the apex bank of the country and provided it with powers to oversee the emerging banking sector. The amended Companies Act included several regulations pertinent to the operation of banking companies. However, there was growing consensus among policymakers that a separate legislation dealing exclusively with the regulation of banking companies was necessary.

Post-Independence Period

One of the first legislations passed after Independence was the Banking Companies Act, 1949, which was subsequently renamed the Banking Regulations Act (BRA). Though enacted post-Independence, the BRA was in continuity of regulatory reforms of the preceding years. Since then, the BRA has been the main legal tool for regulating the formal credit sector. Under this Act, the RBI is given a wide range of regulatory powers over the banking sector, and until the reform era these powers grew with each amendment to the BRA. Cooperative banks were brought under the scope of the BRA in 1965. Every aspect of banking activity, from permission to operate and expand to details regarding the structure and rates of interest, comes under the purview of the RBI due to the various provisions of the BRA. Throughout much of the post-Independence period, the RBI has used these powers to channel credit in the direction commensurate with the socialist principles that governed the thinking of the planning era; it is under this Act that the RBI is able to determine how much of bank lending should go to the priority sector and how many rural branches a bank needs to open. In short, the BRA provides a regulatory framework that has helped consolidate much of the formal credit sector, that is the commercial and cooperative banking sector as well as many NBFCs,[2] under a unified

[2]NBFCs are non-bank financial companies. Their role in the credit market is discussed elsewhere in this volume.

authority. Social control over the banking sector was further consolidated following bank nationalizations in 1969 and again in 1980. It is only recently (after 1991) that the RBI has begun the process of granting banks greater operational discretion and inviting private competition, both domestic and foreign, into the credit markets. Hence the policy approach has once again started shifting in favour of a free-functioning credit market.

While the policy of social control over the banking sector has succeeded in increasing its share in the total lending operations vis-à-vis the informal sector, the latter still caters to a significant population, particularly in the backward rural areas. The regulation of the non-banking and informal sectors—local moneylenders, pawnbrokers, primary agricultural societies, and so on—is placed in the State List of the Constitution and hence falls under the authority of the respective state legislatures. In particular, the issues related to rural indebtedness, perhaps owing to regional variations in agricultural activities, are under states' jurisdiction. There are several laws such as Moneylenders Acts and Debt Relief Acts[3] that are enacted and enforced at the state level for the purpose of controlling private moneylending and redressing rural indebtedness during adverse agricultural shocks.

The line demarcating the states' regulatory powers and those provided by central laws such as the BRA is sometimes fuzzy and that has led to some frictions. Under a provision added to the BRA in 1984 (Section 21-A), courts are precluded from scrutinizing loan contracts by banks to determine whether the interest charged is excessive. Moreover, this provision explicitly overrides the various state laws on this subject. The issue of the primacy of this provision vis-à-vis the states' constitutional prerogative to redress rural indebtedness is far from settled (Tripathi and Jaffree 2000: lvi–lvii). There are differences in opinions given by the various High Courts with regard to this matter. Moreover, with the growing incidence of rural indebtedness and farmer suicides in some states, this issue has gained salience.[4]

Another area of challenge, where the multiplicity of laws has become a hindrance, is the regulation of the emerging micro-finance institutions. While the strategy of using self-help groups (SHGs) and other such channels has received much favourable attention in the policy circles, the magnitude of these activities is still limited and it is still far from clear if their success rate is invariant to scale. The micro-finance sector today operates under a myriad of state and central laws and its successful proliferation will be greatly aided by having a separate Act governing micro-finance institutions.[5]

I have reviewed the laws regulating borrowing and lending and traced their evolution since the pre-British period. However, the efficacy of any law depends on the efficiency of its implementation; indeed, a delay in the delivery of justice is tantamount to its denial. There are monumental hurdles in the legal process of loan recovery. While some of these are placed intentionally with a view to protecting the welfare of the borrower, most are a result of the overload on the Indian court system and impose a hardship on the lender. Moreover, the unpaid debts and non-performing assets (NPAs) deprive other deserving borrowers of a chance to access the much needed credit. An important step towards reducing the backlog of pending debt recovery suits was taken with the passage of the Recovery of Debts due to Banks and Financial Institutions Act, 1993. This Act has helped set up legal machinery, the Debt Recovery Tribunals, to expedite the handling of recovery suits. While the process of legal reform is far from complete, early evidence suggests that it has had a favourable effect on credit market operations (Visaria 2005).

Finally, laws are effective only in so far as they are actually availed of by citizens. Particularly in the backward rural areas, knowledge of and access to the legal system are still limited. This is one of the reasons why rural moneylenders still play an important role in spite of the restrictive regulations intended to curb their usurious practices. Moreover, local powerbrokers and corrupt officials hinder access to the law even when information about it is available to the people. In that sense, the marginalized sections of the rural population are still in the pre-modern paradigm discussed earlier. It can only be hoped that the spread of literacy, local governance, and improved access to the formal as well as regulated micro-finance sector will eventually solve the age-old problem of indebtedness and servitude of the peasant.

MANDAR P. OAK

References

Habib, I. 1964. 'Usury in Medieval India', *Comparative Studies in Society and History*, 6(4): 393–419.

Joshi, S. 2003. 'Politics of Farm Interest Rates', *Hindu Business Line*, Internet Edition.

[3]For example, the Karnataka Prohibition of Exorbitant Interest Act, 2004, and the Maharashtra Debtor's Relief Act, 1976.

[4]In an editorial in *The Hindu* urging state intervention in bank interest rates, a prominent farmers' rights activist asks, 'Do we need a recurrence of Deccan riots to make the Government see reason?' (Joshi 2003).

[5]See http://www.nabard.org/roles/microfinance/index.htm for the views of the NABARD Task Force on Supporting Policy and Regulatory Framework for Micro-finance regarding this matter.

Kane, P.V. 1946. *History of Dharmasastra: Ancient and Medieval Religious and Civil Laws*, Vol. 3, Poona, Bhandarkar Oriental Research Institute.

Kranton, R. and A. Swamy. 1999. 'The Hazards of Piecemeal Reform: British Civil Courts and Credit Markets in Colonial India', *Journal of Development Economics*, 58: 1–25.

Tripathi, G.S.N. and S.I. Jaffree. 2000. *Seth's Commentaries on Banking Regulation Act, 1949 and Allied Banking Laws*, Allahabad, Law Publishers (India) Pvt. Ltd.

Visaria, S. 2005. 'Legal Reform and Loan Repayments: The Microeconomic Impact of Debt Recovery Tribunals in India', Working Paper.

D

■ Dams

At Independence, in 1947, there were fewer than 300 large dams in India. By the year 2000, the number had grown to over 4,000, more than half of them built between 1971 and 1989. India ranks third in the world in dam building, after the US and China. While some of these dams were built primarily for flood control, water supply, and hydroelectric power generation, the primary purpose of most Indian dams (96 per cent) remains irrigation. In fact, large-dam construction has been the main form of investment in irrigation undertaken by the Indian government. But, starting in the 1980s, public investment in large dams in India has been the subject of a sustained controversy—epitomized by the Sardar Sarovar Project—centring on the balance between the social, environmental, and economic costs of dams and their benefits. This entry analyses the economic impact of large irrigation dams in India, focusing on both their aggregate productivity effects and their distributional effects.

Given that the economic gains and losses from dams, like those from many other public investments, often accrue unevenly to different groups in society, one way to begin is to identify the putative winners and losers. Most irrigation dams in India are embankment dams. That is, they consist of a wall built across a river valley to impound water so as to form a reservoir upstream and a system of spillways and gates to bypass the wall so as to maintain normal river flow and convey water to a network of canals feeding irrigated regions downstream. The upstream areas that feed the dam and those submerged by its reservoir make up its 'catchment' area, and the downstream areas fed by its irrigation canals make up its 'command' area. Before any mitigating effects of resettlement and compensation, whether a household stands to gain or lose depends on its location relative to the placement of the dam. People living in the catchment area, who lose property and livelihood but gain little, if anything, from irrigation, tend to lose out, while people living in the command area, who bear little of the social cost but gain the most from irrigation, typically gain.

Proponents of large dams focus on the aggregate productivity benefits, emphasizing the role of dams in enabling irrigation and, even though this is controversial, in recharging the water table, which had been lowered by overuse of underground water sources for irrigation. Between 1951 and 2000, India's production of food grains increased fourfold, from 51 million tonnes to about 200 million tonnes. This not only stopped the importation of food grains, with attendant saving in foreign exchange, but left India with a marginal food grain surplus. Proponents point to the fact that about two-thirds of this increase was in irrigated areas, and that by the year 2000, areas irrigated by dams constituted 35 per cent of irrigated land in India. The most optimistic estimates attribute 25 per cent of the increase in food grain production to dam-irrigated areas. But it is incorrect to attribute the entire production gains in dam-irrigated areas to dams. First, the increase in irrigation coincided with increased uptake of other inputs and technologies, such as high-yielding varieties (HYVs) beginning in the 1960s, fertilizers, machinery, and multicropping. Even though the contribution of these cannot be readily disentangled, we can surmise that it lowers the proportion of the productivity increase due to irrigation alone. Second, there are other methods of harvesting water for irrigation, and so some of the dam-irrigated areas would still have been irrigated even if the dams had not been built.

Indeed, other methods of harvesting water for irrigation, such as groundwater and small dykes, remain pervasive in India. Even so, proponents of large dams have argued that these cannot be relied upon to meet the needs of India's large and growing population. Moreover, it has been argued that these forms of water harvesting are not cost-effective and do not have the added advantages of hydropower generation and flood management.

Opponents of large dams, on the other hand, emphasize the social costs of dams. They point out that the economic gains accrue disproportionately to people living in the command areas. The losses, on the contrary, are suffered disproportionately by people living in the catchment areas. Dam construction and submersion lead to significant loss of arable farmland and forest. Waterlogging and increased salinity reduce agricultural productivity in the vicinity of the reservoir. Policies to ensure adequate flow into the reservoir sometimes prohibit water harvesting in the catchment area, reducing agricultural productivity even more. Large-scale impounding of water increases exposure to vector-borne diseases, such as malaria, schistosomiasis, filariasis, and river blindness. Furthermore, the Indian government's compensation policy towards the displaced remains insufficient in many cases. In particular, since the compensation is based on the amount of land owned, landless households were typically not compensated at all. Nor were people compensated for loss of income or subsistence derived from communal holdings, such as common grasslands and forests. Although dams may also increase economic activity in the catchment area—through construction and economic activity around the reservoir, such as tourism and fishing—these increases are either temporary or depend on the ability to learn new trades, and often cannot compensate for the loss of familiar livelihood.

Ultimately, both the aggregate economic impact of dams and their distributional impact remain complicated empirical questions. As has already been stated, whether a household accrues net losses or gains depends in part on the placement of the dam. That, in turn, depends on several factors including the political and financial power of the local governments; the relative strengths of proponent and opponent civic organizations; and the potential of improved agricultural productivity in the would-be command region. All these factors may have direct impact on both agricultural production and poverty quite independently of the construction of the dam. As such, a simple comparison of the areas in the command or the catchment sites of dams and other areas does not directly inform us about the impact of dams, since these areas are likely to differ along these other salient dimensions, and it is difficult to disentangle their effect and the effect of the dams.

One specific determinant of dam placement, however, is geographic suitability. Dam location is strongly influenced by river gradient. A river flowing at a moderately positive gradient favours irrigation dams; higher water levels upstream facilitate water storage and diversion into irrigation canals. Consequently, within states, new dams tend to be built in those regions that have a river flowing at a moderate incline. After one accounts for the impact of the overall hilliness of the district and the availability of rivers, the gradient of the rivers is unlikely to have a direct impact on changes in agricultural productivity or other district-level outcomes before and after a state builds new dams. It is possible, therefore, to use the variation in dam construction induced by differences in river gradient across districts within Indian states to determine the impact of large dams.

In Duflo and Pande (2005), we use this strategy to estimate the impact of dam construction on district agriculture and poverty outcomes. We find that agricultural productivity in the catchment areas is unaffected, but poverty and vulnerability to rain shocks increase. Poverty increases in terms of both the headcount ratio (the fraction of rural population with consumption levels below the poverty line) and the poverty gap (how much income would be needed to bring the poor to a consumption level equal to the poverty line). In the command areas, irrigation and agricultural productivity increase, and poverty and vulnerability to rainfall shocks decline.

A cost–benefit analysis suggests that dams are, on average, only marginally cost-effective, although there is large variation from dam to dam. We also estimate that large dams increased all-India agricultural productivity by about 9 per cent, a figure close to the World Commission on Dams' estimate of 10 per cent, which has been criticized as too low by proponents of dams.

The increase in poverty in the catchment areas suggests that even though losers are clearly identified as those who live in the vicinity and upstream of the dam, they are rarely adequately compensated. This finding suggests that losers do not have the institutional capacity to negotiate higher compensation. To explore this further, we took a cue from Banerjee and Iyer (2005), who show that Indian districts where the British colonial authorities had delegated the setting and collection of land taxes to a class of landlords tend to have less collective action and public good provision than districts where the individual cultivator paid the taxes directly to the colonial authorities. We found that, while the impact of dams on production is similar in both types of districts, the increase in poverty due to big dams is twice as large in districts where taxation had been delegated to landlords. Our findings are consistent with the view that where the relationship between the elite and the losers is adversarial and where the civic organizations advocating the cause of the losers are relatively weak or non-existent, losers are less likely to have been compensated. The fact that historically disadvantaged groups are disproportionately represented among the displaced (scheduled tribes represent 8 per cent of the population, but 47 per cent of the displaced) also suggests inadequate capacity to negotiate higher compensation. Planning authorities facing groups that have poor capacity to negotiate may not adequately account for the costs of resettlement and compensation, overestimating the economic viability of a dam, which may also increase poverty.

Large dam construction has been an important and expensive undertaking for the Indian government. While dams have enhanced agricultural productivity in India, there is no evidence that they have been very cost-effective, and they have significantly adverse distributional implications. The case of large dams suggests strongly that distributional implications of public policies should be central to any evaluation. Clearly, the case of large dams suggests the need to understand the institutions and power structures that led to the implementation of these projects.

ESTHER DUFLO AND ROHINI PANDE

References

Banerjee, A. and L. Iyer. 2005. 'History, Institutions, and Economic Performance: The Legacy of Colonial Land Tenure Systems in India', *American Economic Review*, 95(4): 1190–213.

Biswas, A. and C. Tortajada. 2001. 'Development and Large Dams: A Global Perspective', *International Journal of Water Resources Development*, 17(1): 9–21.

Duflo, Esther and R. Pande. 2005. 'Dams', mimeo, MIT Poverty Action Lab.

Thakkar, H. 2000. *Assessment of Irrigation in India*, World Commission on Dams.

World Commission on Dams. 2000. *Large Dams: India's Experience*, World Commission on Dams.

V.M. Dandekar

Born in 1920, Vinayak Mahadeo Dandekar grew up in the charged atmosphere of the Indian Freedom Movement. Like other thinkers of his time, he was steeped in Gandhian ideology. However, unlike many of them, Dandekar was first a scientist, then an activist. He questioned everything, even Gandhian principles, and changed his mind frequently as his knowledge of the facts changed. Reading about his life in the many articles that appeared about him in 1995 (when he died), one gets the impression of a sharp and incisive mind put to good use on several of the most important policy problems affecting Indian economic and social life.

Dandekar was not educated formally as an economist—his training was in Statistics at the Indian Statistical Institute in Calcutta, and this is reflected in much of his research on the measurement of national income, rural unemployment, and so on. He was admitted into the Ph.D. programme of the University of London but did not travel there by steamer in protest against the treatment of Indian students (Rath 1995). He was based for most of his professional life at the Gokhalé Institute of Economics and Politics, Pune, and was director of the Institute for 13 years. During much of this period he was also head of the department of economics at Pune University. In 1962 he set up the Indian School of Political Economy at Lonavala, an institute that was designed to train state- and local-level politicians on economic issues. After 1975, however, with the imposition of the Emergency in India, this particular vision of his could not be realized and the institute's main function subsequently has been to bring out a quarterly journal called the *Journal of the Indian Institute of Political Economy* that contains carefully selected works on Indian economics as well as important government documents. He remained editor of the journal till his death in 1995.

Dandekar was a prolific and versatile writer. He wrote on a range of issues from purely measurement related (for example, measurement of national income, anthropometric measurements of Maharashtra, poverty measurement) to purely policy oriented ones (like crop insurance schemes, irrigation in Maharashtra, and the relation between poverty and unemployment).[1]

He started his career with a deep interest in measurement issues: his earliest work was on measuring national income in countries with a large unorganized sector and in the late 1940s he led a large survey of

[1] A full list of his published works is provided in the *Journal of the Indian School of Political Economy*, October–December 1995, 7(4): 671–87.

households at the Gokhale Institute. In 1970 Dandekar became chairman of the autonomous statistical organization, the National Sample Survey Organisation (NSSO), which was responsible for carrying out national sample surveys on a regular basis. From this early base in statistics, he later moved to issues closer to economics.

It would be fair to say that his most widely known research is a monograph entitled 'Poverty in India' (1971), written in collaboration with N. Rath, his colleague at the Gokhale Institute. This piece of research, cited in almost all serious studies of poverty in India, addresses the question of the measurement of poverty by first deriving *poverty lines* for various states, based on the consumption expenditure needed to sustain a minimum caloric intake. Although the natural way to measure poverty lines would be based on income, data on income distribution were hard to come by at that time, so the measurement of poverty was based on expenditure instead. Using an average caloric minimum of 2,250 calories per capita per day, they computed that in rural areas an annual expenditure per household of Rs 170.80 at 1960–1 prices and in urban areas Rs 271.70 would define the respective poverty lines. This was one of the first studies to show that employment and poverty in India were closely linked. The authors then set out to measure the amount of employment that needed to be generated to get rid of poverty. In this study, Dandekar pushed for a rural works programme that would not only generate employment but also be less costly to administer than existing schemes based on household industry. Such a scheme was then launched in Maharashtra, his home state.

Dandekar's other writings on policy issues reflect his innate curiosity and dynamism. Although economics has become much more formal now, his ideas seem to resonate well with contemporary economics and the most recent literature on incentives: for example, his critique of the 'land to the tiller' legislation was based on studying the incentives of landowners before and after the Act and the implications for the optimal use of land. To improve the quality of education at university level, he advocated that fees should be paid by students according to the quality of education they received. Similarly, he advocated labour participation in the form of shareholdings to address the problem of sick textile mills.

Although he started off working as a volunteer for the RSS, a Hindu ideological organization, he did not continue after his university education. Indeed, he wrote a number of articles commenting on the problem of surplus cattle in India, a problem that arose because of the (Hindu) religious ban on cow slaughter. He argued strongly for the culling of unwanted animals, and provoked a huge controversy in the late 1960s. This was ultimately followed by a legal ban on cow slaughter, and hence was, unusually for him, not a very successful endeavour.

He was far from being a purely academic economist—he was deeply committed to the issues he wrote about and actively participated in making those ideas reach fruition through policy changes. His critique of powerful trade unions, his participation in demonstrations, his attack on a leading Hindu organization, and his criticism of the Emergency highlight this particular aspect of his personality.

From all accounts, Dandekar's was a powerful voice in the community of Indian economists, and often a controversial and provocative one. He believed in the importance of debate and was receptive to criticism just as he was very free in criticizing others. In short, he left a rich intellectual legacy for Maharashtra, and indeed for Indian economics.

AMRITA DHILLON

References

Dandekar, V.M. and N. Rath. 1971. 'Poverty in India', mimeo, Indian School of Political Economy, Lonavala.

Rath, N. 1995. 'V.M. Dandekar: Social Scientist with a Difference', *Journal of the Indian School of Political Economy*, October–December, 7(4).

Vaidyanathan, A. 1995. 'V.M. Dandekar', *Economic and Political Weekly*, 19 August, 30(33).

■ M.L. Dantwala

Mohanlal Lallubhai Dantwala was born on 18 September 1909 in Surat (Gujarat). He was a towering personality among the Indian academics of his times. He made the singular contributions to the field of economics in India, particularly agricultural economics, as teacher, researcher, institution builder, and policy advisor.

He had his early education in Dhulia (Maharashtra), and graduated from Wilson College in Bombay. He had a brilliant academic career. He was ranked first among the successful candidates who passed out in the history–economics group of Bombay University which had an extensive jurisdiction, stretching from Sindh to Karnataka. After his graduation, he opted for an active political career and participated in India's freedom struggle, shouldering high organizational responsibility in the Indian National Congress.

During this period, he came in contact with Mahatma Gandhi, and also with socialist stalwarts such as Jaiprakash

Narain, Acharya Narendra Dev, and Ashok Mehta. Gandhi, as well as his socialist friends, had a lasting influence on his thinking and conduct. From Gandhi he imbibed an acute sense of social responsibility and the importance of the purity of means. His association with the leading socialists of his time was reflected in his lifelong commitment to justice and equity. Professor Dantwala was noted for his courage of conviction. He practised what he preached.

After brief stints as a college teacher in Ahmedabad (Gujarat), he joined, at the behest of Professor C.N. Vakil, his academic mentor, the School of Economics and Sociology of Bombay University in 1946 as a lecturer in agricultural economics. He retired as Professor of Economics and Director of the Economics Department of the University in 1973. He taught, influenced, and guided a large number of students for a period stretching over nearly three decades, and set before them high standards of academic excellence and analytical rigour.

Apart from maintaining and enhancing standards of education and research in the Department of Economics, he, along with a few other dedicated leaders in the field, made salutary contributions to make the Indian Society of Agricultural Economics, a premier body of agricultural economists, highly respected within the country and abroad.

Professor Dantwala's research output is marked by his value orientation. His first major contribution as an economist was developing and chiselling Gandhi's idea of property ownership as a 'trust'. His elaboration of the concept of trusteeship was endorsed by Mahatma Gandhi. In the so-called mainstream economic thinking, he made significant contributions in a number of areas. Most of his research was marked by careful marshalling of facts and lucid explanation of complex processes.

Among the leading economists of his times, he was the first to think beyond agricultural growth and take a more comprehensive view of rural development. At a time when a large body of economists were lamenting the discrimination against agriculture, particularly in public investment and pricing policy, ascribing it to 'urban bias', Professor Dantwala disagreed with his colleagues and showed, with facts and figures, that it was the rural areas, rather than agriculture as a sector, that were discriminated against.

At the same time, he favoured faster growth of agriculture, which he thought was important for poverty alleviation. In this regard also, he took a more eclectic stand by laying emphasis not only on the role of economic policy but also on technology and organizational interventions. For example, he appreciated the underlying technological change embodied in the 'Green Revolution', and also supported state-sponsored poverty-alleviation programmes. In all such matters, he took a holistic and comprehensive view.

At the conceptual as well as empirical levels, he made a major contribution to pricing policy. His fundamental concern was 'low' food grain prices, and at the same time, compensating the farmers by increasing productivity levels. In other words, he was in favour of improving income terms of trade rather than relative prices of agricultural produce. For this reason, he laid greater emphasis on the non-price factors and recognized the role of public investment, technology, and organizational improvement. He was not the architect of the price policy hinging on 'minimum support prices for farmers, arrangements for procuring grains available at minimum support prices by public agencies, and distribution of grain through a public distribution system to the poor at below market prices', but, as the first Chairman of the Agricultural Prices Commission, he helped in effectively putting these ideas into practice.

Another area of his concern was rural credit. As a member of the boards of different banks, including the Reserve Bank of India, he was aware of the limitations as well as potential of credit in alleviating rural poverty, which was his major concern. He maintained that credit by itself is not going to make non-viable farming profitable, but without adequate and timely supply of credit, the wheels of development will be choked. He also viewed credit as a powerful instrument for structural change in agriculture, of course in conjunction with land reforms. He examined and approved the role of the Land Development Banks in financing tenants to acquire ownership rights under the 'land to the tiller' programme, which was an early variant of market-based land reforms.

Professor Dantwala made a seminal contribution to understanding the problem of unemployment, especially in rural areas. Rather than taking a generalized view of unemployment, he was in favour of understanding the anatomy of unemployment in a setting characterized by heterogeneity in the composition of rural labour facing different sets of constraints. He advocated a differentiated approach to employment generation in rural areas. Through his earlier writings, and later as Chairman of the Committee of Experts on Unemployment Estimates set up by the Government of India, he significantly influenced the thinking on this subject.

Much before decentralization became an accepted approach in planning and governance, he was advocating devolution of economic powers, including the function of planning, at block level and below. His concept of decentralization was an integrated one, with strong linkages between the different tiers of the structure, that is, village, block, and district. In his later years, he accorded greater importance to civil society institutions in mobilizing people and advocating their rights. He was particularly appreciative of the innovative practices and programmes advocated by some NGOs, and was easily accessible to them for help and advice.

It is true that in his anxiety to protect the poor and the disadvantaged, he sometimes advocated or supported measures which turned out to be counterproductive, for example, his support for zonal restrictions on movement of food grains. Also, on occasion, he advocated 'reforms' in organizations that steered them away from the purposes for which they were set up, a classic example being his plea for relaxing the obligation of the Regional Rural Banks towards their main clientele, the small and marginal farmers. But none of this detracts from the lasting and positive contributions that Professor Dantwala made at the conceptual and policy levels.

A Gandhian to the core and a socialist by conviction, he never lost his sense of realism in discussing the issues facing society and its various institutions. To his redoubtable scholarship he added his innate humanness. For a vast circle of his students, friends, and admirers, he was scholar extraordinaire.

V.S. Vyas

Amiya Dasgupta

In writing even the briefest of biographical sketches, such as this, it is hard to resist the biographer's temptation, of attempting to capture his subject's life in the quintessential phrase. In Amiya Dasgupta's (1903–92) case, the phrase 'child of the 19th-century Indian Renaissance' immediately comes to mind, and I hope his multitude of admirers and students will not take exception to it as encapsulation of a versatile and intellectually adventurous life, deeply committed both to the highest academic principles and to a liberal humanism. The fascinating details of that life, along with warm but insightful personal reminiscences are available in several eminently readable accounts (most notably Sen 1994), and here, as far as the biographical aspects are concerned, I confine myself strictly to the prominent milestones, devoting the major part of the article to a review of his important contributions.

Born in an eastern district of Bengal, Dasgupta was educated at the University of Dhaka and appointed to a lecturing position at the same University even before formally receiving his MA degree—a privilege reserved in those conservative days of British India only for the truly gifted. Dasgupta taught at Dhaka University for two decades (1926–46), and during a two years' residence (1934–6) at the London School of Economics, earned his PhD under the supervision of Lionel Robbins, the then presiding deity of marginalism. He subsequently held academic positions (often allied to onerous official responsibilities) at the Benares Hindu University (1948–58), the National Council of Applied Economic Research (1958–61), the Indian School of International Studies (1961–5), the A.N. Sinha Institute of Social Studies (1965–76), and Jawaharlal Nehru University (1976–81). After his formal retirement in 1981, the rest of his days were spent at Tagore's Shantiniketan—the logical choice of resting place for the true Bengali renaissance spirit.

At the risk of considerable oversimplification, Dasgupta's contributions[1] may be classified into four broad categories:

(i) Theoretical analyses in the areas of microeconomics, macroeconomics, international trade and finance
(ii) Problems of underdevelopment
(iii) Economic thought and political economy
(iv) Contemporary problems and policy issues

While Dasgupta is best remembered as a theorist, 'the alliance of rigour and humanity', which Sen (1994) has so astutely noted in his work, meant that he could not maintain a strict formal aloofness from the reality that confronted him in the contemporary Indian circumstances. As a matter of fact, he devoted a considerable amount of his research effort to analysing both the current issues of the moment, whether it be a Pay Commission award, or war inflation, or a rupee devaluation, as well as endemic issues such as inflation, economic planning, unemployment, and poverty. But what is important to note is that whereas his liberal outlook drew him to the study of these issues, his analysis of them was always based on the strictest principles of economic theory. Nowhere is this 'astute compassion' (to use Sen's phraseology again) more evident than in his *Economics of Austerity* (1975) which attempts to examine several precepts of Gandhian economics from a sympathetic but analytical viewpoint.

Dasgupta made several original contributions to economic theory. Two, in particular, are noteworthy. The first pertains to the so-called Marshall–Graham–Viner

[1]Oxford University Press, India, brought out the complete works of A.K. Dasgupta in three volumes in 2009.

controversy of the 1930s, relating to the dependence of a country's terms of trade on the elasticities of reciprocal demand. While Duncan and Robertson are usually credited with the solution of this controversy around 1938, as noted by Caves (1960), Dasgupta in his PhD thesis *The Conception of Surplus in Theoretical Economics* (approved for the PhD in 1936–7, though published in 1942) had also correctly and independently, resolved this controversy.[2] Dasgupta's second contribution is even more fundamental. In an important article Dasgupta (1954) had presented

> a truly pioneering analysis of the working of underdeveloped economies with surplus labour at about the same time as W.A. Lewis, but this fact has been hardly acknowledged outside India. Dasgupta's lecture on this subject ('Keynesian Economics and Underdeveloped Countries'), delivered in India in 1949, was published in India in 1954—the same year in which W.A. Lewis published in Britain, his well-known paper on 'economic development with unlimited supplies of labour'. (Sen 1994)

Dasgupta also offered several original interpretations, criticisms, and syntheses of classical political economy doctrines.[3] Chief among these would be:

(i) his reconciliation of the various (allegedly inconsistent definitions of *value* in Smith (Dasgupta, *Epochs of Economic Theory*, 1985);
(ii) his strong critique of the Ricardian theory of rent as well as Marshall's defence of the same (Dasgupta, *The Conception of Surplus in Theoretical Economics,* 1942);
(iii) his bringing out of the distinction between Dupuit's *relative utility* as an *objective entity*, and the *subjective nature* of Marshall's *consumer surplus* (Dasgupta, *The Conception of Surplus in Theoretical Economics,* 1942);
(iv) the distinction that he introduces between *frictional* and *dynamic* surplus and his critique of Knight's profit theory as reflecting the former rather than the latter view of surplus, the credit for a truly dynamic theory of profits (in Dasgupta's view) being due to Wicksell (Dasgupta, *The Conception of Surplus in Theoretical Economics,* 1942);
(v) his demonstration that, contrary to the popular view held by modern neoclassicists of Marx as *a minor post-Ricardian* (for example, Samuelson 1972), Marxian *value theory* differs fundamentally from the Ricardian, with the Marxian *rate of exploitation* acting as a *mark-up* in the *transformation problem* (Dasgupta, *Phases of Capitalism and Economic Theory (and Other Essays),* 1983).

Dasgupta's achievements were manifold. He made important contributions to economic theory and gave detailed critiques of classical, neoclassical, and Keynesian economics. His work greatly improved our understanding of the working of less-developed economies. He also deliberated a great deal on the applicability of economic theory, as developed in the West, to problems of less-developed countries. Being an ardent believer in the power of ideas to influence policy in the direction of social welfare, he was also often involved in offering advice to high-level policymaking bodies in India as well as various multilateral agencies. Above all, he was a great teacher and institution builder.

And yet an unhappy constellation of circumstances, including delayed publication schedules, lack of proximity to the centres of academic eminence, and the general indifference of our profession to ideas originating outside the select enclaves of Western scholarship, has denied Dasgupta his rightful place as a leading 20th-century economic theorist. It is to be fervently hoped that a greater familiarity with his work in the West will go some way towards redressing this historical injustice.

DILIP M. NACHANE

References

Caves, R.E. 1960. *Trade and Economic Structure: Models and Methods,* Harvard Economic Studies, Vol. 115, Cambridge, MA, Harvard University Press.

Dasgupta, A.K. 2009. *The Collected Works of A.K. Dasgupta* (3 Volumes), New Delhi, Oxford University Press.

Kemp, M.C. 1956. 'The Relation between Changes in International Demand and the Terms of Trade', *Econometrica,* 24: 41–6.

Samuelson, P.A. 1972. 'The Economics of Marx: An Ecumenical Reply', *Journal of Economic Literature,* 10: 51–7.

Sen, A.K. 1994. 'Amiya Kumar Dasgupta (1903–1992)', *The Economic Journal,* 104: 1147–55.

Data Sets

India stands out among its peers in the breadth and depth of data gathered and disseminated. The richness and credibility of these data is testified by the generations of researchers across the globe who have worked on Indian data. This achievement is rooted in the need, felt in the

[2]The controversy and its resolution are fully discussed in Kemp (1956).

[3]In view of space constraints, I mention only a few of these in brief. All these points, along with several others, are fully developed in my 'Introduction' to Volume I of A.K. Dasgupta's *Collected Works*, referred to in footnote 1.

earliest post-Independence years, for creating a strong statistical system for economic planning (Government of India 2001a). With the establishment of the Central Statistical Unit in 1949 and the Directorate of the National Sample Survey in 1950, India has seen regular, systematic collection of nationwide statistics, often through household and firm surveys. This activity has been remarkable in scale and scope.

In recent years, the availability of these data has improved tremendously. To give an example, any researcher can easily purchase detailed Census or National Sample Survey data, or download the latest agricultural statistics from official websites. In addition to these official data, there is easy access to several data sets which were collected or compiled by other public or private agencies.

Without claiming to be exhaustive, this entry gives a brief outline of these data, focusing on prominent household- and enterprise-level data sets, most of which are in the public domain. Major sources of statistics on wages, prices, production, agricultural conditions, finance, education, health, and nutrition are also discussed. Some of the databases covered here have been dealt with in detail in Chandrashekhar and Tilak (2001).

Household Data

National Sample Survey Organisation (NSSO)

The NSSO is the nodal agency for conducting surveys for the Government of India. The NSSO has conducted nationwide multi-subject integrated socio-economic sample surveys of rural and urban areas since 1950. The wide variety of subjects covered by the NSS can be classified under five broad categories: household surveys covering socio-economic aspects, including the regular employment–unemployment surveys and consumption expenditure surveys; surveys on landholding, livestock, and agriculture; establishment surveys; enterprise surveys; and village surveys (Government of India 2001b). Large, 'thick' sample consumption and employment–unemployment surveys are conducted on a quinquennial basis. Annual surveys involve smaller, 'thin' samples and are based on different sampling designs. Decennial surveys are collected on unorganized enterprises in the non-agricultural sector, landholdings, and livestock enterprises, and on population, births, deaths, disability, morbidity, fertility, maternity and child care, and family planning (Government of India 2001b). Unit-level data sets from 1983 onwards are in the public domain; the data are available after a gap of approximately one–two years. Published reports can be accessed at http://mospi.gov.in.

Consumption Surveys: Consumption surveys form the basis of official poverty estimates in India. Consumption surveys are conducted annually on a small sample basis; larger sample surveys are conducted every five years. The survey collects comprehensive data on a household's consumption of goods and services as well as its socio-economic characteristics. Households are asked to state the value and quantity of goods consumed, as well as the source of consumption. Prior to the 55th round conducted in 1999, these surveys measured consumption using a 30-day recall period for all items of consumption. Since the 55th round, changes in the recall period for low frequency items such as education, health, durables, clothing, and footwear have raised concerns about the comparability of consumption, poverty, and inequality measures over time (see Sen 2000; Sen and Himanshu 2004a, 2004b; Deaton and Drèze 2002; Deaton and Kozel 2005, for further details).

Employment–Unemployment Surveys: These five-yearly surveys canvass household-level data on the employment status and wage labour earnings of individual members, as well as various socio-economic characteristics. The NSSO also collects annual information on employment and unemployment within the annual small sample consumption expenditure surveys. In a number of earlier rounds, the NSSO experimented with concepts and methodologies before settling on their current approach, which has remained more or less unchanged since the 27th round (in 1972–3). Official employment statistics are based on the usual activity principal status approach. Since 1977–8, these surveys have also been the source for the Rural Labour Enquiry and Agricultural Labour Enquiry.

Population Census

The decennial population census of India contains a snapshot of the demographic and socio-economic profile of the population of India. The first census was conducted in 1872; the design, conduct, and scope of the census have altered substantially since its inception and, in particular, since the Census Act of 1948 delegated the responsibility for the systematic collection of population data to the Office of the Registrar General and Census Commissioner. The census collects information on economic activity and socio-economic characteristics and village-level amenities. For the earlier years, detailed tables containing population profiles at a disaggregated level have been published in a hard-copy format. Since 1991 detailed tables have been made available in both soft- as well as hard-copy format. The census has recently released unit-level data at the 5 per cent and 10 per cent sample. Further details can be found at http://www.censusindia.gov.in.

National Council of Applied Economic Research (NCAER)

Additional Rural Incomes Survey (ARIS)/Rural Economic Development Survey (REDS): The ARIS/REDS panel data set covers 259 villages in 17 states between 1969 and 1999. The ARIS data set was designed to constitute a nationally representative sample of Indian households in 1969. It covers 4,756 households for three crop years from 1968–9 and contains questions on economic, demographic, and village-level characteristics. The REDS data, collected in 1982 and 1999, contain more detailed measures of household-level consumption, investment, and income-generating activities, and also a detailed demographic module covering all adult women in the sample. Households in the REDS data can be linked up to those in the 1971 ARIS data to form a panel. The 1999 round of the data set is one of the first to capture all surviving as well as all split-off households. A further unique feature of the 1999 data is the inclusion of a module capturing data on all siblings and children of the household head, whether present in the village or not. The data are available online at http://adfdell.pstc.brown.edu/arisreds_data/.

India Human Development Survey: This household-level nationally representative survey contains a wide range of questions covering social and economic conditions; 41,554 households in 1,503 villages and 971 urban areas are covered; village, school, and medical infrastructure are captured in separate surveys. Household-level data are publicly available online at tp://www.ihds.umd.edu.

International Crop Research Institute in the Semi-Arid Tropics (ICRISAT)

Village Level Studies (VLS) is a high-frequency panel data set initiated in 1975 in six villages in Andhra Pradesh and Maharashtra. The survey was further expanded to include two villages—one in Gujarat (in 1980) and the other in Madhya Pradesh (in 1981). Information from 40 households was collected in each village using 12 questionnaires designed to cover the key aspects of income-generating and consumption activities of agricultural households (Walker and Ryan 1990). Data on transactions, income, and consumption was collected on a three–four weekly basis, whilst data on assets was collected on a yearly basis. Four of the six original ICRISAT villages were revisited in 1992; ICRISAT resumed annual data collection on the six original villages in 2002 and the three–four weekly data collection resumed in 2005, at which point all split-off households were captured. The data are available for download online at www.economics.ox.ac.uk/members/stefan.dercon/icrisat/ICRISAT/usingthedata.html.

National Family Health Survey (NFHS)

Since the first survey conducted in 1992–3, two more rounds of this nationally representative survey have been conducted in 1998–9 and 2005–6. The survey collects information on population, health, and nutrition, with an emphasis on women and young children. NFHS-3 additionally covered HIV/AIDS. State and national-level reports are available in soft- and hard-copy format. The unit-level data are publicly available for download through the Demographic and Health Survey website at www.measuredhs.com.

Living Standards Measurement Survey (LSMS)

The LSMS of household and village characteristics was conducted by the World Bank in 1997–8. A total of 2,250 households were interviewed in 120 villages drawn from a sample of 25 districts in Uttar Pradesh and Bihar (World Bank 1998). A follow-up survey conducted in 2008 covers a sub-sample of the original households in Uttar Pradesh. Household data includes information on economic activities, health, education, expenditures, and production. The data from the first wave are available for download online from the World Bank website at www.worldbank.org/lsms/

Firm Data

Economic Census

The Economic Census enumerates all establishments engaged in the production or distribution of goods and services other than for the sole purpose of self-consumption (Government of India 2005). The census is conducted by the Central Statistical Organisation (CSO), a department in the Ministry of Statistics and Programme Implementation, Government of India. It covers all establishments without hired workers ('Own Account Establishments', or household enterprises), as well as those with hired workers ('Directory and Non-Directory Establishments'), the only major exception being those engaged in crop production and plantation. Since the main purpose of the census is to establish a frame which can be used for more detailed surveys of enterprises, it has a short questionnaire that primarily collects information on enterprises ownership, type of activity, and number of hired and unpaid workers, all disaggregated by gender.

The CSO has conducted five Economic Censuses since 1977. Unit-level data from the Third, Fourth and Fifth Economic Censuses (conducted in 1990, 1998, and 2005, respectively) are publicly available (http://mospi.gov.in/ecdt.htm).

Annual Survey of Industries (ASI)

The ASI is a large plant-level survey conducted nationwide by the CSO. The ASI frame comprises all industrial units ('factories') employing more than 20 workers (or more than 10 workers if they use power) which, as required by the Factories Act, are registered with the Chief Inspector of Factories in each state. Thus, the ASI is representative of manufacturing units registered under the Factories Act, and does not cover the informal manufacturing sector.

The ASI frame is divided into a 'census sector' and a 'sample sector'. All factories employing more than 100 workers are covered in the census sector, and smaller factories are covered in the sample sector. Originally, nearly half of all units in the sample sector were covered every year. This sampling rate dropped to about one-third in 1987–8 and to one-fifth in 2004–5. The sample sector is stratified by state and industry, which ensures that the survey includes factories from more than 3,000 state-industry groups.

Unit-level ASI data sets for the years 1974 through 2000 are in the public domain and are available at http://mospi.nic.in/mospi_asi.htm. New ASI data are usually made available after a lag of two to three years.

Prowess

Prowess is a publicly available panel data set on public limited companies, compiled by the Centre for Monitoring Indian Economy (CMIE). The panel, which begins in 1989, has data on all the companies listed on the major stock exchanges of India, and on large and medium-sized unlisted companies, including central public-sector enterprises. Apart from annual financial data, Prowess has information on plant location, products, inputs, the history of capital changes, bonus and dividends, and stock prices. It also provides descriptive variables such as industry classification, year of incorporation, and group affiliation.

Surveys of Unorganized Manufacturing (NSSO)

A publicly available, unique source of information on informal manufacturing activity in a developing country, the Surveys of Unorganized Manufacturing collect nationally representative data on the 'unorganized manufacturing sector', or all units not registered under the Factories Act (available at http://mospi.nic.in/nsso_4aug2008/web/nsso.htm). By fully covering household enterprises and establishments hiring fewer than 10 workers, they serve to fill the gap in the ASI's coverage of manufacturing activity. Using the Economic Censuses as frames, the NSSO has conducted four such surveys, in 1989, 1994, 2000, and 2005. These surveys sampled enterprises from nearly every district in India by stratifying at the district level and collected data on the nature of activity, revenue, expenses, employment, compensation, fixed assets, and borrowing.

Surveys of Service-sector Enterprises (NSSO)

Apart from Surveys of Unorganized Manufacturing enterprises, the NSSO has periodically used the Economic Census frames to survey service-sector enterprises nationwide. There have been two NSSO 'Surveys of Unorganized Services', in 1979–80 and 2001–2. These surveys covered all household and non-household establishments in the services sector, except those in trade and finance. There have also been three surveys of small trading units, in 1985–6, 1990–1, and 1997. These 'Surveys of Non-Directory and Own Account Trade Establishments' covered all wholesale and retail enterprises employing fewer than six workers, including household enterprises. Unit-level data from all NSSO service-sector surveys conducted in the 1990s and later are available publicly at http://mospi.nic.in/nsso_4aug2008/web/nsso.htm.

World Bank Enterprise Survey

In recent years, the World Bank has conducted standardized 'Enterprise Surveys' in several developing countries, including one in India in 2005 (http://www.enterprisesurveys.org). This publicly available survey covers registered establishments in manufacturing and services. Compared to the ASI, it has a small sample size and limited geographical coverage. However, it collects unique firm-level information on many elements of the 'business climate', such as infrastructure and regulations.

Other Major Data Sources

Agriculture, Climate and the Environment

World Bank India Agricultural and Climate Data: This publicly available data set is a compilation of officially published Government of India statistics, and contains district-level data for the years 1957–8 through 1986–7 (available at http://ipl.econ.duke.edu/dthomas/dev_data/datafiles/india_agric_climate.htm). It covers 271 districts, as defined by 1961 boundaries, in 13 states (Haryana, Punjab, Uttar Pradesh, Gujarat, Rajasthan,

Bihar, Orissa, West Bengal, Andhra Pradesh, Tamil Nadu, Karnataka, Maharashtra, and Madhya Pradesh). It has information on area, production, and prices of 20 crops, including areas under high-yielding varieties of major crops. It also contains data on agricultural wages, and on the price and quantity of agricultural inputs, such as fertilizers, bullocks, and tractors. Soil characteristics and 30-year averages of rainfall and temperature are also included.

'Maryland Indian District Database': This is a similar compilation of district-level data from census and agricultural sources between 1961 and 1991 (available at http://www.bsos.umd.edu/socy/vanneman/districts/index.html).

Environment: Detailed data (starting in 1871) on rainfall, temperature, and other environmental variables by meteorological stations and subdivisions are available at the Indian Institute of Tropical Meteorology (http://www.tropmet.res.in). The Central Groundwater Board publishes estimates of groundwater resources at district level, categorizations of the depletion of groundwater resources at *taluk* level, as well as maps capturing the hydro-geological features of India (http://www.cgwb.gov.in). Further water-related statistics are published by the Central Water Commission (www.cwc.nic.in). The Ministry of Water Resources publishes data on groundwater contamination, river basins, water resources, water pollution, and water quality (http://www.wrmin.nic.in).

Cost of Cultivation Surveys: A continuation of the Farm Management Studies of the 1960s and 1970s, these surveys have been the responsibility of the Directorate of Economics and Statistics in the Ministry of Agriculture since 1971. They collect data by season on 28 crops in 19 states, covering almost 9,000 households (available at http://www.dacnet.nic.in/eands/Activities.htm).

Agricultural and Livestock Census: Since 1970–1, agricultural censuses have been conducted at five-year intervals. The census collects information relating to the number and area of operational holdings, livestock, and agricultural implements and machinery. Census reports are available at http://agcensus.nic.in.

Minor Irrigation Census: The Ministry of Water Resources has conducted three censuses of minor irrigation projects in 1986–7, 1993–4, and 2000–1. Published reports can be found online at http://wrmin.nic.in/.

Educational Statistics

All India School Education Survey (AISES): Conducted by the National Council for Educational Research and Training (NCERT), it covers the availability of schooling facilities in rural habitations, physical and educational facilities in schools, incentive schemes and beneficiaries, medium of instruction and languages taught, enrolment (including that of scheduled castes, scheduled tribes, girls, and educationally-backward minority communities), teachers and their qualifications, library, laboratory, ancillary staff, and subject-wise enrolment at the secondary stage of education. The data as well as published reports are publicly available. The last round for which the data are available is the 2002 (7th) round (http://7thsurvey.ncert.nic.in/index.htm).

District Information System for Education (DISE): Available since 1995, and managed by the National Institute of Educational Planning and Administration (NIEPA), this public data set provides information on schooling characteristics at district level (www.dise.in).

Annual Status of Education Report (ASER): The ASER Centre has been conducting surveys on the learning abilities of primary school children since 2005. State and national report cards are available online at http://www.asercentre.org.

Health and Nutrition (Other than NFHS)

District-level Household and Facility Survey (DLHS): The DLHS is conducted and disseminated by the Ministry of Health and Family Welfare, in collaboration with International Institute of Population Sciences. Previously known as Reproductive and Child Health (RCH) survey, it has information on immunization coverage, institutional delivery, and contraceptive prevalence. Detailed data are made available after the reports are released (http://www.rchiips.org/index.html).

Nutritional and Diet Assessment Surveys: These surveys have been conducted by the National Nutrition Monitoring Board since 1975. Although the detailed data are not in the public domain, the published reports are accessible at http://www.nnmbindia.org.

Price Data

Three consumer price indices and one wholesale price index are available for India.

Wholesale Price Index (WPI): Collected and disseminated by the Office of the Economic Adviser (Ministry of

Commerce and Industry), this is the main source of information on inflation in the Indian economy. The data are available on a weekly basis for various commodity groups, but there is no state- or sector-wise break-up (http://eaindustry.nic.in).

Consumer Price Index for Agricultural Labourers (CPIAL): This index (along with the consumer price index for rural labourers) is brought out by the Labour Bureau on a monthly basis. It is based on price data collected from various rural centres, and is the only price index for rural areas. Recent data can be accessed at www.labourbureau.nic.in.

Consumer Price Index for Industrial Workers (CPIIW): The CPIIW is the urban counterpart of the CPIAL. It is available on a monthly basis for various urban centres, and it is possible to generate state-level indices using centre weights. The CPIAL and CPIIW are also brought out as annual reports, though with a lag. Recent data can be accessed at www.labourbureau.nic.in.

Consumer Price Index for Urban Non-manual Employees (CPIUNME): This is relevant to urban non-manual employees, and can also be used to index the salaries of public-sector employees. It is available on a monthly basis, but stands discontinued since April 2008.

Wage Data Other than the NSS

Wage Rates in Rural India: This new series of wage data is published by the NSSO and Labour Bureau and has been collected since 1986–7, as part of the effort to amass information for the new series of consumer price indices beginning 1986–7. It has been published monthly in the *Indian Labour Journal* since April 1998. The data are presented for eleven agricultural and seven non-agricultural operations, by sex and age group. Annual reports are also available at www.labourbureau.nic.in.

Agricultural Wages in India: The oldest wage series available in India, it is collected and disseminated by the Ministry of Agriculture, and contains district-wise data on wages in various agricultural operations. It is published in a monthly publication of the ministry called *Agricultural Situation in India,* and after scrutiny and verification, in the annual *Agricultural Wages in India.*

CACP (Commission for Agricultural Cost and Prices): In reports on the cost of cultivation, the CACP provides data on wages by crops and agricultural season. Reports are available at www.dacnet.nic.in/cacp.

Other

World Bank India Poverty Data Set: It contains poverty and inequality indicators, along with wages, state domestic product, price indices, and other state characteristics. The series ends in 1993 but is being updated (http://go.worldbank.org/SWGZB45DN0).

National Habitation Survey: Conducted and disseminated by the Department of Water, this survey provides information on various village facilities such as schools and health centres, and on water quality in habitations.

Election Data: Detailed data by constituencies and contestants is available at the Election Commission of India for all the elections since Independence, including state assembly elections (www.eci.gov.in). The Centre for the Study of Developing Societies (CSDS) collects pre- and post-poll data for national- and state-level generation elections (http://www.csds.in/). The CSDS data is not yet in the public domain.

Reserve Bank of India (RBI): The RBI's Database on the Indian Economy (http://dbie.rbi.org.in/) contains macroeconomic time-series data on areas such as money and banking, public finance, consumption, savings, and investment. Also available at the RBI's website are recent issues of several RBI publications containing data on banking. For example, *Statistical Tables Relating to Banks of India* contain data on the number of offices, assets, liabilities, deposits, and advances of banks, disaggregated by state or by rural/urban location. *Branch Banking Statistics* have district-wise data on the number of branches of commercial banks.

Reena Badiani, Siddharth Sharma, and Himanshu

References

Chandrashekhar, C.P. and J.B.G. Tilak. 2001. *India's Socio-economic Database: Surveys of Selected Areas*, New Delhi, Tulika.

Deaton, Angus and Jean Drèze. 2002. 'Poverty and Inequality in India, A Re-examination', *Economic and Political Weekly*, 37(36): 3729–48.

Deaton, Angus and Valerie Kozel. 2005. *The Great Indian Poverty Debate*, New Delhi, MacMillan.

Government of India. 2001a. *Report of the National Statistical Commission.*

——. 2001b. *Concepts and Definitions Used in NSS*, Golden Jubilee Publication, Government of India, Ministry of Statistics and Programme Implementation, National Sample Survey Organisation.

Government of India. 2005. *Economic Census 2005: All India Report*, Government of India, Ministry of Statistics and Programme Implementation, Central Statistical Organisation.

Sen, Abhijit. 2000. 'Estimates of Consumer Expenditure and Its Distribution: Statistical Priorities after NSS 55th Round', *Economic and Political Weekly*, 16–22 December, 35(51): 4499–518.

Sen, Abhijit and Himanshu. 2004a. 'Poverty and Inequality in India-I', *Economic and Political Weekly*, 18 September, 39(38): 4247–63.

——. 2004b. 'Poverty and Inequality in India-II: Widening Disparities in the 1990s', *Economic and Political Weekly*, 2 September, 39(39): 436–75.

Walker, Thomas S. and James G. Ryan. 1990. *Village and Household Economies in India's Semi-arid Tropics*, Baltimore, John Hopkins University Press.

World Bank. 1998. 'Survey of Living Conditions, Uttar Pradesh and Bihar: Introduction to the Datasets'.

Defence Expenditure

India's long-standing tensions with its two largest neighbours—China and Pakistan—with whom it has fought three wars over the past five decades (with China in 1962 and with Pakistan in 1965 and 1971) have made defence spending a matter of priority for the government and the strategic establishment. Since the early 1990s, three related factors have driven spending on the defence forces. One, India's desire to project its military force in the Indian Ocean/Asia region has made the country allocate significant amounts for replacing and augmenting the defence infrastructure. Two, India's decision in 1998 to declare itself a nuclear weapon state has led to a large military acquisition and development programme. Three, the army has been used in a major way to fight separatism and terrorism in Kashmir, and paramilitary forces are being expanded to counter other domestic rebellions, both of which have consumed large human and financial resources.

How large is India's spending on defence? In 2010–11, India's defence spending as officially estimated was placed at Rs 1,55,748 crore (revised estimate) and was budgeted to rise by 8.2 per cent to Rs 1,68,573 crore in 2011–12. As a proportion of the gross domestic product (GDP), India's military expenditure was 2 per cent in 2010–11.

There have always been questions about (i) how much the official data reveal of the true outlay, and (ii) the appropriate measure of defence expenditure. Regarding the first, while India is far more transparent than most countries in presenting statistics on funding of defence, the official numbers on the defence spending–GDP ratio do not cover all military spending. They only include revenue and capital spending under certain budget heads of the Ministry of Defence. They do not include defence pensions—the standard international practice is to include this item in military expenditure—though government documents do provide this information. Second, a significant portion of defence-related expenditure is incurred by other ministries and departments. For instance, paramilitary spending (much of which is spent on patrolling India's external borders) is largely incurred by the Ministry of Home Affairs. Similarly, the outlays on nuclear research and space (which have fed into assembly of fissile material and development of the missile programmes, respectively) are never shown even in part as spending on defence. The decision following the India–US nuclear deal of 2005 to keep 8 of India's 22 nuclear reactors outside international civilian safeguards suggests that more than one-third of the Indian nuclear establishment's expenditure is likely to be oriented towards developing nuclear weapons.

Table 1 presents two different sets of estimates of India's defence expenditure between 1998–9 and 2010–11. The alternative and more inclusive estimate of India's defence outlays is 30–40 per cent higher than the official figure. The alternative estimate is only indicative, but the true level of India's defence spending is likely to be closer to the alternative than the official estimate.

The trend emerging from Table 1 is that India's military spending as a percentage of GDP jumped after the 1998 decision to go nuclear and the Kargil war of 1999, before settling down to around 2.2 per cent in the early and middle part of the first decade of the 21st century. It declined even further thereafter, though this fall also reflects the rapid growth of GDP from 2003–4 onwards.

Going by the official numbers on defence spending, the average annual growth in real terms (at 2004–5 prices) was 5.9 per cent for the period 1998–9/2010–11. This was even higher at 7.1 per cent during 2003–4/2010–11.

Estimates of official outlays on the armed forces over the past three to four decades show defence spending fluctuating between 2.5 and 3.5 per cent of GDP. It jumped after the 1962 war with China and the 1965 conflict with Pakistan, and crossed 3 per cent of GDP in 1971–2 and 1972–3 (during and immediately after the India–Pakistan war of 1971), and then gradually declined over the next decade, touching 2.6 per cent in 1983–4. It rose again on large-scale acquisition of hardware and peaked at 3.4 per cent in 1987–8. Expenditure thereafter slid—partly on account of conditions imposed by the multilateral finance institutions during India's fiscal crisis of the early 1990s—before moving up after the 1998 nuclear tests and the 1999 Kargil war.

Table 1 Defence Spending as a Proportion of GDP and Central Government Expenditure

(in per cent)

Year	As a percentage of GDP		As a percentage of central government expenditure	
	Official	Alternative	Official	Alternative
1998–9	2.3	3.0	14.7	19.4
1999–2000	2.4	3.3	16.1	21.9
2000–1	2.5	3.3	16.3	21.6
2001–2	2.4	3.2	15.7	20.7
2002–3	2.2	3.0	14.1	18.7
2003–4	2.1	2.8	14.3	18.9
2004–5	2.4	3.1	16.5	21.3
2005–6	2.2	2.9	16.4	21.3
2006–7	2.0	2.7	15.1	19.8
2007–8	1.9	2.5	13.3	17.5
2008–9	2.1	2.8	13.0	17.6
2009–10	2.1	2.9	13.7	18.6
2010–11	2.0	2.8	12.8	17.9

Source: Expenditure data from annual budget documents of Government of India, GDP data from the Central Statistical Organisation.
Notes: (i) 'Official' defence expenditure is total spending under budget heads on the army, air force, navy, defence ordinance factories, capital outlay, and research and development. 'Alternative' is official plus defence pensions, budget heads on select paramilitary forces (Ministry of Home Affairs), border roads (Ministry of Surface/Road Transport), 25 per cent of spending on nuclear energy (Department of Atomic Energy), and 25 per cent on space (Department of Space).
(ii) Columns 1 and 2 are based on GDP at current market prices (2004–05 series); GDP figures for 2009–10 are quick estimates and for 2010–11 revised estimates.
(iii) Figures (especially in columns 3 and 4) differ slightly from estimates presented in the entry 'Defence Expenditure' in *The Oxford Companion to Economics in India* (2006), since the numbers here are based on the revised estimates of budget allocations.

While these figures present broad trends in defence spending, it has often been pointed out that the defence expenditure–GDP ratio is of little relevance. Another and perhaps better indicator of the importance a government gives to defence is the defence central government expenditure (CGE) ratio. This would show how much of the resources of the central government are being consumed by spending on the armed forces. The figures (Table 1) for India are revealing. During the period 1998–9/2009–10, defence spending (alternative estimates) was around 19 per cent of CGE. This consistently constituted the second largest item of government spending, exceeded only by interest payments. In 2007–8, defence consumed more than the combined central and state government outlays on health (1.2 per cent of GDP), but it was marginally less than the total funding of education (2.6 per cent of GDP).

Where does India stand globally? The World Bank's compilations of SIPRI[1] data for military expenditure show that in 2009 the defence-CGE percentage for India (16.6) was a little lower than that of Pakistan (18), US (17.8), and Israel (17), but higher than China (16.1 in 2008), Russia (14), and France (5.1).[2] India spends much more than the average for all lower-middle income countries[3] (14.3) and the high-income countries (9.9). The world average (10) was much lower than for India.

Since the mid-1990s, when global debates began to widen the notion of 'national security' beyond the conventional perspective of defence, there have been tentative attempts in wider public discourse to ask if India is spending too much on arms and the armed forces. However, the dominant view remains that defence allocations cannot be fundamentally questioned, especially when India's border dispute with China has not been settled and relations with Pakistan remain uneasy. There are parliamentary debates on defence, media discussions on the choice of equipment, and periodic exposes about kickbacks in procurement. All these interventions have looked at the issue only on the margins; they have not questioned the basic premises of India's military outlays.

But no longer is India's military spending driven only by the state of its relations with its large neighbours. India's 'modernization' drive and its big power ambitions have led to the country becoming a major buyer of arms in the global market for the air force, army, and navy. According to SIPRI, in 2006–10 India was the world's biggest importer of arms ($11.1 billion at constant 1990 US$). This was as much as 9.1 per cent of the world's arms deliveries. Moreover, the volume of transfers of major conventional weapons in 2010 was as much as 259 per cent of the 2006 volume.[4]

India's comfortable balance-of-payments position since the mid-1990s has meant that these purchases have not strained its external finances. This is the opposite of the situation until the late 1980s when India depended

[1]SIPRI's (Stockholm International Peace Research Institute) definition of military expenditure is far more comprehensive than what the official figures would suggest, and is closer to the 'alternative' estimates. SIPRI includes all current and capital expenditure on armed forces (including peace-keeping forces); defence ministries and other government agencies engaged in defence projects; and paramilitary forces and military space activities.
[2]SIPRI's data on military expenditure–GDP ratio for 2009 presents a similar picture, with the figures for India (2.8) being lower than that for US (4.7), Israel (6.3), Russia (4.3), the same as Pakistan (2.8), and higher than that for China (2.2) and France (2.5).
[3]The World Bank places India in the 'lower-middle income' bracket.
[4]This data is part of the Arms Transfers Database of SIPRI, which is based on the volume of arms transfers (as measured by the Trend Indicator Values, expressed in US$ million) and not the financial value of the goods transferred.

on barter/rupee payments to make purchases from the former Soviet Union.

India's major presence in the global market is expected to continue in the second decade of the 21st century as it has announced large plans of acquiring arms from abroad for all the three wings of the defence forces. These include a $8–10 billion contract for purchase of more than 100 fighter aircraft, a $4 billion purchase of transport planes, a $2 billion contract for refitting of an aircraft carrier, a $4–5 billion order for purchase of submarines, and plans for importing combat helicopters, amphibious landing craft, and more.

India's global purchases have been supplemented by a substantial domestic defence production programme that includes developing and testing of short- to medium-range missiles. India has also pushed ahead with developing the medium, intermediate, and intercontinental range of Agni missiles. A new trend is joint programmes: India and Russia have developed the Brahmos missile and have also announced plans to work on a fifth generation fighter aircraft. The country's fairly large domestic arms industry and military research and development have not, however, generated any measurable positive externalities.

In line with its recent transition from one of the largest recipients of aid to an aid donor, India has been providing military aid to neighbouring countries in South Asia. While the estimates for such aid are not reflected in the budget documents of the Ministry of External Affairs, a substantial proportion of the total aid (mostly in the form of grants) to Afghanistan, Bhutan, Myanmar, Sri Lanka, and Nepal (Rs 2,363 crore in 2010–11) is likely to be for defence-related purposes.

India's decision, announced in 1998, to become a nuclear weapon state added a new dimension to the defence programme. A nuclear arsenal is much more than an assembly of nuclear bombs. India's nuclear doctrine of 'no first use' implies developing a second-strike capability that will have a triad of bomb delivery vehicles (aircraft, land and sea-based missiles, and nuclear powered submarines) as well as a sophisticated command, control, communications, and intelligence (C3I) system that can withstand attack and retaliate in the event of a nuclear war. Much of the purchases and development programmes since the late 1990s have to be seen in the context of India's ongoing assembly of a nuclear force. The indigenous missile programme, the acquisition of nuclear delivery capable aircraft and airborne warning and control systems, the development of a missile defence shield, and the launch of a nuclear powered submarine are all expensive components of a second-strike capability infrastructure. A second-strike nuclear force also demands a huge amount of resources. INS Arihant, India's indigenously developed nuclear-powered submarine, took 35 years to be developed and was finally launched in 2009. The cost of developing this submarine was never publicly announced but independent estimates place it at Rs 14,000 crore. India is to build three such submarines at a cost of Rs 3,000 crore each for the additional two vessels.

The government has not made any public assessment of the cost of going nuclear. Independent and conservative estimates place the *incremental* cost of developing a second-strike nuclear weapon capability at 0.5 per cent of GDP a year. Media reports of internal estimates prepared for the Twelfth Finance Commission (2005) confirmed the size of this additional burden of nuclearization.

The acquisition of nuclear weapons is unlikely to reduce spending on conventional arms. In the early years of global nuclear armament it was suggested that the total defence spending would increase more slowly because of the 'bigger bang per buck' that the weapons of destruction could deliver and the presumed strategic value of these arsenals in deterring external threats. Research into arms spending by the established nuclear powers shows no evidence of any such impact on military spending. Conventional arms expenditure has grown alongside nuclear outlays and has contributed to an expansion of the total. In India, neither the government nor the defence forces have discussed a reduction in aggregate expenditure. Spending on conventional arms has increased in real terms since 1998 and this trend is likely to continue.

TANYA SETHI AND C. RAMMANOHAR REDDY

References

Chari, P.R. 2000. *India's Defence Expenditure: Can It be Reduced?*, Colombo, Regional Centre for Strategic Studies Policy Studies 12.

Drèze, Jean and Amartya Sen. 2002. *India: Development and Participation*, New Delhi, Oxford University Press, chapter 8.

Ghosh, Amiya Kumar. 2006. *Defence Budgeting and Planning in India: The Way Forward*, Delhi, Knowledge World.

Navlakha, Gautam. 1999. 'Defence Spending: Cost of Fighting Imaginary Enemies', *Economic and Political Weekly*, 34(18): 1085–8.

Reddy, C. Rammanohar. 2002. 'Nuclear Weapons versus Schools for Children: An Estimate of the Cost of Nuclear Weaponisation', in M.V. Ramana and C. Rammanohar Reddy (eds), *Prisoners of the Nuclear Dream*, New Delhi, Orient Longman.

Singh, Jasjit. 2000. *Reducing Defence Expenditure: Issues and Challenges for South Asian Countries*, Colombo, Regional Centre for Strategic Studies Policy Studies 10.

Singh, Jaswant. 1999. *Defending India*, Bangalore, Macmillan.

■ Defence Strategy

India's posture against external aggression since 1947 can be divided into five broad phases: minimum conventional defence from 1947 to 1962, expanded conventional defence capabilities from 1963 to 1974, strategic deterrence from 1975 to 1998, 'compellence' from 1999 to 2004, and a return to strategic deterrence from 2004 onwards.

Strategy is the art of applying force for the purposes of national security. The challenges of national security are territorial integrity, freedom from interference in the domestic political realm, and balance of power. States must consider the use of force or threat of force to preserve national territory, to remain supreme within that territory, and to ensure a favourable balance of power.

National security can be protected by defence, deterrence, and compellence. *Defence* is the use of force to stop and then repel an invader. *Deterrence* is the threat of military retaliation to prevent an attack. *Compellence* is the threat of force to make an opponent do what it otherwise would not do or to undo something it has already done. While states must prepare in some measure for all three possibilities, at any given time they may well emphasize one posture over the other two.

Minimum Conventional Defence, 1947–62

From 1947 to 1962, India's strategy was one of minimum conventional defence focused on holding territory. Within weeks of Independence, India and Pakistan fought over the state of Jammu and Kashmir, a war that dragged on well into 1948. By the late 1950s, there was a good chance that India would also be involved in a confrontation over the contested border with China. Thus, within a decade, India faced a two-front military problem. Broadly, India's posture in this period was one of stopping attacks on its territory and repelling the invader. India did not expect to fight a long war, in part because it expected the international community to end the fighting and to help India.

Under Prime Minister Jawaharlal Nehru and Defence Minister Krishna Menon, India's strategic posture was one of minimal or defensive defence with conventional weaponry. India's non-aligned foreign policy meant that its military problem was confined to protection of territory (Kashmir and the northern and north-eastern borders with China). New Delhi had no alliance responsibilities. After World War II, and in spite of the division of assets at Partition, India had a robust military force consisting of Anglo-American equipment left over from colonial days and the World War. It also had one of the largest militaries in the world, second only to China in Asia. India inherited most of the imperial ordnance factories and training institutions. Not surprisingly, Nehru and Menon calculated that India was in a comfortable position militarily and that military expenditures could be kept low.

By the mid-1950s, India's complacency had eroded. Pakistan, with US help, had sophisticated tanks and aircraft that were superior to India's World War II equipment. China, after the end of the civil war in 1949, the fight against US forces in Korea, and inflows of Soviet equipment, was a formidable rival. With the border issue on the boil, India's fears of hostilities with China grew. When the Western powers were not terribly helpful in selling India arms, New Delhi turned to the Soviets for virtually all of its arms needs. Nehru and Menon also started augmenting India's indigenous arms production. Finally, Nehru, while opposed to India becoming an overt nuclear weapons power, encouraged Homi Bhabha to pursue research and development in the civilian applications of nuclear energy. Nehru famously declared that whereas he opposed India going nuclear there might come a time when India would take a different view.

Expanded Conventional Defence, 1963–74

The 1962 war with China, which India lost disastrously, shocked the Indian Prime Minister, led to the resignation of Defence Minister Menon, and galvanized public opinion into demanding a more ambitious military programme and posture. India asked the US and UK for military equipment. When Western aid failed to materialize, New Delhi deepened its links with the Soviets, a fundamental decision that was to hold good for the next 20 years.

The grim realities of national security were now upon India and had to be publicly acknowledged. Nehru, to his credit, did so rapidly. He eased Menon out and increased military spending immediately. In the aftermath of the 1962 war, military spending rose from 1.69 per cent of GDP in 1961–2 to 3.84 per cent of GDP in 1963–4.

India's military modernization was quickened by the 1965 war with Pakistan. Indian forces were stretched in the western sector, particularly in Punjab and Kashmir, and there were some anxious strategic moments for the country. India's forces, while much bigger than Pakistan's in aggregate, were divided between the western sector with West Pakistan, the eastern sector with East Pakistan, and the northern sector with China. In the west, India had rough parity with Pakistan, but it was inferior in terms of sophisticated weaponry, particularly tanks and aircraft.

This second military shock in three years once again galvanized India. Military spending in absolute terms continued to rise. Imports from the Soviets rose sharply, as the Western powers continued to deny India weaponry (they had placed an embargo on both India and Pakistan during the 1965 war). India's own arms production was expanded.

By April 1971, with the worsening political crisis in East Pakistan, it was more or less certain that India would be drawn into a third war with Pakistan. In December, hostilities finally broke out culminating in the creation of Bangladesh. Over 90,000 Pakistani troops were taken prisoners of war. In the western sector, India once again made only modest gains. Prime Minister Indira Gandhi claimed that India had no territorial ambitions in the west and had, therefore, agreed to a UN brokered ceasefire as soon as the eastern sector had fallen silent. The fact though was that in three weeks of fighting in the west the Indian military had been blunted by the Pakistanis.

The 1971 war was the first war in which all three of India's forces were significantly involved, with the navy finally coming to play a role, particularly in the western sector where Indian ships bombed Karachi harbour. The war was also crucial from the point of view of military attitudes. It showed that India could win an offensive war and that Indian forces were not restricted to a purely defensive posture. The next time Pakistan attacked, India could take the fight to its opponent and perhaps even destroy the Pakistani military machine if not the Pakistani state. Offensive defence could replace defensive defence.

With China, India had improved the force balance by qualitative improvements in weaponry, better high-altitude equipment and logistics, and a more robust and aggressive military leadership. By the mid-1970s, New Delhi was confident of not only repelling a Chinese attack but also of doing so with some ease. India's posture remained one of defensive defence, though clearly Indian forces were prepared to launch counter offensives using ground forces and air power.

The Bangladesh war suggested that there was another potential danger: the United States. US hostility to India's links with the Soviet Union and India's fear that the US was a fundamentally imperial power were compounded by American unwillingness to side with India over the Bangladesh war. Washington's dramatic diplomatic opening to China, with Islamabad's mediation, in the middle of the Bangladesh crisis, only made matters worse. The presence of an American aircraft carrier in the Bay of Bengal in the closing stages of the 1971 war deepened India's fear that the US might some day be an interventionary force against India.

Indian force planning and acquisitions grew in quantity and quality. After nearly 20 years of exclusive reliance on Soviet equipment, India turned to Britain and France for aircraft, importing both the Jaguar and Mirage fighters in the late 1970s–early 1980s. Finally, alienated from and in fear of Washington after 1971 and unwilling to be permanently tied to the Soviet Union, India speeded up its decision to test a nuclear device which it finally did in May 1974.

Strategic Deterrence, 1975–98

Ever since the Chinese nuclear tests of 1964, New Delhi had been under pressure to go nuclear. For a variety of reasons, including economic constraints and the paucity of nuclear fissile material, India had to wait a decade before it was in a position to test. Though the scientists were prepared to test again, the Indian political leadership refused to do so until May 1998.

While India did not test a nuclear device from 1974 to 1998, nuclear weapons research was carried forward in this period. New Delhi faced a dual nuclear threat. Relations with China were correct but cold until 1988 when Prime Minister Rajiv Gandhi made a path breaking visit to Beijing. The border issue remained unresolved even then, and military tensions along the line of actual control could not be ignored. With Pakistan showing no signs of relenting on issues such as Kashmir and with the advances in the Pakistani nuclear programme after 1972, India had a two-front nuclear problem on its hands. Defence of the border could escalate into a strategic standoff with either China or Pakistan in which no part of India would be safe from nuclear devastation. Defence had to be supplemented by strategic deterrence.

In order to give credibility to its strategic deterrent, India had to acquire strategic delivery capabilities: long-range strike aircraft and ballistic missiles. From the early 1980s onwards, therefore, it focused on inducting both types of delivery vehicles. As noted earlier, it purchased sophisticated aircraft from the Soviets (various MiGs), the French (the Mirages), and the British (the Jaguars). It also increased allocations to rocket and missile programmes. Out of this programme, over the next 20 years, came the *Agni* missiles with ranges of 1,000–2,500 km and various tactical and cruise missiles for both conventional and nuclear warheads. For the future, India has plans for an intercontinental ballistic missile, the *Surya,* with a range of 12,000 km.

Another key area of military investment, both in terms of financial outlays as well as research and development, was the navy. After the 1971war, the Indian Navy grew in confidence and argued that it had a role beyond coastal protection, the three-mile territorial waters limit, and the Exclusive Economic Zone. It added on to its missions the projection of force to more distant theatres. To do this it was necessary to develop a two-carrier force with requisite protective ships and strike aircraft.

In addition, the Navy argued that part of India's nuclear deterrent should be in submarine-launched ballistic missiles (SLBMs), which were supposedly less vulnerable to a first strike. A sea-based deterrent required a nuclear-powered submarine force with at least medium-range if not intercontinental capability. For three years, India leased a Russian *Charlie*-class submarine as part of its acculturation to the rigours of operating a submarine force with a strategic mission. India has been developing its own nuclear-powered submarine since 1985.

India's naval expansion and ambitions came in for criticism in Australia, Southeast Asia, and South Asia. However, by the middle of the 1990s, with the end of the Cold War, improved relations with the US, the growth of Chinese naval capabilities, and the increase in trade and investment in a reforming India, these concerns had largely dissipated.

Ironically, throughout the period from 1982 to 1998, even as its conventional and nuclear capabilities grew, India was faced with serious domestic disorders that threatened security from within. Since Independence, India had been fighting insurgents and separatists in the north-eastern states. By the early 1980s, the situation had worsened. Sikh militants were in full cry in the Punjab. In 1989, Kashmiri militants joined the revolt against the central government. Pakistan supported both militancies, more or less openly. The Sikh movement wound down in the mid-1990s, but the violence in Kashmir grew in intensity as Pakistan concentrated its attention on the Valley.

India's growing conventional military strength and nuclear weapons were irrelevant in terms of dealing with internal violence. As India and Pakistan developed their nuclear deterrents, India's ability to punish Pakistan with conventional weapons declined for fear that a conventional strike against Pakistani forces and territory could escalate to a nuclear confrontation. Military stability at the strategic level had produced greater instability at the sub-conventional level.

Compellence, 1999–2004

Not surprisingly, after the nuclear tests of 1998 India was faced with a series of military crises with Pakistan. In May 1999, India found that Pakistani forces had penetrated the Indian side of Kashmir in the Kargil sector. India responded by using its air power to dislodge Pakistani forces and threatened to cross the line of control if necessary with ground forces, thus indicating it was not going to be constrained by Pakistan's nuclear weapons. In the event, India eventually ousted Pakistani forces on the Kargil heights using conventional force on its own side of the line and by mobilizing international diplomacy. Indian casualties were high and would have been higher still if President Bill Clinton, fearing India would escalate militarily and the subcontinent could explode into nuclear war, had not intervened with the Nawaz Sharif government.

After 1999, the military question before India was how to fight a conventional war in a nuclear environment. What were the limits in terms of military objectives and means? What kinds of strategies and tactics were feasible when the threat of nuclear escalation hung over the battlefield? While Indian commanders insisted that they were prepared to fight in a nuclear environment, it was not clear, at the time, how this could be done.

Unfortunately, India once again had to face up to these questions. In December 2001, after a series of outrageous terrorist attacks on the Jammu and Kashmir Assembly and then Indian Parliament, and perhaps emboldened by the tough US response in Afghanistan after the events of 11 September 2001, Prime Minister Vajpayee ordered the mobilization of Indian troops along the entire boundary with Pakistan. India demanded that Pakistan end its support of terrorism and that it hand over various terrorists to New Delhi. Diplomats were withdrawn, and air and other traffic stopped. War seemed imminent as India engaged in what came to be called 'coercive diplomacy'.

In a reprise of 1999, the Western powers led by the US intervened. By October 2002, the confrontation had ended with an agreement on the withdrawal of forces on both sides. President Pervez Musharraf assured India and the world that terrorist groups would not be allowed to operate from Pakistani territory. The two countries resumed negotiations on Kashmir, security, and six other subjects.

Nevertheless, the Kashmir militancy continued. While the level of cross-border incursions by terrorists subsided, it did not end. India's conventional and nuclear superiority and its willingness to mobilize its forces for a war with Pakistan failed to dissuade militant groups. Clearly, also, Islamabad, although it placed some limits on the activities of militants, has not terminated its patronage of the various Kashmiri groups.

India's decision to adopt a strategy of compellence against Pakistan was at best a limited success. It caused Pakistan to renounce terror in public and to scale down its support to various groups, but it did not stop

Islamabad from using terrorists to destabilize Kashmir and to keep the dispute alive both with India and in international diplomatic forums. The Indian armed forces and security community insist that the events of 1999 and 2002 indicate that India has the ability and willingness to launch punitive military strikes against Pakistan. On the other hand, the fact that India failed to cross the border or line of control shows that New Delhi is in reality much more cautious than its rhetoric would suggest and that it relies on the threat of military escalation to galvanize the international community to intervene against Pakistan.

Strategic Deterrence, 2004 Onwards

The events of 2001–2 caused India to change its emphasis. Compellence against Pakistan gave way to concerns about deterrence against China. While the Indian army continued to work on a punitive strategy for Pakistan, Pakistan's internal political problems and the return of civilian rule in that country caused the Congress-led government to look to diplomacy to deal with Islamabad. Meanwhile, a series of differences and tensions with China dramatized the need to strengthen India's deterrent against its northern neighbour.

Relations with Pakistan were by no means trouble free after 2002 in spite of President Musharraf's promise to rein in terrorism. A series of terrorist strikes within India—in Maharashtra, Delhi, and Uttar Pradesh—culminated in the attack on Mumbai in November 2008. After 2001–2, the Indian Army's diagnosis of the failure of compellence was that the mobilization of force in 2001–2 had been too slow and had allowed Pakistan to counter with its own mobilization. The Army's response was 'Cold Start', an apparently compellent doctrine.

Cold Start envisages a multi-pronged attack on Pakistan, led by several fast-moving armoured battle groups, which would confound Pakistani defences by speed and dispersal. The idea behind Cold Start is to capture up to 50–60 km of Pakistani territory all along the front and to use this to compel Pakistan to come to a final settlement. The calculation is that the penetration along a shallow front will not be provocative enough for Pakistan to resort to nuclear strikes against India's forces but will be punitive enough to get Islamabad to come to the negotiating table.

In the event, however, the Manmohan Singh government did not resort to Cold Start in November 2008. This may have been because the government had not accepted the strategic logic advanced by the Army, doubts on whether or not the Army was truly ready to launch a punitive strike, or in deference to external pressures from the US and other Western powers.

Probably as a result of India's signing a nuclear deal with the United States in March 2006, China's stand towards India hardened. Increasing Chinese armed incursions into Indian territory, a row over Chinese visas to visiting Kashmiris, and growing Chinese assertions that Arunachal Pradesh in India's north-east was part of China led the Indian government to revisit its military preparations in the north-east. Two divisions of additional troops were sent to Arunachal, one squadron of Sukhoi aircraft was moved to Assam, and road work along the border was speeded up.

More important, and not driven by China alone, India increased its arms acquisitions. Buoyed by economic growth, India purchased or was in the market for a large number of weapon systems abroad, including an aircraft carrier, airborne early warning aircraft, light combat training aircraft, heavy lift aircraft, attack helicopters, submarines, destroyers and frigates, tanks, artillery, tactical missiles, and defensive systems. In 2006–10 it was the biggest importer of arms in the world. It is in the process of finalizing its purchase of the next generation of multi-combat role aircraft (MCRA) and has signed an agreement to co-develop a fifth generation fighter aircraft (FGFA) with Russia. In the nuclear and missile field, it has moved ahead to refine the deterrent. While the exact numbers are not known, India may have over 100 nuclear weapons and is continuing to produce weapons grade fissile material. It is testing the longer range *Agni* missiles which can reach the main Chinese cities. It is also making progress on a nuclear-powered and nuclear-armed submarine which will complete its triad of air, land, and sea launched nuclear missiles.

Conclusion

What will India favour in the years to come—defence, deterrence, or compellence? In all likelihood New Delhi will opt for a balanced approach in the years to come, but the accent appears to be on deterrence.

Defence of territory is of course basic. Pakistan and China are the traditional concerns here, and New Delhi will certainly maintain a capability to repel an attack. The chances of large conventional attacks are very slim though given international pressures on Pakistan (read the US), China's obsession with economic modernization, Beijing's military concerns in East Asia (especially Taiwan), and India's nuclear weapons.

Both Pakistan and China have nuclear weapons and, therefore, strategic deterrence is, in India's calculus, inescapable. India's strategic deterrent vis-à-vis Pakistan is more or less assured. It is China that continues to be a challenge. The Chinese nuclear programme runs to

400 strategic and non-strategic weapons. In response, India is adding to its stockpile of weapons grade fissile material (currently estimated as being enough for 100–20 Hiroshima-size weapons), investing in extended range aircraft and mid-air refueling, seeking to produce a ballistic missile capable of reaching Chinese targets, improving command and control, and looking to missile defence (with US cooperation).

Compellence against China being unthinkable (given its size and strength), this strategic posture is only a realistic possibility against Pakistan. Will India persist with the view that it is possible to fight a war under the shadow of nuclear weapons? It seems unlikely that the Indian leadership will repeat the 2002 mobilization effort. The Army's Cold Start doctrine is, therefore, questionable and may serve more as a deterrent than a true compellent threat.

Finally, it bears saying that India's internal violence, particularly the recrudescence of Maoism, continues to be a severe limit on any ambitious war plans and arms acquisitions beyond a point. With instability at home, New Delhi is likely to continue to prefer diplomatic over military instruments, even with Pakistan, to keep military spending to 2.5–3 per cent of GDP, and in any case to emphasize deterrence.

KANTI BAJPAI

References

Cohen, Stephen P. and Sunil Dasgupta. 2010. *Arming without Aiming: India's Military Modernization*, New Delhi, Viking.

Karnad, Bharat. 2009. *India's Nuclear Policy*, Westport, Connecticut, Praeger Security International and New Delhi, Pentagon Press.

Kavic, Lorne. 1967. *India's Quest for Security: Defence Policies, 1947–1965,* Berkeley, CA, University of California Press.

Perkovich, George. 1999. *India's Nuclear Bomb*, New Delhi, Oxford University Press.

Smith, Chris. 1994. *India's Ad Hoc Arsenal: Direction or Drift in Defence Policy?*, New Delhi, Oxford University Press and SIPRI.

Thomas, Raju G.G. 1986. *Indian Security Policy*, Princeton, Princeton University Press.

■ Democracy and Social Welfare

Questions

The relation between democracy and social welfare raises two rather different types of questions. There is, first, the immediately *practical* issue of the pursuit of social welfare: does democracy help that pursuit or hinder the enhancement of social welfare? The second issue is more *conceptual*, and in many ways more difficult. Given the well-known problems in arriving at any cogent and coherent notion of social welfare, we have to ask whether democracy might help to resolve these difficulties.

The last question is almost exactly what Kenneth Arrow asked in his famous book *Social Choice and Individual Values* (1951), as a response to the growing scepticism about not only the cogency but also the reach of what was then ongoing welfare economics, which was well reflected in Jan Graaff's superbly nihilistic assessment in his *Theoretical Welfare Economics* (1947). In fact, however, Arrow's discovery of the famous 'impossibility theorem'—to be discussed presently—added further gloom to pre-existing pessimism, as it seemed to take welfare economics out of an inhospitable frying pan into an annihilating fire. We have to ask whether that pessimism reflected a correct reading of the analytical work of Arrow and also how the relationship between democracy and social welfare now looks, after half a century of active work in social choice theory, to a great extent inspired by Arrow's pioneering move.

These questions are of considerable practical importance for the history of modern India, and, not surprisingly, they have attracted the attention of a great many Indian intellectuals—primarily economists but also others. Following India's independence from British rule in 1947, the newly independent country chose a resolutely democratic constitution. There was, at that time, no other poor country in the world with a democratic political system. The leaders of new India were also much occupied, indeed obsessed, with promoting economic and social development in the country and the idea of social welfare was constantly invoked in direct and indirect ways. It is interesting to ask: how do democracy and development relate empirically as well as conceptually, at the 60th anniversary of the birth of a democratic India?

Practical Connections

While the champions of democracy have been reticent to suggest that Indian democracy would itself promote development and enhancement of social welfare (they saw both as good but separate goals), the detractors of democracy were soon quite willing to diagnose what they saw as serious tensions. The advocates of a practical split—'do you want democracy or do you want development?'—often came from East Asian countries, and their voice grew in influence as several of these countries became immensely successful in promoting economic growth without pursuing democracy. The observation of a handful of such examples led rapidly to something of a general theory: democracies do quite badly in facilitating development, compared with what authoritarian regimes can achieve. Didn't South Korea, Singapore, Taiwan, and Hong Kong achieve astonishingly fast economic progress without fulfilling the basic requirements of democratic governance? And after the economic reforms in China in 1979, didn't authoritarian China fare a lot better in terms of economic growth than democratic India?

To deal with these issues, we have to pay particular attention both to the content of what can be called development and to the interpretation of democracy (in particular to the respective roles of voting and of public reasoning). The assessment of development cannot be divorced from the lives that people can lead and the real freedoms that they enjoy. Development can scarcely be seen merely in terms of enhancement of inanimate objects of convenience, such as a rise in the gross national product (GNP) (or in personal incomes), or industrialization—important as they may be as means to the real ends. Their value must depend on what they do to the lives and freedoms of the people involved, which must be central to the idea of development.

If development is seen in this way, then it becomes immediately clear that the relation between development and democracy has to be seen partly in terms of their constitutive connection, rather than only through their external linkages. Even though the question has often been asked as to whether political freedom is 'conducive to development', we must not miss the crucial recognition that political liberties and democratic rights are *among* the 'constituent components' of development. Their relevance for development does not have to be established indirectly through their contribution to the growth of GNP.

However, after acknowledging this central connection, we also have to subject democracy to consequential analysis, since there are *other* kinds of freedoms as well—other than political liberties and civil rights—to which attention must be paid. We must be concerned, for example, with economic poverty. We do, therefore, have reason to be interested in economic growth, seen even in the rather limited terms of growth of GNP or GDP (gross domestic product) per head, since raising real income can clear the way for the really important achievements. For example, the general connection between economic growth and poverty removal is fairly well established now, supplemented by distributional concerns.

The much articulated scepticism about the compatibility of democracy and rapid economic growth was based on some selected cross-country comparisons, focusing particularly on rapidly growing East Asia, on one side, and India, on the other, with its long history of modest growth of GNP, hovering around 3 per cent per annum. However, fuller cross-country comparisons, for what they are worth (and they cannot be worth less than basing a conclusion on a handful of selected inter-country contrasts), have not provided empirical support for the belief that democracy is inimical to economic growth.[1] And while India used to be cited as living proof that democratic countries are destined to grow much more slowly than authoritarian ones, now that India's economic growth has become much faster (this began in the 1980s but was firmly consolidated through the economic reforms of the 1990s), it becomes hard to use India as the quintessential example of the slowness of economic progress under democratic governance. India is no less democratic today than it was in the 1960s or 1970s. Indeed, the evidence is overwhelming that growth is helped by the supportiveness of the economic climate rather than by the ruthlessness of the political system.

All this challenges the 'development-versus-democracy school', but it would also seem to suggest that there was wisdom in the reticence of the advocates of democracy in India in not basing their case on the contribution of democracy to economic growth, but on the importance of democracy itself as a part of good living. As far as economic growth is concerned, this would call for good economic policies, not bad political fierceness. But what must also be noted here is that despite the dominance of befuddled economic policies in India for many decades, the democratic system itself allowed some of the necessary reforms that could make economic growth much faster.

Furthermore, we have to go beyond economic growth to understand the fuller demands of development and of the economic components of social welfare. Attention must be paid to the extensive evidence that democracy and political and civil rights tend to enhance freedoms of other kinds (such as economic security) through giving voice, at least in many circumstances, to the deprived and the vulnerable. The fact that no major famine has ever occurred in a functioning democratic country with regular elections, active opposition parties, basic freedom of speech, and a relatively free media (even when the country is very poor and in a seriously adverse food situation) merely illustrates the most elementary aspect of the protective power of political liberty. Though

[1]Recent publications by Adam Przeworski and Robert J. Barro easily come to mind.

Indian democracy has many imperfections, the political incentives generated by it have been adequate to eliminate major famines right from the time of Independence (the last famine was four years before that, in 1943), unlike in China which did have the largest famine in recorded history in 1959–62, the mortality from which is estimated to be around 30 million. The history of famines has had close links with colonialism (as in British India or Ireland), one-party states (as in the Soviet Union in the 1930s, or in China or Cambodia later on), and military dictatorships (as in Ethiopia or Somalia). The very recent famines, such as those in North Korea and Sudan, have also occurred in non-democratic authoritarian regimes.

It is worth mentioning in this context that doubts about the reach of this proposition have sometimes been raised by referring to the fact that there have been famines, or at least conditions approximating famines, in a few countries that have started having political elections of a democratic kind. Niger is sometimes cited as an example of this kind of contrary case. The point to recognize here, as *The New York Times* noted in an editorial in August 2005, is that the presumed connection with famine prevention applies specifically to *functioning* democracies; the adoption of a voting format is not itself adequate for the rationale of the process. The direct penalties of a famine are borne only by the suffering public and not by the ruling government. The rulers never starve. However, when a government is accountable to the public, and when there is free news reporting and uncensored public criticism, then the government too has good reasons to do its best to eradicate famines.

The protective power of democracy in providing security is, in fact, much more extensive than famine prevention alone. The poor in booming South Korea or Indonesia may not have given much thought to democracy when the economic fortunes of all seemed to go up and up together in the 1980s and early 1990s, but when the economic crises came (and divided they fell) in the late 1990s, democracy and political and civil rights were desperately missed by those whose economic means and lives were unusually battered. Democracy suddenly became a central issue in these countries, with South Korea taking a major lead, and it led to the consolidation of democracy elsewhere as well, including in Thailand.

India has certainly benefited from the protective role of democracy in giving the rulers excellent political incentive to act supportively when disasters threaten. However, the practice of democracy in India is still quite imperfect. Democracy gives an opportunity to the opposition to press for policy change even when the problem is chronic and has had a long history rather than acute and sudden, as in the case of famines. The weakness of Indian social policies on school education, basic healthcare, elementary nutrition, essential land reform, and gender equity reflects deficiencies of politically engaged public reasoning and social pressure, not just mistaken public policies.

Democratic freedoms can certainly be used to make it more embarrassing for the state and central governments to continue with these neglects. The process, however, is not automatic and requires activism on the part of politically engaged citizens. The connection between democracy and the pursuit of social welfare, while largely positive, cannot be entirely left to institutional virtuosity. It calls for active work of human agency in using the institutional opportunities for pursuing important ends.[2]

Conceptual Links

I turn now to the conceptual linkage between democracy and social welfare, going beyond the empirical connections. Arrow's impossibility theorem was formulated at exactly the time when newly independent India was adopting its democratic constitution. The theorem and related results have fascinated a great many Indian academics (in addition, of course, to academics elsewhere). Arrow (1951) thought it natural to give expression to the basic democratic thought that the assessment of social welfare must be based on individual preferences about alternative states of affairs, and the connection must respect what he took to be some elementary conditions linking the two, such as (1) if everyone prefers some state to another then the former must be higher in social welfare than the latter, (2) if everyone's ranking of two states remains the same, then so must be the social ranking of the two, (3) and no person alone can determine the social ranking irrespective of the preferences of others.[3]

Arrow himself did not draw any clearly anti-democratic conclusion from his analytical findings, but that became the common reading of his mathematical result. Perhaps the most weighty expression of that negative conclusion

[2]These lines of enquiry are pursued further at a conceptual level in Sen (1999) and in the context of India in Basu (2004).

[3]The examples of the conditions imposed by Arrow are made simpler in this statement based on later works, mainly Sen (1970) and Pattanaik (1971). This is an area where the Indian contribution to the global debate and scientific advance has been substantial with contributions from Rajat Deb, Bhaskar Dutta, Ashok Guha, Satish Jain, Tapas Majumdar, Manimay Sengupta, and S. Subramanian. Studies of other economic problems, particularly of development economics, by leading Indian theorists have also been richly informed by social choice perspectives, well illustrated by the works of Kaushik Basu, Ravi Kanbur, Mukul Majumdar, Tapan Mitra, Dilip Mookherjee, and Debraj Ray.

can be found in the writings of William Riker, a leading political analyst in the field of democracy, particularly in his forcefully argued book, *Liberalism against Populism* (1980). Riker argued that there are two rationales for democratic process—what he calls 'populist' and 'liberal'. The former linked democracy to the identification and pursuit of social goals (such as social welfare), and this, Riker argued, has been proved to be incoherent by social choice results, particularly Arrow's. The latter view of democracy (the 'liberal' one, that is), which Riker argued was immune to Arrow's impossibility result, does not seek to establish any general social goal like social welfare, but only demands certain basic processes of making acceptable social decisions, such as removing oppressive authorities. He was, therefore, in favour of delinking democracy and the goal of social welfare, and seeing democracy instead as merely demanding certain basic requirements of social choosability.

The question we have to ask, then, is this: are the impossibility results of social choice theory (Arrow's and related ones) best understood as showing the incoherence of an aggregated ordering (representing social welfare or something like that) based on democratic aggregation of individual preferences? The answer, I fear, is: no, not at all. The first point to note is that even when we drop the idea of social welfare or social good (and what Riker calls 'popular will'), we can get exactly similar impossibility results to Arrow's, merely with the idea that democratic choice should satisfy certain basic conditions of choosability (like Riker's), even without trying to derive a ranking of social welfare. Indeed, Arrow's conditions can be readily translated into such conditions of choosability for democratic governance (closely in line with Riker's 'liberal' requirements) and we would still get an impossibility. It turns out that the idea of a social goal, or that of an aggregate ranking of social welfare, is entirely redundant in getting over the impasse (see Sen 1993).

The second point to note here is that the main contribution of results like Arrow's is to demonstrate the possibility that general principles of social decisions that initially look plausible enough could turn out to be quite problematic since they may, in fact, conflict with the combined consequences *of* other general principles which also look plausible enough. We tend to think—if only implicitly—of principles in terms of their plausibility in a few particular cases which focus our attention on those ideas, but once the principles are formulated in very general terms—covering *inter alia* a great many cases other than those that motivated our interest in those principles—we can run into unforeseen difficulties. We then have to decide what has to give and why. Whether we think of social decisions in terms of some kind of a social ordering or a partial ranking (as in what Riker calls the 'populist' reading—a rather unfortunate term), or in the form of conditions of choosability (what he sees as the 'liberal' reading), we have to face problems of consistency between plausible—or apparently plausible—general principles.

But those conflicts can, of course, be precisely the subject matter of public reasoning. If it turns out, for example, that in order to safeguard the liberties of all, we have to cultivate tolerance of each other, then that is a public-reasoning justification of cultivating tolerance. Democracy is not only an arena of coming to terms with diverse—and possibly conflicting—demands on society and governance, it is also the arena in which such conflicts can be addressed not just through some mechanical procedure of voting, but through interactive societal discussion and public reasoning.

This has a historical connection too. When, in the history of India, visionary political leaders in the form of Emperor Ashoka in the 3rd century BC or Emperor Akbar in the late 16th century argued for public discussion to resolve differences, they certainly were not aware of any 'impossibility results' that would be formulated many centuries later. But they did understand that society cannot work harmoniously, nor can the goals of different members of society all be taken into account, except through interactive public discussion.

If interest in public discussion is strong in Arrow's own work (many of them outside social choice theory),[4] the 18th-century pioneers of mathematical politics, in particular Marquis de Condorcet, were strongly involved in wanting a society with active dialogues and public encounters. Indeed, Condorcet's insistence on the importance of women's education was linked, among other things, to his recognition of the need for women's voice in public affairs. That basic connection between public reasoning, on the one hand, and the demands of democracy, on the other, is central not just to the practical task of making democracy more effective (this was discussed in the last section), but also to the conceptual problem of basing an adequately articulated idea of social welfare on the demands of democratic governance.

The connection between democracy and social welfare—both conceptual and practical—is, thus, not a mechanical entity, but a constructive process that turns critically on the role of inclusive and unfettered public discussion and political action, which is, of course, central to the philosophy of

[4]References must also be made here to the powerful contributions of James Buchanan in emphasizing the role of public discussion and give and take for public choice.

democracy. This is, as should be obvious, an entirely general point, not specific to India at all, and yet, given its history, the connection is particularly significant for India. Its record of successes as well as failures, so far, has been closely linked with the force and effectiveness with which public reasoning has been used in India. There is something of importance here, I would argue, for India's future as well.

AMARTYA SEN

References

Arrow, K.J. 1951. *Social Choice and Individual Values*, New York, Wiley.

Basu, K. (ed.). 2004. *India's Emerging Economy: Performance and Prospects in the 1990s and Beyond*, Cambridge, MA, MIT Press; New Delhi, Oxford University Press.

Graaff, J. de v. 1947. *Theoretical Welfare Economics*, Cambridge, Cambridge University Press.

Pattanaik, P.K. 1971. *Voting and Collective Choice*, Cambridge, Cambridge University Press.

Riker, W.H. 1980. *Liberalism against Populism*, San Francisco, W. H. Freeman.

Sen, A. 1970. *Collective Choice and Social Welfare*, San Francisco, Holden-Day.

——. 1993. 'Internal Consistency of Choice', *Econometrica*, 61(3): 495–521.

——. 1999. *Development as Freedom*, New York, Alfred Knopf; New Delhi, Oxford University Press, 2000.

Demographic Dividend

Over the past four decades India has undergone rapid demographic changes. The onset and speed of demographic transition—a process of change whereby societies move from a situation of high mortality and fertility to one of low mortality and fertility—differs from region to region within India. While the level of fertility in southern Indian states has already reached below replacement, it is still high in many states in north India because, though declining, the decline is at a slower pace. There are two important consequences of demographic transition. The first is population explosion due to a rapid decline in mortality rates amidst the maintenance of a high birth rate. This sudden and sustained increase in population size during the initial phase of demographic transition directly impacts the economy. Another consequence of demographic transition is a shift in the age structure of the population, resulting in broader and long-term age structural transition—changes in cohort sizes as they move through different age groups. In the first phase of the demographic transition the number of children increases both in relative and absolute size due to high fertility levels and a rapid fall in mortality. After some time lag, fertility rate also starts to decline, which then contributes to a decline in the relative share of the young population. The cohort size of the children born during this phase would be smaller than that of children born during the phase of high fertility. As children born during different phases of demographic transition move from youth to adulthood, and to old age, the age structure of the population undergoes major changes reflecting the varying cohort sizes resulting from past changes in fertility and mortality. During this process, there will be a period of 'window of opportunity' where child dependency ratio (ratio of child population to working-age population) declines due to decline in fertility as well as increase in the working-age population as children born during the high fertility regime move into working ages. If this window of opportunity is properly exploited, there is greater potential for demographic dividend through increased savings and investment for economic growth.

The period of 'window of opportunity' can be exploited in three ways to give demographic dividends: (i) *By productive employment of the available labour force, which would raise total gross domestic product (GDP)*. It can also be shown algebraically[1] that output per capita would grow if the growth rate of workers exceeded the growth rate of total population even if the output per worker did not change (Bloom and Williamson 1997; Bhat 2001). (ii) *By directing accumulated wealth and savings into productive investments.* The window of opportunity may give higher incentives to save. Improved health, longevity, and smaller family size make savings easier and more attractive. Households tend to save less when there are more children since a substantial part of the family income is spent on raising them. When fertility declines, the demand on household resources for raising children reduces, allowing households to save more of their income. (iii) *If appropriate investments are made for*

[1] The accounting identity that links income per capita (Y/N) to labour productivity (income per worker) and the labour force is as follows:

$$\frac{Y}{N} = \frac{Y}{L} \times \frac{L}{N}$$

where Y is the income, N is the total population, and L is the total number of workers. By differentiating the above equation, the expression can be converted to growth rates as $g_y = g_z + (g_l - g_n)$ where g_y is the growth rate of per capita income, g_z is the growth rate of income per worker, g_l is the growth rate of labour force, and g_n is the growth rate of total population (for more details, see Bhat 2001).

the formation of large supply of human capital. Fertility decline has immediate and direct impact on the school-going population and provides an opportunity to invest more on their education and health, contributing to better-quality human capital in the future. Women with fewer children are more able and often more willing to participate in remunerative work, and are more likely to invest additional income in the health and education of their children.

This would be a one-time-only opportunity and its length would be determined by the speed of demographic transition. If appropriate interventions are not made during this period, it would have negative implications for the economy and society. Demographic dividend could explain as much as one-third of the per capita GDP growth rate of the East Asian economies during the period of their economic miracle.

'Window of Opportunity' for India

The age structural transition for India since 1950 has been shown graphically in Figure 1. The age structure of the population has been classified according to the life-cycle stages and their impact on the general economy. The broad life-cycle stages are young (age group 0–14), youth (15–24), young working age (25–49), mature working age (50–64), and elderly (65+). As the young population (0–14) is dependent on the adults for their consumption, they incur health and education expenditures in the economy. The youth population (15–24) also consumes health and education; however, the pattern of consumption is likely to be different from that of children (0–14) due to differences in needs and services. The prime working-age population (25–49) saves little. The population in the middle-age group (50–64) is likely to earn higher income because of work experience and also to have a higher saving rate than the population aged 25–49. The elderly would mostly depend on others for their consumption needs such as healthcare and social support. As fertility started declining in India since the 1970s, the share of the population under 15 years of age began to decline and this will continue until 2025–30. The decline is projected to be rapid after 2000. The child dependency ratio is concurrently declining since 1980 and this decline is likely to continue till 2030 due to the continuous decline in fertility and expansion of working-age population (in both absolute and relative terms). This is the greatest opportunity for India to improve the quality of its human capital and this will have greater impact on labour productivity and the economy when it enters into the labour force. Further, it provides the opportunity to raise the saving rate if appropriate policies are pursued to promote it.

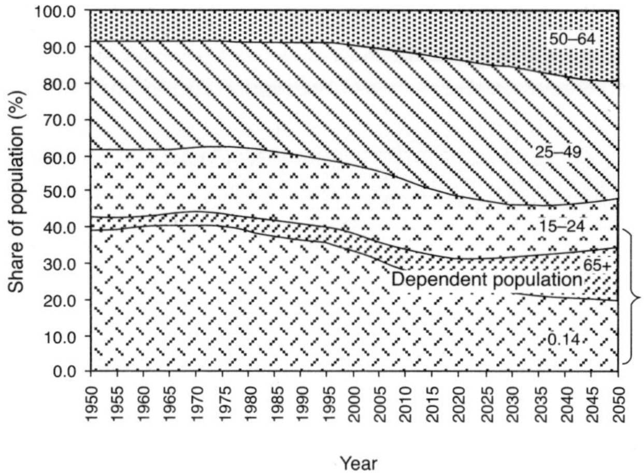

Figure 1 Age Structural Transition for India

Source: Derived from United Nations (1999) and Navaneetham (2004).

The share of the working-age population (15–64) has been increasing since 1980 and is expected to reach its peak by 2025. Generating new employment opportunities to meet the growing working-age population is a major challenge for India. If it is productively employed it will boost the economy. Among the working-age population, the share of the youth segment (15–24) will decrease from now on while that of the mature labour force will be increasing. This is also noted in the rapid decline in the ratio of youth (15–24) to working-age population (25–64) from 2010. This indicates that there will be less pressure on the economy to generate new employment opportunities and that can lead to a possible reduction in unemployment, which can be described as another window of opportunity for India. Further, this would increase the savings ratio as well as tax revenues, which may augment the capacity for investment and funding of social programmes. It is also likely that the increase in the share of middle working-age population (50–64) would contribute to higher saving rates as it tends to have a greater capacity to save due to higher income and reduced consumption. This opportunity would continue even after 2030 and this can be exploited for economic growth.

The size and share of the old-age population will continue to increase during the age structural transition. However, the increase would be greater after 2025. The old dependency ratio would also increase rapidly after 2025 (see Figure 2). Meeting the healthcare and social security needs of the elderly would be a major challenge for India particularly after 2025.

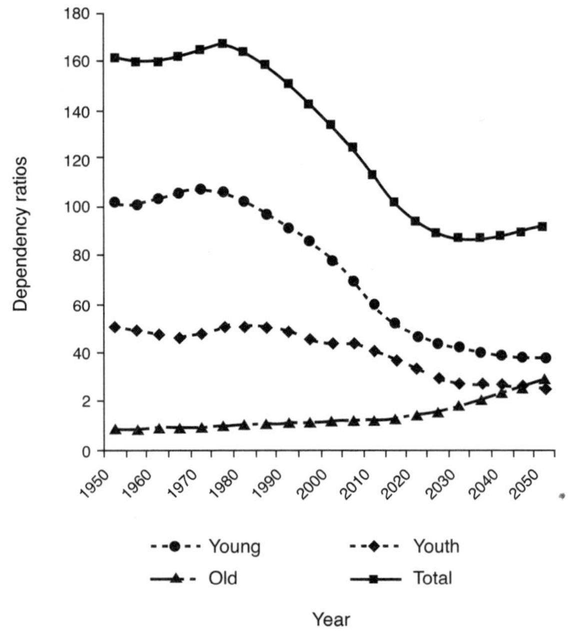

Figure 2 Trends in Dependancy Ratios for India, 1950–2050

Source: Estimated from UN Population Projection (United Nations, 1999, *Long Range Populaton Projection: Based on the 1998 Revision*, New York, United Nations).

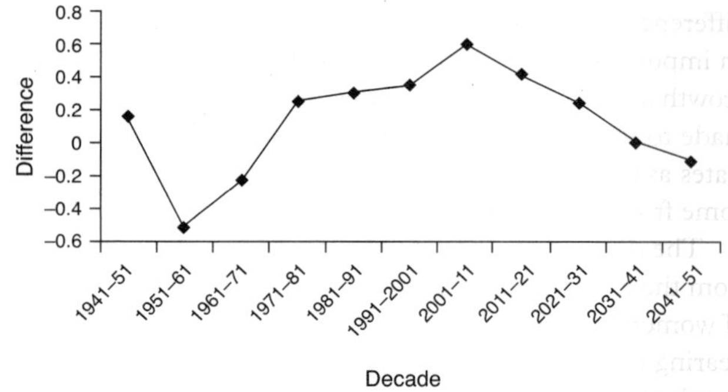

Figure 3 Difference between Growth Rate of Working-age Population and Total Population in India, 1941–2051

Source: P.N.M. Bhat (2001).

Table 1 Difference in the Growth Rate of Population Aged 15–64 and the Growth Rate of Total Population, 1991–2031

State	Decade			
	1991–2001	2001–11	2011–21	2021–31
South				
Kerala	0.50	0.15	–0.20	–0.49
Tamil Nadu	0.77	0.32	–0.14	–0.21
Andhra Pradesh	1.02	0.91	0.11	–0.0
Karnataka	0.67	0.84	0.05	–0.22
West				
Maharashtra	0.69	1.01	0.08	–0.13
Gujarat	0.54	0.80	0.06	–0.26
East				
Orissa	0.40	0.76	0.14	–0.21
West Bengal	0.71	0.88	-0.05	–0.16
Assam	0.70	0.76	0.41	–0.22
North				
Himachal Pradesh	0.58	0.78	0.05	–0.13
Punjab	0.63	0.87	–0.13	–0.21
Haryana	0.47	1.06	0.42	–0.22
Rajasthan	0.38	0.71	0.68	0.14
Madhya Pradesh	0.31	0.79	0.62	0.01
Uttar Pradesh	0.09	0.58	0.58	0.56
Bihar	0.19	0.64	0.64	0.22
All-India	0.35	0.56	0.43	0.07

Source: P.N.M. Bhat (2001).

Estimated Demographic Bonus for India

From the identity equation mentioned in footnote 1, the extent of demographic bonus can be derived from the difference in the growth rate of working-age population and total population. Bhat (2001) estimated that the demographic bonus was negative during the decades 1951–71, as the growth rate of total population was higher than that of working-age population (see Figure 3). After 1971, the growth rate of working-age population was higher than that of total population, resulting in a positive demographic bonus. He also showed that the demographic bonus would be highest during the decade 2001–11—a contribution of 0.6 per cent GDP growth rate in the total per capita GDP growth rate. It is also clear from Figure 3 that the demographic bonus is likely to continue till 2031 and would be negative thereafter. It is also important to note that the extent and the process of age structural transition would be different in different states as the nature of demographic transition is different due to their socio-economic and cultural differences (Table 1). The bonus would be positive till 2011 among the demographically advanced states such as Kerala, Tamil Nadu, and Punjab, and would be negative thereafter. It is interesting to observe that the BIMARU states where the process of demographic transition began later than in other states started getting greater dividend from 2001 and would be likely to continue to do so till 2031. As there are regional differences in age structural transition, internal migration could be of critical importance in the future as young workers move from underdeveloped to developed regions. The regional differences in age structural transition may also play an important role in terms of convergence in economic growth among the states in India, provided efforts are made to invest in human capital among the BIMARU states as a large share of labour supply in the future would come from them.

The demographic dividend is also likely to accrue from the expected increase in labour-force participation of women due to the shortening of the duration of child-bearing years. The total bonus derived from the labour supply during the period 2001–51 is estimated to be 1 per cent, out of which labour supply effect would be 0.2 per cent and the effect of the expected increase in labour-force participation of women would be 0.8 per cent, keeping labour productivity constant (Bhat 2001). The savings ratio would increase from 23 per cent in 2001 to 32 per cent in 2031 due to the expected decline in dependency burden, which would contribute to an increase in economic growth rate. It was estimated that the demographic transition would contribute 40 per cent of the per capita GDP growth rate during the period 2001–51. About 13 per cent of this increase would be due to the increase in labour supply, assuming output per worker remained constant, and the remaining 27 per cent would be due to an increase in the savings ratios, assuming per capita consumption did not change.

India's Response to 'Window of Opportunity'

The age structural transition does not give full dividend automatically and to get economic benefits, it is important to have a favourable economic setting and policy environment. The experience of India so far shows that the 'window of opportunity' has not been exploited though it has become available since the 1980s (Mitra and Nagarajan 2005; Chandrasekhar et al. 2006). It has been argued that the employment growth rate was low during the 1990s, particularly in the rural areas, and consequently the unemployment rate was high (Chandrasekhar et al. 2006). This was the period during which the growth of the youth population was also greater. As new employment opportunities did not grow at the same pace as the numbers of youth, the unemployment rate among the youth increased. But it is encouraging to see that the employment growth rate has increased significantly in both rural and urban areas. It is also likely that the increase in the share of middle working-age population (50–64) would contribute to higher saving rates as it tends to have greater capacity to save due to higher income and reduced consumption. This is likely to continue into the future when the relative share of youth population is expected to decline.

The East Asian success in economic growth was driven by the availability of high-quality human capital at the time when the demographic window of opportunity was emerging, thanks to the concurrently occurring demographic transition (Mason 2003; Navaneetham 2004). The East Asian countries' experience of demographic dividend underscores the importance of the quality of the labour force to maximize the benefits from the demographic transition. But the trend in India is not encouraging on this front. Chandrasekhar et al. (2006) showed that spread of education has been slow in India—the percentage of those with high school and higher educational qualifications has been very low in rural areas and only slightly better in urban areas. The educated unemployment trend among females was also not encouraging during the period 2000–5.

Though healthier populations are more productive and have greater incentives to invest in human capital and save more for their old age, in India, increased longevity may not be accompanied by increased savings due to increase in disease burden across all age groups and the consequent rise in healthcare expenditures (Chandrasekhar et al. 2006). India will also face challenges in the areas of child and reproductive health as the numbers of women in the reproductive age group is projected to increase in the next two decades.

Age structural transition creates different opportunities and challenges across age groups. The relative share of childhood population will decline in the future. This provides an opportunity to improve the human capital through public policy measures with respect to nutrition, education, and healthcare. The relatively rapid growth of the labour force would benefit India, if employment opportunities increased with sufficient speed to match the growth in labour supply, maintained growth in labour productivity, improved public health, and invested in infrastructure. The size and share of the elderly population would increase rapidly after 2031 and this will pose several policy and programme challenges. To meet these challenges effectively there will be need for concerted efforts to devise appropriate public and social policies directed at the provision of social security and healthcare and encouraging the development of social networks. In order to meet the challenges in the future and to prepare for them, it is important for India to exploit the window of opportunity available for a short period, a one-time gift from the demographic transition, with appropriate economic and social policies.

K. Navaneetham

References

Acharya, S. 2004. 'India's Growth Prospects Revisited', *Economic and Political Weekly*, 9 October, 39(41): 4537–42.

Bhat, P.N.M. 2001. 'A Demographic Bonus for India? On the First Consequence of Population Ageing', A Keynote Address Presented on the Occasion of the 10th Anniversary Celebration of the Population Research Centre, University of Groningen, The Netherlands, 22 November.

Bloom, D. and J.G. Williamson. 1997. 'Demographic Transition and Economic Miracles in Emerging Asia', Working Paper 6268, Cambridge, M.A., National Bureau of Economic Research.

Chandrasekhar, C.P., Jayati Ghosh, and Anamitra Roy Choudhury. 2006. 'The Demographic Dividend and Young India's Economic Future', *Economic and Political Weekly*, 9 December, 41(49): 5055–64.

Mason, A. 2003. 'Population Change and Economic Development: What We Have Learned from the East Asia Experience', *Applied Population and Policy*, 1(1): 3–14.

Mitra, S. and R. Nagarajan. 2005. 'Making Use of the Window of Demographic Opportunity: An Economic Perspective', *Economic and Political Weekly*, 10 December, 40(50): 5327–32.

Navaneetham, K. 2004. 'Age Structural Transition and Economic Growth: Evidence from South and Southeast Asia', *Asian Profile*, 32(3).

■ Derivatives

Rise of Derivatives

The global economic order that emerged after the Second World War was a system where many less-developed countries administered prices and centrally allocated resources. Even the developed economies operated under the Bretton Woods system of fixed exchange rates.

The system of fixed prices came under stress from the 1970s onwards. High inflation and unemployment rates made interest rates more volatile. The Bretton Woods system was dismantled in 1971, freeing exchange rates. Less-developed countries like India began opening up their economies and allowing prices to vary with market conditions.

Price fluctuations make it hard for businesses to estimate their future production costs and revenues.[1] Derivative securities provide them a valuable set of tools for managing this risk. This entry describes the evolution of Indian derivatives markets, the popular derivatives instruments, and the main users of derivatives in India. I conclude by assessing the outlook for Indian derivatives markets in the near and medium term.

Definition and Uses of Derivatives

A derivative security is a financial contract whose value is derived from the value of something else, such as a stock price, a commodity price, an exchange rate, an interest rate, or even an index of prices. In the Appendix, I describe some simple types of derivatives: forwards, futures, options, and swaps.

Derivatives may be traded for a variety of reasons. A derivative enables a trader to hedge some pre-existing risk by taking positions in derivatives markets that offset potential losses in the underlying or spot market. In India, most derivatives users describe themselves as hedgers (FitchRatings 2004) and Indian laws generally require that derivatives be used for hedging purposes only. Another motive for derivatives trading is speculation (that is, taking positions to profit from anticipated price movements). In practice, it may be difficult to distinguish whether a particular trade was for hedging or speculation, and active markets require the participation of both hedgers and speculators.[2]

A third type of trader, called arbitrageurs, profit from discrepancies in the relationship of spot and derivatives prices, and thereby help to keep markets efficient. Jogani and Fernandes (2003) describe India's long history in arbitrage trading, with line operators and traders arbitraging prices between exchanges located in different cities, and between two exchanges in the same city. Their study of Indian equity derivatives markets in 2002 indicates that markets were inefficient at that time. They argue that lack of knowledge, market frictions, and regulatory impediments have led to low levels of capital employed in arbitrage trading in India. However, more recent evidence suggests that the efficiency of Indian equity derivatives markets may have improved (ISMR 2004).

Exchange-traded and Over-the-Counter Derivatives Instruments

OTC (over-the-counter) contracts, such as forwards and swaps, are bilaterally negotiated between two parties.

[1] Price volatility may reflect changes in the underlying demand and supply conditions and thereby provide useful information about the market. Thus economists do not view volatility as necessarily harmful.

[2] Speculators face the risk of losing money from their derivatives trades, as they do with other securities. There have been some well-publicized cases of large losses from derivatives trading. In some instances, these losses stemmed from fraudulent behaviour that went undetected partly because companies did not have adequate risk management systems in place. In other cases, users failed to understand why and how they were taking positions in the derivatives.

The terms of an OTC contract are flexible, and are often customized to fit the specific requirements of the user. OTC contracts have substantial credit risk, which is the risk that the counterparty that owes money defaults on the payment. In India, OTC derivatives are generally prohibited with some exceptions: those that are specifically allowed by the Reserve Bank of India (RBI) or, in the case of commodities (which are regulated by the Forward Markets Commission), those that trade informally in *hawala* or forwards markets.

An exchange-traded contract, such as a futures contract, has a standardized format that specifies the underlying asset to be delivered, the size of the contract, and the logistics of delivery. They trade on organized exchanges with prices determined by the interaction of many buyers and sellers. In India, two exchanges offer derivatives trading: the Bombay Stock Exchange (BSE) and the National Stock Exchange (NSE). However, the NSE now accounts for virtually all exchange-traded derivatives in India, at more than 99 per cent of volume in 2003–4. Contract performance is guaranteed by a clearing house, which is a wholly owned subsidiary of the NSE.[3] Margin requirements and daily marking-to-market of futures positions substantially reduce the credit risk of exchange-traded contracts, relative to OTC contracts.[4]

Development of Derivatives Markets in India

Derivatives markets have been in existence in India in some form or other for a long time. In the area of commodities, the Bombay Cotton Trade Association started futures trading in 1875 and by the early 1900s India had one of the world's largest futures industry. In 1952 the government banned cash settlement and options trading and derivatives trading shifted to informal forwards markets. In recent years, government policy has changed, allowing for an increased role for market-based pricing and less suspicion of derivatives trading. The ban on futures trading of many commodities was lifted, starting in the early 2000s, and national electronic commodity exchanges were created.

In the equity markets, a system of trading called *badla* involving some elements of forwards trading had been in existence for decades.[5] However, the system led to a number of undesirable practices and it was prohibited off and on till the Securities and Exchange Board of India (SEBI) banned it for good in 2001. A series of reforms of the stock market between 1993 and 1996 paved the way for the development of exchange-traded equity derivatives markets in India. In 1993, the government created the NSE in collaboration with state-owned financial institutions.

The NSE improved the efficiency and transparency of the stock markets by offering a fully automated screen-based trading system and real-time price dissemination. In 1995, a prohibition on trading options was lifted. In 1996, the NSE sent a proposal to SEBI for listing exchange-traded derivatives. The report of the L.C. Gupta Committee, set up by SEBI, recommended a phased introduction of derivatives products, and bi-level regulation (that is self-regulation by exchanges with SEBI providing a supervisory and advisory role). Another report, by the J.R. Varma Committee in 1998, worked out various operational details such as the margining systems. In 1999, the Securities Contracts (Regulation) Act of 1956, or SC(R)A, was amended so that derivatives could be declared 'securities'. This allowed the regulatory framework for trading securities to be extended to derivatives. The Act considers derivatives to be legal and valid, but only if they are traded on exchanges. Finally, a 30-year ban on forward trading was also lifted in 1999.

The economic liberalization of the early 1990s facilitated the introduction of derivatives based on interest rates and foreign exchange. A system of market-determined exchange rates was adopted by India in March 1993. In August 1994, the rupee was made fully

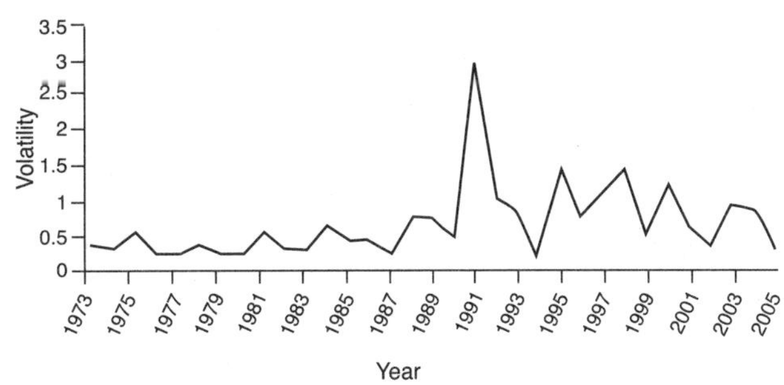

Figure 1 Volatility of Exchange Rate between Indian Rupee and US Dollar

Source: Author's calculations, based on daily exchange-rate data.

[3]A clearing house guarantees performance of a contract by becoming buyer to every seller and seller to every buyer.

[4]Customers post margin (security) deposits with brokers to ensure that they can cover a specified loss on the position. A futures position is marked-to-market by realizing any trading losses in cash on the day they occur.

[5]'Badla' allowed investors to trade single stocks on margin and to carry forward positions to the next settlement cycle. Earlier, it was possible to carry forward a position indefinitely but later the maximum carry forward period was 90 days. Unlike a futures or options, however, in a badla trade there is no fixed expiration date, and contract terms and margin requirements are not standardized.

convertible on current account. These reforms allowed increased integration between domestic and international markets, and created a need to manage currency risk. Figure 1 shows how the volatility of the exchange rate between the Indian rupee and the US dollar has increased since 1991.[6] The easing of various restrictions on the free movement of interest rates resulted in the need to manage interest rate risk.

Derivatives Instruments Traded in India

In the exchange-traded market, the biggest success story has been derivatives on equity products. Index futures were introduced in June 2000, followed by index options in June 2001, and options and futures on individual securities in July 2001 and November 2001, respectively. As of 2005, the NSE traded futures and options on 118 individual stocks and three stock indices. All these derivative contracts are settled by cash payment and do not involve physical delivery of the underlying product (which may be costly).[7]

Derivatives on stock indexes and individual stocks have grown rapidly since inception. In particular, single stock futures have become hugely popular, accounting for about half of the NSE's traded value in October 2005. In fact, the NSE has the highest volume (that is, number of contracts traded) in the single stock futures globally, enabling it to rank 16th among world exchanges in the first half of 2005. Single stock options are less popular than futures. Index futures are increasingly popular, and accounted for close to 40 per cent of traded value in October 2005. Figure 2 illustrates the growth in volume of futures and options on the Nifty index, and shows that index futures have grown more strongly than index options.[8]

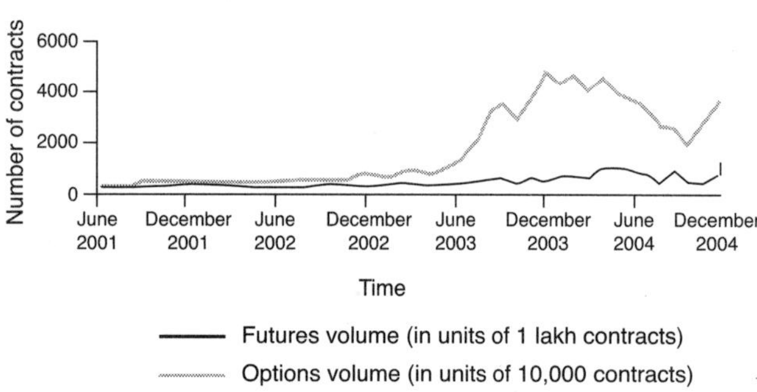

Figure 2 Volume of Futures and Options on Nifty Index

Source: Author's calculations, based on NSE data.

[6]Volatility is measured as the yearly standard deviation of the daily exchange rate series.
[7]Settlement represents the exchange of a security and its payment.
[8]Nifty is an index of 50 stocks comprising 60 per cent of the NSE's total market capitalization as of 31 March 2005.

The NSE launched interest rate futures in June 2003 but, in contrast to equity derivatives, there has been little trading in them. One problem with these instruments was faulty contract specifications, resulting in the underlying interest rate deviating erratically from the reference rate used by market participants. Institutional investors have preferred to trade in the OTC markets, where instruments such as interest rate swaps and forward rate agreements are thriving. As interest rates in India have fallen, companies have swapped their fixed rate borrowings into floating rates to reduce funding costs.[9] Activity in OTC markets dwarfs that of the entire exchange-traded markets, with daily value of trading estimated to be Rs 30 billion in 2004 (FitchRatings 2004).

Foreign exchange derivatives are less active than interest rate derivatives in India, even though they have been around for longer. OTC instruments in currency forwards and swaps are the most popular. Importers, exporters, and banks use the rupee forward market to hedge their foreign currency exposure. Turnover and liquidity in this market has been increasing, although trading is mainly in shorter maturity contracts of one year or less (Gambhir and Goel 2003). In a currency swap, banks and corporations may swap their rupee denominated debt into another currency (typically the US dollar or Japanese yen), or vice versa. Trading in OTC currency options is still muted. There are no exchange-traded currency derivatives in India.

Exchange-traded commodity derivatives have been trading only since 2000, and the growth in this market has been uneven. The number of commodities eligible for futures trading has increased from 8 in 2000 to 80 in 2004, while the value of trading has increased almost four times in the same period (Nair 2004). However, many contracts barely trade and, of those that are active, trading is fragmented over multiple market venues, including central and regional exchanges, brokerages, and unregulated forwards markets. The total volume of commodity derivatives is still small, less than half the size of equity derivatives (Gorham et al. 2005).

Derivatives Users in India

The use of derivatives varies by type of institution. Financial institutions, such as banks, have assets and liabilities of different maturities and in different currencies, and are exposed to different risks of default from their borrowers. Thus they are likely to use derivatives on interest rates and currencies, and derivatives to manage

[9]In an interest rate swap, a company may receive a floating rate (linked to a benchmark rate) and pay a fixed rate. A forward rate agreement allows a company to lock in a particular interest rate.

credit risk. Non-financial institutions are regulated differently from financial institutions, and this affects their incentives to use derivatives. Indian insurance regulators, for example, are yet to issue guidelines relating to the use of derivatives by insurance companies.

In India, financial institutions have not been heavy users of exchange-traded derivatives so far, with their contribution to total value of NSE trades being less than 8 per cent in October 2005. However, market insiders feel that this may be changing, as indicated by the growing share of index derivatives (which are used more by institutions than by retail investors). In contrast to the exchange-traded markets, domestic financial institutions and mutual funds have shown great interest in OTC fixed income instruments. Transactions between banks dominate the market for interest rate derivatives, while state-owned banks remain a small presence (Chitale 2003). Corporations are active in the currency forwards and swaps markets, buying these instruments from banks.

Why do institutions not participate to a greater extent in derivatives markets? Some institutions such as banks and mutual funds are only allowed to use derivatives to hedge their existing positions in the spot market, or to rebalance their existing portfolios. Since banks have little exposure to equity markets due to banking regulations, they have little incentive to trade equity derivatives.[10] Foreign investors must register as foreign institutional investors (FII) to trade exchange-traded derivatives and be subject to position limits as specified by SEBI. Alternatively, they can incorporate locally as a broker-dealer.[11] FIIs have a small but increasing presence in the equity derivatives markets. They have no incentive to trade interest rate derivatives since they have little investment in the domestic bond markets (Chitale 2003). It is possible that unregistered foreign investors and hedge funds trade indirectly, using a local proprietary trader as a front (Lee 2004).

Retail investors (including small brokerages trading for themselves) are the major participants in equity derivatives, accounting for about 60 per cent of turnover in October 2005, according to the NSE. The success of single stock futures in India is unique, as this instrument has generally failed in most other countries. One reason for this success may be retail investors' prior familiarity with badla trades which shared some features of derivatives trading. Another reason may be the small size of the futures contracts, compared to similar contracts in other countries. Retail investors also dominate the markets for commodity derivatives, in part due to their long-standing expertise in trading in the hawala or forwards markets.

In terms of the growth of derivatives markets, and the variety of derivatives users, the Indian market has equalled or exceeded many other regional markets.[12] While the growth is being spearheaded mainly by retail investors, private-sector institutions, and large corporations, smaller companies and state-owned institutions are gradually getting into the act. Foreign brokers such as J.P. Morgan Chase are boosting their presence in India in reaction to the growth in derivatives. The variety of derivatives instruments available for trading is also expanding.

There remain major areas of concern for Indian derivatives users. Large gaps exist in the range of derivatives products that are traded actively. In equity derivatives, NSE figures show that almost 90 per cent of activity is due to stock futures or index futures, whereas trading in options is limited to a few stocks, partly because they are settled in cash and not the underlying stocks. Exchange-traded derivatives based on interest rates and currencies are virtually absent.

Liquidity and transparency are important properties of any developed market. Liquid markets require market makers who are willing to buy and sell, and be patient while doing so. In India, market making is primarily the province of Indian private and foreign banks, with public-sector banks lagging in this area (FitchRatings 2004). A lack of market liquidity may be responsible for inadequate trading in some markets. Transparency is achieved partly through financial disclosure. Financial statements currently provide misleading information on institutions' use of derivatives. Further, there is no consistent method of accounting for gains and losses from derivatives trading. Thus a proper framework to account for derivatives needs to be developed.

Further regulatory reform will help the markets grow faster. For example, Indian commodity derivatives have

[10]Under Reserve Bank of India (RBI) directive, banks' direct or indirect (through mutual funds) exposure to capital markets instruments is limited to 5 per cent of total outstanding advances as of the previous year end. Some banks may have further equity exposure on account of equities collaterals held against loans in default.

[11]In practice, some foreign investors also invest in Indian markets by issuing Participatory Notes to an offshore investor.

[12]Among exchange-traded derivatives markets in Asia, India was ranked second behind South Korea for the first quarter of 2005. How about China, with which India is frequently compared in other respects? China is preparing to develop its derivatives markets rapidly. It has recently entered into joint ventures with the leading US futures exchanges. It has taken steps to loosen currency controls, and the Central Bank has allowed domestic and foreign banks to trade yuan forward and swaps contracts on behalf of clients. However, unlike India, China has not fully implemented necessary reforms of its stock markets, which is likely to hamper growth of its derivatives markets.

great growth potential but government policies have resulted in the underlying spot/physical market being fragmented (for example, due to lack of free movement of commodities and differential taxation within India). Similarly, credit derivatives, the fastest-growing segment of the market globally, are absent in India and require regulatory action if they are to develop.[13]

As Indian derivatives markets grow more sophisticated, greater investor awareness will become essential. The NSE has programmes to inform and educate brokers, dealers, traders, and market personnel. In addition, institutions will need to devote more resources to develop the business processes and technology necessary for derivatives trading.

Appendix: Forwards, Futures, Options, and Swaps

I begin with a description of the simplest types of derivatives: forwards, futures, options, and swaps. To illustrate a forward contract, consider the following example (unless otherwise stated, all prices are in rupees per gram). Jewellery manufacturer Goldbuyer agrees to buy gold at Rs 600 (the forward or delivery price) three months from now (the delivery date) from gold-mining concern Goldseller. This is an example of a forward contract. No money changes hands between Goldbuyer and Goldseller at the time the forward contract is created. Rather, Goldbuyer's pay-off depends on the spot price at the time of delivery. Suppose that the spot price reaches Rs 610 at the delivery date. Then Goldbuyer gains Rs 10 on his forward position (that is, the difference between the spot and forward prices) by taking delivery of the gold at Rs 600.

A futures contract is similar to a forward contract, with some exceptions. Futures contracts are traded on exchange markets, whereas forward contracts are typically traded on OTC markets. Also, futures contracts are settled daily (marked-to-market), whereas forwards are settled only at expiration.

Returning to the example above, suppose that Goldbuyer believes that there is some chance for the spot price to fall below Rs 600, so that he loses on his forward position. To limit his loss, Goldbuyer could purchase a call option for Rs 5 (the option price or premium) at a strike or exercise price of Rs 600 with an expiration date three months from now. The call option gives Goldbuyer the right (but not the obligation) to buy gold at the strike price on the expiration date.[14] Then, if the spot price indeed declines, he could choose not to exercise the option, and his loss would be limited to the purchase price of Rs 5. Alternatively, Goldbuyer may anticipate that the spot gold price is very likely to decline, and attempt to profit from such an eventuality by buying a put option, giving him the right to sell gold at the strike price on the expiration date.

Swaps are derivatives involving exchange of cash flows over time, typically between two parties. One party makes a payment to the other depending upon whether a price is above or below a reference price specified in the swap contract.

ASANI SARKAR

References

Chitale, Rajendra P. 2003. 'Use of Derivatives by India's Institutional Investors: Issues and Impediments', in Susan Thomas (ed.), *Derivatives Markets in India*, New Delhi, Tata McGraw-Hill Publishing Company Limited.

FitchRatings. 2004. Fixed Income Derivatives—A Survey of the Indian Market, available www.fitchratings.com.

Gambhir, Neeraj and Manoj Goel. 2003. 'Foreign Exchange Derivatives Market in India—Status and Prospects', in Susan Thomas (ed.), *Derivatives Markets in India*, New Delhi, Tata McGraw-Hill Publishing Company Limited.

Gorham, Michael, Susan Thomas, and Ajay Shah. 2005. *India: The Crouching Tiger*, Washington DC, Futures Industry Association.

ISMR. 2004. *Indian Securities Market: A Review*, Mumbai, National Stock Exchange of India Limited.

Jogani, Ashok and Kshama Fernandes. 2003. 'Arbitrage in India: Past, Present and Future', in Susan Thomas (ed.), *Derivatives Markets in India*, New Delhi, Tata McGraw-Hill Publishing Company Limited.

Lee, Rupert. 2004. *Seeing Double*, FOW.

Nair, C.G.K. 2004. *Commodity Futures Markets in India: Ready for 'Take Off'*? Mumbai, National Stock Exchange of India Limited.

■ Disaster Management

Definition and Scope

The word 'disaster' has been variously defined in literature, but for the purpose of this entry it is defined

[13]See Chitale (2003) for an assessment of reforms needed for the development of credit derivatives.

[14]The example describes a European option. By contrast, an American option would have allowed the buyer to exercise the option on or before the exercise date.

as a natural or man-made event that negatively affects life, property, livelihood, or employment often resulting in 'permanent or almost irreversible changes' to human societies, ecosystems, and environment. Our planet Earth, formed by cataclysmic events, still has residual violence, as noted by occurences of volcanic eruptions, earthquakes, and so on.

The Chernobyl nuclear accident (26 April 1986) and the Bhopal gas (methyl isothiocyanate) disaster (night of 2 and 3 December 1984) still remain fresh in our memory as the worst among man-made disasters. While man-made disasters are controllable to a large extent by developing foolproof designs and efficient monitoring strategies, natural disasters such as astro-physical, geological, and hydro-meteorological ones are not under human control. The principles of preparedness, early warning, and mitigation become more relevant here. Natural disasters can be divided into astro-physical (for example, meteorite or 'near earth object' (NEA) hitting the planet as happened about 60 million years ago which is reported to have also caused the extinction of dinosaurs), geo-physical (for example, earthquakes and volcanoes), and hydro-meteorological (for example, cyclones/typhoons/hurricanes, floods, and drought) events. Biological disasters are also natural disasters, but unlike astro-physical, geo-physical, and hydro-meteorological events, these are more effectively controllable and treatable due to advances in molecular epidemiology and medicine.

The March 2011 disaster in Japan is unique in the sense that a major earthquake (M~8.9) induced a powerful tsunami and the combined forces of these two resulted in serious structural damage to the nuclear power reactors in Fukushima Daiichi and caused a major nuclear disaster. Explosions in the nuclear reactors led to the release of radionucleides (mainly I^{131} and much less cesium-137) contaminating milk, spinach, and possibly several other food materials. Currently, this is a serious ongoing concern. The Fukushima nuclear disaster is a 'wake-up' call to several nations, particularly India, which require nuclear power for their sustainable development, especially in the coastal regions where the density of human population is very high. The solution does not lie in a negative approach of denial of nuclear power, but in developing necessary technologies for earthquake and tsunami-proof structures and taking adequate precautions to withstand earthquakes, tsunamis, and cyclones. It is noted that the tsunami waves of 26 December 2004 hit the Indira Gandhi Centre for Atomic Research (IGCAR), Kalpakkam, but fortunately, there was no damage to the Madras atomic power plants. So, taking a serious note of the Fukushima nuclear disaster caused by an earthquake and tsunami, M.S. Swaminathan wrote to Jairam Ramesh, the then Minister of State, Ministry of Environment and Forests, Government of India, on 15 March 2011, expressing his concern for the safety of nuclear power plants located along the coast, such as Kalpakkam and Kudangulam in Tamil Nadu. He stated that in addition to necessary technological reinforcements, the bio-shields comprising of mangrove and non-mangrove species in the coastal areas adjoining nuclear power plants should be effectively developed. These would be an effective second-line defence.

Among natural disasters, hydro-meteorological disasters are increasing both in their frequency of occurrence and also in their destructive potential. The data published by the UNEP/DEWA/GRID-Europe 2004 suggest that during 1991–2005, the world distribution of disasters by geological, biological, and hydro-meteorological origin were 10, 14, and 76 per cent, respectively. Hence, the long coastline of about 7,516 km and density of human population of nearly 30 per cent (~ 360 million people) make India particularly vulnerable to hydro-meteorological disasters. Further, a rise in sea level on account of global warming could enhance the risk. Four states (Tamil Nadu, Andhra Pradesh, Orissa, and West Bengal and one union territory, Puducherry) on the east coast, and Gujarat on the west coast, are highly vulnerable to hazards associated with cyclones. Including the less vulnerable ones, there are 13 coastal states and union territories encompassing 84 coastal districts that are affected by tropical cyclones. Broad-scale assessment of the population at risk suggests that an estimated 330 million people out of India's current population of about 1,200 million are directly exposed to the risk of cyclones, tsunamis, and so on, whereas the country as a whole is vulnerable to drought, floods, and such other hydro-meteorological events. Sea level rise due to global warming is yet another hydro-meteorological risk being increasingly faced by coastal communities.

The Orissa super cyclone (1999), the Gujarat earthquake (2001), and the tsunami waves (2004) lashing against the Andaman and Nicobar Islands and the coast of Tamil Nadu have caused over 40,000 deaths and rendered over 10 million people homeless. Many millions of the affected survivors lost their livelihood resource base and suffered from poverty and hunger for months. There were also a few cases of transitional starvation deaths.

The Government of India has been responding to these disasters as promptly as possible with relief and rehabilitation. A paradigm shift in the government's approach to dealing with disasters before they occur than post-disaster management was largely brought about by the 2004 tsunami, and a subsequent article, 'Beyond Tsunami: An Agenda for Action' (Swaminathan 2005). This article emphasized that medium-and long-term rehabilitation demands three initiatives all along the coast: (i) strengthening the ecological foundations of sustainable human security, (ii) rehabilitating livelihoods and fostering sustainable livelihood security, and (iii) putting in place knowledge centres in the vulnerable coastal villages. In other words, this model called for integrating elements of sustainable development in the coastal villages with disaster preparedness, including the early warning system. The enactment of the Disaster Management Act, 2005, marked the paradigm shift from 'post-disaster relief and rehabilitation' to 'improving pre-disaster preparedness', initiating disaster mitigation projects, and strengthening emergency response capacities. The Government of India also established the National Disaster Management Authority (NDMA), chaired by the Prime Minister, as the apex body for disaster management in the country, State Disaster Management Authorities (SDMAs) chaired by respective chief ministers at the state level, and District Management Authorities (DDMAs) chaired by the respective district collectors and co-chaired by the elected representative of the zilla parishad in the respective districts. During the last five years of its existence, NDMA has developed a number of disaster management guidelines for managing floods, cyclones, earthquakes, droughts, biological disasters, nuclear and radiological emergencies, chemical disasters, and disasters caused by terrorist activities, landslides, and snow avalanches. It has also provided guidelines for revamping civil defence, strengthening safety and security for transportation of petroleum, oil and liquid (POL) tankers, medical preparedness, and mass casualty management. These are very detailed guidelines, but these are operationally in a largely 'top–down' approach. Their positive aspect is the emphasis on pre-disaster preparedness in a country where it hardly existed. It also addresses technological, social, and management dimensions. What would, however, be extremely ideal is the integration of the elements of disaster preparedness with those of sustainable rural development, and the blending of the modern early warning system technologies with traditional knowledge of disaster management by indigenous rural communities. It is also essential to provide knowledge and eco-technological empowerment to rural women and men. Further, all these need to be designed and executed in a 'bottom–up' and participatory rather than in a 'top–down' manner. Details of the designs and approaches of these are found in the scientific paper 'Managing Extreme Natural Disasters in Coastal Areas' (Kesavan and Swaminathan 2006).

When the pathways of sustainable rural development are strongly established and rural self-help groups are provided with eco-technological and knowledge empowerment through 'bio-villages' and 'village knowledge centres', they are able to fight the famines of both rural livelihoods and food. Knowledge and technological skills provide the necessary capacity to reduce deaths and devastation by a given disaster and also enhance resilience. Further, satellite and computer-based modern information and communication technologies, when established in all the 638,365 villages in India, will provide almost instantaneously locale-specific, demand-driven information and early warnings on disasters for the resource-poor, vulnerable rural communities. Mobile phones, FM radio, and other modern means of communication, will help in reaching out to the last mile and to the last person. Sustainable development includes sustainable management of natural resources locally available and linking livelihood security with ecological security.

Vulnerability Analysis and Risk Assessment

There are several advantages of preparing vulnerability maps denoting areas with varying levels of proneness to tropical cyclones. Indian coasts are highly vulnerable to tropical cyclones in view of the very nature of the coastlines, coastal bathymetry and tides, and the socio-economic conditions of the coastal populations. Most of the coastal communities consist of resource-poor, small and marginal farming, fishing, and landless families. They are also largely illiterate and unskilled.

The Vulnerability Atlas of India (BMTPC 1997) contains cyclone hazard maps of the country as a whole, depicting the vulnerability of states/UTs to cyclones on a macro scale. Since then, anthropogenic pressure on several fragile coastal ecosystems has greatly increased due to housing, holiday resorts, sand mining, industrial projects, aquaculture enterprises, extraction of coral reefs, and dumping of sewage and toxic wastes. An assessment of the vulnerability at the village level is to be carried out through a community-based strategy and the community's traditional knowledge of risk management. There is the need to develop a 'village information system' using high resolution satellite images/aerial photos and socio-economic data covering natural resources and infrastructure facilities on an appropriate scale (1:10,000/1:8,000) at the survey level using remote sensing and GIS techniques.

Vulnerability to natural hazards like cyclones depends on exposure to the hazard, the coping capacity of the people, and institutional support, such as early warning systems and capacity-building to adapt and reduce adverse impacts. The coping capacity includes appropriate technological and knowledge empowerment of the vulnerable communities, use of defence mechanisms, and access to resources as well as emergency response systems.

Sustainable Preparedness for Disaster Management

The Tenth Five Year Plan document has a detailed chapter on disaster management. The dams and barrages constructed over the past five decades have protected 15 million ha out of a total of 40 million ha prone to severe floods annually. A further recent development is that the Government of India has formed a Central Task Force under the chairmanship of Chairman, Central Water Commission to suggest short- and long-term measures. The Ministry of Home Affairs has initiated a National Disaster Risk Management Programme in all the flood-prone states. Elected representatives and officials, especially of flood disaster-prone states, such as Bihar, Orissa, West Bengal, Assam, and Uttar Pradesh, and representatives of UNDP, USAID, and the European Commission are its members.

So far as earthquake risk mitigation is concerned, the major shortcoming is that there is no technology to provide early warning, and building regulations in the earthquake-prone urban and suburban areas do not necessarily incorporate the codes stipulated by the Bureau of Standards. Use of poor quality material in construction adds to the risk of collapse even during moderate tremors. The mode of construction in the rural areas is no longer the safe mud and thatch one, but brick and concrete, often without proper and secure designs and up-to-date civil engineering inputs. There is a National Core Group for Earthquake Risk Mitigation consisting of experts in earthquake engineering and administrators. Its purpose is provide advice and guidance to states on various aspects of earthquake mitigation and also prepare handbooks/pamphlets/type of designs for earthquake resistant constructions. In addition, there is also a National Programme for Capacity Building of Engineers and Architects in Earthquake Risk Mitigation. Steps are also in progress to mainstream earthquake mitigation in rural development schemes. The Ministry of Rural Development has plans of introducing earthquake/cyclone/flood-resistant designs and features in rural housing and community centres, recreation centres, anganwadi centres, and so on, constructed under the Indira Awas Yojana (IAY).

A National Cyclone Mitigation project, which envisages construction of cyclone shelters, coastal shelter belts/bio-shields consisting of salt-tolerant mangrove or non-mangrove species depending upon hydrological situations together with training, awareness, and capacity-building programmes may be soon cleared by the Planning Commission. Studies by the M.S. Swaminathan Research Foundation (MSSRF) scientists (see *Science* 2005) in 2005 revealed that dense mangrove tree species along the coastline acted as an effective bio-shield and significantly reduced the loss of lives and damage to property and livelihoods on the Tamil Nadu coast when the tsunami waves struck the region in December 2004.

The Government of India has paid special attention to the north-eastern states and Andaman and Nicobar Islands. The adoption of the 'Shillong Declaration', facilitated by the North Eastern Council (NEC), aims at integrating disaster management with development planning. The National Disaster Management Guidelines (Management of cyclones), April 2008, of the NDMA have also emphasized a paradigm shift in disaster management.

While these efforts are laudable, the question remains whether any endeavour *without* a firm foundation that links development, environment, and natural disasters can effectively reduce death and devastation should another Orissa cyclone, Bhuj earthquake, or tsunami occur. Apart from a real focus on sustainable management of natural resources and eco-technological and knowledge empowerment of the local communities in the vulnerable areas, there should also be a conscious paradigm shift from 'top–down' to 'bottom–up' mode of planning and implementation. 'Top–down' approaches, apart from their poor delivery rates, may promote scope for misuse/corruption of funds, as illustrated by Sainath in *Everybody Loves a Good Drought* (1996).

An effective framework for mitigating natural disasters involves sustainable management of natural resources and a system of productivity in perpetuity, awareness, and capacity-building. The local communities are largely poor and illiterate, but research and development endeavours through the bio-villages and rural knowledge centres set up by the M.S. Swaminathan Research Foundation have shown that technological empowerment of rural women and men is achieved through 'techniracy' (a term coined in the 1970s by M.S. Swaminathan to describe 'learning by doing', as against the formal system of education). In addition, MSSRF's knowledge empowerment using modern information and communication technology (ICT) in rural knowledge centres enables local communities access time- and locale-specific, demand-driven, and value-enhanced information. The spectrum of such information content is quite vast, ranging from early warning of impending hydro-meteorological disasters, information on safer locations, first-aid and healthcare, market prices of agricultural produce, rural products manufactured by self-help groups to children's education and youth employment. Integrated into this framework of overall preparedness and sustainable development, there could also be community-centred food, water, and fodder banks as an additional safety net in highly vulnerable areas. These are the 'banks with a difference', developed by MSSRF in the hunger 'hot spots' of Orissa and Tamil Nadu. Essential food grains, fodder, and clean drinking water stored with care (often using the traditional knowledge of rural women and men) help in preventing 'transient' hunger and water-borne diseases. If a disaster, such as cyclone, earthquake, tsunami, or surge storm, hits a cluster of villages, these measures would enable the local governance to cope with it better. Thus air dropping of relief food packets a few days after a disaster might not be required. Disaster reduction is aimed at enhancing awareness, building capacity, and motivating societies at risk to become engaged in the conscious management of risk thereby reducing vulnerability. The needs are greater resilience, a gender-sensitive caring and sharing attitude, awareness, requisite knowledge, and the do-how to combine traditional wisdom and modern technologies to achieve maximum protection of lives and livelihoods.

Village Knowledge Centres (VKCs) in Natural Disaster Management

Guided by the foresight that satellite and computer-based, geo-spatial ICT would be of immense help in providing locale and time-specific, demand-driven information and in overall knowledge empowerment of the rural women and men, MSSRF set up a few modern ICT-based village knowledge centres (VKCs) in the union territory of Puducherry in early 1998. The resource-poor, marginal farming, fishing, and landless rural families could access VKCs without any discrimination on the basis of class, caste, creed, and gender. One of the VKCs established in the fishing village of Veerampattinam became globally acknowledged as early as 1998 for its great service in providing information on sea wave heights well in advance of an impending storm and rise of sea waves to dangerous heights of toppling the country rafts in which the resource-poor marginal fishermen venture for fishing in the deep sea. The women of fishing families, in particular, have expressed their gratitude for saving the lives of their fishermen. The collection of data on sea wave heights involves use of hi-tech, but the dissemination of the information/warning about the sea wave heights in the local vernacular (Tamil) is by relatively low-tech loudspeakers.

The positive impact of VKCs triggered the idea of 'Mission 2007: Every Village a Knowledge Centre' at the beginning of this century and millennium. The aim of this programme is bridging the urban–rural digital-divide and harnessing ICT for addressing major problems like poverty, famine of livelihoods, illiteracy, lack of skills, lack of technological support, prevalence of social and gender inequities, ignorance, credulity, and helplessness of rural India. With this aim, the goal was to set up VKCs in all the 600,000 plus villages of India. Since this is a stupendous task, a national alliance, which now has over 400 members drawn from private, public, academic, civil society, and financial sectors has been set up. The alliance is supported by a UN International Support Group, bilateral agencies, and private-sector corporations. Since 2007, this movement is called the 'Grameen Gyan Abhiyan' (rural knowledge movement). A cluster of VKCs is connected with a village resource centre (VRC) established with the help of the Indian Space Research Organisation (ISRO). VRCs have satellite connectivity and tele-conferencing facilities to provide early warning, e-health, e-commerce, and other demand-driven and dynamic services.

With particular reference to the dissemination of early warning alarms and other demand-driven and dynamic services, VRCs and VKCs play a significant role at the level of a group of villages and a single individual village, respectively. The last mile and last person connectivity is achieved through the integrated use of internet and cellular phones or FM radio or the public address system. With increasing numbers of rural people possessing mobile phones, the last person connectivity is expected to become far more effective.

VRCs and VKCs provide information on ocean state forecast and potential fishing zones—for example, location of fish shoals—to fisherfolk with the support of the Indian National Centre for Ocean Information Services (INCOIS). The ocean state forecast (wind direction, sea wave height, weather, and so on) helps fisherfolk in avoiding disasters, saving fuel, and preventing economic loss due to damage to fishing nets and smaller fibre reinforced plastic (FRP) fishing boats.

VRCs and VKCs also provide specific Integrated Agromet Advisory Services (IAAS) based on weather conditions to the farmers with the help of universities, the India Meteorological Department, Krishi Vigyan Kendras, and so on. The purpose of providing locale-specific weather advisories is to sensitize the farmers about the positive impact of agro-climatic conditions on field crops and guide them in adopting necessary agronomic and plant protection practices for obtaining maximum yields. The weather advisories mainly focus on pest and diseases management, crop growth based on agronomic practices (fertilizer application), and water management (irrigation). Information on temperature (minimum, maximum), humidity, rainfall, and cloud conditions is also disseminated regularly. The weather-based agro-advisories are useful for inter-cultural operations like weeding, fertilizer application, irrigation, plant protection measures, anticipation of possible pest and disease attacks in various crop fields, and necessary vaccinations for livestock to protect them from weather-influenced diseases. Weather-based agro-advisories pertaining to each district are provided based on the cropping pattern and crop calendar.

The integration of ICT-based rural knowledge centres with a system of coastal bio villages for sustainable livelihoods and ecological security is the key for achieving a steady state of preparedness against all natural disasters in vulnerable areas. The bio-villages (bios=living) are villages where eco-technologies (that is, the result of modern technologies blended with traditional wisdom and ecological prudence) with their pro-nature, pro-poor, and pro-women orientation help in the sustainable management of locally available natural resources and in creating market-driven rural eco-enterprises. Many eco-technologies such as production of bio-fertilizers, bio-pesticides, oyster mushrooms, ornamental fish, fish pickles, and paper and board from agricultural waste involve tools, techniques, and principles of classical biotechnology. It is done with the reason that a combination of ICT and traditional biotechnology through the integration of rural knowledge centres and bio-villages elevates the level of local development in social, economic, environmental, and technological dimensions. *The Global Environment Outlook 3* (GRID-Arendal 2002) observes that the level of development is directly proportional to the severity of deaths and destruction due to a natural disaster. It has estimated that the average number of people dying per reported disaster is 22.5, 145.0, and 1,052 for countries with high-, medium-, and low-level development, respectively. Within India, the urban–rural divide in terms of available amenities and technological development is enormous. It is also known that natural disasters cause more deaths and destruction in rural areas. The knowledge and technological empowerment of women and the weakest among the poor is crucial for achieving an appreciable level of rural development for coping with and mitigating natural disasters.

Climate Change and Food Security

The data and interpretations pertaining to climate change, global warming, sea-level rise, and so on, of the Intergovernmental Panel on Climate Change (IPCC) mainly implicate human activities (that is, anthropogenic) in the nature of emission of heat-trapping greenhouse gases (for instance, carbon dioxide, methane, nitrous oxide). Therefore, the role of mitigation mainly aimed at reducing greenhouse gases and sequestration/absorption of carbon dioxide is greatly emphasized. However, elaborate scientific studies conducted by the Non-governmental International Panel on Climate Change (NIPCC), published in August 2010 by the Heartland Institute, Chicago, suggest that natural causes are very likely to be the dominant cause of global warming and climate change. The Heartland Institute made a summary of its findings for policymakers in 2008 under the title, 'Nature, Not Human Activity Rules the Planet' (Singer 2008). Yet, both IPCC and NIPCC agree that climate change is real and a matter of serious concern. The average global temperature has already increased by 0.78°C and the CO_2 concentration now is about 398 ppm as compared to about 280 ppm in the late 18th century.

Apart from acute and extreme hydro-meteorological events, chronic and subtle adverse effects of global warming, especially on monsoon, biodiversity, fresh water resources, and productivity of crops and farm animals are quite considerable. Studies in the 1980s by M.S. Swaminathan and his associates revealed that a rise of 0.5°C in the night temperature reduces the duration of wheat by a week and consequently, the yield by about 450 kg per ha. Plantation crops would need upward movement to cooler altitudes. This means the destruction of natural biodiversity occurring at the higher altitudes in order to make land available for plantation crops. Coral reefs would suffer varying levels of bleaching that would greatly diminish breeding and replenishment of several edible fish. Degradation of mangroves in the estuaries is known to adversely affect the breeding and development of several species of fish, crabs, prawns, and so on.

Milk production in cows and buffaloes would also be adversely affected directly due to increase in the incidence of parasitic diseases and indirectly due to decreased supply of nutritious fodder and forage.

Livelihoods, especially of resource-poor farming and fishing families could come under severe stress. The dreadful combination of short supply (that is, inadequate availability) and diminished access to food would enhance food insecurity at the individual household level.

India's Action Plan on Climate Change: Prime Minister's Council on Climate Change

One of the major principles of the National Action Plan on Climate Change is to protect the poor and vulnerable sections of society through an inclusive and sustainable development strategy, which is sensitive to climate change. The focus is on promoting basic understanding of climate change, adaptation and mitigation, energy efficiency, and natural resource conservation. There are eight national missions which form the core of the National Action Plan, and these represent multi-pronged, long-term, and integrated strategies for achieving key goals in the context of climate change. The eight national missions are National Solar Mission, National Mission for Enhanced Energy Efficiency, National Mission on Sustainable Habitat, National Water Mission, National Mission for Sustaining the Himalayan Ecosystem, National Mission for a Green India, National Mission for Sustainable Agriculture, and National Mission on Strategic Knowledge for Climate Change, and their major goals have been identified as mitigation, adaptation, and risk management. These deal more directly with climate risk management over a period of time. It is noted that climate change risk consists of an acute, sudden burst of hydro-meteorological extreme events with high destructive potential (for example, cyclones, cloud-burst, and floods) and chronic and not-so-readily discernible events, such as slow ingression of sea water into coastal land and aquifers, global warming adversely impacting the yield of agricultural/horticultural and marine production systems, and development of new diseases and pests.

These eight missions seem to have their base in the concept of an 'evergreen revolution' proposed and developed by M.S. Swaminathan two decades ago. It envisages achieving productivity in perpetuity without accompanying ecological harm; it also encompasses sustainable management of natural resources, developing rural livelihoods for poverty-reduction, and food security on the principles of ecology, economics, and equity in the social and gender dimensions. Thus, the basic components of evergreen revolution are: (i) eco-agriculture to achieve productivity in perpetuity without accompanying ecological harm, (ii) linking ecological security with livelihood security which, in the coastal areas, involves maintenance of mangrove as well as non-mangrove bio-shields, (iii) eco-technological and knowledge empowerment of the resource-poor, marginal farming, fishing, and landless rural families, and (iv) reinforcing social, economic, and gender equities in access to natural resources and benefit sharing.

Coastal Regulation Zone (CRZ) Notification—2010

The CRZ Notification 2010 is a revision of the CRZ Notification 1991. It has new inclusions such as an 'Aquatic' part (that is, sea area up to 12 nautical miles and water area of 'tidal influenced water bodies') in its jurisdiction, action plans for control of pollution in the nature of discharge of untreated waste, effluents, and sewage including solid waste in a time bound manner, classification of erosion-prone areas in the coastal zones for appropriate regulatory and control measures depending upon the extent of erosion, and new hazard mapping based on tides, waves, sea level rise, and shoreline changes as impacts of a rise in sea level. The new classification recognizes five coastal regulation zones based on ecological sensitivity: (CRZ-I), built-up municipal area (CRZ-II), rural areas whether developed or undeveloped (CRZ-III), aquatic area from the low tide line to 12 nautical miles on the seaward (CRZ-IV) and areas requiring special consideration, such as the islands of Lakshadweep and Andaman and Nicobar (CRZ-V). The broad principle of CRZ is ensuring livelihood security to fisher communities and other local communities living in the coastal areas; conserving and protecting coastal stretches, their unique environment, and marine area; and promoting development through a sustainable manner based on scientific principles while taking adequate steps to meet the dangers of natural hazards in the coastal areas, sea level rise due to global warming, and so on. It is not easy to reconcile development for livelihood needs with adequate disaster preparedness in the highly vulnerable coastal zones. However, CRZ 2010 is a step towards this goal.

In conclusion, disaster management in India is rapidly evolving into an effective system integrating technological, social, gender, and policy dimensions. Among the different kinds of disasters, hydro-meteorological disasters such as cyclones, floods, and droughts are of particular concern from the point of view of agriculture, animal husbandry, fisheries, and national food security.

P.C. Kesavan and M.S. Swaminathan

References

Building Materials and Technology Promotion Council (BMTPC). 1997. *The Vulnerability Atlas of India*, New Delhi, Ministry of Housing & Urban Poverty Alleviation, Government of India.

GRID-Arendal. 2002. *The Global Environment Outlook 3: Natural Disasters*, available at http://www.grida.no/geo/geo3/english/448.htm.

Kesavan, P.C. and M.S. Swaminathan. 2006. 'Managing Extreme Natural Disasters in Coastal Areas', *Philosophical Transactions of the Royal Society A*, 364(1845): 2191–216.

Sainath, P. 1996. *Everybody Loves a Good Drought*, New Delhi, Penguin Books India (P) Ltd.

Science. 2005. Vol. 310, No. 643.

Singer, Fred. 2008. *Nature, Not Human Activity Rules the Planet*, Chicago, IL, The Heartland Institute.

Swaminathan, M.S. 2005. 'Beyond Tsunami: An Agenda for Action', *The Hindu*, 17 January.

Discretionary Centre–State Transfers

The allocation of grants from central to sub-national governments has always been an important issue of fiscal federalism. Central government grants help to break the linkage between revenue and expenditure assignments by levels of government, and permit the Centre to pursue various objectives. While the traditional literature on fiscal federalism assumes that the central government is a 'benevolent planner', interested in maximizing social welfare, the more recent literature on political economy emphasizes that political considerations may influence the pattern of central grants to the states.

Case (2001) uses data on social assistance block grants from the central government to communes in Albania and concludes that politics does matter in determining the pattern of block grants. Johanssen (2003) analyses data on grants from the central government to municipalities in Sweden and finds limited support for the hypothesis that intergovernmental grants are influenced by political considerations. In the Indian context, Dasgupta et al. (2004), Khemani (2003), and Rao and Singh (2004) analyse whether *discretionary* grants—that is grants that are not governed by explicit formulae—are related to political considerations. The Indian evidence is discussed in greater detail here.

In India, there are *three* major channels through which the Centre transfers funds to state governments. These are: (i) tax devolution and grants through the Finance Commissions; (ii) grants and loans given by the Planning Commission; and (iii) transfers or various central-sector and centrally sponsored schemes by different central ministries.

The Indian Constitution specifies that the states are entitled to a share of the tax revenues collected by the Centre. The aggregate share as well as the distribution amongst the states is decided by Finance Commissions appointed at periodic intervals. Successive Finance Commissions recommend explicit formulae to determine the allocations amongst states. While Finance Commission awards have also been criticized from time to time, it is generally agreed that the formulae are *not* influenced by political considerations.

A sizeable proportion of grants and loans is also channelled through the Planning Commission. From 1969, plan transfers have been carried out on the basis of a formula decided by the National Development Council. Since transfers on account of state plan schemes are based on this consensus formula, it is tempting to exclude them from the category of discretionary grants to the states. However, discretionary elements can enter into the determination of these grants for two reasons. First, while each state proposes its plan size to the Planning Commission, the final approval of the size rests with the Commission. So there is some scope for negotiation and 'persuasion'. Second, the formula explicitly sets aside 7.5 per cent of the grants on account of 'special' problems of states. Again, this allows for some subjectivity to creep into the determination of grants for state plan schemes.

The transfers given to states through central plan schemes and centrally sponsored schemes have attracted the sharpest criticism because these are essentially completely discretionary. Central plan schemes are funded entirely by the Centre, the states merely exercising an agency role in executing these programmes. Centrally sponsored programmes involve some element of cost sharing between the Centre and the concerned state.

Are central government transfers to state governments in India really motivated by political considerations? In order to examine this question, it is crucial to incorporate the fact that different political parties may be in control of government at different levels. This is important since the state government stands 'between' the central government and the voters in the state. Central grants relax the budget constraints of state governments and permit state governments to increase their expenditure. The increased expenditure in any state generates goodwill amongst the voters in the state. To the extent that voters in the state are unsure about how the additional expenditure is financed, the party in power in the state also benefits from increased central grants. So if the Congress Party is in power at the Centre, and the BJP in a particular state, then at least some of the benefits of central transfers 'leak' to the BJP.

Of course, if the incumbents in the state and the Centre happen to be the same party (that is, the state government is *aligned* with the central government), then that party derives the entire electoral benefit of any additional expenditure in the state. This suggests that the 'alignment effect'—the ruling parties (or coalition) being 'aligned' at the Centre and in the state—should result in the aligned states receiving a disproportionately larger share of discretionary grants. Rao and Singh (2004) find some evidence in support of this hypothesis.

Dasgupta et al. (2004) propose a variant of the alignment hypothesis. Suppose the objective of the central incumbent is to maximize the *number of states* it can win, and it uses discretionary grants to further this objective. Assume that there are only two major parties or coalitions. They define a state to be *partisan* if one of the parties has a devoted 'vote bank' that constitutes more than half the electorate. In such states, there is no electoral compulsion to 'buy' votes since a majority of voters are *committed* to one of the parties. States that are not partisan are called *swing* states. The election is expected to be 'close' in these swing states, and so the marginal benefit from buying the extra vote is also correspondingly larger. Of course, the swing states that are aligned are in a particularly advantageous position. Dasgupta et al. (2004) find strong empirical support for the *aligned swing* effect.

Dasgupta et al. (2004) also focus on the possible influence of lobbying by Members of Parliament (MPs). More specifically, they assume that lobbying power is restricted to members of the ruling party. That is, if the BJP is in power at the Centre, then MPs elected from say Uttar Pradesh and belonging to the BJP can exert pressure to get additional grants to their constituencies. Members of the opposition parties have less lobbying power because Cabinet Ministers perceive no benefit in increasing expenditure in constituencies where the incumbent belongs to the opposition. There is also some support for the lobbying hypothesis—ceteris paribus, states that elect relatively more MPs from the ruling party get higher discretionary grants.

BHASKAR DUTTA

References

Case, Anne. 2001. 'Election Goals and Income Redistribution: Recent Evidence from Albania', *European Economic Review*, 45: 405–23.

Dasgupta, S., A. Dhillon, and B. Dutta. 2004. 'Electoral Goals and Center–State Transfers: A Theoretical Model and Empirical Evidence from India', mimeo, University of Warwick.

Johanssen, Eva. 2003. 'Intergovernmental Grants as a Tactical Instrument: Some Empirical Evidence from Swedish Municipalities', *Journal of Public Economics*, 87: 883–915.

Khemani, Stuti. 2003. 'Partisan Politics and Intergovernmental Transfers in India', mimeo, Development Research Group, World Bank.

Rao, M. Govinda and Nirvikar Singh. 2004. 'The Political Economy of Center–State Fiscal Transfers in India', mimeo, University of California at Santa Cruz.

■ Disinvestment, The Economics of

Public debates about economic policies in India have been very controversial ever since the early 1990s when India embarked on the reform process. Every major change has been intensely contested by opposition parties, professional economists, and trade unions. Even against this background, the discussions about the desirability of disinvestment of government holdings in public-sector enterprises stand out because they have been particularly heated. Is it sensible for the government to go in for privatization or should the public sector be allowed to survive 'as is'? If disinvestment is the right approach, what is the appropriate mechanism for the sale of shares? And how should the government utilize the revenues collected through disinvestment? Each of these aspects of disinvestment has been the subject of intense scrutiny.

The entire debate on disinvestment would have been only of academic interest if India did not have such a large public sector. The public sector played a central role under Nehruvian socialism and was instrumental in building up the economy in post-Independence India, in particular the heavy industrial base of the Indian economy. It is debatable whether private entrepreneurs would have shouldered the huge risks associated with setting up heavy industries in the immediate post-Independence period when the economy was in a fledgling state—the small size of the domestic market would have acted as a deterrent since the private sector would necessarily take uncoordinated decisions. Conceptually, centralized planning has tremendous advantage because the government can take *coordinated* decisions so that the steel industry demands the products of the capital goods industry while the capital goods industry demands the output of the steel industry. In other words, the simultaneous creation of several giant firms can circumvent the problem of small markets because each small firm would demand the products of the other firms.

In principle, centralized planning does not necessarily imply the existence of public-sector enterprises if the government has sufficient regulatory instruments allowing it to control the private sector. However, it is obviously easier to control the allocation of resources if the public sector occupies the commanding heights of the economy, and this provided the rationale for the emergence of the public sector in India.

Nation-building was the primary if not the only goal of the public sector. In particular, public-sector enterprises never had to achieve any hard financial targets. While this made sense in the initial stages of development, the absence of a stringent adherence to financial discipline was to prove disastrous for many public-sector enterprises in the long run. Even a cursory look at the balance sheets of these enterprises suggests that they produce paltry returns on the capital invested in them, and most of them are not commercially viable. Several of these units are now in sunset industries or operate with rundown machinery and obsolete technology, and only massive infusions of capital can possibly restore their viability.

The initial rationale for the growth of the public sector is no longer valid since the Indian economy now has a strong industrial base. So the continued existence of the public sector must depend largely on whether it utilizes scarce resources more efficiently than the private sector. Of course, even die-hard supporters of the public sector will concede that the public sector does not perform very well on the criterion of productive efficiency. Since they still believe that the public sector has a useful role to play in the Indian economy, it is important to examine possible objections to the use of (relative) productive efficiency as the principal criterion for the survival of the public sector in India. Much of the subsequent discussion focuses on the issue of whether it is right to use productive efficiency as the principal criterion in judging whether the government should go in for privatization of various public-sector enterprises. Before one does that, it is expedient to dispose of a relatively minor issue—there are a *few* sectors of tremendous strategic importance that should be outside the purview of the 'productive efficiency' criterion. The ordnance industry is an obvious example.

Perhaps, the *strongest*—though not necessarily *soundest*—opposition to the 'productive efficiency' criterion comes from the belief that the government should not sell its shares in *profitable* public-sector enterprises. The economic logic underlying this belief has never been very clearly spelt out, although analogies have often been drawn to the foolishness of selling off the family silver. Such analogies are misplaced because the proceeds from the sale of these enterprises can of course be used to build up other national assets such as economic and social infrastructure.

Perhaps a better or more appropriate analogy is to view the government's ownership of these enterprises as national assets. An owner often changes the composition of his portfolio of assets, selling off some assets in order to finance the purchase of others. This is very common practice, and no one labels the reallocation of asset portfolios as necessarily foolish or economically unsound. The correct principle here is that investment be changed in favour of assets that promise higher future social returns. Why should the government continue to own (say) Indian Airlines when private-sector airlines are offering the same type of service? Would it not be better for the government to use the proceeds from the sale of Indian Airlines to modernize Indian ports or build new highways?

Another strand of the arguments against disinvestment of profitable public-sector enterprises runs along the following lines. Public-sector enterprises have been built up with taxpayers' money, often in areas where the private sector would simply not have entered because of the initial risks associated with these ventures. If there are sectors and enterprises that are now profitable, then the public sector should be allowed to reap these profits. Why should the government allow private individuals to 'capture' the profits of enterprises built with public money?

However, the fallacy with this argument is that no one is advocating that the profitable public-sector enterprises be handed over on a platter to the private sector. The higher the prospective returns from a project, the greater is the present discounted value of the project. Hence the market value of an asset promising a million rupees every year is several times higher than that of an asset promising an annual return of only a few hundred rupees. Of course, this discrepancy in market valuations does not induce anyone to claim that the former asset should not change ownership. It simply means that the more profitable asset should be sold at significantly higher prices. Similarly, the more profitable the public-sector enterprise, the higher the price at which it can be sold. So the government loses nothing by selling off a profitable enterprise provided it extracts an *appropriate* price from the buyer.

The price that can be extracted from prospective buyers is also linked to the *mode* of disinvestment. First, *when* should the actual sale take place? G.V. Krishnamurthy, Chairman of the erstwhile Disinvestment Commission, had argued that restructuring of the public-sector enterprises must precede any attempt at disinvestment. The rationale for this was that these enterprises would not find any takers unless they were first nursed back to health. Although there is some sense in this argument, the problem is that public management may never be capable of reviving the enterprises. External circumstances also influence the optimum time for disinvestment. The government should not attempt to sell its shares when the share market is in a slump. Indeed, the depressed state of the share market during the East Asian meltdown was a principal reason behind the United Front government's disinclination to proceed with disinvestment.

Second, *how* should the shares be sold? One school believes that there should be an immediate sale to a strategic partner, who would then obtain management control. The rationale behind this view is that the offer of management control would make the enterprises significantly more valuable to prospective bidders, and hence improve marketability of the enterprise. In other words, the offer of management control would enable the government to maximize the proceeds from disinvestment.

The downside to this argument is that in some sectors—petroleum being a prime example—economies of scale imply that there are only a few enterprises. Thus the strategic sale option carries with it the danger that the process will result in a couple of business houses capturing an entire sector. For instance, fears were expressed that the Reliance group would become a gigantic monopoly in the entire oil sector if the government had gone ahead with the privatization of HPCL and BPCL. Others feared that multinational groups such as Shell would capture the oil sector and hold the economy to ransom.

Those who hold these fears advocate a different route to disinvestment. They prefer the direct sale of shares in giant public-sector enterprises to retail or small investors, with the government retaining management control at least in the initial stages. This procedure will inevitably result in lower sale proceeds to the government because of the widely held belief that the government is less efficient in running businesses than the private sector. So these are very different policy options involving possible trade-offs—a potential loss of wealth in the form of lower sale proceeds versus benefits accruing from the prevention of private monopolies. However, both the central and state governments in India are armed with a diverse set of regulatory controls, and it is questionable whether a couple of giant business houses can hold the economy to ransom. This suggests the desirability of the strategic sale option.

The public sector has played a crucial role in building up the Indian economy. But the private sector has now come of age. If economic logic rather than nostalgia is to guide economic policies, then it is time for the government to privatize public-sector enterprises in a large number of areas. The mode of disinvestment also involves important policy choices since this influences the prices at which the government can sell its shares.

BHASKAR DUTTA

■ Doctoral Education

In the Ancient and Universal Company of Scholars

During graduation ceremonies in many universities in the United States, after doctorate degrees have been conferred upon the candidates, the university's president or the graduate school's dean adds a comment signifying the profession's high calling: '*Welcome to the ancient and universal company of scholars*', or '*Welcome into the society of educated men and women*'. These words signify the calling of the *doctorate*, the highest academic degree, which is commonly referred to as the *PhD* (*Philosophiae Doctor,* or, *DPhil, Doctor of Philosophy*). Its primary purpose is training professors and other researchers who would act as recipients and keepers of vast knowledge handed down from the past, creators of new knowledge through research, and disseminators of knowledge through teaching.

What is doctoral education? There is a tongue-in-cheek saying: 'In graduate study, you learn more and more about less and less, so that in the limit you know nothing'.[1] Jokes aside, a PhD requires years of intense

[1]In the United States and many other countries, a bachelor's degree is referred to as the undergraduate degree, and master's and doctoral degrees are considered graduate degrees. By

study and research in minute detail in some area of human knowledge and writing a dissertation based on the findings. In its ideal form, a PhD is free from encumbrances that may characterize research done in industry, government agencies, or think tanks, such as pressures to turn a profit, diktats to work on specific subjects or promote a certain ideology, and strictures to meet deadlines. Doctoral research, which is conducted in universities or university-like research institutions, is a unique privilege and an extraordinary pursuit.[2]

Consequently, doctoral education may seem relevant only for developed countries. However, developing countries sorely need high-quality PhDs. Cornell University President Emeritus Professor Frank Rhodes (2001) opined that 'doctoral education is one of the most important of all tasks of the university because it is the foundation for the nation's research and development enterprise'.

Complexities and Challenges

PhD eludes simple descriptions. Rhodes (2001) characterizes doctoral education as:

1. *Variable.* A PhD is flexible and loosely structured to allow creative student–teacher interaction; a PhD experience varies from institution to institution, from department to department, and even from professor to professor.
2. *Vulnerable.* Funding depends on diverse sources like the government, the university, private charities and foundations, industry, as well as personal resources.
3. *Expensive.* Typically students receive stipends and do not pay tuition. Highly educated and trained professors spend long hours supervising a student's research and dissertation writing. Research equipment and material are costly.
4. *Wasteful.* After wasting substantial time and effort, a research project can come to a dead end. Attrition rate is high—many students do not graduate.
5. *Long lasting.* A PhD has a longer duration than other degrees. Although students in front-ranked universities often finish in four to six years, instances of people taking much longer, even 10 to 15 years, are not uncommon.
6. *Ambiguous.* There is considerable disagreement about a PhD's purposes like: (a) preparing future university teachers, (b) training for and initiation into the conduct of research, (c) conducting independent research that is a substantial contribution to the general pool of knowledge, and (d) producing 'trained minds' to meet the fundamental need to address the larger issues of contemporary society.

Doctoral education in developed countries has been carefully studied and efforts have been made to improve it.[3] In a major book entitled *In Pursuit of the PhD* (1992), former Princeton University President and Andrew W. Mellon Foundation President Emeritus Professor William G. Bowen and Harvard University President Emeritus Professor Neil L. Rudenstine found students in humanities also had high attrition rates and took a long time to finish their PhDs. They identified inadequate financial support as a cause but argued that simply increasing funding would not be enough—the department must be involved, students should compete for funding, and funding must be 'conditional' on performance. Bowen and Rudenstine stressed the importance of *departmental organization and culture* and identified obstacles for students like 'unclear expectations about how long it "should" take to earn the degree, the absence of timetables, a proliferation of course options, elaborate and sometimes conflicting requirements, intermittent (or insufficient) advising and monitoring, disagreements among faculty members about epistemological fundamentals and thus about what doctoral programs should teach'. Fellowship recipients at smaller departments were found to perform better than their counterparts in larger departments.

In 1991, the Mellon Foundation launched a 10-year project 'Graduate Education Initiative' (GEI) whereby 10 major universities in the US were provided a total of $80.5 million to systematically improve 'the structure and organization of PhD programs in the humanities and related social sciences'. Influenced by Bowen and Rudenstine's findings, the bulk of the programme money went to the departments. GEI modestly improved both the rate of completion and time-to-degree, which illustrated how hard it is to improve PhD education (in advanced nations). But several other factors like a department's clear expectations and a faculty member's interest in a student's work were also found to be significant.

contrast, the United Kingdom, India, and most Commonwealth nations consider the completion of a bachelor's degree as graduation and studying for a master's or doctoral degree as postgraduate studies.

[2]Rosovsky (1990) observed that '... training of Ph.D.'s is a necessary condition for university status ... Without a graduate school of arts and sciences, a university would be a college.'

[3]The discussion in this and the following paragraph and all quotes therein are based on Ehrenberg et al. (2010).

Faculty and PhD Students in Academia

Professors in major universities are evaluated in terms of three criteria, which in decreasing order of importance are—*research, teaching,* and *academic service* (such as administrative jobs, committee work, and editing of professional journals). Significant differences exist among the faculty—some love teaching while some others dislike it, some do research alone, some do research in collaboration with colleagues and postdoctoral collaborators, and some work with PhD students and find teaching and training of their intellectual 'children and heirs' a deeply satisfying professional experience.[4] The following exemplify two extreme views:

- Two-time Nobel Prize winning chemist Frederick Sanger focused only on research. He wrote in his autobiography (1980) on Nobelprize.org: 'I had remained in Cambridge concentrating only on basic research and avoiding as far as possible teaching or administrative responsibilities.' Sanger thanked 'excellent collaborators' and stated that 'most of these have been students and postdoctoral fellows spending a few years in the laboratory and bringing their experience and ideas with them, but I feel particularly indebted to my more permanent colleagues ...'
- Nobel laureate physicist Richard P. Feynman stitched teaching and research together:

> In any thinking process there are moments when everything is going good and you've got wonderful ideas. Teaching is an interruption ... And then there are the longer period of time when not much is coming to you. ... If you're teaching a class, you can think about the elementary things that you know very well. These things are kind of fun and delightful. ... They [students] often ask profound questions that I've thought about at times and then given up on, so to speak, for a while. ... The students may not be able to see the thing I want to answer, or the subtleties I want to think about, but they remind me of a problem by asking questions in the neighborhood of that problem. (Feynman et al. 1986)

Feynman lambasted the 'great minds at the Institute for Advanced Study [Princeton] ... now given this opportunity to sit in this lovely house by the woods there, with no classes to teach, with no obligations whatsoever' who still run out of ideas due to lack of 'enough real activity and challenge' like 'contact with the experimental guys' and not thinking about 'how to answer questions from the students'. (Following Feynman, it is pertinent to ask the staff of myriads of narrowly focused 'research' institutes in India: What do these people do? Do they add real value? At least, they can be engaged to teach.)

Faculty members need academia to effectively function and reach their full potential. In this context, *The New Oxford Dictionary of English* (1998) defines 'academia' as 'the environment or community concerned with the pursuit of research, education, and scholarship'. Also needed is an 'academic marketplace' where professors would be evaluated on the basis of their tangible and intangible academic contributions (in terms of excellence in the three criteria mentioned earlier, with 'learning' being the common thread linking them all) and be rewarded accordingly with tangible and intangible benefits. Talented faculty members who have realized their potential are essential for doctoral education to thrive.

Academia and an academic marketplace exist in their highest form in the United States, where 17 of the world's top 20 universities are located (see entry on 'Academic Research' by Chatterjea and Moulik, this volume). Unfortunately, academia exists only in isolated pockets in India; an academic marketplace is non-existent. Let's take a bird's eye view of the history of PhD education in India before delving into today's problems.

A Promising Start of Doctoral Education in Colonial India

The first modern universities in Asia were established in 1857 in Calcutta, Bombay, and Madras. However, they were modelled after the University of London and set up as affiliating universities that merely conducted examinations and granted degrees to students who were taught in affiliated colleges. Changes began under the dynamic vice chancellor of the University of Calcutta, Sir Asutosh Mookerjee. He declared in the 1907 convocation address: 'From now on the University is not just an institution issuing certificates, nor is it even a conglomeration of colleges.... This will be a centre of learning and the expansion of the frontiers of knowledge. This is precisely the true ideal of the university' (see Bose 1964).

Sir Asutosh pursued his dreams in right earnest. He started departments for postgraduate study in various disciplines, a move that was quickly followed by other universities.[5] He raised funds to create new chairs, hired

[4]Rosovsky comments: 'In Germany, the professor who guides a Ph.D. dissertation is called a *Doktorvater* (doctor–father) and that aptly describes the ideal'.

[5]Until 1915, India had only five universities—the Universities of Calcutta, Bombay, Madras, Punjab, and Allahabad.

outstanding professors in diverse fields from different parts of India, and supported graduated students in their efforts to pursue advanced research. Meghnad Saha and Sisir Mitra, who were among the earliest doctorates of Indian universities, achieved one of the world's highest scientific honours by becoming Fellows of the Royal Society (FRS) of England.[6]

One of Sir Asutosh's recruits was Sir C.V. Raman who became Asia's first Nobel Prize-winning scientist. As a professor, hands-on researcher, and mentor, Raman attracted and trained many distinguished scientists. In the meetings of the Indian Science Congress in 1917, he observed that 'a real school of physics has grown up in Calcutta the like of which does not exist in any other Indian University and which even now will not compare very unfavourably with those existing in European and American Universities' (see Ghatak et al. 1976). But it was not just physics—colonial India succeeded in developing outstanding scholars in many different fields of knowledge who worked and trained doctoral students in universities across the land. Full professorships were usually reserved for top academics, pay was good for those high up in the academic pyramid, and potentially serious scholars pursued PhDs. Academic culture seemed to prevail in India; a rich history of doctoral education gave the country a head start over most other Asian nations except Japan.

Doctoral Education in Independent India

Independent India saw rapid expansion in education. Higher education, which was previously a state subject, was increasingly brought under the central government's control. The Ministry of Human Resource Development (MoHRD) was created in 1985 to integrate 'all relevant instruments and agencies contributing to or responsible for' to 'ensure all-round development' of Indian citizens.[7] One of MoHRD's two departments, the Department of Higher Education, runs India's vast higher education system. This department is sub-divided into several sectors that include: (a) university and higher education, (b) technical education, (c) organizations promoting different languages, (d) various scholarship and educational loan schemes, (e) 'open and distance learning system' (which includes the vast Indira Gandhi National Open University that serves over 3 million students; it even has PhD programmes tucked inside it!), (f) a book promotion body, (g) the copyright office, (h) special provisions for the education of scheduled castes/scheduled tribes and minorities, and (i) the Indian National Commission for Cooperation with UNESCO (United Nations Educational, Scientific and Cultural Organization).

Doctoral programmes in India primarily belong to the first two of these categories:

- *University and higher education* includes the University Grants Commission, the Association of Indian Universities, Councils, other institutes of higher learning, and the National Assessment and Accreditation Council. The number of conventional universities has grown since 1947. *India 2010: A Reference Annual* notes that 'Universities and university-level institutions in India include 20 central universities, 215 state universities, 100 deemed universities, 5 institutions established under State Act and 13 institutes of national importance'.
- *Technical education* received particular attention in independent India. Many institutes with relatively narrower research and teaching interests were set up with the aim of making them centres of excellence. These include the 'Indian Institutes' like the renowned institutes of technology (the IITs) and management (the IIMs), the 'National Institutes' (which even include an institute of homoeopathy), and many others.

Many of the universities and institutes support advanced research and doctoral student training. Table 1 gives the discipline-wise break-up of the total number of doctorates granted in India for select years in the new millennium. The number rose from 11,534 PhDs in 2000–1 to 17,898 in 2004–5 and then shrply fell during 2006–7 and 2007–8. UGC Annual Report 2008–09 does not ascribe any particular reason for this steep decline.

Degree granting in India is regulated by the University Grants Commission (UGC), a statutory organization that was established in 1953 by an Act of Parliament. The UGC: (a) provides grants to eligible universities and colleges, (b) is responsible for 'the coordination, determination and maintenance of standards of university education', and (c) 'advises the Central and State Governments on the measures which are necessary for the development of higher education'. Renowned educator Professor Amrik Singh observed (2004) that Indian universities had more autonomy at the time of Independence; moreover, in the second capacity, no other federal country gives a single agency more power over

[6]Saha and Mitra received the Doctor of Science degree from the University of Calcutta in 1918 and 1919, respectively.
[7]Unless noted otherwise, the discussion in this section is based on data retrieved from MoHRD's website http://www.education.nic.in/ (accessed on 13 September 2011).

Table 1 Faculty-wise Number of Doctorate Degrees Awarded for Select Years in the New Millennium

Faculty	Number of doctorate degrees awarded					
	2000–1	2001–2**	2003–4**	2004–5**	2006–7	2007–8
Arts	4,398	4,545	7,473	7,532	4,752	4,405
Science	3,727	4,012	5,612	5,549	4,098	4,514
Commerce/ Management	621	704	1,096	1,010	882	873
Education	399	427	613	491	423	425
Engineering/ Technology	778	747	882	968	844	1,427
Medicine	221	192	317	456	319	277
Agriculture	889	781	1,026	888	664	664
Veterinary Science	110	90	116	132	161	123
Law	105	108	144	179	137	127
Others*	296	293	574	693	493	402
Total	11,534	11,899	17,853	17,898	12,773	13,237

Source: 2000–1 and 2001–2 data obtained from http://www.ugc.ac.in/, accessed on 26 January 2006; 2003–4 and 2004–5 and 2006–7 and 2007–8 from available UGC Annual Reports for 2005–6 and 2008–9, respectively, available at http://www.ugc.ac.in/pub/index.html, accessed on 15 September 2011.

Notes: * Others includes Music/Fine Arts, Library Science, Physical Education, Journalism, and Social Work.

** Provisional

the universities. However, he noted that the UGC has no strategy for handling PhD education and has left it largely untouched.

There are two approaches to doctoral studies in India. The first is the European-influenced PhD, which is prevalent in Continental Europe, the United Kingdom, and many Commonwealth universities, where doctoral students start doing research from the beginning. This has been the traditional approach to doctoral education in India. The second approach is the American-influenced PhD, a relatively recent development that is gaining ground in India, where students take courses in general and special areas, pass appropriate qualifying examinations, and then start research and thesis writing.

Direct immersion into research is an attractive proposition. However, in reality, this often leads to poorly trained PhDs who study on a part-time basis while working full time in other jobs. The UGC is discouraging this practice by granting scholarships to doctoral students so that they can focus full time on research. Moreover, the first approach forces students to become overly dependent on their PhD supervisors, making it hard to change advisors even in cases of breakdown in relationships.

By contrast, the second approach helps students build a record trail indicating progress, which reduces their vulnerability to the idiosyncrasies of a single professor. However, the second approach could be more expensive because institutions will have to allocate faculty resources for teaching various graduate-level courses and it may take students longer to complete their degrees.

The quality of doctoral education is a serious concern. Consider the latest issue (2010) of the highly influential global league table of universities, the 'Academic Ranking of World Universities' (ARWU) developed by scholars at China's Shanghai Jiao Tong University. ARWU places no Indian institution among the world's top 300 universities, one (Indian Institute of Science, Bangalore) among 301 to 400, and one (IIT Kharagpur) among 401 to 500 (see entry on 'Academic Research', this volume). Doesn't this reflect an overall failure of today's Indian educational institutions to do high-quality academic research, publish in top-notch journals, and train world class PhD students?

Challenges, Problems, and Some Policy Recommendations

When informed about a US-based prospective hire whose research record outshone that of his peers in India, the head of the institution shrugged off the suggestion with a bureaucratic reply, 'He must apply'. An MA in social sciences who has no serious research publications became a 'director-grade scientist'. Practitioners with no research publications have been granted full professorships. Most foreign qualified PhDs in India cannot or did not get permanent professorships at strong universities in the US or Western Europe; even dropouts from foreign PhD programmes have become professors in India. After a PhD thesis examination committee gets selected, clerks take months to send out notification letters to the prospective committee members.

These illustrate some of the maladies afflicting academic institutions affecting doctoral education in India. Some problems, like the last one, have easy solutions that provide immediate efficiency gains. Most problems, however, are complex and defy easy explanations.

Next, we consider some challenges and problems and provide some policy recommendations.

1. *Attracting and engaging high-quality faculty*. Former Dean of Harvard University's Faculty of Arts and Sciences Professor Henry Rosovsky recounted (1990) 'a wooing session' where his job was to convince a young philosopher to accept a full professorship. He commented in this regard: '...

nothing that I will do today matters more. Whenever an opportunity exists to raise average quality, a dean's heart beats faster ...' He also warned senior administrators not to get too excited over the nice treatment that they received as part of their job: 'Do not consider these tokens of honor as personal recognition; those go to thinkers, creators, and other great researchers. Our recognition is entirely derived'. The old Sanskrit saying 'Svadeshe pujyate raja vidwan sarvatra pujyate' (a king is worshipped in his own land; a scholar is worshipped everywhere) also suggests the supremacy of scholars.

It is the quality of the faculty that draws doctoral students.[8] Unfortunately, a majority of outstanding as well as high-quality Indian professors work abroad these days. Consequently, a major problem for India is to recruit, seek return of, and retain talented faculty in universities and institutes.

The best universities attract outstanding faculty by carefully creating a package that may include a higher salary, a lower teaching load, support for PhD students, generous research budgets and facilities, creation of an academic centre to support research, an opportunity to build the department, good office location, spousal job opportunities, help in locating housing, and so on. By contrast, highly bureaucratic Indian universities have little flexibility—the professors get paid according to the same salary scale, no matter what they contribute in terms of research, teaching, and academic service. Moreover, Indian educational institutions suffer from resource limitations and poor quality academic administration, and are plagued by many other problems (see entry on 'Academic Research', this volume).

Perhaps something similar to a tenure system of US universities is needed. For start, distinguished professors like fellows of the Indian National Science Academy may be granted tenure—perhaps retirement at the age of 75 or 80 years, provided they can discharge their academic duties while they hold their jobs. Others would also be eligible for tenure. Tenured faculty's compensation package should be completely negotiable.

2. *Attracting high-quality students.* PhD students in the world's top universities are culled from all corners of the globe through a keenly competitive process. Like many other nations, India faces the 'brain drain' problem. India should make efforts to attract high-quality PhD students both domestically and from other nations. This is extremely important because India has significantly expanded its higher education during recent years creating a huge demand for talented professors.
3. *Financial support.* Recall our earlier discussion on the critical role that financial support plays for doctoral students. Currently, PhD students in elite Indian institutions receive Rs 15,000 to Rs 20,000 as stipend per month plus a contingency grant plus other benefits like subsidized housing and medical care. Value of the financial aid package is comparable to what students receive in the world's major universities after purchasing power adjustment.
4. *Academic opportunities.* A comparison of the resources, facilities, and opportunities granted to doctoral students in elite Indian universities and institutes with those at the world's best programmes, typically located in the United States,[9] indicates that this is a major shortcoming. By contrast, PhD students in the finest universities get excellent academic opportunities—chance to be mentored by high-quality faculty, access to editors of major academic journals, opportunity to attend major research conferences, and so on. Such opportunities are largely absent in India.
5. *Creating academia.* This is the hardest problem—a multi-pronged attack in all the dimensions discussed in this entry and also in Chatterjea and Moulik (this volume) will be needed. A necessary condition would be attracting a highly research active faculty who would train PhDs in India. Practices like inbreeding (hiring of one's own students as faculty members), parochialism (hiring people who speak the same language, reside in the same state, belong to the same community, and so on), and nepotism (giving jobs to one's friends and relatives) must end.
6. *Institutional changes.* First, the current plan to give autonomy to elite Indian institutions, though attractive in many ways, is unlikely to improve them. Giving all authority to faculty is like a fox guarding the hen house; this is particularly problematic due to the academic weakness of the faculty in India. In the US, academics run academic functions of the university where they enjoy near-complete freedom. But, the overall functioning of the university is placed in the hands of a board of trustees where faculty members

[8]Didn't students come from faraway places to study under renowned masters at the great Buddhist universities of India of yesteryears?

[9]The 2010 ARWU rankings place 17 US universities among the world's top 20 universities. Academic opportunities granted to PhD students at the other three top 20 universities (Cambridge, Oxford, and Tokyo) are largely similar.

have scant representation. The board typically begins with benefactors of a new private (but non-profit) university, and government appointed as well as elected members at a public (government) university. Then, over time, it gets filled with alumni members who contribute to the university in various ways. Designing appropriate board structures is critical for the proper functioning of any organization—unfortunately, this concept is absent in government-run Indian academic institutions.

Second, there is a need for the right kind of persons who could manage the change. Harvard's Rosovsky advises using academics for running academic institutions (and, by an extension of the argument, running different aspects of higher education) because technical skills of an executive 'are trivialities compared to understanding the fundamental nature of the university. And this has to come from inside experience acquired by long hours in library, laboratory, and with students'.

Third, India needs to move away from the flawed model of building institutes and towards creating great multi-product research universities. In such universities, faculty members are subject to more extensive scrutiny, have to compete for resources from other academic areas, have opportunity to do interdisciplinary research, and so on, all of which are beneficial in the long run.

For this:

- The government can initiate a dialogue between billionaires in Bangalore and faculty members at Indian Institute of Science and explore how different faculties like arts and sciences, law school, undergraduate studies, and so on, can be added to make it a great multi-product research university.
- A similar approach may be taken with respect to the seven major IITs by initiating a dialogue between alums, faculty members, and wealthy Indians who would be potential donors. This would create something similar to the Ivy League in the US and prestigious (one time) imperial universities in Japan.
- With patronage from the house of Tatas, the Tata Institute of Fundamental Research may be developed into Tata University. This could be an example for Indian billionaires and other very wealthy people to emulate.

Once these institutions are established, they can be released from UGC's oversight and other governmental controls.[10] Perhaps then academia would be built in India and an academic marketplace would develop. Improved doctoral education would follow.

Arkadev Chatterjea

[10]Central and state governments can have one board member each to keep them abreast of the developments.

References

Bose, Satyendra Nath. 1964. 'The Problem of Education in Bengal and Asutosh', in Santimay Chatterjee et al. (eds), *S N Bose: The Man and His Work; Part II: Life, Lectures and Addresses, Miscellaneous Pieces,* Calcutta, S.N. Bose National Centre for Basic Sciences, 1994.

Bowen, William G. and Neil L. Rudenstine. 1992. *In Pursuit of the PhD*, Princeton, New Jersey, Princeton University Press.

Ehrenberg, Ronald G., Harriet Zuckerman, Jeffrey A. Groen, and Sharon M. Brucker. 2010. *Educating Scholars: Doctoral Education in the Humanities*, Princeton, New Jersey, Princeton University Press.

Feynman, Richard P., Ralph Leighton, and Edward Hutchings (eds). 1986. *'Surely You're Joking Mr. Feynman!' Adventures of a Curious Character*, New York, Bantam Books.

Ghatak, U.R., S.C. Mukherjee, A.K. Chaudhuri, S.B. Banerjee, S.N. Bhattacharya, S.P. Ghosh, and M.N. Bagchi. 1976. *Indian Association for the Cultivation of Science: A Century*, Kolkata, Indian Association for the Cultivation of Science.

The New Oxford Dictionary of English. 1998. New York, Oxford University Press.

Rhodes, Frank H.T. 2001. *The Creation of the Future*, Ithaca, New York, Cornell University Press.

Rosovsky, Henry. 1990. *The University: An Owner's Manual*, New York, W. W. Norton & Company.

Singh, Amrik. 2004. *Fifty Years of Higher Education in India: The Role of the University Grants Commission*, New Delhi, Sage Publications.

Dowries

For most Indian parents, the cost of a daughter's marriage is the single largest expense of their lives. In one rural sample the average cost of a daughter's marriage was six times the parents' annual income and, consequently, a cause of indebtedness and destitution (Rao 1993). This expense is often labelled 'dowry'.

The term 'dowry', however, has many different meanings. It is a gift made to cement bonds between two families—usually given in the form of jewellery or clothing. It is an investment to assist the newly-weds in setting up their home—in the form of durable goods or contributions towards a new business venture. It is a 'pre-mortem' bequest to a daughter—enabling her to obtain a *stridhan* that she would not customarily be entitled to on the death of her father. It is a symbolic expense used to celebrate the marriage in an appropriate manner. And it is a 'groom price'—a transfer made to the groom's parents as an inducement to agree to the marriage. The academic and popular discourses on dowries both tend to confuse these different meanings, but they have extremely different implications for marital incentives, household bargaining, and the status of women.

Dowry as 'Groom Price'

The last category of dowry as 'groom price' is of primary concern because several scholars have noted that groom prices in South Asia have risen over the last six decades, vastly exceeding general price inflation. It is for this reason that we have a 'dowry problem', and a host of related social problems such as discrimination against girl children and violence against women. Why dowries exist and why they have risen are among the most interesting questions in Indian social science, and have generated a large body of scholarship. There is little disagreement that there are some fundamental patriarchal conditions that lie at the root of the problem.

1. A woman's primary role is as a mother and daughter with limited options outside marriage.
2. A daughter who stays unmarried beyond a certain age and her parents face high social costs.
3. Divorce is practically non-existent.
4. Women are customarily denied inheritance rights.
5. Marriages are arranged between the parents of brides and grooms to largely reflect the interests of parents.

These conditons tell us why dowries might exist in the first place, but theories of why groom prices have risen have to focus on changes that may have taken place to reduce the relative worth of women in the marriage market. On this subject, economists have provided two major explanations, one demographic and the other status based.[1] The demographic explanation, originally proposed by demographer Jack Caldwell and developed by Rao (1993), lays the blame on population growth. A sharp decline in mortality, first noticed in the Indian subcontinent in the 1920s, resulted in increases in population growth because fertility did not decline at the same pace. High rates of population growth resulted in a pyramidical age structure—that is each year more babies were born than in the previous year so there were always more young people than older people. Since men typically marry women who are five to ten years younger than them, this means that there were always more women in the 'marriage market' than men, creating a 'marriage squeeze'. Counteracting this effect was the fact that in India there are more boys than girls of the *same age*—a consequence of the famous 'missing women' phenomenon. However, till very recently the 'marriage squeeze' overwhelmed the 'missing women' effect resulting in about 1.2 women for every man in the marriage market. This has been shown to be correlated with the rise in dowries (Rao 1993, 2000).

If women had options outside marriage, the marriage squeeze would have not led to an increase in dowries. Women who had better opportunities in the labour market or benefited from more favourable inheritance laws could choose to not get married or stay unmarried for a longer time. This would have reduced the demand for grooms and also the surplus supply of brides of marriageable age. The key issue, therefore, is not the effect of population growth alone, but its interaction with the patriarchal context prevalent in the Indian subcontinent.

An alternative explanation for the rise in dowries puts the blame on the drive towards social status. The original variant—proposed by sociologist M.N. Srinivas—argued that Brahmins had always paid dowries in their marriage rituals. Low-caste groups, in an attempt to acquire higher social status, started emulating Brahmins in a process he called 'Sanskritization', and started to pay dowries. This explanation has two problems. First, it falls into the common trap of confusing the various types of transactions that fall under dowry and there is little evidence that most Brahmins paid a groom price. Second, it does not seem plausible that Brahmin-emulation is any longer an important goal for lower castes.

Anderson (2003) has proposed a related but different theoretical explanation that focuses on the search for status in a developing economy. Considerations of caste-based status matter a great deal in India, along with economic motives, in driving marriage choices and marriages are almost always arranged within endogamous caste groups. To remove any marriage squeeze considerations, Anderson assumes that there are equal numbers of men and women in the marriage market. Potential brides would prefer, if possible, to marry higher-caste grooms because caste is patrilineally determined. Anderson argues that the development process makes incomes more unequal, even within caste groups, and high-caste brides would prefer rich high-caste grooms to poor ones. But prices paid for poor high-caste grooms will not fall below

[1] There is also a third, much earlier, explanation by Rajaraman (1983) which lays the blame on the relative increase in economic opportunities in favour of men over women in the labour market. While interesting, the claim is difficult to justify on empirical grounds.

a reserve price. This is because low-caste brides would be willing to pay a premium to marry high-caste grooms, even if they were poor. Since it would be unacceptable for a high-caste bride to marry a low-caste groom, this potential competition from low-caste brides would force high-caste brides to match their price. Thus the groom price that a low-caste bride would pay for a poor high-caste groom would provide a floor below which the price of high-caste grooms could not fall. However, development would produce more rich grooms who would command high dowries. Thus the average price of higher-caste grooms would rise. Since there is a large hierarchy of castes in India and most castes are ranked higher than some other caste, the average price of grooms would rise.

The marriage squeeze and status explanations for the rise in groom price are not incompatible because the marriage squeeze would simply exacerbate status competition. However, they have different prognoses for the future of groom prices. Population growth rates in India are declining sharply and at the same time the number of missing women is increasing with worsening population sex ratios. Cohorts born in this vastly different demographic regime will soon reach marriageable age, and this will cause a sharp reversal in the marriage squeeze. Therefore, if the marriage squeeze explanation for the rise in dowries is valid, this should cause groom prices to stop their rise and possibly even fall or turn into bride prices—men would pay women for the privilege of their hand. On the other hand, if groom prices are primarily driven by status competition, they will continue to rise with increased economic growth, unless there is a fundamental change in the relationship between caste and marriage.

Wedding Celebrations

Groom prices, as noted earlier, represent only one part of the burden at marriage, albeit a very important one. Wedding celebrations are getting increasingly lavish and their costs are now almost as large as groom prices, but the economics of wedding celebrations are rather different. This is because they are not a transfer from one family to another, but a symbolic expense that mainly serves a signalling function—rather like burning expensive firecrackers. What drives these large wedding celebrations? Bloch et al. (2004) ask this question in the context of poor families in rural Karnataka where marriage celebrations mimic urban patterns. Like Anderson, they argue that the primary motive is social status, but the mechanism driving it is rather different. Signalling has to serve the function of transmitting information. There is no point showing off if no one is watching. If wedding celebrations are a signal for social status then it must be the case that families that have newly acquired a higher social status should, everything else being equal, celebrate more lavish weddings if other people in the community are not aware of this higher status.

To test this hypothesis Bloch et al. (2004) utilize a natural experiment—the rules of village endogamy which assert that some families have to marry spouses from outside their home village, while others are required to marry spouses from the same village. If the spouse is from another village then the village will know less about him than if the spouse is from the same village. Thus a lavish celebration can communicate information. However, if a desire for social status is driving celebrations then it is only when the spouse is from a high-status family, *and* from an outside village, that it will be worth signalling via a lavish wedding celebration. What the data show is that marriage signals are at their most lavish, other things held constant, when the new spouse is rich and the kinship rule forces him/her to be from another village. By marrying a man from a rich family the bride's family has acquired a higher social status, and because the new in-laws are from another village the bride's home village would not be aware of this. Hence the result demonstrates that status signalling drives particularly lavish wedding celebrations.

Dowries and Domestic Violence

High dowries do not merely have an economic impact but can also raise the risk of domestic violence, as numerous newspaper articles on 'dowry violence' have outlined over the years. But the logic of this is unclear. Why would a man beat his wife in order to extract a higher dowry? Wouldn't this be self-destructive? Is domestic violence an entirely irrational act, or is it driven by an element of rationality? These questions are investigated by Bloch and Rao (2002) using a 'participatory econometric' approach of mixing anthropological and economic methods with data from rural Karnataka. The model they develop has the following logic. Since men and women cannot get divorced, the only way that a man can end the union is by committing an extreme act of violence—murder. The model assumes that there are two types of husbands—those who are capable of committing murder and those who are not. Since marriages are arranged, often with limited information, wives do not really know which type of husband they have married. There is a cost to violence in the form of legal and social sanctions, so a rational husband would weigh the costs and benefits of violence before beating his wife.

If the husband chooses to beat his wife, he is revealing to her that he is a violent type who is capable of resorting to murder. Thus violence is also a signal—communicating information about the type of husband and thereby instituting a 'regime of terror'. Given the possibility of this extreme threat, the wife's parents are then forced to acquiesce to the demands of a violent husband in order to prevent him from exercising the ultimate threat of murder. Husbands who are capable of violence weigh the costs and benefits of being violent, and will only beat their wives when the benefits of doing so—extracting resources from the wife's family—outweigh the costs of social and legal sanctions. The model, therefore, predicts that, other things being equal, wives who come with lower dowries are more likely to be beaten because husbands who received high dowries would be relatively more satisfied than those who received low dowries. It also predicts that husbands with richer in-laws would be more likely to beat their wives than those who have married women from poorer families, because violent husbands can extract more resources from rich in-laws than poor ones. Both predictions are borne out by the data.

The article by Bloch and Rao focuses on the economic rationality underlying dowry-based violence but, of course, there are many other, less economically rational, reasons why men beat their wives. Alcoholism, a desire to control behaviour, sexual infidelity, age, social norms and sanctions, the internalization of unequal power relations, all contribute to the risk of violence and have been the focus of a large body of research by social anthropologists and public health scholars (Karlekar 2003).

Given the importance of dowry as a social problem in India, the economics literature on it is rather small. There are many important questions that remain to be answered. What is the relationship between changing kinship structures and dowry payments? Who owns the dowry and do these patterns of ownership affect the risk of violence and the allocation of resources within the family? Is the reduction in the marriage squeeze having a significant impact on the size of groom prices? As caste-based marriage breaks down, will the size of the groom prices decrease? Furthermore, all the data that have been collected on dowries show that there are substantial exchanges made on both sides of the transaction. That is, gift exchanges are central to marriage transactions. What happens to marriages that have relatively smaller gift exchanges during the wedding? Who 'owns' these gifts and what proportion of them constitute a groom price? What are the implications of this for the status of women and for informal insurance?

One reason for the small economics literature on the subject is the relative unwillingness of economists to spend a substantial amount of time in the field collecting data that are not available in conventional surveys. While this is changing, if economists are to study important but understudied topics such as this, a more anthropologically informed approach to data collection would be required.

VIJAYENDRA RAO

References

Anderson, Siwan. 2003. 'Why Dowry Payments Declined with Modernization in Europe but Are Rising in India', *Journal of Political Economy*, 111(2): 269–310.

Bloch, Francis and Vijayendra Rao. 2002. 'Terror as a Bargaining Instrument: A Case Study of Dowry Violence in Rural India', *American Economic Review*, September, 92(4): 1029–43.

Bloch, Francis, Vijayendra Rao, and Sonalde Desai. 2004. 'Wedding Celebrations as Conspicuous Consumption', *Journal of Human Resources*, 39(3): 675–95.

Karlekar, Malavika. 2003. 'Domestic Violence', in Veena Das (ed.), *Oxford Companion to Sociology and Social Anthropology*, New Delhi, Oxford University Press.

Rajaraman, Indira. 1983. 'Economics of Brideprice and Dowry', *Economic and Political Weekly*, 18(8): 275–8.

Rao, Vijayendra. 1993. 'The Rising Price of Husbands: A Hedonic Analysis of Dowry Increases in Rural India', *The Journal of Political Economy*, August, 101(4): 666–77.

——. 2000. 'The Marriage Squeeze Interpretation of Dowry Inflation: Response', *Journal of Political Economy*, December, 108(6).

E

■ Education and Religious Minorities

Religious group affiliation is very clearly associated with different educational outcomes in contemporary India. The smaller minorities—Jains, Christians, Sikhs, and Buddhists—generally have more schooling and are more likely to be recorded as literate in the census than the majority Hindu population, but the indicators for Muslims are worse than those for Hindus as a whole. The generalized stereotype of Muslim Indians is that they are 'backward'; that their lack of educational achievements is their own 'fault'; that Muslims are committed to a conservative view of Islam; and that their religious beliefs lead them to turn to madrasahs instead. This entry considers how far such views accord with reality.[1] Using data from a small-scale study I will also explore how current policy changes are affecting educational experiences for Muslim and Hindu children in western Uttar Pradesh.

The 2001 Census results on literacy and religious-group affiliation are summarized in Table 1; holding sex and residence constant, Muslim literacy rates are below those of Hindus. National Sample Survey (NSS) data show similar patterns, with relatively small differences between male and female schooling achievements in rural areas, compared to urban areas. In general, however, the Muslims are catching up with the Hindu population, since the rate of change is fastest for Muslims, then for Hindus, and then Christians (NSSO 2002: 24, 26, 28). Similar data from the 1994 National Council for Applied Economic Research (NCAER) data set on human development in rural India suggest that Muslim households spend the least on education per student, at all income levels, followed by Hindu households, Christians, and finally other minorities (Tilak 2002: 24). These data also suggest that less might be spent on Muslim girls than on girls from other religious backgrounds, though this is not statistically significant (ibid.: 68). This finding is unexpected, since the differences between Muslim and Hindu female literacy rates are relatively small and noticeably smaller than those

Table 1 Literacy of Population Aged 7 and above by Religion, for Persons, Males, and Females, India, 2001

(per cent)

Religious group	Persons	Males	Females
Others	47.02	60.80	33.19
Muslims	59.13	67.56	50.09
Religion not stated	61.34	71.23	50.31
Hindus: of which	65.09	76.16	53.21
Scheduled castes	45.20	55.10	34.62
Other Hindu	71.32	82.74	59.06
Sikhs	69.45	75.23	63.09
Buddhists	72.66	83.13	61.69
Christians	80.25	84.37	76.19
Jains	94.08	97.41	90.58
All religions	64.84	75.26	53.67

Source: Census of India, 2001, Tabulations made available.
Note: The 'Other Hindus' are derived by subtracting scheduled castes (SCs) from 'Hindus'. Some SCs are non-Hindu, but this is unlikely to lead to significant errors.

[1]Another useful discussion of these issues can be found in Borooah and Iyer (2005).

for males, whether or not scheduled castes (SCs) are included in the 'Hindu' total.

Table 2 shows considerable variations across India in literacy for Hindu and Muslim women. Rural literacy rates for Hindu and Muslim women in Bihar are only about one-third of those in Kerala. In almost all urban areas, Muslim women are less likely to be literate than Hindu women (Tamil Nadu being the sole exception), but in seven states rural Muslim women are *more* likely to be literate than are rural Hindu women (Orissa, Gujarat, Maharashtra, Madhya Pradesh, Karnataka, Andhra Pradesh, and Tamil Nadu). Table 2 also brings out the extent to which, in rural areas, three states (Jammu and Kashmir, Assam, and Delhi) skew the overall results.

After the 2004 national elections, the Congress-led government made minorities, especially girls from minority groups, a focus for its educational concerns. Is there any point? What explains poor Muslim educational achievements? In part, Muslims invest less in boys' schooling because the returns are below those for other groups. In urban UP, for example, Muslim parents' motivation to acquire schooling for their children might be adversely affected by wage and job discrimination, though the data are not conclusive (Kingdon 1998: 49). If the beliefs and practices of the Muslim population, or

Table 2 Literacy of Females Aged 7 and above, by Religion and Residence, India and Major States, 2001

(per cent)

States	Urban Hindu	Urban Muslim	Urban Difference	Rural Hindu	Rural Muslim	Rural Difference
Jammu and Kashmir	77.4	52.4	25.0	52.0	29.7	22.3
Uttar Pradesh	67.9	47.3	20.6	37.7	31.6	6.1
West Bengal	78.3	59.2	19.1	55.7	47.9	7.8
Assam	82.6	65.6	17.0	56.9	38.4	18.5
Delhi	76.0	59.5	16.5	68.2	48.8	19.4
Rajasthan	66.3	50.4	15.9	37.2	31.2	6.0
India	73.9	63.2	10.7	45.7	42.7	3.0
Bihar	63.8	56.7	7.1	29.9	27.9	2.0
Orissa	73.1	66.3	6.8	46.9	59.6	–12.7
Gujarat	74.8	68.0	6.8	47.1	57.1	–10.0
Maharashtra	79.6	74.7	4.9	58.0	62.2	–4.2
Madhya Pradesh	70.2	65.9	4.3	42.3	49.5	–7.2
Karnataka	74.2	70.6	3.6	47.4	52.0	–4.6
Kerala	90.8	87.2	3.6	85.2	84.9	0.3
Andhra Pradesh	68.7	66.9	1.8	43.0	48.5	–5.5
Tamil Nadu	74.7	77.9	–3.2	53.8	71.8	–18.0

Source: Census of India, 2001; tabulations made available electronically.

their employment opportunities, are the major reasons behind the picture outlined here, then government policy might be fruitless; but if government policy (in how it is implemented or in how it is framed) is part of the problem, then change is essential.

Data from our study of Bijnor district can help answer some of these questions (Jeffery et al. 2006a; Jeffery et al. 2006b).[2] A 2001 database of primary schools shows that schools near Muslim villages, or with high proportions of Muslim pupils, had fewer teachers, higher pupil–teacher ratios, and worse facilities than other schools. When faced with choices about which new school proposals to accept, or which schools to invest in, officials put schools serving Muslims down the list. When teachers have a choice of schools to work in, they vote with their feet, avoiding Muslim-dominated schools if they can. One result of this 'everyday' communalism is to increase Muslim girls' disadvantage. General problems of girls' access to education are exacerbated for Muslims when there are few schools in Muslim-dominated villages or *muhallas* and women teachers (predominantly Hindu) are scarce, because parents hesitate to enrol their daughters.

Accessibility is, however, only the start. In most schools in UP—whether government, government-aided, or Hindu-dominated private ones—the vernacular non-elite forms of Hindi spoken by most poor villagers, Hindu and Muslim alike, are marginalized and denigrated by the dominance of Sanskritized Hindi. For Muslims, vocabulary and grammatical issues are compounded by those of script: Urdu facilitates children's access to Islam, but hinders access to the Hindi-based public sphere. Despite the constitutional guarantee of 'mother tongue' primary schooling for minorities, Urdu is marginalized in school curricula and, as a medium of instruction, is now largely restricted to madrasahs. Moreover, the formal and informal curricula in most UP schools (except the 'minority' institutions) presume that pupils are Hindu. Hindi literature courses contain narratives of Indian history and mythology in which Muslims are portrayed in a negative light. Hindu iconography and Sanskritized Hindi dominate daily assemblies and other functions. And teachers—not only those in Arya Samaj or Rashtriya Swayamsevak Sangh (RSS) schools—are often very unsympathetic to Muslim pupils and their concerns.

In sum, the education sector shows long-standing class, gender, and locational exclusionary biases that

[2]The research in Bijnor was carried out with Patricia Jeffery and Craig Jeffery and was funded by the Economic and Social Research Council in 2000–2 [Grant no. Rooo238495]; additional funding came from the Ford Foundation and the RGS/IGB: none of these bears any responsibility for the views expressed here.

are especially disadvantageous to Muslims. However strongly Muslim parents in UP want to provide for their children's education, most have inadequate opportunities and resources to do so. How do Muslim parents try to provide their children with education in such situations? The answer is not straightforward: urban and rural, rich and poor, girls and boys, and low- and high-caste Muslim children follow different trajectories.

In villages and in some poor urban neighbourhoods, Muslim children are increasingly attending madrasahs, but in varying ways. Sometimes madrasahs teach children outside official school hours, and children move between schools and madrasahs: some pupils attend madrasahs full-time. Often boys are outnumbered by girls in the lower classes, though some madrasahs are restricted to boys only. Increasingly, boarding madrasahs are springing up to provide higher Islamic education for girls. But madrasahs can go only some way towards addressing Muslim children's lack of access to formal education. Madrasah funding is erratic and unpredictable, most are poorly resourced, and this (rather than hostility from teachers or managers) explains why few madrasahs teach Hindi and other subjects. Most madrasahs charge no fees for teaching the Islamic curriculum, but they usually charge for 'secular' subjects—a serious deterrent for poor parents. Few madrasahs can contemplate 'modernizing' their curricula by introducing science and computing, purchasing teaching materials, or employing well-trained staff. Consequently, most madrasahs fail to equip Muslim children with the credentials and skills necessary in the local labour market. Muslim parents understand the costs of illiteracy: better, they say, a madrasah education than no education at all; better one that imparts Islamic values than one that marginalizes Muslims. Muslim parents' preference for madrasahs rests on their accessibility and low cost, their safe, user-friendly environment and conscientious teaching, as well as Islamic 'moral education'.

But madrasahs are only a part of the story of Muslim education in Bijnor. Some prominent Muslims simultaneously manage schools and madrasahs, and teachers in schools and madrasahs have similar educational philosophies and pedagogies. Most Muslim schoolchildren attend supposedly 'secular' schools. But most Muslim secondary schoolchildren do not follow an Islamic curriculum. In Bijnor town, schools established by Muslims teach the UP Hindi-medium curriculum, some offering Urdu as an optional subject, none teaching in Urdu. They recruit fair numbers of SC children—but very few pupils from other groups. Most urban Muslim children, however, go elsewhere, disproportionately to poorly funded government middle schools, leaving Muslim children under-represented in the better-funded, more expensive, competitive-entry government and aided intermediate colleges.

Muslim girls attend schools—especially single-sex institutions—in large numbers, but nearly three times as many Muslim boys as Muslim girls attend English-medium schools. Almost exactly the same number of Muslim boys and Muslim girls attend private Hindi-medium schools, but almost all the Muslim girls are in Muslim-run schools.

Middle-class Muslim boys, especially those in urban areas, are likely to continue in formal 'secular' education at least through secondary schooling. They might seem the most likely to integrate successfully into the Indian 'mainstream'—but they do not enter the labour market on completely equal terms with comparable Hindus. They face additional hurdles in accessing white-collar employment: they need 'pioneers' who can sponsor them, and Muslim kinship- and trust-based networks less often lead into such work, though they may help with obtaining comparable work in the Gulf states.

Poor Muslim parents rarely spend their scarce resources on educating their children in inadequate or failing schools: they know their children will not obtain credentials. These parents lack the social and financial resources to ease their children through a successful transition into employment. Their children rarely complete Class 5, let alone Classes 8, 10, or 12, and they will barely cope with the public sphere of newspapers, government offices, and so on. In most respects, Muslim boys leaving schools and those leaving local madrasahs are in very similar circumstances, and they usually move straight into work that does not depend on paper qualifications—for example, the occupations of their fathers (farming, small businesses, or artisanal positions), apprenticeships for craft skills, or work as unskilled labourers. Some boys follow existing migration chains to places such as Delhi, Surat, or Kashmir. Here, poor Muslims seem to operate at a relative advantage compared to equivalent Hindus in Bijnor.

The few who take advanced Islamic training in Bijnor madrasahs often compete for admission to one of the larger Islamic seminaries (in Deoband or Saharanpur), where higher training may lead to respected (though not lucrative) careers as maulwis or imams. Other graduates from these seminaries then gain alternative credentials, or enter family enterprises. In general, these seminaries offer a learned and genteel Muslim alternative identity to 'secular' options, thereby making a public statement of commitment to Islam, and an implicit critique of Westernization, consumerism, and modern India—perhaps this is why they provoke such hostility.

The hostility that madrasahs often face should not distract attention from the widespread and established processes of social and economic exclusion of Muslims, to which madrasahs themselves have been one response. Muslim parents enrol their children in schools, if they can afford to, if the schools are accessible and non-threatening for their children, and if there are realistic chances of schooling leading to good jobs. Muslim-friendly schools—in the right places, with sufficient facilities and committed staff, and with the worst excesses of saffronization removed—draw in Muslim children.

On 30 November 2006, the Justice Sachar Committee reported on the position of Muslims in India, and confirmed that Muslims in much of north India have lower levels of educational enrolment, largely as the result of state actions (or inaction). Segregation in school is growing, and non-state institutions are beyond the pockets of most north Indian Muslim parents. The Committee made a series of suggestions for reform. However, even if these proposals are all implemented, Muslim children will not immediately overcome the social and economic exclusion that perpetuates inequalities through the generations. Meanwhile, in the face of consumerism and with problematic access to employment, they are likely to be increasingly disaffected that the prizes of modernity and money elude them.

ROGER JEFFERY

References

Borooah, V.K. and S. Iyer. 2005. 'Vidya, Veda and Varna: The Influence of Religion and Caste on Education in Rural India', *Journal of Development Studies* 41(8): 1369–1404.

Jeffery, P.M., R. Jeffery, and C. Jeffrey. 2006a. 'Investing in the Future: Education in the Social and Cultural Reproduction of North Indian Muslims', in M. Hasan (ed.), *The Future of Muslims in India*, New Delhi, Manohar.

———. 2006b. 'Patterns and Discourses of the Privatisation of Secondary Schooling in Bijnor, UP', in K. Kumar and J. Oesterheld (eds), *Education in South Asia*, New Delhi, Orient Longman.

Kingdon, G. 1998. 'Education of Females in India: Determinants and Economic Consequences: A Case-study of Urban Uttar available at Pradesh', available at http://www.economics.ox.ac.uk/Members/geeta.kingdon/Discussion Papers/min amarareport98.pdf, accessed on 21 November 2005.

National Sample Survey Organisation (NSSO). 2002. *Employment and Unemployment Situation among Religious Groups in India, 1999–2000*, New Delhi, NSSO Report No. 468.

Tilak, J.B.G. 2002. 'Determinants of Household Expenditure on Education in Rural India', New Delhi, NCAER Working Paper 88.

Elections and Political Business Cycles

What determines the economic policies of a government? While traditional economics textbooks answer this question from alternative perspectives, it is always assumed that the government is the equivalent of a benevolent social planner, interested in maximizing the representative citizen's welfare. In contrast, the recent literature in political economics argues that policymakers are typically politicians and, frequent protestations notwithstanding, benevolence is not an accurate summary of politicians' motives. Therefore, economic policies that are undertaken reflect both the *intrinsic desires* of politicians (I shall discuss what these might be) and the *institutional constraints* under which policies are formulated. At times, this political economics approach permits us to rationalize regularities in the real world data that would otherwise remain inscrutable.

Consider democratic polities wherein periodic elections determine the fate of incumbent governments. Substantial anecdotal and econometric evidence suggests that such polities are witness to the following data pattern: certain economic variables (for example, tax revenues collected, public expenditures incurred, money growth, and unemployment rate) experience systematic dips or spurts around election time. In other words, elections *independently induce* movements in these economic variables. I shall refer to each such causal connection as a *political business cycle*. This entry deals with the phenomenon of political business cycles and is built around three themes. First, I describe two models that furnish theoretical arguments for why such cycles crop up at all. The theoretical literature on this topic is both vast and expanding; the models that I discuss are amongst the most influential in this genre. Second, I survey and interpret the empirical literature on political business cycles in India. Third, I suggest avenues for further research using Indian data.

Models of the Political Business Cycle

Any model of the political business cycle must begin by specifying the motives of its central actors, that is, the politicians. One class of models maintains that politicians are *partisan* or ideological: they simply implement their favoured policies once in office. I shall not discuss partisan political business cycles since most political parties in

India are impossible to place on a conventional left–right scale. Instead, the two models that I outline below assume that politicians are *opportunistic* or self-interested: they care about being in office per se and implement policies to further that goal.

In a seminal contribution, Nordhaus (1975) considered a polity in which elections are held at fixed intervals. During an election, the votes received by the incumbent government are presumed to depend on its economic performance in the recent past. The performance measure, in turn, is posited to be a decreasing function of the inflation and unemployment rates. How does an incumbent government behave? When an election is imminent, the economy is stimulated (that is, unemployment rate lowered) by sudden injections of money. The post-election rise in inflation rate is controlled by engineering a recession in response! Notice that the political business cycle generated by Nordhaus turns on a crucial, but controversial, assumption. Evaluations of the incumbent government during election time should surely depend on what it can deliver in the future. Why, then, is voting based on past performance instead?

Rogoff and Sibert (1988) demonstrate that election-year policy manipulations (namely, tax revenue declines and spikes in public expenditure) can occur even when voters are fully rational. Since I shall refer repeatedly to this paper, it is useful to sketch the story involved. An incumbent government provides certain fixed services to citizens. To pay for these services, revenues must be raised through any combination of non-distortionary taxes (that voters observe immediately) and distortionary taxes (that voters observe with a lag). Now, in terms of administrative capability, the incumbent government can be either competent or incompetent. To provide the given services, a competent government naturally requires less tax revenues in total than an incompetent government. Suppose the incumbent government is actually competent. In an election year, it convinces the initially ill-informed electorate of its competency by lowering the level of visible non-distortionary tax revenues. Why do voters believe that such revenue decreases are proof of government competency? The rough idea is that it is difficult for an incompetent government to both balance the budget and provide the observed revenue cuts. The argument for election-year increases in public expenditures, omitted for brevity, is identical in spirit to that for the tax revenues case.

Interestingly, the approach of Rogoff and Sibert (1988) can be extended to predict election-induced alterations in the composition of public spending. Suppose an incumbent government is allowed to incur expenditures of two sorts: public consumption and public investment. Since voters likely observe the effects of public investment with a lag, the incumbent government establishes its competency by shifting expenditures in favour of consumption and against investment.

Empirical Evidence from India

Does empirical evidence from India comport with the theories outlined above? Chaudhuri and Dasgupta (2006) and Khemani (2004) examine the fourteen major states of India over, respectively, 21 and 33 financial years and ask the following question: does the proximity of a state legislative assembly (that is, Vidhan Sabha) election temper the fiscal policy choices of state governments? Before presenting their findings, a methodological point needs to be made. Vidhan Sabha election dates are of course somewhat flexible. The Constitution of India mandates that a state legislative assembly have a normal term of five years from the date appointed for its first sitting. However, *mid-term* (that is, early) elections are a regular feature of the political history of Indian states. State governments, for example, may, and frequently do, voluntarily petition the governor of a state to hold mid-term elections. Rather than considering ways of dealing with mid-term election years, the aforementioned papers instead distinguish between *scheduled* election years and all other years.

There is *clear* evidence that politics matters. First, consider the tax revenue raised by state governments. Commodity tax revenues, the most important component of state governments' own tax revenue, are lowered around the time of scheduled elections. Khemani (2004) probes this finding further by examining the three most significant sources of commodity tax revenues: state sales taxes on items of mass consumption, state excise duties (levied on producers of alcoholic beverages and products containing alcohol or opium), and producer taxes on inter-state trade of goods. Surprisingly, electoral cycles crop up only in the latter two categories! Note, therefore, that scheduled elections are not associated with broad-based tax reductions; rather, tax breaks are given to a small set of producers. Second, consider the current account expenditure of state governments. Despite containing a large public-consumption component, the evidence *suggests* that such expenditures are actually lowered during scheduled election years! What drives this result? State governments' current account expenditures are of three types: developmental spending, non-developmental spending, and grants to local bodies and Panchayati Raj institutions. Chaudhuri and Dasgupta (2006) show that the electoral cycle in current account expenditure is based on electoral cycles in one component of non-developmental spending (namely, outlays on fiscal and administrative services) and grants to local bodies and Panchayati Raj institutions. In other words, during a scheduled election year, the incumbent government does not tinker with explicit subsidies or wages to public-sector employees (these are items in the developmental spending category); rather, current account expenditures are pruned at the expense of local bodies and by organizing the functioning of government at a lower cost. Third, consider the capital account expenditure of state governments. This mainly entails the discharge of internal debt, the repayment of loans to the central government, and the provision of loans for assorted purposes. However, a proportion of capital account expenditure (namely, developmental spending) is devoted to the creation of physical assets. During scheduled election years, total capital account expenditure as well as its developmental component experience a slight increase.

How does one *interpret* the evidence? Khemani (2004) dismisses the relevance of the Rogoff–Sibert electoral cycles models. Instead, she argues that the election-year tax breaks given to specific producers and the rise in public investment spending point to a story wherein narrow interest groups are favoured in exchange for campaign support. Perhaps so, but more evidence is surely required to buttress these claims! Consider, for example, the documented shift in public spending in favour of investment and against consumption. It may be that the type of investment taking place around election time is of the most visible variety. If so, investment cycles can be rationalized by the Rogoff–Sibert theories, the essence of which distinguishes between immediately observed and partially unobserved forms of public spending. Summing up, researchers have yet to conclusively identify the economic mechanism(s) responsible for election-year policy changes in the states of India.

Are there electoral cycles in central governments' economic policies in India? For a review of the literature addressing this question, the reader is referred to Chaudhuri and Dasgupta (2005). Here, I highlight the main findings. First, there is no evidence that aggregate central tax revenue is responsive to the timing of national legislative assembly (that is Lok Sabha) elections. On the other hand, revenues from the central excise tax are significantly lower when Lok Sabha elections loom large. Recall that election-induced tinkering with *certain* tax revenue components is what state governments in India do as well! Second, there is some evidence *suggesting* that Lok Sabha elections alter the composition of public spending in favour of consumption and against investment. Chaudhuri and Dasgupta (2005) examine three public infrastructure variables: per capita schools (primary and secondary), kilometres per capita of highways, and kilometres per capita of railway tracks. It turns out that the construction of schools and highways declines around election time. On the other hand, while the evidence for electoral cycles in broad components of current account expenditure is weak, prominent cycles show up in certain highly visible components of current account spending (namely, the per capita fertilizer subsidy and the per capita amount of food grains that are publicly distributed through fair-price shops or as part of the Food-for-Work Programme). Third, the growth rate of real money supply and the central bank's discount rate do not change during Lok Sabha election years. Hence Nordhaus's (1975) prediction that governments use monetary policy to manufacture economic booms in election years is refuted by the data. A caveat is in order here: the findings that I have reported should be viewed with caution. This is because data sets used to study central government behaviour in India have barely fifty annual observations and less than a dozen Lok Sabha election years. Naturally, the degrees-of-freedom problem limits the extent to which econometric concerns are addressed.

Further Research Questions

The empirical evidence from India shows that governments manipulate economic policy variables during election years. On the other hand, I have argued that identifying the mechanism(s) driving the results is, at best, difficult: there are simply too many internally consistent stories that can account for the observed data patterns. Given this, it may be worthwhile to test for the predictive validity of the *entire* class of political business cycle models.

Consider, for example, the following amendment to the politico-economic models of government behaviour. Since policy manipulation, whatever be the underlying model, is likely to be costly (for example, there may be loss of reputation), the extent of government manoeuvring will depend on the value of the marginal vote. Thus safe elections should not witness policy distortions. Indian state-level data provide an ideal testing ground for this idea. The electoral history of India neatly divides into two distinct phases: a pre-1967 period during which state legislative assembly elections were dominated by the Congress party, and a post-1967 era that beheld lively inter-party competition for assembly seats. Electoral cycles in economic policies, which are sometimes present in the post-1967 data, *should* disappear completely during the years of Congress party hegemony.

Finally, let me point out a curious lacuna in all of the empirical papers dealing with political business cycles in India: while governments' pre-electoral behaviour is extensively studied, voting patterns are left unexamined. But a government tinkers with economic policies before an election precisely because electoral fortunes are viewed as being contingent on these variables. Hence it is critical to ask the following question: Does the Indian electorate condition its vote, at least at the margin, on economic policies? I mention two recent papers that address *related* questions. Using a comprehensive data set consisting of all candidates contesting the 2009 Lok Sabha elections, Gupta and Panagariya (2010) demonstrate that economic growth at the state level significantly enhances the victory prospects of candidates contesting on the ticket of the party in power in the state. Cole et al. (2008) analyse Vidhan Sabha election data over a 23 year period. The authors show that voters punish the incumbent ruling party in the state for adverse but exogenous weather events. Importantly, the degree of punishment depends on the responsiveness of the ruling party: those distributing greater amounts of disaster relief suffer smaller subsequent electoral losses. More research on voter behaviour (for example, whether governments' fiscal and monetary policies impact election returns) is clearly warranted.

SUGATO DASGUPTA

References

Chaudhuri, K. and S. Dasgupta. 2005. 'The Political Determinants of Central Governments' Economic Policies in India: An Empirical Investigation', *Journal of International Development*, 17(7): 1–22.

——. 2006. 'The Political Determinants of Fiscal Policies in the States of India: An Empirical Investigation', *Journal of Development Studies*, 42(4): 640–61.

Cole, S., A. Healy, and E. Werker. 2008. 'Do Voters Appreciate Responsive Governments? Evidence from Indian Disaster Relief', Harvard Business School and Loyola Marymount University, Mimeo.

Gupta, P. and A. Panagariya. 2010. 'India: Election Outcomes and Economic Performance', ICRIER and Columbia University, Mimeo.

Khemani, S. 2004. 'Political Cycles in a Developing Economy: Effect of Elections in the Indian States', *Journal of Development Economics*, 73(1): 125–54.

Nordhaus, W. 1975. 'The Political Business Cycle', *Review of Economic Studies*, 42(2): 169–90.

Rogoff, K. and A. Sibert. 1988. 'Elections and Macroeconomic Policy Cycles', *Review of Economic Studies*, 55(1): 1–16.

Employment

Why Employment?

Expert evaluation of national economic performance tends to leave the common man cold. To argue about data on the growth rate or foreign exchange reserves or the Sensex is all very well, but such data scarcely address the economic concerns of the masses directly, and may be not indirectly either. As a result, there could be contradictions that are somewhat cruel for many. It may happen that the country's net national product (NNP) per capita, that is, its average income per head, is accelerating and at the same time unemployment is rising. If such is the case, can we really say that the economy is doing better? It is hard to deny that in a straightforward sense an aggregate employment index will better reflect the condition of the average Indian than does NNP per capita. Employment generation is central to the pursuit of inclusive growth.

What's Been Happening?

The years since 1992 have been the best years for India as far as NNP growth is concerned. This is evident from the data provided by the annual *Economic Survey* of the Government of India. For 2002–7, real NNP at factor cost grew at 7.8 per cent and per capita NNP grew at 6.1 per cent. This is certainly an improvement over that obstinate 3.5 per cent 'Hindu rate of growth' that dogged our fortunes right up to the end of the 1970s and led to per capita income growing at hardly 1.5 per cent. There is no doubt that in terms of raw growth, India is doing much better now than ever before.

And yet, though growth has been high on the quantity index, there have been doubts about its quality. Concern that growth has not been 'inclusive' and has not 'trickled down' have become quite widespread. A major reason for this is that the improved growth performance has not been accompanied by sufficient employment generation. The high output growth of the 1990s was accompanied by a sharp fall in employment growth. Using National Sample Survey (NSS) data, while for 1983 to 1993–4, employment grew at 2.72 per cent per annum, the corresponding figure for 1993–4 to 1999–2000 was only 1.02. This sharp drop in employment growth led to an *increase* in unemployment from 20 million in 1993–4 to nearly 27 million in 1999–2000. The deceleration in employment was especially sharp in the rural sector. During 1993–4 to 1999–2000, employment in the agricultural sector grew at an insignificant 0.01 per cent compared to the comfortable 2.59 per cent over the period 1983–4 to 1993–4. The policy response to this has been the Mahatma Gandhi National Rural Employment Guarantee Scheme of 2005.

In 1999–2000 to 2004–5 employment growth did pick up, with the growth rate for the rural sector rising to 1.97 per cent and that for the urban sector rising to 3.22 per cent per annum. However, the latest figures on employment are less encouraging. If one considers the entire period from 1999–2000 right up to 2007–8, figures for employment growth turn out to be lower, being 1.27 per cent for the rural sector and 2.64 for the urban sector respectively. Clearly the rate of growth of employment has fallen during 2004–5 to 2007–8, despite the fact that GDP, or gross output, grew at more than 9 per cent per annum. More telling is the finding that unemployment was higher in 2007–8 as compared to 1993–4 as data from successive rounds of surveys carried out by the National Sample Survey Office (NSSO) show.

Features of Unemployment

India has been a late industrializer, and still has miles to go. The share of organized manufacturing in the total labour force has been roughly constant for the last 40 years. In comparison to Thailand and Indonesia, India had a larger proportion of the workforce engaged in the organized manufacturing sector in 1970. However, by 1995, in Thailand the ratio was three times more and in Indonesia 2.3 times more. India remains predominantly rural and overpopulated. Despite 50 years of development policies, a majority of Indians—more than 60 per cent—are still sustained by agriculture and allied activities. At the same time, the labour absorption capacity of the agricultural sector has long since been exhausted. This is not the same thing as output stagnation; improvements in infrastructure and technology can be expected to boost output growth in agriculture. However, it is not exactly clear that such changes, unless they are land extending, will lead to significant increases in rural employment.

That being the case, the problem of rural unemployment in India is a problem of inadequate demand for unskilled labour in non-rural activities. At the same time contemporary growth is being driven by the growth of the service sector, which typically requires *skilled* labour and has no place for surplus rural labour. The *potential* for absorption of unskilled labour should be quite high in the organized manufacturing industry. However, though employment in the organized manufacturing sector grew at 7.5 per cent per annum between 2003–4 and 2008–9, as data from the Central Statistical Organisation (CSO) and the Annual Survey of Industries show, this has not been sufficient to reduce rural unemployment.

The increase in employment in the organized sector at the national level is not the result of a shift to labour-intensive activities but a result of the flexibility of enforcing labour laws in some Indian states. Inter-state data suggest that increases in organized employment are linked to the extent of labour reforms undertaken.

The other development on the employment front is the increase in casual employment, as opposed to regular employment, and an increase in the size of the informal or unregistered sector. Growing employer preference for casual employment and contract labour in the face of labour market rigidities is plain.

Employment and Irreversibility

The ostensible reason for the slowdown in organized manufacturing employment in some states, such as West Bengal, Delhi, Jharkhand, and Kerala, may appear to be comparatively low profitability. This, in turn, may have something to do with the perception of investors that labour productivity in organized manufacturing is low.

But low profitability may not be *the* reason. A somewhat more subtle reason is irreversibility as the following argument shows. Market demand is volatile and market preferences are fluid, especially in global markets. Moreover, technological change has speeded up the rate of obsolescence under compulsions of creative destruction. To grab the best opportunities, investors need to move quickly, exiting one industry and entering another. However, the industry-wise composition of the organized workforce is not that malleable. Actually, employment in the organized manufacturing sector is largely *irreversible* in the absence of labour reforms. Giving employment is a bit like buying specialized equipment for which there is no second-hand market, but with one important difference: while equipment can be abandoned, it is much more difficult to desert the workforce. That is what creates exit barriers. Given such barriers, investors would not like to get stuck with a workforce which they may like to trim down later. Hence, even if it is profitable by current calculations to increase employment, uncertainties of future demand, cost, and innovations may induce new capital to seek other more malleable pastures. The problem of exit inhibits entry. This explains why states such as Uttarakhand and Himachal Pradesh that adopted flexible practices with respect to enforcing labour laws were also successful in achieving very high rates of growth in organized sector employment.

This argument simultaneously offers one possible explanation for the observed increase in casual labour and growth of the informal sector in recent times. As for rapid growth of the skill-intensive services sector, the problem of irreversibility is less serious since skilled labour in the private sector is not that organized. It is less difficult to trim down skilled labour than it is to trim down unskilled labour. The exception to this rule is of course the highly organized skilled and semi-skilled manpower in the extended government sector.

One reason frequently cited for fall in employment growth in the organized sector during the 1990s is curtailment of recruitment in the public sector and in public administration. Such stringency is part of the reforms agenda and is sought to reduce the government's fiscal deficit. Policymakers no longer regard employment in the government sector as producing useful social products. Such employment is now seen as causing a net drain on financial resources. This is in contrast to the planning agenda of earlier periods. What went wrong with the earlier policy stance on employment?

Employment per se, Government, and Keynes

Employment generation cannot be left to the care of the market. For private producers, employment is simply a side-effect; labour is useful only to the extent that it generates marketable output and profits. Despite theoretical assertions to the contrary, the profit motive has turned out to be grossly negligent in addressing problems of unemployment, inequality, and poverty. Employment is a social good. It is valuable not merely because it produces consumable output for the market and profits for an enterprise but because it generates purchasing power for the poor and removes the stigma that goes with being unemployed. In view of the market's failure to generate full employment, the government cannot simply sit back. It has to intervene in employment creation. The obvious action plan is for the government to directly create more jobs.

The government sector itself, including the public sector and public institutions, would seem to be the first arena for job creation given the objective of *employment for the sake of employment*. Policymakers may have become wary of creating jobs in the government sector now but this was not always the case. The economically difficult period of the late 1960s gave rise to the feeling that the Five Year Plans had become politically costly as they were not producing results fast enough; hence policy prerogatives shifted from long-term development to quick measures of poverty removal (*Garibi Hatao*). Employment in the government sector, public administration, and public sector was expanded not because of the compulsions of increased market demand, but because employment created income and helped meet livelihood requirements. This policy of employment for employment's sake continued through the 1980s.

The emphasis on the income-creating role of employment that this policy stance embodies is central to short-run macroeconomics and dates from John Maynard Keynes' powerful 1930s work. In Keynesian theory, unemployment is the result of inadequate market demand for final goods; it calls for a policy of active state intervention that stimulates demand. There is an interesting question of causation here. While it stands to reason that more employment will lead to more demand, Keynes and his followers were stressing the fact that more employment requires more demand *in the first place*. The Keynesian proposal was to focus on employment generation *for its own sake*—digging holes and filling them up—to kick-start the process. Once some initial demand is created, the production response to it creates income. That stimulates further demand and sets off a chain reaction that snowballs into what has come to be known as the *multiplier process*. The beauty of the multiplier argument is that it may not require state intervention on a massive scale, calling for gigantic budgets. The eventual increase in aggregate expenditure is many times the initial spurt and the government need only give the starting push. According to textbook calculations, in a country with a saving ratio of 25 per cent, the ultimate increase in demand is predicted to be 400 per cent the initial impetus.

To what extent can this argument be applied to unemployment in India? First, demand-led solutions to unemployment may not work if there are other bottlenecks to increasing production. This could be the case in the agricultural sector. Second, to have a significant impact, additional incomes in the multiplier chain must be directed to goods which intensively use unskilled labour and where existing units of production are not plagued by pre-existing underemployment of such labour. If that is not the case, additional demand will not create additional incomes or employment, but simply lead to better utilization of the workforce already on the payrolls. At this stage the multiplier process will come to a halt.

There is a more fundamental problem with the Keynesian proposal. This has to do not with the chain reaction but with the starting point itself. It is one thing to argue that employment is good in its own right and employment is just about the most desirable of policy objectives. It is quite another to claim that it does not matter *what* is produced and whether there is demand for that output. It will be argued here that deliberate employment creation with no regard to demand and productivity conditions can actually hurt the cause of aggregate employment. What is good for an individual job seeker can be severely detrimental to an entire generation of job seekers.

What's Wrong with Job Creation?

If the policy is to create employment for its own sake, it is easiest to do this in the government sector. The objection to deliberate job creation in the government sector is that this tends to engender adverse productivity effects that spread far and wide. Once the profit motive is jettisoned and meeting consumer demand is not a compulsion, it becomes hard to define accountability and productivity norms. In the absence of these norms, one can hardly have a system of rewards and incentives. It is no wonder that in the government sector promotions are based not on performance but on seniority, and the compensation for modest salary scales is job security.

The problem with having a larger than necessary workforce is that the productivity consequences of this have a habit of spilling over. Attitudes to work tend to spread like epidemics. The advantage that I personally enjoy—of having a salary but not enough work to do—tends to generate negative 'neighbourhood effects' on the productivity of *others* who *do* have work to do. The malaise spreads out in concentric circles like an epidemic and plays havoc with the work environment of an entire region. The effect of the epidemic is devastating for new investment in the era of global capital mobility. Investors have a choice. Capital stays away from the labour-wise less malleable organized sector. As a consequence there is an *overall* cut-back in existing and potential employment. The potential jobs that are lost vastly outnumber those that are forcibly created in the short run.

The Policy Dilemma

There is no doubt that a sincere policymaker will be trapped in a dilemma. Ironically, the low-productivity epidemic—which is bad for employment—is the result of *commitment* to reduce unemployment; it is a result of trying to do good. Because such an attitude will be seen as a virtue, it can hardly be an obvious target to attack. Moreover, trying to denigrate an attitude *because* it is socially committed, is likely to cause outrage among responsible citizens. This is what makes the epidemic so hard to tackle.

AMITAVA BOSE

References

Keynes, J.M. 1936. *The General Theory of Employment, Interest and Money*, London, Macmillan.

Ministry of Finance. 2011. *Economic Survey 2010–11*, New Delhi, Government of India.

National Sample Survey Office. *Employment and Unemployment Survey*, various rounds, New Delhi, Ministry of Statistics and Programme Evaluation.

■ Employment Guarantee Scheme

In the semi-arid region to which Maharashtra belongs, agriculture is a highly seasonal activity. During the lean periods, large sections of rural households eke out a bare subsistence through short spells of mostly unremunerative employment. Motivated by this concern, V.C. Page launched the Employment Guarantee Scheme (EGS) experimentally in 1965. It was subsequently expanded as part of an integrated rural development project, culminating in the EGS Act (No. XX of 1978), and its implementation in Maharashtra in 1979. From a modest beginning, EGS expanded rapidly into the most important poverty alleviation programme in Maharashtra.

Inspired by EGS, Food-for-Work (FFW) programmes were introduced in the 1970s, mainly to mitigate the distress resulting from natural calamities, such as droughts, floods, and earthquakes. These are a special case of rural public works (RPW), such as the Jawahar Rozgar Yojana (JRY), as they are tied to the provision of food. In 2001, FFW became a component of the Employment Assurance Scheme (EAS) in some states. Soon after, motivated by considerations of cost-effectiveness, EAS, Jawahar Gram Samrudhi Yojana (JGSY—a redesigned version of the JRY), and FFW were merged into the Sampoorna Grameen Rozgar Yojana (SGRY). But this new version continued to be referred to as FFW. The performance of FFW programmes ranged from unsatisfactory to dismal.

As EGS was hailed as the most innovative anti-poverty intervention in the developing world, it is reviewed in this entry. In particular, careful attention is accorded to some distortions that crept into EGS over time and the lessons that follow for designing and implementing an employment guarantee scheme at the national level. This is followed by a selective review of its successor, the National Rural Employment Guarantee Scheme (NREGS).

Salient Features

The scheme guaranteed that every adult who wanted a job in rural areas will be given one, preferably within a radius of 8 km, provided that the person was willing to do unskilled manual work on piece-rate basis. Failure to provide work within 15 days entitled the person to an unemployment allowance. Self-selection of the poor was built into EGS. No choice of work was offered. Until 1988, the wage rate was usually below the agricultural wage rate. The projects were selected on the basis of their labour intensity (that is, the ratio of labour costs to other costs must be 51:49) and their productiveness (that is, whether they contribute to production directly or indirectly). Most EGS activity was concentrated in agricultural slack periods.

Recent Developments

Over the 1980–97 period, there was a sharp decline in EGS participation—the person days of employment fell from 20.55 crore to 9.01 crore. The expenditure also fell—from Rs 30.17 crore to Rs 24.66 crore (at constant prices). Although participation fluctuated, following the EGS wage hike in 1988, there was a sharp reduction in 1989. Between 1987 and 1989, there was a reduction in person days of employment of over 5.50 crores, with a large part due to rationing (Gaiha 1997a). The brunt of the reduction was borne by the poor (Gaiha 1997a). Soon after there was a gradual rise in EGS participation until 1993, followed by a steady decline in subsequent years.

Over the 1991–6 period, the composition of EGS expenditure also changed. The share of (usual) EGS projects fell slightly from 74 per cent to about 70 per cent; that of the Shram Shaktidware Gram Vikas (SSGV)—village development through labour—halved from about 12 per cent to about 6 per cent; while that of Jawahar Wells rose sharply from over 13 per cent to about 23 per cent. These compositional changes weakened the poverty-reducing effect of EGS. Replacement of community assets with individual assets diverted the benefits of EGS away from the poorest landless households to the moderately poor or relatively affluent landowning ones (Gaiha 2005).

Benefits

In principle, EGS conferred transfer and stabilization benefits. The transfer benefits can be direct—gross earnings of participants less any cost they incur in participating, or indirect—including the share of the poor in the extra income generated by the scheme's output, and any other second round effects from other income sources (for example, higher agricultural wage rates). The stabilization benefits arise mainly from the scheme's effect on the risk faced by the poor of a decrease in consumption.

While detailed estimates of these benefits are not available, some pieces of illustrative evidence, based mainly on the International Crops Research Institute for the Semi-Arid Tropics (ICRISAT) panel survey and a survey designed and implemented by the author in two villages in Ahmadnagar district, are now cited.

1. *Transfer Benefits*: Targeting accuracy is closely linked to transfer benefits. The share of the poor among EGS participants closely followed their corresponding share in the labour force in both 1979 and 1989. In fact, the former turned out to be lower than the latter in both years (over 48 per cent as against about 54 per cent in 1979, and over 27 per cent as against over 29 per cent in 1989), implying that the participation of the poor in EGS was slightly less than their participation in the labour force. Had EGS been well targeted, a significantly higher participation of the poor would have been observed. Although relative to their participation in the labour force there was no deterioration in the targeting of EGS during 1979–89, the fact that the share of the non-poor among EGS participants increased from about 52 to over 70 per cent suggests that there was marked deterioration in targeting over this period (Gaiha 1997a). Evidence from two extremely poor villages in Ahmadnagar in 1999–2000 is, however, more favourable. About half of the EGS participants were extremely poor. Moreover, the (net) direct transfer benefit was as much as 60 per cent of EGS earnings among the poorest.

   Much of the evidence on the benefits from EGS assets is sparse and dated. A detailed survey carried out by the Planning Commission in 1977 revealed that a large share of the benefits from EGS assets accrued to large landowners (Gaiha 1997a). A similar finding is obtained from a review of EGS assets in Ahmadnagar (Gaiha 2005).

   Another significant indirect transfer benefit is the effect of EGS on agricultural wage rates. Specifically, if EGS wages increase by a rupee, agricultural wages would rise by about 17 paise in the short term and by about 28 paise in the long term (Gaiha 1997b). The mechanisms through which EGS influenced agricultural wages include: (i) gains in agricultural productivity through EGS assets (for example, percolation tanks); and (ii) a higher reservation wage as a consequence of a 'guaranteed' employment option in slack periods.
2. *Stabilization Benefits*: Comparisons of income variability with and without EGS in the ICRISAT sample confirm the income-stabilizing role of this scheme. This effect is captured more vividly in the

Ahmadnagar sample. Without EGS, the prospects of making ends meet for a majority of the participants were grim. Failure to secure employment of any kind involved cuts in food expenditure, liquidation of assets, and loans at exorbitant rates of interest. The stabilizing role of EGS through income and consumption smoothing is thus a significant one (Gaiha 2005).

3. *Promotional and Protective Roles*: The protective and promotional roles of EGS are distinct—the first focuses on whether the vulnerable were prevented from falling into poverty, and the second on whether the poor were enabled to move out of poverty. Simulations with the ICRISAT panel data show that these effects are significant when substantially larger EGS outlays are combined with maximum participation of the poorest (Gaiha and Imai 2002). There are three important implications: (i) the proposed nationwide scheme must be confined to the most backward regions; (ii) a (relatively) low wage must be maintained to attract the poorest; and (iii) the scheme should operate only during seasonal slacks.

(Dis)Incentives

There is often a presumption that public support (for example, guaranteed employment) discourages job search and makes the poor dependent on it. Evidence based on ICRISAT, however, does not corroborate this. Many of the poor withdrew from EGS when farm and non-farm employment opportunities expanded. As a result, a sizeable section became better-off (Gaiha 1996). Another related finding is that switches into EGS are positively linked to the EGS/agricultural wage ratio (Scandizzo et al. 2009). This further reinforces the case for lowering the EGS wage.

National Rural Employment Guarantee Scheme

As an extension of EGS, the National Rural Employment Guarantee Act (NREGA) of 2005 is the most significant social policy initiative in India in the last decade.[1] Its main objective is to enhance the 'livelihood security of people in rural areas by guaranteeing hundred days of wage employment in a financial year to a rural household whose adult members volunteer to do unskilled manual work', at the minimum wage, on demand, within 15 days of asking for employment (Ministry of Rural Development). Some of its unique features include a time-bound employment guarantee and wage payment, prohibition of private contractors and machinery, and a mandatory 33 per cent participation of women. The programme was rolled out in stages, starting with the 200 poorest districts in the first stage followed by another 130 districts in 2007–8, and it now covers the entire country. In 2010–11, the scheme's budget was Rs 4.01 trillion (Shankar et al. 2011).

Based on household surveys in three Indian states (Rajasthan, Maharashtra, and Andhra Pradesh) in 2007–8, the targeting accuracy was unsatisfactory or dismal. Rajasthan was the best performer, as half the participants there were poor. In Andhra Pradesh and Maharashtra, however, 70 and 72 per cent respectively, were non-poor. A weakening of the self-selection mechanism through high NREGS wages relative to agricultural wages was a key contributory factor. Another contributory factor was limited awareness of the benefits of this scheme. Individuals from households that belonged to social networks (self-help groups, credit and cooperative groups, or trade unions) were more likely to participate in NREGS, as well as those who lived in villages with high attendance in public meetings (for example, gram sabha or village assembly meetings) (Shankar et al. 2011).

Using BMI (weight in kilograms/[height in metres]^2) as a nutritional criterion, individuals in the Rajasthan sample (2009–10) were classified into underweight, normal, and overweight. Cross-classifying them into acutely poor, moderately poor, moderately non-poor, and affluent, the proportion of underweight fell while that of normal increased across these groups.

Over 81 per cent of the male participants and about 71 per cent of the female participants in NREGS were normal while most of the remaining were underweight. In a piece-rate system, the earnings are likely to be much higher for normal participants even if the days worked do not vary much, mainly because rewards for physical dexterity and stamina are greater. To the extent that acutely poor overlap with the underweight, as they do, their prospects of climbing out of poverty are bleak (Jha et al. 2011a).

As a common fallacy in assessing benefits to the participants is equating them to their earnings from NREGS, net transfer benefits (NREGS earnings – opportunity cost of time or wages from alternative employment in the absence of NREGS) were computed.[2] An analysis with household data in Andhra Pradesh, Rajasthan, and Maharashtra further confirms varying but

[1]It was subsequently renamed the Mahatma Gandhi National Rural Employment Guarantee Scheme by the Government of India through a notification on 31 December 2009.

[2]For a succinct exposition, see Basu (2008).

generally low benefits to the poor. Maharashtra had the lowest share of net transfer benefit in NREGS earnings for the poor (about 7.5 per cent), followed by Rajasthan (about 10 per cent), and then Andhra Pradesh with the highest share (about 17 per cent). The underlying reasons (for example, limited awareness, rampant corruption, and work-sites scattered over long distances) raise concerns amenable to policy intervention. While corruption takes many different forms (low fractions of wages paid because of collusion between village councils and bank officials), evidence shows the considerable potential of participation in village assembly meetings in curbing this (Jha et al. 2011b; Shankar et al. 2011).

Current debates on wage hikes seem misplaced, especially when the benefits to the poor and undernourished are so small. Legislating higher wages risks greater distortions. Careful attention to enhancing awareness about some components of NREGS (for example, wage payments), proper maintenance of muster rolls, and social audits may do more to transform the lives of the poor than misguided social activism.

RAGHAV GAIHA

References

Basu, K. 2008. 'Not Much of a Guarantee', *The Times of India*, 19 December.

Gaiha, R. 1996. 'How Dependent are the Rural Poor on the Employment Guarantee Scheme in India?', *Journal of Development Studies*, 32(5): 669–94.

———. 1997a. 'Rural Public Works and the Poor: The Case of the Employment Guarantee Scheme in India', in S. Polacheck (ed.), *Research in Labour Economics*, Vol. 16, Connecticut, JAI Press.

———. 1997b. 'Do Rural Public Works Influence Agricultural Wages? The Case of the Employment Guarantee Scheme in India', *Oxford Development Studies*, 25(3): 301–14.

———. 2005. 'Does the Employment Guarantee Scheme Benefit the Rural Poor in India? Some Recent Evidence', *Asian Survey*, 45(6): 949–69.

Gaiha, R. and K. Imai. 2002. 'Rural Public Works and Poverty Alleviation—The Case of the Employment Guarantee Scheme in Maharashtra', *International Review of Applied Economics*, 16(2): 131–51.

Jha, R., R. Gaiha, and M. Pandey. 2011a. 'Body Mass Index, Participation, Duration and Earnings under NREGS: Evidence from Rajasthan', ASARC Working Paper 2011/06, Canberra, Australian National University.

———. 2011b. 'Net Transfer Benefits under India's Rural Employment Guarantee Scheme', forthcoming in *Journal of Policy Modelling*.

Ministry of Rural Development. Available at http://www.nrega.nic.in/-netnrega/home.aspx, accessed on 1 February 2010.

Scandizzo, P., R. Gaiha, and K. Imai. 2009. 'Option Values, Switches and Wages—An Analysis of the Employment Guarantee Scheme in India', *Review of Development Economics*, 13(2): 248–63.

Shankar, S., R. Gaiha, and R. Jha. 2011. 'Information, Access and Tageting: The National Rural Employment Guarantee Scheme in India', *Oxford Development Studies*, 39(1): 69–95.

■ Employment and Poverty

India has the dubious distinction of having the largest share of the world's poor. According to Ravallion and Chen (2007), in 2004, 969 million people lived under $1 a day while the corresponding figure for $2 a day was 2.5 billion. In India 371 million lived under $1 day and 868 million lived under $2 a day. Taking the $2 a day poverty line, India had 80.36 percentage of its own population living under the poverty line while the corresponding figure for China was 35 per cent. In most OECD (Organisation for Economic Co-operation and Development) countries, the percentage of population living under the poverty line of $2 a day is essentially zero. No matter what we say about the arbitrariness of the poverty measure, by international standards much of India's population is poor. Being a populous country, India is also home to a vast percentage of the world's poor.

Most of the debates about the extent of India's poverty have in fact used a much lower poverty line of Rs 328 per month or little over Rs 10 a day. Henceforth, in this entry, the term 'poor' refers to those under this lower poverty line. In 2004–5, 28.7 per cent of the rural population and 25.9 per cent of the urban population was living under poverty, with the corresponding all-India figure being 27.9 per cent (Himanshu 2007).

At this level of poverty, an individual is caught in a vicious cycle from which escape is very difficult. Poverty results in malnutrition and low levels of education. In turn, the lack of physical strength and education lowers the chances of employment with reasonable remuneration. What makes this problem worse is that the poor have more children. Given that the poor have little access to sound healthcare, infant mortality rates are high among them. They overcompensate and end up having large families with more mouths to feed. Poverty thus begets poverty.

Who are the poor? According to the 61st round of the National Sample Survey (NSS), in 2004–5, agricultural labourers and self-cultivating farmers constituted 42 and 27 per cent of the rural poor respectively. Thus, the poor eke out a living as unskilled labourers and marginal farmers.[1]

It is also important to realize that urban poverty is nothing but rural poverty spilled into cities. The urban ghettos are made up of rural migrants looking for work in the informal sector in cities. If the rural economy prospers, the flow of migration to cities will slow down and wages in the informal sector in cities will increase, reducing urban poverty. Also, the wages of unskilled workers in the non-farm sector, whether in informal trade and retail or some other employment, are related to agricultural wages because agriculture is the residual employment sector. In other words, you cannot lure someone away from agriculture unless you pay him at least what he can get in agriculture. It is, therefore, not surprising that agricultural wages exhibit a strong negative correlation with poverty. Thus, in order to understand why India has such extreme poverty we have to understand why agricultural wages are so low in the country.

How are agricultural wages determined? Of course, there are many instances of exploitation of labour in some pockets of India where employment relations are feudal (for example, the indentured labour system in certain tribal areas). Yet, in most of rural India, labour markets do respond to the changing conditions of demand and supply. Though these markets are far from being perfect, the prevailing wages have a strong positive relationship with the wages that competitive markets would set. The demand and supply factors that would make market wages go up and down would have similar effects on the observed wages. Therefore, it is fruitful to understand how different demand and supply factors affect market wages.

An employer is willing to hire an extra worker provided he or she contributes a value that exceeds the wage. Thus, the contribution of the marginal worker is a good approximation of the wage. On a given plot of land, if you add more and more workers, each will contribute marginally less and thus the wages will increase with productivity and with the land-to-labour ratio. Areas with high agricultural productivity and high land-to-labour ratios (for example, Punjab and Haryana) have higher wages and vice versa (for example, Bihar and Orissa). Productivity is determined by technology—the seeds, irrigation, fertilizers, and so on. Land-to-labour ratio is determined by the size of the agricultural labour force that the land has to support. Areas with high population density, that is, areas that have experienced high rates of population growth for a long time, will have low land-to-labour ratios and hence low wages. Also, if the economy is characterized by well-developed manufacturing and service sectors so that there is significant employment outside agriculture, then correspondingly there is less labour in agriculture and hence wages are high. This is the key link between employment patterns and poverty.

If we scan the sectoral composition of labour across countries we find that developed countries with high wages are typically also those which have a very small percentage of labour force in agriculture. For example, even land-abundant countries like the US, Canada, and Australia have less then 5 per cent of their labour working in agriculture. In contrast, poor countries like Afghanistan, Nepal, and Niger have more then 70 per cent of their labour force in agriculture. Clearly, countries that have drawn labour away from agriculture into other sectors are the ones that have managed to raise the wages of their labour. What is true across countries is true of different states in India; in 2004–5, 49 per cent of India's male labour force was in agriculture. In Punjab and Bihar, it was about 38 and 64 per cent, respectively (Eswaran et al. 2009).

Two centuries ago, most economies were largely agrarian, with a significant part of their populations engaged in activities closely related to agriculture. What brought about the transformation that shifted their labour forces to industry and services? A self-contained or a closed economy (that is, not trading with other economies) produces to meet the demands generated by its own population. To some extent, our demands are biologically determined. For example, at low levels of income, our top priority is to first satisfy our basic needs like food and shelter. Thus, at low levels of productivity most of our labour will go into producing food. In terms of whole economies, at low levels of productivity a significant part of the labour force is engaged in agriculture. As the agricultural productivity increases, people whose food needs are satisfied start demanding other things and this can lead to the expansion of the non-farm sector. Wages first increase in response to a rise in agricultural productivity and subsequently due to employment opportunities in other sectors (thus causing an increase in the land-to-labour ratio). Agricultural productivity increase is thus a key to wage growth.[2]

However, this is not the only way that wages can increase. If an economy trades with other areas it has the option of moving a significant part of its labour force to non-farm activities (for example, industry) and importing its food needs in exchange for its industrial exports. Agricultural wages can increase due to an increase in

[1]The figures in this paragraph are from Eswaran et al. (2009).

[2]This paragraph is entirely based on the theory presented in Eswaran and Kotwal (1994).

the land-to-labour ratio that is brought about without any accompanying increase in agricultural productivity. Instead, its ability to export industrial products (that is, its comparative advantage in industrial production) can come about as a result of an increase in its industrial productivity. Thus, for a trading economy, an increase in industrial productivity can also bring about an increase in agricultural wages and thereby a decrease in poverty. East Asia's success in reducing poverty has to a large extent been based on this process. China had 75 per cent of its labour force in agriculture in 1982; in 2000 it had only 47 per cent. Poverty fell from 53 to 8 per cent during the same period (Ravallion and Chen 2004).

It is also possible that an increase in industrial or service productivity makes industrial goods and services cheaper and thus helps shift expenditures away from agricultural goods. A demand shift will be followed by a supply shift, thus causing the agricultural labour force to shrink and the wages to rise. The possibilities of such substitution between food and non-agricultural consumption are, however, quite limited.

Over the last two decades, the Indian economy has grown at a fast rate of over 6 per cent per year. Much has been written about its software and biotech sectors. India and China are discussed in the foreign press as posing a real challenge to the long-held Western advantage in industrial technology. It is interesting to ask whether the fast growth and success in certain sectors have had a significant impact on India's poverty.

The answer lies in the changes in employment patters across sectors over the time period in question. Eswaran et al. (2009) examine how the employment patterns changed from 1983 to 2004. It is remarkable how little the percentage of labour force in agriculture changed over these years of fast growth. At the national level, it went down from 59.6 per cent to 48.6 per cent for males and from 74.4 per cent to 68.1 per cent for females. The absolute size of the agricultural labour force was in fact greater in 2004 than in 1983 despite a decline in its percentage share of the total labour force. Thus, the land-to-labour ratio in Indian agriculture (in all states except four) was in fact smaller in 2004 than in 1983. If agricultural productivity had not increased during this time, the wages would actually have declined, increasing the number below the poverty line. However, agricultural wages increased in real terms by about 68 per cent during these 21 years and poverty declined. But how much of the credit for this can be given to productivity growth in the non-farm sectors (that is, industry and services) is an interesting question. Indeed, if no increase in non-farm employment had taken place during this period, the increase in labour force would have ended up in agriculture thereby lowering the land-to-labour ratio and hence the wages significantly. That this did not happen has to be credited to the creation of non-farm employment. However, what caused the increase in non-farm employment is an open question.

It is interesting to note that the only sectors whose share in the total labour force grew are three service sectors: trade, transportation, and construction. The share of manufacturing remained unchanged at around 12 per cent (Eswaran et al. 2009). This picture is very different from what happened in East Asia. The service sectors where employment growth took place in India are mostly non-traded services for domestic consumption. It is likely that those who experienced income growth increased their demand for some of these services, which in turn increased the demand for labour in these sectors. Software engineers in Bangalore and managers in Gurgaon spent their income gains on travel, restaurants, and construction of houses. A small component of these additional expenditures filtered down to the unskilled poor who are employed in these activities. The extent to which this process reduced the labour force that would otherwise be dependent on agricultural employment was the extent of 'trickle down' to the poor from the income growth of the elite. In India today, the low levels of employment created during the present growth episode indicate that the trickle down has been very small. The onus for reducing poverty in India is still very much on improving agricultural productivity.

ASHOK KOTWAL

References

Eswaran, M. and A. Kotwal. 1994. *Why Poverty Persists in India*, New Delhi, Oxford University Press.

Eswaran, M., A. Kotwal, B. Ramaswami, and W. Wadhwa. 2009. 'Sectoral Labour Flows and Agricultural Wages in India, 1983–2004: Has Growth Trickled Down?', *Economic and Political Weekly*, January, 44(2): 46–55.

Himanshu. 2007. 'Recent Trends in Poverty and Inequality: Some Preliminary Results', *Economic and Political Weekly*, February, 42(6): 497–508.

Ravallion, M. and S. Chen. 2004. 'Learning from Success: Understanding China's (Uneven) Progress against Poverty', *Finance and Development*, December, 41(4): 16–19.

——. 2007. 'Absolute Poverty Measures for the Developing World, 1981–2004', World Bank Policy Research Working Paper No. 4211, April.

■ Employment Trends

Employment has featured as an important priority in the development agenda in India. Approaches to it have, however, varied in different periods over the more than 50 years of Independence. In the initial years of development planning, unemployment was not expected to emerge as a major problem; yet some thought was given to ensure the generation of employment of a fair magnitude in the development process to productively employ the growing labour force. A reasonably high rate of economic growth combined with an emphasis on labour-intensive sectors like small-scale industry was envisaged to achieve this goal. The rate and structure of growth rather than technology were seen as the instruments of employment generation. Thus while granting that in 'an economy with relative abundance of labour, a bias in favour of comparatively labour-intensive techniques is both natural and desirable', it was clearly recognized that 'considerations of size and technology should not be set aside to emphasise employment' (Planning Commission 1956: 112–13). Unemployment was estimated to be relatively low, as also the growth rate of the labour force, and a targeted economic growth rate of 5 per cent with some emphasis on labour-intensive consumer goods sectors was expected to generate enough employment over the years to prevent any increase in unemployment.

These assumptions and expectations continued from one Five Year Plan to the next during the 1950s and 1960s. Meanwhile the magnitude and rate of unemployment increased significantly. The economy grew at a rate of around 3.5 per cent as against the planned rate of 5 per cent per annum. Yet employment grew at a relatively high rate of 2 per cent per annum. However, since labour force growth was much higher at 2.5 per cent as against the less than 2 per cent per annum envisaged, the result was an increase in unemployment. The magnitude of unemployment had almost doubled during 1956–72, from around 5 to 10 million, and the unemployment rate from 2.6 to 3.8 per cent (Papola 1992). These figures are, however, only approximations as detailed data on employment and unemployment started becoming available from the National Sample Survey Organisation (NSSO) through its quinquennial surveys starting with 1972–3. They, nevertheless, do indicate overall trends during the first two decades of planned development in India.

With the availability of comprehensive data on levels of consumption, employment, and unemployment for 1972–3 which revealed a high incidence of poverty (54 per cent rural and 41 per cent urban) and high unemployment rates (8.4 per cent on current daily status [CDS] and 4.3 per cent on currently weekly status [CWS] basis), the official approach to the employment problem underwent a change in the mid-1970s. The Fifth Five Year Plan (1974–9) sought to address the employment issue by reorienting the pattern of growth in favour of employment-intensive sectors. At the same time, a strong view was emerging to suggest that growth alone cannot solve the problems of poverty and unemployment and, therefore, a number of special employment and poverty alleviation programmes were launched. They were mostly of two kinds: providing financial and other assistance for productive self-employment, and offering supplementary wage employment to the underemployed. Over the years, these programmes have been continued in one form or another with modifications or integrations, or new ones have been started while some old ones have been discontinued. The latest in the series is the National Rural Employment Guarantee Programme which aims at legally guaranteeing employment of up to 100 days annually to every rural household, under an Act of Parliament.

While these programmes seem to have been able to reduce the degree of underemployment to a certain extent, the open unemployment rates have not declined over the years. This can be discerned from unemployment rates on CDS basis, which includes both open and under employment and on CWS and usual principal status (UPS) bases given in Table 1. During the period 1993–4 to 1999–2000, however, unemployment rates, including those based on CDS, have increased.

Table 1 Unemployment Rates (% of labour force)

Year	UPS	UPSS	CWS	CDS
1972–3	3.80	1.61	4.32	8.35
1977–8	4.23	2.47	4.48	8.18
1983	2.77	1.90	4.51	8.28
1987–8	3.77	2.62	4.80	6.09
1993–4	2.56	1.90	3.63	6.03
1999–2000	2.81	2.23	4.41	7.32

Notes: UPS: Usual Principal Status. A person is considered unemployed according to this concept if available for but without work for major part of the year.
UPSS: Usual Principal and Subsidiary Status includes, besides UPS, those available but unable to find work on a subsidiary basis, during a year.
CWS: Current Weekly Status. A person is unemployed if available for but unable to find work for even one hour during the reference week.
CDS: Current Daily Status measures unemployment in terms of person-days of unemployment of all persons in the labour force during the reference week.

Looking at different rates of unemployment, it is clear that underemployment is a problem of much larger magnitude than open unemployment. For example, in 1999–2000, the UPS unemployment rate was estimated to be only 2.81 per cent as compared to a CDS rate of 7.32 per cent. The problem, however, is not confined to these time-criterion-based rates; a large part of the employed people work at very low levels of income, as indicated by a much higher incidence of poverty (26 per cent in 1999–2000) than of unemployment. Thus the employment challenge in India consists not only of creating jobs for the unemployed, and providing additional work to the underemployed, but, to a much larger extent, of enhancing productivity and income levels of a large mass of the 'working poor'.

It is against this background that this entry presents an account of the trends in employment during the period 1973–2000 for which data are available from the quinquennial surveys of the NSSO. Besides the slow growth rates of employment and its deceleration with higher economic growth in recent years, there are several other disquieting features of the Indian employment scene that are also covered briefly. They include a slow change in employment structure by sectors of economic activity, predominance of self-employment and increase in the share of the casual category of workers, predominance of the unorganized sector and stagnation and decline in organized-sector employment, and the issue of quality of employment which seems to have undergone a deterioration, in general, in recent years. The entry finally ventures to assess the prospects of employment growth and its qualitative aspects in the medium term.

Table 2 Employment Growth, 1972–3 to 1990–2000 (% per annum)

Sector	1972–3 to 1977–8	1977–8 to 1983	1983 to 1987–8	1987–8 to 1993–4	1993–4 to 1999–2000
Agriculture	2.32	1.20	0.04	2.39	0.06
Mining	4.68	5.85	6.16	2.09	–3.27
Manufacturing	5.10	3.75	2.10	1.45	2.05
Construction	1.59	7.45	13.59	–1.10	6.61
Elasticity, gas, water supply	12.23	5.07	4.64	3.39	–5.25
Transport	4.85	6.35	2.67	3.58	5.28
Trade	3.71	4.12	4.42	3.20	6.20
Services	3.67	4.69	3.92	3.76	0.55
Total	2.82	2.22	1.55	2.37	1.02

Note: Growth rates are on UPSS basis, which defines a person as employed if carrying out economic activity on main or subsidiary basis during a year.

Employment Growth

As noted earlier, employment growth has been over 2 per cent for almost 30 years since the early 1950s. In fact, it is recorded to be much higher during the 1970s. But since the 1980s there has been a declining trend in the growth rate of employment.

As Table 2 shows, the growth rate of employment declined continuously from one quinquennium to the next except for the period 1987–8 to 1993–4. Higher growth during the 1987–8 to 1993–4 period seems primarily to have been contributed by agriculture which has otherwise experienced a generally low and rapidly declining employment growth. Among other major sectors, manufacturing has also experienced a declining trend in employment growth, but construction, trade, and transport have had fluctuating trends and have recorded relatively high employment growth even during 1994–2000 when overall employment growth has been the lowest. In fact, the non-agricultural sectors together have registered a relatively high employment growth of 2.69 per cent during the 1994–2000 period, but because of a low growth of 0.06 per cent in agriculture, which had a weight of 60 per cent in total employment, the aggregate employment growth works out to be only 1.02 per cent. Construction, trade, and transport recorded employment growth rates of 6.61, 6.20, and 5.58 per cent, respectively, and manufacturing 2.05 per cent during 1994–2000.

What is particularly intriguing is the fact that while employment growth was reasonably high at around 2 per cent with a GDP growth rate of just around 3.5 per cent during the earlier decades, with GDP growth at over 6 per cent, employment growth has been much lower since the 1980s, particularly during the period 1994–2000. It must, however, be clarified that with the large weight of agriculture, overall employment growth has been mainly influenced by employment growth in that sector. Thus, even though employment growth in construction, trade, transport, and manufacturing has improved, aggregate employment growth has significantly declined during 1994–2000 as compared to 1988–94 due to a steep fall in employment growth rate in agriculture (and to a certain extent a decline in the growth rate of employment in community, social, and personal services). Slowdown in employment growth in agriculture has been a result both of a low GDP growth and a decline in employment elasticity (ratio of employment growth to GDP growth).

Employment content of growth as measured by employment elasticity has been declining over the entire period since 1972–3, but has seen a particularly sharp decline during 1994–2000 (Table 3). Manufacturing, on

Table 3 Employment Elasticities in Major Sectors, 1972–3 to 1999–2000

	1972–3 to 1977–8	1977–8 to 1983	1983 to 1987–8	1987–8 to 1993–4	1993–4 to 1999–2000
Agriculture	0.64	0.49	0.36	0.50	0.02
Mining	0.95	0.67	0.85	0.33	–0.63
Manufacturing	0.55	0.42	0.40	0.25	0.28
Construction	0.35	1.00	1.00	–1.10	1.00
Elasticity, gas, water supply	1.0	0.74	0.48	0.63	–0.76
Transport	0.76	0.92	0.45	0.64	0.56
Trade	0.78	0.75	0.70	0.58	0.68
Services	0.80	0.99	0.42	0.51	–0.06
All	0.61	0.55	0.38	0.41	0.15

the other hand, had a reasonably high elasticity to begin with, but has shown a continuous decline with slight increase during 1994–2000. Construction, transport, and trade have maintained relatively high elasticities, and have even shown an increase during 1994–2000 when aggregate elasticity is estimated to have sharply declined. Elasticity in other services has continuously declined over the years but the decline has been very sharp during the last quinquennium. It may be noted that the non-agricultural sectors on average have shown an employment elasticity of 0.35, as against 0.02 in agriculture and 0.15 in aggregate.

Employment Structure

With differential growth of employment among different sectors of the economy, there have obviously been changes in the structure of employment. Among the three major sectors by broad division of economic activity, namely, agriculture, industry, and services, there has been a decline, as expected, in the share of agriculture and increase in the share of industry and services in total employment. The structural changes have, however, been slow. In a period of 27 years, from 1973 to 2000, the share of agriculture has declined by 17 percentage points only from 74 to 57 per cent. The share of industry has increased from 11 to 18 per cent and that of services has risen faster from 15 per cent in 1972–3 to 26 per cent in 1999–2000, growing particularly fast during 1987–8 to 1999–2000 (Table 4).

The slow change in employment structure assumes the nature of a problem particularly when seen along with the change in the structure of the national gross domestic product. During the period when the share of employment in agriculture declined from 74 per cent to 57 per cent, its contribution in GDP declined from over 40 per cent to

Table 4 Employment Shares of Major Sectors, 1972–3 to 1999–2000 (per cent)

	1972–3	1977–8	1983	1987–8	1993–4	1999–2000
Agriculture	74.0	72.3	68.4	65.5	60.38	56.70
Industry	11.4	12.3	13.7	15.5	15.82	17.56
Services	14.6	15.4	17.5	18.4	23.80	25.74

22 per cent; and while the share of the services sector in employment increased from 15 to 26 per cent, its contribution to GDP increased much faster from around 30 per cent to 52 per cent. As a result the asymmetry between the income and employment shares among different sectors has sharply increased, particularly between the agricultural and non-agricultural sectors. A sharper decline in the contribution of agriculture in GDP than in its share in employment implies a decline in its relative productivity and increase in income differentials between agriculture and the non-agricultural sectors. An opposite trend is seen in services, where the increase in GDP share has been faster than in employment, while industry has retained its position in respect of relative productivity. That there would be a decline in the share of agriculture in GDP was expected, but a continuance of the heavy dependence of workers and population on agriculture as a source of income and livelihood is a matter of concern from the viewpoints of poverty and inequality. One hopes that a relatively higher employment growth in manufacturing, construction, transport, and services like trade, as experienced in recent years, will lead to some correction in this increasing imbalance.

Increasing Casualization

Another aspect of employment trends and structure that is of interest in a developmental context is the distribution of workers by employment category as self-employed, regular wage, and salaried workers, and casual wage earners. It has been generally expected that with shift of workers from agriculture to non-agricultural activities and from footloose to enterprise-based employment, there will be an increase in the proportion of workers employed on a regular wage and salary basis. As Table 5 shows, there has been a decline, albeit slow, in the share of the self-employed, from 61 per cent in 1972–3 to 53 per cent in 1999–2000. The share of regular wage-salaried workers has, however, stagnated at around 14 per cent, while that of casual workers has increased from 23 to 33 per cent.

This situation has generally been interpreted to mean an increasing 'casualization' of workforce. Insofar as the term describes an increase in the share of casual workers,

Table 5 Employment Status by Category of Employment, 1972–3 to 1999–2000

	1972–3	1977–8	1983	1987–8	1993–4	1999–2000
Self-employed	61.4	58.9	57.4	56.0	54.8	52.9
Regular wage/ salaried workers	15.3	13.9	13.9	14.4	13.2	13.9
Casual wage workers	23.3	27.2	28.7	29.6	32.0	33.2

it is factually true. But if it is meant to imply a process of 'regular' workers turning 'casual', or a decline in employment and earnings, the trend needs to be carefully analysed. The shift is seen from the self-employed to casual workers category and most of it has taken place in rural areas, from agriculture to non-agricultural activities such as construction, trade, and services. There has, no doubt, been displacement of workers from large industries in urban areas, reducing regular workers to the status of casual workers. But the magnitude of such change has not been very significant in relation to the total numbers involved.

The phenomenon of casualization, therefore, needs to be seen in the overall perspective of employment trends in the economy. Agriculture is increasingly unable to productively absorb the growing rural labour force. At the same time, there has been some growth of non-agricultural activities in rural areas in construction, trade, and services which have generally offered better earnings than agriculture. Most of these employment opportunities have been of temporary and casual nature. But they have provided either full-time or supplementary employment, adding to the incomes of rural households. On the other hand, regular jobs have hardly increased in urban areas; in fact, there is evidence to show that such jobs have declined due to redundancy caused by technological and competitive compulsions in the larger industrial enterprises. So part of the regular workforce has been rendered casual and most new jobs have been in the casual category.

The increasing proportion of casual workers in total employment is thus mostly a result of structural shifts taking place in rural areas. To some extent, it is distress-driven, small and marginal landholders and the landless not finding gainful work in agriculture and taking up whatever work they find in the non-agricultural activities, irrespective of earnings. But there is evidence to suggest that many are opting for non-farm work due to more regular employment and better earnings. This has been possible partly on account of various state-sponsored employment programmes, and partly because of an increase in the demand for labour in expanding construction, trade, and service activities in rural areas. In other words, 'casualization' of the nature observed does not necessarily imply a deterioration in the quality of employment. A small part of the real casualization that has taken place due to displacement of regular workers from large enterprise in urban areas, no doubt, indicates such a deterioration.

Slow growth of employment in the organized sector has been a major factor in stagnancy in the proportion of regular wage and salary earners. This sector consisting of public services and enterprises and large private firms is the one that offers regular jobs. Employment growth in this sector has been just about 0.5 per cent during 1994–2000. In the post-2000 period, organized-sector employment has, in fact, shown an absolute decline—declining by about 1 million from around 28 million to 27 million during 2000–3 (GoI 2005a). Of around 21 million new employment opportunities generated during 1994–2000, only about 4 per cent have been in the organized sector and the remaining 96 per cent in the unorganized sector (Planning Commission 2002). As a result, the share of the unorganized sector in total employment has increased from around 92 per cent to 93 per cent. The high and increasing preponderance of the unorganized sector has been a matter of anxiety from the viewpoint of quality of employment as workers in this sector suffer from poor conditions of work, low earnings, and lack of employment and social security.

Employment Prospects

What are the prospects for growth and quality of employment in India in the near future? The fact that a high economic growth rate has not been able to generate high employment growth, and it has, in fact, been accompanied by a slowdown in employment growth in recent years, has led many economists and others concerned to describe the recent experience as one of 'jobless growth'. A brief look at the performance of different sectors as attempted earlier, however, shows that but for the almost negligible employment growth in agriculture, growth in the non-agricultural sector has not really been jobless. Yet employment elasticities have declined in most sectors, though in some sectors like construction, trade, and transport, they continue to be relatively high (Table 5). And a faster growth of these sectors will lead to an increase in overall employment growth. Their share in employment, however, is still small as compared to manufacturing which has shown a relatively low employment growth and low and declining employment elasticity. Yet manufacturing still has an employment elasticity of around 0.3 and there are indications to suggest that it may improve. For example, its export-oriented sub-sectors have recently experienced higher employment growth and employment elasticity. During the 1990s, employment in export-oriented industries grew at 3.36 per cent per annum and showed an employment elasticity of 0.48 (Goldar 2003). A faster growth of manufactured exports, which now constitute over 75 per cent of total exports, as compared to 58 per cent in 1980, therefore, promises to be an important factor in reversing the declining trend in employment growth.

Employment growth is a function of growth of GDP and employment elasticity. The Indian economy has sustained a relatively high growth of over 6 per cent for about two decades and is expected to grow at that, if not a higher, rate in the coming years. There are indications towards a reversal of the declining trend in employment elasticities, particularly in manufacturing, and expectations of a growth structure in which sectors with higher employment elasticity will grow faster. Thus overall employment elasticity is likely to increase from the low of 0.15 experienced during 1994–2000. There is, therefore, a strong likelihood of the growth rate of employment getting restored to over 2 per cent during the first decade of this century. In fact, the evidence from the limited sample survey of the NSSO suggests a reversal of the trend already during 2000–4 when employment growth is estimated to be around 2.70 per cent. This, however, is still to be validated by the results of the larger sample survey (GoI 2005b).

The recent experience, however, suggests that most of the new employment opportunities are likely to be generated in the unorganized sector and will be characterized by poor conditions of work and lack of employment and social security. Even within the organized sector an increasing number of workers are being employed in a 'flexible' manner on casual or contract basis, without the social security benefits available to regular workers. Also, the problem of the 'working poor', namely, of those fully engaged in work but earning less than poverty-line income, will persist. Thus the challenge of quality of work, in terms of earnings and social security, will continue. Tightening of the labour market with increase in the demand for labour may lead to improved earnings over time, but a vast majority of workers will continue to have no social protection against the risks of work-related hazards, unemployment, sickness, maternity, and old age. A measure of security against these risks is currently available to workers in the organized sector. With a decline in its share and increase in that of the unorganized sector, the share of unprotected workers will increase. Provision of a minimum social protection to this large mass of workers is, therefore, likely to emerge as a much greater challenge than that of expanding employment opportunities. It will require special attention of the state and society at large in coming years, as the market-driven high growth, even if accompanied by an expansion in employment opportunities, may not by itself be adequate to address the issue of social protection.

T.S. Papola

References

Goldar, B.N. 2003. 'Trade Liberalisation and Manufacturing Employment: The Case of India', Employment Paper 2002/3, 4, Geneva, International Labour Office.

Government of India (GoI). 2005a. *Economic Survey, 2004–2005*, New Delhi, Government of India, Ministry of Finance, Economic Division.

——. 2005b. *Employment and Unemployment Situation in India: January–June 2004*, National Sample Survey Organisation, Report No. 506.

Papola, T.S. 1992. 'The Question of Unemployment', in Bimal Jalan (ed.), *The Indian Economy: Problems and Prospects*, New Delhi, Viking.

Planning Commission. 1956. *Second Five Year Plan*, New Delhi, Government of India.

——. 2002. *Report of the Special Group on Targeting Ten Million Employment Opportunities*, New Delhi, Government of India.

■ Energy

The role of energy in India's economic growth and its importance to Indian society has undergone substantial changes since India attained independence in 1947 when its total installed capacity for power generation was a mere 1,362 megawatts. Electricity was unavailable in many towns and cities, and rural areas certainly could not aspire to receiving any form of electric power. The transport sector consisted largely of bicycles, bullock carts, and horse-drawn carriages although most inter-city and long-distance travel was undertaken on a relatively modern and extensive railway system. Cooking fuel in most households included fuel-wood, charcoal, and to a lesser extent kerosene oil. Since then, urban and peri-urban areas have witnessed a major expansion in electricity supply based on a rapid growth in the use of modern fuels, but rural areas are still characterized by an overwhelming dependence on biomass fuels, particularly for cooking. In assessing the role of energy in India's current economy and society, it is important to understand the structural relationship between energy and other activities in the economy, and the challenge of providing modern forms of energy for a large part of the population which has no access to commercial forms even today, over 63 years after India attained independence.

There are clear linkages between energy trends and global as well as national economic growth indicators. With the recent global economic crisis, global oil demand registered negative growth for two consecutive years in 2008 and 2009, for the first time since the early 1980s. The role of energy in economic growth and development drew the attention of a number of economists, such as Dale Jorgenson and E.W. Berndt (1990), after the oil price shock of 1973–4. The emphasis on economic studies was largely on the formulation of production functions and empirical estimation of relationships, on the basis of which future predictions could be made and policy options evaluated. A number of engineering studies also analysed energy on the basis of bottom–up models linking energy consumption with production and consumption activities based on specified technologies for processes as well as energy-using devices.

Recent energy research has revisited some of this work in an attempt to understand the contribution of energy in driving economic growth. The International Energy Agency's (IEA) World Energy Outlook (WEO 2004) suggested that energy as a factor of production is a complement to capital in the short run, but over a period of time it is generally a substitute. This is precisely what economists and analysts had concluded in the 1980s and 1990s. It is notable, however, that the path traversed by different countries over time in terms of their energy–GDP relationships has been and continues to be highly variable (Figure 1). The countries that industrialized earlier pursued a highly energy-intensive pattern of growth, largely because emphasis was placed on exploitation of basic mineral resources and heavy industry based on energy-intensive technologies in the initial stages. It was only later that the services sector, which largely exhibits lower energy intensity, grew and developed, thereby leading to a decline in energy intensity of GDP. Countries that industrialized later had the benefit of more energy-efficient technology options, the choice of which is determined by relative energy prices as well as domestic resource endowments. National decision-making has generally tended to favour the exploitation of local energy resources rather than relying on large-scale imports for reasons of energy security.

As the Indian economy grows, the country's primary energy consumption is expected to register a steep increase but its energy intensity (unit of energy used per unit of GDP) will gradually reduce (Figure 2). According to analysis undertaken by The Energy and Resources Institute (TERI), under the 'Sustainable Energy Scenario', where energy security concerns are held paramount and there is a concerted push for renewable sources (nuclear energy and new technologies), the country would be able to significantly cut its energy intensity in comparison to the 'Reference Energy Scenario' where business as usual

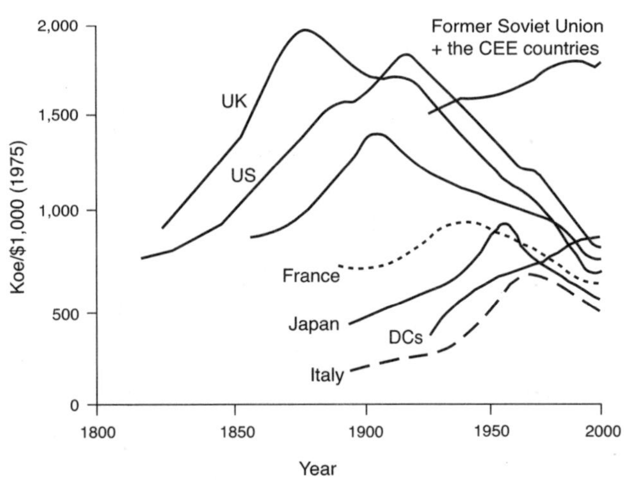

Figure 1 Energy–GDP Relationship

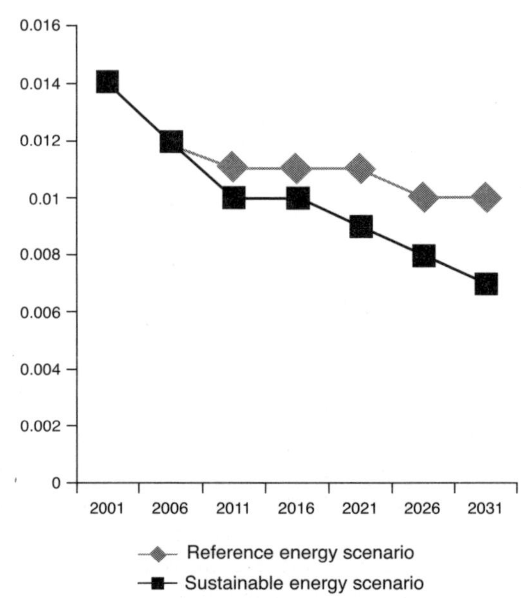

Figure 2 Energy Intensity (kgoe/Rs GDP)

persists and efficiency of energy is determined by market considerations alone.

There are still several prevailing myths about linkages between energy consumption and economic growth driven by an aggregation of solely quantitative models that view the amount of energy required for economic activities as fixed for specific levels of production. In actual fact, a country has many choices, not only in devising policies that would result in a specific mix of economic activities, but also in a range of technologies that would provide an input in the sectors that are favoured for production and consumption. Opportunities exist not only for substitution between capital, labour, energy, and the use of raw materials in the exercise of long-term decisions but also in the choice of energy sources used as inputs for preferred sets of economic activities. These could be achieved as a result of proactive measures encompassing incentives and disincentives that government policies could provide, as well as through regulatory measures mandating technological benchmarking and efficiency standards. Energy policy is not merely an aggregation of policies for supply of power, petroleum, natural gas, and so on, but a clearly defined integrated approach for influencing choices for the use of energy versus other factors of production as well as for choices involving different forms of energy. In today's context, the Indian energy scene shows several examples of this reality. For instance, the failure of supply of electric power in the requisite quantity and quality leads to consumers setting up their own diesel-based power-production units of various sizes, ranging from small generating devices installed by shopkeepers and households to large captive power-generation units installed by industry. The cumulative effect of these individual decisions has generally been a greater dependence on oil products. Hence, in a situation where consumers, including those involved in manufacturing activities can make choices of this nature, the state of supply of one form of energy has implications for other forms as well.

For several years there was a lack of a composite energy policy in India. Attempts were made by several committees established by the Government of India to articulate a comprehensive energy policy, such as the Fuel Policy Committee of 1973–4, the Working Group on Energy Policy in 1977–9, and then the Advisory Board on Energy (1983–6), which reported directly to the Prime Minister. However, the implementation of an integrated policy remained an elusive goal. To alleviate this concern, the Planning Commission, Government of India, drafted and released the Integrated Energy Policy in 2006, which provides a set of guidelines for envisioning the country's energy future. The underlying rationale of the policy was the substitutability of one energy source with another for consumption and production processes. The policy sought to address fragmentation that had crept into energy decision-making with separate ministries dealing with power, petroleum and natural gas, coal, new and renewable sources, and atomic energy. It provided an overview of the energy supply and demand situation in the country and defined policy interventions in the areas of regulation, pricing, taxation, and institutions. Since a comprehensive energy policy needs to cover the major energy-consuming sectors of the economy, the Integrated Energy Policy lays emphasis on demand-side management. It recommends policy options to promote efficient use of energy in major consuming sectors, including the transport and residential sectors (Figure 3). An Energy Coordination Committee, chaired by the Prime Minister, with members drawn from among ministers dealing with various aspects of energy and major consuming sectors, is already in place as a centralized authority to review and refine energy decision-making. While many recent policy initiatives have been directed at adopting and implementing the recommendations put forth in the Integrated Energy Policy, it remains to be seen whether this effort will result in the desired long-term energy development pathway.

As climate considerations come to influence India's energy choices, in conjunction with the Integrated Energy Policy, the National Action Plan on Climate Change (NAPCC) put forth by the Prime Minister's Council on Climate Change in 2008, also provides a new set of considerations in establishing a framework for the energy sector. The NAPCC focuses in particular on an ambitious uptake of solar energy, the building

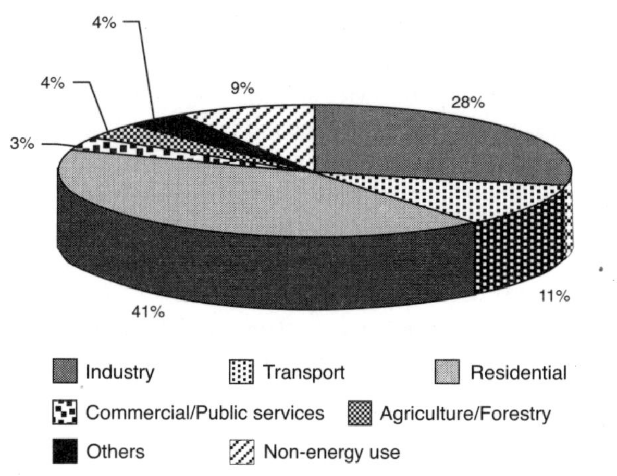

Figure 3 Sector-wise Share in Final Energy Consumption

Source: IEA Statistics 2008.

of sustainable habitats, and improvements in energy efficiency. The document underscores the importance of pursuing policy initiatives that bring co-benefits in terms of both energy security and climate change mitigation. The National Mission on Enhanced Energy Efficiency approved by the cabinet in June 2010, for instance, includes the Perform, Achieve, and Trade (PAT) mechanism under which 700 of the most energy-intensive power stations and industry units in the country would be given a mandate to reduce their energy consumption by a unique specified percentage respectively. Savings in excess of the mandated requirement will make them eligible for energy savings certificates that are tradable amongst select entities.

In light of the energy challenges that the country faces, several objectives need to define India's energy future. The most important of these would be providing adequate energy for all at the least cost and facilitating energy access for the country's entire population. This would require major reforms of energy supply utilities and organizations, involving major restructuring and opening up of these organizations to competitive forces to bring about efficiency improvements. There would also be need for ensuring access to global opportunities and the removal of barriers that in the past have provided protection to domestic industry in developments related to coal as well as oil and natural gas. In this context, opportunities for supply of natural gas from countries such as Iran and/or Turkmensitan would be of great value, particularly given some of the physical constraints in mining of coal and the implied cost of transporting it from domestic coal mines to major consuming sectors. Also, the New Exploration and Licensing Policy (NELP) put in place in 1998 made exploration blocks offered by the government open for a transparent competitive bidding process, allowing foreign companies to own 100 per cent equity in oil and gas projects. Progressive rounds of NELP have seen an increase in the number of private-sector participants but have fallen short of expectations. Possibilities for exploring shale gas could also influence hydrocarbon supply, but as yet there are no firm estimates available on the potential of shale gas in India.

In today's context, and to effectively address future prospects, India's energy policy should be guided by the following objectives:

1. Ensuring secure supply of hydrocarbon fuels. This would require a shift to natural gas and ownership or control of oil resources in other parts of the world combined with a move towards greater efficiency gains in their use. This would require, for instance, a major shift in current developments in the transport sector.
2. Early reforms of the energy supply industry, particularly the power sector, throughout the country, such that it is able to attract private capital in different segments of the industry and by which it is able to provide adequate and reliable power for all customers. Reforms in the power sector have been dragging and are now long overdue. The competitiveness of Indian industry is likely to be adversely affected unless some resolute steps are taken to bring about higher efficiency and operational improvements in the power sector, for which restructuring of this industry and some institutional innovations are essential.
3. The lack of a far-sighted rural energy policy has resulted in prolonged dependence on the consumption of poor-quality biomass for cooking purposes not only in rural areas, but also in the slums of towns and cities. Quite apart from the hardships that this imposes on women for collection of fuel-wood, burning of inferior biomass in ill-designed stoves has harmful health effects, particularly for women and children, due to heavy exposure to harmful emissions from cooking.
4. A mix of effective regulation and market signals through appropriate pricing is required to ensure efficient use of energy and the adoption of appropriate technologies in the major energy-consuming sectors of the economy, such as in the case of transport and the rapidly growing construction and housing sectors. In the area of transport, mechanisms need to be devised for expansion of public transport for intra-city travel and upgrade of Indian Railways for inter-city travel. As a result of the stagnation in the railway system, the share of both freight and passenger transport has been shifting from rail to road for several decades now with adverse implications for the efficiency of energy use, and with serious effects on air quality.

These objectives, if properly incorporated in decision making, would require a fiscal regime involving appropriate taxation and pricing measures. These would then result in overall efficiency gains for the Indian economy and an effective lowering of costs of energy as a factor of production. In a rapidly globalizing world, if India has to register high rates of growth, low cost of energy would be an important prerequisite and imperative. So would be a diversification of sources, particularly for guarding against threats to energy security that could affect the country in the not-too-distant future. And finally, an essential step for enhancing human welfare in the country is the articulation and widespread implementation of initiatives and measures to ensure energy access for all, such that modern and non-polluting forms of energy can benefit all sections of society.

R.K. PACHAURI AND DEEPTI MAHAJAN

References

Dale W. Jorgenson. 1990. 'Productivity and Economic Growth', in E. Berndt and J. Triplett (eds), *Fifty Years of Economic Measurement, Studies in Income and Wealth*, Vol. 54, Chicago, IL, University of Chicago Press, available at http://post.economics.harvard.edu/faculty/jorgenson/colwork/prods2.html.

IEA. 2004. *World Energy Outlook 2004: Energy and Development*, Paris, IEA.

——. 2009. *World Energy Outlook 2009*, Paris, IEA.

The Oxford Institute for Energy Studies. 2010. 'International Developments in Oil and Natural Gas Markets and Their Impact on Arab Countries', paper presented at Ninth Arab Energy Conference, 9–12 May, Doha.

Pachauri, R.K. 1983. 'Third World Energy Policies: The Urban–Rural Divide', *Energy Policy*, September, 11(3): 217—24.

Planning Commission. 2006. *Integrated Energy Policy: Report of the Expert Committee*, New Delhi, Government of India.

Prime Minister's Council on Climate Change. 2008. *National Action Plan on Climate Change*, New Delhi, Government of India.

TERI. 2002. *Defining an Integrated Energy Strategy for India: Ensuring Security, Sufficiency, and Sustainability*, New Delhi, TERI.

——. 2009. 'India's Energy Security: New Opportunities for a Sustainable Future', Paper submitted to the Hon'ble Prime Minister of India, New Delhi, TERI.

■ Entrepreneurs in India and Abroad

Each year the best of India's higher education system, the top engineering, science, medical, and management institutes, graduate over 30,000 high-quality professionals. Many of them go abroad to pursue advanced degrees, especially to the United States where the universities offer generous financial assistance. Till a few years ago, on completing their studies, most Indian students worked for businesses in the US that hire foreigners. There are two main reasons for these hiring practices—first, foreigners are cheaper and, second, they usually stay with the employer, irrespective of working conditions, till they secure a permanent work visa, currently up to nine years of waiting for a computer engineer. Migrant professionals, including those directly recruited from India, are in turn looking for higher incomes, more comfortable lifestyles, and better career prospects than they find in India.

While working in the US, some Indian professionals gain enough confidence in their business skills to give up their jobs and risk setting up an enterprise. The rapidly evolving information technology business has been an especially fertile area. For instance, in the late 1990s in California's Silicon Valley, it was estimated that well over 1 per cent of professionals of Indian origin had started their own companies.[1] This vast move into entrepreneurship was fuelled by the frenzy to set up an internet company, take it public, and get rich quickly. Since the mid-2000s, there has been another wave of Silicon Valley based Indian professionals turning into entrepreneurs, this time chasing the boom in social networking and other web-based businesses. Indian professionals outside the Silicon Valley in the US have also set up several successful businesses, mostly in high technology, especially in the Boston–Washington DC corridor.

At the other end of the spectrum, and rarely publicized, is the existence of several companies started by Indians in the US that secure contracts set aside for racial minorities and women by government and quasi-government operations as well as regulated businesses like telephone and power companies. Claiming that they are handicapped by ethnicity and colour, these Indian men and women, including from the upper castes and educated at top institutions in India and in the US, bid against African Americans, Hispanics, and American Indians, some of whom may be more deserving of such contracts.

Indians have also set up enterprises abroad which are not based on skilled intellectual labour. Then there are companies started by Indians from the traditional business communities and castes in a number of countries, including the US and the UK. While successful Indian entrepreneurs abroad get wide media coverage, the failure rate amongst start-ups is very high for Indians and non-Indians alike in the US and elsewhere. Some studies point out that the chances of a new enterprise succeeding are less than one in ten.

Even if the figure for entrepreneurship amongst Indian professionals in the US is conservatively assumed to be a third of the 1990s internet bubble, it is still a big number compared to the situation in India. Overall, several thousand professionals of Indian origin in the US have started enterprises. Successful companies founded by them in the 1990s include

[1]This estimate is inferred from data listed in Saxenian (2000).

Cascade Communications, TIBCO Software, Junglee and Sycamore Networks, and since the mid-2000s, Flingo, Posterous, and Lattice Engines.

Some Indian entrepreneurs in the US have gone on to becoming venture capitalists. They include Promod Haque, an electrical engineer from Delhi University and an MBA from Northwestern University's Kellogg School. Haque has invested in more than 60 companies and created $60 billion in exit values since joining Northwest Venture Partners in 1990. Vinod Khosla, an electrical engineer from the Indian Institute of Technology Delhi and an MBA from Stanford University, was one of the founders of Sun Microsystems in 1982. Khosla joined venture capitalist Kleiner Perkins Caufield & Byers in 1986 where his successes include Cerent, which was sold to Cisco Systems for $7 billion, and failures include Dynabook.

As with entrepreneurs anywhere, Indians in the US are motivated by the business challenge as well as the fact that they want to become rich. An indication of the wealth accumulated by Indians in America, though of a far wider group than entrepreneurs, is a 2002 study by stock broker Merrill Lynch which estimated that over 50,000 Indians in the US then had a personal net worth exceeding 1 million dollars.

A striking aspect about Indian professionals turned entrepreneurs in the US is that many of them are first generation businessmen and women, coming from non-business families as well as those not born into traditional business castes and communities.[2] Their advanced skills and habits of hard work, when coupled with a perceptive grasp of potential demand for a product or service, give them a major edge in starting businesses based on intellectual content. Often the initial capital used to set up such enterprises is relatively small, in some cases a few thousand dollars.

Among the venture capitalists riding the recent social networking wave is Naval Ravikant, who grew up with little money in Delhi and then New York and washed dishes to support himself through Dartmouth College. In 2009 he co-founded AngelList, a website that has enabled over 200 start-ups to get funding by linking them to over 1,300 investors, including major venture capitalists. Ravikant helped found successful websites—epinions.com and vast.com, and was an early investor in Twitter and Foursquare. 'I'm always rooting for the small guy…call it growing up as a poor, fat, immigrant kid…', he told *The New York Times* (7 March 2011).

In the US, the initial funding may come from several sources and in several rounds, including from friends and family, angel investors, venture capitalists, and investment banks. They all expect to get wealthy by exchanging their low-cost private holdings for stock in an initial public offering, which on average involves a wait of about eight years from the start. So Indian as well as non-Indian professionals in the US leap from well paying jobs into the risk of starting an enterprise because they know that, if the business shows signs of success, there is a very high probability that they can get wealthy as well as raise more capital for growth through a stock market listing.

India too has examples of professionals turned first generation entrepreneurs, including the huge success of Infosys Technologies and Biocon. But the proportion, and perhaps even the total number, of professionals starting enterprises in India is far lower than in the US. This is in a way reflected in the IT industry itself, the breeding ground for many Indian entrepreneurs in the US. Anecdotal evidence suggests that most such companies in India are controlled by business families and foreign entities, including Indian professionals turned entrepreneurs from the US.

One major reason for the absence of a vibrant culture of entrepreneurship among professionals in India is the relatively high level of unemployment and therefore lack of easy job mobility, especially for mid-career professionals. This makes it difficult for professionals in India to find jobs, or at least those paying the same wages and offering similar career paths as their current jobs, in case they leave to start an enterprise and it fails.

A second big hurdle is the dominance of well-entrenched families and related groups over most major Indian businesses as well as access to capital. Many foreign investors as well as publications like *The Financial Times* have recently started referring to these families as the Indian oligarchs, stressing the similarity with the oligarchs who control much of the Russian economy and who actively prevent local and foreign competitors from entering their businesses. Even with the liberalization and reforms of the Indian economy since the 1980s, the same families remain in control.[3]

The third major obstacle for entrepreneurs, with no ties to Indian oligarchs or key politicians, is raising capital since a financing chain, with a stock market as

[2]For some profiles of Indian entrepreneurs in the US, see Chithelen and Souza (2005).

[3]At recent Indian investment conferences in New York and other global financial centres, most questions are about finding reliable partners, securing return of investments and profits, and getting full and timely payments for products and services from India. For an empirical study that shows the continued dominance of the major business families, see Alfaro and Chari (2009).

the pivot, largely does not exist for them. The Bombay Stock Exchange, founded in 1875, historically served in part as a mechanism for the subsidiaries of multinational corporations to share some of their profits with the Indian elite. In 1994 the electronic National Stock Exchange was set up and it now links to over 230,000 terminals. It has some 2,700 listings with a total market capitalization of over $1.5 trillion, with many major companies also listing on the Bombay Stock Exchange. Today, while most companies on the two exchanges are Indian owned, the ones that dominate major businesses are mainly controlled by oligarchs, multinational corporations, and government-owned entities. Even in the highly entrepreneur fertile IT industry, two of the three biggest public companies are family controlled—Tata Consultancy Services and Wipro Technologies—while the third is Infosys.

In India there are also socio-cultural reasons, reflecting the age-old caste-based division of labour. Educated professionals, who are mostly from the middle class and from non-business castes and communities, have the importance of getting and holding onto a good job for life ingrained in them since early childhood. Parents push them to study hard, do well in the exams, get into a good engineering, medical, management, or science school, and then hold on to a steady job for life. In contrast, most wealthy business owners in India ignore this grueling, competitive path of seeking the lottery of economic well-being through higher education.[4] Instead, they focus on retaining and growing their wealth on grounds that if you have the money you can always hire a good manager or engineer or accountant.

Socio-cultural factors do not appear to be as big a burden on Indians in the US. One reason these factors dissolve is because the safety net of job security, as in a job for life, does not exist. In the US there is also greater job mobility for mid-career professionals and a business culture that celebrates both getting rich through entrepreneurship as well as failing in a business and applying the lessons learned to another successful venture or job.

Typically, professionals in India with business ideas continue working at their jobs, rather than leave to start a venture and risk facing future financial ruin. Some of them convince their employers while a few may join other companies which want to pursue their business ideas. In return, some enterprising employees may be fortunate to get bigger salaries and bonuses. But most of them get no major financial rewards, even if their business ideas generate huge profits, since they do not have the savings to hire good lawyers and wage a lengthy legal fight.

Since the late 1990s several factors have made it more conducive for professionals in India to start their enterprises. The rapid growth in the Indian economy has boosted all businesses. On top of this, in the IT industry, demand surged due to widespread fear that computer systems worldwide would fail on 1 January 2000—the so-called Y2K issue which turned out to be a non-problem—and the outsourcing of the contracts to solve the problem, mostly to India.[5] Then, after the internet bubble collapsed in 2000, IT jobs were slashed in the US and there was another wave of work outsourced to India.

On the labour side, during and after the 2000–2 and the 2007–9 recessions in the US, the recruitment of fresh Indian graduates dropped sharply. As a result, thousands of fresh graduates, as well as unemployed Indian professionals in the US, returned home to India for jobs. Seeking to replicate what they saw in the US, some of them have helped start and fund new enterprises.

Over the past decade or so, while Infosys and other established IT companies have grown rapidly, several Indian professionals have also started new businesses and ridden the outsourcing waves. For instance, MindTree was set up in 1999 by former employees of Wipro, from humble backgrounds, by raising funds from angel investors and venture capitalists. Based in Bangalore, like a quarter of the Indian IT companies, MindTree went public on the National Stock Exchange in 2007 and now has a market capitalization of $360 million.

Entrepreneurial opportunities for professionals in India are very large given the wide range of businesses in which intellectual labour is the key component and the initial capital required for start-ups is relatively small. In addition to information technology, professionals have a clear advantage in areas like education, engineering and medical research and services, equity brokerage, money management, media and publishing, web-based information, retailing, financial, and other services.

India has major success stories like Infosys, founded in 1981 by seven IT engineers with $250 in capital. It

[4]The leakage of question papers in advance of tests for admission to top educational institutes in India, while devastating to honest, hardworking students, chips away at the reputation of the institutions. The *Wall Street Journal* (30 June 2004) prominently displayed a long article 'India Battles Entrance Exam Thefts', covering the leakage of questions for 10 major entrance examinations in recent years, including for the Indian Institutes of Management and the All India Pre-Medical Test.

[5]The outsourcing boom in India has led to a shortage of qualified professional staff, spike in wages, and high employee turnover (see Chithelen 2004).

now has a market capitalization of $37 billion, making N.R. Narayana Murthy and other founders celebrated billionaires. Kiran Mazumdar-Shaw founded the biotechnology company Biocon with $1,000 in 1978 to export a plant enzyme used in the brewing industry. In fiscal 2011 Biocon's sales were $625 million. Shantanu Prakash's founding of the New Delhi-based Educomp Solutions is another example of a professional seizing an edge in an intellectual capital-based business and growing big, before some of the oligarchs entered the business. Prakash started his company as a supplier of computer services to schools in 1994, six years after graduating from the Indian Institute of Management Ahmedabad. Today Educomp serves 3.6 million students and educators across 6,400 schools in India, Singapore, and the US and has a stock market value of over $1.1 billion.

Some of the founders of Infosys, as well as Vinod Khosla, are members of TiE—The IndUS Entrepreneurs—a loose-knit worldwide networking organization of professionals and entrepreneurs of mostly Indian origin with chapters in several Indian cities. Other efforts to promote new ventures include the business incubator founded in 1999 at the Indian Institute of Technology Bombay. One start-up it spawned is ThinkLABS Technosolutions which is using robotics systems in the field of education.

A few companies like Infosys are offering stock options to retain key employees in India, some of whom may be tempted to set up competing businesses. While options may buy loyalty for the short term, any wealth it creates will free more professionals to risk starting their own enterprises.

There are major foreign venture and private equity funds operating in India, including Sequoia Capital and Warburg Pincus. Venture capitalists are estimated to have invested roughly 1 billion dollars in India in the year ending June 2010, according to Ernst & Young. But the bulk of such foreign capital appears to be going to businesses controlled by oligarchs.

ICICI Bank, IDBI Bank, and others like them are semi-government owned financial institutions which are a chief source of capital and loans for the major families, state-run enterprises, and multinational corporations. Through policy measures and political pressure, these financial giants should be pushed to seed more entrepreneurs, including professionals and help them raise additional capital by listing on the Over-the-Counter Exchange of India and thereby broaden and deepen a crucial part of the capital raising chain. The exchange, set up in 1990 to help entrepreneurs raise capital, failed to take off and currently lists only 62 companies. This is in stark contrast to the success of the National Stock Exchange, especially given that both exchanges were set up by ICICI, IDBI, and others, under orders from the Government of India.

Some professionals turned entrepreneurs in India are funding philanthropies seeking sustainable, long-term solutions to widen the availability of good quality public education, from early schooling to postgraduate levels. So while not a cure for India's poverty, illiteracy, and malnutrition, spread of entrepreneurship will be a force for positive change.

IGNATIUS CHITHELEN AND SHANKAR PARAMESHWARAN

References

Alfaro, Laura and Anusha Chari. 2009. 'India Transformed? Insights from the Firm Level 1988–2005', Harvard Business School Working Paper, October.

Chithelen, Ignatius. 2004. 'Outsourcing to India: Causes, Reaction and Prospects', *Economic and Political Weekly*, 6 March, 39(10): 1022–4.

Chithelen, Ignatius and Val Souza. 2005. 'Public Capital Markets and New Generation of Entrepreneurs—Success of Indians in the US and Potential in India', *Economic and Political Weekly*, 1 October, 40(40): 4373–86.

Saxenian, AnnaLee. 2000. *The Bangalore Boom: From Brain Drain to Brain Circulation?*, available at www.sims.berkeley.edu.

Entrepreneurship

Definition of an Entrepreneur

It is to Joseph Schumpeter, the Austrian economist at Harvard, that we owe our contemporary use of the word 'entrepreneur'. Schumpeter took an old word from the economics dictionary and used it to describe what he believed to be the secret of the capitalist system. Capitalism is dynamic and brings growth, he explained, because the entrepreneur introduces technological or organizational innovations, which bring new or cheaper ways of making things. These innovations create a flow of income, which cannot be explained either by labour or capital. The new process enables the innovating capitalist to produce at a lower cost, which increases his profit until other capitalists learn the same trick. Schumpeter's great insight was that this new profit does not come from inherited or God-given advantages but springs from the will and intelligence of the entrepreneur.

On the heels of the innovator, says Schumpeter, come a swarm of imitators, and soon everyone wants to invest in the new idea. Banks get busy giving loans to the imitators, everyone begins to talk of a boom, and there is a rash of capital spending. As with all booms, supply soon gets ahead of demand, and suddenly there is huge excess capacity. Prices are forced down, profits begin to decline, and business becomes a routine. As profits disappear, so does investment, and this leads to a bust. Schumpeter's entrepreneur falls as well, squeezed by the very dynamic that he set in motion. Schumpeter called this process 'creative destruction'. The individual that emerges from this vision is a romantic, almost tragic figure. He is not a 'normal' businessman, following established practices and norms; nor is he representative of a social class. Yet, he craves for social esteem and respect.

Indian Entrepreneurship Originated in the Trading Castes

Despite Schumpeter's attempt to differentiate the entrepreneur from the established business class, the word is commonly used to designate somebody who sets up a commercial enterprise to make a profit. By this definition entrepreneurship began in the innovations within merchant families. In India too innovations, both organizational and technical, began with merchants in their trading practices within the Bania or Vaishya families. In *Origins of the Modern Indian Business Class*, D.R. Gadgil points out that India's traditional trading castes in early modern times were predominantly Aggarwals and Guptas in the north, Chettiars in the south, Parsees, Gujarati, Jains and Banias, Muslim Khojas, and Memons in the west, and Marwaris across the country. In addition, Khatris were a vigorous, urban Hindu community engaged in trading activity in Punjab, Afghanistan, and Central Asia. Of these, Marwaris have been amongst the most successful.

Marwari Magic

In 1997, 15 out of the 20 largest industrial houses were from Vaishya trading castes; of these eight were Marwaris (*Business Today*, 22 August 1997). Of the 128 merchant Marwari sub-castes in Rajasthan, which James Tod mentions in his *Annals and Antiquities of Rajasthan*, only five became big and prominent in national commerce. These were the Maheshwaris, Oswals, Aggarwals, Porwals, and Khandelwals. For centuries Marwaris were bankers and helped finance the great trade route which passed through northern Rajasthan. During the Mughal days, they were financiers to princes, including the Emperor. Jagat Seth, a Marwari Oswal, who was banker to the Nawabs of Bengal, also befriended Clive in the conspiracy at Plassey, and thus helped change the history of India and Britain.

James Tod notes that in 1832 'nine-tenths of the bankers and commercial men of India are natives of Maroo des, and these chiefly of the Jain faith'. With the coming of the railway, there was a huge migration of Marwari traders into India's remotest villages. The migrants began as petty shopkeepers and graduated to moneylending, and financed commercial crops like opium and cotton. Some became hugely successful, creating large firms, such as Tarachand Ghanshyamdas, under whose umbrella the Birlas got started in Calcutta at the beginning of the 20th century. It had branches in Bombay and Calcutta, on the river ports along the Ganges, and throughout the opium and cotton growing areas. The firm took deposits, gave loans, engaged in the wholesale trade of commodities, transferred funds for clients to distant cities, cashed bills of trade, insured shipments, and speculated on commodity futures. These 'great firms', also lent money to the princely families. For example, Bhagoti Ram Poddar, the founder of Tarachand Ghanshyamdas, was a banker to the royal families of Jaipur, Bikaner, and Hyderabad.

The Marwaris achieved their biggest success in Calcutta, where they became brokers and agents to the British. Nathuram Saraf, for example, began as a clerk in Ramdutt Goenka's firm and graduated to becoming a 'banian' to British firms. He opened a free hostel for migrants from the Shekhavati area of Rajasthan, and this helped spawn many entrepreneurial careers. The Delhi–Calcutta railway in the 1860s quickened the Marwari migration to Calcutta. By the end of the 19th century, they had become dominant in the jute and cotton trade. In the First World War they made spectacular profits, which laid the foundation of many industrial careers after the War.

Why the Marwaris turned out to be so spectacularly successful had a lot to do with their support system, explains Tom Timberg in his book, *The Marwaris*. When a Marwari travelled on business, his wife and children were cared for in a joint family at home. Wherever he went in search of trade, he found shelter and good Rajasthani food in a *basa*, a sort of collective hostel run on a cooperative basis or as philanthropy by local Marwari merchants. G.D. Birla's grandfather, Shiv Narian settled in a basa when he first went to Bombay in the 1860s. When the Marwari needed money, he borrowed from another Marwari trader on the understanding that the loan was payable on demand. This promise was invariably fulfilled. His sons and nephews were apprenticed to other Marwari traders, where they earned their 'salaries' through profit sharing, learned business skills, and accumulated capital to start their own businesses when they were ready.

Marwaris scored over other Bania castes because they had a stronger stomach for risk. Their biggest fortunes were made during the First World War in extremely speculative forward trading. They were also ruthless and did not stop at anything to stop a rival.

Industrial Entrepreneurship Came after the First World War

India's industrial entrepreneurs thus rose from the bazaar. In Bombay and Ahmedabad in western India, where the cotton textile mills came up in the last half of the 19th century, it was the trading communities who became entrepreneurs and industrialists—they were Parsees, Khojas, and Bhatia traders of Bombay and Jain Banias in Ahmedabad. Serious industrialization, however, only picked up after the First World War, as G.D. Birla, Kasturbhai Lalbhai, and others, who had made huge trading profits during the War, reinvested them in setting up industries. Rajat Ray tells us in *Entrepreneurship and Industry in India 1800–1947* that between 1913 and 1938, manufacturing output grew 5.6 per cent a year, well ahead of the world average of 3.3 per cent. By 1947, the share of industry had doubled to 7.5 per cent of national output from 3.4 per cent. But it was not enough to broadly transform the agricultural society, as modern industry employed only 2.5 million people out of 350 million people.

But Thwarted after Independence by Nehru's 'Mixed Economy'

After Independence, Jawaharlal Nehru and his planners attempted an industrial revolution through the agency of the state. They did not trust the private individual, so they made the state the entrepreneur. Private industrialists, who had naively proposed a vigorous but enabling role for the state in the 'Bombay Plan', were increasingly thwarted in their ambitions by the controls of the 'mixed economy'. They were denied access to global technology; they were told to import substitutes and forced to 'reinvent the wheel'; they became victims of a Kafkaesque nightmare of red tape based on a case-by-case review; most damagingly, they were denied the pressures of global competition, which ultimately forces companies to upgrade their skills. Instead, the system spawned monopolies and rewarded the corrupt. Indira Gandhi's government in the 1970s became even more rigid and introduced more controls, such as the Monopolies and Restrictive Trade Practices (MRTP). It nationalized banks, discouraged foreign investment, and further diminished competition in the marketplace. As a result, productivity of entrepreneurs plunged even further, as Isher Ahluwalia has pointed out. To top that, they increasingly faced a hostile and pampered organized labour.

Aditya Birla was India's most dynamic entrepreneur during this 'dark' period. He succeeded, however, because he took many of his operations out of India. He became the world's largest producer of viscose staple fibre and palm oil; the world's third largest maker of insulators; and the sixth largest of carbon black. During his 52 years, he built 70 factories in six countries, and by 1991 he had achieved sales of Rs 16,500 crore and net profits of Rs 1,500 crore, more than half emanating from overseas. He said famously, 'We produce staple fibre in Thailand, for which we buy pulp in Canada. This Thai made fibre goes to Indonesia for converting to yarn in our unit there. The yarn is then exported from Indonesia to Belgium, where it is made into carpets, and finally the carpet is exported to Canada.' Although he was an Indian, India did not figure in his global value-added chain because India was hostile to private investment.

Unlike Aditya Birla who succeeded by going out, Dhirubhai Ambani rose by manipulating the Licence Raj within India. He created an integrated petrochemicals company from scratch, which grew at a scorching pace to become India's largest company and among the world's top five producers of polyester, polypropylene, PTA, polyethylene, the world's largest maker of paraxylene, and the world's largest integrated producer of PET. By 1991, he had 2.4 million shareholders—more than any company in the world—and held his annual general meetings in a football stadium. In the 1990s, he set up the world's largest multi-feed refinery. Apart from his skills in manipulating the system to his advantage, his success lay in relentless focus. When other Indian business houses were diversified hopelessly in dozens of business activities, Reliance focused on adding value to a single product's vertical chain—petroleum.

Liberation Came with the Reforms in 1991

Forty years of Nehruvian socialism or state capitalism was not able to destroy India's legendary entrepreneurship even though it distorted its behaviour. With the reforms in 1991, Indian entrepreneurs began to be liberated from industrial licensing, import licensing, MRTP, high taxes and tariffs, and a host of other controls. The reforms were incremental and slow—painfully slow—but the remarkable thing is that all governments after 1991 engaged in these slow reforms. And even slow reforms add up and they added up to make India the second fastest major economy in the world in the first decade of the 21st century.

Initially, many businesses did not know how to respond to the new competitive climate. Like hungry children, many responded by setting up ventures with foreigners promiscuously, without a thought to their own capabilities, and expanded capacities unthinkingly. They had a 'factory mindset' when the increasingly competitive market demanded customer service and technology. When the recession came in 1997, supply was hopelessly ahead of demand and they were in trouble. The joint ventures began to come apart as foreigners realized that their Indian partners were not up to scratch—they had neither the competence nor the capital. As a result, the 'Bombay Club' led by Rahul Bajaj redoubled its clamour for protection.

Over the next five years, the best Indian companies went through a trial by fire, re-invented themselves and emerged globally competitive. The case of Rahul Bajaj illustrates this. In 1991, Bajaj was the market leader in India, the world's second largest maker of scooters. With massive economies of scale, he was also the world's lowest cost producer. He had a rugged product for Indian roads and twice the dealer and after-sales service network of any of his competitors. He sold everything he produced. Indeed, there was a ten-year waiting list for his scooters, which sold in the black market at a 40 per cent premium. He made more profit than all his Indian competitors put together. Despite these advantages, he did not have the confidence to take on the Japanese.

Before the reforms, no one would have criticized Bajaj for not thinking globally. Government rules did not permit him to expand production at will, or buy new technology without a lengthy approval process, or import components or machines with a reasonable customs duty. He also suffered from high costs of steel and power. Thus, he had a purely 'local' mindset of a shortage economy, with little marketing or product development skills. The legacy of 40 years of a closed economy had caught up with him, and he was the symbol of an India hobbled by poor infrastructure, obstructionist bureaucrats and inspectors, and high tariffs and interest costs.

By the end of the century Rahul Bajaj loomed large on the Indian industrial horizon like a tragic figure. Having built a fine company, he was losing share rapidly to Hero Honda, in part because consumer preference had turned against scooters and in favour of motor cycles. He reflected the mood of India Inc., which was floundering in progressively competitive markets. Yet within a few years, not only Bajaj but a host of Indian companies responded to the competitive challenge, and emerged stronger and globally competitive. One of these was Bharat Forge, which became a significant supplier to the world's automobile majors, and a symbol of reinvigorated Indian entrepreneurship. Bharat Forge was one of a number of auto component companies that went on to become globally competitive, as India became one of the fastest growing markets for automobiles in the following decade. These competitive companies rose to the challenge by getting the basics right—recruiting and developing talent, investing in R&D, and becoming more customer-focused.

Indian Entrepreneurship is Still Family-based

Apart from the new firms in the knowledge economy, Indian companies continued to be run largely by families. This is not surprising. Even in the US, the most 'professionalized' business nation, 40 per cent of the GNP is created by family companies and more than 80 per cent of all enterprises are family-run. The private sectors of France, Italy, and China are still dominated by smaller, family-owned and managed businesses. Thus, being a family firm per se is not a disadvantage—it is even an advantage in certain circumstances. What small companies give up in financial clout, technological resources, and staying power, they gain in flexibility, lack of bureaucracy, and speed of decision making. For that to happen, however, a family firm must be able to professionalize.

Indian companies have been transitioning to greater professionalism ever since 1991. Because of competitive pressures, they have realized that entrepreneurial companies are built by entrepreneurial talent. There has thus been a huge scramble to find talented individuals and to retain them. They are painfully coping with the problem of incompetent family members at the top, and reluctantly, they have started handing over management to outside professionals. Slowly and very reluctantly the good ones have made the mental leap to separate ownership and management.

Traditional Strengths and Failings of Indian Entrepreneurs

The traditional strengths of Indian companies are financial acumen, a propensity to take calculated risks, an ability to accumulate and manage capital, and an austere lifestyle. The Birla companies were famous for monitoring the performance of their numerous enterprises across the world on a daily basis. The Ambanis single-handedly created 'the equity cult' among the Indian middle class by building a 2 million shareholder base in the 1980s, one of the largest for any company in the world. Because many Indian industries had been under severe price control in the past 40 years, entrepreneurs were forced to become low-cost producers in order to survive. When the economy opened up to competition in 1991, these constituted significant strengths, and provided a basis for competitive advantage as India joined the global economy.

However, Indian family companies continue to have numerous weaknesses. Although these have been diminishing since 1991, the four most important ones are: the difficulty in separating the family's interests from the interest of the business; a lack of focus on a clear business strategy; a short-term approach to business, leading to an absence of investment in employees and in product development; and insensitivity to the customer, largely because of uncompetitive markets, but resulting in weak marketing skills. These weaknesses were reinforced during 1950–90 by a closed economy, which discouraged competition. And as a result of these weaknesses, many business houses collapsed in the 1990s. The successful ones, however, were able to overcome these failings in the next two decades and emerged stronger.

Is it Realistic to Expect Indian Entrepreneurs to Follow a Strategy Other than Cost Leadership?

There are only three ways to build competitive advantage—through superior costs, superior service, or superior technology. It is unrealistic to expect Indian companies to become technology leaders in the near term. This is not because Indian scientists are not capable, but because Indian companies will take time to mobilize the power of science and develop a technology-driven culture. Most Indian firms have adopted a cost leadership strategy. This, however, does not mean that they can ignore quality or service. To be a player at all in the global market, they have to be capable of delivering global thresholds of quality and service. But they have decided that their differentiator will be cost in order to derive competitive advantage.

The essential question is whether Indian companies can realistically adopt another strategy besides cost leadership. Anyone who has shopped in a sari store or eaten in an Udipi restaurant knows the Indian entrepreneur's ability to deliver superior service. The employee in a typical sari store opens a hundred saris in an attempt to sell a single one; the waiter in a typical *dhaba* delivers a *thali* in two minutes. Among larger companies, HDFC and Sriram Finance are good examples of superior service. Moreover, a strategy based on superior service can be especially powerful when delivered by highly trained 'knowledge' workers—scientists, engineers, market researchers, lawyers. Commitment to a service strategy, however, implies that one hires new employees on the basis of their attitude and trains them on skills. Most companies do the opposite. Although, a service strategy is practically 'free' compared to the other two, it is surprising that Indian companies with global ambitions have not yet excelled in it.

Emerging Global Players Share Common Virtues

It is hard to believe that many of the large, successful Indian companies in 2010 were small firms when the reforms began. In 1992, for example, Infosys had a turnover of less than Rs 10 crore; in 2010, it was Rs 27,500 crore. Bharti Airtel was a tiny company in 1992, struggling to make fax machines and fixed line handsets, but in 2010, its turnover was Rs 39,615 crore. Even the more established Tata Steel had sales of only Rs 2,066 crore in 1990 compared to Rs 1,04,269 in 2010; and Reliance Industries' sales were Rs 2,016 crore compared to Rs 2,58,651 in 2010. This is only one measure of the 'scorching rate of growth' of the best Indian companies in the two decades after the reforms.

When the Indian reforms began the world economy also changed to India's advantage. It changed from an industrial age to an information economy. Although a broad industrial revolution continues to elude India, its companies appeared to be swimming nicely in the knowledge sectors—software, IT-related services, generic pharmaceuticals, and telecom.

In recent lists of Indian billionaires, there have been plenty of first generation entrepreneurs, with a majority who had made their fortunes in knowledge industries. They did not inherit wealth, nor did they have a family name. They reflected a new social ethos of post-reform India where talent, hard work, and managerial skills had replaced inherited wealth.

Successful Indian companies with global ambitions shared a number of virtues: (a) they had developed competence in a core area—for example, Infosys in software, Bharti in telecom, Indigo in civil aviation, HDFC and Axis in banking; (b) they had leveraged their pre-eminent position to become even stronger in the domestic market, despite tougher global competition—for example, Asian Paints in paints, Reliance in petrochemicals, Maruti in automobiles, and Hero and Bajaj in two-wheelers; (c) they had achieved low-cost producer status in their respective product categories and have leveraged it in the world market—for example, Tata Steel, Tata Consultancy (TCS), Hindalco; (d) they had used the large Indian market to set up world scale plants—for example, Reliance; (e) they have become sub-contractors to foreign majors—for example, auto component companies like Bharat Forge; (f) they had shown surprisingly appetite and ambition to acquire foreign companies to make India Inc. one of the largest in global M&As between 2000–10; and (g) they had responded quickly to the infrastructure deficit in the country to throw up competitive infrastructure companies—L&T, Punj, IVRCL, etc.

Conclusion

Over 60 countries embarked upon the same reforms as India between 1985 and 2005, but why did India become the second fastest growing economy in the world? Why did India produce the maximum number of globally competitive companies? No one knows for sure but one might speculate: If reforms occur in a society where there are groups or communities which know how to conserve capital, then the reforms are likely to gain a 'bigger bang for the buck' (as the Americans say). India is fortunate to have had plenty of Vaishya and Bania communities—Marwaris, Chettiars, Khojas, Jains, Aggarwals, Guptas, etc—who have learned to accumulate capital over the centuries. Hence, it is not surprising to find that more than 50 per cent of the names on the Forbes 2007 list of Indian billionaires still had Vaishya/Bania surnames. Ironically, India's much reviled caste system may have contributed to the country's competitive advantage!

At the moment of revising this essay in 2011, there were approximately 30 Indian companies that had become globally competitive, and another 20 were on the way. Freed of the shackles of Licence Raj, the best Indian entrepreneurs had responded beyond even the most optimistic hopes of the reformers. Gone was the protectionist rhetoric of the 'Bombay Club', and the best firms were benchmarking with the best in the world. The distractions of family feuds had also receded. Many houses had collapsed, of course, but the successful ones had learned to separate the family from the company interest. The biggest surprise was that some of the best and most innovative firms were members of old business houses like the Tatas.

Some commentators have suggested that Indian entrepreneurship is still controlled by a handful of family-run conglomerates that are quick to use their political and financial muscle to move into any sector that shows promise and close the path for competitors. This is clearly inaccurate. Only 9 out of 30 companies, which constituted the 1990 Sensex of the Bombay Stock Exchange, were still in the 2010 Sensex. This constitutes a very large churn, and shows the vigorous competitive entrepreneurial climate today. The nine survivors are Hindustan Lever, Hindalco, ITC, L&T, Mahindra, Reliance Industries, Tata Steel, Tata Motors, and Tata Power. While it is true that India has its fair share of crony capitalism, it is wrong to state that India is dominated by a handful of business oligarchs with political connections who wreck competition. The story of 20 years of reforms is that newcomers keep breaking into the top 30 with surprising regularity.

Literature is about passion. But, so is entrepreneurship, and in this respect Schumpeter was correct. Since 1991, thousands of otherwise sensible Indians have responded to the reforms, pulling out their hard-earned savings and starting new businesses. Not surprisingly many failed. The remarkable thing about a competitive economy is the very high failure rate of entrepreneurs. In India, there is also the indignity of having to still grovel before a dozen inspectors. Some might call this courageous, others stupidity. It is not only greed but passion which inspires it.

GURCHARAN DAS

■ Environment and Law

The interface between and law and environment in India is a fascinating exploration in the issues relating to constitutional doctrines of separation of powers and issues in development policy. The role played by the judiciary takes us into domains of policy and governance that are unique in the democratic world. It is a story that can be told in roughly three phases. Starting with a period of relative unconcern on environmental matters, there followed a period of law making but weak implementation, culminating in the Bhopal Gas Tragedy. The final period is one in which we see increased judicial activism.

Till around 1972 there was a complete neglect of environmental matters. The few interventions that had occurred were largely in the context of matters like occupational safety as in the Factories Act. In 1972 we see a shift in perceptions, the Stockholm Conference on Environment and Development in 1972 playing a major role in this change in attitudes. The major developments included an amendment to the Constitution providing for Article 48A in the directive principles and Article 51A(g) in the newly created fundamental duties to provide for environmental protection; the passage of the Wildlife (Protection) Act in 1972, the Water (Prevention and Control of Pollution) Act in 1974, the Forest (Conservation) Act in 1981, and the Air (Prevention and Control of Pollution) Act in 1981; and the creation of institutions such as the Central and State Pollution Control Boards for implementing the provisions of these Acts. These laws and institutions were to play a major role in the judicial interventions of the last decade of the 20th century.

The major event shaping legal attitudes to environmental matters was clearly the Bhopal Gas Tragedy. The immediate response was to try to seek a remedy in US courts as they had a well-established system of tort liability. However, in 1986, the New York courts dismissed the case on the grounds of *forum non conveniens.*

The matter then shifted to Indian courts. However, the legal response to Bhopal was poor, as the matter was settled and so there was no opportunity to develop a jurisprudence on mass torts with multinational firms. But the incident both raised public concern as well as highlighted the failure of the existing legal regulatory framework for taking remedial steps. This then laid the ground for a number of public interest litigations (PILs) that were filed on various environmental matters.

The PIL had originated earlier in the late 1970s, in a series of cases. The Supreme Court enlarged its reach and jurisdiction in two ways. First, by moderating the ancient requirement of locus standi (standing and interest) for access to judicial remedies and redress, it eased access to the Court for the affected people, social workers, or even journalists. And, second, it re-interpreted the Constitution to expand the scope and content of various fundamental rights. Thus, in *Francis Coralie Mullin* vs *The Administrator, Union Territory of Delhi*, Justice Bhagwati, speaking for the Supreme Court, stated that 'a constitutional provision must be construed, not in a narrow and constricted sense, but in a wide and liberal manner so as to anticipate and take account of changing conditions and purposes so that the constitutional provision does not get atrophied or fossilized'. This was to have a major impact as the Court was to read the right to clean air and water into the right to life. Thus we see that in *Subhash Kumar* vs *State of Bihar*, the Court observed:

> The right to live is a fundamental right under Article 21 of the Constitution, and it includes the right of enjoyment of pollution-free water and air for full enjoyment of life. If anything endangers or impairs that quality of life in derogation of laws, a citizen has the right to have recourse to Article 32 of the Constitution.

This type of reasoning played an important role in the environmental PILs of the 1980s and 1990s. So, for instance, in *Vellore Citizens Welfare Forum* vs *Union of India and Others*, the Supreme Court in 1996, citing the Stockholm Declaration of 1972, constitutional and statutory provisions, and common law to protect a person's right to fresh air, clean water and pollution-free environment, endorsed the concept of sustainable development, 'the precautionary principle', and 'the polluter pays principle'.

The early PILs were by quarry workers, prisoners, and other marginalized groups on account of human rights violations. The Bhopal tragedy, however, led to an increase in PILs being filed on environmental matters. The range of issues included in these litigations is vast—from coastal zone regulation and river pollution (Ganga and Yamuna) to the operations of tanneries and slaughter houses. It is not possible to give a comprehensive account of this phenomenon.[1] Instead, I will illustrate the issues and problems through two influential examples, the Delhi Air Pollution case (*M.C. Mehta* vs *Union of India* writ petion(civil) 130295 of 1985) and the Forest case (*T.N. Godavarman Thirumalpad* vs *Union of India* writ petition (civil) No. 202 of 1995).

In 1985, concerned with Delhi's growing pollution problems, M.C. Mehta filed a writ petition to direct the Delhi government to implement the Air Act. This petition led to a series of inquiries by the court on what was being done in this regard. In the early stages of the litigation, the impact was primarily to push the executive into formulating measures for pollution control. These measures were ineffective due to poor implementation. This poor progress led the court to push the administration into creating an authority to monitor progress and implementation. This authority was further assisted by the court in that a number of its decisions were made into court orders so that violation/non-implementation of the order opened the door for a charge of contempt of court. These court orders include restrictions on the plying of all commercial vehicles (including taxis) which are over 15 years old; ban on the supply of loose 2T oils at petrol stations and service garages; augmentation of public transport (stage carriage) to 10,000 buses; elimination of leaded petrol from the NCT of Delhi; replacement of all pre-1990 auto rickshaws and taxis with new vehicles on clean fuels; steady conversion of the entire city bus fleet (DTC and private) to single fuel mode on CNG; new Inter State Bus Terminals to be built at entry points in the north and south-west to avoid pollution due to entry of inter-state buses. The orders were not limited to pollution matters; after a horrible accident involving a school bus, the court passed orders on safety standards in school buses. As one can see, the orders get into complex executive decisions on technology, urban development, and modes of transport.[2]

In a similar manner, a PIL was filed in 1995 on account of excessive logging and diversion of forest land in the Nilgiris. In course of hearing the PIL, it became clear that the matter had wider import. The Supreme Court in a landmark order of 12 December 1996 expanded the definition of forests for the purposes of the Forest Act and gave a number of specific directions which had far-reaching impact. The immediate effect was to

[1] A dated though comprehensive coverage is in Ahuja (1997); see also the discussion in Sathe (2002).

[2] For a detailed discussion, see Bell et al. (2004).

virtually halt all felling of trees in forests. Subsequently orders were passed on diverting forest land for mining or other industrial purposes. As with the Delhi case, these orders were based on earlier executive decisions that were not being implemented. For instance, there was a clear rule that felling in forests would be in accordance with the approved Working Plan as provided in the Forest Conservation Act. Further, there were provisions on replantation. All of these were being violated. In the course of the PIL, it became clear that significant ongoing executive direction would be needed, so the Court ordered the creation of a special empowered committee as per the provisions of the Environment Protection Act. This committee then functioned in the nature of an executive arm of the Court. Directions of the committee are converted into court orders through the vehicle of an Intervention Application. The format leads to continuous involvement of the Court to adjudicate and pronounce on a number of decisions. Thus, for instance, a review of the Court's daily orders shows that the forest case was heard 26 times in 2005 till the end of September. Similarly, the Delhi Vehicular Air Pollution case came up for hearing 10 times in the same period in 2005.

This formulation is not unique, since in virtually all of these PILs the Court constitutes an executive office either through the vehicle of amicus curiae, or commissioners, or by directing the creation of an appropriate authority. This has created a novel experiment of amalgamation of judicial and executive authority. The legal instrument of implementing this is the concept of 'continuing mandamus'. Under this system the executive reports compliance with court orders and seeks further orders based on implementation experience. The environmental benefits of this experiment are indisputable; evidence on Delhi air pollution or forest cover has shown significant improvements or at least a reversal of trend. The problems are more in the realm of separation of powers, especially in so far as they relate to the authority of the legislature or the problem of democratic control. One facet of this is the emerging conflict on the rights of tribals located in or near forest land. In this case, two different arms of the government concerned with tribal welfare and forests, respectively, have conflicting views on the best way to proceed. A separate problem arises due to the fact that in forests the benefit of conservation is to the wider ecosystem whereas the costs are disproportionately borne by the concerned state governments. The framers of the Indian Constitution did not formulate a strict doctrine of separation of powers but envisaged a system of checks and balances. In practice, the amalgamation of legislative and executive authority has vitiated some of these checks. In particular, it was clear that executive decision-making was subordinated to political expediency. The vehicle of executive action through judicial support has sought to correct this weakness. This, however, is fraught with its own risks of legitimacy and effectiveness. To illustrate, the vehicle pollution case has focused on Delhi and, with some high courts following the example of the Supreme Court, on major metros. However, air pollution and in fact other forms of pollution are of nationwide concern. In the forest case, the management task extends to remote areas of the country and a variety of different bio-geographical zones. The ability of an already overburdened judiciary to monitor these challenges is doubtful. Thus, while the amalgamation of judicial and executive authority may have had a short-run beneficial impact, its long-run viability needs to be assessed. What is clear is that there is urgent need to question some of the simplified assumptions of separation of powers that have governed the development dialogue till now.[3]

T.C.A. Anant

References

Ahuja, Sangeeta. 1997. *People, Law and Justice,* vols I and II, New Delhi, Orient Longman.

Anant, T.C.A. and Jaivir Singh. 2002. 'An Economic Analysis of Judicial Activism', *Economic and Political Weekly,* 26 October, 37(43): 4433–9.

____. 2006. 'Structuring Regulation: The Constitutional and Legal Frame in India', *Economic and Political Weekly,* 14 January, 41(2): 121–7.

Bell, R.G., K. Mathur, U. Narain, and D. Simpson. 2004. 'Clearing the Air: How Delhi Broke the Logjam on Air Quality Reforms', *Environment,* 46(3), April: 22–39.

Sathe, S.P. 2002. *Judicial Activism in India,* New Delhi, Oxford University Press.

Singh, Jaivir. 2004. '(Un)Constituting Property: The Deconstruction of the '"Right to Property" in India', Centre for the Study of Law and Governance Working Paper Series, CSLG/WP/04–05, Jawaharlal Nehru University.

Environment Policy

India has achieved notable economic growth during the last six decades. However, as the country enters the new millennium poised to attain gross domestic product (GDP) growth in excess of 8 per cent per annum, it is

[3]Different facets of this problem can be seen in Anant and Singh (2002 and 2005) and Singh (2004).

confronted with the spectre of environmental pollution and natural resource degradation.

Environmental pollution refers to release of pollutants, which are unwanted by-products of production processes, in water, air, or on land, in quantities in excess of the assimilative capacity of the receiving media. Natural resource degradation refers to the decrease in the quality or quantity of nature's services. It is associated with deforestation, soil erosion, land degradation, erosion of wetlands, mangroves and coastal ecosystems, threat to wildlife, and loss of biodiversity. Environmental policy collectively refers to strategies and actions needed to address these distinct but related problems. In addition to these immediate and direct problems, it also refers to steps necessary to address the threat of global warming in the coming decades. This entry traces the evolution of policy in respect of environmental pollution.

During the first 25 years after Independence, environmental concerns got neglected due to the perceived need of urgent industrialization. Environmental policymaking began in earnest only in the 1970s when disappearing forests and the deteriorating quality of water and air compelled attention. The first systematic assessment of India's environment was undertaken by the Planning Commission in 1971. This was in part spurred by a request from the UN to its members to report on the state of their environment in preparation for the Stockholm Conference in 1972. As a follow up, the government set up the National Committee on Environment Planning and Coordination. This was possibly the first institutional arrangement for formally addressing environmental concerns. It is interesting to note, in passing, that the Indian Constitution did not originally contain explicit provisions on environmental protection. It was amended in 1976, and by way of the 42nd Amendment, it made environmental protection a fundamental duty of citizens and an obligation on the part of the state. To address a wider set of emerging problems, the Department of Environment was established in 1980, and a full-fledged Ministry of Environment and Forests (MOEF) in 1985. This ministry is currently the apex body for making policy and initiating supportive legislation in respect of environmental matters. Dwivedi (1997) gives a detailed description of the evolution of early thinking and institutions on environmental policy.

The first major environmental legislation was the Water (Prevention and Control of Pollution) Act of 1974. It led to the establishment of State Pollution Control Boards (SPCBs) to set and enforce effluent standards. A Central Pollution Control Board (CPCB) was set up to coordinate the activities of state boards and to advise the central government. The Act made it mandatory for industries which were likely to discharge effluents in water bodies to obtain consent from the SPCBs prior to being set up. Defaulters could be punished with fines, imprisonment, or orders to close down. A tax was levied on the use of water in specified industries, under the Water (Pollution and Control) Cess Act of 1977, to raise financial resources for the boards and to help conserve water. Subsequently, the Air (Prevention and Control of Pollution) Act of 1981 extended the regulatory framework of water pollution to cover air pollution. It became obligatory for industries operating within specified air pollution control areas to obtain prior consent.

The regulatory framework for water and air pollution control proved to be quite ineffective. The SPCBs were perpetually short of funds. They lacked technical expertise and manpower to effectively monitor pollution. Many of them did not even have access to laboratories for testing of water samples. They basically aimed at end-of-the-pipe treatment through installation of specific devices. Often it was enough for a polluting entity just to instal a device to demonstrate compliance. It did not matter whether it actually worked or not. The financial and political clout of polluters also made enforcement difficult. Not surprisingly, these boards could launch very few successful prosecutions against the defaulters in the first decade of their existence. Over time, the volume of pollution increased manifold and its nature became more complex. New sources and newer forms of pollutants, particularly hazardous chemicals, emerged which were dangerous even in miniscule quantities. With restrictions on release in air and water, pollutants started getting diverted to land posing threat to underground water. Soon, the SPCBs found themselves incapable of handling the situation. The Bhopal gas tragedy of 1984 demonstrated this in a dramatic way.

The Environment Protection Act of 1986 (EPA) was enacted to deal with the new catastrophic reality brought home by that tragedy. It was a significant piece of legislation in many ways. It extended the authority of the central government to legislate for the entire country. It took a comprehensive view of the environment and extended the scope of regulation to cover almost all forms of pollution. The government used the Act to frame wide-ranging laws for pollution control, hazardous substance regulation, environmental impact assessment, and the protection of the coasts and other ecologically fragile areas. For pollution control, the government notified detailed standards for discharge of effluents, emissions, and noise. Hazardous waste management rules were designed to fix responsibility on persons generating the waste which, therefore, required a permit to regulate its handling and disposal. For a specified list of industries, government made Environment Impact Assessment (EIA) mandatory prior to their being set up. This would involve, apart from submission of an environment management plan, the holding of a public hearing where affected parties got a chance to voice their concerns. The government also notified specific prohibitions and regulations concerning development in ecologically sensitive areas. For example, Coastal Zone Regulations were notified to control development activity, including tourism, within a strip of 500 m from the sea shore, along the entire Indian coast. The Act gave the SPCBs vast administrative powers to compel compliance with the laws directly instead of having to go to courts as previously. It also gave the CPCB overriding authority over the SPCBs. A development of the utmost importance was that the Act gave citizens the right to initiate proceedings against the defaulting industries and the boards. Divan and Rosencrantz (2001) provide a detailed and a very lucid description of the evolution of environmental policy from a legal point of view.

By the end of the 1980s, India had an extensive body of laws and rules on environment protection. It also had an elaborate institutional set-up in place. However, these were unable to arrest the deteriorating trend in environment. This was due both to the nature of the regulatory regime and poor enforcement of laws. Even though the EPA considerably expanded the scope of regulation, it in effect continued to be an extension of water and air pollution control. The basic approach continued to be technological fixes, which were ex post in nature and, consequently, tended to take care of the symptoms rather than the causes. Polluters were viewed as adversaries and compliance was enforced through coercion rather than cooperation. Policies were often ad hoc responses to problems that were neglected till they became unbearable or precipitated a crisis. It is ironical that even though the country had a very comprehensive framework for investment planning, environmental considerations were not integrated into it. In the late 1960s an industrial estates programme was started, where clusters of industries could share infrastructural facilities. It is a telling example of lack of foresight that, in many of them, no provision was made for common effluent treatment plants. An oft-cited explanation for poor performance of environmental laws has been lack of adequate funds given the size of the problem. Multiplicity of jurisdiction has also been cited as a source of delays in taking timely action.

At a more basic level, the poor performance of environmental laws, as all other laws, has been attributed to India being a 'soft state', a state characterized by weak institutions, a high degree of corruption, and absence of well-developed social norms. In such a state, decisions that go against the vested interests of industry, bureaucracy, or politicians are hard to make and do not get implemented.

However, contrary to the above pessimistic assessment, solutions have in fact been found to many seemingly impossible problems. This is thanks to the Indian judiciary, which has played a critical role in giving teeth to environmental law and in ensuring administrative accountability. Political scientists call this a case of third-party enforcement. The Supreme Court in particular has intervened in environmental matters by allowing citizens' initiatives in the form of public interest litigation and also by taking suo moto cognizance of actions injurious to environment. Not confining itself to mere interpretation of laws, it has at various times stepped in directly to compel enforcement on a variety of issues. It has ordered stretches of rivers to be cleaned up by installation of effluent treatment plants and polluting factories to be shut down or moved out of urban areas. To combat noise pollution, it has imposed restrictions on use of loudspeakers even from religious places, a very thorny issue politically. In one of the more dramatic cases, in the highly polluted capital city of New Delhi, it successfully forced the entire diesel-based public transport system to switch to compressed natural gas. This was a technologically complex and politically difficult problem that had defied solution for long. To inculcate social norms it has directed that ecology and environment be taught in schools and colleges. Judicial activism has often been criticized for intruding into executive territory. Yet it has been so effective that when the SPCBs found themselves powerless against influential people, they actually encouraged public interest litigation. Unfortunately, there are diminishing returns to judicial intervention. While the air in Delhi got cleaned in response to its intervention, the water in the river Yamuna did not. Ten years ago the Supreme Court had ordered installation of common effluent treatment plants. The order was complied with. The plants were installed but not put into operation. They have since been rusting. The greatest contribution of judicial intervention has been a heightened awareness of environmental problems in the society. There are now a large number of citizens and non-governmental organizations (NGOs) who are exerting pressure on state agencies through media and the courts.

The effect of this pressure is visible, at least on paper, in the policy statements issued by the Government of

India in recent years. The Policy Statement on Pollution released in February 1992 acknowledged the increasing trend in pollution. It also recognized the limitations of the earlier piece-meal approach in arresting it. In its place, it advocated integration of environmental considerations into decision making at all levels. It promised to move towards prevention of pollution at source, making polluters pay for the pollution and for the clean-up costs, and encouraging public participation in decision making. In the Environmental Action Plan of 1993, the government took this commitment a step further by identifying priority areas for industrial pollution, with emphasis on reduction and management of wastes through technological upgradation. The latter would be achieved through enforcement of stricter standards and by giving fiscal and other incentives. The plan lays emphasis on decentralized decision-making and strengthening of organizations at all levels. As suggested in the beginning, environment policy is not confined to pollution alone. Consequently, the National Conservation Strategy and Policy Statement on Environment and Development, released in 1992, has a much broader scope. Following the principles agreed upon at the Rio conference, it declared the government's commitment to a policy of sustainable development. To achieve that goal, it promised to reorient policies and actions in different sectors such as agriculture, forestry, and industrial development, keeping in mind the environmental perspective. Realizing that mere passing of laws was not enough, it laid stress on the joint role of the government, NGOs, industries, public, and particularly women in preserving and protecting the environment. The statement also outlined strategies and action plans for protection of wildlife and preservation of biodiversity.

Recently a National Environmental Policy (NEP 2004) draft has been circulated by the MOEF for public debate. This is the most comprehensive and detailed policy statement on environment issues so far. Apart from elaboration of many sector-specific issues, covered in the statements mentioned in the preceding paragraph, it proposes a major rationalization of environmental laws and policies in India. In particular it promises to review procedures for granting environmental and forest clearances for development projects. These have been a source of delay for and a cause of complaints by investors in the past. The review will also extend to rules relating to development activities along the coasts to remove anomalies arising from their application in varying local conditions.

The NEP marks a major departure from the earlier policy framework in emphasizing increasing use of economic principles in environmental decision-making. This implies that the costs associated with degradation and depletion of natural resources be reflected in the decision making of economic actors to prevent their overexploitation. Extending this to the macro level, it proposes to institute a system of natural resource accounting so that macro aggregates like gross domestic product give a truer picture of economic growth.

The NEP promises to replace adversarial relationships in environmental management with cooperative ones. These would be based on partnerships between public agencies and local communities. This has special relevance to forestry. It advocates complementing and, wherever possible, replacing the fiat-based instruments for environmental compliance with economic instruments. In order to make compliance more effective, it advocates greater reliance on civil law in place of criminal law.

The draft NEP has brought to the fore the competing pulls of the economic and ecological approaches to environmental policy. Ecologists have faulted the policy draft for diluting concerns for biodiversity. Civil society groups have complained of inadequate provisions for protection of cultural identities, knowledge systems, and livelihood of indigenous communities that are directly dependent on ecological resources. Critics have derisively described it as a policy not on environment but an 'investor-friendly' policy on 'sustainable development'. Policymakers have used the same two terms with a sense of self-congratulation. A more valid criticism of the draft would be that it promises action on too many things in very general terms and fails to specify an enforceable agenda.

PURAN MONGIA

References

Divan, Shyam and Armin Rosencrantz. 2001. *Environment Law and Policy in India*, New Delhi, Oxford University Press.

Dwivedi, O.P. 1997. *India's Environmental Policies, Programmes and Stewardship*, New York, St. Martin's Press.

Government of India. 2004. Ministry of Environment and Forests, National Environment Policy, Draft for Comments, New Delhi, October, available at http://www.envfor.nic.in.

■ Equity Premium

Equity premium is the return earned by a risky security, such as a stock, in excess of that earned by a risk-free security, such as a treasury bill (T-bill). It is a crucial input in financial decisions such as asset allocation, capital budgeting, and planning for retirement.

Table 1 US Returns, 1802–2004

(per cent)

	Mean real return		
Period	Market index	Relatively riskless Security	Risk premium
1802–2004	6.9	2.9	4.0
1889–2004	7.5	1.0	6.5
1926–2004	8.0	0.7	7.3
1947–2000	7.5	0.5	7.0

Historical data provide a wealth of evidence that over long periods of time, stock returns have been considerably higher than returns for T-bills. As Table 1 shows, the average annual real return (that is, the inflation-adjusted return) on the US stock market for the past 115 years has been about 7.5 per cent. In the same period, the real return on a relatively riskless security was a paltry 1 per cent.

The difference between these two returns, 6.5 percentage points, is the equity premium. This statistical difference has been even more pronounced in the post-Second World War period. Data on US stock and bond returns going back to 1802 reveal a similar, although somewhat smaller, premium for the past 200 years.

Furthermore, this pattern of excess returns to equity holdings is not unique to US capital markets. Table 2 documents that equity returns in other developed countries also exhibit this historical regularity when compared with the return to riskless debt holdings.

The annual return on the UK stock market, for example, was 5.7 per cent in the post-Second World War period, an impressive 4.6 per cent premium over the average bond return of 1.1 per cent. Similar statistical differences have been documented for France, Germany, and Japan. Together, the United States, the United Kingdom, Japan, Germany, and France account for more than 85 per cent of capitalized global equity value.

Table 2 Returns for Selected Developed Countries

(per cent)

		Mean real return		
Country	Period	Market index	Relatively riskless security	Risk premium
United Kingdom	1947–99	5.7	1.1	4.6
Japan	1970–99	4.7	1.4	3.3
Germany	1978–97	9.8	3.2	6.6
France	1973–98	9.0	2.7	6.3
Sweden	1919–2003	11.1	5.6	5.5
Australia	1900–2000	13.3	4.6	8.7

Table 3 shows the equity premium for India in the 'post-liberalization' period, using both the Bombay Stock Exchange (BSE) 100 and the Sensex as a proxy for the return on equity. Since participation in the T-bill market was highly regulated before 2000, the equity premium is calculated relative to the bank deposit rate, using the latter as a proxy for the return on a risk-free security.

For the period prior to 1991, reliable data on dividend yields are not available. Table 4 gives the equity premium using the average annual stock price index as documented and reported by the Reserve Bank of India (RBI).

The dramatic investment implications of the differential rates of return are illustrated in Tables 5 and 6. Table 5 shows the enormous disparity in capital appreciation of $1 invested in different assets in the US for various time periods.[1] Table 6 displays a similar analysis for India.

Table 3 India Returns, 1991–2004

(per cent)

	Relatively riskless security	BSE 100	Equity premium (BSE 100)	Sensex	Equity premium (Sensex)
Mean real return	1.28	12.6	11.3	11.0	9.7
Standard deviation	1.73	37.2	37.7	32.6	33.2

Table 4 India Returns 1984–1991

(per cent)

	Relatively riskless security	BSE 100	Equity premium (BSE 100)
Mean real return	1.13	22.4	21.3
Standard deviation	0.74	28.1	27.9

Table 5 Real Terminal Value of $1 Invested

Investment period	Stocks	T-bills	Ratio
1889–2004	$4092.36	$3.14	1303.30
1926–2004	$407.56	$1.67	244.05
1947–2004	$61.70	$1.33	46.39

Table 6 Real Terminal Value of Re 1 Invested

Investment period	Stocks (BSE 100)	Bank deposit	Ratio
1984–2004	Rs 19.25	Rs 1.28	15.04
1991–2004	Rs 4.68	Rs 1.18	3.97

[1]The calculations in Table 5 assume that all payments to the underlying asset, such as dividend payments to stocks and interest payments to bonds, were reinvested and that no taxes were paid.

One can gain additional insights by examining what these differential rates imply for the time it takes to double one's money. Using rates in India over the 1991–2004 period, the doubling period for investments in stocks is about six years compared to fifty-five years for investments in a risk-free asset. This kind of long-term perspective underscores the remarkable wealth-building potential of equity premium and highlights why it is of central importance in portfolio allocation decisions, in making estimates of the cost of capital, and in the current debate about the advantages of investing social security trust or retirement funds in the stock market.

A Premium for Nearing Risk?

Why has the rate of return on stocks in India and other countries been significantly higher than the rate of return on relatively risk-free assets? An intuitive answer is that stocks are 'riskier' than bonds and investors require a premium for bearing this additional risk. Indeed, the standard deviation of the returns to stocks in India (about 30 per cent a year historically) is larger than that of the returns to T-bills (about 2 per cent a year), so obviously stocks are considerably riskier than bills.

But are they? Figure 1 illustrates the variability in the annual real rate of return on the BSE 100 index while Figure 2 shows the variability of a relatively risk-free security over the 1991–2004 period.

To enhance our understanding of the risk–return trade-off in the pricing of financial assets, let us make a detour into modern asset pricing theory and look at why different assets yield different rates of return. The deux ex machina of this theory is that assets are priced such that, ex ante, the loss in marginal utility incurred by sacrificing current consumption and buying an asset at a certain price is equal to the expected gain in marginal utility contingent on the anticipated increase in consumption when the asset pays off in the future.

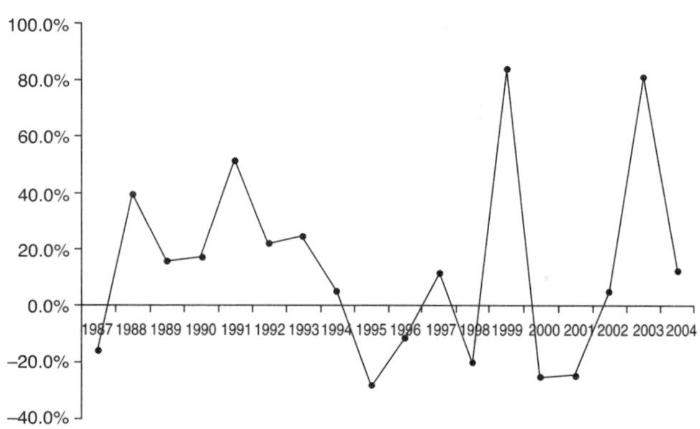

Figure 1 Annual Real Rate of Return—BSE 100

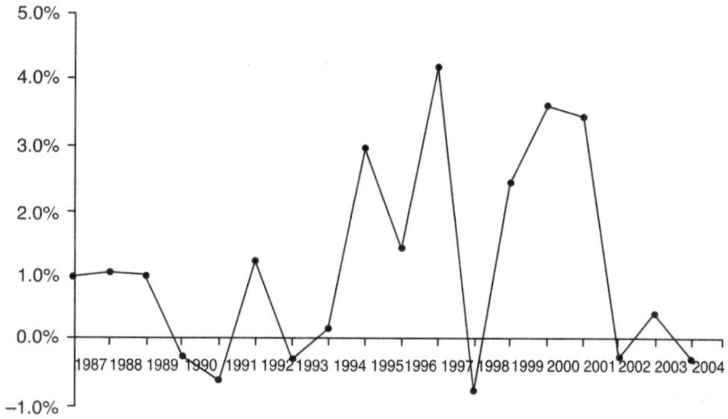

Figure 2 Commercial Bank Deposit Rate

The operative emphasis here is the *incremental loss* or *gain* in well-being due to incremental consumption, which must be differentiated from the incremental consumption itself. This is because the *same* amount of incremental consumption may result in different degrees of well-being at different times. A five-course dinner after a heavy lunch, for example, yields considerably less satisfaction than a similar dinner when one is hungry!

As a consequence, assets that pay off when times are good and consumption levels are high, that is, when the incremental value of additional consumption is low, are less desirable than those that pay off an equivalent amount when times are bad and additional consumption is both desirable and more highly valued.

Let us illustrate this principle in the context of the standard popular paradigm, the Capital Asset Pricing Model (CAPM). This model postulates a linear relationship between an asset's 'beta', a measure of systematic risk, and expected return. Thus high beta stocks yield a high expected rate of return. That is so because in the CAPM, good times and bad times are captured by the return on the market. The performance of the market as captured by a broad-based index acts as a surrogate indicator for the relevant state of the economy. A high beta security tends to pay off more when the market return is high, that is, when times are good and consumption is plentiful; as discussed earlier, such a security provides less incremental utility than a security that pays off when consumption is low, is less valuable to investors, and consequently sells for less. Thus assets that pay off in states of low marginal utility will sell for a lower price than similar assets that pay off in states of high marginal utility. Since rates of return are inversely proportional to asset prices, the latter class of assets will, on average, give a lower rate of return than the former.

Another perspective on asset pricing emphasizes that economic agents prefer to smooth patterns of consumption over time. Assets that pay off a relatively larger amount at times when consumption is already high, 'destabilize' these patterns of consumption, whereas assets that pay off when consumption levels are low, 'smooth' out consumption. Naturally, the latter are more valuable and thus require a lower rate of return to induce investors to hold these assets. (Insurance policies are a classic example of assets that smooth consumption. Individuals willingly purchase and hold them, in spite of their very low rates of return.)

To return to the original question: are stocks so much riskier than bills as to justify a 7 per cent differential in their rates of return as observed in the US?

What came as a surprise to many economists and researchers in finance was the conclusion of a research paper that Edward Prescott and I wrote in 1979. Stocks and bonds pay off in approximately the same states of nature or economic scenarios and hence, as argued earlier, they should command approximately the same rate of return. In fact, using standard theory to estimate risk-adjusted returns, we found that stocks in the US on average should command, at most, a 1 per cent return premium over bills. Since, for as long as we had reliable data (about a 100 years), the mean premium on stocks over bills was considerably and consistently higher, we realized that we had a puzzle on our hands. It took us six more years to convince a sceptical profession and for our paper 'The Equity Premium: A Puzzle' to be published (Mehra and Prescott 1985).

For the purposes of this entry, I have done a similar analysis for India using the data in Table 7, which contains the sample statistics for the Indian economy for the 1991–2004 period.

Table 7 Indian Economy Sample Statistics, 1991–2004

Statistic	Value
Risk-free rate, R_f	1.0128
Mean return on equity, $E(R_e)$	1.126
Mean growth rate of consumption, $E(x)$	1.0227
Standard deviation of growth rate of consumption, $\sigma(x)$	0.0224
Mean equity premium, $E(R_e)–R_f$	0.113

My finding is that the theoretical equity premium should be in the range 0.02 per cent to 0.16 per cent if the coefficient of risk aversion is varied from 2 to 10. Since the observed risk premium in India is of a higher order of magnitude, there is a puzzle with respect to Indian data as well.

I want to emphasize that the equity premium puzzle is a *quantitative* puzzle. Standard theory is qualitatively consistent with the notion of risk: stocks do, on average, return more than bonds in the theoretical model. The puzzle arises from the fact that the quantitative predictions of the theory are of an order of magnitude different from what has been historically documented. The puzzle cannot be dismissed lightly because much of our economic intuition and policy directives are based on the very class of models that fall short so dramatically when confronted with financial data. It underscores the failure of paradigms central to financial and economic modelling to capture the characteristic that appears to make stocks comparatively so risky. Hence the viability of using this class of models for any quantitative assessment—for example, to gauge the welfare implications of alternative stabilization policies—is thrown open to question.

For this reason, over the past 20 years or so, attempts to resolve the puzzle have become a major research impetus in finance and economics. Several generalizations of key features of the Mehra–Prescott (1985) model have been proposed to reconcile observations with theory, including alternative assumptions about preferences, modified probability distributions to admit rare but disastrous events, survivorship bias, incomplete markets, and market imperfections. None has satisfactorily resolved the puzzle.

Recently some researchers and analysts have argued that ex-ante equity premium is likely to be low. The data used to document equity premium (over the past 100 years in some instances) represent as reliable an economic data set as analysts have, and 100 years is a long series when it comes to economic data. Before the equity premium is dismissed, not only do researchers need to understand the observed phenomena, but they also need a plausible explanation as to why the future is likely to be any different from the past. Demographic shifts and changes in participation in equity markets will, of course, impact on the equity premium in India over time. For instance, greater stock market participation in particular by the younger generation is likely to reduce the equity premium. However, before these demographic factors play a role, on the basis of what is currently known, I make the following assertion: the equity premium in the future is likely to be similar to what it has been in the past and returns to investment in equity will continue to substantially dominate returns to investment in T-bills for investors *with long planning horizons*.

RAJNISH MEHRA

References

Cochrane, J.H. 1997. 'Where is the Market Going? Uncertain Facts and Novel Theories', *Economic Perspectives*, November, 21(6): 3–37.

Constantinides, G.M. 2002. 'Rational Asset Prices', *Journal of Finance*, August, 57(4): 1567–91.
Kocherlakota, N.R. 1996. 'The Equity Premium: It's Still a Puzzle', *Journal of Economic Literature*, March, 34(1): 42–71.
Mehra, R. 2003. 'The Equity Premium: Why is It a Puzzle?', *Financial Analysts Journal*, January/February, 59: 54–69.
———. 2006. *Handbook of Investments: Equity Risk Premium*, Amsterdam, North Holland.
Mehra, R. and E.C. Prescott. 1985. 'The Equity Premium: A Puzzle', *Journal of Monetary Economics*, March, 15(2): 145–61.
———. 2003. 'The Equity Premium in Retrospect', in G.M. Constantinides, M. Harris, and R. Stulz (eds), *Handbook of the Economics of Finance*, Amsterdam, North Holland.

Exchange Rates

As India becomes more open and increasingly integrated into the world economy, the rupee's exchange rate is likely to play a very important role in defining the competitiveness of Indian goods and services in international markets.

A bilateral exchange rate, say of the rupee against the US dollar, is an incomplete measure of competitiveness for two reasons. First, a bilateral exchange rate only considers fluctuations against a single currency, whereas most open economies trade with many countries. Second, it does not adjust for the fact that the evolution of prices and costs in the home country could be quite different from that in the trading partners. To deal with this, economists compute 'effective exchange rates' (EERs). The nominal effective exchange rate (NEER) is a weighted average of various bilateral nominal exchange rates with the choice and associated weights of the bilateral rates depending upon the economic issue being analysed (for example, competitiveness in international markets, determinants of domestic inflation, and demand for financial assets). The real effective exchange rate (REER) is the nominal effective exchange rate deflated by a similarly weighted average of foreign prices or costs, relative to those in the home country.

The construction of an EER depends on the definition of the exchange rate, the averaging techniques, and the weighting scheme used (see, for instance, Zanello and Desruelle 1997). To fix ideas, define an exchange rate as the rupee price of a unit of foreign currency. Let us suppose that India trades with n foreign countries and the exchange rate for the *ith* foreign currency at time t is given by E_{it}, $i = 1, 2,\ldots, n$; for each currency, an exchange rate index $E^{*}_{it} = (E_{it}/E_{i0})$ is constructed relative to a base period ($t = 0$). For a given set of weights, w_i, $i = 1, 2,\ldots, n$, we could use an arithmetic, a harmonic, or a geometric average to construct an NEER using the exchange rate indices for the n trading partners. The geometric mean is generally used because it treats appreciations and depreciations symmetrically. The weights w_i can be, for example, the share of India's exports going to country i, or the share of India's imports from country i, or a weighted average of Indian export and import shares, or something rather more complex, depending on the issue being studied. For India, the International Monetary Fund (IMF) uses weights based on trade in manufactured goods, primary commodities, and tourism services over the period 1988–90. The weights generally reflect both direct and third market competition, that is, the weights take into account competition between exported and imported goods and their Indian substitutes, and competition in third markets between Indian exports and the exports of other countries.

The NEER for India measures how India's exchange rate has changed vis-à-vis its trading partners relative to a particular base year. It is expressed as an index number relative to the base year, and using the geometric averaging method it is written as

$$\text{NEER} = 100\cdot\prod_{i=1}^{n}\left(E^{*}_{it}\right)^{w_i}. \tag{1}$$

Movements in the NEER do not tell us anything about how the purchasing power of the rupee may have changed over time, because the evolution of prices in India and its trading partners could have been very different. For example, if the Indian price level has risen vis-à-vis its trading partners, then one rupee will buy relatively more abroad (compared to the base year) than in India, and India's exports will have become more expensive relative to those of its trading partners. In this case, we say that the rupee has become overvalued, and this may have adverse consequences for India's competitiveness in world markets. To this end, economists calculate the REER index which is the NEER index deflated by a measure of relative price movements. Movements in the REER compared to the base period measure the effective change in national price or cost levels using a purchasing power standard. The REER index is defined as

$$\text{REER} = 100\cdot\prod_{i=1}^{n}\left(\frac{E^{*}_{it}}{P^{*}_{it}}\right)^{w_i} \tag{2}$$

where P^{*}_{it} is the ratio of the price index of the *i*th trading partner in period t to the Indian price index in period t

(with the base year being the same as that used for the exchange rate indices).

What price measure should one use to compute the REER? The options fall into two broad categories: those based on aggregate price indices and those based on wage costs. There are four aggregate price indices that are commonly used to compute REERs—the consumer price index (CPI), the wholesale price index (WPI), the producer price index (PPI), and the GDP deflator. The REER-CPI is most commonly used and offers several advantages. The consumer price index is designed to reflect changes in the cost of living by comparing over time the cost of a fixed basket of goods purchased by a typical urban consumer. It is, by and large, comparable across countries and provides a relatively accurate measure of domestic price developments. Compared to other aggregate price series, the data is readily available and up to date. A disadvantage is that movements in the CPI could reflect price developments that are unrelated to the costs of production. For example, an increase in the price of electricity supplied to households may affect the CPI, but may have less of a direct effect on the cost of intermediate and capital goods used in production.

As an alternative to the CPI-based measure, REER indices based on the wholesale price index and the producer price index are also frequently computed. The main advantage is that these price series provide a closer approximation to tradable goods prices than the CPI. However, a number of disadvantages limit their usefulness. The data quality is often poor and not comparable across countries. In some countries, there is an emphasis on commodities and semi-manufactured goods that may not be traded. The REER can also be computed using the GDP deflator, which provides a broad measure of aggregate domestic costs. But the downside is that the data on deflators are available with a much greater time lag than for the CPI and is subject to more frequent revisions.

Because labour costs represent such a large share of the costs of production, the unit labour cost (ULC)-based REER measure is often preferred as a measure of competitiveness. Changes in unit labour costs are seen as having a direct effect on profitability. This interpretation of the REER-ULC index is based on two assumptions. First, the price of traded goods is equal across countries (so that increases in unit labour costs imply a direct and one-to-one decline in profits from production) and, second, there is no change in capital–labour ratios or in the share of non-traded intermediate inputs. Unit labour costs can change owing to changes in productivity or the structure of production; under such circumstances, the relationship between changes in ULC and profitability may be difficult to decipher (see Lipschitz and McDonald 1992). A further drawback stems from the fact that unit labour cost data is often available across countries for only the manufacturing sector and, hence, manufacturing goods are used as a proxy for traded goods. With the growing international trade in services, this assumption may not be appropriate for many countries, including India. Another issue to keep in mind when using unit labour costs is the variation over the business cycle.

In general, interpretation of changes in the REER-ULC requires an understanding of the underlying products and markets. For example, excess wage demands could lead to increasing prices, with a negative effect on the ability to compete in international markets. In contrast, wage and price increases because of innovation and a move into higher-value-added goods could be a positive development. In any event, a suitable unit labour cost data series is not yet available for India, and the IMF only calculates the REER-CPI.

Table 1 lists the currency regimes used by India in the last hundred years. Till 1975, with the exception of a brief period in 1971 when it was fixed to the US dollar, the Indian rupee was pegged to the pound sterling. Once afloat, the rupee had a de facto crawling band around the pound sterling between 1975 and 1979, and then a de facto crawling band around the US dollar between 1979 and 2003. India has had a managed float with no pre-announced path for the exchange rate since the beginning of 2004.

For the first five decades of Independence, a binding foreign exchange constraint was a constant feature of the Indian macroeconomic environment. It began to really bite as early as the Second Five Year Plan (1955–60), during which India's ambitious import-substitution strategy was unleashed. Draconian industrial and foreign exchange controls could not prevent the emergence of a shortage of foreign exchange, and a high parallel market premium remained in place during 1957–91. The premium reached a peak before the sharp devaluation in 1966, remained high and volatile till the rupee was floated in 1975, and only came down substantially after the financial crisis of 1991 (see Figure 1).

India's economic performance has been hampered by the reluctance of policymakers to vary the nominal exchange rate. External balance was maintained through import restrictions, concessional finance, and a build-up of external debt. This was most evident in the first half of the 1960s and the 1980s. During periods of rapid growth and export expansion in the 1970s and 1980s, India's REER depreciated substantially: in the 1974–9 period, the REER (adjusted for export subsidies) depreciated by

Table 1 India: Exchange Rate Arrangements 1914–2005

Date	Classification: Primary/secondary/tertiary	Comments
August 1914	Peg to pound sterling	Convertibility into sterling is suspended
22 March 1927	Peg	Gold standard
24 September 1931	Peg to pound sterling	Suspension of gold standard adherence to sterling area
3 September 1939	Peg to pound sterling	Capital controls are introduced
November 1941	Peg to pound sterling/freely falling	
November 1943	Peg to pound sterling	
1 October 1965	De facto band around pound sterling/parallel market There are multiple exchange rates	Band width is +/– 5%
6 June 1966	Peg to pound sterling	
23 August 1971	Peg to US dollar	
20 December 1971	Peg to pound sterling	
25 September 1975	De facto crawling band around pound sterling	Band width is +/– 2%. Officially pegged to a basket of currencies
March 1979	Managed floating	
August 1979	De facto crawling band around US dollar	Band width is +/–2%. Officially pegged to a basket of currencies
August 1989	De facto crawling peg to US dollar	
August 1991	De facto peg to US dollar	One devaluation on March 1993; parallel market premium rose to 27% in preceding February
July 1995	De facto crawling peg to US dollar	During this period, the parallel market premium has consistently been in single digits
January 2004	Managed float with no pre-announced path for the exchange rate	
30 April 2008	Floating	The change reflects only a methodological modification and does not imply a judgement that there has been a substantive alteration in the exchange arrangement or other policies

Sources: Reinhart and Rogoff (2004); IMF (2009).

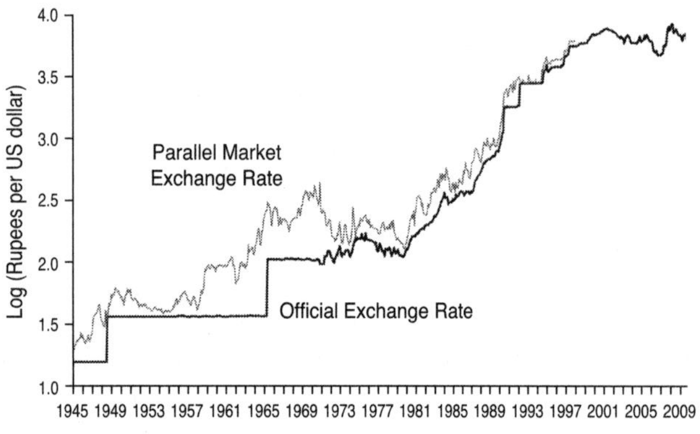

Figure 1 India: Official and Market-determined Exchange Rates

Sources: Background Materials from Reinhart and Rogoff (2004); International Financial Statistics, IMF.

about 30 per cent; and during 1984–9, the fall was by about 40 per cent (Joshi and Little 1994).

Since the crisis of 1991, India's de facto exchange rate strategy has been one of keeping the REER stable; Figure 2 shows that the REER-CPI has fluctuated in a relatively tight band. In the last 15 years, India has seen a marked acceleration in export growth with a broadening of the export base, including services, and a diversification of trading partners. Despite increases in productivity, India's export performance has lagged behind that of China and other Asian countries, and its share of global exports remains low. Most commentators agree that poor infrastructure and a high regulatory burden have prevented India from capturing a greater share of world exports.

India removed all restrictions on the current account and accepted its obligations under Article VIII of the IMF's Articles of Agreement in 1994 (IMF 2009). Since the mid-1990s, it has also embarked on a strategy of gradually removing impediments to foreign direct investment and other capital flows (Ahluwalia 2002; Panagariya 2008). More recently, even though integration with international financial markets has increased considerably and gross cross-border capital flows have more than doubled in the last decade, in terms of both de jure and de facto measures, India's financial openness is

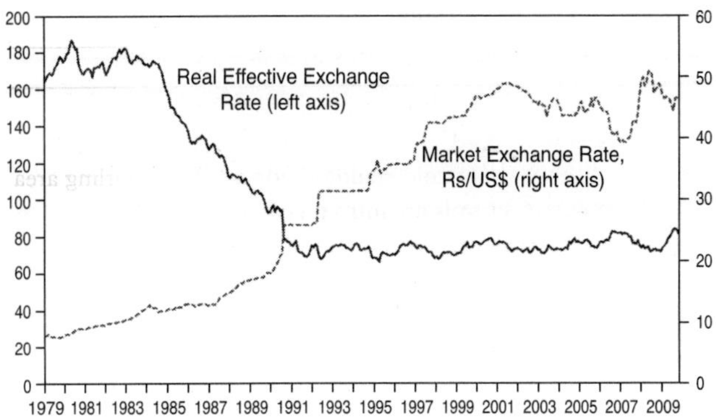

Figure 2 India: Real Effective Exchange Rate CPI-based Weights, 1990 = 100

Source: International Financial Statistics, IMF.

well below the levels attained by other emerging market economies, including Brazil, China, and Russia. While full capital account convertibility is not a priority per se, India continues to be opportunistic in taking advantage of opportunities for facilitating greater openness (see, for example, Prasad and Rajan 2008, Reddy 2008, Mohan 2008, and Prasad 2009).

Greater nominal exchange rate flexibility and the cautious path to capital account liberalization adopted by the Indian authorities has served the economy well in promoting growth as well as handling the contagion from the global financial crisis of 2007–10. The market exchange rate appreciated before the onset of the global crisis and then depreciated as foreign capital withdrew from India. Faced with a resurgence of capital flows starting in mid-2008, the Reserve Bank has allowed the market exchange rate to appreciate again. This has contributed to containing domestic inflation as well as serving as a measure to staunch the inflow of hot money. For now, as of October 2010, India has a comfortable foreign exchange reserve buffer for managing a relatively flexible exchange rate that is likely to be an increasingly important element of monetary policy and part of the toolkit for sustaining the increased outward orientation of the Indian economy.

SUNIL SHARMA

References

Ahluwalia, Montek S. 2002. 'Economic Reforms in India since 1991: Has Gradualism Worked', *Journal of Economic Perspectives*, Summer, 16(3): 67–88.

International Monetary Fund. 2009. Annual Report on Exchange Arrangements and Exchange Restrictions, Washington DC, International Monetary Fund.

Joshi, Vijay and Ian M.D. Little. 1994. *India: Macroeconomics and Political Economy, 1964–1991*, Washington DC, World Bank.

Lipschitz, Leslie and Donogh McDonald. 1992. 'Real Exchange Rates and Competitiveness: A Clarification of Concepts, and Some Measurements for Europe', *Empirica*, 19(1): 37–69.

Mohan, Rakesh. 2008. 'Capital Flows to India', BIS Paper No. 44, Basel, Bank for International Settlements.

Panagariya, Arvind. 2008. *India: The Emerging Giant*, Oxford, UK, Oxford University Press.

Prasad, Eswar. 2009. 'India's Approach to Capital Account Liberalization', IZA Discussion Paper No. 3927, Bonn, Institute for the Study of Labour.

Prasad, Eswar and Raghuram Rajan. 2008. 'A Pragmatic Approach to Capital Account Liberalization', *Journal of Economic Perspectives*, 69: 5–50.

Reddy, Y.V. 2008. 'Management of the Capital Account in India: Some Perspectives', Address at the Annual Conference of the Indian Econometric Society, Hyderabad, 3 January.

Reinhart, Carmen M. and Kenneth S. Rogoff. 2004. 'The Modern History of Exchange Rate Arrangements: A Reinterpretation', *Quarterly Journal of Economics*, CXIX(1): 1–48.

Zanello, Alessandro and Dominique Desruelle. 1997. 'A Primer on the IMF's Information Notice System', IMF Working Paper WP/97/71, Washington DC, International Monetary Fund.

Exogamy and Endogamy

Marriage patterns can broadly be classified into two categories: exogamous and endogamous. These represent rules or customs that define marriage partners. In addition, each type can further be classified into homogamous and heterogamous marriages, where homogamy refers to marriages where the partner is chosen from a similar background and/or interest.

Exogamy (endogamy) refers to rules or customs that require people to marry outside (within) certain groups/ communities or localities. The concepts of exogamy and endogamy are, therefore, very broad and their scope depends on what one considers to be a community or locality. Endogamy that requires the marriage partner to belong to the same village is village endogamy, and a marriage can similarly be district endogamous. Endogamy could also be at community level such as marriage between relatives who are related by marriage and/or by blood. Examples of these types of endogamy are marriage between first and second cousins or between uncles and nieces. Another widespread custom in India is marriage within a caste (caste endogamy). In spite of this wide scope in definition, to all intents and purposes, the form of endogamy that receives most attention is marriage between relatives.

Many social and economic reasons have been offered for the prevalence of endogamy, especially consanguineous marriages: strengthening of family ties, reducing financial uncertainties in marriage decisions, reduction of the burden of dowry, reduction of violence against wives, keeping wealth within families, and so on.

India poses an extremely interesting case study of exogamy and endogamy both in terms of prevalence and distribution as well as in terms of trends over time. There is usually a social taboo against consanguineous unions among the Hindu population in northern India, but not so among Hindus in the south. The Hindu Marriage Act of 1955 banned uncle–niece marriages, a practice that is still followed in some regions in the south. Among north Indian Hindus, marriages between relatives up to seven generations are generally frowned upon in order to avoid any chances of consanguinity. The north–south difference in the practice is rather sharp. The percentages of consanguineous marriages in total marriages were approximately 31 and 30 in the southern states of Andhra Pradesh and Karnataka, respectively, in the year 1992 (Bittles 2002). Even in the south, the rural–urban divide is significant. For example, during 1969–74, where in the rural areas of Tamil Nadu the percentage of consanguineous marriages was 46, the figure for urban areas was 29 (Rao and Inbaraj 1977). Kerala, which has a large Christian population, is an exception with only 7.5 per cent of marriages being consanguineous. In contrast to the south, the incidence of endogamy is very small in the north. Less that 1 per cent of marriages in Punjab and Haryana are consanguineous. For Uttar Pradesh, which has a significant Muslim population, the figure is still only 7.5 per cent. The east–west comparison is also interesting. Whereas about 5 per cent of marriages are consanguineous in the eastern states of West Bengal, Bihar, and Orissa, for the state of Maharashtra in the west the figure is 21 per cent (Bittles 2002).

The practice of endogamy is also very different among Hindus and Muslims. Even in the north and the east, first-cousin marriages are quite common among Muslims (the Koran prohibits uncle–niece marriages). For example, in the city of Lucknow in Uttar Pradesh, the incidence of consanguineous marriages during the period 1981–4 was only 0.1 per cent, among Hindus, but 17 per cent among Muslims (Agarwal et al. 1991). In the city of Mumbai, the figures for Hindus and Muslims were 8 per cent and 22 per cent, respectively (Sanghvi et al. 1956). The interaction between the north–south and Hindu–Muslim dimensions of endogamy is also interesting. In Karnataka the incidence of consanguineous marriages was higher among Hindus (34 per cent) than among Muslims (24 per cent) during 1980–9 (Bittles et al. 1991).

The practice of consanguineous marriages in India seems to be highest in rural areas and among poorer and less-educated people. However, sometimes even wealthy families practice endogamy as a means of keeping wealth within families. The overall trend in consanguineous marriages in India seems to indicate that its practice has declined over time (Audinarayana and Krishnamoorthy 2000). However, this decline seems more apparent among Hindus in southern India than among Muslims (Bittles and Hussain 1976). The fact that in Tamil a wife typically calls her husband '*Athan*' (father's sister's son) regardless of whether the husband is actually her father's sister's son related by blood implies that the practice of marrying one's father's sister's son was extremely widespread in the past for women in some regions of the south.

There could be many implications of endogamous unions, and these can be socio-economic, genetic, and fertility related. While the general consensus is that higher levels of fertility are found among consanguineous couples, there is no such consensus as far as the genetic mortality and morbidity consequences are concerned. However, since the genetic bond between an uncle and his niece is much stronger than that between first cousins, the ill effects of inbreeding are more likely to affect Hindus in the south than Muslims. There is some evidence for increased post-natal morbidity and mortality among women in consanguineous marriages.

As far as the socio-economic consequences of endogamy and exogamy are concerned, not much has been written. However, exogamy, when interacting with certain socio-cultural practices prevalent in India, can also have implications for the way young girls are treated within a family vis-à-vis young boys. One such practice is that of the extended family system. According to this system, once daughters are married, they leave the parents' house and live with their in-laws. Any income of the daughter after marriage becomes a property of the in-laws' family. Sons continue to live with parents after getting married and the income of a son and his wife becomes part of the income of the parents' family. In such situations, when a marriage is exogamous, parents of brides and grooms are more often than not unknown to each other when those brides and grooms were younger. These parents, therefore, are unlikely to coordinate among themselves and take the future income of daughters-in-law into consideration when making decisions on intra-family distribution of resources, leading to bias against young girls in education and in healthcare (Lahiri and Self 2007). In contrast, one would expect more coordination in societies where endogamy is practised and thus less bias against daughters.

SAJAL LAHIRI AND SHARMISTHA SELF

References

Agarwal, S.S., U. Singh, P.S. Singh, S.S. Singh, V. Das, and A. Sharma. 1991. 'Prevalence and Spectrum of Congenital Malformations in a Prospective Study at a Teaching Hospital', *Indian Journal of Medical Research*, 94: 413–9.

Audinarayana, N. and S. Krishnamoorthy. 2000. 'Contribution of Social and Cultural Factors to the Decline in Consanguinity in South India', *Annals of Human Biology*, 27(2): 163–71.

Bittles, A.H. 2002. 'Endogamy, Consanguinity, and Community Genetics', *Journal of Genetics*, 81: 91–8.

Bittles, A.H. and R. Hussain. 1976. 'An Analysis of Consanguineous Marriage in the Muslim Population at Regional and State Levels', *Human Heredity*, 26(2): 131–6.

Bittles, A.H., W.M. Mason, J. Greene, and N. Appaji Rao. 1991. 'Reproductive Behavior and Health in Consanguineous Marriages', *Science*, 252: 789–94.

Lahiri, S. and S. Self. 2007. 'Gender Bias in Education: The Role of Inter-household Externality, Dowry and Other Social Institutions', *Review of Development Economics*, 11(4): 591–606.

Rao, P.S.S. and S.G. Inbaraj. 1977. 'Inbreeding Effects on Human Reproduction in Tamil Nadu of South India', *Annals of Human Genetics*, 41: 87–98.

Sanghvi, L.D., D.S. Varde, and H.R. Master. 1956. 'Frequency of Consanguineous Marriages in Twelve Endogamous Groups in Bombay', *Acta Genetica et Statistica Medica*, 6: 41–9.

Exports and Export Policy

Exports typically refer to goods and services produced within a country, but consumed elsewhere in the rest of the world. For the past few decades, issues related to export promotion, growth, and export-led development strategies have been occupying centre stage in discussions on policymaking everywhere in the world. This has widely influenced theoretical and empirical literature in international trade and development. Primarily, the impetus for assigning a prime role to export-related strategies in the developing world comes from the tremendous achievement of East and Southeast Asian countries in expanding their exports and gross domestic product (GDP) growth rates. While there was a setback for some of them in the 1990s due to the well-known 'Asian crisis', their performance since the 1970s has been truly commendable. This entry takes a panoramic view of the theoretical aspects of export-promotional strategies, elaborates a few key concepts of export-related problems of the developed and developing countries, and subsequently analyses the contemporary Indian scenario in a little more detail.

Export-promotion Theory

Traditional trade theory suggests that left to themselves atomistic exporters within a country are going to export too much, adversely affecting the country's terms of trade. The nation as a whole should act like a monopolist in the world market and restrict its exports accordingly. Thus, an export tax is prescribed (Caves et al. 2002). Such a theoretical assertion seems to be inconsistent with the actual policy scenario, since countries always pursue proactive export policies and what we observe are export subsidies, not taxes. James Brander and Barbara Spencer (1985) have argued that in an oligopolistic market structure, countries will subsidize exports to shift profits away from their rivals. For example, the US and European Union blame each other for providing fiscal support to the two large airline-manufacturing giants, Boeing of the US and Airbus of France. Although such a policy is justified from the perspective of one particular exporting industry, it is not clear whether such subsidies are beneficial for the entire nation. Subsequently, it has also been pointed out that by restricting imports of a particular good, say automobiles, one could in fact push down its cost of production and increase exports to other markets.

Another aspect of the export-promotion strategy is related to its growth-augmenting impact. The earlier export pessimism, which was apprehensive of export-led growth of primary products because of low elasticity of demand and the resultant decline in terms of trade, has been convincingly dispelled thanks to the success of some of the Asian countries in the last few decades. Major expansion of manufacturing exports has been strongly correlated with growth in productivity and diversity of export items. Product differentiation, economies of scale, and growth in infrastructure have all led to a sustained growth in export and real incomes. However, in spite of numerous efforts to prove the causal relation between export and GDP growth, no one knows for sure which way the causality goes.[1]

[1]Francisco Rodriquez and Dani Rodrik provide an elegant analysis of the existing literature on trade and growth in one of their NBER Working Papers.

Relatively recent literature on productivity and export focuses on the relationship between firm and productivity and the ability to export. Typically, it is shown that the most productive firms are likely to be exporters in a particular industry. Productivity-driven exports also features in the analysis of intra-industry trade. Among labour-intensive products differentiated according to quality, the exported goods are likely to be more capital-intensive and of better quality than those made available to the local market. This suggests that even relatively labour-abundant countries can export capital-intensive goods, contrary to the conventional view. Hence, a relatively capital-abundant country can export labour-intensive goods. More recent treatment of factors determining the pattern of exports takes into account the remarkable developments in the field of information technology (IT) and virtual trade across naturally separated time zones.

Key Export-related Arrangements

Voluntary Export Restraint

Unrestricted competitive exports can lead to serious problem in the importing countries. The recent public opinion in the US against the import of cheap garments from China, earlier against cars from Japan, and also fairly recently against outsourced services from India, are some well-known examples. With Japan, the US arranged a system called voluntary export restraints or VERs. VER is a policy which voluntarily restricts exports and raises the local price of exports relative to the world price. However, such a premium, interpreted as rent from imposing the export quota, goes to the exporting country. In case of an import tax, the importing country appropriates the margin.

Export-processing Zones

Another often-quoted term concerning exports from the developing world seems to be export-processing zones (EPZs). In their drive to promote exports, developing countries have built special zones where export-oriented industries are granted special favours in terms of duty exemption on imported materials and other tax deductions. Such an effort has paid off well in China whereas in India it has not done so well. EPZs have recently lost some significance as tariffs and taxes have been declining all around and therefore special favours to some regions do not make much sense. However, EPZs are still thought to be a way of attracting foreign investment and export-oriented business in India.

Multi-fibre Agreements

Multi-fibre agreements (MFAs) refer to the export quota on textiles imposed to protect the textile industry in developed countries. Textile-exporting countries have specified quotas beyond which they are not allowed to export. MFA has been criticized time and again as a severe protectionist device to block exports from developing countries. For India these are related to a product group that accounts for around one-third of its exports. Interestingly, there is a feeling that the Chinese entry into the World Trade Organization (WTO) might make it difficult for other exporting nations to fulfil their quotas.

Anti-dumping Disputes

Disputes regarding the anti-dumping duties imposed to prevent exporters from selling cheap in the foreign markets relative to their local markets are quite common these days. The multilateral trade negotiations initiated by WTO have generally accepted the abolition of non-tariff barriers, such as quantitative restrictions or non-price restrictions, but have allowed the provision that in case exporters are dumping their products in foreign markets, that is, selling at a price lower than their average cost they can be subjected to anti-dumping duties. This has hurt exporters from the developing world since they have to prove that their prices are legitimate in the sense that they are not artificially lowering prices to deter the entry of locals. In any case, local cost and price estimates are hotly debated issues. Also such duties are often used as clear protection devices either to delay the entry of products or to force the exporters into arriving at some sort of settlement with local entities. In recent times, India has successfully defended quite a few anti-dumping proceedings against European and American companies. But given the current scenario and the competitive edge possessed by the cheap labour-abundant developing world, anti-dumping will be the most sought-after protection device in developed countries for years to come, notwithstanding the fact that it is local consumers or users who always suffer because of such duties.

The Indian Scenario

After Independence, India pursued a strategy of import substitution with a focus on self-reliance up to the mid-1980s. High import tariffs, both on final goods and intermediates, essentially taxed exports by channeling resources towards import substitutes and by making imported capital goods, technology, and raw materials quite expensive to use for potential exports. Since the mid-1980s, and especially since the early 1990s, there has been a radical change in India's external economic policies with increasing emphasis on export promotion and import competition. Substantial reduction in tariff and quantitative restrictions on imports have effectively made resources available for the export sector. A more flexible exchange rate policy, duty draw back on exportables, tax break for 100 per cent export-oriented units in software-related services, and rationalization of bureaucratic procedures are some of the policies that have positively impacted exports. India's volumes of trade and exports have grown commendably over the last decade (Marjit and Raychaudhuri 1997; Sinha Roy 2005). The resilient nature of our export growth is reflected in the fact that although in the last two years the Indian rupee has experienced substantial appreciation, exports have not faltered both due to sustained world demand and easing out of tariffs on imported intermediates. As suggested in theory, tariffs of various kinds do act as a tax on exports and, therefore, even if no proactive measures are taken for exports, liberalization of trade itself acts as an incentive. However, non-price factors seem to have constrained export growth to some extent (Marjit 1998; Sinha Roy 2005).

The positive effects of liberalization have not remained within the purview of traditional industries. Growth of software and/or IT-related exports has been quite impressive. India was ranked 2 in 2008 in the export of computer and information services; her share in export of software services in 2008–9 was 45.5 per cent and the compound annual growth rate (CAGR) stood at 30.5 from 2000–1 to 2006–7. However, the impact of global recession was also visible on services export which had a negative growth rate of 21.4 per cent in 2009–10[2] compared to a growth rate of 27.6 per cent for the corresponding period of the previous year. While the share of agriculture and allied products in total exports went down from 44 per cent in 1960–1 to 15 per cent in 1999–2000, the share of manufacturing exports increased from 45 per cent to 80 per cent. One can clearly associate a substantial jump in the average of growth of exports during 1985–99 (11 per cent) from 1973–84 (6 per cent) and 1960–72 (4 per cent), with policies directed towards a liberal trade regime.

Two major supply-side factors continue to adversely affect India's performance as an exporter. The first has to do with bureaucratic control and transaction costs related to procedural complexities and regulatory problems. These were reduced to some extent in the 1990s but some problems persist.

The second has to do with infrastructural bottlenecks. Indian ports are rare examples of overutilized capacities. The loading and offloading of items, connection of ports to the hinterland, and roads and related transportation logistics usually create severe problems for small exporters (Marjit 1998). A natural comparison between India and China is quite relevant here. Both have cheap labour and huge production capacity and both seem to be doing well on the export front. China is well on its way to becoming the largest production hub in the world because of its infrastructure and labour-related costs of production; this is yet to happen in India. The Chinese advantage over India is also reflected in the fact that many Indian producers are setting up business in China. On the demand side, it is felt that while Indian products have been doing well in spite of the appreciation of the Indian rupee, the pattern of India's exports does not really match with the transforming global demand—that is, the pattern of growth in demand for various products at the world level does not match with the pattern of growth in our exportables. There are also some genuine concerns regarding the desirability of export of agricultural goods when poor farmers are net buyers of food.

The following issues have often come up for debate in the public domain:

1. Is India's growth performance related to growth in exports? This is an unresolved issue. Working with data till the mid-1990s, Marjit and Raychaudhuri (1997) argue that exports are essentially residuals when we consider the overall growth in GDP and that growth in GDP was not caused by export growth. However, the IT sector now commands a substantial fragment of our national income and therefore export growth in that segment is bound to boost our growth rate to some extent. One point to be noted here is that when we compare the Indian case with that of other successful nations in Asia, a striking dissimilarity is the very high rates of savings and investments in most of these countries and a relatively stagnant rate of investments in India. Such information tends to blur the relationship between exports and growth unless one finds a link between exports and the rate of investment. Apart from growth through increased exports, the Indian economy also benefited from sizeable measured productivity gains by obtaining access to new products or new varieties of existing products. The benefits obtained from international trade through increased access to previously unavailable inputs generate static gains from trade. Access to these new imported inputs in turn enables firms to expand their domestic product range through the introduction of new varieties which generate dynamic gains from trade. Goldberg et al. (2008) argue that trade reforms have benefited Indian firms by providing access to more and cheaper variety of input goods. They effectively explain that lower tariff rates (as a result of liberalization in 1991) increased the availability of new imported inputs at a cheaper rate which led to an increase in the number of

[2]Estimates are for April to September.

products manufactured by Indian firms during the immediate post-liberalization phase. Moreover, the indirect benefit of this whole production process ultimately accrued to the consumers who became well-off. Lower import tariffs also increased R&D expenditures albeit with some amount of heterogeneity across firms (Goldberg et al. 2009).

2. Does an increase in exports widen the income gap between the rich and the poor in India? This is related to the popular debate on globalization and inequality. Increasing international trade and investment seem to have widened the skilled–unskilled wage gap almost everywhere in the world. Although no definitive empirical evidence points to trade as the only causal factor, there is a feeling that new technology enriches those who have the required human capital to absorb such technology and therefore it also leads to widening inequality. There is some evidence in India that the rising wage gap has coincided with the ongoing phase of economic reforms. But the issue is still wide open.

Financial Crisis and India's Exports

The decade 1980–1 to 1990–1 was marked by the low growth syndrome of the Indian economy from which it emerged in the late 1990s. According to WTO's 2007 trade statistics, India's share in merchandise exports increased from 0.4 per cent in 1981 to 0.91 per cent in 2006 and India's services exports increased from 0.59 per cent of world services exports in 1991 to 2.32 per cent in 2006. This growth continued more or less unhindered till 2007, when it was jolted by the sub-prime crisis in the US which led to a full blown global recession. Owing to this worldwide crisis, India's export growth decelerated from a 20 per cent plus growth rate in 2002–3 to a 3.6 per cent growth rate in 2008–9. However, the crisis seemed to have weakened by early 2010 with India's exports picking up again. The CAGR for India's merchandise exports for 2004–5 to 2008–9 increased from 14 to 23.8 per cent. Though India's export growth rate marginally declined from 21.4 per cent in 2007 to 20.4 per cent in 2008, and –18.4 per cent in 2009,[3] it must be noted that India's share in world merchandise exports over the same period mostly remained the same (1.1 per cent in 2007 and 2008) with a slight increase in 2009[4] (1.2 per cent).

SUGATA MARJIT

[3]Estimates are for January to June.
[4]Estimates are for January to June.

References

Brander, J. and B. Spencer. 1985. 'Export Subsidies and International Market Share Rivalry', *Journal of International Economics*, 18: 83–100.

Caves, R.E., J. Frankel, and R.W. Jones. 2002. *World Trade and Payments* (9th edition), Reading MA, Addision-Wesley.

Goldberg P., A. Khandelwal, N. Pavcnik, and P. Topalova. 2008. 'Imported Intermediate Inputs and Domestic Product Growth: Evidence from India', *Quarterly Journal of Economics*.

——. 2009. 'Trade Liberalization and New Imported Inputs', *American Economic Review*, 99(2): 494–500.

Marjit, S. 1998. 'Transaction Costs of India's Exports—An Analysis', Occasional Paper No. 64, Export-Import Bank of India.

——. 2007. 'Trade Theory and Role of Time Zones', *International Review of Economics and Finance*, 16: 153–60.

Marjit, S. and A. Raychaudhuri. 1997. *India's Exports—An Analytical Study*, New Delhi, Oxford University Press.

Sinha Roy, S. 2005. 'Factors in the Determination of India's Exports', Unpublished PhD Thesis, Centre for Development Studies, Thiruvananthapuram.

■ External Debt

The Current Debt Situation

From being on the brink of defaulting on its debt in 1991, India has very significantly improved its creditworthiness. Key indicators in Table 1 show that India's debt-carrying capacity has strengthened even though external debt in US dollar terms has more than trebled in the past two decades. In fact, much of the increase in total external debt has been over the past five years with an almost doubling of the debt since 2004–5. However, over the years the economy's resource potential to repay the debt has grown faster than the debt. As a result, debt-to-gross domestic product (GDP) has come down to around 20 per cent and, more markedly, debt-to-external current receipts (excluding official transfers) declined from 323 per cent in 1990–1 to 76 per cent in 2009–10. Measures of liquidity, such as the debt service ratio (DSR) (interest and principal payments as a proportion of exports of goods and services) and the extent of short-term debt in relation to foreign exchange reserves, also show a substantial improvement.

How does India compare with other countries? India ranks fifth among the debtor countries in the world by size of debt, but the burden of external debt depends less on its size than on a country's ability to service it. On such measures, India compares favourably with

Table 1 Key External Debt Indicators, 1990–1 to 2009–10

As in end-March	CAB/GDP %	Total debt $ bn	Debt/GDP (%)	Debt/curr rec. (%)	DSR (%)	Short-term debt/total debt (%)	Short-term debt/foreign exchange reserves (%)
1990–1	−3.0	83.8	26.4	323.0	34.6	10.2	146.5
1991–2	−0.4	85.3	31.9	307.1	29.7	8.3	76.7
1992–3	−1.4	90.0	36.7	319.2	27.2	7.0	64.5
1993–4	−0.4	92.7	33.6	272.6	25.1	3.9	18.8
1994–5	−1.0	99.0	30.6	233.5	25.6	4.3	16.9
1995–6	−1.7	93.7	26.3	187.6	26.0	5.4	23.2
1996–7	−1.2	93.5	24.1	168.3	22.8	7.2	25.5
1997–8	−1.3	93.5	22.8	158.7	19.4	5.4	17.2
1998–9	−1.0	96.9	23.3	161.3	18.7	4.4	13.2
1999–2000	−1.0	98.3	21.8	144.8	17.0	4.0	10.3
2000–1	−0.6	101.3	22.0	130.4	16.5	3.6	8.6
2001–2	0.7	98.8	20.7	121.4	13.6	2.8	5.1
2002–3	1.3	104.9	20.7	109.6	15.9	4.5	6.1
2003–4	2.3	112.7	18.8	94.0	16.0	3.9	3.9
2004–5	−0.3	134.0	18.6	86.6	5.9	13.2	12.5
2005–6	−1.2	139.1	16.6	71.4	10.0	14.0	12.9
2006–7	−1.0	172.4	18.2	70.8	4.7	16.3	14.1
2007–8	−1.3	224.4	18.3	71.2	4.7	20.4	14.8
2008–9 (R)	-2.4	224.5	18.5	63.7	4.4	19.3	17.2
2009–10 (PR)	-2.9	261.2	19.9	76.1	5.5	20.0	18.8

Source: Reserve Bank of India, *Handbook of Statistics on the Indian Economy 2009–10*; Ministry of Finance, *India's External Debt Status Reports*.
Note: DSR for 2008–9 is partially revised (PR) and 2009–10 are quick estimates (QE).

Table 2 Key Indebtedness Indicators, 2007–9

Country	Total external debt, 2009 ($ bn)	Ratio of present value of debt to GNI (%)	Ratio of present value of debt to to exports of goods and services (%)	Debt service to XGS (%)	Short-term debt/total debt (%)	Short-term debt/foreign exchange reserves (%)
China	428.4	9	25	2.9	56	10
Russian Federation	381.3	26	74	17.7	8	14
Brazil	276.9	17	125	23.4	14	6
Turkey	251.4	35	144	41.6	16	2
India	237.7	17	71	5.9	18	7
Mexico	192.0	18	61	16	18	4
Indonesia	157.5	30	99	18.4	12	4
Argentina	120.2	41	156	17.3	16	2
Romania	117.5	53	166	31.4	18	2
Kazakhstan	109.9	96	157	80.2	8	3
Ukraine	93.2	62	123	36.2	21	1
Chile	71.6	43	84	22.6	24	1
Malaysia	66.4	31	27	5.2	36	4
Philippines	62.9	35	90	18.5	6	11
Thailand	58.8	22	28	6.8	47	5

Source: World Bank (2011).

other countries, as may be seen in Table 2. Since some (currently down to about 16 per cent) of India's debt outstanding is contracted on concessional terms, the nominal or face value of the debt overestimates the debt burden. Therefore, for comparability across countries, the present value (PV) of debt is used, which takes into account the degree of concessionality of the debt by discounting the future stream of debt service obligations at a market interest rate. Some indicators of what is considered a sustainable debt threshold for low-income countries are: PV of debt to exports of 150–200 per cent, and debt service to exports of around 20–25 per cent. By these yardsticks, India is clearly comfortable.

Borrowing Used to Enhance Growth Rate

Countries generally borrow when they are developing and industrializing and their investment needs exceed their domestic savings. As long as the rate of return on investment exceeds the interest rate at which they borrow, the capacity of the economy is enhanced and the debt is serviceable. Countries, such as the United States and the United Kingdom also relied extensively on external borrowings during earlier periods in their economic history. Britain financed much of its industrial revolution in the 19th century with borrowings from cash-rich Holland. Then Britain itself became a lender and financed much of the economic expansion of the United States, which in turn became a net lender only towards the middle of this century. Of course, countries also borrow to finance consumption. But then, unless the economy is growing at a rate faster than the real interest rate, it may run into a 'debt trap'.

In national accounting terms, the excess of a country's expenditure over national income is reflected in its current account deficit in the balance of payments (BOP), which in turn is financed by recourse to foreign savings either by way of non-debt-creating flows, such as foreign investment or by way of debt flows in the form of bonds, loans, and deposits. The actual transfer of resources from the rest of the world is the current account deficit before interest payments. Conversely, a primary (non-interest) current account surplus signifies a transfer of resources to the rest of the world.

An important issue here has to do with the availability of foreign exchange. The government may be able to raise sufficient resources to service its debt but might not be able to transform them into foreign currency assets. If the exchange rate is inconvertible and there are insufficient foreign exchange reserves, it could lead to foreign exchange scarcity, as happened in 1991. Or, if the exchange rate is over-valued then there could be a speculative attack on the exchange rate resulting in a sharp loss of reserves, as happened in East Asia. If the exchange rate is managed flexibly, then imbalances in demand and supply for foreign exchange translate into exchange rate movements rather than foreign exchange shortages.

'Too Little' Borrowing?

For more than three decades India pursued extremely conservative borrowing policies. This was a direct outcome of the development strategy adopted after Independence, which was based on self-reliance and import-substitution, whereby investments were almost entirely financed through domestic savings, with recourse to foreign flows only at the margin. The government accessed the International Monetary Fund (IMF) facilities to meet extraordinary needs, such as drought and oil shocks. Therefore, until the 1980s, the government borrowed mostly from official sources, bilateral and multilateral, and mainly on concessional terms. While this was a prudent debt policy given the limited capacity to repay foreign currency loans, the inward-oriented approach was arguably at the cost of growth and poverty reduction, as GDP growth averaged a lacklustre 3.6 per cent between 1965 and 1980.

Too Much Borrowing Relative to Capacity to Repay

On the other hand, during the 1980s borrowing accelerated and the cost of borrowing rose. The decade saw a large increase in public-sector deficit and a widening current account deficit. As aid inflows declined, the country turned to commercial sources of financing and the government started borrowing from private creditors, including raising non-resident Indian (NRI) deposits at a higher cost. External debt quadrupled in 10 years to $83.8 billion in 1990–1. Almost 40 per cent of the debt was owed to private creditors, up from negligible levels 10 years previously.

A significant part of this increase during the late 1980s was short-term debt, in particular short-term NRI deposits. The East Asian financial crisis has shown that even if the total external debt burden is not high, the composition of debt is important. The greater the amount of short-term debt over and above trade credit, the greater is the vulnerability of the economy to external shocks and sudden reversals in capital flows. In 1990–1, $8.5 billion of short-term debt had accumulated. This was 147 per cent of the foreign exchange reserves. In fact, by the end of January 1991, foreign exchange reserves had been depleted to a mere $1 billion (equivalent to two weeks' imports). Throughout these difficulties India maintained full debt servicing, but it did so by various forms of financing, including by pledging its gold reserves and by an administrative squeeze on imports.

What were the fundamental causes of the crisis? Besides the rapid increase in the amount and cost of debt, there were other major problems that led to its unsustainability. First, the borrowing was driven by expanding government deficits, in large part due to a growth in unproductive expenditures. The fiscal deficit rose sharply due to an increase in current expenditures, not investments. The consolidated central and state government deficits increased from an average of 5.4 per cent of GDP in the second half of the 1970s to 10 per cent of GDP in the second half of the 1980s. Current expenditures rose by almost 7 per cent of GDP, outstripping the increase in revenues of 2 percentage points, whereas investment remained about the same—at 7 per cent of GDP—over the same period. Thus, the additional borrowing was not used to finance investment in growth-enhancing activities that would eventually help to repay the debt, but rather for expenditures, such as subsidies and wage payments. Borrowing for consumption purposes cannot be sustained for a long time.

Second, the economy was still relatively closed and uncompetitive, mired in inefficiencies, notwithstanding the step up in the economic growth rate to 5.5 per cent in the 1980s. Until 1985 there was complete stagnation of exports, in turn largely the result of an inappropriate exchange rate policy and limited deregulation of the industrial and trade regimes. The exchange rate became increasingly over-valued, rendering exports uncompetitive. Exports rebounded in the second half of the 1980s as the exchange rate policy became more flexible and the exchange rate depreciated in real terms. But by then it was insufficient to offset the impact of rising interest payments on external debt and the rapid growth in imports induced by fiscal deterioration. Once the external finances had become so fragile, the country was vulnerable to exogenous shocks, such as the Gulf War and concomitant oil price hike and disruption in worker remittances. Political uncertainties and a sovereign rating downgrade then precipitated a drying up of commercial financing, and ultimately a severe liquidity crisis ensued.

Reforms and External Debt Management Strategy

Reforms were initiated in the fiscal and industrial policies, the financial sector, and—perhaps mostly extensively of all—in the external sector, to make better use of resources, including foreign borrowings. The framework for the reforms of the external sector was provided by the Report of the High Level Committee on Balance of Payments chaired by Dr C. Rangarajan. External sector reforms included exchange rate devaluation and the introduction of a market-determined exchange rate, reduction of anti-export bias through trade reforms, and policies to encourage foreign direct investment (FDI) and portfolio flows through foreign institutional investors (FIIs).

Besides emphasizing non-debt-creating capital flows, the external debt management policies since 1991 have focused on reducing the cost of debt, encouraging long maturity loans, and controlling volatile components, such as commercial borrowings as well as short-term debt. Accordingly, high-cost multilateral and bilateral loans were prepaid. This was facilitated by foreign exchange reserves increasing and interest rates declining globally and domestically. The interest rates on NRI deposits were rationalized and the schemes streamlined. Short-term debt was brought down and restricted to trade-related purposes, with NRI deposits of less than one year maturity phased out. Medium-term borrowing from private commercial sources was subject to annual caps, minimum maturity requirements, and end-use stipulations. Foreign exchange reserves were built up. In addition, external debt statistics were substantially improved in terms of coverage, classification, and consistency, consequent upon the recommendations of a Policy Group and Task Force on External Debt Statistics in 1992. Indeed, it is only thereafter that a reliable debt series is available.

Some Debt Management Issues and Challenges

The composition of external debt is changing, with borrowing increasingly by the private sector and from private creditors. Non-government debt expanded from 40 per cent in 1990–1 to almost 75 per cent in 2009–10. The rapid growth in the debt since 2004–5 has been driven by the (non-financial) private sector, which together with short-term debt (mostly trade credits), accounted for 80 per cent of the increase. As a result, the private non-financial sector now comprises over 37 per cent of the debt and the public sector a steady 7.5 per cent, whereas the financial sector accounts for 29 per cent, down from 50 per cent in 2005. Improved access of corporates to international capital markets, underpinned by some liberalization of the external commercial borrowing policy, have raised commercial borrowings sharply.

Private-sector borrowing brings in its wake different risks. As witnessed in the East Asian crisis, excessively risky private-sector behaviour can precipitate a crisis. This has been guarded against in India to a large extent by stipulations on the end use of such borrowing as well as annual borrowing limits and all-in-cost ceilings. Thus, the rapid accumulation of debt by the private sector between 2005 and 2010 was mainly to finance investment (imports of equipment). Another, perhaps more likely, risk is the impact of exchange rate depreciation on the repayment of foreign currency loans. Since the exchange rate has been fairly stable or has even appreciated over the recent past, much of this borrowing may have been unhedged. If, therefore, the rupee depreciates, debt servicing will become more costly and if the private-sector borrower does not generate adequate foreign exchange earnings, it will have a net adverse impact on its profitability and ability to repay.

A second issue relates to the costs of excessive reserve accumulation. The large build-up of foreign exchange reserves over the past few years has certainly improved the country's creditworthiness, reduced vulnerability to external shocks and possible abrupt reversals of capital flows, and provided liquidity in exchange rate management. However, the current level of foreign exchange reserves exceeds, by a large margin, the conventional measures of reserve adequacy. As against a rule of thumb of a three-to-six-month import cover, India's foreign exchange reserves (excluding gold) covered 10.4 months of merchandise imports (or 8.7 months of imports of goods and services). Moreover, the reserves exceed five times over the stock of short-term debt. Indeed, RBI's foreign currency assets provided a cover of around 97.5 per cent of the *total* external debt outstanding at end-March 2010. This means that India is barely a net debtor as net debt (foreign debt *minus* foreign assets) is negligible.

A debate has been ongoing about whether India should hold such large reserves when our investment financing needs, especially for infrastructure, are so high. In addition, there are also significant costs in holding the reserves: these are the difference between what the foreign currency reserve assets earn and what the RBI must pay on domestic securities issued to offset their expansionary monetary impact.

A third, and related, issue is to consider a broader definition of external liabilities for monitoring volatile capital flows. Some economists and policymakers have pointed out that while equity flows provide a means of reducing debt levels, proper debt management should involve ensuring the cost effectiveness and sustainability of a stock of liabilities which include both debt and non-debt elements. In particular, as foreign portfolio flows have become significant and they are relatively volatile, it is arguable whether foreign exchange reserves should also cover for a sudden outflow of such capital. Even if the stock of portfolio investment brought in cumulatively by FIIs is taken into account as well as short-term debt, the level of our existing foreign exchange reserves is more than necessary.

RITU ANAND

References

Acharya, Shankar. 2002. 'Macroeconomic Management in the Nineties', *Economic and Political Weekly*, 20 April, 37(16): 1515–38.

Government of India. 2010. *India's External Debt: A Status Report 2009–10,* September.

——. 2011. *India's External Debt as at End-December 2010,* March.

Joshi, Vijay and I.M.D. Little. 1992a. *Report of the High Level Committee on Balance of Payments.*

——. 1992b. *Report of Policy Group and Task Force on External Debt Statistics of India.*

——. 1994. *India: Macroeconomics and Political Economy, 1964–1991,* New Delhi, Oxford University Press.

——. 1998. *Report of the Technical Committee on External Debt*, May.

Reserve Bank of India. 2010. *Handbook of Statistics on the Indian Economy 2009–10,* Mumbai, RBI.

Vasudevan, A. (ed.). 1999. *External Debt Management: Issues, Lessons and Preventive Measures*, Mumbai, Reserve Bank of India.

World Bank. 2011. *Global Development Finance*, Washington DC, World Bank

F

Famines

Famine is one of the oldest scourges of mankind. Fortunately, in India today, we can claim with a reasonable degree of assurance that 'famine is history'—at least so it has been for over half a century. In spite of this success, or perhaps because of it, the study of Indian famines remains a matter of immense interest for a number of reasons.

First and foremost, the rich and varied literature that has emerged out of the study of Indian famines constitutes a valuable resource for advancing our understanding of how famines occur and how they can be prevented, relevant not just for those parts of the world where famines remain a recurrent scourge, for instance, in large parts of Africa, but also for India itself, where, although famine might be history, sadly the threat of famine is not.

Second, the fierce debates that raged between the nationalist and colonial commentators over the famines that occurred during the British colonial period are singularly relevant for our understanding of the impact of colonial rule on the economic and social evolution of India. Third, the early colonial discourse on what would constitute an appropriate famine policy in India involved an intriguing interplay between economic theory and public policy that provides a striking example of how knowledge can be pressed into the service of power. Fourth, recent studies on the interaction between famine and epidemics in India shed valuable light on the nutrition–infection nexus—the synergistic relation that nutritionists believe to exist between food deprivation and infection. Finally, the study of Indian famines has great potential to contribute to the current research on famine demography—the study of the consequences of famine for fertility, mortality, and population growth.

Aetiology of Famines

The record of famines in ancient and medieval India is scant, although old literary sources and religious scriptures do testify that major famines occurred from time to time. More is known about famines that occurred after the onset of Muslim rule in the 12th century, the major recorded ones being those in 1396 (in the Deccan and lasting 12 years), 1596 (almost the whole of India, and other parts of Asia, lasting three to four years), and 1660 (all of Aurangzeb's empire, excluding Bengal and Bombay).

Famines became more frequent with the advent of British rule. Soon after the East India Company established its dominion over Bengal in 1757, a severe famine decimated Bengal in 1769–70. This was followed by another major famine in 1803–4, which devastated most of India, excluding Bengal and the Deccan. The intensity and frequency of famines increased sharply in the second half of the 19th century, culminating in the Great Famines of 1896–1900, which engulfed almost all of India, and is known to be the greatest famine ever recorded in this land (Bhatia 1967). The situation improved in the 20th century, but the improvement was rudely interrupted by the Great Bengal Famine of 1943—the last famine of the British period. Since Independence in 1947, India has managed to avoid a famine, despite a few close calls—Bihar in 1965–6, Maharashtra in 1972–3, and the whole of north India in

1979–80. Of the regions that were parts of British India, only Bangladesh has suffered a famine (in 1974) in the post-colonial period.

It is interesting that no major famine is recorded in Bengal until the arrival of the British. Bengal was often exempt when most of India was ravaged, as in 1660, and in 1343 during Mohammad-bin Tughlak's time people migrated to Bengal from the famine-stricken province of Delhi. All that was to change, however, after the British acquired the *Diwani* (revenue rights) of Bengal in the 1760s.

Until that time, the modus operandi of the Company was to purchase Indian commodities in exchange for precious metals imported from England and to sell them in international markets for profit. The acquisition of revenue rights in Bengal enabled the Company to enhance its profits enormously. Instead of using their own precious metals, they could now use the tribute collected from the peasants of Bengal to purchase the commodities for export, making the purchase virtually costless. Profits now consisted of the whole of the sales proceeds (minus trading costs), and not just the difference between selling price and purchase price. In a bid to maximize these profits, the Company set about extorting tributes at exorbitant rates. On paper, these rates were no different from the ones imposed earlier by the Muslim rulers, but the British collected the tribute more efficiently and more ruthlessly, with scant regard for the condition of the peasantry. They did not relent even after harvest failed repeatedly in the late 1760s, thereby reducing the peasants to a state of utter penury. This is what precipitated the famine of 1769–70, which killed nearly one-third of the population of Bengal, followed by another in 1783–4 and again in 1787–8. These famines were created not so much by the parsimony of nature as by the greed and callousness of men.

As famines and starvation ravaged Bengal, realization dawned on the British rulers that they were actually harming their own long-term future by killing the goose that laid the golden egg. Beyond a point, not much tribute could be extracted from a ruined peasantry, howsoever ruthlessly. This realization led eventually to the institution of the Permanent Settlement in eastern India and *ryotwari* settlement in the south, whose objective was to trade off some land revenue in the short run in the hope of collecting more revenue from commerce in the long run. These institutions in turn had profound impact on the evolution of agrarian relations in India, with implications for not just the social and economic structures that emerged but also for the political alignments that characterized the nationalist movement in the later part of British rule. In this sense the Bengal famines of the early colonial era can be said to have played a catalytic role in shaping the entire course of Indian colonial history.

After the early shocks, Bengal was spared a major famine for nearly a century, but other parts of India continued to be ravaged. Indeed, famines became more frequent and more virulent in the second half of the 19th century. This was deeply embarrassing for the British government, as the period of more frequent famines started almost immediately after the East India Company's rule was replaced with direct rule by the Crown in 1858. Colonial administrators and other British commentators sought desperately to give a positive spin to this coincidence by describing the famines as an inevitable, if sad, by-product of their benevolent rule! To this end, the ideas of classical political economy, especially those of Malthus, were frequently invoked. Of the three positive checks—namely, war, disease, and famine—that, according to Malthus, kept population down to the feeding capacity of land, the British claimed to have eliminated the first two through good governance. As a result, so the argument went, famines remained the only mechanism of nature to maintain parity between people and land. Famine was inevitable, the argument added, in the absence of preventive checks, in the form of conscious fertility control, allegedly not being practised by the Indians.

This view was hotly contested by the nationalist scholars (for example, Dutt 1904) as well as some sympathetic British commentators. They argued that famines had become more frequent because British rule had actually reduced the living standards of the majority of Indians, making them more vulnerable than ever before to the vagaries of nature. Thus emerged a prolonged and heated debate on the economic impact of British rule in India whose reverberations can be felt even today (Habib 1985). The critics identified a number of policies that had exacerbated the vulnerability of Indian masses.

The most culpable of all was land tax policy. The example of the Permanent Settlement that was introduced in eastern India as a means of keeping land revenue down to a permanently fixed level was not followed elsewhere. Even the ryotwari system that was instituted in the south with a similar objective was subsequently modified to allow for more intensified extraction of rent. Thus the general experience of peasantry in most parts of India was one of high and uncertain demand for rent, which left it barely at the edge of survival.

No less pernicious was the policy of unrequited transfer of tribute to England. In the earlier era, when the rulers extracted tribute from the peasantry they used to spend most of it on local crafts and services. This had spawned a sizeable urban-based industrial and services sector during the Mughal period. The policy of unrequited transfer during the British period ensured that this particular source of demand for industrial products and services dried up, setting in motion a secular process of deindustrialization and deurbanization.

This process was further exacerbated by the trade and industrial policy pursued by the colonial administration in support of the Industrial Revolution in England. First, it allowed free import of English cotton yarn, which destroyed the local spinning industry, and subsequently the British government imposed tariffs on the import of Indian cloth into England, which weakened the weaving industry as well (although the weaving industry revived somewhat in the 20th century for other reasons).

The combined effect of these policies was to not only destroy existing jobs in the urban areas but also the possibility of absorbing surplus rural labour into off-farm activities. Thus, while, on the one hand, the peasantry was impoverished through rack-renting, it was at the same time deprived of the opportunity of escaping from rural misery by working outside. The result was a marked increase in rural landlessness, accompanied by declining real wages. It was little wonder that vulnerability to famine should have increased under these circumstances.

The problem was compounded by the unanticipated side effects of the expansion of irrigation and railways. By obstructing the natural flow of water, these developments created a serious waterlogging problem, resulting in mosquito infestation and the spread of malaria. Repeated bouts of malarial fever combined with food deprivation to create a malnutrition–infection nexus, leading to serious debilitating effects. Modern research has demonstrated how this nexus contributed to raising the level of excess mortality when famines struck repeatedly in the late 19th century (Maharatna 1996).

Two hundred years of British rule in India started with a famine in Bengal and ended with another—the Great Bengal Famine of 1943. The principal proximate cause of this famine, which took at least 1.5 million lives, was inflationary financing of India's involvement in the Second World War. The price spiral seriously eroded the purchasing power of the impoverished segments of the population—landless agricultural labourers and all others who had to buy food from the market. As Amartya Sen has noted, the famine struck not so much because overall food availability had declined, but because millions of people had lost their 'entitlement to food' through loss of purchasing power (Sen 1981). The problem was aggravated by the government's failure to protect the entitlements of vulnerable groups through provision of work or food.

Sen's analysis of the 1943 famine led to the emergence of the celebrated entitlement approach to famine, which focuses on food entitlements instead of overall food availability as the chief explanatory variable in a famine analysis. Empirically, there has been some debate as to whether decline in food availability was a contributory factor or not in the famine of 1943. On the theoretical front, however, Sen's entitlement-focused analysis has made a lasting contribution to our understanding of famines in at least two ways. First, it has shown that famine can occur even without a decline in overall food availability—that is, the Malthusian route is not the only one through which famine might strike. Second, even when decline in food availability plays a role, it is still necessary to look at the entitlements of different segments of population in order to understand why it is that in times of famine only some groups of people suffer while others do not, at least not to the same extent. At policy level too, the entitlement approach offers critical insights, as discussed in the following section.

Famine Policy

Public policy towards famines in India has undergone remarkable metamorphosis over the centuries. In the pre-British period, the rulers would typically respond to famines by adopting various kinds of interventionist policies—for example, debt forgiveness for poor farmers, importation of food grains, and fixation of maximum prices. During the first half of British rule, however, a deliberate hands-off policy became the norm. The government would neither intervene in the market for food grains to relieve scarcity in the afflicted areas, nor would it take measures to provide subsidized food to the famine victims. Ostensibly, the rationale for this laissez faire policy was drawn from the doctrines of classical political economy (Ambirajan 1978).

The ideas of Adam Smith and John Stuart Mill were repeatedly invoked to justify the policy of non-intervention in the market for food grains. It was argued that the only sensible way of dealing with a situation of scarcity was to allow prices to rise, for any attempt to artificially keep prices down would only serve to prolong the period of scarcity as lower prices would discourage private traders from bringing additional food from outside. The faith in the ability of the private sector to deal with the problem was founded on the assumption of a competitive market, for which the existence of a very large number of small traders was adduced as evidence. The flaw with this argument was that a large number of traders was but one condition out of many that were needed for a market to function efficiently. Faced with serious transport bottlenecks and credit constraints, it was practically impossible for small traders to move large amounts of food grains from one part of the country to another quickly enough, even if they had the incentive to do so. As a result, even if the market behaved efficiently at normal times, it was bound to fail in times of acute scarcity. And so it did, costing millions of lives.

The non-interventionist approach extended to the issue of relief as well. Drawing inspiration from classical political economy's aversion to the Poor Laws in England, it was argued that giving charity to the famine victims was not going to help in the long run, as it would only prolong the imbalance between population and food supply, which eventually must take its toll. The only tangible effect of charity would be to create a culture of dependency.

Apart from doctrinal influences, practical financial considerations also played a role in predisposing policy towards non-intervention. This became obvious during the famine that struck Madras and Bombay presidencies in 1875. Budgetary resources were dwindling at that time because of silver depreciation as well as repeal of certain import duties under pressure of British manufacturing industry. Severely handicapped by shortage of cash, and faced with the enormity of the famine, Governor General Lytton categorically declared that saving lives at any cost was not the responsibility of the government.

Within the general approach of non-intervention, the only action that the colonial government countenanced with some favour was providing temporary employment to famine victims. Contemporary analyses of famines had made it clear that the reason people suffered when harvests failed was not so much that there was not enough food around (in the country as a whole) as that they found themselves without work and thus without the purchasing power to buy food. As Baird Smith, commenting on the North Western Provinces Famine of 1860–1, put it in 1861, the famines in India were 'rather famines of work than of food'[1]—a clear precursor of the entitlement approach to famine that was to emerge later.

After much vacillation, the principle of providing work as a means of famine relief was operationalized under a system of 'Famine Codes' built on the suggestions of the Famine Enquiry Commission of 1880. Even here, however, the bias towards minimalist intervention was manifest in at least two ways. First, workers were to be paid strictly in cash, not in food, so that the government did not have to intervene in the grain market to procure the necessary food. Second, the wage rate was to be kept as low as possible consistent with survival. This was meant to act as a self-selection mechanism of targeting relief to the neediest of people, helping to keep expenditure down (Loveday 1914).

It would appear that, for all its limitations, the Famine Codes were reasonably successful in dealing with, and even preventing, famines during the subsequent seven decades of British rule, with two major exceptions. The first exception was the Great Famines of 1896–1900 and the second the Bengal famine of 1943. Each of these exceptions offers important lessons for famine policy. The famines of 1896–1900 demonstrate the folly of dogmatic refusal on the part of government to intervene in the grain market. Harvest failure was so widespread that unlike in earlier crises overall food production had declined drastically, so much so that private traders were simply unable to cope. In the absence of government efforts to augment food supply, provision of employment alone was not enough to stave off crisis, especially in view of the stinginess shown with respect to wages and the debilitating effects of the malnutrition–infection nexus referred to earlier.

The Bengal famine of 1943 highlights the political preconditions necessary for successful implementation of famine policy. Despite clear signs of distress before the famine became full-blown, the British government deliberately ignored the Famine Codes for political reasons. It was loath to acknowledge that its War efforts were creating vulnerabilities through inflation, nor was it willing to set aside resources for relief operations at the expense of War-related expenditure. It was only after Independence and the establishment of a democratic polity that the principles embodied in the Famine Codes became fully operational in India. Every time a crisis loomed, the government intervened in multiple ways—by providing employment, importing food grains, and activating the public food grain distribution system—to forestall a full-blown famine (Drèze 1990). The existence of a democratic polity—characterized by electoral accountability, multi-party politics, and a free press—ensured that the government would spring into action to keep famines at bay by protecting the entitlements of vulnerable groups. Two major lessons regarding famine prevention thus emerge from the experience of Indian famines. First, governments must intervene actively to protect the entitlements of vulnerable people quite early in a crisis and, second, governments are more likely to do so in the presence of some form of effective accountability. These lessons remain valid as much for India today as for the rest of the world.

S.R. Osmani

[1]Quoted in Loveday (1914).

References

Ambirajan, S. 1978. *Classical Political Economy and British Policy in India*, Cambridge, Cambridge University Press.

Bhatia, B.M. 1967. *Famines in India: A Study in Some Aspects of the Economic History of India 1860–1965*, Delhi, Asia Publishing House.

Drèze, J. 1990. 'Famine Prevention in India', in J. Drèze and A. Sen (eds), *The Political Economy of Hunger*, Vol. II, Oxford, Clarendon Press.

Dutt, R.C. 1904. *The Economic History of India*, London, Routledge and Kegan Paul.

Habib, I. 1985. 'Studying a Colonial Economy—Without Perceiving Colonialism', *Modern Asian Studies*, 19(3): 355–81.

Loveday, A. 1914. *The History and Economics of Indian Famines*, London, A.G. Bell & Sons.

Maharatna, A. 1996. *The Demography of Famines: An Indian Historical Perspective*, New Delhi, Oxford University Press.

Sen, A. 1981. *Poverty and Famines: An Essay on Entitlement and Deprivation*, Oxford, Oxford University Press; New Delhi, Oxford University Press, 1998.

■ Farmers' Distress and Suicides

Background

The agrarian structure in India has undergone three significant phases of change during the last six decades. First, the land reforms across the country helped to correct some of the land market distortions albeit with diverse results. The issues governing land in the country underwent significant changes and while solving many of the ulcerating problems, generated a few new ones. Reverse and/or hidden tenancy, high density of non-viable holdings, and imperfections in the land market are the prominent fallouts among these. Second, the seed–water–fertilizer technology 'Green Revolution' of the mid-1960s helped overcome food insecurity and brought in a new production culture. Specifically, this increased the need for the cash component in the cost of cultivation and introduced a strong tilt towards commercialization. Farmers' incomes were not sufficient to generate the needed investment and, as a result, they had to seek help from the credit market. Formal and informal credit markets flourished in rural areas with amplified aspirations of the new generation of farmers. Third, with the commercialization of agriculture, the new generation of the ambitious entrepreneurial farmers turned towards new/commercial crops. Among the entrepreneurial farmers, the group that had easy access to the needed resources (especially cash resources) succeeded. The other vulnerable (on count of resources and market) but ambitious farmers could not reap the benefits. The process of commercialization intensified under the influence of a new trade wave, but received little support from reforms in agricultural markets (land, labour, inputs, and products). With these factors, the sector could not overcome its proverbial constraints, which deepened as there was little attention to basic reforms. The distress in the sector began intensifying and was compounded by the phases of stagnation in the sector and externalities due to the changing policy scenario in the other sectors.

In the Indian context, farmers have always been at the receiving end in the factor, credit, as well as product markets. The 1990s witnessed a spate of stagnation compounded by the failure of policy to meet the challenges. The intermittent phases of stagnation in the 1990s weakened the vulnerable farmers, making them increasingly sensitive even to the slightest economic shocks. The situation had become worse by the end of the 1990s, when the central government issued a first ever 'hold-all' agricultural policy document comprising mostly all perceivable 'catch phrases' without even consulting the state governments. The vulnerability of agriculture during the 1990s was quite disturbing in Karnataka, Andhra Pradesh, Maharashtra, and Punjab. Agricultural production in these states stagnated along with prices causing stagnation in net real incomes. As the distress in the sector became acute the spate of farmers' suicides was noted in these states. Among other factors, the emergence of WTO, GM varieties, and spurious seeds also became prominent stressors. Certainly the accumulation of distress through all these is a genuine cause of increasing stress but connecting it directly to suicides in every case may not be analytically correct.

Distress among farmers in the country is genuine and it was acute during 1998 to 2004 (Figure 1, data from Government of India 1998–2010, 2010). The situation

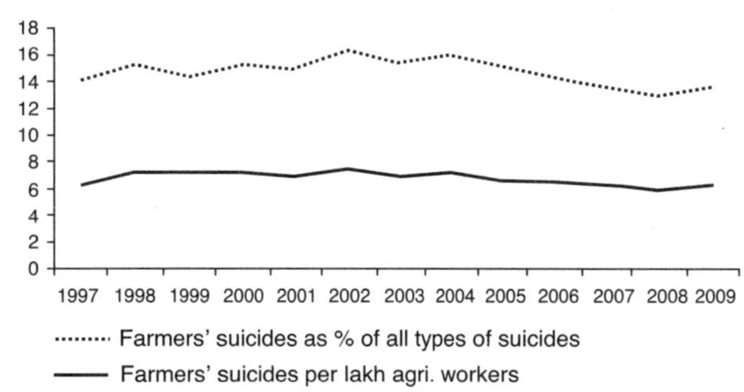

Figure 1 Percentage Share of Farmers' Suicides and SMR for Farmers

was, however, quite depressing in Andhra Pradesh, Karnataka, Maharashtra, Punjab, and Madhya Pradesh (Nagaraj 2008).

Theoretical Scaffolding

Most of the studies on suicides failed to look at the phenomenon from an interdisciplinary perspective. Confronting pure psychological theories, Durkheim (1952) categorized suicides as *egoistic, altruistic, anomic*, and *epidemiological*, based on the social response theory to distress. An egoistic person is more prone to suicide and this is exactly the case in northern Karnataka, Telangana, and Rayalseema in Andhra Pradesh), and Vidarbha in Maharashtra. The *altruistic* characteristics involve idealistic persons who confront inequality between their expectations and capability. Anomic suicides are due to the process of individualization of farmers under the pressure of commercialization and collapse of the village as an institution of social protection. The epidemiological explanation of suicides refers to a psychological trait, which is referred to as an 'imitation effect' or the 'Werther effect'. The process of commercialization, market imperfections, stagnation in productivity, vulnerability to natural calamities, and overall agrarian changes aggravate conditions of stress. These factors alienated the farmers in village society and led to forced individualization without effective/timely safety nets and state policy to protect them.

Behavioural scientists' way of analysing the causes of suicides requires understanding the incidence as culmination of four factors: 'events', 'stressors', 'actors', and 'triggers'. This categorization stems from the mental set-up of the victims (Deshpande 2002). Among the 'events', crop loss, failure of borewells, price crashes, daughters' marriage, family problems, and property disputes are included. Some of these become acute 'stressors' (stress creators). Further, 'actors/catalysts' create a sense of 'insecurity' or 'insult' to potential victims. These include moneylenders, bankers, spouses, relatives, and close friends. They instigate the final act by forcing an occasion to be the 'trigger' for the unfortunate incident. Therefore, a simple explanation of the phenomenon is a naïve attempt and largely takes only the triggers into consideration.

Agricultural economists deal with a vulnerability analysis of the sector. Farmers, as an occupational group, face high risk and uncertainty in income flows world over (Malmberg and Hawton 1999). In the factor market, a farmer has to pay the prices dictated by the suppliers, whereas in the product market, the purchasers determine the prices with a farmer remaining a mute observer. The role of a farmer in influencing the prices in either market is astonishingly minimal. Thus, farmers not only face weather risks along with constraints on access to inputs (water, fertilizers, pesticides, or seeds) but also perpetual price uncertainty. This is compounded by spurious inputs and domestic market imperfections. Further, even though farming is a free enterprise, state policies largely dictate its course of development. This is compounded by social stress caused by the collapse of the village as an institution and the strong current of commercialization. We have to look for a holistic policy that impacts the very roots of the vulnerability confronted by farmers.

Empirical Evidence

India's agricultural sector is passing through testing times and the fear of stagnation in productivity as well as in prices is real and looming large. Farmers today have become increasingly vulnerable even to the slightest economic shocks. Certainly, the current agrarian crisis has its roots in the nature of the agricultural sector and the failure of policy response (Suri 2006). The situation is quite grave in some of the states. The 1990s witnessed a phase of complacency at the policy level. Technological optima was almost reached with no new technological breakthrough in sight. On one hand, the fragmentation of holdings caused reduction in the average farm size, increasing the number of small and marginal farms. On the other hand, more farmers got into the unviable size of holdings. The proverbial agricultural backward districts still continue in the same state of hierarchy. Rainfed farming still dominates the farm sector and the policy has failed the rainfed farmers as also farmers with unviable farm sizes. The situation is quite alarming in Karnataka, Maharashtra, Andhra Pradesh, Madhya Pradesh, Punjab, and Rajasthan (Table 1). The spate of suicides that emerged in these states was associated with the performance of the agricultural sector.

Table 1 SMR of Persons Self-employed in Agriculture

States	2006	2007	2008	2009
Andhra Pradesh	19.6	12.1	14.7	16.6
Karnataka	14.1	17.4	14.2	18.7
Madhya Pradesh	21.4	20.0	18.1	15.3
Maharashtra	28.7	27.9	26.5	20.1
Punjab	11.0	10.4	7.6	11.5
Rajasthan	09.3	13.4	15.4	16.8
Uttar Pradesh	13.3	12.4	18.2	15.8
India	**14.4**	**13.6**	**13.0**	**13.7**

Source: Govt of India (for years mentioned), Accidental Deaths and Suicides in India, National Crime Records Bureau, Ministry of Home, New Delhi.

Average farm business income of 14 states (deflated by the consumer price index for agricultural labourers [CPIAL]) grew at 1.02 per cent per annum during 1990–1 to 1999–2000 as against 3.21 per cent per during 1983–4 to 1990–1 (Sen and Bhatia 2004: 241). The picture looks quite dismal when one plots the CPIAL along with the index of farm business income with the same base. As a result, a farmer would have to borrow to meet the increased cost of cultivation or investment, while the shrinking net income will result in non-repayment and indebtedness. During the 1990s, indebtedness in the farm sector increased substantially. Non-viability due to the increased cash component in the cost and size of holdings meant that the farmers opted for non-institutional credit. The share of cooperative credit plummeted and that was not compensated for by commercial banks or regional rural banks. As a result, indebtedness became a major cause of distress and was quite erroneously treated as one of the policy correction points. Actually it was the erosion of the repaying capacity of a farmer due to shrinking net incomes that caused the distress and needed attention.

Studies conducted on farmers' suicides in India can be grouped into three broad groups (Deshpande and Arora 2010; Mishra 2007; Sainath 2005a, 2005b, 2007). The first group includes the reports of some committees prepared to assist the state in policy formulations. Such reports are available for Karnataka, Andhra Pradesh, Punjab, and Maharashtra. These reports essentially focus on the causes of suicides and the policy needed to alleviate the distress in farming communities. Karnataka's report focuses on the 'Farmer Consultation Centre' approach to deal with the 'welfare domain', whereas the Andhra Pradesh report highlights inadequate public investment and need for an Agriculture Technology Mission. Maharashtra's report emphasizes on the credit market, mitigating price risk, and post-suicide compensation. The second group of studies include citizens reports which are guided by ideological moorings and focus on policy lapses. The third group includes those studies conducted by individual researchers, mostly using socio-anthropological methods. With the help of a few case studies these authors argue in the same tune. Indebtedness, borrowing from moneylenders, externalities of the new technology, blind commercialization, crop failures due to spurious seeds and inputs, increased cost of production, over-exploitation of natural resources, absence of safety nets, and collapse of the village as an institution are some of the causes pointed out in these studies (Deshpande and Arora 2010). This really says that all is not well in the sector. But rarely do these studies suggest a feasible policy to mitigate the problems.

Towards a Policy Frame

Locating the reasons for the spate of suicides has two objectives. First, to locate the probable areas and issues causing distress and, second, to provide a policy frame to reduce the intensity of such distress. One can broadly group policy initiatives into four groups. First, the 'production sub-system' includes correcting product market imperfections, diversifying farm activities, providing non-farm production systems, promoting agro-processing, and upgrading technology. The 'input sub-system' includes amendments to legal impediments that include liberalizing the tenancy market, fixing the lower size of holdings to arrest marginalization of ownership holdings, high density sustainable agriculture, regular supply of electricity, and quality monitoring of other inputs. The 'input support system' includes providing information to farmers on a day-to-day basis through established Farmer Consultation Centres even by internalizing and training input dealers. The 'welfare sub-system' for the farmers includes creating a farmers' welfare fund, a nodal department for farmers, and a wide-ranging social security system with facilities for pensions for aged farmers. These are being considered seriously in Karnataka. Safety nets, such as health and crop insurance and a single window credit system, will go a long way in strengthening the support system. Finally, the falling viability of small and marginal farmers due to their size of operations and weak bargaining powers should be addressed through a group approach to farming.

R.S. Deshpande

References

Deshpande, R.S. 2002. 'Suicide by Farmers in Karnataka', *Economic and Political Weekly*, 37(26): 2601–10.

Deshpande, R.S. and Saroj Arora. 2010. *Agrarian Crisis and Farmer Suicides*, New Delhi, Sage Publications, pp. 1–42.

Durkheim, Emile. 1952. *Suicide: A Study in Sociology*, translated by John A. Spaulding and George Simpson, London, Routledge and Kegan Paul.

Government of India. Issues 1998–2010. *Accidental Deaths and Suicides in India*, New Delhi, National Crime Records Bureau, Ministry of Home Affairs.

———. 2010. *Agricultural Statistics at a Glance 2010*, New Delhi, Directorate of Economics and Statistics, Ministry of Agriculture.

Malmberg, Sue Simkin and Keith Hawton. 1999. 'Suicides in Farmers', *British Journal of Psychitry*, 175: 103–5.

Mishra, Srijit. 2007. *Suicides of Farmers' in Maharashtra* (Research Report), Mumbai, Indira Gandhi Institute of Development Research.

Nagaraj, K. 2008. *Farmers' Suicides in India: Magnitudes, Trends and Spatial Patterns*, Madras, Madras Institute of Development Studies, March.
Sainath, P. 2005a. 'Six Out of Ten?', *The Hindu*, 31 May.
——. 2005b. 'Vidharbha: Whose Suicide Is It Anyway?', *The Hindu*, 25 June.
——. 2007. 'As You Sow, So Shall You Weep', *The Hindu*, 30 June.
Sen, Abhijit and M.S. Bhatia. 2004. *State of the Indian Farmer: A Millennium Study—Cost of Cultivation and Farm Income*, Vol.14, New Delhi, Academic Foundation.
Suri, K.C. 2006. 'Political Economy of Agrarian Distress', *Economic and Political Weekly*, 22 April, 41(16): 1523–9

■ Finance and Law

The history of organized financial markets in India can be traced back to the year 1875 when the Bombay Stock Exchange (BSE) was founded, soon to be followed by two other stock exchanges in Calcutta and Delhi. However, for a century to follow, these establishments largely resembled clubs with privileged membership. Trading was primarily controlled by a handful of brokers, membership to the exchanges was fairly limited, and so were new issues, even in the post-Independence era.[1] Limited membership of the brokerage firms (which mostly run on a partnership basis), long settlement cycles, lack of transparency in trading, and absence of alternative stock exchanges exposed ordinary investors to risks attributable to illiquid markets and information monopoly of the brokers and traders. The absence of a mandatory requirement of information disclosures by listed firms added to the severity of the problem of informational asymmetry between a firm and its dispersed shareholders. Without a central and functionally independent body for overseeing activities of stock exchanges, small investors were left unprotected from losses due to both the selection of stocks and the process of trading in them. This, in turn, discouraged small investors from participating in equity markets. At the same time, under the licensing regime of the post-Independence period, which prevailed into the mid-1980s, companies were restricted from freely entering the market to raise funds. Even for firms lucky enough to obtain a permit, it was not easy to raise finance because the office of the Controller of Capital Issues (CCI) determined the price of initial public offerings (IPOs) and monitored the number of shares issued, without paying much heed to informational issues that could hurt small investors. The yearly long-term capital raised by companies between 1957 and 1980 hovered around Rs 150 crore. The thinness of the market was reflected in a meagre stock market capitalization to gross national product (GNP) ratio of 5 per cent in 1980. Apart from stock market investors, creditors to firms were equally vulnerable due to a very time-consuming process for the resolution of bankruptcy as well as inflexible and archaic laws that prevailed during most of the post-Independence era.

Major legal, operational, and institutional changes began in the late 1980s. This entry will primarily concentrate on the relationship between the legal environment and financial markets in the pre- and post-reform periods and evaluate the performance of stock markets and bankruptcy procedures on the basis of some objective criteria that will shortly be outlined. It will also, in the Indian context, shed some light on the current debate in academics that makes a connection between legal origins of a country and finance.

Markets and Regulatory Reforms

There were two major developments in the late 1980s and early 1990s that altered the functioning of the stock markets in India. First, in 1992, the government set up the Securities and Exchange Board of India (SEBI) with enhanced statutory authority to enable it to perform a wide variety of functions. These ranged from checking information disclosure by firms and setting guidelines for other financial institutions like mutual funds to investigating insider trading and related fraudulent transactions in the market. Second, a National Stock Exchange (NSE) was established with the objective of reaching investors who are scattered geographically through a computerized trading system. An alternative to the BSE, the NSE offered a wide range of choices to investors including screen-based transactions that increased the transparency in trades. It also offered to become either a buyer or a seller, thereby assuring completion of trades, and helped in the floating of new financial products such as derivatives and futures to cater to the various needs of corporations and investors.

Informational asymmetry between investors and the possibility of default in transactions are two major impediments to the development of any financial market. Prior to the 1990s, Indian stock exchanges were monopolized by a few participants who had captured enough informational rent from the prevailing system and were naturally very resistant to changes in daily business practices. The launching of the NSE directly created

[1] In 1981, the BSE's annual turnover was Rs 4 million a day with 517 brokers. The corresponding figures in 1991 were Rs 23 million and 550 respectively. See Singhal (2004).

competition for other stock exchanges and left them with no option but to follow new trading practices in order to retain their clientele. At the same time, the creation of SEBI together with its added emphasis on disclosures of information was a step towards resolving the concerns of small dispersed investors due to informational asymmetry. Hence the introduction of a new and modern stock exchange curbed the monopoly power of brokers and the initiation of a coordinating body sent a strong message to participants against manipulating markets or trading and booking profits based on their privileged information. These changes, together with the abolition of industrial licences and permits, created a flurry of activity in the stock market almost immediately. The number of shareholders and investors in mutual funds rose from 2 to 40 million between 1980 and 1993, the turnover of shares increased from Rs 130 million in 1981 to Rs 3,700 million in 1994. While Rs 929 million was raised through corporate securities in 1981, the figure reached Rs 225 billion by 1993–4 and out of nearly 1,700 companies that raised funds in the equity market in 1994–5, 369 were new.[2] Although such phenomenal growth in numbers decelerated later, primarily due to recessions, it is on the rise again in recent years.

Contrary to the experience with regulations, the pace of legal and legislative/political reforms in the context of the credit market is slow and laws and institutions that are relevant for bankruptcy and reorganization of firms have been weak. Prior to the 1990s, the quasi-judicial body responsible for overseeing liquidation or reorganization was primarily the Board of Industrial and Finance Reconstruction (BIFR), instituted by the Sick Industrial Companies (SIC) Act of 1985. Due to the tremendous rise in volume of bad debts as well number of sick organizations, a new Act came into force in 1993 that allowed a creditor with more than Rs 1 million outstanding debt to appeal to a Debt Recovery Tribunal (DRT) for the speedy recovery of loans. Then again, in 2002, there was an amendment to the Companies Act that sought to streamline the procedures of bankruptcy and reorganization. Hence, currently, the BIFR and DRT, together with the Company Law Board and High Courts, define the legal jurisdiction of bankruptcy procedures.

Evaluation Criteria

In order to evaluate the impact of legal systems and institutions on financial markets, one needs some objective criteria. Since there have not been any extensive studies on the effects of reforms, I will resort to a combination of casual empiricism and some datum for evaluation and will use the following yardsticks for such judgements.

Efficiency

The legal system must ensure that it does not interfere with ex-post efficient outcomes and at the same time must ensure ex-ante efficiency. Early detection of insider trading in the stock market, and the assignment of more power to banks to investigate whether borrowers have violated covenants are examples of ex-ante efficiency. Further, creditors should be able to get early redress from the legal system if debtor firms engage in activities that violate bond indenture agreements, such as payment of dividends. Ex-ante efficiency can be measured by the combination time (and/or costs) spent in detecting such unlawful activities. That is, the longer it takes to detect occurrences of insider trading or fraudulent activity by controlling shareholders, the greater the inefficiency.

On the other hand, the concept of ex-post efficiency deals with the issue of resolution of a crisis once it has taken place. An obvious example is when a debtor firm has already defaulted on loans. The major question is whether the firm should be liquidated or its assets and liabilities be organized for continuation as an economic entity. The legal framework must forestall liquidation when continuation is feasible and vice versa. In the context of equity markets, an example could be ex-post default on delivery of shares on a large scale, and whether the government would bail out or punish?

Fairness

The legal system should also ensure that minority shareholders and public debt holders' wealth is not expropriated by dominant insiders via either direct or indirect methods of coercion leading to violation of contractual agreements. Such a transfer of wealth could be the outcome of either privileged information of dominant stakeholders or loopholes in the legal system or both. Again, this issue is more important during unusual activities within a firm such as mergers and acquisitions and/or bankruptcy. For example, if there are different classes of creditors, fairness requires payments to senior and secured creditors first during bankruptcy.

However, it is not always easy to achieve efficiency and fairness because at times there could be a trade-off between ex-post efficiency and fairness as illustrated by the following simple example. Suppose that a firm has failed to repay a loan of Rs 600 and liquidation value is Rs 300 and this sum will go to the creditor in the event the business of the firm gets wrapped up and assets are sold in the market. Alternatively the firm could have a

[2]See Singh (2003) and Singhal (2004) for details.

new project that could generate a cash flow (cash available to its investors) of either Rs 800 or Rs 1200 and each could occur with equal probability. This project needs an investment of Rs 600 and the firm is cash starved. If the firm is allowed to raise finance for this project by issuing new debt and this debt is granted seniority over old debt, then it violates the seniority of old debt and could be unfair from the point of view of old creditors. On the other hand, if the project begins with new debt, old creditors could get either Rs 200 or Rs 600 with equal probability so that the expected value of what they might receive in the continuation of the firm is Rs 400 that exceeds their pay-off in liquidation. Though efficient, continuation of the firm violates original priority of payments. This simple example illustrates conflicts between fairness and efficiency. Of course, in the real world the problem is more complex but nevertheless, one could use this simple case to highlight problems that arise due to asymmetric information as well as from conflicts of interests between various parties in a legal dispute. For example, the dominant shareholders or managers may know more about the probability of success in the new project or the liquidation value of assets than the bank or the legal authority. In that case, a legal solution leads to an outcome which is both inefficient and unfair. Conflicts of interests could arise due to the presence of many classes of creditors such as senior and secured and the agents could play the game of chicken in which one class of agents expects the others to concede first. This results in a suboptimal outcome for everyone.

The Indian Financial Market Context

Though there are a series of reforms in the stock-market rules and regulations, insider trading leading to default is still a nagging problem. The recent liquidity crisis of the Calcutta Stock Exchange offers evidence of serious violations of trading norms still going undetected ex ante. SEBI has undertaken a series of investigations in recent times against irregularities in trading and there has been a sharp rise in the number of investigations, prosecutions, and penalties. In the year 2003–4, SEBI initiated 287 enquiry proceedings against intermediaries compared to a figure of 185 in the preceding year with a concurrent 168 per cent increase in arbitration for imposing monetary penalties. The figures cited by SEBI are of course very insignificant in comparison to the overall volume of trading or potential violations. The main problems still lie with manipulation of the market, rigging of prices, and insider trading and it is still not clear on what basis SEBI undertakes investigation. No comprehensive study exists so far to gauge the effect of efficient and fair handling of malpractices but indirect evidence points to an overall positive effect of the reforms. A wide variety of indicators suggests a positive connection between legal reforms and overall activity of the stock market. These include confidence of foreign mutual funds marked by large-scale entry (SEBI website), improved corporate governance norms for companies that have more than 25 per cent insider holdings, intensive monitoring of domestic financial institutions (Sarkar and Sarkar 2000), and overall increase in market capitalization.

However, similar changes in laws dealing with bankruptcy and reorganization pertaining to credit markets were very slow and had often led to both inefficient and unfair outcomes. As of March 2001, 3317 firms defaulted on loans equal to Rs 258 billion, which is nearly 2 per cent of the gross domestic product (GDP) (Kang and Nayar 2004). The definition of industrial sickness by the BIFR precluded the existence of ex-ante inefficiency. According to the BIFR, the process of reorganization should begin once a registered company's accumulated losses exceed their net worth by the end of the year. Such a definition of sickness leaves no room for detection of financial trouble before companies lose their value. Hence a majority of the firms that appealed to the BIFR were liquidated and not reorganized. For example, out of 1,711 active cases in 2002, liquidation was proposed for 63 per cent and only 22 per cent were successfully reorganized. The picture is even worse in the preceding decades. Second, huge delays in the resolution of bankruptcy hurt everyone except for the controlling shareholders and managers. In 2002, the BIFR's decision to reorganize took seven years and it recommended liquidation after 6.5 years.[3] Even a casual empiricism suggests that such a long time for resolution of bankruptcy and reorganization very often leads either to a drastic fall in net worth or in liquidation value of the firm and provides a sanctuary for the entrenched management or other parties with vested interests to keep the firm alive even when it should have been wrapped up. Hence the whole system has a bias towards ex-post inefficiency and unfairness. Though the Act of 2002 promised to deal with this situation, its effectiveness is yet to be assessed or seen.

An Academic Debate

The discussion has so far highlighted the uneven pace of legal reforms relevant to transactions in the debt and equity markets. To what extent is performance linked to the legal origins of the country? Much of India's legal

[3]See Kang and Nayar (2004) for details on bankruptcy procedures and relevant data for India.

framework had its origin in the English Common Law due to the colonial legacy. An influential body of empirical research links a country's legal origin and development of its financial markets because of the influence that the legal structure exerts on shaping contractual arrangements between outside investors and insiders of a firm. A spate of works, starting with La Porta et al. (1997, 1998), primarily made the distinction between the various legal regimes which had their origins in one of the following customs: (i) English Common Law; (ii) French Civil Law; (iii) German Civil Law; and (iv) Scandinavian Civil Law.

According to La Porta et al. (1997, 1998), the English Common Law fares better in protecting small investors against the risk of appropriation by dominant shareholders and other influential insiders, in comparison with other legal systems. A major testable implication of this assertion is that in countries that adopted French or Scandinavian Civil Law, poor protection of investors must have led to costly outside financing as investors would factor out consequences of such poor protection and demand higher returns. Moreover, costly outside financing also prompts excessive concentration of equity in the hands of the insiders of a firm, causing them to bear huge risks. This, in turn, discourages formation of entrepreneurial activities. Finally, dense concentrations in holding of equity by a few major players create poor liquidity in the secondary market since insiders' holdings of stock are very infrequently traded.

Hence, according to La Porta et al. (1997, 1998), poorer investor protection and inefficient legal systems put brakes on economic development as they make outside financing expensive, contribute to the thinness of the stock market, and act as an impediment to the formation of an entrepreneurial class. Based on this argument, La Porta et al. (1997, 1998) have run tests on many countries and have ranked their performance in terms of various indices. According to them, average creditors' rights index in countries with English Common Law is 3.11 and is the highest among the four systems, the same index for the French Civil Law countries being 1.58. In their measures of shareholders' protection, such as the anti-director rights index, common law countries score higher (4.0) than, say, French Civil Law countries (2.33).

Though an important piece of work, La Porta et al.'s classification could be overly simplistic because countries with similar legal origins vary significantly with respect to the workings of financial markets such as equity and credit markets. Second, La Porta et al.'s empirical assertions could be interpreted as too deterministic because while 'legal origin' of a country can be treated as an 'initial condition', development of and compliance with laws over time certainly depend upon the economic environment that determines the incentives of the various parties to implement or even change the law through political processes. Hence, the view that 'initial condition' dominates the dynamic interactions of agents in terms of the implementation of rules as well as incentives to change laws is certainly a very strong assertion. In the Indian context, there has not been much change in the last 15 years in the legal structure which is of English origin, but big bang reforms such as the introduction of the NSE and SEBI have had far-reaching impact on the equity market while things have remained more or less stationary in credit markets due to the absence of such reforms. My conjecture or maintained hypothesis regarding such uneven changes is that the introduction of strong legal institutions in one market has altered the incentives or even aligned the incentives of various parties while the lack of such changes in other markets has caused the status quo to prevail.

To sum up, though India's legal origin is in the English Common Law, its structure and effectiveness are not uniform across all markets. The World Bank Index of 'closing a business' for 2005 states that it takes almost 10 years to resolve bankruptcies in India with 9 per cent cost of estate values, and the recovery rate is 12.8 cents a dollar. Similar figures for the Southeast Asia region and the Organisation for Economic Co-operation and Development (OECD) countries are 4.2 years, 7.3 per cent, and 19.7 cents and 1.5 years, 7.4 per cent, and 73.8 cents, respectively. On the other hand, in the investors' protection index, primarily for shareholders' benefit, India's position is much higher and is comparable to that of the OECD countries. This index is 6 for India, 5 for the region, and 5.9 for the average OECD country. Though India has made significant gains in implementing legal and institutional reforms in the stock market, weak legal organization, lack of coordination with the labour laws, and overlapping jurisdiction of different statutory bodies are the primary weaknesses of the legal system. Two major deficiencies in India's legal reforms are worth mentioning. First, the reluctance to use market information contained in prices for the purpose of curbing illegal economic activities. For example, SEBI could use the information content of changes in price of stock induced by a huge volume of buying and selling, which could be either an outcome of pure information-based trading or a result of market manipulation. SEBI could announce and commit to investigation if the movements of prices cross a threshold limit. That is, combining information contained in price with its own information would not only reduce costs of investigation but also provide incentives to participants not to engage in market manipulation and rigging of prices. Second, the legal system and regulatory bodies very often ignore economic incentives of various individuals to engage in negotiations to make a deal to resolve financial crisis. Allowing agents to negotiate or renegotiate initial contracts implies flexibility and promotes efficiency. The legal authority could then intervene only to check whether renegotiation of contracts has led to unfair outcomes for a third party. This is very relevant for financially distressed firms that could float a new security (that could be traded in financial markets) while replacing old securities such as bonds. However, this requires a comprehensive change in the structure of bankruptcy and labour laws.

Sanjay Banerji

References

Kang, N. and N. Nayar. 2004. 'The Evolution of Corporate Bankruptcy Law in India', *ICRA Bulletin, Money and Finance*, 3 October–4 March.

La Porta, R., F. Lopez-de-Silanes, A. Shleifer, and R. Vishny. 1997. 'Legal Determinants of External Finance', *Journal of Finance*, 52: 1131–50.

——. 1998. 'Law and Finance', *Journal of Political Economy*, 106: 1113–55.

Sarkar, J. and S. Sarkar. 2000. 'Large Shareholder Activism in Corporate Governance in Developing Countries: Evidence from India', *International Review of Finance*, 1(3): 161–94.

Singh, Ajit. 2003. 'Corporate Governance, Corporate Finance and Stock Markets in Emerging Countries', Working Paper 258, ESRC Centre for Business Research, University of Cambridge.

Singhal R. 2004. 'Financial Sector Reform in India: Is There a Grand Design?', Occasional Paper Number 16, Centre for the Advanced Study of India, University of Pennsylvania.

Finance Commissions

The framers of our Constitution wanted that the country should be one common economic space, unhindered, as far as possible, by internal tax barriers. But they also recognized that the state governments, being closer to the people and more immediately answerable to them, would be better aware of their needs and aspirations. They, therefore, assigned the major taxation powers under the Constitution to the union and most of the responsibilities in the social and economic spheres to the states. This resulted in a mismatch between the resources and the responsibilities assigned to each of the two levels. To correct this, they provided for the constitution of a Finance Commission (FC), not later than every fifth year, to periodically review the financial position of the union and the states and recommend transfer of resources from the union to the states and between the states. This process of periodic matching and realignment of resources and responsibilities is somewhat similar to the introduction of an intercalary year in a lunar calendar to periodically bring it into greater alignment with the solar calendar.

Thirteen Commissions have so far given their recommendations. The union government has always accepted the recommendations of the Commissions, except in the case of the Third Commission, when that Commission had included plan grants. An FC is assigned two main functions under Article 280 (1). One, to determine the share of the states in the tax receipts of the union with respect to those taxes which are shareable with them under the Constitution. Two, to distribute the total states' share so determined, as among the various states. The former is described as vertical distribution and the latter as horizontal distribution. Initially, only income taxes and union excise duties were covered under this Article. But after the 89th Constitutional Amendment in 2000, the proceeds of all union taxes are covered by it.

There has not been much controversy, either political or academic, about the vertical distribution between the union and the states. The devolution by the FCs of the tax proceeds of the union has never come down, but has gone up from 10 per cent of total union tax receipts in the 1950s to 25 per cent in the 1990s and 29.5 per cent by the Eleventh Commission. Over and above this, the states receive about another 10 per cent as central grants. It is generally agreed that the scope for further transfers from the union to states is limited, notwithstanding a pro forma demand made by some states for a devolution of 50 per cent of total union tax receipts.

Most states have not had much grievance about the horizontal distribution amongst the states of the total amount devolved. Each state compares its own *inter se* position after each Commission's report with its position under the previous Commission's report. Even those states whose position might have come down do not make much of an issue of it because it might reflect on their own performance during the intervening period. After the Eleventh Commission's report, some states, which considered themselves to be efficient, represented to the Commission that efficiency should be given greater weightage and that a premium should not be placed on backwardness. Every Commission, including the Eleventh, had taken both efficiency and equity into consideration, though each may have given different weights to these factors. They had to bear in mind that economic efficiency was as much a function of the level of development of the state as of its effort. Assisting backward states could not be construed as rewarding backwardness. The Special Category States, which include Kashmir, Assam, and the north-eastern states, get an even more beneficial treatment. As Austin (1999: 222) put it in the Constituent Assembly, 'If federalism means anything, it means that there should be a transfer of wealth from the richer to the poorer provinces.' In any case, these arguments had some relevance when the more developed states could be shown to be the more financially prudent. Now, with the finances of all states being in bad shape, it becomes a moot question whether imprudence should not be penalized more in the case of the advanced states than the poorer ones.

The criticisms about the horizontal distribution by the FCs have come mostly from academic fiscal experts, despite one or more of them having been members of every Commission. These criticisms fall broadly under four categories. First, that the *inter se* financial or developmental position of the states has not changed. The states that were poor at the time of Independence continue to be poor, while those that were prosperous continue to prosper. The FCs have tried to address this problem by evolving various criteria that reflect the level of economic development and social infrastructure in each state and by modulating financial transfers on that basis. It is generally agreed that these criteria are more progressive than the Gadgil Formula of the Planning Commission. There is no lack of ingenuity on the part of economists in evolving formulae. The problem arises from the fact that the initial regional disparities were so large, and arose out of such diverse socio-economic factors, that mere financial transfers were not adequate to tackle them. More comprehensive planning and action were required for this purpose, which was the function of the Planning Commission and not the FCs. The removal, or at least reduction, of such regional disparities is the direct concern of the Planning Commission. The FCs have to take them into account only to the extent that differences in levels of economic development, on the one hand, affect the ability of a state to raise its own resources and, on the other, determine the need for greater devolution of finances.

Arising from this is the second criticism that backward states can be better helped differentially by giving greater weightage to grants than to devolution in the transfer of funds. Grants have generally constituted 10 to 14 per cent of the total devolutions. This is because the states themselves want larger transfers by way of devolutions, as these arise out of their constitutional right to a share in the tax revenues of the union. Further, devolutions have the same buoyancy as the union taxes, while grants are fixed amounts. The criteria built into the formulae for devolution may reflect some conditionality; but beyond the formula devolutions are unconditional. Grants, on the other hand, have come with continuing conditions and monitoring. Even the poorer and smaller states, therefore, prefer devolutions to grants.

The third criticism is that the FCs have not adopted a 'normative' approach in assessing either the resources or the needs of the states. Every Commission has, in fact, adopted some norms for projecting the needs of the states during the 'forecast period'. These norms have been improved over time as more data and better techniques became available. The limitation has been the complexity of the issues involved and the great differences in the conditions of different states. The criticism, however, is that the FCs have accepted the actual position for the base year, instead of calculating this on the basis of the norms of the previous Commission. This is not entirely correct. The base year actuals have been corrected on the basis of a judgement of the Commission. For instance, the FCs have assumed certain water rates for this year based on previous norms. They could not, however, adopt a full-fledged normative basis for this year as they had to recognize the prerogative of the state governments in respect of certain political decisions, such as the introduction of prohibition of liquor. The FCs also had to recognize the effect on the states' finances of certain decisions by the Centre, such as on pay revision. The FC is required, by its terms of reference, to take into account the 'Committed Expenditure' of the plans. The FCs had to, therefore, recognize the actual situation on the ground at the beginning of their exercise. The FCs are accused of having become irrelevant because their forecasts have, in the event, been proved to be wrong. Had they adopted a normative approach for the base year also, the divorce from reality would have been complete. FCs have recommended grants to states to 'fill the gap in resources' as determined by them, on the basis of the above exercises. Experts have derogatively described this as a 'gap-filling exercise' which, according to them, has condoned financial imprudence and encouraged profligacy. It is the duty of an FC under Article 280 to recommend 'the principles which should govern the grants-in-aid of the revenues of the States'. This presumes that the states will require grants-in-aid in addition to their own revenue. The various formulae devised by the FCs are meant to make this determination as objective and rigorous as possible. Nevertheless, the exercise itself may have inadvertently helped enlarge the need. All offer of assistance has this danger. The plan exercises have condoned even greater gaps, both in resources and performance, despite the Planning Commission being a continuing body. At least 'an FC dispensation is like the Catholic Confessional; it condones past sins subject to certain penitence. The Planning Commission approving a Plan with a deficit is the Pontiff approving continued sinning' (Vithal and Sastri 2001: 273).

The exclusion of plan revenue expenditure from the purview of the FCs has also been widely criticized. The Constitution does not recognize the distinction between plan and non-plan revenue expenditure. However, from the Fourth Commission onwards the FCs have accepted this exclusion as inevitably arising out of the division of functions between the Finance and Planning Commissions. The Ninth Commission once again examined the legal aspects and took the view that the FCs could take into account plan revenue expenditure also and recommended grants accordingly. After the Eleventh Commission, the union government has accepted this position, perhaps because revenue deficits had become a common feature of both plan and non-plan budgets. In practice this has meant that the FC makes a certain calculation of plan expenditures for the forecast period and recommends plan grants also accordingly. The Planning Commission has, however, taken this only as the base and has not allowed it to inhibit it from drawing up larger plans, even if it does not identify any additional resources!

The general view, at present, is that there are advantages in the FCs being periodically constituted. Continuing bodies in India, whether statutory or regulatory, seem to acquire vested interests more quickly than expertise or wisdom. With this their stature and utility get diminished. There has been continuous debate about whether it was right to have two commissions dealing with devolution of union finances to the states. It is generally recognized that the planning function, in its entirety, cannot be discharged by the Finance Commission and that, therefore, it is necessary to have a separate Planning Commission. It is also generally recognized that there are advantages in not having this body as a constitutional authority. Working under the National Development Council and being answerable to it have given the Planning Commission a special position in Centre–state relations.

The other issue is whether the FC should be a continuing body and whether it should deal with all revenue expenditure, including plan revenue expenditure, as in the case of the Eleventh and Twelfth Commissions. In that case, should the Planning Commission deal only with the capital plan? As long as providing social infrastructure remains the basic duty of the state, plans will inevitably have a large revenue component. The plans will, therefore, have to have both capital and revenue components. This means that the coexistence between a statutory, but periodic, Finance Commission and a continuing, but non-statutory, Planning Commission that has worked smoothly for over half a century will have to continue.

As explained earlier, the framers of the Constitution had provided for a Finance Commission because they were aware that they had built in a mismatch between the allocation of resources and functions to the union, on the one hand, and the states, on the other. The revenue surplus of the union did not necessarily indicate financial prudence nor did the deficits of the states indicate profligacy. However, in the new millennium the financial position of both the union and the states so deteriorated that both were having revenue deficits. Financial devolution became an act of balancing deficits.

Both the union and the states then accepted the need to balance the revenue budgets and agreed to legislative constraints on themselves, through Fiscal Responsibility Acts. This required that road maps be prepared to indicate the action to be taken and its time-schedule so as to facilitate monitoring the achievement of the goals as prescribed in the respective Fiscal Responsibility Acts. This task was assigned to the Thirteenth Commission.

This Commission was also asked to study other issues such as the impact of the goods and services tax, including on 'foreign trade', the need to manage ecology and climate change, and so on. The task of preparing road maps for achieving the goals of Fiscal Responsibility Acts falls more squarely under the duties and functions of the Finance Commission under Art. 280, as originally envisaged, than the other miscellaneous tasks assigned to the Thirteenth Commission, which figure perhaps because they are currently internationally in vogue!

The provocation for this wide-ranging extension of functions seems to have been that the Commission, like all other Finance Commissions, had eminent experts with wisdom and ingenuity. The Planning Commission also has such experts, but it is like a Messiah always available for supplication and redemption. In our country availability, like familiarity, erodes faith in capacity. The Finance Commissions, on the other hand, arise only periodically, like avatars, dispense justice, restore order, and cease to exist. Hope then rests on the next avatar, which the Constitution guarantees.

B.P.R. Vithal

References

Austin, Granville. 1999. *The Indian Constitution: Cornerstone of a Nation*, New Delhi, Oxford University Press.

Vithal, B.P.R. and M.L. Sastri. 2001. *Fiscal Federalism in India*. New Delhi, Oxford University Press.

Financial Crisis

A financial crisis is seen as occurring when the inability of one or a group of economic agents to meet commitments to creditors or investors in financial instruments leads to bankruptcies and/or the sale of assets, which in turn results in the collapse of asset prices and threatens the financial viability of related enterprises. Most often the event is accompanied by a freezing or slowing of the flow of credit that adversely affects the real economy. There have been a number of instances of financial crises throughout the history of capitalism. But concern over the phenomenon has increased substantially over the last three decades as a result of an increase in the periodicity and intensity of such crises when compared to the period between the Second World War and the early 1980s. While India has not faced financial difficulties since the debt-driven balance-of-payments crisis (BOP) it experienced in 1991, it has recently been adversely affected by the global financial crisis and sections of its financial sector do show signs of fragility.

A financial crisis could take many forms. It could, for example, take the form of a run on a group of banks resulting from a collapse of confidence in their ability to redeem deposits on demand because of the weaknesses of their balance sheets. It could appear in the form of a dramatic collapse in stock market valuations because of a flight out of equity, most often in the wake of an equally dramatic boom in stock values. It could be reflected in the actual or potential default on interest and amortization payments due on the external debt owed by a country or its private sector. Or, it could entail the collapse of a currency because of a speculative attack triggered by signs of difficulty a country is facing in obtaining the foreign exchange needed to meet commitments denominated in those currencies.

These crises have been experienced in rich, middle-income, and poor countries alike, belying the perceptions of some that, unlike in the period prior to the Second World War, the problem is one that is particularly acute in the so-called 'emerging markets'. In fact, a study of banking crises from the early 19th to the early 21st century (Reinhart and Rogoff 2008) found that the incidence of such crises was similar in the high to middle-to-low income countries, with the tally being particularly high for the world's financial centres', that is, the United Kingdom, the United States, and France.

The inter-temporal experience has also been characterized by much variation, as illustrated by the financial history of the US. For example, over the period 1955–81, failures of US banks averaged 5.3 per year, excluding banks kept from going under by official open-bank assistance. On the other hand, during 1982–90 failures averaged 131.4 per year or 25 times as during 1955–81 (Kareken 1992). Since then the US financial system has seen a variety of financial crises, culminating in the crisis of 2007–9 which was triggered by the sub-prime mortgage collapse.

Crises and Regulation

The sharp increase in the number of failures has been traced to the shift in the regulatory regime in the United States starting in the 1970s. Prior to that banking in the US was highly regulated and shaped by the Glass-Steagall Act of 1933. That regulatory framework limited competition with deposit insurance, interest rate regulation, and entry barriers which together rendered any bank as good as any other in the eyes of the ordinary depositor. This pre-empted the tendency to push up deposit rates to attract depositors that would require risky lending and investment to match returns with costs. The regulatory framework went even further and imposed restrictions on investments that banks or their affiliates could make, limiting their activities to provision of loans and purchases of government securities. There was a ban on banks underwriting securities and serving as insurance underwriters or agents, besides limits on outstanding exposure to a single borrower and lending to sensitive sectors like real estate.

Even though this regulatory framework was directed at and imposed principally on the banking sector, it implicitly regulated the non-bank financial sector as well. It is not often recognized that the size, degree of diversification, and level of activity of the non-bank financial sector depends on the degree to which institutions in that sector can leverage their activity with credit delivered directly or indirectly from the banking system. Banks being the principal depository institutions are the first port of call for a nation's savings. So if direct or indirect bank involvement in a range of non-bank financial activities was prohibited, as was true under Glass-Steagall, then the range and scope of those activities are bound to be limited. Not surprisingly, even by the 1950s, banking activity in the US constituted

80–90 per cent of that in the financial sector and trading on the New York Stock Exchange was limited to a daily average of three million shares as compared to as much as 160 million shares per day during the second half of the 1980s, when leverage became possible (Sametz 1992).

The regulatory shift began in the 1980s and the era of deregulation of interest rates and banking activity followed. The institutional landscape of the financial sector also changed. Initially money market funds grew in importance and stock market activity increased. The process of dismantling of the Chinese Walls separating different segments of the financial sector began in 1982, culminating in the Gramm-Leach-Bliley (or Financial Services Modernization) Act of 1999, which dismantled Glass-Steagall.

The transformation of the financial framework which followed had many features. To start with, banks extended their activity beyond conventional commercial banking into merchant banking and insurance. Second, within banking, there was a gradual shift in focus from generating incomes from net interest margins to obtaining them in the form of fees and commissions charged for various financial services. Third, related to this was a change in the focus of banking activity as well. While banks did provide credit and create assets that promised a stream of incomes into the future, they did not hold those assets any more. Rather, they structured them into pools, 'securitized' those pools, and sold these securities for a fee to institutional investors and portfolio managers. Banks transferred the risk for a fee, and those who bought into the risk looked to the returns they would earn in the long term. This implied a shift from a 'buy and hold' to an 'originate and distribute' model of banking and meant that those who originated the credit assets tended to understate or discount the risks associated with them. Finally, financial liberalization increased the number of layers in an increasingly universalized financial system, with the extent of regulation varying across the layers. Where regulation was light, as in the case of investment banks, hedge funds, and private equity firms, financial companies could borrow huge amounts based on a small amount of own capital and undertake leveraged investments to create complex products that were often traded over the counter rather than through exchanges. The system was one which put a premium on proliferating risk for profit.

Thus, by adopting a range of measures, the US state and federal governments and the Federal Reserve dismantled during the 1980s and 1990s the system of regulation and financial structure created by the policy framework put in place during and after the Great Depression. Threatened by regulatory arbitrage and the dynamic image of Wall Street, the United Kingdom and other countries followed the United States in liberalizing their financial sectors to differing degrees. The net result was an increasing proneness to crises, as illustrated starkly by the savings and loan crisis and the financial crisis triggered by the collapse of sub-prime mortgage market.

Developing Country Experience

The experience in developing countries has been similar though not the same. Since the 1980s they too have been drawn into the world of global finance. Till the early 1970s the private international financial system played only a limited role in recycling financial surpluses to the developing countries. The period immediately after the first oil shock saw a dramatic change in this scenario. Since oil surpluses were held in the main as deposits with the international banking system controlled in the developed world, the private financial system there became the powerful agent for recycling surpluses. This power was indeed immense. Expenditure fuelled by credit in the developed and developing world generated surpluses with the oil producers, who then deposited these surpluses with transnational banks, that, in turn, could offer further doses of credit. As a consequence, there was a massive expansion of the international financial market.

Two other developments contributed to the increase in international liquidity during the 1970s and 1980s. First, the United States had built up large international liabilities during the Bretton Woods years, including those resulting from expenditures on the Vietnam War and its policing efforts elsewhere in the world (Sweezy and Magdoff 1972). The explosion of the Eurocurrency market in the 1970s reflected this. This was sustained by the confidence in the dollar stemming from the immediate post-War hegemony of the US, which made it as good as gold.

Second, the demographic structure in most of the advanced countries was changing, with baby boomers reaching the age when they would emphasize personal savings for retirement. This led to the accumulation of investible resources in pension funds, mutual funds, and the like, and created demand for greater variety in savings instruments as well as higher returns.

From the point of view of the developing countries, this growth in international finance appeared positive. Needing liquidity to finance their BOP deficits, they found it easier to negotiate with a relatively atomistic private financial system that could not openly impose conditions rather than with centralized multilateral financial institutions like the International Monetary Fund (IMF). This encouraged developing countries to liberalize their capital accounts and financial markets to attract such capital.

India too attempted to exploit this opportunity to 'escape' from the development impasse of the mid-1960s and after. The government opted to pump prime the system with deficit-financed spending and prevented this from spilling over in the form of an inflationary crisis or BOP crisis by borrowing from the international markets to import commodities in domestic short supply and finance the higher current account deficit that accompanied higher growth. The country's external debt to gross domestic product (GDP) ratio doubled during the 1980s, with short-term debt accounting for a rising share. However, creditors were soon reluctant to roll over past debt and provide new debt resulting in a collapse of reserves and a crisis which led to the reforms adopted in the early 1990s. The liberalization that followed resulted in an increase in inflows of portfolio capital into India's equity and debt markets, besides flows of foreign direct investment and commercial bank credit.

Though India has not faced a severe financial crisis since then, financial crises have been the norm in other developing countries that were discovered as 'emerging markets' by international financial capital.' This suggests that India too is vulnerable. There is an additional problem. If international finance is to use these markets as new avenues for investment and as a hedge against the risks in its own markets, the rules of the game in these 'emerging markets' have to correspond to those in their own markets. It was this which made financial liberalization of a kind that seeks to replicate the Anglo-Saxon 'model' a key demand of international finance. An excess of capital in the form of debt and equity investments began to flow into countries which were willing to change the regulatory regime applicable to the financial sector (including the entry and operations of international financial agents).

In India too, there are three broad forms that the process of financial liberalization has taken: (i) it has opened the country to new forms and larger volumes of international financial flows, in order to attract a part of the substantially increased flows of financial capital to the so-called 'emerging markets' since the late 1970s; (ii) to facilitate these inflows it has liberalized to differing degrees the terms governing outflows of foreign exchange in the form of current account investment income payments and in the form of capital account transfers for permitted transactions; and (iii) it has transformed the structure of the financial sector and the nature and operations of financial firms in a manner that makes the financial system resemble that in countries like the US and the UK.

However, while financial liberalization began early in the 1990s, the surge in foreign investment flows occurred much later. Liberalization was a necessary condition for such inflows, but not a sufficient one. Until 2003, net inflows were relatively low, reaching a maximum of $8.2 billion in 2001–2. This rose to $15.7 billion in 2003–4, partly encouraged by tax concessions offered to foreign investors in that year. Thereafter India was 'discovered' by foreign investors and effectively became the target of a capital investment surge. Foreign investment flows to India more than doubled from $29.2 billion in 2006–7 to $61.8 billion in 2007–8, even as capital was fleeing other Asian emerging markets (RBI 2009a).

Capital inflows rose also due to large increases in commercial borrowing by private-sector firms. As constraints on external commercial borrowing by domestic companies were relaxed and because interest rates ruled higher in the domestic market, large Indian firms at the margin took the syndicated loan route to borrow money abroad at relatively lower interest rates. They engaged in a version of the carry trade, borrowing money in foreign exchange from the international markets where interest rates were lower and making investments in India (besides financing investments abroad).

Not surprisingly, the 2007–8 crisis resulted in a sharp outflow of capital, especially capital brought into the stock market by foreign institutional investors (FIIs). Needing cash to meet commitments and cover losses at home, these FIIs were selling out in Indian markets and repatriating capital abroad (RBI 2009a, 2009b). One consequence of the capital outflow was a collapse of India's stock markets, just as the earlier capital inflows had triggered a speculative bubble in both stock and real estate markets. They had caused an unprecedented rate of asset price inflation in India's stock markets and substantially increased volatility in the movements of the Bombay Stock Exchange's (BSE) Sensitive Index (Sensex).

Another route through which integration has influenced the way in which the global crisis has affected India is its impact on the role played by credit in financing private consumption and investment. Three trends in the domestic credit market following internal financial liberalization are of note. The first was the scorching pace of expansion of total bank credit from 2005, at more than double the rate of increase of nominal GDP. The second was the evidence of a sharp increase in the retail exposure of the banking system, with personal loans increasing from 12.2 per cent of advances in 2000–1 to

22.3 per cent in 2006–7 (RBI 1993–2007). A significant but as yet unknown proportion of this expansion in retail lending could be 'sub-prime' in nature. Finally, the Indian financial sector too had begun securitizing personal loans of all kinds so as to transfer the risk associated with them to those who could be persuaded to buy into them. As the US experience shows, this tends to slacken diligence when offering credit, since risk does not stay with those originating retail loans.

Thus India could experience its own financial crisis for two reasons. First, there is the fragility that comes out of opening up its capital account to encourage the inflow of capital. Second, by institutionally transforming the financial sector it has unleashed a dynamic that endows the financial system with a poorly regulated, oligopolistic structure, which could again increase the fragility of the system. Greater freedom to invest, including in sensitive sectors such as real estate and stock markets, ability to increase exposure to particular sectors and individual clients, freedom to expand exposure to retail credit markets for purchases of housing, automobiles and durables, and increased regulatory forbearance could all lead to financial failure.

C.P. Chandrasekhar

References

Kareken, John H. 1992. 'Regulation of Commercial Banking in the United States', in Peter Newman, Murray Millgate, and John Eatwell (eds), *The New Palgrave Dictionary of Money and Finance*, Vol. 3, London, Macmillan, pp. 315–19.

Reinhart, Carmen M. and Kenneth S. Rogoff. 2008. 'Banking Crises: An Equal Opportunity Menace', Working Paper 14587, National Bureau of Economic Research, Cambridge, MA, available at http://www.nber.org/papers/w14587, accessed on 1 August 2009.

Reserve Bank of India (RBI). 1993–2007. *Basic Statistical Returns of Scheduled Commercial Banks in India*, Mumbai, Reserve Bank of India.

——. 2009a. 'India's Overall Balance of Payments in Dollars', available at http://rbidocs.rbi.org.in/rdocs/Bulletin/DOCs/T43_TradeBal.xls, accessed on 21 March 2009.

——. 2009b. 'International Investment Position (IIP) of India as at the End of September 2008', available at http://rbidocs.rbi.org.in/rbiadmin/scripts/BS_PressReleaseDisplay.aspx?prid=20357, accessed on 21 March 2009.

Sametz, A.W. 1992. 'Financial Innovation and Regulation in the United States', *Palgrave Dictionary of Finance*, London, Macmillan, pp. 71–5.

Sweezy, Paul M. and Harry Magdoff. 1972. *The Dynamics of US Capitalism*, New York, Monthly Review Press.

Financial Inclusion

In a far flung village of Andhra Pradesh, Achhamma was forced to hide her hard-earned money under the kitchen stove so that her drunkard husband could not get his hands on it. When first introduced to ICT-based banking, with some trepidation she asked, 'Can anyone take away my money from my bank account without my knowing it?' When it was carefully explained to her that due to the use of biometric devices for unique identification, no one other than her could touch the money in the bank, she was comforted enough to deposit all her savings in the bank. And today Achhamma runs a small business making pickle and is aspiring to expand the enterprise.

Half the world's population—about 2.5 billion—does not use formal financial services to save or to borrow. The bulk of these—about 2.2 billion—live in Africa, Asia, Latin America, and the Middle East.[1] Achhamma's story highlights that the poor have the inclination and ability to save, even though these savings may be small and irregular. Her story is also an illustration of how financial inclusion can enfranchise the poor in a powerful way.

Why is Financial Inclusion Important?

Why is financial inclusion important? It is important simply because it is a necessary condition for sustaining equitable growth. There are few, if any, instances of an economy transiting from an agrarian system to a post-industrial modern society without broad-based financial inclusion. As people having comfortable access to financial services, we all know from personal experience that economic opportunity is strongly intertwined with financial access. Such access is especially powerful for the poor as it provides them opportunities to build savings, make investments, and avail credit. More important, access to financial services also helps the poor insure themselves against income shocks and equips them to meet emergencies such as illness, death in the family, or loss of employment. Needless to add, financial inclusion protects the poor from the clutches of the usurious money lenders.

There is another benefit of financial inclusion which we have yet to fully appreciate let alone exploit. Financial inclusion will make it possible for governments to make payments, such as social security transfers and National Rural Employment Guarantee Programme (NREGA) wages, into the bank accounts of beneficiaries through the 'Electronic Benefit Transfer' (EBT) method. This will minimize transaction costs including leakages. In parts of the country where such EBT has already

[1]See Chaia et al. (2009).

taken off, the results are impressive and the experience of both payers and recipients very encouraging.

There are enormous benefits at the aggregate level too. The first and more obvious benefit is that financial inclusion provides an avenue for bringing the savings of the poor into the formal financial intermediation system and channel them into investment. Second, the large number of low-cost deposits will offer banks an opportunity to reduce their dependence on bulk deposits and help them to better manage both liquidity risks and asset-liability mismatches.

What is Financial Inclusion?

Financial inclusion can mean different things at different stages of economic development. In advanced economies, financial inclusion is more about the knowledge of fair and transparent financial products and a focus on financial literacy. In emerging economies, it is a question of both access to financial products and knowledge about their fairness and transparency. In India, financial inclusion is defined as 'the process of ensuring access to appropriate financial products and services needed by vulnerable groups, such as weaker sections and low-income groups, in a fair and transparent manner by mainstream institutional players'.

Financial Exclusion in India

Financial exclusion is caused by multiple barriers, both the price and non-price variety. Price barriers come by way of transaction costs in terms of money, time, and labour. Non-price barriers come in a variety of ways: discrimination on the basis of gender, caste, and religion; financial illiteracy; lack of confidence and lack of empathy on the part of bank staff. Access to the financial sector, as we would expect, is directly proportional to income—the poorer a person is, the more difficult is the access to mainstream financial sources. Overcoming the above barriers is, in a nutshell, the challenge of financial inclusion.

The extent of financial exclusion in India is staggering. Here are some figures for 2009/2010:

- There was only one bank branch per 14,000 people.
- Only 55 per cent of the population had deposit accounts and 9 per cent had credit accounts with banks.[2] Consequently, a significant portion of the population is forced to depend on informal sources of finance (Table 1).
- Only a little less than 20 per cent had some kind of life insurance.[3]

Table 1 Percentage Share of Household Debts from Various Sources

Source	Rural	Urban
Formal sources	**57.1**	**75.1**
Of which,		
Commercial banks	24.5	29.7
Informal sources	**42.9**	**24.9**
Of which,		
Professional moneylenders	19.6	13.2
Traders	2.6	1.0
All sources	**100.0**	**100.0**

Source: All India Debt and Investment Survey, 2002–03.

- Just 19 per cent had debit cards and less than 2 per cent had credit cards.[4]

The disparity in financial exclusion is even more striking at disaggregated levels.

(a) *Rural–Urban Divide*: Access to financial services is significantly worse in rural India than in urban India (Figure 1) implying that rural people rely more on informal sources of finance. Even as urban India is better, there are disparities in access to finance even here, and as we would expect, slum-dwellers, hawkers, informal sector workers, and migrant labourers form the bulk of the excluded.

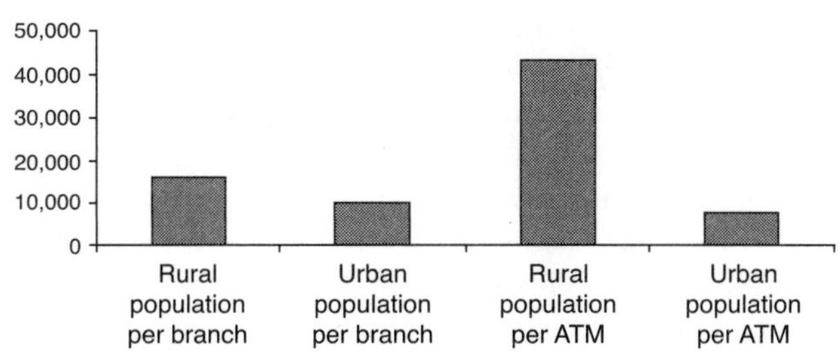

Figure 1 Rural–Urban Divide in Banking, 2010

Source: *Report on Trend and Progress of Banking in India* (2010).

(b) *Geographical Divide*: In a large and heterogeneous country like India, the fault lines across geographic regions in access to banking services are significant. The western, southern, and northern regions have traditionally been ahead of the north-eastern, eastern, and central regions. The disparity shows up both in terms of branch intensity and per capita deposit/credit (Table 2).

(c) *Asset Class Divide*: A comparison based on asset class shows that small farmers borrow less from banks

[2]Calculated from *Basic Statistical Returns of Scheduled Commercial Banks in India—2009*.
[3]IRDA (2010).

[4]Calculated on the basis of data from Census of India 2010–11 and *RBI Bulletin*, September 2011.

Table 2 Indicators of Banking Outreach across Geographical Regions

Region	Population per bank branch ('000)	Amount of deposits per capita (Rs)	Amount of credit per capita (Rs)
North-eastern region	19.8	17,775	6,119
Central region	18.0	17,183	8,028
Eastern region	18.5	20,413	10,267
Southern region	10.3	39,870	36,778
Northern region	10.7	63,766	47,554
Western region	12.9	86,393	67,171
All-India	13.9	38,833	28,232

Source: *Report on Trend and Progress of Banking in India* (2010).

than large farmers. Farmers operating with less than 0.4 hectares, for instance, reported only about 20 per cent of their total debt from commercial banks, while farmers with more than 10 hectares of land reported 43 per cent of their total debt from banks (NSSO 2005).

(d) *Gender Divide*: Estimates for 2009 show that for every 100 individual deposit accounts held by men, only 32 were held by women.[5] The disparity is greater for loans. For every 100 loan accounts held by men, only 16 were held by women.

These statistics, staggering as they are, do not convey the true extent of financial exclusion. Even where bank accounts are claimed to have been opened, verification has shown that these accounts are dormant. Few conduct any banking transaction and even fewer receive any credit. Millions of people across the country are thereby denied the opportunity to harness their earning capacity and entrepreneurial talent, and are condemned to marginalization and poverty.

Financial Inclusion in India: The Shift to a Focus on Households and Individuals

Effort at financial inclusion is not new; both the government and the Reserve Bank of India (RBI) have been pursuing this goal over the last several decades. The precise strategy changed with the changing environment and on the basis of experience. The strategy was building the rural cooperative structure in the 1950s, social contract with banks in the 1960s, and the expansion of bank branch networks in the 1970s and 1980s. The large-scale branch expansion resulted in a significant drop in the benchmark index of population per bank branch from 63,000 in 1969 to 14,000 in 2010. The policy of mandating priority-sector lending targets for banks channelled bank credit into agriculture and small-scale industries. All through, the approach to inclusive finance remained focused more on specific sectors and less on households and individuals (RBI 2008).

This approach changed in 2005, reflecting the lessons of experience. Currently, RBI is focused on reducing the extent of exclusion at the household and individual levels. This synchronizes the policy of inclusion with the ongoing process of financial liberalization and aims to achieve inclusion through a mix of development initiatives and relaxation in regulatory dispensation. Banks are expected to be at the forefront of reaching unserved and underserved clients at the bottom of the pyramid. In due course, banks should walk the last mile too and replace micro-finance institutions (MFIs), and MFIs should replace the moneylender in offering consumption smoothing by extending small amounts of credit to borrowers to meet their lifecycle needs.

The current approach of RBI towards financial inclusion is multi-pronged. At the aggregate level, it focuses on creating an enabling environment for flow of credit to first generation entrepreneurs and small enterprises. On the individual consumer side, the focus is on adopting new tools and technology to bring every household into the banking fold and helping educate them to be financially literate. The following is a listing of some major initiatives.

- RBI has advised banks to adopt policies in support of financial inclusion with new financial product offerings such as zero or minimal balance 'no frills' accounts.
- RBI has liberalized regulations of bank branch expansion. Banks are now free to open branches in population centres below tier II (population less than 50,000). They are also advised to open 25 per cent of all new branches in unbanked villages with population of less than 10,000.
- There is a comprehensive plan to provide banking access to all villages with population over 2,000 by March 2012. About 70,000 villages fall into this category. The access can be either through a brick and mortar branch or through a business correspondent (BC).
- The BC model is gaining popularity and credibility. There are plans to train all BCs so as to make them efficient, effective, and customer friendly.
- RBI's regulation is being tailored to encourage innovation in financial inclusion through hand-held machines, mobile phones, ATM machines, and so on.
- Banks have been advised to draw up board-approved Financial Inclusion Plans (FIPs) for a period of three

[5]Calculated based on data from *Basic Statistical Returns of Scheduled Commercial Banks in India—2009.*

years up to March 2013, which should be integrated with the business plan of the bank. A uniform model has not been imposed so that each bank can build its strategy in line with its business model and comparative advantage. The key features of the Financial Inclusion Plans (FIPs) are discussed in Box 1.

Box 1 FIPs—A New Approach to Financial Inclusion

In 2010, the Reserve Bank of India (RBI) asked all banks to prepare a Financial Inclusion Plan (FIP) and have it approved by their respective boards. The idea was to allow flexibility to banks to draw up a plan consistent with their business plans and comparative advantage. This greater ownership of the plan will also help in its effective implementation.

The FIP should ensure that every account holder has access to a minimum of four banking products: a savings-cum-overdraft account, a pure savings account, a remittance product, and an entrepreneurial credit facility like General Credit Card (GCC) or Kisan Credit Card (KCC).

As the involvement of the field staff is crucial in achieving the objectives of the FIPs, banks have been advised to make 'work done with regard to financial inclusion' a criterion in evaluating the performance of their field staff.

The FIPs have delineated goalposts for implementation. Banks are expected to have Core Banking Solutions (CBS) in their own rural branches and also in their sponsored regional rural banks (RRBs), along with a strategy for BCs. The plan also furnishes annual goals for inclusion of villages with a population above 2,000 and outlines the bank's strategies for including urban centres and adoption of the Unique Identity (UID) project.

- Banks have been asked to include performance on financial inclusion in the performance evaluation of their field staff.
- State governments are encouraged to shift to EBT, that is, all benefits and wages paid by the government to people should be remitted directly to the bank accounts of the beneficiaries.
- In order to further financial literacy, RBI has established centres focused on financial education in its regional offices in Chandigarh, Pune, and Bangalore. Commercial banks have been encouraged to set up financial literacy and credit counselling centres to help people develop better financial planning skills and learn of the opportunities available in the financial sector. Most important, RBI is encouraging both central and state government to include financial literacy in school and college curriculum so that the next generation enters the adult world financially literate.

Challenges for Financial Inclusion

As much as there is greater awareness of the benefits of financial inclusion, and there is enthusiasm for furthering it, there are many challenges ahead. Let us look at the important ones:

Viability of Financial Inclusion as a Business Model

For financial inclusion to become a viable business proposition, the mindset of the banks needs to change. Currently, because of low volumes, banks feel that extending financial services is not cost effective. Banks must look at financial inclusion as a business opportunity and not as an obligation. The key to this lies in moving from a cost-centric model to a revenue-generating model in which customers will get quality banking services at their door step and at the same time generate business opportunities for the banks. In this context, credit linkage of deposits mobilized through financial inclusion initiatives become imperative.

The BC model is becoming popular because it is cost-effective. But a BC cannot fully substitute a physical bank branch and there is much to be said for face-to-face contact between the bank and the first generation low-income account holder. Banks should accordingly maintain a viable balance between brick and mortar branches and BCs. Now technologies and business processes offer a low-cost model for a brick and mortar branch with minimum infrastructure and staff.

Because volumes are currently low, there are also concerns about whether the BC model is sustainable. The lasting solution lies in expanding volumes, training BCs, and giving them constant back-stop support.

Suitable and Appropriate Delivery Models

Improving the access of common people to suitable financial products using appropriate delivery models requires a two-pronged action: first, to devise fair and simple financial products and services and, second, to adopt an appropriate cost-effective delivery platform. At the outset, as enumerated in the FIP, delivery of services, at the minimum, should include four products: (i) a savings cum overdraft account, (ii) a remittance product for EBT and other remittances (iii) a pure savings product, ideally a recurring deposit scheme, and (iv) entrepreneurial credit in the form of GCC or KCC.

It is also important to adapt the existing Information and Communication Technology (ICT) to not only innovate but also deliver these financial products. A minimum prerequisite for this is for all the branches of a bank to be on the Core Banking Solution (CBS) platform. Seamless integration of the ICT-based devices/servers with the CBS needs to be ensured to minimize glitches. The technology adopted should aim at ensuring economies of scale by enabling the delivery of small-ticket transactions in large numbers. The recently launched Unique Identity (UID) project has immense potential to improve the delivery of social security benefits and financial services. Apart from technology, harnessing community-based products and delivery models that are in tune with the existing socio-cultural milieu will go a long way in faster expansion of the financial network.

Need for Financial Literacy

Spreading financial literacy and awareness is another important task in ensuring universal financial inclusion since it helps increase the demand for such financial services. It is important to design innovative knowledge programmes and capsules that make the public aware of the various products and services available as well as their risks and returns. Awareness programmes should also educate the public about how to use these products and caution them against financial fraud. The financial literacy drive needs to be spearheaded by banks in continuous coordination with the governments, educational institutions, and civil society organizations. Efforts to impart financial education to customers on a continuous basis would help reduce the inhibitions of new customers in interacting with the banking system.

The gender gap needs to be bridged too through efforts to devise innovative financial literacy programmes targeted at women. There are already some successful experiments such as the financial counselling training service for poor self-employed women started by Self-Employed Women's Association (SEWA). These need to be scaled up across the country.

Creating Infrastructure

The last challenge relates to the development of physical and social infrastructure which would directly facilitate financial inclusion and indirectly create demand for financial products by increasing the absorptive capacity of the region.

Outreach Programme

Last year, RBI celebrated its Platinum Jubilee. The flagship of the celebrations, one which will possibly have the most enduring value, has been the outreach programme. The outreach programme was focused on taking forward the twin pillars of financial inclusion and financial literacy. The motivation behind this venture was for the RBI, as an institution, to connect with ordinary people of the country. The odyssey took all the top management of RBI to villages across the country—typically off-main road, away from urban influence, unbanked villages—to see and understand how grass-roots institutions (self-help women's groups, micro-finance institutions, non-government organizations, rural cooperatives, rural branches of regional and mainstream commercial banks) operate, and to listen first-hand to the hopes and aspirations of village India. In return, the RBI top brass got an opportunity to explain to people what RBI does, and how it touches their everyday life. Because of the rich dividends, it has been decided to continue this as a permanent programme.

In Conclusion

Let me end by quoting from my personal experience. In 2010, I visited Jalanga village in Orissa as part of the outreach programme. I was very impressed by the women's self-help groups—small groups of women who get together, pool their savings, and give loans to their members—and how these groups have empowered the women. This empowerment came by way of several things: rising aspirations, opportunities to fulfil those aspirations, confidence to take advantage of those opportunities, and determination and hard work.

I visited the same village again this year. The experience was indeed heartening. Subsequent to my visit, a bank branch was set up. This resulted in a huge increase in banking outreach, particularly within the village. Deposit mobilization increased by a whopping 140 per cent in 2010. Credit disbursal also increased, albeit at a slower pace of 20 per cent. But what was more impressive was the increase in financial awareness not only in Jalanga, but also in the neighbouring villages. In fact, people from the neighbouring villages were quite vocal in their demand for bank branches in their own villages, which is a clear pointer to increased financial literacy in Jalanga and its neighbourhood and the domino effect that such outreach activities could trigger.

The village visits gave me confidence that banking on the poor can actually be a rich banking proposition. Financial inclusion is a win–win opportunity for the poor, for the banks, and for the nation. Due to growing incomes and improving awareness levels, the aspirations of the poor are on the rise. We will not be forgiven if we do not rise to meet these aspirations because of the poverty of our imagination. It is for the banks to convert what they see as a dead-weight obligation into an exciting opportunity and to move aggressively on financial inclusion.

D. SUBBARAO

References

Chaia, Alberto, Aparna Dalal, Tony Goland, Maria Jose Gonzalez, Jonathan Morduch, and Robert Schiff. 2009. 'Half the World is Unbanked', Financial Access Framing Note, October.

Insurance Regulatory Authority of India. 2010. *Annual Report—2009–10*, available at www.irda.org.in.

National Sample Survey Organisation. 2005. *Situation Assessment Survey of Farmers—Indebtedness of Farmer Households*, Report No. 498, New Delhi.

Reserve Bank of India (RBI). 2008. *Report on Currency and Finance 2006–8*, Mumbai, RBI.

——. 2009. *Basic Statistical Returns of Scheduled Commercial Banks in India—2009*, Mumbai, RBI.

——. 2010. *Report on Trend and Progress of Banking in India—2009–10*, Mumbai, RBI.

■ Financial-sector Reforms*

Finance and Development

It is broadly recognized in economic literature that efficient and developed financial markets can lead to increased economic growth by improving the efficiency of allocation and utilization of savings in the economy. Better functioning financial systems ease the external financing constraints that impede firm and industrial expansion. There is a growing body of empirical evidence across countries that prove this strong, positive link between the functioning of the financial system and long-term economic growth.

Growing Importance of Finance in India

The Indian economy has grown sharply in recent years and has enjoyed a high rate of savings and investments. This has inevitably involved a substantial role for finance as the intermediary between household and firms. Over the last 10 plus years, India went from being medium size developing country, with an aggregate GDP of $396 billion in 1998–9, to being a member of the G-20 with an aggregate GDP of $1.13 trillion in 2009–10.[1] This is a rough tripling of the aggregate GDP. Alongside this, the savings rate went up dramatically from 24.13 per cent to 34.65 per cent. This combination gave a 4.64 times increase in gross domestic savings. The Indian financial system which used to handle a flow of $91 billion of savings in 1998–9 was handling $390 billion of savings by 2008–9. In addition, the private corporate sector which is the focus of the formal financial system came to play a bigger role in investment. Gross capital formation by the private corporate sector grew from 7.67 per cent of GDP to 14.53 per cent of GDP over this decade. There was a rise of 5.71 times: investment went from $29 billion in 1998–9 to $153 billion in 2008–9.

As a result of all this, the financial system has begun to play a more prominent role in the economy and the significance of financial reforms has risen. With $390 billion of household savings being produced a year, and $153 billion of private corporate investment taking place a year, modest improvement in the capability of the financial system would help accelerate growth.

Evolution of India's Financial System

India has undertaken major financial sector reforms in the last 20 plus years. Developments in each sub-sector of the Indian financial system and the unfinished agenda is briefly described and analysed in the following sections.

Equity Markets

Though India has, in the Bombay Stock Exchange (BSE), one of the oldest stock exchanges in Asia and the world, the country's modern securities market history really starts only in the 1990s. With the establishment of the Securities and Exchange Board of India (SEBI) as its regulator, establishment of many new institutions, and extensive use of technology and IT in the markets starting in the mid-1990s, the Indian securities market has had many 'firsts' to its credit including:

- establishing one of the first demutualized exchange in the world and
- corporatization and demutualization of all stock exchanges.

According to the *Global Stock Markets Factbook* (2009), India ranked 13 in the world in terms of total market capitalization (US$645 billion) and total value traded (US$1,050 billion) in 2008. The explosive growth of the Indian equity markets is well captured in the market capitalization to GDP ratio which stood at 92.64

*The views expressed are personal and not attributable to the Government of India or the Prime Minister's Economic Advisory Council.

[1]All conversions from Indian rupees to US dollars for a particular year are made at the exchange rate prevailing on 31 December of that year for calendar year data and 31 March for financial year data.

per cent as at end December 2010. What these numbers do not adequately capture is the rapid evolution of a modern securities market in India and the emergence of SEBI as a tough and effective regulator over a rather short period of time. The initial hard work of institution and capacity building is now clearly showing in the form of good quality orders, which is the heart and soul of financial sector supervision.

Equity Derivatives Markets

India's introduction of exchange-traded equity derivatives began only in this century. Trading first commenced in index futures contracts, followed by index options in June 2001. Since then, equity derivatives have come a long way, as evident from the fact that the derivatives turnover on the National Stock Exchange of India (NSE) has surpassed the equity market turnover within four years of the introduction of derivatives. The turnover of derivatives (on the NSE and BSE) increased from Rs 40,380 million (US$ 0.87 billion) in 2000–1 to Rs 292,483,750 million (US$ 6,551 billion) in 2010–11.

However, despite being one of the most successful developing countries in terms of a vibrant market for exchange-traded equity derivatives on the general issue of risk mitigation products (of which equity derivatives are just one example), it is poignant to note that 'innovations' have appeared in the country only after years of toil and waiting. Stock index futures took five years to be offered to the investors, from the time they were conceived. Exchange traded funds for gold took four years to become a reality. Interest rate derivatives though launched in 2003, did not take off mainly due to constraints on the participation of banks in this market and had to be re-launched in 2009. These experiences highlight the adverse environment for financial innovation in the country.

Money Markets

India had a reasonably vibrant bond market till the financial markets scam of the early 1990s, popularly known as the Harshad Mehta scam. An immediate consequence of the scam was a clamp down which took many years to overcome. But in comparison to the period before that, money markets are currently better in terms of depth, and as a result of various policy initiatives, activity in all the segments has increased significantly, especially during the last five years. The average monthly turnover in the money market which was $1,118 million in 2001–2 reached $2,782 million in March 2010. With the development of market repo and collateralized borrowing and lending obligation segments, the call money market has been transformed into a pure interbank market since August 2005. Volatility in call rates has declined over the years, especially after the introduction of the liquidity adjustment facility. There has also been a reduction in bid ask spread in the overnight rates, which indicates that the Indian money market has become reasonably deep, vibrant, and liquid.

However, though the money market is free from interest rate ceilings, structural barriers and institutional factors continue to create distortions in the market. Apart from the overnight interbank (call market) rate, the other interest rates in the money market are sticky and appear to be set in customer markets rather than auction markets. A well-defined yield curve, therefore, does not exist in the Indian money market.

Government Securities Markets

As a result of the many developmental measures undertaken from 1992 onwards, the volume of transactions in government securities has increased manifold over the past decade. Secondary market transactions in government securities increased from a turnover of $29,093 million in the year 2000 to $770,614 million over January to June 2009. The investor base, which was largely determined by mandated investment requirements before reforms, has expanded slightly with the voluntary holding of government securities. Accordingly, the share of commercial banks in holding government securities has declined marginally from about 41.5 per cent in 2007 to 38.85 per cent in 2009.

However, a number of problems continue to confront these markets. Liquidity of the markets is poor. This impedes the development of a benchmark yield curve that can be reliably used to price all cash flows off the curve. Only a handful of securities account for the bulk of trading. There are isolated pockets of liquidity for very short-term and very long-term securities. In addition, there are limits on foreign institutional investor (FII) investments in government securities, which limit voluntary demand for them from abroad.

A key issue for government securities markets as of now is that the central bank is also the manager of public debt in the country. The existing arrangement leads to a series of conflicts between setting the short-term interest rate and selling bonds for the government. In addition, the Reserve Bank of India (RBI) administers the operational system for these markets, leading to a situation where the owner–administrator of these systems is also a participant in the market. This is now set to change with the proposed sitting up of an independent debt management office (DMO).

Corporate Debt Markets

Private bond market capitalization as percentage of GDP was 0.4 per cent for India in 2001, increasing to 5.83 per cent in 2009. The public bond market capitalization as a percentage of GDP was 23 per cent and 29.58 per cent for these years, respectively. These figures indicate underdeveloped bond markets when compared to other emerging markets with similar financial sector development. Financial institutions and government or government-guaranteed instruments dominate most of the issuance in the corporate bond market in India, with a share of 8 per cent and 90 per cent of the total issuance as of the end of March 2009, respectively.

A well-functioning bond market provides for financial diversification and facilitates financing for corporations and infrastructure development. However, as noted earlier, this market remains practically non-existent in India, imposing an avoidable constraint on India's ability to finance its growing need for debt, particularly for infrastructure development. The lack of depth in the government bond market and the absence of a yield curve for government bonds, which could serve as a benchmark for corporate bonds; a cumbersome primary issuance mechanism (to some extent addressed by recent changes in the regulations by the market regulator, the Securities and Exchange Board of India); the absence of sufficiently diversified long-term investors; and chronic illiquidity caused inter alia by absence of derivative instruments are some the factors leading to underdeveloped bond markets. There are also limits on FII investments in corporate debt.

Foreign Exchange Markets

The most important measures undertaken to reform these markets were the move towards a market-based exchange rate regime in 1993 and the subsequent adoption of current account convertibility. Allowing greater autonomy for banks in their foreign exchange operations, admitting new players into the markets, and permitting limited introduction of new products have been other important reforms.

As a result of these measures, the annual turnover in the foreign exchange market increased more than eightfold, from $1,305 billion in 1997–8 to $10,355 billion in 2009–10. During this period, there has been a steady but slow fall in the share of spot transactions in total turnover in the foreign exchange markets, implying an increase in gross turnover in the over-the-counter (OTC) derivative (swaps and forwards) segment of currency markets. Activity in this segment has picked up, particularly from late 2007 onwards, following increased volatility in the US dollar–rupee exchange rate. The current average daily turnover calculated on a monthly basis is a little over $21 billion.

While OTC foreign exchange markets have been in existence for a while, the exchange-traded currency futures market was only introduced in August 2008. This market, as it exists today, is limited to a few currencies with low position limits and a ban on trading by non-residents, including FIIs. Despite these limitations, the currency futures market has seen a steady growth in liquidity and now matches the spreads that are seen on their OTC forwards counterparts. There is considerable scope for further development of these markets by removing the aforementioned restrictions.

Banking Sector

Between 1992 and 2010, from a limited predominantly government-owned banking system, India moved towards a more competitive system with the entry of foreign and new private banks, and the reduction of public ownership in public-sector banks by allowing them to raise capital from equity markets up to 49 per cent of paid up capital. Alongside, interest rates have been largely deregulated with a few exceptions. However the statutory pre-emption is yet to come down appreciably. With the enactment of the Securitization and Reconstruction of Financial Assets and Enforcement of Securities Interest Act, 2002 (SARFAESI Act, 2002), and subsequent amendments, a market for distressed assets got created. As a result of regulatory and policy changes the average capital to risk (weighted) assets ratio (CRAR) of all banks increased from 9.2 per cent as of 31 March 1994 to 13.2 per cent as of 31 March 2009. With the global range for CRAR being 10.2 to 13.2 per cent, the capital adequacy of Indian banks is comparable to those at the international level. Similarly the ratio of gross NPAs to gross advances for the banking system, which was 14.4 per cent in March 1998, decreased to 2.33 per cent in March 2009. During the same period, the ratio of net NPAs to net advances declined from 7.3 per cent to 1.05 per cent. The reform measures have also resulted in an improvement in the profitability of banks. The return of assets of all banks in India rose from 0.4 per cent in 1991–2 to 1.0 per cent in 2008. The return on assets of Indian banks is in the range 0.1 to 2.1 per cent, which is comparable to the levels in other EMEs. However, these profitability figures mask an important fact—that India is hugely under-banked and needs more banks. This is likely to be marginally remedied with the likelihood of the RBI licensing a few more banks soon. Nevertheless, private credit (called non-food credit in India) remains a small fraction, as a percentage of GDP, when compared even with countries at similar levels of development.

Insurance Sector

The life insurance business (measured in the context of first-year premiums) registered a year-on-year growth of 94.96 per cent in 2006–7 and 25.84 per cent in 2009–10.

The gross direct premium of non-life insurers registered a growth of 13.96 per cent in 2009–10 (versus 21.51 per cent achieved in 2006–7). The industry has witnessed a slow increase in insurance penetration across the country. Insurance penetration for the year 2007 stood at 4 per cent for life insurance and had reached 4.6 per cent in 2009. Non-life insurance penetration has been stagnating at around 0.6 per cent for the past few years. The growth in the insurance industry has been spurred by product innovation, active distribution channels coupled with targeted publicity, and promotional campaigns by the insurers. Despite all this, India has low insurance density. One-third of all paid workers have some life insurance protection. However, only 14 per cent of people in the lowest income quartile and 26 per cent in the second quartile have life insurance, compared to 69 per cent of those in the highest income quartile.

The insurance industry also continues to face some basic problems. One of these is that a large part of the sale of 'insurance' products is merely tax arbitrage, where a fund management product is given preferential tax treatment under the garb of a minimal insurance cover. A related issue is that much of the growth in insurance penetration is as a result of selling products such as unit linked insurance plans (ULIPs), which are essentially a mutual fund type of securities market product and about the 'pushy' sales practices that are widely prevalent in the insurance industry.

Way Ahead

Regulatory Architecture

The current financial regulatory system involves half a dozen apex regulatory agencies, apart from several ministries in the government that retain direct regulatory powers. This structure leads to major regulatory overlaps and gaps. Sometimes this structure can also lead to regulatory arbitrage as similar financial services may be offered by institutions that come under different regulators and are, therefore, subject to different regulatory requirements. The overlapping regulatory structure also becomes a barrier to innovation as any new product might need approval from more than one regulator. Hence regulatory structures need to be streamlined to avoid regulatory inconsistencies, gaps, overlap, and arbitrage. Besides this, there is also a need to review financial regulations, which tend to be 'rule based' and overly prescriptive, inserting every minute detail into the basic legislation and supplemented by detailed subordinated rules and regulations. The suggestion here is to move towards more principle-based regulation to promote financial innovation and avoid the mistake of over-regulation. The recently constituted Financial Sector Legislative Reforms Council (FSLRC) has been tasked with rewriting financial sector laws with a view to remedying these defects.

Financial Inclusion

A robust financial system is not as socially relevant if most people in the country do not have access to it. India's poor, many of whom work as agricultural and unskilled or semi-skilled wage labourers, micro-entrepreneurs, and low-salaried workers, are largely excluded from the formal financial system. Financial inclusion is, therefore, a key priority for India, both for the urban and rural poor. Focus on merely opening bank accounts for the 'excluded' is, however, likely to be inadequate as there is a need to understand the myriad financial product requirements of the 'excluded' and allow innovative solutions to emerge. This will be a huge regulatory challenge given that the regulatory system is generally over cautious and risk averse.

Competition

Lack of sufficient competition in parts of the financial services industry, the pervasiveness of public ownership, and the over-compartmentalization of sub-sectors have resulted in suboptimal performance by existing market players. Competition needs to be across larger (in terms of capital), more capable players rather than among a plethora of small, weak, undercapitalized players that cannot capture economies of scale or make the kind of investments in people, training, technology, and research into product development that supports innovation.

Financial Stability and Regulatory Coordination

Financial stability is the key to the sound functioning of the financial markets and the economy itself. By definition, this is a multi-agency function. Though not explicitly located by law in any agency, the task of maintaining financial stability in India lay with the inter-regulatory body known as the HLCCFM (High Level Coordination Committee on Financial Markets) and the RBI. The newly created Financial Sector Development Council (FSDC) chaired by the Finance Minister is now formally vested with this as well as the responsibility for regulatory coordination. The FSDC now has to embark on an ambitious agenda of working out its operational protocols, role clarity of individual agencies, and methods of enforcement while retaining operational autonomy of regulators.

Conclusion

Financial sector reforms in India which began in the early 1990s now need to move faster. Over this period, a variety of financial sector reform measures have been undertaken in India, with many important successes. These reforms can be broadly classified as steps taken towards

- liberalizing the overall macroeconomic and regulatory environment within which financial sector institutions function,
- strengthening the institutions and improving their efficiency and competitiveness, and
- establishing and strengthening the regulatory framework and institutions for overseeing the financial system.

A key feature of these reforms has been the attempt of the authorities to align the regulatory framework with international best practices, keeping in view the needs of the country and domestic factors.

A question which comes up in all contemporary discussions on the subject is whether the global financial crisis necessitated a change in India's approach and commitment to financial sector development? The Indian approach to the development of financial markets has focused on a gradual, phased, and calibrated opening of the domestic financial and external sectors, taking into account reforms in other sectors of the economy. This continues to be the overall stand on reforms, even after the global crisis, though policies for the financial sector seem to be a little more cautious. However, given that a lot of the agenda of financial sector reforms in India has consisted of permitting formerly banned financial markets, strengthening regulation, plugging regulatory gaps, and strengthening regulatory coordination, recent global developments have in no way diluted this agenda.

K.P. KRISHNAN

■ Fiscal Deficit*

The *gross fiscal deficit* (GFD) of the government is the excess of its total expenditure, current and capital, including loans net of recovery, over revenue receipts (including external grants) and non-debt capital receipts. It measures the government's overall financing and borrowing needs. Some related measurements are useful: *net fiscal deficit* is the gross fiscal deficit less net lending by the government; *revenue deficit* is the excess of revenue expenditures over revenue receipts; *primary deficit* is gross fiscal deficit less interest payments.

When the government runs a gross fiscal deficit, it has four main ways to finance it: (i) borrowing from the central bank by printing new currency (and benefiting from 'seignorage'), and the central bank thereby monetizing the newly issued debt; (ii) raising reserve requirements on banks, where they are made to hold additional reserves in the form of cash balances with the central bank or eligible government securities; (iii) domestic open-market borrowing, where government debt is issued (and held by the banks or the public); and (iv) external borrowings. On the financing side, the role of the central bank is important and usefully measured by the net credit extended to the government; it represents the sum of changes in the central bank's holdings of: (i) government dated securities, (ii) treasury bills, (iii) rupee coins, and (iv) loans and advances from the central bank to the government (adjusted for changes in cash balances).

The manner in which the government finances its deficit has potentially profound, albeit differential impacts on the economy. While the size of these impacts remains a matter of debate, the nature of expected impacts is relatively well-understood. If the government relies on creating money to finance the deficit, it is essentially an 'inflation tax' because monetization will result in higher inflation. If the government finances the deficit by forcing banks to hold more securities, the impact is of taxing financial intermediaries. If it relies on borrowing from the market, the impact is the 'crowding out' of private investment. If the government borrows abroad, then it risks unanticipated pro-cyclical shocks from capital inflows, exchange rate changes, and creditworthiness assessments. Each of these financing options thus creates vulnerabilities, and there is no easy way to sustain a persistently high fiscal deficit and the resulting public debt—as interest costs and rates rise with higher deficit and debt, and growth itself begins to slow down. However, two caveats should be noted. The first is counter-cyclical fiscal policy—the scope for such action is dictated by starting fiscal positions, and is another reason for governments to reduce fiscal deficit (and debt) during 'good' times. The second is that the effectiveness of public spending matters a great deal for the sustainability of the fiscal deficit (and debt), that is, whether such spending generates higher social and economic rates of return than the cost of borrowing, and crowds-in rather than crowds-out private spending and growth.

India's Fiscal Deficit

Five different periods of India's fiscal deficit and debt are identifiable (Figure 1). The first period covers the three decades after Independence, when deficits and debt remained relatively prudent. The second is rapid deterioration in the 1980s at the central government

*In the original edition, this entry was provided by the late Professor Amaresh Bagchi. Our entry is a tribute to him.

level, culminating in the 1990–1 balance-of-payments crisis. The third is persistently high deficits in the 1990s, coinciding with sweeping economic reforms to open the economy, which nevertheless resulted in the fiscal deficit and debt coming to another head by 2001–1 (especially among state governments). The fourth is a phase of successful fiscal consolidation (both of central and state governments) till 2007–8 in response to the deterioration. The fifth is the current phase, relatively novel in modern India, when the country was forced to undertake a sharp counter-cyclical fiscal policy during the unprecedented global financial crisis of 2008–9; this immediately resulted in a jump in the deficit, but provided a floor to the slowdown in growth. Renewed fiscal consolidation is, however, important and underway.

Phase 1: The First Three Decades. Fiscal deficit remained within manageable limits for the first three decades after Independence. Largely, current receipts were used to finance current expenditure and capital expenditure was usually financed by relatively limited borrowings. Despite the rapid increase in expenditure due to the growth of the public sector, the combined GFD of the Centre and states generally did not exceed 4 per cent of GDP (Bagchi 2007; Ministry of Finance 2004). In 1973–4, the central government had a revenue surplus of 0.36 per cent of GDP and a gross fiscal deficit of 2.61 per cent of GDP (see Figure 1). By 1978–9, however, events had started unraveling, as the second oil shock hit India. The central government's revenue surplus fell to 0.26 per cent of GDP, while the fiscal deficit increased to 5.13 per cent. The state governments, fortunately, continuously ran revenue surpluses from 1974–5 to 1983–4, saving the situation.

Phase 2: Fiscal Deterioration of the 1980s. The situation started changing rapidly in the 1980s. Public expenditure grew rapidly while revenues did not. The combined GFD as a percentage of GDP reached a record high of 9.78 per cent in 1986–7, while the Centre's GFD was 8.37 per cent in the same year. Climbing revenue deficits were the reason: the Centre's revenue deficit reached 2.48 per cent in 1988–9. The combined (Centre plus states) revenue deficit climbed from 0.22 per cent in 1982–3 to 3.2 per cent in 1989–90, even as capital expenditure was

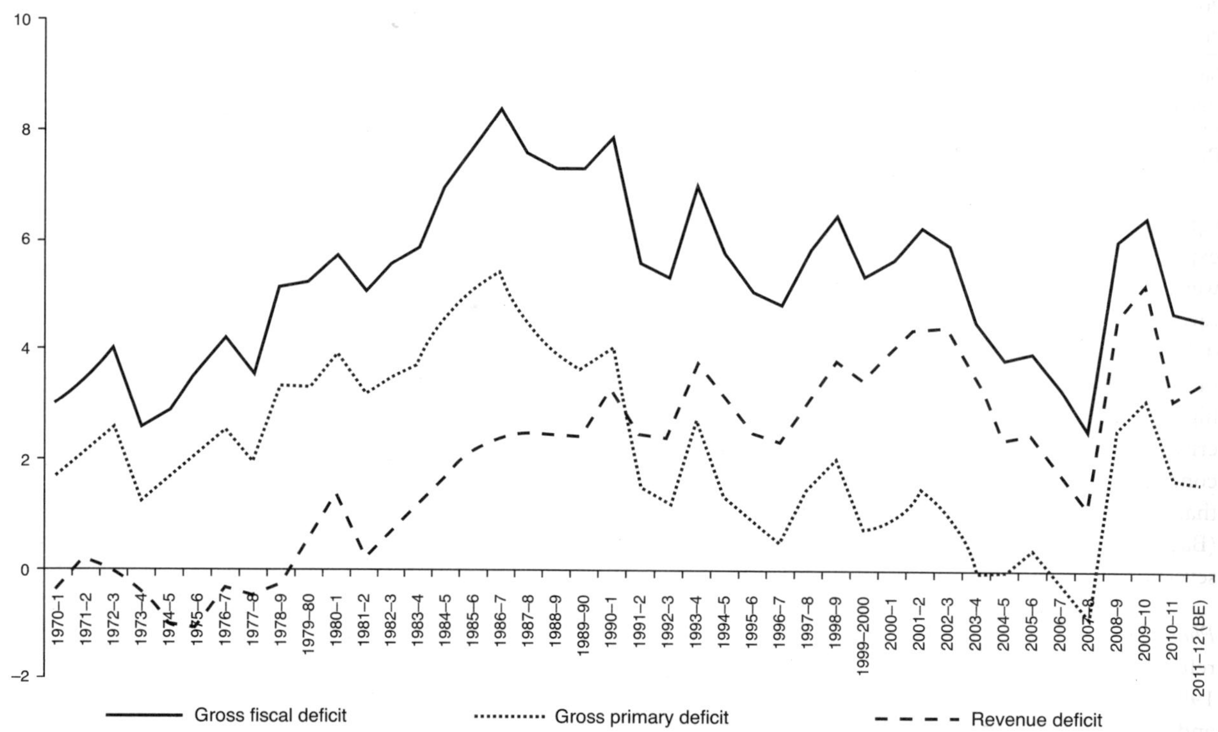

Figure 1 Deficits of the Central Government, 1970–1 to 2011–12

Source: Reserve Bank of India database (available at http://dbie.rbi.org.in) for all data, except provisional (unaudited) accounts from Comptroller General of Accounts for 2010–11, and Union Budget 2011–12, for 2009–10 and 2011–12.

Table 1 Deficits of the Central and State Governments as Percentage of GDP (Selected Years)

Year	Centre			States			Combined		
	Gross fiscal deficit	Gross primary deficit	Revenue deficit	Gross fiscal deficit	Primary deficit	Revenue deficit	Gross fiscal deficit	Gross primary deficit	Revenue deficit
1970–1	3.04	1.74	-0.35	1.95	1.09	0.04			
1973–4	2.61	1.28	-0.36	2.21	1.38	0.18			
1978–9	5.13	3.35	-0.26	2.37	1.52	-1.02			
1980–1	5.71	3.92	1.4	2.55	1.71	-1.02	7.42	5.38	0.38
1981–2	5.07	3.2	0.23	2.38	1.54	-0.81	6.21	4.01	-0.58
1982–3	5.56	3.5	0.68	2.61	1.72	-0.46	5.82	3.39	0.22
1986–7	8.37	5.43	2.47	2.94	1.64	-0.05	9.78	6.4	2.42
1989–90	7.31	3.67	2.44	3.16	1.69	0.75	8.84	4.63	3.2
1990–1	7.84	4.06	3.26	3.3	1.78	0.93	9.41	5.02	4.19
1993–4	6.96	2.72	3.78	2.35	0.53	0.45	8.17	3.2	4.23
1996–7	4.84	0.53	2.37	2.65	0.81	1.22	6.28	1.21	3.59
1998–9	6.47	2.03	3.82	4.19	2.16	2.54	8.91	3.62	6.36
2001–2	6.19	1.47	4.4	4.14	1.43	2.65	9.86	3.65	7.05
2003–4	4.48	-0.03	3.57	4.38	1.46	2.3	8.42	2.03	5.87
2005–6	3.95	0.37	2.49	2.43	0.16	0.19	6.46	0.96	2.68
2007–8	2.56	-0.89	1.06	1.53	-0.49	-0.87	4.12	-1.13	0.19
2008–9	6.05	2.6	4.55	2.63	0.72	-0.19	8.5	3.35	4.14
2009–10	6.4	3.1	5.2	3.2	1.33	0.52	9.59	4.29	5.06
2010–11	4.7	1.7	3.1						
2011–12	4.6	1.6	3.4						

Source: For central government, Reserve Bank of India database (available at http://dbie.rbi.org.in) for all data, except provisional (unaudited) accounts from Comptroller General of Accounts for 2010–11, and Union Budget 2011–12, for 2009–10 and 2011–12 (BE). From RBI database for states and combined deficit. Figures for 2008–9 are RE and those for 2009–10 are BE. RE: Revised Estimates, BE: Budget Estimates.

squeezed, and interest payments took a larger share of the expenditure.[1] After dipping a little, the combined GFD went up to 9.41 per cent in 1990–1 with a combined revenue deficit of 4.19 per cent, and a combined primary deficit that exceeded 5 per cent of GDP. Moreover, much of the deficit was being monetized, with persistently high inflation—all factors paving the way for the 1990–1 crisis. There were proximate causes that immediately contributed to the crisis, most notably the first Gulf War that caused a jump in the oil bill, with reserves plunging (Bagchi 2007). But the fiscal deficit contributed to the severity of the crisis (Table 1).

Phase 3: Resurgence of Deficits in the 1990s. Wide-ranging reforms were undertaken by the new government after the 1990–1 crisis to open the economy (by reducing tariffs and improving exchange rate management), and to spur private investment by dismantling the 'licence-raj' system of bureaucratic controls. Fiscal reforms also figured prominently (Bagchi 2007): (i) stopping the automatic monetization of the deficit, reducing inflation, and shifting to domestic market borrowing; and (ii) cutting back on current spending, while improving the tax administration. The initial results were favourable as the combined GFD fell back to 6.28 per cent by 1996–7 and inflation moderated to about 5 per cent. However, the combined gross fiscal deficit surged again thereafter and reached a new peak of 9.86 per cent by 2001–2. Soaring state government deficits, which nearly doubled, was a major reason, but central government deficits also remained stubbornly high at about 6 per cent of GDP. The result was another sharp increase in the government combined debt–GDP ratio, which now exceeded 80 per cent of GDP (Figure 2).

The impact on the balance of payments was, however, modest and the situation was very different in this respect from the 1990–1 crisis episode—rapid export growth (including services) as well as remittances contained

[1]As a percentage of total disbursements, the capital component fell from around 34 per cent in 1981–2 to 21.7 per cent by 1989–90, while the interest part rose from 8.45 to 14.14 per cent across the same period.

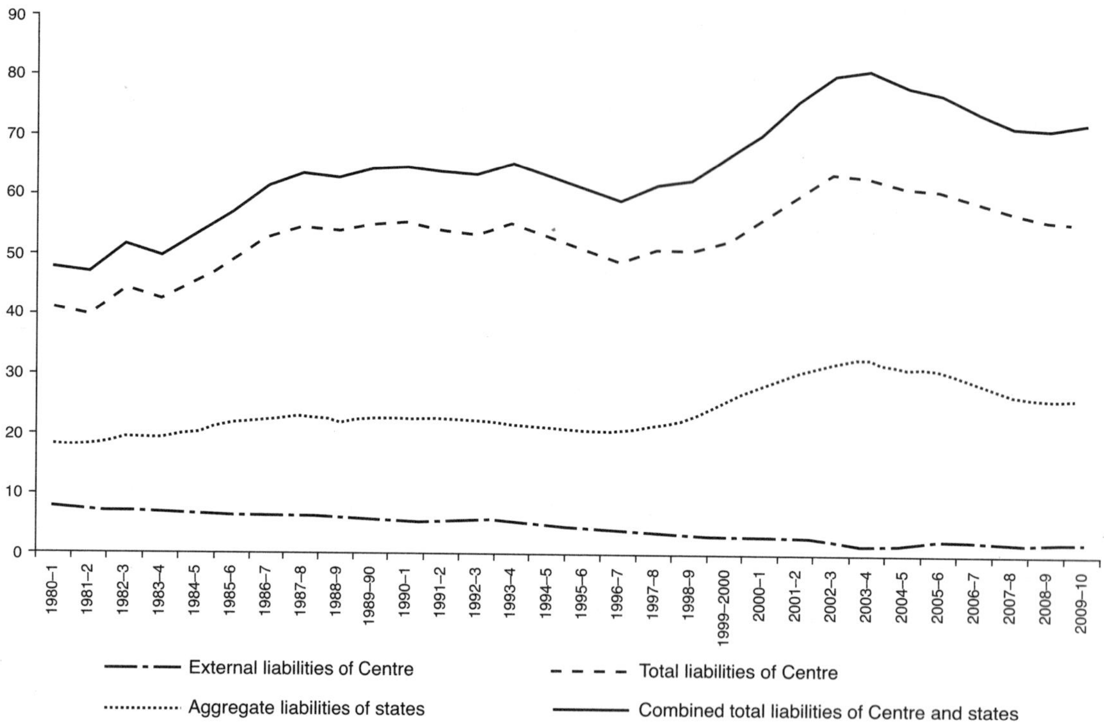

Figure 2 Liabilities of the Centre and the States as Percentage of GDP, 1980–1 to 2009–10

Source: Reserve Bank of India database (available at http://dbie.rbi.org.in).

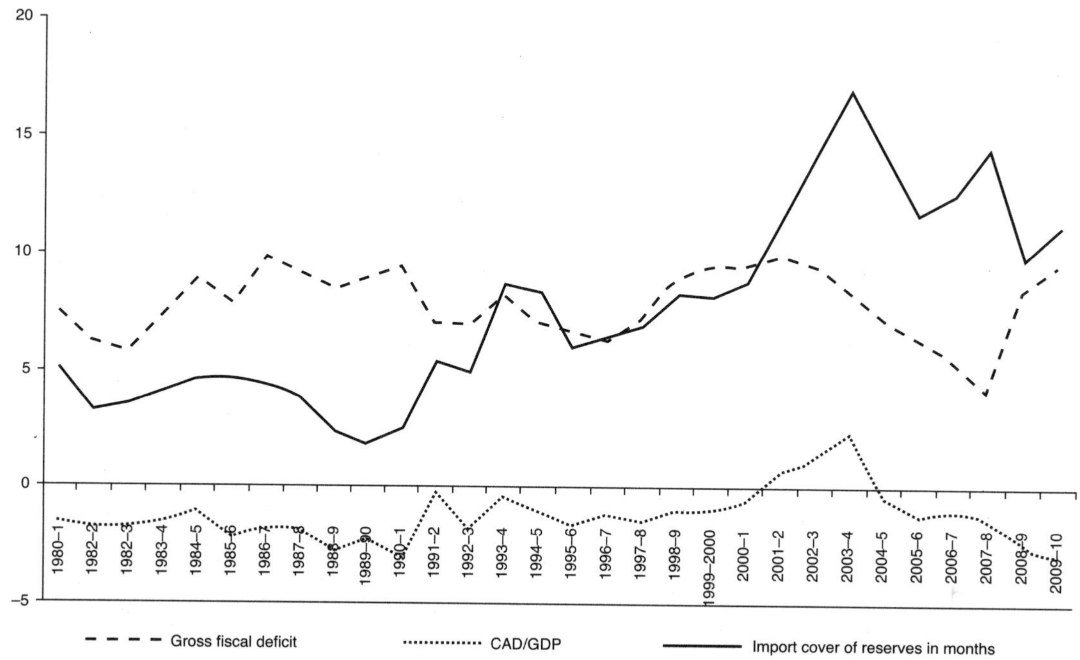

Figure 3 Combined Gross Fiscal Deficit (as Percentage of GDP) and Balance of Payments, 1980–1 to 2009–10

Source: Reserve Bank of India database (available at http://dbie.rbi.org.in).

the current account deficit (CAD) to very modest levels (and even some surpluses), while reserves were also much higher and relatively comfortable (Figure 3). Nevertheless, the large fiscal deficit and rising debt, much of it because of rising revenue deficit to finance current spending and rising interest expenditure, rang alarm bells domestically. A slowing economy was one factor, but the underlying factors were clearly structural: rising and inflexible wages, salaries and pensions, a major pay revision following the recommendations of the Fifth Pay Commission, which the states followed on the heels of adjustments by the Centre, and rising subsidy bills, especially for electricity utilities at the state-level, and food, fertilizer, and fuels at the Centre. On the revenue side, the loss of trade taxes following the reforms was yet to be made up by other taxes, despite remarkable improvements in tax collections from direct taxes.

Phase 4: Successful Fiscal Consolidation from 2003 till 2007–8. Given the imperatives, a political consensus was achieved on improved, target-based fiscal management, and several sweeping initiatives of fiscal reforms came together. First, the central Fiscal Responsibility and Budget Management (FRBM) Act was enacted in August 2003. It mandated a reduction in fiscal and revenue deficits. Second, a value-added tax (VAT) was finally agreed on, which was adopted by virtually all the states and by the Centre by 2004. Third, measures were adopted to improve the tax administration and widen the tax base, especially with electronic information systems. Finally, expenditure on subsidies and other current spending was sought to be much more tightly constrained, following the agreed FRBM Act, not only at the Centre, but also at the state level, as many states (26) too adopted FRBM legislations to take advantage of debt relief concessions offered by the central government (Thirteenth Finance Commission 2009).

Under the 'rules-based' targeting of FRBM (with similar provisions at the state level), the annual minimum revenue deficit reduction at the Centre was targeted at 0.5 per cent of GDP while the annual fiscal deficit reduction was set at a minimum of 0.3 per cent of GDP. The fiscal deficit was sought to be reduced below 3 per cent of GDP by 31 March 2008. (Ministry of Finance 2004). While FRBM targets have not always been strictly adhered to, it appears to have guided policy towards a more responsible fiscal stance.

The results were evident: fiscal year 2007–8 was the 'golden year' of fiscal discipline with the central government's GFD being brought down to 2.56 per cent and the revenue deficit to 1.06 per cent of GDP. Faced with a tighter fiscal policy framework and revenue gains from the implementation of the state VAT, the states also performed well. From a fiscal deficit of 4.38 per cent and a revenue deficit of 2.3 per cent of GDP in 2003–4, the states' GFD came down to 1.53 per cent of GDP in 2007–8 with a revenue surplus of 0.87 per cent. The combined central and state GFD thus fell to 4.12 per cent with a combined revenue deficit of 0.19 per cent of GDP. It contributed to a benign macroeconomic atmosphere with high growth, investment, and moderate inflation. The combined debt–GDP ratio was lowered by some 10 percentage points during the same period, a remarkable gain. Whether endogenous or otherwise, faster growth was achieved and it helped: GDP growth surged to above 9 per cent of GDP annually between 2004–5 and 2007–8.

Phase 5: Global Financial Crisis and Counter-cyclical Fiscal Policy. India was thus much better placed in 2008–9 than at any time during the previous three decades in terms of its fiscal situation. It, therefore, had more room for counter-cyclical action. In the event, the severe global financial crisis contributed to fiscal actions that countered the previous trend of fiscal consolidation. Indeed, it was fortuitous that in the 2008–9 Budget, the central government had already planned an expansionary fiscal stance with the sizeable expansion of the National Rural Employment Guarantee Act, the implementation of another round of pay increases (following the Sixth Pay Commission recommendations) for its employees, and additional subsidies and farm loan waivers (Mundle et al. 2011). With the rapid onset of the global crisis, the government was thus able to expand spending quickly, and also put in place three rounds of additional fiscal stimulus characterized by further targeted expenditure and lowering of indirect taxes. As a result, the combined GFD shot up to 8.5 per cent of GDP in 2008–9. While the Centre's GFD went up to 6.05 per cent with a revenue deficit of 4.55 per cent of GDP, the states had a GFD of 2.63 per cent and a revenue surplus of 0.19 per cent in that fiscal.

The most important impact of this sharp expansion in fiscal spending and reduced taxes, estimated at over 3 per cent of GDP, was to set a floor to the drop in India's growth consequent to the global crisis. In the event, GDP growth moderated to about 6.8 per cent in 2008–9, a much smaller decline than feared earlier, thanks to counter-cyclical fiscal actions (as well as monetary policies that cut policy rates aggressively and injected large liquidity). Moreover, the dip in growth was short: GDP growth quickly recovered to 8 per cent in 2009–10 and 8.5 per cent in 2010–11.

Two challenges now confronted policymakers: returning back to a medium-term path of fiscal consolidation at a pace that maintained the growth recovery, while also moderating inflation, which shot up suddenly (led by escalating food prices) in 2009–10 to over 11 per cent in the wake of a severe drought, and remained persistently high through 2010–11. The government announced a medium-term fiscal consolidation path (and ensuing Budgets), largely in line with the recommendations of the Thirteenth Finance Commission. Faster growth, a successful strategy of disinvestment, and enhanced proceeds from a new round of 3G telecommunication spectrum licences and broadband fees helped the central government achieve a faster than planned reduction in its fiscal deficit in 2010–11 to 4.7 per cent, with a target of 4.6 per cent for 2011–12, as compared to an over 6 per cent deficit in 2008–9, and better than the targets provided by the Thirteenth Finance Commission.

Institutionally, the recommendations of the Thirteenth Finance Commission remain important. Entrusted with the responsibility of devolution of central taxes and review of the fiscal adjustment process for both the Centre and the states, the Thirteenth Finance Commission provided a fiscal consolidation roadmap for both. It was keenly aware that FRBM targets had been missed by the central government due to the global financial crisis. However, it also acknowledged the fiscal progress and debt reduction at the state level.

The Thirteenth Finance Commission charted a phased withdrawal from the expansionary fiscal stance necessitated by the global financial crisis. For the central government, it set a revenue deficit of 4.8 per cent and a fiscal deficit of 6.8 per cent of GDP for 2009–10, to be brought down to a revenue surplus of 0.5 per cent and a fiscal deficit of 3 per cent by 2014–15 (Thirteenth Finance Commission 2009). To ensure monitoring and compliance, it recommended that the central government set net borrowing limits for states on the basis of the mandated deficit paths. There have been views, which aver that the Thirteenth Finance Commission's norms reduce the fiscal flexibility of the states (Chakraborty 2011). But given the 'common pool' resources problem facing a federal system, this may well be a neat scheme for ensuring fiscal discipline, not only in terms of expenditure management but also in engendering greater revenue efforts.[2]

Being aware of the importance of revenue reforms the Thirteenth Finance Commission also strongly recommended a goods and services tax (GST) 'grand bargain' between the Centre and the states. The combined prescriptive framework of the FRBM Act and the Thirteenth Finance Commission seems to have played a role in instilling greater fiscal discipline. The Union Budget of 2011–12 clearly attempts to bring the central government back to a path of fiscal prudence. In addition, the central government also pushed hard to reach an accord with the states, including a required constitutional change, for adopting GST, which promises to potentially add substantial gains in revenues (of some 1–1.4 per cent of GDP) in the medium term, and also announced a direct tax code to be implemented shortly—a consensus and enactment of both are still pending.

Lessons Learned and Challenges

India's fiscal policymakers, at both the Centre and the states, have learnt many lessons from the experiences of the past several decades, especially after the wide-ranging reforms of 1990–1. At the same time, some challenges have remained unresolved.

There appears to be a wider realization than earlier that *fiscal consolidation matters* and, more important, delivers better results in terms of faster growth, lower inflation, and more spending ability ultimately, as faster growth revs up the revenue base. The experiences of both the fiscal crises of the early 2000s and the successful fiscal consolidation in 2003–8 have also again critically reinforced the consensus that fiscal consolidation matters and delivers far better results for growth, poverty reduction, and social spending.

The second important lesson, at least in the case of India, is that *raising revenues through broadening the tax base, lowering and simplifying rates, reducing exemptions, and improving tax administration* can work very effectively. The emphasis in a rich country with relatively high taxes may well be on cutting expenditures as the main path to sustainable fiscal consolidation, but in a fast-growing and modernizing economy such as India, there may be much more room for improving revenues as an instrument of fiscal consolidation.

The third important lesson, still in the early stages, is the potentially important role for counter-cyclical fiscal policy and related to that, the ability to quickly revert back to fiscal prudence once the goal of stabilization has been achieved. This is not easy both because automatic fiscal stabilizers (such as unemployment insurance) are unavailable, and because other expenditures are often difficult to design flexibly.

The fourth important lesson is the success with *private provision of public services*, especially in physical

[2]See Hausmann and Purfield (2004) for a description of the 'multiple common pool problems' facing the Indian federal system.

infrastructure, which has allowed a huge degree of freedom for budget-framers.

But some things have not yet been fully resolved. There is realization that public spending on welfare activities and subsidies is characterized by 'leakages'. As a result, reforms have begun, towards better targeting, more reliable technology-based identification of the poor, and a shift towards cash-based income support, rather than in-kind support.

A second challenge is how to *price public services better*—everything from water, to power, fuels, fertilizer, and other public services, such as tertiary education and health. Perhaps a shift to private service provision is a feasible answer. Part of the problem is also the low quality of public services and the lack of accountability.

The third challenge that follows is improving *service delivery and accountability by decentralizing public services* and related budgets and budgetary management. This is likely to be a long haul, but a vital one for improved fiscal management.

DIPAK DASGUPTA AND SUPRIYO DE

References

Bagchi, Amaresh. 2007. 'Fiscal Deficit', in Kaushik Basu (ed.), *The Oxford Companion to Economics in India,* New Delhi, Oxford University Press.

Chakraborty, Pinaki. 2011.'Deficit Fundamentalism *vs* Fiscal Federalism: Implications of 13th Finance Commission's Recommendations', Working Paper No. 2011–81, National Institute of Public Finance and Policy, New Delhi, available at http://www.nipfp.org.in.

Hausmann, Ricardo and Catriona Purfield. 2004. 'The Challenge of Fiscal Adjustment in a Democracy: The Case of India', Working Paper No. WP/04/186, International Monetary Fund, available at http://www.imf.org/external/pubs/ft/wp/2004/wp04168.pdf.

Ministry of Finance. 2004. *Report of the Task Force on Implementation of the Fiscal Responsibility and Budget Management Act, 2003*, New Delhi, Government of India.

———. 2011. 'Budget at a Glance', in *Union Budget 2011–12,* New Delhi, Government of India, available at http://www.finmin.nic.in.

Mundle, Sudipto, M. Govinda Rao, and N.R. Bhanumurthy. 2011.'Stimulus, Recovery and Exit Policy', Working Paper No. 2011–85, National Institute of Public Finance and Policy, New Delhi, available at http://www.nipfp.org.in.

Reserve Bank of India. 'Database on the Indian Economy', available at: http://dbie.rbi.org.in, accessed on 9 May 2011.

Thirteenth Finance Commission. 2009. *Thirteenth Finance Commission, 2010–15. Volume 1: Report.*

■ Fiscal Federalism

India has 28 states governed by their own elected parliaments. It has seven union territories which come under the jurisdiction of the central government. Fiscal relations between the Centre and the states are shaped by the Seventh Schedule in the Indian Constitution which describes the legislative, executive, and judicial powers of the Centre and states through the *Union*, *State*, and *Concurrent* lists. The division of revenue and expenditure powers between the Centre and states is specified by: (a) the Union List, which states the powers that are exclusively under the purview of the central government and (b) the State List, which gives those powers exclusively under the state government. All residual powers rest with the Centre.

Most taxes with a broad tax base are assigned to the Centre—for example, income and wealth tax from non-agricultural sources, corporation tax, and customs and excise duties. Sales taxes, land revenue, alcohol excises, and agricultural income taxes are with state governments.

Out of these, sales tax is the most significant source of revenue for states. An important recent milestone has been the adoption of VAT by 21 states in 2005. On the expenditure side, the Centre spends on defence and infrastructure while state governments spend mainly on internal security, law and order, and social and economic services. Among social services the largest proportion goes to education, public health, and family.

In 1992, the 72nd and 73rd Constitutional Amendments introduced a third tier of fiscal authority, giving constitutional validity to existing rural and urban local governments. Till that time, local governments acted as agencies of state governments. Panchayati Raj Institutions (PRIs) in the villages informally provided basic community and judicial services, while in urban areas this purpose was fulfilled by municipal authorities. The constitutional amendments of 1992 gave these institutions an elective status and gave them powers to impose taxes—usually property taxes in urban areas. Education, housing, and land use; development of industrial and commercial estates; and electricity distribution are some of the functions that have been decentralized in urban areas.

Traditionally, there are high deficits at both the central and state levels: in 2004–5 the central deficit was about 4.1 per cent of GDP. State level deficits are similar. The deficits can be traced back to the political unwillingness of governments to improve the limited tax base and flexibility. As a result, fiscal responsibility laws have been enacted: the Fiscal Responsibility and Budget

Management Act (FRBMA) was enacted in 2003 by the central government and has been followed by a number of states.

There is a well-documented vertical imbalance between the Centre and the states: in 2005–6, on average, the state governments raised about 37 per cent of total revenues but accounted for 57 per cent of the expenditures. This imbalance has grown worse over the years: in 1955–6 these figures were 41 and 59 per cent, respectively. The imbalance was a direct result of the types of taxes that were assigned to the Centre and the bias in favour of the Centre, which was a legacy of the colonial system and the subsequent emphasis on planned development and reducing inequalities between states. The Constitution recognized this imbalance and provided for assigning revenues between the Centre and the states as well as for the sharing of revenues from the proceeds of certain centrally levied taxes. In addition to this, the Constitution provides for grants from the Centre to the states.

The President of India appoints the Finance Commission, an independent body, to determine the share of the Centre and the states in shared central revenues and their allocation between states. The Finance Commission was responsible for about 60 per cent of the total transfers from the Centre to the states in 2002–7; this figure increased to 68 per cent in 2005–9. Till 2010, there have been 13 Finance Commissions. The members of the Finance Commission include academics and retired administrators. The Finance Commission also recommends grants to states in need on the basis of a formula that weights different states according to their population, income, area, infrastructure, tax effort, and fiscal discipline. After the 72nd and 73rd Amendments to the Constitution, State Finance Commissions were set up analogous to the Finance Commission at the national level. Similar to the asymmetry between the Centre and the states, there is a marked asymmetry between states' and local governments' revenue-raising powers. If decentralization has taken place, it is more at the level of expenditure than at the level of revenue generation. A disproportionate share of expenditure at the local level is incurred by urban local bodies compared to rural areas. Rural local bodies have so far mostly implemented grants from central ministries, usually in poverty alleviation and social and community services, but are heavily circumscribed by state governments and have yet to fulfil their potential as independent tiers of the government.

To finance their deficits, state governments can rely on both tax and non-tax revenue sources. The latter comprise interest receipts from loans issued by state governments, dividends and profits from public-sector undertakings owned by the states, and revenue from state lotteries. The Thirteenth Finance Commission recommended that states' share of central taxes should increase to 32 per cent while grants to states accounted for 11 per cent of the total revenues. Hence states' dependence on central transfers is very high and causes many problems of fiscal indiscipline and low tax effort. This is improving now due to the introduction of tax efforts in the formula recommended by the Finance Commission.

Transfers from the Centre to state governments have been criticized for displaying a political bias. This criticism is especially directed towards *discretionary* transfers although even formula-based transfers have been suspect. The proportion of discretionary transfers has been increasing over time. There are three major channels through which the Centre transfers funds to state governments:

(i) Tax devolution and grants through the Finance Commissions (approximately 62 per cent of total transfers in 2002–7).

(ii) Grants and loans given by the Planning Commission (approximately 32 per cent of total transfers in 2002–7).

(iii) Transfers for various central-sector and centrally sponsored schemes by various central ministries (approximately 4.32 per cent of total transfers in 2000–1). From 1969, plan transfers (that is, transfers determined by the Planning Commission) have been effected on the basis of a formula called the 'Gadgil Formula' after the first chairman of the National Development Council. The formula is based on population, per capita income and its deviation from an average of all states as well as from the highest per capita income, fiscal performance, and 'special problems'. The decision-making body is the National Development Council, which is chaired by the Prime Minister, and contains all cabinet ministers at the Centre, chief ministers of states, and members of the Planning Commission. These are called transfers on account of *state plan schemes*. Although these transfers are based on a consensus formula, discretionary elements can enter into the determination of these grants for two reasons. First, while each state proposes its plan size to the Planning Commission, the final approval of the size rests with the Commission. Hence, there is some scope for negotiation and 'persuasion'. Second, the formula explicitly sets aside 7.5 per cent of the grants on account of *special problems* of states. This allows for some subjectivity to creep into the determination of grants for state plan schemes. In addition to grants, the Planning Commission also gives assistance in the form of loans. Major states get 70 per cent of all transfers by the Planning Commission at present; out of this 70 per cent is in the form of loans and the rest is in the form of grants.

Central plan schemes are funded entirely by the Centre, with the states merely exercising an agency role in executing these programmes. Centrally sponsored programmes involve some element of cost sharing between the Centre and the concerned state. In principle, discretionary grants are meant to provide flexibility and responsiveness to states' contingencies. However, they have often been criticized for the political bias displayed in the disbursement of such grants. Indeed, the scope for politics to play a role in disbursement has only been increasing as the discretionary component of grants has grown at the expense of formula-based grants.

The transfers given to the states through central plan schemes and centrally sponsored schemes have attracted the sharpest criticism because these are essentially completely discretionary. In financial year 1996–7, states' share of central taxes accounted for 23.3 per cent of the states total revenues, while grants on account of state plan schemes, centrally sponsored schemes, and central plan schemes (that is items (ii) and (iii)) jointly amounted to 15.9 per cent of the states' total revenues (averaged over 15 major states). Political favouritism in discretionary grants may work through different channels. There may be favouritism by the incumbent party at the Centre which is interested in furthering its re-election prospects, both at the central and state levels. Transfers in this model are akin to 'pork' or targeted spending aimed at maximizing electoral support. There may also be lobbying by state governments, so that states with a higher representation in decision-making bodies get a favourable treatment. Both models predict that *alignment* matters—that is, it matters whether the incumbent party at the state level is the same as the ruling party at the Centre. The first type of model (see Dasgupta et al. 2004) predicts that the proportion of 'floating' voters in a state matters as well—this is the *swing* effect. Intuitively, a resource-constrained party that is interested in maximizing its electoral prospects can decide to focus either on its core support group or on voters who are most easily 'bribed'. Dasgupta et al. (2004) show that swing states which are aligned get more grants—the logic underlying this result is that transfers that add directly to the states' budget may not be attributed to the central ruling party, unless the two governments are aligned. The lobbying model (for example, Rao and Singh 2002) predicts that states with higher representation in the central Parliament get more transfers—hence that the *degree* of alignment should matter. Biswas and Marjit (2000) study a similar problem for loans from the Centre to the states which are often at highly subsidized rates. Finance Commission transfers have mostly been immune to such criticisms. Khemani (2003), however, shows that Finance Commission transfers tend to compensate for the political bias in other transfers. Since the early 1990s, however, the assumption that there is a unitary incumbent has been challenged by the large number of coalition governments at the Centre. Rodden and Wilkinson (2004) argue that theories of legislative bargaining are more suited to the current scenario. They find that in line with this theory, states that have powerful bargaining positions or are pivotal in some way in the coalition receive disproportionate allocations. This is true also for states that have a larger number of party members supporting the central coalition from outside, even though they are not formally members of the coalition.

The other notable feature of Indian fiscal federalism is the inter-state inequalities in revenue capacity and per capita expenditures. This is a natural consequence of the huge differences in per capita incomes between states, which are, moreover, increasing over time: in 1980–1, Punjab, the richest state, had a per capita income which was about three times that of Bihar, the poorest state, while in 1998–9 Punjab's per capita income was five times that of Bihar. Hence, differences in the ability to raise revenue have also increased over time. Per capita expenditures were 44 per cent higher than the all-India average in the high-income states while they were 36 per cent lower than the average in low-income states in 2000–1. Part of the rationale for transfers by the Centre to the states was to reduce the horizontal imbalance. Empirical evidence on the issue of whether Finance Commission transfers have resulted in lower inequality is ambiguous at best.

AMRITA DHILLON

References

Biswas, R. and Sugata Marjit. 2000. 'Political Lobbying and Discretionary Finance in India: An Aspect of Regional Influence in a Representative Democracy', mimeo, Center for Studies in Social Sciences, Calcutta.

Dasgupta, S., A. Dhillon, and B. Dutta. 2004. 'Electoral Goals and Centre–State Transfers: A Theoretical Model and Empirical Evidence from India', mimeo, University of Warwick.

Khemani, S. 2003. 'Partisan Politics and Intergovernmental Transfers in India', mimeo, Development Research Group, World Bank.

Rao, M.G. 2000. 'Fiscal Decentralisation in Indian Federalism', mimeo, Institute for Social and Economic Change, Bangalore.

——. 2004. 'Changing Contours in Fiscal Federalism in India', mimeo, National Institute of Public Finance, New Delhi.

Rao, M.G. and Nirvikar Singh. 2002. 'The Political Economy of Center–State Fiscal Transfers in India', mimeo, University of California, Santa Cruz.

Rodden, J. and S. Wilkinson. 2004. 'The Shifting Political Economy of Redistribution in the Indian Federation', MIT mimeo, available at web.mit.edu/jrodden/www/materials/rodden.wilkinson.isnie2004.pdf.

■ Fiscal Policy Reforms since 1991

India practises fiscal federalism with distinct demarcation of powers between the central and state governments. Since 1991, both the Centre and states have initiated significant fiscal reforms as an integral part of the ongoing initiatives launched in the aftermath of the balance-of-payments crisis in 1990. The reforms aim at improving efficiency, productivity, and competitiveness of Indian industries and imparting dynamism to the overall growth process.

The initial fiscal reforms were guided by the following factors and motivations:

- Large fiscal deficits and automatic monetization of fiscal deficits leading to high inflation and interest rates and crowding out private investment.
- High and irrational tax rates and tariff walls leading to industrial inefficiency, lack of competitiveness, high-cost economy, non-optimal allocation of resources, low compliance rate, and high degree of tax evasion.
- Large variance and multiplicity of tax rates on the basis of end-uses leading to weak tax administration and rent seeking.
- A narrow tax base and low buoyancy and elasticity of both direct and indirect taxes.
- Complicated tax structure, laws, rules, and procedures.
- Emphasis on social services and safety nets.
- Need for reforms of public-sector enterprises and disinvestments of government equity.
- Integration of fiscal, monetary, exchange rate, and trade policies.
- Demographic transition with an increase in life expectancy requiring old-age social security and healthcare and reforms in pensions and provident and insurance funds.

The basic objective of fiscal reforms since 1991 has been to reduce fiscal deficits to sustainable levels by expenditure management and resource mobilization through rationalization of taxes and duties, widening of the tax base, modernizing the tax administration, focusing attention on contingent liabilities, and improving Centre–state fiscal relations.

Like any other reforms, fiscal policies have perforce to be based on a gradual and step-by-step approach, rather than a big bang or shock therapy approach, and need to have a strong emphasis on the human face and a bias towards poverty reduction and employment generation. Over the years, the government has reduced its scope and gradually withdrawn from commercial sectors where private initiatives are more productive and efficient. But the need for enhanced public expenditure remains for the development of social and physical infrastructure. The government is also encouraging public–private partnership, including foreign investment in crucial sectors. It is restructuring public pension systems and insurance and provident funds with private participation so that these contractual savings with long-term maturity can be utilized for financing infrastructure projects. The government has increased allocations for poverty-alleviation and employment-generation programmes to fulfil its commitments under the UN millennium development goals.

Central Tax Reforms

Direct Taxes

Direct tax rates were gradually brought down over the years with reduction in the peak rate of personal income tax from 56 per cent in 1991–2 to 40 per cent in 1995–6, that of corporate tax from 57.5 per cent to 43 per cent, and that of surcharge from 15 per cent to 7.5 per cent over the same period. The Union Budget 1997–8 was a landmark in fiscal reforms in attempting to align Indian tax rates with those in other developing countries. The maximum marginal tax rate for personal income was reduced to 30 per cent and that for corporate income to 35 per cent for domestic companies[1] and 48 per cent for foreign companies. Since then, the emphasis on the direct tax front has been to continue with moderate tax rates, widening the tax base, simplifying and rationalizing tax rules and procedures, continuing incentives for infrastructure and housing, reviving the capital market, and strengthening enforcement and tax compliance.

[1] In the 2005–6 Budget, the corporate tax rate was reduced to 30 per cent.

Indirect Taxes

With respect to indirect taxes, the focus was on reducing the multiplicity of duty rates by abolishing end-use specifications, moving towards ad valorem rates, rationalizing the tax structure, and drastically curtailing the scope for discretion by abolishing the power to grant ad hoc duty exemptions except for charitable purpose or strategic reasons. In the 1998–9 Budget, 11 major ad valorem duty rates were reduced to three, namely, a central rate of 16 per cent, a merit rate of 8 per cent, and a demerit rate of 24 per cent. Customs duty rates were also rationalized and simplified from seven to five ad valorem rates ranging from 5 per cent to 40 per cent.

These reforms resulted in reduction of peak rate of customs duty in a phased manner from 150 per cent in 1991–2 to 10 per cent in 2004–5 to make Indian industry globally competitive.

MODVAT

A modified value-added tax called MODVAT was introduced in 1986 for reducing industrial costs and prices by relieving taxes on inputs, thereby mitigating the cascading effect on final products. Since 1986, the MODVAT scheme has undergone significant changes and is presently known as CENVAT (central value-added tax) and extends to almost all commodities and input tax credit is available across goods and services.

Service Tax

The tax net was widened by introducing tax on a select number of services in 1994. With the share of the services sector growing in the gross domestic product (GDP), the coverage of the service tax has been widened to ensure greater equity and diversity in the tax system.

Fiscal Incentives

India provides fiscal incentives for the development of industry, infrastructure, and technology, which are equally applicable to both domestic and foreign companies. Tax holidays up to 15 years are allowed for industries set up in backward regions and for infrastructure projects set up anywhere in India. Incentives are given to exporters, for research and development (R&D) activities, and to units located in special economic zones (SEZs), export processing zones (EPZs), and science and technology parks. A number of incentives such as capital subsidy, tax breaks, exemption from state duties, and concessional land and power are also provided by the states. Regulatory authorities for telecom, ports, and power determine tariffs that are important for enhancing the financial health of public-sector enterprises within these sectors.

India allows World Trade Organization (WTO)-compatible tax exemption for exports, lower interest rates for export credits, and duty drawback on inputs used for exports. However, tax exemptions on exports are being phased out over time. Producers are allowed duty-free imports of capital goods subject to export obligations. Exporters of food grains are given WTO-compatible subsidies. India is a member of the Multilateral Investment Guarantee Agency and has signed comprehensive treaties for avoidance of double taxation with many countries. The so-called tax expenditures (that is, revenue foregone for most of these fiscal incentives) are being estimated in the Receipts Budget since 2007–8.

Public Debt Management

The outstanding domestic liabilities of the central government increased from 49.8 per cent of GDP at end March 1991 to 54.4 per cent of GDP at end March 2009, and are estimated at 48 per cent at end March 2011, while the book value of outstanding external debt declined from 5.5 per cent to 2.2 per cent of GDP over the same period and is budgeted at 2.1 per cent of GDP at end March 2011. An encouraging feature in recent years has been a decline in interest payment from 53.4 per cent of revenue receipts in 2001–2 to 35.6 per cent in 2008–9; it is budgeted at 36.4 per cent in 2010–11. The average interest rate on outstanding domestic liabilities declined from 7.7 per cent in 2001–2 to 7 per cent in 2005–6. It is budgeted at 7.9 per cent for 2010–11.

The combined public debt of the general government (Centre and states) as a percentage of GDP increased by 7.5 percentage points from 64 per cent at end March 1991 to 71.5 per cent of GDP at end March 2009 and is budgeted at 77 per cent of GDP estimated for 2009–10 (budget estimate, BE). However, outstanding guarantees of the general government declined from 13.4 per cent at end March 1993 to 2 per cent at end March 2009. The government is pursuing an active debt management policy with emphasis on appropriate maturity and interest rate minimization. It pre-paid $7.2 billion worth of high-cost external debt during 2002–3 and 2003–4.

Until 1990, India adopted a development strategy based on the predominant role of a public sector. Unlimited borrowings from the Reserve Bank of India (RBI) at subsidized rates enabled the government to finance large fiscal deficits. The government initiated reforms in 1992 with the auction of government securities at market-determined rates, followed by gradual withdrawal of RBI support and cessation of automatic monetization of government deficit. The government also strengthened institutional infrastructure and the legal and regulatory set-up for the government securities market. The active public debt management strategy comprised minimizing refinancing risk and avoidance of issuing floating rate and short-term and foreign currency-denominated debt.

These policies, together with external sector policies, which aimed at a gradual and sequenced liberalization of the capital account, paid dividends and protected India from the contagion effect of the East Asian crisis in 1997–2000. There was significant improvement in external debt indicators with external debt–GDP ratio declining from 38.7 per cent at end March 1992 to 20.5 per cent at end March 2009 and the debt service ratio declining from 35.3 per cent in 1990–1 to 4.4 per cent in 2008–9. As per the classification in the World Bank's Global Development Finance, India is now a 'low indebted' country.

Central Fiscal Responsibility and Budget Management (FRBM) Act, 2003

The central government enacted the Fiscal Responsibility and Budget Management (FRBM) Act, 2003, for fiscal consolidation. The FRBM Act, 2003, and FRBM Rules 2004 came into force with effect from 5 July 2004. The Act mandates the central government to eliminate revenue deficit by March 2009 and to reduce fiscal deficit to 3 per cent of GDP by March 2009. Under the Act, the central government is required to lay before both Houses of Parliament a Medium-term Fiscal Policy Statement, a Fiscal Policy Strategy Statement, and a Macroeconomic Framework Statement, along with the Annual Financial Statement and Demand for Grants.

The FRBM Rules 2004 specify reduction of revenue deficit by 0.5 per cent of GDP or more and reduction of gross fiscal deficit by 0.3 per cent of GDP or more every year; there is no assumption of additional debt exceeding 9 per cent of GDP for 2004–5; progressive reduction of this limit by at least one percentage point of GDP in each subsequent year; and no central government guarantee in excess of 0.5 per cent of GDP in any financial year. The Rules also require quarterly review of the fiscal situation, greater transparency in the budgetary process, rules, accounting standards and policies, and projection of four fiscal indicators (revenue deficit, fiscal deficit, tax revenue, and total debt as a proportion of GDP) for the medium term.

The Rules mandate the central government to take appropriate corrective action in case the revenue and fiscal deficits exceed 45 per cent of the budget estimates, or total non-debt receipts fall short of 40 per cent of the budget estimates at the end of the first half of the financial year.

The government undertook several measures during 2004–5 to 2007–8 to realize the objectives under the FRBM Act. The targets set for the period ending 2007–8 are given in Table 1. Up to 2007–8, necessary fiscal space was created for undertaking social sector expenditure and funding the creation of essential infrastructure with higher public outlays. In tune with the philosophy of inclusive growth and sustainable development, the reforms laid emphasis on improving fiscal discipline without restricting the much-needed social sector expenditure. However, the fiscal consolidation was primarily revenue driven. The central government's gross tax revenue increased from 9.4 per cent of GDP in 2004–5 to 11.9 per cent in 2007–8 and is budgeted for 2010–11 at 9.5 per cent of GDP as per the advance estimate of GDP. This was achieved through the widening of the tax base, modernization of the tax administration, and rationalization of various taxes and duties. The overall tax structure underwent a significant change during 2007–8 when, for the first time, direct tax collection as a percentage of GDP exceeded indirect tax collection as a percentage of GDP. This implied a more progressive tax structure in the country. Tax rates and slabs were further moderated during this period. A new Direct Tax Code was prepared. This was placed in the public domain in August 2009 and, once enacted into law, will carry forward the reforms of the tax structure and the administration.

Table 1 Medium-term Rolling Targets for Fiscal Indicators as Percentage of GDP at Current Market Prices

Items	2009–10 RE	2010–11 BE	2011–12 Target	2012–13 Target
1. Revenue deficit	5.3	4.0	3.4	2.7
2. Fiscal deficit	6.7	5.5	4.8	4.1
3. Gross tax revenue	10.3	10.8	11.5	11.8
4. Year-end debt stock	51.5	51.1	50.0	48.2

Note: RE stands for revised estimate and BE stands for budget estimate.

The share of indirect taxes in the overall tax revenue has gradually come down. Peak rate of custom duty was reduced in a phased manner to bring it in line with the rates existing in ASEAN countries. The mean CENVAT rate was also gradually reduced. More services were included in the list of taxed services and contribution of service tax in the overall indirect taxes increased significantly during this period.

In 2005–6 Budget, the focus on expenditure management shifted from outlays to outcomes. The composition of expenditure also changed, albeit marginally, towards developmental expenditure during the FRBM Act regime. Fiscal deficit was reduced from 3.9 per cent of GDP in 2004–5 to 2.5 per cent in 2007–8. It is placed at 6.3 per cent of GDP for 2009–10 (Prov.) and budgeted at 5.5 per cent of GDP for 2010–11. Central government debt as percentage of GDP reduced from 61.6 per cent in 2004–5 to 56.9 per cent in 2007–8 and is budgeted at 50.1 per cent for 2010–11.

States Finances

Side by side, there is growing awareness that improvement in the economic management of the states is also critical for the country to sustain high rates of economic growth and accelerate the pace of poverty reduction. India's central challenge lies in more effective management of public finances at all levels of government. States have become more important in a liberalized environment. While the specific issues and remedies may differ between central and state governments, fiscal challenge and prudence are relevant for the states as well.

A state-level value-added tax (VAT) was introduced from 1 April 2005 to create a uniform, self-sustaining, and transparent tax system for the whole country. Haryana started implementing VAT from 1 April 2003. Sixteen states and four union territories started implementing VAT from 1 April 2005. Assam and Meghalaya joined the VAT states from 1 May 2005. Two union territories, Andaman and Nicobar Islands and Lakshadweep, do not have any sales tax or VAT.

The central government is playing the role of facilitator for the successful implementation of this significant reform by agreeing to bear the loss in revenue collection, if any, by the states. The government desires to move towards a uniform goods and services tax (GST), applicable to the whole country with a central share and a state share.

The incentives provided through the Twelfth Finance Commission recommendations had helped in significant fiscal consolidation at the state level during 2005–10. All but two states have enacted fiscal reform legislations. Most of the state governments were able to achieve the targets and the consolidated fiscal deficit of the state governments was below 3 per cent of GDP by 2005–6. The consolidated revenue account of all the state governments showed a surplus.

Impact of the Global Crisis—Fiscal Expansion

The year 2008–9 witnessed an unprecedented crisis in the world economy. Though the crisis emanated from developments in the advanced economies, it forced Indian authorities to make changes in the fiscal policy stance so that the Indian economy was protected from the adverse impact of the crisis.

The central government undertook fiscal expansionary measures to provide stimulus to the economy. These measures resulted in reversal of the fiscal consolidation process. Fiscal deficit of the central government increased to 6 per cent of GDP in 2008–9. This increase could be explained by lower tax to GDP ratio due to reduction in taxes and duties as well as moderation in growth in the economy and higher expenditure by the government. Government investment was increased to compensate for the decline in investment from the private sector. These measures, along with monetary measures taken by the central bank and other administrative measures, helped the Indian economy to grow at 6.8 per cent in 2008–9. The policy of fiscal expansion was continued in 2009–10 in view of the uncertainties prevailing in the world economy. The stimulus policies, both on the tax and the expenditure sides, were largely continued in 2009–10. Fiscal deficit at 6.6 per cent of GDP was higher than the level in 2008–9. Indirect taxes as a percentage of GDP fell significantly due to the combined impact of moderation of growth and reduction in rates of taxes and duties. Looking back, the decision to pause the fiscal consolidation process clearly helped in achieving the desired objective. The Indian economy grew at 8 per cent in 2009–10 and at 8.9 per cent in the first half of 2010–11. The outlook for 2010–11 looks good and the economy is estimated to grow at 8.6 per cent during 2010–11(advance estimates by CSO).

Like the other economies of the world, India has also started the process of unwinding from fiscal expansion. During the crisis period, states were allowed to have higher fiscal deficits for incurring capital expenditure. However, states were more prudent and the fiscal deficit for 2008–9 and 2009–10 remained below the authorized limit.

The Thirteenth Finance Commission has recommended the following measures for fiscal consolidation:

- Fiscal deficit to GDP for the Centre be targeted at 3 per cent, and of the states at 2.4 per cent.
- Revenue deficit of the Centre and states be reduced to zero by 2014–15.
- Combined debt of the Centre and states should be reduced to below 68 per cent by 2014–15.

With fiscal consolidation and states adhering to the consolidation path suggested by the Thirteenth Finance Commission, debt stock as a percentage of GDP for the central and state governments is estimated to decline to less than 45 per cent and 25 per cent, respectively, in 2014–15. The consolidated general government debt is estimated to decline to about 65 per cent of GDP by 2014–15.

A new road map for fiscal consolidation has been announced. Accordingly, the fiscal deficit for 2010–11 is estimated to be brought down from 6.3 per cent of GDP in 2009–10 to 5.5 per cent of GDP in 2010–11 (this stands revised to 4.8 per cent of GDP as per the advance estimate of GDP at current market price for 2010–11). The stated policy of the government is to reduce the fiscal deficit further to 4.8 per cent, 4.1 per cent, 3.5 per cent, and 3 per cent in the four years ending 2014–15. Central government debt as a percentage of GDP is estimated to decline from 50.5 per cent in 2009–10 to 43 per cent in 2014–15.

Perspectives—Fiscal Consolidation to Value for Money

The process of fiscal consolidation needs to be sustained over the medium term. The concept of a counter-cyclical policy should be applied both during bad as well as 'good' years. Only this will help in creating the necessary fiscal space for undertaking unconventional measures during crisis periods. Developing economies like India have enormous demands on the expenditure side to fulfil the gap in the provision of physical as well as social infrastructure. However, with scarce and limited resources available with the government, the focus should be on just allocation and closer monitoring of deliverables. Outcomes should get more emphasis than mere outlays and financial expenditures. The concept of the 'government as a whole' needs to permeate the decision-making process and the concept of incremental allocation of resources to all the sectors needs to be looked at afresh. There is no second argument about having good social safety nets for the poor and the vulnerable. But there must be clarity on 'who is really poor' and 'who is really vulnerable'. In India, the outlays on social sector schemes along with those on subsidies should be redesigned to have a larger positive impact on the quality of life of the entire mass of people who constitute this nation.

Fiscal policy is not only about correcting fiscal imbalances but also about developing and strengthening institutions and designs of expenditure programmes. There is need to promote competitive and efficient delivery in these programmes, where possible, so as to reduce delivery costs and improve quality. It is also essential to establish systems that allow options for beneficiaries and promote transparent, accountable, and locally managed services. The role of grass-roots institutions such as panchayats and dynamic non-governmental organizations (NGOs) in the management of the development process should be emphasized. Empowerment of panchayats, capacity building at the local level, and greater transparency, accountability, and participation in programmes are essential for improving the effectiveness of development funding.

Nevertheless, efforts must continue towards the goal of ensuring that expenditures, subsidies, and transfers reach the intended beneficiaries by targeting subsidies to the poor and making the rest pay for the cost of public goods and services, cutting leakages, and reducing administrative overheads. There is also a need for concerted efforts to increase both the investment and savings rates to attain a consistent high-growth path.

P. CHIDAMBARAM

■ Food and Nutrition

According to Pierre Mac Orlan, artist and writer, 'Humanity is first and foremost a stomach'. The statement is based on Mac Orlan's personal experience of hunger during his childhood in France, but it would not be difficult to substantiate it in the Indian context. Folk songs, historical records, direct observation, consumer expenditure surveys, and a host of other sources point to the absorbing role of food in Indian culture. This popular concern, however, goes hand in hand with an extraordinary neglect of nutrition issues in public policy, in spite of the democratic nature of India's political institutions. Even the basic facts are poorly understood.

The Nutrition Situation

The first point to note about the food situation in India is that undernutrition levels are extremely high. To illustrate, according to the second National Family Health Survey (NFHS–2, conducted in 1998–9), 47 per cent of all Indian children below age three are underweight, 52 per cent of all adult women are anaemic, and 36 per cent have a 'body mass index' below the cut-off of 18.5 commonly associated with chronic energy deficiency (International Institute for Population Sciences 2000). This humanitarian catastrophe is not just a loss for the persons concerned, but also a tragedy for the nation as a whole. A decent society cannot be built on the ruins of hunger, malnutrition, and ill health.

Few countries fare so badly in this field. According to the *Human Development Report 2005*,[1] only two countries (Bangladesh and Nepal) have a higher proportion of underweight children than India, and another two (Sudan and Yemen) have a higher proportion of infants with low birth weight. Even after taking into account various gaps and inaccuracies in the international data, there is no

[1]UNDP 2005, New York.

doubt that undernutrition levels in India are among the highest in the world.

A wealth of further evidence on different aspects of the nutrition situation in India is available from NFHS–2. Consumption data, for instance, bring out the frugal nature of food intakes for a majority of the population. Only 55 per cent of adult women in India consume milk or curd at least once a week, only 33 per cent eat a fruit at least once a week, and only 28 per cent get an egg. The evidence on child morbidity is no less sobering. Among children under the age of three years, 30 per cent had fever during the two weeks preceding the survey, 19 per cent had diarrhoea, and another 19 per cent had symptoms of acute respiratory infection (International Institute for Population Sciences 2000). Even after allowing for some overlap between these different groups, this suggests that at least half of all Indian children below the age of three suffer from one of these conditions within any given interval of two weeks.

All these figures are national averages. It goes without saying that the situation gets worse—far worse—as we consider the poorer states (for example, Jharkhand or Orissa), and the more deprived regions within these poorer states (for example, Palamau in Jharkhand or Kalahandi in Orissa), not to speak of the poorer communities within these deprived regions. Among the Sahariyas, Musahars, Kols, Bhuiyas, and other marginalized communities, the nutritional situation can only be described as a permanent emergency. To illustrate, in a recent survey of 21 randomly-selected households in a Bhuiya hamlet of Palamau district in Jharkhand, 20 reported that they had to 'skip meals regularly' (Bhatia and Drèze 2002). At the time of the survey, most of the households in this hamlet survived on *chakora* (a local spinach) and *gheti* (a wild root), supplemented with some broken rice on lucky days. Some had nothing to eat but plain chakora.

Trends over Time

Recent nutrition trends in India present some interesting puzzles. Starting with anthropometric indicators, the situation seems to be improving, though rather slowly. For instance, anthropometric data from the National Nutrition Monitoring Bureau (NNMB) suggest a slow increase in the heights and weights of Indian children in the 1980s and 1990s, as well as a reduction in the proportion of adults with low 'body mass index'. The first two rounds of the National Family Health Survey (1992–3 and 1998–9) point in the same direction. To illustrate, the proportion of underweight children came down by about one percentage point per year between the two surveys—from 53 to 47 per cent. Both sources (NNMB and NFHS) suggest similar rates of reduction of undernutrition over time.

While anthropometric data present a fairly consistent picture of slow improvement, food intake data are harder to interpret. There has been much debate, for instance, about the steady decline in cereal intake. According to National Sample Survey (NSS) data, average cereal intake declined from 14.8 kg per month to 12.5 kg per month between 1983–4 and 2000–1 in rural areas, and from 11.4 to 10.2 kg per month in urban areas (Deaton 2006). The decline was particularly sharp among the higher income groups. For instance, among the top 20 per cent of the rural population in terms of monthly per capita expenditure (MPCE), cereal consumption declined from 18.8 to 13.4 kg per month in this period. Among the poorest 20 per cent, cereal consumption remained virtually unchanged (about 11.5 kg per capita per month in both years).

The issue is whether the decline of cereal consumption is a matter of concern. This decline has been associated with substantial increases in intakes of non-cereal food items such as milk, oil, fish, meat, eggs, and fruits, not just among the rich but also among the poor. Some experts have argued that this gradual substitution from cereal to non-cereal foods is a positive development. Indeed, a similar 'diversification' of food intake, away from cereals, has been observed in many other countries as levels of living improve.

What is puzzling, however, is that the diversification of food intake in India does not seem to be associated with an increase in nutrient intakes. According to NSS data, per capita calorie intake in rural India declined from 2221 kcal/day in 1983–4 to 2149 kcal/day in 1999–2000 (NSSO 2001). In fact, per capita intake of most nutrients declined in that period, with a few exceptions such as Vitamin C (Sharma 2006). This trend is broadly consistent with independent evidence from the National Nutrition Monitoring Bureau (see Table 1). Here again, the decline was particularly sharp among higher MPCE groups, but it is fairly broad-based, and even among the poorer groups there is little indication of a significant rise in nutrient intakes in the 1980s and the 1990s.

The simultaneous decline of cereal and nutrient intakes has been interpreted by some commentators as a symptom of the 'impoverishment' of the rural population. This interpretation, however, leads to further paradoxes and unresolved puzzles. First, there is little evidence of sustained, widespread impoverishment of the rural population in the 1980s and 1990s. This is particularly true of the 1980s (poverty trends in the 1990s are more controversial), when poverty indexes and related social

Table 1 Basic Nutrition Indicators

Year	Average energy/protein consumption (per 'consumer unit' per day)		Proportion (%) of adults with 'body mass index' (BMI) below 18.5	Proportion (%) of underweight children, age 1–5 years
	Energy (kcal)	Protein (g)		
1988–90	2283	58.4	49.2	66.6
1996–7	2108	53.7	46.8	62.4
2000–1	1954	50.7	38.6	60.1
2004–5*	1907	48.8	35.5	54.5

Source: National Nutrition Monitoring Bureau (partially published data kindly supplied by Dr G.N.V. Brahman, Deputy Director).
Note: *Provisional. The reference region consists of Andhra Pradesh, Gujarat, Karnataka, Kerala, Madhya Pradesh, Maharashtra, Orissa, Tamil Nadu, and West Bengal. The 1988–90 and 1996–7 figures exclude Madhya Pradesh and West Bengal; the 2004–5 figures exclude Gujarat.

indicators were steadily improving. Yet the decline of cereal and nutrient intakes was already in full swing in that decade. Second, this explanation jars with the fact that the decline of nutrient intakes has occurred mainly in the higher MPCE groups. There is strong evidence that these groups have enjoyed sustained increases in living standards in the 1980s and 1990s. Clearly, something else than impoverishment (for example, a reduction in nutrient requirements associated with reduced activity levels or better health) needs to be invoked to explain the decline of nutrient intakes among these groups. And it is quite possible that this hidden factor, whatever it was, also played a role in the stagnation of nutrient intakes among lower-income groups. Third, if impoverishment is the reason for the stagnation of nutrient intakes among lower-income groups, it is not clear why the consumption of superior foods such as milk, oil, eggs, and meat should have increased in the same period (changes in relative prices are unlikely to provide an adequate explanation).

As things stand, both the 'diversification' view and the 'impoverishment' view of recent trends in food intake leave important questions unanswered. The diversification view, which regards the substitution from cereals to non-cereals as a positive development, has to be reconciled with the decline of nutrient intakes. The impoverishment view, for its part, is hard to square with other recent evidence on food intakes and living standards.

A related puzzle is the relation between cereal intake and per capita income (the 'Engel curve' for cereals). NSS data suggest that cereal intake rises steadily with per capita income (more precisely, per capita expenditure). According to NNMB data, however, this Engel curve is more or less flat, and, if anything, downward sloping except at very low levels of per capita income. The NNMB pattern is much easier to reconcile with recent changes over time—rising incomes and declining cereal intake. If this pattern applies, the decline of cereal intake over time may not be a matter of concern. On the other hand, it would also mean that there is something wrong with the NSS food consumption estimates, and cast doubt on a good deal of 'conventional wisdom' based on these estimates.

This is an important area for further research. Meanwhile, two useful lessons emerge from this debate. First, our understanding of 'nutrient requirements' seems to call for reappraisal. Food intake studies in India are typically based on rigid norms (such as the Indian Council of Medical Research's 'recommended daily allowances') that make little allowance for possible changes in activity levels, epidemiological environments, and so on. The steep decline in nutrient intakes among the better-off sections of the rural population in recent years suggests that nutrient requirements may, in fact, be highly context-specific. This would also help to explain related 'anomalies' in food consumption data, such as Kerala's very low calorie-intake levels, combined with excellent health and nutrition indicators.

Second, the fact that anthropometric indicators have apparently improved without any increase in average nutrient intakes draws attention to the role of 'non-food factors' in nutritional achievements—basic education, antenatal care, clean water, and sanitation, among others. There is strong evidence, for instance, that maternal education is one of the major determinants of child nutrition. Similarly, there is increasing recognition of the crucial role of appropriate breastfeeding and weaning for healthy child growth. Effective nutrition policies call for paying much greater attention to these non-food factors, along with a better understanding of the food factors.

Food Policy Reconsidered

Until recently, food policy in India was mainly geared towards promoting higher cereal consumption. This was based on a particular interpretation of the food problem, which might be called the 'naive economic perspective'. In this perspective, calorie deficiency is taken to be the most important form of nutritional deprivation. Further, cereals are held to be the cheapest source of calories. From this it appears that the main issue is to raise calorie intake, and that raising cereal intake is the best means of achieving that goal.

This perspective translated into various policies aimed at boosting cereal intake. One example is state promotion of the Green Revolution, which led to major increases in the production of rice and wheat and helped to make cereals more affordable. India's public distribution system (PDS) also focused on subsidizing the consumption of cereals. Even child nutrition programmes such as the Integrated Child Development Services (and, later on, mid-day meals in primary schools), in spite of their formal recognition of the need for an 'integrated' approach to child nutrition, quickly drifted in the direction of providing cereal-based food supplements to young children.

The preceding discussion raises important questions about this whole approach. Indeed, the evidence suggests that recent improvements in nutrition indicators have little to do with increases in cereal consumption. And there is a real possibility that further improvements depend overwhelmingly on food and non-food factors other than cereal intake. This does not detract from the usefulness of, say, subsidizing cereal consumption through the PDS, as a form of income support or social security. But it does suggest that the sharp focus on cereal intake as a means of nutritional improvement may be misplaced, and that more attention needs to be paid to other means of removing malnutrition: qualitative dietary improvements, better antenatal care, the promotion of effective breastfeeding, and the prevention of infectious diseases, to cite a few examples.

The naive economic perspective has been associated with another major bias in food policy: an excessive focus on households rather than individuals. If cereal intake is the main issue, focusing on household entitlements seems appropriate, since the intra-household distribution of cereal intake is hard to influence through public policy. But if nutrition is influenced by a wide range of food and non-food factors, the scope for individual intervention is likely to be much larger. This broader perspective draws our attention, in particular, to the possibility of intervening in early childhood. In India, the nutritional status of children deteriorates sharply between the ages of six months and two years, and this 'early childhood dip', which is very hard to reverse, has a lasting impact on nutrition and health achievements. Yet, little effort has been made to reach out to this crucial age group. There are well-known means of doing so, notably by expanding and revamping the Integrated Child Development Services—a national programme of integrated health, nutrition and pre-school education services for children under the age of six years (Drèze 2006). Bringing young children (and their mothers) closer to the centre of attention would be a major step towards more effective nutrition policies in India.

Switching, then, to my activist hat, I cannot resist concluding with a reference to the case for a 'rights approach' to food and nutrition policies in India (Drèze 2004). The ability of the rights approach to bring about practical change in this field has been well demonstrated in recent years, notably with the mandatory introduction of mid-day meals in primary schools, the enactment of the National Rural Employment Guarantee Act, and, more recently, the gradual 'universalization' of ICDS. There is much scope for further extension of this approach, especially by putting in place legal safeguards for children's right to food.

Recent Developments

If anything, recent evidence has reinforced the concerns discussed in this entry, and thrown some new puzzles.

India has consolidated its position at the rock bottom of the international scale in terms of nutrition indicators. For instance, according to *World Development Indicators* 2010, no country in the world (not even Bangladesh or Nepal) has a higher proportion of underweight children than India. Bangladesh is now doing better than India in terms of a wide range of nutrition and health indicators, in spite of much slower economic growth and lower baseline incomes. Nepal, for its part, is more or less at par with India—a sobering pattern considering that Nepal's per capita income (in terms of 'PPP international dollars') is barely *one-third* of India's.

The findings of the third National Family Health Survey (NFHS-3, conducted in 2005–6) have also come as a rude shock: they point to very slow improvements, if any, of nutrition indicators between 1998–9 (the reference year for NFHS-2) and 2005–6. For instance, there was a marginal decline in the proportion of underweight children in that seven-year period: from 47 per cent in 1998–9 to 46 per cent in 2005–6 based on 'NCHS standards', and from 42.7 per cent to 40.4 per cent based on 'WHO standards'. Similarly, the proportion of adult women (more precisely, ever-married women in the age group of 15–49 years) with 'low body mass index' was much the same in both years—36 per cent in 1998–9 and 33 per cent in 2005–6. Anaemia levels, for their part, were *higher* in 2005–6 than in 1998–9, by a few percentage points, for both women and young children (International Institute for Population Sciences 2007). These alarming trends are yet to be adequately understood, discussed, and confronted.

Meanwhile, changes in consumption patterns have continued, more or less in line with earlier trends, including some further decline in per capita cereal consumption and calorie intake (Deaton and Drèze 2009). This has led to a lively debate around different interpretations of these trends, notably in the columns of *Economic and Political Weekly*. The jury is still out on these matters.

While there is plenty of scope for further debate, what is not in doubt is that the nutrition situation in India is both extremely alarming and nowhere near being addressed with adequate resolve and resources. The proposed National Food Security Act (NFSA) was an opportunity to make a new departure in this field. Alas, at the time of writing, the draft NFSA is little more than a consolidation of the status quo in food policy.

JEAN DRÈZE

References

Bhatia, Bela and Jean Drèze. 2002. 'Still Starving in Jharkhand', *Frontline*, 16 August.

Deaton, Angus. 2006. Special Tabulations of National Sample Survey Data, Department of Economics, Princeton University.

Deaton, Angus and Jean Drèze. 2009. 'Food and Nutrition in India: Facts and Interpretations', *Economic and Political Weekly*, 14 February, 44(7): 42–65.

Drèze, Jean. 2004. 'Democracy and the Right to Food', *Economic and Political Weekly*, 24 April, 39(17): 1723–31.

———. 2006. 'Universalization with Quality: ICDS in a Rights Perspective', *Economic and Political Weekly*, 26 August, 41(34): 3706–15.

International Institute for Population Sciences (IIPS). 2000. *National Family Health Survey 1998–9 (NFHS-2): India*, Mumbai, IIPS.

———. 2007. *National Family Health Survey 2005–6 (NFHS-3): India*, Mumbai, IIPS.

NSSO. 2001. 'Nutritional Intake in India, 1999–2000', Report 471, National Sample Survey Organisation, New Delhi.

Sharma, Rekha. 2006. 'Quantifying Malnutrition in India', PhD thesis, Delhi School of Economics.

Food Procurement Policy

The Indian government's food procurement policy is geared towards achieving the twin objectives of serving consumers through price subsidy and supporting the price for producers.[1] The policy has come under criticism not only for the increasing fiscal burden that it causes but also for administrative inefficiencies and creating market distortions. This entry provides a brief overview of the functioning of the food grain procurement system, examines the roles of the public and private sectors in a scenario of restrictions on domestic and international trade, and comments on related policy changes under liberalized external trade. It ends with suggestions for directions of change.

Price and Distribution Controls in the Food Grains Market

The major elements of the food policy are procuring grain at the minimum support price (MSP), maintaining buffer stocks, and distributing grains at subsidized rates through the public distribution system (PDS). The Government of India (GoI)[2] allocates grains to states at the central issue price (CIP) for distribution to consumers. The Food Corporation of India (FCI), a GoI agency, handles procurement, storage, and transportation of grains to states. The states in turn distribute grains to consumers at subsidized prices through a network of some 500,000 fair price shops (FPSs). The 'food subsidy' comprises the cost of procurement incurred by GoI net of sales realization (for rice, wheat, and sugar) and the carrying costs for maintaining the central pool of buffer stock incurred by FCI and reimbursed by GoI.

The concept of MSP was adopted for paddy, wheat, and various other crops in the early 1990s. The policy is still effective for rice and wheat in major surplus states. For wheat, the government offers to buy all grain that comes forth for sale at the announced MSP. In the case of rice, part of the procurement is in the form of paddy at the MSP, which is custom milled, and the rest, which is the major part, is procured as rice through a statutory levy imposed by all major rice-producing states on rice millers/dealers. The levy percentage varies widely from 10 per cent in Puducherry to 75 per cent in major surplus states, such as Haryana, Punjab, and Uttar Pradesh. Rice millers are paid levy rice prices fixed by the state government. The Commission for Agricultural Costs and Prices (CACP) recommends levels at which the MSP should be fixed based on several considerations. These include cost of cultivation, the overall shortage of grains as reflected by the trend in wholesale prices, and the need to keep in check the rate of inflation in the consumers' interest.

In practice, the actual price offered is influenced by high expectations of rich farmers represented by politically strong farm lobbies. The MSP was higher than the cost of production in the 1990s. It is estimated that between 2004–5 and 2010–11, the MSP of paddy, wheat, and pulses went up by as much as 75 to 125 per cent. This increased profitability of these crops and

[1]In this entry, 'food' refers largely to grains, mainly rice and wheat and to some extent coarse grains.

[2]Alternatively referred to as the central government or just the government.

motivated farmers to shift a greater area to these crops from coarse cereals (mainly consumed by the poor) and oilseeds (for which India has large import dependence), thereby putting upward pressure on their prices. Price distortions in the output market combined with distorted prices of inputs such as fertilizers, power, and irrigation have had an added detrimental effect not only on the production of other crops but also on the environment, such as a decline in water tables.

Setting MSPs at levels higher than normal market clearing prices and world prices have disconnected them from market realities (Jha et al. 2007). In the early 2000s, exorbitantly high MSPs resulted in the government buying up most of the marketable surplus, raising budgetary costs and reducing incentives for private-sector agents. The credit blocked in these stocks put pressure on interest rates and possibly crowded out more productive investments. At the same time, lower availability of grains in the market, coupled with inefficient subsidized distribution, raised their prices even further and adversely affected consumers. Moreover, income transfers from higher MSPs accrued disproportionately to large farmers confined mainly to surplus states.

These adverse implications led to increased recognition of the need to reform farm support policies (see, among others, GoI 2001 and 2002). As a short-term measure to reduce the physical and fiscal burden of storage, the government released stocks at subsidized prices to exporters, revived the PDS, and introduced other food-based programmes. Recommendations were made to reduce the MSP so that it served as a price stabilization mechanism and not as an income guarantee to farmers and to cover only the variable costs, namely, the costs of inputs and wages (including family labour). The High-level Committee on Long-term Grain Policy (GoI 2002) examined the cost effectiveness and liabilities arising from some alternative programmes to support farmers in lieu of the MSP scheme (Box 1). Among other things, the Committee proposed the removal of both the rice levy and restrictions on grain trade, limiting their use to emergencies.

These measures were partly responsible for bringing the stocks-to-norm ratio to reasonable levels in the mid-2000s (Figure 1). However, global food and economic crises reversed this effect, making many of the above recommendations valid once again as of end-2010. As

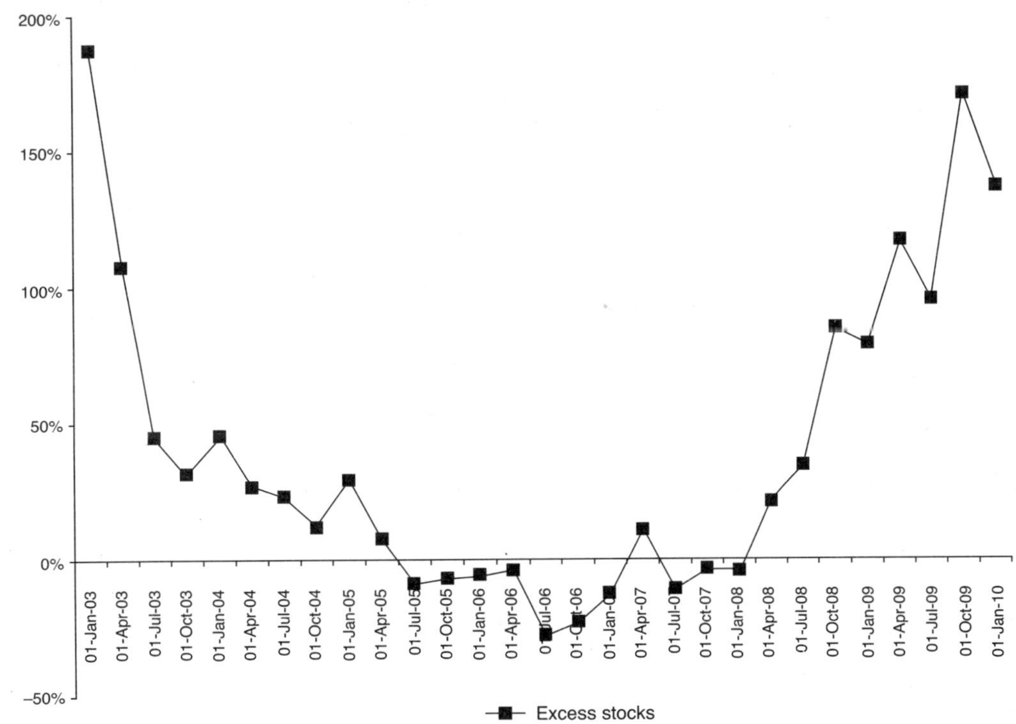

Figure 1 Excess of Actual Stock over Minimum Buffer Stock Norms (%)

Source: Annual Report 2009–10, Department of Food and Public Distribution, Ministry of Consumer Affairs, Food and Public Distribution, Government of India.

food prices began to shoot up in 2008, the government procured ever larger amounts of grain to calm down market prices through subsidized sales. However, the policy led to an unwarranted accumulation of buffer stocks which was more than twice the minimum norm in 2008 and almost thrice in 2009. Indeed, the government has faced a repeat of the situation that occurred in the early 2000s, namely, a problem of 'plenty', as its stocks once again crossed 60 million tonnes in 2010. Beginning from 2005, buffer stock norms were raised as well. The average annual minimum stock to be held increased by about 11 million tonnes between 2004 and 2009, with 1 January levels rising by as much as 32 million tonnes.

Even as world prices fell following the 2008 global price spikes, domestic market prices of food in India increased rapidly as large supplies were stacked away in buffer stocks (resulting from remunerative farm prices). Efforts to protect consumers from rising prices led to a 35 per cent increase in the food subsidy bill between April and September 2009. To keep the bill under check, other distortionary policies were adopted, including a selective ban on exports and futures trading, zero import duty on key food items, and licensing and restrictions on stocks and movements of food articles across state boundaries. A by-product of some of these policies was higher global prices of grains, especially rice, in which India is a large trader.

Box 1 Selected Recommendations of the High-level Committee on Long-term Grain Policy (GoI 2002)

- MSP policy should extend to all regions.
- MSP should be the national-level floor price, rather than remaining confined to surplus regions.
- MSP should be reduced to levels of average capital costs (that is, all costs including imputed costs of family labour, owned capital, and rental on land).
- Procurement should be at market prices and levy procurement of rice should be eliminated.
- MSP should be supplemented with a variable import and export tariff for effective price stabilization.
- When market price is greater than the MSP, the government should import or make open market purchases.
- There should be a stable and predictable policy regarding open market sales.
- Private trade should be encouraged.

Roles of the Public and Private Sectors

To serve the government's procurement policy, the private sector has traditionally been controlled through formal and informal restrictions on trading, storage, and inter-state movement of grains. Restrictions, such as limits on stocks under the Essential Commodities Act and selective credit controls, increase the cost of operations for private traders. Harassment by officials, corruption, and bribery add to the costs of marketing and trading, making domestic prices internationally uncompetitive. High levels of grain stored by government agencies further reduce incentives for private storage. In spite of such drawbacks, private traders operate with lower trade and marketing costs than the post-procurement costs incurred by the FCI.

The government plays a major role in the food grain marketing system. FCI undertakes near monopoly procurement and moves more than 20 million tonnes of grain annually or 400,000 bags daily from surplus to deficit areas by rail, road, and inland waterways. In the last two and a half decades, procurement has increased from 4 million tonnes to about 50 million tonnes per annum. The share of official agencies in market arrivals has steadily increased. In recent years, rice and wheat procurement has amounted to 17 to 25 per cent of food grain production. Several factors caused the downtrend in private share in grain markets: lower rate of increase in retail than procurement and wholesale prices, expectations of low future prices due to a large build-up of public stocks, and subsidized sale from stocks for exports and for open market sales. Private traders found it more attractive to buy grain from government agencies than from the market.

However, government operations have proved to be costly. Labour, interest, and administration costs constitute a significant proportion of FCI costs. Procurement incidentals and distribution, administration, and carrying costs put together form a high percentage of the actual purchase cost of grain. FCI's storage facilities are inadequate and grain losses are reported to be large due to pilferage and damage under storage as well as during transit. Excessive costs also arise from inefficiencies in operations, diversion of grain to the open market due to lack of transparent and accountable delivery systems, and multiple movements of grain back and forth between storage and distribution points to cater to deficit areas (see, for example, Drèze 2001, Deininger and Deininger 2001, Jha and Ramaswami 2010).

The move to decentralize procurement operations to states was in part meant to rectify these problems. Under the decentralized procurement scheme, state governments purchase, store, and distribute grains locally according to their requirements while their related expenditures are met by the central government. Procurement of rice under the scheme multiplied from 4 million tonnes in

2002–3 to about 13 million tonnes in 2008–9. FCI's share in rice procurement for the central pool declined from 40 per cent in 2005–6 to 8 per cent in 2008–9.

Procurement Policy under External Trade Liberalization

Being a signatory to the World Trade Organization (WTO), India has tried to move towards more open trade in agriculture. This brings new opportunities as well as challenges to the food security system. The challenges are in terms of making appropriate changes in policy and developing appropriate marketing infrastructure and institutions to deal with trade in agricultural commodities. Liberalized external trade provides opportunities for reduced dependence on buffer stocks for price stabilization and in turn reduced government costs. It also provides incentives to deregulate the domestic market and increase the role of private traders in the marketing of food grains.

Under a regime of liberalized trade, the domestic buffer stock policy is closely related to the external trade policy. Appropriate policy changes are required to avoid situations such as the following. In the post-WTO period[3] international prices of rice and wheat plunged to the lowest levels while domestic prices in India rose upward largely due to continued hike in the support price. Since India was an exporter of rice and an occasional importer of wheat, lower world wheat prices made it profitable to import wheat but lower world rice prices adversely affected rice exports. As a consequence of this, according to an estimate, private traders imported 1.33 million tonnes of wheat during 1999–2000 despite record buffer stock levels in the country (Chand 2002). To counter this tendency, in 2000–1 the government introduced a 50 per cent tariff on imports of wheat and 80 per cent on import of rice without any exemption even to official agencies. Moreover, further decline in international prices and increase in domestic prices made it difficult to dispose of large public stocks for export at the acquisition cost. The government was thus forced to subsidize grain export even though it charged domestic consumers a much higher price. For instance, in 2002–3 the government sold wheat to exporters for less than the procurement price and covered transport, storage, and other handling costs. A side effect of this policy was that stocks sold for exports at a subsidized price were diverted back to the domestic market, fetching traders a higher price and bringing larger supplies for government purchase at the MSP. In 2000–1, as against the release of 1.6 million tonnes of wheat for export, actual export was estimated to be only 0.682 million tonnes.

Liberalization of exports again suffered a setback in 2007–8 when export controls were restored as a response to the global price spike. As external trade is liberalized, the government can use new instruments such as variable tariffs to stabilize prices and depend less on physical procurement and storage of grains.

Recent Policy Initiatives and the Steps Forward

In the last few years, the government has initiated steps to encourage private participation in grain markets. FCI's role is proposed to be restricted to timely sales and purchases to maintain stability in food prices. However, in a scenario of trade liberalization this needs to be complemented with appropriate trade and tariff policies. Apart from plans to promote exports through long-term credit, removal of export restrictions, and establishment of agricultural export zones, it is also important to improve facilities for grading and measuring standards as well as address quality problems. To take full advantage of growing export markets, exporters would need to have better ports and other domestic infrastructure facilities, which are currently very meagre. The ports are highly congested, have obsolete equipment, are managed by government-controlled port trusts, and are marred by bureaucracy. Undertaking reforms in these areas would allow India to take on competition from major exporting countries such as Thailand, Vietnam, and Pakistan for rice and the United States for wheat.

The National Food Security Mission was launched in 2007–8 to enhance the production of rice, wheat, and pulses by 10 million tonnes, 8 million tonnes, and 2 million tonnes, respectively, by the end of the Eleventh Plan. The Food Security Bill proposed in 2010 endeavours to give every household below the poverty line legal right to 25 kg of rice or wheat per month at Rs 3/kg. This would be distributed under the targeted PDS through fair price shops. However, this poses a significant challenge of identifying and counting the poor families. In particular, switching to poverty lines that show much higher poverty rates than previously accepted would put further pressure on public agencies to procure larger fractions of total production and add to fiscal costs.

Domestic marketing reforms also need to be undertaken so that there is one integrated market for food within India and restrictions do not prevent inter-regional flows in a timely and efficient manner. The private sector should be allowed to operate more freely based on its expectations from the market. It would also benefit from

[3]1996 was the first year after implementation of the Uruguay Round Agreement and formation of the WTO.

abolition of statutory and non-statutory charges that add to transaction costs and discourage free movement of grains domestically. The public sector needs to play a facilitating role by providing the appropriate economic environment and creating a level playing field for private operators and traders.

The high costs of maintaining public stocks can be reduced through encouraging private storage, which plays a complementary role to public storage. Instead of setting it at unduly high levels, the MSP should be fixed such that it provides protection against distress sales during surplus situations and not a guarantee for fixed returns on the costs incurred. FCI's costs of operation can be reduced by expanding decentralized procurement to the local market, carrying out storage operations at the state level, and by avoiding cross hauling of grain in the centralized system (Jha and Srinivasan 2004). Decentralization would help ensure market efficiency and reduce the economic costs of running the PDS. Reforms to the GoI's food procurement policy in these directions would help achieve its twin objectives more effectively.

SHIKHA JHA

References

Chand, R. 2002. 'Government Intervention in Food Grain Markets in the New Context', Report prepared for the Ministry of Consumer Affairs, Food and Public Distribution, New Delhi, National Centre for Agricultural Economics and Policy Research.

Deininger, D. Umali, and K.W. Deininger. 2001. 'Towards Greater Food Security for India's Poor: Balancing Government Intervention and Private Competition', *Agricultural Economics*, 25: 321–35.

Drèze, J. 2001. 'Starving the Poor', *The Hindu*, 26 and 27 February.

Government of India (GoI). 2001. *Report on Food Security, Expenditure Reforms Commission*, Chairman: K.P. Geethakrishnan.

——. 2002. *Report of the High-level Committee on Long-term Grain Policy*, Chairman: Abhijit Sen.

Jha, Shikha and Bharat Ramaswami. 2010. 'How Can Food Subsidies Work Better? Answers from India and the Philippines', Economics Working Paper Series No. 221, Asian Development Bank, Manila.

Jha, Shikha and P.V. Srinivasan. 2004. 'Achieving Food Security in a Cost Effective Way: Implications of Domestic Deregulation and Reform under Liberalized Trade', MTID Discussion Paper No. 67, International Food Policy Research Institute, available at http://www.ifpri.org/divs/mtid/dp/mtidp67.htm.

Jha, Shikha, P.V. Srinivasan, and Maurice Landes. 2007. 'Indian Wheat and Rice Sector Policies and Implications of Reform', Economic Research Report No. 41, Economic Research Service, US Department of Agriculture, Washington DC.

■ Food Security

Food security has emerged as a serious concern for policymakers the world over. Globally, food security is under serious threat, raising the very real fear that the millennium development goal (MDG) of halving the proportion of hungry people during 1990–2015 may not be met. According to the Global Hunger Index (GHI) 2010, the number of undernourished people exceeded 1 billion in 2009.

Unfortunately, India's high economic growth in the past decade has not been matched by a commensurate improvement in the health of its people, with 20 per cent of its population still undernourished. Better health is an important goal by itself. But its role as an 'economic engine' provides an additional compelling rationale for public policy to support well-targeted nutrition-improving interventions.

This entry focuses on two aspects of food security: food availability and access to food. The first aspect is explored by examining food production trends and the per capita availability of food grains and the second aspect by examining various schemes currently in force to enable poor and vulnerable groups to access food at affordable costs.

Conceptualizing Food Security

Though food security is a national problem, it is now undisputedly accepted as an international responsibility. As a concept, food security has evolved from being traditionally defined in terms of food availability and price stability to more recent definitions that encompass economic access and nutritional balance.

The first comprehensive definition of food security emerged at the 1974 World Food Summit which emphasized availability of adequate food supplies to sustain a steady rise in consumption and offset production and price fluctuations. Subsequent definitions introduced the distinction between chronic food insecurity and 'transitory' food insecurity, incorporating both as important public policy concerns for achieving food security. In the 1990s, in addition to food availability and access, a third dimension was included in the definition of food security—nutritional balance. A working definition by Edward Clay (2002) which captures all these dimensions is: 'Food security exists when all people, at all times, have physical, social and economic access to sufficient, safe and nutritious food which meets their dietary needs and food preferences for an active and healthy life.'

There is an alternative conceptual framework (Gross et al. 2000) that emphasizes the difference between 'food security' and 'nutrition security'. This framework argues that the final goal of public policy on food is to achieve a certain nutritional status for the population that translates into positive health outcomes, enabling countries to utilize their human resources optimally for economic development. In this framework the nutritional status is a function of both food intake and the health status. The former depends on food availability and access, which constitute 'food security' while the latter depends on access to health services and access to complementary civic services. In the rest of this entry the discussion is restricted to 'food security' and it focuses on the two building blocks, that is, availability and access.

Availability of Food

The first building block to 'food security' is adequate availability of food in the economy. The term 'food' ideally encompasses all items which add up to a balanced diet required to prevent malnutrition and disease. Such a diet would consist of all the food groups—carbohydrates, proteins, fats, and minerals/vitamins. In terms of food articles, this would translate to wheat, rice, pulses, milk, edible oils, fruits, vegetables, and meat/poultry. However, we restrict ourselves to the production and availability of cereals, especially wheat and rice, with some comments on the total food grains, including pulses.

In 2008–9, India witnessed a record food grain production of 234.47 million tonnes. The subsequent drought in the 2009–10 kharif season resulted in an output decline of 16 million tonnes but in 2010–11 the total food grain output bounced back to reach 235.88 million tonnes (3rd Advance Estimates). Since wheat, rice, and pulses constitute more than 80 per cent of this output, this analysis is restricted to these three crops. Since 2004–5 wheat production has been steadily increasing, crossing the 80 million tonne mark in 2008–9. There was no decline in output in the drought year of 2009–10, and 2010–11 is expected to witness an all-time high production of 84.27 million tonnes. In the case of rice, with only 57 per cent of the area under irrigation (in 2007–8), the steady increase in output since 2004–5 was interrupted by a 10 million tonne production decline in 2009–10, which will only be partially made up in 2010–11 with output estimated at 94.11 million tonnes. The production of pulses, which has been stagnating for a while at around 14 million tonnes, is estimated to increase by 18 per cent to reach 17.29 million tonnes in 2010–11, driven mainly by price signals both in the open market and the increase in the minimum support price by the government.

Table 1 Trend Growth Rate of Food Grain Production

	1970–1 to 1979–80	1980–1 to 1989–90	1990–1 to 1999–2000	2000–1 to 2009–10
Rice	1.9	3.6	2.0	1.6
Wheat	4.2	3.5	3.5	1.9
Pulses	-0.4	1.5	0.85	2.7
Total food grains (including coarse cereals)	2.1	2.7	2.1	1.88

Source: Calculations based on Ministry of Agriculture statistics.

Looking at long-term trends, the growth rate in production has come down since the 1980s except in the case of pulses. Both rice and wheat have decelerated with growth rates halving from around 3.5 per cent in 1980–1 to 1989–90 to less than 2 per cent in 2000–1 to 2009–10 (Table 1). A concerted effort is called for to reverse the declining trend.

In addition to aggregate domestic production numbers, it is important to explore trends in per capita availability of food grains, since 'food security' is a concept that relates to an individual's access to food. The net per capita availability of food grains[1] increased from 394 grams per day in 1951 to 510 grams per day in 1991 but has since declined by 13 per cent to 444 grams per day. The sharpest fall at 20 per cent was in coarse cereals followed by a 15 per cent decline in rice and 11 per cent decline in pulses. In the case of wheat, the decline was less at around 7 per cent. An explanation for the decline in net per capita availability of food grains since 1991, despite food grain production exceeding the population growth rate, can be found in the trends in net imports and changes in the government stock of food grains. In the period 1991–2 to 2008–9, in a number of years, a combination of high exports and a simultaneous increase in government stock reduced net per capita availability. A case in point is the year 2007–8 when net imports were at (–) 14.4 million tonnes while government stocks increased by 17 million tones, leading to a 31.4 million tonnes reduction in net availability.

According to the National Nutrition Monitoring Bureau, the recommended dietary allowance (RDA) for Indians is 400 gm of cereals per capita and 35 gm of pulses per capita per day.[2] In 2009, the per capita availability of cereals at 407 gm per capita and 37 gm per capita for

[1]The net availability of food grains is estimated to be gross production (–) seed, feed, and wastage (–) exports (+) imports (+/–) change in stocks. This is divided by population estimates multiplied by 365 to give net per capita availability. These figures are not strictly representative of consumption as they do not take into account private change in stocks.
[2]These are broad averages. There will be variations in RDA depending on age, gender, and occupation.

pulses was in line with the RDA, but this does not take into account the distribution of food grains, which is skewed against the poor and vulnerable groups. The declining trend in per capita cereal consumption is discernible in most states, including the agriculturally prosperous ones of Punjab and Haryana. The decline in cereal consumption has been attributed to changes in consumers' tastes and preference from food to non-food items and within food groups, from cereals to non-cereal food items, and from coarse to fine cereals (Radhakrishna and Ravi 1992).

Access to Food

Adequate availability of food at the national level does not automatically translate into equitous availability at the household level. Low incomes, inadequate purchasing power, and high food prices often constrain households from obtaining the desired quantity of food grains. To ensure access to poor and vulnerable groups, governments across the globe have designed safety net programmes ranging from direct cash transfers, income-based programmes, employment generation schemes, and food coupons to subsidized food distribution programmes.

Policy initiatives taken by successive governments in India can be broadly categorized into two sets—measures to increase food availability and measures to improve access through employment generation programmes and providing physical access to food to vulnerable sections. Starting with the Green Revolution, input subsidies on fertilizers, water and electricity, irrigation projects, and the more recent Rashtriya Krishi Vikas Yojana and the National Food Security Mission have all helped boost agricultural production and increase food availability. The other set of interventions to improve access have inter alia included National Rural Employment Guarantee Act, Swarna Jayanti Grameen Swarozgar Yojana, Essential Commodities Act, Integrated Child Development Scheme (ICDS), Antyodaya Anna Yojana (AAY), Mid-Day Meal Scheme for school-going children, and most important, the Public Distribution System (PDS), one of the largest safety net programmes in the world in terms of the population it covers for physical distribution of food grains. Besides this, a recent initiative of the government is the proposed National Food Security Act, which aims to provide the poor a legal entitlement to food.

Public Distribution System

Food grain shortages due to war and famines in the 1940s led to government intervention in their distribution. This was the beginning of the Public Distribution System in the country. A major milestone in the evolution of PDS was in the 1960s when there was a clear recognition that the national food policy must be based on domestic production. Fortunately, this became possible thanks to the Green Revolution. The policy was to be implemented using the strategy of public procurement of food grains, setting up of a public distribution system, and building a buffer stock. To operationalize this, the Food Corporation of India (FCI) was set up in 1965.[3] These three strategies are the foundation of India's food policy till date. The early focus of PDS was on ensuring access to food and maintaining price stability in urban areas. Over time, as food production increased, the scope of PDS was expanded in the 1970s and 1980s to cover tribal blocks and areas of high incidence of poverty. However, the major focus continued to be urban areas.[4]

In January 1992, against the background of hunger deaths, especially in the tribal areas of Orissa and Madhya Pradesh and large food stocks with FCI, the government expanded the PDS and launched the Revamped Public Distribution System (RPDS). The RPDS sought to strengthen, streamline, and increase the outreach of the PDS by adopting an area-based approach. The central idea was to identify, in consultation with the states, areas which had a disadvantageous geographical location, a weak PDS network, and low purchasing power. For implementing RPDS, 1,750 plus blocks—mainly located in tribal, hilly, and drought-prone areas and home to a substantial section of the poor—were identified. However, to improve the focus of food distribution to the vulnerable sections in the country as a whole, the Targeted Public Distribution System (TPDS) was launched in 1997. According to PEO (2005), TPDS targets subsidized provision of food grains to the 'poor in all areas' as opposed to the RPDS which catered to 'all in poor areas'.

The TPDS envisaged that the central government would be responsible for the availability and affordability of food grains while the state governments would be responsible for ensuring accessibility through a network of fair price shops (FPS) (PEO 2005). Currently there are nearly half a million FPS in the country. TPDS initially proposed issuing 10 kg of subsidized food grain (subsequently increased to 35 kg) to below poverty line (BPL) households. Grain allocations to the states were based on the average offtake of the previous 10 years. After meeting the entitlements of the BPL population,

[3]Several states set up civil supplies corporations which helped in the distribution of the PDS items.

[4]According to the Report of the Study Group on Public Distribution System for Areas other than Metropolitan Cities, 1986, roughly 46 per cent of the entire food grains allotted in 1983 from the central pool went to just three states that had metropolitan cities and to Delhi (excluding the quantity allocated to Kerala) (K.R.Venugopal 2010).

the remaining grain was issued to the APL population but at a price that was not subsidized (the price is now subsidized but the issue price for APL is above that for BPL). Macro estimates of the BPL population in a state were fixed according to the poverty estimates of the Planning Commission,[5] while the actual identification of the beneficiaries was to be done by the states. This led to an anomalous situation with the Planning Commission capping the BPL households at 65.2 million[6] and state governments issuing 111.2 million BPL ration cards (as on January 2010). The largest variations were in Tamil Nadu, Andhra Pradesh, Karnataka, Orissa, and Madhya Pradesh.

In December 2000, in a further effort to address acute hunger, the government identified 1 crore 'poorest of poor' families within the BPL category, and launched the Antyodaya Anna Yojana (AAY) which supplied 25 kg (subsequently increased to 35 kg) of wheat and rice per household at a highly subsidized rate (Rs 2 per kg for wheat and Rs 3 per kg for rice). The scheme has been subsequently expanded and currently caters to 24.3 million families.

A number of studies have been commissioned by the government to evaluate the performance of TPDS. The general conclusion is that the identification of beneficiaries has been quite unsatisfactory with large-scale inclusion and exclusion errors. A case in point is Jharkhand, where, according to a study by NCAER, 80 per cent of the poor are excluded from TPDS and 20–40 per cent of the non-poor are included. Besides, there is large-scale leakage of grain and according to some estimates almost 54 per cent of the grain released by FCI under TPDS did not reach the intended beneficiaries in 2004–5 (Himanshu and Sen 2011). These problems have often been used as an argument to dismantle targeting and adopt a 'universal PDS'. However the point that such arguments miss is that the solution for improving access for the poor lies in better governance of the PDS and precise identification rather than a 'universal' PDS that subsidizes the non-poor.

Identification of BPL Families under TPDS

The TPDS, India's largest safety net programme for food security, uses the official measure of poverty to identify the poor and direct its benefits. In India, the poverty line is an exogenously determined normative consumption expenditure, which divides the population into poor and non-poor. Since Independence, there have been a number of official studies on this subject; the initial ones pegged the poverty line on calorie norms and assigned it monetary values from the NSS-based consumption expenditure surveys. Two recent studies have suggested methodologies to update these to yield inter-temporal estimates of poverty. The Expert Group under the Chairmanship of Professor D.T. Lakdawala[7] used the calorie-based poverty line defined by the earlier study group[8] as the base line. These national poverty lines were disaggregated into state-specific poverty lines and then updated using the relevant consumer price indices for rural and urban areas. This was changed by an Expert Group under the Chairmanship of Professor Suresh D. Tendulkar, which accepted the urban poverty line and the associated poverty ratios but changed the methodology for computing the rural poverty line. The all-India poverty ratio in 2004–5 was estimated at 37.2 per cent, with the rural poverty ratio at 41.8 per cent and the urban poverty ratio at 25.7 per cent. These have now been accepted as the official estimates of poverty and will be used to deliver targeted benefits under several safety net programmes, including the TPDS.

The poverty lines and ratios in India have been subject to a lot of debate. There are two main criticisms of which the first is the use of a calorie-based, fixed consumption basket using the 1973–4 consumption survey to generate the monetary value of the poverty line. Even though the link between the poverty line and calorie norms is somewhat tenuous now, this consumption basket still underlies poverty estimates. The second criticism has centred around the divergence between the consumption expenditure generated by NSS on which the present estimates depend and the national accounts statistics. The divergence between the two series has increased and there is an urgent need to address this issue.

National Food Security Bill

India's determination to eliminate hunger has translated into a proposal to grant the poor a legal entitlement to food through an appropriate enactment. Currently a Bill drafted by the National Advisory Council (NAC) is under the consideration of the government. The salient features of the National Food Security Bill (NFSB) proposed by NAC are:

- Legal entitlement to subsidized food grains to be extended to 72 per cent of the population in the first phase and 75 per cent in the final phase.

[5] Based on the methodology of the Expert Group on Estimation of Proportion and Number of Poor, chaired by Late Professor Lakdawala.

[6] Using the methodology of the Expert Group chaired by Professor Lakdawala.

[7] Submitted its report in 1993, and till recently formed the basis of the official poverty estimates in India.

[8] Task force under the Chairmanship of Dr Y.K. Alagh which pegged the poverty lines at Rs 49.09 in rural areas and Rs 56.64 in urban areas at 1973–4 prices.

- Priority households (46 per cent in rural areas and 28 per cent in urban areas) to have a monthly entitlement of 35 kg (equivalent to 7 kg per person) at a subsidized price of Re 1 per kg for millets, Rs 2 per kg for wheat, and Rs 3 per kg for rice.
- General households (39 per cent rural and 12 per cent urban in phase 1 and 44 per cent rural and 22 per cent urban in the final phase) to have a monthly entitlement of 20 kg (equivalent to 4 kg per person) at a price not exceeding 50 per cent of the current minimum support price for millets, wheat, and rice.
- Legal entitlements for child and maternal nutrition, destitute, and other vulnerable groups.

The NAC has estimated the food grain requirement for phase 1 at 49.36 million tonnes and for the final phase at 55.59 million tonnes (Table 2). These estimates are based on population projections for October 2010 and on the assumption of 85 per cent offtake of food grains during phase 1 and 90 per cent offtake of food grains during the final phase. The food grain requirement projected by NAC is somewhat underestimated and we need to use population projections pertaining to the year for which the phases are to be implemented to obtain more realistic estimates[9] and increase the offtake to 100 per cent (since NFSA provides a legal entitlement). By this calculation the estimated food grain requirement increases to 58.76 million tonnes and 63.98 million tonnes for the two phases (Table 2). Adding 8 million tonnes for other welfare programmes[10] and 2 million tonnes for buffer stock, the total food grain requirement increases to 68.76 million tonnes in phase 1 and 73.98 million tonnes in the final phase. The subsidy implications for the entitled food grain are Rs 855,840 million in phase I and Rs 920,600 million in the final phase.

As against these requirements the maximum public procurement of wheat and rice was 59.07 million tonnes for the production year 2008–9 (33 per cent of production). In subsequent years, the procurement has been lower. Projections about the availability of food grains for NFSB, based on past performance and on a best effort basis, works out to 56.35 million tonnes in the first phase and 57.61 million tonnes in the final phase. The underlying assumption is that the average procurement will be around 30 per cent, which translates to about 50 per cent of the marketable surplus. A higher level of procurement without increase in production levels will be potentially inflationary and hit the poor adversely since the most vulnerable sections depend on the market for 25–30 per cent of their consumption requirements for wheat and rice.[11] At this level of procurement, NAC's recommendations cannot be implemented for either phase.

Table 2 Food Grain Requirement for Implementing the Proposed NFSB

(million tonne)

	NAC* projections scenario 1		Updated** projections	
	Phase 1	Final Phase	Phase 1	Final Phase
Priority households	34.40	36.42	40.96	41.93
General households	14.96	19.17	17.80	22.05
Sub-total	49.36	55.59	58.76	63.98
Other welfare schemes	8.00	8.00	8.00	8.00
Buffer stock	-		2.00	2.00
Total food grains	57.36	63.59	68.76	73.98

Note: * Population—October 2010.
** Population—Phase 1: October 2011; Phase 2: October 2013.

The Expert Committee appointed by the Prime Minister to examine the implications of NFSB felt that given the feasible level of procurement, it is best to restrict the legally assured delivery of food grains at Rs 2 per kg for wheat and Rs 3 per kg for rice to the really needy households and cover the rest through an executive order with a varying quantum depending on the availability of food grains. 'Really needy households' can be defined as those falling below the official poverty line plus 10 per cent of the BPL population which translates to 46 per cent rural and 28 per cent urban population. These percentages are the same as those recommended by NAC for categorization as 'priority' households and capture not only the poor but also some at the margin. The total food grain requirement for the entitled population, buffer stocks, and other welfare programmes will be 50.96 million tonnes in phase 1 and 51.93 million tonnes in the final phase. In this option, after meeting statutory entitlements, the balance 5 million tonne of grain can be used for distribution to the remaining population at an issue price higher than that of the entitled category. As production and procurement improve, coverage can be increased. However, if all the available procurement is to be distributed, it is possible to increase the population coverage to 54 per cent rural and 34 per cent urban, with a total population coverage of 48 per cent. Alternatively, besides the preferred category, legal coverage too can

[9]October 2011 for phase 1 and October 2013 for the final phase. October population projections have been used as these can be used as a proxy for the average of the relevant financial year.
[10]Government programmes—Mid-Day Meal Scheme, ICDS, Social Welfare Hostels, and Natural Calamities.

[11]Based on NSSO surveys.

be extended to the general category with a much lower entitled quantity.

Reformed PDS

Besides the entitlement, the other important element in implementing a food security system is the distribution of food grains. The PDS with its network of about half a million FPS is the most obvious choice. However, in its current form, the PDS is inefficient with large-scale leakages, unviable FPS creating perverse incentives for diversion, and general lack of accountability. There is a need for major systemic reforms in the PDS. Two interventions which can make the maximum impact are comprehensive computerization of the PDS and introduction of smart cards to the beneficiaries. The government has already undertaken a number of initiatives for computerizing PDS operations but each of these target a part of the system and are not comprehensive and replicable at the all-India level. The computerization of the PDS network starting from the allocation of the grain to the final delivery to the targeted beneficiary is crucial for creating an efficient distribution system if food security is to be ensured.

As an improvement to the existing PDS, we may switch over to the use of smart cards. Keeping the current method of food grain allocation to FPS unchanged we can introduce smart cards for the beneficiaries. These biometric cards may simply contain details of the beneficiary and his entitlement. Only when the beneficiary swipes the card at an FPS, will it be deemed that the targeted grain has been delivered. Allocations to FPS will depend on electronic proof of delivery of the grain to the targeted beneficiary. This will prevent large-scale leakages of food grains which happen under the present system of manual record keeping at FPS. These cards can initially be linked to an FPS mandated to service the beneficiary and as the system stabilizes, the beneficiary may be permitted to use the smart card at any convenient FPS. The advantage of this will be the introduction of some competition amongst FPS making it easy for the migrant poor to access the entitled food grains irrespective of their location. The UID project which would make the unique identification of each beneficiary possible is currently underway. It is extremely important to explore the synergies between these two programmes which will go a long way in streamlining the food delivery mechanism.

C. Rangarajan

References

Clay, Edward. 2002. *FAO Expert Consultation on Trade and Food Security—Conceptualizing the Linkages*, chapter 2.

Gross, Rainer, Hans Schoeneberger, Hans Pfeifer, and Hans-Joachim A. Preuss. 2000. *The Four Dimensions of Food and Nutrition Security: Definitions and Concepts.*

Himanshu and Abhijit Sen. 2011. 'Why Not a Universal Food Security Legislation', *Economic and Political Weekly*, XLVI(12): 38–47.

Kumar, Parmod and Sudhir Kumar Singh. 2008. 'Concurrent Evaluation of Targeted Public Distribution System', New Delhi, NCAER.

Ministry of Agriculture. 2010. *Agricultural Statistics at a Glance*, available at www.agricoop.nic.in.

Radhakrishna, R. and C. Ravi. 1992. 'Effects of Growth, Relative Price and Preferences on Food and Nutrition', *Indian Economic Review*, 27: 303–23.

Venugopal, K.R. 2010. 'A Note on the National Food Security (NFS) Act, 2010.'

■ Foreign Direct Investment

Foreign direct investment (FDI) involves foreign investors taking a controlling and lasting stake in productive enterprises. This is unlike foreign portfolio investments that represent minor equity or debt holdings through stock markets by foreign investors only to seek returns on investments and not management control. FDI inflows are generally associated with multinational enterprises (MNEs) that have operations and production facilities across the world. FDI flows generally come as capital bundled with technology, skills, and sometimes even market access. Therefore, they are widely perceived as important resources for expediting the industrial development of receiving (or host) countries. Most developing countries, therefore, have a welcoming attitude towards MNEs and FDI. India's case is atypical in this context. After following a somewhat restrictive policy towards FDI in the first 40 years of Independence, India has liberalized her FDI policy regime considerably since 1991, besides opening new sectors to FDI, such as mining, banking, insurance, telecommunications, airlines, construction and management of ports, harbours, roads and highways, and defence equipment. With the build-up of foreign exchange reserves, the limits for outward investments have been gradually relaxed since 1991 and Indian enterprises are now permitted to invest up to 100 per cent of their net worth on automatic basis abroad. This liberalization has been accompanied by increasing inflows. It has also been accompanied by changes in the sectoral composition, sources, and entry modes of FDI. The increasing recognition of India's locational advantages in knowledge-based industries among MNEs has also led to increasing investments by them in software development and in global R&D centres set up in India to exploit these advantages. Another trend in recent years has been of increasing outward FDI from India that attracts attention given its developing country status. This entry is a brief overview of the trends, patterns, and impact of FDI in and out of India in the context of reforms.

Reforms and FDI Flows

With a progressively liberalized FDI policy regime since 1991 and a large and growing domestic market, among other advantages, the investment climate has steadily improved with India moving up in the A.T. Kearney FDI Confidence Index, from fifteenth in 2002 to sixth in 2003; it was only behind China and the US in 2005 and has stayed within the top three ranks since then. FDI inflows received by India have shown a marked increase since the 1991 liberalization, especially since 2001 as the Indian economy has picked up growth momentum. The big turnaround came in 2006 when the magnitude of FDI nearly tripled from $7.6 billion in 2005 to $20 billion. The inflows peaked at $40 billion in 2008 before declining to $35 billion in 2009 under the shadow of the global financial crisis.

The magnitude of FDI inflows received by India would appear small, especially if compared with inflows received by other countries in the region, such as China (around US$ 100 billion in recent years). However, the difference in the FDI to gross domestic product (GDP) ratio narrows if underestimation of FDI in India due to measurement problems and overestimation of FDI in China due to round tripping of Chinese capital are taken into account. The latter covers domestic Chinese investment registering as FDI through Hong Kong, Macau, or other countries to take advantage of a more favourable tax treatment of foreign investors. The ratio of FDI inflows as a percentage of gross fixed capital formation for India more than tripled from 3 per cent in 2005 to 9.6 per cent in 2008. But it is still lower than the developing countries' average at 12.8 per cent indicating the potential of the country to receive greater magnitudes of FDI in the future. An analysis of the role of liberalization in explaining the rising FDI inflows suggests that only a part of the increase in FDI inflows in the 1990s could be attributed to liberalization, as the sharp expansion in the global scale of FDI flows also played a role. Further analysis suggests that liberalization of the FDI policy may be necessary but not sufficient for expanding FDI inflows. The overall macroeconomic performance continues to exercise a major influence on the magnitude of FDI inflows by acting as a signalling device for foreign investors about the growth prospects of the potential host economy. Hence, paying attention to macroeconomic performance indicators, such as growth rates of industry through public investments in socio-economic infrastructure and other supportive policies, and creating a stable and enabling environment would crowd in FDI inflows. There has also been a discussion on the quality of FDI inflows in the post-reforms period. A substantial proportion of FDI in the post-reforms period has gone to services, infrastructure, and relatively low-technology intensive consumer-goods manufacturing industries largely oriented to India's domestic market and very little to export-oriented production. As much as 40 per cent of FDI in the late 1990s in India also took the route of acquisitions rather than greenfield ventures. In China, in contrast, FDI is concentrated in export-oriented and high-technology manufacturing industry and has come largely in the form of greenfield ventures.

Another important trend is India's emergence as a significant source of FDI flows. Although Indian companies have been investing abroad since the early 1970s, the magnitude of investments was quite small until the mid-1990s. However, the magnitude as well as the number of outward investments started increasing since 2000 to around $1.5 billion per annum jumping to nearly $5 billion in 2005–6 and then to $14 billion in 2006–7. In 2007–8 the value increased to $19 billion, before moderating slightly to $16 billion in the following year in the wake of the global financial crisis. In particular, involvement of Indian companies in large cross-border acquisitions, for example, Tata Steel-Corus, Hindalco-Novelis, and Tata Motors-Jaguar/Land Rover, among others, have helped in focusing attention on their emergence on the global scene. The recent spurt in the outward FDI activity of Indian enterprises reflects the change in motivation from purely market-seeking to also seeking strategic assets such as global brand names and marketing networks, proprietary technology, and other resources to jump-start their internationalization. Their ability to acquire much larger enterprises in the developed world despite their origins in a low-income country reflects their new found confidence in managing the acquired entities successfully. It has been argued that the source of their ownership or competitive advantage which enables such acquisitions lies in their accumulation of skills for managing large multi-location operations across diverse cultures in India and in their ability to deliver value for money with their 'frugal engineering skills' honed up while catering to the larger part of the income pyramid in India.

Impact of FDI and the Role of Government Policies

Although the importance of FDI as a source of capital and output generation increased in the 1990s, its impact on domestic investment and growth is mixed as some FDI inflows possibly crowd in domestic investments while some others crowd it out. One way to maximize the contribution of FDI to host development is to improve the chances of FDI crowding in domestic investments and minimizing the possibilities of it crowding out domestic investments. In this context, the experiences of Southeast Asian countries such as Malaysia, Korea, China, and Thailand in channelling FDI into export-oriented manufacturing through selective policies and export performance requirements imposed at the time of entry deserve careful consideration. Export-oriented FDI minimizes the possibilities of crowding out of domestic investment and generates favourable spillovers for domestic investment by creating demand for intermediate goods. India's experience with respect to fostering export-oriented industrialization with the help of FDI has also been much poorer than that of East Asian economies. However, recent analysis suggests that MNEs are beginning to take a serious look at India's potential as a base for export-oriented manufacture.

Another policy that can help in maximizing the contribution of FDI inflows is to push them to newer areas where local capabilities do not exist as that minimizes the chances of conflict with domestic investment, as was done by Malaysia through pioneer industry programmes. Similarly, because MNE entry through acquisition of domestic enterprises is likely to generate less favourable externalities for domestic investment than greenfield investments, some governments discourage acquisitions by foreign enterprises. Governmental intervention may also foster diffusion of knowledge brought in by foreign enterprises by promoting vertical inter firm linkages with domestic enterprises through various means, such as local content regulations or by creating sub-national or sub-regional clusters that facilitate the spillovers of knowledge through informal and social contacts among the employees besides traditional buyer–seller links. India is also attracting increasing attention from MNEs as a base for their knowledge-based activities, such as software development and global R&D activity. Studies suggest that India's success owes largely to the cumulative investments made by the government over the past five decades in building what is now termed as national innovation systems, including higher education and centres of excellence, among other initiatives. Finally, in light of all this, it is clear that it is of critical importance for host governments to preserve policy flexibility to pursue selective policy or impose performance requirements on FDI, if necessary. Some of the performance requirements have already been outlawed by the World Trade Organization's (WTO) Trade Related Investment Measures (TRIMs) Agreement. Attempts have been made by developed countries to expand the scope of international trade rules beyond what is covered under TRIMs and the General Agreement on Trade in Services (GATS) and further limit the policy flexibility available to developing countries by creating a WTO multilateral framework on investment. However, due to resistance by developing countries, investment has been dropped from the ongoing Doha Round of WTO negotiations.

NAGESH KUMAR

References

Kumar, Nagesh. 2002. *Globalization and the Quality of Foreign Direct Investment*, New Delhi, Oxford University Press.

——. 2005. 'Liberalization, Foreign Direct Investment Flows and Development: Indian Experience in the 1990s', *Economic and Political Weekly*, 40(14): 1459–69.

——. 2008. 'Internationalization of Indian Enterprises: Patterns, Strategies, and Ownership Advantages and Implications', *Asian Economic Policy Review*, 3: 242–61.

——. 2010. 'Capital Flows and Development: Lessons from South Asian Experiences', ESCAP/MPDD Working Papers, WP/10/11, UN-ESCAP, Bangkok.

Kumar, Nagesh and Jaya Prakash Pradhan. 2005. 'Foreign Direct Investment, Externalities and Economic Growth in Developing Countries: Some Empirical Explorations', in Edward M. Graham (ed.), *Multinationals and Foreign Investment in Economic Development*, New York, Palgrave Macmillan.

UNCTAD. 2010. *World Investment Report 2010*, New York, United Nations.

Foreign Direct Investment for Media

The electronic media in India has rapidly expanded since it was opened up to the private sector in the early 1990s. The growth has been particularly pronounced in television. The GDP from radio and broadcasting was Rs 980 crore in 2001–2, sixteen times of that in 1990–1. Foreign direct investment (FDI) in the media was also first permitted in TV and cable and more recently in newspapers. There are, however, limits on the equity that foreigners can hold in the media. Restrictions on foreign control of 'current affairs and news' and cultural aspects may be justified, but foreign equity limits can be liberalized taking account of these.

Role of Media

A competitive, wisely regulated media can play a role in the dissemination of global knowledge. India has a dynamic comparative advantage in the media, which can be translated into trade competitiveness, given a competitive environment. Among its strengths are:

- Facility with English, the language of global commerce and trade in services.
- The advantages of a free and open society—the freedom of information, thought, and expression.
- Cultural diversity. This can be exploited to give a unique product, if merged skilfully with the basic cultural and society-specific characteristics of the target audience (artistic joint product/venture).

The current position with respect to FDI in Indian media is shown in Table 1.

Table 1 FDI in Media: Foreign Equity Limits

	Limit (per cent)	Conditions
Broadcasting		
TV software production	100	
Uplinking, HUB, etc.	49	includes FII
Cable network	49	includes FII
DTH	49	s.t. 20% for individual
Terrestrial broadcast FM	20	FII only
Print media		
Science/professional journals	100	
Newspapers	26	
Periodicals		
News and current affairs	26	
Others	100	

Note: FII = Foreign institutional investors (portfolio investment).

Reciprocity Principle

We should have no objection in principle to publications on culture, society, and entertainment being published and sold in India as long as this is not at the expense of Indian culture and social norms and practices. Globalization of culture must, however, be a two-way street, with the rest of the world having the same access to Indian culture as we do to theirs (reciprocity). This has two aspects:

C1: Exploring Exports

Every foreign entrant must explore the possibility of exporting Indian cultural publications and programmes. This could be done, for example, by having at least one full-time marketing person assigned to exploration of markets for Indian output in the rest of the world.

C2: Content

Globalization of media cannot simply mean that all the existing cultural (for example, soap operas) and nationalistic (for example, war news) content created in democratic USA, UK, and other English-speaking countries is transferred to India. Globalization must also mean that the cultural and nationalistic content created by the one-sixth of humanity living in democratic India is brought to a global audience (in due course).

Two criteria which could define globalization of publishing are: country maximum and India minimum.

C2*a: Country Maximum*: This would mean that content from the USA (22 per cent), Japan (8 per cent), China (11 per cent), Germany (5 per cent), and the UK (3 per cent) could not exceed their respective shares in world GDP measured at purchasing power parity (PPP). The idea is to ensure cultural diversity and discourage a homogenization of culture based on world media oligopoly.

Publishers should be allowed to offset any divergence from this criterion by a point-for-point increase in the share of Indian content. For instance, if the publication has only 2 per cent content on China, the remaining 9 per cent can be substituted by Indian content.

C2*b: India Minimum*: This would mean that Indian content must be greater than India's share in world GDP at PPP (about 4.5 per cent) in the third year after entry and rise to India's share in world population (17 per cent) by the tenth year of production. The content referred to here can be interpreted liberally to *include* any non-Indian content provided by any author/writer of Indian origin (up to children of parents who once held Indian passports). Again the idea is to ensure cultural diversity and that the Indian cultural perspective is fully reflected in this diversity.

Culture

The reciprocity principle can be applied to the areas of media impacting on culture. FDI in scholarly and semi-scholarly books and journals providing analysis and information, on food, popular music, and films, up to 74 per cent could be permitted subject to criteria C1 and C2b and up to 51 per cent subject to C1 alone (automatic route). Higher foreign equity could be considered based on formal commitment to export or provide Indian content. FDI in entertainment (popular novels, magazines, and comic books) up to 74 per cent could be granted automatically subject to criteria C1 and C2 and up to 51 per cent subject to C1 and C2b. The Foreign Investment Portfolio Board (FIPB) could consider relaxation of C2 (if it cannot be met) by substituting it with formal export commitment.

Current Affairs and News

The globalization criteria (C1 and C2) can also be applied to foreign entrants in the field of current affairs and news programmes, along with a third one. The need for this clause arises because reporting of international affairs is strongly influenced by nationality, as demonstrated by the build-up to and aftermath of the Afghanistan and Iraq wars and non-reporting of Pakistan as the training ground for global terrorists and nuclear proliferation till the September (9/11) attack on the USA.

C3: Editorial Control

Editorial control (policy and content) must vest with Indian nationals. The business managers and those who control commercial decisions can, however, be foreigners. There could also be a grace period during which editorial policy is completely under the control of foreign editors.

Foreign entry into publishing of newspapers and news magazines dealing with current affairs and news can be allowed, subject to criteria C1, C2, and C3. This could be done through the FIPB route subject to a maximum of 49 per cent foreign equity.

TV and Radio

There should be free entry, including 100 per cent FDI, into the setting up of public broadcasting facilities like radio and TV stations based on the public carrier principle (open access on non-discriminatory terms). Use of these facilities for public broadcasting will require a public broadcasting licence.

Specialized channels focusing on nature, geography, classical music, children's education, or educational topics should be allowed foreign equity up to 100 per cent. Foreign equity up to 49 per cent in public broadcasting in news and popular culture could be allowed, subject to the three criteria (C1, C2, C3). Permission would, however, be given on a case-by-case basis by a Public Broadcasting Authority set up to regulate the content of public broadcasts.

ARVIND VIRMANI

Foreign Exchange Markets

Introduction

During 2003–4 the average monthly turnover in the Indian foreign exchange market touched about US$ 175 billion. Since then, the foreign exchange market activity has increased almost six times in as many years with the average monthly turnover reaching US$ 1,016 billion in March 2010, about eight times the monthly turnover at the National Stock Exchange and the Bombay Stock Exchange for all cash, derivatives, and debt instruments combined. As in the rest of the world, in India too, foreign exchange constitutes the largest financial market by far. And it has been growing at a breakneck pace, faster than its worldwide growth rate. In 1998, rupee-related transactions accounted for 0.05 per cent of the world's currency transactions. By 2010 the figure had risen nine-fold to 0.45 per cent.

Liberalization has radically changed India's foreign exchange sector. Indeed the liberalization process itself was sparked by a severe balance-of-payments and foreign exchange crisis. Since 1991, the rigid, four-decade old, fixed exchange rate system replete with severe import and foreign exchange controls and a thriving black market is being replaced with a less regulated, 'market-driven' arrangement. While the rupee is still far from being 'fully floating' (many studies indicate that the effective pegging is no less marked after the reforms than before), the nature of interventions and range of independence tolerated have both undergone significant changes. With the security of foreign exchange reserves to over a quarter trillion US dollars (the fifth largest in the world), imports are no longer viewed with fear and scepticism. The Reserve Bank of India (RBI) and its allies now intervene occasionally in foreign exchange markets more often to avoid an appreciation in their value. Full convertibility of the rupee is clearly visible on the horizon. The effects of these developments are palpable in the explosive growth in the foreign exchange markets in India.

Foreign Exchange Markets in India—A Brief Background

Foreign exchange markets in India started in earnest slightly over three decades ago when in 1978 the government allowed banks to trade foreign exchange with one another. Today over 65 per cent of the trading in foreign exchange continues to take place in the inter-bank market. The market consists of over 90 authorized dealers (mostly banks) who transact currency among themselves and come out 'square' or without exposure at the end of the trading day. Trading is regulated by the Foreign Exchange Dealers Association of India (FEDAI), a self-regulatory association of dealers. Since 2001, clearing and settlement functions in the foreign exchange markets are largely carried out by the Clearing Corporation of India Limited (CCIL) that handles transactions of approximately US$ 3.5 billion a day, about 80 per cent of the total transactions.

The liberalization process has significantly boosted foreign exchange markets in the country by allowing both banks and corporations greater flexibility in holding and trading foreign currencies. The Sodhani Committee set up in 1994 recommended greater freedom to participating banks, allowing them to fix their own trading limits, interest rates on FCNR deposits, and the use of derivative products.

The growth of foreign exchange markets in the last few years has been nothing less than momentous. In the last five years, from 2004–5 to 2009–10, trading volume in foreign exchange markets (including swaps, forwards, and forward cancellations) has more than *tripled*, growing at a compounded annual rate exceeding 26 per cent. Figure 1 shows the growth of foreign exchange trading in India between 1999 and 2010. The inter-bank forex trading volume continued to account for the dominant share (over 74 per cent) of total trading over this period, though there is an unmistakable downward trend in that proportion. (Part of this dominance, though, results from double-counting since purchases and sales are added separately, and a single inter-bank transaction leads to a purchase as well as a sales entry.) This is in keeping with global patterns.

In March 2010, about half (51 per cent)of the transactions were spot trades, while swap transactions (essentially repurchase agreements with a one-way transaction—spot or forward—combined with a longer-horizon forward transaction in the reverse direction) accounted for 30 per cent, and forwards and forward cancellations made up 12 and 7 per cent, respectively. About two-thirds of all transactions had the rupee on one side. In 2010, the Indian rupee featured in the 19th rank among all currencies in terms of being on one side of all foreign transactions. Since 1998 it has overtaken the Brazilian real, Danish krone, and the South African rand in this respect. The USD/INR currency pair is the 20th most exchanged currency pair. As a host of foreign exchange trading activity too, India ranked 20th among all countries covered by the BIS survey in April 2010.

Features of the Forward Premium on the Indian Rupee

The Indian rupee has had an active forward market for some time now. The forward premium or discount on the rupee (vis-à-vis the US dollar, for instance) reflects the market's beliefs about future changes in its value. The strength of the relationship of this forward premium with the interest rate differential between India and the

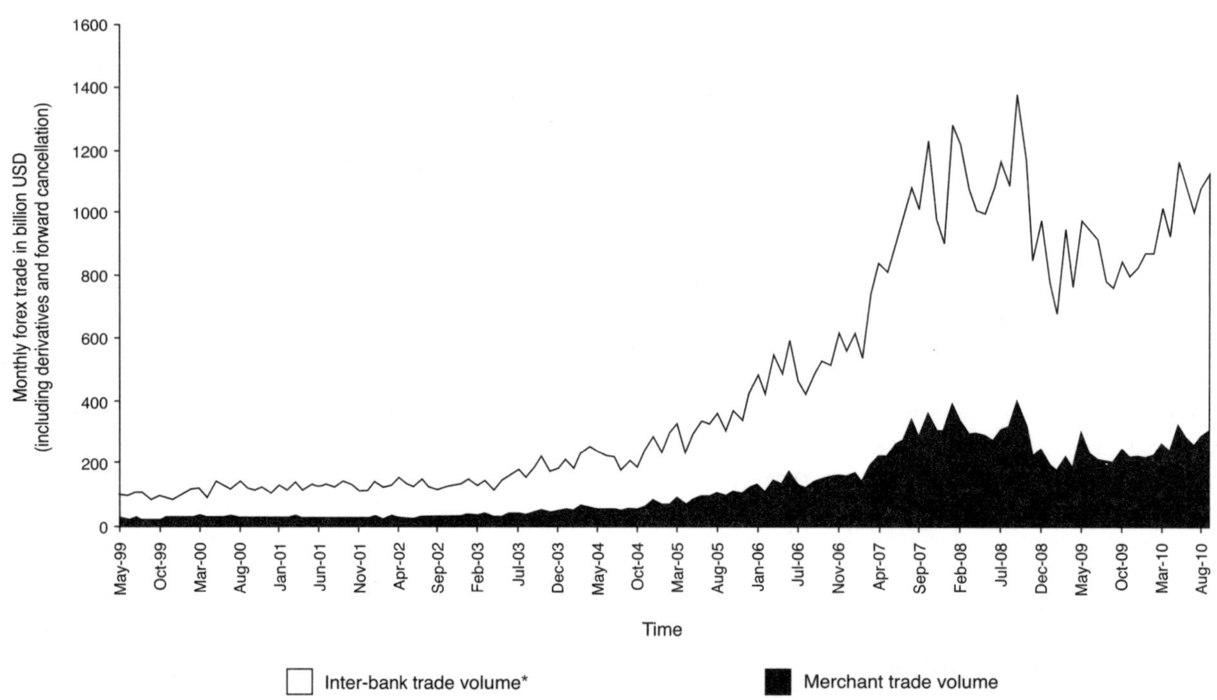

Figure 1 Forex Trading Activity

Source: *RBI Bulletin* (various years).
Note: *Not corrected for double counting.

US—the covered interest parity (CIP) condition—gives us a measure of India's integration with global markets. The CIP is a no-arbitrage relationship that ensures that one cannot borrow in a country, convert to and lend in another currency, insure the returns in the original currency by selling the anticipated proceeds in the forward market and make profits without risk through this process.

Chakrabarti (2006) reports that between late 1997 and mid-2004 the average discount on the rupee was about 4 per cent per annum. During the period the average difference between 90–180 day bank deposit rates in India and the inter-bank USD offer rate was about 4.5 per cent for a three-month and 3.5 per cent for a six-month period. With these two figures in the same ballpark (particularly given that bank deposit rates and inter-bank rates are not strictly comparable), annual averages of interest rate differences and the forward exchange premium also indicate a moderate degree of co-movement between the two variables. The interest rate differential explains about 20 per cent of the total variation in the forward discount. The deviation of the Indian rupee–US dollar from the covered interest parity, however, exhibits long-lived swings on both sides of the zero line. This would indicate arbitrage opportunities and market imperfections provided we could be sure of the comparability of the interest rates considered. Therefore, while the behaviour of the forward premium on the Indian rupee is broadly in lines with CIP, more careful empirical analysis involving directly comparable interest rates is necessary to measure the strength of the covered interest parity condition and the efficiency of foreign exchange markets.

Under market efficiency, the forward exchange rate is considered to be an unbiased predictor of the future spot rate, with random prediction errors. Dua and Ranjan (2010) report that the predictive ability of forward rates on future spot rates has improved over time.

Intervention in Foreign Exchange Markets

The two main functions of foreign exchange markets are to determine the price of the different currencies in terms of one another and to transfer currency risk from more risk-averse participants to those more willing to bear it. As in any market, essentially the demand and supply for a particular currency at any specific point in time determines its price (exchange rate) at that point. However, since the value of a country's currency has significant bearing on its economy, foreign exchange markets frequently witness government intervention in one form or another, to maintain the value of a currency at or near its 'desired' level. Interventions can range from quantitative restrictions on trade and cross-border transfer of capital to periodic trades by the central bank of the country or its allies and agents so as to move the exchange rate in the desired direction. In recent years, India has witnessed both kinds of intervention though liberalization has implied a long-term policy push to reduce and ultimately remove the former kind. It is safe to say that over the years since liberalization, India has allowed restricted capital mobility and followed a 'managed float' type exchange rate policy.

During the early years of liberalization, the Rangarajan Committee recommended that India's exchange rate be flexible. Officially speaking, India moved from a fixed exchange rate regime to a 'market determined' exchange rate system in 1993. The overt objective of India's exchange rate policy, according to various policy pronouncements, has been to manage 'volatility' in exchange rates without targeting any specific levels. This has been hard to do in practice.

Till the mid-2000s the Indian rupee had a remarkably stable relationship with the US dollar. Meanwhile the dollar appreciated against major currencies in the late 1990s and then went into an extended decline, particularly during 2003 and 2004. The lock-step pattern of the US dollar and the rupee is best reflected in the movements in the two currencies against a third currency like the euro. The correlation of the exchange rates of the two currencies against the euro during 1999–2004 was 0.94. Several studies have established the pegged nature of the rupee in recent years (see Chakrabarti 2006 for a more detailed discussion). Based on volatility, India had a de facto crawling peg to the US dollar between 1979 and 1991 which changed to a de facto peg from mid-1991 to mid-1995, with a major devaluation in March 1993. From mid-1995 to end-2001, the rupee reverted to a crawling peg arrangement in practice. An analysis of the ratio of the variance of the exchange rate to the sum of the variances of the interest rate and the foreign exchange reserves reveals a move even closer to the fixed exchange rate system. A comparison of the sensitivity (beta) of the dollar–rupee rate with the euro–rupee rate for a three-year period (1999 through 2001), indicates that India had a dollar beta of 1.01—tenth highest among the 53 countries considered. More important, the US dollar–euro exchange rate explained about 97 per cent of all movements in the Indian rupee–euro exchange rate—the *highest* among all the 53 countries considered. Clearly the Indian rupee has been an excellent 'tracker' of the US dollar.

It is instructive to consider the rupee–dollar exchange rate in the light of the purchasing power parity (PPP) holding that the exchange rate between the two currencies should equal the ratio of price *levels* in the two countries. In its dynamic form, PPP holds that that the rate of depreciation of a currency should equal the excess of its inflation rate to that in the other country. Over a reasonably long period of time, the devaluation in the Indian rupee, vis-à-vis the US dollar does seem to have an association with the difference in the inflation rates in the two countries. Between 1991 and 2003, the two variables had visible co-movements with a correlation of about 0.57 (Chakrabarti 2006). This may be a result of Indo-US trade flows dominating the exchange rate markets but it is perhaps more likely that it reflects the exchange rate management principles of monetary authorities.

The situation changed considerably after 2004 as a surge in foreign portfolio flows tended to steadily appreciate the rupee, despite RBI's best efforts to contain the rise, till by December 2007, the rupee had reached 39 per dollar and it was expected to rise up to 35. However, 2008 brought the economic crisis to India and as the flows turned the rupee crashed to 52 before slowly firming up again to the mid-40s during 2009 and 2010. All through, India refrained from using capital controls, on outflows or inflows, bringing credibility to its commitment to a freer capital flow regime.

The RBI has used a varied mix of techniques in intervening in foreign exchange markets—indirect measures such as press statements (sometimes called 'open mouth operations' in central bank speak) and, in more extreme situations, monetary measures to affect the value of the rupee as well as direct purchase and sale in foreign exchange markets using spot, forward, and swap transactions (see Ghosh 2002). Till around 2002, the measures were mostly in the nature of crisis management of saving-the-rupee kind and sometimes the direct deals would be repeated over several days till the desired outcome was accomplished. Other public-sector banks, particularly the State Bank of India, often aided or veiled the intervention process.

The exact details of the interventions are shrouded in mystery, not unusual for central banks ever wary of disclosing too much of their hand to currency speculators. The Tarapore Committee report had urged more transparency in the intervention process and recommended, in 1997, that a 'Monitoring Exchange Rate Band' of ± 5 per cent be used around an announced neutral real effective exchange rate (REER), with weekly publication of relevant figures, something yet to be implemented.

Intervention has become a greater challenge for RBI since 2004 when capital flows to India surged. In order to arm RBI with further government bonds to enable sterilization of interventions to temper the increase in the rupee the government started the market stabilization scheme (MSS). However, within three years, even that proved insufficient to stem the tide of capital inflows till the crisis arrived to take the rupee on an opposite swing.

In a recent survey on interventions in foreign exchange markets in emerging markets, the Bank for International Settlements (BIS 2005) found that out of 11 emerging market countries considered, India gave out most complete information on its intervention *strategy* (along with three others); no information on *actual* interventions (five others did the same), and did not cover foreign exchange interventions in annual reports (like two other countries). On the whole it ranked as the fourth most opaque in matters of foreign exchange interventions among the 11 countries compared.

Regulation of Cross-border Currency Flows

A feature of the economy that is intricately related with the exchange rate regime that is followed is the freedom of cross-border capital flows. This relationship comes from the so-called 'impossible trinity' or 'trilemma' of international finance, which essentially states that a country may have any two but not all of the following three things—a fixed exchange rate, free flow of capital across its borders, and autonomy in its monetary policy. Since liberalization, India has been having close to a de facto peg to the dollar and simultaneously has been liberalizing its foreign currency flow regime.

Close on the heels of the adoption of a market-determined exchange rate (within limits) in 1993 came current account convertibility in 1994. In 1997, the Tarapore Committee on Capital Account Convertibility defined the concept as 'the freedom to convert local financial assets into foreign financial assets and vice versa at market determined rates of exchange' and laid down fiscal consolidation, a mandated inflation target, and strengthening of the financial system as its three main preconditions. Meanwhile, capital flows have been gradually liberalized, allowing, on the inflow side, foreign direct and portfolio investments, and tapping foreign capital markets by Indian companies as well as considerably better remittance privileges for individuals; and on the outflow side, international expansion of domestic companies. In 2000, the infamous Foreign Exchange Regulation Act (FERA) was replaced with the much milder Foreign Exchange Management Act (FEMA) that gave participants in foreign exchange markets a much greater leeway.

By the late 1990s, the ultimate goal of capital account convertibility seemed to be in the government's sights and 2009 was set by the Tarapore Committee as the year by which it should happen, though the issue continued to be strongly debated. Closer to the date, however, the convergence towards convertibility appeared to be slower than initially expected. Williamson (2006), for instance, pointed out that with a public-sector deficit of 7.6 per cent of the GDP and the ratio of public debt to GDP of over 83 per cent in 2005–6, India was far from fulfilling at least one of the three major preconditions to capital account convertibility set out by the Tarapore Committee—fiscal discipline. Finally, of course, the global economic crisis in 2008 led to the shelving of all such plans indefinitely.

Advocates of convertibility cite the 'consumption smoothing' benefits of global funds flow and point to improved macroeconomic discipline owing to external monitoring by the global financial markets, greater domestic investment and growth because of easier and cheaper financing, and greater efficiency in the banking and financial systems. However, premature adoption of convertibility as a source of problems is also well recognized. Prasad and Rajan (2008) argue that convertibility should not be a priority till the policy and institutions in a country are well developed and properly aligned.

It is generally held that it was, in fact, the *lack* of convertibility that protected India from contamination during the Asian contagion in 1997–8. In the wake of the global financial crisis, RBI's approach of cautious gradualism received much praise and as of now the policy debates do not signal a likelihood of early adoption of convertibility.

The Dynamics of Swelling Reserves

An important corollary of India's foreign exchange policy has been the quick and significant accumulation of foreign currency reserves in the past few years. Starting from a situation in 1990–1 with the foreign exchange reserves level barely enough to cover two weeks of imports, and about $35 billion at the beginning of 2000, India's foreign exchange position rocketed to one of the largest in the world with over $298 billion in November 2010. Since 2000, this implies a compounded annual growth rate of about 23 per cent with the years 2003 and 2008 having the most stunning increases at 32 and 36 per cent, respectively. During these two years the US dollar fell against the euro by 19 per cent and against the rupee by 9 per cent. Without RBI intervention, the latter figure is likely to have been larger and the reserves accumulation less spectacular.

A sizeable foreign exchange reserve acts as a liquidity cover and protects against a run on the country's currency, and reduces the rate of interest on Indian debt in the world market by lowering the country risk perception by international rating agencies. However, beyond a point, it begins to affect the money supply in the country, and also interest rates. A small part of the reserves have been used to fund infrastructure projects.

Outlook

Liberalization has transformed India's external sector and a direct beneficiary of this has been foreign exchange markets in India. From a foreign exchange-starved, control-ridden economy, India has moved on to a position of $298 billion plus in international reserves with a confident rupee and drastically reduced foreign exchange control. As foreign trade and cross-border capital flows continue to grow, and the country moves towards capital account convertibility, foreign exchange markets are poised to play an even greater role in the economy, but are unlikely to be completely free of RBI interventions any time soon.

RAJESH CHAKRABARTI

References

Bank for International Settlements (BIS). 2005. 'Foreign Exchange Market Intervention in Emerging Markets: Motives, Techniques and Implications', BIS Paper No. 24, Basel, Switzerland.

Chakrabarti, Rajesh. 2006. *The Financial Sector In India: Emerging Issues*, New Delhi, Oxford University Press.

Dua, Pami and Rajiv Ranjan. 2010. 'Exchange Rate Policy and Modelling in India', Department of Economic Analysis and Policy, Reserve Bank of India, Study No. 33.

Ghosh, Soumya Kanti. 2002. 'RBI Intervention in the Forex Market: Results from a Tobit and Logit Model Using Daily Data', *Economic and Political Weekly*, 15 June, 37(49): 2333–48.

Prasad, Eswar S. and Raghuram G. Rajan. 2008. 'A Pragmatic Approach to Capital Account Liberalization', *Journal of Economic Perspectives*, 22(3): 149–72.

Williamson, John. 2006. 'Why Capital Account Convertibility in India is Premature', *Economic and Political Weekly*, 13 May, 41(19): 1848–50.

Foreign Exchange Reserves

Any discussion of India's foreign exchange reserves immediately brings back unsavoury memories of April 1991 when India's foreign exchange reserves plummeted to $4.9 billion, which would suffice for barely two weeks of merchandise imports and brought the country to the precipice of an external payment default. Reserve Bank of India (RBI) had to physically airlift the required quantities of gold to London to ensure that credits were rolled over and the default avoided. Emergency access to standby facility with the International Monetary Fund (IMF) in June 1991 followed by wide-ranging structural reforms that included steep currency devaluation provided the much-needed breathing space and started the process of rebuilding the foreign exchange reserves. The traumatic events of 1991 have ensured that the economic policy stance has been focused on maintaining healthy external-sector balances in subsequent years. This is amply evident in foreign exchange reserves having risen to $309.7 billion by the end of 2007 and reaching a peak level of $314.6 billion in May 2008. While these reserves declined somewhat sharply in the wake of the Lehman Brothers collapse and the ensuing global financial meltdown and economic downturn, they provided the much-needed security to the Indian economy and helped it weather the storm without any palpable difficulties. By the end of July 2009 when the economic recovery was clearly visible both globally and in India, foreign exchange reserves (see Figure 1) were $271.6 billion. The decline of $43.0 billion from their peak in May 2008 was to a large extent due to valuation effects with the dollar having appreciated against the rupee as with other major currencies during this period.

It can be argued that India and the rest of the Asian economies were spared the more serious effects of the unprecedented global crisis of 2008–9, the worst since the Great Depression, primarily on account of the self-insurance that they had achieved by building up their foreign exchange reserves. This is in contrast to the Asian experience in the late 1990s and to the current experience of the East European and Baltic economies which did not have the comfort of large reserves and had to rush to the IMF for large-scale emergency assistance. The

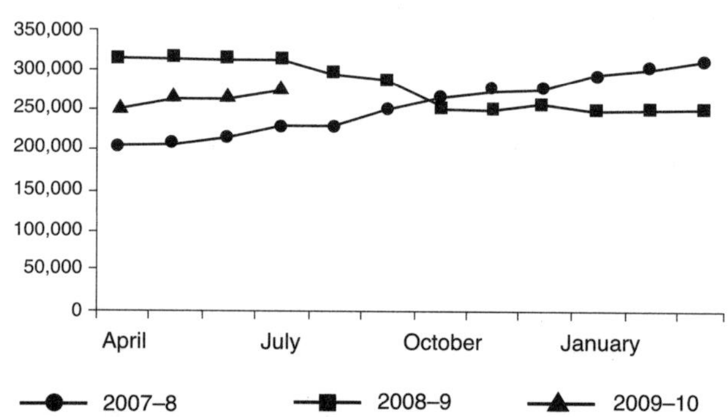

Figure 1 Stock of Foreign Exchange Reserves (US$ million)

Source: RBI.

experience of the Asian economies in the late 1990s and that of the East Europeans in the present downturn will reinforce the global trend towards building up national foreign exchange reserves as a self-insurance against acute external shocks. This is not a healthy development as these reserves represent a cost that could be avoided with the presence of an efficient multilateral agency that could be depended upon for bailing out countries during such emergencies. It is to be hoped that the IMF in its latest avatar, and armed with emergency and flexible credit facilities that can disburse urgent relief without conditionalities, will encourage its member countries to minimize the use of foreign exchange reserves for self-insurance. The question of the optimum level of foreign exchange reserves, which has been raised in the literature (Sen Gupta 2008), that provide a country with the required level of insurance is a difficult one as the answer clearly depends on the exchange rate policy (whether fixed, floating, or managed peg), the composition of the country's foreign exchange reserves, and the overall macroeconomic stability that determines the foreign investors' stance and the consequent stability of foreign capital flows to and from the country. I address these issues in the Indian context later in this entry.

India's experience since 1991 has helped refute the earlier held belief that a country's economic vulnerability increases with greater openness and higher levels of integration with the global economy. As Table 1 shows, the share of external-sector transactions (exports and imports of merchandise goods and invisibles) in the gross domestic product (GDP) has increased from a low 27 per cent in 1991–2 to 35 per cent in 2000–1 and further to 60 per cent in 2008–9.

With a more than doubling of the external sector's presence in the economy, its resilience to external shocks has grown manifestly. Several measures are used for estimating the economy's resilience to external shocks. The ratio traditionally used is to estimate the cover provided by the foreign exchange reserves (or reserves) for total annual requirements of merchandise imports. This has improved from five months of import cover in 1991–2 to ten months in 2008–9. The second measure used is to estimate the cover offered by the reserves against not only merchandise imports but against total imports of both goods and services. On this count too, the cover has improved (Table 2).

Table 3, in addition, provides the factor income payments which is largely the interest payments on India's external debt during this period. Adding factor income payments to total imports of goods and services yields an estimate of expected current account liabilities facing the economy. As Table 2 shows, the foreign exchange cover

Table 1 India's External Trade (US$ million)

Year	Merchandise exports	Merchandise imports	Invisibles exports	Invisibles imports	Total exports (2+4)	Total imports (3+5)	Total trade (6+7)	GDP	Trade as % of GDP (8/9)*100
1	2	3	4	5	6	7	8	9	10
1991–2	18,266	21,064	9,502	7,882	27,768	28,946	56,714	209,677	27.0
1992–3	18,869	24,316	9,334	7,413	28,203	31,729	59,932	240,942	24.9
1993–4	22,683	26,739	11,319	8,422	34,002	35,161	69,163	275,976	25.1
1994–5	26,855	35,904	15,554	9,874	42,409	45,778	88,187	322,516	27.3
1995–6	32,310	43,670	17,664	12,217	49,974	55,887	105,861	346,962	30.5
1996–7	34,133	48,948	21,405	11,209	55,538	60,157	115,695	383,855	30.1
1997–8	35,680	51,187	23,244	13,236	58,924	64,423	123,347	386,671	31.9
1998–9	34,298	47,544	25,770	16,562	60,068	64,106	124,174	412,678	30.1
1999–2000	37,542	55,383	30,312	17,169	67,854	72,552	140,406	447,663	31.4
2000–1	45,452	57,912	32,267	22,473	77,719	80,385	158,104	450,753	35.1
2001–2	44,703	56,277	36,737	21,763	81,440	78,040	159,480	466,998	34.2
2002–3	53,774	64,464	41,925	24,890	95,699	89,354	185,053	516,695	35.8
2003–4	66,285	80,003	53,508	25,707	119,793	105,710	225,503	634,048	35.6
2004–5	85,206	118,908	69,533	38,301	154,739	157,209	311,948	719,783	43.3
2005–6	105,152	157,056	89,687	47,685	194,839	204,741	399,580	804,113	49.7
2006–7	128,888	190,670	114,558	62,341	243,446	253,011	496,457	947,167	52.4
2007–8	166,163	257,789	148,604	74,012	314,767	331,801	646,568	1,181,293	54.7
2008–9	175,184	294,587	162,556	72,970	337,740	367,557	705,297	1,179,882	59.8

Source: RBI.

Table 2 Reserve Cover for Total Imports (Goods and Services)

Year	Merchandise imports (US$ million)	Imports of goods and services (US$ million)	Reserves (US$ million)	Reserve cover (in months) (3/4)
1	2	3	4	5
1991–2	21,064	24,879	9,220	4
1992–3	24,316	27,917	9,832	4
1993–4	26,739	31,469	19,254	7
1994–5	35,904	41,437	25,186	7
1995–6	43,670	51,214	21,687	5
1996–7	48,948	55,696	26,423	6
1997–8	51,187	59,297	29,367	6
1998–9	47,544	58,565	32,490	7
1999–2000	55,383	67,028	38,036	7
2000–1	57,912	72,488	42,281	7
2001–2	56,277	70,093	54,106	9
2002–3	64,464	81,584	76,100	11
2003–4	80,003	96,727	112,959	14
2004–5	118,908	146,731	141,514	12
2005–6	157,056	191,545	151,622	9
2006–7	190,670	234,981	199,179	10
2007–8	257,789	310,301	309,723	12
2008–9	294,587	345,993	251,735	9

Source: RBI.

on this basis increased from four months import cover in 1992–3 to thirteen months in 2003–4 before declining to a comfortable eight months in 2008–9.

The Asian financial crisis of the late 1990s demonstrated that countries which did not have sufficient reserves to cover their debt servicing and portfolio investment liabilities (for example, Indonesia) suffered a serious capital flight. Portfolio investment is distinct from foreign direct investment (FDI) because investors can encash and liquidate their portfolio holdings even while

Table 3 External Payments (US$ million) and Reserve Cover (in months)

Year	Merchandise imports	Service imports	Factor income payments	Stock of FII investment	Foreign exchange reserves	Reserve cover (in months) (6)/(2+3+4)
1	2	3	4	5	6	7
1992–3	24,316	3,601	3,799	4.2	9,832	4
1993–4	26,739	4,730	3,665	1,638.3	19,254	7
1994–5	35,904	5,533	4,317	3,166.6	25,186	7
1995–6	43,670	7,544	4,634	5,202.3	21,687	5
1996–7	48,948	6,748	4,380	7,634.2	26,423	5
1997–8	51,187	8,110	5,081	9,284.3	29,367	5
1998–9	47,544	11,021	5,479	8,898	32,490	6
1999–2000	55,383	11,645	5,490	11,371.3	38,036	6
2000–1	57,912	14,576	7,686	13,531.4	42,281	6
2001–2	56,277	13,816	7,585	15,370.7	54,106	8
2002–3	64,464	17,120	6,968	15,936.3	76,100	10
2003–4	80,003	16,724	8,409	25,941.7	112,959	13
2004–5	118,908	27,823	9,572	36,293.2	141,514	11
2005–6	157,056	34,489	12,263	45,656.5	151,622	9
2006–7	190,670	44,311	16,639	52,477	199,179	9
2007–8	257,789	52,512	19,185	68,918.5	309,723	11
2008–9	294,587	51,406	18,818	59,081.1	251,735	8

Source: RBI and Securities and Exchange Board of India (SEBI).

suffering an exchange loss if they are even slightly unsure of receiving their payments in light of the 'insufficient reserves holdings of the country'. Thus, in a world of self-insurance, central banks would be better off keeping an eye on their reserves position even in relation to portfolio investment liabilities that could be cashed at any point with foreign investors willing to bear the exchange rate loss that would invariably have to be incurred in such an eventuality. This leads us to also estimate the cover provided by reserves in relation to the total annual debt servicing requirements (included in factor income payments) and the stock of foreign institutional investments (FIIs, also referred to as portfolio inflows). As Table 3 shows, the stock of FII into India increased from a mere $4 million in 1992–3 to $68.9 billion in 2007–8 before declining to $59.1 billion in 2008–9. With liberalization and reforms, the growth in reserves ensured that by 2006–7, they had reached 220 per cent of the total debt servicing and portfolio investment liabilities and thus provided the much-needed insurance against any external shock and consequent run on the currency. This ratio has gone up to 352 per cent in 2007–8 primarily because of the rapid build-up of reserves in that year. The build-up in reserves ensured that the economy could absorb, without much difficulty, a net outflow of nearly $10 billion from portfolio investments in 2008–9. As a result of these outflows, the ratio of foreign exchange reserves to total debt servicing and portfolio investment liabilities actually decreased to 323 per cent in 2008–9. It is thus evident that while the size of Indian reserves is much smaller than China's ($1.76 trillion), it has afforded India the necessary cushion against external shocks.

It is perhaps useful to point out that unlike in the case of China, whose current account surplus has contributed significantly to the reserves build-up, India has built up its reserves exclusively with the help of a surplus on the capital account. As Table 4 shows, during 1991–2 to 2008–9, as also in previous decades, India's external sector has been characterized by a persistent current account deficit. In only three years (2001–2 to 2003–4) did India manage to generate a current account surplus over this period. India was successful in attracting sufficiently large capital inflows to generate a capital account surplus in every year since 1991–2. This has been steadily increasing and it peaked at 9 per cent of the GDP in 2007–8 when India added $110 billion to its reserves holdings.

The composition of capital inflows used to build up the foreign exchange reserves is important in ensuring that these do not result in an unsustainable accumulation of external debt especially short-term debt. Table 5, therefore, gives us the annual stock of external debt in India including the share of short-term debt defined as debt of less than one year's duration. It is important to note that unlike many other emerging economies, India has managed to restrain the share of its short-term debt to less than 20 per cent of its total external debt. This gives the needed degree

Table 4 Current and Capital Account Balance (as per cent of GDP)

Year	Current account balance	Capital account balance
1	2	3
1991–2	–0.6	1.9
1992–3	–1.5	1.6
1993–4	–0.4	3.2
1994–5	–1.0	2.6
1995–6	–1.7	1.2
1996–7	–1.2	3.1
1997–8	–1.4	2.5
1998–9	–1.0	2.0
1999–2000	–1.0	2.3
2000–1	–0.6	2.0
2001–2	0.7	1.8
2002–3	1.2	2.1
2003–4	2.2	2.6
2004–5	–0.3	3.9
2005–6	–1.2	3.2
2006–7	–1.0	4.8
2007–8	–1.4	9.1
2008–9	–2.5	0.8

Source: RBI.

of comfort. More important, short-term debt has declined from nearly 93 per cent of total foreign exchange reserves in 1991–2 to less than 9 per cent by 2007–8 before rising to 18 per cent in 2008–9 when reserves declined in the aftermath of the global recession.

It is, therefore, evident that India today enjoys a comfortable foreign exchange reserve position in relation to all relevant parameters. Its reserves are, however, only a fraction of the total reserves held by other Asian economies like China and Japan, or even much smaller economies like Taiwan and South Korea (see Figure 2). But these comparisons are not particularly relevant because the accumulation of reserves in other Asian economies has been primarily on account of pursuing an export-oriented strategy which has generated large current account surpluses that have to be absorbed through reserve accretion. The flip side of this strategy has been an imbalanced growth that has seen low levels of private consumption and extraordinarily high levels of savings in the economy. As the current global crisis has amply demonstrated, these imbalances, which are unsustainable, are having to be corrected and will force Asian economies to rely more on domestic sources of demand in the coming years.

India, having successfully overcome its bias against exports and greater economic openness, has to persist

Table 5 External Debt and Foreign Exchange Reserves (US$ million)

Year	Total debt	Short-term debt	Foreign exchange reserves	Short-term debt as % of foreign exchange reserves (3/4)*100
1	2	3	4	5
1991–2	83,801	8,544	9,220	92.7
1992–3	85,285	7,070	9,832	71.9
1993–4	90,023	6,340	19,254	32.9
1994–5	92,695	3,627	25,186	14.4
1995–6	99,008	4,269	21,687	19.7
1996–7	93,730	5,034	26,423	19.1
1997–8	93,470	6,726	29,367	22.9
1998–9	93,531	5,046	32,490	15.5
1999–2000	96,886	4,274	38,036	11.2
2000–1	98,263	3,936	42,281	9.3
2001–2	101,326	3,628	54,106	6.7
2002–3	98,843	2,745	76,100	3.6
2003–4	104,914	4,669	112,959	4.1
2004–5	111,645	4,431	141,514	3.1
2005–6	132,973	17,723	151,622	11.7
2006–7	138,133	19,539	199,179	9.8
2007–8	169,669	26,376	309,723	8.5
2008–9	221,212	44,313	251,735	17.6

Source: RBI.

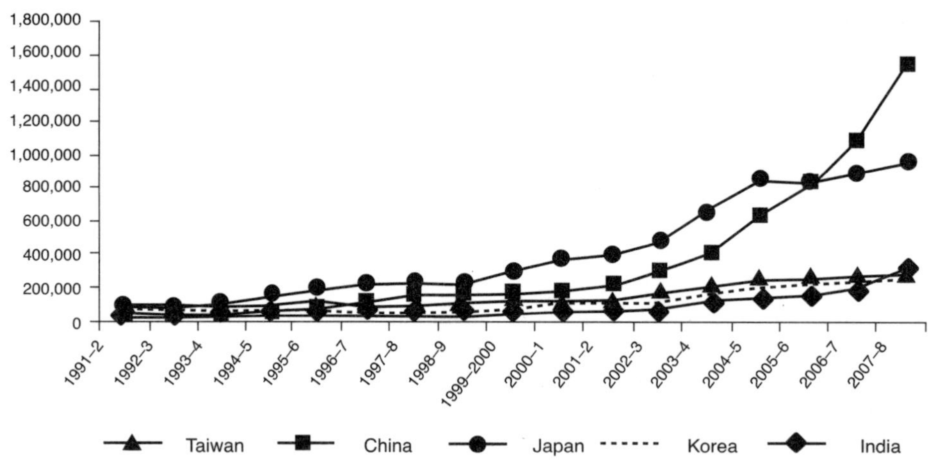

Figure 2 Foreign Exchange Reserves of Selected Countries (US$ million)

Source: IMF and RBI.

with making its economy even more deeply integrated with global flows and further sharpen its competitive advantage to make better use of external demand. Its current growth strategy that has resulted in net exports (of goods and services) contributing –10.5 per cent to GDP growth between 2001/2–2007/8 also needs to be rebalanced so that net exports and external demand can be relied upon to a greater extent as a driver of growth. This is clearly feasible, given that India's present share in world trade of goods is 1.3 per cent and in services is 2.5 per cent. A higher contribution of net exports to GDP growth (or in other words a smaller negative contribution than at present) combined with policy initiatives to make India an even more attractive destination for FDI will ensure that the country's overall external balance-of-payments position, which is summarily represented in the level of foreign exchange reserves, remains on a sound footing in the coming years.

RAJIV KUMAR*

References

Acharya, Shankar. 2008. 'India's Macroeconomic Performance and Policies since 2000'.

Ahluwalia, M.S. 2002. 'India's Vulnerability to External Crisis', in M.S. Ahluwalia, S. Tarapore, and Y.V. Reddy (eds), *Macroeconomics and Monetary Policy: Issues for Reforming the Economy*, Oxford University Press.

*Research assistance from Ritika Tewari and review by ICRIER colleagues is gratefully acknowledged. Mistakes are the author's responsibility.

Burke, D. and P. Lane. 2001. 'The Empirics of Foreign Reserves', *Open Economics Review*, 12(4): 423–34.

Department of Investment Services, Taiwan.

Financial Statistics of the Central Bank of China, Republic of China.

IMF, International Financial Statistics.

Ministry of Finance, India.

Reserve Bank of India (RBI). 2009. *Handbook of Statistics and Bulletin*, September.

Sen Gupta, Abhijit. 2008. 'Cost of Holding Excess Reserves: The Indian Experience', March.

Foreign Institutional Investment

In 2004–5 portfolio investments in India accounted for about 62 per cent of total foreign investment in the country and at about 1.29 per cent of the gross domestic product (GDP) well exceeded the current account deficit (0.95 per cent of GDP). Foreign Institutional Investors' (FIIs) investments accounted for about 97.5 per cent of this. Ever since the opening of the Indian equity markets to foreigners, FII investments have steadily grown from about Rs 2,600 crore in 1993 to over Rs 48,000 crore in 2005. At the end of June 2006, the cumulative FII flows to India accounted for a little over 9 per cent of the Bombay Stock Exchange (BSE) market capitalization.

While it is generally held that portfolio flows benefit the economies of recipient countries, policymakers worldwide have been more than a little uneasy about such investments. Often referred to as 'hot money', they are known to stampede out at the slightest hint of trouble in the host country leaving an economic wreck in their wake, like in Mexico in 1994. They have been blamed for exacerbating small economic problems in a country by making large and concerted withdrawals at the first sign of economic weakness. They have also been held responsible for spreading financial crises—causing 'contagion' in international financial markets.

International capital flows and capital controls have emerged as important policy issues in the Indian context as well. The danger of abrupt reversals and their destabilizing effects on equity and foreign exchange markets are always a concern. Nevertheless, in recent years, the government has been making strong efforts to increase FII flows in India. Some scholars (Rakshit 2006) have argued that, far from being healthy for the economy, FII inflows have actually imposed certain burdens on the Indian economy. Understanding the determinants and effects of FII flows and devising appropriate regulation, therefore, constitute an important part of economic policymaking in India.

Foreign Institutional Investors—A Brief Introduction

Entities covered by the term 'FII' include

> Overseas pension funds, mutual funds, investment trust, asset management company, nominee company, bank, institutional portfolio manager, university funds, endowments, foundations, charitable trusts, charitable societies, a trustee or power of attorney holder incorporated or established outside India proposing to make proprietary investments or investments on behalf of a broad-based fund (i.e., fund having more than 20 investors with no single investor holding more than 10 per cent of the shares or units of the fund). (GoI 2005)

FIIs can invest their own funds as well as invest on behalf of their overseas clients registered as such with the Securities and Exchange Board of India (SEBI). These client accounts that the FII manages are known as 'sub-accounts'. A domestic portfolio manager can also register itself as an FII to manage the funds of sub-accounts.

A few large FIIs (less than 3 per cent of all registered ones, according to GoI 2005), issue derivative instruments called 'participatory notes' that are registered and traded overseas, backed by the FIIs' holdings of Indian securities. This arrangement has raised some concerns in regulatory circles since it makes it difficult to trace the ultimate beneficiary in the funds and may be used to bring in 'unclean' funds (funds generated out of illegal activities) into the Indian markets.

As of mid-July 2006, there were 932 FIIs registered with SEBI, of which 115 were registered in the first half of 2006 itself. US-based funds accounted for 39 per cent of all registered FIIs, followed by UK (16 per cent), Luxembourg (7 per cent), and Singapore (5 per cent) based ones. In terms of net cumulative investment, US-based funds accounted for 29 per cent at the end of October 2005 (GoI 2005) followed by UK-based ones at 17 per cent.

Though initially restricted to investing only in listed company stocks, FIIs are now allowed to invest in equity, bonds, and derivative instruments in India subject to limits of foreign ownership for various sectors as well as ceilings on total investment per FII. Regular FIIs follow what has come to be known as the '70:30 rule', that is, they must invest no less than 70 per cent of their funds in equity-related instruments and may invest the remainder in debt-related instruments. There are also some FIIs that are registered as '100 per cent debt-fund FIIs' that are permitted to invest exclusively in debt instruments. Although equity holdings of FIIs have received maximum attention from the press, researchers, and policymakers alike, the debt holdings of FIIs are not wholly insignificant. As of 21 July 2006, the regular FIIs held US$ 224.25 million (about Rs 1,009 crore) in government securities/treasury bills and US$ 82.02 million (about Rs 369 crore) in corporate debt. At the end of June 2006, the open interest of FIIs in stock and index futures and options exceeded Rs 22,000 crore.

What We Know about FII Flows to India

Over the last few years, research has brought to light a few important features of FII flows to India. The key question has been the relationship between FII flows and returns in the Indian markets shown in Figure 1. Clearly FII

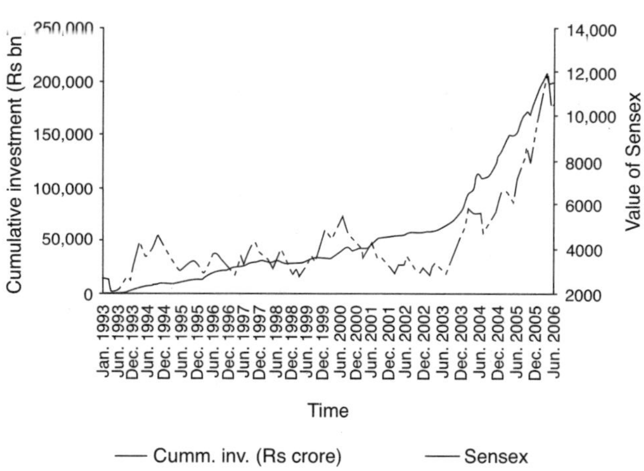

Figure 1 Cumulative FII Investment and the Sensex

Source: www.equitymaster.com.

equity investments and stock market performance in India have been very closely interlinked. Also, both variables experienced a sharp break around April 2003, after which they ramped up steeply. The association is unmistakable—the correlation of monthly net FII equity inflows and monthly Sensex returns is 0.61 since April 2003 and 0.33 in the overall sample.

FII flows are routinely depicted as a major driver of Indian stock market return in the financial press. However, research seems to suggest they are more of an effect than a cause of stock market performance. Analysing daily flow data during 1999, Chakrabarti (2001) concludes that in the post-Asian crisis period, stock market performance has been the sole driver of FII flows, though monthly data in the pre-Asian crisis period may suggest some reverse causality. This return-chasing behaviour has been confirmed using daily data during 1999–2002 in Mukherjee et al. (2002), who also find that the sales of Indian securities by FIIs are affected by returns but not purchases. On the other hand, Gordon and Gupta (2003) analyse monthly data over the period 1993–2000 to conclude that FII flows are *negatively* related to lagged stock market returns, suggesting negative feedback trading. There are, however, issues about the appropriateness of using monthly data in this analysis (Rakshit 2006). In any case, given that there is a structural break in the data around April 2003, careful analysis of more recent data would be instructive in understanding the nature of the relationship and causality, if any, between these two variables.

The largest single-month pull-out of FII funds happened in May 2006 when the FIIs withdrew over $1.7 billion (Rs 8247 crore) followed by May 2004 ($719 million, Rs 3250 crore). These were also the months with the fourth largest and the largest single-month per cent decline in the Sensex, respectively (15.8 per cent and 18.8 per cent), in the post-reforms era.

As for other features, Chakrabarti (2001) finds no evidence of any informational disadvantage for foreign investors vis-à-vis their domestic counterparts. The Asian crisis marked a regime shift in determining FII flows. In the pre-crisis period, the beta (or co-movement) of the Indian market with the American S&P 500 index seemed to inversely affect FII flows to India, but the effect disappeared in the post-crisis period. India's country risk rating did not seem to affect FII flows. Mukherjee et al. (2002) have questioned the diversification motive behind FII flows to India and report auto-correlation or inertia in the flows. Gordon and Gupta (2003) report that FII flows are sensitive to the London Inter-bank Offer Rate (LIBOR) as well as India's macroeconomic fundamentals. Coondoo and Mukherjee (2004) argue that both the stock market as well as FII flows in India have high and related volatility. Finally, in their analysis of the effects of regulatory measures on FII flows, Bose and Coondoo (2004) find that liberalizing policy changes have had expansionary effect on FII flows while restrictive measures aimed at giving regulators greater control over FII flows do not necessarily dampen them.

Government Policy Regarding FII Flows

In policy circles in India, FII flows are believed to have a positive impact on the country's development; so much so that encouraging FII flows—while reducing the financial sector's vulnerability to speculative capital flows—constitutes an objective of the National Common Minimum Programme. Accordingly, an expert group was set up in 2004 (in addition to a committee in 2002 which reported in 2004) to suggest ways to accomplish this goal. The group submitted its report in November 2005 (GoI 2005). Its rationale for encouraging FII flows is that such flows can increase domestic investment without increasing foreign debt. They can raise stock prices, lower cost of equity, stimulate investment by Indian firms, and lead to improvements in securities market design and corporate governance.

In order to further stimulate FII flows, the expert group has suggested setting FII investment caps, if any, over and above the foreign direct investment (FDI) sectoral limits. In cases where the limits have to be combined, they should be set at sufficiently high levels. Another recommendation is to increase the supply of 'good-quality equities' through disinvestment in the public sector and through encouraging companies with large projects like those in the infrastructure and telecom sectors to raise money in the domestic markets.

As for the companion objective of reducing the market's vulnerability to speculative flows, the group recommends participation of domestic institutional investors like pension funds in the equity markets. Entities from 'tax haven' countries should be barred from registering as FIIs. The practice of participatory notes (PNs) is acceptable provided SEBI has the powers to track down the final beneficiary for investigation or surveillance by making it obligatory for the FIIs to provide such information. PNs should not be issued to entities not regulated anywhere in the world and FIIs must follow the 'know-your-client' principle. Existing non-eligible PNs should be allowed to expire or wound down within five years, whichever is earlier. Further, to avoid abuse of the sub-account route to circumvent investment limits, the FII limits should be applied to total investments managed by an FII—directly and through its sub-accounts.

Rakshit (2006) has questioned the basic premise of beneficial effects of FII flows in India as well as the expert group's recommendations. Apart from the risks of financial instability, which he views as underestimated by the expert group, Rakshit (2006) points out that during the 1992–2002 period there has been little relationship between the capital account balance and aggregate investment in India and, except for a couple of years, the latter has exceeded the current account balance in all years since liberalization began. This indicates that FII flows are contributing primarily to the amassing of huge foreign exchange reserves at the Reserve Bank of India (RBI) rather than to real investment in the economy. Further, this accretion of reserves implies significant costs for the economy in terms of a fall in RBI profits through holding of lower-yielding reserves, loss of seignorage revenue, and the costs of sterilizing the inflows. In the presence of demand deficiency in the economy, the real effects of enhanced FII flows are likely to be far from positive. Thus FII flows should be viewed not in isolation but as part of an integrated policy package for all capital receipts keeping in mind their role in the overall macroeconomic structure.

RAJESH CHAKRABARTI

References

Bose, Suchismita and Dipankar Coondoo. 2004. 'The Impact of FII Regulations in India', *Money and Finance*, July–December.

Chakrabarti, Rajesh. 2001. 'FII Flows to India: Nature and Causes', *Money and Finance*, October–December. Reprinted in *The Financial Sector in India: Emerging Issues*, New Delhi, Oxford University Press, 2006.

Coondoo, Dipankar and Paramita Mukherjee. 2004. 'Volatility of FII in India', *Money and Finance*, October–March.

Gordon, James and Poonam Gupta. 2003. 'Portfolio Flows into India: Do Domestic Fundamentals Matter?', IMF Working Paper No. 03/20.

Government of India (GoI), Ministry of Finance. 2005. Report of the Expert Group on Encouraging FII Flows and Checking the Vulnerability of Capital Markets to Speculative Flows, New Delhi, November.

Mukherjee, Paramita, Suchismita Bose, and Dipankar Coondoo. 2002. 'Foreign Institutional Investment in the Indian Equity Market', *Money and Finance*, April–September.

Rakshit, Mihir. 2006. 'On Liberalising Foreign Institutional Investments', *Economic and Political Weekly*, 18 March: 991–8.

Forest Policy

Forest policy in India faces a complex set of challenges. Massive deforestation in the past has drastically reduced the capacity of forests as a source of timber and other industrial raw materials. Further, degradation of standing forests has created serious ecological problems like soil erosion, reduction in the ability of soil to retain moisture, excessive water run-off during the monsoons, siltation of rivers, and the possibility of cycles of drought and flood. More critically, it has put at risk the livelihood of millions of people, particularly tribals, living within or around forests, who have for generations depended on forests for food, fuelwood, and fodder.

This state of Indian forests, and the ensuing policy dilemmas, can in part be traced to the advent of commercial forestry in India and the laws and policies initiated by the British in the 19th century. The British appropriated all forests which were not on private lands for state use. This step was motivated by revenue considerations and to ensure sustained supply of timber for shipbuilding and railway sleepers. The establishment of state control ended traditional property rights of village communities which had been in place for centuries. The resulting alienation and resentment ended the customary care of forests by these communities which had been part of their culture. They responded by non-cooperation in forest protection and, in many instances, even by hostile acts aimed at harming the state-owned forests.

Independent India inherited and continued with the colonial forest policy. In the Indian Constitution forests were originally placed in the state list of subjects. They were managed by the forest departments of respective states through laws enacted by them under the Indian Forest Act of 1927. This was a slightly amended version of a similar Act of 1878 conceived to assert exclusive state right on protection, production, and management of forests. The Act empowered state governments to declare forests on specified non-private lands reserved forests. This declaration had the effect of extinguishing any existing private rights of access to forests and their resources. From within these reserved forests, the state could declare certain areas village forests, where village communities had access to specified forest resources in exchange for forest protection duties. This access was a matter of privilege and not a right. The government could also declare certain areas on private lands protected forests where felling of trees, quarrying, and removal of forest produce were prohibited. The net result of these laws was that traditional forest dwellers came to be looked upon as encroachers on forest lands.

The Government of India announced a National Forest Policy in 1952. This policy did, in principle, recognize the ecological functions of forests. It stressed that at least one-third of the country's land area be brought under forests, partly in an effort to repair the extensive damage to forests in the inter-War period, primarily, however, to ensure the supply of timber and other raw materials for the emerging industrialization programme. It placed restrictions on grazing, shifting cultivation, and other local uses to promote conservation. Chopra (1995) recounts how, with regard to the needs of the local people, this was more restrictive even than the colonial forest policy of 1894, which had placed local interests above revenue needs.

The following two decades witnessed massive deforestation, as states were unable or unwilling to protect forests in the face of perceived needs of development. Major expansion of forest-based industries, aided by subsidized wood prices, put great stress on forests. Forests were cleared for cultivation, for extraction of timber, for mining and quarrying, to make way for industrial projects, and for construction of dams. As a result, forest cover was reduced to less than one-fifth of geographical area as against the recommended one-third. Apart from seriously endangering the ecological balance, it resulted in widespread uprooting of forest dwellers from their habitats.

An important development from the point of view of forest policy was the transfer of forests from the State to the Concurrent List through the 42nd Amendment to the Constitution in 1976. This empowered the central government to act directly in the management of forests. To check rapid deforestation, it enacted the Forest Conservation Act in 1980. The Act mandated prior approval of the central government before a state government could de-reserve a reserved forest, use forest land for non-forest purposes, or assign forest land to a private person or corporation. The transfer of responsibility to the central government did not significantly improve the situation. At its core, forest policy still consisted of fencing off forests to protect them from the people! Over time, with the growth in population, scarcity of fuel and fodder assumed crisis proportions in different parts of the country and led to organized protests. It became clear that a policy based on centralized policing would be impossible to implement effectively.

The central government announced a new National Forest Policy in 1988. This policy marked a significant departure from the past in respect of conservation strategy. It stressed that henceforth forests would be maintained only for ecological functions and for meeting the subsistence needs of the people. It recommended that industry must meet its needs from farm forestry rather than from clear felling of forests. Most significantly, it recognized people's rights over forest resources. It suggested that forest departments should work together with village communities and voluntary agencies for management of forests. Following guidelines issued by the central government in 1990, most state governments took steps to establish Joint Forest Management (JFM) groups. Under the JFM programme, village communities were given conditional access to forest products like fuelwood, fodder, and non-timber products. In return, village communities undertook to protect the forests against encroachment, poaching, and timber smuggling. JFM programmes have met with a fair degree of success. Apart from their geographical spread and increase in numbers, there is evidence that forest cover is beginning to respond.

But new sources of tension have emerged. While the earlier policy was production oriented, the new policy has tended to move too much towards conservation. It has led to resentment among states that are rich in forest cover but find that their development is hampered by not allowing forests to be cleared. They want compensation for providing the ecological benefits that accrue to the nation or even the globe.

As in the case of environmental policy, the Supreme Court has played a critical role in enforcing forest protection policies. Divan and Rosencranz (2001: 294–304) recount judgement in a forest conservation case that has had far-reaching consequences. A recent court order has the potential to make diversion of forest land for non-forest activities costlier and more difficult. The users must now pay an amount that must include, apart from the price of land and value of trees felled, the net present value (NPV) of a stream of ecological benefits, like soil protection, carbon sequestration, and flood and drought prevention, which would accrue in the future.

The conflict between the need for conservation and the needs of local people immediately affected by the policy persists. A proposed Scheduled Tribes (Recognition of Forest Rights) Bill has generated a lot of controversy. This Bill seeks to accord legal recognition to the rights of tribals to forest lands and their produce. The Ministry of Environment considers this Bill an obstacle in the way of forest protection. The Ministry of Tribal Affairs and social activists consider it necessary to 'undo the historical injustice done' to tribal population and believe that it will ensure the survival and sustainability of forest ecosystems. There is clearly still a long way to go.

PURAN MONGIA

References

Chopra, Kanchan. 1995. 'Forests and Other Sectors: Critical Role of Government Policy', *Economic and Political Weekly*, 24 June: 1480–2.

Divan, Shyam and Armin Rosencranz. 2001. *Environment Law and Policy in India*, New Delhi, Oxford University Press.

G

■ G-20 and Multilateral Economic Cooperation

MFIs and Developing Countries

India has a long association with multilateral financial institutions (MFIs), the most prominent of which are the World Bank and the International Monetary Fund (IMF), frequently referred to as the 'Bretton Woods Institutions'. India was one of the few developing countries that participated in the Bretton Woods Conference, which set up these institutions after the Second World War, even before India formally gained Independence. Its role in multilateral economic cooperation, however, is more recent. Being a less developed country, India's association with multilateral financial institutions, as also its bilateral cooperation with Organisation for Economic Co-operation and Development (OECD) countries generally, was mostly as an aid recipient and borrower. Although India was the fifth largest shareholder in the IMF and World Bank till the early 1970s, their governance structure is dominated by developed, rich donor countries. Originally set up to facilitate the post-War reconstruction of Europe, their role subsequently evolved into providing aid and technical assistance to developing countries.

The 'two-gap model' was for long a core assumption in traditional developmental economics. According to this, the twin deficits of capital (a deficit of domestic savings relative to domestic investment needs) and foreign exchange (the counterpart of the first gap, since the savings gap needed to be bridged through net capital inflows) are amongst the chief constraints on growth in developing countries. The World Bank over time came to augment the savings gap in developing countries, whereas the IMF provided emergency balance-of-payment (BOP) support, since developing countries were always hard currency constrained and, therefore, vulnerable to external shocks. The economies and, macroeconomic, frameworks of developing countries were also considered to be more unstable. Both the IMF and World Bank, therefore, provided technical advice, and also linked their assistance to policy reforms. The IMF also had a surveillance role to anticipate and forestall external shocks and crises.

However, the last two decades have transformed the global economic landscape and thrown up a number of macroeconomic anomalies as a result of which both the World Bank and IMF were beginning to lose their relevance.

Rise of Big EMEs

First, over the last few decades some Emerging Market Economies (EMEs), mostly small economies, started growing at rates much faster than OECD countries on a sustained basis, even as OECD growth rates began to decline. Over the last couple of decades the really big economies—Brazil, Russia, India, and China (BRIC)—also increased their trend growth to levels significantly above OECD rates. Consequently, the relative share of EMEs in global GDP, which had been declining ever since the Industrial Revolution, started increasing rapidly. The changing economic weights in the global economy are best captured in GDP (gross domestic product) on PPP (purchasing power parity) basis rather than in

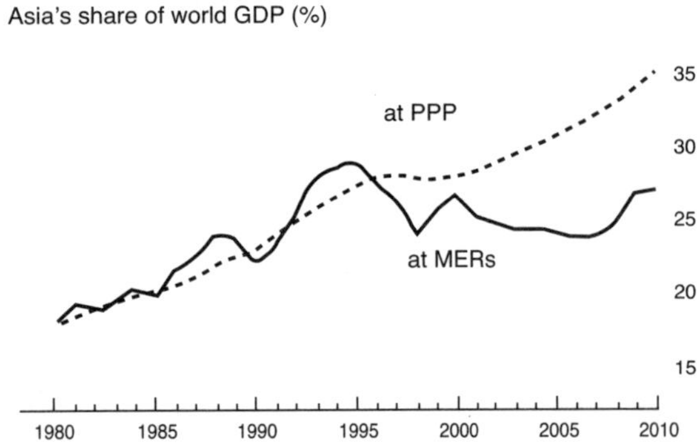

Figure 1 Asia's Share of Global GDP

Source: *The Economist*, 27 February–5 March 2010, p. 71.

terms of market exchange rates (MER). While both GDP MER and PPP captured the changing economic weights, reflected in growth differentials, in the global economy right up to the time of the East Asian Crisis, volatilities in MERs and consequential accumulation of hard currency reserves following the crisis makes the GDP PPP measure the appropriate measure to capture the continuing shifts in economic gravity. This emerges very clearly from Figure 1. While GDP is a flow measure and reserves are a stock measure, the difference in valuation between PPP and MER would be substantially made good if the accumulated stock of foreign exchange reserves are taken into consideration.

By 2007 the share of BRIC countries in global GDP slightly exceeded that of the US in terms of PPP. Both Goldman Sachs (2003) and PricewaterhouseCoopers (Hawkson and Cookson 2007) have projected that at current differential rates of growth, both the Chinese and Indian economies would soon rival the US economy in aggregate GDP at PPP (although the gap in per capita GDP would remain significant in the foreseeable future). The current crisis may have advanced the parity point by several years. Their contribution to global growth is even larger. BRIC accounted for 43 per cent of global growth at PPP in 2008. In 2009, their contribution was 372 per cent, which meant that their growth substantially compensated for the decline that occurred elsewhere. Be it as it may, what the international financial crisis has brought out in strong relief, manifest in the leading role the G-20 is playing in formulating a coordinated global response, is that the participation of these new systemically important economies is essential to manage an open, globalized economy, and that their role in global economic governance needs to be enhanced.

Second, developing countries started running huge current account surpluses and became net savers, exporting rather than importing capital. This was reflected in their huge reserve build-ups. Even some developing countries, like India, that retained a domestic savings gap (admittedly a modest one in the case of India) built up large foreign currency reserves that cushioned them against sudden capital stops/external shocks. It is a moot point whether this reserve build-up was the result of a conscious insurance mechanism based on experience gained during the East Asian Crisis, or the by-product of an export-led model based on holding down exchange rates in what is sometimes described as 'Bretton Woods II'. There is a widely held view that it was this 'imbalance', or net export of capital from developing countries that ramped up leveraged consumption in developed countries, which: (i) sustained high growth rates based on external demand in several developing countries and (ii) lowered the cost of capital and led to many of the financial excesses leading up to the global financial meltdown. The recent crisis has changed the prevailing view that IMF lending was solely for developing countries. Post-crisis the largest borrowers from the Fund are in developed countries, including those in the Euro area, a measure of how the world has changed.

The outcome of these developments was that IMF started running out of clients, and World Bank lending started shrinking in relative terms. The decline in IMF lending was more of a demand-side problem, as private capital flows plugged whatever foreign currency gaps several developing countries had, except in those conflict-ridden/failed states from where private capital shied away. In the case of the World Bank, however, it was more of a supply-side issue. India has always had, and continues to have, a huge pipeline of infrastructure projects which World Bank lending has been unable to saturate.

MFIs and the Global Financial Crisis

The response to the recent global crisis under the aegis of the G-20 expanded the roles of the World Bank, particularly that of IMF. World Bank lending was expected to expand to plug the investment gap left by the withdrawal of private capital, while IMF was expected to increase its war chest to address BOP crises caused by the flight of foreign capital.

As things turned out, while IMF's resources were trebled to address external shocks more effectively, the permanent increase in World Bank resources was modest. There were perhaps two reasons for this. First, the traditional donors and majority shareholders were in a fiscal crisis as a fall-out of the global financial crisis. Second, the major recipients of international assistance, such as China and India, were on a fast growing trajectory. It appears that the World Bank is being repositioned to provide assistance to smaller and poorer developing countries. Therefore, while India will continue to remain one of the biggest borrowers from multilateral development banks in the foreseeable future by virtue of its size, its developmental needs, and low per capita income, these institutions are unlikely to significantly contribute to the country's resource mobilization efforts. This could change, however, if multilateral development banks are substantially recapitalized to enable them to intermediate global savings for infrastructure investment in fast-growing emerging markets on a large scale. India's bilateral cooperation with OECD countries, meanwhile, has also shifted from aid to investment.

On the IMF side, however, the position is quite different. India has built up huge foreign currency reserves which cushioned it from the twin shocks of a sharp increase in the current account deficit and reversal in capital flows during the recent crisis. The magnitude of the external shock was perhaps greater than in the early 1990s which led to a major BOP crisis. Over the longer term, capital flows into India are expected to fully finance its current account deficits, while its sizeable reserves would insulate it from periodic sudden stops. Given India's long-term growth prospects, she may expect to continue being a major recipient of capital inflows. India is, therefore, more likely to be a contributor to IMF's resources in the future through its substantial reserves rather than a borrower. India contributed about $14 billion dollars to the recent increase in IMF's resources.

EMEs and Global Governance

It was becoming abundantly clear even prior to the recent crisis that growing trade and investment linkages were blunting time-tested macroeconomic policy tools through spillover effects; that globalization needed new and appropriate policy tools, institutional structures, and coordinated action for its effective management; and that the bigger, fast-growing EMEs needed to be given a greater voice in global economic governance. Outside the European Union (EU), policy coordination was limited to informal consultations amongst the G-7, comprising a small club of major developed countries, and the OECD, which accounted for a major share of global GDP. While The World Trade Organization (WTO) and Multilateral Investment Guarantee Agency (MIGA) coordinated trade and investment policies, including binding legal commitments, international financial institutions like the IMF and the World Bank, and global standards setting bodies, like the Financial Stability Forum, the Basel Committee on Banking Supervision, the International Audit Standards Board, and International Organization of Securities Commission (IOSCO), were exclusive clubs of G-8/OECD countries that set their agenda.

The G-8 nevertheless felt the need to invite the big emerging countries to their summits as special invitees through what came to be known as the 'Heiligendamm process'. This initiative that sought to institutionalize a high-level dialogue between the G-8 and the five most important emerging economies known as the O-5 (Outreach-5)—China, Mexico, India, Brazil, and South Africa. Following the institutionalization of the G-20 at the summit level this process has become defunct. Separately, BRIC also started meeting at the summit level to coordinate policies and emerged as a sort of counter to the G-8. This acronym for Brazil, Russia, India, and China (BRIC) was originally devised by the investment bank Goldman Sachs to describe the block of large developing economies with the greatest potential. Since 2009, BRIC has been meeting annually at the summit level. In 2011, BRIC was enlarged to BRICS with the inclusion of South Africa.

The global financial crisis has put the rise of major developing countries in sharper relief. They were less affected by the crisis, and have returned to former levels of high trend growth, even as recovery in OECD countries is weak and fraught with serious downside risks. Their fiscal and monetary frameworks are under pressure, even as the frameworks in major developing countries have held up well. The global financial crisis has, therefore, underscored the need to associate major developing countries in global economic governance on an equal footing.

Rise of the G-20

This transnational consultative process is spearheaded by the G-20, comprising systemically important developed and developing economies on an equal footing, and representing over 80 per cent of global income, trade (including intra-EU trade), investment flows, greenhouse emissions, and population. Its decisions, therefore, have the potential to influence global outcomes. Set up as a multilateral finance ministers' forum during the East Asian Crisis, it is only over the last few years, in the wake of the recent global financial crisis, that it has started becoming abundantly clear that the G-20, or a similar inclusive group, was likely to emerge as the premier forum of international economic dialogue, policy coordination, and decision making even beyond the crisis. A formal declaration to that effect was made at the third G-20 summit in Pittsburgh, USA, in 2009. G-20 leaders will now meet each year at the summit level. The bigger EMEs have now become too systemically important to be excluded from any meaningful or effective international economic consultative process to manage globalization. India is one of the bigger economies within the G-20.

The new G-20 style of global economic governance is to take up important issues and engage in a policy dialogue through working and expert groups, with technical inputs from relevant international institutions such as IMF, the World Bank, WTO, Financial Stability Board (FSB), and OECD, who attend G-20 meetings, and arrive at a consensus. These institutions were always expected to scrutinize the policy frameworks of both developed and developing countries, but the main focus was on developing countries as the prevailing orthodoxy was that they were the sources of instability in the global economy, and on account of the governance structure of the IMF in which the majority shareholders were from developed countries, and the borrowers from developing countries. The governance structure of the G-20 is very different, as it operates through consensus rather than vote share. Such surveillance, henceforth, is likely to be more even handed, especially since the source of the recent crisis lay in developed rather than developing countries, and because developed and developing countries are equally represented. Unlike the Article IV process, which is internal to IMF, G-20 surveillance is member country led and owned by the group, with IMF providing technical inputs and advice.

G-20 Governance and Decision Making

The G-20 is a self-styled informal grouping of countries. Unlike in WTO or the UN, its policy recommendations are non-binding consensus documents that all G-20 countries commit to feed into domestic policy. This rather loose and flexible style of governance proved surprisingly effective in the matter of coordinated stimulus measures to combat the recent crisis, where the G-20 arrived at a consensus on what needed to be done collectively. Each country went back and did what was appropriate for its circumstances. While no specific country commitment was asked for, or given, this consensus fed into domestic policy, and all countries used both monetary and fiscal policies on an unprecedented scale and in a coordinated manner. In this way the G-20 may have averted a second great depression. In the matter of raising resources, where commitments are made, these are on a purely voluntary basis and according to country circumstances as interpreted by each country, and through moral suasion.

Coordination beyond this, to addressing long-standing structural problems in the global economy, is more challenging, and may seem too ambitious presently for countries may find it difficult to give forward-looking policy commitments. They would first need to navigate domestic legislative processes and independent regulators, including central banks and judicial authorities, over which governments have little control. Countries can only commit to what has already been successfully navigated through these processes. Seeking firm, forward-looking commitments, or pointed criticism of policy frameworks of other countries on the lines of the EU, or even the OECD style of functioning, may be difficult and divisive at this stage. In this sense, the G-20, and the full welfare benefits of globalization are still hostage to sovereignty associated with the Westphalian notion of the nation-state, even as globalization is fast undercutting its economic rationale. That political integration lags far behind economic integration is painfully apparent even in the EU, which has travelled farthest in the direction of policy coordination, where the lag in fiscal integration, one of the last major symbols of sovereignty, threatens the integrity of monetary integration.

While a more ambitious style of global governance will take some time to take shape, the G-20 is a major advance from the time when there was little communication, and much acrimony, between the G-8 and the G-77. At this stage the issue really is monitoring and assessing whether the general direction of G-20 member country policies is heading in a mutually consistent and agreed fashion over the medium to long term, and how the G-20 processes can help countries navigate their domestic legislative, regulatory, and judicial processes such that mutually agreed policies are adopted. It is important to bear in mind that commitments in the G-20 are broad and do not constitute legally binding treaties.

Major governance reforms in international financial and regulatory bodies, such as the World Bank, IMF, and the FSB, are being made to accommodate major fast-growing developing countries. However, until these countries are adequately accommodated in important institutions of global governance in a manner resembling the G-20 it is difficult to see G-20 countries developing the level of mutual trust that would allow them to cede sovereign space on the lines of the EU, or even the OECD. The Bretton Wood twins reflect the economic reality prevailing at the end of the Second World War and major governance issues need to be sorted out if they are to regain global pre-eminence. The voice and participation reforms in the World Bank and IMF recently done under the aegis of the G-20 are relatively too modest to induce major developing countries to assume equal responsibility for global outcomes. There is presently some concern that the expanding agenda in the G-20 mostly reflects the concerns and perspectives of developed countries; and that negotiations that are stalled in more inclusive and legally binding bodies such as WTO and UN organizations are double tracked in the G-20.

Beyond the Washington Consensus

To carry its global reform agenda forward, the G-20 has tasked international financial, regulatory, and code-setting bodies to formulate appropriate best practices in their respective areas; it has also initiated a mutual assessment process to make global growth more balanced, sustainable, and strong in going forward and also to prevent similar crises in future. This growing G-20 macroeconomic policy and regulatory consensus, which incorporates the perspective of major developing countries, is recasting the old and largely G-8 centric Washington Consensus reflected in the documentation of the IMF, World Bank, and the OECD.

What this new consensus will be remains to be seen. Through its various working groups, workstreams, and communiqués the G-20 is slowly but surely developing an OECD-like 'acquis' that reflects the current consensus amongst major developed and developing countries on critical global economic issues. The G-20 has to a great extent delivered on its promises on the crisis resources front and, through international code-setting bodies like the FSB and the Basel Committee on Banking Supervision (BCBS), is contributing substantially to arriving at a consensus on revamping financial sector regulations. It is less clear how much of this would be eventually implemented, since nothing is legally binding, and there is no global super-regulator. Financial sector regulation will be nationally legislated and implemented for the foreseeable future. Likewise, both monetary and fiscal policies are crafted and implemented nationally even though global consensus and coordination on their general direction is being attempted through the G-20. The third G-20 leaders' summit at Pittsburgh also put in place a peer review of macroeconomic frameworks of their economies to abate global imbalances and to raise and sustain global growth. It is, however, still to be seen how effective the peer review process would be.

The credibility and future of the G-20 grouping now seems to rest substantially on the perception of its ability to deliver on its own ambitious and rapidly expanding agenda that, encouraged by its success in delivering in crisis situations, may presently be racing ahead of the nation-state. The G-20 leaders' declarations and working group recommendations are consensus documents, the products of long, hard-nosed negotiations, whose careful choice of words and constructive ambiguities frequently mask underlying stresses and geopolitical undercurrents. As a result, the G-20 track record on reaching agreements was good, even as its track record in implementing what was agreed on was not. There are clearly divided developed and developing country perspectives on reforms of the Bretton Woods institutions, especially between the Europeans and the bigger EMEs. There are also nuanced differences between the Anglo-Saxon model of a relatively lightly regulated market capitalism with low tax rates, and the more Statist, tightly regulated social capitalism based on automatic stabilizers and higher tax rates that has led to differing perceptions on discretionary fiscal stimulus and the extent of regulatory reforms required. The regulatory reforms' priorities in developed countries are pitted against the developmental priorities in developing countries. Most important, there is the tension between the United States and China on the issue of global imbalances, exchange rates, and the global reserve currency. These differences need to be harmonized for the G-20 to emerge as the new institutional structure to coordinate macroeconomic policies, address structural

Table 1 The G-20

G-20 country	Gross domestic product PPP* 2010 (%Share)	Rank	MER** 2010 (%Share)	Rank
EU	20.43	1	25.88	1
USA	19.74	2	23.30	2
China	13.58	3	9.34	3
Japan	5.80	4	8.68	4
India	5.47	5	2.44	11
Germany	3.96	6	5.27	5
Russia	2.99	7	2.33	12
UK	2.93	8	3.57	7
Brazil	2.92	9	3.32	8
France	2.89	10	4.11	6
Italy	2.39	11	3.27	9
Mexico	2.11	12	1.65	14
Korea	1.96	13	1.60	15
Canada	1.79	14	2.50	10
Indonesia	1.39	15	1.12	17
Turkey	1.29	16	1.18	16
Australia	1.19	17	1.96	13
Argentina	0.87	18	0.59	19
Saudi Arabia	0.84	19	0.71	18
South Africa	0.71	20	0.57	20

Source: IMF (2011).
Note: * Purchasing Power Parity; **Market Exchange Rate.

problems in the global economy, and collectively assume responsibility for global outcomes.

ALOK SHEEL

References

Goldman Sachs. 2003. 'Dreaming with BRICs: The Path to 2050', Global Economics Paper No. 99.

Hawkson, John and Gordon Cookson. 2007. *The World in 2050. Beyond the BRICS: A Broader Look at Emerging Market Growth Prospects*, PricewaterhouseCoopers.

International Monetary Fund. 2011. World Economic Outlook Data Bank, IMF, April.

■ Indira Gandhi

Indira Gandhi was born in Allahabad on 19 November 1917. She became the third Prime Minister of independent India, 48 years later, on 19 January 1966. By then, she was a well-known figure on the Indian political scene. She had been a minister (holding the portfolio of Information and Broadcasting) in her predecessor Lal Bahadur Shastri's cabinet from June 1964 to January 1966. Prior to that, in 1959, she had been elected President of the ruling Congress Party. However, a much more important political consideration among the leaders of the party in electing her Prime Minister was her popularity in the country as the daughter and companion of her father Jawaharlal Nehru, the first Prime Minister of independent India. Nehru was an iconic figure, who was universally admired for his leadership during India's long freedom struggle against colonial rule in close association with Mahatma Gandhi.

Indira Gandhi was Prime Minister for as many as 16 years in two spells—from 19 January 1966 to 23 March 1977, and from 14 January 1980 until her death on 31 October 1984. Both politically and economically, the 16 years of her rule were probably the most eventful years in India's post-Independence history. Politically, the pre-eminent political party, the Congress, split in 1969 as a result of internal differences. India was faced with severe crises in several states, particularly Kashmir, Punjab, Assam, and Kerala. Border tensions with Pakistan had also become intense particularly during the Bangladesh war of independence in 1971. Relations with the United States had deteriorated sharply after the war with Pakistan in 1965. As a punitive measure, the US had decided to suspend aid to India during one of the worst droughts and balance-of-payments crises in the mid-1960s.

Worst of all, Mrs Gandhi decided to promulgate, by Ordinance, an internal Emergency in June 1975 without adequate cause and without any prior consultations with the ruling party or Parliament. The Emergency deprived Indians of all their fundamental freedoms. Press censorship was imposed, the Constitution was amended to make the government and its leaders unaccountable for their actions, and political leaders in opposition were put behind bars. Fortunately for India and its people, the Emergency ended in 1977 after fresh national elections were announced. In March 1977, the ruling Congress Party was decisively defeated as a result of public anger against the excesses of the Emergency. The new government that came into power in 1977, however, did not last long because of internal dissensions. Mrs Gandhi became Prime Minister again after elections in January 1980.

From an economic policy point of view, the two periods of Indira Gandhi's rule (that is 1966–77 and 1980–4) were vastly different. The first period was perhaps the darkest in India's history. In addition to repeated droughts in the mid-1960s, India was also trapped in severe and prolonged balance-of-payments crises. It did not have sufficient access to external and other capital flows due to suspension of US assistance and the impact of the US decision on other bilateral and multilateral donors. In order to cope with the extremely difficult economic situation, the wide-ranging government controls on the economy were further intensified and expanded to banking, insurance, real estate, and several other sectors. One of the most significant steps, which was taken at the initiative of the Prime Minister despite the opposition of the then Finance Minister Morarji Desai, was the nationalization of 14 commercial banks by an ordinance. This move set the pace for further expansion of government ownership in the economy through takeover of weak or sick private-sector units and nationalization in strategic areas, including wholesale trade in food grains (which had to be reversed after only a few days). Import, export, production, and investment controls became all pervasive. Even the most inconsequential economic activity required specific government approval.

The economic consequences of expansion and intensification of government controls were far-reaching. The annual growth rate during the first period of Mrs Gandhi's regime was less than 3 per cent and population growth was more than 2 per cent. As a result, there was very little growth in per capita incomes. The pace of industrialization plummeted and balance-of-payments crisis became even more severe. The rate of growth in industrial output was virtually half of the growth rate of

8 per cent registered during the previous 15 years (1950–65). One bright spot in the economy was agriculture. Due to the efforts of India's agricultural research institutes and excellent leadership in the scientific field, the Green Revolution had become a reality and there was substantial increase in yields.

The second period of Indira Gandhi's Prime Ministership (1980–4) was, however, remarkably different and progressive (compared to the earlier period). Controls on industrial production and investment in industry were loosened; the import licensing system was liberalized; the rigidity of price and distribution controls was reduced, and tax rates on personal and corporate incomes were lowered. The economic effects of these liberalization measures were highly positive. The growth rate of the economy increased to about 6 per cent per annum. Growth of industrial production also accelerated and was more than 7 per cent during the 1980s.

After the severe oil crisis of 1979, India was able to access a structural adjustment loan of $5 billion from the International Monetary Fund (IMF). This was an unusually high figure of IMF credit for that time and enabled India to achieve relative viability in its external accounts. In fact, progress in this direction was faster than envisaged (partly because of oil discovery at Bombay High), and India was able to terminate the IMF credit without utilizing the full amount.

An interesting question to ponder is: why were Indira Gandhi's economic policies so different in the second period of her Prime Ministership as compared to the first? As of now, there is no firm verdict by professional historians or her biographers. It seems to me that the answer is to be found in the very different political situations and ideologies prevailing in the country during the two periods, and India Gandhi's own personal political position. She was not the unanimous choice of her party when she first became Prime Minister in 1966. In fact, she was supposed to be inexperienced and weak, and got elected as Prime Minister due to the backing of the so-called 'syndicate' consisting of a few important leaders of her party. They were suspicious of her opponent Morarji Desai, who was an established political figure with strong views.

Unfortunately, soon after she became Prime Minister, she also had to approve the proposal to devalue the rupee by 57.5 per cent against the dollar in view of the prevailing payments crisis and pressure of international financial institutions. The devaluation of the rupee was a highly unpopular measure within her party, the media, opposition parties, and among people in general. The devaluation also did not result in any substantial increase in aid which was expected. As a result, Indira Gandhi's political position and popularity were at their lowest during the first year of her Prime Ministership. To overcome this, with the backing of some leftist ministers in her cabinet and personal advisers, she decided to embark on a 'socialist' and interventionist economic programme, including the nationalization of insurance and banks. This programme, despite its unfavourable economic consequences, was politically highly popular. By the end of 1969, she was able to split the Congress Party and emerge as the undisputed leader of her section of the party with a majority in Parliament.

In 1980, when she became Prime Minister for the second time, she was a much-chastened person, but also a very confident one. She was rudely shaken by her defeat in 1977 after the Emergency. However, in view of serious internal differences within the Janata Dal government which succeeded her and several short-sighted steps taken by them (including putting her in jail), she soon regained the lost political ground. She came back to power with a resounding electoral victory, and there was practically no credible political opposition to her leadership either within her party or outside. India's poor economic record, as compared to its East Asian neighbours and Japan, had led to the emergence of a different development paradigm than that of the 1960s or the 1970s. There was also a change in the economic orientation of her personal advisors. The most important was the entry into politics of her son, Rajiv Gandhi. Rajiv was young. He was generally in favour of liberalization of the economy with export orientation. In 1981, she appointed a new Finance Minister, Pranab Mukherjee, who was not politically very powerful, but enjoyed her trust.

Soon after she had come back to power in 1980, the political situation in the north-east and Punjab had become very tense, and there was widespread discontent with the functioning of government in Kashmir. These political problems occupied much of her time, and she largely left the task of economic policy formulation to her ministers and the new set of advisors. The Left parties, particularly the Communist Party of India (Marxist), were strongly opposed to liberalization and the loan from the IMF. However, by and large, there was considerable public support for a more liberal economic policy in view of India's poor record as compared to some other developing countries. Against this background, Indira Gandhi decided to go along with the economic advice rendered by her advisors to loosen controls and encourage investment in order to accelerate industrial growth.

Politics was the primary driver of Indira Gandhi's economics. To understand the economics of her time, as also the impact of her policies on India's development, it is necessary to pay attention to the conflicting pulls and pressures at different points of time in India's political evolution.

BIMAL JALAN

References

Frank, Katherin. 2002. *Indira—The Life of Indira Nehru Gandhi*, London, HarperCollins.
Butler, Francelia. 1986. *Indira Gandhi*, Chelsea House.
Gandhi, Indira. 1980. *My Truth*, Grover Press.
Rodrik, Dani and Arvind Subramanian. 2004. 'From Hindu Growth to Productivity Surge', NBER Working Paper No. 10376.

■ Mahatma Gandhi

Mohandas Karamchand Gandhi, or Mahatma Gandhi, as he is generally known, was born on 2 October 1869 at Porbandar in western India. He studied law at the University of London. After a brief and unsuccessful stint as a lawyer in India, in 1893 he left for Natal, South Africa, as a lawyer for a business firm. There he acquired political prominence by organizing the Indians against racially discriminatory South African laws. He returned to India from South Africa in 1915. Soon he plunged himself in the Indian struggle for freedom from British rule and became the leading figure in the non-violent Indian resistance to British rule in India, which finally resulted in India's freedom in 1947. He was assassinated on 30 January 1948.

Though Gandhi was influenced by the writings of Ruskin, Tolstoy, and Thoreau, his economic and social thinking was primarily based on his extensive and close observation of the life of the masses in India. He wrote widely on numerous economic problems in India. Here I highlight a few salient features of his economic thinking.

Machines and labour: Gandhi believed that the traditional village crafts, rather than modern machines and industrialization, constituted the solution for the widespread poverty, unemployment, and disguised unemployment in rural India. While he advocated a range of products that can be produced in villages, including hand-ground flour, hand-pressed oil, *gur* (jaggery), and leather, the central place in his plan for village industries was reserved for hand spinning and weaving. He believed that *charkha* (the spinning wheel) and *khaddar* (hand-spun and hand-woven cloth) could provide supplementary income to millions of people and restore their dignity by giving them gainful employment. His persistent emphasis on the charkha and khaddar and his strongly expressed reservations about machines often led some sections of the intelligentsia to believe that he was making a cult of the charkha. It is true that Gandhi never missed an opportunity to stress the importance of charkha and khaddar and that some of Gandhi's writings about industrialization and cities remind one of Tolstoy's idealization of peasant life. It should not, however, be forgotten that many of Gandhi's views about village crafts including khaddar were based, at least partly, on his pragmatic conviction that labour-intensive village industries, especially khaddar, constituted the best method of providing productive employment to a huge rural population unemployed for a large part of the year. In a famous response to Rabindranath Tagore's reservations about Gandhi's overwhelming emphasis on khaddar, Gandhi wrote, 'Machinery has its place; it has come to stay. But it must not be allowed to displace the necessary human labour' (Gandhi 1925: 425–30). He elaborated his position: 'Mechanization is good when the hands are too few for the work intended to be accomplished. It is an evil when there are more hands than required for the work, as is the case in India' (Gandhi 1934: 355–7).

Conception of economic development: Gandhi's view of economic development went much further than the generation of employment and income for the poor in India. Long before the conception of people's living standards in terms of 'real' indicators, such as nutritional intake, education, and health, came to be widely used by social scientists, Gandhi thought of economic development in rural India in these terms rather than in terms only of income. He was, therefore, deeply concerned about diet, education, and hygiene in villages and often recommended dietary and hygienic practices in surprisingly minute detail.

Trade: Gandhi's views about domestic and foreign trade tended to be influenced by his vision of villages as more or less self-sufficient economic units. For example, with respect to *khadi*, the ideal was that 'just enough *khadi* for local requirement should be produced in each village' (see Tendulkar 1962: 306). Gandhi would allow for some departure from this ideal by letting excess supply of khadi in one area to be diverted to meet the excess demand in another area, but he would not like such trade to take place beyond a district or 'province at the utmost' (ibid.). Regarding foreign trade, he often tended to be protectionist. In the specific case of cloth, he declared that, if he had the power to do so, he would resort to import duties to stop the import of foreign cloth into India (see Tendulkar 1961: 198). He wanted to mobilize opinion against 'immoral' competition and wanted competition to be 'fair'. However, he did not quite spell out his notion of 'unfair' competition. In fact, sometimes he seemed to think that the inability of a domestic industry to withstand foreign competition could be, in itself, a justification for protecting the industry. For example, while discussing the need for supporting village industries, Gandhi (1934a: 293–4) wrote that if the textile or sugar or rice mills in India were in danger of becoming extinct because of foreign competition, then they would deserve support, but they did not actually need such support since they were doing well despite foreign competition. The underlying suggestion seems to be that the inability of a domestic industry to face foreign competition is, by itself, adequate justification for protecting it. It may be worth noting that, when on 1 April 1938 the Working Committee of the Indian National Congress passed a resolution, which was notably suspicious of foreign capital and which laid down guidelines (see Ganguli 1973: 263) to determine when foreign capital should be allowed to operate in India, Gandhi approved it.

Capitalism and workers: Gandhi's attitude towards capitalism and capitalists was ambivalent. On the one hand, he blamed capitalism for the change in the economic life of India, which, he felt, had shifted the focus from the village to the city and had 'virtually ... converted' the village into 'a slum'. On the other hand, he also called upon Indian capitalists to take charge of the industrial development of India as 'trustees and servants' of the poor. The apparent inconsistency is explained when one notes Gandhi's belief that the capitalist could be taught and transformed so that he would consider himself to be a trustee of the society and would use his capital and intelligence for the benefit of society.[1] Gandhi preferred a system where capitalists acted as trustees of society to direct state ownership of industries because he shared with Tolstoy and Thoreau a distrust of the state. At the same time, he was realistic enough to see that capitalists might not be willing to work as trustees of society. In that case, he felt, the state would have to confiscate their possessions 'with the minimum exercise of violence'. In some of his writings, Gandhi advocated the use of heavy income tax and death duties to reduce inequalities in the distribution of income and wealth.

Gandhi was in favour of ensuring a living wage for workers. In the specific case of spinning, he urged that a living wage be paid to spinners even if that increased the price of khadi and reduced its demand. Gandhi felt that industrial workers in India were unorganized and this put them at a disadvantage vis-à-vis employers. He urged the unionization of industrial workers but was firmly against violent or coercive action by unionized workers. He felt that if industrial workers could unite and work towards settling disputes in a non-violent fashion, their power would be much more than that of the employers. In the case of strikes by workers, the employers should give the workers what informed public opinion considered just. Gandhi was a firm believer in arbitration as a method for resolving disputes between employers and workers.

As may be seen from the brief account given here, Gandhi's thoughts on economic issues did not constitute an integrated system. His thinking evolved over a long period, often in response to specific situations. It is not, therefore, difficult to find in his writings, strands that are not entirely consistent with each other. Also, some of his thinking, such as his conception of the role of capitalists as trustees of society, may be considered utopian by many people. However, the depth of his insight into the economic realities of rural India in his time is undeniable and many of his ideas for economic development in villages seem to be relevant even now.

PRASANTA K. PATTANAIK

References

Gandhi, M.K. 1925. 'The Poet and the Charkha', *Young India*, 5 November; reproduced in *The Collected Works of Mahatma Gandhi*, Vol. 28, Delhi, Publications Division, Ministry of Information and Broadcasting, Government of India, 1968.

——. 1934. 'Village industries', *Harijan*, 16 November; reproduced in *The Collected Works of Mahatma Gandhi*, Vol. 59, New Delhi, Publications Division, Ministry of Information and Broadcasting, Government of India, 1974.

——. 1934a. 'Swadeshi', *Harijan*, 10 August; reproduced in *The Collected Works of Mahatma Gandhi*, Vol. 58, New Delhi, Publications Division, Ministry of Information and Broadcasting, Government of India, 1974.

Ganguli, B.N. 1973. *Gandhi's Social Philosophy: Perspective and Relevance*, Delhi, Vikas.

Tendulkar, D.G. 1961. *Mahatma*, Vol. 2, revised edition, New Delhi, Publications Division, Ministry of Information and Broadcasting, Government of India.

——. 1962. *Mahatma*, Vol. 6, revised edition, New Delhi, Publications Division, Ministry of Information and Broadcasting, Government of India.

[1]For an illuminating discussion of Gandhi's ambivalent attitude towards capitalists and his 'trusteeship theory', see Ganguli (1973: chs XII and XIII).

Gender and Empowerment

There is no doubt that power differs by gender. Men have greater ability to make decisions that impinge on one's well-being and that of others than women even in the developed countries. It is much more so in developing countries, and certainly so in India. By gender empowerment, in this entry, I mean the facilitation of greater autonomy for women, so that they will have more say in matters important to them. Since the household is the primary institution within which the autonomy of women is weak (relative to men's), the primary focus here will be on empowering women within the household.

Economists' approach to autonomy is through bargaining models. In these models, it is presumed that women's ability to dictate decisions depends on the bargaining power they wield within households vis-à-vis husbands and their husbands' families (because, when they marry, women leave their natal families and live with their husbands' families). But how is this bargaining power determined?

One of the most widely used frameworks to analyse this is the Nash bargaining model. Consider this model as applied to a husband and wife couple. It is assumed that each wants to maximize her/his own well-being, but with the recognition that they need to cooperate to achieve this. Furthermore, assume that they make decisions in such a way that there is no wastage of resources. In other words, for a given level of well-being achieved by the husband, say, that achieved by the wife is the maximum possible, and vice versa. The fact that they behave in a cooperative manner by no means implies, however, that they achieve roughly identical levels of well-being. It is quite possible—as may well be the case in India—that men typically enjoy a larger share of the benefits to cooperation within the household. What determines how these benefits are shared between the couple?

The Nash bargaining model demonstrates that the crucial determinant is the level of well-being that the wife and the husband can assure themselves of in the event that cooperation between them breaks down. This scenario is referred to as the 'threat outcome'. The member who is better off in the threat outcome can assure himself or herself of a greater share of the benefits to cooperating. The person who has less to lose in the event of a breakdown of cooperation gets a better deal in the (cooperative) bargaining outcome.

Women in India lack autonomy, then, because their bargaining power within the household is undermined by potentially poor threat outcomes for them. What is this threat outcome defined by? One extreme scenario that is perhaps not as relevant for India (especially in rural areas) is divorce. A more appropriate threat outcome is that in which the couple remain married but do not cooperate in making decisions. The wife's threat well-being will be determined by how well off she is in this (non-cooperative) outcome. This is the nub of the issue of female empowerment: What would a woman's level of well-being be if the couple abandoned the attempt to make decisions cooperatively and behaved non-cooperatively?

There can be many factors that impinge on the threat level of well-being of women. In a landmark paper, Dyson and Moore (1983) drew attention to the fact that many demographic statistics (like sex ratios and infant mortality) were worse in the northern Indian states than in the southern ones. They claimed that this was because women in the northern states had less autonomy than their southern counterparts. Among the reasons they offered, differences in kinship relationships and various cultural practices were deemed important. In the north, marriages tend to be exogamous (that is spouses reside outside the village) and to individuals who are unrelated by blood. In the south, marriages are less exogamous and marriages between some types of blood relatives (such as uncles and nieces) are not taboo. These differences mean that, upon marriage, women in the north move into an alien family in a different village. This would be expected—in the context of the Nash bargaining model—to undermine their threat level of well-being, because their entire support group is lost when they move into their in-laws' home. In the south, in contrast, women do not necessarily have to leave their native village and they do not necessarily marry into an unknown family. As a result, their support group would be still available to them after marriage and their threat options would be better than for their northern counterparts.

Rahman and Rao (1994) recently subjected the Dyson–Moore hypothesis to a test by comparing the autonomy of women in the northern Indian state of Uttar Pradesh and women in the southern Indian state of Karnataka. Their results do not confirm some aspects of the Dyson–Moore hypothesis. First, exogamy was practised as much in the southern state as in the northern. Exogamy did not seem to restrict the free mobility of women, whereas the Dyson–Moore hypothesis would suggest that it should (by reducing women's autonomy). The practices of *purdah* and *ghunghat*, however, are indicators of weaker female autonomy as the Dyson–Moore hypothesis would suggest. Rahman and Rao also find that marriage between relatives (uncles–nieces or cross-cousins) does not necessarily increase women's autonomy, possibly because it perpetuates existing hierarchies. It appears that women in Uttar Pradesh exert control over different spheres (for example, household expenditures) than do women in Karnataka (for example, fertility and children's health and education). Rahman and Rao find that women in villages with higher female wages exhibit greater autonomy. It may well be true that culture is an important determinant of the bargaining power of women. But then so is economics.

Greater economic independence for women would lead to greater autonomy because their threat level of well-being would be higher. Economic independence can come about in broadly two ways. One is by owning assets (like land) with which women can earn an income on which they can rely in the event cooperation with their husbands breaks down. Another is by earning an income through their labour or by having the potential to earn such income if needed. Anything that enhances the (potential) income of women through either of these avenues would increase their autonomy. For example, inheritance laws that are egalitarian would go some distance in this direction by providing asset income to women. Greater education that improves women's access to gainful employment would do the same.

The work of Basu (2006), however, cautions us that the causality may not merely go from earnings to autonomy but also operate in the reverse direction. A husband who currently has greater bargaining power than his wife, in the anticipation that her earnings would increase her bargaining power, may exercise this power to prevent his wife from gaining employment. The exercise of current bargaining power by one member of the couple may thwart the economic activities of the other that would increase her autonomy.

If governments are to empower women, it is important to know whether labour income would increase their autonomy by more than would unearned (asset) income or vice versa. At first glance, it might appear that asset income would be the more efficacious route. This is because asset income does not come at the expense of current leisure, whereas earned income does. This would suggest that a given increase in unearned income would increase a woman's threat well-being by more than would the same increase in earned income. However, as argued in Anderson and Eswaran (2005), this is not necessarily so. While both earned and unearned incomes would very likely make women better-off, there is an asymmetry in the manner in which they impinge on the threat well-being of their spouses. Earning an independent income commits a woman's time outside the house. So, if the couple's cooperative behaviour were to break down, this diversion of time to outside work would curtail the amount of housework she could do. Since household services are a public good that both husband and wife consume, the effect would be to *reduce* the husband's threat well-being. So, although a woman's earned income comes at the expense of her leisure, it may actually provide her with greater bargaining power than unearned income in the cooperative endeavour by adversely affecting the husband's well-being in the non-cooperative outcome.

Anderson and Eswaran (2005) provide empirical evidence for this contention using data from the Matlab area of Bangladesh. In these data, the effect of earned income on a woman's decision-making power appears to be of a greater magnitude than that of unearned income.[1] Although in South Asia income earned by a wife may be handed over in large part to her husband, there is nevertheless greater scope for her to control and possess income when she actually earns it. It is this that seems essential to empowering women. Kantor (2003) arrives at a similar conclusion by using data on women in the textile sector of Ahmedabad.

Greater empowerment of women in India would not only improve their well-being but it would also be what a social planner would deem appropriate if he/she gives equal weightage to the well-being of all individuals in society. In patriarchal societies, men have greater say in household decisions but women often end up bearing a greater share of the costs associated with these decisions. Fertility decisions are an example of this. Whenever the people making the decisions are not bearing a commensurate share of the costs, the decisions are suboptimal from society's point of view. Both women and society would be better served if couples had fewer children. The decline in fertility in India would be one of the major developmental benefits of empowering women.

It is important, however, to note that empowerment cannot be divorced from the cultural context of a society. The cultural environment may be such that greater empowerment of women may occasionally have some adverse consequences in some spheres. An example of this is in the realm of fertility. When women are empowered, especially through their access to the labour market, couples would have fewer children. Now in the Indian context, it is only male children who provide old-age security to parents. It is well known that this cultural norm is responsible for discrimination against female children in terms of education, access to healthcare, nutrition, and so on. So even when couples opt to have fewer children on average, their preference for male children may remain

[1] And this is after the reverse causality pointed out by Basu (2006) has been accounted for.

intact. With lower fertility, it would become important for them to ensure that a higher proportion of surviving children are male. Consequently, their discrimination against female children may increase in relative terms. This would be particularly so for daughters of higher parity (second, third, and so on, daughters). Eswaran (2002) has formally demonstrated this possibility theoretically.

Das Gupta (1987) has provided some evidence from the district of Ludhiana in the Punjab. While the families of women with higher education levels (who may be construed to have greater autonomy) in this sample exhibited reduced child mortality rates, they also showed higher disparities between the mortality rates of female children of high order and the remaining children.[2] For the empowerment of women to have entirely benign effects in these circumstances, however, it is important that female autonomy must extend beyond the household: it must enable daughters to be of assistance to their aged parents or militate against the cultural preference for sons.

MUKESH ESWARAN

References

Anderson, S. and M. Eswaran. 2005. 'What Determines Female Autonomy: Evidence from Bangladesh', University of British Columbia, mimeo.

Basu, K. 2006. 'Gender and Say: A Model of Household Behavior with Endogenously-determined Balance of Power', *The Economic Journal*, April, 116: 558–80.

Das Gupta, M. 1987. 'Selective Discrimination against Female Children in Rural Punjab, India', *Population and Development Review*, 13: 77–100.

Das Gupta, M. and P.N. Mari Bhat. 1997. 'Fertility Decline and Increased Manifestation of Sex Bias in India', *Population Studies*, 51: 307–15.

Dyson, M. and M. Moore. 1983. 'On Kinship Structure, Female Autonomy, and Demographic Behaviour in India', *Population and Development Review*, 9: 35–60.

Eswaran, M. 2002. 'The Empowerment of Women, Fertility, and Child Mortality: Towards a Theoretical Analysis', *Journal of Population Economics*, 15: 433–54.

Kantor, P. 2003. 'Women's Empowerment through Home-based Work: Evidence from India', *Development and Change*, 34(3): 425–45.

[2]The argument is also consistent with the more recent evidence of Das Gupta and Mari Bhat (1997): in India (1981–91), the ratio of male births to female births has increased despite a reduction in fertility rates. The phenomenon of an increase in the sex ratio in favour of male children accompanying a decline in fertility is also observed in Southeast Asian countries.

Rahman, L. and V. Rao. 1994. 'The Determinants of Gender Equity in India: Examining Dyson and Moore's Thesis with New Data', *Population and Development Review*, 30: 239–68.

■ Gender Inequality

Gender inequality, compared with other forms of inequality such as class or race, has some distinct features. It dwells not only outside the home but also centrally within it. It stems not only from differences in economic endowments between women and men but also from social norms and perceptions, that is, the inequalities are ideologically embedded. While norms and perceptions also affect other inequalities like race and caste, gendered norms and perceptions cut across these categories and exist additionally. Moreover, gender inequality not only pre-exists, new forms can arise from the foundations of the old ones. For instance, those with prior advantage can formulate rules that perpetuate that advantage, such as rules governing new institutions now being promoted to manage common pool resources. These can effectively exclude significant sections, such as women, from their decision making and their benefits. In other words, gender inequality, unless specifically addressed, can be in the process of constant recreation in new dimensions.

In India, gender inequality is manifest in multiple forms, including basic survival (female adverse sex ratios); literacy and education; nutrition and healthcare (revealed especially in anthropometric indices and hospital admissions); employment (especially in the formal sector); wage rates and earnings; political participation and holding office; legal rights, especially in marriage and inheritance; and most particularly in command over property, and in social perceptions and social norms (Agarwal 1994, 1997; Drèze and Sen 2002). The geographic variability of these inequalities is also notable (Raju et al. 1999).

Some of these aspects are well studied, others remain neglected or hidden. In particular, inequality in command over property remains largely neglected, and the workings of social perceptions and norms are often hidden, albeit with visible economic outcomes. This entry focuses on these dimensions that are rather little addressed by economists. The former constitutes a significant material form of inequality, the latter a significant ideological form. Examining their interaction can illuminate the process of inequality creation, as also the means of its alleviation. The bargaining approach provides a promising analytical framework for understanding how both the material and the ideological aspects of gender inequality can be challenged, within the multiple arenas they are constituted—the family, the community, the market, and the state.

Command over Property

Inequality in command over property is one of the most important forms of persisting economic inequalities between women and men, with a critical bearing not only on women's economic well-being but also on their social and political status.

The idea of 'command' over property implies not merely rights in law, but also effective rights in practice. Equality in legal rights to own property need not guarantee equality in actual ownership. The gap between inheritance law and its practice is especially wide. Indian women legally enjoy significant inheritance rights (even if unequal to men's). In practice, only a small percentage inherit. This is especially true of immovable property such as land or a house. A 1991 survey of rural widows by development sociologist Martha Chen found that only 13 per cent of the surveyed women with landowning fathers inherited any land as daughters; and only 51 per cent of widows whose deceased husbands owned land, inherited any (calculated by Agarwal: see Agarwal 1994).

Command over property also implies effective control. Ownership alone does not guarantee control, given social and legal obstacles. Moreover, command over property relates not only to private property but also to public property. A notable gender inequality lies in men as a gender (albeit not all men as individuals) largely controlling wealth-generating public property as managers of large corporations or heads of bureaucracies. In addition, those commanding property often control the instruments through which existing property advantages get perpetuated, such as parliaments and law courts that enact and implement property laws; the mechanisms of recruitment into bodies which control property; and the institutions that shape ideas about gender, such as the media, and educational and religious bodies. Predominantly male control over these bodies can perpetuate negative ideas and assumptions about women's needs, work roles, and capabilities, which, in turn, affect women's economic outcomes.

Which form of property is important for economic and social security, however, can differ by context. In agrarian contexts, arable land has a pre-eminent position. In urban and industrialized contexts, housing and financial assets gain prominence.

In India, with its vast agrarian population, arable land is still the most valued form of property. It is wealth creating, livelihood sustaining, and status enhancing. For most rural households it provides security against poverty. Traditionally, it has been the basis of political power and social status. For many, it is linked with personal identity and rootedness. And it has a permanence that few other assets possess.

However, large-scale surveys such as the Agricultural Census and the National Sample Survey do not collect gender-disaggregated data on land or other assets. Hence no comprehensive gender-specific assessment of access to these assets is possible. But small-scale surveys and village studies are indicative: they show that few women own arable land; even fewer effectively control any. Underlying this inequality is male bias in inheritance; in government land transfers largely to male household heads under various poverty-alleviation and resettlement schemes; and in women's restricted market access to land, especially due to financial constraints.

The welfare and efficiency implications of this inequality are wide-ranging. Many million rural women depend critically on land-based livelihoods. More men than women have moved to non-farm jobs, leaving women disproportionately dependent on farming. Relative to 53 per cent of male workers, 75 per cent of female workers are in agriculture. Over 1988–94, while 29 per cent of rural male additions to the labour force in the 15+ age group were absorbed into non-agriculture, less than 1 per cent of the additional female workers were so absorbed. And the gender gap is growing, as are de facto female-headed households, estimates for which range between 20 and 35 per cent. Many of these women bear primary responsibility for farming, but are constrained by their lack of independent land rights in their ability to procure secure livelihoods, or obtain production credit and inputs.

Without their own land, rural women face high risks of poverty in case of desertion, divorce, or widowhood. Propertylessness can also reduce entitlement to kin support. Many elderly people recognize that without property children do not look after their parents well. In contrast, having land enhances the probability of getting supplementary employment and higher wages. Even a small plot can prove critical in a *diversified livelihood system*, by providing the means to grow crops, vegetables, fodder, or trees (for fruit or firewood), or to establish a micro-enterprise. The landed earn more than the landless, even in non-farm activity.

Moreover, assets in women's hands benefit the whole family. Women spend substantially more of their earnings on family needs than men. Children are found more likely to attend school and get medical care if the mother has assets, and to be better nourished where she cultivates a home garden and controls its produce. The best social indicators on health and education are found in Kerala (as also in neighbouring Sri Lanka) where many women historically enjoyed significant rights in immovable property.

Gender-equal land rights can also enhance production efficiency through better cross-farm distribution of inputs and incentive effects. On the latter, research on India is lacking but that from other countries is indicative. In Kenya, for instance, the introduction of new weeding technology raised crop yields by 56 per cent on women's plots, the output of which they controlled, but only by 15 per cent on men's plots where too women weeded but men controlled the proceeds (Elson 1995).

Land also empowers women socially, adding to their self-confidence and voice. This was graphically illustrated in the 1970s Bodhgaya movement in Bihar. When landless women in two villages received titles after an extended struggle, they movingly recounted: 'Now that we have the land, we have the strength to speak and walk.' Recent empirical work in Kerala also shows a significantly lower probability of marital violence if women own land or a house, than if they own neither (Panda and Agarwal 2005).

In private property, land and house appear key to women's economic and social security. In public property, decision-making control is critical, be it in government- or community-run institutions.

Social Perceptions

The second major source of gender inequality, largely neglected by economists, is ideological, embedded in social perceptions and norms. There is often a divergence between what a person actually contributes, needs, or is able to do, and perceptions about her contributions, needs, or abilities. In particular, women's contributions and needs are usually undervalued. In the labour market, for instance, the work women do is often labelled as 'unskilled' and that which men do as 'skilled', even if both require equal skill. Or women are perceived as having lesser ability or commitment, or as being supplementary earners and men as the breadwinners.

Such assumptions underlie many discriminatory hiring and pay practices, with women not being hired or being paid less than men with the same abilities, for the same tasks.

Perceptions also guide intra-family allocations. Home-based or unwaged work done mostly by women is less valued than work that is more 'visible' in physical or monetary terms. Women and girls also do more poorly in nutrition and healthcare, because they are perceived as contributing less ('perceived contribution response': Sen 1990) or as needing less ('perceived need response': Agarwal 1997).

Perceptions similarly hinder women's community participation. They are often excluded from community decision-making bodies, such as for forest management, because men perceive them as making little contribution, or on the grounds that they are illiterate. Since the men who support such exclusion are themselves often illiterate (Agarwal 2001), their response has rather more to do with their *perceptions* about women's abilities than with *actual* gender differences in abilities.

Public policy is likewise influenced by perceptions. For instance, that the government transfers land almost solely to men, even when women are significant farmers, has much to do with perceptions about, rather than the universal fact of, male responsibility and female dependency. Indeed perceptions underlie many assumptions in economic analysis and policy.

Social Norms

Gendered social norms, like perceptions, embody an important ideological inequality and touch virtually every activity. They define housework and childcare as mainly women's work and, in rural areas, also firewood collection and cattle care. Hence firewood or fodder shortages adversely affect women more than men. In north India, norms determine that males eat first and/or get more and better-quality food. This makes for gender differences in nourishment and growth. In most regions, social norms discourage women from asserting their property rights, by dictating, for instance, that 'good' sisters should forfeit their claims in parental property in favour of brothers.

Outside the household again, social norms restrict women's earning options by discouraging them from working outside the home, limiting the range of tasks they may perform, placing double work burdens on them, institutionalizing lower wages for them, having them relocate with husbands on marriage or job shifts, and so on. In rural north India, women of 'good character' are expected to avoid spaces where men congregate. Hence, while male farmers can sit in market spaces and strike deals with other men for hiring labour or selling crops, women farmers are socially restricted.

Social norms also affect economic outcomes by governing female behaviour. Women fish traders in parts of south India, if found haggling loudly, risk being dubbed 'masculine' and losing social status. Women attending public meetings are expected to listen rather than speak, even when livelihood or resource distribution issues that centrally affect them are discussed.

Basically gendered social perceptions and social norms embody inequalities that are largely invisible and difficult to quantify. Yet they centrally affect economic outcomes for women in multiple ways.

Emergent Inequalities: Community Forestry

Gender inequalities in property endowments, norms, and perceptions form the bedrock of pre-existing material and ideological disadvantage. And their persistence can create new inequalities, as revealed, for instance, by my recent research, based on extensive fieldwork, on community forest management (Agarwal 2001). Forests and commons are important sources of firewood, fodder, and other basic items for rural households. And since women usually lack private property resources such as land, and social norms make firewood and fodder collection mainly their responsibility, their dependence on the commons is greater than men's.

Traditionally, access to community resources such as local forests was based on village citizenship, thus mitigating,to some degree, inequalities in private property. Today, community forestry groups (CFGs), mostly falling under the state-initiated Joint Forest Management (JFM) programme launched in 1990, in which governments and villagers share the costs and benefits from protection, are largely excluding women from their decision making and benefit sharing.

There are over 65,000 JFM groups today. Their typical two-tier management structure has a general body (GB), meant to draw members from the whole village, and an executive committee (EC) of 9–15 persons. Both bodies, interactively, define the rules for forest use, the punishments for abuse, and the methods of protection and benefit distribution. Who has a voice in the GB and EC bears centrally on who gains or loses from these initiatives.

In many states the criteria for GB membership is one person per household. Although technically gender-neutral, usually only men—seen as the household heads—join. But even where women can become members, few attend or speak up at meetings due to restrictive social norms and perceptions. These 'participatory exclusions', that is, exclusions within seemingly participative institutions, have other negative consequences. The rules framed for forest use, for instance, take little account of women's concerns.

CFGs typically ban or severely restrict forest entry. In some regions women's firewood collection time and distance travelled have doubled as a result. Everywhere women have switched in varying degrees to inferior fuels such as crop waste, which take more time to ignite and keep alight, and seriously increase smoke-related health risks, both for women and infants playing in smoky kitchens. Despite substantial forest regeneration, firewood extractions remain exceedingly low, sometimes less than 10–15 per cent of sustainable limits. Thus, despite several years into protection, firewood shortages persist, often to serious extent.

Benefits from the regenerated resource are, however, largely male controlled. In particular, any cash generated typically goes into a community fund, which is usually spent on items that bring women little benefit and do little to alleviate their fuel or fodder shortages. The new arrangements are thus creating a system of property rights in communal land which, like existing rights in privatized land, are strongly male centred and inequitable.

Here new gender inequality has emerged through male control of public property and the rules that govern its use. Gender-neutral rules become unequal when filtered through the prism of pre-existing inequalities. Hence membership by one person per household translates to one man per household. Women's lack of private property increases their dependence on common property, with associated fallouts. Both norms and perceptions restrict women's participation in rule making and implementation. And this remains largely invisible, since most evaluations deem the CFGs as success stories of decentralized management and participative community involvement.

Enhancing Bargaining Power

Women's ability to reduce these inequalities is likely to depend on their bargaining power with the state, the community, the market, and the family, as the case may be. Traditionally, economists have applied ideas about bargaining within the game-theoretic mode and with little attention to gender. Recent interest in intra-household gender dynamics has yielded interesting formulations of bargaining models, as also of the less formal bargaining *approach* which extends the standard ideas to take account of qualitative factors. Unconstrained by the structure that formal modelling requires, a bargaining approach also allows freer application of concepts such as bargaining power to new arenas such as the state and the community.

What affects women's bargaining power? The determinants can vary by context and would include women's command over economic resources, support from external agents such as the state and non-governmental organizations (NGOs), and pre-existing social norms and perceptions (Agarwal 1997, 2001). For community forestry (as an illustration), two factors appear especially important: external agent support and women's group strength. Pressure from NGOs, donors, and key individuals has helped reshape JFM membership rules. Several states have instituted that one man and one woman per household or all village adults can be members of the GB. Here village women did not need to bargain explicitly for change. External support gave them implicit bargaining power vis-à-vis the state.

However, bargaining with the community would require village women's more direct involvement. Ground experience suggests that for them to have more voice within mixed community forums would need, for a start, a critical mass of vocal women, and a sense of group identity.

On these counts women's credit and self-help groups have had mixed results. On the one hand, such groups enhance women's self-confidence and collective identity; improve male perceptions about women's capabilities through a demonstration effect; weaken restrictive social norms; and increase women's intra-family bargaining power. On the other hand, such groups often remain segregated from mixed gender forums such as mixed CFGs. Strategic interventions, as attempted by some NGOs, appear necessary to integrate separate women's groups into mixed groups and change the latter's gender dynamics. Also, a deeper structural change appears necessary to uproot certain social norms, such as the gender division of domestic work, and to reduce gender inequalities in command over property.

In sum, gender inequality takes both material and ideological forms. A critical material form is embedded in who commands private and public property. Critical hidden dimensions of the ideological form are social norms and perceptions. The interactive effects of these pre-existing gender disadvantages can create new inequalities. Enhancing women's bargaining power could help challenge and undermine both forms of inequality.

Bina Agarwal

References

Agarwal, Bina. 1994. *A Field of One's Own: Gender and Land Rights in South Asia*, Cambridge, Cambridge University Press.

———. 1997. '"Bargaining" and Gender Relations: Within and Beyond the Household', *Feminist Economics*, 3(1): 1–50.

———. 2001. 'Participatory Exclusions, Community Forestry and Gender: An Analysis and Conceptual Framework', *World Development*, 29(10): 1623–48.

Drèze, Jean and Amartya Sen. 2002. *India: Development and Participation*, New Delhi, Oxford University Press.

Elson, D. 1995. 'Gender Awareness in Modelling Structural Adjustment', *World Development*, 23(11): 1851–68.

Panda, P. and Bina Agarwal. 2005. 'Marital Violence, Human Development and Women's Property Status in India', *World Development*, 33(5): 823–50.

Raju, Saraswati, Peter J. Atkins, Naresh Kumar, and Janet G. Townsend. 1999. *Atlas of Women and Men in India*, New Delhi, Kali for Women.

Sen, Amartya K. 1990. 'Gender and Cooperative Conflicts', in Irene Tinker (ed.), *Persistent Inequalities: Women and World Development*, New York, Oxford University Press, pp. 123–49.

■ Genetically Modified Crops

In common usage, 'genetically modified' crops means those crops produced by genetic engineering, a suite of techniques widely used in medicine, pharmaceuticals, agriculture, and other industries. Many cultivars bred with molecular techniques contain traits produced by genes from other species, and are, therefore, more precisely called transgenic crops. Recombinant DNA (rDNA) breeding in agricultural crops has created political controversy and subsequently special surveillance and regulations that are absent in applications of genetic engineering in other fields.

Definitions of what constitutes a 'genetically modified crop' are thus critical determinants of the acceptability of plants with new traits and their diffusion in Indian agriculture. Forms of genetic modification of crops other than rDNA techniques, such as inducement of mutations by radiation or chemical mutagens, are not subject to special regulation in India. India has 259 irradiated mutagenic cultivars registered with the International Atomic Energy Agency. Among these is one of only five mutagenic brinjals registered globally, transformed by gamma radiation for solasodine production: *Dehra Dun local*, introduced in 1975. That cultivar required no special regulation since the form of genetic modification did not involve engineering at the individual gene level. In contrast, a transgenic (Bt) brinjal developed in 2002 did require approval by statutory regulators in Delhi (the Genetic Engineering Approval Committee) for commercialization. Bt brinjal passed biosafety scrutiny by scientific panels, but failed to receive approval from the Ministry of Environment as of April 2011.

India began formal institutional development of indigenous capacity in this field with the establishment of a Department of Biotechnology (DBT), under the Ministry of Science and Technology in 1986. Then Prime Minister Atal Bihari Vajpayee stated on 7 September 2001 that the national policy envisioned biotechnology as 'a premier precision tool of the future for creation of wealth and ensuring social justice—especially for the welfare of the poor'. Biotechnology was to be developed to fight obdurate diseases, increase agricultural production, combat nutritional deficiencies, and protect the environment. There is empirical evidence that these goals are within the potential of genetic engineering (Herring 2007).

Despite the ambitious goals set for the national policy, the history of genetically modified crops in India to date largely revolves around two crops: cotton and brinjal, though other crops are at the testing and development stages. The brinjal case illustrates the intersection of political, regulatory, and scientific positions that determine the diffusion of transgenic crops in many countries, as well as India's particularities.

As of April 2011, only one transgenic crop had been approved for commercialization in India. Bt cotton was approved on 26 March 2002, when India became the 16th country in the world to commercialize a genetically engineered cultivar. Bt cotton hybrids diffused rapidly and widely on farms and in commercial firms' offerings. India ranked fourth in the world in area under transgenic crops in 2010, following the United States, Brazil, and Argentina, and ahead of Canada and China according to data from the International Service for the Acquisition of Agri-biotech Applications. However, such data understate Indian acreage as illicit seeds continue to circulate in unknown quantities. Cotton yields have increased significantly along with aggregate production, currently standing at about 339 lakh bales. India recently surpassed the United States as the second-largest cotton-producing nation, behind China.

Biosafety

Transgenics, but not crops modified by different technologies, such as mutagenesis, are governed by the Environmental Protection Act of 1986, Rules of 1989, and specifically Notification No. GSR 1037 E dated 5 December 1989. This institutional arrangement empowers the Ministry of Environment and Forests over other ministries with interests in agricultural technology, such as the ministries of agriculture and science and technology.

As in other countries, regulation of transgenics in India is theoretically based on 'incremental risk', that is, risk added by the transgenic that is not present in the isogenic variety of the same plant. Assessment of trial data and biosafety regulations has by statute rested with the Genetic Engineering Approval Committee (GEAC) of the Ministry of Environment. Institutional capacity to regulate transgenic crops was called into question when illegal Bt cotton—undetected by both state and civil society—was discovered growing in Gujarat in September 2001. GEAC ordered destruction of the crop, creating a conflict with farmers' representatives and state governments. Banning the successful Bt hybrid Navbharat 151 led to a 'cottage industry' of stealth Bt cotton seed breeding and production, especially in Gujarat. Official reduction in the trait value of Bt cotton seeds by state governments in 2006 reduced prices of government-approved hybrids by 40–60 per cent, thus reducing incentives for underground breeders. Nevertheless, both counterfeit and stealth seeds have had significant impacts on Bt cotton diffusion.

Bt Cotton

India has more land under cotton than any other country; but yields have historically been among the lowest in the world. Bt technology was meant to reduce losses to pests—hence improving yields—while reducing pesticide use, resulting in improvement of farmers' incomes and ecological integrity. These outcomes are widely documented in peer-reviewed literature.

Bt cotton was produced by inserting the gene of a common soil bacterium—*Bacillus thuringiensis*, hence 'Bt'—into cotton hybrids. This transgene enables plants to produce a protein (*cry1Ac*) in their own tissues, a protein which is lethal to Lepidopterans, most importantly for farmers the indigenous 'American' bollworm (*Helicoverpa armigera*), which often causes heavy crop damage. The technology was developed by Mahyco-Monsanto Biotech Limited (MMB) and subsequently licensed to other seed firms. In 2002, only three Bt hybrids were legally available; in 2010 there were 779 approved Bt hybrids and one transgenic variety (from the public sector). Early hybrids contained a single transgene; beginning in 2006, a 'stacked gene' technology produced hybrids with two transgenes (*cry1Ac* and *cry2Ab*) to expand insect control. By 2009 more hybrids incorporated the stacked gene technology than the first-generation single-gene technology. Pending commercialization is a three-gene technology that includes *cry* genes for insect control and a gene for resistance to the herbicide glyphosate (*cp4-epsps*). By 2010, Bt cotton hybrids accounted for about 94 lakh hectares (lh) of the approximately 110 lh planted with cotton in India. Within the Bt acreage, 'stacked gene' technology covered about 66 lh.

Bt Brinjal

The first food crop based on transgenic technology in India was a brinjal (*Solanum melongena*; *baingan* in Hindi, aubergine or eggplant in English), engineered to be resistant to insects. It was developed in 2002 by the Maharashtra Hybrid Seeds Company (MAHYCO) using technology similar to that of the first-generation Bt cotton. The insect-resistance trait was created by insertion of genetic Event EE-1, based on the Bt *cry1Ac* gene.

India is the world's second largest producer of brinjals, after China. The crop is widely distributed in both production and consumption and ideally suited to small-scale labour-intensive production. But the yields suffer from extensive insect damage. The fruit and shoot borer (FSB, *Leucinodes orbonalis*) damages crops both by boring into stems, weakening the plant, and by damaging fruits, reducing market acceptability and the prices received by farmers. Insecticides to protect brinjals are costly, often ineffective, destroy beneficial insects, promote resistance in FSB, and leave residues (some of which are unregulated and toxic) on marketed fruits. Farmer incomes suffer from extensive crop losses, which vary with season and area, and pesticide costs. FSB is not well-controlled by insecticides because of its reproductive biology: sprays cannot reach the plant's interior tissue, which larvae penetrate soon after hatching. Because there is evidently no resistance to FSB in the brinjal genome, conventional breeding cannot produce an effective insect-resistance trait. Genetic engineering is widely employed in this situation; insect resistance is produced with a transgene.

GEAC evaluated Bt brinjal by considering nine years of study, laboratory, and fields trials involving 11 government departments and institutions. They reported that the Bt protein provided effective control of target insects; as a result, insecticides were significantly reduced in field trials. Field trials also indicated that yields of top-grade marketable crops roughly doubled in comparison with non-Bt controls. These trials suggested even larger reductions in pesticide application and harvestable yields than did Bt-cotton trials. Tests for pollen flow, weediness, growth, toxicity, nutrition, composition, and allergenicity detected no incremental risk in comparison with existing brinjal cultivars. These results for hybrids permitted public-sector institutions to begin field trials of their transgenic open-pollinated varieties (OPVs) beginning in 2007.

In October 2009, GEAC concluded that the insect-resistant trait in brinjals, for both hybrids and open-pollinated varieties, was 'effective in controlling target pests, safe to the environment, non-toxic as determined by toxicity and animal feeding tests, nonallergenic and has potential to benefit the farmers'.

Bio-property

Gobal transgenic crop development has been concentrated in the hands of multinational life-science corporations, of which Monsanto is the most notable. In recent years, public-sector development of genetically engineered crops has increased globally, with China the clear leader. MMB enjoyed privileged market position for Bt cotton in India because of biosafety regulations, and not property law. There was no patent on Bt cotton, but their hybrids were for some time the only ones legally approved for sale by GEAC.

Brinjal presented a different property configuration. About 40 per cent of brinjal farmers grow hybrids and 60 per cent OPVs. Beginning in 2003, market segmentation facilitated a unique public–private collaboration. MAHYCO shared its technology with public-sector institutions in India, as well as in Bangladesh and the Philippines, for developing transgenic varieties. Public institutions in India developed locally popular varieties with the trait donated by MAHYCO. Different cultivars were developed for different regions. The Tamil Nadu Agricultural University developed four transformed varieties for southern India. The University of Agricultural Sciences, Dharwad developed six for southwest India. The Indian Institute of Vegetable Research in Varanasi developed both hybrids and OPVs for the northern and eastern regions. MAHYCO continued to concentrate on hybrids, assuming that many farmers would eventually favour them for their yield advantage.

In contrast to Bt cotton, more brinjal OPVs from the public sector than hybrids from the private sector were planned for release. For farmers, this would mean a choice between two types of insect-resistant cultivars: the lower-cost and savable seeds of varieties, or the higher-yielding, more expensive hybrid seeds. This unique arrangement of bio-property was not, however, widely understood; much public discourse at all levels continued to emphasize Monsanto and foreign control of the food system, reflecting the distinctive nature of politics around transgenic crops.

Bio-politics

Transgenic crops face not only different regulatory control in comparison to crops modified by different means, but raise distinctive politics as well. Approval of Bt brinjals by GEAC in 2009 was overturned by Jairam Ramesh, the Minister of Environment and Forests in 2010. The minister endorsed the claims of inadequate official science and hypothetical environmental risks, as well as the threat of foreign control over India's food supply raised by civil society organizations. Political arithmetic worked against Bt brinjal. Most brinjal farmers grow multiple crops, precluding collective action to form an effective producers' lobby. There are only 14 lakh brinjal farmers, controlling about 5.5 lakh hectares of land. There are 63 lakh cotton farmers for 94 lakh hectares. Cotton has weighty forward linkages in the economy and earns significant export revenues.

Politics will decide much of the future of genetically modified crops in India. Despite endorsement of the GEAC position on the safety of Bt brinjal by six of India's leading science academies in 2010, the moratorium on approval holds indefinitely. Minister of Agriculture Sharad Pawar publically expressed concern that unilateral rejection of scientific conclusions in the brinjal case would discourage ongoing research in Indian public institutions on transgenic potato, tomato, rice, mustard, chickpea, groundnut, and pigeon pea. GEAC has been demoted in anticipation of a new comprehensive regulatory authority for biotechnology, but continues to function. Except for the ruling Congress Party, all political parties had opposed 'genetically modified organisms' in their 2009 election manifestoes. Some states have declared themselves 'GMO-free' and announced bans on field testing of transgenic crops. As agriculture is a state subject in the Indian Constitution, divergent positions of different states complicate announced national policy goals in agricultural biotechnology.

RONALD J. HERRING

References

Herring, Ronald J. ed. 2007. *Transgenics and the Poor: Biotechnology and Development Studies,* Oxon/London, Routledge (paperback 2008).

———. 2008. 'Whose Numbers Count? Probing Discrepant Evidence on Transgenic Cotton in the Warangal District of India', *International Journal of Multiple Research Approaches,* October, 2(2).

Herring, Ronald J. and Milind Kandlikar. 2009. 'Illicit Seeds: Intellectual Property and the Underground Proliferation of Agricultural Biotechnologies', in Sebastian Haunss and Kenneth C. Shadlen (eds), *The Politics of Intellectual Property: Contestation over the Ownership, Use, and Control of Knowledge and Information,* Cheltenham, Edward Elgar.

Narayanamoorthy, A. and S.S. Kalamkar. 2006. 'Is Bt Cotton Cultivation Economically Viable for Indian Farmers? An Empirical Analysis', *Economic and Political Weekly,* 41: 2716–24.

Rao, N. Chandrasekhara and S. Mahendra Dev. 2010. *Biotechnology in Indian Agriculture: Potential, Performance and Concerns,* New Delhi, Academic Foundation.

Subramanian, Arjunan and Matin Qaim. 2009. 'Village-wide effects of Agricultural Biotechnology: The Case of Bt Cotton in India', *World Development,* 37(1): 256–67.

———. 2010. 'The Impact of Bt Cotton on Poor Households in Rural India', *Journal of Development Studies,* 46(2): 295–311.

Global Warming

Global warming refers to the likely rise in annual average global surface temperature due to increase in the concentration of greenhouse gases (GHGs) in the atmosphere. Important anthropogenic GHGs are Carbon dioxide (CO_2), Methane (CH_4), and Nitrous Oxide (N_2O). These gases are emitted due to the use of fossil fuels in the energy sector, certain agricultural and industrial practices, and deforestation. Their concentration in the atmosphere traps outgoing radiation from the earth leading to surface warming.

According to the Government of India, total emission of all GHGs from India, expressed in CO_2 equivalent terms, was 1,228 million metric tonnes (mmt), in the reference year 1994. Of this, emission of CO_2 itself, not counting the amount absorbed by forests and other sinks, was 793 mmt, or 65 per cent of the total. This made India, in absolute terms, the fifth largest emitter of CO_2 in the world. In per capita terms, at 0.87 tonnes, or 4 per cent of emissions from the USA, it was amongst the lowest in the world. Approximately 85 per cent of CO_2 emissions came from the energy sector, 13 per cent from industrial processes, and the remaining 2 per cent from land use, including changes therein. Methane accounted for 31 per cent of total GHGs. Its major source was rice cultivation, enteric fermentation by cattle, energy sources such as biomass burning, coal mining and handling, flaring of natural gas, and waste-disposal activities. Nitrous oxide formed 4 per cent of total GHGs originating in agriculture, fuel combustion, industrial processes, and waste and biomass burning.

Climate change models predict that, in line with changes worldwide, average temperatures in India will rise by 2 to 5 degrees celsius during the next 50 to 100 years. This is likely to lead to the following important developments: a change in the pattern and intensity of rainfall, an increase in the rate of melting of glaciers, a rise in sea level, and possibly an increase in the frequency of extreme weather phenomena. Together, they are likely to lead to an increase in the intensity of floods and severity of drought in different parts of the country. Thus global warming will have an adverse impact on the water balance in the country. The quality of water is also likely to be adversely affected by saline intrusion into coastal aquifers due to rise in sea level.

A rise in sea level will have more direct and drastic consequences. It will lead to submergence of vast stretches of heavily populated coastal land, along with infrastructure like roads and buildings. It is estimated that a 1 m rise in sea level will displace approximately 7.1 million people and lead to a loss of over 5,000 sq km of land. It will also seriously endanger coastal ecosystems like mangroves.

Surface warming, along with altered water balance, will affect the productivity of different crops. It is possible that some crops may actually benefit from increased CO_2 in the atmosphere. However, the overall effect is expected to be a decrease in agricultural productivity, with significant regional variations. This, combined with increase in the frequency of extreme weather phenomena, can seriously threaten India's food security. There will be important changes in the forest ecosystems in the form of shift in forest boundaries and changes in forest types. In the transient phase, there can be loss of forests and potential loss or significant change in biodiversity. Together these changes may further accentuate the existing regional disparities.

There is a lot of uncertainty associated with the degree and timing of global warming. It is also impossible to precisely estimate the likely sectoral, regional, or aggregate effects. Yet, following the precautionary principle, actions to mitigate its effects and adaptation to inevitable changes cannot be postponed. These entail significant social and economic costs and raise important questions of sharing responsibility domestically and internationally.

In the international climate policy debates, India has stressed that the present problem is caused by past accumulations of GHGs, mainly due to actions of developed countries. It has advocated the principle of common but differentiated responsibility for reducing future emissions by countries based on their levels of development and per capita emissions. At Kyoto in 1997, an agreement was reached, by which the so-called Annexe 1 (mainly developed) countries were obliged to reduce their CO_2 emissions by 5.2 per cent during the period 2008–12, compared to base-year 1991 levels. At present India, in common with other developing countries, is not committed to any emission-reduction targets. However, this position has not found favour with USA, the largest contributor to CO_2 emissions on total and per capita basis. It has opted out of the Kyoto Protocol, insisting that developing countries, mainly India and China, undertake some emission reductions. There is pressure from the European Union too on this score. Therefore, in the not too distant future India may be forced to take on some commitments. That requires serious appraisal of India's options and strategies.

Since the bulk of CO_2 emissions originate in the energy sector, major policy initiatives will have to focus on this sector. The following facts constrain India's ability to reduce CO_2 emissions. A growing population and the national commitment to remove poverty and raise the standard of living of people need economic growth to be accelerated and sustained over a long period of time. Energy consumption in per capita terms is among the lowest in the world. Therefore, drastic reductions in energy consumption cannot be contemplated without seriously compromising development goals. As incomes rise, there is progressive shift from traditional fuels like biomass to modern fuels like electricity. The energy resource base of India is dominated by coal with relatively small endowments of oil and natural gas. Within the energy sector, more than 50 per cent of emissions are due to coal-based electricity generation. Massive fuel switching cannot be resorted to without jeopardizing the balance of payments. Therefore, in the near future, energy consumption and CO_2 emissions are actually expected to go up. However, India can take steps to moderate the growth of emissions where they are consistent with reductions in local pollution and other development goals. For this the available options are: (i) switching from coal to oil and natural gas, (ii) increasing the use of renewable energy sources like hydro, solar, and wind, (iii) adoption of more efficient energy supply and energy use technologies, and (iv) undertaking sustainable forestry projects on a large scale to help control carbon. The capital requirements and financial and economic costs of these alternatives can be substantial. According to some estimates they may be as much as 1 to 2 per cent of GDP. It has been felt that these steps cannot be undertaken without major international transfers of resources and technologies.

The Kyoto Protocol envisaged a clean development mechanism (CDM), whereby the developed countries could invest in carbon-abatement projects in developing countries and claim certified emission-reduction (CER) credits. These would be tradable among the developed countries. Neither the mechanism nor the Indian position on participation in CDM projects is as yet fully clear. Indian industry has tended to view them as a source of additional revenue, sometimes mistakenly as 'manna from heaven'. NGOs have tended to view these projects suspiciously, fearing that they would foster technological dependence. They have also cautioned about unfavourable terms at which CERs would get sold. In the meanwhile, the Government of India has gone ahead with setting up a facilitation mechanism hoping that many of the carbon abatement projects will help reduce local pollution in the form of urban smog and acid rain. The immediate challenge before the policymakers is to work out in detail alternative adaptation strategies including short-run catastrophic changes like tsunami not necessarily related to global warming.

PURAN MONGIA

References

Government of India. 2004. *India's Initial National Communication to the United Nations Framework Convention on Climate Change*, New Delhi, Ministry of Environment and Forests.

Mongia, Nandita, R. Bhatia, J. Sathaye, and Puran Mongia. 1991. 'Cost of Reducing CO_2 Emissions from India: Imperatives for International Transfer of Resources and Technologies', *Energy Policy*, 19(10): 977–86.

■ Globalization and the Poor

Globalization and economic reform have enormous potential for economic growth and poverty reduction. But there are at least three troubling features of these phenomena that have emerged over the last two decades—technical change which is biased in favour of capital and skilled labour, increased vulnerability and exposure to economic risks, and a shift of economic power towards more mobile factors of production. The benefits and the costs of globalization are seen in the ground-level experiences of SEWA, which is primarily a movement of self-employed women workers, arising out of a confluence of three movements—the labour movement, cooperative movement, and women's movement based on a Gandhian philosophy.

We take as an example SEWA's experience in the construction sector. SEWA has many thousands of members in the construction sector, most of them in Ahmedabad city. These women are mainly 'unskilled' construction workers, working as casual labour. Here is how the issue appears to Madhuben Maganbhai, a 35-year-old construction worker, in her own words:

> I started at the age of 15 and first carried loads of concrete on my head. Then I learnt to carry twelve bricks at a time. Later, I learnt to lay concrete and then do plastering. When I first started working we were attached to a contractor and would get work everyday. We only had one holiday on *amavas* (no-moon day). However, in the last 10–12 years, the numbers of workers increased with the closure of the textile mills and the printing factories. Then workers started competing with each other, and we no longer had regular work. We all had to stand at the *kadiya-naka* [roadside site for construction workers] and contractors came and hired us by the day. Still, I used to get about 20 days of work a month. However, over the last five years things have become especially bad. I hardly get six- to seven-days' work a month. This is the situation with all of us who stand at the kadiya-naka. Why? I don't know why. The work seems to have decreased overall. Some say it is due to recession. Others say it is due to new machines which have come in. In some of the bigger sites now, I have seen that all digging is done by machines, and even carrying bricks that we used to do, is now done by machines, and in some sites whole walls are made elsewhere and brought to the site.

The experience of Madhuben is multiplied manifold among the members of SEWA, across the many sectors in which SEWA works, and is documented in many detailed and rigorous studies. For example, take home-based garment workers. The products in the market have been changing rapidly. A decade ago, women were mainly making petticoats and children's wear for the local market. Now the demand is for more sophisticated items in the national and international markets, which they do not know how to stitch. Earlier, cotton cloth was the main raw material, but now there is a variety of synthetic materials including satin and velvet. These materials do not stitch well on the older sewing machines owned by the women. Most women have the simplest machines, and although many women have fitted these machines with motors, they still remain low in productivity. They would like to move to the next level of sewing machines but cannot afford the capital to do so. In addition, many types of work that used to be done by hand, such as making buttonholes and hemming, are now done by machines, or by add-ons to existing machines. One of the major problems of the garment workers is the lack of capital to expand their business if they are self-employed, or to upgrade the quality of their sewing machines.

SEWA's poor women members have always had tremendous vulnerabilities in their lives—the risks of accidents and illness, fire and theft, and periodic unemployment and loss of income through the vagaries of product and labour markets. In the late 1990s, the Indian Parliament passed an Act allowing private insurance companies into the sector. Once the Act was passed, SEWA was keen to launch its own insurance company in the form of a cooperative. However, it was not allowed to do so because the Act seemed only to be promoting very large companies. The minimum capital required to register a company under the Act was Rs 100 crore for life insurance, and for general insurance. SEWA argued with the government that an insurance company for the poor did not require such a large capital base, and that Rs 30 crore would guarantee the safety and stability of such a company. However, this argument is not being heard and so far only the very large companies are being allowed to enter the market.

What can be done to help Madhuben, her sisters in SEWA, and the poor in India generally—to prepare her for the opportunities of globalization and economic reform, and to protect her against their ravages? Maximizing the benefits and minimizing the costs require active management of the process of globalization and economic reform with the outcomes for the poor in mind. A hands-off policy is not an option. Strategies for management should be developed by listening to the experiences of the poor and to their representatives. The actions need to address the three problems highlighted at the beginning—skills, vulnerability, and organization. Managing and mitigating the negative consequences of liberalization will require direct interventions to enhance the skills of the poor, and to develop insurance tools to manage the risks they face. Detailed policy recommendations on these, including, for example, reform of the national framework for skill training, and reform of the structure of insurance regulations to allow micro-insurance to expand, are presented in several SEWA policy papers.

These interventions need to combine government action and action by organizations of the poor. The poor, and especially unskilled poor women, need organization to counteract the growing economic power of capital and skilled labour as a result of their greater national and global mobility. Organization is also the sine qua non for representation of the interests of poor women in local, national, and global policymaking councils. Public policy can help by developing an enabling legal and regulatory environment in which membership-based organizations of the poor can represent their interests and provide them with services they need.

RENANA JHABVALA AND RAVI KANBUR

■ Government Subsidies

The term 'subsidy' is sometimes used to describe a financial transfer, for example, scholarships to students, and sometimes to mean the unrecovered cost of publicly provided goods and services (henceforth collectively referred to as 'services'), that is, the difference between the cost of providing a service and revenues realized from the provision of that service that is absorbed by the government budget. For purposes of this entry, we find it useful to make a distinction between transfers and subsidies, which are here interpreted to mean the unrecovered cost of publicly provided services. Such unrecovered costs can be calculated at conventional prices prevailing in the market or they can be calculated at their economic value, that is, the outputs forgone on account of the inputs used up in the provision of the relevant service, what economists call 'opportunity cost' or 'shadow price'. Hence a further distinction has to be made between 'financial subsidies' computed at market prices and 'economic subsidies' computed in 'shadow prices'. Here we will mainly be discussing the volume and composition of financial subsidies in India.

A clarification is required here regarding the kind of publicly provided services for which unrecovered costs can be considered subsidies. At one end of the spectrum there are pure 'public services' that cannot be supplied by the market because they are characterized by 'non-rivalry' and 'non-excludability' in consumption. Non-rivalry implies that the service in question is jointly available to all consumers, and its consumption by one consumer does not reduce the supply available for other consumers. A good example is defence services that provide the same security to all citizens of a country simultaneously. The enjoyment of such security by one citizen does not reduce the security available for other citizens. Citizens are not rivals competing for the enjoyment of such security. It is also evident that once such security is provided to the nation, it is not possible to exclude any citizen from this benefit. This non-excludability makes it impossible to 'sell' such a service to individual citizens at a price, since citizens know that once such security is provided to the nation they cannot be excluded from enjoying it even if they do not pay for it, that is, they can free ride.

Such pure public services can only be provided by the government, and they have to be financed out of its general revenues. The question of recovering the cost of these services through user charges does not arise. Hence the concept of 'subsidies' as defined here will also not apply. Defence, maintenance of law and order, and general administrative services are typical examples of such pure public services. At the other end of the spectrum are pure private services, characterized by 'rivalry' and excludability' in consumption, that are generally provided by the market, though it may happen that these are also sometimes provided by the government. In between these two polar categories is also a range of quasi-public services that combine some characteristics of public services with some characteristics of private services. They are characterized by rivalry and excludability in consumption, and could therefore be supplied by the market. However, the market-determined supply may not be optimal for a variety of reasons that economists call 'externalities'. This is later discussed in greater detail. The concept of 'subsidy' applies only to the unrecovered cost of quasi-public and private services.

Unless such subsidies can be explicitly justified, they should be phased out or reduced as they lead to several undesired consequences. A large volume of subsidies generates macroeconomic pressures via its impact on the budget. Subsidies affect relative prices, thereby altering market signals and the allocation of resources via the market. Subsidies also alter the distribution of income since they enhance the effective income of beneficiaries relative to others in the economy, and this could be iniquitous. However, under some conditions subsidies are justifiable and desirable. First, there are services with positive externalities, where the social benefit of a service exceeds the private benefit accruing to the immediate beneficiary. In such cases, the cost of these services may have to be subsidized to increase the level of private demand for these services to the socially optimal level. Second, there may be services where unit costs decline as supply increases because of economies of scale in production or distribution. Costs would be minimized in such cases if a single 'natural monopolist' supplies the entire market. However, the 'natural monopolist' would be interested in maximizing profits not minimizing costs, and may have to be regulated as well as subsidized to minimize costs. Technological developments that enable unbundling of many such services and multiple-part pricing options have reduced the challenge of natural monopolies. Nevertheless, scale economies remain a valid justification for subsidies in some cases. Third, there may be 'missing markets' for some products that need to be nurtured and grown or a missing technology, for example, cost-effective solar power, where subsidies may be justified.

Since subsidies affect income distribution, sometimes subsidies are provided for distributional reasons. However, as noted earlier, transfer payments are an alternative policy instrument for meeting this goal. If there is a social/political choice to support the income of a particular target group, for example, the unemployed, this may be better accomplished by income transfers through the budget. Compared to subsidies they are more transparent, with less leakages to non-target groups, they do not distort relative prices, and do not encourage excess consumption of any particular service as a subsidy would.[1] A qualification arises in the case of some very basic needs of the poor such as food grains, potable water, basic education, or primary healthcare. Society may wish to ensure provision of a minimal quantity of these specific 'merit' items to everyone regardless of their income or personal preference. In such cases a subsidy would be preferred to a transfer payment. Finally, even when transfers are preferable to subsidies, policymaking has to be based on ground realities, including a history of widespread use of subsidies for distributional reasons. Hence, often the practical policy option is to gradually phase out inefficient subsidies and replace them by transfers wherever feasible.

Perhaps the most striking feature of government subsidies in India is their very large scale. The total volume of government financial subsidies was estimated for the first time for financial year 1987 by Mundle and Rao (1991) at the National Institute of Public Finance and Policy (NIPFP).[2] They calculated the unrecovered costs (including annualized capital costs) of 86 out of 123 major categories of public services provided by the federal and state governments. This calculation excluded 37 major services treated as pure public services, that is, general administrative services in the functional classification of government expenditure, relief on account of natural calamities, general secretariat expenses of departments providing social and economic services, and compensation and assignment to local bodies and Panchayati Raj Institutions. The authors also netted out pure transfer payments, and then arrived at an estimate of Rs 423 billion or 14.4 per cent of the gross domestic product (GDP) as the total volume of government financial subsidies, reflecting an underlying cost recovery rate of only 32 per cent for social and economic services. Of this, Rs 161 billion or 5.5 per cent of GDP was provided by

[1]Atkinson and Stiglitz (1976) also argued that under a set of strong assumptions direct transfers are superior to subsidies.

[2]Subsidy in a specific service (j) can be obtained by,

$S_j = R_j + i\,(K_j + L_j + Z_j) + d\,K_j - y_j - r_j - t_j$

S_j is the subsidy;

R_j is the variable cost or revenue expenditure on the services;

K_j is the capital stock in the sector;

L_j is the stock of loans advanced for the service;

Z_j is the stock of equity and loans advanced to public enterprises classified within the service category;

i is an imputed interest rate representing the opportunity cost of money for government;

d is the depreciation rate;

y_j is revenue receipt by the sector;

r_j is income by way of interest or dividend on loans and equity; and

t_j is a transfer payment from the sector to individual agents.

the federal government and Rs 262 billion or 8.9 per cent of GDP was provided by all the state governments taken together.

These estimates have turned out to be quite robust. In an updated NIPFP estimate for the financial year 1994, Srivastava and Sen (1997) arrived at the same subsidy–GDP ratio of 14.4 per cent despite some changes in method and coverage. Unfortunately, combined estimates for the federal and state governments are not available for any other year. However, NIPFP estimates of federal government subsidies based on a broadly similar method are available for six additional years up to the financial year 2003 and indicate that federal government subsidies have generally varied within a narrow range of 4–5 per cent of GDP since the financial year 1987. Since there have been no marked changes in the cost recovery policy of most state governments during this period, it is possible that the total volume of subsidies has remained in the ball park of 14–15 per cent of GDP. However, with no actual estimates available after the financial year 1994, this is a hypothesis that has to be tested. It would be very useful if the periodic updates of estimates of federal-level subsidies undertaken by the NIPFP at the behest of the Finance Ministry could be complemented by similar updated estimates of state government subsidies.

In their study Mundle and Rao (1991) noted that subsidies in social services, with an underlying cost recovery rate of less than 4 per cent, accounted for 40 per cent of total subsidies while economic services, with an underlying recovery rate of around 44 per cent, accounted for 60 per cent of total subsidies. They pointed out that less than 30 per cent of this large volume of subsidies was provided as visible subsidies and the rest was non-transparent, making it extremely difficult to identify the beneficiaries or assess whether these subsidies are justifiable in terms of the rationale outlined earlier. Based on a detailed analysis of the allocation of subsidies across social groups, sectors, and states they concluded that the distribution of subsidies was quite regressive, and that 'with greater transparency and better targeting it should be possible to increase the flow of services as well as subsidies to disadvantaged groups without any increase, perhaps even with a reduction, in the total bill of subsidies.'

Subsequent exercises have confirmed these broad conclusions. In their study Srivastava and Sen (1997) aggregated surplus-generating and deficit sectors separately to get a full measure of subsidy flowing in subsidized sectors without surplus offsets. They also introduced the concept of 'merit subsidies', which subsidies might be justified, and attempted to get at least a rough measure of the volume of 'unjustified' subsidies. They concluded that even non-merit services had an average recovery rate of less than 9 per cent and that 'non-merit' subsidies amounted to nearly 11 per cent of the GDP, the implication being that elimination of these unjustifiable subsidies could wipe out India's entire fiscal deficit. They also concluded that the overall allocation of subsidies was distributionally quite regressive. Brent (1995) used the Mundle–Rao state-level estimates to compare cost recoveries with his measure of socially desirable user charges in a cost–benefit analysis framework, and concluded that 'the application of the cost–benefit framework to India's state user price experience does therefore on the whole, support the Mundle–Rao conjecture that it is hard to justify the limited use of user pricing for government services in India'.

Available studies of government subsidies in India thus confirm that the total volume of such subsidies is very large, approaching around 15 per cent of GDP, that most of it is difficult to justify as 'merit goods' or in a social cost–benefit analysis framework, and that the incidence of subsidies is regressive and difficult to justify even on distributional considerations. This calls for a significant reform of subsidy policy in India. At the same time, in identifying a road map for subsidy policy reform that is feasible, it is important to recognize political economic ground realities. It is important to first freeze, and then reduce in a phased manner, subsidies that cannot be justified as 'merit subsidies' to both reduce the fiscal burden of unwarranted subsidies and also the distorting effects on resource allocation. Second, wherever feasible, subsidies should be substituted by other policy instruments that are less distorting for resource allocation, for example, two-part or multiple-part pricing. Third, subsidies given for distributional reasons should be substituted by pure transfer payments that are more visible and, therefore, can be better targeted, and that also do not distort price signals that impact on resource allocation. Finally, the shift to alternative policy instruments should be introduced alongside the phased reduction of subsidies so as to make these policy packages politically feasible.

SUDIPTO MUNDLE AND HIRANYA MUKHOPADHYAY

References

Atkinson, A.B. and J.E. Stiglitz. 1976. 'The Design of Tax Structure: Direct Versus Indirect Taxation', *Journal of Public Economics*, 6: 55–75.

Brent, R. J. 1995. 'Cost–Benefit Analysis, User Prices, and State Expenditures in India', *Public Finance*, 50(3): 327–41.

Mundle, S. and M.G. Rao. 1991. 'The Volume and Composition of Government Subsidies in India', *Economic and Political Weekly*, 4 May, 26(18): 1157–72.
Srivastava, D.K. and Tapas Sen. 1997. *Government Subsidies in India*, New Delhi, National Institute of Public Finance and Policy.

Green Revolution

The term 'Green Revolution' in India suggests two images. In the popular mind it is associated with a period in which India crossed the hump in terms of shortages of, and external dependence for, its grain and food requirements. The second more technical perception of the Green Revolution is one of a productivity breakthrough emerging from the high-yielding variety (HYV) of seeds in food grains, particularly wheat and then rice. These seeds, initially imported from Mexico for wheat, were adapted, replicated, and developed by Indian scientists. On account of their photo-insensitivity properties, they were shorter-duration crops as compared to the earlier varieties, and this property by itself led to more intensive use of land, in addition to water and nutrients. Technology and productivity improvement became the driving force in the Green Revolution areas. The Green Revolution in India is seen as spanning four epochs (Alagh 2004). The first phase of the introduction of the high-yielding technology is attributed to the initiative of political leader C. Subramaniam and civil servant B. Sivaraman in the second half of the mid-1960s, a 'ship-to-mouth' phase of grain shortage and large grain imports as PL 480 aid from the US. They took the risk of importing the dwarf varieties of wheat from the International Wheat Research Institute (IWRI) in Mexico and were assisted by Indian scientist M.S. Swaminathan and the Indian Council of Agricultural Research (ICAR) teams in replicating the seeds.

The second phase was one in which the technology was internalized in what is called the favoured region, favoured crop period in the 1970s. However, in the early 1970s there was still considerable pessimism about the growth potential of Indian agriculture. Paddock and Paddock, in *Famine 1975*, argued:

> Today, India absorbs like a blotter 25 per cent of the entire American wheat crop. No matter how one may adjust present statistics and allow for future increase in the American wheat crop ... it will be beyond the US to keep famine out of India during 1970. The reason? Of all the national leadership the Indian comes close to being the most childish and inefficient, perversely determined to cut the country's economic throat. (Paddock and Paddock 1968: 217)

This assessment was from a larger canvas. Other think tanks—the Hudson Institute, Keith Griffin, Francine Frankel, the Bretton Woods institutions, and Paul Streeten and Michael Lipton at the Institute of Development Studies (IDS), Sussex—all had a dim view of India's agricultural prospects and some argued that India also did not have medium-term growth prospects since poor agriculture would lead to a wage goods constraint. The initial spurt of grain growth had petered out and the Green Revolution was seen as a misnomer. India's grain production after reaching 108 million tonnes in 1971, ranged between 101 and 104 million tonnes in the early 1970s. The World Bank, and in fact even the Indian Finance Ministry, felt that India would not achieve its target of 125 million tonnes of grain by 1978–9; estimates ranged between 118 and 120 million tonnes. It was at this time that policymaking in India focused on resource allocation and policy support to agriculture with priorities set by the then Prime Minister Indira Gandhi who saw food security as a central issue. The Planning Commission produced its first agricultural sub-model (with the present author organizing the effort) and this model made conservative assumptions on land reserves and productivity assumptions so that resource allocation for agriculture, particularly irrigation, got high priority in the investment budget. Interestingly, public-sector capital formation of Rs 5,566 crore at 1993–4 prices in 1976–7 was not reached in any year in the 1990s, reflecting the lack of strategic policymaking for agriculture in the reform period. By 1978–9, India was producing 127 million tonnes and was a net exporter of grains. In the late 1960s, it was the received wisdom from studies, amongst others by Keith Griffin, to state that the Green Revolution strategy would not impact on small farms and also that such farms would not participate in diversified agriculture. In a large sample study of Haryana agriculture, G.S. Bhalla produced the counter-factual. Bhalla, an economist of avowed Marxist persuasion, hypothesized that small farms would not access the new technology, but since his data rejected the hypothesis, it showed that the class of adopters was more equal than that of non-adopters (Bhalla 1974: survey in 1971). At roughly the same time, economist Vijai S. Vyas, with his team at Vallabh Vidyanagar, showed with a field survey in the Charotar that small farms were viable in the sense that if given necessary support, they could generate incomes above the poverty line. This was at that time, like all new ideas, neither intuitively felt nor accepted and yet soon became the orthodoxy at home and abroad. They also argued that with the support of technology and credit, more small farmers would cross the poverty line, but there would be some families left below the poverty line and a non-land-based non-farm growth programme was necessary for them (Vyas et al. 1969). Policymaking was to follow. Meanwhile in the 1980s, in the third phase, Indian agriculture was growing faster and, as the economy picked up, non-food grains were leading. The growth rate accelerated in new crops, particularly rice, cotton, and oilseeds, and in new regions. The larger picture in terms of output and productivity growth and the shift away from food grains is shown in the estimates in Table 1. Output growth rate went up since the 1980s for the agricultural sector as a whole. Output is now rising at 3.37 per cent compound annual as compared to 2.46 per cent earlier.

Table 1 Average Annual Growth Rates in Index of Area and Production

	1950/1–1996/7		1950/1–1979/80		1980/1–1996/7	
	All crops	Non-food grains	All Crops	Non-food grains	All-crops	Non-food grains
Prod.	2.7	2.99	2.46	2.70	3.37	4.39
Area	0.61	1.22	0.86	1.17	0.27 (NS)	2.02

Source: M. Alagh (2004).
Notes: Estimated by semi-log regressions on time. Estimates significant at 99 per cent confidence levels. (NS) implies not significant.

The contribution of area went down, yield being the major source of growth in the second phase. Growth of output in the non-food grains sector was only marginally higher than for the entire sector for the period up to 1980. However, since then the non-food grains sector has grown at 4.39 per cent annual, which is significantly higher than the growth of the sector as a whole. This also led to a change in the structure of employment. A comparison of the 1999–2000 estimates with those of 1961 brings out this shift (Table 2).

Table 2 Structural Change in Workforce in India, 1961–2000

Sector	Per cent of workforce 1961	1999–2000
1. Agriculture, forestry, and fishing	75.9	59.9
2. of which crop production	73.5	54.3
3. Livestock	2	4.1
4. Agricultural services	0	0.9
5. Logging forestry and fishing	0.5	0.5

Source: Census of India 1961; NSSO 2000, as quoted in Y.K. Alagh (2004: 32).

Three points are notable. The first is that decline in the workforce engaged in crop production is higher than that in the agricultural sector as a whole. The second is that the increase in employment based on livestock is high. The third is that forestry is not absorbing a larger share of the workforce, because policies are not conducive to giving rise to a dynamic local production sector. These trends are more pronounced in some fast-growing areas since either the share of non-farm employment is much lower than the national average and has fallen, or the decline is faster than in the country as a whole, as the estimates in Table 3 show.

Table 3 Shift in Employment in the 1990s

S. No.	State	Share of agricultural sector in employment 1991	2001
1.	Gujarat	56.3	51.0
2.	Haryana	57.8	51.6
3.	Karnataka	63.1	55.9
4.	Punjab	55.3	39.4
5.	Tamil Nadu	59.5	49.5
6.	India	64.8	58.4

Source: Y.K. Alagh (2004: 32).

Since the mid-1990s, in the fourth epoch, the agricultural growth rate went down and employment growth in agriculture was low. Profitability of agriculture fell by 14.2 per cent during this decade. Public capital formation fell initially and as anticipated by the present author, private investment also stagnated in response to the declining profitability of the sector. Irrigation and fertilizer growth slackened.

These negative trends outlined by Indian economists were noted in the Mid-Term Appraisal of the Tenth Plan and the government gave a high priority to agriculture arising from the Mid-Term Review of the Tenth Plan and in the Eleventh Plan. This led to a substantial revival of public capital formation in agriculture. This period also saw an improvement in the terms of trade for agriculture and a revival of private investment. Table 4 shows a distinct improvement in the profitability of Indian agriculture.

Agricultural capital formation as a percentage of agricultural GDP increased from 14.07 per cent in 2004–5 to a high of 21.31 per cent in 2008–9, increasing both in the public and private sector according to recent estimates at 2004–5 prices. According to the new series of CSO estimates, private agricultural capital formation as a percentage of agricultural GDP (at 2004–5 prices) fell from 12.41 per cent in 2005–6, to 11.58 per cent in 2006–7, but

Table 4 Agriculture Terms of Trade based on GDP Implicit Price Deflators

Year	Terms of trade for agriculture
2004–5	93.4
2005–6	96.8
2006–7	97.7
2007–8	101.4
2008–9	103.4

Source: Estimated based on National Accounts Statistics, CSO.
Note: GDP implicit price deflators for agriculture and non-agriculture are used to derive agricultural terms of trade.

preliminary estimates show an increase to an impressive rate of 17.55 per cent in 2008–9. More generally, it was argued in the low capital formation phase that a gross rate of capital formation of about 12 per cent of agricultural GDP was necessary to support an agricultural growth rate of around 3.5 to 4 per cent annually and this rate was not being achieved then. For example:

> It would be naïve to plan agricultural growth and policies with low incremental capital–output ratios (ICORs). In terms of gross capital formation, past ICORs are estimated as follows:
>
> | Period | ICOR |
> |---|---|
> | 1978/79 to 1986/87 | 4.37 |
> | 1987/88 to 1991/92 | 3.32 |
>
> Agricultural gross fixed investment is around two-thirds of agricultural gross investment. It would be imprudent plan for an ICOR of less than 3 for agricultural fixed capital formation. (Alagh 1997: 283)

This kind of investment levels have been consistently exceeded, but the agricultural growth rate does not show the resilience that a 20 per cent capital formation would provide. This in turn raises in a fundamental way questions of productivity of investment and non renewable resource constraints of land and water. Real resource scarcities remain. Cropped area, earlier a constant, was falling whilst the area under irrigation was a matter of concern. There was recognition that faster diversification of the sector was required to achieve growth objectives, and this required policies relating to market reforms and infrastructure in the context of the rural–urban continuum (Alagh 2011). Since widespread growth was required, a policy of 'walking on two legs' was needed with improved productivity of cereal producing areas allowing land to be released for high-value crops. In the short run, technology and input intensification were seen as the source of growth as policies of land and water management took effect. Institutional reforms of markets, empowerment of small farmers to leverage their assets for strategic partnerships with corporates, new technology and market linkages, and establishing farmer groups and local institutions to build up the support bases for emerging Indian agriculture have all been advocated.

The 'big-ticket' central sector plan schemes now demand responsibility and empowerment mechanisms at local levels as preconditions (for details, see, Alagh 2009; FAO 2008).

There has been a revival of these ideas in the Eleventh Plan. Many of the Eleventh Plan's blue ribbon schemes are in the agro-climatic mould. An important innovation during the Eleventh Plan is the new Rashtriya Krishi Vikas Yojana (RKVY), designed to give more flexibility to states and provide incentives for them to spend more on agriculture and to do so on the basis of properly designed district and state plans. The state agricultural plan, it said, should be based on (these initial) district plans, subject to reasonable resources from its own plan and adding those available from the Centre, aimed at achieving the state's agricultural growth objective, keeping in view the sustainable management of natural resources and technological possibilities in each agro-climatic region. This plan should then determine each district's final resource envelope, their production plan, and the associated input plan.

The recent Mid-Term Appraisal of the Eleventh Plan has a sober review of this approach:

> States like Madhya Pradesh, Uttarakhand, Kerala, Tripura, Punjab, and West Bengal have adopted the approach to some extent while others are still dragging their feet in this regard. Comprehensiveness and convergence was the other important objective of C-DAP preparation. Madhya Pradesh, Uttarakhand, Haryana, Andhra Pradesh, Himachal Pradesh have achieved this objective to some extent. But convergence of non-governmental programmes has been invariably omitted by the states. (GoI 2010: 76)

The National Food Security Mission (NFSM) is a new centrally sponsored scheme, which was launched starting with rabi 2007–8. This scheme included three components: NFSM-rice, NFSM-wheat, and NFSM-pulses. The main objectives of NFSM are to increase the production of rice, wheat, and pulses through area expansion and productivity enhancement in a sustainable manner in certain identified districts of the country. The results are again uneven.

A rudimentary district agricultural plan exists for each district. But an IRMA (Institute of Rural Management Anand) State of Panchayats Report for 2008–9 did not find any district very savvy on such a plan. So there maybe some disconnects to remedy.

With regard to banking finance for projects in the agro-climatic approach, NABARD had introduced a concept of agro-climatic planning in its lending in 1990 but that was allowed to get into disuse. This concept is being reintroduced. NABARD was to write its annual report on financing agro-climatic plans in 1990, but under the V.P. Singh and Narasimha Rao governments the entire system was dismantled. The earlier NABARD report was in the old style, funding each programme. NABARD's new thinking is state of the art in the rural development game. It sees its role as developing refinancing for financial products to suit each region's agricultural priorities leaving the state funding to the plan. This is fascinating and can really go far. Very few private and no foreign banks, apart from the Dutch Coop Rabo, go where no man has gone before. Some states have worked it out. For example, Maharashtra has an easy scheme to finance watershed development, ridge furrows, seeds for tree crops, even expensive ones as in Bt, drips, and for the tree-growing cycle for horticulture, but that is an exception. There can be many new needs. Fodder crops, money for innovative water management, combinations of farm ponds and drips, piped delivery systems, certifying organics, meeting the preliminary costs of leaching the soil of accumulated muck, and so on. The usual examples are to the contrary in many states. Producer groups incorporated in the Companies Act do not get working capital since the rules are there only for cooperatives.

Technology is going to be the kingpin of solutions. Since the high rate of capital formation in India agriculture (21 per cent of agricultural GDP) is not leading to a commensurate increase in agricultural growth, those groups which are pushing technology should be in the driver's seat and with performance markers. Since the land base has stopped growing, productivity growth will have to be much higher. At the request of the present author, an Indian Statistical Institute team (Mukherjee et al. 2001) worked out that the past growth of productivity in agriculture was 1.62 per cent per annum in 1981–90 and 1.55 per cent per annum in 1991–2000. This growth will have to be 1.72 to 2.08 per cent per annum in 2001–20 if agriculture grows at roughly 3.5 to 4 per cent per annum and 1.9 to 2.5 per cent per annum if agriculture grows at 3.8 to 4.8 per annum in 2001–20. Thus, to source higher growth, factor productivity will have to rise at least by a third, which is difficult in agriculture. A discussion of agro-climatic planning and policies highlights the importance of holistic approaches given the resource endowments of a region. These would include agricultural diversification, including animal husbandry and the neglected sector of tree crops and forestry.

The technology interface is important, both for land and water management and for cropping and non-crop farm systems that are optimal in this class of issues. While a lot of research has been done and is available, the real issues are policy rules for fast replicability of existing knowledge and success stories. Community institutions have to be at the heart of this process. The successful projects that have been examined have varied considerably. Watershed development for settled agriculture, alternative tree crops, reclamation of saline lands, lower-level irrigation systems run by farmers, aquifer management in difficult situations, like coastal aquifers, tribal irrigation cooperatives, and tank irrigation have all been reported as success stories and studied. The question is replicability on a larger scale. We have (Alagh 2003) tried to set out some policy rules, which we argued may reverse the tide if applied in functioning policies. Progress has recently been reviewed (Planning Commission 2008).

The producers' company legislation now on the statute book provides an important method of strengthening farmers' groups to take advantage of strategic alliances for growth, following the cooperative principle. The cooperative principle is alive and kicking, if we have the strength to adapt and innovate. It is early hours yet and the mixture of public and private initiatives in strategic organizations is a question with experimental possibilities. In the forthcoming period, farmers groups, and stakeholder organizations and cooperatives, apart from playing a larger role themselves, will also play a larger role in strategic partnerships with business groups. Otherwise interaction between atomistic peasants and large companies may create problematic situations. However, the more we encourage organizations of smaller producers to organize their interests and strategize their relations with large companies, the better and more enduring will be the systems that we will create.

YOGINDER K. ALAGH

References

Alagh, M. 2004. 'Aggregate Agricultural Supply Function in India', *Economic and Political Weekly*, 10 January, 39(2): 202–6.

Alagh, Yoginder. K. 1997. 'Agricultural Investment and Growth', Inaugral Address of the 56th Annual Conference of the Indian Society of Agricultural Economics, *Indian Journal of Agricultural Economics*, April–June, pp. 279–87.

——. 2001. *Sustainable Development India: 2020,* UNU/IAS. (also see by Yoginder K. Alagh, 'India 2020', *Journal of Quantitative Economics*, January 2006, pp. 1–14).

——. 2003. 'Emerging Institutions and Organisations: Some Aspects of Sustainable Rural Development', in K. Chopra, C.H. Hanumantha Rao, and R.P. Sengupta (eds), *Water:*

Resources, Sustainable Livelihoods and Eco-system Services*, Delhi, Concept.
——. 2004. *State of the Indian Farmer—A Millennium Study: An Overview*, New Delhi, Academic Press.
——. 2009. *Evaluation Report of FAO Cooperation with India: 2003–2008*, Rome, FAO.
——. 2011. 'Agriculture in a Rural Urban Continuum', *Indian Journal of Agricultural Economics*, April–June, pp. 165–77.
Bhalla, G.S. 1974. *Changing Agrarian Structure in India*, Delhi, Minakshi.
FAO. 2008. *Accelerating Agricultural Growth in India*, New Delhi, Ministry of Agriculture, Government of India.
Mukherjee, Robin, Manabendhu Chattopadhyay, and Chiranjib Neogi. 2001. *Productivity, Human Development and Basic Needs in India*, Calcutta, Indian Statistical Institute.
Paddock, William and Paul Paddock. 1968. *Famine 1975, America's Decision: Who Will Survive*, Boston, Little Brown & Co.
Planning Commission, Government of India. 2008. *Eleventh Five Year Plan: 2007/2012*, New Delhi, Oxford University Press.
——. 2010. *Mid-Term Appraisal of Eleventh Plan*, available at www.planningcommission,nic.in.
Vyas, V.S., D.S. Tyagi, and V.N. Misra. 1969. *Significance of the New Strategy of Agricultural Development for Small Farmers*, Vallabh Vidyanagar, Agro-Economic Research Centre

Growth Experience[1]

India's economic performance during the first three decades since Independence was christened the 'Hindu' rate of growth, a term connoting a disappointing but not disastrous outcome, and playing on the cliché of acquiescence in the present that the religion supposedly imparts, because of a greater emphasis on the hereafter.

That cliché, of course, is gradually lapsing into disuse thanks to the remarkable transformation in India during the last 25 years. Since 1980, its economic growth rate has more than doubled, rising from 1.7 per cent (in per capita terms) in 1950–80 to nearly 4 per cent thereafter. Shackled by the socialist policies and the 'license-permit-quota raj' (to use Rajaji's memorable phrase) of the past, India used to serve as an exemplar of development strategies gone wrong. It has now become the latest poster child for how economic growth can be unleashed with a turn towards free markets and open trade. India has yet to catch up with China's growth rates (or China's level of income), but thanks to its solid democratic institutions and impressive performance in information technology, the country is increasingly vying with China as the country of the future.

This entry describes and analyses the Indian growth experience from two perspectives. First, it documents the facts on India's *aggregate* growth performance over time and presents a view on when and why it turned around. Second, it lists the facts relating to *growth across the states* within India, and offers explanations for the variation in state-level economic growth. Lastly, it raises some questions for the future, relating to aggregate and state-level growth.

Aggregate Growth

The most striking fact about India's growth has been the remarkable turnaround in nearly all measures of growth performance since 1980 (Figure 1). Output per capita, output per worker, as well as total factor productivity accelerated sharply after 1980. For example, total factor productivity (TFP), which grew at about 0.3 per cent per annum during the 1960–80 period, grew at close to 2 per cent per annum in the following two decades.

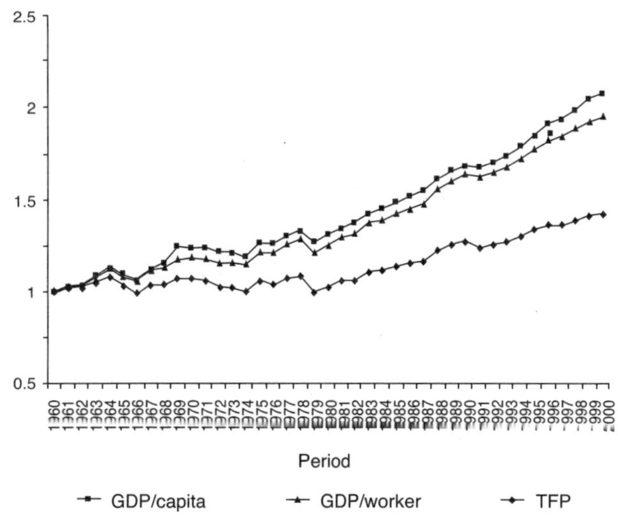

Figure 1 Economic Performance in India, 1960–2000 (log scale, 1960=1)

Source: Rodrik and Subramanian (2005).

A growth accounting decomposition also shows that the contribution of growth of TFP to overall labour productivity growth, which was meagre prior to 1980, was exceptionally high—about 60 per cent—between 1980 and 2000, a performance that was only surpassed by China (Table 1). Indian per capita income growth since 1980 has, therefore, been extensive—motored by productivity—and hence sustainable in the future, rather than based on capital accumulation (or deferred gratification), which

[1]This entry draws extensively upon Rodrik and Subramanian (2004, 2005) and Kochhar et al. (2006).

Table 1 India: Aggregated and Sectoral Growth Accounting (annual average growth rates, unless otherwise specified)

	1960–70	1970–80	1980–90	1990–9
Bosworth–Collins (B–C)				
Output	3.84	2.98	5.85	5.59
Output per worker (Q/L)	1.87	0.69	3.90	3.27
Capital per worker	0.83	0.61	1.06	1.32
Education	0.29	0.58	0.32	0.34
Total factor productivity (TFP)	0.74	–0.50	2.49	1.57
IMF				
Output	3.75	3.16	5.64	5.61
Output per worker	1.77	0.86	3.69	3.30
Total factor productivity 1/	1.17	0.47	2.89	2.44
Total factor productivity 2/	–0.94	–2.07	1.28	0.94
Disaggregated growth of Q/L based on current employment shares				
Agriculture 3/	1.20	0.13	2.57	1.29
Manufacturing 4/		2.00	6.30	6.00
Services (B–C) 5/		2.12	6.32	6.57
Services (IMF) 6/		3.14	5.30	6.69
Growth rate of aggregate Q/L with base-period employment share as weights				
Aggregate (B–C)		0.69	3.66	3.08
Aggregate (IMF)		0.86	3.49	3.11
Contribution of labor-shifts to aggregate Q/L growth				
Aggregate (B–C)	n.a.		0.24	0.19
Aggregate (IMF)	n.a.		0.20	0.19
Employment Share 7/		1975	1985	1995
Agriculture		70.8	64.4	60.8
Industry		12.4	15.2	15.8
Services		16.8	20.4	23.4

Source: Rodrik and Subramanian (2005).
1. Based on labour force.
2. Based on average years of schooling of population above 15 years of age.
3. From World Bank's World Development Indicators.
4. For 1980s and 1990s, data from IMF Working Paper; for 1970s, estimate based on Ahluwalia (1995).
5. Calculated as a residual by deducting weighted average sectoral productivity growth rates from B–C agg. Q/L growth rate.
6. Calculated as a residual by deducting weighted average sectoral productivity growth rates from IMF agg. Q/L growth rate.
7. Obtained from Ghose (1999). His number for 1977–8 is extrapolated backward to 1975 by applying the trend between 1977–8 and 1983 and his number for 1993–4 is extrapolated forward to 1995 by applying the trend between 1987–8 and 1993–4.
Note: Bosworth–Collins (B–C) is from Bosworth and Collins (2003).

runs into the limits imposed by diminishing returns to capital. From being a caricature of inefficiency, India has become the model for high and efficient growth.

This turnaround has also been true at the level of the three major sectors, especially manufacturing and services (Table 1). Agricultural growth accelerated by about 2.7 per cent between the 1970s and 1980s, and manufacturing and services posted growth rates of over 6 per cent in the 1980s and 1990s, compared to about 2–3 per cent in the years before that.

The surge in Indian growth after 1980 was accompanied by a reduction in the instability of growth. The standard deviation in the growth of output per worker which was 3.7 pre-1980 declined sharply to 1.9 per cent thereafter, a performance that surpassed that of nearly every other country. Thus, in the period after 1980, India has had very high but also very stable growth.

The improvement in India's performance since the 1980s is also confirmed by cross-national evidence in the form of Barro-type cross-country growth regressions for the periods 1960–80 and 1980–99. These regressions suggest that, after controlling for policies, endowments, and initial income, India grew 0.7 per cent per year slower than the average country in the 1960–80 period, but grew 2.1 per cent per year faster than the average country in the 1980–99 period. These results indicate that India's turnaround is not a consequence merely of catching up. In the cross-section, the magnitude of overperformance in the latter period has been substantial and exceeds the magnitude of underperformance in the 1960–80 period (Rodrik and Subramanian 2005).

How can this 'reversal of fortune' around 1980 be explained, especially since in the conventional rendition of the Indian economic story, serious reforms and the break with the dirigiste past occurred when India experienced a serious external crisis in 1991, at least 10 years after the turnaround?

A number of plausible explanations can easily be ruled out. External liberalization could not have been a factor because the Indian trade regime actually became more restrictive during the 1980s, and the full impact of trade reforms implemented in the 1990s was only felt at the end of the 1990s. Very little internal reform, of product and labour markets, was witnessed in the 1980s, and the only serious effort in this area—the delicensing of Indian manufacturing—started late in the 1980s and was fairly limited in scope; in other words, it was 'too little, too late' to explain the turnaround in performance.

Another strand of opinion (Ahluwalia 2000; Srinivasan and Tendulkar 2003) downplays what happened in the 1980s, arguing that 'the fiscal expansionism of the 1980s, accompanied by some liberalization of controls on economic activity, generated real GDP growth of more than 5.8 per cent a year. This expansionism, however, was not sustainable and led to the macroeconomic crisis of 1991' (Srinivasan and Tendulkar 2003: 9).

This Keynesian-run-amok explanation is, at first blush, supported by the data. During the 1970s, the average consolidated government deficit averaged 5 per cent of GDP. During the 1980s, this had soared to 9 per cent, an annual increase of 4 percentage points. But it is not clear how demand (fiscal) expansion can explain a large and sustained rise in *trend productivity*. After all, Latin America went on a fiscal binge in the 1970s without experiencing a corresponding improvement in supply-side performance.

The only possible explanation would rely on sustained differences in capacity utilization across time. One way to control for such a demand-induced increase in productivity is to compute the productivity aggregates incorporating changes in capacity utilization. One consistent estimate for the 1970s and 1980s (World Bank 1995) implies an increase in capacity utilization of about 2.7 per cent, which would have the effect of reducing measured TFP growth in the 1980s by about 1 per cent per year. Even on the strong assumption that all this change in capacity is demand-induced, the turnaround in TFP growth between the 1970s and 1980s would remain substantial (about 2–2.2 per cent per year).

An alternative explanation comprises three elements. First, there was an attitudinal change on the part of the government in the 1980s, signalling a shift in favour of the private sector, with this shift validated in a very haphazard and gradual manner through actual policy changes. Second, this shift and the limited policy changes were *pro-business* rather than *pro-competition*, aimed primarily at benefiting incumbents in the formal industrial and commercial sectors. Third, these small shifts elicited a large productivity response because India was far away from its income possibility frontier.

Sometime in the early 1980s there was a significant attitudinal change towards the private sector on the part of the national government, led by Indira Gandhi's Congress Party. The Congress went from being hostile to private business to mildly supportive, and eventually quite supportive. This change was inaugurated with the return of a much-chastened Indira Gandhi to political power in the 1980s after a three-year rule by the Janata Party.

As already noted, there were few significant policy changes in the early 1980s, and the changes later on (beginning in 1985) were restricted largely to some internal liberalization relating to the relaxation of industrial licensing. The limited nature of these changes, as well as the form that they took, is best understood by appreciating the political logic of Indira Gandhi's (and later Rajiv Gandhi's) efforts. These were aimed to gather support from the business establishment rather than to alienate it. Hence there was more action where business support existed—for example, in reducing taxes, easing access to imported capital inputs, or liberalizing capacity restrictions—than where it did not—for example, in external liberalization.

I make a distinction here between a *pro-market* and *pro-business* orientation. The former focuses on removing impediments to markets and aims to achieve this through economic liberalization. It favours entrants and consumers. A pro-business orientation, on the other hand, is one that focuses on raising the profitability of the established industrial and commercial establishments. It tends to favour incumbents and producers. Nevertheless, this shift towards a pro-business orientation was the essential trigger that set off the boom of the 1980s.

That an attitudinal change on the part of the national leadership could have such a strong impact on growth is in turn grounded in India's initial conditions. India has very strong political and economic institutions for a country at its income level. It is a democracy where the rule of law generally prevails and property rights are adequately protected. Judged by cross-country norms, it ought to have a level of income that is several times higher (see Rodrik and Subramanian 2004: Table 3). The implication is that relatively minor changes in the policy environment can produce a large growth impact. The suspension of the national government's hostility to the private sector could be interpreted as one such change, something that left little paper trail in actual policies but had an important impact on investors' psychology.

State-level Growth

Prior to 1980, the growth rate of the Indian states was mediocre but relatively uniform. After 1980, however, the fortunes of the states diverged considerably (Ahluwalia 2000). Figure 2 plots the log of per capita GDP for all states for every 10 years beginning in 1960. From 1980 onwards, there is both an upward trend in the average as well as a wider spread in the distribution of incomes. A more formal test of convergence between states for the four decades suggests that there is clear evidence of fortunes diverging in the 1980s but especially in the 1990s and beyond.

What explains this divergent pattern of growth across states in India? Prior to 1960, it is difficult to explain this variation because economic decision-making was largely centralized. After 1980, however, some clearer patterns become evident. It appears that two sets of factors played a role. First, different states had different pre-existing capabilities. But these remained latent and could not find expression until the economic environment changed. The trigger—the second set—was the liberalization that began in 1980, and especially the decentralization of economic power that was forced by the changing political landscape after 1980. Thus it was the interaction between pre-existing capabilities and the twin triggers of liberalization and decentralization that explains how the different states fared.

What was this pre-existing capability? It turns out that this capability was something more than a state's level of development or educational level or geography. It is best captured by how diversified a state's manufacturing base was. This diversified base is probably a proxy for some generalized capability—human capital, entrepreneurial spirit, organizational capital—that could exploit a favourable economic environment.

Figure 3 illustrates this capability at work. It plots the Herfindahl coefficient of concentration within manufacturing in the different states in the early 1980s against their subsequent overall growth rates. The relationship is strongly negative, that is, the less concentrated the manufacturing base to begin with (or the more diversified it was), the faster the subsequent growth. This relationship is confirmed more formally in Kochhar et al. (2006).

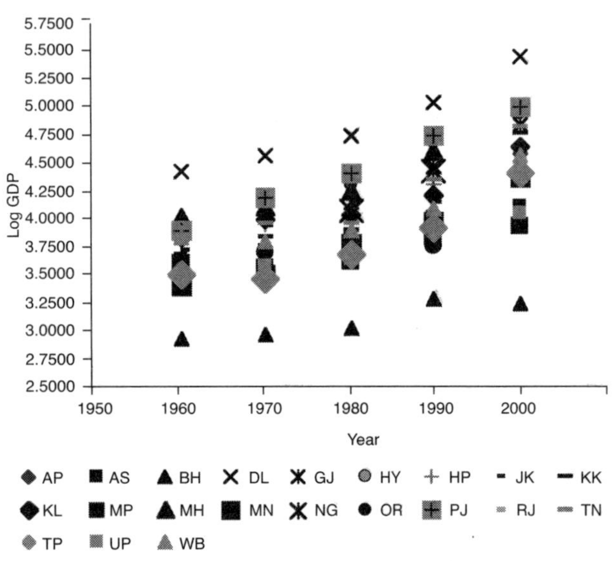

Figure 2 Divergence across States, 1960–2000

Source: Rodrik and Subramanian (2005).

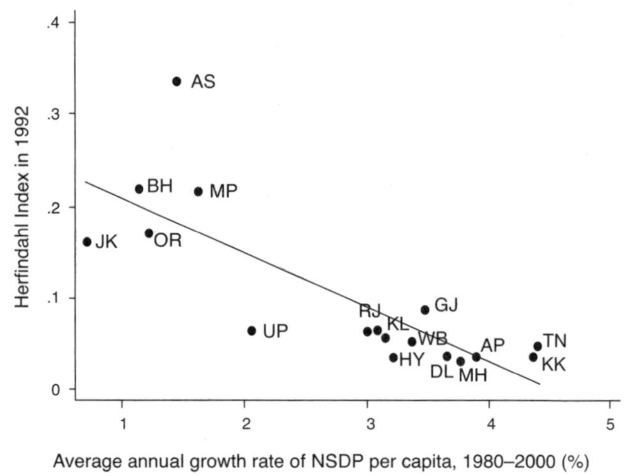

Figure 3 Diversification and States' Growth

Source: Kochhar et al. (2006).
Notes: NSDP is the net state domestic product. For each state, the Herfindahl Index measures concentration of value added across three-digit industries in 1982; the lower the index, the lower the concentration, or the higher the diversification.

Consider next the triggers of liberalization and decentralization. While the formal reforms at the Centre received tremendous publicity, perhaps less noticed was the growing decentralization of policy. The Congress Party had held power without a break at the Centre since Independence, but the aura of invincibility surrounding it started waning soon after Indira Gandhi lost the post-Emergency election in 1977. Also, even though the Congress Party returned to power at the Centre through much of the 1980s, a number of states were captured by the opposition, often by regional or even single state parties.

No longer could a regional leader be confident that the Centre—especially if the party in power was different from that running the state—would dole out its bounty fairly across states, and over time. Also, the parties in power could change, so that implicit agreements reached by prior governments might not be honoured by subsequent governments. Simply put, the centrifugal forces created by the dispersion of political power in India did not sit well with the enormous centralization of economic power, and the inter-state cross-subsidies the Centre effected through its investment strategy. Something had to give, and it was the centralization of economic power.

Greater economic decentralization meant states could differentiate themselves, not least in their ability to attract private-sector investment. This was, of course, facilitated by the gradual dismantling of the industrial licensing system that used regional equity as one of the primary criteria guiding industrial investments. Further contributing to differentiation over this period was the rising trend in private investment, as well as the falling trend in public investment, with private investment likely to be more sensitive to differences in policies across states.

The decentralization dynamic is most visible in the divergence in economic performance across states that was illustrated in Figure 2. The decentralization dynamic can be seen in yet another way: if decentralization was indeed important, then states' economic performance should be more closely tied to state-level policies and institutions in the post-1980s period than before. After all, if the pre-1980s era was about the Centre deciding, for example, where and how much electricity capacity to instal, there is little that the states could have done to affect economic performance within their borders. This is exactly what the evidence shows. For example, when state-level growth is related to state-level policies and institutions, the latter are found to have no role in explaining growth prior to 1980 but a robust role in explaining post-1980s, especially post-1990s, growth. This is illustrated in Figure 4.

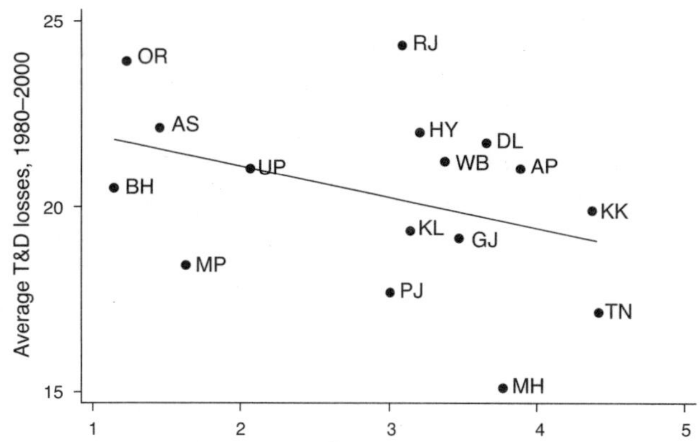

Figure 4 Institutions and States' Growth

Source: Kochhar et al. (2006).
Notes: NSDP is the net state domestic product. Institutions are proxied by transmission and distribution losses (T&D) of the State Electricity Boards, which is the fraction of electrical power generated but not paid for, measured as a per cent of availability.

As a measure of state policies and institutions affecting the quality of infrastructure and the business environment, the transmission and distribution losses (T&D losses) of State Electricity Boards (as a fraction of generating capacity) are used. T&D losses refer to power that is generated but not paid for—in part because some of it is lost naturally along power lines in the process of T&D, but also in part because it is stolen. In areas where T&D losses are high, the quality of power, as reflected in the voltage as well as reliability, is low. Thus T&D losses are not directly related to capacity, but are determined by state-level political decisions. They broadly reflect the quality of both infrastructure and institutions (politicians turning a blind eye to power theft by their constituencies, or politicians' unwillingness to enforce laws, as well as viability and level of corruption in State Electricity Boards).

As Figure 4 shows, there is a negative correlation between the average T&D losses in 1980–2000 in a state and its growth during that period. Formal regression analysis confirms this tighter relationship between state-level institutions and state-level performance for the 1990s (Kochhar et al. 2006).[2]

[2]The relationship between state-level growth and institutions is robust to alternative ways of measuring the quality of institutions (see Kochhar et al. 2006).

Economic development results from the interaction of growth triggers with the right fundamentals that allow the triggers to be exploited. In the conventional view of the Indian development process, there was a long and dark period—the period of controls and import substitution—followed by the burst of sunlight and reforms since 1991. The boom in the IT sector first awakened observers to the fact that the dark age was not all dark, that important cumulative elements (the fundamentals) were being built up that yielded rewards with a lag, and that these fundamentals were as important as the triggers that sparked the IT boom.

The fundamentals were not just the pools of skilled human capital built through the technology, management, and research institutes—a sort of import substitution effort in skilled human capital development—that were integral to the Nehruvian vision. They went beyond and consisted of the meta institutions of democracy, rule of law, free press, and technocratic bureaucracy that recent research shows are crucial to economic development.

Looking ahead, a big uncertainty relates to the quality of these institutions. While the scope of state activities is desirably shrinking, there are core functions that need an effective, competent state. The Nehruvian meta institutions have been buffeted and weakened by the vicissitudes of vested interests, time, and politics. While transparency has increased dramatically, there seems to be less and less accountability of key public institutions.

Institutional decline will not just need to be averted at the national level but also at the level of the states. Higher growth in India is leading to more divergent growth, with some key states—Bihar, Uttar Pradesh, Rajasthan, and Madhya Pradesh—lagging considerably behind. These are also the most populous states and any large divergence between political and economic power will assert itself—negatively—for example, through demands for inefficient distribution.

So a key question is how the process of divergence within India can be reversed. In theory, free mobility of capital and labour should facilitate convergence. But capital will not flow into the lagging states, which are stuck in a governance trap. Because basic state functions such law and order, an efficient bureaucracy, and competent courts have not been provided, they have remained poor, which in turn has led to exit of the middle class and the skilled, leading to a further hollowing out of state capabilities. If this continues, the process of arresting divergence could take the form of large labour *outflows* from the backward states. This would create its own tensions. Averting them by creating the conditions for greater economic convergence across states and skill groups will be a big challenge for India in the years ahead.

ARVIND SUBRAMANIAN

References

Ahluwalia, Montek. 2000. 'Economic Performance of States in the Post Reforms Period', *Economic and Political Weekly*, 6 May, 35(19): 1637–48.

Bosworth, B. and S. Collins. 2002. 'Economic Reforms in India since 1991: Has Gradualism Worked', *Journal of Economic Perspectives*, 16(7): 67–88.

——. 2003. 'The Empirics of Growth: An Update', Brookings Paper on Economic Activity, Brookings Institution.

Ghose, A.K. 1999. 'Current Issues of Employment Policy in India', *Economic and Political Weekly*, 4 September, 34(36): 2592–608.

Rodrik, Dani and Arvind Subramanian. 2004. 'Why India Can Grow at 7 per cent a Year or More? Projections and Reflections', *Economic and Political Weekly*, 17 April, 39(16): 1591–6.

——. 2005. 'From Hindu Growth to Productivity Surge: The Mystery of the Indian Growth Transition,' *IMF Staff Papers*, 52(2).

Kochhar, Kalpana, Utsav Kumar, Raghuram Rajan, Arvind Subramanian, and Ioannis Tokatlidis. 2006. 'India's Pattern of Development: What Happened, What Follows', *Journal of Monetary Economics*, 53(5): 981–1019.

Srinivasan, T.N. and S. Tendulkar. 2003. *Reintegrating India with the World Economy*, Washington DC, Institute for International Economics.

World Bank. 1995. 'India: Recent Economic Developments and Prospects', Country Report, Washington DC.

■ Low-carbon Growth and Development

Introduction: The Global Problem

Unless the world embarks now on a new energy and industrial revolution and a transition to a low-carbon economy and society, it will be very difficult to manage the huge risks of climate change. Continuing with 'business-as-usual' (BAU) for the next few decades will bring grave risks. Greenhouse gas (GHG) concentrations (or stocks) have increased to around 445 parts per million (ppm) of carbon-dioxide-equivalent (CO_2e). If we continued with BAU for a century we would likely add at least 300 ppm,[1] taking concentrations to around

[1]Concentrations are now rising at a rate of about 2.5 ppm p.a. and that rate is rising.

750 ppm CO_2e or higher around the end of this century. Even if concentrations were stabilized in the next century at 750 ppm, such a path would bring somewhere in the region of a 50–50 chance[2] of a warming of more than 5°C[3] above the mid-19th century, a temperature not seen on Earth for more than 30 million years. *Homo sapiens* have experienced nothing like this, being present for only around 200,000 years. Our own civilization, with the cultivation of cereals and other crops, and the potential for non-agricultural and village and town life it brought, dates from the period after the last ice age, around 10,000 years ago—after warming up following the ice age, global average temperatures appear to have stayed in a narrow range, around plus or minus 1.5°C from the 19th century. We are already 0.8°C above the 19th century average global temperature.

The rise in temperatures would likely cause large-scale disruption to local habitats and climates, for example, through flooding, desertification, and water scarcity. Hundreds of millions of people would have to move, with the associated risks of severe and extended conflict. These impacts would put at risk the great advances in development and inclusion of the last few decades, which have seen hundreds of millions rise out of income poverty, great improvements in health and life expectancy, major advances in education and literacy, and increased participation in society, especially for women.

While none of the predictions can be made with certainty, it is clear that the potential risks are huge and the probabilities are not small. India is especially vulnerable to the impacts of climate change with its large fraction of the population near the coast, its pressures on water supply, its dependence on the Himalayan region as a water source and on the patterns of monsoons, and the location of the many populous countries along its northern borders.

Given the risks, a high-carbon growth strategy is unsustainable and not a serious medium- or long-term option for the world or any major part of it. A transition to low-carbon growth and the new energy and industrial revolution is a far more attractive path. The history of past waves of technological change suggests the transition will be a dynamic period full of innovation, creativity, opportunity, and growth. And the low-carbon economy and society is likely to be cleaner, quieter, safer, more energy-secure and more bio-diverse.

[2]It is difficult to be precise about these probabilities, but the risk is clearly substantial.

[3]This warming would be lagged several decades behind the increases in GHG level.

Low-carbon growth is necessary for the next two or three decades in the developing world if we are to rise to the two defining challenges of our century: overcoming poverty and managing climate change. Failure on one implies failure on the other: unmanaged climate change risks irretrievably damaging prospects for development and greater inclusion over the course of the century, and action on climate change which hinders development and inclusion can never build the global coalition on which effective, efficient, and equitable action depends.

Scale of the Challenge: Mitigation and Global Targets

To manage the risks of climate change, the world must act together and achieve major reductions in emissions. Greater understanding has emerged in recent years, guided by the science, around the scale of the reductions necessary.

Figure 1 illustrates global emission paths consistent with limiting (with around a 50 per cent probability) average global temperature increases to no more than 2°C, the level above which is taken in international negotiations and by most countries to be dangerous. Whilst there are some, albeit limited, options on timing of reductions, global emissions paths that can achieve a 50–50 chance of meeting the 2°C goal would need to peak within 10 years.

Starting at the current (2010) global level of 47 billion tonnes of CO_2e p.a., the most plausible paths pass well below 35 billion tonnes of CO_2e in 2030, and well below

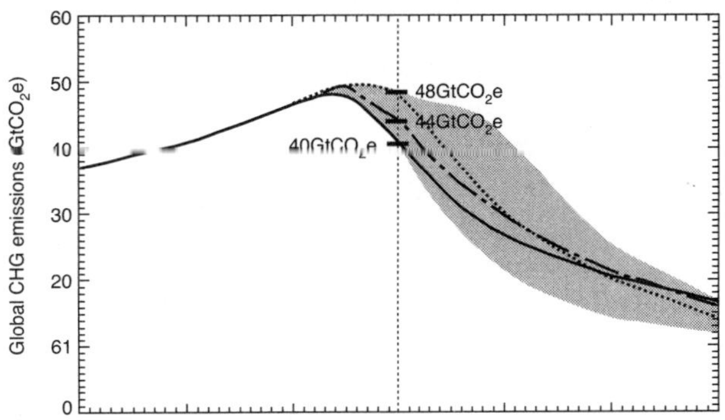

Figure 1 Paths for Global Annual Emissions that Lead to a Reasonable Chance of a Temperature Rise of No More than 2°C

Source: Bowen and Ranger (2009).

Note: The shaded area represents the range of emission paths that are consistent with a reasonable chance, around 50–50, of the 2°C goal and the three lines show specific paths within this range.

20 billion tonnes of CO_2e in 2050. These numbers, 35 billion tonnes in 2030 and 20 billion tonnes in 2050, are crucial. If we are serious about achieving a reasonable chance of holding to 2°C they must be understood as essentially global constraints. If we break them as a world, it will be very difficult to catch up later. We cannot negotiate with the laws of physics and chemistry.

Delay is dangerous: the flow-stock process and the difficulty of removing GHGs means there is a ratchet effect. And lock-in of infrastructure and capital equipment exacerbates the dangers of delay. If we do not act strongly over the coming few years we will likely miss the opportunity of a reasonable chance of holding temperature increases to 2°C.

Sustainability and the Relationship between Mitigation, Adaptation, and Development

We discuss sustainability here primarily in terms of actions and policies to reduce emissions and support the transition to low-carbon growth. But actions and policy to promote sustainability must go much further than simply reducing emissions. The notion of sustainability is usually understood as 'sustaining the opportunities' of the next generation so that their freedoms are no less than those we enjoy. This could include a notion of a duty to preserve key aspects of our planet, such as the environment and other species, for our descendants to understand and appreciate. The implications of such a notion suggest a more holistic approach to policy for sustainability is warranted rather than solely emission reductions. It would encompass a wide range of actions including on climate change, water management, land and air pollution, waste management, forests, oceans, biodiversity, and natural resources. Indeed these are all intimately related. Policies to make progress in one of these areas are likely to help with others. For example, policy to reduce landfill waste may involve the capture of methane, a potent GHG, to generate low-carbon electricity; sound forest management may help manage water and biodiversity; and so on. Given these relationships and interactions, we need to pay very careful attention to make sure policy is designed appropriately in relation to sustainability interpreted broadly.

No matter how successful we are with actions and policies to reduce emissions and to promote the transition to low-carbon growth, we are committed over the next few decades to substantial climate change due to past and future emissions. That means countries will have to adapt. The challenge is particularly difficult and urgent for developing countries, including India, as they are likely to be hit earliest and hardest. Adaptation is essentially development in a more hostile climate. It is an intricate part of the low-carbon development story and its importance should not be underestimated or overlooked. It clearly makes no sense to plan and act as if climate is stable when there is powerful evidence that it is changing.

Development in a more hostile climate will be more difficult and costly. The first priority is to understand the risks, and this will require detailed and collaborative analysis involving those with detailed local knowledge of developing countries and those working on world-level modelling and analysis. The second priority is to understand how climate change and its local effects should affect development strategy, including infrastructure (water, road transport, flood protection, power, and so on), the planning and protection of cities, and rural policy, including the promotion of agricultural practices and investments that are more climate-resilient. Disaster protection, insurance, and risk-sharing must all be examined. All countries should integrate such analyses into their investments and development planning.

Such an understanding underscores the importance of integrating development, mitigation, and adaptation. For example, low-till agriculture can reduce emissions from soil. But there are also significant co-benefits in that low-till agriculture saves water (it enhances water retention in the soil and slows evaporation, reducing the need for irrigation), energy, labour, and maintenance. Low-till also protects topsoil in the face of more hostile weather conditions, leading to enhanced yields and less chemical run-off into water supplies. Policies that recognize these links and co-benefits will not only succeed in reducing emissions, but also assist communities to adapt and develop. The importance of integrating action across development, mitigation, and adaptation also suggests that funding across these areas should be integrated.

Equity and the Relationship between Rich and Poor Peoples

Emission paths in the centre of the range illustrated in Figure 1 correspond to emissions per capita of around 7 tonnes per capita in 2010, 6 in 2020, 4 in 2030, and 2 in 2050, since world population is close to 7 billion now and is likely to rise to around 9 billion in 2050. For comparison, the US, Canada, and Australia are currently well over 20 tonnes per capita p.a. CO_2e, Europe and Japan 10–12, China close to 7, India below but close to 2, and much of Sub-Saharan Africa below 1. This is a story of strong inequality in current emissions and an even stronger story of inequality in the history of emissions, with the rich countries (currently around 1 billion population) responsible for more than 60 per cent of current concentrations.

Many of the poorest people in the world will be the most exposed and vulnerable to the impacts of climate change that will occur over the next few decades. These are also the people who are least able to afford the costs of adaptation, and who have contributed much less than those in the rich world to the current levels of GHGs in the atmosphere. There is a fundamental double inequity here and a strong moral imperative for the rich countries to provide more funds to developing countries, in addition to current development commitments, to fund the extra costs created by climate change. This is also in the direct interest of rich countries: as Archbishop Desmond Tutu argued 'the problems of the poor will arrive at the doorstep of the wealthy, as the climate crisis gives way to despair, anger and collective security threats'.

There are powerful arguments that funding for adaptation should be additional to, but not separated from, current commitments on Overseas Development Assistance (ODA), given that many of these commitments were made before those working on development were fully aware of the scale of the problems of climate change. As we look forward to the challenges the developing world faces beyond 2015, and we should already be examining and formulating the successors to the millennium development goals (MDGs) beyond 2015, we must take careful account of the tasks of both mitigation and adaptation and other integration with development.

From this perspective, targets for support from the public budgets of rich countries are likely to be closer to 1.0 per cent of GDP rather than 0.7 per cent for the coming two decades.

The High-Level Advisory Group on Climate Change Financing, established by the Secretary-General of the UN following the United Nations Framework Convention on Climate Change (UNFCCC) Conference of the Parties (COP 15) in Copenhagen in 2009, examined possible funding sources. AGF (2010) reported on options for generating, by 2020, US$ 100 billion per year, including both public and private resources, as flows from developed to developing countries in order to support adaptation and mitigation activities. The establishment of the Green Climate Fund in 2010 at the UNFCCC, COP 16, in Cancun, Mexico, was a further positive and complementary step. This fund will aim to generate and mobilize funding for developing countries. Note that the inequity should be recognized through funding and technology. There is no way of achieving global averages of less than 4 tonnes per capita in 2030, and 2 tonnes per capita in 2050, unless the 7 billion out of 8 billion people in developing countries in 2030, and 8 billion out of 9 billion in 2050, have averages close to these levels.

The New Energy–Industrial Revolution and Low-carbon Growth

If world economic growth increases at around 3 per cent p.a., on average, in the next 40 years, that is, output expands by around a factor of 3, then emissions per unit of output must be cut by a factor of at least 8 by 2050 for global emissions to be consistent with a 2°C path. We cannot achieve this change if any major economy and sector is left out. Indeed, change on this scale means an energy–industrial revolution.

The transition to low-carbon growth and the new energy and industrial revolution looks like a far more attractive path than an attempt at high-carbon growth and the destruction it risks. Past periods of economic and social transformation, for example, steam and railways, electricity and steel, suggest that this transition is likely to be a period of transformation with two or more decades of strong innovation, creativity, investment, and growth, with investment flowing to the pioneers. It is likely to involve disruption of some current structures and methods, indeed that is the point. This is 'creative destruction' (in the Schumpeterian sense), where new firms and ideas drive out the old, generating a dynamic period of innovation, opportunity, and economic growth. This idea of 'creative destruction', combined with modern growth theories that incorporate endogenous technical change and learning-by-doing, is likely to be central to analyses and understanding of this concept of dynamic and transformative growth (see, for example, Aghion and Howitt 1998).

Many of the actions and policies such as off-grid solar energy, better managed forests, and more careful use of energy and water are likely to involve greater economic and social inclusion. And low-carbon growth, when achieved, will be more energy-secure, cleaner, quieter, safer, and more bio-diverse than its predecessors.

A 'green race' has already begun with, for example, South Korea, China, some parts of Europe, and California moving into the lead. The flow of ideas from industry and research institutions over the last few years has been remarkable. These range from the refinement of existing technologies that has lowered costs and improved effectiveness (solar energy, hybrid cars, cellulosic ethanol), to new and more speculative ideas concerning nanotechnology (including for electricity storage), algae, and so on. Ten to fifteen years from now, countries that choose to go slowly and be left behind are likely to face strong pressure to more rapidly reduce emissions and transform their economies, which could prove substantially more disruptive and expensive than measured and strong action starting now. Such countries may also see their industries shut out of important markets, may be left with stranded high-carbon assets, and may experience significant reputational damage.

China's example is clearly of great importance given its size, rate, and pattern of growth. Its plans, actions, and policies are often poorly understood around the world. China is committed to, and is already planning for, the transition to a low-carbon economy. Their green stimulus of 2008–9, involved strong investment in rail transport and in an advanced, flexible, and interconnected electricity transmission network/grid. It is committing along these lines together with rapid growth in production and use of renewables, regulation of vehicle emissions, reforestation, strong emission intensity, and energy efficiency targets. These are all evidence of a commitment to a changed pattern of growth from that followed over the past two or three decades.

China's Twelfth Five Year Plan, 2011 to 2015, is designed to take this commitment forward and to accelerate the transition to a low-carbon economy. The plan embodies fundamental structural change designed to place China at the forefront of the new energy–industrial revolution.

China will promote seven strategic industries including energy saving and environmental protection, new energy, clean-energy vehicles, next generation information technology, biotechnology, high-end manufacturing, and new materials. China plans to increase the share of GDP in these industries from around 3 per cent today to 15 per cent by 2020. Likely investment in these industries will probably average in the region of half a trillion dollars or more per annum in this decade and see output in these industries increase from around $US 150 billion today to around $US 1.5 to 2 trillion in 2020 (Stern 2011). The Twelfth plan also sets a target for reductions in emissions per unit of output (emissions intensity) of 17 per cent and reductions in energy per unit of output (energy efficiency) of 16 per cent over the plan period. These targets are likely to fall short of what is necessary for a global 2°C path. However, it is possible that the learning from this plan period could allow further acceleration. Understanding of China's action is crucial to an assessment of world prospects on climate change.

Challenges and Opportunities for India

India's development challenges include: improving standards in human health and well-being, improving income inequality, managing water and food security, managing forests and natural ecosystems, and maintaining regional security. These areas are likely to be severely affected by the impacts of climate change, which will make development, greater inclusion, and equality much more difficult to achieve.

Poverty remains widespread with around three-quarters of the total population (around 850 million people) living on less than $2 a day (2005), compared to 85 per cent (around 650 million people) in 1983 (World Bank 2011).[4] The lives of many of these poor people are closely linked to climate-sensitive sectors or problems such as agriculture, drought and water availability, and threats from floods and storms.

There is already evidence of impacts from more intense heatwaves, cyclones, and floods. For example, a recent study of climate variability in the state of Karnataka found that the year-to-year variability in monsoon rainfall shows evidence of more extreme droughts and floods, and that this may be reducing agricultural output (BCCI-K 2011). These impacts are likely to intensify without strong action to manage climate change.

With unmanaged climate change, that would see significant probabilities of global temperatures increasing by around 4–5°C, or higher, on 19th-century levels, the likely impacts could involve: high risks of large increases in disease, morbidity, and mortality due to the compound effects of a more hostile climate and food and water insecurity; significant falls in agricultural output; internal tensions from population movements; threats to regional security due to climate-induced cross-border migration; and tensions over water sharing between neighbouring countries such as Pakistan, Bangladesh, Nepal, and China.

These impacts are likely to threaten and severely disrupt livelihoods, making development much more difficult with the risks of reversal of the advances of the last few decades. The prospects for higher living standards and security for hundreds of millions of people would be put at risk.

[4]Percentage of population living below $2 per day (PPP) at 2005 international prices. (The comparison between periods is illustrative only. There are problems in comparison with earlier periods due to PPP revisions.)

We must recognize that rising material living standards, including having energy and food, are essential for overcoming poverty. Thus growth is necessary for the next two or three decades in the developing world, including India. The most sensible and attractive path over the next two to three decades that will allow developing countries to overcome poverty, raise overall living standards, and allow prosperity for further and sustainable advance is low-carbon growth.

The transition to low-carbon growth and the new energy–industrial revolution holds great promise and opportunity for India, especially for local communities and the poorest in Indian society. For example, at a local level, rapid cost reductions and technological advances in solar power present a real opportunity to bring electricity to the 400 million or so people in India who are currently without power. Decentralized solar power avoids many of the costs of traditional high-carbon infrastructure such as grid connection. Those who control the grid have substantial power over those connected, and local people and communities are vulnerable to exploitation. Renewable power provides both low-carbon electricity and empowers local communities. It can enable both children and adults to study at night. It can enable women to establish businesses. We should not pretend that such changes would be easy. There are many barriers, including vested interests, to the necessary changes. However, none is insurmountable, and overcoming these obstacles is part and parcel of the transition towards a more sustainable low-carbon development path.

Renewable energy investment in India in 2010 was around $3.8 billion (including $3.6 billion in wind and $400 million on solar), an increase of 25 per cent on 2009 (UNEP 2011). This compares with $49 billion of investment in China, $35 billion in Europe, $30 billion in North America, and $3.6 billion in Africa. This rapid growth in India was promoted by tax breaks for wind, the Government's Solar Mission (which aims to achieve 1.1 GW of installed on-grid capacity by 2013), and the Renewable Energy Certificate and Renewable Purchase Obligation Schemes (UNEP 2011).

However, India's investment levels are far lower than required to meet national solar capacity targets. Chakraborty (2011) indicates that $110 billion in investment is required over the next decade to meet the Solar Mission target of 20 GW by 2020, close to triple the current rate of investment. And much of this investment in solar power is and will be on-grid, which will miss the opportunities available from decentralized low-carbon power. India's total investment in renewable energy is also low relative to its main competitors, especially China, which is beginning to take advantage of advances in low-carbon technologies and rapidly falling capital costs of renewable energy to accelerate progress towards low-carbon growth.

The opportunities for India for more inclusive, equitable, and sustainable development from a low-carbon development path are immense. A high-carbon growth path has no future. It will kill itself. First on high prices for hydrocarbons and the risk of being left behind and shut out of key markets, and second and fundamentally on the hostile climate it will create that will disrupt development. It is not a serious medium- or long-term option.

India's National Policies: Recent Progress and the Twelfth Five Year Plan

India has publicly confirmed support for the 2°C target and the need for a global agreement to reduce emissions accordingly (see Major Economies Forum (MEF) Leaders Declaration signed at the G8 Summit, L'Aquila, Italy, 2009).

At the national level, India has made a number of voluntary emission reduction commitments, including the declaration, made by India's Prime Minister in June 2007, that India's per capita emissions level will never exceed the average per capita emissions of developed countries. A voluntary target of a reduction in emissions intensity (emissions per unit of output) of 20–25 per cent over the period 1990 to 2020 was also announced in relation to the Copenhagen Accord (December 2009), and the Cancun agreement at UNFCCC (COP16), December 2010.

India's first major plan on climate change was announced in June 2008. The National Action Plan on Climate Change (NAPCC) aims to promote development and achieve mitigation and adaptation objectives. The plan comprises eight comprehensive 'national missions' including: solar (achieve 20 GW of installed capacity by 2020); enhanced energy efficiency; sustainable habitat; water; sustaining the Himalayan ecosystem; green India; sustainable agriculture; and strategic knowledge for climate change. Progress to date on these national missions has been varied and the development of state action plans is proving a very slow process.

At the international level, India has played a far more constructive role in recent international climate change negotiations. Following the disappointing meeting at

UNFCCC COP15 in Copenhagen in 2009, India sent a more prepared, cohesive, and purposive delegation to UNFCCC COP16 in Cancun in 2010. India's delegation was instrumental in both setting a better atmosphere for discussion and in achieving progress on specific issues, especially on Monitoring, Reporting and Verification (MRV); developing countries agreed to produce biennial update reports on their GHG emissions, which will be reviewed under an international consultation and analysis (ICA) process.

India's focus in coming months will be on preparing its Twelfth Five Year Plan, to be released on 1 April 2012, which will run from 2012 to 2017. Ahluwalia (2011) identifies four critical challenges for the Twelfth Five Year Plan, all of which relate to climate change. These are: managing energy requirements, water economy, addressing problems that could arise from rapid urbanization, and ensuring protection of the environment in a manner that can facilitate rapid growth.

In May 2011, the Planning Commission of India released the interim report from the Expert Group on Low-Carbon Strategies for Inclusive Growth. This report will assist in the development of a low-carbon growth strategy that will form part of the Twelfth Plan. It sets out options and policies for reducing emissions intensity across the power, transport, industry, buildings, and forestry sectors. The analysis indicates India may be able to reduce the emission intensity of GDP by around 25 per cent over the period 2005–20. India's emissions intensity of GDP is (2005) around 760 tonnes of CO_2e per million dollars of GDP (World Resources Institute 2011).[5] This is only slightly higher than the US at around 600 tonnes but well below China at around 1,400 tonnes. It is far above Japan and Germany at around 350 tonnes.

While much further work will be undertaken prior to the release of the Twelfth Plan, this report is a positive development and demonstrates India's increasing recognition of the importance of, and opportunities available from, pursuing a low-carbon growth path, together with the dangers if the world goes the other way. Support from developed countries, on both finance and technology, will help India strengthen and achieve its low-carbon objectives, although India is also likely to contribute strongly to the world in technological advances. India has a unique opportunity in the Twelfth Plan to lay strong foundations for the transition to a far more attractive model of growth and development, in terms of overall living standards, social inclusion, and the environment.

[5]Emissions (tonnes of CO_2e) per unit of GDP (millions of International dollars, constant 2005 PPP).

Conclusion

The two defining challenges of our century are overcoming world poverty and managing climate change. We succeed or fail on both together. India, due to the size of its emissions and population, and its vulnerability to the impacts of climate change, will play a role of fundamental importance.

The risks from unmanaged climate change are immense. Over the coming few years the world must embark on a transition to low-carbon growth and a new energy–industrial revolution. The transformation will not only involve strong action to reduce emissions but also represents a far more attractive low-carbon development path. High-carbon growth is not a serious future option. Delay is dangerous: if we do little over the next 10 or 15 years we will likely lose the opportunity of having a reasonable chance of holding temperature increases to 2°C.

The opportunities from the transition to low-carbon growth are attractive and exciting and, with careful planning, could bring several decades of more inclusive, equitable, and sustainable growth across the world, both for developing and developed countries. The transition has already begun. Global investment in low-carbon technologies is already substantial and continues to grow strongly, despite the financial and political crises around the world. The transition, for those who embrace it, will be dynamic, innovative, full of opportunity, and will drive more sustainable growth across the whole economy.

India's constructive participation in international negotiations was key to progress during the recent international negotiations in Cancun in 2010. India's intentions, plans and voluntary targets, and its aim to include a more ambitious strategy for low-carbon growth in its Twelfth Five Year Plan, can add further to India's standing in the international community and increase its positive influence in moving forward international collaboration and agreement. The example of other major developing countries, including China and Brazil, can provide further momentum and encourage other countries to follow. The alternative is to ignore the risks or place the onus on others to act. This would be a profound misjudgement for any country due to the scale of the challenges we face as a world and the profound limitations of high-carbon growth.

Nicholas Stern, Ruth Kattumuri, and James Rydge

References

Aghion, Philippe and Peter Howitt. 1998. *Endogenous Growth Theory*, MIT Press.

Ahluwalia, Montek S. 2011. 'Prospects and Policy Challenges in the Twelfth Plan', *Economic and Political Weekly*, (46)21: 88–105.

Bangalore Climate Change Initiative—Karnataka (BCCI—K). 2011. *Karnataka Climate Change Action Plan*, an analytical report submitted to the government of Karnataka, available at http://www2.lse.ac.uk/asiaResearchCentre/_files/KarnatakaCCactionPlanFinal.pdf.

Bowen, Alex and Nicola Ranger. 2009. 'Mitigating Climate Change through Reductions in Greenhouse Gas Emissions: The Science and Economics of Future Paths for Global Annual Emissions', Policy Brief, December, Centre for Climate Change Economics and Policy, and Grantham Research Institute on Climate Change and the Environment, available at http://www2.lse.ac.uk/GranthamInstitute/publications/Policy/docs/PBMitigatingBowenRangerDec09.pdf.

Chakraborty, Shruti. 2011. 'India's Solar Mission on Track, But Needs More Props', *The Wall Street Journal*, 31 May 2011, available at http://online.wsj.com/article/SB100014240527023037453045763567401703230 36.html?mod=googlenews_wsj.

Planning Commission, Government of India. 2011. *Low-carbon Strategies for Inclusive Growth—An Interim Report*, Interim Report of the Expert Group on Low Carbon Strategies for Inclusive Growth Chaired by Kirit Parikh, available at http://moef.nic.in/downloads/public-information/Interim%20Report%20of%20the%20Expert%20Group.pdf.

Stern Nicholas. 2011. 'Raising Consumption, Maintaining Growth and Reducing Emissions', Paper for China Development Forum, Beijing, March 2011 Session on Strategic Emerging Industries for Economic Restructuring, Centre for Climate Change Economics and Policy, and Grantham Research Institute on Climate Change and the Environment.

Stern Nicholas, Ruth Kattumuri, and Nandan Nilekani. 2010. 'A Global Deal on Climate Change: A Possible Role for India', in Shankar Acharya and Rakesh Mohan (eds), *India's Economy: Performance and Challenges—Essays in Honour of Montek Singh Ahluwalia*, New Delhi, Oxford University Press.

UNEP, Bloomberg New Energy Finance. 2011. 'Global Trends in Renewable Energy Investment 2011: Analysis of Trends and Issues in the Financing of Renewable Energy', Frankfurt School, UNEP Collaborating Centre for Climate and Sustainable Energy Finance.

World Bank Development Indicators. 2011. 'Poverty Headcount Ratio at $2 a Day (PPP) (% of Population)', available at http://data.worldbank.org/indicator/SI.POV.2DAY?page=1.

World Resources Institute. 2011. Climate Analysis Indicators Tool (CAIT) Version 8.0, Washington DC, World Resources Institute.

India's Growth Turnaround

From 1950 to 1980, Indian real gross domestic product (GDP) grew at an annual average rate of 3.6 per cent (1.5 per cent in per capita terms). From 1990 to 2007 the growth rate averaged 6.4 per cent (4.1 per cent in per capita terms).[1] The shift to a higher growth path during the course of the 1980s is referred to as the Indian growth turnaround. Fast growth in India since the early 1980s has placed it amongst the top nine rapidly growing economies in the world (Ahmed and Varshney 2009).[2]

India's growth turnaround is illustrated in Figure 1. This plots aggregate real GDP growth from 1950 to 2008 against the estimated probability of being in a high growth regime using Hamilton's (1994) Markov Switching Model.[3] The model estimates two distinct regimes: a first sub-period from 1950 to 1981 over which the estimated average real GDP growth rate is 3.7 per cent; and a second regime during which the estimated average growth rate is 6 per cent. The model suggests that there was a relatively short transition period in the early 1980s, with an estimated 100 per cent probability of being in the high growth regime by the mid-1980s. More recently, between 2003–4 and 2007–8, real GDP growth increased further, averaging 8.8 per cent.[4]

The identification of a turnaround in the early 1980s by the Hamilton model is consistent with a range of studies using aggregate data (see Rodrik and Subramanian 2005; Balakrishnan and Parameswaran 2007). More recent work using disaggregated data (Ghate and Wright 2009) points to a rather later data in the mid-1980s, suggesting a conflict between both approaches. We discuss the contrast between these two attempts to time the turnaround in more detail later; but the key issue on which all studies agree is that, at some point during the 1980s, there was an increase in growth,

[1]These numbers reflect simple averages and are measured in 1999–2000 prices. The per capita averages for the 1990–2007 period are until 2004, the latest year for which population numbers are available on the Penn World Tables.

[2]Brad De Long at UC Berkeley first pointed out that India's growth acceleration started in the early 1980s. Subsequently, there was a race to explain this acceleration.

[3]Regimes are generated using a Markov switching model (see Hamilton 1994). The model was estimated using EM algorithm-based GAUSS codes by Hamilton. We use the Markov switching model as an illustrative technique.

[4]The year 1980–1 is also identified as a breakpoint when we undertake the same exercise with real GDP measured in 1993–4 prices. This suggests that India's growth transition in the early 1980s does not depend on the price series one uses. Interestingly, 1991–2 is not identified as a breakpoint using 1993–4 prices, although it is using 1999–2000 prices.

which, from the 1990s, was not only of statistical but also of massive economic significance. What has puzzled many contributors to the literature is that analysis of aggregate data suggests a pickup in growth during the early 1980s, *before* most of the major policy changes.[5]

The low growth in the first phase is pejoratively referred to as the Hindu rate of growth, a period in which import duties were among the highest in the world, foreign direct investment (FDI) was prohibited in many sectors of the economy, and there was extensive regulation of interest rates. During this period Indian GDP per capita growth was, at best, in line with the long-run average growth rates in most rich countries: there was minimal, if any, tendency to converge. While this performance was better than many African countries, it was clearly in marked contrast to the extremely rapid rates of convergence of the East Asian Tigers during this period.

The upward shift in India's growth path during the 1980s is significant for two reasons: the turnaround happened well before the BOP crisis of 1991 and the large-scale macroeconomic reforms that ensued.

The second puzzling aspect about India's growth turnaround is that it was not driven by manufactured exports and, therefore, has little in common with the East Asian economic miracle. In particular, there was no industrial policy targeted towards developing specific industries. It was the service sector that led the increase in the overall growth rate in the early 1980s. Since many components of services are income-related (such as financial services, business services, and hotels and restaurants) and begin to increase only after a certain stage in development, the fact that India's service sector created the impulse for the growth turnaround is puzzling.

While there is a reasonable degree of consensus amongst economists on the timing of India's growth turnaround, there is less agreement about its causes. What is indisputable is that something happened during the 1980s that opened the door to a rise in growth. The challenge facing growth economists is to weave a logically consistent story on the timing and causes of India's growth turnaround.

Total Factor Productivity (TFP) or Policies?

In an influential paper, Rodrik and Subramanian (2005) argue that Indira Gandhi, substantially chastened by her 1977 electoral defeat, became significantly more 'pro-business' after coming back to power in 1980. This 'attitudinal shift' led to more investment which increased manufacturing output dramatically. This led to a growth pickup in 1980. In their view, aggregate productivity measured by TFP growth is driven by an attitudinal shift towards pro-business policies. This contrasts with the role that directly observable policies, such as trade liberalization, would have on a growth shift.[6] The Rodrik–Subramanian story is essentially a manufacturing sector–driven explanation of India's growth turnaround.

The above story, however, is generally known to be problematical. This is because of the unlikely finding that a small manufacturing sector (roughly 9 per cent of GDP in the early 1980s) would raise the aggregate growth rate by 2 percentage points. The implied multiplier effects would have to be fantastically large for this to occur. This seems highly implausible, especially since the share of registered manufacturing to GDP in the early 1980s was very small (roughly 8 per cent of GDP).

Balakrishnan and Paramewswaran (2007) use the multiple structural break test approach of Bai and Perron (1998) to look at breaks in sectoral growth rates since 1950. They find that agriculture growth increases (permanently) during the mid-1960s. This is followed by a take-off in the service sector in the mid-1970s. Finally, manufacturing output growth breaks in 1982–3, after the break in overall growth which they place as early as 1979. Based on the timing of these recursive sectoral breaks, they suggest that the manufacturing sector is not responsible for a shift to a higher growth path, rather it is has been led by growth shifts in other sectors.[7] This discussion suggests that framing the debate on India's growth turnaround as driven either by

[5]While a few significant pro-market reforms took place in the mid-1980s, the bulk of economic reforms—which shifted India to an outward-looking, incentive-based private-sector economy—were enacted after the balance-of-payments (BOP) crisis of 1991.

[6]Rodrik and Subramanian distinguish between pro-business policies and pro-market policies. Examples of pro-business polices are easing restrictions on capacity expansion for incumbents, removing price controls, and reducing corporate taxes; trade liberalization is an example of a market-oriented policy. They conclude that a shift towards a pro-business orientation can be an essential trigger that sets off growth accelerations.

[7]Balakrishnan and Parameswaran argue that because of the drought of the mid-1960s, there was a huge decline in food grain production. There was also extremely poor management of the macro-economy leaving little foreign exchange to import food. The crisis ultimately induced a Green Revolution and saw large public investments in the agriculture sector. The resource flow into the sector led to a growth shift in agriculture. This explains the impulse in agriculture in the mid-1960s. The problem with this narrative is that it does not address the endogeneity problem surrounding public investment. An interesting open research question is whether intersectoral linkages from the manufacturing sector are greater than those from the service sector.

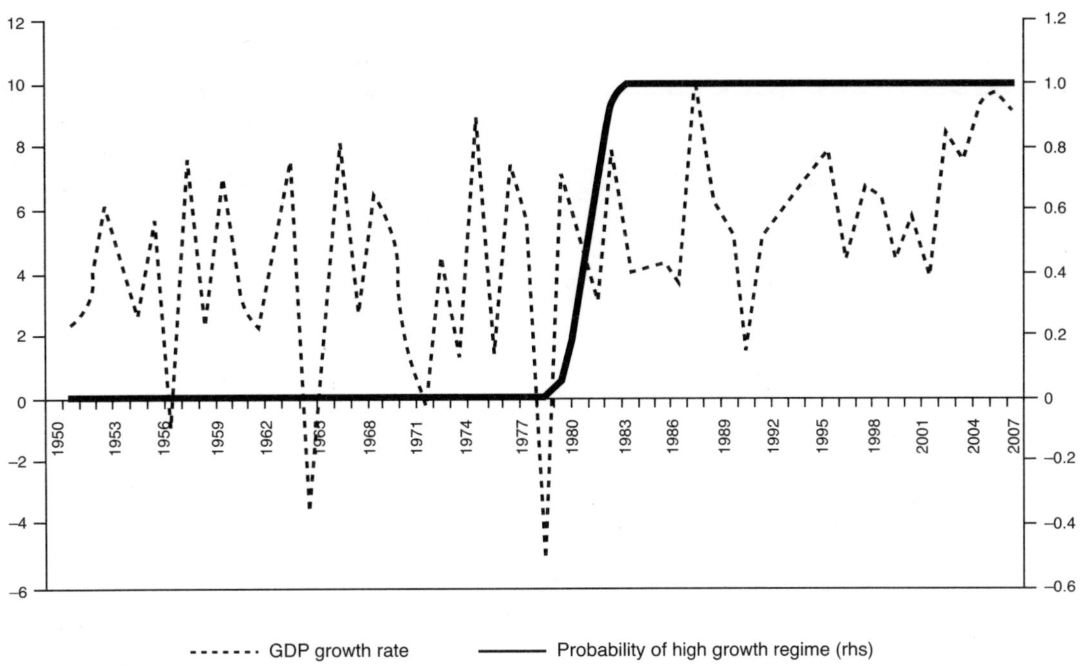

Figure 1 Indian GDP Growth Rate against the Probability of a High GDP Growth Regime

TFP shifts or a change in policies is problematical. The shift in manufacturing growth occurring after the shift in overall growth is also verified by Figure 2: using the regime switching approach, the break in manufacturing occurs in 1986–7, well after the estimated upward shift in aggregate growth (see Figure 1), with the growth rate of manufacturing output amounting to 4.8 per cent in the period 1964–86 and 6.5 per cent between 1987 and 2007 (and before 1964).[8]

Balakrishnan and Parameswaran's approach for determining turning points is (itself) not without criticism. Basu (2008) argues that a common problem that applies to the existing empirical literature on the Indian growth turnaround is the special nature of the period 1979–80, which saw a sharp contraction in Indian real GDP growth (–5.2 per cent). The approach followed by Balakrishnan and Parameswaran (2007)—by essentially fitting linear segments to a fluctuating growth pattern—would find a propensity for the break to appear before 1979–80.[9]

A possible reconciliation of the TFP versus policy debate is that while a few key trade reforms were legislatively enacted in the mid-1980s, they started to get debated in the early 1980s. Because investment is forward looking, the anticipated effects of policy changes led to India's growth turnaround prior to the enactment of the reforms. For instance, the removal of capacity constraints would allow firms to produce at higher or full capacity with the same inputs, leading to an increase in the rate of growth of productivity. The need for future research is to understand more clearly the disaggregated mechanisms that induced the Indian growth turnaround.[10]

The V Factor

Recent work by Ghate and Wright (2009) suggests that the turning point in Indian growth was not in the early 1980s, as most other studies have assumed, but in the mid-1980s. In this respect the Ghate and Wright approach

[8]Both Rodrik and Subramanian (2005) and Balakrishnan and Parameswaran (2007) use the multiple structural break tests of Bai and Perron (1998). This possibly explains why they obtain a similar breakpoint (early 1980s) in aggregate real GDP growth.

[9]Basu (2008) finds that if 1979–80 is discounted, the break in trend occurs in 1975–6. This suggests that the 1979–80 breakpoint is a statistical construct without much policy significance.

[10]In an interesting discussion, Kotwal et al. (2009) suggest that technology transfers in the early and mid-1980s allowed cheaper and easier access to imported machinery made possible by trade liberalization, unleashing a process of creative destruction in which the efficient firms—who upgraded their technology—drove out the inefficient firms. This raised the overall productivity of factors in the economy as factors got reallocated more productively. Rising industrial and service-sector productivity also had secondary effects: it attracted labour from agriculture. This raised wages for the workers left behind in agriculture.

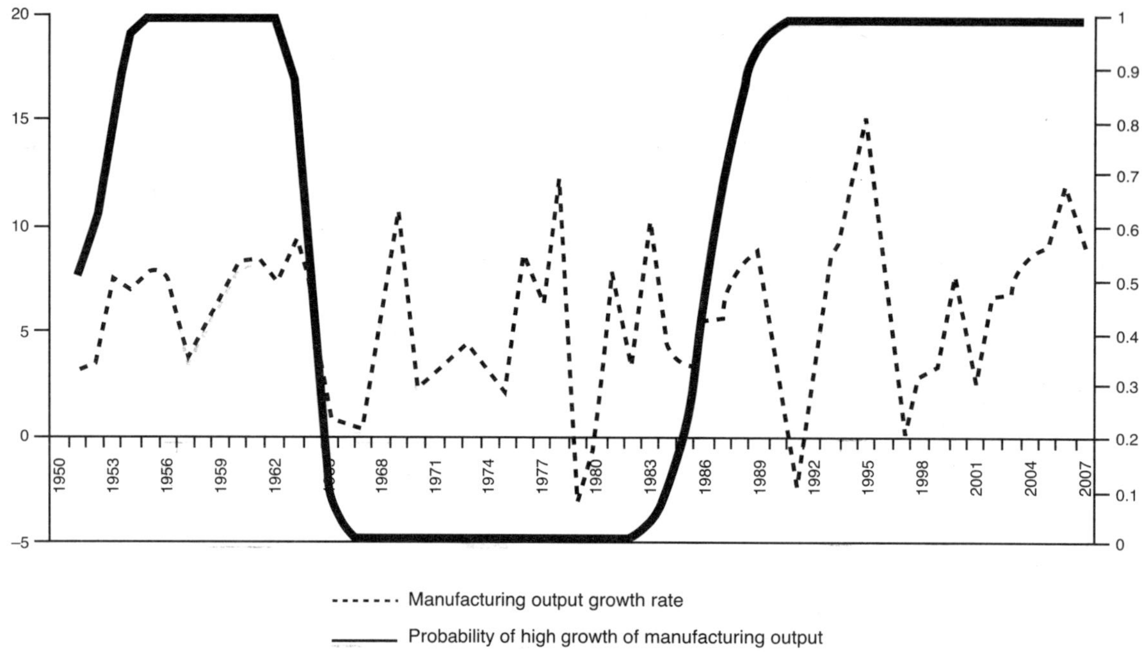

Figure 2 Growth Rate of Manufacturing Output against the Probability of High Growth of Manufacturing Output

appears to resolve the puzzle discussed by Rodrik and Subramanian (2005), who, using aggregate data, concluded that the turnaround in growth came in the early 1980s, well before any observable shift in policy. Instead of using an aggregate GDP series, Ghate and Wright use factor analysis on state-level sectoral time series data for 14 sectors in 15 states—at 1993–4 prices—to identify common patterns in the growth shifts of Indian states. A significant advantage of the common factor representation is that one does not need to impose a particular date for the turnaround in growth. Nor does one need to impose that it be a deterministic shift, as in standard econometric representations of structural breaks; nor even that all series participate in the shift at identical dates.

Apart from random fluctuations, Ghate and Wright find that two factors drive these time series: one is a nearly deterministic straight-line growth factor, and the other exhibits a V shape, which the authors refer to as the V factor. The apex of the V is in 1987 when reforms to open up the economy started.[11] In fact, the time profile of the V is strongly correlated with the pattern of trade liberalization, as summarized by the effective tariff rate (see Ghate and Wright 2009: Figure 7).[12]

While the common nature of the growth turnaround, as identified by the V factor, appears to correspond to a common shift in trade policy, the disparate impact of the V factor across major Indian states presents something of a puzzle. Table 1 examines this issue by showing correlations between identifiable state characteristics shortly before the turnaround, and their estimated V factor loadings. The table provides both negative and some (weaker) positive results. On the negative side, it allows us to dispose of some candidate explanations: (i) the turnaround in growth was not restricted to a club of richer states: initial income levels were unrelated to the magnitude of the response to the V factor; (ii) explanations based on differences in key magnitudes in a standard Solow-style growth model (saving, investment population growth rate and level) also do not show any systematic differences (the sign of the

[11]Figure 1 shows that up until at least the mid-1980s growth of GDP remained within the range of variation observed in the first regime. Aggregate data do not, therefore, appear to conflict markedly with the null hypothesis that the switch actually occurred as late as, say, 1987, the date identified by Ghate and Wright (2009), using disaggregated data.

[12]Other major internal liberalization measures that were implemented in 1985 and 1986 involved (a) eliminating the licensing of 25 categories of industries, (b) extending de-licensing to large companies in 22 industries that were previously restricted by the Monopolies and Restrictive Trade Practices Act and Foreign Exchange Regulation Act, and (c) allowing companies that had reached 80 per cent capacity utilization to expand their capacity up to 133 per cent of that reached in any of the previous years (see Rodrik and Subramanian 2005).

Table 1 State Characteristics and State V Factor Loadings

State characteristics	Correlation with average state V factor loading
A Rich State Club?	
Log real ouput per capita, 1985	–0.07
Solow Variables	
Fixed investment, % of NSDP, 1981	–0.42
Log population, 1981	0.09
Population growth, 1971–81	–0.22
Public Spending	
Development expenditures as a percentage of NSDP, 1981	0.17
Supply-side Characteristics	
Share of registered manufacturing, 1985	0.18
Electricity generation, kwh per capita, 1981	–0.19
Share of agriculture, % 1985	–0.68
Literacy rate, 1981	0.49
Urban population, %	0.32

Note: NSDP is net state domestic product.

investment correlation is perverse—the correlation with population growth is of the correct sign but very low); (iii) the direct contribution of the public sector to the turnaround appears to have been at best weak, and possibly perverse: there was essentially a zero correlation between the initial values of development spending and the subsequent impact of the V factor; and (iv) total public spending actually had a V factor loading which was somewhat negatively correlated with the overall state loading (that is, 'V states'—those with a positive loading on the V factor—tended if anything to have slowdowns in growth of public spending after the turnaround in overall growth).

The bottom block of the table provides evidence of some proxies for supply-side characteristics of individual states. The table shows that 'V states' tended to be somewhat more literate and somewhat more urbanized, and (the strongest correlation shown) had lower shares of agriculture.

Table 1 also shows that there was essentially no link between V factor loadings and the share of registered manufacturing, which played an important role in Rodrik and Subramanian's (2005) explanation of the turnaround. This suggests that while registered manufacturing may, in line with Rodrik and Subramanian's analysis, have been a catalyst for growth in the early 1980s, it was far from being an engine of growth over the longer term.

The Growth Turnaround and Implications for Divergence

The V factor provides evidence of a highly pervasive, but by no means universal shift in behaviour in India during the course of the 1980s. Can we reconcile this evidence with any underlying economic model? One way to think about this is to consider a general model of convergence of the form

$$\Delta(y^{i}_{t+1} - y^{US}_{t+1}) = \alpha_i (y^{US}_{t} + s_{it} + s^{India}_{t} - y_{it}) + \Delta TFP^{i}_{t+1} - \Delta TFP^{US}_{t+1} + \varepsilon_{it+14}$$

where y_{it} is log output per capita for state *i*, the s_{it} and s^{India}_{t} variables captures factors that determine steady-state output relative to the frontier represented by y^{US}_{t}; log output per capita in the United States, for individual states and for India as a whole; TFP_{it} and TFP^{US}_{t} is growth rate of TFP in state *i* and in the United States and ε_{it} captures short-run cyclical factors.

The simple framework of the equation offers a range of possible ways of accounting for the all-India pattern. It seems reasonable to argue that the sum of the last three terms on the right-hand side of the above equation is unlikely to provide an adequate explanation of longer-term trends. In standard Cobb-Douglas type technology models TFP growth shocks are common across all economies and hence cancel out precisely. But even if they are country-specific, such relative shocks might reasonably be assumed to have a stationary distribution. The same applies to the short-term error term, (ε_{it}). Thus we need to look for an explanation somewhere in the first term.

One possible interpretation of the earlier period was that the bracketed 'convergence' term (the term multiplied by α_i) was on average close to zero—that is, most, or possibly all, Indian states were conditional upon the s_{it} and s^{India}_{t} processes, fairly close to their steady-state values. The downward drift in most states' relative output levels would, according to this interpretation, be understood either as a succession of bad relative TFP growth shocks, or possibly as a downward drift in s^{India}_{t}.

It is harder to continue the logic of this explanation after the growth turnaround. The evidence of the V factor, and its correlation with the measure of trade liberalization in Ghate and Wright (2009), suggests very strongly that the impetus for the turnaround was common across all states, hence it is reasonable to attribute it to changes in the common Indian steady state factor, s^{India}_{t}. Given the subsequent dramatic changes in rates of convergence, then, conditional upon a reasonable degree of stability in the other elements on the right-hand side of the equation, the implied changes in s_t^{India} must have been quite dramatic. Rodrik and Subramanian (2005) argue that this is plausible because India was well away from its production possibility frontier.

But since these changes were common across states, the puzzle presented by the differential impact of the V factor is why any such shift in s_t^{India} did not have largely symmetric effects across the states. There is one possible explanation which reconciles both the all-India and state-wise evidence. The analysis of these shifts has implicitly assumed that the state-specific rates of convergence, α_i, were both strictly positive and reasonably similar across states. But an alternative explanation would attribute the pattern of the evidence largely to the α_i themselves. According to this interpretation, and consistent with the arguments of Rodrik and Subramanian, the bracketed expression in the first term was *not* necessarily close to zero in the first period; but failure to converge to the global frontier was largely due to the a_i being so close to zero that differences between actual and steady state income levels had essentially no impact. The turnaround in growth and its differential pattern would then be attributed to some combination of a common shift in s_t^{India} and state-wise differences in the α_i. A differential impact of the all-India shock might be attributed to different values of α_i; with non-V states, by implication, having α_i values extremely close to zero, thus closing off any convergence response.

Agenda for Future Research

Research on India's growth turnaround needs to move beyond its empiricist nature and towards a theoretical model of India's growth pattern. Given India's economic planning history and the empirical evidence it would be natural to think of the main counterfactual as openness to trade, that is, what would India's growth path have looked like if the many opportunities for trade had been acted upon? However, an alternative counterfactual relates to India's abysmal record in primary education to which the Mahalanobis plan gave little attention (Balakrishnan 2008). The rate of growth induced by higher human capital accumulation might have vastly changed the growth pattern of India.

Looking forward, probably the most crucial factor is whether the Indian turnaround is sufficiently robust that it will be sustained, and whether India will follow the East Asian precedent of rapid convergence (albeit from a very low base) towards per capita income levels of rich countries at the technological frontier. To the extent that, for example, while the 'V factor' of Ghate and Wright (2009) appears strongly correlated with tariff reductions, there are arguably only modest further gains that can arise from this source, since tariffs are now steadily approaching the levels in most OECD countries. The key issue looking forward, therefore, is that having shifted to a higher growth path (whatever the initial impetus or catalyst may have been), will this growth path prove self-sustaining?

CHETAN GHATE, STEPHEN WRIGHT, AND TATIANA FIC*

References

Ahmed, Sadiq and A. Varshney. 2009. 'Battles Half Won: The Political Economy of India's Growth and Economic Policy since Independence', Commission on Growth and Development, Working Paper No. 15.

Bai, Jushan and P. Perron. 1998. 'Estimating and Testing Linear Models with Multiple Structural Changes', *Econometrica*, 66(1): 47–78.

Balakrishan, Pulapre. 2008. 'Visible Hand: Public Policy and Economic Growth in the Nehru Era', *The Indian Economic Journal*, April–June, 56(1): 11–35.

Balakrishnan, Pulapre, and M. Parameswaran. 2007. 'Understanding Economic Growth in India: A Prerequisite', *Economic and Political Weekly*, 42(27–8): 2915–22.

Basu, Kaushik. 2008. 'The Enigma of India's Arrival: A Review of Arvind Virmani's "Propelling India: From Social Stagnation to Global Power",' *Journal of Economic Literature*, 46(2): 396–406.

Ghate, Chetan and S. Wright. 2009. 'The V-Factor: Distribution, Timing, and Correlates of the Great Indian Growth Turnaround', *Jena Economic Research Papers in Economics 2009–10*, Max Planck Institute of Economics.

Hamilton, James. 1994. *Time Series Analysis*, Princeton University Press.

Kotwal, Ashok, B. Ramaswami, and W. Wadhwa. 2009. 'Economic Liberalization and Indian Economic Growth: What's the Evidence?', mimeo, Indian Statistical Institute, Delhi Centre.

Rodrik, Dani and A. Subramanian. 2005. 'From Hindu Growth to Productivity Surge: The Mystery of the Indian Growth Transition', *IMF Staff Papers*, 52(2): 193–228.

*We are grateful to Kaushik Basu and Pulapre Balakrishnan for helpful comments.

H

■ Handicrafts

In today's developed nations, few traditional craft producers survive. In India, however, millions of people possessing traditional skills and knowledge of traditional techniques still make a living by producing handcrafted goods. Handicrafts have not only been an important part of the economy, but have also played an important role in the formation of the ideology of development in the region. In the early 20th century, it was argued by the nationalist critics of British colonial rule in India that the 19th-century globalization and industrialization had destroyed traditional industry in India. This view eventually gave rise to a package of measures designed to protect these industries from global and domestic competition. Another contemporary view held that globalization had, in fact, helped some handicrafts access markets that valued consumer goods intensive in craftsmanship. More recently, this latter view has gained ground, partly in response to the export success of handicrafts in the post-reform trade regime in India.

In 1750, India supplied about a quarter of the world's industrial output, and possibly a larger percentage of world textile exports. The entire output of textiles came from handlooms, which in turn used yarn from hand-driven spinning machines. By 1800, the export trade in textiles was dwindling. The demand for handicrafts from the older political elite, whom the new British rulers suppressed, also dwindled. All of these factors may have combined to reduce the extent of Indian handicraft textiles in the early 19th century. This phenomenon is known as 'de-industrialization' and is believed to have pushed many industrial workers into other low-paying occupations. While a large number of jobs were indeed lost in handicraft textiles in the 19th century, we cannot be sure when and how large the phenomenon was. Nor can we assert if there was a large income loss as a result, for many among those who lost their livelihoods had worked only part-time inside households without wage or for very low wage.

From the late 19th century, there was a general expansion in the major handicrafts, chiefly handloom weaving. Several factors contributed to this 're-industrialization'. First, consumer demand for craft skills was strong in the domestic market, especially in textiles. Such traditional markets grew when incomes of peasants and workers increased, which they did significantly in some regions. Second, globalization helped these industries by creating new markets for crafts abroad, and by cheapening raw materials such as cotton yarn, raw silk, dyes and chemicals, and metal sheets that were now mass produced and/or imported. Third, new markets and trade opportunities enabled capital accumulation. Capital and labour became more mobile, giving rise to large urban centres of production and to organizational change from the household to factory. Urbanization and new organizations helped many artisan capitalists experiment with new technologies. Labour productivity increased.

Craft Policy

Despite this resurgence, which, if properly used, might have contributed to export-driven industrialization in post-War India, on independence from British rule (1947), the nationalist legacy took India along a different course. The memory of de-industrialization was a more powerful ideological force than the ongoing re-industrialization, which only a small band of provincial officers and economists understood and wrote about. M.K. Gandhi's idea that the Indian village needed to be strong and self-sufficient, which called for an accent on rural handicrafts, joined with the prevailing nationalist view that the British commercial policy had killed Indian handicrafts. While India's policymakers adopted as the foundation a Soviet-style capital-intensive industrialization model, better known as the Nehruvian model, they made a significant concession to the Gandhian ideal by offering a package of state aid to handicrafts. Handicrafts and the handloom-weaving industry, thus, began to occupy a central place in the discourse on national development. But they entered development policy through the presumption that they were obsolete and weak, destined to disappear without state aid, and worthy of support only because they represented a good ideal. Craft policy was driven by the perceived weakness of the crafts, rather than by their economic strengths. Craft policy, thus, relied upon fiscal concessions and subsidies far more heavily than upon technological and skill development or market access abroad. The inefficient and the obsolete were protected while the efficient and the contemporary were left out in the cold. The rationale for policy became a cultural one.

The ideological and policy upheaval in the 1990s changed the situation. On the one hand, both the Gandhian and the Nehruvian ideals in their pure forms lost in popularity, and the economy was exposed to world market forces. This was bad news for handicrafts, which lost their symbolic status in the new regime. On the other hand, as international trade opened up, crafts seemed to jump out of the world of emotions on to commercial centre stage. They became an export success. The world market for ethnic goods rediscovered Indian designs and products. In this process, a large number of new stakeholders emerged—non-government organizations, private firms, designers—who are now fashioning a different discourse on crafts. There is demand for information on the present status of these industries, and also demand for a policy based on the strengths of the handicrafts rather than their weaknesses, that is, based on building capability rather than on protecting the weak from extinction. Recent studies, done partly in response to this new interest, help us build a profile of handicrafts in present times.

Profile at Present

Characterizing handicrafts and their output presents some difficulty. There are many different definitions. Perhaps the most defensible one would use a combination of four features: (i) manual labour with minimal or no input from machines; (ii) a substantial level of skill or expertise; (iii) a significant element of tradition; and (iv) a history of survival on a significant scale. Today, the major industry groups that satisfy these criteria are handloom weaving, hand embroidery, hand-printed textiles, knotted carpets, engraved metalware, and jewelry. Handicrafts employ 8–9 million persons. In the last decade and a half, they have roughly maintained their presence in the manufacturing sector at about 5 per cent of all manufacturing employment.

Exports increased from Rs 10 billion in 1991 to more than a 100 billion in 2001. In the export market, there was significant gain in employment and labour productivity per worker. There have been regional shifts too. Craft concentration has moved from south India, which was the main handloom centre, to western India which is a major hub of tourism and trade in ethnic goods. Compared to the export market, growth was considerably slower in the segment catering to the domestic market. Generally speaking, handicrafts making utility goods, handloom weaving, and earthenware have declined in the last 20 years, whereas crafts with design capability that has a potential urban demand have grown.

In terms of scale, the five most important handicrafts in India are handloom weaving, printed textiles, embroidered textiles, art metalware, and carpets. These 'big five' employ an overwhelmingly large percentage of handicraft workers. A recent census of handloom weavers estimated 3.47 million individual weavers still working at a total of 3 million active looms. This is almost certainly an overestimate, but survival on a significant scale cannot be disputed. A segment in the handloom industry remains capable of generating high profits and wages thanks to the demand for high-quality bordered *saris*. In recent times, there has been a decline in domestic demand for saris in general, though the demand for designed saris remains strong. There are also a certain number of handlooms engaged in ethnic furnishing and garment fabrics for which export demand grew in the 1990s.

Indian hand-printed cloth has two major distinctions: a strong craftsmanship tradition and, in at least some cases, the use of environmental friendly natural dyes. These features have enabled printed textiles to emerge as a major export item. Until recently, all printing was done with hand-carved wooden blocks. Today, the technology is more mixed. Once widely spread out, the largest clusters now are found in western India, including the Rajasthan towns of Sanganer, Bagru, Pali, and Jodhpur, and the Gujarat centres of Ahmedabad, Jetpur, and Dhamadka. There are numerous embroidery traditions in India. Some of the most well known are centred in Gujarat (in Banaskantha and Kutch districts), in western Rajasthan, in western Uttar Pradesh, and in West Bengal. Of these, the most successful in export have been the western Indian crafts. Until recently, women among rural communities practised embroidery to supply local demand. In the last 10–15 years, embroidery has found a growing urban market.

Carpets and art metalware have long been established as craft exports. Cast metal objects with designs engraved on them by hand, a process known as *meenakari*, is concentrated in Moradabad. The styles and finesse involved in the engraving craft are highly evolved and distinctively Indian. The export trade in hand-knotted carpets, though an old one, was relatively small until the Iranian Revolution in 1979, after which the demand for carpets made in South Asia increased rapidly. The areas of manufacture are eastern Uttar Pradesh (around Benares, Mirzapur, Bhadohi towns), Jaipur, and Kashmir.

Problems

As the foregoing description shows, handicrafts have a potentially large and growing market, but these industries also suffer from a variety of deficiencies. The problems can be classified under two broad heads: poor market access and innovation capability.

A hundred years ago, many of these goods were sold locally. Market access was not a problem. Today rural crafts are either sold in the cities or exported abroad. And there is a wedge between the producers and the market in the current scenario. Physical access is often difficult because of dispersed location. While buying goods from the well-trodden tourist routes such as the 'golden triangle' of Jaipur, Agra, and Delhi, the problem may not appear to be a serious one. But to reach a craft cluster outside these routes, chances are that one would travel for hours on poor roads to a small town without safe food or water, schools or hospitals, and assured supply of electricity. The generally poor level of education of the artisans creates information gaps. Their poor level of empowerment despite decades of Gandhian policies exposes them to harassment by the tax–labour–customs inspectors, on the one side, and by mafia and cartels, who try to control the lucrative export trade, on the other. There are large transactions costs in doing this business, which keep artisans outside the mainstream commercial infrastructure even as their goods become globalized. While the export business is profitable on average, the gap between producer price and retail price in the international market is very wide. A second set of problems arises from the fact that even though handicrafts do not face unqualified obsolescence, in order to survive, old skills need to study, target, and adapt to new buyers and what they want. Where such adaptation has been done with some degree of skill and sophistication, the outcome has been striking commercial success. But such instances remain scarce in relation to the scale of the industry because access to technical knowledge and information, capital, and learning is still very inadequate.

TIRTHANKAR ROY

References

Haynes, D. 2001. 'Artisan Cloth-producers and the Emergence of Powerloom Manufacture in Western India 1920–1950', *Past and Present*, 172: 170–98.

Liebl, M. and T. Roy. 2003. 'Handmade in India: Status Report on Indian Artisans', *Economic and Political Weekly*, 38(51): 5366–76.

Roy, T. 1999. *Traditional Industry in the Economy of Colonial India*, Cambridge, Cambridge University Press.

Health Indicators

Introduction

The health sector as it exists in India today has many features that are a result of active planning; it also has some other features which have resulted from omission, rather than commission. These features have, in turn, created a situation where the health outcomes are extremely heterogeneous, depending on the parameters being used and the units being analysed.

The health system as a whole, with its infrastructure, key inputs, and resources going into the health sector affect the health outcomes of the population to a large extent. Thus, while health outcomes are of interest in understanding how India has performed over the years, a full discussion on the determinants of health outcomes would require an analysis of all the components that go into defining a health system.

This entry does not attempt to analyse the various correlates of health outcomes; instead, it presents a brief overview, based on selected indicators, of the current health status of the population, the areas of concern, and the progress that India has made in the recent past, especially in light of the millennium development goals (MDGs).

Health Data in India

Health outcomes can be measured by a variety of indicators, but different mortality and morbidity rates, defined across age, gender, residence, and economic categories are often the best indicators for understanding the health status of populations.

India has a few reliable sources of information on the health outcomes of the population. Birth and death rates, as well as infant and under-five mortality are based on the Census of India and the Sample Registration System (SRS), which is implemented by the Office of the Registrar General, under the Ministry of Home Affairs. The SRS is considered the most reliable source for fertility and mortality estimates in India.

India has also carried out three rounds of the National Family Health Survey (NFHS), under the Ministry of Health and Family Welfare (MoHFW). The NFHS is a large-scale, multi-round survey conducted in a representative sample of households throughout India. The survey provides state and national information on fertility, infant and child mortality, the practice of family planning, maternal and child health, reproductive health, nutrition, anaemia, and utilization and quality of health and family planning services.

In addition to NFHS, MoHFW also initiated the District Level Household Survey (DLHS) in 1997 to provide district-level estimates on health indicators. The objective was to assist policymakers and programme administrators in decentralized planning, monitoring, and evaluation. Three such surveys have been conducted so far.

Besides these sources, India also has health surveys conducted by the National Sample Survey Organisation (NSSO) under the Ministry of Planning and Programme Implementation. The surveys are at the household level, and collect information on morbidity and mortality along with many socio-economic correlates.

In the analysis presented here, information has been drawn from a variety of primary and secondary sources on the indicators of interest.

Trend in Health Outcomes

While birth and death rates are important indicators of population dynamics, the health status of a population is better understood from different measures of mortality rate: infant mortality rate (IMR), under-five mortality rates, and maternal mortality rate (MMR). The other key variable that reflects long-term improvements in health outcomes is life expectancy (LE) at birth.

IMR is the number of children dying before age one divided by the number of live births in that year. It is expressed as the number of infant deaths per 1,000 live births. The under-five mortality rate (per 1,000 live births) is defined as the probability of dying between birth and exactly five years of age, expressed per 1,000 live births. Life expectancy at birth (years) is defined as the number of years a newborn infant would live if the prevailing patterns of age-specific mortality rates at the time of birth were to stay the same throughout the child's life. MMR is defined as the number of maternal deaths per 100,000 live births.

Table 1 presents trends in these indicators over the last 20 years. Table 2 presents comparisons with four neighbouring South Asian countries (Bangladesh, Nepal, Pakistan, and Sri Lanka) to better understand the relative position of India in the region.

Table 1 Trend in Selected Demographic and Health Indicators in India

Indicators	1990	2000	2009
Life expectancy (2001–6)	60.3 (1991–5)	62.4 (1998–2002)	65
IMR	84	68	50
Under-five mortality rate	118	94	66
MMR	-	540*	230

Source: Planning Commission (2009); SRS (various issues); WHO (2011a).
Note: * This number pertains to 2000.

LE at birth was 30 years at the time of Independence. Since then India has made rapid progress with LE increasing significantly between the 1980s and 1990s, but the improvement slowed down subsequently. While countries like Japan and Australia lead the world in life expectancy (with values of 83 and 82, respectively), there are many other countries in the developing world that are doing much better than India in terms of improving the longevity of their populations. China and Sri Lanka, for instance, have LE of 74 and 71, respectively (Table 2), indicating that there is a lot of room for further improvement in this core parameter. This is also clear from the fact that the average life expectancy at birth of the global population in 2009 was 68 as reported by WHO's Global Health Observatory (WHO 2011a).

Table 2 Demographic and Health Indicators in India and Selected Countries, 2009

	Under-five mortality rate	Infant mortality rate	Life expectancy at birth	Maternal mortality rate
Bangladesh	52	41	65	340
China	19	17	74	38
India	66	50	65	230
Nepal	48	39	67	380
Pakistan	87	70	63	260
Sri Lanka	16	13	71	39

Source: WHO (2011a).

As for IMR, there has been significant improvement since the 1990s, with a slowing down in the rate of improvement in the early part of this decade. Since then there has been a quickening of pace, though India still has a long way to go when compared to its other neighbours. While it will be difficult to match Sri Lanka and China's IMRs of 13 and 17, respectively, any time soon, India is doing even worse than its immediate neighbours Bangladesh (41) and Nepal (39). The same picture emerges when one looks at under-five mortality rates, where, with the exception of Pakistan, all the neighbouring countries are performing much better.

MMR of 230—while down substantially from earlier very high figures—remains at unacceptable levels when compared to what China and Sri Lanka have been able to achieve (38 and 39, respectively). MMR has a direct impact on infant mortality rates: according to the United Nations Children's Fund (UNICEF), 'babies whose mothers die during the first 6 weeks of their lives are far more likely to die in the first two years of life than babies whose mothers survive.'[1]

The MDG goals are directly relevant for the discussion here. Goals 4 and 5 are reducing child mortality and maternal health with specific indicators on IMR, the under-five mortality rate, and maternal mortality rate among a few others. Specifically, the goal is to reduce the under-five mortality rate by two-thirds and MMR by three-quarters between 1990 and 2015. The *India Country Report 2010* on the MDG goals (GoI 2009) clearly brings out that India is not going to be able to meet its MDG targets by 2015, especially in child mortality rates. High infant deaths continue to be a major source of concern in the country with many states lagging behind on this front. India's target is to reduce its IMR to 26.7 per 1,000 live births by 2015. The current trend of decline since 1990, if continued, can achieve a rate of only about 46 by 2015, which is far short of the target.

The picture is slightly better for MMR, which has shown a sharper decline between 1997 and 2005, compared to the preceding eight years from 1990 to 1997; despite this, India will fall short of the MDG target, though not by as much as in the case of under-five mortality rates.

Since inter-state variations are critical to such an analysis, a quick state-level status is now given. Table 3 gives selected indicators for selected Empowered Action Group (EAG)[2] states, and major states besides those included in the EAG group, one state from the north-east (NE)—Assam,[3] and India.

Statistics indicate that there are significant inter-state variations in health outcomes: for example, while Kerala has an IMR of 12, Madhya Pradesh has an IMR of 67. The averages over all indicators for EAG states are much worse than for other major states as well as for India. Among the north-eastern states Assam is also faring poorly in all the indicators.

An effective immunization programme can eradicate much of the infant and childhood morbidities and mortalities. Table 3 also gives the percentage of eligible children fully immunized in the country. The numbers indicate very clearly that India is unlikely to achieve universal immunization any time soon. Currently about 61 per cent of all children are immunized fully in the country, with significant state-level variations. As expected, the EAG states fare much worse than the other major states.

Institutional deliveries and births assisted by skilled personnel have a direct impact on mothers' health and MMR and indirectly on the health of newborns. Table 3 shows the variation in the percentage of institutional deliveries; while currently the all-India average is much improved at 73 per cent as compared to earlier years, the inter-state variations are stark; for example, Bihar has a value of less than 50 per cent, Jharkhand has a value of 40 per cent, whereas the figure for Nagaland is about 30 per cent (not shown in Table 3). As before, EAG states generally have worse MMR as compared to other states.

Finally, the annual average exponential growth in population is presented in the last column of Table 3 to indicate that all the concerns are aggravated with high rates of growth in population; the poorest states, which are also experiencing rapid population growth, will contribute an even higher share of the country's population, and it is the performance of these states that would determine whether and when India can expect to achieve the MDG targets. The EAG states, which comprise almost half of India's population, are unlikely to be able to contribute enough to ensure a reduction of MMR by 50 per cent in the next five years (Deolalikar 2005).

The discussion on these basic health indicators would be incomplete without mentioning the status with respect to place of residence and gender. Table 4 presents the rural–urban and male–female scenario with respect to the key indicators.

There are significant differences between IMR and under-five mortality rates between rural and urban

[1]See http://www.unicef.org/india/health.html.

[2]The EAG includes eight states: Bihar, Chhattisgarh, Rajasthan, Jharkhand, Madhya Pradesh, Odisha, Uttarakhand, and Uttar Pradesh.

[3]Comparable data do not exist for the other north-eastern states.

Table 3 Demographic and Health Indicators across States in India

States	IMR	Under-five MR	MMR	LE at birth	Institutional deliveries	Full immunization	Annual growth in population (%)
Selected EAG states							
Bihar	52	75	312	61.6	48.3	49	2.5
Madhya Pradesh	67	92	335	58	81	42.9	2.18
Uttar Pradesh	63	91	440	60	62.1	40.9	2.3
EAG average	**56**	**81**	**358**	**60**	**60**	**54**	**2.1**
Selected other major states							
Andhra Pradesh	49	58	154	64.4	94.3	68	1.3
Haryana	51	65	186	66.2	63.3	71.7	2.47
Kerala	12	14	95	74	99.9	81.5	0.9
Maharashtra	31	41	130	67.2	81.9	78.6	2.04
Tamil Nadu	28	36	111	66.2	98.4	77.3	1.06
West Bengal	33	42	141	64.9	69.5	64.9	1.64
Average—other major states	**37**	**47**	**154**	**67**	**81**	**73**	**1.6**
Selected north-eastern state							
Assam	**61**	**88**	**480**	**58.9**	**64.4**	**59.1**	**1.73**
All-India	50	69	254	63.5	72.9	61	1.93

Source: Planning Commission (2009); SRS (2009).

Table 4 Rural–Urban and Male–Female Differences in Selected Indicators

	Rural		Urban		Total	
	Male	Female	Male	Female	Male	Female
Infant mortality rate (2009)	54	56	32	35	49	52
Under-five mortality rate (2008)	71	81	41	46	64	73
Life expectancy at birth (2001–6)					63.9	66.9

Source: Planning Commission (2008); SRS (2009); WHO (2011a).

India, and also between males and females. For example, IMR in rural males is 54 versus 32 among urban males India (67 and 72). Similarly, urban under-five mortality for males is 41 versus 71 for rural males. As for gender differentials, rural IMR among females is 56 as against 54 among rural males. In fact, rural–urban differences are much more striking than male–female differences, and raise concerns about the uneven pace of development in the country.

The gender difference in life expectancy is a very important marker of inequities that may exist between males and females in health and other related social well-being indicators. In countries with the highest life expectancies, women tend to outlive men by 5 to 8 years; this difference is only 0 to 3 years in countries where life expectancy is low, as is the case with India, where female LE is only about 3 years more than male LE. In Sri Lanka, the numbers are 76 and 65 for females and males, respectively. India also has an adverse sex ratio with only 933 women per 1,000 men. It is of even more concern that the child sex ratio (ages 0–6) declined sharply from 962 in 1981 to 927 in 2001 (Planning Commission 2008).

There are other pieces of evidence that indicate that India continues to grapple with reproductive and child health issues. NFHS-III data shows that women with a body mass index categorized as below normal and with anaemia are 35.6 and 55.3 (among ever-married women) per cent, respectively. Also, the percentage of underweight children under 3 years born to ever-married women was 40.4 per cent.

This analysis on vital statistics and other basic indicators of the health status of the population indicates that there is immense scope for improvement. Compared to earlier decades there has been considerable progress, but there is still a long way to go, if one looks at other countries, especially in the Southeast Asia region. The uneven geographical pace of improvement, rural–urban variations, and gender inequities continue to be the major feature of these health outcomes, making it difficult for India to meet its MDG goals.

This discussion can be put in a proper perspective by adding an analysis of the burden of diseases in the country.

Disease Burden in India

India has made progress in eliminating and controlling diseases such as small pox, leprosy, and polio. However, the disease burden continues to be high in the aggregate with a burden profile typical of an economy that is characterized by progress as well as poverty and underdevelopment. As the Eleventh Five Year Plan states 'India is in the midst of an epidemiological and demographic transition with increasing burden of chronic diseases, decline in mortality and fertility rates, and ageing of the population' (Planning Commission 2008).

The latest available data on burden of diseases (BoD) is from the *Global Burden of Disease—2004 Update* report compiled and published in 2008 by the World Health Organization (WHO 2008a). This report—built on an earlier WHO report on BoD in 2002—uses the disability adjusted life years (DALYs) as a metric for estimating BoD for diseases, injuries, and risk factors. The global burden of disease (GBD) cause categories are divided in a three-step classification—group, sub-group, and diseases. The three major groups are: (i) communicable, maternal, perinatal, and nutritional conditions, (ii) non-communicable diseases, and (iii) injuries. Table 5 presents these statistics for India and India's share in the world in DALYs lost.

India contributes around one-fifth to the total DALYs lost globally, with almost an equivalent proportion of DALYs lost due to communicable, maternal, perinatal, and nutritional conditions as well as injuries (22 per cent); India's contribution in non-communicable diseases is slightly lower at 18 per cent. The burden of disease due to both communicable and non-communicable categories is around 43 per cent in India. Among communicable diseases, while the share of burden due to infectious and parasitic diseases is more or less the same in the country as well as in the world (around 20 per cent), there is a disproportionate share in the world DALY of other diseases like perinatal conditions, respiratory infections, maternal conditions, and nutritional deficiencies (21–28 per cent). Overall, the top five causes among infectious and parasitic diseases and respiratory infections by estimated DALYs lost are lower respiratory infections, diarrhoeal diseases, childhood-cluster diseases, tuberculosis (TB), and HIV/AIDS. More recent government estimates also indicate that the acute respiratory infections and acute diarrhoeal diseases comprise a major share of communicable diseases (GoI 2011).

Table 5 DALYs ('000) by Major Causes in India and World, 2004

Cause	India*	Proportion in world DALY
Communicable, maternal, perinatal, and nutritional conditions	43.9	22.2
Infectious and parasitic diseases	19.3	19.5
Perinatal conditions	11.6	28.1
Respiratory infections	7.1	22.2
Nutritional deficiencies	3.2	25.5
Maternal conditions	2.7	21.1
Non-communicable diseases	43.0	17.9
Neuropsychiatric conditions	11.8	18.1
Cardiovascular diseases	9.5	19.1
Sense organ diseases	6.3	22.1
Respiratory diseases	3.7	19.0
Digestive diseases	2.9	20.5
Malignant neoplasms	2.8	10.9
Other**	6.1	16.3
Injuries	13.0	21.2
Unintentional injuries	10.5	23.1
Intentional injuries	2.5	15.8
All Causes	100	20.0

Source: Gupta and Guin (2010).

Among the various communicable diseases reported by the states/union territories during 2010, pulmonary TB accounted for the maximum number of reported deaths (GoI 2010). WHO reports indicate that India is among five countries in the organization's Southeast Asia region (along with Bangladesh, Indonesia, Myanmar, and Thailand) that account for 95 per cent of all cases in the region. This group is also among the 22 countries with the highest burdens of TB globally (WHO 2011b). India accounts for nearly one-third of the global incidence of tuberculosis, with an estimated prevalence of 1.4 per cent (Tenth Plan, Planning Commission). The emergence of the HIV–TB co-infection (it is the leading opportunistic infection among those infected with HIV) and multi-drug resistant TB has added to increased concern about TB in the country.

As for non-communicable diseases (NCDs), available estimates indicate that India contributes substantially to their global burden. In 1990, India accounted for 16 per cent of all NCD deaths in the world (Murray and Lopez 1996). It is estimated that the overall NCD burden will rise sharply by 2020 in India, imposing significant economic burden from mortality from NCDs. The higher burden from NCDs in the developing world is attributable to relative early manifestations of NCDs in younger populations due to exposure to risk factors, changing lifestyles, and various environmental factors. The specific features that characterize NCD in India are—wide consumption of tobacco in various forms, indoor pollution due to use of wood and dung cakes for cooking, impaired fetal nutrition, and high fat and low-fibre diet (Goyal and Yusuf 2006; Mishra 2003; Stein et al. 1996). The main NCDs in India are neuropsychiatric conditions and cardiovascular diseases (WHO 2004). Other conditions like diabetes and cancer are spreading alarmingly fast in the population. It is estimated that 700,000–900,000 cases of cancer occur every year in India, with tobacco-related cancers comprising almost half of all such cases (Planning Commission 2008).

The important point to note is that as is commonly assumed, NCDs are no longer confined to only the rich and affluent; there is mounting evidence that NCDs are impacting on the socio-economically lower rungs of the society as well (Gupta 2009).

India has also seen the emergence of newer and re-emerging diseases. While HIV/AIDS has been around now for more than two decades, it is relatively new compared to many other diseases like TB and malaria that have been around for a much longer time. While the newer estimates of HIV/AIDS indicate that India is probably not facing as much of a threat as was perceived earlier, concerns remain around its spread due to its close connection with socio-economic vulnerabilities. The dual burden of HIV and TB also adds to concerns around the HIV epidemic. The HIV/AIDS epidemic has brought to the forefront concerns around human and legal rights, especially of marginalized and vulnerable population groups.

Another worrying trend in India has been the spread of Hepatitis B. WHO classifies countries based on the prevalence of Hepatitis B carrier state in the general population: countries are classified as having high (8 per cent or more), intermediate (2–7 per cent), or low (less than 2 per cent) HBV endemicity. According to WHO, India has intermediate endemicity of Hepatitis B, with Hepatitis B surface antigen (HBsAg) prevalence between 2–10 per cent among the populations studied (WHO 2008b). The number of HBsAg carriers in India is estimated to be over 40 million. Hepatitis B is vaccine preventable and an efficient universal immunization programme can prevent substantial morbidity and mortality due to this disease.

Finally, there has been a resurgence of vector-borne diseases like malaria and dengue. About two-thirds of the reported cases of malaria in WHO's South and Southeast Asian region are from India, which reported 1.5 million confirmed cases in 2008 (WHO 2011c). Malaria is endemic in India, and five states account for 60 per cent of the total cases—Orissa, Chhattisgarh, Madhya Pradesh, Jharkhand, and West Bengal, with Orissa accounting for the most number of deaths. Other highly endemic states include Arunachal Pradesh, Assam, Meghalaya, and Tripura. Young children and pregnant mothers are at special risk from malaria and while early treatment can tackle it effectively, growing resistance to anti-malarial medicines has spread very rapidly, undermining malaria control efforts, especially in developing countries such as India.

As for dengue and dengue hemorrhagic fever, it is endemic in most of the countries in Southeast Asia, including India. WHO categorizes India as a Category B country along with Bangladesh and Maldives, where cyclical epidemics are becoming more frequent, multiple virus serotypes are circulating, and where the diseases are seen to be expanding geographically within the country (WHO 2007). While not yet resulting in very high mortality or morbidity, the dengue scare in India is happening with an alarming regularity each year, especially after the monsoons are over, giving rise to concerns of a much more rapid spread.

There are other newer diseases that, while not endemic or leading to significant morbidities, create concerns and fear due to uncertainties around detection and treatment: one example is that of the H1N1 influenza virus that caused a major scare worldwide, including in India in 2009. It is important to note that urban areas are equally prone to these viral and vector-borne diseases, making prevention efforts more challenging.

Overall, the health situation in India seems to be pointing towards a mixed scenario. While significant progress has been made since Independence, this progress has been neither spectacular nor equitable. India remains in the group of low achievers, and has been unable to step up the rate of improvement or even distribute this modest improvement fairly across regions and groups. The less developed states, rural areas, the poor, the marginalized groups, and women continue to have adverse health outcomes, which are made worse by their poor access to healthcare. While there are fewer studies on the urban poor, the rapid urbanization and emergence of numerous slums across the major cities, indicate that the urban poor are now a constituency that needs urgent focus as well. With countries like Sri Lanka and China galloping ahead, and even some other less developing countries catching up and overtaking India, it is clear that major rethinking in terms of strategies is required to jump to the next level in terms of health outcomes. The challenges of preventing and controlling communicable, non-communicable, new, and re-emerging diseases are acute. This brief overview of health outcomes in India is meant to lead researchers, policymakers, and those concerned with the well-being of the population to ask the right questions: what are the critical factors that determine how quickly health outcomes can improve, and how best to distribute those gains in a manner that is consistent with the goals of equity and welfare.

INDRANI GUPTA

References

Deolalikar, Anil. 2005. 'Attaining the Millennium Development Goals in India: Reducing Infant Mortality, Child Malnutrition, Gender Disparities and Hunger-Poverty and Increasing School Enrollment and Completion', Washington DC, World Bank.

Government of India (GoI). 2009. *Millennium Development Goals: India Country Report*, New Delhi, Central Statistical Organisation, Ministry of Statistics and Programme Implementation.

———. 2010. *National Health Profile 2010*, New Delhi, Ministry of Health and Family Welfare.

———. 2011. *National Health Profile 2010* (January to December), Ministry of Health and Family Welfare, Directorate of Health Services, and Central Bureau of Health Intelligence.

Goyal, A. and S. Yusuf. 2006. 'The Burden of Cardiovascular Disease in the Indian Subcontinent', *Indian Journal of Medical Research*, 124: 235–44.

Gupta, Indrani. 2009. 'Potential Impact on Health and Economic Inequality from Cardiovascular Diseases and Diabetes in India: Evidence from the National Sample Survey', IEG Discussion Paper Series No. 136/2009.

Gupta, Indrani and Pradeep Guin. 2010. 'Communicable Diseases in the South-East Asia Region of the World Health Organization: Towards a More Effective Response', *Bulletin of the World Health Organisation*, 88(3).

Mishra, V. 2003. 'Effects of Indoor Air Pollution from Biomass Combustion on Prevalence of Asthma in the Elderly', *Environmental Health Perspective*, 111: 71–8.

Murray, C.J. and A.D. Lopez. 1996. *The Global Burden of Disease*, Harvard University Press.

Planning Commission. 2002. *National Human Development Report 2001*, New Delhi, Planning Commission, Government of India.

———. 2008. *Eleventh Five Year Plan (2007–2012): Inclusive Growth*, New Delhi, Oxford University Press.

———. 2009. Government of India. http://planningcommission.nic.in/data/datatable/index.php?data=datatab

Sample Registration System (SRS). 2004. *Statistical Report 2002*, Report No. 3 of 2004, New Delhi, Office of the Registrar General.

———. 2009. *Statistical Report 2008*, Report No. 1 of 2009, New Delhi, Office of the Registrar General.

Stein, C.E., C.H.D. Fall, K. Kumaran, C. Osmond, V. Cox, and D.J.P. Barker. 1996. 'Fetal Growth and Coronary Heart Disease in South India', *The Lancet*, 348: 1269–73.

World Health Organization (WHO). 2007. 'Situation of Dengue/Dengue Haemorrhagic Fever in South-East Asia Region', available at http://www.searo.who.int/en/Section10/Section332_1100.htm.

———. 2008a. 'Global Burden of Disease: 2004 Update', available at http://www.who.int/healthinfo/global_burden_disease/GBD_report_2004update_full.pdf.

———. 2008b. 'Hepatitis B: Core Programme Clusters, Family and Community Health', available at http://www.whoindia.org/en/section6%5Csection8.htm.

———. 2011a. 'Global Health Observatory', available at http://www.who.int/gho/countries.

———. 2011b. 'Communicable Diseases: TB in South East Asia', available at http://www.searo.who.int/en/Section10/Section2097/Section2100_10641.htm.

———. 2011c. 'Malaria Situation in SEAR Countries. India', available at http://www.searo.who.int/en/Section10/Section21/Section340_4021.htm, accessed on 24 January 2011.

■ Higher Education

Higher education in India has been, in Stanley Wolpert's evocative words, 'the swiftest elevators to the pinnacles of modern Indian power and opportunity'. At the time of Independence, while small relative to its population, India already had one of the largest and most sophisticated higher education systems among developing countries. Since then the system has expanded rapidly, with student enrolment growing at about two-and-half times the population growth rate, a result of both a population bulge in lower age cohorts as well as increased demand for higher education. By 2009, India had nearly 26,000 colleges and about 14 million students. India's gross enrolment ratio in tertiary education was approximately 13 per cent of the age cohort, considerably lower than China (22 per cent) and much lower than OECD countries. Enrolment ratios vary across Indian states, with the southern and western states faring better than their eastern and northern counterparts.

Women constitute about 41 per cent of enrolments (compared to just 10 per cent in 1950), varying from less than a quarter in Bihar to a high of three-fifths in Kerala. There has been a gradual increase in the enrolment of India's most marginalized social groups. While overall participation rates for socially marginalized groups (SCs, STs, OBCs, and Muslims) are lower than the average, for the eligible population (that is, in the college-going age group), flow measures show that conditional on completing high school there is rough parity in the likelihood of students from a marginalized or a non-marginalized group going to college suggesting a trend towards convergence across all groups (Basant and Sen 2010). The bulk of students (about two-thirds) are enrolled in arts and science, with roughly another fifth in commerce/management. Recent growth—driven by the private sector—has been much greater in professional colleges (especially engineering, management, and medicine), as well as in private vocational courses. Even as political parties rail against *de jure* privatization, *de facto* privatization continues unabated (Kapur and Mehta 2008).

There are considerable misconceptions regarding India's misplaced emphasis on higher education in the early decades after Independence. There is no evidence that the neglect of primary and secondary education, however unconscionable, was *because of* an overemphasis on higher education. Higher education expenditure as a share of gross national product (GNP) declined from nearly 1 per cent during the 1970s to just 0.35 per cent in the mid-1990s before increasing modestly to 0.6 per cent by the end of the decade. Government expenditure on higher education as a percentage of total education expenditure declined from an average of 15 per cent during the 1980s to about 10 per cent during the 1990s. Since this occurred at a time when enrolment was rapidly increasing, the result was a sharp decline in real spending per pupil. A striking feature of higher education expenditure is that most of it goes to salaries resulting in poor infrastructure and intense competition for scarce resources resulting in greater politicization.

Indian higher education continues to be one of the most regulated sectors. *Dirigisme* and the *licence raj* may have been dismantled in industry, but they are flourishing in higher education. The principal regulators are the University Grants Commission (UGC), the All India Council for Technical Education (AICTE), and for specialized professional courses such as medicine, law, and accountancy, the respective professional bodies—the Medical Council of India (MCI), Bar Council of India (BCI), and the Institute of Chartered Accountants of India (ICAI). Although higher education is a concurrent subject, private universities (as distinct from private colleges) have required approval from the federal regulator, UGC. Although this was tested by the state of Chhattisgarh in 2002, the Supreme Court upheld the UGC's monopoly. The basic thrust of regulation is a deep reluctance to grant institutions the autonomy over the academic criteria that determine whom they wish to educate. Regulation has increased the cost of supplying education and resulted in adverse selection by deterring genuine educationists from investing, while encouraging those who are adept at manipulating the licence quota raj in the system, one reason why many private colleges are run by politicians or their affiliates. A perceived need to curb 'exploitation' because of high fees has led to fee-caps instead of empowering students directly by enhancing scholarships and loans. User costs (or costs recovered from students) have remained at roughly 5 per cent (compared to about a quarter in East Asia). Coupled with severe fiscal constraints facing the state, the fee-caps simply diminish the supply and quality of education rather than help the poor.

In 1948, the Radhakrishnan Commission had cautioned that the exclusive control of education by the state was a recipe for 'totalitarian tyrannies'. That warning went unheeded. From the 1980s, while the state maintained tight official control over higher education, actual provisioning shifted to the private sector, a trend that accelerated in the 1990s. This de facto privatization was not a result of changing ideological commitments of the key actors—the state, the judiciary, or India's propertied classes—but instead resulted from a breakdown of the state system and an exit of Indian elites from public institutions, to both private-sector institutions within the country as well as abroad. The mushrooming of private higher education institutions (with the largest number in the southern states and in Maharashtra) has been driven by four factors: fiscal exhaustion, diffusing the reservation conundrum by expanding supply, and, with earlier sources of patronage exhausted, the search for new sources of patronage. A fourth factor is inter-state competition and policy diffusion as states like Kerala and West Bengal realized that their students were fleeing—and spending large amounts of money—in neighbouring states. There is little doubt that while the mushrooming of private colleges has been driven by profit motives, it has helped bring dynamism to the economy over the long run. States that moved early in this direction (like Karnataka) benefited from this supply shock, whereas states, such as Kerala whose basic educational attainments garner so much attention, languished because of the limited supply of higher education (although this has been changing in recent years).

The political economy of higher education defies easy explanations. Ideological considerations have played an important role. Rapid expansion without regard to quality has led to several low level traps. One, it has a diminishing signalling effect. With university degrees serving as formal minimal requirements but little else, competitive exams have virtually replaced performance at the university level as a passport to further education or jobs. Consequently, there is no compelling demand for quality improvement in the bulk of higher education. Resources have shifted to those arenas which perform signalling functions: entrance exams, competitive tests, and so on, and those who can afford it have seceded from the system through a combination of private tuitions, private professional education, and study abroad. Although the last is relatively small in number (about 1 per cent of tertiary education), the financial implications are more than an order of magnitude greater with estimates suggesting that expenditure on overseas consumption of education is to the tune of several billion dollars annually.

Second, even as private expenditures have increased dramatically, officially there continues to be an enormous reluctance to see education as an industry or business or even as a service sector. Public institutions face numerous hurdles in mobilizing private resources in any form—higher fees, licensing arrangements, or philanthropy. Prior to Independence private philanthropy in higher education played a critical role in its growth. This support not only built some of India's best liberal arts colleges and technology institutes but it also supported public institutions in significant ways. With private initiatives hostage to the discretionary actions of the state, private philanthropy's share in public higher education institutions withered, falling from 17 per cent just after Independence to less than 2 per cent half a century later. Although this share would decline as government expanded its role in higher education, the extent is striking. Moreover, philanthropy became increasingly conflated with creating not-for-profit, but financially sustainable institutions, with beneficiaries charged for the services provided to them rather than funded through financial contributions of donors.

The proliferation of private institutions has been largely in the area of professional education driven by entrepreneurial activities of politicians. However, these private colleges are subject to roughly the same curricular guidelines as public institutions and hence lack pedagogical innovation or excellence associated with private initiative, even while they retain the money-making focus of the private sector. The result is a regulatory environment where the private sector will not be deregulated, foreign institutions will not be permitted, the state sector is strapped for resources because of the government's fiscal constraints, and public education cannot mobilize higher funds because of ideological fetters.

Third, the higher education policy is being driven less by a clear ideological vision or class interest than by the state's own interest (or perhaps its own ideological whims). While ideological battles over the curriculum in history capture attention, state bodies have sought to increase administrative control over institutions of higher education through a web of regulations—the setting up of an institution requires a gamut of clearances and is required to conform to a set of norms set by state bodies. Over the course of the 1970s and 1980s, politicians acquired a great vested interest in the affairs of universities, seeing them as possible sites for not just political recruitment, but expanding patronage. The direct interference of the state has implied that in most states, universities have become appendages of government offices.

As with other aspects of India's reforms, courts have played an important role in shaping the political economy of higher educational reforms, imperfectly filling in for the government and the statutory authorities who have been reluctant to clean up the Augean stables. In a series of judgements in the 1990s, the court affirmed the state's right to interfere in admission policies and the fee structures of private professional institutions on the grounds that education, being a fundamental right, could not be the object of a profit-seeking activity. As a result, poor service in education was effectively not justiciable in consumer courts with the courts and the Monopolies and Restrictive Trade Practices Commission (MRTP) holding that education was not a service because the courts defined 'service' as covering only commercial transactions. More recently, there has been a distinct shift in the Supreme Court's stance, from an undisguised suspicion of the private sector, to a grudging acceptance. In its landmark 'Inamdar' judgement in 2005, the Supreme Court reversed its earlier stance unshackling institutions that do not receive state funding from state diktats. However, this immediately prompted the Parliament to swiftly pass the 104th Constitution Amendment Bill that would allow for reservations in all private educational institutions.

The court's interventions have been driven by an attempt to reconcile disparate principles of merit and social justice focusing more on the procedural aspects of equality and less on enabling higher education to be more widely available or on improving quality. Like the government, courts have been reluctant to sanction fee hikes in public institutions reinforcing a peculiar public–private split. While the primary and secondary school sector has been left replete with freedoms, higher education is regarded as the arena where a formal principle of equality of opportunity is most vigorously asserted. The political and legal energies have overwhelmingly focused on professional and technical education (medicine, engineering, pharmacy, management), neglecting both a majority of the students enrolled in traditional science and arts courses as well as vocational training institutions. India has a sizeable system of industrial training institutes (ITIs), with enrolments of roughly three-quarters of a million. Most ITIs are of very poor quality, though there have been attempts to revive them through public–private partnerships. But ITIs remain a neglected sector of higher education, with the result that the system is skewed towards degrees rather than skills.

India's higher education system remains neither fish nor fowl—suspended between over-regulation by the state, on the one hand, and a discretionary privatization that is unable to mobilize private capital in productive ways, on the other. The success of narrow professional schools masks a deep crisis. The veneer of the few institutions of excellence masks the reality that the median higher education institutions in India have become incapable of producing students who have skills and knowledge. A few of the top institutions like IITs can free ride on the fact that they have little competition and can, therefore, get the best students out of a very large pool of available talent. But the bulk of the system does not provide adequate screening or signalling. Consequently, students are forced to spend more years (and, increasingly, large resources) in acquiring some sort of postgraduate professional qualification as they desperately seek ways to signal their qualities to potential employers. It would not be an exaggeration to say that India's current system of higher education is centralized and politicized, and militates against producing broad analytical skills. The fact that the system nonetheless produces a noticeable number of high-quality students has to do with the sheer number of students and the Darwinian struggle at the high school to get admission into the few good institutions.

The core problem in the sector is the mismatch of supply and demand and poor standards. The pressure on the state to expand higher education has been largely expressed as a demand for more seats rather than as a demand for higher quality or greater expenditure. There are too few institutions compared to the size of the demand, the supply is locked into programmes that have not kept with changing demands in labour markets, and even fewer quality institutions. Over the long run, internal incentives and adverse selection effects within universities have undermined autonomy and professionalism.

The public-sector supply which was stagnant since the early 1980s is, however, poised for significant expansion if the targets announced for the Eleventh Plan come to pass. It has targeted a GER of 15 per cent (21 million students), implying an annual growth rate of nearly 9 per cent or an additional enrolment of 870,000 students in universities and about 6 million in colleges in this period. To this end the central government intends setting up and funding 14 new central 'innovation' universities across the country along with ambitious plans in 'Technical Education' (this includes setting up eight new IITs, seven Indian Institutes of Management [IIMs], five Indian Institutes of Science and Engineering Research [IISERs], two Schools of Planning and Architecture [SPAs], 10 National Institutes of Technology [NITs], 20 Indian Institutes of Information Technology [IIITs], and 50 Centres for Training and Research in frontier areas.

The most acute weakness plaguing India's higher education is a crisis of accountability at all levels of the system, the result of a deeply flawed regulatory environment. The prevailing political ideological climate in which elite institutions are seen as being anti-democratic, finds its natural response in political control to influence admission policies, internal organization, the structure of courses, and funding. With even flagship institutions like the IITs and IIMs suffering from growing shortfalls of faculty, pressures to adjust to the increasingly global market for talent have been mounting. The travails of Indian universities have compounded the problems resulting from the decision to separate research from teaching in the 1950s.

Nonetheless, Indian research in science and technology fields has improved considerably (as measured by publications) since 2003 and is evenly distributed between the physical and life sciences. The number of papers filed from India increased from 18,911 in 2002 to 36,261 in 2008 (the corresponding figures for China were 38,206 and 104,968) (UNESCO 2010), but the role of Indian universities has been modest. And except for a few elite institutions, the quality of teaching remains poor. Rigid regulations and underinvestment have ensured that there is not enough quality education to meet the skill demands of the economy. Nonetheless, skill development and knowledge creation is occurring, but outside traditional universities—in narrow specialized institutions (so-called 'deemed-to-be-universities'), workforce training within firms, through purely commercial ventures, and purchase of higher education abroad. These second best solutions have worked reasonably well, but at a cost. Wage premiums are higher, few faculty are being trained (with implications for higher education in the future), and disciplines outside the professions (especially in the liberal arts) are collapsing (Kapur 2010).

Ironically, even as India is positioning itself as global service provider, it is becoming an ever larger consumer of overseas education in higher education. In recent years, there has been a considerable debate on regulatory reforms. Some of the proposed interventions aim at introducing accountability by strengthening accrediting systems. Others aim at regulatory reforms, including a new regime for allowing foreign institutions to operate in India. The progress on these interventions is very slow and it is not yet clear that the overall architecture will be a great improvement on the present system. But in some ways, these regulatory proposals sidestep two important bottlenecks in the expansion of quality higher education. The first is the availability of adequately trained researchers and teachers. The second bottleneck stems from the reality that setting up universities and colleges requires a whole range of intermediate permissions, including permissions on land use. In short, this expansion could still be stymied by bottlenecks outside of education. India will need a regulatory revolution to take full advantage of the knowledge economy but the political economy of the reforms of higher education poses more severe challenges than almost any other sector.

DEVESH KAPUR AND PRATAP BHANU MEHTA

References

Basant, Rakesh and Gitanjali Sen. 2010. 'Who Participates in Higher Education in India? Rethinking the Role of Affirmative Action', *Economic and Political Weekly*, XLV(39): 62–70.

Kapur, Devesh. 2010. 'Indian Higher Education', in Charles Clotfelter (ed.), *American Universities in a Global Market*, NBER, University of Chicago Press, pp. 305–34.

Kapur, Devesh and Pratap Bhanu Mehta. 2008. 'Mortgaging the Future? Indian Higher Education,' *Brookings–NCAER India Policy Forum*, 4: 101–57.

UNESCO. 2010. *UNESCO Science Report 2010: The Current Status of Science around the World*, UNESCO Publishing.

Higher Education: Regulation and Control

The term higher education needs to be defined. It is not school education. Nor is it vocational education, administered primarily, but not exclusively, through industrial training institutes (ITIs). Higher education is largely university education, delivered through universities and colleges and covering bachelor's (undergraduate), master's (postgraduate), and doctoral or pre-doctoral (MPhil) degrees. But it also includes technical education, where undergraduate and postgraduate diplomas (rather than degrees) are offered.

Although the Ministry of Human Resource Development is directly or indirectly involved, there are multiple layers in higher education. First, there are 18 central universities, funded by the union government, and these include the Indira Gandhi National Open University (IGNOU), established in 1985 with a focus on distance education. Second, there are institutions, often with a narrower teaching focus but with emphasis also on research, that have been declared deemed universities under Section 3 of the UGC Act of 1956. The Constitution of India is federal in character. Article 246 of the Constitution specifies areas the Parliament (the central government) can legislate on, and areas that are under the jurisdiction of state legislatures. There is a Seventh Schedule to the Constitution that lists out these areas. List I in the Seventh Schedule is a Union (central government) List, List II is a State List, and List III is a Concurrent List, listing areas that both the Centre and the states can legislate on. These lists have not remained constant and have been changed through constitutional amendments from time to time. Till 1976–7, higher education was in the State List of the Constitution. In 1976–7, education was moved to the Concurrent List. Entry 25 of the Concurrent List now reads, 'Education, including technical education, medical education and universities, subject to the provisions of entries 63, 64, 65 and 66 of List I (the Union list)'. The most important of these entries in the Union List is 66, which states, 'co-ordination and determination of standards in institutions for higher education or research and scientific and technical institutions' is a central responsibility. This is done through the University Grants Commission (UGC), set up in 1952 and with statutory backing granted in 1956. Third, there are state universities, and coordination between the Centre and states is ensured through the Central Advisory Board of Education (CABE). Some universities are affiliating, others are unitary. Some are single campus, others are multi-campus. Fourth, technical education is supervised by assorted statutory councils like the All India Council for Technical Education (AICTE), the Bar Council of India, the Medical Council of India, the Indian Council for Agricultural Research (ICAR), and the National Council for Teacher Education

(NCTE). The AICTE is the most important. It was established as an advisory body in 1945, but became statutory in 1987.

The evolution of higher education in India can be traced back to 1857, when the first Indian universities were set up. Earlier, Indian colleges were affiliated to British universities. Between 1857 and 1947, 18 universities were set up, the ones in Bombay, Calcutta, and Madras providing the models, with an emphasis on liberal arts. There were also nationalist attempts, like the National College set up in 1906 in Calcutta, with Sri Aurobindo as principal. At the time of Independence, there were 20 universities, 500 colleges, and 100,000 students. The number of students (per 100,000 population) was 80 in 1951. However, very few women, or scheduled caste and scheduled tribe students, were enrolled, or graduated. By the end of the Ninth Plan (March 2002), there were 133 central and state universities, 27 deemed universities, 12,342 colleges, 1,500 women's colleges, and 7,500,000 students, that is, 717 students per 100,000 population. And the trend since March 2002 is nothing short of exponential. By the time of the Mid-Term Appraisal of the Tenth Plan in 2004–5, there were 229 central and state universities, 95 deemed universities, 16,000 colleges, 1,650 women's colleges, and 9,228,000 students, that is, 854 students per 100,000 population. No data on the number of teachers are available after 2000 and the 2000 figure is 0.331 million. The figures are no less impressive for technical education.

Yet the problems with the higher education system have also been repeated ad nauseam, going as far back as the Radhakrishnan Commission on University Education (1947), the Education Commission (1966), and in more recent times the National Policy on Education (1986) or the Mid-Term Appraisal of the Tenth Five Year Plan (1997–2002). The UPA (United Progressive Alliance) government's National Common Minimum Programme (NCMP) promised a National Commission on Education and this has been set up as the Knowledge Commission, under the Chairmanship of Sam Pitroda. No doubt, the Knowledge Commission will also revisit these issues.

First, the point is made that returns on investments in higher education are high. This may well be true, although figures on what these returns are never surface in government documents. Nor are there estimates on how these returns compare with investments in school (primary and secondary) or vocational education. Second, as a corollary, it is argued that enrolment of the population in the 18–23 age group must be increased from 6 per cent at the start of the Tenth Plan to 10 per cent by the end of 2007. The choice of 10 per cent seems to be based on the fact that many countries in Southeast and East Asia have this kind of enrolment figure. India's 6 per cent enrolment also needs qualification. The explosion since March 2002 has already been mentioned, particularly through the open and distance education route. The present enrolment ratio is more like 8 per cent and the 10 per cent target in 2007 is eminently reachable. Third, the point is made that there must be more colleges and universities and institutes imparting technical education so that access ratios can further increase. As a general point, this is unexceptionable. After all, Census 2001 shows that India has more places of worship (2.4 million) than schools and colleges (1.5 million) and hospitals (0.5 million) combined. But one should also note that there is considerable excess capacity in the higher education system. Some back-of-the-envelope figures will demonstrate this point, based on the figures for universities, deemed universities, and colleges mentioned earlier. Whatever be the average number of students a college/deemed university or university can cater to, the present enrolment of 9,228,000 is far short of capacity. One forms an impression of excess demand based on admission problems at better higher education institutes. However, on a macro basis, there is still excess supply.

Fourth, this leads to the obvious point that there is a serious quality issue. Barring the IITs and IIMs, one often argues that few of India's institutes of higher education figure in global lists. During the Tenth Plan, the UGC has also picked five universities (Jawaharlal Nehru University, Hyderabad, Madras, Jadavpur, Pune) for pushing as universities with potential for excellence. However, all this is about the better Indian institutes for higher education. The more serious issue is that quality is poor in the worse-off ones. Fifth, there is an argument that there are disparities in access to higher education, among women, SCs/STs, and even backward regions within the country. While inequity in access does exist, this inequity is no more than in other socio-economic indicators and there is enough anecdotal evidence to indicate that disparities based on criteria other than merit are becoming less. IIT admissions and the emergence of Kota in Rajasthan as a training centre for IIT admissions are cases in point.

Sixth, it is argued that public expenditure on higher education must increase. After all, the National Policy on Education (1986) had the target of increasing public expenditure on education to 6 per cent of GDP (the present figure is 3.74 per cent). This is reiterated by the NCMP, with the stipulation that out of 6 per cent, at least half will be spent on primary and secondary education. Ipso facto, the remainder will be spent on other forms of education, including higher education (higher education's present share is around 0.5 per cent of GDP), and this has also been reflected in the use of the 2 per cent education cess, imposed on all central taxes since 2004. But this argument needs further elaboration. The expression 'public good' is used in a loose sense. In its technical sense, higher education is not a public good, even though there may be positive externalities. Higher education is a private good. It may be a merit good, warranting public subsidization for those who deserve such subsidies, as opposed to the present system of subsidizing across the board, with fees progressively declining, the higher one moves up the education ladder. One must remember that the share of student fees, endowments, and other sources of income in funding of higher education has progressively declined. However, public financing of higher education is not identical with public provisioning of higher education. The presumption that greater supply, better quality, and reduced inequity have to be solved through public provisioning is not axiomatic. There is also the issue of imparting greater efficiency to public expenditure. For instance, more than 80 per cent of current expenditure on higher education is on salaries. In the 1990s, two committees specifically examined issues of funding higher education, the M.S. Swaminathan Committee (High Power Committee for Mobilization of Additional Resources for Technical Education, AICTE, 1994) for technical education and the Punnayya Committee (Committee on UGC Funding of Institutions of Higher Education, UGC, 1993) for central universities. In general, both suggest better cost recovery through hikes in fees, student loans and means-based scholarships, and reduction or elimination of maintenance grants or subsidies on maintenance. The point that subsidies to institutes are not identical with subsidies to poor students should be reiterated.

This debate about higher education reform takes place against the background of certain other developments. First, there are global commitments in the services sector through the WTO (World Trade Organization). Of particular interest is service-sector delivery through Mode 3, that is, commercial presence of the service provider in India. Under the Uruguay Round agreement, India has no commitments in higher education. However, in the ongoing request-offer stage of service-sector negotiations, to be eventually formalized through the DDA (Doha Development Agenda), higher education, training services, and testing services are on the request lists of other countries. Therefore, these are likely to be eventually opened up to foreign service providers. Second, a large number of Indian students head overseas for higher education, not just to the United States. This, de facto, amounts to India subsidizing human resource development in developed countries. But, more pertinently, such exit options are only available to better-off students from relatively richer segments. Third, there has been a simultaneous decline in the number of overseas students (from neighbouring countries in Asia and from Africa) who come to India to study. Fourth, because of a grey area in the law, some foreign universities already operate in India, with degrees ostensibly awarded abroad. But this only brings the relatively lesser-known institutes to India. Is it not better to broaden access across all economic classes by permitting foreign higher educational institutes to legitimately operate in India?

This presupposes legitimate private-sector entry, not just from foreign providers but also from domestic ones. The Private Universities (Establishment and Regulation) Bill has been pending since 1995. There is also a Private Professional Educational Institutions (Regulation of Admission and Fixation of Fee) Bill, 2005. However, the issue that arises is one of regulation vis-à-vis control. Be it through the UGC and AICTE Acts and associated rules, or these two proposed Bills, the emphasis is on control. Output prices (student fees) will be fixed. Input costs (salaries of teachers) will be fixed. Standards will be ensured through norms. This planning mindset was given up for manufacturing in the 1990s and consumers have not suffered. Yet it continues for higher education. And the effective licensing is reflected in shortages, manifest in capitation fees and donations. To compound matters, an artificial distinction is created between professional/technical education and colleges/universities and higher education as a profit-making venture is anathema. It is far better to give up this control mindset in its entirety. Beyond private-sector entry, there is an issue of reforming existing public institutes. The same principles can apply to these also. The present attempts at granting autonomy to selected colleges are half-hearted moves, since they are restricted to methods of teaching and designing syllabi. In a phased fashion, it is far better to give such public institutions complete autonomy (including on so-called input and output prices) and confront them with hard budget constraints, with public subsidies directed at students.

Competition removes shortages through supply-side adjustments and ensures better quality. This does not imply absence of regulation, since higher education, like many other sectors, is characterized by asymmetry of information. The oft-cited experience of Chhattisgarh through the Chhattisgarh Niji Vishwavidyala Adhiniyam (University Act) of 2002 merely reinforces the point. The debate should be about the content of regulation and about appropriate disclosure norms. The Chhattisgarh Private Universities (Establishing and Functioning) Bill of 2005 mentions some possible disclosure norms. Insistence on disclosure norms is not the same as an attempt to monitor quality. The latter is best left to competition and the market and rankings of institutes of higher education also evolve through the market, provided the requisite information is available. The UGC and AICTE have outlived their purpose. The National Higher Education Commission, a super-regulator that the Ministry of Human Resource Development is now pushing through a new Bill, is not the answer.

Bibek Debroy

References

Indian National Commission for Cooperation with UNESCO. 1998. 'Higher Education in India', Vision and Action Country Paper, UNESCO World Conference on Higher Education in the Twenty-first Century, Indian National Commission for Cooperation with UNESCO, Paris, October, available at http://education.nic.in/htmlweb/unhighedu.htm.

Planning Commission. 2005. *Mid-Term Appraisal of Tenth Five Year Plan (2002–2007)*, Government of India, June.

■ HIV/AIDS, Economics of

India's response to the challenges posed by HIV/AIDS will have far-reaching consequences for the success of the global response to the epidemic. India has a growing global presence, encompassing more than 15 per cent of the world's population and presenting considerable economic potential. Any significant economic effects of the epidemic in India could, therefore, have substantial economic repercussions worldwide.

The first serological evidence of an HIV infection in India appeared in 1986, and since then HIV cases have been detected in almost all of India's 35 states and union territories. Although infections for the most part are contained within 'high-risk' population groups, in seven Indian states the prevalence of HIV among women attending ante-natal clinics exceeds 1 per cent, putting those infections and states in the 'generalized' epidemic category. According to the National AIDS Control Organisation (NACO), in 2008 there were an estimated 2.27 million people in India living with HIV/AIDS, which translates into an adult prevalence rate of 0.29 per cent (NACO 2010). This is a substantially lower figure than previous estimates of the HIV-infected population of India, which exceeded 5 million (NACO 2004). This downward revision reflects improved methods of estimation that rely less on sentinel surveillance of women in ante-natal clinics and more on population-based surveys such as the National Family Health Survey, the most recent round of which was conducted in 2005–6. Despite this dramatic reduction in estimates of India's HIV-infected population, HIV prevalence is still large enough to constitute a continuing and significant public health challenge. Since halting and reversing the advance of the HIV/AIDS epidemic is entrenched in the United Nations millennium development goals, this cause is also a prime source of international donor-funding and a powerful driver of socio-economic reforms.

Traditional thinking about HIV/AIDS has focused on its biomedical aspects, including the structure of the HIV virus, mechanisms of transmission, the management of opportunistic infections, and the quest to develop an effective vaccine. Yet, the effects of HIV/AIDS clearly extend far beyond physical health. HIV/AIDS has profoundly impacted human rights and ethics frameworks, and has catalysed powerful debates on prevention and treatment strategies. In assessing the implications of the epidemic, it is important to note its disproportionate impact on high-risk, vulnerable groups, such as sex workers and their clients, or injecting drug users and their partners. The structural determinants associated with HIV/AIDS, such as poverty and unequal access to health services, are particularly important in the case of developing countries like India. Social and cultural norms have led to a reluctance to acknowledge the spread of HIV/AIDS, leading to mental health problems associated with a stigmatized disease and hesitance to take preventive measures. Women are particularly vulnerable due to their limited decision-making powers, extending even to a lack of ability to negotiate safe sex.

When evaluating the economic impacts of HIV/AIDS, it is important to note that the disease appears to be spreading without significant limit. Given the lack of a cure for AIDS in the near future, each new case represents irreversible economic loss for a particular household, albeit with variable time lags from diagnosis to the onset of illness and ultimately death. When transmitted sexually—the dominant mode in most of India—HIV adversely affects economically productive age groups. Families and dependants in turn are at high risk of infection, amplifying this negative economic impact. Given this compounded family burden, treatment costs can be exorbitant, especially in a country such as India where the great majority of healthcare is paid for out of pocket (Bloom et al. 2004).

Impacts of HIV/AIDS

Sectoral Impacts

There are few studies and thus limited information on sectoral impacts of HIV/AIDS in South Asia. Migrant workers, who constitute an important part of the unskilled labour force in both rural and urban areas, are at increased risk of HIV infection, presumably due to living far from their families with income to spare, compounded by their low levels of education and awareness of HIV transmission risks (Gupta and Singh 2002). Sectors relying heavily on unskilled labour, such as construction, may face greater economic challenges from AIDS. Nevertheless, India's vast pool of underemployed labour means that the threat to economic sectors that rely heavily on unskilled labour is not likely to be significant in the near future.

To the extent that HIV/AIDS is associated with declines in the rate of growth of per capita income, it is natural to suppose it will also thwart any decline in poverty. Cross-country evidence suggests that both economic inequality and the poverty rate (defined as the proportion of the population living on less than US$ 1 per day) are positively correlated with HIV prevalence (Bloom et al. 2001). A causal impact of HIV on poverty or inequality has not been empirically demonstrated thus far in the Indian context, although it has been suggested that healthcare costs play a critical role in driving populations into poverty (Selvaraj and Karan 2009).

There is reasonable micro-evidence to support the assertion that the poor and less educated are at greater risk of infection than other groups (Bloom et al. 2001). It is likely that the poor disproportionately bear the economic consequences of AIDS, contributing both to increased poverty as well as worsening overall economic inequality. Though the exact extent of the effects of HIV/AIDS is still to be measured, it seems inevitable that the disease will contribute to increased poverty among already low-income, high-risk groups in India, particularly sex workers, truck drivers, and unskilled migrant workers, and especially in states where there are localized sub-epidemics. Stigma and discrimination faced by these groups are likely to act as further barriers to confronting challenges of HIV/AIDS (Mawar et al. 2005).

Individual households may experience severe health crises differently from the social sectors to which they belong. In some cases, previously unemployed members of the labour force may take over from household members or extended family that are rendered unable to work. In addition, NGO networks and industries may offer some limited mechanisms (such as orphanages and care services) to mitigate sustained household-level impacts. The National Council on AIDS has also recently attempted to mobilize a multi-sectoral response for addressing household and community-level impacts.

Macro-level Impacts

Analysing the broad impact of HIV/AIDS on economic growth and productivity is difficult because this impact depends largely on which demographic groups are most affected by HIV/AIDS. Anand et al. (1999) estimated that HIV/AIDS would cost India roughly 1 per cent of GDP per year through lost productivity and treatment of secondary infections. More recent estimates of the impact of HIV/AIDS on India's aggregate economic performance suggest that the impact will be small, perhaps resulting in a loss of no more than 0.16 per cent of GDP per capita each year, reflecting the low HIV prevalence in the country (Haacker 2009).

Though reported HIV prevalence is marginally higher in urban areas than in rural areas, the number of rural dwellers affected by the disease is higher. This implies that an abundant labour supply could fill any labour gap and lower the aggregate economic impact of HIV/AIDS. However, if the epidemic were to affect greater numbers of young, educated, urban professionals, the economic costs would be much higher, especially given the premium placed on skilled labour. Most notably, by curtailing adult lifespans, a widespread HIV epidemic alters the calculus of investment in education and technical skills, thereby undermining the process of investment in human capital (Bloom and Mahal 1997). In addition, burgeoning HIV prevalence could affect international decisions regarding direct foreign investment, technology transfer, and personnel allocation in countries perceived to be of high health risk, in effect cutting off afflicted locales from the benefits of globalization. The long-term economic impact of such a shift could be more significant than even the constraints imposed by an epidemic on local labour supplies or savings.

An alternative approach to assessing the macroeconomic impact of HIV/AIDS is to estimate the aggregate welfare loss to Indian households due to the infection. In one study that sought to do this, Das et al. (2009) estimated the magnitude of the monetary transfers required to compensate households for HIV infection among their members and associated negative impacts on schooling, health, and consumption. The authors concluded that the resulting welfare loss would be monetarily equivalent to about Rs 65,000 per person and that in the aggregate, household welfare losses would total about 7 per cent of GDP annually, which is substantially greater than the estimates for national output losses.

Impacts of Urbanization and Migration

Though the effects of HIV/AIDS on Indian economic growth are likely to be modest, the epidemic has a complex relationship with economic development. The implications of economic growth and changes in economic priorities and investments, such as those initiated by the liberalization policies adopted in the 1990s have likely affected the spread of the epidemic. In particular, the fallout of India's market-driven development policies are visible in both rural to urban and international migration, in increasing and unregulated urbanization, in a rise in incomes in certain sections of society, and in stagnant living standards for a large swath of Indians.

India has a large migrant population, both internal and international. The floating population of migrant workers in India is significant, as is rural to urban migration, especially in Maharashtra, Tamil Nadu, and West Bengal. India is also experiencing substantial cross-border population movements with Bangladesh and Nepal, as well as strong migration flows to and from the Middle East and a growing influx of tourists and foreign business people. Ongoing economic reform is likely to further augment this movement of people. Increasing economic inequality, another correlate of economic growth in its early stages, is also likely to contribute to increased risk of HIV transmission among Indians.

Mobility and migration can aggravate the spread of HIV from high-risk groups, such as truck drivers, migrants, and refugees, to the wider community. Mobile populations with disposable cash, such as migrant labourers and possibly tourists, are especially likely to demand commercially available sex or engage in multiple-partner sex (Bloom et al. 2004). The behaviour of migrants is not easily subject to monitoring by their families and communities, and migrants may be more inclined to seek out the sex industry due to separation from their partners. Moreover, economic deprivation exacerbates the vulnerability of certain groups who provide these services. For example, the supply side of the sex industry naturally attracts poor women and girls and renders them a high-risk group for HIV infection.

A focus on the economic and political roots of the epidemic, coupled with a study of cultural and individual risk behaviour, therefore, has a potentially vital role in promoting our understanding of the spread of HIV/AIDS and in designing policies that most efficiently limit its impact (Bloom et al. 2004).

The Role of Economic Analysis

By clarifying the underpinnings of risk behaviours for HIV infection, economic analysis has also helped explain individuals' perspectives in a way that can provide policy insights. Consider a policy of isolating or imprisoning HIV-positive commercial sex workers, as India did some years ago in a highly publicized case. Policies such as this fail on two counts: they do not influence the demand side of the market for commercial sex, and they neglect the deeper economic roots of the supply of commercial sex workers. Under the prevailing economic conditions in India, the demand for commercial sex will be satisfied by a newly migrating group of women; frequent arrests of commercial sex workers, and their consequent withdrawal from the market, will only enhance work opportunities for new entrants into the industry. Moreover, the incarceration of sex workers in rehabilitation homes and prisons is likely to result in the industry remaining 'underground', which will hinder sex workers from accessing public health messages. Without access to information on HIV prevention or the power to negotiate the use of condoms, new migrants, too, will become infected and in turn infect their partners (Bloom et al. 2001, 2004).

Economic approaches to policymaking, starting with understanding the economic roots of undesirable outcomes, underlie effective policy design and implementation. They also highlight the fact that many practical policies for AIDS prevention may conflict with other social goals and policies. For example, decriminalizing the use and possession of drugs and needles may conflict with social goals of limiting drug use. In addition, attempts in India to disseminate information about safe sex, condom use, and the use of condoms in brothels have been controversial and have elicited moral postures and cultural justifications intended to resist such policy interventions.

Evaluation of the Health System's Response to AIDS

The Indian government's response to HIV/AIDS came soon after the detection of the first AIDS case with the formation of the National AIDS Committee (NACO) in 1986. The Committee was part of the Ministry of Health and Family Welfare and initially focused on data gathering in what were then perceived as high-risk areas (Chandrasekaran et al. 2006). The first National AIDS Control Programme was launched and NACO was subsequently established to implement the programme, with assistance from the World Bank.

NACO aims to increase awareness and to promote condom usage among teenagers and other vulnerable or high-risk sections of the population. This programme itself requires much greater resources than the funds presently earmarked by the Indian government to combat HIV/AIDS. Until about 2003, treatment with antiretroviral (ARV) drugs was relatively limited and mostly provided by the private sector (Gupta et al. 2009). In 2004, following a grant from the Global Fund for AIDS, Tuberculosis and Malaria (GFATM), the Indian government began providing free access to ART (antiretroviral treatment) to individuals with HIV who sought care through the public system. However, the general inadequacies of the health system, including the lack of coordination between various agencies and levels of health services delivery, have been reflected in India's HIV/AIDS programmes.

The challenges and limitations posed by the existing surveillance resources at the national and state levels, such as the unequal distribution of sentinel sites and the inability of ante-natal clinics to provide extensive HIV prevalence data, have been important constraints in managing AIDS. Coordination has been poor between state health departments and state-level public hospitals that provide central-government-funded ART services. The goals of HIV/AIDS programmes are often insufficiently aligned with either the resources or objectives of state-level health departments. And despite healthcare being free, private costs of accessing ART treatment amount to about 70 per cent of the costs of ART (Gupta et al. 2009). There have been some efforts to overcome these limitations: the Indian government recently initiated an effort focused on district-level projects in areas of low awareness, integrating its activities with the National Rural Health Mission, reproductive health programmes, and tuberculosis control programmes. ARV drugs have also been marketed at considerable price reductions, although not in all regions and populations (Godbole and Mehendale 2005).

The non-government sector has also sought to address the HIV/AIDS epidemic. Some international agencies and partnerships have been influential in shaping the priorities of HIV/AIDS programmes, particularly around prevention. Of particular note is the influence of Avahan, the India-based AIDS initiative founded in 2003 by the Bill and Melinda Gates Foundation, which focuses on prevention programmes in high-risk groups, such as female sex workers, high-risk men, and injecting drug users. The Gates Foundation provided additional financial support of $338 million in 2009 for prevention services. These large financial aid flows have attracted criticism due to their narrow focus on knowledge and information and their neglect of the broader social determinants of HIV/AIDS in India. Factors such as unequal access to health services due to socio-economic factors like gender, educational attainment, and wealth need to be emphasized equally in policy solutions.

In order to curb the HIV/AIDS epidemic in the near future India will need a dramatic shift in its present approaches and priorities. In the face of continued widespread HIV infection, current health services are inadequate, and the cost of education and treatment programmes is steadily rising. Despite growing concern among policymakers, the sheer numbers of the population affected by the epidemic, health system resource constraints, widespread ignorance about HIV/AIDS, cultural taboos and stigmas related to the disease, and differences in priorities between levels of government complicate the challenge of curbing HIV/AIDS. While recent estimates show a drop in infections in the southern states, there has been no significant decline in the north or north-eastern states. If necessary research is conducted, economists can contribute usefully to thinking about the determinants of transmission and potential economic impacts of the HIV/AIDS epidemic in India, thereby aiding the development of strategies to address this immense challenge.

BHARGAVI RAO, AJAY MAHAL, KAVITA SIVARAMAKRISHNAN, AND DAVID E. BLOOM

References

Anand, K., C.S. Pandav, and L.M. Nath. 1999. 'The Impact of HIV/AIDS on the National Economy of India', *Health Policy*, 47: 195–205.

Bloom, D. and Ajay Mahal. 1997. 'Does the AIDS Epidemic Threaten Economic Growth?', *Journal of Econometrics*, 77: 105–24.

Bloom, D., Ajay Mahal, Jaypee Sevilla, and River Path Associates. 2001. 'AIDS and Economics', Harvard School of Public Health, Department of Population and International Health.

Bloom, D., Ajay Mahal, Larry Rosenberg, Jaypee Sevilla, David Steven, and Mark Weston. 2004. *Asia's Economies and the Challenge of AIDS*, Manila, Asian Development Bank.

Chandrasekaran P., G. Dallabetta, V. Loo, S. Rao, H. Gayle, and A. Alexander. 2006. 'Containing HIV/AIDS in India: The Unfinished Agenda', *Lancet Infectious Diseases*, 6: 508–21.

Das, Sanghamitra, Abhiroop Mukhopadhyay, and Tridip Ray. 2009. 'Economic Cost of HIV and AIDS in India', in Markus Haacker and Mariam Claeson (eds), *HIV and AIDS in India: An Economic Development Risk*, Washington DC, World Bank, pp. 123–54.

Godbole, S. and S. Mehendale. 2005. 'HIV/AIDS Epidemic in India: Risk Factors, Risk Behaviour & Strategies for Prevention & Control', *Indian Journal of Medical Research* 121(4): 356–68.

Gupta, Indrani, Mayur Trivedi, and Subodh Kandamuthan. 2009. 'Recurrent Costs of India's Free ART Program', in Markus Haacker and Mariam Claeson (eds), *HIV and AIDS in India: An Economic Development Risk*, Washington DC, World Bank, pp. 191–237.

Gupta, K. and S.K. Singh. 2002. *Social Networking, Knowledge of HIV/AIDS and Risk-taking Behaviour among Migrant Workers*, Mumbai, Indian Institute of Population Sciences.

Haacker, Markus. 2009. 'Development Impact of HIV and AIDS in South Asia', in Markus Haacker and Mariam Claeson (eds), *HIV and AIDS in India: An Economic Development Risk*, Washington DC, World Bank, pp. 75–121.

Mawar, N., S. Sahay, A. Pandit, and U. Mahajan. 2005. 'The Third Phase of HIV Pandemic: Social Consequences of HIV/AIDS Stigma & Discrimination & Future Needs', Review Article, *Indian Journal of Medical Research*, 122: 471–84

National AIDS Control Organisation (NACO). 2004. *Annual Report*, New Delhi, NACO.

——. 2010. Department of AIDS Control. *Annual Report 2009–2010*, Ministry of Health and Family Welfare, Government of India, available at http://www.nacoonline.org/.

Selvaraj, S. and A.K. Karan. 2009. 'Deepening Health Insecurity in India: Evidence from National Sample Surveys since 1980s', *Economic and Political Weekly*, 44(40): 55–60.

Home-based Work

Home-based work is generally defined as an economic activity undertaken within the periphery of the producer/worker's residence. The range of activities it encompasses is rather large; home-based workers 'sew garments, embroider, make lace, roll cigarettes, weave carpets, peel shrimp, prepare food, polish plastic, process insurance claims, edit manuscripts, and assemble artificial flowers, umbrellas, and jewelry' (Prugl 1999). In fact, the range is much larger.

Within this rather broad characterization of home-based work, a variety of economic relationships are included, from independent production for sale to the consumer, to subcontracting that may be horizontal or vertical in nature. Subcontracting itself is mostly of the type where production occurs as per the specifications of the buyer. In home-based subcontracting in India, the buyer mostly provides the necessary inputs or credit, but that is not essential. Subcontracting also may be of the vertical type where the buyer is primarily a downstream manufacturer/seller, or horizontal where the buyer is engaged in a similar activity as the home-based worker.

Home-based workers constituted 20.9 per cent of the total non-agricultural workforce in India in 1999–2000. Almost half (about 9 per cent) of the non-agri workforce was subcontracted, the rest being independent sellers not tied to a particular buyer. Home-based work is much more important in the case of female workers. About 45 per cent of the non-agri female workforce is engaged in home-based work. Slightly more than 18 per cent were in dependent subcontracting relationships. Though there has been a rise in the absolute numbers of home-based workers, as a percentage of workforce there has been a slight fall in the post-reform years (Unni and Rani 2005).

On the one hand, home-based work allows a high degree of flexibility, reduces production costs, is low on transaction costs, and is in many cases an economically efficient and low-cost method of production. To that add income generation for large numbers who would otherwise not be able to take up income-earning activities, and the resultant personal and household benefits that are generated (Bhandari 2005). On the other hand, there has been much concern about the low wages, poor working conditions, child labour, and exploitative relationships in home-based work in India (see for instance Carr et al. 2000).

Women home-based workers appear to suffer most from such poor conditions since a large section of female home workers are in vertical subcontracting relationships. According to Unni and Rani (2005), while 12 per cent of the non-agri male workers were engaged in home-based horizontal subcontracting relationships, only 6 per cent of the women were so engaged. In contrast, while only about 22 per cent of the male dependent producers were in vertical subcontracting, women constituted 47 per cent of such workers. There is also substantial evidence to show that children are significant components of the home-based work economy (Burra 2005).

The work conditions, from all available evidence, are quite poor (NCAER 2001): low rates, lower than minimum wages, lower incomes than those required to sustain minimum consumption requirements, uncertainty in incomes, exploitative informal contracts, little investment in improving work conditions on the part of the contractor, unethical practices, little regard for basic labour and work-related laws, and so on (see, for instance, Menon-Sen and Kumar 2001 and Singh et al. 2002).

Home-based work typically occurs where (i) there is little need for expensive capital equipment that has to be shared between workers and, therefore, production economies of scale are not there; (ii) there exist strong social networks that prevent individual workers from reneging on contracts; this also facilitates lower transactions costs; (iii) the output is standardized and observable by both buyer and seller so that compensation can be output-based. One more characteristic that is not essential but facilitates informal contracts is that of repeated transactions between the same parties.

Though much has been written about the exploitative conditions, how and why they come about, and their consequences, little attention has been paid to the nature of the contract between the home-based worker and the contractor. The key characteristic is that of informality in the sense that the contract is not explicit or coded; it is based on an understanding between the parties. While in itself informality in contracts is not bad and can be beneficial to all concerned, it does have negative ramifications if outside options for the home-based worker, or an impartial enforcing entity, are missing. This is the crux of the problem. Given the poor economic conditions, it is unlikely that significant enough other options can be generated. Moreover, given our experience with government functionaries, it is also unlikely that rapid and impartial justice can be expected.

Many call for a government-backed solution where some mechanism is set up, backed by explicit laws as well as adequate enforcement powers. The problem here is not so much with the intentions but the ability of the government to implement such a policy. A better solution which now appears to be gathering momentum is that of collectivized bargaining. Improvements in conditions can best be achieved if communities of home-based workers gather and bargain collectively with the contractors. This is, in a sense, a non-policy solution with little need for government to institute a new set of laws that it will anyway be unable to implement.

Home-based work in itself can be an economically efficient means of production; it also provides incomes directly to otherwise unskilled women. Therefore, it should be *encouraged* provided, of course, that basic minimum work conditions and compensations are met.

LAVEESH BHANDARI

References

Bhandari, Laveesh. 2005. 'Economic Efficiency of Subcontracted Home-Based Work', in Bibek Debroy and P.D. Kaushik (eds), *Reforming the Labour Market*, New Delhi, Academic Foundation.

Burra, Neera. 2005. 'Crusading for Children in India's Informal Economy', EPW Special Articles, *Economic and Political Weekly*, 3 December.

Carr, Marilyn, Martha Alter Chen, and Jane Tate. 2000. 'Globalization and Home-Based Workers', *Feminist Economics*, 6(3): 123–42.

Menon-Sen, Kalyani and A.K. Shiva Kumar. 2001. 'Women in India: How Free? How Equal?' Report Commissioned by the Resident Coordinator India, United Nations/UNDP, New Delhi.

National Council of Applied Economic Research. 2001. 'Outsourcing of Manufacturing to Households: Sub-contracted Home-based Work in India: A Study of Three Sectors, Agarbathi, Bidi and Zardosi', New Delhi, NCAER, unpublished.

Prugl, Elisabeth. 1999. *The Global Construction of Gender: Home-based Work in the Political Economy of the 20th Century*, Columbia, Columbia University Press.

Singh, Ruma Ghosh, Nikhil Raj, and Helen R. Sekar. 2002. 'Hard Labour at a Tender Age—Child Labour in the Home-Based Industries in the Wake of Legislation', NOIDA, V.V. Giri National Labour Institute.

Unni, Jeemol and Uma Rani. 2005. 'Impact of Recent Policies on Home-based Work in India', Discussion Paper Series 10, Human Development Resource Center, UNDP.

Household Welfare and Decision Making

The nature of decision making within the household crucially affects what happens beyond it. In a variety of areas such as child labour, child schooling, and poverty and inequality estimation, this has considerable policy significance. However, following the 'unitary household' framework of Samuelson and Becker, the economics literature has traditionally treated the household, rather than the individuals residing in it, as the decision-making unit. Consequently, while topics such as household formation and dissolution, the 'power' of members in influencing household decisions, and gender inequality in intra-household resource allocation have figured prominently in demography, sociology, and anthropology, their absence, until recently, has been conspicuous in the economics literature.

The treatment of the household as a 'black box' in economics has also been necessitated by the absence of consumption data at the individual level. An early consequence of this was seen in the estimation of the 'equivalence scale' which measures the impact of household composition changes on welfare. Following Engel, Prais, Houthakker, Rothbarth, and Barten, applied demand analysts, making heroic behavioural assumptions, have avoided the requirement of individual consumption data and estimated the 'scale' using available household-level data. Subsequent empirical studies have, almost invariably, rejected these behavioural assumptions.

With increasing realization among economists that an understanding of intra-household decision-making is crucial for policy analysis, the 'unitary model' has recently received considerable critical attention and its limitations examined. Following the work of Chiappori, Browning, Bourguignon, and others, the unitary model has given way to the 'collective household model', which defines household welfare as a weighted average of the individual members' utilities. Consequently, the 'collective approach' allows each individual household member to influence household decisions, with the nature and extent of that influence dependent on her/his bargaining power vis-à-vis other household members. This is seen as a significant improvement over the unitary framework which views the household head as the sole decision maker. Basu (2006) has extended the collective model by allowing the members' bargaining power to be affected by the household's behaviour with significant implications for modelling adult and child labour supply.

A key behavioural assumption of the unitary model that is restrictive and adds to its unattractiveness is that the members pool their individual incomes, so that the household's expenditure outcomes are invariant to the identity of the income recipient. This assumption has been tested and rejected in several studies using the 'collective approach' including Bourguignon et al. (1993) on France, Maitra and Ray (2003) on South Africa, and Lancaster et al. (2006) on India.[1]

The Indian Evidence

Does the 'power' of an individual in influencing household decisions have an impact on its expenditure pattern and, if so, how? What are the principal determinants of the bargaining power variable, which is measured as the individual's share of household earnings? These questions have recently been investigated using Indian budget data by Lancaster et al. (2006). The study finds that changing power relations within the household, generally, have significant effects on expenditure outcomes. The relationship between an item's budget share and the individual's share of earnings is mostly non-monotonic and varies between items. As a spouse's bargaining power increases from insignificance to dominance, household preferences switch from luxuries to necessities and then switch back to the former. In other words, the budget share of the necessities is at its peak when the bargaining power is spread evenly between the spouses. Since 'necessities', which are jointly consumed, are more likely to be child-centred than 'luxuries', this result suggests that child welfare is better protected in households where neither spouse enjoys an overwhelmingly dominant position in decision making. Consistent with this result, this study also finds that the income-pooling assumption of the unitary model, which ensures the irrelevance of the intra-household 'power' variable, is less likely to be rejected when neither spouse dominates the decision making than when one of them does. The study also finds an inverted U-shaped relationship between the adult male's share of household earnings and his corresponding share of the household's educational experience.

The Indian evidence is also one of sharp differences between states reflecting regional heterogeneity in the household structure, making generalized statements hazardous. For example, the matriarchal structure in Kerala contrasts sharply with the patriarchal structure in northern Indian states. The changes to these structures over time and their implications for household behaviour should not be underestimated. For example, as Kodoth (2004) notes, land reforms in Kerala have strengthened the patriarchal conjugal framework of property relations in the state, thereby weakening women's independent right to property and, consequently, their ability to influence household decisions.

The inadequacy of the unitary model in portraying household behaviour is also evident from its failure to detect gender bias even in societies where such bias is known to exist. In an extension of their 2006 study, Lancaster et al. show the usefulness of the collective model in detecting widespread prevalence of gender bias in resource allocation in India. The results point to significant pro-boys gender bias in educational expenditure in several regions, especially in the backward states. The results also show that the gender bias tends to weaken or disappear as the adult literacy level of the household improves.

Further evidence on the impact of women's 'power' in decision making on household behaviour in India has been presented by Lisa Smith and Elizabeth Byron (2005), who report that an increase in women's influence in household decisions leads to better nutritional and schooling outcomes for the children. However, they also find that an increase in women's influence does not necessarily lead to a weakening of bias against girls in resource allocation. In some cases, the bias actually worsens reflecting sociological factors such as son preference in patriarchal societies. This suggests policy responses such as increasing the

[1]The interested reader is also referred to the special issue of the *Journal of Human Resources*, 25, 1990, for a comprehensive treatment.

economic returns to the girl child, altering inheritance laws in favour of the girl, and the strengthening of anti-dowry legislation.

This entry argues that household decisions have implications that extend far beyond the household. The policy implications are immense, as discussed by Linda Mayoux (2004). She also highlights the differences in women's role in decision making between India and other developing countries.

Let us conclude by listing some of the mechanisms by which a better understanding of household decision-making, via the collective household approach, will aid in devising better policies:

(i) prevent mis-targeting of assistance in poverty interventions through over- or under-estimating poverty levels of individuals within the household;
(ii) promote gender equity within the household;
(iii) reduce intra-household inequalities that may adversely affect the effectiveness of policy interventions; and
(iv) design more effective policies to combat child labour and promote child schooling.

In the current debate in India on the proposed 'employment guarantee' legislation, the literature on intra-household decision-making and its impact on household welfare may provide guidelines on where to enforce such legislation and whom to target for the employment guarantees. The resource constraints on anti-poverty programmes make selective targeting essential, as several commentators have already noted.

RANJAN RAY

References

Basu, K. 2006. 'Gender and Say: A Model of Household Behaviour with Endogenously Determined Balance of Power', *The Economic Journal*, 116: 558–80.

Bourguignon, F., M. Browning, P.A. Chiappori, and V. Lechene. 1993. 'Intra Household Allocation of Consumption: Some Evidence on French Data', *Annales d' Economia et de Statistique*, 29: 137–56.

Kodoth, P. 2004. 'Gender, Property Rights and Responsibility for Farming in Kerala', *Economic and Political Weekly*, 29(19): 1911–20.

Lancaster, G., P. Maitra, and R. Ray. 2006. 'Endogenous Intra-household Balance of Power and Its Impact on Expenditure Patterns: Evidence from India', *Economica*, 73(291): 435–60.

Maitra, P. and R. Ray. 2003. 'The Effect of Transfers on Household Expenditure Patterns and Poverty in South Africa', *Journal of Development Economics*, 71: 23–49.

Mayoux, Linda, 2004. 'Intra-Household Impact Assessment Issues and Participatory Tools', available at www.lindaswebs.info.

Smith, Lisa and Elizabeth Byron. 2005. 'Is Gender Decision Making Power of Women Associated with Reduced Gender Discrimination in South Africa', IFPRI Discussion Paper No. 200, August.

■ Housing Finance

Since the turn of the 20th century, home loans have grown at a rapid pace in India. The majority of the country's billion-plus population continues to live in rural areas where expansion of existing village homes has mostly serviced the needs of the expanding population. For a variety of reasons India has had a slower rate of urbanization than most developing economies, and certainly so relative to China. The 2001 Census of India found that 27.8 per cent of the population lived in urban areas, a modest increase from 25.7 per cent in 1991 and 23.3 per cent a decade earlier. By contrast, China saw urbanization rise from 26.9 per cent in 1991 to 41.8 per cent in 2004. However, even with the slower pace of urbanization, the need for new housing is large. The Planning Commission had estimated that during the Tenth Plan period (2002–7) there would be a need for constructing more than 22 million dwelling units.

In India, prior to the reforms of 1991, provision of housing was seen as part of the many social obligations of the government and accordingly the agencies entrusted with the task were State (Provincial) Housing Boards and City Development Authorities. These agencies were specially mandated to service the needs of the lower-income sections of society. As a result, numerous small, congested, and aesthetically unappealing apartment blocks arose across the country, variously categorized as *janata* (people's), low-, and middle-income housing. That section of the middle class that did not qualify on the income criterion did have the option to buy housing plots from official agencies and build houses upon them or, since the late 1970s, to purchase ready-built apartments from the same agencies. While many of the apartments constructed under the lower-income schemes were pre-financed by state agencies with easy repayment terms, the relatively higher-income middle-class home buyer had to primarily rely on his or her personal financial resources once the considerable challenge of securing an allotment was overcome. Some financing from a variety of state agencies was, however, available for cooperative purchases, which was particularly useful for accommodating employees of the government, including the armed and police services.

In 1970, the central government set up the Housing and Urban Development Corporation (HUDCO) which was mandated to finance the construction of urban economic infrastructure and also support housing schemes. The state-owned Life Insurance Corporation (LIC) and General Insurance Corporation (GIC) were also mandated to provide support for housing finance. This mandate was discharged indirectly by lending to social schemes that included housing and subsequently, since the late 1980s, directly, by the establishment of subsidiary housing finance companies.

The first private company established to provide home finance was the Housing Development and Finance Corporation (HDFC) set up in 1977. Historically in post-Independence India, both the legislation and legal system were not amenable to executing foreclosure, irrespective of the documentation securing the loan. To complicate matters, much of the property in the faster-growing urban areas was leasehold, with the state agency that was lessor having enjoined special prohibitions on resale. Under these circumstances, the mortgage of housing property at most served the role of a negative lien—prohibiting the borrower from selling the property without prior assent of the lender. The dread with which many Indians view their country's legal system was an added deterrent to the extent that most individuals would assess their own ability to navigate the court system very poorly compared to a corporation with its much greater resources.

The HDFC chose to focus on the salaried section of prospective home buyers, for that resolved several issues all at once. It immediately determined the income status of the borrower and subjected him/her to the additional discipline of the authority of his or her employer. The social reality was also that this section of Indian society was intrinsically risk-averse and hence loan-averse, with great fear of the social humiliation perceived to be associated with being named a defaulter and dragged to court. This made for a business where the borrower was most likely to have little or no debt other than the home loan and was under several obligations to observe the covenants of the loan. The economic environment of the era with its widespread shortages meant that the market price of the housing asset was always increasing and thereby the proportion of home equity (the difference between market price and the outstanding loan) was continually rising as a proportion of the outstanding loan.

It was, therefore, not surprising that the HDFC had assets with an enviable delinquency record and an even better loan loss record. Since the mid-1980s other non-banking finance companies (NBFCs) also began to enter the market and the delinquency rates for individual salaried home owners continued to be sterling, with loan losses mostly restricted to credits given to companies in the construction business.

In the years after 1991, a market for personal loans began to rapidly develop, primarily focusing on the financing of cars. Foreign banks and some NBFCs that took the initiative found that the combination of credit discipline of one section of borrowers and the legislative initiatives easing repossession made for a business with fairly low likely loan losses compared to the relatively higher yields prevalent. State-owned commercial banks, which had previously stayed away from personal finance, were increasingly attracted to it, and this at a time when their corporate portfolio was coming under considerable pressure. At the beginning of the second half of the 1990s, the personal finance business, and in particular home finance, was set to expand rapidly.

It needs to be remembered that India is a relatively under-leveraged economy. The proportion of bank credit to gross domestic product (GDP) at current market prices was 21.4 per cent in fiscal year 1995–6, which has since increased to 42.7 per cent in 2005–6. This is in considerable contrast to China, for instance, where the bank credit to GDP ratio at the end of calendar year 2005 was 136.2 per cent. In the USA, bank credit as a proportion of GDP is 56 per cent, up from 48 per cent a decade earlier. However, banks form a smaller source of credits in the US economy and the total outstanding debt of households was 85 per cent in 2005, with home loans at 64 per cent of the GDP.

In India, at the end of March 1996, home loans issued by banks amounted to a mere 0.6 per cent of the GDP, which has since risen to 4.1 per cent at the end of 2004–5 and 5.3 per cent in 2005–6, forming about half of the stock of personal loans and little over 12 per cent of outstanding bank credit. In addition there are the independent housing finance companies and the small amount of mortgage-backed securitized (MBS) paper that is outside the balance sheet of the loan-originating institutions. The total of mortgage assets on the books of the banks, independent housing finance companies, and investing institutions was close to 8 per cent of the GDP at the end of 2005–6, compared to less than 0.7 per cent a decade earlier.

The environment of declining interest rates since 2001 helped the home finance business push out credit by making terms very attractive to prospective home buyers with variable rates as low as 6.5 per cent. The business, however, was careful in preferentially selling variable interest products and has thus largely excluded interest risk from its balance sheet. Some of the growth in the period 2001 to 2004 was due to refinancing of high-cost previously contracted debt, which added to business volumes. It also lowered perceived risk with previously existing lenders profiting from pre-payment fees and new lenders obtaining access to seasoned assets. The increase in interest rates in 2005 and 2006 is likely to curb the growth of the business, as home buyers find loan conditions becoming more expensive with interest rates on home loans having risen by 30 to 40 per cent in recent years. However, the pace of urban growth does not yet pose a serious downside risk on property prices and to that extent point to significant erosion of home equity. However, if property prices were to decline significantly following a severe economic downturn or some other crisis, pressure on delinquency is inevitable. Offsetting this is the fact that as loans mature, along with more stable loan growth, the loan-to-value ratio would also ease, thereby reducing vulnerability.

The tightening of interest rates has energized the expected process of consolidation with marginal players choosing to exit from the loan-origination market. The four biggest players, namely, ICICI, HDFC, State Bank of India, and LIC Housing, have well over 40 per cent market share; the next four have about 9 per cent market share. The concentration of the larger players is likely to increase in the next phase of expansion, which with high interest rates is likely to see slower growth and more cost pressure on margins.

The home finance business has also benefited from fiscal and regulatory encouragement. In 1999, the government provided an income tax shelter for interest payments of up to Rs 150,000 on housing loans. Initially designed to be operational for a few years, the provision continues to be in force. At about the same time, housing loans extended by a bank, subject to loan size limits, were also qualified to count towards the bank's obligation under mandated priority-sector credit. The risk weight for purposes of computing capital adequacy of banks is set at 75 per cent, which is less than general commercial credits (100 per cent risk weight). The National Housing Bank (NHB), a wholly owned subsidiary of the Reserve Bank of India (RBI), acts as regulator and a source of refinancing for housing finance companies. However, by far the larger part of the business is with the commercial banks and remains regulated by the RBI.

Housing loans grew by 21 per cent in 1997–8 and maintained an average annual rate of expansion of 45 per cent over the next seven years to 2004–5. The year 2003–4 was the high point when housing credit grew by 74 per cent. The sharp expansion in housing credit (along with other retail loans) helped fuel the expansion of bank credit in 2002–3 and 2003–4 and contributed to lifting the pace of overall economic expansion. In 2004–5 and 2005–6, while retail loans including bank credit continued to play an important role, they yielded considerable ground to conventional industrial and infrastructure borrowing.

The delinquency and loan loss record of the housing finance business reveals many things. First that, as was expected, the generation of non-performing assets (NPAs) was low, estimated at 0.2 to 0.6 per cent (per annum) for established players. The overall stock of gross NPAs is estimated at around 2 per cent of outstanding advances on an average basis. Since the length of the asset is long and a large proportion of the loans are fresh, the possibility does exist that delinquencies will rise in coming years. While the careful way of feeling around credit quality of the 1980s may have been excessive, the rapid and competitive expansion of recent years may have imparted a certain amount of avoidable credit risk. It is believed that some agencies, particularly in the state-owned sector, incurred above-average NPAs owing in part to inadequate credit selection resources and in part to collusive inaccurate documentation. On a static basis, that is, over the lifetime of the credit, it is believed that the existing pool of mortgage credits would have loan losses of 3 to 5 per cent.

Initially there was little differentiation in interest spreads among customers of varying credit quality and the spreads in general were possibly thinner than what the credit risk should have implied. However, over the past couple of years, major lenders have been able to put in place differential pricing that is a more accurate reflection of the loan-adjusted profitability of the business, which is expected to be strengthened in the forthcoming period likely to be characterized by tighter monetary conditions and stable loan growth.

The home finance market in India is yet to penetrate the sub-prime markets in any significant fashion. Geographically too it has been concentrated in the larger cities, with metropolitan centres accounting for 47 per cent of outstanding loans in March 2005, and other urban centres another 27 per cent. Both vertical and horizontal expansion of the business is likely to increase the inherent credit risk, given continued weakness in institutional support for foreclosure. The further expansion of the business may encourage the development of innovations which try and get around the problems posed by the combination of sub-prime credit and the relative illiquidity of the underlying asset.

SAUMITRA CHAUDHURI

References

ICRA Limited. 2004. 'Mortgage Loan Market', *ICRA Rating Feature*, October.

Karnad, Renu S. 2004. 'Housing Finance and the Economy: Regional Trends in South Asia—Perspectives', International Union for Housing Finance, 25th World Congress, June, Brussels.

Moody's Investors Service. 2005. 'A Primer on the US Residential Mortgage Market for Banks and Thrift Investors', *Global Credit Research*, March.

Reserve Bank of India (RBI). Various issues. *Banks Statistical Returns*, Mumbai, RBI.

———. 2005. *Report on Trends and Progress of Banking in India 2004–5* (also previous issues), Mumbai, RBI.

Human Development Index

The term 'human development' entered the lexicon of development economics in 1990 through the first *Human Development Report* (HDR) published by the United Nations Development Programme (UNDP). The concept, developed by Mahbub ul Haq and Amartya Sen, was originally defined as 'the process of enlarging people's choices'. In 2010, the definition was refined as: 'Human development is the expansion of people's freedoms to live long, healthy and creative lives; to advance other goals they have reason to value; and to engage actively in shaping development equitably and sustainably on a shared planet'. People are considered both the beneficiaries and drivers of human development, as individuals and in groups. Economic growth is considered only a means for expanding capability and not as an end in itself.

The Human Development Index (HDI), used in the HDRs to compare countries in the world, has been designed as an alternative to per capita gross domestic product (GDP), the single most commonly used measure to evaluate development outcomes. The index includes three important choices—to lead a long and healthy life, to acquire knowledge, and to have a decent standard of living. The distinguishing feature of HDI is that while developed as an alternative to the use of per capita income for evaluating development outcomes, it does not ignore the income dimension itself.

With respect to HDI, several crucial decisions were taken by Mahbub ul Haq and Amartya Sen, the principal architects of the HDI. The first was that it should reflect human capabilities. Second, it should include only a limited number of variables to keep it 'simple and manageable'. Third, a composite index rather than several separate indices would be prepared. Fourth, HDI would cover both social and economic aspects and, finally, the coverage and methodology of HDI would be kept flexible (Haq 1995).

Three features of HDI—its simplicity, universality, and plurality—have contributed to the emergence of HDI as a strong alternative evaluative measure of development outcomes.

Methodology

Dimensions and Indicators

Since HDI is an evaluation of development outcomes, it focuses on attainments in the realms of education, health, and real GDP per capita. Longevity is measured by life expectancy at birth. The dimension of knowledge is measured using two indicators: (i) adult literacy rate, which is a crude reflection of access to education and (ii) combined primary, secondary, and tertiary enrolment, with the former having a two-thirds weight and the latter, a one-third weight The third dimension, command over resources needed for a decent living, is represented by per capita GDP. In order to reflect the diminishing returns that accrue while transforming income into human capabilities, the logarithm of per capita GDP is used as an indicator. However, to enable cross-country comparisons, per capita income is adjusted for purchasing power parity (PPP) reflecting the relative purchasing power of the currency; this is expressed in US dollars. It is important to understand here that the income indicator represents a bundle of goods and services needed for the best use of human capabilities. All three dimensions are given equal weights as they are considered equally valuable in ensuring well-being.

While the basic dimensions used in the index have remained unchanged since 1990, some of the indicators underwent refinements in 2010. Longevity continues to be measured in terms of life expectancy at birth. However, the indicators for knowledge and command over resources for decent living have been modified. Knowledge is now measured in terms of: (i) mean years of adult education, which is the average number of years of education received by people aged 25 years and above and (ii) expected years of schooling for children of school-entrance age, which is the total number of years of schooling that a child of school-entrance age can expect to receive if prevailing patterns of age-specific enrolment rates stay the same throughout the child's life. This change was necessary as the discriminatory power of the indicators used in the earlier approach had diminished, as countries at the higher end of the HDI spectrum had achieved high levels of combined gross enrolment ratios and adult literacy rates.

Standard of living or command over resources is now measured by gross national income (GNI) per capita in PPP US dollars instead of the erstwhile GDP per capita. GNI is a better measure in a globalized economy as it accounts for in-income flows, such as remittances across countries.

Index Construction

In order to combine the three indicators, a dimension index is prepared for each indicator using maximum and minimum values. Since 1995, fixed goal posts have been used, which are a minimum of 25 years and a maximum of 85 years for life expectancy, zero and 100 for adult literacy, combined primary, secondary, and tertiary enrolment, and purchasing power adjusted to US$ 100 and U$ 40,000 for per capita income.

Performance in each dimension is expressed as a value between 0 and 1 applying the following general formula:

Dimension Index = [actual value – minimum value] / [maximum value – minimum value].

HDI is then calculated as a simple average of the dimension indices. The values of HDI vary between 0 and 1.

HDR 2010 presented HDI with a different methodology; the index used observed minimum and maximum values for all the indicators.

In 2010 there was also a change in the method of aggregation. HDI was previously calculated as an *arithmetic mean* of the dimension indices; in 2010 a multiplicative method of aggregation using *geometric mean* was used to construct the index. This methodology is superior to the previous one as it reduces the substitutability between the dimensions. For example, previously deprivation on one dimension could be compensated for in HDI calculations by high achievement in the other dimension; the new methodology ensures that this will not happen and a 1 per cent decline in, for example, life expectancy at birth, will have the same impact on HDI as a 1 per cent decline in education or income.

The differences in indicators and methodology used for calculating HDI prior to 2010 and in 2010 are summarized in Table 1.

In order to account for inequalities in achievements across the various HDI dimensions, the 2010 HDR introduced an inequality adjusted HDI which takes into account inequality in all three dimensions of HDI by 'discounting' each dimension's average value according to its level of inequality. HDI is thus a measure of the average level of human development that a country has achieved in the three HDI dimensions, given the existing inequality in distribution of achievements, and the level of aversion to inequality.

Critique

As is evident, the index is simple to compute and has a strong appeal as it advocates the cause of 'well-being' rather than only income. However, the index has been

Table 1 Summary of HDI Reforms

Dimensions	Previous			2010		
	Indicators	Transformation		Indicators	Transformation	
		Minimum	Maximum value		Minimum	Maximum (observed values)
Health	Life expectancy at birth (years)	25	85	Life expectancy at birth (years)	20	83.2
Knowledge	Adult literacy rate (%)	0	100	Expected years of schooling	0	20.6
	Combined gross enrolment ratio (%)	0	100	Mean years of schooling	0	13.2
Standard of living	GDP per capita (PPP US$)	100	40,000 (capped)	GNI per capita (PPP US$)	163	108,211
Aggregation	Arithmetic mean			Geometric mean		

Source: Compiled by Human Development Report Office, UNDP.

subject to much criticism both on conceptual and methodological grounds. Conceptually, the very simplicity of the index, which has made it so successful, is its failing, for the expanse of the concept of human development is not fully captured by HDI. Human development is increasingly being identified with improved education and health attainments alone. Important indicators like political and social freedom, participation in community life, environmental concerns, and crime and violence that could jeopardize the quest for sustainable development are excluded from HDI.

More important, though it is positioned as an alternative approach, the focus continues to be on *average* levels of attainment; distributional concerns are bypassed. This has been remedied to an extent in HDR 2010 where better averaging techniques like the geometric mean are used in conjuncture with the crafting of the Inequality Adjusted Human Development Index.

It has also been observed that there is a high correlation between the three components with per capita income, explaining much of the variation in HDI values across countries and rendering HDI less useful as a replacement to GDP per capita. However, it has been observed that this applies only for middle-income countries where the differential between the economic and social attainments is higher than in either the high-income or low-income countries.

HDI is also criticized for including both stock variables, such as adult literacy and life expectancy and flow variables, such as income per capita and gross enrolment ratios rendering difficult the evaluation of impact of policies on attainments within a short period.

India

In India, HDI was officially calculated for the states by the Planning Commission in the first *Human Development Report* (2001). HDI was computed separately for rural and urban areas for all the states for 1981 and 1991 and for select states for 2001. While the methodology used was similar to that of UNDP in terms of the dimensions used, process indicators—intensity of education to supplement adult literacy rate in the knowledge dimension, infant mortality rate to supplement life expectancy in the health dimension, and inequality adjusted per capita consumption expenditure in the standard of living dimension—were used in each of the dimensions to enable frequent monitoring of HDI within the country.

Several state-level HDRs have also been prepared in India, all of which compute district-level HDI. This level of disaggregation and the limitations of data have required some substitution and modification of indicators to compute district-level HDI. Most often, the infant mortality rate is substituted for life expectancy and per capita GDP is reflected through per capita district domestic product. The computation of district-level HDI has shown severe data gaps and spurred efforts towards district-level estimation of district domestic product, poverty, and demographic indicators.

Policy Impact

Despite its many limitations, HDI has proved to be very useful as a tool for policy analysis. It has enabled several developing countries in Asia, Africa, and Latin America to take explicit cognizance of human development issues and enabled a move away from excessively growth-centred strategies. HDI has governed resource allocation strategies in countries, for example, Egypt and Philippines and in the states of Madhya Pradesh and Maharashtra within India. It has enabled examination of inter- and intra-country disparities with respect to HDI rankings, which, in turn, has spurred competition among countries and regions within a country to improve HDI rankings giving rise to support for social sectors. This has been particularly valuable at a time when countries have been undergoing the process of economic reforms which typically lead to reduction in public resource allocation to these sectors. HDI has also been a powerful advocacy tool and has rekindled debate and dialogue among various groups of people on the relevance of various development strategies and has spurred research on newer indicators and indices that are more relevant in capturing the multi-dimensional nature of development.

To quote Amartya Sen (2000), 'It would be a great mistake to concentrate on the Human Development Index. These are useful indicators in rough and ready work: but the real merit of the human development approach lies in the plural attention it brings to bear on development evaluation, not in the aggregative measures it presents as an aid to diverse statistics.'

K. Seeta Prabhu

References

Haq, Mahbub ul. 1995. *Reflections on Human Development*, Oxford University Press, (chapter 4) also reprinted in Fukuda Parr-Sakiko and A.K. Shiv Kumar (eds), *Readings in Human Development* (2003), New Delhi, Oxford University Press.

Planning Commission. 2002. *Human Development Report 2001*, New Delhi, UNDP.

Sen, Amartya. 2000. 'A Decade of Human Development', *Journal of Human Development*, 1(1): 17–23.

United Nations Development Programme (UNDP). 1990. 'Defining and Measuring Human Development', *Human Development Report*, chapter 1.

____. 2010. 'Technical Note', in *Human Development Report 2010: The Real Wealth of Nations*.

Websites

http://hdrc.undp.org.in
http://undp.hdro.org

Human Rights

To have a 'right' means to have a claim to something of value on other people, institutions, the state, or the international community, which in turn have the obligation of providing or helping to provide that something of value (CDHR 2004: 47). As Amartya Sen put it, 'rights are *entitlements*[1] that require *correlated duties*. If a person A has a right to some X, then there has to be some agency, say B, that has the duty to provide A with X' (Sen 2000: 228). Right holders could be individuals, or groups behaving like individuals, capable of ordering 'things' or 'objects' in terms of 'value', 'utility', or 'preference'. Duty bearers are agents whose actions or behaviours can influence or fulfil the enjoyment of those rights. Establishing this relationship between a right holder and one or more duty bearers is important for all rights—moral, legal, contractual, or any others—because rights imply accountability. The matching of rights with duties could be explained in terms of the Kantian concept of *perfect* and *imperfect obligations*.[2] Someone having a right does not mean anything unless agent-specific duties and ways of fulfilling the obligation of duty bearers can be identified. When such duties can be specified precisely for a particular agent responsible for the realization of a right, it is subjected to *perfect obligations* and could be legally enforced if that right is recognized in law. However, the duty bearers would have imperfect obligations wherein claims are addressed to anyone who can help without specifying the action that would deliver the rights. Thus imperfect obligations are essentially moral obligations that duty bearers ought to fulfil by trying to help but that cannot always be legally enforced.

This discussion on rights thus brings to the fore two crucial issues with respect to the realization of a right. These are: identification of the duty pertaining to a right and identification of the duty holders for that right.

However, identifying a duty corresponding to a particular right essentially presumes that the realization of that right is feasible. For if it were not feasible, there could be no duty that would lead to the realization of that right. So, in order to translate an aspiration or something that is desirable into a right with correlated duties, it would be necessary to establish that such a right is 'feasible' and that taking some measure or creating some enabling conditions, by some agency in society, could pave the way for feasibly realizing the right.[3]

Thus, if we consider 'development' as a process of realizing all the rights and fundamental freedoms, then for development to be considered a right, it must be 'feasible', which implies that it should be possible to design a social arrangement to enable the claimants to enjoy those rights. Obviously, such development has to be 'progressively' realized as a process in time, as the instantaneous or immediate realization of all (or even most) of the rights will not be feasible. The obligation of the policymakers or the state authorities would be to expedite to the maximum extent the process of progressive realization of as many rights as possible depending upon the constraints of resources and institutions in a country. However, the process of progressive realization should not be at the cost of a denial or violation of any other rights that are inherent to human existence and dignity.

With regard to the identification of different duty bearers to specific duties, it deserves to be mentioned that it may not always be the case that identifying a duty with respect to a right would automatically lead to unequivocal identification of the bearers of that duty. Sometimes more than one agency may need to

[1]Entitlement, as explained by Amartya Sen, is a very general concept. It implies the totality of things which a person can have by virtue of his rights. The 'things' referred to here need not be commodities but anything that a person can conceivably wish to have like non-molestation in the streets, or the freedom to lecture on the immorality of the modern age, or adequate means of livelihood (Sen 1982: 343–60).

[2]See *Stanford Encyclopedia of Philosophy*, 'Kant's Moral philosophy', available at http://plato.stanford.edu/entries/kant-moral.

[3]'It is quite possible that at a particular point of time or in a given state of affairs a right is not "feasible" to be realized, unless appropriate changes in the institutions and social arrangements are introduced. Feasibility would then imply that there exists a set of actions or policies adopted by the duty-bearers that will change the institutions and make it possible to realize the right. In other words, changing the institutions, or what is sometimes referred to as institutionalizing the right would be a part of the obligations of the duty-bearers' (Sengupta 2004: 188).

perform the same duty in parts or complementary to each other. Sometimes one agency may be the primary duty bearer, having the primary responsibility of carrying out the duty while others may have shared responsibility. These would in turn be contingent upon the institutional arrangements for exercising the rights. But until the duty bearers can be specified and the duties corresponding to a right assigned to specific agencies, a right holder's claim cannot be regarded as a right.[4]

Recognizing a 'right' as a 'human right' essentially lifts the status of the right to one with universal applicability to all human beings and at all places and articulates a set of norms governing the action by states and non-state actors, of individuals and groups, on which that claim is made. Realizing human dignity is the essential concern of human rights, which confers on the implementation of these rights a first-priority claim[5] and also obliges the state and non-state actors including the international community to take all steps to implement those rights. The most important characteristics of human rights as recognized by the international law of human rights are that they are universal, inviolable, indivisible, and interdependent.

Human Rights in International Instruments

The Universal Declaration of Human Rights (UDHR), adopted in 1945 by all members of the United Nations, including India, is the first declaration where an attempt has been made to encompass most of the human rights within its ambit. The UDHR lays down principles or standards of achievement to be followed by all nations and has been regarded as a benchmark in setting up the constitutional and legal systems of many countries including India. The UDHR has been followed by the adoption of a plethora of international instruments that seek to address issues relating to specific themes or sections of people. Out of these, six instruments that deserve special mention are as follows:

- International Covenant on Civil and Political Rights[6] (ICCPR)
- International Covenant on Economic, Social, and Cultural Rights[7] (ICESCR)
- Convention on the Elimination of all forms of Discrimination against Women (CEDAW)
- Convention on the Elimination of all forms of Racial Discrimination (CERD)
- Convention on the Rights of the Child (CRC)
- Convention against Torture and Other Cruel, Inhuman, or Degrading Treatment or Punishment (CAT)

Development and Human Rights

The traditional development discourse evolved through various phases, focusing on maximizing gross national product (GNP), satisfying 'basic needs', incorporating 'structural adjustment', and so on. However, a focus on 'rights' was missing. The definition of 'development' earlier had a primary focus on 'economic growth' and material prosperity to the exclusion of the freedom, dignity, and overall 'well-being' of the people, and development was not usually linked to human rights standards.

The concept of 'Right to Development' (RTD)[8] provided the missing link between 'development' and 'human rights' discourses. The former Independent

[4]In the case of development, 'the primary duty-bearer will have to be the state-authorities who are in the position to design appropriate development policies and implement them. There will be other duty-bearers who will have responsibilities with respect to different aspects of development—taxpayers must pay taxes, multi-nationals must follow the appropriate conduct and the international community must cooperate. But the state-party would have the responsibility to ensure that these other duty-bearers fulfill their obligations. When these duty-bearers are subject to their domestic legal and administrative forces, the national states could hold them accountable. When the duty-bearers are other sovereign states and institutions, the national states will have to persuade them to cooperate to carry out those duties. But in either case, the exact responsibilities with respect to the different aspects of the development policies will have to be assigned to these duty-bearers. The design of the development policies must incorporate such assignments of specific responsibilities to all the different agents and methods of monitoring and enforcing the accountabilities' (Sengupta 2004: 201).

[5]In human rights discourse, a human right is a higher-order right with the expectation that it carries a peremptory character similar to John Rawl's idea of 'priority of liberty' or Ronald Dworkin's 'rights as trumps' that sets limits on state action whenever it encroaches upon individual liberty. Thus 'the fulfilment of such human rights gets overwhelming priority in the use of resources and public policy' (Sengupta 2004: 189).

[6]Civil rights basically guarantee a person's liberty and equality. Political rights allow people to participate in the political life of their community and society by voting in their representatives, throwing them out, and restricting those elected in what they can do while they are in power.

[7]Economic and social rights guarantee the basic necessities of life like food, shelter, clothing, work, and social security. Cultural rights allow people to participate in cultural life of the community and in various traditional and cultural practices.

[8]The Senegalese jurist Keba M'Baye has coined the term in 1972 and it has been debated extensively in various international fora. On 4 December 1986, the United Nations General Assembly formally adopted the Declaration on the Right to Development.

Expert on RTD[9] delineated the essence of RTD as the '*right to a process*[10] *of development*' where all human rights and fundamental freedoms are realized. He further clarified that the right to development as the *right to a process of development* is not just an umbrella right or the sum of a set of rights. It is the right to a process that expands the capabilities or freedom of individuals to improve their well-being and to realize what they value. He underscores that both the *outcomes* of the process and the *process* of development itself are human rights, which entail obligations.

The realization of the different rights (civil and political rights and economic, social, and cultural rights) is the specific outcome of several policy programmes. But the right to those outcomes is not the same thing as the right to the process that produces those outcomes. In the RTD approach, the '*process*' is as important as the '*outcome*'. Just as different specific rights require specific policies to be implemented as obligation of the different duty bearers, the primary duty bearer being the state, the process requires designing and implementing appropriate programmes of coordinated policies of realizing the rights over the target period.

India's International Commitments on Human Rights Protection[11]

Of the six principal international human rights instruments, India has signed as well as ratified[12] five. Table 1 indicates India's status of ratification of the principal human rights instruments.[13]

Table 1 India's Status of Ratification of the Principal International Human Rights Treaties

Convention	Signature	Ratification/ Accession	Entry into force
ICESCR	–	10 April 1979 (a)	10 July 1979
ICCPR	–	10 April 1979 (a)	10 July 1979
CERD	2 March 1967	3 December 1968 (r)	4 January 1969
CEDAW	30 July 1980	9 July 1993 (r)	8 August 1993
CRC	–	11 December 1992 (a)	11 January 1993
CAT	14 October 1997	–	–

Source: Treaty Body Database of the Office of the UN High Commissioner for Human Rights.

India, however, has not maintained a good record of reporting to the human rights treaty bodies[14] as mandated by the ratification of the instruments, as can be seen from Table 2. Apart from the CRC, for which it has submitted all its reports, India is lagging behind in its reporting commitments to all the other treaty bodies.

With reference to the Five Year Implementation Review of the Vienna Declaration and Programme of Action,[15] the Government of India reaffirmed its commitment to the promotion and protection of human rights through national efforts and international cooperation. In the statement submitted for the Secretary General's report on the review in 1998,[16] India views

[9]A/55/306, 'Second Report of the Independent Expert (Arjun Sengupta) to the Human Rights Commission', 17 August 2000, para 22 [republished in *Franciscans International* (2003): 160–85].

[10]The *process* is a phased realization of the targeted outcomes with a corresponding programme or plan executed over time maintaining consistency and sustainability, which is expected to lead to the realization of the outcome [E/CN.4/1999/WG.18/2, 'First Report of the Independent Expert (Arjun Sengupta) to the Human Rights Commission', 27 July 1999, para 47–56, republished in *Franciscans International* (2003): 146–9].

[11]This section draws on CDHR (2004: ch. 4, 123–6).

[12]'Ratification' denotes an international act whereby a state indicates its consent to be bound to a treaty. 'Signature' merely expresses the willingness of the signatory state to continue the treaty-making process, though it does create an obligation to refrain, *in good faith*, from acts that would defeat the object and the purpose of the treaty.

[13]The six major international human rights treaties discussed here in the section on international instruments contain arrangements for a reporting system to monitor the way in which a government is fulfilling its treaty obligations. States party to these treaties are required to submit a report to the relevant supervisory committee every four or five years (the reporting period for the Convention on the Elimination of All Forms of Discrimination is every two years). Such a state report should contain detailed information on the efforts the government of a state is making to respect of the human rights contained in the treaty, what progress has been made, and what obstacles and problems the state has encountered. After considering a state party's report, the committee will adopt so-called 'Concluding Observations', a public document that comments on the state's performance, recognizing positive developments, highlighting areas of concern, and providing suggestions and recommendations on specific issues.

[14]A committee of independent experts appointed to monitor the implementation by state parties of the core international human rights treaties. They are called 'treaty bodies' because each is created in accordance with the provisions of the treaty that it oversees. In many important respects, they are independent of the United Nations system, although they receive support from the United Nations Secretariat and report of the General Assembly. Also referred to as the 'committee' or 'treaty-monitoring body'.

[15]In 1993, at the World Conference on Human Rights held at Vienna, the Vienna Declaration and Programme of Action re-emphasized the status of the RTD as a universal and inalienable human right.

[16]See website: www.indianembassy.org/policy/Human_Rights/vdpa_india.html.

Table 2 India's Status of Reporting to the Human Rights Treaty Bodies

ICESCR		
Report number	Due	Submitted
4.	30 June 2001	*Awaited*
3.	30 June 1996	*Awaited*
2.	30 June 1991	*Awaited*
1.	NA, 1 September 1983, 1 September 1979	5 January 1989, 16 December 1985, 30 May 1983
ICCPR		
Report number	Due	Submitted
4.	31 March 2001	*Awaited*
3.	31 March 1992	29 November 1995
2.	9 July 1985	12 July 1989
1.	9 July 1980	4 July 1983
CERD		
Report number	Due	Submitted
17.	4 January 2002	*Awaited*
16.	4 January 2000	*Awaited*
15.	4 January 1998	*Awaited*
10, 11, 12, 13, 14.	4 January 1988	10 November 1994
8, 9.	4 January 1984	26 June 1986
7.	4 January 1982	16 August 1982
6.	4 January 1980	8 June 1981
5.	4 January 1978	5 March 1979
4.	4 January 1976	18 July 1977
CEDAW		
Report number	Due	Submitted
3.	8 August 2002	*Awaited*
2.	8 August 1998	*Awaited*
1.	8 August 1994	2 February 1999
CRC		
Report number	Due	Submitted
2.	10 January 2000	10 December 2001
1.	10 January 1995	19 March 1997

Source: Treaty Body Database of the Office of the UN High Commissioner for Human Rights.

the RTD Declaration as 'an integral link between the UDHR and the *Vienna Declaration and Programme of Action* through its elaboration of a holistic view integrating economic, social and cultural rights with civil and political rights' (para 14). The statement further adds that India agreed with the Office of the High Commissioner of Human Rights that the RTD has the potential of providing the homogenous and integrated approach to human rights that the international community has been searching for over five decades, and that 'it bears all the necessary components to guide the human rights system into the new millennium' (para 15).

Framework for Human Rights Protection in India

The Constitution

Most human rights, which are identified in the UDHR and the main international covenants, are protected under the Constitution of India. Some of them are guaranteed as Fundamental Rights (Part III) and some form a part of the Directive Principles of State Policy (Part IV). The Fundamental Rights can be divided into six broad groups: right to equality; right to particular freedoms; right against exploitation; freedom of religion; cultural and educational rights; and right to constitutional remedies. The Directive Principles of State Policy (DPSP) set out certain socio-economic goals for the country and require that the state must make efforts to achieve these goals through its policies and laws. While the Fundamental Rights are enforceable in a court of law, the goals in the DPSP are not.

The Judiciary

A citizen of India whose rights have been violated has the right to directly approach the Supreme Court and the High Courts for judicial intervention for redressal under Articles 32 and 226 of the Constitution.

The role of the judiciary since its inception has undergone a sea change, witnessing its emergence as a dynamic institution pioneering the expansion of the scope and content of individual and collective rights of the citizens. This changing role has evolved by virtue of a series of developments primarily through the innovation of public interest litigation[17] as an instrument to achieve social objectives by facilitating easy access to courts, particularly for the economically and socially disadvantaged sections of the community, through relaxation of the rules of standing and procedure as mandated by an ordinary litigation and freeing the litigants from the complexities of formal law. Some notable developments that evince the emergence of a more progressive judiciary are:

[17]Public interest litigation (PIL), in simple words, means litigation filed in the court of law for the protection of public interest such as pollution, terrorism, road safety, and constructional hazards. Public interest litigation is not defined in any statute or in any Act. Although the main and only area of PIL is 'public interest', there are various areas where a PIL can be filed. These includes among others: violation of basic human rights of the poor, content or conduct of government policy, violations of religious rights, and compelling municipal authorities to perform a public duty.

- The declaration of the indivisibility of the fundamental rights, on the one hand, and the DPSPs, on the other. The Supreme Court underscored: 'In building up a just social order it is sometimes imperative that the fundamental rights should be subordinated to the directive principles'[18] and that both are complementary, 'neither part being superior to the other'.[19]
- Attempts by the court in early PIL cases to rescue bonded labour from dehumanizing conditions of work,[20] ensuring availability of free legal aid to destitute undertrial prisoners,[21] protecting rights of pavement dwellers to due process while facing forced evictions.[22] More recently, the courts have been instrumental in specifying binding guidelines to deal with the problem of sexual harassment at the workplace,[23] have catalysed changes in law and policy relating to education in general and primary education in particular,[24] have delineated the right to emergency medical care for accident victims as forming a core minimum of the right to health,[25] and have emphasized the right of access to food supplies as bare non-derogable minimum and crucial to preserve human dignity.[26]
- Broadened interpretation of existing rights through judicial activism. For instance, the most fundamental human right—right to life and liberty—was widened in *Francis Coralie Mullin* vs *Administrator, Union Territory of Delhi*[27] in 1981 with the Supreme Court observing that 'the right to life includes the right to live with human dignity and all that goes along with it, namely the bare necessaries of life such as adequate nutrition, clothing and shelter and facilities for reading, writing and expressing oneself in diverse forms'. Similarly, in *Bandhua Mukti Morcha* vs *Union of India* in 1984,[28] the Supreme Court held that the 'right to life' must include protection of the health and strength of workers, men and women, and of the tender age of children against abuse, opportunities and facilities for children to develop in a healthy manner and in conditions of freedom and dignity, educational facilities, just and humane conditions of work and maternity relief. Neither the central government nor any state government has the right to take any action which will deprive a person of the enjoyment of these basic essentials.

Despite its substantial autonomy and independence, the Indian judiciary has been plagued by innumerable problems that have dampened its effective functioning. There is paucity of courts, judges, and physical infrastructure. As a result, almost all courts have a huge backlog of cases. The National Commission to Review the Working of the Constitution (2001) notes that delayed hearings are 'a serious infraction of the right to speedy trials', and tantamount to violation of human rights.

Human Rights Commissions[29]

Human Rights Commissions have been established to protect human rights of the people in the country and to facilitate creation of an environment conducive to respect and understanding of human rights. The National Human Rights Commission (NHRC) was set up by the Protection of Human Rights Act, 1993. The Commission is an autonomous statutory body enjoying considerable operational independence. It has the powers of a civil court trying a case under the Civil Procedure Code, 1908. Thus it has some degree of investigative power, can issue notices to people, can summon witnesses, and so on.[30]

The NHRC can inquire into complaints of violations of human rights or abetment in, and failure to prevent, such violations by a public servant. It can also intervene in any court proceeding involving an allegation of violation of human rights. The Commission has powers of reviewing the constitutional, statutory, and international safeguards for the protection of human rights. It has the power to recommend measures for their effective implementation, though it does not have the power to enforce its orders. The NHRC also undertakes and promotes research in the field of human rights and works towards spreading human rights literacy.

The Commission has, in its various recommendations relating to specific cases, urged the government to

[18]*Kesavananda Bharati* vs *State of Kerala* (1973) 4 SCC 879.
[19]*State of Kerala* vs *N.M. Thomas* (1978) 2 SCC 310.
[20]*Bandhua Mukti Morcha* vs *Union of India* 1984 (Supp) 3 SCC 161.
[21]*Hussainara Khatoon* vs *State of Bihar* (1980) 1 SCC 81.
[22]*Olga Tellis* vs *Bombay Municipal Corporation* (1985) 3 SCC 545.
[23]*Vishaka* vs *State of Rajasthan* (1997) 6 SCC 241.
[24]*Unnikrishnan JP* vs *State of Andhra Pradesh* (1993) 1 SCC 645.
[25]*Paschim Banga Khet Majoor Samity* vs *State of West Bengal* (1996) 4 SCC 37.
[26]*Peoples Union of Civil Liberty (PUCL)* vs *Union of India* (2001) Indlaw SCC 196.
[27](1981) 2 SCR 516.
[28]*Kesavananda Bharati* vs *State of Kerala*.

[29]This section draws on CDHR (2004): 128–9.
[30]For detailed information on the NHRC, see website http://www.nhrc.nic.in.

formulate policies that are responsive to the needs of the most vulnerable in society. Such action includes provision of free and compulsory education up to the age of 14 years, primary health facilities, potable drinking water, basic levels of maternal- and child-welfare facilities, and food and nutritional standards essential to fulfilling the potential of the human being.

The Protection of Human Rights Act, 1993, also mandated the establishment of human rights commissions in each state. A State Human Rights Commission (SHRC) can inquire into violation of human rights only in respect of matters in the State List (issues on which only state governments can take action) and Concurrent List (subjects on which both the Centre and the states can take action) of the Constitution. Only 12 states have so far set up SHRCs. They are Assam, Chhattisgarh, Himachal Pradesh, Jammu and Kashmir, Kerala, Madhya Pradesh, Maharashtra, Manipur, Punjab, Rajasthan, Tamil Nadu, and West Bengal. Some SHRCs have taken up matters relating to food, education, and health.

Human Rights Courts[31]

The Protection of Human Rights Act, 1993, also stipulates the setting up of Human Rights Courts for providing speedy trial in cases of alleged human rights violations. In each district, a sessions court is to act as a Human Rights Court. The Court will have a public prosecutor or appoint an advocate who has been practising for not less than seven years, as a special public prosecutor for conducting cases in that Court. The state governments of Assam, Andhra Pradesh, Sikkim, Tamil Nadu, Uttar Pradesh, Meghalaya, Himachal Pradesh, Goa, Madhya Pradesh, and Tripura have notified Human Rights Courts.

National Commission for Women[32]

The National Commission for Women (NCW) was set up as a statutory autonomous body in January 1992 under the National Commission for Women Act, 1990.[33] The mandate of the NCW is, among other things, to review the constitutional and legal safeguards for women; recommend remedial legislative measures; facilitate redressal of grievances; advise the government on all policy matters affecting women; investigate complaints; undertake promotional and educational research; inspect places of custody of women; and fund litigation. The NCW is, however, a purely recommendatory body with no powers to enforce its orders.

National Commission for Minorities[34]

The National Commission for Minorities is a statutory autonomous body set up under the National Commission for Minorities Act, 1992. The central government has notified five communities as 'minority communities': Muslims, Christians, Sikhs, Buddhists, and Zoroastrians. A prominent member of each community is appointed to the Commission. The Commission's brief is to evaluate the progress of the development of the minority communities; to monitor the working of the safeguards provided in the Constitution and in laws; to recommend the implementation of safeguards for the protection of the interests of minorities; to investigate specific complaints regarding deprivation of rights of the minorities and take up such matters with the appropriate authorities; to undertake studies into problems arising out of any discrimination against minorities and related issues; and to recommend appropriate measures in respect of any minority to be undertaken by the central or state government. The Commission has all the powers of a civil court trying a suit but does not have the power to enforce its recommendations.

National Commission for Children[35]

The setting up of a National Commission for Children is also in the offing. The idea of a Children's Commission was proposed in 1998 and has been debated since then. The Department of Women and Child Development prepared the draft National Commission for Children Bill[36] in 2001.

The Commission is supposed to work as a statutory body for the protection of children's rights and also as an independent ombudsman for children, dealing exclusively with the status and development needs of children. The Commission will be a seven-member statutory body comprising specialists in the field of child welfare and headed by a retired judge of the Supreme Court, a sitting High Court judge, or a person of eminence in the field of child rights. It will be mandated to safeguard the interests of children, guide government policy on child-related issues, and review the laws and programmes relating to children's development.

ARJUN K. SENGUPTA AND KAUSHIK RANJAN BANDYOPADHYAY

[31]This section draws on CDHR (2004): 130–1.
[32]This section draws on CDHR (2004): 131.
[33]For more information on the NCW, see website http://www.nationalcommissionforwomen.org.
[34]This section draws on CDHR (2004): 131–2.
[35]This section draws on CDHR (2004): 133.
[36]For the text of the National Commission for Children Bill, see http://wcd.nic.in/ncchildren.htm.

References

Centre for Development and Human Rights (CDHR). 2004. *The Right to Development: A Primer*, New Delhi, Sage Publications.

Franciscans International. 2003. 'The Right to Development: Reflections on the First Four Reports of the Independent Expert (Arjun Sengupta) on Right to Development', Franciscans International, Geneva.

Sen, Amartya. 1982. 'The Right Not to Be Hungry', *Contemporary Philosophy: A New Survey*, The Hague, Martinus Nijhoff.

——. 2000. *Development as Freedom*, Oxford, Oxford University Press; New Delhi, Oxford University Press, 2000.

Sengupta, Arjun. 2004. 'The Human Right to Development', *Oxford Development Studies*, 32(2): 179–203.

Contributors
(with Entries)

Bina Agarwal (*Gender Inequality*)
Director and Professor of Economics, Institute of Economic Growth, Delhi, India

Isher Judge Ahluwalia (*Industry*)
Chairperson, Board of Governors, Indian Council for Research on International Economic Relations (ICRIER), New Delhi, and Vice Chairperson, Global Development Network, New Delhi, India

Montek S. Ahluwalia (*Planning*)
Deputy Chairman, Planning Commission, Government of India

Yoginder K. Alagh (*Green Revolution*)
Chancellor, Nagaland University; Chairman, Institute of Rural Management Anand (IRMA); and Vice-Chairman, Sardar Patel Institute of Economics & Social Research, Ahmedabad, India

Mukesh Anand (*Pensions*)
Assistant Professor, National Institute of Public Finance and Policy (NIPFP), New Delhi, India

Ritu Anand (*External Debt*)
Group Head—Policy and Chief Economist, Infrastructure Development Finance Company Ltd. (IDFC), Mumbai, India

T.C.A. Anant (*Environment and Law*)
Chief Statistician of India, Ministry of Statistics and Programme Implementation, Government of India, and Professor of Economics, Delhi School of Economics, University of Delhi, Delhi, India

Reena Badiani (*Data Sets, co-authors Siddharth Sharma and Himanshu*)
PhD Student, Economic Growth Centre, Yale University, USA

Amiya Kumar Bagchi (*State Bank of India*)
Director, Institute of Development Studies Kolkata, India

Jugnu Bagga (*Rent Control Acts, co-author Shubhashis Gangopadhyay*)
Formerly with India Development Foundation, Gurgaon, India

Kanti Bajpai (*Defence Strategy*)
Professor, Department of Politics and International Relations, School of Interdisciplinary Area Studies, University of Oxford, UK

G. Balachandran (*Reserve Bank of India, co-author T.C.A. Srinivasa-Raghavan*)
Professor of International History and Politics, Graduate Institute of International Studies, Geneva, Switzerland

Kaushik Ranjan Bandyopadhyay (*Human Rights, co-author Arjun K. Sengupta*)
Associate Professor, Department of Policy Studies, TERI University, New Delhi, India

TAMAL BANDYOPADHYAY (*Interest Rates; Repo Market*)
Deputy Managing Editor, *Mint*, HT Media Business Paper, India

ABHIJIT V. BANERJEE (*Public Goods*)
Professor, Department of Economics, Massachusetts Institute of Technology, Cambridge, USA

ANIRVAN BANERJI (*Business and Growth Rate Cycles, co-author Pami Dua*)
Co-founder and Chief Research Officer, Economic Cycle Research Institute (ECRI), New York, USA

SANJAY BANERJI (*Finance and Law*)
Reader in Finance, Essex Business School, University of Essex, UK

RASHMI BANGA (*Wage Inequality*)
Senior Economist, United Nations Conference on Trade and Development (UNCTAD)—India Program, New Delhi, India

ARINDAM BANIK (*Technology Transfer, co-author Pradip K. Bhaumik*)
Professor of Economics, International Management Institute, New Delhi, India

PRANAB BARDHAN (*Political Economy*)
Professor of Economics, University of California, Berkeley, USA

ALAKA MALWADE BASU (*Infant and Child Mortality; Population Policy*)
Professor of Demography, Department of Sociology, Cornell University, New York, USA

ARNAB BASU (*National Rural Employment Guarantee Act, co-authors Nancy H. Chau and Ravi Kanbur*)
Professor, Asian and Middle Eastern Studies, Global Studies, College of William and Mary, Williamsburg, VA, USA

KAUSHIK BASU (*Inflation: Experience and Policy*)
Chief Economic Adviser, Ministry of Finance, Government of India, and C. Marks Professor, Department of Economics, Cornell University, New York, USA

SUMAN BERY (*NCAER's Household Survey*)
Director-General, National Council of Applied Economic Research (NCAER), New Delhi, India

LAVEESH BHANDARI (*Home-based Work*)
Director, Indicus Analytics, New Delhi, India

VINAY BHARAT-RAM (*Manufacturing Hub*)
Chairman and Managing Director, DCM Group, India

ANURADHA BHASIN (*Tourism*)
Consultant, National Council of Applied Economic Research (NCAER), New Delhi, India

ADITYA BHATTACHARJEA (*Antitrust Law*)
Professor, Department of Economics, Delhi School of Economics, University of Delhi, Delhi, India

RUCHIRA BHATTAMISHRA (*Tribal Development*)
PhD Student, Department of Economics, Cornell University, New York, USA

PRADIP K. BHAUMIK (*Technology Transfer, co-author Arindam Banik*)
Professor of Quantitative Techniques & Operations Management, International Management Institute, New Delhi, India

SHARIT K. BHOWMIK (*Street Vendors*)
Dean and Professor, School of Management and Labour Studies, Tata Institute of Social Sciences (TISS), Mumbai, India

DAVID E. BLOOM (*HIV/AIDS, Economics of, co-authors Bhargavi Rao, Ajay Mahal, and Kavita Sivaramakrishnan; Urbanization and Its Management, co-authors Jennifer O'Brien and Marija Ozolins*)
Clarence James Gamble Professor of Economics and Demography, Department of Global Health and Population, Harvard School of Public Health, Boston, Massachusetts, USA

VANI K. BOROOAH (*Religion and Economic Well-being*)
Professor of Applied Economics, University of Ulster, Jordanstown, Northern Ireland, UK

AMITAVA BOSE (*Employment*)
Professor of Economics, Indian Institute of Management Calcutta, Kolkata, India

SUMIT BOSE (*Public-sector Enterprises, co-author Sharat Kumar*)
Secretary, Department of Expenditure, Ministry of Finance, Government of India

RAJESH CHAKRABARTI (*Foreign Exchange Markets; Foreign Institutional Investment*)
Assistant Professor of Finance, Indian School of Business, Hyderabad, India

RUPA CHANDA (*Services-led Growth*)
Professor of Economics and Social Sciences, Indian Institute of Management Bangalore, India

PANKAJ CHANDRA (*Textile and Apparel Industry*)
Director and Professor of Operations and Technology Management, Indian Institute of Management Bangalore, India

C.P. CHANDRASEKHAR (*Financial Crisis*)
Professor, Centre for Economic Studies and Planning, School of Social Sciences, Jawaharlal Nehru University, New Delhi, India

A.V. CHARI (*Licensing*)
Associate Economist at RAND, USA

ARKADEV CHATTERJEA (*Academic Research, co-author Satya Priya Moulik; Doctoral Education*)
Research Fellow, Center for Excellence in Investment Management, Kenan-Flagler Business School, University of North Carolina at Chapel Hill, and Affiliated Faculty, Cornell Higher Education Research Institute (CHERI), Cornell University, USA

MIRAI CHATTERJEE (*Social Protection for Informal-sector Workers*)
Director, Social Security, Self-Employed Women's Association (SEWA), Ahmedabad, India

NANCY H. CHAU (*National Rural Employment Guarantee Act, co-authors Arnab Basu and Ravi Kanbur*)
Professor, Charles H. Dyson School of Applied Economics and Management, Cornell University, New York, USA

BASUDEB CHAUDHURI (*Regional Disparities, co-author Velayoudom Marimoutou*)
Director, Centre de Sciences Humaines, New Delhi, India, and Associate Professor of Economics, CREM, University of Caen, Caen, France

MRINAL DATTA CHAUDHURI (*V.K. Ramaswami*)
Former Professor, Delhi School of Economics, University of Delhi, Delhi, India

SAUMITRA CHAUDHURI (*Housing Finance*)
Member, Economic Advisory Council to the Prime Minister; and Member, Planning Commission, New Delhi, India

SUDIP CHAUDHURI (*Pharmaceutical Industry*)
Professor of Economics, Indian Institute of Management Calcutta, Kolkata, India

P. CHIDAMBARAM (*Fiscal Policy Reforms since 1991*)
Union Minister of Home Affairs, Government of India

IGNATIUS CHITHELEN (*Entrepreneurs in India and Abroad, co-author Shankar Parameshwaran*)
Managing Partner, Banyan Tree Capital Management, New York, USA

DEB KUSUM DAS (*Trade Barriers in Manufacturing*)
Reader, Department of Economics, Ramjas College, University of Delhi, Delhi, India

GURCHARAN DAS (*Entrepreneurship*)
Author, Commentator, and Public Intellectual, and former CEO, Procter & Gamble India

JISHNU DAS (*Chronic Illnesses, co-author Jeffrey S. Hammer; Medical Care, Quality of, co-author Jeffrey S. Hammer*)
Senior Economist, Development Economics Research Group, World Bank, Washington DC, USA, and Visiting Scholar at Center for Policy Research, New Delhi, India

MAUSUMI DAS (*Prashanta Chandra Mahalanobis*)
Reader, Department of Economics, Delhi School of Economics, University of Delhi, Delhi, India

MONICA DAS GUPTA (*Public Health*)
Senior Demographer, Development Research Group, World Bank, Washington DC, USA

ARINDAM DAS-GUPTA (*Corruption*)
Professor, Goa Institute of Management, India

ASIM K. DASGUPTA (*Value-added Tax in the States*)
Former Finance Minister, West Bengal, India

DIPAK DASGUPTA (*Fiscal Deficit, co-author Supriyo De*)
Principal Economic Adviser, Ministry of Finance, Government of India

SUGATO DASGUPTA (*Elections and Political Business Cycles*)
Professor, Centre for Economic Studies and Planning, Jawaharlal Nehru University, New Delhi, India

SUPRIYO DE (*Fiscal Deficit, co-author Dipak Dasgupta*)
Officer on Special Duty to the Chief Economic Adviser, Ministry of Finance, Government of India

BIBEK DEBROY (*Higher Education: Regulation and Control; Law and Legal System in India*)
Professor, Center for Policy Research, New Delhi, India

ASHOK V. DESAI (*Convertibility*)
Consultant Editor, *Business World*, New Delhi, India

NITIN DESAI (*Sustainable Development*)
Honorary Professor, Indian Council for Research in International Economic Relations (ICRIER), New Delhi, India

SONALDE DESAI (*Middle Class*)
Professor of Sociology, University of Maryland, USA

ASHWINI DESHPANDE (*Affirmative Action; Caste; Women in the Labour Force; Caste*)
Professor, Department of Economics, Delhi School of Economics, University of Delhi, Delhi, India

R.S. DESHPANDE (*Farmers' Distress and Suicides*)
Director, Institute for Social and Economic Change (ISEC), Bangalore, India

S. MAHENDRA DEV (*Agriculture Development*)
Director (Vice Chancellor), Indira Gandhi Institute of Development Research (IGIDR), Mumbai, India

AMRITA DHILLON (*V.M. Dandekar; Fiscal Federalism*)
Professor, Department of Economics, University of Warwick, UK

ASHUTOSH DIKSHIT (*Tax System and Reform, co-authors Sunil Mitra and Vivek Johri*)
Joint Secretary (TPL-I), Central Board of Direct Taxes, Department of Revenue, Ministry of Finance, Government of India

RAFIQ DOSSANI (*IT-enabled Sectors*)
Senior Research Scholar and Director, Center for South Asia, Stanford University, Stanford, California, USA

JEAN DRÈZE (*Food and Nutrition; Ashok Rudra, co-author Suman Sarkar*)
Visiting Professor, Department of Economics, University of Allahabad, Allahabad, India

PAMI DUA (*Business and Growth Rate Cycles, co-author Anirvan Banerji*)
Professor and Head, Department of Economics, Delhi School of Economics, University of Delhi, Delhi, India, and Senior Research Scholar, Economic Cycle Research Institute, New York, USA

ESTHER DUFLO (*Dams, co-author Rohini Pande*)
Abdul Latif Jameel Professor of Development Economics and Poverty Alleviation, Massachusetts Institute of Technology, Cambridge, Massachusetts, USA

BHASKAR DUTTA (*Discretionary Centre–State Transfers; Disinvestment, The Economics of*)
Professor of Economics, Department of Economics, University of Warwick, UK

INDRANIL DUTTA (*Inequality; co-author Ajit Mishra*)
Research Associate, Brooks World Poverty Institute, The University of Manchester, UK

MUKESH ESWARAN (*Gender and Empowerment*)
Professor of Economics, Department of Economics, University of British Columbia, Canada

TATIANA FIC (*India's Growth Turnaround, co-authors Chetan Ghate and Stephen Wright*)
Senior Research Officer, National Institute of Economic and Social Research, London, UK

GARY S. FIELDS (*Income Mobility*)
Professor of Labor Economics and and the John P. Windmuller Chair of International and Comparative Labor, Cornell University, New York, USA

RAGHAV GAIHA (*Employment Guarantee Scheme*)
Professor, Faculty of Management Studies, University of Delhi, Delhi, India

IRA N. GANG (*Small-scale Industries, co-author Mihir Pandey*)
Professor, Department of Economics, Rutgers University, USA

SHUBHASHIS GANGOPADHYAY (*Rent Control Acts, co-author Jugnu Bagga*)
Director, India Development Foundation, Gurgaon, India

MAITREESH GHATAK (*Land Reform*)
Professor, Department of Economics, London School of Economics, UK

CHETAN GHATE (*India's Growth Turnaround, co-authors Stephen Wright and Tatiana Fic*)
Associate Professor, Planning Unit, Indian Statistical Institute, Delhi Centre, New Delhi, India

AJIT K. GHOSE (*Informal Labour*)
Senior Economist, Economic and Labour Market Analysis Department, International Labour Organization, Geneva, Switzerland

SAIBAL GHOSH (*Banking, co-authors Dilip M. Nachane and Partha Ray*)
Assistant Adviser, Department of Economic Analysis and Policy, Reserve Bank of India, Mumbai, India

SUBIR GOKARN (*Railways*)
Deputy Governor, Reserve Bank of India, Mumbai, India

OMKAR GOSWAMI (*Corporate Governance*)
Chairman, CERG Advisory Pvt. Ltd, New Delhi

ASHIMA GOYAL (*International Finance*)
Professor of Economics, Indira Gandhi Institute of Development Research (IGIDR), Mumbai, India

ASHOK GUHA (*International Trade*)
Professor, School of International Studies, Jawaharlal Nehru University, New Delhi, India

ASHOK GULATI (*Agribusiness*)
Director, International Food Policy Research Institute (IFPRI), New Delhi, India

MUKESH GULATI (*Industrial Clusters, co-author Amar Singh*)
Executive Director, Foundation for MSME (micro, small and medium enterprises) Clusters, New Delhi.

INDRANI GUPTA (*Health Indicators*)
Professor and Head, Health Policy Research Unit, Institute of Economic Growth, Delhi

JEFFREY S. HAMMER (*Chronic Illnesses, co-author Jishnu Das; Medical Care, Quality of, co-author Jishnu Das*)
Charles and Marie Robertson Visiting Professor in Economic Development, Woodrow Wilson School of Public and International Affairs, Princeton University, USA

RONALD J. HERRING (*Genetically Modified Crops*)
Professor, Department of Government, Cornell University, New York, USA

HIMANSHU (*Data Sets, co-authors Reena Badiani and Siddharth Sharma*)
Assistant Professor, Centre for the Study of Regional Development, School of Social Sciences, Jawaharlal Nehru University, New Delhi, India

NARENDRA JADHAV (*B.R. Ambedkar*)
Member, Planning Commission, Government of India

BIMAL JALAN (*Indira Gandhi*)
Former Governor, Reserve Bank of India

ROGER JEFFERY (*Education and Religious Minorities*)
Professor of Sociology of South Asia, School of Social and Political Studies, University of Edinburgh, Edinburgh, Scotland, UK

SHIKHA JHA (*Food Procurement Policy*)
Principal Economist, Economics and Research Department, Asian Development Bank

RENANA JHABVALA (*Globalization and the Poor, co-author Ravi Kanbur*)
National Coordinator, Self-Employed Women's Association (SEWA), Ahmedabad, India

VIVEK JOHRI (*Tax System and Reform, co-authors Sunil Mitra and Ashutosh Dikshit*)
Joint Secretary (TRU-I), Central Board of Excise and Customs, Department of Revenue, Ministry of Finance, Government of India

PRITAL SAILESH KADAKIA (*Roads*)
Department of Economics, Harvard University, Cambridge, Massachusetts, USA

RAVI KANBUR (*Globalization and the Poor, co-author Renana Jhabvala; National Rural Employment Guarantee Act, co-authors Arnab Basu and Nancy H. Chau*)
T.H. Lee Professor of World Affairs and Economics, Cornell University, New York, USA

MILIND KANDLIKAR (*Outsourcing, co-author Ashok Kotwal*)
Assistant Professor, Centre for India and South Asia Research (Institute of Asian Research) and Liu Institute for Global Studies, University of British Columbia, Vancouver, Canada

DEVESH KAPUR (*Higher Education, co-author Pratap Bhanu Mehta; International Migration from India: Economic Impact*)
Director, Center for the Advanced Study of India, University of Pennsylvania, USA

SANDEEP KAPUR (*Literacy, co-author Mamta Murthi*)
Professor of Economics, Department of Economics, Mathematics and Statistics, Birkbeck, University of London, UK

RUTH KATTUMURI (*Low-carbon Growth and Development, co-authors Nicholas Stern and James Rydge*)
Co-Director, India Observatory, London School of Economics (LSE), UK

P.C. KESAVAN (*Disaster Management, co-author M.S. Swaminathan*)
Emeritus Professor, Indira Gandhi National Open University (IGNOU), New Delhi, and Distinguished Fellow, M.S. Swaminathan Research Foundation, Chennai, India

DEENA KHATKHATE (*I.G. Patel*)
Former Assistant Director, International Monetary Fund and Managing Editor, *World Development*

SUNIL KHILNANI (*Jawaharlal Nehru*)
Director and Professor of Politics, India Institute, King's College, London, UK

GEETA KINGDON (*Secondary Education*)
Chair, Education Economics and International Development, Institute of Education, University of London, UK

STEFAN KLONNER (*Non-banking Financial Companies*)
Professor of Development Economics, South Asia, Südasien Institut, Ruprecht Karls Universität Heidelberg, Germany

ANJINI KOCHAR (*Primary Education*)
Director, India Program, and Senior Research Scholar, Stanford Center for International Development (SCID), Stanford Institute for Economic Policy Research (SIEPR), Stanford University, Stanford, California, USA

ASHOK KOTWAL (*Employment and Poverty; Outsourcing, co-author Milind Kandlikar*)
Professor of Economics and Director, Centre for India and South Asia Research, Institute of Asian Research, University of British Columbia, Vancouver, Canada

K.L. KRISHNA (*National Income*)
Chairman, Centre for Economic and Social Studies (CESS), Hyderabad, India

VIJAY KRISHNA (*Raj Krishna*)
Professor of Economics, Penn State University, University Park, Pennsylvania, USA

K.P. KRISHNAN (*Financial-sector Reforms*)
Secretary, Prime Minister's Economic Advisory Council, Government of India

K.S. KRISHNASWAMY (*Krishna Raj*)
Former Deputy Governor, Reserve Bank of India

MEDHA MALIK KUDAISYA (*G.D. Birla*)
Associate Professor, Department of History, National University of Singapore, Singapore

A.K. SHIVA KUMAR (*Millennium Development Goals*)
Visiting Professor, Institute for Human Development, New Delhi, India, and Adviser to UNICEF India

NAGESH KUMAR (*Foreign Direct Investment*)
Chief Economist and Director, Macroeconomic Policy and Development Division (MPDD), United Nations Economic and Social Commission for Asia and the Pacific (UN-ESCAP)

RAJIV KUMAR (*Foreign Exchange Reserves*)
Secretary General of the Federation of Indian Chambers of Commerce and Industry (FICCI), New Delhi, India

SHARAT KUMAR (*Public-sector Enterprises, co-author Sumit Bose*)
Economic Adviser, Department of Public Enterprises, Government of India

AMITABH KUNDU (*Mobility of Population*)
Professor of Economics, Centre for the Study of Regional Development and Dean, School of Social Sciences, Jawaharlal Nehru University, New Delhi, India

ASHOK K. LAHIRI (*Monsoon*)
Former Chief Economic Adviser, Ministry of Finance, Government of India

SAJAL LAHIRI (*Exogamy and Endogamy, co-author Sharmistha Self*)
Vandeveer Professor of Economics, Department of Economics, Southern Illinois University Carbondale, Carbondale, Illinois, USA

DEEPTI MAHAJAN (*Energy, co-author R.K. Pachauri*)
Area Convenor, Centre for Research on Energy Security, The Energy Research Institute (TERI), New Delhi, India

AJAY MAHAL (*HIV/AIDS, Economics of, co-author Bhargavi Rao, Kavita Sivaramakrishnan, and David E. Bloom*)
Adjunct Associate Professor of International Health Economics, Department of Global Health and Population, Harvard School of Public Health, Boston, Massachusetts, USA

DIPJYOTI MAJUMDAR (*Teacher Absenteeism*)
Professor, Department of Economics, Concordia University, Montréal (Québec), Canada

PAYAL MALIK (*Power Sector and Regulation*)
Associate Professor of Economics, University of Delhi, Delhi, India

VELAYOUDOM MARIMOUTOU (*Regional Disparities, co-author Basudeb Chaudhuri*)
Director and Professor, Institut Français de Pondicherry, Pondicherry, India

SUGATA MARJIT (*Exports and Export Policy*)
Director and Reserve Bank of India Professor of Industrial Economics, Centre for Studies in Social Sciences, Kolkata, India

R.A. MASHELKAR (*Intellectual Property Rights*)
National Research Professor, CSIR Bhatnagar Fellow and President, Global Research Alliance, Pune, India

J.V. MEENAKSHI (*Undernutrition*)
Professor, Department of Economics, Delhi School of Economics, University of Delhi, Delhi, India

RAJNISH MEHRA (*Equity Premium*)
E.N. Basha Arizona Heritage Chair, Professor of Finance and Economics, W.P. Carey School of Business, Arizona State University, USA

PRATAP BHANU MEHTA (*Higher Education, co-author Devesh Kapur*)
President, Centre for Policy Research, New Delhi

GAYATRI AMBIKA MENON (*Slums*)
Visiting Assistant Professor of Sociology, Department of Sociology, Franklin & Marshall College, Lancaster, PA, USA

DIVYA MINISANDRAM (*Brain Drain*)
Graduate, Harvard University, Cambridge, Massachusetts, USA

AJIT MISHRA (*Inequality, co-author Indranil Dutta*)
Senior Lecturer, Economics and International Development, University of Bath, Bath, UK

ASHOK MITRA (*Sachin Chaudhuri*)
Former Minister of Finance, West Bengal, India

SUNIL MITRA (*Tax System and Reform, co-authors Ashutosh Dikshit and Vivek Johri*)
Former Union Finance Secretary and Revenue Secretary, Government of India

PURAN MONGIA (*Environment Policy; Forest Policy; Global Warming*)
Former Professor of Economics, Centre for Development Economics, Delhi School of Economics, University of Delhi, Delhi, India

DILIP MOOKHERJEE (*Panchayats*)
Professor of Economics and Director, Institute for Economic Development, Boston University, Massachusetts, USA

SEBASTIAN MORRIS (*Infrastructure*)
Professor of Economics, Indian Institute of Management Ahmedabad, India

SATYA PRIYA MOULIK (*Academic Research, co-author Arkadev Chatterjea*)
Fellow of the Indian National Science Academy and UGC Emeritus Scientist

PRANAB MUKHERJEE (*Budget Making*)
Union Minister of Finance, Government of India

HIRANYA MUKHOPADHYAY (*Government Subsidies, co-author Sudipto Mundle*)
Public Management Economist, Asian Development Bank, Manila, Philippines

SUDIPTO MUNDLE (*Government Subsidies, co-author Hiranya Mukhopadhyay*)
Emeritus Professor, National Institute of Public Finance and Policy (NIPFP), New Delhi, India

KAIVAN MUNSHI (*Technology Diffusion*)
Professor of Economics, Department of Economics, Brown University, Rhode Island, USA

KARTHIK MURALIDHARAN (*Teacher and Medical Worker Incentives*)
Assistant Professor of Economics, University of California, USA

MAMTA MURTHI (*Literacy, co-author Sandeep Kapur*)
Sector Manager, Education, Europe and Central Asia Region, World Bank, Washington DC, USA

N.R. NARAYANA MURTHY (*Software and Services Exports*)
Founder-Chairman, Infosys, Bangalore, India

DILIP M. NACHANE (*Amiya Dasgupta; Banking, co-authors Saibal Ghosh and Partha Ray*)
Professor Emeritus, Indira Gandhi Institute of Development Research (IGIDR), Mumbai, India

R. NAGARAJ (*Industrial Growth; Trade Unions*)
Professor, Indira Gandhi Institute of Development Research, Mumbai, India

REEMA NANAVATY (*Self-Employed Women, The Organization of*)
Director, Economic and Rural Development, Self-Employed Women's Association (SEWA), Ahmedabad, India

D. NARAYANA (*Self-help Groups*)
Reserve Bank of India Chair Professor, Centre for Development Studies, Thiruvananthapuram, India

SUDHA NARAYANAN (*Contract Farming*)
PhD Student, Department of Applied Economics and Management, College of Agriculture and Life Sciences, Cornell University, New York, USA

K. NAVANEETHAM (*Demographic Dividend*)
Professor, Centre for Development Studies, Thiruvananthapuram, India

PULIN B. NAYAK (*Sukhamoy Chakravarty; Privatization*)
Professor of Economics, Delhi School of Economics, University of Delhi, Delhi, India

DEEPAK NAYYAR (*International Migration*)
Professor of Economics, Jawaharlal Nehru University, New Delhi, India, and Distinguished University Professor of Economics at the New School for Social Research, New York, USA

S. NEELAKANTAN (*Land Rights and Acquisition*)
Professor of Economics, Madras Institute of Development Studies, Chennai, India

NANDAN NILEKANI (*Unique Identification*)
Chairman, Unique Identification Authority of India (UIDAI)

T.N. NINAN (*Dhirubhai Ambani and Reliance Industries*)
Editorial Director and Chairman of Business Standard Ltd, India

MANDAR P. OAK (*Credit Market Regulation, Evolution of*)
Assistant Professor of Economics, Department of Economics, Williams College, Williamstown, Massachusetts, USA

JENNIFER O'BRIEN (*Urbanization and Its Management, co-authors David E. Bloom and Marija Ozolins*)
Harvard School of Public Health, Boston, Massachusetts, USA

S.R. OSMANI (*Famines*)
Professor of Developmental Economics, School of Economics and Politics, University of Ulster, Jordanstown Campus, UK

MARIJA OZOLINS (*Urbanization and Its Management, co-authors David E. Bloom and Jennifer O'Brien*)
Harvard School of Public Health, Boston, Massachusetts, USA

R.K. PACHAURI (*Energy, co-author Deepti Mahajan*)
Director-General, The Energy Research Institute (TERI), New Delhi

ARVIND PANAGARIYA (*World Trade Organization*)
Professor of Economics and Jagdish Bhagwati Professor of Indian Political Economy, Columbia University, New York, USA

ROHINI PANDE (*Dams, co-author Esther Duflo; Rural Credit*)
Mohammed Kamal Professor of Public Policy, Harvard Kennedy School, Harvard University, Cambridge, Massachusetts, USA

MIHIR PANDEY (*Small-scale Industries, co-author Ira N. Gang*)
Associate Professor in Economics, Ramjas College, University of Delhi, Delhi

T.S. PAPOLA (*Employment Trends*)
Honorary Professor, Institute for Studies in Industrial Development, New Delhi, India

SHANKAR PARAMESHWARAN (*Entrepreneurs in India and Abroad, co-author Ignatius Chithelen*)
Associate Editor of India Knowledge@Wharton

KIRIT S. PARIKH (*Petroleum Product Pricing*)
Former Member, Planning Commission, and Chairman, Integrated Research and Action for Development (IRADe), New Delhi, India

ILA PATNAIK (*Tariffs*)
Professor, National Institute of Public Finance and Policy (NIPFP), New Delhi, India

PRABHAT PATNAIK (*Krishna Bharadwaj; Inflation*)
Retired Professor, Centre for Economic Studies and Planning, Jawaharlal Nehru University, New Delhi, India

UTSA PATNAIK (*Bonded Labour*)
Retired Professor, Centre for Economic Studies and Planning, Jawaharlal Nehru University, New Delhi, India

PRASANTA K. PATTANAIK (*Mahatma Gandhi*)
Emeritus Professor, Department of Economics, University of California, Riverside, USA

ANANDITA PHILIPOSE (*Child Malnutrition and Feeding Practices*)
Cornell Institute of Public Affairs, Cornell University, New York, USA

K. SEETA PRABHU (*Human Development Index*)
Senior Assistant Country Director, United Nations Development Programme, New Delhi, India

ANINDITA PUJARI (*Constitution and Economic Reforms*)
Advocate, Supreme Court of India

DHUSHYANTH RAJU (*Worker Benefits*)
Senior Economist, South Asia Education Department, World Bank, Washington DC, USA

MIHIR RAKSHIT (*Oil Price Shocks*)
Director, Monetary Research Project, Information and Credit Rating Agency (ICRA), Kolkata, India

BHARAT RAMASWAMI (*Public Distribution System; Unemployment, The Measurement of, co-author Wilima Wadhwa*)
Professor, Planning Unit, Indian Statistical Institute, Delhi, India

C. RANGARAJAN (*Food Security*)
Chairman, Economic Advisory Council to the Prime Minister, India

BHARGAVI RAO (*HIV/AIDS, Economics of, co-author Ajay Mahal, Kavita Sivaramakrishnan, and David E. Bloom*)
Clinical Specialist, Harvard Medical School (Division of AIDS), Boston, Massachusetts

C.N.R. RAO (*Scientific Research*)
National Research Professor and Honorary President & Linus Pauling Research Professor, Jawaharlal Nehru Centre for Advanced Scientific Research, Bangalore, India

S.L. RAO (*V.K.R.V. Rao*)
Former Chairman, Institute for Social and Economic Change (ISEC), Bangalore, India

U.R. RAO (*Space Satellites*)
Chairman, Governing Council, Department of Space, Physical Research Laboratory, Ahmedabad, India

VIJAYENDRA RAO (*Dowries; Sex Work, co-author Manisha Shah*)
Lead Economist, Development Research Group, World Bank, Washington DC, USA

PARTHA RAY (*Banking, co-authors Dilip M. Nachane and Saibal Ghosh*)
Adviser to Executive Director (India), International Monetary Fund (IMF), Washington DC, USA

RANJAN RAY (*Household Welfare and Decision Making*)
Professor of Economics, School of Economics and Finance, University of Tasmania, Australia

C. RAMMANOHAR REDDY (*Defence Expenditure, co-author Tanya Sethi*)
Editor, *Economic and Political Weekly*, Mumbai

Y.V. REDDY (*Monetary Policy*)
Former Governor, Reserve Bank of India

TIRTHANKAR ROY (*Handicrafts; Industrialization*)
Reader in Economic History, London School of Economics and Political Science, UK

JAMES RYDGE (*Low-carbon Growth and Development, co-authors Nicholas Stern and Ruth Kattumuri*)
Research Officer, Grantham Research Institute on Climate Change and the Environment, London School of Economics (LSE), UK

ABHIRUP SARKAR (*Monsoon and Economic Activity; Special Economic Zones*)
Professor of Economics, Economic Research Unit, Indian Statistical Institute, Kolkata, India

ASANI SARKAR (*Derivatives*)
Research Officer, Federal Reserve Bank of New York, New York, USA

JAYATI SARKAR (*Corporate Ownership and Performance, co-author Subrata Sarkar*)
Associate Professor, Indira Gandhi Institute of Development Research (IGIDR), Mumbai

SUBRATA SARKAR (*Corporate Ownership and Performance, co-author Jayati Sarkar*)
Professor, Indira Gandhi Institute of Development Research (IGIDR), Mumbai

SUMAN SARKAR (*Ashok Rudra, co-author Jean Drèze*)
Professor, Visva-Bharati University, Santiniketan, India

N.C. SAXENA (*Land Acquisition for Industry*)
Member, National Advisory Council, Government of India

SHARMISTHA SELF (*Exogamy and Endogamy, co-author Sajal Lahiri*)
Associate Professor, Department of Economics, Missouri State University, Springfield, MO, USA

AMARTYA SEN (*Democracy and Social Welfare*)
Thomas W. Lamont University Professor and Professor of Economics and Philosophy, Harvard University, USA

ANINDYA SEN (*Business Policy*)
Professor of Economics, Indian Institute of Management Calcutta (IIMC), Kolkata, India

LATE ARJUN K. SENGUPTA (*Human Rights, co-author Kaushik Ranjan Bandyopadhyay*)
Member of Parliament (Rajya Sabha), India

RAMPRASAD SENGUPTA (*Power Industry; Steel Industry*)
Professor of Economics at Centre for Economic Studies and Planning, Jawaharlal Nehru University, New Delhi, India

TANYA SETHI (*Defence Expenditure, co-author C. Rammanohar Reddy*)
Assistant Editor, *Economic and Political Weekly*

AJAY SHAH (*Securities Markets; Stock Market Indexes, co-author Susan Thomas*)
Professor, National Institute of Public Finance and Policy (NIPFP), New Delhi, India

MANISHA SHAH (*Sex Work, co-author Vijayendra Rao*)
Assistant Professor of Economics, Department of Economics, University of California-Irvine, USA

KAMESHWARI SHANKAR (*Labour Turnover in the High-technology Sector*)
Assistant Professor of Economics, City College of New York, USA

SIDDHARTH SHARMA (*Data Sets, co-authors Reena Badiani and Himanshu*)
Research Analyst, Middle East and North Africa Region, World Bank, Washington DC, USA

SUNIL SHARMA (*Exchange Rates; IMF Conditionality*)
Director, IMF–Singapore Regional Training Institute, Singapore

ALOK SHEEL (*G-20 and Multilateral Economic Cooperation*)
Joint Secretary, Department of Economic Affairs, Government of India

PARTHASARATHI SHOME (*Savings and Investment*)
Director and Chief Executive, Indian Council for Research on International Economic Relations (ICRIER), New Delhi, India

AMAR SINGH (*Industrial Clusters, co-author Mukesh Gulati*)
Deputy General Manager, Foundation for MSME (micro, small and medium enterprises) Clusters, New Delhi

JAIVIR SINGH (*Labour Laws*)
Associate Professor, Centre for the Study of Law and Governance, Jawaharlal Nehru University, New Delhi, India

KANHAIYA SINGH (*Oil*)
Senior Fellow, National Council of Applied Economic Research (NCAER), New Delhi, India

NIRVIKAR SINGH (*Call Centres; Telecommunications*)
Professor, University of California, Santa Cruz, USA

RAM SINGH (*Liability Rules*)
Associate Professor, Department of Economics, Delhi School of Economics, University of Delhi, Delhi, India

ANUP KUMAR SINHA (*Corporate Ethics*)
Professor, Management Information Systems, Indian Institute of Management Calcutta (IIMC), Kolkata, India

U.K. SINHA (*Stock Exchange*)
Chairman, Securities and Exchange Board of India (SEBI)

KAVITA SIVARAMAKRISHNAN (*HIV/AIDS, Economics of, co-author Bhargavi Rao, Ajay Mahal, and David E. Bloom*)
Research Fellow, Harvard Center for Population and Development Studies, Harvard School of Public Health, Boston, Massachusetts, USA

E. SOMANATHAN (*Biodiversity*)
Professor, Planning Unit, Indian Statistical Institute, Delhi, India

ROHINI SOMANATHAN (*Poverty and Exclusion*)
Professor, Department of Economics, Delhi School of Economics, Delhi University, Delhi, India

KALA SEETHARAM SRIDHAR (*Cities*)
Head, Public Affairs Centre (PAC), Bangalore, India

T.C.A. Srinivasa-Raghavan (*Aviation; Ports and Shipping; Reserve Bank of India, co-author G. Balachandran*)
Associate Editor, *Business Line*, India

Nicholas Stern (*Low-carbon Growth and Development, co-authors Ruth Kattumuri and James Rydge*)
IG Patel Chair and Director, London School of Economics (LSE) Asia Research Centre, UK

D. Subbarao (*Financial Inclusion*)
Governor, Reserve Bank of India (RBI)

Arvind Subramanian (*Growth Experience*)
Senior Fellow jointly at the Peterson Institute for International Economics and the Center for Global Development, Washington DC, USA

Dilip Subramanian (*Voluntary Retirement Schemes*)
Professor, Reims Management School, Reims, France

S. Subramanian (*Poverty*)
Professor, Madras Institute of Development Studies, Chennai, India

M.S. Swaminathan (*Disaster Management, co-author P.C. Kesavan*)
Chairman, M.S. Swaminathan Research Foundation, Chennai, India

Madhura Swaminathan (*Child Labour*)
Professor, Indian Statistical Institute, Kolkata, India

Ratan Tata (*Tata, The House of*)
Chairman, Tata Group, Mumbai, India

Suresh D. Tendulkar (*National Sample Surveys*)
Former Professor of Economics, Delhi School of Economics, University of Delhi, Delhi, India and Chairman, National Statistical Commission, Government of India

Susan Thomas (*Stock Market Indexes, co-author Ajay Shah*)
Assistant Professor, Indira Gandhi Institute of Development Research (IGIDR), Mumbai, India

Jeemol Unni (*Agricultural Labour*)
RBI Chair Professor in Rural Economics, Institute of Rural Management Anand (IRMA), India

A. Vaidyanathan (*Irrigation; Water*)
Honorary Fellow of the Centre for Development Studies, Thiruvananthapuram, India, and a member of the Central Board of Directors, Reserve Bank of India

Arvind Virmani (*Balance of Payments; Foreign Direct Investment for Media*)
Executive Director, International Monetary Fund (IMF)

B.P.R. Vithal (*Finance Commissions*)
IAS (Retired); Member, Tenth Finance Commission, India

V.S. Vyas (*M.L. Dantwala*)
Professor Emeritus, Institute of Development Studies, Jaipur, India

Wilima Wadhwa (*Unemployment, The Measurement of, co-author Bharat Ramaswami*)
Director, Statistics, Assessment Survey Evaluation Research Centre, New Delhi, India

Jayashree Watal (*Patents*)
Adjunct Professor of Law; Counsellor, Intellectual Property Division, World Trade Organization, Geneva, Switzerland

Stephen Wright (*India's Growth Turnaround, co-authors Chetan Ghate and Tatiana Fic*)
Professor of Economics, Department of Economics, Mathematics and Statistics, Birkbeck College, University of London, UK

Name Index

(Note: Page numbers in bold type indicate authors' entries or biographical entries)

Subject Index

(Note: Page numbers in bold type indicate entries)

'For years to come, this book
anyone seeking to understand
and political economy

'Kaushik Basu has done a g
broader scope and assembling
accessible style. —P

'...a unique and important
economy, and also a collection
of the world's true exp

'...an indispensable and inno
economics, not only for econo
are affected by eco

'The volume is a unique exp
a variety of themes penned
A must-buy for each and every
libr
—*Busi*

'This is a dictionary that exp
leaves it for readers to expl
engaging and useful res

'Too many economists may
can certainly produce a good e
Ou

'India's first companion to
the more impressive additio
encyclopedias. —